A HISTORY OF WESTERN SOCIETY

FIFTH EDITION

A History of Western Society

✦ **Volume I** *From Antiquity to the Enlightenment*

John P. McKay
University of Illinois at
Urbana–Champaign

Bennett D. Hill
Georgetown University

John Buckler
University of Illinois at
Urbana–Champaign

HOUGHTON MIFFLIN COMPANY
Boston   Toronto
Geneva, Illinois   Palo Alto
Princeton, New Jersey

Sponsoring Editor: Sean W. Wakely
Basic Book Editor: Elizabeth Welch
Associate Editor: Jeffrey Greene
Senior Manufacturing Coordinator: Priscilla Bailey
Marketing Manager: Pamela Shaffer

Credits: Pages 13, 14, and 21: excerpts from The Sumerians: Their History, Culture and
Character by S. N. Kramer. Copyright © 1963 by University of Chicago Press. Pages
43–46: Abridged and adapted from The Holy Bible. Copyright © 1974 The Gideons
International. Page 74: Sappho by Willis Barnstone. Copyright © 1965 by Willis
Barnstone. Page 75: Poem by Tyrtaeus. Reprinted by permission of the publishers
and the Loeb Classical Library from J.M. Edmonds, Greek Elegy and Iambus,
Cambridge, Mass.: Harvard University Press, 1931. Pages 285–286: The Muslim
Discovery of Europe by B. Lewis. Copyright © 1982 by W.W. Norton. Pages 359–
360: Poem by Bertran de Born. This material originally appeared in *Lyrics of the
Middle Ages. An Anthology* by J.J. Wilhem, ed. Copyright © 1993 by Garland
Publishing, Inc. Reprinted by permission. Page 329: "Life of Thomas Beckett" by
William fitz. Stephen from *English Historical Documents II,* by D.C. Douglas and G.E.
Greenaway, eds. Copyright © 1961 by Eyre and Spottiswoode. Page 550: Poem by
Joost van den Vondel quoted from *Europe in the Seventeenth Century* by D. Maland.
Copyright © 1967 by A & C Black, Ltd.

Cover designer: Harold Burch, Harold Burch Design, New York, New York
Cover image: Hans Memling. Man with a Coin, 15th c. Koninklijk Museum voor Schone
Kunsten, Plaatsnijdersstraat 2–B–2000, Antwerp, Belgium.

Printed in the U.S.A.
Library of Congress Catalog Card Number: 94-76525
ISBN Student Text: 0–395–70842–7
ISBN Examination Copy: 0–395–71720–5
123456789-VH–98 97 96 95 94

About the Authors

John P. McKay Born in St. Louis, Missouri, John P. McKay received his B.A. from Wesleyan University (1961), his M.A. from the Fletcher School of Law and Diplomacy (1962), and his Ph.D. from the University of California, Berkeley (1968). He began teaching history at the University of Illinois in 1966 and became a professor there in 1976. John won the Herbert Baxter Adams Prize for his book *Pioneers for Profit: Foreign Entrepreneurship and Russian Industrialization, 1885–1913* (1970). He has also written *Tramways and Trolleys: The Rise of Urban Mass Transport in Europe* (1976) and has translated Jules Michelet's *The People* (1973). His research has been supported by fellowships from the Ford Foundation, the Guggenheim Foundation, the National Endowment for the Humanities, and IREX. His articles and reviews have appeared in numerous journals, including *The American Historical Review, Business History Review, The Journal of Economic History,* and *Slavic Review.* He edits *Industrial Development and the Social Fabric: An International Series of Historical Monographs.*

Bennett D. Hill A native of Philadelphia, Bennett D. Hill earned an A.B. at Princeton (1956) and advanced degrees from Harvard (A.M., 1958) and Princeton (Ph.D., 1963). He taught history at the University of Illinois at Urbana, where he was department chairman from 1978 to 1981. He has published *English Cistercian Monasteries and Their Patrons in the Twelfth Century* (1968) and *Church and State in the Middle Ages* (1970); and articles in *Analecta Cisterciensia, The New Catholic Encyclopaedia, The American Benedictine Review,* and *The Dictionary of the Middle Ages.* His reviews have appeared in *The American Historical Review, Speculum, The Historian, The Catholic Historical Review,* and *Library Journal.* He has been a fellow of the American Council of Learned Societies and has served on committees for the National Endowment for the Humanities. Now a Benedictine monk of St. Anselm's Abbey, Washington, D.C., he is also a Visiting Professor at Georgetown University.

John Buckler Born in Louisville, Kentucky, John Buckler received his B.A. (*summa cum laude*) from the University of Louisville in 1967. Harvard University awarded him the Ph.D. in 1973. From 1984 to 1986 he was an Alexander von Humboldt Fellow at the Institut für Alte Coschichte, University of Munich. He has lectured at the Fondation Hardt at the University of Geneva, and has participated in numerous international conferences. He is currently the professor of Greek history at the University of Illinois. In 1980 Harvard University Press published his *The Theban Hegemony, 371–362 BC.* He has also published *Philip II and the Sacred War* (Leiden 1989), and co-edited *BOIOTIKA: Vorträge vom 5. International Böotien-Kolloquium* (Munich 1989). He has assisted the National Endowment for the Humanities, and reviews articles for journals in the United States and Europe. His articles have appeared in journals both here and abroad, including the *American Journal of Ancient History, Classical Philology, Rheinisches Museum für Philoloqie, Classical Quarterly, Wiener Studien, Symbolae Osloenses,* and many others.

Contents in Brief

Contents

✥ CHAPTER 1
Near Eastern Origins   3

✥ CHAPTER 2
Small Kingdoms and Mighty Empires in the Near East   37

✥ CHAPTER 3
The Legacy of Greece   63

Maps

Timelines/Genealogies

* The comparative timeline, *A History of Western Society: A Brief Overview,* can be found on page 588

Listening to the Past

Preface

A History of Western Society grew out of the authors' desire to infuse new life into the study of Western civilization. We knew full well that historians were using imaginative questions and innovative research to open up vast new areas of historical interest and knowledge. We also recognized that these advances had dramatically affected the subject of European economic, intellectual, and, especially, social history, while new research and fresh interpretations were also revitalizing the study of the traditional mainstream of political, diplomatic, and religious development. Despite history's vitality as a discipline, however, it seemed to us that both the broad public and the intelligentsia were generally losing interest in the past.

It was our conviction, based on considerable experience introducing large numbers of students to the broad sweep of Western civilization, that a book reflecting current trends could excite readers and inspire a renewed interest in history and our Western heritage. Our strategy was twofold. First, we made social history the core element of our work. Not only did we incorporate recent research by social historians, but also we sought to recreate the life of ordinary people in appealing human terms. At the same time we were determined to give great economic, political, intellectual, and cultural developments the attention they unquestionably deserve. We wanted to give individual readers and instructors a balanced, integrated perspective so that they could pursue—on their own or in the classroom—those themes and questions that they found particularly exciting and significant. In an effort to realize fully the potential of our fresh, yet balanced approach, we made many changes, large and small, in the three editions that followed.

Changes in the New Edition

In preparing the fifth edition we have worked hard to keep our book up-to-date and to strengthen our distinctive yet balanced approach. Six main lines of revision guided our many changes.

Updated Approach to Social History.   First, in a thorough revision of social developments, we have given greater attention to cultural and intellectual life, and somewhat reduced the quantitative and demographic aspects. Increased emphasis on culture and attitudes invigorates our social history core and accurately reflects current scholarship and changing interests within the historical profession. Accordingly, this edition has expanded discussions of religious life including popular religion in Mesopotamia (Chapter 1), classical Greece (Chapter 3), and revolutionary France (Chapter 21); the evolution of Jewish religion (Chapter 2), Eastern monasticism (Chapter 7), and Calvin's Geneva (Chapter 14); and religious revival in the twentieth century (Chapter 28). Consistently greater attention to popular culture includes new sections on medieval music, troubadour poets, and recreation in Chapters 11 and 12; community values in the eighteenth-century (Chapter 20); and the counterculture in the 1960s (Chapter 30). New material on health and health care features recent research on medieval practices (Chapter 10), early hospitals and the Black Death (Chapter 12), and eighteenth-century practitioners (Chapter 20). Interactions between cultures have also been highlighted, as, for example, the relations between Egyptians and Nubians (Chapter 1), pagans and Christians (Chapter 6), Muslims and Christians (Chapter 7), and educated elites and popular classes (Chapters 18 and 20). In addition, we have carefully revised sections on the life of the people to set social developments consistently in their larger historical context. For example, Chapters 18 through 21 provide a dynamic, thoroughly updated treatment of the eighteenth century that interrelates cultural change, economic expansion, social life, and political revolution.

Integrated Treatment of Women and Gender. Second, we have broadened our treatment of women's history and gender issues and integrated it into the main narrative, rather than reserving it for separate sections. This approach also reflects current scholarly thinking. For example, the updated discussion of Hellenistic women has been integrated into the central narrative (Chapter 4); new material on women in agriculture and commerce during the Middle Ages (Chapters 10 and 11), and on gender roles in the arts (Chapter 15) has been appropriately positioned; elite women in the Enlightenment and peasant women in village communities have been reconsidered in context (Chapters 18 and 20); and women in twentieth-century dictatorships have been compared systematically (Chapter 29). The contemporary women's movement receives expanded separate analysis (Chapter 31) because it emerged as a major cultural and political force.

Organizational Changes. Third, our integrated treatment of women's history is one of several organizational improvements. In addition to the revision of Chapters 18 through 21, Chapter 15 has been thoroughly revised to relate sixteenth-century social and cultural changes consistently to political and religious developments. Chapters 30 and 31 have been completely recast, interrelating political, economic, social, and cultural developments from the new edition's post-Cold War perspective. Chapter 1 has been reorganized to clarify the chronology and the role of writing in Sumerian civilization. The early development of the Kievan principality has been relocated to Chapter 8 to maintain the chronology, and to highlight the integral role of the eastern Slavs in early medieval Europe.

Incorporation of Recent Scholarship. Fourth, every chapter has been carefully revised to reflect recent scholarship. Because the authors are committed to a balanced approach, we have continued to incorporate important new findings on political, economic, and intellectual developments in this edition. Revisions of this nature include the Babylonian Captivity (Chapter 2), democratic ideology in Athens and political background to Plato and Aristotle's thought (Chapter 3), and Roman commerce and frontier relations between Romans and Germans (Chapter 6). Similar revisions in Chapters 7 through 16 incorporate new material on the Spanish *reconquista* (Chapter 7), the medieval origins of the modern state and the power of the church in private life (Chapter 9), economic causes for Magna Carta (Chapter 11), and political violence (Chapter 12). There is new material on banks in continental industrialization and the early labor movement (Chapter 22); the role of class conflict in nineteenth-century domestic politics, imperialism, and the origins of World War One (Chapters 25-27); educational reforms and political culture in Republican France (Chapter 25); Nietzsche and his influence (Chapter 28); and the Nazi state and the origins of Italian fascism (Chapter 29). In short, recent research keeps the broad sweep of our history fresh and up-to-date.

New "Problems of Historical Interpretation." Fifth, the addition of more "problems of historical interpretation" in the fourth edition was well received, so we have increased their number again in this edition. We believe that the problematic element helps our readers develop the critical-thinking skills that are among the most precious benefits of studying history. New examples of this more open-ended, interpretive approach include the debate over the origins of Rome (Chapter 5), the impact of the Renaissance on the lives of ordinary and elite women (Chapter 13), the motives and legacy of Christopher Columbus (Chapter 15), popular reading habits and their significance (Chapter 20), social tensions and the origins of World War One (Chapter 27), and the nature of twentieth-century dictatorships (Chapter 29).

Revised Full-Color Art and Map Programs. Finally, the illustrative component of our work has been carefully revised. We have added many new illustrations to our extensive art program, which includes nearly two hundred color reproductions, letting great art and important events come alive. As in earlier editions, all illustrations have been carefully selected to complement the text, and all carry captions that enhance their value. Artwork remains an integral part of our book; the past can speak in pictures as well as in words. The use of full color throughout this edition also serves to clarify the maps and graphs and to enrich the textual material. The maps and map captions have been updated to correlate directly to the text.

Distinctive Features

Distinctive features, both new and revised, guide the reader in the process of historical understanding. Many of these features also show how historians sift through and evaluate evidence. Our goal is to suggest how historians actually work and think. We want the reader to think critically and to realize that history is neither a list of cut-and-dried facts nor a senseless jumble of conflicting opinions.

New Primary-Source Chapter Feature.   To help students and instructors realize this goal, we have added a two-page excerpt from a primary source at the end of each chapter in the fifth edition. This important new feature, entitled "Listening to the Past," extends and illuminates a major historical issue considered in the chapter. For example, in Chapter 4, a selection from *Plutarch's Lives* recounts the sacrifice of a famous queen for her people, while Chapter 9 presents a mind-opening Arab account of the First Crusade. Crime in medieval England is examined through criminal case reports in Chapter 12, and the German traveler Olearius provides a fascinating and influential picture of the Russian state and society in Chapter 17. Writer Stephan Zweig probes the sexuality of young men and women in nineteenth-century Vienna in Chapter 24, and a Jewish doctor who survived Auschwitz describes the horrible inhumanity of Nazi death camps in Chapter 29.

Each primary source opens with a problem-setting introduction and closes with "Questions for Analysis" that invite students to evaluate the evidence as historians would. Drawn from a range of writings addressing a variety of social, cultural, political, and intellectual issues, these sources promote active involvement and critical interpretation. Selected for their interest and importance and carefully fitted into their historical context, these sources do indeed allow the student to "listen to the past" and to observe how history has been shaped by individual men and women, some of them great aristocrats, others ordinary folk.

Improved Chapter Features.   Distinctive features from earlier editions have been revised and improved in the fifth edition. To help guide the reader toward historical understanding, we pose specific historical questions at the beginning of each chapter. These questions are then answered in the course of each chapter, and each chapter concludes with a concise summary of its findings. All of the questions and summaries have been reexamined and frequently revised in order to maximize the usefulness of this popular feature.

In addition to posing chapter-opening questions and presenting more problems in historical interpretation, we have quoted extensively from a wide variety of primary sources in the narrative, demonstrating in our use of these quotations how historians evaluate evidence. Thus primary sources are examined as an integral part of the narrative as well as presented in extended form in the new "Listening to the Past" chapter feature. We believe that such an extensive program of both integrated and separate primary source excerpts will help readers learn to interpret and think critically.

Each chapter concludes with carefully selected suggestions for further reading. These suggestions are briefly described to help readers know where to turn to continue thinking and learning about the Western world. Also, chapter bibliographies have been revised and updated to keep them current with the vast amount of new work being done in many fields.

Revised Timelines.   The timelines appearing in earlier editions have been substantially improved in this edition. In addition to revising the timelines placed within many chapters, we have expanded the comparative timelines previously dispersed throughout the fourth edition and placed them in a unified format in an appendix at the end of the book. Comprehensive and easy to locate, this useful timeline allows students to compare simultaneous political, economic, social, cultural, intellectual, and scientific developments over the centuries.

Flexible Format.   Western civilization courses differ widely in chronological structure from one campus to another. To accommodate the various divisions of historical time into intervals that fit a two-quarter, three-quarter, or two-semester period, *A History of Western Society* is being published in four versions, three of which embrace the complete work:

- One-volume hardcover edition, A HISTORY OF WESTERN SOCIETY
- Two-volume paperback, A HISTORY OF WESTERN SOCIETY *Volume I: From Antiquity to the Enlightenment* (Chapters 1–17), *Volume II: From Absolutism to the Present* (Chapters 16–31)
- Three-volume paperback, A HISTORY OF WESTERN SOCIETY *Volume A: From Antiquity to 1500* (Chapters 1–13), *Volume B: From the Renaissance to 1815* (Chapters 12–21), *Volume C: From the Revolutionary Era to the Present* (Chapters 21–31)
- A HISTORY OF WESTERN SOCIETY *Since 1400* (Chapters 13–31), for courses on Europe since the Renaissance

Note that overlapping chapters in both the two- and the three-volume sets permit still wider flexibility in matching the appropriate volume with the opening and closing dates of a course term.

Ancillaries

Learning and teaching ancillaries, listed below, also contribute to the usefulness of the text.

- *Study Guide*
- *Computerized Study Guide*
- *Instructor's Resource Manual*
- *Test Items,*
- *Computerized Test Items*
- *Map Transparencies*
- *Videodisc*
- *Videodisc Guide*

The excellent *Study Guide* has been thoroughly revised by Professor James Schmiechen of Central Michigan University. Professor Schmiechen has been a tower of strength ever since he critiqued our initial prospectus, and he has continued to give us many valuable suggestions as well as his warmly appreciated support. His *Study Guide* contains learning objectives, chapter summaries, chapter outlines, review questions, extensive multiple-choice exercises, self-check lists of important concepts and events, and a variety of study aids and suggestions. The fifth edition also retains the study–review exercises on the interpretation of visual sources and major political ideas as well as suggested issues for

discussion and essay, chronology reviews and sections on studying effectively. These sections take the student through reading and studying activities like underlining, summarizing, identifying main points, classifying information according to sequence, and making historical comparisons. To enable both students and instructors to use the *Study Guide* with the greatest possible flexibility, the guide is available in two volumes, with considerable overlapping of chapters. Instructors and students who use only Volumes A and B of the text have all the pertinent study materials in a single volume, *Study Guide, Volume 1* (Chapters 1–21); likewise, those who use only Volumes B and C of the text also have all the necessary materials in one volume, *Study Guide, Volume 2* (Chapters 12–31). The multiple-choice sections of the *Study Guide* are also available in a *Computerized Study Guide,* a tutorial version that tells students not only which response is correct but also why each of the other choices is wrong; it also provides the page numbers in the text where each question is discussed. These "rejoinders" to the multiple-choice questions also appear in printed form at the end of the *Study Guide.* The *Computerized Study Guide* is available for IBM® computers.

The *Instructor's Resource Manual,* prepared by Professor John Marshall Carter contains instructional objectives, annotated chapter outlines, suggestions for lectures and discussion, paper and class activity topics, primary source exercises, map activities, and lists of audio-visual resources. The accompanying *Test Items,* by Professor Charles Crouch of Georgia Southern University offer identification, multiple-choice, map, and essay questions for a total of approximately 2000 test items. These test items are available to adopters in both IBM® and Macintosh versions, both of which include editing capabilities. To add an exciting multimedia component to lectures and learning laboratories, we have created *The History of Western Civilization Videodisc/Videotape/Slide* program. The program allows the instructor to create customized multimedia classroom presentations using this rich collection of visual images. The program is divided into five chronological periods (ancient, medieval, early modern, modern, and Twentieth Century) and contains over 165 still images, 30 animated maps, and motion footage accompanied by period music. A companion *Videodisc/Videotape* instructor's guide provides descriptions, printed bar codes, bar code stickers to create customized lectures, and numeric codes. The program is available at no cost to adopters of the book. Please contact your local Houghton Mifflin representative for more information about this innovative and exciting multimedia program.

In addition, a set of full-color *Map Transparencies* of all the maps in the text is available on adoption.

Acknowledgments

It is a pleasure to thank the many instructors who have read and critiqued the manuscript through its development:

Anthony Cardoza
Loyola University

Jack Cargill
Rutgers University

Stephanie Christelow
Idaho State University

Jessica Coope
University of Nebraska

George Early
Black Hills State University

Charles Evans
Northern Virginia Community College

Keith Francis
Pacific Union College

David Graf
University of Miami

Barbara Hanawalt
University of Minnesota

Paul Harvey
Penn State University

Charles Ingrao
Purdue University

Gary Johnson
University of Southern Maine

Ellen Kittell
University of Idaho

Harry Liebersohn
University of Illinois

James Masschaele
Rutgers University

Mavis Mate
University of Oregon

Kathryn Norberg
Univlersity of California, Los Angeles

Kathleen Paul
University of South Florida

William M. Reddy
Duke University

Raymond Sickinger
Providence College

Sherill Spaar
East Central University

Ruth Suyama
Mission College, Los Angeles

Bruce Taylor
University of Dayton

Marilyn Yancey
Virginia Union University

It is also a pleasure to thank our editors at Houghton Mifflin for their effort and support over many years. To Elizabeth Welch, Senior Basic Book Editor, who has skillfully guided and encouraged our work since the third edition, we owe a special debt of gratitude and admiration. To Jean Woy, Editor-in-Chief for Social Sciences, who has led us onward for more than a decade, and to Sean Wakely, Sponsoring Editor for History, we express our sincere appreciation. And we thank Leslie Anderson Olney and Carole Frohlich for their contributions in production and photo research.

Many of our colleagues at the University of Illinois continued to provide information and stimulation for our book, often without even knowing it. N. Frederick Nash, Rare Book Librarian, made many helpful suggestions for illustrations, and the World Heritage Museum at the University allowed us complete access to its sizable holdings. James Dengate kindly supplied information on objects from the museum's collection and Caroline Buckler took many excellent photographs of the museum's objects. Such wide-ranging expertise was a great asset for which we are very appreciative. Bennett Hill wishes to express his sincere appreciation to Ramón de la Fuente for his support, encouragement, and research assistance in the preparation of this fifth edition.

Each of us has benefited from the generous criticism of his co-authors, although each of us assumes responsibility for what he has written. John Buckler has written the first six chapters; Bennett Hill has continued the narrative through Chapter 16; and John McKay has written Chapters 17 through 31. Finally, we continue to welcome the many comments and suggestions that have come from our readers, for they have helped us greatly in this ongoing endeavor.

J. P. M.   B. D. H.   J. B.

A HISTORY OF WESTERN SOCIETY

1

Near Eastern Origins

✤ The culture of the modern Western world has its origins in the ancient Near East, a region that includes the lands bordering the Mediterranean's eastern shore, the Arabian peninsula, and parts of northeast Africa. In these areas human beings abandoned their life of roaming and hunting to settle in stable agricultural communities. From these communities grew cities and civilizations, societies that invented concepts and techniques that have become integral parts of contemporary life. Fundamental to the development of Western culture was the invention of writing by the Sumerians of Mesopotamia, which allowed knowledge of the past to be preserved and facilitated the spread and accumulation of learning, lore, literature, and science. Mathematics, astronomy, and architecture were also innovations of the ancient Near Eastern civilizations. So, too, were the first law codes, as well as religious concepts that still permeate daily life.

But how do we know and understand these things? Before embarking on the study of history, it is necessary to ask, "What is it?" Only then can the peoples and events of tens of thousands of years be placed into a coherent whole. Once the nature of history is understood, further questions can be asked and reasonably answered. Specifically for this chapter,

✤ ✤ ✤ ✤ ✤ ✤ ✤ ✤ ✤

A group of votive statuettes from the Abu Temple, Square Temple of the god Abu, Tell Asmar, 2700–2600 B.C. *(Source: Courtesy of The Oriental Institute of the University of Chicago. Victor J. Boswell, photographer)*

- How did nomadic hunters become urban dwellers?
- How did Western culture originate in Mesopotamia, and what caused Mesopotamian culture to become predominant throughout most of the ancient Near East?
- How did the Egyptians contribute to this vast story?
- What did the arrival of the Hittites on the frontiers of Mesopotamia and Egypt mean to the more advanced cultures of their new neighbors?

These are the questions we will explore in this chapter.

✤ WHAT IS HISTORY AND WHY?

History is the effort to reconstruct the past to discover what people thought, what they did, and how their beliefs and actions continue to influence human life. In order to appreciate the past fully, we must put it into perspective so that we can understand the factors that have helped to shape us as individuals, the society in which we live, and the nature of other peoples' societies. Why else should we study civilizations as separated from ours through time, distance, and culture as classical Greece, medieval Germany, and modern Russia? Although many of the people involved in these epochs are long dead, what they did has touched everyone alive today.

Historians begin to reconstruct the past by posing questions about it. How and why, for example, did cities emerge? How did the political system of a particular society evolve? How did people create an economic system to sustain a complex society? What were a society's religious beliefs, and how did they influence daily life? These are just a few of the kinds of questions that historians ask to guide their research and focus their approach to the past.

To answer these questions historians examine primary sources, the firsthand accounts of people who lived through the events, people who were in the best position to know what happened. Thus, historians most commonly rely on the written record of human experience because, no matter how extensive a civilization's physical remains may be, its history largely remains a mystery if it has not left us records that we can read. Until we are able to decipher the written texts left us by the ancient civilization of Minoan Crete, for example, we can draw only vague conclusions about its history. Nonetheless, it is the historian's responsibility to examine all of the evidence left by the past, and this includes visual evidence. Examined properly, visual sources provide a glimpse of the world as contemporaries saw it. Especially in conjunction with written documents, art can be a singularly valuable and striking means of understanding the past. Similarly, archaeology has proved a valuable avenue to the past, whether the excavation uncovers an ancient Greek city, a medieval church, or a modern factory building. Things as dissimilar as beautiful paintings and ordinary machines tell historians much about the ways in which people have lived and worked.

In the fifth century B.C., a Greek named Herodotus wrote the first true history of people and events in an effort to understand a great conflict between the Persians and the Greeks.* Herodotus, the "father of history," wrote that he was publishing his "inquiry" into the past. The Greek word that he used for "inquiry" was *historia,* from which we derive the word *history.* The two concepts of inquiry and history, first joined by Herodotus, became inseparable, and their connection is as valid today as when Herodotus wrote.

When studying sources—the most basic activity in research—historians must assess the validity and perspective of each account. They try to determine whether their sources are honest and accurate, generally by comparing and contrasting the testimony of several different observers. They criticize sources both externally—to attempt to uncover forgeries and errors—and internally—to find the author's motives for writing, inconsistencies within the document, biases, even cases of outright lying. In some instances, especially in ancient and medieval history, contemporary written accounts have been lost; they are known to posterity only through people who later read the originals and incorporated the information into their own writings. Although historians must analyze the viewpoints and accuracy of such derivative, or secondary, sources very carefully, these writings have preserved much history that otherwise would have been lost. For the modern period historians have a vast supply of contemporary accounts of events, memoirs, personal letters, economic statistics, and government reports, all of them useful for an understanding of the past.

Once historians have pieced together what happened and have determined the facts, they must interpret what they have found. Understanding the past does not necessarily come easily, which is one of the joys and frustrations of history. Unlike the exact physical sciences, history cannot reproduce experiments under controlled conditions, because

*The authors follow the traditional practice in the West of expressing historical dates in relation to the birth of Jesus Christ. Dates before his birth are labeled B.C. (for *Before Christ*), and dates after his birth are labeled A.D. (*Anno Domini,* Latin for "in the year of the Lord"). A widely used alternative system refers to these dates as B.C.E. (Before the Common Era) and C.E. (Common Era).

no two historical events are precisely alike. People cannot be put into test tubes, and they are not as predictable as atoms or hydrocarbons. That is hardly surprising, for history is about people, the most complex organisms on this planet.

To complicate matters, for many epochs of history only the broad outlines are known, so interpretation is especially difficult. For example, historians know that the Hittite Empire collapsed at the height of its power, but interpretations of the causes of the catastrophe are still speculative. On the other end of the spectrum, some developments are so vast and complex that historians must master mountains of data before they can even begin to interpret them properly. Events as diverse as the end of the western Roman Empire, the origins of the Industrial Revolution, and the causes of the French Revolution are very complicated because so many people brought so many different forces to bear for so many different reasons. In such cases, there can never be one simple explanation that will satisfy everyone, and this fact in itself testifies to the complexity of life in developed societies.

Still another matter complicates an accurate understanding of the past. The attempt to understand history is uniquely human. Interpretations of the past sometimes change because people's points of view change in the course of life. The values and attitudes of one generation may not be shared by another. Despite such differences in interpretation, the effort of historians to examine and understand the past can give them a perspective that is valuable to the present. It is through this process of analysis and interpretation of evidence that historians come to understand not only the past but its relation to life today.

Social history, an important subject of this book, is itself an example of the historian's reappraisal of the meaning of the past. For centuries people took the basic facts, details, and activities of life for granted. Obviously, people lived in certain types of houses, ate certain food that they either raised or bought, and reared families. These matters seemed so ordinary that few serious historians gave them much thought. Yet within this generation a growing number of scholars have demonstrated that studies of the ways in which people have lived over the years deserve as much attention as the reigns of monarchs, the careers of great political figures, and the outcomes of big battles.

The topics of history and human societies lead to the question, "What is civilization?" *Civilization* is a word easier to describe than to define. It comes from the Latin adjective *civilis,* which refers to a citizen. Citizens willingly and mutually bind themselves in political, economic, and social organizations in which individuals merge themselves, their energies, and their interests in a larger community.

In the course of time, civilization has come to embrace not only a people's system of social and political organization but also their particular shared way of thinking and believing, their art, and other facets of their culture—the complex whole that sets one people apart from other peoples who have different shared values and practices. One way to understand this idea is to observe the origins and development of the chief Western civilizations, analyzing similarities and differences among them. The term *Western* in this context means the ideas, customs, and institutions that developed primarily in Europe, the Americas, and their colonies throughout the world. These ideas, customs, and institutions set Western civilization apart from other civilizations, such as the African and Asian, that developed their unique way of life as a result of different demands, challenges, and opportunities, both human and geographical. Yet no civilization stands alone. Each influences the others, all the while preserving the essentials that make it distinctive.

At the fundamental level, the similarities of Western civilization are greater than the differences. Almost all people in Europe and the Americas share some values, even though they may live far apart, speak different languages, and have different religions and political and social systems. These values are the bonds that hold a civilization together. By studying these shared cultural values, which stretch through time and across distance, we can see how the various events of the past have left their impression on the present and even how the present may influence the future.

 ## THE FIRST HUMAN BEINGS

On December 27, 1831, young Charles Darwin stepped aboard the H.M.S. *Beagle* to begin a voyage to South America and the Pacific Ocean. In the course of that five-year voyage, he became convinced that species of animals and human beings had evolved from lower forms. At first Darwin was reluctant to publicize his theories because they ran counter to the biblical account of creation, which claimed that God had made Adam in one day. Finally, however, in 1859 he published *On the Origin of Species*. In 1871 he followed it with *The Descent of Man*, in which he argued that human beings and apes are descended from a common ancestor. Even before Darwin had proclaimed his theories, evidence to support them had come to light. In 1856 the fossilized bones of an early form of man were discovered in the Neander valley of Germany. Called "Neanderthal Man" after the place of his discovery, he was physically more primitive than modern man (*Homo sapiens*, or thinking man). But he was clearly a human being and not an ape. He offered proof of Darwin's theory that *Homo sapiens* had evolved from less developed forms.

The theories of Darwin, supported by the evidence of fossilized remains, ushered in a new scientific era in which scientists and scholars have reexamined the very nature of human beings and their history. Men and women of the twentieth century have made many discoveries and solved some old problems, but raised many new ones. Although the fossil remains of primitive unicellular organisms can be dated back roughly two and a half billion years, the fossil record is far from complete. Thus the whole story of evolution cannot yet be known.

Ever since Darwin published his theories of evolution, scholars have tried to find the "missing link" to the one fossil that would establish the point from which human beings and apes went their own different evolutionary ways. However, recent finds have caused them to question the very concept of the missing link and its implications. Fossil remains in China suggest that evolution was more complicated than paleoanthropologists—scientists who study early human beings—previously thought and even that human beings may not have originated in Africa. It is not simply that paleoanthropologists, like historians, must interpret their data; they must rethink everything that they have discovered in the light of their latest findings.

Many contemporary paleoanthropologists now suggest that the search for a missing link is a blind alley. Given the small numbers of these primates and the extent of the globe, there is an almost infinitesimal chance of finding a skeleton that can be considered the missing link between other primates and human beings. Instead, they stress the need to study all of these fossil remains to open new vistas for the understanding of evolution. That conclusion should not be surprising. In 1969, Loren Eiseley, a noted American anthropologist, offered the wisest and humblest observation: "The human interminglings of hundreds of thousands of years of prehistory are not to be clarified by a single generation of archeologists."[1]

Despite the enormous uncertainty surrounding human development, a reasonably clear picture can be drawn of two important early periods: the Paleolithic or Old Stone Age, and the Neolithic or New Stone Age. The immensely long Paleolithic Age, which lasted from about 400,000 to 7000 B.C., takes its scholarly name from the crude stone tools the earliest hunters chipped from flint and obsidian, a black volcanic rock. During the much shorter Neolithic Age, which lasted from about 7000 to 3000 B.C., human beings began using new types of stone tools and, more important, pursuing agriculture.

✤ THE PALEOLITHIC AGE

Paleolithic peoples hunted a huge variety of animals, ranging from elephants in Spain to deer in China. The hunters were thoroughly familiar with the habits and migratory patterns of the animals on which they relied. But success in the hunt also depended on the quality and effectiveness of the hunters' social organization. Paleolithic hunters were organized—they hunted in groups. They used their knowledge of the animal world and their power of thinking to plan how to down their prey. Paleolithic peoples also nourished themselves by gathering nuts, berries, and seeds. Just as they knew the habits of animals, so they had vast knowledge of the plant kingdom. Some Paleolithic peoples even knew how to plant wild seeds to supplement their food supply. Thus they relied on every part of the environment for survival.

The basic social unit of Paleolithic societies was probably the family, but family bonds were no doubt stronger and more extensive than those of families in modern, urban, and industrialized societies. It is likely that the bonds of kinship were strong not just within the nuclear family of father, mother, and children but throughout the extended family of uncles, aunts, cousins, nephews, and nieces. People in nomadic societies typically depend on the extended family for cooperative work and mutual protection. The ties of kinship prob-

✤ **Paleolithic Cave Painting** All Paleolithic peoples relied primarily on hunting for their survival. This scene, painted on the wall of a cave in southern France, depicts the animals that this group normally hunted. Paleolithic peoples may have hoped that by drawing these animals they gained a magical power over them. *(Source: Douglas Mazonowicz/Gallery of Prehistoric Art)*

ably also extended beyond the family to the tribe. A tribe was a group of families, led by a patriarch, a dominant male who governed the group. Tribe members considered themselves descendants of a common ancestor. Most tribes probably consisted of thirty to fifty people.

As in the hunt, so too in other aspects of life—group members had to cooperate to survive. The adult males normally hunted abroad and between hunts made stone weapons. The women's realm was primarily the camp, but they too ranged through the neighborhood gathering nuts, grains, and fruits to supplement the group's diet. The women's primary responsibility was the bearing of children, who were essential to the continuation of the group. Women also had to care for the children, especially the infants. Part of women's work, too, was tending the fire, which served for warmth, cooking, and protection against wild animals.

Some of the most striking accomplishments of Paleolithic peoples were intellectual. They used reason to govern their actions. Thought and language permitted the lore and experience of the old to be passed on to the young. An invisible world also opened up to *Homo sapiens*. The Neanderthals developed the custom of burying their dead and leaving offerings with the body, perhaps in the belief that somehow life continued after death.

Paleolithic peoples produced the first art. They decorated cave walls with lifelike paintings of animals and scenes of the hunt. Located deep in the caves, some of these paintings still survive, such as those at Altamira in Spain and Lascaux in France. Paleolithic peoples also began to fashion clay models of pregnant women and of animals. By portraying the animals as realistically as possible, the artist-hunters may have hoped to gain power over them. The statuettes of pregnant women seem to express a wish for fertile women to have babies and thus ensure the group's survival. The wall paintings and clay statuettes of Paleolithic peoples represent the earliest yearnings of human beings to control their environment.

✤ THE NEOLITHIC AGE

Hunting is at best a precarious way of life, even when the diet is supplemented with seeds and fruits. Paleolithic tribes either moved with the herds and adapted themselves to new circumstances or perished. Several long ice ages—periods when huge glaciers covered vast parts of Europe—subjected the small bands of Paleolithic hunters to extreme hardship.

Not long after the last ice age, around 7000 B.C., some hunters and gatherers began to rely chiefly on agriculture for their sustenance. Others continued the old pastoral and nomadic ways. Indeed, agriculture itself evolved over the course of time, and Neolithic peoples had long known how to grow crops. The real transformation of human life occurred when huge numbers of people began to rely primarily and permanently on the grain they grew and the animals they domesticated. Agriculture made possible a more stable and secure life. Neolithic peoples flourished, fashioning an energetic, creative era. They were responsible for many fundamental inventions and innovations that the modern world takes for granted. First, obviously, is systematic agriculture—that is, the reliance of Neolithic peoples on agriculture as their primary, not merely subsidiary, source of food. Thus they developed the primary economic activity of the entire ancient world and the basis of all modern life. With the settled routine of Neolithic farmers came the evolution of towns and eventually cities.

Neolithic farmers usually raised more food than they could consume, and their surpluses permitted larger, healthier populations. Population growth in turn created an even greater reliance on settled farming, as only systematic agriculture could sustain the increased numbers of people. Since surpluses of food could also be bartered for other commodities, the Neolithic era witnessed the beginnings of large-scale exchange of goods. In time the increasing complexity of Neolithic societies led to the development of writing, prompted by the need to keep records and later by the urge to chronicle experiences, learning, and beliefs.

The transition to settled life also had a profound impact on the family. The shared needs and pressures that encourage extended-family ties are less prominent in settled than in nomadic societies. Bonds to the extended family weakened. In towns and cities, the nuclear family was more dependent on its immediate neighbors than on kinfolk.

However, the nomadic way of life and the family relationships it nurtured continued to flourish alongside settled agriculture. Dramatic evidence of this fact came to light on September 19, 1991, when a hiker in the Tyrolean Alps in Italy discov-

❖ **Return of the Iceman** This scene captures the discovery of a Neolithic herdsman who was trapped in the ice about 5,300 years ago. The discovery was made by chance in September 1991. In an ancient accident, he was sealed in ice with all of his tools, thus providing modern scholars with a unique view of the past. The discovery is so important that scientists have not yet done an autopsy on the corpse. *(Source: Paul Hanny/Liaison)*

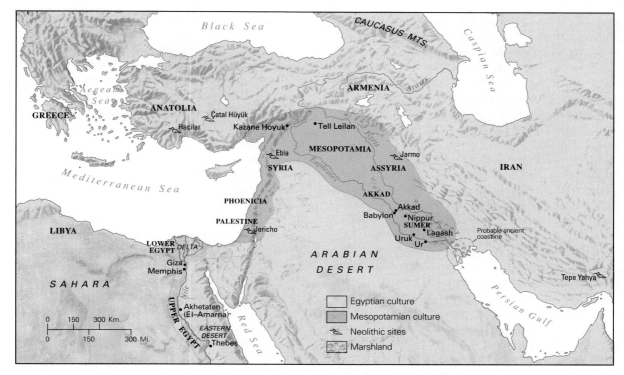

✦ **MAP 1.1 Spread of Cultures in the Ancient Near East** This map illustrates the spread of Mesopotamian and Egyptian culture through a semicircular stretch of land often called the "Fertile Crescent." From this area knowledge and use of agriculture spread throughout the western part of Asia Minor.

ered the frozen body of a Neolithic herdsman. The corpse is the oldest found intact, and its preservation results from the man having been covered for some 5,300 years by glacial ice. Although the discoverers unfortunately did irreparable damage to the site, enough remains to give a unique impression of European nomadic life and a surprising glimpse of its sophistication. The "Iceman," as he is now called, was found equipped with the implements of everyday life. Among them are advanced bows and arrows that prove a remarkable knowledge of ballistics. A number of tools, some of bone, wood, and even copper, show that European people were making the transition from the Neolithic Age to the time when they relied primarily on metals for their tools. Dental evidence suggests that the Iceman's diet consisted of milled grain. These findings strongly suggest that the Iceman was a hunter and gatherer, but also that he and his society depended on tilled grain as a vital part of their diet. The Iceman proves that nomadic and pastoral life could and did coincide peacefully with

the emerging agricultural settlements. Often farmers and nomads bartered with one another, each group trading its surpluses for those of the other. Although nomadic peoples continued to exist throughout the Neolithic period and into modern times, the future belonged to the Neolithic farmers and their descendants. While the development of systematic agriculture may not have been revolutionary, the changes that it ushered in certainly were.

Until recently, scholars thought that agriculture originated in the ancient Near East and gradually spread elsewhere. Contemporary work, however, points to a more complex pattern of development. For unknown reasons people in various parts of the Near East all seem to have begun domesticating plants and animals at roughly the same time, between 8000 and 3500 B.C. Four main points of origin have been identified. In the Near East, the inhabitants of sites as far apart as Tepe Yahya in modern Iran, Jarmo in Iraq, Jericho in Palestine, and Hacilar in modern Turkey (Map 1.1) raised wheat, barley, peas, and lentils. They also kept herds of sheep, pigs, and possibly goats.

Once people began to rely on farming for their livelihood, they settled in permanent villages and built houses. The location of the village was crucial. Early farmers chose places where the water supply was constant and adequate for their crops and flocks. At first, villages were small, consisting of a few households. By about 7000 B.C., however, as the population expanded and prospered, villages usually developed into walled towns. Walls offered protection and permitted a more secure, stable way of life than that of the nomad. They also prove that towns grew in size, population, and wealth, for these fortifications were so large that they could have been raised only by a large labor force. They indicate, moreover, that towns were developing social and political organization. The fortifications, the work of the whole community, would have been impossible without central planning.

One of the major effects of the advent of agriculture and settled life was a dramatic increase in population. No census figures exist for this period, but the number and size of the towns prove that Neolithic society was expanding. Early farmers found that agriculture provided a larger and much more dependable food supply than hunting and gathering. No longer did the long winter months mean the threat of starvation. Farmers learned to store the surplus for the winter. Because the farming community was better fed than ever before, it was also more resistant to diseases that kill people suffering from malnutrition. Thus Neolithic farmers were healthier and longer-lived than their predecessors.

Agricultural surplus also made possible the division of labor. It freed some members of the community from the necessity of raising food. Artisans and craftsmen devoted their attention to making the new stone tools farming demanded—hoes and sickles for fieldwork and mortars and pestles for grinding the grain. Other artisans began to shape clay into pottery vessels, which were used to store grain, wine, and oil and to serve as kitchen utensils. Still others wove baskets and cloth. People who could specialize in particular crafts produced more and better goods than any single farmer could.

Until recently it was impossible to say much about these goods. But in April 1985, archaeologists announced the discovery near the Dead Sea in modern Israel of a unique deposit of Neolithic artifacts. Found buried in a cave were fragments of the earliest cloth yet discovered, the oldest painted mask, remains of woven baskets and boxes, and jewelry. The textiles are surprisingly elaborate, some woven in eleven intricate designs. These artifacts give eloquent testimony to the sophistication and artistry of Neolithic craftsmen.

Prosperity and stable conditions nurtured other innovations and discoveries. Neolithic farmers improved their tools and agricultural techniques. They domesticated bigger, stronger animals, such as the bull and the horse, to work for them. To harness the power of these animals they invented tools such as the plow, which came into use by 3000 B.C. The first plows had wooden shares and could break only light soils, but they were far more efficient than stone hoes. By 3000 B.C., the wheel had been invented, and farmers devised ways of hitching bulls and horses to wagons. These developments enabled Neolithic farmers to raise more food more efficiently and easily than ever before, simply because animals and machines were doing a greater proportion of the work.

In arid regions such as Mesopotamia and Egypt, farmers learned to irrigate their land and later to drain it to prevent the buildup of salt in the soil. By diverting water from rivers, they were able to open new land to cultivation. River waters flooding the fields deposited layers of rich mud, which increased the fertility of the soil. Thus the rivers, together with the manure of domesticated animals, kept replenishing the land. The results included a further increase in population and wealth. Irrigation, especially on a large scale, demanded group effort. The entire community had to plan which land to irrigate and how to lay out the canals. Then everyone had to help dig the canals. The demands of irrigation underscored the need for strong central authority within the community. Successful irrigation projects in turn strengthened such central authority by proving it effective and beneficial. Thus corporate spirit and governments to which individuals were subordinate—the makings of urban life—began to evolve.

The development of systematic agriculture was a fundamental turning point in the history of civilization. Farming gave rise to stable settled societies, which enjoyed considerable prosperity. Farming made possible an enormous increase in population. Some inhabitants of the budding towns turned their attention to the production of goods that made life more comfortable. Settled circumstances and a certain amount of leisure made the accumu-

SIGNIFICANT EVENTS IN MESOPOTAMIAN HISTORY

Period	Event
ca 3000 B.C.	Sumerians become prevalent in southern Mesopotamia
ca 2600 B.C.	Spread of Mesopotamian Culture to northern Mesopotamia
ca 2331 B.C.	Sargon captured Sumer and created the new kingdom of Akkad
ca 1792 B.C.	Hammurabi wins control of Mesopotamia; Babylon the new capital of Mesopotamia
ca 1595 B.C.	Hittites and Kassites destroyed Hammurabi's dynasty

lation and spread of knowledge easier. Finally, sustained farming prepared the way for urban life.

✥ MESOPOTAMIAN CIVILIZATION

Mesopotamia is the Greek name for the land between the Euphrates and Tigris rivers. Both rivers have their headwaters in the mountains of Armenia in modern Turkey. Both are fed by numerous tributaries, and the entire river system drains a vast mountainous region. Overland routes in Mesopotamia usually follow the Euphrates because the banks of the Tigris are frequently steep and difficult. North of the ancient city of Babylon the land levels out into a barren expanse. The desert continues south of Babylon, and in 1857 the English geologist and traveler W. K. Loftus depicted it in grim terms:

There is no life for miles around. No river glides in grandeur at the base of its [the ancient city of Uruk] mounds; no green date groves flourish near its ruins. The jackal and the hyena appear to shun the dull aspect of its tombs. The king of birds never hovers over the deserted waste. A blade of grass or an insect finds no existence there. The shrivelled lichen alone, clinging to the weathered surface of the broken brick, seems to glory in its universal dominion upon those barren walls.[2]

Farther south the desert gives way to a 6,000-square-mile region of marshes, lagoons, mud flats, and reed banks. At last, in the extreme south the Euphrates and the Tigris unite and empty into the Persian Gulf.

This forbidding area became the home of many folk and the land of the first cities. The region around Akkad (or Agade, probably located somewhere near modern Baghdad) was occupied by bands of Semitic nomads, people linked by the fact that their languages all belonged to the group of languages known as Semitic, a group that includes Hebrew and Arabic. The Sumerians established themselves in the south, perhaps migrants from the east. Their origins are still uncertain, and they were not the only people to inhabit Mesopotamia. By 3000 B.C., however, they had established a number of cities in the southernmost part of Mesopotamia, which became known as Sumer. The Sumerians soon changed the face of the land and made Mesopotamia the "cradle of civilization" (see Map 1.1).

The Role of Environment

From the outset geography had a profound effect on the evolution of Mesopotamian civilization. In this region agriculture is possible only with irrigation and good drainage. Consequently, the Sumerians and later the Akkadians built their cities along the Tigris and Euphrates and the branches of these rivers. Some major cities, such as Ur and Uruk, took root on tributaries of the Euphrates, while others, notably Lagash, were built on branches of the Tigris. The rivers supplied fish, a major element of the city dwellers' diet. The rivers also provided reeds and clay for building materials. Since this

Meaning	Pictograph	Ideogram	Phonetic sign
A Star			
B Woman			
C Mountain			
D Slave woman			
E Water In			

Figure 1.1 Sumerian Writing (*Excerpted from S. N. Kramer,* The Sumerians: Their History, Culture and Character, *University of Chicago Press, Chicago, 1963, pp. 302–306*)

entire area lacks stone, mud brick became the primary building block of Mesopotamian architecture.

Although the rivers sustained life, they also destroyed it by frequent floods that ravaged entire cities. Moreover, they restrained political development by making Sumer a geographical maze. Among the rivers, streams, and irrigation canals stretched open desert or swamp where nomadic tribes roamed. Communication among the isolated cities was difficult and at times dangerous. Thus each Sumerian city became a state, independent of the others and protective of its independence. Any city that tried to unify the country was resisted by the other cities. As a result, the political history of Sumer is one of almost constant warfare. Although Sumer was eventually unified, unification came late and was always tenuous.

The Invention of Writing and the First Schools

The origins of writing probably go back to the ninth millennium B.C., when Near Eastern peoples used clay tokens as counters for record keeping. By the fourth millennium people had realized that drawing pictures of the tokens on clay was simpler

than making tokens. This breakthrough in turn suggested that more information could be conveyed by adding pictures of still other objects. The result was a complex system of pictographs, in which each sign pictured an object. These pictographs were the forerunners of a Sumerian form of writing known as *cuneiform*, from the Latin term for "wedge-shaped," used to describe the strokes of the stylus.

How did this pictographic system work, and how did it evolve into cuneiform writing? At first, if a scribe wanted to indicate a star, he simply drew a picture of it (line A of Figure 1.1) on a wet clay tablet, which became rock-hard when baked. Anyone looking at the picture would know what it meant and would think of the word for star. This complicated and laborious system had serious limitations. It could not represent abstract ideas or combinations of ideas. For instance, how could it depict a slave woman?

The solution appeared when the scribe discovered that signs could be combined to express meaning. To refer to a slave woman the scribe used the sign for woman (line B) and the sign for mountain (line C)—literally, "mountain woman" (line D). Because the Sumerians regularly obtained their slave women from the mountains, this combination of signs was easily understandable.

The next step was to simplify the system. Instead of drawing pictures, the scribe made conventionalized signs that were generally understood to represent ideas. Thus the signs became *ideograms*: they symbolized ideas. The sign for star could also be used to indicate heaven, sky, or even god.

The real breakthrough came when the scribe learned to use signs to represent sounds. For instance, the scribe drew two parallel wavy lines to indicate the word *a* or "water" (line E). Besides water, the word *a* in Sumerian also meant "in." The word *in* expresses a relationship that is very difficult to represent pictorially. Instead of trying to invent a sign to mean in, some clever scribe used the sign for water because the two words sounded alike. This phonetic use of signs made possible the combining of signs to convey abstract ideas.

The Sumerian system of writing was so complicated that only professional scribes mastered it, and even they had to study it for many years. By 2500 B.C. scribal schools flourished throughout Sumer. Most students came from wealthy families and were male. Each school had a master, teachers, and monitors. Discipline was strict, and students were caned for sloppy work and misbehavior. One graduate of a scribal school had few fond memories of the joy of learning:

My headmaster read my tablet, said:
"There is something missing," caned me.
. . . .
The fellow in charge of silence said:
"Why did you talk without permission," caned me.
The fellow in charge of the assembly said:
"Why did you stand at ease without permission,"
   caned me.[3]

The Sumerian system of schooling set the educational standards for Mesopotamian culture, and the Akkadians and, later, the Babylonians adopted its practices and techniques. Mesopotamian education always had a practical side because of the economic and administrative importance of scribes. Most scribes took administrative positions in the temple or palace, where they kept records of business transactions, accounts, and inventories. But scribal schools did not limit their curriculum to business affairs. They were also centers of culture and scholarship. Topics of study included mathematics, botany, and linguistics. Advanced students copied and studied the classics of Sumerian literature. Talented students and learned scribes wrote compositions of their own. As a result, many literary, mathematical, and religious texts survive today, giving a full picture of Mesopotamian intellectual and spiritual life.

Mesopotamian Thought and Religion

The Mesopotamians made significant and sophisticated advances in mathematics using a numerical system based on units of sixty, ten, and six. They developed the concept of place value—that the value of a number depends on where it stands in relation to other numbers. Mesopotamian mathematical texts are of two kinds: tables and problems. Scribes compiled tables of squares and square roots, cubes and cube roots, and reciprocals. They wrote texts of problems, which dealt not only with equations and pure mathematics but also with concrete problems, such as how to plan irrigation ditches. The Mesopotamians did not consider mathematics a purely theoretical science. The building of cities, palaces, temples, and canals demanded practical knowledge of geometry and trigonometry.

Mesopotamian medicine was a combination of magic, prescriptions, and surgery. Mesopotamians believed that demons and evil spirits caused sickness and that magic spells could drive them out. Or, they believed, the physician could force the demon out by giving the patient a foul-tasting prescription. As medical knowledge grew, some prescriptions were found to work and thus were true medicines. Surgeons practiced a dangerous occupation, and the penalties for failure were severe. One section of Hammurabi's law code (see page 18) decreed: "If a physician performed a major operation on a seignior with a bronze lancet and has caused the seignior's death, or he opened up the eye-socket of a seignior and has destroyed the seignior's eye, they shall cut off his hand."[4] No wonder that one medical text warned physicians to have nothing to do with a dying person.

Mesopotamian thought had a profound impact in theology and religion. The Sumerians originated many beliefs, and their successors added to them. The Mesopotamians believed that many gods run the world, but they did not consider all gods and goddesses equal. Some deities had very important jobs, taking care of music, law, sex, and victory, while others had lesser tasks, overseeing leatherworking and basketweaving. The god in charge of metalworking was hardly the equal of the god of wisdom.

Mesopotamian gods lived their lives much as human beings lived theirs. The gods were anthropomorphic, or human in form. Unlike men and women, they were powerful and immortal and could make themselves invisible. Otherwise, Mesopotamian gods and goddesses were very human: they celebrated with food and drink, and they raised families. They enjoyed their own "Garden of Eden," a green and fertile place. They could be irritable, vindictive, and irresponsible.

The Mesopotamians considered natural catastrophes the work of the gods. At times the Sumerians described their chief god, Enlil, as "the raging flood which has no rival." The gods, they believed, even used nature to punish the Mesopotamians. According to the myth of the Deluge, which gave rise to the biblical story of Noah, the god Enki warned Ziusudra, the Sumerian Noah:

A flood will sweep over the cult-centers;
To destroy the seed of mankind . . .
Is the decision, the word of the assembly of the
   gods.[5]

❖ **Sumerian Ram** In the art of many Near-Eastern cultures, animals served as symbols of fertility, linked to the gods. Here a ram is depicted in a thorn bush, an obvious symbol of a deity who has taken the form of an animal. *(Source: Courtesy of the Trustees of the British Museum)*

The Mesopotamians did not worship their deities because the gods were benevolent. Human beings were too insignificant to pass judgment on the conduct of the gods, and the gods were too superior to honor human morals. Rather, the Mesopotamians worshiped the gods because they were mighty. Likewise, it was not the place of men and women to understand the gods. The Sumerian equivalent to the biblical Job once complained to his god:

The man of deceit has conspired against me,
And you, my god, do not thwart him,
You carry off my understanding.[6]

The motives of the gods were not always clear. In times of affliction one could only pray and offer sacrifices to appease them.

The Mesopotamians had many myths to account for the creation of the universe. According to one Sumerian myth (echoed in Genesis, the first book of the Bible), only the primeval sea existed at first. The sea produced heaven and earth, which were united. Heaven and earth gave birth to Enlil, who separated them and made possible the creation of the other gods. Babylonian beliefs were similar. In the beginning was the primeval sea, the goddess Tiamat, who gave birth to the gods. When Tiamat tried to destroy the gods, Marduk, the chief god of the Babylonians, proceeded to kill her and divide her body and thus created the sky and earth. These myths are the earliest known attempts to answer the question, "How did it all begin?" The Mesopotamians obviously thought about these matters, as about the gods, in human terms. They never organized their beliefs into a philosophy, but their myths offered understandable explanations of natural phenomena. The myths were emotionally satisfying, and that was their greatest appeal.

Mesopotamian myths also explained the origin of human beings. In one myth the gods decided to make their lives easier by creating servants, whom they wanted to have made in their own image. Nammu, the goddess of the watery deep, brought the matter to Enki. After some thought, Enki instructed Nammu and the others:

Mix the heart of the clay that is over the abyss.
The good and princely fashioners will thicken the clay.
You, do you bring the limbs into existence.[7]

In Mesopotamian myth, as in Genesis, men and women were made in the divine image but without godlike powers. The Mesopotamians believed it their duty to supply the gods with sacrifices of food and drink and to house them in fine temples. In return, they hoped that the gods would be kind.

One of the Mesopotamians' oldest deities was Inanna, a complicated goddess who represented the passions of love and war. Although she could be kind, she could also be harsh. She took many forms, one of the most important being the symbol of mother-earth who gave birth to everything in the world. Inanna was also worshiped by the Semites as Ishtar, and her cult lasted into Roman times.

In addition to myths, the Sumerians produced the first epic poem, the *Epic of Gilgamesh*, which evolved as a reworking of at least five earlier myths (see Listening to the Past). An epic poem is a narration of the achievements, labors, and sometimes the failures of heroes that embodies a people's or a nation's conception of its own past. Historians can use epic poems to learn about various aspects of a society, and to that extent epics can be used as historical sources. The Sumerian epic recounts the wanderings of Gilgamesh—the semihistorical king of Uruk—and his companion Enkidu, their fatal meeting with the goddess Ishtar, after which Enkidu dies, and Gilgamesh's subsequent search for eternal life. Although Gilgamesh finds a miraculous plant that gives immortality to anyone who eats it, a great snake steals it from him. Despite this loss, Gilgamesh visits the lower world to bring Enkidu back to life, thereby learning of life after death. The *Epic of Gilgamesh* is not only an excellent piece of literature but also an intellectual triumph. It shows the Sumerians grappling with such enduring questions as life and death, mankind and deity, and immortality. Despite its great antiquity, it addresses questions of importance to people today.

Sumerian Society

Their harsh environment fostered a grim, even pessimistic, spirit among the Mesopotamians. The Sumerians sought to please and calm the gods, especially the patron deity of the city. Encouraged and directed by the traditional priesthood, which was dedicated to understanding the ways of the

✦ **Aerial View of Ur** This photograph gives a good idea of the size and complexity of Ur, one of the most powerful cities in Mesopotamia. In the lower right-hand corner stands the massive ziggurat of Umammu. *(Source: Georg Gerster/Comstock)*

gods, the people erected shrines in the center of each city and then built their houses around them. The best way to honor the gods was to make the shrine as grand and as impressive as possible, for gods who had a splendid temple might think twice about sending floods to destroy the city.

The temple had to be worthy of the gods, a symbol of their power, and it had to last. Special skills and materials were needed to build it. Only stone was suitable for its foundations and precious metals and colorful glazed tiles for its decoration. Since the Mesopotamians had to import both stone and metals, temple construction encouraged trade. Architects, engineers, craftsmen, and workers had to devote a great deal of thought, effort, and time to build the temple. By 2000 B.C. the result was Mesopotamia's first monumental architecture—the ziggurat, a massive stepped tower that dominated a city.

Once the ziggurat was built, the traditional priesthood assumed the additional duty of running it and performing the gods' rituals. The people of the city met the expenses of building and maintaining the temple and its priesthood by setting aside extensive tracts of land for that purpose. The priests took charge of the produce of the temple lands and the sacred flocks. Part of the yield went to feeding and clothing the priests and temple staff and for offerings to the gods. Part was sold or bartered to obtain goods needed for construction, maintenance, and ritual.

Until recently, the dominant position and wealth of the temple led historians to consider the Sumerian city-state an absolute theocracy, or government by an established priesthood. It is now known that the temple owned a large fraction, but not all, of the city's territory and did not govern the city. A king (lugal) or local governor (ensi) exercised political power, and most of the city's land was the property of individual citizens.

Sumerian society was a complex arrangement of freedom and dependence, and its members were divided into four categories: nobles, free clients of the nobility, commoners, and slaves. The nobility consisted of the king and his family, the chief priests, and high palace officials. Generally, the king rose to power as a war leader, elected by the citizenry, who established a regular army, trained it, and led it into battle. The might of the king and the frequency of warfare quickly made him the supreme figure in the city, and kingship soon became hereditary. The symbol of royal status was the palace, which rivaled the temple in grandeur.

The king and the lesser nobility held extensive tracts of land that were, like the estates of the temple, worked by slaves and clients. Clients were free men and women who were dependent on the nobility. In return for their labor, the clients received small plots of land to work for themselves. Although this arrangement assured the clients of a livelihood, the land they worked remained the possession of the nobility or the temple. Thus, not only did the nobility control most—and probably the best—land, they also commanded the obedience of a huge segment of society. They were the dominant force in Mesopotamian society.

Commoners were free citizens. They were independent of the nobility; however, they could not rival the nobility in social status and political power. Commoners belonged to large patriarchal families who owned land in their own right. Commoners could sell their land, if the family approved, but even the king could not legally take their land without their approval. Commoners had a voice in the political affairs of the city and full protection under the law.

Until comparatively recent times, slavery has been a fact of life throughout the history of Western society. Some Sumerian slaves were foreigners and prisoners of war. Some were criminals who had lost their freedom as punishment for their crimes. Still others served as slaves to repay debts. These were more fortunate than the others, because the law required that they be freed after three years. But all slaves were subject to whatever treatment their owners might mete out. They could be beaten and even branded. Yet they were not considered dumb beasts. Slaves engaged in trade and made profits. Indeed, many slaves bought their freedom. They could borrow money and received at least some legal protection.

✤ THE SPREAD OF MESOPOTAMIAN CULTURE

The Sumerians established the basic social, economic, and intellectual patterns of Mesopotamia, but the Semites played a large part in spreading Sumerian culture far beyond the boundaries of Mesopotamia. The interaction of the Sumerians and Semites, in fact, gives one of the very first glimpses of a phenomenon that can still be seen today. History provides abundant evidence of peoples of different origins coming together, usually on the borders of an established culture. The result was usually cultural change, outweighing any hostility, for each side learned from the other. The outcome in these instances was the evolution of a new culture that consisted of two or more old parts. Although the older culture almost invariably looked on the newcomers as inferior, the new just as invariably contributed something valuable to the old. So it was in 2331 B.C. The Semitic chieftain Sargon conquered Sumer and created a new empire. The symbol of his triumph was a new capital, the city of Akkad. Sargon, the first "world conqueror," led his armies to the Mediterranean Sea. Although his empire lasted only a few generations, it spread Mesopotamian culture throughout the Fertile Crescent, the belt of rich farmland that extends from Mesopotamia in the east up through Syria in the north and down to Egypt in the west (see Map 1.1).

Sargon's impact and the extent of Mesopotamian influence even at this early period have been dramatically revealed at Ebla in modern Syria. In 1964 archaeologists there unearthed a once-flourishing Semitic civilization that had assimilated political, intellectual, and artistic aspects of Mesopotamian culture. In 1975 the excavators uncovered thousands of clay tablets that proved that the people of Ebla had learned the art of writing from the Mesopotamians. Eblaite artists borrowed heavily from Mesopotamian art but developed their own style, which in turn influenced Mesopotamian artists. The Eblaites transmitted the heritage of Mesopotamia to other Semitic centers in Syria.

Further evidence of these developments came to light in November 1993, when American and Turkish archaeologists reported evidence of Sumerian influences far removed from Mesopotamia. At Tell Leilan in northern Syria and at Kazam Hoyuk in southern Turkey, researchers found proof of large urban centers that shared Sumerian culture as early as ca 2600 B.C. Finds included evidence of widespread literacy, a functioning bureaucracy, and links with Ebla and Mesopotamia. These discoveries also point to another conclusion. These frontier cities came under Sumerian influence not by conquest but because they found Mesopotamian culture attractive and useful. In this process, a universal culture developed in the an-

cient Near East, a culture basically Mesopotamian but fertilized by the traditions, genius, and ways of many other peoples.

The question to answer is why Mesopotamian culture had such an immediate and wide appeal. In the first place it was successful and enjoyed the prestige of its success. Newcomers wanted to find a respectable place in this old and venerated culture. It also provided an easy means of communication among people on a broad scale. The Eblaites could efficiently deal with the Mesopotamians and others who embraced this culture in ways that all could understand. Culture ignores borders. Despite local variations, so much common ground existed that similar political and economic institutions, exchange of ideas and religious beliefs, methods of writing, and a shared etiquette served as links among all who embraced Mesopotamian culture.

The Triumph of Babylon

Although the empire of Sargon was extensive, it was short-lived. The Akkadians, too, failed to solve the problems posed by Mesopotamia's geography and population pattern. Most scholars have attributed the fall of the Akkadian empire to internal problems and external invasions. Yet dramatic discoveries announced in August 1993 suggest strongly that climate also played a role in the demise of Akkadian power. Archaeologists have found evidence of a long, harsh drought, perhaps lasting as long as 300 years, that struck the northern regions of the empire. The areas most severely affected were in modern Iraq, Syria, and parts of southern Turkey. Abandonment of the northern cities led to a stream of refugees to the south, overtaxing the economic resources of the cities there and straining their social and political structures. Cuneiform tablets had earlier mentioned this migration. The turmoil that resulted from this large influx of peoples may have contributed to the fighting that consumed the Akkadian empire.

It was left to the Babylonians to unite Mesopotamia politically and culturally. The Babylonians were Amorites, a Semitic people who had migrated from Arabia and settled on the site of Babylon along the middle Euphrates, where that river runs close to the Tigris. Babylon enjoyed an excellent geographical position and was ideally suited to be the capital of Mesopotamia. It dominated trade on

❖ **Stele of Naramsin** Naramsin, the grandson of
Sargon, was one of the greatest of the Akkadian
kings. The topmost figure on this stele, or commemorative tablet, he displays his power by defeating his enemies in battle. Naramsin's horned
crown suggests that he considered himself divine.
(Source: Louvre © Photo R.M.N.)

the Tigris and Euphrates rivers: all commerce to
and from Sumer and Akkad had to pass by its walls.
It also looked beyond Mesopotamia. Babylonian
merchants followed the Tigris north to Assyria and
Anatolia. The Euphrates led merchants to Syria,
Palestine, and the Mediterranean. The city grew

great because of its commercial importance and
soundly based power.

Babylon was also fortunate to have a farseeing
and able king, Hammurabi (r. 1792–1750 B.C.).
Hammurabi set out to do three things: make Baby-
lon secure, unify Mesopotamia, and win for the
Babylonians a place in Mesopotamian civilization.
The first two he accomplished by conquering
Assyria in the north and Sumer and Akkad in the
south. Then he turned to his third goal.

Politically, Hammurabi joined in his kingship the
Semitic concept of the tribal chieftain and the
Sumerian idea of urban kingship. Culturally, he
encouraged the spread of myths that explained
how Marduk, the god of Babylon, had been
elected king of the gods by the other Mesopotamian deities. Hammurabi's success in making
Marduk the god of all Mesopotamians made Babylon the religious center of Mesopotamia. Through
Hammurabi's genius the Babylonians made their
own contribution to Mesopotamian culture—a
culture vibrant enough to maintain its identity
while assimilating new influences. Hammurabi's
conquests and the activity of Babylonian merchants
spread this enriched culture north to Anatolia and
west to Syria and Palestine.

Life Under Hammurabi

One of Hammurabi's most memorable accomplishments was the proclamation of a law code that
offers a wealth of information about daily life in
Mesopotamia. Hammurabi's was not the first law
code in Mesopotamia; indeed, the earliest goes
back to about 2100 B.C. Like earlier lawgivers,
Hammurabi proclaimed that he issued his laws on
divine authority "to establish law and justice in the
language of the land, thereby promoting the welfare of the people." Hammurabi's code inflicted
such penalties as mutilation, whipping, and burning. Despite its severity, a spirit of justice and a
sense of responsibility pervade the code. Hammurabi genuinely felt that his duty was to govern the
Mesopotamians as righteously as possible. He tried
to regulate the relations of his people so that they
could live together in harmony.

The Code of Hammurabi has two striking characteristics. First, the law differed according to the
social status of the offender. Aristocrats were not
punished as harshly as commoners, nor commoners as harshly as slaves. Second, the code demanded
that the punishment fit the crime. It called for "an

eye for an eye, and a tooth for a tooth," at least among equals. However, an aristocrat who destroyed the eye of a commoner or slave could pay a fine instead of losing his own eye. Otherwise, as long as criminal and victim shared the same social status, the victim could demand exact vengeance.

Hammurabi's code began with legal procedure. There were no public prosecutors or district attorneys, so individuals brought their own complaints before the court. Each side had to produce written documents or witnesses to support its case. In cases of murder, the accuser had to prove the defendant guilty; any accuser who failed to do so was put to death. This strict law was designed to prevent people from lodging groundless charges. The Mesopotamians were very worried about witchcraft and sorcery. Anyone accused of witchcraft, even if the charges were not proved, underwent an ordeal by water. The gods themselves would decide the case. The defendant was thrown into the Euphrates, which was considered the instrument of the gods. A defendant who sank was guilty; a defendant who floated was innocent. Another procedural regulation covered the conduct of judges. Once a judge had rendered a verdict, he could not change it. Any judge who did so was fined heavily and deposed. In short, the code tried to guarantee a fair trial and a just verdict.

Consumer protection is not a modern idea; it goes back to Hammurabi's day. Merchants and businessmen had to guarantee the quality of their goods and services. A boat builder who did sloppy work had to repair the boat at his own expense. A boatman who lost the owner's boat or sank someone else's boat replaced it and its cargo. Housebuilders guaranteed their work with their lives. Careless work could result in the collapse of a house and the death of its inhabitants. If that happened, the builder was put to death. A merchant who tried to increase the interest rate on a loan forfeited the entire amount. Hammurabi's laws tried to ensure that consumers got what they paid for and paid a just price.

Crime was a feature of Mesopotamian urban life just as it is in modern cities. Burglary was a serious problem, hard to control. Because houses were built of mud brick, it was easy for an intruder to dig through the walls. Hammurabi's punishment for burglary matched the crime. A burglar caught in the act was put to death on the spot, and his body was walled into the breach the burglar had made. The penalty for looting was also grim: any-

❖ **Dedication to the Sumerian Goddess Inanna** This alabaster and gold votive figurine dates to ca. 2850 B.C., and is typical of many other figures dedicated to the gods. This one was found in the excavation of a temple of the goddess Inanna at Nippur. *(Source: Iraq National Museum)*

one caught looting a burning house was thrown into the fire.

Mesopotamian taverns were notorious haunts of criminals, who often met there to make their plans. Tavernkeepers were expected to keep order and arrest anyone overheard planning a crime. Taverns were normally run by women, and they also served

Law Code of Hammurabi Hammurabi ordered his code to be inscribed on a stone pillar and set up in public. At the top of the pillar Hammurabi is depicted receiving the scepter of authority from the god Shamash. *(Source: Himer Verlag München)*

as houses of prostitution. Prostitution was disreputable but neither illegal nor regulated by law. Despite their social stigma, taverns were popular places, for Mesopotamians were fond of beer and wine. Tavernkeepers made a nice profit, but if they were caught increasing their profits by watering drinks, they were drowned.

Because farming was essential to Mesopotamian life, Hammurabi's code dealt extensively with agriculture. Tenant farming was widespread, and tenants rented land on a yearly basis. Instead of money they paid a portion of their crops as rent. Unless the land was carefully cultivated, it quickly reverted to wasteland. Therefore tenants faced severe penalties for neglecting the land or not working it at all. Since irrigation was essential to grow crops,

tenants had to keep the canals and ditches in good repair. Otherwise the land would be subject to floods and farmers to crippling losses. Anyone whose neglect of the canals resulted in damaged crops had to bear all the expense of the lost crops. Tenants who could not pay the costs were sold into slavery.

Sheep raising was very lucrative because textile production was a major Mesopotamian industry. The shepherd was a hired man with considerable responsibility. He was expected to protect the flock from wild animals, which were a constant problem, and to keep the sheep out of the crops. This strict regulation of agriculture paid rich dividends. The Mesopotamians often enjoyed bumper crops, which fostered a large and thriving population.

Hammurabi gave careful attention to marriage and the family. As elsewhere in the Near East, marriage had aspects of a business agreement. The prospective groom and the father of the future bride arranged everything. The man offered the father a bridal gift, usually money. If the man and his bridal gift were acceptable, the father provided his daughter with a dowry. After marriage the dowry belonged to the woman (although the husband normally administered it) and was a means of protecting her rights and status. Once the two men agreed on financial matters, they drew up a contract; no marriage was considered legal without one. Either party could break off the marriage, but not without paying a stiff penalty. Fathers often contracted marriages while their children were still young. The girl either continued to live in her father's house until she reached maturity or went to live in the house of her father-in-law. During this time she was legally considered a wife. Once she and her husband came of age, they set up their own house.

The wife was expected to be rigorously faithful. The penalty for adultery was death. According to Hammurabi's code: "If the wife of a man has been caught while lying with another man, they shall bind them and throw them into the water."[8] The husband had the power to spare his wife by obtaining a pardon for her from the king. He could, however, accuse his wife of adultery even if he had not caught her in the act. In such a case she could try to clear herself before the city council that investigated the charge. If she was found innocent, she could take her dowry and leave her husband. If a woman decided to take the direct approach and kill her husband, she was impaled.

The husband had virtually absolute power over his household. He could even sell his wife and children into slavery to pay debts. Sons did not lightly oppose their fathers, and any son who struck his father could have his hand cut off. A father was free to adopt children and include them in his will. Artisans sometimes adopted children to teach them the family trade. Although the father's power was great, he could not disinherit a son without just cause. Cases of disinheritance became matters for the city to decide, and the code ordered the courts to forgive a son for his first offense. Only if a son wronged his father a second time could he be disinherited.

Law codes, preoccupied as they are with the problems of society, provide a bleak view of things. Other Mesopotamian documents give a happier glimpse of life. Although Hammurabi's code dealt with marriage in a hard-fisted fashion, a Mesopotamian poem tells of two people meeting secretly in the city. Their parting is delightfully romantic:

Come now, set me free, I must go home,
Kuli-Enlil . . . set me free, I must go home.
What can I say to deceive my mother?[9]

Countless wills and testaments show that husbands habitually left their estates to their wives, who in turn willed the property to their children. All this suggests happy family life. Hammurabi's code restricted married women from commercial pursuits, but financial documents prove that many women engaged in business without hindrance. Some carried on the family business, while others became wealthy landowners in their own right. Mesopotamians found their lives lightened by holidays and religious festivals. Traveling merchants brought news of the outside world and swapped marvelous tales. Despite their pessimism, the Mesopotamians enjoyed a vibrant and creative culture, a culture that left its mark on the entire Near East.

✤ EGYPT, THE LAND OF THE PHARAOHS (3100–1200 B.C.)

The Greek historian and traveler Herodotus in the fifth century B.C. called Egypt the "gift of the Nile." No other single geographical factor had such a fundamental and profound impact on the shaping of Egyptian life, society, and history as the

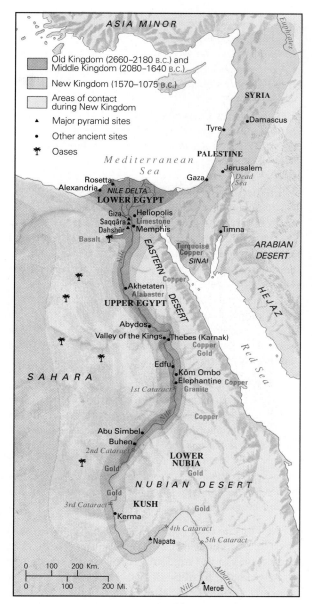

MAP 1.2 Ancient Egypt Geography and natural resources provided Egypt with centuries of peace and abundance.

Nile (Map 1.2). Unlike the rivers of Mesopotamia it rarely brought death and destruction by devastating entire cities. The river was primarily a creative force. The Egyptians never feared the relatively tame Nile in the way the Mesopotamians feared the Tigris. Instead, they sang its praises.

*Hail to thee, O Nile, that issues from the earth and
comes to keep Egypt alive! . . .
He that waters the meadows which Re created,
He that makes to drink the desert . . .
He who makes barley and brings emmer [wheat]
into being . . .
He who brings grass into being for the cattle . . .
He who makes every beloved tree to grow . . .
O Nile, verdant art thou, who makest man and cat-
tle to live.*[10]

In the mind of the Egyptians the Nile was the
supreme fertilizer and renewer of the land. Each
September the Nile floods its valley, transforming
it into a huge area of marsh or lagoon. By the end
of November the water retreats, leaving behind a
thin covering of fertile mud ready to be planted
with crops.

The annual flood made the growing of abundant
crops almost effortless, especially in southern
Egypt. Herodotus, used to the rigors of Greek
agriculture, was amazed by the ease with which the
Egyptians raised crops:

*For indeed without trouble they obtain crops from the
land more easily than all other men. . . . They do not
labor to dig furrows with the plough or hoe or do the
work which other men do to raise grain. But when the
river by itself inundates the fields and the water re-
cedes, then each man, having sown his field, sends
pigs into it. When the pigs trample down the seed, he
waits for the harvest. Then when the pigs thresh the
grain, he gets his crop.*[11]

As late as 1822, John Burckhardt, an English
traveler, watched nomads sowing grain by digging
large holes in the mud and throwing in seeds. The
extraordinary fertility of the Nile valley made it
easy to produce an annual agricultural surplus,
which in turn sustained a growing and prosperous
population.

Whereas the Tigris and Euphrates and their
tributaries carved up Mesopotamia into isolated
areas, the Nile unified Egypt. The river was the
region's principal highway, promoting easy communication throughout the valley. As individual
bands of settlers moved into the Nile valley, they
created stable agricultural communities. By about
3100 B.C. there were some forty of these communities in constant contact with one another. This
contact, encouraged and facilitated by the Nile,
virtually ensured the early political unification of
Egypt.

Egypt was fortunate in that it was nearly self-
sufficient. Besides the fertility of its soil, Egypt
possessed enormous quantities of stone, which
served as the raw material of architecture and
sculpture. Abundant clay was available for pottery,
as was gold for jewelry and ornaments. The raw
materials that Egypt lacked were close at hand. The
Egyptians could obtain copper from Sinai and timber from Lebanon. They had little cause to look
to the outside world for their essential needs, a fact
that helps to explain the insular quality of Egyptian
life.

Geography further encouraged isolation by closing Egypt off from the outside world. To the east
and west of the Nile valley stretch grim deserts.
The Nubian Desert and the cataracts of the Nile
discourage penetration from the south. Only in the
north did the Mediterranean Sea leave Egypt exposed. Thus geography shielded Egypt from invasion and from extensive immigration. Unlike the
Mesopotamians, the Egyptians enjoyed centuries
of peace and tranquillity during which they could
devote most of their resources to peaceful development of their distinctive civilization.

Yet Egypt was not completely sealed off. As early
as 3250 B.C., Mesopotamian influences, notably
architectural techniques and materials and perhaps
even writing, made themselves felt in Egyptian life.
Still later, from 1680 to 1580 B.C., northern Egypt
was ruled by foreign invaders, the Hyksos. Infre-
quent though they were, such periods of foreign
influence fertilized Egyptian culture without
changing it in any fundamental way.

The God-King of Egypt

The geographical unity of Egypt quickly gave rise
to political unification of the country under the
authority of a king whom the Egyptians called
"pharaoh." The details of this process have been
lost. Although some scholars have recently suggested that the origins of Egyptian kingship can be
found in Nubia, to the south of Egypt, the evidence is against the idea. First, the concept of
kingship is an early and virtually world-wide political notion. Second, the Nubian artifacts so far
found can be dated only by Egyptian archaeological finds. That suggests that the Nubians borrowed
and adapted some of the symbols of the pharaoh
and other aspects of Egyptian culture. What little
is known of Nubian kingship indicates typical rule
of a single region, in this case much of it moun-

❖ **Narmer Palette** This ceremonial object celebrates the deeds of Narmer, but it also illustrates several of the attributes of the pharaoh in general. On left at top, the conquering pharaoh views the decapitated corpse of an unknown enemy, showing his duty to defend Egypt by defeating its enemies. This same theme recurs on the right where the pharaoh—also represented by the falcon, symbol of Horus—is about to kill a captive. (*Source: Jean Vertut*)

tainous. In contrast, Egyptian kingship is intimately connected with the Nile valley. The pharaoh was the king of both Upper and Lower Egypt, a geographical situation that did not exist in Nubia.

Most probably, as was the case with the Mesopotamians and the Eblaites, the Egyptians and Nubians enjoyed a long period of mostly peaceful relations during which each learned from the other. Such exchanges of ideas involve the adaptation of certain aspects of culture to fit new, particular, and local circumstances. This situation is precisely what one routinely finds on frontiers. In these cases, all parties bring new ideas and customs together. As a result, they all assimilated what they desired and rejected what they found unnecessary. Although the Nubian concept of kingship did not apply to

Egyptian geographical conditions, the cultural bonds between the two peoples became so strong that they remained even after the Roman conquest of Egypt centuries later.

The Egyptians themselves told of a great king, Menes, who united Egypt into a single kingdom around 3100 B.C. Thereafter the Egyptians divided their history into dynasties, or families of kings. For modern historical purposes, however, it is more useful to divide Egyptian history into periods (see page 00). The political unification of Egypt ushered in the period known as the Old Kingdom, an era remarkable for prosperity, artistic flowering, and the evolution of religious beliefs.

In religion, the Egyptians developed complex, often contradictory, ideas about an afterlife. These

PERIODS OF EGYPTIAN HISTORY

Period	Dates	Significant Events
Archaic	3100–2660 B.C.	Unification of Egypt
Old Kingdom	2660–2180 B.C.	Construction of the pyramids
First Intermediate	2 80–2080 B.C.	Political chaos
Middle Kingdom	2080–1640 B.C.	Recovery and political stability
Second Intermediate	1640–1570 B.C.	Hyksos "invasion"
New Kingdom	1570–1075 B.C.	Creation of an Egyptian empire Akhenaten's religious policy

beliefs were all rooted in the environment. The climate of Egypt is so stable that change is cyclical and dependable: though the heat of summer bakes the land, the Nile always floods and replenishes it. The dry air preserves much that would decay in other climates. Thus there was an air of permanence about Egypt; the past was never far from the present.

This cyclical rhythm permeated Egyptian religious beliefs. According to the Egyptians, Osiris, a fertility god associated with the Nile, died each year, and each year his wife Isis brought him back to life. Osiris eventually became king of the dead, and he weighed human beings' hearts to determine whether they had lived justly enough to deserve everlasting life. Osiris's care of the dead was shared by Anubis, the jackal-headed god who annually helped Isis resuscitate Osiris. Anubis was the god of mummification, so essential to Egyptian funerary rites.

The focal point of religious and political life in the Old Kingdom was the pharaoh, who commanded the wealth, resources, and people of all Egypt. The pharaoh's power was such that the Egyptians considered him to be the falcon-god Horus in human form. The link between the pharaoh and the god Horus was doubly important. In Egyptian religion Horus was the son of Osiris (king of the dead), which meant that the pharaoh, a living god on earth, became one with Osiris after death. The pharaoh was not simply the mediator between the gods and the Egyptian people. Above

all, he was the power that achieved the integration between gods and human beings, between nature and society, that ensured peace and prosperity for the land of the Nile. The pharaoh was thus a guarantee to his people, a pledge that the gods of Egypt (strikingly unlike those of Mesopotamia) cared for their people.

The king's surroundings had to be worthy of a god. Only a magnificent palace was suitable for his home; in fact, the very word *pharaoh* means "great house." The king's tomb also had to reflect his might and exalted status. To this day the great pyramids at Giza near Cairo bear silent but magnificent testimony to the god-kings of Egypt.

The religious significance of the pyramid is as awesome as the political. The pharaoh as a god was the earthly sun, and the pyramid, which towered to the sky, helped him ascend the heavens after death. The pyramid provided the dead king with everything that he would need in the afterlife. His body had to be preserved from decay if his *ka*, an invisible counterpart of the body, was to survive. So the Egyptians developed an elaborate process of embalming the dead pharaoh, wrapping his corpse in cloth, and carving a statue of him in stone. The need for an authentic likeness of the pharaoh accounts for the naturalism of Egyptian portraiture. Artistic renderings of the pharaohs combine accuracy and the abstract in the effort to capture the essence of the living person. This approach produced that haunting quality of Egyptian sculpture—portraits of lifelike people imbued with a solemn, ageless, serene spirit.

The Pharaoh's People

Because the common folk stood at the bottom of the social and economic scale, they were always at the mercy of grasping officials. The arrival of the tax collector was never a happy occasion. One Egyptian scribe described the worst that could happen:

And now the scribe lands on the river-bank and is about to register the harvest-tax. The janitors carry staves and the Nubians rods of palm, and they say, Hand over the corn, though there is none. The cultivator is beaten all over, he is bound and thrown into a well, soused and dipped head downwards. His wife has been bound in his presence and his children are in fetters.[12]

That was an extreme situation. Nonetheless, taxes might amount to 20 percent of the harvest, and tax collection could be brutal.

On the other hand, everyone, no matter how lowly, theoretically had the right of appeal, and the account of one such appeal, "The Tale of the Eloquent Peasant," was a favorite Egyptian story. The hero of the tale, Khunanup, was robbed by the servant of the high steward, and Khunanup had to bring his case before the steward himself. When the steward delayed his decision, Khunanup openly accused him of neglecting his duty, saying, "The arbitrator is a spoiler; the peace-maker is a creator of sorrow; the smoother over of differences is a creator of soreness."[13] The pharaoh himself ordered the steward to give Khunanup justice, and the case was decided in the peasant's favor.

Egyptian society seems to have been a curious mixture of freedom and constraint. Slavery did not become widespread until the New Kingdom. There was neither a caste system nor a color bar, and humble people could rise to the highest positions if they possessed talent. On the other hand, most ordinary folk were probably little more than serfs who could not easily leave the land of their own free will. Peasants were also subject to forced

❖ **The Pyramids at Giza** Giza was the burial place of the pharaohs of the Old Kingdom and of their aristocracy, whose rectangular tombs are visible behind the middle pyramid. The small pyramids at the foot of the foremost pyramid probably belong to the pharaohs' wives. *(Source: Hirmer Verlag München)*

❖ **Hippopotamus Hunt** This wall painting depicts the success of two men in a small boat who have killed a hippopotamus, seen in the lower right-hand corner. Behind the hippopotamus swims a crocodile hoping for a snack. *(Source: Egyptian Museum SMPK, Berlin/Bildarchiv Preussischer Kulturbesitz)*

labor, including work on the pyramids and canals. Young men were drafted into the pharaoh's army, which served both as a fighting force and as a labor corps.

The vision of thousands of people straining to build the pyramids and countless artists adorning the pharaoh's tomb brings to the modern mind a

distasteful picture of oriental despotism. Indeed, the Egyptian view of life and society is alien to those raised on the Western concepts of individual freedom and human rights. To ancient Egyptians the pharaoh embodied justice and order—harmony among human beings, nature, and the divine. If the pharaoh was weak or allowed anyone to challenge his unique position, he opened the way to chaos. Twice in Egyptian history the pharaoh failed to maintain rigid centralization. During those two eras, known as the First and Second Intermediate periods, Egypt was exposed to civil war and invasion. Yet the monarchy survived, and in each period a strong pharaoh arose to crush the rebels or expel the invaders and restore order.

The Hyksos in Egypt (1640–1570 B.C.)

While Egyptian civilization flourished behind its bulwark of sand and sea, momentous changes were taking place in the ancient Near East, changes that would leave their mark even on rich, insular Egypt. These changes involved enormous and remarkable movements, especially of peoples who spoke Semitic tongues.

The original home of the Semites was perhaps the Arabian peninsula. Some tribes moved into northern Mesopotamia, others into Syria and Palestine, and still others into Egypt. Shortly after 1800 B.C. people whom the Egyptians called Hyksos, which means "Rulers of the Uplands," began to settle in the Nile Delta. Many scholars have sought the origins of the Hyksos. The evidence available indicates that they entered Egypt from the areas of modern Israel and Lebanon. Yet that is only a partial explanation. The movements of the Hyksos were in fact part of a larger pattern of migration of peoples during this period. The history of Mesopotamia records many such wanderings of people in search of better homes for themselves. Such nomads normally settled in and accommodated themselves with the native cultures. The process was mutual, for each group had something to give and to learn from the other.

So it was in Egypt, but Egyptian tradition, as later recorded by the priest Manetho in the third century B.C., depicted the coming of the Hyksos as a brutal invasion:

In the reign of Toutimaios—I do not know why—the wind of god blew against us. Unexpectedly from the regions of the east men of obscure race, looking for-

ward confidently to victory, invaded our land, and without a battle easily seized it all by sheer force. Having subdued those in authority in the land, they then barbarously burned our cities and razed to the ground the temples of the gods. They fell upon all the natives in an entirely hateful fashion, slaughtering them and leading both their children and wives into slavery. At last they made one of their people king, whose name was Salitis. This man resided at Memphis, leaving in Upper and Lower Egypt tax collectors and garrisons in strategic places.[14]

Although the Egyptians portrayed the Hyksos as a conquering horde, they were probably no more than nomads looking for good land. Their entry into the delta was probably gradual and generally peaceful. The Hyksos "invasion" was one of the fertilizing periods of Egyptian history; it introduced new ideas and techniques into Egyptian life.

The Hyksos brought with them the method of making bronze and casting it into tools and weapons that became standard in Egypt. They thereby brought Egypt fully into the Bronze Age culture of the Mediterranean world, a culture in which the production and use of bronze implements became basic to society. Bronze tools made farming more efficient than ever before because they were sharper and more durable than the copper tools they replaced. The Hyksos' use of bronze armor and weapons as well as horse-drawn chariots and the composite bow, made of laminated wood and horn and far more powerful than the simple wooden bow, revolutionized Egyptian warfare. However much the Egyptians learned from the Hyksos, Egyptian culture eventually absorbed the newcomers. The Hyksos came to worship Egyptian gods and modeled their monarchy on the pharaonic system.

The New Kingdom: Revival and Empire (1570–1200 B.C.)

Politically, Egypt was only in eclipse. The Egyptian sun shone again when a remarkable line of kings, the pharaohs of the Eighteenth Dynasty, arose to challenge the Hyksos. These pharaohs pushed the Hyksos out of the delta, subdued Nubia in the south, and conquered Palestine and parts of Syria in the northeast. They fought inconclusively with the Hurrians, who had migrated into the upper Euphrates from the north and created there the new Hurrian kingdom of Mitanni. In this way, Egyptian warrior-pharaohs inaugurated the New Kingdom—a period in Egyptian history characterized by enormous wealth and conscious imperialism. During this period, probably for the first time, widespread slavery became a feature of Egyptian life. The pharaoh's armies returned home leading hordes of slaves, who constituted a new labor force for imperial building projects.

The kings of the Eighteenth Dynasty created the first Egyptian empire. They ruled Palestine and Syria through their officers and incorporated into the kingdom of Egypt the neighboring region of Nubia. Egyptian religion and customs flourished in Nubia, making a huge impact on African culture there and in neighboring areas. The warrior-kings celebrated their success with monuments on a scale unparalleled since the pharaohs of the Old Kingdom had built the pyramids. Even today the colossal granite statues of these pharaohs and the rich tomb objects of Tutankhamen ("King Tut") testify to the might and splendor of the New Kingdom.

One of the most extraordinary of this unusual line of kings was Akhenaten (r. 1367–1350 B.C.), a pharaoh more concerned with religion than with conquest. Nefertiti, his wife and queen, encouraged his religious bent. The precise nature of Akhenaten's religious beliefs remains debatable. The problem began during his own lifetime. His religion was often unpopular among the people and the traditional priesthood, and its practice declined in the later years of his reign. After his death, it was condemned and denounced; consequently, not much is known about it. Most historians, however, agree that Akhenaten and Nefertiti were monotheists; that is, they believed that the sun-god Aton, whom they worshiped, was universal, the only god. They considered all other Egyptian gods and goddesses frauds and disregarded their worship. Yet their belief suffered from an obvious flaw. The pharaoh himself was considered the son of god, and monotheism obviously cannot have two gods. What Akhenaten meant by monotheism is that only Aton among the traditional Egyptian deities was god.

The religious notions and actions of Akhenaten and Nefertiti were in direct opposition to traditional Egyptian beliefs. The Egyptians had long worshiped a host of gods, chief among whom was Amon-Re. Originally Amon and Re had been two distinct sun-gods, but the Egyptians merged them and worshiped Amon-Re as the king of the gods. Furthermore, many Egyptians were sincerely devoted to their older gods, whom they thought had preserved Egypt and would grant them life after death.

To genuine religious sentiments were added the motives of the traditional priesthood. Although many priests were scandalized by Akhenaten's brand of monotheism, many others were concerned more about their own welfare. By deposing the old gods Akhenaten destroyed the priests' livelihood and their reason for existence. On grounds of pure self-interest, the established priesthood opposed Akhenaten. Opposition in turn drove the pharaoh to intolerance and persecution. With a

 Akhenaten and Aten This relief shows the pharaoh and his family giving offerings to Aten, who is represented as the sun. It also demonstrates a new realism in Egyptian art. *(Source: Egyptian Museum, Cairo)*

vengeance he tried to root out the old gods and their rituals.

Akhenaten's monotheism, imposed from above, failed to find a place among the people. The prime reason for Akhenaten's failure is that his god had no connection with the past of the Egyptian people, who trusted the old gods and felt comfortable praying to them. Average Egyptians were no doubt distressed and disheartened when their familiar gods were outlawed, for those gods were the heavenly powers that had made Egypt powerful and unique. The fanaticism and persecution that accompanied the new monotheism were in complete defiance of the Egyptian tradition of tolerant polytheism, or worship of several gods. Thus, when Akhenaten died, his religion died with him.

✚ THE HITTITE EMPIRE

At about the time the Hyksos entered the Nile Delta, the Hittites, who had long been settled in Anatolia (modern Turkey), became a major power in that region and began to expand eastward (Map 1.3). The Hittites were an Indo-European people. The term *Indo-European* refers to a large family of languages that includes English, most of the languages of modern Europe, Greek, Latin, Persian, and Sanskrit, the sacred tongue of ancient India. During the eighteenth and nineteenth centuries, European scholars learned that peoples who spoke related languages had spread as far west as Ireland and as far east as central Asia. In the twentieth century, linguists deciphered the language of the Hittites and the Linear B script of Mycenaean Greece. When both languages proved to be Indo-European, scholars were able to form a clearer picture of these vast movements. Archaeologists were able to date the migrations roughly and put them into their historical context.

The Rise of the Hittites

Until recently, scholars thought that as part of these vast movements the Hittites entered Anatolia around 1800 B.C. Current archaeological work and new documents, however, prove that Hittites had settled there at least as early as 2700 B.C. Nor did they overrun the country in a sweeping invasion, burning, looting, and destroying. Their arrival and diffusion seem in fact to have been rather peaceful,

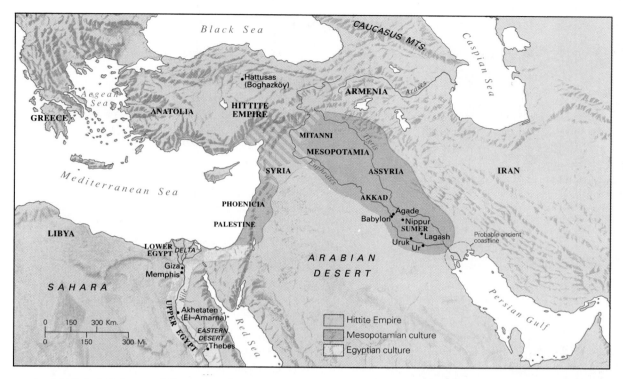

✦ **MAP 1.3 Balance of Power in the Near East** This map shows the regions controlled by the Hittites and Egyptians at the height of their power. The striped area represents the part of Mesopotamia conquered by the Hittites during their expansion eastward.

accompanied by intermarriage and alliance with the natives.

The rise of the Hittites to prominence in Anatolia is reasonably clear. During the nineteenth century B.C. the native kingdoms in the area engaged in suicidal warfare that left most of Anatolia's once-flourishing towns in ashes and rubble. In this climate of exhaustion the Hittite king Hattusilis I built a hill citadel at Hattusas, the modern Boghazköy, from which he led his Hittites against neighboring kingdoms. Hattusilis's grandson and successor, Mursilis I (ca 1595 B.C.), extended the Hittite conquests as far as Babylon. With help from the Kassites, a people who had newly settled along the upper reaches of the Euphrates River, Mursilis captured the city and snuffed out the dynasty of Hammurabi. While the Hittites carried off Babylonian loot, the Kassites took control of the territory. Upon his return home, the victorious Mursilis was assassinated by members of his own family, an act that plunged the kingdom into confusion and opened the door to foreign invasion. Mursilis's career is representative of the success and weakness of the Hittites. They were extremely vulnerable to attack by vigilant and tenacious enemies. Yet, once they were united behind a strong king, the Hittites were a power to be reckoned with.

Hittite Society

The geography of central Anatolia encouraged the rise of self-contained agricultural communities. Each was probably originally ruled by a petty king, but under the Hittites a group of local officials known as the "Elders" handled community affairs. Besides the farming population, Hittite society included a well-defined group of artisans who fashioned pottery, cloth, leather goods, and metal tools. Documents also report that traveling merchants peddled goods and gossip, reminding individual communities that they were part of a larger world. Like many other societies, ancient and modern, the Hittites held slaves, who nonetheless enjoyed certain rights under the law.

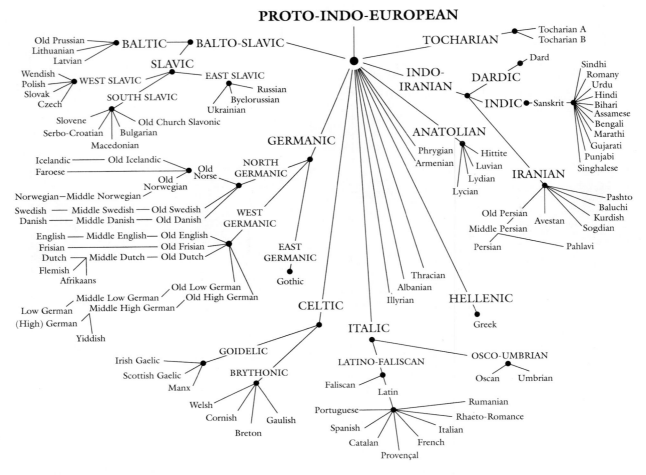

 Indo-European Languages This schematic tree of the Indo-European languages demonstrates at a glance the richness, complexity, and relationships of the major Western languages. From the original Proto-Indo-European language to English, French, and Italian is a long way. Yet after centuries of careful research, linguists have been able to demonstrate their common features as well as their differences. *(Source: The American Heritage Dictionary. American Heritage Publishing Co., Inc. and Houghton Mifflin Company: 1973, inside back cover)*

At the top of Hittite society was the aristocracy, among whom the relatives of the king constituted a privileged group. The king's relations were a mighty and often unruly group who served as the chief royal administrators. Hittite nobles often revolted against the king, a tendency that weakened central authority and left Hittite society open to outside attack. Below the nobles stood the warriors, who enjoyed the right to meet in their own assembly, the *pankus*. The pankus met to hear the will of the king, but it could not itself vote on policy. It was, however, a court of law, with the authority to punish criminals.

Just as the aristocracy stood at the head of society, so the king and queen stood above the aristocracy. The king was supreme commander of the army, chief judge, and supreme priest. He carried on all diplomatic dealings with foreign powers and in times of war personally led the Hittite army into the field. The queen, who was highly regarded, held a strong, independent position. She had important religious duties to perform, and some queens even engaged in diplomatic correspondence with foreign queens.

The Hittites are typical of many newcomers to the ancient Near East in that they readily assimi-

✦ **Hittite Sphinx Gate** Little praise can be heaped upon Hittite art, but this sphinx was a symbol of divine protection of the city of Alaca Hüyük. It was common in much of the Near East to use ferocious-looking animals at the city gates to ward off evil. *(Source: Antonello Perissinotto, Padua)*

lated the cultures that they found. Soon they fell under the powerful spell of the more advanced Mesopotamian culture. The Hittites adopted the cuneiform script for their own language. Hittite kings published law codes, just as Hammurabi had done. Royal correspondence followed Mesopotamian forms. The Hittites delighted in Mesopotamian myths, legends, epics, and art. To the credit of the Hittites, they used these Mesopotamian borrowings to create something of their own.

The Era of Hittite Greatness (ca 1475–ca 1200 B.C.)

The Hittites, like the Egyptians of the New Kingdom, eventually produced an energetic and capable line of kings who restored order and rebuilt Hittite power. They did so by controlling the aristocracy, securing central Anatolia, and regaining Syria.

Around 1300 B.C. the Hittites stopped the Egyptian army of Rameses II at the battle of Kadesh in Syria. Having fought each other to a standstill, the Hittites and Egyptians first made peace, then an alliance. Alliance was followed by friendship, and friendship by active cooperation. The two greatest powers of the early Near East tried to make war between them impossible.

They next included the Babylonians in their diplomacy. All three empires developed an official etiquette in which they treated one another as "brothers." They made alliances for offensive and defensive protection, and swore to uphold one another's authority. These contacts facilitated the exchange of ideas throughout the Near East. Furthermore, the Hittities passed much knowledge and lore from the Near East to the newly arrived Greeks in Europe (see Chapter 3). The details of Hittite contact with the Greeks are unknown, but enough literary themes and physical objects exist to prove the connection.

✦ THE FALL OF EMPIRES (CA 1200 B.C.)

Like the Hittite kings, Rameses II (ca 1290–1224 B.C.) used the peace after the battle of Kadesh to promote the prosperity of his own kingdom. Free from the expense and waste of warfare, he concentrated the income from the natural wealth and the foreign trade of Egypt on internal affairs. In the age-old tradition of the pharaohs, he began new building projects that brought both employment to his subjects and grandeur to Egypt. From Nubia to the delta of the Nile he bedecked his kingdom with grand, new monuments. Once again, Egypt was wealthy and secure within its natural boundaries. In many ways, he was the last great pharaoh of Egypt.

This stable and generally peaceful situation endured until the late thirteenth century B.C., when both the Hittite and the Egyptian empires were destroyed by invaders. The most famous of these marauders, called the "Sea Peoples" by the Egyptians, remain one of the puzzles of ancient history. Despite much new work, modern archaeology is still unable to identify the Sea Peoples satisfactorily. The reason for this uncertainty is that the Sea Peoples were a collection of peoples who went their own, individual ways after their attacks on the Hittities and Egyptians. It is known, however, that their incursions were part of a larger movement of peoples. Although there is serious doubt about whether the Sea Peoples alone overthrew the Hittites, they did deal both the Hittites and the Egyptians a hard blow, making the Hittites vulnerable to overland invasion from the north and driving the Egyptians back to the Nile Delta. The Hittites fell under the external blows, but the Egyptians, shaken and battered, retreated to the delta and held on.

SUMMARY

For thousands of years Paleolithic peoples roamed this planet seeking game. Although many groups of Paleolithic peoples relied partly on agriculture, they lived a largely nomadic life. Only in the Neolithic Age—with the invention of new stone tools, a reliance on sustained agriculture, and the domestication of animals—did people begin to live in permanent locations. These villages evolved into towns, where people began to create new social bonds and political organizations. The result was economic prosperity.

The earliest area where these developments led to genuine urban societies is Mesopotamia. Here, the Sumerians and then other Mesopotamians developed writing, which enabled their culture to be passed on to others. The wealth of the Mesopotamians made it possible for them to devote time to history, astronomy, urban planning, medicine, and other arts and sciences. Mesopotamian culture was so rich and advanced that neighboring peoples eagerly adopted it, thereby spreading it through much of the Near East.

Nor were the Mesopotamians alone in advancing the civilization of the day. In Egypt another strong culture developed, one that made an impact in Africa, the Near East, and, later, in Greece. The Egyptians too enjoyed such prosperity that they developed writing of their own, mathematical skills, and religious beliefs that influenced the lives of their neighbors. Into this world came the Hittites, an Indo-European people who were culturally less advanced than the Mesopotamians and Egyptians. The Hittites learned from their neighbors and rivals, but they also introduced their own sophisticated political system for administering their empire, a system that in some ways influenced both their contemporaries and later peoples.

NOTES

1. L. Eiseley, *The Unexpected Universe* (New York: Harcourt Brace Jovanovich, 1969), p. 102.
2. W. K. Loftus, *Travels and Researches in Chaldaea and Susiana* (New York: R. Carter & Brothers, 1857), p. 163.
3. Quoted in S. N. Kramer, *The Sumerians* (Chicago: University of Chicago Press, 1964), p. 238. John Buckler is the translator of all uncited quotations from a foreign language in Chapters 1–6.
4. J. B. Pritchard, ed., *Ancient Near Eastern Texts*, 3d ed. (Princeton, N.J.: Princeton University Press, 1969), p. 175. Hereafter called ANET.
5. ANET, p. 44.

6. ANET, p. 590.
7. Kramer, p. 150.
8. ANET, p. 171.
9. Kramer, p. 251.
10. ANET, p. 372.
11. Herodotus, *The Histories* 2.14.
12. Quoted in A. H. Gardiner, "Ramesside Texts Relating to the Taxation and Transport of Corn," *Journal of Egyptian Archaeology* 27 (1941): 19–20.
13. A. H. Gardiner, "The Eloquent Peasant," *Journal of Egyptian Archaeology* 9 (1923): 17.
14. Manetho, *History of Egypt,* frag. 42.75–77.

SUGGESTED READING

Those interested in the tangled and incomplete story of human evolution will be rewarded by a good deal of new work, much of it difficult. C. E. Oxnard, *Fossils, Teeth and Sex* (1987), concludes that the search for the "missing link" is the wrong approach because the question is ultimately impossible to answer. I. Rouse, *Migrations in Prehistory* (1989), studies population movements using information from cultural remains. A broad study about women's role in these events comes from M. Ehrenberg, *Women in Prehistory* (1989).

Some very illuminating general studies of Near Eastern developments have recently reached print. H. W. F. Saggs, *Civilization before Greece and Rome* (1989), provides a fresh analysis of the period that incorporates archaeological and literary evidence to discuss the many achievements of ancient Eastern societies. Similar in nature is A. B. Knapp, *The History and Culture of Ancient Western Asia and Egypt* (1988), a good synthesis by an able scholar. H. J. Nissen examines a broad range of subjects in *The Early History of the Ancient Near East* (1988), which covers the period from 9000 to 2000 B.C., and in *Archaic Bookkeeping* (1993), which discusses both the development of early writing and its use in the administration of the ancient economy. Most welcome is the publication of D. Schmandt-Besserat's two-volume work on the origins of writing: *Before Writing,* vol. I (1992), which explores the development of cuneiform writing, and vol. II (1992), which provides the reader with the actual evidence. There is nothing to match it on the topic.

H. Crawford, *Sumer and the Sumerians* (1991), gives a fresh appraisal of the Sumerians and poses some intriguing questions. In a very ambitious and thoughtful book, G. Algaze, *The Uruk World System* (1993), examines how the early Mesopotamians expanded their civilization. Older, but still valuable, is H. W. F. Saggs, *Everyday Life in Babylonia and Assyria* (1965), which offers a delightful glimpse of Mesopotamian life. G. Pettinato, the excavator of Ebla, gives the most thorough description of the site and its importance in *Ebla* (1991).

N. Grimal, *A History of Ancient Egypt* (1992), provides the most recent reassessment of Egyptian history. A bit older but still useful is C. G. Kemp, *Ancient Egypt: Anatomy of a Civilization* (1988), a comprehensive study of Egyptian society. A. Blackman, *Gods, Priests and Men* (1993), is a series of studies in the religion of pharaonic Egypt. B. S. Lesko, *The Remarkable Women of Ancient Egypt,* 2d ed. (1987), is a brief survey of aristocratic and ordinary women that concludes that Egyptian women led freer lives than women of the Greco-Roman period. G. Robins, *Women in Ancient Egypt* (1993), which is richly illustrated, adds visual information to the literary sources. W. L. Moran, *The Amarna Letters* (1992), has translated the Egyptian documents that are so important to the understanding of events in the New Kingdom. Moran also includes a commentary to the documents that explains their significance. D. B. Redford, *Akenaten: The Heretic King* (1984), puts Akhenaten into his historical context, both political and religious. The title of L. Manniche, *Sexual Life in Ancient Egypt* (1987), aptly describes the book's subject. M. Lichtheim, *Ancient Egyptian Literature,* 3 vols. (1975–1980), is a selection of readings covering the most important periods of Egyptian history.

O. R. Gurney, *The Hittites*, 2d ed. (1954), is still a fine introduction by an eminent scholar. Good also is J. G. MacQueen, *The Hittites and Their Contemporaries in Asia Minor,* 2d ed. (1986). J. P. Mallory, *In Search of the Indo-Europeans* (1989), uses language, archaeology, and myth to study the Indo-Europeans. The 1960s were prolific years for archaeology in Turkey. A brief survey by one of the masters of the field is J. Mellaart, *The Archaeology of Modern Turkey* (1978), which also tests a great number of widely held historical interpretations. The Sea Peoples have been recently studied by T. and M. Dothan, *People of the Sea* (1992), who concentrate their work on the Philistines.

A truly excellent study of ancient religions, from Sumer to the late Roman Empire, is M. Eliade, ed., *Religions of Antiquity* (1989), which treats concisely but amply all of the religions mentioned in Chapters 1 through 6.

LISTENING TO THE
PAST

A Quest for Immortality

The human desire to escape the grip of death, to achieve immortality, is one of the oldest wishes of all peoples. The Sumerian Epic of Gilgamesh *is the earliest recorded treatment of this topic. The oldest elements of the epic go back at least to the third millennium B.C. According to tradition, Gilgamesh was a king of Uruk whom the Sumerians, Babylonians, and Assyrians considered a hero-king and a god. In the story Gilgamesh and his friend Enkidu set out to attain immortality and join the ranks of the gods. They attempt to do so by performing wondrous feats against fearsome agents of the gods, who are determined to thwart them.*

During their quest Enkidu dies. Gilgamesh, more determined than ever to become immortal, begins seeking anyone who might tell him how to do so. His journey involves the effort not only to escape from death but also to reach an understanding of the meaning of life.

The passage begins with Enkidu speaking of a dream that foretells his own death.

Listen, my friend [Gilgamesh], this is the dream I dreamed last night. The heavens roared, and earth rumbled back an answer; between them I stood before an awful being, the sombre-faced man-bird; he had directed on me his purpose. His was a vampire face, his foot was a lion's foot, his hand was an eagle's talon. He fell on me and his claws were in my hair, he held me fast and I smothered; then he transformed me so that my arms became wings covered with feathers. He turned his stare towards me, and he led me away to the palace of Irkalla, the Queen of Darkness [the goddess of the underworld; in other words, an agent of death], to the house from which none who enters ever returns, down the road from which there is no coming back.

At this point Enkidu dies, whereupon Gilgamesh sets off on his quest for the secret of immortality. During his travels he meets with Siduri, the wise and good-natured goddess of wine, who gives him the following advice.

Gilgamesh, where are you hurrying to? You will never find that life for which you are looking. When the gods created man they allotted to him death, but life they retained in their own keeping. As for you, Gilgamesh, fill your belly with good things; day and night, night and day, dance and be merry, feast and rejoice. Let your clothes be fresh, bathe yourself in water, cherish the little child that holds your hand, and make your wife happy in your embrace; for this too is the lot of man.

Ignoring Siduri's advice, Gilgamesh continues his journey, until he finds Utnapishtim. Meeting Utnapishtim is especially important because, like Gilgamesh, he was once a mortal, but the gods so favored him that they put him in an eternal paradise. Gilgamesh puts to Utnapishtim the question that is the reason for his quest.

Oh, father Utnapishtim, you who have entered the assembly of the gods, I wish to question you concerning the living and the dead, how shall I find the life for which I am searching?

Utnapishtim said "There is no permanence. Do we build a house to stand forever, do we seal a contract to hold for all time? Do brothers divide an inheritance to keep forever, does the flood-time of rivers endure? . . . What is there between the master and the servant when both have fulfilled their doom? When the Anunnaki [the gods of the underworld], the judges, come together, and Mammetun [the goddess of fate] the mother of destinies, together they decree the fates of men. Life and death they allot but the day of death they do not disclose.

Then Gilgamesh said to Utnapishtim the Faraway, "I look at you now, Utnapishtim, and your appearance is no different from mine; there is nothing strange in your features. I thought I should find you like a hero prepared for battle, but you lie here taking your ease on your back. Tell me truly, how was it that you came to enter the company of the gods and to possess everlasting life?" Utnapishtim said to Gilgamesh, "I shall reveal to you a mystery, I shall tell you a secret of the gods."

Utnapishtim then tells Gilgamesh of a time when the great god Enlil had become angered with the Sumerians and encouraged the other gods to wipe out humanity. The god Ea, however, warned Utnapishtim about the gods' decision to send a great flood to destroy the Sumerians. He commanded Utnapishtim to build a boat big enough to hold his family, various artisans, and all animals in order to survive the flood that was to come. Although Enlil was infuriated by the Sumerians' survival, Ea rebuked him. Then Enlil relented and blessed Utnapishtim with eternal paradise. After telling the story, Utnapishtim foretells Gilgamesh's fate.

Utnapishtim said, ". . . The destiny was fulfilled which the father of the gods, Enlil of the mountain, had decreed for Gilgamesh: In nether-earth the darkness will show him a light: of mankind, all that are known, none will leave a monument for generations to compare with his. The heroes, the wise men, like the new moon have their waxing and waning. Men will say, Who has ever ruled with might and power like his? As in the dark month, the month of shadows, so without him there is no light. O Gilgamesh, this was the meaning of your dream [of immortality]. You were given the kingship, such was your destiny, everlasting life was not your destiny. Because of this do not be sad at heart, do not be grieved or oppressed; he [Enlil] has given you power to bind and to loose, to be the darkness and the light of mankind. He has given unexampled supremacy over the people, victory in battle from which no fugitive returns, in forays and assaults from which there is no going back. But do not abuse this power, deal justly with your servants in the palace, deal justly before the face of the Sun."

✢ Gilgamesh, from decorative panel of a lyre unearthed at Ur. (*Source: The University Museum, University of Pennsylvania*)

Questions for Analysis

1. What does *The Epic of Gilgamesh* reveal about Sumerian attitudes toward the gods and human beings?

2. At the end of his quest, did Gilgamesh achieve immortality? If so, what was the nature of that immortality?

3. What does the epic tell us about Sumerian views of the nature of human life? Where do human beings fit into the cosmic world?

Source: THE EPIC OF GILGAMESH, translated by N. K. Sanders. Copyright © 1972 by Penguin Books, Ltd.

2

Small Kingdoms and Mighty Empires in the Near East

✥ The migratory invasions that brought down the Hittites and stunned the Egyptians in the late thirteenth century B.C. ushered in an era of confusion and weakness. Although much was lost in the chaos, the old cultures of the ancient Near East survived to nurture new societies. In the absence of powerful empires, the Phoenicians, Syrians, Hebrews, and many other peoples carved out small independent kingdoms, until the Near East was a patchwork of them. During this period Hebrew culture and religion evolved under the influence of urbanism, kings, and prophets.

In the ninth century B.C. this jumble of small states gave way to an empire that for the first time embraced the entire Near East. Yet the very ferocity of the Assyrian Empire led to its downfall only two hundred years later. In 550 B.C. the Persians and Medes, who had migrated into Iran, created a "world empire" stretching from Anatolia in the west to the Indus valley in the east. For over two hundred years the Persians gave the ancient Near East peace and stability.

- How did Egypt, its political greatness behind it, pass on its cultural heritage to its African neighbors?

- How did the Hebrew state evolve, and what was daily life like in Hebrew society?

- What forces helped to shape Hebrew religious thought, still powerfully influential in today's world?

- What enabled the Assyrians to overrun their neighbors, and how did their cruelty finally cause their undoing?

- Last, how did Iranian nomads create the Persian Empire?

✥ ✥ ✥ ✥ ✥ ✥ ✥ ✥ ✥

Reconstruction of the "Ishtar Gate," Babylon, early sixth century, B.C. In the Berlin Museum. *(Source: Staatlich e Museen zu Berlin)*

✤ EGYPT, A SHATTERED KINGDOM

The invasions of the Sea Peoples brought the great days of Egyptian power to an end. The long wars against invaders weakened and impoverished Egypt, causing political upheaval and economic chaos. One scribe left behind a somber portrait of Egypt stunned and leaderless:

The land of Egypt was abandoned and every man was a law to himself. During many years there was no leader who could speak for others. Central government lapsed, small officials and headmen took over the whole land. Any man, great or small, might kill his neighbor. In the distress and vacuum that followed . . . men banded together to plunder one another. They treated the gods no better than men, and cut off the temple revenues.[1]

No longer able to dream of foreign conquests, Egypt looked to its own security from foreign invasion. Egyptians suffered a four-hundred-year period of political fragmentation, a new dark age known to Egyptian specialists as the Third Intermediate Period (eleventh–seventh centuries B.C.).

The decline of Egypt was especially sharp in foreign affairs. Whereas the pharaohs of the Eighteenth Dynasty had held sway as far abroad as Syria, their weak successors found it unsafe to venture far from home. In the wake of the Sea Peoples, numerous small kingdoms sprang up in the Near East, each fiercely protective of its own independence. To them Egypt was a memory, and foreign princes often greeted Egyptian officials with suspicion or downright contempt. In the days of Egypt's greatness, petty kings would never have dared to treat Egyptian officials in such a humiliating fashion.

Disrupted at home and powerless abroad, Egypt fell prey to invasion by its African neighbors. Libyans from North Africa filtered into the Nile Delta, where they established independent dynasties. Indeed, from 950 to 730 B.C. northern Egypt was ruled by Libyan pharaohs. The Libyans built cities, and for the first time a sturdy urban life grew up in the delta. Although the coming of the Libyans changed the face of the delta, the Libyans genuinely admired Egyptian culture and eagerly adopted Egypt's religion and way of life.

In southern Egypt, meanwhile, the pharaoh's decline opened the way to the energetic Nubians, who extended their authority northward throughout the Nile valley. Nubian influence in these years was pervasive but not destructive. Since the imperial days of the Eighteenth Dynasty (see pages 27–28), the Nubians, too, had adopted many features of Egyptian culture. Now Nubian kings and aristocrats embraced Egyptian culture wholesale. The thought of destroying the heritage of the pharaohs would have struck them as stupid and barbaric. Thus the Nubians and the Libyans repeated an old Near Eastern phenomenon: new peoples conquered old centers of political and military power but were assimilated into the older culture.

The reunification of Egypt occurred late and unexpectedly. With Egypt distracted and disorganized by foreign invasions, an independent African state, the kingdom of Kush, grew up in the region of modern Sudan with its capital at Nepata. Like the Libyans, the Kushites, worshiped Egyptian gods and used Egyptian hieroglyphs. In the eighth century B.C. their king, Piankhy, swept through the entire Nile valley from Nepata in the south to the delta in the north. United once again, Egypt enjoyed a brief period of peace during which Egyptians continued to assimilate their conquerors. In the kingdom of Kush, Egyptian methods of administration and bookkeeping, arts and crafts, and economic practices became common, especially among the aristocracy. Nonetheless, reunification of the realm did not lead to a new Egyptian empire. In the centuries between the fall of the New Kingdom and the recovery of Egypt, several small but vigorous kingdoms had taken root and grown to maturity in the ancient Near East. By 700 B.C. Egypt was once again a strong kingdom, but no longer a mighty empire.

Yet Egypt's legacy to its African neighbors remained vibrant and rich. By trading and exploring southward along the coast of the Red Sea, the Egyptians introduced their goods and ideas as far south as the land of Punt, probably a region on the Somali coast. As early as the New Kingdom, Egyptian pharaohs had exchanged gifts with the monarchs of Punt, and contact between the two areas persisted. Egypt was the primary civilizing force in Nubia, which became another version of the pharaoh's realm, complete with royal pyramids and Egyptian deities. Egyptian religion penetrated as far south as Ethiopia. Just as Mesopotamian culture enjoyed wide appeal throughout the Near East, so Egyptian culture had a massive impact on northeastern Africa. Nor was Egyptian influence limited to Africa. Through earlier military, economic, and diplomatic contacts with Palestine and Syria, Egyptian ideas and beliefs later found their way to Europe.

✤ THE CHILDREN OF ISRAEL

The fall of the Hittite Empire and Egypt's collapse created a vacuum of power in the western Near East that allowed for the rise of numerous small states. No longer crushed between the Hittites in the north and the Egyptians in the south, various peoples—some of them newcomers—created homes and petty kingdoms in Syria, Phoenicia, and Palestine. After the Sea Peoples had raided Egypt, a branch of them, known in the Bible as Philistines, settled along the coast of Palestine (Map 2.1). Establishing themselves in five cities somewhat inland from the sea, the Philistines set about farming and raising flocks.

Another sturdy new culture was that of the Phoenicians, a Semitic-speaking people who had long inhabited several cities along the coast of modern Lebanon. They had lived under the shadow of the Hittites and Egyptians, but in this period the Phoenicians enjoyed full independence. Unlike the Philistine newcomers, who turned from seafaring to farming, the Phoenicians took to the sea and became outstanding merchants and explorers. In trading ventures they sailed as far west as modern Tunisia, where in 813 B.C. they founded the city of Carthage, which would one day struggle with Rome for domination of the western Mediterranean. Phoenician culture was urban, based on the prosperous commercial centers of Tyre, Sidon, and Byblos. The Phoenicians' overwhelming cultural achievement was the development of an alphabet: they, unlike other literate peoples, used one letter to designate one sound, a system that vastly simplified writing and reading. The Greeks modified this alphabet and then used it to write their own language.

South of Phoenicia arose another small kingdom, the land of the ancient Jews or Hebrews. It is difficult to say precisely who the Hebrews were and what brought them to this area because virtually the only source for much of their history is the Bible, which is essentially a religious document. Even though it contains much historical material,

✤ **MAP 2.1 Small Kingdoms of the Near East**
This map illustrates the political fragmentation of the Near East after the great wave of invasions that occurred during the thirteenth century B.C.

it also contains many Hebrew myths and legends. Moreover, it was compiled at different times, with the earliest parts dating to between about 950 and 800 B.C.

Earlier Mesopotamian and Egyptian sources refer to people called "Hapiru," which seems to mean homeless, independent nomads. According to Hebrew tradition, the followers of Abraham migrated from Mesopotamia, but Egyptian documents record Hapiru already in Syria and Palestine in the second millennium B.C. The Hebrews were probably a part of them. Together with other seminomadic peoples they probably migrated into the Nile Delta seeking good land. According to the Bible the Egyptians enslaved them. One group, however, under the leadership of Moses, perhaps a

❖ **Standing Sphinx** The sphinx was both a decorative and protective figure in ancient art and society. This ivory is a splendid illustration of the sphinx itself—part human, part bird, and part lion. This sphinx also displays the richness of Phoenician art at this period. *(Source: Iraqi National Museum, Baghdad)*

semimythical figure, left Egypt in what the Hebrews remembered as the Exodus. From Egypt they wandered in the Sinai peninsula, until they settled in Palestine in the thirteenth century B.C. Their arrival was by no means peaceful. In a series of vicious wars and savage slaughters they slowly won a place. Success was not automatic, and the Hebrews suffered defeats and setbacks, but gradually they spread their power northward. Archaeology testifies that the thirteenth century B.C. in Palestine was a time of warfare and disruption. It also shows that the situation in Palestine was far more complicated than the Bible suggests.

In Palestine the Hebrews encountered the Philistines; the Amorites, relatives of Hammurabi's Babylonians; and the Semitic-speaking Canaanites. Despite the numerous wars, contact between the

Hebrews and their new neighbors was not always hostile. The Hebrews freely mingled with the Canaanites, and some went so far as to worship Baal, an ancient Semitic fertility god represented as a golden calf. Archaeological research supports the biblical account of these developments. In 1990 an expedition sponsored by Harvard University discovered a statue of a golden calf in its excavations of Ashkelon in modern Israel. Despite the anger expressed in the Bible over Hebrew worship of Baal, there is nothing surprising about the phenomenon. Once again, newcomers adapted themselves to the culture of an older, well-established people.

The greatest danger to the Hebrews came from the Philistines, whose superior technology and military organization at first made them invincible. In Saul (ca 1000 B.C.), a farmer of the tribe of Benjamin, the Hebrews found a champion and a spirited leader. In the biblical account, Saul carried the war to the Philistines, often without success. Yet in the meantime he established a monarchy over the twelve Hebrew tribes. Thus, under the peril of the Philistines, the Hebrews evolved from scattered, independent units into a centralized political organization in which the king directed the energies of the people. From this period derives the name *Israelites* for these erstwhile nomads.

Saul's work was carried on by David of Bethlehem, who in his youth had followed Saul into battle against the Philistines. Through courage and cunning, David pushed back the Philistines and waged war against his other neighbors. To give his kingdom a capital he captured the city of Jerusalem, which he enlarged, fortified, and made the religious and political center of his realm. David's military successes won the Hebrews unprecedented security, and his forty-year reign was a period of vitality and political consolidation. His work in consolidating the monarchy and enlarging the kingdom paved the way for his son Solomon.

Solomon (ca 965–925 B.C.) applied his energies to creating a nation out of a collection of tribes ruled by a king. He divided the kingdom, for purposes of effective administration, into twelve territorial districts cutting across the old tribal borders. To Solomon the twelve tribes of Israel were far less important than the Hebrew nation. To bring his kingdom up to the level of its more sophisticated neighbors, he set about a building program to make Israel a respectable Near Eastern state. Work was begun on a magnificent temple in Jerusalem, on cities, palaces, fortresses, and roads. Solomon worked to bring Israel into the commercial mainstream of the world around it and kept up good relations with Phoenician cities to the north. To finance all of the construction and other activities that he initiated, Solomon imposed taxes far greater than any levied before, much to the displeasure of his subjects.

Solomon dedicated the temple in grand style and made it the home of the Ark of the Covenant, the cherished chest that contained the holiest of Hebrew religious articles. The temple in Jerusalem was intended to be the religious heart of the kingdom and the symbol of Hebrew unity. It also became the stronghold of the priesthood, for a legion of priests was needed to conduct religious sacrifices, ceremonies, and prayers. Yet Solomon's efforts were hampered by strife. In the eyes of some people, he was too ready to unite other religions with the worship of the Hebrew god Yahweh, and the financial demands of his building program drained the resources of his people. His use of forced labor for building projects further fanned popular resentment. However, Solomon turned a rude kingdom into a state with broad commercial horizons and greater knowledge of the outside world. At his death, the Hebrews broke into two

political halves (see Map 2.1). The northern part of the kingdom of David and Solomon became Israel, with its capital at Samaria. The southern half was Judah, and Solomon's city of Jerusalem remained its center. With political division went a religious rift: Israel, the northern kingdom, established rival sanctuaries for gods other than Yahweh. The Hebrew nation was divided, but at least it was divided into two far more sophisticated political units than before the time of Solomon. Nonetheless, war soon broke out between them, as recorded in the Bible. Unexpected and independent evidence of this warfare came to light in August 1993, when an Israeli archaeologist found an inscription that refers to the "House of David," the royal line of Israel. The stone celebrates an Israelite victory from the early ninth century B.C. This discovery is the first mention of King David's royal family outside the Bible and helps to confirm the biblical account of the fighting between the two kingdoms.

Eventually, the northern kingdom of Israel was wiped out by the Assyrians, but the southern kingdom of Judah survived numerous calamities until the Babylonians crushed it in 587 B.C. The survivors were sent into exile in Babylonia, a period commonly known as the, "Babylonian Captivity."

Nomadic Semitic Tribe This Egyptian fresco captures the essentials of nomadic life. These Semites have captured a gazelle and an ibex. The four men behind the leaders are portrayed with their weapons, a bow and spears, which were used for both hunting and defense. Bringing up the rear is a domesticated burro. *(Source: Erich Lessing Culture and Fine Arts Archive)*

❖ **Aerial View of Hazor** This sweeping scene illustrates the strength and the economic basis of a Jewish citadel. At the left is the fortified upper city and in the background the agricultural land that sustained it. *(Source: Zev Radovan, Jerusalem)*

From 587 B.C. until 538 B.C., men known as the prophets kept Yahweh's religion alive in the midst of far older Babylonian religious practices. They predicted that Yahweh would permit their return to their homeland, if they only remained true to him. In 538 B.C. the Persians under their king Cyrus the Great permitted some 40,000 exiles to return to Jerusalem. During and especially after the "Babylonian Captivity" the exiles redefined their beliefs and practices, and thus established what they believed was the law of Yahweh. Those who lived by these precepts can be called *Jews*.

The Evolution of Jewish Religion

Hand in hand with their political evolution from fierce nomads to urban dwellers, the Hebrews were evolving spiritual ideas that still permeate Western society. Their chief literary product, the Hebrew Bible, has fundamentally influenced both Christianity and Islam and still exerts a compelling force on the modern world.

Fundamental to an understanding of Jewish religion is the concept of the Covenant, a formal agreement between Yahweh and the Hebrew people. According to the Bible, the god Yahweh, the Christian "Jehovah," appeared to Moses on Mount Sinai. There Yahweh made a covenant with the Hebrews that was in fact a contract: if the Hebrews worshiped Yahweh as their only god, he would consider them his chosen people and protect them from their enemies. The Hebrews believed that Yahweh had led them out of bondage in Egypt and had helped them to conquer their new land, the promised land. In return, the Hebrews worshiped Yahweh and Yahweh alone. They also obeyed Yahweh's Ten Commandments, an ethical code of conduct revealed to them by Moses.

Yahweh was unique because he was a lone god. Unlike the gods of Mesopotamia and Egypt, Yahweh was not the son of another god, nor did he have a divine wife or family. Initially anthropomorphic, Yahweh gradually lost human form and became totally spiritual. Although Yahweh could assume human form, he was not to be depicted in any form. Thus the Hebrews considered graven images—statues and other physical representations—idolatrous.

At first Yahweh was probably viewed as no more than the god of the Hebrews, who sometimes faced competition from Baal and other gods in Palestine. Enlil, Marduk, Amon-Re, and the others sufficed for foreigners. In time, however, the Hebrews came to regard Yahweh as the only god. This was the beginning of true monotheism.

Yahweh was considered the creator of all things; his name means "he causes to be." He governed the cosmic forces of nature, including the movements of the sun, moon, and stars. His presence filled the universe. At the same time, Yahweh was a personal god. Despite his awesome power, he was neither too mighty nor too aloof to care for the individual. The Hebrews even believed that Yahweh intervened in human affairs.

Unlike Akhenaten's monotheism, Hebrew monotheism was not an unpopular religion. It became the religion of a whole people, deeply felt and cherished. Some might fall away from Yahweh's worship, and various holy men had to exhort the Hebrews to honor the Covenant, but on the whole the people clung to Yahweh. Yet the Hebrews did not consider it their duty to spread the belief in the one god. The Hebrews rarely proselytized, as later the Christians did. As the chosen people, their chief duty was to maintain the worship of Yahweh as he demanded. That worship was embodied in the Ten Commandments, which forbade the Hebrews to steal, murder, lie, or commit adultery. The Covenant was a constant force in Hebrew life (see Listening to the Past), and the Old Testament records one occasion when the entire nation formally reaffirmed it:

And the king [of the Jews] stood by a pillar, and made a covenant before the lord, to walk after the lord, and to keep his commandments and his testimonies and his statutes with all their heart and all their soul, to perform the words of this covenant that were written in this book [Deuteronomy]. And all the people stood to the covenant.[2]

❖ **The Golden Calf** According to the Hebrew Bible, Moses descended from Mt. Sinai, where he had received the ten commandments, to find the Hebrews worshiping a golden calf, which was against Yahweh's laws. In July 1990 an American archaeological team found this model of a gilded calf inside a pot. The figurine dates to about 1550 B.C., and proves the existence of the cult represented by the calf in Palestine. *(Source: Courtesy of the Leon Levy expedition to Ashkelon/Carl Andrews)*

From the Ten Commandments evolved Hebrew law, a code of law and custom originating with Moses and built on by priests and prophets. The earliest part of this code, the Torah or Mosaic law, was often as harsh as Hammurabi's code, which had a powerful impact on it. Later tradition, largely the work of prophets who lived from the eleventh to the fifth centuries B.C., was more humanitarian. The work of the prophet Jeremiah (ca 626 B.C.) exemplifies this gentler spirit. According to Jeremiah, Yahweh demanded righteousness from his people and protection for the weak and helpless.

Jeremiah's emphasis is on mercy and justice, on avoiding wrongdoing to others because it is displeasing to Yahweh. These precepts replaced the old law's demand for "an eye for an eye." Jeremiah's message is thus representative of a subtle and positive shift in Hebrew thinking. Jeremiah proclaimed that the god of anger was also the god of forgiveness: "Return, thou backsliding Israel, saith the lord; and I will not cause mine anger to fall upon you; for I am merciful, saith the lord, and I will not keep anger forever."[3] Although Yahweh would punish wrongdoing, he would not destroy those who repented. One generation might be punished for its misdeeds, but Yahweh's mercy was a promise of hope for future generations.

The uniqueness of this phenomenon can be seen by comparing the essence of Hebrew monotheism with the religious outlook of the Mesopotamians. Whereas the Mesopotamians considered their gods capricious, the Hebrews knew what Yahweh expected. The Hebrews believed that their god would protect them and make them prosper if they obeyed his commandments. The Mesopotamians thought human beings insignificant compared to the gods, so insignificant that the gods might even be indifferent to them. The Hebrews, too, considered themselves puny in comparison to Yahweh. Yet they were Yahweh's chosen people, whom he had promised never to abandon. Finally, though the Mesopotamians believed that the gods generally preferred good to evil, their religion did not demand ethical conduct. The Hebrews could please their god only by living up to high moral standards as well as worshiping him.

Many parts of the Old Testament show obvious debts to Mesopotamian culture. Nonetheless, to the Hebrews goes the credit for developing a religion so emotionally satisfying and ethically grand that it has not only flourished but also profoundly influenced Christianity and Islam. The religious standards of the modern West are deeply rooted in Judaism.

Daily Life in Israel

Historians generally know far more about the daily life of the aristocracy and the wealthy in ancient societies than about the conditions of the common people. Jewish society is an exception simply because the Bible, which lays down laws for all Jews, has much to say about peasants and princes alike.

Comparisons with the social conditions of Israel's ancient neighbors and modern anthropological work among Palestinian Arabs shed additional light on biblical practices. Thus the life of the common people in ancient Israel is better known than, for instance, the lives of ordinary Romans or ancient Chinese.

The nomadic Hebrews first entered Palestine as tribes, numerous families who thought of themselves as all related to one another. At first, good farmland, pastureland, and water spots were held in common by the tribe. Common use of land was—and still is—characteristic of nomadic peoples. Typically each family or group of families in the tribe drew lots every year to determine who worked which fields. But as formerly nomadic peoples turned increasingly to settled agriculture, communal use of land gave way to family ownership. In this respect the experience of the ancient Hebrews seems typical of that of many early peoples. Slowly the shift from nomad to farmer affected far more than just how people fed themselves. Family relationships reflected evolving circumstances. With the transition to settled agriculture, the tribe gradually becomes less important than the extended family. With the advent of village life and finally full-blown urban life, the extended family in turn gives way to the nuclear family.

For women, however, the evolution of Jewish society led to less freedom of action, especially in religious life. At first women served as priestesses in festivals and religious cults. Some were considered prophetesses of Yahweh, although they never conducted his official rituals. In the course of time, however, the worship of Yahweh became more male-oriented and male-dominated. Increasingly, he also became the god of holiness, and to worship him people must be pure in mind and body. Women were seen as ritually impure because of menstruation and childbirth. Because of these "impurities," women now played a much reduced role in religion. Even when they did participate in religious rites, they were segregated from the men. For the most part, women were largely confined to the home and the care of the family.

Marriage was one of the most important and joyous events in Hebrew family life. The typical marriage in ancient Israel was monogamous, and a virtuous wife was revered and honored. Perhaps the finest and most fervent song of praise to the good wife comes from the book of Proverbs in the Bible:

Who can find a virtuous woman? for her price is far above rubies. . . . Strength and honour are her clothing; and she shall rejoice in time to come. She openeth her mouth with wisdom; and in her tongue is the law of kindness. She looketh well to the ways of her household, and eateth not the bread of idleness. Her children arise up, and call her blessed; her husband also, and he praiseth her. . . . Favour is deceitful, and beauty is vain: but a woman that feareth the lord, she shall be praised.[4]

The commandment "honor thy father and thy mother" was fundamental to the Mosaic law. The wife was a pillar of the family, and her work and wisdom were respected and treasured.

Betrothal and marriage were serious matters in ancient Israel. As in Mesopotamia, they were left largely in parents' hands. Boys and girls were often married quite early, and the parents naturally made the arrangements. Rarely were the prospective bride and groom consulted. Marriages were often contracted within the extended family, commonly among first cousins—a custom still found among Palestinian Arabs today. Although early Jewish custom permitted marriage with foreigners, the fear of alien religions eventually led to restrictions against mixed marriages.

The father of the groom offered a bridal gift to the bride's father. This custom, the marriage price, also existed among the Mesopotamians and still survives among modern Palestinian Arabs. The gift was ordinarily money, the amount depending on the social status and wealth of the two families. In other instances, the groom could work off the marriage price by performing manual labor. At the time of the wedding the man gave his bride and her family wedding presents; unlike Mesopotamian custom, the bride's father did not provide her with a dowry. A dowry is meant to protect the position of the wife, and the lack of it in Israel made it easier for the husband to divorce his wife without financial loss.

Divorce was available only to the husband. He could normally end the marriage very simply and for any of a number of reasons. The right to initiate a divorce was denied the wife. Even adultery by the husband was not necessarily grounds for divorce, although Jewish law, like the Code of Hammurabi, generally punished *women's* adultery with

death. Overall, Jewish custom frowned on divorce, and the typical couple entered into marriage fully expecting to spend the rest of their lives together.

The newly married couple was expected to begin a family at once. Children, according to the book of Psalms, "are an heritage of the lord: and the fruit of the womb is his reward."[5] The desire for children to perpetuate the family was so strong that if a man died before he could sire a son, his brother was legally obliged to marry the widow. The son born of the brother was thereafter considered the offspring and heir of the dead man. If the brother refused, the widow had her revenge by denouncing him to the elders and publicly spitting in his face.

Sons were especially desired because they maintained the family bloodline and kept the ancestral property within the family. The first-born son had special rights, honor, and responsibilities. At his father's death he became the head of the household and received a larger inheritance than his younger brothers. Daughters were less valued because they would eventually marry and leave the family. Yet in Jewish society, unlike other cultures, infanticide was illegal; Yahweh had forbidden it.

The Bible often speaks of the pain of childbirth. Professional midwives frequently helped during deliveries. The newborn infant was washed, rubbed with salt, and wrapped in swaddling clothes—bands of cloth that were wrapped around the baby. Normally the mother nursed the baby herself and weaned the infant at about the age of three. The mother customarily named the baby immediately after birth, but children were free to change names after they grew up. Eight days after the birth of a son, the ceremony of circumcision—removal of the foreskin of the penis—took place. Circumcision signified that the boy belonged to the Jewish community; according to Genesis, it was the symbol of Yahweh's covenant with Abraham. Although this practice was common among the Egyptians, it took on a special significance among the Jews.

As in most other societies, in ancient Israel the early education of children was in the mother's hands. She taught her children right from wrong and gave them their first instruction in the moral values of society. As boys grew older, they received more education from their fathers. Fathers instructed their sons in religion and the history of their people. Many children were taught to read and write, and the head of each family was probably able to write. Fathers also taught sons the family craft or trade. Boys soon learned that inattention could be painful, for Jewish custom advised fathers to be strict: "He that spareth his rod hateth his son: but he that loveth him chasteneth him betimes."[6]

Once children grew to adulthood, they entered fully into economic and social life. For most that meant a life on the farm, whose demands and rhythm changed very little over time. Young people began with the lighter tasks. Girls traditionally tended flocks of sheep and drew water from the well for household use. The well was a popular meeting spot, where girls could meet other young people and even travelers passing through the country with camel caravans. After the harvest, young girls followed behind the reapers to glean the fields. Even this work was governed by law and custom. Once the girls had gone through the fields, they were not to return, for Yahweh had declared that anything the gleaners left behind belonged to the needy.

Boys also tended flocks, especially in wild areas. Like the young David, they practiced their marksmanship with slings and entertained themselves with music. They shared the lighter work, such as harvesting grapes and beating the limbs of olive trees to shake the fruit loose. Only when they grew to full strength did they perform the hard work of harrowing, plowing, and harvesting.

The land was precious to the family, not simply because it provided a living, but also because it was a link to the past. Ironically, the success of the first Hebrew kings endangered the future of many family farms. With peace, more settled conditions, and increasing prosperity, some Jews began to amass larger holdings by buying out poor and struggling farmers. Far from discouraging this development, the kings created their own huge estates. In many cases slaves, both Jewish and foreign, worked these large farms and estates shoulder to shoulder with paid free men. In still later times, rich landowners rented plots of land to poor, free families; the landowners provided the renters with seed and livestock and normally took half the yield as rent. Although many Bible prophets denounced the destruction of the family farm, the trend continued toward large estates that were worked by slaves and hired free men.

The development of urban life among the Jews created new economic opportunities, especially in crafts and trades. People specialized in certain occupations, such as milling flour, baking bread, making pottery, weaving, and carpentry. All these crafts were family trades. Sons worked with their father; daughters with their mother. If the business prospered, the family might be assisted by a few paid workers or slaves. The practitioners of a craft usually lived in a particular section of the town, a custom still prevalent in the Middle East today.

Commerce and trade developed later than crafts. In the time of Solomon, foreign trade was the king's domain. Aided by the Phoenicians, Solomon built a fleet to trade with Red Sea ports. Solomon also participated in the overland caravan trade. Otherwise, trade with neighboring countries was handled by foreigners, usually Phoenicians. Jews dealt mainly in local trade, and in most instances craftsmen and farmers sold directly to their customers. Many of Israel's wise men disapproved of commerce and considered it unseemly and immoral to profit from the work of others.

These social and economic developments also left their mark on daily life by prompting the compilation of two significant works, the Torah and the Talmud. The Torah is basically the Mosaic law, or the first five books of the Bible. The Talmud is a later work, begun during the "Babylonian Captivity" and completed by the end of the sixth century B.C. The Talmud records civil and ceremonial law and Jewish legend. The dietary rules of the Jews provide an excellent example of both the relationship between the Torah and the Talmud and their effect on ordinary life and culture. According to the Torah, people were not to eat meat that they found in the field. This very sensible prohibition protected them from eating dangerous food. Yet if meat from the countryside could not be eaten, then some rules were needed for meat in the city. The solution found in the Talmud was a set of regulations for the proper way to conduct ritual slaughter. Some of these rules were very burdensome. The ritual defined the knife to be used in the slaughter and the way in which it was to be used. Accompanying these precise acts were prayers to be given when the animal's throat was cut. So too with the Torah's prohibition against cooking a kid in its mother's milk. This interpretation of Mosaic law went to such lengths that milk and meat could not be eaten at the same table, and different bowls must be used to serve them. Even different towels must be used to cleanse them. What had begun as simple and sensible dietary rules had become a complicated ritual, but one that many Orthodox Jews follow today.

Between the eclipse of the Hittites and Egyptians and the rise of the Assyrians, the Hebrews moved from nomadism to urban life and full participation in the mainstream of ancient Near Eastern culture. Developing their unique religion and customs, they drew from the practices of other peoples and contributed to the lives of their neighbors.

✥ ASSYRIA, THE MILITARY MONARCHY

Small kingdoms like those of the Phoenicians and the Hebrews could exist only in the absence of a major power. The beginning of the ninth century B.C. saw the rise of such a power: the Assyrians of northern Mesopotamia, whose chief capital was at Nineveh on the Tigris River. The Assyrians were a Semitic-speaking people heavily influenced, like so many other peoples of the Near East, by the Mesopotamian culture of Babylon to the south. They were also one of the most warlike peoples in history, largely because throughout their history they were threatened by neighboring folk. Living in an open, exposed land, the Assyrians experienced frequent and devastating attacks by the wild, war-loving tribes to their north and east and by the Babylonians to the south. The constant threat to survival experienced by the Assyrians promoted political cohesion and military might. Yet they were also a mercantile people who had long pursued commerce both with the Babylonians in the south and other peoples in the north.

The Power of Assyria

For over two hundred years the Assyrians labored to dominate the Near East. In 859 B.C. the new Assyrian king Shalmaneser unleashed the first of a long series of attacks on the peoples of Syria and Palestine. Year after relentless year, Assyrian armies hammered at the peoples of the west. These ominous events inaugurated two turbulent centuries marked by Assyrian military campaigns, constant efforts by Syria and the two Jewish kingdoms to maintain or recover their independence, and eventual Assyrian conquest of Babylonia and northern Egypt. In addition, periodic political instability occurred in Assyria itself, which prompted stirrings of freedom throughout the Near East.

Under the Assyrian kings Tiglath-pileser III (774–727 B.C.) and Sargon II (r. 721–705 B.C.), both mighty warriors, the Near East trembled as

✥ **Siege of a City** Art here serves to glorify horror. The Assyrian king Tiglath-pileser III launches an assault on a fortified city. The impaled bodies shown at center demonstrate the cruelty of Assyrian warfare. Also noticeable are the various weapons and means of attack used against the city. (*Source: Courtesy of the Trustees of the British Museum*)

never before under the blows of Assyrian armies. The Assyrians stepped up their attacks on Anatolia, Syria, and Palestine. The kingdom of Israel and many other states fell; others, like the kingdom of Judah, became subservient to the warriors from the Tigris. In 717 to 716 B.C., Sargon led his army in a sweeping attack along the Philistine coast into Egypt. He defeated the pharaoh, who suffered the further ignominy of paying tribute to the foreign conquerors. Sargon also lashed out at Assyria's traditional enemies to the north and then turned south against a renewed threat in Babylonia. By means of almost constant warfare, Tiglath-pileser III and Sargon carved out an Assyrian empire that stretched from east and north of the Tigris River to central Egypt (Map 2.2). Revolt against the Assyrians inevitably promised the rebels bloody battles, prolonged sieges accompanied by starvation, plague, and sometimes even cannibalism, and finally surrender followed by systematic torture and slaughter.

Though atrocity and terrorism struck unspeakable fear into Assyria's subjects, Assyria's success

was actually due to sophisticated, farsighted, and effective military organization. By Sargon's time the Assyrians had invented the mightiest military machine the ancient Near East had ever seen. The mainstay of the Assyrian army, the soldier who ordinarily decided the outcome of battles, was the infantryman armed with spear and sword and protected by helmet and armor. The Assyrian army also featured archers, some on foot, others on horseback, still others in chariots—the latter ready to wield lances once they had expended their supply of arrows. Some infantry archers wore heavy armor. These soldiers served as a primitive field artillery, whose job was to sweep the enemy's walls of defenders so that others could storm the defenses. Slingers also served as artillery in pitched battles. For mobility on the battlefield, the Assyrians organized a corps of chariots.

Assyrian military genius was remarkable for the development of a wide variety of siege machinery and techniques, including excavation to undermine city walls and battering rams to knock down walls and gates. Never before in the Near East had any-

❖ **MAP 2.2 The Assyrian Empire** The Assyrian Empire at its height (ca 650 B.C.) included almost all of the old centers of power in the ancient Near East. As Map 2.3 shows, however, its size was far smaller than that of the later Persian Empire.

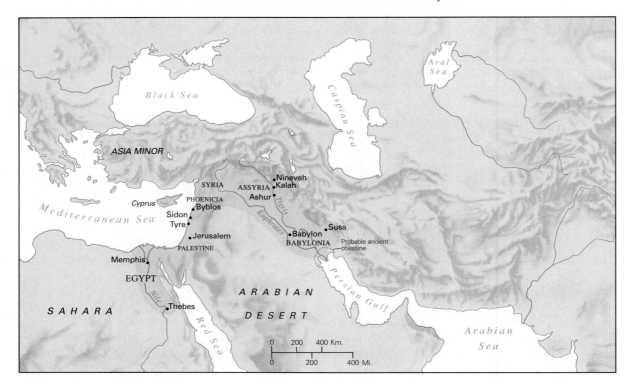

one applied such technical knowledge to warfare. The Assyrians even invented the concept of a corps of engineers, who bridged rivers with pontoons or provided soldiers with inflatable skins for swimming. Furthermore, the Assyrians knew how to coordinate their efforts, both in open battle and in siege warfare. King Sennacherib's account of his siege of Jerusalem in 701 B.C. is a vivid portrait of the Assyrian war machine in action:

As to Hezekiah, the Jew, he did not submit to my yoke, I laid siege to 46 of his strong cities, walled forts and to the countless small villages in their vicinity, and conquered them by means of well-stamped earth-ramps, and battering rams brought thus near to the walls combined with the attack by foot soldiers, using mines, breaches as well as sapper work. . . . Himself I made prisoner in Jerusalem, his royal residence, like a bird in a cage. I surrounded him with earthwork in order to molest those who were leaving his city's gate. . . . Hezekiah himself, whom the terror-inspiring splendor of my lordship had overwhelmed and whose irregular and elite troops which he had brought into Jerusalem, his royal residence, in order to strengthen it, had deserted him, did send me, later, to Nineveh, my lordly city, together with 30 talents of gold . . . and all kinds of valuable treasures.[7]

Hezekiah and Jerusalem shared the fate of many a rebellious king and capital and were indeed lucky to escape severe reprisals. The Assyrians were too powerful and well organized and far too tenacious to be turned back by isolated strongholds, no matter how well situated or defended.

Assyrian Rule and Culture

Not only did the Assyrians know how to win battles, they also knew how to use their victories. As early as the reign of Tiglath-pileser III, the Assyrian kings began to organize their conquered territories into an empire. The lands closest to Assyria became provinces governed by Assyrian officials. Kingdoms beyond the provinces were not annexed but became dependent states that followed Assyria's lead. The Assyrian king chose their rulers either by regulating the succession of native kings or by supporting native kings who appealed to him. Against more distant states the Assyrian kings waged frequent war in order to conquer them outright or make the dependent states secure.

Royal roads and swift mounted messengers linked the Assyrian Empire, and Assyrian records describe how these royal messengers brought the king immediate word of unrest or rebellion within the empire. Because of good communications, Assyrian kings could generally move against rebels at a moment's notice. Thus, though rebellion was common in the Assyrian Empire, it rarely got the opportunity to become serious before meeting with harsh retaliation from the king.

In the seventh century B.C. Assyrian power seemed secure. Yet the downfall of Assyria was swift and complete. Babylon finally won its independence in 626 B.C. and joined forces with a newly aggressive people, the Medes, an Indo-European-speaking folk from Iran. Together the Babylonians and the Medes destroyed the Assyrian Empire in 612 B.C., paving the way for the rise of the Persians. The Hebrew prophet Nahum spoke for many when he asked: "Nineveh is laid waste: who will bemoan her?"[8] Their cities destroyed and their power shattered, the Assyrians disappeared from history, remembered only as a cruel people of the Old Testament who oppressed the Hebrews. Two hundred years later, when the Greek adventurer and historian Xenophon passed by the ruins of Nineveh, he marveled at the extent of the former city but knew nothing of the Assyrians. The glory of their empire was forgotten.

Yet modern archaeology has brought the Assyrians out of obscurity. In 1839 the intrepid English archaeologist and traveler A. H. Layard began to excavate Nineveh, then a mound of debris beside the Tigris. His findings electrified the world. In the course of a few years, Layard's discoveries shed remarkable new light on Assyrian history and had an equally stunning impact on the history of art. Layard's workers unearthed masterpieces, including monumental sculpted figures—huge winged bulls, human-headed lions, and sphinxes—as well as brilliantly sculpted friezes. Equally valuable were numerous Assyrian cuneiform documents, which ranged from royal accounts of mighty military campaigns to simple letters by common people.

Among the most renowned of Layard's finds were the Assyrian palace reliefs, whose number has been increased by the discoveries of twentieth-century archaeologists. Assyrian kings delighted in scenes of war, which their artists depicted in graphic detail. By the time of Ashurbanipal (r. 668–633 B.C.), Assyrian artists had hit on the idea of portraying a series of episodes—in fact, a visual narrative of events that had actually taken place. Scene followed scene in a continuous frieze, so that

Royal Lion Hunt This relief from the palace of Ashurbanipal at Nineveh, which shows the king fighting a lion, is a typical representation of the energy and artistic brilliance of Assyrian sculptors. The lion hunt, portrayed in a series of episodes, was a favorite theme of Assyrian palace reliefs. *(Source: Courtesy of the Trustees of the British Museum)*

the viewer could follow the progress of a military campaign from the time the army marched out until the enemy was conquered. So, too, with another theme of the palace reliefs, the lion hunt. Hunting lions was probably a royal sport, although some scholars have suggested a magical significance. They argue that the hunting scenes depict the king as the protector of his people, the one who wards off evil. Here, too, the viewer proceeds in sequence, from preparations for the chase through the hunting itself to the killing of the lions.

Assyrian art, like much of Egyptian art, was realistic, but the warmth and humor of Egyptian scenes are absent from Assyrian reliefs. Assyrian art is stark and often brutal in subject matter, yet marked by an undeniable strength and sophistication of composition. Assyrian realism is well represented by the illustration above, which portrays the climax of the royal lion hunt. The scene is like a

photograph snapped at the height of the action. The king, mounted on horseback, has already fired arrows into two lions, who nonetheless are still full of fight. The wounded lion on the left has just pounced on a riderless horse, which in a moment will fall mortally wounded. Meanwhile, the king thrusts his spear into another lion, which has begun its spring. The artistic rendering of the figures is exciting and technically flawless. The figures are anatomically correct and in proper proportion and perspective. The whole composition conveys both action and tension. Assyrian art fared better than Assyrian military power. The techniques of Assyrian artists influenced the Persians, who adapted them to gentler scenes.

In fact, many Assyrian innovations, military and political as well as artistic, were taken over wholesale by the Persians. Although the memory of Assyria was hateful throughout the Near East, the fruits of Assyrian organizational genius helped en-

have conquered peoples shown such gratitude to their conquerors. Cyrus's benevolent policy created a Persian Empire in which the cultures and religions of its members were respected and honored. Seldom have conquerors been as wise, sensitive, and farsighted as Cyrus and his Persians.

Thus Spake Zarathustra

Iranian religion was originally simple and primitive. Ahuramazda, the chief god, was the creator and benefactor of all living creatures. Yet, unlike Yahweh, he was not a lone god. The Iranians were polytheistic. Mithra the sun-god, whose cult would later spread throughout the Roman Empire (see Chapter 6), saw to justice and redemption. Other Iranian deities personified the natural elements: moon, earth, water, and wind. As in ancient India, fire was a particularly important god. The sacred fire consumed the blood sacrifices that the early Iranians offered to all of their deities.

Early Iranian religion was close to nature and unencumbered by ponderous theological beliefs. A priestly class, the Magi, developed among the Medes to officiate at sacrifices, chant prayers to the gods, and tend the sacred flame. A description of this early worship comes from the German historian Eduard Meyer:

Iranian religion knew neither divine images nor temples. On a hilltop one called upon god and his manifestations—sun and moon, earth and fire, water and wind—and erected altars with their eternal fire. But in other appropriate places one could, without further preparation, pray to the deity and bring him his offerings, with the assistance of the Magi.[9]

In time the Iranians built fire temples for these sacrifices. As late as the nineteenth century, fire was still worshiped in Baku, a major city on the Russian-Iranian border.

Around 600 B.C. the religious thinking of Zarathustra—Zoroaster, as he is better known—breathed new meaning into Iranian religion. So little is known of Zoroaster that even the date of his birth is unknown, but it cannot be earlier than around 1100 B.C. Whatever the exact dates of his life, his work endured long afterward. The most reliable information about Zoroaster comes from the *Zend Avesta*, a collection of hymns and poems, the earliest part of which treats Zoroaster and primitive Persian religion. Zoroaster preached a novel concept of divinity and human life. Life, he

taught, is a constant battleground for two opposing forces, good and evil. Ahuramazda embodied good and truth but was opposed by Ahriman, a hateful spirit who stood for evil and falsehood. Ahuramazda and Ahriman were locked together in a cosmic battle for the human race, a battle that stretched over thousands of years. But, according to Zoroaster, people were not mere pawns in this struggle. Each person had to choose which side to join—whether to lead a life of good behavior and truthful dealings with others or one of wickedness and lies.

Zoroaster emphasized the individual's responsibility in this decision. He taught that people possessed the free will to decide between Ahuramazda and Ahriman and that they must rely on their own conscience to guide them through life. Their decisions were crucial, Zoroaster warned, for there would be a time of reckoning. He promised that Ahuramazda would eventually triumph over evil and lies, and that at death each person would stand before the tribunal of good. Ahuramazda, like the Egyptian god Osiris, would judge whether the dead had lived righteously and on that basis would weigh their lives in the balance. In short, Zoroaster taught the concept of a Last Judgment at which Ahuramazda would decide each person's eternal fate.

In Zoroaster's thought the Last Judgment was linked to the notion of a divine kingdom after death for those who had lived according to good and truth. They would accompany Ahuramazda to a life of eternal truth in what Zoroaster called the "House of Song" and the "Abode of Good Thought." There they would dwell with Ahuramazda forever. Liars and the wicked, denied this blessed immortality, would be condemned to eternal pain, darkness, and punishment. Thus Zoroaster preached a Last Judgment that led to a heaven or a hell.

Though tradition has it that Zoroaster's teachings originally met with opposition and coldness, his thought converted Darius (r. 521–486 B.C.), one of the most energetic men ever to sit on the Persian throne. The Persian royal family adopted Zoroastrianism but did not try to impose it on others. Under the protection of the Persian kings, Zoroastrianism swept through Iran, winning converts and sinking roots that sustained healthy growth for centuries. Zoroastrianism survived the fall of the Persian Empire to influence religious thought in the age of Jesus and to make a vital

✣ **Darius the Great and Ahura Mazda** In this rock-carving Darius, king of the Persians, in the eyes of the god Ahura Mazda and with his blessing, triumphs over lesser and sometimes rebellious kings. The scene asserts the divine approval of Darius' right to rule. *(Source: Robert Harding Picture Library)*

contribution to nicheanism, a theology that was to spread through the Byzantine Empire and pose a significant challenge to Christianity. A handful of the faithful still follow the teachings of Zoroaster, whose vision of divinity and human life has transcended the centuries.

Persia's World Empire

Cyrus's successors rounded out the Persian conquest of the ancient Near East. In 525 B.C. Cyrus's son Cambyses (r. 530–522 B.C.) subdued Egypt. Darius (r. 521–486 B.C.) and his son Xerxes (r. 486–464 B.C.) invaded Greece but were fought to a standstill and forced to retreat (see pages 78–79); the Persians never won a permanent foothold in Europe. Yet Darius carried Persian arms into India. Around 513 B.C. western India became the Persian satrapy of Hindush, which included the valley of the Indus River. Thus within thirty-seven years (550–513 B.C.) the Persians transformed themselves from a subject people to the rulers of an empire that included Anatolia, Egypt, Mesopotamia, Iran, and western India. They had created a "world empire" encompassing all of the oldest and most honored kingdoms and peoples of the ancient Near East. Never before had the Near East been united in one such vast political organization (see Map 2.3).

The Persians knew how to use the peace they had won on the battlefield. Unlike the Assyrians, they did not resort to royal terrorism to keep order. Like the Assyrians, however, they employed a number of bureaucratic techniques to bind the empire together. The sheer size of the empire made it impossible for one man to rule it effectively. Consequently, the Persians divided the empire into some twenty huge satrapies measuring hundreds of square miles apiece, many of them kingdoms in themselves. Each satrapy had a governor, usually drawn from the Median and Persian nobility and often a relative of the king; the governor, or *satrap,* was directly responsible to the king. Others were local dynasts subject to the Persian king. An army officer, also responsible to the king, commanded the military forces stationed in the satrapy. Still another official collected the taxes. Moreover, the king sent out royal inspectors to watch the satraps and other officials, a method of surveillance later used by the medieval king Charlemagne.

Effective rule of the empire demanded good communications. To meet this need the Persians established a network of roads. The main highway, known as the Royal Road, spanned some 1,677 miles from the Greek city of Ephesus on the coast of Asia Minor to Susa in western Iran. The distance was broken into 111 post stations, each equipped with fresh horses for the king's messengers. Other roads branched out to link all parts of the empire from the coast of Asia Minor to the valley of the Indus River. This system of communications enabled the Persian king to keep in intimate touch with his subjects and officials. He was able to rule efficiently, keep his ministers in line, and protect the rights of the peoples under his control. How effective Persian rule could be, even in small matters, is apparent in a letter from King Darius to the satrap of Ionia, the Greek region of Anatolia. The satrap had transplanted Syrian fruit trees in his province, an experiment Darius praised. Yet the governor had also infringed on the rights granted to the sanctuary of the Greek god Apollo, an act that provoked the king to anger:

The King of Kings, Darius the son of Hystaspes says this to Gadatas, his slave [satrap]. I learn that you are not obeying my command in every particular. Because you are tilling my land, transplanting fruit trees from across the Euphrates [Syria] to Asia Minor, I praise your project, and there will be laid up for you great favor in the king's house. But because you mar my dispositions towards the gods, I shall give you, unless you change your ways, proof of my anger when wronged. For you exacted payment from the sacred gardeners of the temple of Apollo, and you ordered them to dig up secular land, failing to understand the attitude of my forefathers towards the god, who told the Persians the truth.[10]

Fruit trees and foreign gods—even such small matters as these were important to the man whom the world called "The Great King, King of Kings, King of Countries, containing all kinds of men, King in this great earth far and wide."[11] This document alone suggests the efficiency of Persian rule and the compassion of Persian kings. Conquered peoples, left free to enjoy their traditional ways of life, found in the Persian king a capable protector. No wonder that many Near Eastern peoples were, like the Jews, grateful for the long period of peace they enjoyed as the subjects of the Persian Empire.

Lion Weight This formidable lion was a standard weight used to weigh taxes paid in silver and gold. The lion was a royal symbol, and the taxes were sent to the royal treasury at Susa for the costs of administering the Persian Empire. *(Source: Louvre © Photo R.M.N.)*

❖ **The Royal Palace at Persepolis**   King Darius began and King Xerxes finished building a grand palace worthy of the glory of the Persian Empire. Pictured here is the monumental audience hall, where the king dealt with ministers of state and foreign envoys. *(Source: George Holton/Photo Researchers)*

SUMMARY

During the centuries following the Sea Peoples' invasions, Egypt was overrun by its African neighbors, but its long and rich traditions and culture, its firmly established religion, and its administrative techniques became the heritage of these conquerors. The defeat of Egypt also led to conditions that allowed the Hebrews to create their own state. A series of strong leaders fighting hard wars won the Hebrews independence and security. In this atmosphere Hebrew religion evolved and flourished,

thanks to priests, prophets, and common piety among the people. Daily life involved the transition from nomad to farmer, and people's lives revolved around the religious and agricultural year.

In the eighth century B.C. the Hebrews and others in the ancient Near East fell to the onslaught of Assyria, a powerful Mesopotamian kingdom. The Assyrians combined administrative skills, economic acumen, and wealth with military organization to create an aggressive military state. Yet the Assyrians' military ruthlessness and cruelty raised powerful enemies against them. The most important of these enemies were the Iranians, who created the Persian Empire. The Persians had migrated into Iran, settled the land, and entered the cultural orbit of the Near East. The result was rapid progress in culture, economic prosperity, and increase in population, which enabled them to create the largest empire yet seen in the Near East. Unlike the Assyrians, however, they ruled mildly and gave the Near East a long period of peace.

NOTES

1. James H. Breasted, *Ancient Records of Egypt* (Chicago: University of Chicago Press, 1907), vol. 4, para. 398.
2. 2 Kings 23:3.
3. Jeremiah 3:12.
4. Proverbs 31:10, 25–30.
5. Psalms 128:3.
6. Proverbs 13:24.
7. J. B. Pritchard, ed., *Ancient Near Eastern Texts,* 3d ed. (Princeton, N.J.: Princeton University Press, 1969), p. 288.
8. Nahum 3:7.
9. E. Meyer, *Geschichte des Altertums,* 7th ed., vol. 4, pt. 1 (Darmstadt: Wissenschaftliche Buchgesellschaft, 1975), pp. 114–115. John Buckler is the translator of all uncited quotations from foreign languages in Chapters 1–6.
10. R. Meiggs and D. M. Lewis, *A Selection of Greek Historical Inscriptions* (Oxford: Clarendon Press, 1969), no. 12.
11. R. G. Kent, trans., *Old Persian,* 2d ed. (New Haven: Yale University Press, 1953), p.138.

SUGGESTED READING

Although late Egyptian history is still largely a specialist's field, K. A. Kitchen, *The Third Intermediate Period in Egypt* (1973), is a sturdy synthesis of the period from 1100 to 650 B.C. Valuable, too, is M. L. Bierbrier's monograph, *Late New Kingdom in Egypt,* c. 1300–664 B.C. (1975). D. B. Redford, *Egypt, Canaan, and Israel in Ancient Times* (1992), is an excellent study of relations among the three states. G. Herm, *The Phoenicians* (1975), treats Phoenician seafaring and commercial enterprises.

The Jews have been one of the best-studied people in the ancient world, so the reader can easily find many good treatments of Jewish history and society. E. Anati, *Palestine before the Hebrews* (1962), though dated, still provides a sound historical treatment of life in Palestine from human origins to the conquest of Canaan. More recent is G. Alon, *The Jews in Their Land* (1989), which covers the Talmudic age. H. Shanks, ed., *The Rise of Ancient Israel* (1991), is a collection of papers that treat numerous aspects of the period. R. Tappy, *The Archaeology of Israelite Samaria* (1993), studies the archaeological remains of the period. S. Niditch, *War in the Hebrew Bible* (1992), addresses the ethics of violence in the Bible. A general introduction to the Bible is B. M. Mezter and M. D. Coogan, eds., *The Oxford Companion to the Bible* (1993). H. W. Attridge ed., *Of Scribes and Scrolls* (1990), gives a fascinating study of the Hebrew Bible and of Christian origins. Turning to politics, M. Smith, *Palestinian Parties and Politics That Shaped the Old Testament,* 2d ed. (1987), takes a practical look at events. G. W. Ahlstrom, *Royal Administration and National Religion in Ancient Palestine* (1982), treats secular and religious aspects of Hebrew history. W. D. Davis et al., *The Cambridge History of Judaism,* vol. I (1984), begins an important new synthesis with work on Judaism in the Persian period. R. Hachlili, *Ancient Jewish Art and Archaeology in the Land of Israel* (1988), attempts to trace the development and meaning of Jewish art in its archaeological context.

The Assyrians, despite their achievements, have not attracted the scholarly attention that other Near Eastern peoples have. Even though woefully outdated, A. T. Olmstead, *History of Assyria* (1928), has the merit of being soundly based in the original sources. H. W. F. Saggs, *Everyday Life in Babylonia and Assyria,* rev. ed. (1987), offers a general and well-illustrated survey of Mesopotamian history from 3000 to 300 B.C. Those who appreciate the vitality of Assyrian art should start with the masterful work of R. D. Barnett and W. Forman, *Assyrian Palace Reliefs,* 2d ed. (1970), an exemplary combination of fine photographs and learned, but not difficult, discussion.

Several new works on ancient Iran have lately appeared. A comprehensive survey of Persian history is given by one of the leading scholars in the field, R. N. Frye, *History of Ancient Iran* (1984). I. Gershevitch, ed., *The Cambridge History of Iran,* vol. II (1985), provides the reader with a full account of ancient Persian history, but many of the chapters are already out of date. E. Herzfeld, *Iran in the Ancient East* (1987), puts Persian history in a broad context. Most welcome is M. A. Dandamaev, *A Political History of the Achaemenid Empire* (1989), which discusses in depth the history of the Persians and the organization of their empire. Finally, M. Boyce, a leading scholar in the field, provides a sound and readable treatment of the essence of Zoroastrianism in her *Zoroastrianism* (1979).

LISTENING TO THE
PAST

The Covenant Between Yahweh and the Hebrews

These passages from the Hebrew Bible address two themes important to Hebraic thinking. The first is the meaning of kingship; the second, the nature of the covenant between the Hebrews and the Lord, Yahweh. The selection also raises the difficult question of how much of the Hebrew Bible can be accepted historically. As we discussed in this chapter, the Hebrew Bible is not a document that we may accept as literal truth, but it does tell us a great deal about the people who created it. From the following passages we may discern what the Hebrews thought about their own past and religion.

The background of the excerpt is a political crisis that has some archaeological support. The war with the Philistines put a huge strain on Hebrew society. A new and effective political and military leadership was needed to meet the situation. The elders of the tribes had previously chosen judges to lead the community only in times of crisis. The Hebrews, however, demanded that a kingship be established, even though Yahweh was their king. They turned to Samuel, the last of the judges, who anointed Saul as the first Hebrew king. In this excerpt Samuel reviews the political, military, and religious situation confronting the Hebrews, reminding them of their obligation to honor the covenant and expressing hesitation in being named king.

Then said Samuel to the people, Come, and let us go to Gilgal, and renew the kingdom there. And all the people went to Gilgal; and there they made Saul king before the Lord in Gilgal; and there they sacrificed sacrifices of peace offerings before the Lord; and there Saul and all the men of Israel rejoiced greatly.

And Samuel said unto all Israel, Behold, I have hearkened unto your voice in all that you said to me, and have made a king over you. And now, behold, the king walks before you; and I am old and gray-headed; and behold,

my sons are with you: and I have walked before you from my childhood until this day. Behold, here I am: witness against me before the Lord, and before his anointed: whose ox have I taken? or whose ass have I taken? or whom have I defrauded? whom have I oppressed? or of whose hand have I received any bribe to blind my eyes with it? and I will restore it to you.

And they said, You have not defrauded us, nor oppressed us, neither have you taken anything from any man's hand. And he said to them, the Lord is witness against you, and his anointed is witness this day, that you have not found anything in my hand. And they answered, he is witness.

At this point Samuel reminds the Hebrews of their covenant with Yahweh. He lists a number of cases in history in which the Hebrews had broken that covenant. Stinging under the rebuke, they lament. Then Samuel gives them stern advice, capped by a threat about any future disobedience.

Now therefore behold the king whom you have chosen, and whom you have desired! and behold, the Lord has set a king over you. If you will fear the Lord, and serve him, and obey his voice, and not rebel against the commandment of the Lord, then shall both you and also the king who reigns over you continue following the Lord your God: But if you will not obey the voice of the Lord, but rebel against the commandment of the Lord, then shall the hand of the Lord be against you, as it was against your fathers. Now therefore stand and see this great thing, which the Lord will do before your eyes. Is it not wheat harvest today? I will call to the Lord, and he shall send thunder and rain; that you may perceive and see that your wickedness is great, which you have done in the sight of the Lord, in asking you a king. So Samuel called to the

Lord; and the Lord sent thunder and rain that day: and all the people greatly feared the Lord and Samuel. And all the people said to Samuel, pray for your servants to the Lord your God, so that we will not die: for we have added to all of our sins this evil, to ask us for a king. And Samuel said to the people, Fear not: you have done all this wickedness; yet turn not aside from following the Lord, but serve the Lord with all your heart; And do not turn aside; for then should you go after vain things, which cannot profit nor deliver; for they are vain. For the Lord will not forsake his people for his great name's sake: because it pleases the Lord to make you his people. Moreover, as for me, God forbid that I should sin against the Lord in ceasing to pray for you: but I will teach you the good and the right way: Only fear the Lord, and serve him in truth with all your heart: for consider how great things he has done for you. But if you shall still act wickedly, you will be consumed, both you and your king.

✤ Art of the Covenant, depicted in a relief from Capernaum Synagogue, 2nd century A.D. *(Source: Ancient Art and Architecture Collection)*

Questions for Analysis

1. How did Samuel explain his anointment of a king?

2. What was Samuel's attitude toward kingship?

3. What were the duties of the Hebrews toward Yahweh?

4. Might those duties conflict with those toward the secular king? If so, in what ways, and how might the Hebrews avoid the conflict?

Source: Abridged and adapted from *The Holy Bible.* Copyright © 1974 The Gideons International.

CHAPTER

3

The Legacy of Greece

✤ The rocky peninsula of Greece was the home of the civilization that fundamentally shaped Western civilization. The Greeks were the first to explore most of the questions that continue to concern Western thinkers to this day. Going beyond mythmaking and religion, the Greeks strove to understand, in logical, rational terms, both the universe and the position of men and women in it. The result was the birth of philosophy and science—subjects that were far more important to most Greek thinkers than religion. The Greeks speculated on human beings and society and created the very concept of politics.

While the scribes of the ancient Near East produced king lists, the Greeks invented history to record, and understand, how people and states functioned in time and space. In poetry the Greeks spoke as individuals. In drama they dealt with the grandeur and weakness of humanity and with the demands of society on the individual. The greatest monuments of the Greeks were not temples, statues, or tombs, but profound thoughts set down in terms as fresh and immediate today as they were some 2,400 years ago.

The history of the Greeks is divided into two broad periods: the Hellenic period (the subject of this chapter), roughly the time between the arrival of the Greeks (approximately 2000 B.C.) and the victory over Greece in 338 B.C. by Philip of Macedon; and the Hellenistic period (the subject of Chapter 4), the age beginning with the remarkable reign of Philip's son, Alexander the Great (336–323 B.C.) and ending with the Roman conquest of the Hellenistic East (200–148 B.C.).

Bronze statue of Poseidon (Zeus?), fifth century B.C. *(Source: Ancient Art & Architecture Collection)*

- What geographical factors helped to mold the evolution of the city-state and to shape the course of the Greek experience?

- What was the nature of the early Greek experience, and how did the impact of the Minoans and Mycenaeans lead to the concept of a heroic past?

- How did the Greeks develop basic political forms, forms as different as democracy and tyranny, that have influenced all of later Western history?
- What did the Greek intellectual triumph entail, and what were its effects?
- Last, how and why did the Greeks eventually fail?

These profound questions, which can never be fully answered, are the themes of this chapter.

HELLAS: THE LAND

Hellas, as the ancient Greeks called their land, encompassed the Aegean Sea and its islands as well as the Greek peninsula (Map 3.1). The Greek peninsula itself, stretching in the direction of Egypt and the Near East, is an extension of the Balkan system of mountains. Perhaps the best and most eloquent description of Greece comes from the eminent German historian K. J. Beloch:

Greece is an alpine land, which rises from the waters of the Mediterranean Sea, scenically probably the most beautiful region in southern Europe. The noble contours of the mountains, the bare, rocky slopes, the dusty green of the conifer forests, the white cover of snow that envelops the higher summits for the greatest part of the year, added to which is the profound blue surface of the sea below, and above everything the diffused brightness of the southern sun; this gives a total picture, the charm of which impresses itself unforgettably on the soul of the observer.[1]

The rivers of Greece are never more than creeks, and most of them go dry in the summer. Greece is, however, a land blessed with good harbors, the most important of which look to the east. The islands of the Aegean serve as steppingstones between the peninsula and Asia Minor.

Despite the beauty of the region, geography acted as an enormously divisive force in Greek life. The mountains of Greece dominate the landscape, cutting the land into many small pockets and isolating areas of habitation. Innumerable small peninsulas open to the sea, which is dotted with islands, most of them small and many uninhabitable. The geographical fragmentation of Greece encouraged political fragmentation. Furthermore, communications were extraordinarily poor. Rocky

tracks were far more common than roads, and the few roads were unpaved. Usually a road consisted of nothing more than a pair of ruts cut into the rock to accommodate wheels. These conditions discouraged the growth of great empires.

THE MINOANS AND MYCENAEANS (CA 1650–CA 1100 B.C.)

The origins of Greek civilization are obscure. Neither historians, archaeologists, nor linguists can confidently establish when Greek-speaking peoples made the Balkan peninsula of Greece their homeland. All that can now safely be said is that by about 1650 B.C. Greeks had established themselves at the great city of Mycenae in the Peloponnesus and elsewhere in Greece. Before then, the area from Thessaly in the north to Messenia in the south was inhabited by small farming communities. Quite probably the Greeks merged with these natives, and from that union emerged the society that modern scholars call "Mycenaean," after Mycenae, the most important site of this new Greek-speaking culture.

Of this epoch the ancient Greeks themselves remembered almost nothing. The *Iliad* and the *Odyssey*, Homer's magnificent epic poems (eighth century B.C.), retain some dim memory of this period but very little that is authentic. One of the sterling achievements of modern archaeology is the discovery of this lost past. In the nineteenth century Heinrich Schliemann, a German businessman, fell in love with the *Iliad* and decided to find the sites it mentioned. He excavated Troy in modern Turkey, Mycenae, and several other sites in Greece to discover the lost past of the Greek people. At the turn of this century, the English archaeologist Sir Arthur Evans uncovered the remains of an entirely unknown civilization at Cnossus in Crete, and he gave it the name "Minoan" after the mythical Cretan king Minos. Scholars since then have further illuminated this long-lost era, and despite

MAP 3.1 Ancient Greece In antiquity the home of the Greeks included the islands of the Aegean and the western shore of Turkey as well as the Greek peninsula itself.

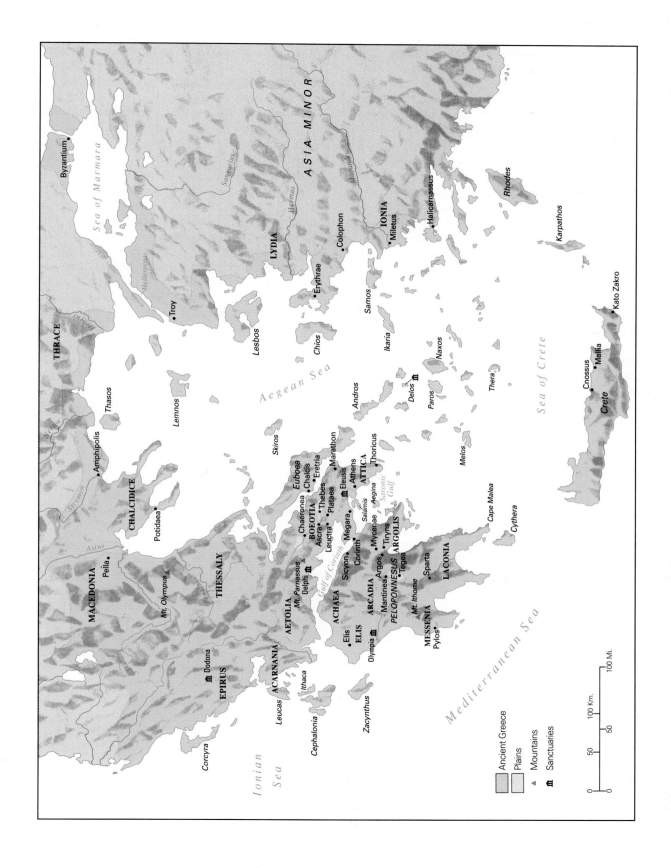

THRACE

Byzantium

Sea of Marmara

Hellespont

Sangarius

ASIA MINOR

Troy

LYDIA

Hermus

Colophon

Erythrae

IONIA

Miletus

Halicarnassus

Rhodes

Karpathos

Lesbos

Chios

Samos

Ikaria

Naxos

Paros

Thera

Sea of Crete

Kato Zakro

Mallia

Cnossus

Crete

Aegean Sea

Skiros

Andros

Delos

Melos

THRACE

Amphipolis

CHALCIDICE

Potidaea

Thasos

Lemnos

Strymon

Axius

MACEDONIA

Pella

Mt. Olympus

THESSALY

Penius

Euboea

Chaeronea

Chalcis

Eretria

Marathon

Thebes

BOEOTIA

Ascra

Plataea

Eleusis

Athens

Thoricus

Leuctra

ATTICA

Megara

Salamis

Aegina

Saronic Gulf

AETOLIA

Mt. Parnassus

Delphi

Gulf of Corinth

Sicyon

Corinth

Mycenae

Tiryns

ARGOLIS

ACHAEA

Argos

ARCADIA

Mantinea

Tegea

PELOPONNESUS

Sparta

LACONIA

Mt. Ithome

Elis

ELIS

Olympia

MESSENIA

Pylos

Cape Malea

Cythera

Mediterranean Sea

Leucas

ACARNANIA

Ithaca

Dodona

EPIRUS

Aous

Cephalonia

Zacynthus

Corcyra

Ionian Sea

Ancient Greece

Plains

▲ Mountains

♨ Sanctuaries

50   100 Km.

0   50   100 Mi.

many uncertainties a reasonably clear picture of the Minoans and Mycenaeans has begun to emerge.

By about 1650 B.C. the island of Crete was the home of the flourishing and vibrant Minoan culture. The Minoans had occupied Crete from at least the Neolithic period. They had also developed a script, now called "Linear A" (and yet to be deciphered), to express their language in writing. Because Linear A is still a riddle, it is as yet worthless to historians as a literary source and can provide no information on the status of men and women in society and politics or any idea of the course of Minoan history. Only archaeology and art offer clues to Minoan life. The symbol of Minoan culture was the palace. Around 1650 B.C. Crete was dotted with palaces, such as those at Mallia on the northern coast and Kato Zakro on the eastern tip of the island. Towering above all others in importance was the palace at Cnossus. The palace was the political and economic center of Minoan society, which, like many ancient Near Eastern societies, was rigorously controlled from above. Few specifics are known about Minoan society except that at its head stood a king and his nobles, who governed the lives and toil of Crete's farmers, sailors, shepherds, and artisans. The implements of the Minoans, like those of the Mycenaeans, were bronze, so archaeologists have named this period the "Bronze Age." Minoan society was wealthy and, to judge from the absence of fortifications on the island, peaceful. Enthusiastic sailors and merchants, the Minoans traded with Egypt and the cities of the area known today as the Middle East, Levant. Their ships also penetrated the Aegean Sea, throughout which they established trading posts. Their voyages in this direction brought them into contact with the Mycenaeans on the Greek peninsula.

By about 1650 B.C. Greek speakers were firmly settled at Mycenae, which became a major city and trading center. Later, other Mycenaean palaces and cities developed at Thebes, Athens, Tiryns, and Pylos. As in Crete, the political unit was the kingdom. The king and his warrior-aristocracy stood at the top of society. The seat and symbol of the king's power and wealth was his palace, which was also the economic center of the kingdom. Within its walls royal craftsmen fashioned jewelry and rich ornaments, made and decorated fine pottery, forged weapons, prepared hides and wool for clothing, and manufactured the other goods needed by the king and his retainers. Palace scribes kept records in Greek with a script known as "Linear B," which was derived from Minoan Linear A. The scribes kept account of taxes and drew up inventories of the king's possessions. From the palace, as at Cnossus, the Mycenaean king directed the lives of his subjects. Little is known of the king's subjects except that they were the artisans, traders, and farmers of Mycenaean society. The Mycenaean economy was marked by an extensive division of labor, all tightly controlled from the palace. At the bottom of the social scale were the slaves, who were normally owned by the king and aristocrats but who also worked for ordinary craftsmen.

Contacts between the Minoans and Mycenaeans were originally peaceful, and Minoan culture flooded the Greek mainland. But around 1450 B.C. the Mycenaeans attacked Crete, destroying many Minoan palaces and taking possession of the grand palace at Cnossus. For about the next fifty years the Mycenaeans ruled much of the island until a further wave of violence left Cnossus in ashes. These events are more disputed than understood, and the fate of Cnossus in particular has sparked controversy. Theories that Cnossus was destroyed by natural catastrophe have long since been disproved. Without doubt, human beings were responsible for the conflagration. Archaeologists cannot, however, determine who was responsible—whether the Mycenaeans at Cnossus were attacked by other Mycenaeans or whether the conquered Minoans rose in revolt.

Whatever the answer, the Mycenaean kingdoms in Greece benefited from the fall of Cnossus and the collapse of its trade. Mycenaean commerce quickly expanded throughout the Aegean, reaching as far abroad as Anatolia, Cyprus, and Egypt. Throughout central and southern Greece Mycenaean culture flourished as never before. Palaces became grander, and citadels were often protected by mammoth stone walls. Prosperity, however, did not bring peace, and between 1300 and 1000 B.C. kingdom after kingdom suffered attack and destruction.

Later Greeks accused the Dorians, who spoke a particular dialect of Greek, of overthrowing the Mycenaean kingdoms. Yet some modern linguists argue that the Dorians dwelt in Greece during the Mycenaean period. Archaeologists generally conclude that the Dorians, if not already present, could have entered Greece only long after the era of destruction. Furthermore, not one alien artifact

✤ **Minoan Naval Scene** This fresco, newly discovered at Thera, probably depicts the homecoming of a Minoan fleet of warships. Though later Greeks thought that the Minoans had ruled the sea, fleets such as the one pictured here probably protected Minoan maritime interests and suppressed piracy. Despite its military nature, the scene displays a general air of festivity, characteristic of Minoan art. *(Source: National Archaeological Museum, Athens/Ekdotike Athenon)*

has been found on any of these sites; thus there is no archaeological evidence for outside invaders. Normally, foreign invaders leave traces of themselves—for example, broken pottery and weapons—that are different from those of the attacked. We can conclude, therefore, that no outside intrusion destroyed the Mycenaean world. In fact, the legends preserved by later Greeks told of grim wars between Mycenaean kingdoms and of the fall of great royal families. Apparently Mycenaean Greece destroyed itself in a long series of internecine wars, a pattern that later Greeks would repeat.

The fall of the Mycenaean kingdoms ushered in a period of such poverty, disruption, and backwardness that historians usually call it the "Dark Age" of Greece (ca 1100–800 B.C.). Even literacy, which was not widespread in any case, was a casualty of the chaos. Yet even this period was important to the development of Greek civilization. It was a time of widespread movements of Greek-speaking peoples. Some Greeks sailed to Crete, where they established new communities. A great wave of Greeks spread eastward through the

Aegean to the coast of Asia Minor. These immigrations turned the Aegean into a Greek lake. The people who stayed behind gradually rebuilt Greek society. They thus provided an element of continuity, a link between the Mycenaean period and the Greek culture that emerged from the Dark Age.

✤ HOMER, HESIOD, AND THE HEROIC PAST (1100–800 B.C.)

The Greeks, unlike the Hebrews, had no sacred book that chronicled their past. Instead they had the *Iliad* and the *Odyssey* to describe a time when gods still walked the earth. And they learned the origin and descent of the gods from the *Theogony*, an epic poem by Hesiod (ca 700 B.C.). Instead of authentic history the poems of Homer and Hesiod offered the Greeks an ideal past, a largely legendary Heroic Age. In terms of pure history these poems contain scraps of information about the Bronze Age, much about the early Dark Age, and some about the poets' own era. Chronologically, then, the Heroic Age falls mainly in the period between the collapse of the Mycenaean world and the rebirth of literacy.

The *Iliad* recounts an expedition of Mycenaeans, whom Homer called "Achaeans," to besiege the city of Troy in Asia Minor. The heart of the *Iliad*, however, concerns the quarrel between Agamemnon, the king of Mycenae, and Achilles, the tragic hero of the poem, and how their quarrel brought suffering to the Achaeans. Only when Achilles put away his anger and pride did he consent to come forward, face, and kill the Trojan hero Hector. The *Odyssey*, probably composed later than the *Iliad*, narrates the adventures of Odysseus, one of the Achaean heroes who fought at Troy, during his voyage home from the fighting.

The splendor of these poems does not lie in their plots, although the *Odyssey* is a marvelous adventure story. Rather, both poems portray engaging but often flawed characters who are larger than life and yet typically human. Homer was also strikingly successful in depicting the great gods, who generally sit on Mount Olympus and watch the fighting at Troy like spectators at a baseball game, although they sometimes participate in the action. Homer's deities are reminiscent of Mesopotamian gods and goddesses. Hardly a decorous lot, the Olympians are raucous, petty, deceitful, and splendid. In short, they are human.

Homer at times portrayed the gods in a serious vein, but he never treated them in a systematic fashion, as did Hesiod, who lived somewhat later than Homer. Hesiod's epic poem, the *Theogony*, traces the descent of Zeus. Hesiod was influenced by Mesopotamian myths, which the Hittites had adopted and spread to the Aegean. Hesiod's poem claims that in the beginning there was chaos, the "yawning deep." From chaos came Gaea (Earth), who gave birth to Uranus (Heaven). Gaea and Uranus then gave birth to Cronus and Ocean (the deep-swelling waters). Cronus, the son of Earth and Heaven, like the Mesopotamian Enlil, separated the two and became king of the gods.

Like the Hebrews, Hesiod envisaged his cosmogony—his account of the way the universe developed—in moral terms. Zeus, the son of Cronus, defeated his evil father and took his place as king of the gods. He then sired Lawfulness, Right, Peace, and other powers of light and beauty. Thus, in Hesiod's conception, Zeus was the god of righteousness, who loved justice and hated wrongdoing.

In another epic poem, *Works and Days*, Hesiod wrote of his own time and his own village of Ascra in Boeotia, a scenic place set between beautiful mountains and fertile plains. In his will, Hesiod's father had divided his lands between Hesiod and his brother, Perses. Perses bribed the aristocratic authorities to give him the larger part of the inheritance and then squandered his wealth. Undaunted by the injustice of the powerful, Hesiod thundered back in a voice reminiscent of Khunanup, the "Eloquent Peasant" (see page 25):

Bribe-devouring lords, make straight your decisions,
Forget entirely crooked judgments.
He who causes evil to another harms himself.
Evil designs are most evil to the plotter.[2]

The similarities are striking between the fictional Khunanup and Hesiod, both of whom were oppressed by the rich and powerful. Yet the differences are even more significant. Hesiod, unlike Khunanup, did not receive justice from the political authorities of the day, but he fully expected divine vindication. Hesiod's call for justice has gone ringing through the centuries, its appeal as fresh today as when he first uttered it more than two millennia ago. Hesiod spoke of Zeus as Jeremiah had spoken of Yahweh, warning that Zeus would see that justice was done and injustice punished. He cautioned his readers that Zeus was angered by those who committed adultery, harmed orphans, and offended the aged. Hesiod's ethical concepts and faith in divine justice were the product of his belief that the world was governed by the power of good.

✤ THE POLIS

After the upheavals that ended the Mycenaean period and the slow recovery of prosperity during the Dark Age, the Greeks developed their basic political and institutional unit, the *polis* or city-state. The details of this development are largely lost, but by the end of the Dark Age the polis was common throughout Greece. Rarely did there occur the combination of extensive territory and political unity that allowed one polis to rise above others. Only three city-states were able to muster the resources of an entire region behind them (see Map 3.1): Sparta, which dominated the regions of Laconia and Messenia; Athens, which united the large

✦ **The Polis of Argos** This view, taken from the east of modern Argos, remarkably illustrates the structure of an ancient polis. Atop the hill in the background are the remains of the ancient acropolis. At its foot to the right are foundations of ancient public and private buildings. In the foreground are modern houses, situated just where ancient homes were located. *(Source: John Buckler)*

peninsula of Attica under its rule; and Thebes, which in several periods marshaled the resources of the fertile region of Boeotia. Otherwise, the political pattern of ancient Greece was one of many small city-states, few of which were much stronger or richer than their neighbors.

Physically the term *polis* designated a city or town and its surrounding countryside. The people of a typical polis lived in a compact group of houses within the city. The city's water supply came from public fountains and cisterns. By the fifth century B.C. the city was generally surrounded by a wall. The city contained a point, usually elevated, called the *acropolis*, and a public square or marketplace (*agora*). On the acropolis, which in the early

period was a place of refuge, stood the temples, altars, public monuments, and various dedications to the gods of the polis. The agora was originally the place where the warrior assembly met, but it became the political center of the polis. In the agora were porticoes, shops, and public buildings and courts.

The unsettled territory of the polis was typically its source of wealth. This territory consisted of arable land, pastureland, and wasteland. Farmers left the city each morning to work their fields or tend their flocks of sheep and goats, and they returned at night. On the wasteland men often quarried stone, mined for precious metals, and at certain times of the year obtained small amounts of fodder. Thus the polis encompassed a combination of urban and agrarian life.

The size of the polis varied according to geographical circumstances. Population figures for Greece are mostly guesswork, because most city-states were too small to need a census. The philosopher Plato thought that five thousand citizens constituted the ideal population of a polis. The intimacy of the polis was an important factor, one hard for modern city dwellers to imagine. The small population enabled Greeks to see how the individual fitted into the overall system—how the human parts made up the social whole.

The average polis did not have a standing army. Instead it relied on its citizens for protection. Very rich citizens often served as cavalry, which was, however, never as important as the heavy-armed infantry or *hoplites*. These were the backbone of the army. They wore metal helmets, body armor, carried a heavy, round shield, and armed themselves with a spear and sword. They provided their own equipment and were basically amateurs. In the Classical period (ca 500–338 B.C.) they were generally wealthy landowners who were accustomed to outdoor labor. When in battle, they stood in several dense lines, in which cohesion and order became as valuable as courage. This effort also gave them a sense of comradship and pride. Poor men made up the light-armed infantry. Usually wielding only a javelin or two, they used their mobility in rough areas to harass hoplites. In some instances the citizens of a polis hired mercenaries to fight their battles. Mercenaries were expensive, untrustworthy, and willing to defect to a higher bidder. Even worse, they sometimes seized control over the polis that had hired them.

Regardless of its size or wealth, the polis was fundamental to Greek life. The polis was far more than a political institution. Above all, it was a community of citizens, and the affairs of the community were the concern of all. The customs of the community were at the same time the laws of the polis. Rome later created a single magnificent body of law, but the Greeks had as many law codes as they had city-states. Though the laws of one polis might be roughly similar to those of another, the law of any given polis was unique simply because the customs and the experience of each one had been unique.

The polis could be governed in any of several ways. First, it could be a *monarchy*, a term derived from the Greek for "the rule of one man." A king could represent the community, reigning according to law and respecting the rights of the citizens. Second, the *aristocracy* could govern the state. Third, the running of the polis could be the duty and prerogative of an *oligarchy*, which literally means "the rule of a few"—in this case a small group of wealthy citizens, not necessarily of aristocratic birth. Or the polis could be governed as a *democracy*, through the rule of the people, a concept which in Greece meant that all citizens, without respect to birth or wealth, administered the workings of government. How a polis was governed depended on who had the upper hand. When the wealthy held power, they usually instituted oligarchies; when the people could break the hold of the rich, they established democracies. In any case, no polis ever had an ironclad, unchangeable constitution. Still another form of Greek government was *tyranny*. Under tyranny the polis was ruled by a tyrant, a man who had seized power by unconstitutional means, generally by using his wealth to gain a political following that could topple the existing government.

Ironically, the very integration of the polis proved to be one of its weaknesses. Because the bonds that held the polis together were so intimate, Greeks were extremely reluctant to allow foreigners to share fully in its life. An alien, even someone Greek by birth, could almost never expect to be made a citizen. Nor could women play a political role. Women participated in the civic cults and served as priestesses, but the polis had no room for them in state affairs. Thus the exclusiveness of the polis doomed it to a limited horizon.

Although each polis was normally jealous of its independence, some Greeks banded together to create leagues of city-states. Here was the birth of Greek federalism, a political system in which several states formed a central government while remaining independent in their internal affairs. United in a league, a confederation of city-states was far stronger than any of its individual members and better able to withstand external attack.

Yet even federalism could not overcome the passionate individualism of the polis, which proved to be a serious weakness. The citizens of each polis were determined to remain free and autonomous. Rarely were the Greeks willing to unite in larger political bodies. The political result in Greece, as in Sumer, was almost constant warfare. The polis could dominate, but unlike Rome it could not incorporate.

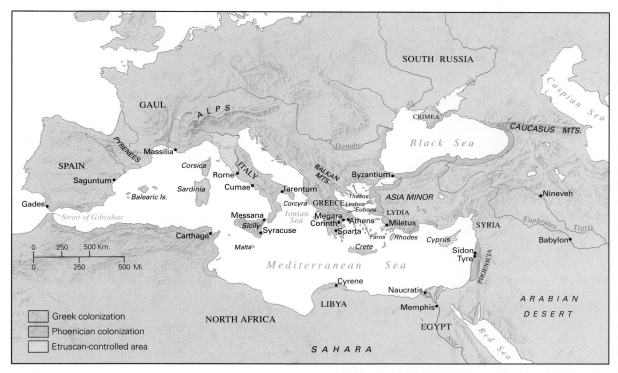

✤ **MAP 3.2 Colonization of the Mediterranean** Though the Greeks and Phoenicians colonized the Mediterranean basin at about the same time, the Greeks spread over far greater areas.

✦ THE LYRIC AGE (800–500 B.C.)

The maturation of the polis coincided with one of the most vibrant periods of Greek history, an era of extraordinary expansion geographically, artistically, and politically. Greeks ventured as far east as the Black Sea and as far west as Spain (Map 3.2). With the rebirth of literacy, this period also witnessed a tremendous literary flowering as poets broke away from the heroic tradition and wrote about their own lives. Politically these were the years when Sparta and Athens—the two poles of the Greek experience—rose to prominence.

Overseas Expansion

During the years 1100–800 B.C., the Greeks not only recovered from the breakdown of the Mycenaean world but also grew in wealth and numbers. This new prosperity brought with it new problems. Greece is a small and not especially fertile country. The increase in population meant that many men and their families had very little land or none at all. Land hunger and the resulting social and political tensions drove many Greeks to seek new homes outside of Greece. Other factors, largely intangible, played their part as well: the desire for a new start, a love of excitement and adventure, and natural curiosity about what lay beyond the horizon.

The Mediterranean offered the Greeks an escape valve, for they were always a seafaring people. To them the sea was a highway, not a barrier. Through their commercial ventures they had long been familiar with the rich areas of the western Mediterranean. Moreover, the geography of the Mediterranean basin favored colonization. The land and climate of the Mediterranean region are remarkably uniform. Greeks could travel to new areas, whether to Cyprus in the east or to Malta in the west, and establish the kind of settlement they had known in Greece. They could also raise the same crops they had raised in Greece. The move to a new home was not a plunge into totally unknown

❖ **Early Corinthian Vase** This vase shows all of the vivacity of Greek art. It also illustrates the Greek use of foreign artistic motifs on traditional pieces of pottery. *(Source: Courtesy of the Trustees of the British Museum)*

conditions. Once the colonists had established themselves in new homes, they continued life essentially as in Greece.

From about 750 to 550 B.C., Greeks from the mainland and from Asia Minor poured onto the coasts of the northern Aegean, the Ionian Sea, and the Black Sea and into North Africa, Sicily, southern Italy, southern France, and Spain (see Map 3.2). Just as the migrations of the Dark Age had turned the Aegean into a Greek lake, this later wave of colonization spread the Greeks and their culture throughout the Mediterranean.

In the process the Greek world itself changed. When the Greeks came into contact with other

peoples, they encountered new ideas and customs. They also established new economic links. As the eminent German scholar Walter Burkert has recently demonstrated, the Greeks grafted some foreign ideas and artistic styles from the Near East and Egypt onto their own culture. In vase painting the Greeks began to decorate their pots with exotic monsters derived from Eastern models, but they did so on existing types of vases. Something similar occurred with sculpture. The Egyptians had a long tradition of carving statues of people in a stylized postion. The Greeks adapted that style to their own tradition of sculpture that blended realism and idealism. They then spread their increasingly cosmopolitan art and culture beyond the Aegean to Italy and Carthage in the west.

In economic terms the expansion of the Greeks created a much larger market for agricultural and manufactured goods. From the east, especially from the northern coast of the Black Sea, came wheat in a volume beyond the capacity of Greek soil. In return flowed Greek wine and olive oil that could not be produced in the harsher climate of the north. Greek-manufactured goods, notably rich jewelry and fine pottery, circulated from southern Russia to Spain. Thus, Greek culture and economics, fertilized by the influences of other societies, spread throughout the Mediterranean basin.

Colonization presented the polis with a huge challenge, for it required organization and planning on an unprecedented scale. The colonizing city, called the *metropolis* or mother-city, first decided where to establish the colony, how to transport colonists to the site, and who would sail. Then the metropolis collected and stored the supplies that the colonists would need both to feed themselves and to plant their first crop. The metropolis must also provide adequate shipping for the voyage. All preparations ready, a leader, called an *oikist*, ordered the colonists to sail. From then the oikist was in full command of the band until the colony was established in its new site and capable of running its own affairs. A significant aspect of colonizing ventures is that colonists sailed as equals, and as equals they set about building a new life together.

Once the colonists landed, the oikist laid out the new polis, selected the sites of temples and public buildings, and established the government. Then he surrendered power to the new leaders. The colony was thereafter independent of the metropolis. For the Greeks, colonization had two important aspects. First, it demanded that the polis assume a much greater public function than ever before, thus strengthening the city-state's institutional position. Second, colonization spread the polis and its values far beyond the shores of Greece. Even more important, colonization on this scale had a profound impact on the course of Western civilization. It meant that the prevailing culture of the Mediterranean basin would be Greek, the heritage to which Rome would later fall heir.

One man can in many ways stand as the symbol of the vital and robust era of colonization. Archilochus was born on the island of Paros, the bastard son of an aristocrat. He knew that because of his illegitimacy he would never inherit his father's land, and this knowledge seems to have made him self-reliant. He was also a poet of genius, the first of the lyric poets who left an indelible mark on this age. Unlike the epic poets, who portrayed the deeds of heroes, Archilochus sang of himself. He knew the sea, the dangers of sailing, and the price that the sea often exacted. He spoke of one shipwreck in grim terms and even treated the god of the sea with irony: "Of fifty men gentle Poseidon left one, Koiranos, to be saved from shipwreck."

Together with others from Paros he took part in the colonization of Thasos in the northern Aegean. He described the island in less than glowing terms: "Like the spine of an ass it stands, crowned to the brim with a wild forest." His opinion of his fellow colonists was hardly kinder: "So the misery of all Greece came together in Thasos." Yet at Thasos he fell in love with a woman named Neoboule. They did not marry because her father opposed the match. In revenge, Archilochus seduced Neoboule's younger sister, railed at the entire family, and left Thasos to live the life of a mercenary.

His hired lance took him to Euboea, and he left a striking picture of the fighting there:

Not many bows will be strung, nor slings be slung
When Ares begins battle in the plain.
There will be the mournful work of the sword:
For in this kind of battle are the spear-famed
Lords of Euboea experienced.[3]

❖ **Greek Influence Abroad** This stunning gold comb is a remarkable combination of Greek and eastern details. The art is almost purely Greek. The mounted horseman is clothed with largely Greek armor, but he attacks an eastern enemy. The horseman's companion is also eastern. This splendid piece of art testifies to the exchange of artistic motifs and styles in the eastern Mediterranean basin. *(Source: Hermitage, Leningrad)*

Archilochus exemplifies the energy, restlessness, self-reliance, and sense of adventure that characterizes this epoch. People like him broke old ties, faced homelessness and danger, and built new homes for themselves. They made the Mediterranean Greek.

Lyric Poets

Archilochus the colonist and adventurer is not nearly as important as Archilochus the lyric poet, whose individualism set a new tone in Greek literature. For the first time in Western civilization, men and women began to write of their own experiences. Their poetry reflected their belief that they had something precious to say about themselves. To them poetry did not belong only to the gods or to the great heroes on the plain of Troy. Some lyric poets used their literary talents for the good of their city-states. They stood forth as individuals and in their poetry urged their countrymen to be patriotic and just.

One of the most unforgettable of these writers is the poet Sappho. Unlike Archilochus, she neither

✦ Mosaic Portrait of Sappho The Greek letters in the upper left corner identify this idealized portrait as that of Sappho. The mosaic, which was found at Sparta, dates to the late Roman Empire and testifies to Sappho's popularity in antiquity. *(Source: Caroline Buckler)*

braved the wilds nor pushed into the unknown, yet she was no less individual than he. Sappho was born in the seventh century B.C. on the island of Lesbos, a place of sun, sea, and rustic beauty. Her marriage produced a daughter, to whom she wrote some of her poems. Sappho's poetry is personal and intense. She delighted in her surroundings, which were those of aristocratic women, and celebrated the little things around her. Hers was a world of natural beauty, sacred groves, religious festivals, wedding celebrations, and noble companions. Sappho fondly remembered walks with a woman friend:

How we went to every hill, brook,
And holy place, and when early spring
Filled the woods with noises of birds
And a choir of nightingales—we two
In solitude were wandering there.[4]

Sappho is best known for erotic poetry, for she expressed her love frankly and without shame. She was bisexual, and much of her poetry dealt with her homosexual love affairs. In one of her poems she remembered the words of her lover:

Sappho, if you do not come out,
I swear, I will love you no more.
O rise and free your lovely strength
From the bed and shine upon us.
Lifting off your Chian nightgown, and
Like a pure lily by a spring,
Bathe in the water.[5]

In antiquity Sappho's name became linked with female homosexual love. Today the English word *lesbian* is derived from Sappho's island home. The Greeks accepted bisexuality—that men and women could enjoy both homosexual and heterosexual lovemaking. Homosexual relationships normally carried no social stigma. In her mature years Sappho was courted by a younger man who wanted to marry her. By then she had already proclaimed her love for several girls, yet the young man was not troubled by these affairs. As it turned out, Sappho refused to marry because she was past child-bearing age.

In their poetry Archilochus and Sappho reveal two sides of Greek life in this period. Archilochus exemplifies the energy and adventure of the age, while Sappho expresses the intensely personal side

✤ **The Hoplite Phalanx** When the Greeks adopted heavy armor, weapons, and shields, their lack of mobility forced them to fight in several dense lines, each behind the other. Cohesion and order became as valuable as courage. To help the hoplites maintain their pace during the attack, a flute player here plays a marching tune. *(Source: Villa Giulia Museum/Gabinetto Fotografico Nazionale)*

of life. The link connecting the two poets is their individualism, their faith in themselves, and their desire to reach out to other men and women in order to share their experiences, thoughts, and wisdom.

The Growth of Sparta

During the Lyric Age the Spartans expanded the boundaries of their polis and made it the leading power in Greece. Like other Greeks, the Spartans faced the problems of overpopulation and land hunger. Unlike other Greeks, the Spartans solved these problems by conquest, not by colonization. To gain more land the Spartans set out in about 735 B.C. to conquer Messenia, a rich, fertile region in the southwestern Peloponnesus. This conflict, the First Messenian War, lasted for twenty years and ended in a Spartan triumph. The Spartans appropriated Messenian land and turned the Messenians into *helots* or state serfs.

In about 650 B.C., Spartan exploitation and oppression of the Messenian helots led to a helot revolt so massive and stubborn that it became known as the Second Messenian War. The Spartan poet Tyrtaeus, a contemporary of these events, vividly portrayed the ferocity of the fighting:

For it is a shameful thing indeed
When with the foremost fighters
An elder falling in front of the young men
Lies outstretched,
Having white hair and grey beard,
Breathing forth his stout soul in the dust,
Holding in his hands his genitals
stained with blood.[6]

Confronted with such horrors, Spartan enthusiasm for the war waned. Finally, after some thirty years of fighting, the Spartans put down the revolt. Nevertheless, the political and social strain it caused led to a transformation of the Spartan polis.

It took the full might of the Spartan people, aristocrat and commoner alike, to win the Second Messenian War. After the victory the non-nobles, who had done much of the fighting, demanded rights equal to those of the nobility. They had taken their place in the battle line next to their aristocratic neighbors but lacked the social prestige and political rights of their noble companions. The agitation of these non-nobles disrupted society until the aristocrats agreed to remodel the state.

Although the Spartans later claimed that the changes brought about by this compromise were the work of Lycurgus, a legendary, semidivine lawgiver, they were really the work of the entire Spartan people. The "Lycurgan regimen," as these reforms were called, was a new political, economic, and social system. Political distinctions among the Spartans were eliminated, and all citizens became legally equal. In effect, the Lycurgan regimen abolished the aristocracy and made the government an oligarchy. Actual governance of the polis was in the hands of two kings, who were primarily military leaders. The kings and twenty-eight elders made up a council that deliberated on foreign and domestic matters and prepared legislation for the assembly, which consisted of all Spartan citizens. The real executive power of the polis was in the hands of five *ephors*, or overseers, elected from and by all the people.

To provide for their economic needs the Spartans divided the land of Messenia among all citizens. Helots worked the land, raised the crops, provided the Spartans with their living, and occasionally served in the army. The Spartans kept the helots in line by means of systematic terrorism, hoping to beat them down and keep them quiet. Spartan citizens were supposed to devote their time exclusively to military training.

In the Lycurgan system every citizen owed primary allegiance to Sparta. Suppression of the individual together with emphasis on military prowess led to a barracks state. Family life itself was sacrificed to the polis. Once Spartan boys reached the age of twelve, they were enrolled in separate companies with other boys of their age. They slept outside on reed mats and underwent rugged physical and military training until age twenty-four, when they became front-line soldiers. For the rest of their lives, Spartan men kept themselves prepared for combat. Their military training never ceased, and the older men were expected to be models of endurance, frugality, and sturdiness to the younger men. In battle Spartans were supposed to stand and die rather than retreat. An anecdote about one Spartan mother sums up Spartan military values. As her son was setting off to battle, the mother handed him his shield and advised him to come back either victorious, carrying the shield, or dead, being carried on it. In the Lycurgan regimen Spartan men were expected to train vigorously, disdain luxury and wealth, do with little, and like it.

Similar rigorous requirements applied to Spartan women, who may have been unique in all of Greek society. They were prohibited from wearing jewelry or ornate clothes. They too exercised strenuously in the belief that hard physical training promoted the birth of healthy children. Yet they were hardly oppressed. They enjoyed a more active and open public life than most other Greek women, even though they could neither vote nor hold office. They were far more emancipated than many other Greek women in part because Spartan society felt that mothers and wives had to be as hardy as their sons and husbands. Sparta was not a place for weaklings, male or female. Spartan women saw it as their privilege to be the wives and mothers of victorious warriors, and on several occasions their own courage became legendary. They had a reputation for independent spirit and self-assertion. This position stemmed from their genuine patriotism, but also from their title to much Spartan land. For all of these reasons, they shared a footing with Spartan men that most other Greek women lacked in their own societies.

Along with the emphasis on military values for both sexes, the Lycurgan regimen had another purpose as well: it served to instill in society the civic virtues of dedication to the state and a code of moral conduct. These aspects of the Spartan system were generally admired throughout the Greek world.

The Evolution of Athens

Like Sparta, Athens faced pressing social and economic problems during the Lyric Age, but the Athenian response was far different from that of the Spartans. Instead of creating an oligarchy, the Athenians extended to all citizens the right and duty of governing the polis. Indeed, the Athenian democracy was one of the most thoroughgoing in Greece.

The late seventh century B.C. was for Athens a time of turmoil, the causes for which are virtually unknown. In either 632 or 636 B.C., Cylon, an Athenian aristocrat, seized the Acropolis in an effort to become tyrant. Rushing immediately into the city, peasants foiled Cylon's attempt. In 621 B.C., Draco, an Athenian aristocrat, doubtless under pressure from the peasants, published the first law code of the Athenian polis. His code was thought harsh, but it nonetheless embodied the ideal that the law belonged to the citizens. Nevertheless, peasant unrest continued.

By the early sixth century B.C., social and economic conditions led to another explosive situation. The aristocracy still governed Athens as oppressively as the "bribe-devouring lords" of Boeotia against whom Hesiod had railed. The aristocrats owned the best land, met in an assembly to govern the polis, and interpreted the law. Noble landowners were forcing small farmers into economic dependence. Many families were sold into slavery; others were exiled and their land pledged to the rich. Poor farmers who had borrowed from their wealthy neighbors had to put up their land as collateral. If a farmer was unable to repay the loan, his creditor put a stone on the borrower's field to signify his indebtedness and thereafter took one-sixth of the annual yield until the debt was paid. If the farmer had to borrow again, he pledged himself and sometimes his family. If he was again unable to repay the loan, he became the slave of his creditor. Because the harvests of the poor farmer were generally small, he could usually raise enough to live on but not enough to repay his loan.

In many other city-states conditions like those in Athens led to the rise of tyrants. One person who recognized these problems clearly was Solon, himself an aristocrat and poet, and a man opposed to tyrants. He was also the one man in Athens who enjoyed the respect of both aristocrats and peasants. Like Hesiod, Solon used his poetry to condemn the aristocrats for their greed and dishonesty. Solon recited his poems in the Athenian agora, where everyone could hear his relentless call for justice and fairness. The aristocrats realized that Solon was no crazed revolutionary, and the common people trusted him. Around 594 B.C. the nobles elected him *archon*, chief magistrate of the Athenian polis, and gave him extraordinary power to reform the state.

Solon immediately freed all people enslaved for debt, recalled all exiles, canceled all debts on land, and made enslavement for debt illegal. He also divided society into four legal groups on the basis of wealth. In the most influential group were the wealthiest citizens, but even the poorest and least powerful group enjoyed certain rights. Solon allowed them into the old aristocratic assembly, where they could take part in the election of magistrates.

In all his work Solon gave thought to the rights of the poor as well as the rich. He gave the commoners a place in government and a voice in the political affairs of Athens. His work done, Solon insisted that all swear to uphold his reforms. Then, because many were clamoring for him to become tyrant, he left Athens.

Although Solon's reforms solved some immediate problems, they did not bring peace to Athens. Some aristocrats attempted to make themselves tyrants, while others banded together to oppose them. In 546 B.C. Pisistratus, an exiled aristocrat, returned to Athens, defeated his opponents, and became tyrant. Pisistratus reduced the power of the aristocracy while supporting the common people. Under his rule Athens prospered, and his building program began to transform the city into one of the splendors of Greece. His reign as tyrant promoted the growth of democratic ideas by arousing in the Athenians rudimentary feelings of equality.

Athenian acceptance of tyranny did not long outlive Pisistratus, for his son Hippias ruled harshly, committing excesses that led to his overthrow. After a brief period of turmoil between factions of the nobility, Cleisthenes, a wealthy and prominent aristocrat, emerged triumphant in 508 B.C., largely because he won the support of the people. Cleisthenes created the Athenian democracy with the full knowledge and approval of the Athenian people. He reorganized the state completely but presented every innovation to the assembly for discussion and ratification. All Athenian citizens had a voice in Cleisthenes' work.

Cleisthenes created the *deme*, a local unit, to serve as the basis of his political system. Citizenship was tightly linked to the deme, for each deme kept the roll of those within its jurisdiction who were admitted to citizenship. Cleisthenes also created ten new tribes as administrative units. All the demes were grouped in tribes, which thus formed the link between the demes and the central government. The central government included an assembly of all citizens and a new council of five hundred members. Cleisthenes is often credited with the institution of *ostracism*, a vote of the Athenian people by which the man receiving the most votes went into exile. The goal of ostracism was to rid the state peacefully of a difficult or potentially dangerous politician.

The democracy functioned on the idea that all full citizens, the *demos*, were sovereign. Yet not all citizens could take time from work to participate in government. Therefore, they delegated their power to other citizens by creating various offices meant to run the democracy. The most prestigious of them was the board of ten archons, who were charged with handling legal and military matters. Six of them oversaw the Athenian legal system. They presided over courts, fixed dates for trials, and ensured that the laws of Athens were consistent. They were all elected for one year. After leaving office, they entered the *Areopagos*, a select council of ex-archons who handled cases involving homicide, wounding, and arson.

Legislation was in the hands of two bodies, the *boule*, or council, composed of five hundred members, and the ecclesia, the assembly of all citizens. The boule, separate from the Areopagos, was perhaps the major institution of the democracy. By supervising the various committees of government and proposing bills to the assembly, it guided Athenian political life. It received foreign envoys and forwarded treaties to the assembly for ratification. It oversaw the granting of state contracts and was responsible for receiving many revenues. It held the democracy together. Nonetheless, the assembly had the final word. Open to all male citizens over eighteen years of age, it met at a specific place to vote on matters presented to it. The assembly could either accept, amend, or reject bills put before it. Every member could express his opinion on any subject on the agenda, and a simple majority vote was needed to pass or reject a bill.

Athenian democracy was to prove an inspiring ideal in Western civilization. It demonstrated that a large group of people, not just a few, could efficiently run the affairs of state. By heeding the opinions, suggestions, and wisdom of all its citizens, the polis enjoyed the maximum amount of good counsel. Because all citizens could speak their minds, they did not have to resort to rebellion or conspiracy to express their desires.

Athenian democracy must not, however, be thought of in modern terms. In Athens democracy meant a form of government in which poor men as well as rich enjoyed political power and responsibility. In practice, though, most important offices were held by aristocrats. Furthermore, Athenian democracy denied political rights to many people, including women and slaves. Foreigners were seldom admitted to citizenship. Unlike modern democracies, Athenian democracy did not mean that the citizen would vote for others who would then run the state. Instead, every citizen was expected to be able to perform the duties of most magistrates. In Athens citizens voted and served. The people were the government. They enjoyed equal rights under the law, and the voice of the majority determined law. It is this union of the individual and the state—the view that the state exists for the good of the citizen, whose duty it is to serve it well—that has made Athenian democracy so compelling an ideal.

✤ THE CLASSICAL PERIOD (500–338 B.C.)

In the years 500 to 338 B.C., Greek civilization reached its highest peak in politics, thought, and art. In this period the Greeks beat back the armies of the Persian empire. Then, turning their spears against one another, they destroyed their own political system in a century of warfare. Some thoughtful Greeks felt prompted to record and analyze these momentous events; the result was the creation of history. This era saw the flowering of philosophy, as thinkers in Ionia on the western coast of Asia Minor and on the Greek mainland began to ponder the nature and meaning of the universe and human experience; they used their intellects to explain the world around them and to determine humanity's place in it. The Greeks invented drama, and the Athenian tragedians Aeschylus, Sophocles, and Euripides explored themes that still inspire audiences today. Greek architects reached the zenith of their art and created buildings whose very ruins still inspire awe. Because Greek intellectual and artistic efforts attained their fullest and finest expression in these years, this age is called the "classical period." Few periods in the history of Western society can match it in sheer dynamism and achievement.

The Persian Wars (499–479 B.C.)

One of the hallmarks of the Classical period was warfare. In 499 B.C. the Ionian Greeks, with the feeble help of Athens, rebelled against the Persian Empire. In 490 B.C. the Persians struck back at Athens but were beaten off at the Battle of Marathon, a small plain in Attica (see Map 3.3). This failure prompted the Persians to try again. In 480 B.C. the Persian king Xerxes led a mighty invasion force into Greece. Facing this emergency, many of the Greeks united and pooled their resources to resist the invaders. The Spartans provided the overall leadership and commanded the Greek armies. The Athenians, led by the wily Themistocles, provided the heart of the naval forces.

The first confrontations between the Persians and the Greeks occurred at the pass of Thermopylae and in the waters off Artemisium, the northern tip of Euboea. At Thermopylae the Greek hoplites, heavily armed foot soldiers, showed their mettle. Before the fighting began, a report came in that when the Persian archers shot their bows the arrows darkened the sky. One gruff Spartan replied merely, "Fine, then we'll fight in the shade." The Greeks at Thermopylae fought heroically, but the Persians took the position. In 480 B.C. the Greek fleet, inspired by the energetic Themistocles, met the Persian armada at Salamis, an island just west of Athens. Though outnumbered by the Persians, the Greek navy won an overwhelming victory (see Listening to the Past). The remnants of the Persian fleet retired, and with them went all hope of Persian victory. In the following year, a coalition of Greek forces, commanded by the Spartan Pausanias with assistance from the Athenian Aristides, smashed the last Persian army at Plataea, a small polis in Boeotia. Greece remained free.

By defeating the Persians, the Greeks ensured that Oriental monarchy would not stifle the Greek achievement. The Greeks were thus able to develop their particular genius in freedom. These decisive victories meant that Greek political forms and intellectual concepts would be the heritage of the West.

Growth of the Athenian Empire (478–431 B.C.)

For the Greeks the Persian wars were a beginning, not an end. Before them was a novel situation: the

❖ **The Persian Wars** This vase dates to the early fifth century B.C. It depicts fighting between a heavily-armed Greek hoplite on the left, carrying a shield and spear, against an Asian soldier who is less heavily armed. *(Source: The Metropolitan Museum of Art, Rogers Fund, 1906 (06.1021.117))*

defeat of the Persians had created a power vacuum in the Aegean. The state with the strongest navy could turn the Aegean into its lake. In 478 B.C., to take advantage of this situation, the Athenians and their allies, again led by Aristides, formed the Delian League, a grand naval alliance aimed at liberating Ionia from Persian rule. The league took its name from the small island of Delos, on which stood a religious center sacred to all parties. The Delian League was intended as a free alliance under the leadership of Athens. Athenians provided most of the warships and crews and determined how many ships or how much money each member of the league should contribute to the allied effort.

The Athenians, supported by the Delian League and led by the young aristocrat Cimon, carried the war against Persia. But Athenian success had a sinister side. While the Athenians drove the Persians out of the Aegean, they also became increasingly imperialistic, even to the point of turning the Delian League into an Athenian empire. Athens began reducing its allies to the status of subjects. The Athenians sternly put down dissident or rebellious governments, replacing them with trustworthy puppets. Tribute was often collected by force, and the Athenians placed the economic resources of the Delian League under tighter and tighter control.

Athens justified its conduct by its successful leadership. In about 467 B.C. Cimon defeated a new and huge Persian force at the Battle of the Eurymedon River in Asia Minor, once again removing the shadow of Persia from the Aegean. But as the threat from Persia waned and the Athenians treated their allies more harshly, major allies such as Thasos revolted (ca 465 B.C.), requiring the Delian League to use its forces against its own members. The expansion of Athenian power and the aggressiveness of Athenian rule also alarmed Sparta and its allies. While relations between Athens and Sparta cooled, Pericles (ca 494–429 B.C.) became the leading statesman in Athens. Like the democracy he led, Pericles, an aristocrat of solid intellectual ability, was aggressive and imperialistic. At last, in 459 B.C., Sparta and Athens went to war over conflicts between Athens and some of Sparta's allies. Though the Athenians conquered Boeotia, Megara, and Aegina in the early stages of the war, they met defeat in Egypt and later in Boeotia. The war ended in 445 B.C. with no serious damage to either side and nothing settled. But this war divided the Greek world between the two great powers.

During the 440s and 430s, Athens continued its severe policies toward its subject allies and came into conflict with Corinth, one of Sparta's leading supporters (see Map 3.3). In 433 B.C. Athens sided with Corcyra against Corinth in a dispute between the two. Together with the Corcyraean fleet, an Athenian squadron defeated the Corinthian navy in open combat. The next year Corinth and Athens collided again, this time over the Corinthian colony of Potidaea, in a conflict the Athenians also won. In this climate of anger and escalation, Pericles took the next step. To punish Megara for alleged sacrilege Pericles in 432 B.C. persuaded the Athenians to pass a law, the Megarian Decree, which excluded Megarians from trading with Athens and its empire. In response the Spartans convened a meeting of their allies, whose complaints of Athenian aggression ended with a demand that Athens be stopped. Reluctantly the Spartans agreed to declare war. The real reason for war, according to the Athenian historian Thucydides, was very simple: "The truest explanation, though the one least mentioned, was the great growth of Athenian power and the fear it caused the Lacedaemonians [Spartans], which drove them to war."[7]

The Peloponnesian War (431–404 B.C.)

At the outbreak of this conflict, the Peloponnesian War, the Spartan ambassador Melesippus warned the Athenians: "This day will be the beginning of great evil for the Greeks." Few men have ever prophesied more accurately. The Peloponnesian War lasted a generation and brought in its wake fearful plagues, famine, civil wars, widespread destruction, and huge loss of life.

After a Theban attack on the nearby polis of Plataea, the Peloponnesian War began in earnest. In the next seven years, the army of Sparta and its Peloponnesian allies invaded Attica five times. The Athenians stood behind their walls, but in 430 B.C. the cramped conditions nurtured a dreadful plague, that killed huge numbers, eventually claiming Pericles himself. The death of Pericles opened the door to a new breed of politicians, men who were rash, ambitious, and more dedicated to themselves than to Athens. One such was Cleon, a very daring and in some ways a very capable man. To divert the constant Spartan invasions of Attica, Cleon proposed a counterattack at Pylos, a rocky peninsula in Messenia immediately opposite the Spartan-occupied island of Sphacteria. Spartan forces were defeated, yet the outcome failed to bring peace. Instead, the energetic Spartan commander Brasidas widened the war in 424 B.C. by

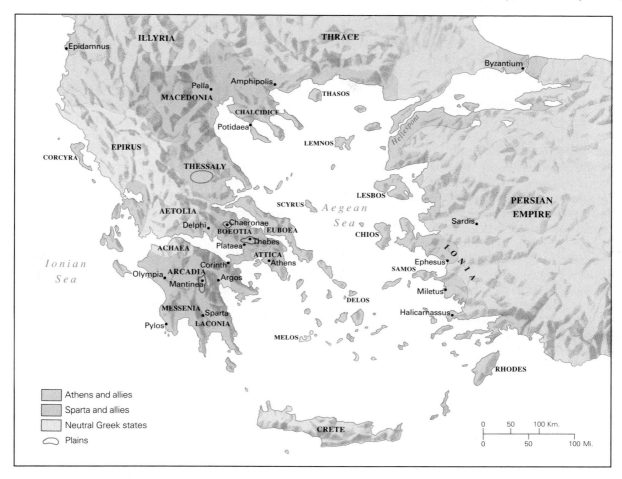

❖ MAP 3.3 The Peloponnesian War This map, which shows the alignment of states during the Peloponnesian War, vividly illustrates the large scale of the war and its divisive impact.

capturing Amphipolis on the northern coast of the Aegean, one of Athens's most valuable subject states. Two years later, both Cleon and Brasidas were killed in a battle to recapture the city. Recognizing that ten years of war had resulted only in death, destruction, and stalemate, Sparta and Athens concluded the Peace of Nicias in 421 B.C.

The Peace of Nicias resulted in a cold war. But even cold war, as the people of the twentieth century know so well, can bring horror and misery. Such was the case when in 416 B.C. the Athenians sent a fleet to the neutral island of Melos with an ultimatum: the Melians could surrender or perish. The motives of the Athenians were frankly and

brutally imperialistic. The Melians resisted. The Athenians conquered them, killed men of military age, and sold women and children into slavery.

The cold war grew hotter, thanks to the ambitions of Alcibiades (ca 450–404 B.C.), an aristocrat, kinsman of Pericles, and student of the philosopher Socrates. A shameless opportunist, Alcibiades widened the war to further his own career and to increase the power of Athens. He convinced the Athenians to attack Syracuse, the leading polis in Sicily. The undertaking was vast, requiring an enormous fleet and thousands of sailors and soldiers. Trouble began at the outset. Alcibiades' political enemies indicted him, whereupon he fled to Sparta rather than stand trial. Meanwhile, in 414 B.C. the Athenians laid siege to Syracuse. The Syracusans fought back bravely, and even a huge Athenian relief force failed to conquer the city. Finally, in 413 B.C. the Syracusans counterattacked, completely crushing the Athenians. Thucydides wrote the epitaph for the Athenians: "Infantry, fleet, and everything else were utterly destroyed, and out of many few returned home."[8]

The disaster in Sicily ushered in the final phase of the war, which was marked by three major developments: the renewal of war between Athens and Sparta, Persia's intervention in the war, and the revolt of many Athenian subjects. The year 413 B.C. saw Sparta's declaration of war against Athens and widespread revolt within the Athenian empire. Yet Sparta still lacked a navy, the only instrument that could take advantage of the unrest of Athens's subjects, most of whom lived either on islands or in Ionia. The sly Alcibiades, now working for Sparta, provided a solution: he engineered an alliance between Sparta and Persia. The Persians agreed to build a fleet for Sparta. In return, the Spartans promised to give Ionia back to Persia. Now equipped with a fleet, the Spartans challenged the Athenians in the Aegean, the result being a long roll of inconclusive naval battles.

The strain of war prompted the Athenians in 407 B.C. to recall Alcibiades from exile. He cheerfully double-crossed the Spartans and Persians, but even he could not restore Athenian fortunes. In 405 B.C. Athens met its match in the Spartan commander Lysander, a man whose grasp of strategy, politics, and diplomacy easily rivaled Alcibiades'. Lysander destroyed the last Athenian fleet at the Battle of Aegospotami, after which the Spartans blockaded Athens until it was starved into submission. After twenty-seven years the Peloponnesian War was over, and the evils prophesied by the Spartan ambassador Melesippus in 431 B.C. had come true.

The Birth of Historical Awareness

One positive development grew out of the Persian and Peloponnesian wars: the beginnings of historical writing. Herodotus (ca 485–425 B.C.), known as the "father of history," was born at Halicarnassus in Asia Minor. As a young man he traveled widely, and later he migrated to Athens, which became his intellectual home.

In his book *The Histories*, Herodotus chronicled the rise of the Persian Empire, sketched the background of Athens and Sparta, and described the land and customs of the Egyptians and the Scythians, who lived in the region of the modern Crimea. The sheer scope of this work is awesome. Lacking newspapers, sophisticated communications, and easy means of travel, Herodotus nevertheless wrote a history that covered the major events of the Near East and Greece.

Perhaps Herodotus's most striking characteristic was his curiosity. He loved to travel, and like most travelers he accumulated a stock of fine stories. But tales and digressions never obscure the central theme of his work. Herodotus diligently questioned everyone who could tell him anything about the Persian wars. The confrontation between East and West unfolds relentlessly in *The Histories*, reaching its climax in the great battles of Salamis and Plataea.

The outbreak of the Peloponnesian War prompted Thucydides (ca 460-ca 400 B.C.) to write a history of its course in the belief that it would be the greatest war in Greek history. An Athenian politician and general, Thucydides saw action in the war until he was exiled for a defeat. Exile gave him the time and opportunity to question eyewitnesses about the details of events and to visit battlefields. Since he was an aristocrat and a prominent man, he had access to the inner circles, the men who made the decisions.

Thucydides was intensely interested in human nature and how it manifested itself during the war. When the terrible plague struck Athens in 430 B.C., Thucydides described both the symptoms of the plague and the reactions of the Athenians in the same clinical terms. He portrayed the virtual breakdown of a society beset by war, disease, desperation, and despair. Similarly, he chronicled the bloody civil war on the island of Corcyra. Instead of condemning the injustice and inhumanity of the fighting, in which citizen turned on citizen and people ruthlessly betrayed their friends, he coolly observed that such things are normal, human nature being what it is.

Thucydides saw the Peloponnesian War as highly destructive to Greek character. He noted—with a visible touch of regret—that the old, the noble, and the simple fell before ambition and lust for power. He firmly rejected any notion that the gods intervened in human affairs. In his view the fate of

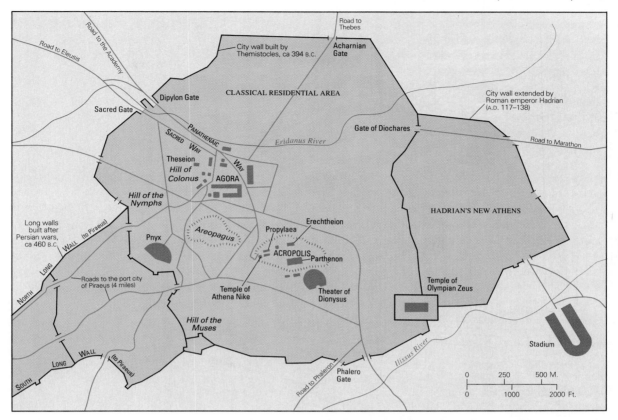

❖ **MAP 3.4 Ancient Athens** By modern standards the city of Athens was hardly more than a town, not much larger in size than one square mile. Yet this small area reflects the concentration of ancient Greek life in the polis.

men and women was, for good or ill, entirely in their own hands.

Athenian Arts in the Age of Pericles

In the last half of the fifth century B.C., Pericles turned Athens into the showplace of Greece. He appropriated Delian League funds to pay for a huge building program, planning temples and other buildings to honor Athena, the patron goddess of the city, and to display to all Greeks the glory of the Athenian polis. Pericles also pointed out that his program would employ many Athenians and bring economic prosperity to the city.

Thus began the undertaking that turned the Acropolis into a monument for all time. Construction of the Parthenon began in 447 B.C., followed by the Propylaea, the temple of Athena Nike (Athena the Victorious), and the Erechtheum

(Map 3.4). Even today in their ruined state they still evoke awe. Even the pollution of modern Athens, although it is destroying the ancient buildings, cannot rob them of their splendor and charm.

The planning of the architects and the skill of the workmen who erected these buildings were both very sophisticated. Visitors approaching the Acropolis first saw the Propylaea, the ceremonial gateway, a building of complicated layout and grand design whose Doric columns seemed to hold up the sky. On the right was the small temple of Athena Nike, whose dimensions harmonized with those of the Propylaea. The temple was built to commemorate the victory over the Persians, and the Ionic frieze above its columns depicted the struggle between the Greeks and the Persians. Here for all the world to see was a tribute to Athenian and Greek valor—and a reminder of Athens's part in the victory.

❖ **Sectional View of the Parthenon** This figure both indicates what the Parthenon looked like in antiquity and explains the complex nature of Greek temple-building. As the illustration shows, the Parthenon's apparently simple façade is a work of great architectural sophistication. *(Source: Guide to Sculptures of the Parthenon, a British Museum publication)*

To the left of the visitors, as they passed through the Propylaea, stood the Erechtheum, an Ionic temple that housed several ancient shrines. On its southern side was the famous Portico of the Caryatids, a porch whose roof was supported by statues of Athenian maidens. The graceful Ionic columns of the Erechtheum provided a delicate relief from the prevailing Doric order of the massive Propylaea and Parthenon.

As visitors walked on, they obtained a full view of the Parthenon, thought by many to be the perfect Doric temple. The Parthenon was the chief monument to Athena and her city. The sculptures that adorned the temple portrayed the greatness of Athens and its goddess. The figures on the eastern

pediment depicted Athena's birth, those on the west the victory of Athena over the god Poseidon in their struggle for the possession of Attica. Inside the Parthenon stood a huge statue of Athena, the masterpiece of the great sculptor, Phidias.

In many ways the Athenian Acropolis is the epitome of Greek art and its spirit. Although the buildings were dedicated to the gods and most of the sculptures portrayed gods, these works nonetheless express the Greek fascination with the human and the rational. Greek deities were anthropomorphic, and Greek artists portrayed them as human beings. While honoring the gods, Greek artists were thus celebrating human beings. In the Parthenon sculptures it is visually impossible to distinguish the men

❖ **The Athenian Acropolis** This painting, though made only in the nineteenth century, gives a vivid impression of what the buildings and their entire setting looked like in antiquity. It demonstrates the artistic appeal of these buildings, both then and now, and proves what Plutarch wrote of them: "Each of them is always in bloom, maintaining its appearance as though untouched by time, as though an evergreen breath and undecaying spirit had been mixed in its construction." *(Source: Neue Pinakothek, München)*

and women from the gods and goddesses. The Acropolis also exhibits the rational side of Greek art. Greek artists portrayed action in a balanced, restrained, and sometimes even serene fashion, capturing the noblest aspects of human beings: their reason, dignity, and promise.

Other aspects of Athenian cultural life were as rooted in the life of the polis as were the architecture and sculpture of the Acropolis. The development of drama was tied to the religious festivals of the city. The polis sponsored the production of plays and required that wealthy citizens pay the expenses of their production. At the beginning of the year, dramatists submitted their plays to the archon. He chose those he considered best and

assigned a theatrical troupe to each playwright. Although most Athenian drama has perished, enough has survived to prove that the archons had superb taste. Many plays were highly controversial, but the archons neither suppressed nor censored them.

The Athenian dramatists were the first artists in Western society to examine such basic questions as the rights of the individual, the demands of society on the individual, and the nature of good and evil. Conflict is a constant element in Athenian drama. The dramatists used their art to portray, understand, and resolve life's basic conflicts.

Aeschylus (525–456 B.C.), the first of the great Athenian dramatists, was also the first to express the agony of the individual caught in conflict. In his trilogy of plays, *The Oresteia*, Aeschylus deals with the themes of betrayal, murder, and reconciliation. *Agamemnon*, the first play, depicts Agamemnon's return from the Trojan War and his murder by his wife, Clytemnestra, and her lover, Aegisthus. In the second play, *The Libation Bearers*, Orestes, the son of Agamemnon and Clytemnestra, avenges his father's death by killing his mother and her lover. The last play of the trilogy, *The Eumenides*, works out the atonement and absolution of Orestes. The Furies, goddesses who avenged murder and unfilial conduct, demand Orestes' death. When the jury at Orestes' trial casts six votes to condemn and six to acquit him, Athena casts the deciding vote in favor of mercy and compassion. Aeschylus used *The Eumenides* to urge reason and

justice to reconcile fundamental conflicts. The play concludes with a prayer that civil dissension never be allowed to destroy the city and that the life of the city be one of harmony and grace.

Sophocles (496–406 B.C.) also dealt with matters personal and political. In *Antigone* he examined the relationship between the individual and the state by exploring a conflict between the ties of kinship and the demands of the polis. In the play Polynices has attacked his own state, Thebes, and has fallen in battle. Creon, the Theban king, refuses to allow Polynices' body to be buried. Polynices' sister, Antigone, is appalled by Creon's action because custom demands that she bury her brother's corpse. Creon is right in refusing to allow Polynices' body to be buried in the polis but wrong to refuse any burial at all. He continues in

❖ **"Procession of the Horsemen" from the Parthenon Frieze**   The great temple of Athena on the Acropolis, the Parthenon, was decorated by a band of sculpture depicting the religious procession to celebrate the festival of the payathena. Artists took their subjects from the actual procession. Here an Athenian artist has caught the young riders trying to restrain their unruly horses. The entire frieze also blends idealism and realism in its depiction of human activity. (*The British Museum*)

his misguided and willful error. As the play progresses, Antigone comes to stand for the precedence of divine law over human defects. Sophocles touches on the need for recognition of the law and adherence to it as a prerequisite for a tranquil state.

Sophocles' masterpieces have become classics of Western literature, and his themes have inspired generations of playwrights. Perhaps his most famous plays are *Oedipus the King* and its sequel, *Oedipus at Colonus*. *Oedipus the King* is the ironic story of a man doomed by the gods to kill his father and marry his mother. Try as he might to avoid his fate, Oedipus's every action brings him closer to its fulfillment. When at last he realizes that he has carried out the decree of the gods, Oedipus blinds himself and flees into exile. In *Oedipus at Colonus* Sophocles dramatizes the last days of the broken king, whose patient suffering and uncomplaining piety win him an exalted position. In the end the gods honor him for his virtue. The interpretation of these two plays has been hotly debated, but Sophocles seems to be saying that human beings should obey the will of the gods, even without fully understanding it, for the gods stand for justice and order.

Euripides (ca 480–406 B.C.), the last of the three great Greek tragic dramatists, also explored the theme of personal conflict within the polis and sounded the depths of the individual. With Euripides drama entered a new, in many ways more personal, phase. To him the gods were far less important than human beings. Euripides viewed the human soul as a place where opposing forces struggle, where strong passions such as hatred and jealousy conflict with reason. The essence of Euripides' tragedy is the flawed character—men and women who bring disaster on themselves and their loved ones because their passions overwhelm reason. Although Euripides' plays were less popular in his lifetime than those of Aeschylus and Sophocles, Euripides was a dramatist of genius whose work later had a significant impact on Roman drama.

Writers of comedy treated the affairs of the polis bawdily and often coarsely. Even so, their plays, too, were performed at religious festivals. The comic playwrights dealt primarily with the political affairs of the polis and the conduct of its leading politicians. Best known are the comedies of Aristophanes (ca 445–386 B.C.), an ardent lover of his city and a merciless critic of cranks and quacks. He

lampooned eminent generals, at times depicting them as morons. He commented snidely on Pericles, poked fun at Socrates, and hooted at Euripides. He saved some of his strongest venom for Cleon, a prominent politician. It is a tribute to the Athenians that such devastating attacks could openly and freely be made on the city's leaders and foreign policy. Even at the height of the Peloponnesian War, Aristophanes proclaimed that peace was preferable to the ravages of war. Like Aeschylus, Sophocles, and Euripides, Aristophanes used his art to dramatize his ideas on the right conduct of the citizen and the value of the polis.

Perhaps never were art and political life so intimately and congenially bound together as at Athens. Athenian art was the product of deep and genuine love of the polis. It aimed at bettering the lives of the citizens and the quality of life in the state.

Daily Life in Periclean Athens

In sharp contrast with the rich intellectual and cultural life of Periclean Athens stands the simplicity of its material life. The Athenians—and in this respect they were typical of Greeks in general—lived very happily with comparatively few material possessions. In the first place, there were very few material goods to own. The thousands of machines, tools, and gadgets considered essential for modern life had no counterparts in Athenian life. The inventory of Alcibiades' goods, which the Athenians confiscated after his desertion, is enlightening. His household possessions consisted of chests, beds, couches, tables, screens, stools, baskets, and mats. Other common items of the Greek home included pottery, metal utensils for cooking, tools, luxury goods such as jewelry, and a few other things. These items they had to buy from craftsmen. Whatever else they needed, such as clothes and blankets, they produced at home.

The Athenian house was rather simple. Whether large or small, the typical house consisted of a series of rooms built around a central courtyard, with doors opening onto the courtyard. Many houses had bedrooms on an upper floor. Artisans and craftsmen often set aside a room to use as a shop or work area. The two principal rooms were the men's dining room and the room where the women worked wool. Other rooms included the kitchen and bathroom. By modern standards there was not much furniture. In the men's dining room were couches, a sideboard, and small tables. Cups and other pottery were often hung on the wall from pegs. Other household furnishings included items such as those confiscated from Alcibiades after his desertion.

In the courtyard were the well, a small altar, and a washbasin. If the family lived in the country, the stalls of the animals faced the courtyard. Country dwellers kept oxen for plowing, pigs for slaughtering, sheep for wool, goats for cheese, and mules and donkeys for transportation. Even in the city, chickens and perhaps a goat or two roamed the courtyard together with dogs and cats.

Cooking, done over a hearth in the house, provided welcome warmth in the winter. Baking and roasting were done in ovens. Food consisted primarily of various grains, especially wheat and barley, as well as lentils, olives, figs, and grapes. Garlic and onion were popular garnishes, and wine was always on hand. These foods were stored at home in large jars; with them the Greek family sometimes ate fish, chicken, and vegetables. Women ground wheat into flour, baked it into bread, and on special occasions made honey or sesame cakes. The Greeks used olive oil for cooking, as families still do in modern Greece; they also used it as an unguent and as lamp fuel.

By American standards the Greeks did not eat much meat. On special occasions, such as important religious festivals, the family ate the animal sacrificed to the god and gave the god the exquisite delicacy of the thighbone wrapped in fat. The only Greeks who consistently ate meat were the Spartan warriors. They received a small portion of meat each day, together with the infamous Spartan black broth, a ghastly concoction of pork cooked in blood, vinegar, and salt. One Greek, after tasting the broth, commented that he could easily understand why the Spartans were so willing to die.

In the city a man might support himself as a craftsman—a potter, bronzesmith, sailmaker, or tanner—or he could contract with the polis to work on public buildings, such as the Parthenon and Erechtheum. Men without skills worked as paid laborers but competed with slaves for work. Slaves—usually foreigners, barbarian as well as Greek—were paid the same amount for their employment as were free men.

Slavery was commonplace in Greece, as it was throughout the ancient world. In its essentials Greek slavery resembled Mesopotamian slavery. Slaves received some protection under the law and could buy their freedom. On the other hand, masters could mistreat or neglect their slaves, although killing them was illegal. Most slaves in Athens served as domestics and performed light labor around the house. Nurses for children, teachers of reading and writing, and guardians for young men were often slaves. The lives of these slaves were much like those of their owners. Other slaves were skilled workers, who could be found working on public buildings or in small workshops.

The importance of slavery in Athens must not be exaggerated. Athenians did not own huge gangs of slaves as did Roman owners of large estates. Slave labor competed with free labor and kept wages down, but it never replaced the free labor that was the mainstay of the Athenian economy.

Most Athenians supported themselves by agriculture, but unless the family was fortunate enough to possess holdings in a plain more fertile than most of the land, they found it difficult to reap a good crop from the soil. Many people must have consumed nearly everything they raised. Attic farmers were free and, though hardly prosperous, by no means destitute. They could usually expect yields of five bushels of wheat and ten of barley per acre for every bushel of grain sown. A bad harvest meant a lean year. In many places farmers grew more barley than wheat because of the nature of the soil. Wherever possible, farmers also cultivated vines and olive trees.

For sport both countryman and city dweller often hunted for rabbits, deer, or wild boar. A successful hunt supplemented the family's regular diet. Wealthy men hunted on horseback; most others hunted on foot with their dogs. Hunting also allowed a man to display to his fellows his bravery and prowess in the chase. If wild boar were the prey, the sport could be dangerous, as Odysseus discovered when a charging boar slashed open his thigh.

The social condition of Athenian women has been the subject of much debate and little agreement. One of the difficulties is the fragmentary nature of the evidence. Women appear frequently in literature and art, often in idealized roles, but seldom in historical contexts of a wider and more realistic nature. This is due in part to the fact that most Greek historians of the time recounted primarily the political, diplomatic, and military events of the day, events in which women seldom played a notable part. Yet that does not mean that women were totally invisible in the life of the polis. It indicates instead that ancient sources provide only a glimpse of how women affected the society in which they lived. Greek wives, for example, played an important economic and social role by their management of the household. Perhaps the best way to describe the position of the free woman in Greek society is to use the anthropologist's term *liminal*, which means in this case that although women lacked official power, they nonetheless played a vital role in shaping the society in which they lived. The same situation had existed in Hammurabi's Babylonia, and it would later recur in the Hellenistic period. The mere fact that Athenian and other Greek women did not sit in the assembly does not mean that they did not influence public affairs.

The status of a free woman of the citizen class was strictly protected by law. Only her children, not those of foreigners or slaves, could be citizens. Only she was in charge of the household and the family's possessions. Yet the law protected her primarily to protect her husband's interests. Raping a free woman was a lesser crime than seducing her, because seduction involved the winning of her affections. This law was not concerned with the husband's feelings but with ensuring that he need not doubt the legitimacy of his children.

Women in Athens and elsewhere in Greece received a certain amount of social and legal protection from their dowries. Upon marriage, the bride's father gave the couple a gift of land or money, which the husband administered. However, it was never his; and in the rare cases of divorce, it returned to the wife's domain. The same is often true in Greece today among the upper class.

Ideally, respectable women lived a secluded life in which the only men they saw were relatives. How far this ideal was actually put into practice is impossible to say. At least Athenian women seem to have enjoyed a social circle of other women of their own class. They also attended public festivals, sacrifices, and funerals. Nonetheless, prosperous and respectable women probably spent much of their time in the house. A white complexion—a sign that a woman did not have to work in the fields—was valued highly.

Courtesans lived the freest lives of all Athenian women. Although some courtesans were simply

Women Working The scene on this vase represents the women of the household at work. It shows how they produced woolen cloth, from the spinning of yarn to the completion of the cloth itself, here held by two women. *(Source: The Metropolitan Museum of Art, Fletcher Fund, 1931)*

prostitutes, others added intellectual accomplishments to physical beauty. In constant demand, cultured courtesans moved freely in male society. Their artistic talents and intellectual abilities appealed to men who wanted more than sex. The most famous of all courtesans was Aspasia, mistress of Pericles and supposedly a friend of Socrates. Under Pericles' roof, she participated in intellectual discussions equally with some of the most stimulating thinkers of the day. Yet her position, like that of most other courtesans, was precarious. After Pericles' death, Aspasia fended for herself, ending her days as the madam of a house of prostitution.

A woman's main functions were to raise the children, oversee the domestic slaves and hired

✦ **Golden Chariot** By the classical period the Greeks had stopped using horse-drawn chariots in warfare. Yet they remained a symbol of aristocracy and a memory of the heroic past. Very few ancient artifacts capture that spirit as well as this chariot and its team, which is still trying to win the race. *(Source: Museum of Fine Arts, Boston)*

labor, and together with her maids work wool into cloth. The women washed the wool in the courtyard and then brought it into the women's room, where the loom stood. They spun the wool into thread and wove the thread into cloth. They also dyed wool at home and decorated the cloth by weaving in colors and designs. The woman of the household either did the cooking herself or directed her maids. In a sense, poor women lived freer lives than did wealthier women. They performed manual labor in the fields or sold goods in the agora, going about their affairs much as men did.

A distinctive feature of Athenian life and of Greek life in general was acceptance of homosexuality. The Greeks accepted the belief that both homosexual and heterosexual practices were normal parts of life. They did not think that these practices created any particular problems for those who engaged in them.

No one has satisfactorily explained how the Greek attitude toward homosexual love developed or determined how common homosexual behavior was. Homosexuality was probably far more common among the aristocracy than among the lower classes. Even among the aristocracy, attitudes toward homosexuality were complex and sometimes conflicting. Most people saw homosexual love affairs among the young as a stage in the development of a mature heterosexual life. Warrior-aristocracies generally emphasized the physical side of the relationship in the belief that warriors who were also lovers would fight all the harder to impress and to protect each other. Whatever their intellectual content, homosexual love affairs were also overtly sexual.

Greek Religion

Greek religion is extremely difficult for modern people to understand, largely because of the great differences between Greek and modern cultures. In the first place, it is not even easy to talk about "Greek religion," since the Greeks had no uniform faith or creed. Although the Greeks usually worshiped the same deities—Zeus, Hera, Apollo, Athena, and others—the cults of these gods and goddesses varied from polis to polis. The Greeks had no sacred books such as the Bible, and Greek religion was often a matter more of ritual than of belief. Nor did cults impose an ethical code of conduct. Greeks did not have to follow any particular rule of life, practice certain virtues, or even live decent lives in order to participate. Unlike the Egyptians and Hebrews, the Greeks lacked a priesthood as the modern world understands the term. In Greece priests and priestesses existed to care for temples and sacred property and to conduct the proper rituals, but not to make religious rules or doctrines, much less to enforce them. In short, there existed in Greece no central ecclesiastical authority and no organized creed.

Although temples to the gods were common, they were unlike modern churches or synagogues in that they were not normally places where a congregation met to worship as a spiritual community. Instead, the individual Greek either visited the temple occasionally on matters of private concern or walked in a procession to a particular temple to celebrate a particular festival. In Greek religion the altar, which stood outside the temple, was important; when the Greeks sought the favor of the gods, they offered them sacrifices. Greek religious observances were generally cheerful. Festivals and sacrifices were frequently times for people to meet together socially, times of high spirits and conviviality rather than of pious gloom. By offering the gods parts of the sacrifice while consuming the rest themselves, worshipers forged a bond with the gods.

Besides the Olympian gods, each polis had its own minor deities, each with his or her own local cult. In many instances Greek religion involved the official gods and goddesses of the polis and their cults. The polis administered the cults and festivals, and all were expected to participate in this civic religion, regardless of whether they even believed in the deities being worshiped. Participating unbelievers, who seem to have been a small minority, were not considered hypocrites. Rather, they were seen as patriotic, loyal citizens who in honoring the gods also honored the polis. If this attitude seems contradictory, an analogy may help. Before baseball games Americans stand at the playing of the national anthem, whether they are Democrats, Republicans, or neither, and whether they agree or disagree with the policies of the current administration. They honor their nation as represented by its flag, in somewhat the same way an ancient Greek honored the polis and demonstrated solidarity with it by participating in the state cults.

Some Greeks turned to mystery religions like those of the Eleusinian mysteries in Attica and of Trophonios in Boeotia. These mystery religions in some ways foreshadowed aspects of early Christian practices by their rites of initiation and their acceptance of certain doctrines. The basic concept of these cults was to unite individuals in an exclusive religious society with particular deities. Those who joined them went through a period of preparation in which they learned the essential beliefs of the cult and its necessary rituals. Once they had successfully undergone initiation, they were forbidden to reveal the secrets of the cult. Consequently, modern scholars know comparatively little about their tenets. Although the mystery religions were popular until the coming of Christianity in the Roman Empire, relatively few except the wealthy could afford the luxuries of time and money to join them.

For most Greeks religion was quite simple and close to nature. They believed in the supernatural and the primitive. The religion of the common people was a rich combination of myth, ritual, folklore, and cult. They believed in a world of deities who were all around them. The goddess Hestia oversaw the sanctity of the hearth, various nymphs resided at clear springs, and Pan, the lover of wild things and places, protected the herds and flocks. Deities and human beings shared their world so intimately that they could change places within it. An excellent example comes from the myth of Zeus, the Olympian god, who could change his shape into that of a bull in order to carry Europa, the daughter of a Phoenician king, to Crete. Having borne Zeus several children, she herself became a goddess, for whom the continent of Europe is named.

So much of popular religion was taken for granted that comparatively little of it is now known. Two examples from two very different people, however, give an idea of the nature of this religion, its bond with nature, and its sense of ethics and propriety. Probably no one today thinks much about wading across a stream, unless it is too deep. That attitude would have horrified the Boeotian farmer and poet Hesiod, who would have considered it sacrilegious. Instead, he advises the traveler who encounters a stream:

Never cross the beautifully flowing water of an
overflowing river on foot,
until having looked into the lovely stream and hav-
ing washed your hands in the very lovely, clear
waters,
you offer a prayer. Whoever crosses a river and
with hands unwashed of evil,
to him the gods will wreak vengeance and will give
him pain.[9]

This is an unaffected example of ritual purification, but no temple or sanctuary is needed for it. Even Plato's Socrates, the supreme rationalist, shared these ordinary beliefs (see page 00). In the *Phaedrus,* one of the grandest of the Socratic dialogues, Socrates and a friend sit in the shade of a grove and pass the afternoon in serious philosophical discussion. They finish their conversation after the heat of the day has abated. When they rise to leave, Socrates suggests that they offer a prayer to the local deities, to which his friend agrees. Socrates then addresses the gods:

O friend Pan and all the other gods here, please give me beauty within me and of the things outside that I have, may they be in concord with those within me.[10]

Socrates was not being a hypocrite. He, like most other Greeks, shared their world with many invisible beings, not all of them hostile or unpleasant. In that respect ordinary Greek religion kept itself in tune with the natural world. The Olympian deities and the mystery religions had their honored places within this scheme of religion, but average Greeks held simpler beliefs.

Though Greek religion in general was individual or related to the polis, the Greeks also shared some pan-Hellenic festivals, the chief of which were held at Olympia in honor of Zeus and at Delphi in honor of Apollo. The festivities at Olympia included the famous games, athletic contests that have inspired the modern Olympic games. Held every four years, these games were for the glory of Zeus. They attracted visitors from all over the Greek world and lasted well into Christian times. The Pythian games at Delphi were also held every four years, but these contests differed from the Olympic games by including musical and literary contests. Both the Olympic and the Pythian games were unifying factors in Greek life, bringing Greeks together culturally as well as religiously.

The Flowering of Philosophy

The myths and epics of the Mesopotamians are ample testimony that speculation about the origin of the universe and of mankind did not begin with the Greeks. The signal achievement of the Greeks was the willingness of some to treat these questions in rational rather than mythological terms. Although Greek philosophy did not fully flower until the Classical period, Ionian thinkers had already begun in the Lyric Age to ask what the universe was made of. These men are called the Pre-Socratics, for their work preceded the philosophical revolution begun by the Athenian Socrates. Though they were keen observers, the Pre-Socratics rarely undertook deliberate experimentation. Instead, they took individual facts and wove them into general theories. Despite appearances, they believed, the universe was actually simple and subject to natural laws. Drawing on their observations, they

speculated about the basic building blocks of the universe.

The first of the Pre-Socratics, Thales (ca 600 B.C.), learned mathematics and astronomy from the Babylonians and geometry from the Egyptians. Yet there was an immense and fundamental difference between Near Eastern thought and the philosophy of Thales. The Near Eastern peoples considered such events as eclipses to be evil omens. Thales viewed them as natural phenomena that could be explained in natural terms. In short, he asked why things happened. He believed the basic element of the universe to be water. Although he was wrong, the way in which he had asked the question was momentous: it was the beginning of the scientific method.

Thales' follower Anaximander continued his work. Anaximander was the first of the Pre-Socratics to use general concepts, which are essential to abstract thought. One of the most brilliant of the Pre-Socratics, a man of striking originality, Anaximander theorized that the basic element of the universe is the "boundless" or "endless"—something infinite and indestructible. In his view, the earth floats in a void, held in balance by its distance from everything else in the universe. Anaximander even concluded that mankind had evolved naturally from lower organisms: "In water the first animal arose covered with spiny skin, and with the lapse of time some crawled onto dry land and breaking off their skins in a short time they survived."[11] This remarkable speculation corresponds crudely to Darwin's theory of evolution of species, although it predated Darwin by two and a half millennia.

Another Ionian, Heraclitus (ca 500 B.C.), declared the primal element to be fire. He also declared that the world had neither beginning nor end: "This world, the world of all things, neither any god nor man made, but it always was and it is and it will be: an everlasting fire, measures kindling and measures going out."[12] Although the universe was eternal, according to Heraclitus, it changed constantly. An outgrowth of this line of speculation was the theory of Democritus that the universe is made of invisible, indestructible atoms. The culmination of Pre-Socratic thought was the theory that four simple substances make up the universe: fire, air, earth, and water.

Not all of these early philosophers devoted their attention to pure philosophy or natural science. Aesop (d. 564 B.C.) devoted his attention to ethics, the treatment of moral behavior. A slave endowed with a keen mind, Aesop made his points by using fables, which were as popular in antiquity as they still are today. Fables make their points metaphorically, often using animals instead of people as the main characters. His tales spread throughout Greece, survived in medieval and modern Europe, and not only can still be enjoyed in books today but also sometimes even form the plot line of Bugs Bunny cartoons. They are a reservoir of good sense and simple patterns of behavior. A few examples will illustrate Aesop's method of conveying his message. In one of his fables Aesop tells of a hungry fox who encounters sun-ripened grapes in a vineyard. Try as he might, he cannot reach them. In disgust he leaves, muttering that they were probably sour and wormy anyway, whence comes our expression "sour grapes." The moral is that all fools can criticize what they cannot get. In another fable Aesop tells of a good-natured farmer whose dog falls into a well. The farmer climbs into the well to retrieve the dog only to be bitten on the hand. Greatly angered, the farmer throws the dog back into the well. The moral is again simple: "don't bite the hand that feeds you." Many people who never read the writings of philosophers learned from such fables as Aesop's something about life and ethics.

With this impressive heritage behind them, the philosophers of the Classical period ventured into new areas of speculation. This development was partly due to the work of Hippocrates (second half of the fifth century B.C.), the father of medicine. Like Thales, Hippocrates sought natural explanations for natural phenomena. Basing his opinions on empirical knowledge, not on religion or magic, he taught that natural means could be employed to fight disease. In his treatise *On Airs, Waters, and Places*, he noted the influence of climate and environment on health. Hippocrates and his followers put forward a theory that was to prevail in medical circles until the eighteenth century. The human body, they declared, contains four humors, or fluids: blood, phlegm, black bile, and yellow bile. In a healthy body the four humors are in perfect balance; too much or too little of any particular humor causes illness. But Hippocrates broke away from the mainstream of Ionian speculation by declaring that medicine was a separate craft—just as ironworking was—that had its own principles.

The distinction between natural science and philosophy on which Hippocrates insisted was also promoted by the Sophists, who traveled the Greek world teaching young men. Despite differences of opinion on philosophical matters, the Sophists all agreed that human beings were the proper subject of study. They also believed that excellence could be taught, and they used philosophy and rhetoric to prepare young men for life in the polis. The Sophists laid great emphasis on logic and the meanings of words. They criticized traditional beliefs, religion, rituals, and myth and even questioned the laws of the polis. In essence, they argued that nothing is absolute, that everything is relative. Hence more traditional Greeks considered them wanton and harmful, men who were interested in "making the worse seem the better cause."

One of those whose contemporaries thought him a Sophist was Socrates (ca 470–399 B.C.), who sprang from the class of small artisans. Socrates spent his life in investigation and definition. Not strictly speaking a Sophist, because he never formally taught or collected fees from anyone, Socrates nonetheless shared the Sophists' belief that human beings and their environment are the essential subjects of philosophical inquiry. Like the Sophists, Socrates thought that excellence could be learned and passed on to others. His approach when posing ethical questions and defining concepts was to start with a general topic or problem and to narrow the matter to its essentials. He did so by continuous questioning, a running dialogue. Never did he lecture. Socrates thought that by constantly pursuing excellence, an essential part of which was knowledge, human beings could approach the supreme good and thus find true happiness. Yet in 399 B.C. Socrates was brought to trial, convicted, and executed on charges of corrupting the youth of the city and introducing new gods.

Socrates' student Plato (427–347 B.C.) carried on his master's search for truth. Unlike Socrates, Plato wrote down his thoughts and theories and founded a philosophical school, the Academy. Most people rightly think of Plato as a philosopher. Yet his writings were also literary essays of great charm. They drew out characters, locales, and scenes from ordinary life that would otherwise be lost to posterity. In addition, Plato even used satire, irony, and comedy to relay his thoughts. Despite all the reverence that people normally pay to Plato, they can also read him for the sheer fun of it. Behind the elegance of his literary style, however, stand the profound thoughts of a brilliant mind that grappled with the problems of his own day and the eternal realities of life. The destruction and chaos of the Peloponnesian War prompted him to ask new and different questions about the nature of human society. He pondered where, why, and how the polis had gone wrong. Thus, he gave serious thought to the very nature of the polis and what was the best form that it should take. In these considerations Plato was not only a philosopher but a political scientist and a utopian, a man who genuinely thought that he could create a form of government that would give people the most ethical and satisfying way of life. He spent his entire life trying to determine the ideal polis.

The ideal polis could exist only when its citizens were well educated. Plato tried to show that a life of ignorance was wretched. From education came the possibility of determining an all-comprising unity of virtues that would lead to an intelligent, moral, and ethical life. Yet can virtue be taught? Plato never satisfactorily answered his own question. He concluded that only divine providence could guide people to virtue. In his opinion, divine providence was one intelligible and individualistic being. In short, he equated god with the concept of good. Plato's tool was mathematics as the servant of education. Human life is transitory, but ideas are permanent. If people could master the essential ideas, guided by mathematics, their souls would become immortal. Here is where the state helped people to reach this goal. It was the highest duty of true statesmen to educate their people so that they could reach this goal.

Plato developed the theory that all visible, tangible things are unreal and temporary, copies of "forms" or "ideas" that are constant and indestructible. Only the mind, not the senses, can perceive eternal forms. In Plato's view the highest form is the idea of good. He discussed these ideas in two works. In *The Republic* Plato applied his theory of forms to politics in an effort to describe the ideal polis. His perfect polis was utopian; it aimed at providing the greatest good and happiness to all its members. Plato thought that the ideal polis could exist only if its rulers were philosophers. He divided society into rulers, guardians of the polis, and workers. The role of people in each category would be decided by the education, wisdom, and ability of the individual. In Plato's republic men and women would be equal to one another, and women could become rulers. The utopian polis would be a balance, with each individual doing what he or she could to support the state and with

each receiving from the state his or her just due. In *The Laws*, however, he drew a more authoritarian picture of government and society, one not so very different from that of twentieth-century dictatorship. If Plato ultimately failed to realize his utopia, he at least introduced to others the concept that they could strive to shape an ideal society.

Aristotle (384–322 B.C.) carried on the philosophical tradition of Socrates and Plato. A student of Plato, Aristotle went far beyond him in striving to understand the universe. The range of Aristotle's thought is staggering. Everything in human experience was fit subject for his inquiry. In *Politics* Aristotle followed Plato's lead by writing about the ideal polis. Yet Aristotle approached the question more realistically than Plato and criticized *The Republic* and Plato's other writings on many points. In his Politics and elsewhere, Aristotle stressed moderation, concluding that the balance of his ideal state depended on people of talent and education who could avoid extremes.

Aristotle also tried to understand the changes of nature—what caused them and where they led. Hence, he was both a philosopher and a scientist. He became increasingly interested in the observation and explanation of natural phenomena. The range of his interests was stunning, embracing logic, dialectic, ethics, natural sciences, politics, poetry, and art. He used logic as his method of scientific discussion. His method was the syllogism, whereby he reasoned from a general statement to a particular conclusion. His thinking was so different from Plato's that he established his own school. He held lectures in a gymnasium, and afterward discussed topics with students while walking under the eaves of the building. From that practice his school gained the name *Peripatos*, which literally means "to walk around" (and is related to our modern English word *peripatetic*).

Aristotle also attempted to bridge the gap that Plato had created between abstract truth and concrete perception. He argued that the universe is finite, spherical, and eternal. Here he discusses an immaterial being that is his conception of god. Yet his god neither created the universe nor guided it. The inconsistencies of Aristotle on these matters are obvious. His god is without purpose. Yet for him scientific endeavor, the highest attainable form of living, reaches the divine.

Aristotle expressed the heart of his philosophy in two masterful works, *Physics* and *Metaphysics*. In them he combined empiricism, or observation, and

PERIODS OF GREEK HISTORY

Period	Significant Events	Major Writers
Bronze Age 2000–1100 B.C.	Arrival of the Greeks in Greece Rise and fall of the Mycenaean kingdoms	
Dark Age 1100–800 B.C.	Greek migrations within the Aegean basin Social and political recovery Evolution of the polis Rebirth of literacy	Homer Hesiod
Lyric Age 800–500 B.C.	Rise of Sparta and Athens Colonization of the Mediterranean basin Flowering of lyric poetry Development of philosophy and science in Ionia	Archilochus Sappho Tyrtaeus Solon Anaximander Heraclitus
Classical Age 500–338 B.C.	Persian wars Growth of the Athenian Empire Peloponnesian War Rise of drama and historical writing Flowering of Greek philosophy Spartan and Theban hegemonies Conquest of Greece by Philip of Macedon	Herodotus Thucydides Aeschylus Sophocles Euripides Aristophanes Plato Aristotle

speculative method. In *Physics* he tried to explain all of nature to how natural physical phenomena worked on one another and how these actions lead to the results that people actually see around them daily. He postulated the four principles of matter, form, movement, and goal. A good analogy is a seed. It possesses both matter and an encoded form. Form determines whether the plant will be a rose or poison ivy. Growth represents movement, and the mature plant the goal of the seed. Although Aristotle considered nature impersonal, he also felt that it had its own purposes. In a sense, this is a rudimentary ancestor of the concept of evolution.

In *On the Heaven* Aristotle took up the thread of Ionian speculation. His theory of cosmology added ether to air, fire, water, and earth as building blocks of the universe. He concluded that the universe revolves and that it is spherical and eternal. He wrongly thought that the earth is the center of the universe, with the stars and planets revolving

around it. The Hellenistic scientist Aristarchus of Samos later realized that the earth revolves around the sun, but Aristotle's view was accepted until the time of the sixteenth-century astronomer Nicolaus Copernicus.

Aristotle possessed one of the keenest and most curious philosophical minds of Western civilization. While rethinking the old topics explored by the Pre-Socratics, he also created whole new areas of study. In short, he tried to learn everything possible about the universe and everything in it. He did so in the belief that all knowledge could be synthesized to produce a simple explanation of the universe and of humanity.

The Final Act (404–338 B.C.)

The end of the Peloponnesian War only punctuated a century of nearly constant warfare that lasted from 421 to 338 B.C. The events of the fourth century demonstrated that no single Greek

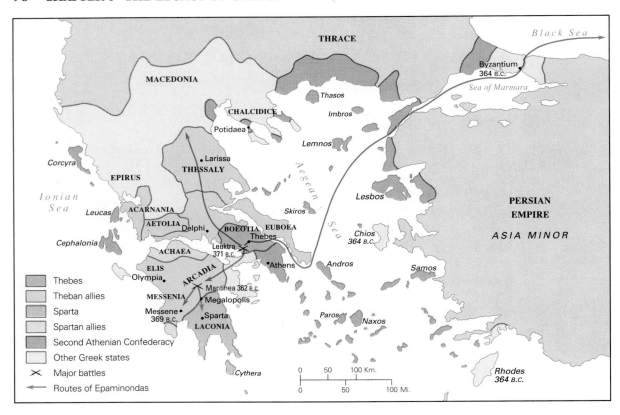

❖ **MAP 3.5 Greece at 362 B.C.** The fourth century B.C. witnessed the rapid growth of Greek federalism as states sought allies to gain security from rival powers.

state possessed enough power and resources to dominate the others. There nevertheless ensued an exhausting struggle for hegemony among the great powers, especially Sparta, Athens, and Thebes (Map 3.5). Immediately after the Peloponnesian War, with Athens humbled, Sparta began striving for empire over the Greeks. The arrogance and imperialism of the Spartans turned their former allies against them. Even with Persian help Sparta could not maintain its hold on Greece. In 371 B.C. the Spartans met their match on the plain of Leuctra in Boeotia. A Theban army under the command of Epaminondas, one of Greece's most brilliant generals, destroyed the flower of the Spartan army on a single summer day. The victory at Leuctra left Thebes the most powerful state in Greece. Under Epaminondas the Thebans destroyed Sparta as a first-rank power and checked the ambitions of Athens, but they were unable to bring peace to Greece. In 362 B.C. Epaminondas was killed in

battle, and a period of stalemate set in. The Greek states were virtually exhausted.

The man who turned the situation to his advantage was Philip II, king of Macedonia (359–336 B.C.). Throughout most of Greek history Macedonia, which bordered Greece in the north, in modern Greece and Serbia, had been a backward, disunited kingdom, but Philip's genius, courage, and drive turned it into a major power. One of the ablest statesmen of antiquity, Philip united his powerful kingdom, built a redoubtable army, and pursued his ambition with drive and determination. His horizon was not limited to Macedonia, for he realized that he could turn the rivalry and exhaustion of the Greek states to his own purposes. By clever use of his wealth and superb army Philip won control of the northern Aegean and awakened fear in Athens, which had vital interests there. Demosthenes, an Athenian patriot and a fine orator, warned his fellow citizens against Philip. Others, too, saw Philip as a threat. A comic playwright depicted one of Philip's ambassadors warning the Athenians:

Do you know that your battle will be with men
Who dine on sharpened swords,
And gulp burning firebrands for wine?
Then immediately after dinner the slave
Brings us desert—Cretan arrows
Or pieces of broken spears.
We have shields and breastplates for
Cushions and at our feet slings and arrows,
And we are crowned with catapults.[20]

Finally the Athenians joined forces with Thebes, which also appreciated the Macedonian threat, to stop Philip. In 338 B.C. the combined Theban-Athenian army met Philip's veterans at the Boeotian city of Chaeronea. Philip's army won a hard-fought victory: he had conquered Greece and put an end to Greek freedom. Because the Greeks could not put aside their quarrels, they fell to an invader.

SUMMARY

The mountainous geography of Greece divides the land into small pockets, so that at first small settlements were the natural pattern of human inhabitation. Never cut off from one another, these settlements evolved a common political and social institution, the polis. Although the causes for this common development are still unknown, the polis proved basic to Greek life. It was far different from the political institutions of the earlier Minoan and Mycenaean kingdoms, which did, however, leave all Greeks the heritage of a heroic past. Through the poetry of Homer and the monumental ruins of the Bronze Age, later Greeks remembered a time when great kings ruled the land. The polis, however, was a dramatic break with this past, and in this atmosphere the Greeks developed basic political forms that are still alive in the contemporary world. The Greeks gave serious thought to the relationship between society and the polis and the nature of political rights. From these thoughts, which they put into practice, developed concepts like democracy and tyranny. The Greek passion for open debates and exchange of ideas was also important to the intellectual explosion of Greek phi-

The Lion of Chaeronea This stylized lion marks the mass grave of nearly 300 elite Theban soldiers who valiantly died fighting the Macedonians at the Battle of Chaeronea. After the battle, when Philip viewed the bodies of these brave troops, he said: "May those who suppose that these men did or suffered anything dishonorable perish wretchedly." *(Source: Caroline Buckler)*

losophy. Not bound to religion, Greek philosophy considered the human mind to be a sufficient tool to understand the cosmos. This very line of thinking underlies modern scientific thought. In view of all their great achievements, it seems incomprehensible that the Greeks and their polis could fail. Yet the desire of several powerful city-states to dominate the others led to years of warfare that eventually weakened them all and left them vulnerable to the successful invasion of the Macedonian king, Philip II.

NOTES

1. K. J. Beloch, *Griechische Geschichte*, vol. 1, pt. 1 (Strassburg: K. J. Trübner, 1912), p. 49. John Buckler is the translator of all uncited quotations from a foreign language in Chapters 1–6.
2. Hesiod, *Works and Days* 263–266.
3. F. Lasserre, *Archiloque* (Paris: Société d'Edition "Les Belles Lettres," 1958), frag. 9, p. 4.
4. W. Barnstable, *Sappho* (Garden City, N.Y.: Doubleday, 1965), frag. 24, p. 22.
5. Ibid., frag. 132, p. 106.
6. J. M. Edmonds, *Greek Elegy and Iambus* (Cambridge, Mass.: Harvard University Press, 1931), I.70, frag. 10.
7. Thucydides, *History of the Peloponnesian War* 1.23.
8. Ibid., 7.87.6.
9. Hesiod, *Works and Days* 737–741.
10. Plato, *Phaedrus* 279.
11. E. Diels and W. Krantz, *Fragmente der Vorsokratiker*, 8th ed. (Berlin: Weidmannsche Verlagsbuchhandlung, 1960), Anaximander frag. A30.
12. Ibid., Heraclitus frag. B30.

SUGGESTED READING

Translations of the most important writings of the Greeks and Romans can be found in the volumes of the Loeb Classical Library published by Harvard University Press. Paperback editions of the major Greek and Latin authors are available in the Penguin Classics. Recent translations of documents include C. Fornara, *Translated Documents of Greece and Rome*, vol. 1 (1977), and P. Harding, vol. 2 (1985).

Among the many general treatments of Greek history is that of H. Bengtson, *History of Greece* (English trans. 1988). Also good is J. Fine, *The Ancient Greeks* (1984).

A number of books on early Greece are available in addition to those cited in the Notes. A careful and learned synthesis can be found in Lord W. Taylour, *The Mycenaeans*, rev. ed. (1983). R. Castledon, *Minoans* (1993) uses archaeology, not always successfully, in an attempt to recreate the life of Bronze Age Crete. C. G. Thomas, *Myth Becomes History* (1993), is an excellent treatment of early Greece and modern historical attitudes toward it. R. Drews, *The Coming of the Greeks* (1988), puts the movement of the Greeks in the broader context of Indo-European migrations. No finer introduction to the Lyric Age can be found than A. R. Burn's *The Lyric Age* (1960). Its sequel, *Persia and the Greeks*, 2d ed. (1984), which is still unsurpassed, carries the history of Greece to the defeat of the Persians in 479 B.C. More recent is J. Boardman et al., *The Cambridge Ancient History*, 2d. ed., vol. 4 (1988), but the coverage is very uneven. A. J. Graham, *Colony and Mother City in Ancient Greece*, rev. ed. (1984), gives a good but somewhat dated account of Greek colonization. The same can be said of C. Roebuck, *Economy and Society in the Early Greek World* (1984). R. Osborne, *Classical Landscape with Figures* (1985), looks at the relation of the polis to its surrounding landscape. R. A. Tomlinson, *From Mycenae to Constantinople* (1992), is a broad study of the evolution of the city in the Greek and Roman world.

W. Burkert, *The Orientalizing Revolution* (1992), is a masterful discussion of Near Eastern influence on early Greek culture. A good survey of work on Sparta is P. Cartledge, *Sparta and Lakonia* (1979). J. F. Lazenby, *The Spartan Army* (1985), studies the evolution of the Spartan army and hoplite warfare. The Athenian democracy and the society that produced it continue to attract scholarly attention. Interesting and important are M. Ostwald, *From Popular Sovereignty to the Sovereignty of Law* (1986); M. H. Hansen, *The Athenian Assembly* (1987); and J. Ober, *Mass and Elite in Democratic Athens* (1989).

The history of the fifth century B.C. and the outbreak of the Peloponnesian War are treated in M. McGregor, *The Athenians and Their Empire* (1987); G. E. M. de Ste. Crois, *The Origins of the Peloponnesian War* (1972), despite its defects; A. Ferrill, *The Origins of War* (1985), chap. 4; and E. Badian, *From Plataea to Potidaea* (1993), a collection of essays on major aspects of the period.

The fourth century has been one of the most fertile fields of recent research. G. Proietti, *Xenophon's Sparta* (1987), and P. Cartledge, *Agesilaos and the Crisis of Sparta* (1987), both treat Spartan government and society in its period of greatness and collapse. J. Buckler, *The Theban Hegemony, 371–362 B.C.* (1980), examines the period of Theban ascendancy, and his *Philip II and the Sacred War* (1989) studies the ways in which Philip of Macedonia used Greek politics to his own ends. J. Cargill, *The Second Athenian League* (1981), a significant study, traces Athenian policy during the fourth century. G. Cawkwell, *Philip of Macedon* (1978), analyzes the career of the great conqueror, and R. M. Errington, *A History of Macedonia* (English trans., 1990), is the best general treatment of the topic published in recent years.

Greek social life has recently received a great deal of attention, constituting a theme of continuing interest among classical scholars. R. Just, *Women in Athenian Law and Life* (1988), explores such topics as daily life, the family, and women's role in society. W. K. Lacey, *The Family in Classical Greece* (1984), treats ordinary family relations. N. Loraux, *The Children of Athena* (1993), examines Athenian myths to explore the ideas about citizenship and the status of women in Athenian life. M. Golden, *Children and Childhood in Ancient Athens* (1993), studies a neglected topic. D. Cohen, *Law, Sexuality, and Society* (1992), discusses what the Athenians thought was proper moral behavior and how they tried to enforce it. J. J. Winkler, *The Constraints of Desire* (1989), examines the anthropology of sex and gender in ancient Greece. S. Isager and J. E. Skydsgaard, *Ancient Greek Agriculture* (1992), endorses the theory that agriculture was the main source of wealth in ancient Greece. D. Sansone, *Greek Athletics and the Genesis of Sport* (1988), well illustrated, provides a good and far-ranging treatment of what athletics meant to the classical Greek world. The topic of slavery is addressed in Y. Garlan, *Slavery in Ancient Greece* (1988); and in the more adventur-

ous E. M. Wood, *Peasant-Citizen and Slave* (1988), which links the two groups to the founding of Athenian democracy.

For Greek literature, culture, and science, see A. Lesky's classic *History of Greek Literature* (English trans., 1963), and for drama, H. C. Baldry, *The Greek Tragic Theater* (1971). Still unsurpassed in Greek philosophy is J. Burnet, *Greek Philosophy* (1914), and in science B. Farrington, *Greek Science,* 2 vols. (reprint, 1949). More recent is M. Clagett, *Greek Science in Antiquity* (1971). M. Ferejohn, *The Origins of Aristotelian Science* (1991), discusses earlier Greek scientific thought and Artistotle's response to it. Two new works explore medicine: M. D. Grmek, *Diseases in the Ancient Greek World* (1991), and J. Longrigg, *Greek Rational Medicine* (1993), which emphasizes the importance of Greek physicians who concentrated on natural causes of illness and their cure rather than on magic and religion.

Studies of Greek religions and myth include J. D. Mikalson, *Athenian Popular Religion* (reprint, 1987), which opens a valuable avenue to the understanding of Greek popular religion in general. P. N. Hunt, ed., *Encyclopedia of Classical Mystery Religions* (1993), provides more than 1,000 entries on mystery religions. It also discusses the later competition between them and Christianity. In a classic book, E. R. Dodds, *The Greeks and the Irrational* (1951), discusses a hitherto neglected side of intellectual history. In general, W. Burkert, *Greek Religion* (1987), gives a masterful survey of ancient religious beliefs. Last, K. Dowden, *The Uses of Greek Mythology* (1992), is a systematic study of the importance of mythology to Greek history, which explores its originality and its relation to Greek culture in general.

PAST

A Veteran's Account of the Battle of Salamis

The battle of Salamis in 480 B.C. was the turning point in the Greek victory over the Persians. One man serving in the Greek fleet that day was the great Athenian dramatist Aeschylus. In his play The Persians *he gave a poetic account of the action. His was the first complete account of a major battle in Greek history, and his historical play was one of the earliest in Attic drama. Though giving few details of the naval maneuvers, which Herodotus recorded later, Aeschylus left a vivid sketch of the battle as seen through the eyes of a veteran.*

The Persian fleet was at sea to prevent the Greeks from escaping from the bay of Salamis (west of Athens), where they had anchored. At dawn the Greek ships lured the Persians into the bay, which became the scene of a furious naval battle.

Aeschylus produced The Persians *probably in 472 B.C., when most of those in the Greek audience could remember these events. The scene begins with a Persian herald reporting news of the battle to the queen, whose husband has not yet returned from the war. One of the remarkable aspects of this play is that Aeschylus uses a Persian in the royal court to praise Greek valor. The herald begins by describing the first movements of the Persian fleet, which expected the Greeks to flee.*

Herald: When the glare of sunlight died, and night
　　Came on every [Persian] man was at his oar,
　　Every man at arms who knew them.
　　Rank encouraged rank, and long-boats sailed
　　To stations each had been assigned.
　　All night the captains kept the fleet awake;
　　And night ran on. No Greek army set
　　Secret sail; but when the steeds of day,
　　White and luminous, began to cross

The sky, a song-like, happy tumult sounded
From the Greeks, and island rocks returned
The high-pitched echo. Fear fell among us,
Deceived in hope; for they (and not as if to flee)
A solemn paean chanted, and to battle
　　Rushed with fervent boldness: trumpets flared,
Putting every Greek aflame. At once
　　Concordant strokes of oars in dissonance
Slapped the waters' depths: soon we saw
　　Them all: first the right wing led in order,
Next advanced the whole fleet:
　　A great concerted cry we heard: "O Greek
Sons, advance! Free your fathers' land,
　　Free your sons, your wives, the sanctuaries
Of paternal gods, the sepulchers
Of ancestors. Now the contest is drawn:
All is at stake!" And babel Persian tongues
Rose to meet it: no longer would the action
Loiter. Warships struck their brazen beaks
Together: a Greek man-of-war began
The charge, a Phoenician-ornamented stern
Was smashed; and another drove against another.
First the floods of Persians held the line,
But when the narrows choked them, and rescue hopeless,
Smitten by prows, their bronze jaws gaping,
Shattered entire was our fleet of oars.
The Greek warships, calculating, dashed
Round, and encircled us: ships showed their belly:

No longer could we see the water,
  charged
With ships' wrecks and men's blood.
Corpses glutted beaches and the rocks.
Every warship urged its own anarchic
Rout; and all who survived that expedi-
  tion,
Like mackerel or some catch of fish,
Were stunned and slaughtered, boned
  with broken oars
And splintered wrecks: lamentations, cries,
Possessed the open sea, until the black
Eye of evening, closing, hushed them.
  The sum
Of troubles, even if I should rehearse
  them
For ten days, I could not exhaust. Rest
Content: never in a single day
So great a number died.
  . . .

Queen: Oh wretched am I alas! What doom
Destroyed them?

Herald: There is an island fronting Salamis,
Small, scarce an anchorage for ships,
Where the dancer Pan rejoices on the
  shore;
Whither Xerxes [the Perian king] sent
  those men to kill
The shipwrecked enemies who sought the
  island
As a refuge (easily, he thought,
  the Greek arms would be subdued);
He also bid them rescue friends. He
  conned [studied]
The future ill. For when a god gave
  Greeks
The glory, that very day, fenced in bronze,
They leaped ashore, and drew the circle
  tight
At every point: mewed up, we could not
  turn.
Many rattled to the ground, whom stones
Had felled, and arrows, shot by bowstring,
Others killed; and in a final rush,
The end: they hacked, mangled their
  wretched limbs,
Until the life of all was gone.
Xerxes mourned, beholding the lowest
  depths
Of woe, who, seated on a height that near
The sea commanded all his host, his robes
Destroying (and his lamentations shrill),
Dispatched his regiments on land: they
  fled

Bust of Aeschylus, from the Musei Capi-
tolini, Rome. *(Art Resource, NY)*

Orderless. Now you may lament their fate,
Added to the others' summed before.

Questions for Analysis

1. Why did Aeschylus use a Persian herald to narrate the events of the battle at the Persian court?

2. What inspired the Greeks to mount a defense against the Persian invasion?

3. What was the Greek attitude toward the victory? Are there any religious overtones to the passage? If so, describe and explain them.

Source: *The Complete Greek Tragedies,* vol. 1, edited by D. Grene and R. Lattimore, Copyright © 1959 by University of Chicago Press. Reprintd by permission.

4

Hellenistic Diffusion

Two years after his conquest of Greece, Philip of Macedon fell victim to an assassin's dagger. Philip's twenty-year-old son, historically known as Alexander the Great (r. 336–323 B.C.), assumed the Macedonian throne. This young man, one of the most remarkable personalities of Western civilization, was to have a profound impact on history. By overthrowing the Persian Empire and by spreading *Hellenism*—Greek culture, language, thought, and the Greek way of life—as far as India, Alexander was instrumental in creating a new era, traditionally called "Hellenistic" to distinguish it from the Hellenic. As a result of Alexander's exploits, the individualistic and energetic culture of the Greeks came into intimate contact with the venerable older cultures of the Near East.

The impact of Philip and Alexander was so enormous that the great German historian Hermann Bengtson has commented:

Philip and his son Alexander were the ones who opened the door of the world to the Macedonians and Greeks. With Macedonian imperialism was joined the diffusion of the Greek spirit, which permeated the entire ancient world. Without the achievement of these two kings, neither the Roman Empire nor the diffusion of Christianity would have been conceivable.[1]

- Is this estimation correct, or is it mere rhetoric?
- What did the spread of Hellenism mean to the Greeks and the peoples of the Near East?
- What did the meeting of West and East hold for the development of economics, religion, philosophy, women's concerns, science, and medicine?

These are the questions we will explore in this chapter.

Wall-painting from Pompeii of Pelias and his daughters. *(Source: Museo Nazionale Naples)*

ALEXANDER AND THE GREAT CRUSADE

In 336 B.C. Alexander inherited not only Philip's crown but also his policies. After his victory at Chaeronea, Philip had organized the states of Greece into a huge league under his leadership and announced to the Greeks his plan to lead them and his Macedonians against the Persian Empire. Fully intending to carry out Philip's designs, Alexander proclaimed to the Greek world that the invasion of Persia was to be a great crusade, a mighty act of revenge for the Persian invasion of Greece in 480 B.C. It would also be the means by which Alexander would create an empire of his own in the East.

Despite his youth, Alexander was well prepared to lead the attack. Philip had groomed his son to

Bust of Alexander This Roman portrait of Alexander the Great is a copy of a Greek original. Alexander's youth and self-confidence are immediately apparent. Yet the style is surprisingly simple for a bust of someone who had conquered the Persian Empire. The Greek inscription is equally simple: "Alexander, the son of Philip, Macedonian." *(Source: Louvre/Girandon/Art Resource)*

become king and given him the best education possible. In 343 B.C. Philip invited the philosopher Aristotle to tutor his son. From Aristotle, Alexander learned to appreciate Greek culture and literature, and the teachings of the great philosopher left a lasting mark on him. Alexander must also have profited from Aristotle's practical knowledge, but he never accepted Aristotle's political theories. Philip appointed Alexander regent of Macedonia at the age of sixteen, and two years later at the Battle of Chaeronea Alexander helped defeat the Greeks. By 336 B.C. Alexander had acquired both the theoretical and the practical knowledge to rule peoples and lead armies.

In 334 B.C. Alexander led an army of Macedonians and Greeks into Asia Minor. With him went a staff of philosophers and poets, scientists whose job was to map the country and study strange animals and plants, and the historian Callisthenes, who was to write an account of the campaign. Alexander intended not only a military campaign but also an expedition of discovery.

In the next three years Alexander won three major battles at the Granicus River, Issus, and Gaugamela. As Map 4.1 shows, these battle sites stand almost as road signs marking his march to the East. After his victory at Gaugamela, Alexander captured the principal Persian capital of Persepolis, where he performed a symbolic act of retribution by burning the buildings of Xerxes, the invader of Greece. In 330 B.C. he took Ecbatana, the last Persian capital, and pursued the Persian king to his death.

The Persian Empire had fallen and the war of revenge was over, but Alexander had no intention of stopping. He dismissed his Greek troops but permitted many of them to serve on as mercenaries. Alexander then began his personal odyssey. With his Macedonian soldiers and Greek mercenaries, he set out to conquer the rest of Asia. He plunged deeper into the East, into lands completely unknown to the Greek world. Alexander's way was marked by bitter fighting and bloodshed. It took his soldiers four additional years to conquer Bactria and the easternmost parts of the now-defunct Persian Empire, but still Alexander was determined to continue his march.

In 326 B.C. Alexander crossed the Indus River and entered India. There, too, he saw hard fighting, and finally at the Hyphasis River his

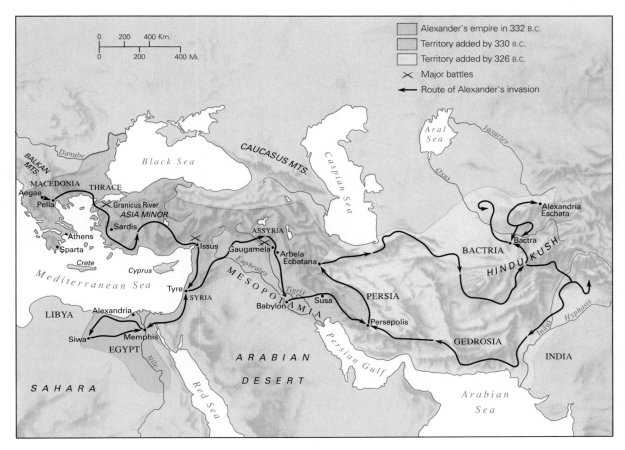

 MAP 4.1 Alexander's Conquests This map shows the course of Alexander's invasion of the Persian Empire and the speed of his progress. More important than the great success of his military campaigns was his founding of Hellenistic cities in the East.

troops refused to go farther. Alexander was enraged by the mutiny, for he believed he was near the end of the world. Nonetheless, the army stood firm, and Alexander had to relent. Still eager to explore the limits of the world, Alexander turned south to the Arabian Sea. Though the tribes in the area did not oppose him, he waged a bloody, ruthless, and unnecessary war against them. After reaching the Arabian Sea and turning west, he led his army through the grim Gedrosian Desert. The army suffered fearfully, and many soldiers died along the way; nonetheless, in 324 B.C. Alexander reached his camp at Susa. The great crusade was over, and Alexander himself died the next year in Babylon.

ALEXANDER'S LEGACY

Alexander so quickly became a legend during his lifetime that he still seems superhuman. That alone makes a reasoned interpretation of him very difficult. Some historians have seen him as a high-minded philosopher, and none can deny that he possessed genuine intellectual gifts. Others, however, have portrayed him as a bloody-minded autocrat, more interested in his own ambition than in any philosophical concept of the common good. Alexander is the perfect example of the need for the historian carefully to interpret the known facts.

The historical record shows that Alexander in a drunken brawl murdered the friend who had saved

❖ **Alexander at the Battle of Issus**   At left, Alexander the Great, bareheaded and
wearing a breastplate, charges King Darius, who is standing in a chariot. The moment marks the turning point of the battle, as Darius turns to flee from the attack.
(Source: National Museum, Naples/Alinari/Scala/Art Resource)

his life at the Battle of the Granicus River. Alexander also used his power to have several other
trusted officials, who had done nothing to offend
him, assassinated. Other uglier and grimmer facts
argue against the view that Alexander was a humane and tolerant man. In eastern Iran and India
he savagely and unnecessarily slaughtered peoples
whose only crime was their desire to be left in
peace.

The only rationale to support those who see
Alexander as a philosopher-king comes from a banquet held in 324 B.C. at the end of his career of
carnage. This event is very important for a variety
of reasons. It came immediately on the heels of a
major Macedonian mutiny. The veteran and otherwise loyal Macedonians resented Alexander's new
policy of giving high offices to Persians, people
whom they had conquered after great suffering.
Alexander realized that his Macedonians were too
few to administer his new empire and that he

needed the ability and experience of the Persians.
As a gesture of reconciliation and to end the mutiny, Alexander named the entire Macedonian army
his kinsmen and held a vast banquet to heal
wounds. He reserved the place of honor for the
Macedonians, giving the Persians and others positions of lesser status. At the banquet Alexander
offered a public prayer for harmony and partnership between the Macedonians and the Persians,
and this prayer has been interpreted as an expression of deep philosophical views. But far from representing an ideal desire for the brotherhood of
man, the gesture was a blatant call for Macedonians and Persians to form a superior union for the
purpose of ruling his new empire. It is undeniably
true that the concepts of universal harmony and
the brotherhood of man became common during
the Hellenistic period, but they were the creations
of talented philosophers, not the battle-hardened
king of Macedonia.

Alexander was instrumental in changing the face of politics in the eastern Mediterranean. His campaign swept away the Persian Empire, which had ruled the East for over two hundred years. In its place he established a Macedonian monarchy.

More important in the long run was his founding of new cities and military colonies, which scattered Greeks and Macedonians throughout the East. Thus the practical result of Alexander's campaign was to open the East to the tide of Hellenism.

The Political Legacy

In 323 B.C. Alexander the Great died at the age of thirty-two. The main question at his death was whether his vast empire could be held together.

The answer became obvious immediately. Within a week of Alexander's death, a round of fighting began that was to continue for forty years. No single Macedonian general was able to replace Alexander as emperor of his entire domain. By 275 B.C. three officers had divided it into large monarchies (Map 4.2). Antigonus Gonatas became king of Macedonia and established the Antigonid dynasty, which ruled until the Roman conquest in 168 B.C. Ptolemy, son of Lagus, made himself king of Egypt, and his descendants, the Ptolemies, assumed the powers and position of pharaohs. Seleucus, founder of the Seleucid dynasty, carved out a kingdom that stretched from the coast of Asia Minor to India. In 263 B.C. Eumenes, the Greek ruler of Pergamum, a city in western Asia Minor, won his independence from the Seleucids and cre-

❖ **MAP 4.2 The Hellenistic World** After Alexander's death, no single commander could hold his vast conquests together, resulting in the empire's breakup into several kingdoms and leagues.

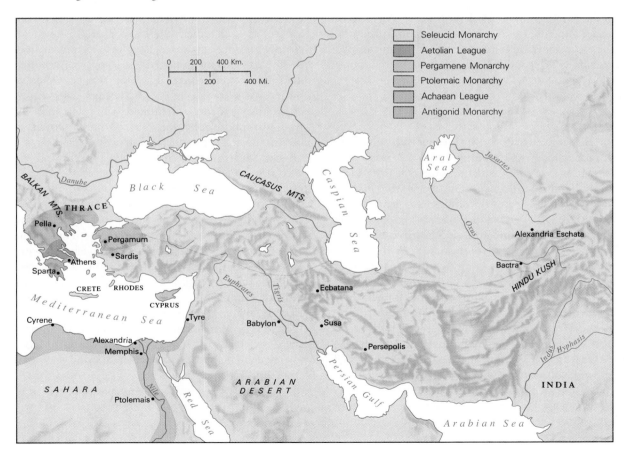

ated the Pergamene monarchy. Though the Seleucid kings soon lost control of their easternmost provinces, Greek influence in this area did not wane. In modern Turkestan and Afghanistan another line of Greek kings established the kingdom of Bactria and even managed to spread their power and culture into northern India.

The political face of Greece itself changed during the Hellenistic period. The day of the polis was over; in its place rose leagues of city-states. The two most powerful and extensive were the Aetolian League in western and central Greece and the Achaean League in the Peloponnesus. Once-powerful city-states like Athens and Sparta sank to the level of third-rate powers.

The political history of the Hellenistic period was dominated by the great monarchies and the Greek leagues. The political fragmentation and incessant warfare that marked the Hellenic period continued on an even wider and larger scale during the Hellenistic period. Never did the Hellenistic world achieve political stability or lasting peace. Hellenistic kings never forgot the vision of Alexander's empire, spanning Europe and Asia, secure under the rule of one man. Try though they did, they were never able to re-create it. In this respect, Alexander's legacy fell not to his generals but to the Romans of a later era.

The Cultural Legacy

As Alexander waded ever deeper into the East, distance alone presented him with a serious problem: how was he to retain contact with the Greek world behind him? Communications were vital, for he drew supplies and reinforcements from Greece and Macedonia. Alexander had to be sure that he was never cut off and stranded far from the Mediterranean world. His solution was to plant cities and military colonies in strategic places. In these settlements Alexander left Greek mercenaries and Macedonian veterans who were no longer up to active campaigning. Besides keeping the road open to the West, these settlements served the purpose of dominating the countryside around them.

Their military significance apart, Alexander's cities and colonies became powerful instruments in the spread of Hellenism throughout the East. Plutarch described Alexander's achievement in glowing terms: "Having founded over 70 cities among barbarian peoples and having planted Greek magistracies in Asia, Alexander overcame its wild and savage way of life."[2] Alexander had indeed opened the East to an enormous wave of immigration, and his successors continued his policy by inviting Greek colonists to settle in their realms. For seventy-five years after Alexander's death, Greek immigrants poured into the East. At least 250 new Hellenistic colonies were established. The Mediterranean world had seen no comparable movement of peoples since the days of Archilochus (see page 73), when wave after wave of Greeks had turned the Mediterranean basin into a Greek-speaking region.

One concrete and almost exotic example of these trends comes from the newly discovered Hellenistic city of Ay Khanoum. Situated on the borders of Russia and Afghanistan and not far from China, the city was predominantly Greek. It had the typical Greek trappings of a gymnasium, various temples, and administration buildings. It was not, however, purely Greek. It also contained an Oriental temple and artistic remains that prove that the Greeks and the natives had already embraced aspects of each other's religion. One of the most curious discoveries was a long inscription written in Greek verse by Clearchus, a pupil of Aristotle. The inscription, carved in stone, was set up in a public place for all to see. Clearchus had simply copied the precepts of famous Greeks. The inscription was philosophy for the common people, a contribution to popular culture. It provided the Greeks with a link to their faraway homeland. It was also an easy way to make at least some of Greek culture available to natives.

The overall result of Alexander's settlements and those of his successors was the spread of Hellenism as far east as India. Throughout the Hellenistic period, Greeks and Easterners became familiar with and adapted themselves to each other's customs, religions, and ways of life. Although Greek culture did not completely conquer the East, it gave the East a vehicle of expression that linked it to the West. Hellenism became a common bond among the East, peninsular Greece, and the western Mediterranean. This pre-existing cultural bond was later to prove supremely valuable to Rome—itself heavily influenced by Hellenism—in its efforts to impose a comparable political unity on the known world.

✣ **Ay Khanoum** This view of a Greek palaestra was found at Ay Khanoum, a city located in modern Afghanistan. The palaestra and other buildings are mute evidence
of how the Greeks took their culture with them no matter how far from home.
(Source: French Archaeological Delegation, Afghanistan)

✤ THE SPREAD OF HELLENISM

When the Greeks and Macedonians entered Asia
Minor, Egypt, and the more remote East, they
encountered civilizations older than their own. In
some ways the Eastern cultures were more advanced than the Greek, in others less so. Thus this
third great tide of Greek migration differed from
preceding waves, which had spread over land that
was uninhabited or inhabited by less-developed
peoples.

What did the Hellenistic monarchies offer Greek
immigrants politically and materially? More
broadly, how did Hellenism and the cultures of the
East affect one another? What did the meeting of
East and West entail for the history of the world?

Cities and Kingdoms

One of the major developments of these new kingdoms was the resurgence of monarchy, which had
many repercussions. For most Greeks monarchs
were something out of the heroic past, something
found in Homer's *Iliad* but not in daily life. Furthermore, most Hellenistic kingdoms embraced
numerous different peoples who had little in common. Hellenistic kings thus needed a new political
concept to unite them. One solution was the creation of a ruler cult that linked the king's authority
with that of the gods. Thus, royal power had divine
approval and was meant to create a political and
religious bond between the kings and their subjects. These deified kings were not considered gods

as mighty as Zeus or Apollo, and the new ruler cults probably made little religious impact on those ruled. Nonetheless, the ruler cult was an easily understandable symbol of unity within the kingdom.

Monarchy also included royal women, who began to play an active part in political and diplomatic life (see Listening to the Past). Some of them did so in their own right, others by manipulating their husbands. Many Hellenistic queens were depicted as willful or ruthless, especially in power struggles over the throne. In some cases those charges are accurate. Yet for the most part, they served as examples that women too were capable of shouldering vast responsibilities and performing them successfully.

Although Alexander's generals created huge kingdoms, the concept of monarchy, even when combined with the ruler cult, never replaced the ideal of the polis. Consequently, the monarchies never won the deep emotional loyalty that Greeks had once felt for the polis. Hellenistic kings needed large numbers of Greeks to run their kingdoms. Otherwise royal business would grind to a halt, and the conquerors would soon be swallowed up by the far more numerous conquered population. Obviously, then, the kings had to encourage Greeks to immigrate and build new homes. The Hellenistic kings thus confronted the problem of making life in the new monarchies resemble the traditional Greek way of life. Since Greek civilization was urban, the kings continued Alexander's policy of establishing cities throughout their kingdoms in order to entice Greeks to immigrate. Yet the creation of these cities posed a serious political problem that the Hellenistic kings failed to solve.

To the Greeks civilized life was unthinkable without the polis, which was far more than a mere city. The Greek polis was by definition *sovereign*— an independent, autonomous state run by its citizens, free of any outside power or restraint. Hellenistic kings, however, refused to grant sovereignty to their cities. In effect, these kings willingly built cities but refused to build a polis.

Hellenistic monarchs gave their cities all the external trappings of a polis. Each had an assembly of citizens, a council to prepare legislation, and a board of magistrates to conduct the city's political business. Yet, however similar to the Greek polis they appeared, these cities could not engage in diplomatic dealings, make treaties, pursue their own foreign policy, or wage their own wars. None

could govern its own affairs without interference from the king, who, even if he stood in the background, was the real sovereign. In the eyes of the king the cities were important parts of the kingdom, but the welfare of the whole kingdom came first. The cities had to follow royal orders, and the king often placed his own officials in the cities to see that his decrees were followed.

A new Hellenistic city differed from a Greek polis in other ways as well. The Greek polis had enjoyed political and social unity even though it was normally composed of citizens, slaves, and resident aliens. The polis had one body of law and one set of customs. In the Hellenistic city Greeks represented an elite citizen class. Natives and non-Greek foreigners who lived in Hellenistic cities usually possessed lesser rights than Greeks and often had their own laws. In some instances this disparity spurred natives to assimilate Greek culture in order to rise politically and socially. Other peoples, such as many Jews, firmly resisted the essence of Hellenism. The Hellenistic city was not homogeneous and could not spark the intensity of feeling that marked the polis.

In many respects the Hellenistic city resembled a modern city. It was a cultural center with theaters, temples, and libraries. It was a seat of learning, home of poets, writers, teachers, and artists. It was a place where people could find amusement. The Hellenistic city was also an economic center that provided a ready market for grain and produce raised in the surrounding countryside. The city was an emporium, scene of trade and manufacturing. In short, the Hellenistic city offered cultural and economic opportunities but did not foster a sense of united, integrated enterprise.

There were no constitutional links between city and king. The city was simply his possession. Its citizens had no voice in how the kingdom was run. The city had no rights except for those the king granted, and even those he could summarily take away. Ambassadors from the city could entreat the king for favors and petition him on such matters as taxes, boundary disputes, and legal cases. But the city had no right to advise the king on royal policy and enjoyed no political function in the kingdom.

Hellenistic kings tried to make the kingdom the political focus of citizens' allegiance. If the king could secure the frontiers of his kingdom, he could give it a geographical identity. He could then hope that his subjects would direct their primary loyalty to the kingdom rather than to a particular city. However, the kings' efforts to fix their borders led only to sustained warfare. Boundaries were determined by military power, and rule by force became the chief political principle of the Hellenistic world.

Border wars were frequent and exhausting. The Seleucids and Ptolemies, for instance, waged five wars for the possession of southern Syria. Other kings refused to acknowledge boundaries at all. They followed Alexander's example and waged wars to reunify his empire under their own authority. By the third century B.C., a weary balance of power was reached, but only as the result of stalemate. It was not based on any political principle.

Though Hellenistic kings never built a true polis, that does not mean that their urban policy failed. Rather, the Hellenistic city was to remain the basic social and political unit in the Hellenistic East until the sixth century A.D. Cities were the chief agents of Hellenization, and their influence spread far beyond their walls. These cities formed a broader cultural network in which Greek language, customs, and values flourished. Roman rule in the Hellenistic East would later be based on this urban culture, which facilitated the rise and spread of Christianity. In broad terms, Hellenistic cities were remarkably successful.

The Greeks and the Opening of the East

If the Hellenistic kings failed to satisfy the Greeks' political yearnings, they nonetheless succeeded in giving them unequaled economic and social opportunities. The ruling dynasties of the Hellenistic world were Macedonian, and Greeks filled all important political, military, and diplomatic positions. They constituted an upper class that sustained Hellenism in the barbarian East. Besides building Greek cities, Hellenistic kings offered Greeks land and money as lures to further immigration.

The opening of the East offered ambitious Greeks opportunities for well-paying jobs and economic success. The Hellenistic monarchy, unlike

Theater of Orchomenus This theater was discovered at Orchomenus in Boeotia, Greece in 1973. A small gem, it is complete with remains of the stage building in the foreground, the orchestra, and behind it the seats. Besides its many architectural refinements, it is of interest because most Greek plays were staged in small theaters such as this. Yet few others have survived as well. *(Source: John Buckler)*

❖ **Old Shepherdess** Daily life for the poor and elderly was as hard in the Hellenistic period as in other times. Here a tough, old, scantily clothed shepherdess brings a sheep to market. Such scenes were common during the period; but art, not written sources, has preserved them for posterity. *(Source: Alinari/Art Resource)*

the Greek polis, did not depend solely on its citizens to fulfill its political needs. Talented Greeks could expect to rise quickly in the governmental bureaucracy. Appointed by the king, these administrators did not have to stand for election each year, as had many officials of a Greek polis. Since they held their jobs year after year, they had ample time to evolve new administrative techniques. Naturally they became more efficient than the amateur officials common in Hellenic Greek city-states. The needs of the Hellenistic monarchy and the opportunities it offered thus gave rise to a professional corps of Greek administrators.

Greeks and Macedonians also found ready employment in the armies and navies of the Hellenistic monarchies. Alexander had proved the Greco-Macedonian style of warfare to be far superior to that of the Easterners, and Alexander's successors, themselves experienced officers, realized the importance of trained Greek and Macedonian soldiers. Moreover, Hellenistic kings were extremely reluctant to arm the native populations or to allow them to serve in the army, fearing military rebellions among their conquered subjects. The result was the emergence of professional armies and navies consisting entirely of Greeks and Macedonians.

Greeks were able to dominate other professions as well. The kingdoms and cities recruited Greek writers and artists to create Greek literature, art, and culture on Asian soil. Architects, engineers, and skilled craftsmen found their services in great demand because of the building policies of the Hellenistic monarchs. If Hellenistic kingdoms were to have Greek cities, those cities needed Greek buildings—temples, porticoes, gymnasia, theaters, fountains, and houses. Architects and engineers were sometimes commissioned to design and build whole cities, which they laid out in checkerboard fashion and filled with typical Greek buildings. An enormous wave of construction took place during the Hellenistic period.

New opportunities opened for women as well, owing in part to the examples of the queens. Especially in social and economic pursuits women played an expanded role. More women than ever before received educations that enabled them to enter medicine and other professions. Literacy among women increased dramatically, and their options expanded accordingly. Some won fame as poets, while others studied with philosophers and contributed to the intellectual life of the age. As a rule, however, these developments touched only wealthier women, and not all of them. Although some poor women were literate, most were not.

The major reason for the new prominence of women was their increased participation in economic affairs. During the Hellenistic period some women took part in commercial transactions. They still lived under legal handicaps; in Egypt, for example, a Greek woman needed a male guardian to buy, sell, or lease land, to borrow money, and to represent her in other transactions. Yet often such a guardian was present only to fulfill the letter of the law. The woman was the real agent and handled the business being transacted. In Hellenistic Sparta, women accumulated large fortunes and vast amounts of land. As early as the beginning of the Hellenistic period, women owned two-fifths of the land of Laconia. Spartan women, however, were exceptional. In most other areas, even women who were wealthy in their own right were formally under the protection of their male relatives.

Women also began to participate in politics on a limited basis. They served in civil capacities, for which they often received public acknowledgment. Women sometimes received honorary citizenship from foreign cities because of aid given in times of crisis. Few women achieved these honors, however, and those who did were from the upper classes.

Despite the opportunities they offered, the Hellenistic monarchies were hampered by their artificial origins. Their failure to win the political loyalty of their Greek subjects and their policy of wooing Greeks with lucrative positions encouraged a feeling of uprootedness and self-serving individualism among Greek immigrants. Once a Greek had left home to take service with, for instance, the army or the bureaucracy of the Ptolemies, he had no incentive beyond his pay and the comforts of life in Egypt to keep him there. If the Seleucid king offered him more money or a promotion, he might well accept it and take his talents to Asia Minor. Why not? In the realm of the Seleucids he, a Greek, would find the same sort of life and environment that the kingdom of the Ptolemies had provided him. Thus professional Greek soldiers and administrators were very mobile and apt to look to their own interests, not their kingdom's.

One result of these developments was that the nature of warfare changed. Except in the areas of Greece and to some extent Macedonia, Hellenistic soldiers were professionals. Unlike the citizen hoplites of classical Greece, these men were regular soldiers capable of intricate maneuvers. Hellenistic kings paid them well, often giving them land as an incentive to remain loyal. Only in Macedonia among the kingdoms was there a national army that was devoted to its land, homes, and monarchy. The loyalty, skill, and bravery of Macedonian soldiers made them the most formidable in the Hellenistic world.

As long as Greeks continued to replenish their professional ranks, the kingdoms remained strong. In the process they drew an immense amount of talent from the Greek peninsula, draining the vitality of the Greek homeland. However, the Hellenistic monarchies could not keep recruiting Greeks forever, in spite of their wealth and willingness to spend lavishly. In time, the huge surge of immigration slowed greatly. Even then, the Hellenistic monarchs were reluctant to recruit Easterners to fill posts normally held by Greeks. The result was at first the stagnation of the Hellenistic world and finally, after 202 B.C., its collapse in the face of the young and vigorous Roman republic.

Greeks and Easterners

The Greeks in the East were a minority, and Hellenistic cities were islands of Greek culture in an Eastern sea. But Hellenistic monarchies were remarkably successful in at least partially Hellenizing Easterners and spreading a uniform culture throughout the East, a culture to which Rome eventually fell heir. The prevailing institutions, laws, and language of the East became Greek. Indeed, the Near East had seen nothing comparable since the days when Mesopotamian culture had spread throughout the area.

Yet the spread of Greek culture was wider than it was deep. At best it was a veneer, thicker in some places than in others. Hellenistic kingdoms were never entirely unified in language, customs, and thought. Greek culture took firmest hold along the shores of the Mediterranean, but in the Far East, in Persia and Bactria, it eventually gave way to Eastern cultures.

The Ptolemies in Egypt made no effort to spread Greek culture, and unlike other Hellenistic kings they were not city builders. Indeed, they founded only the city of Ptolemais near Thebes. At first the native Egyptian population, the descendants of the pharaoh's people, retained their traditional language, outlook, religion, and way of life. Initially untouched by Hellenism, the natives continued to be the foundation of the state: they fed it by their labor in the fields and financed its operations with their taxes.

Under the pharaohs, talented Egyptians had been able to rise to high office, but during the third century B.C. the Ptolemies cut off this avenue of advancement. They tied the natives to the land ever more tightly, making it nearly impossible for them to leave their villages. The bureaucracy of the Ptolemies was ruthlessly efficient, and the native population was viciously· and cruelly exploited. Even in times of hardship the king's taxes came first, although payment might mean starvation for the natives. Their desperation was summed up by one Egyptian, who scrawled the warning: "We are worn out; we will run away."[3] To many Egyptians, revolt or a life of brigandage was certainly preferable to working the land under the harsh Ptolemies.

Throughout the third century B.C., the Greek upper class in Egypt had little to do with the native

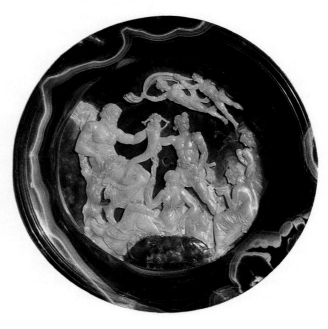

❖ **Tazza Farnese Bowl** This exquisite cameo bowl from Hellenistic Egypt dates to ca. 125 B.C.. The figure on the left represents the Nile pouring out the horn of plenty. The other figures also personify the deities who gave Egypt its great richness. *(Source: National Museum, Naples/Wim Swaan)*

population. Many Greek bureaucrats established homes in Alexandria and Ptolemais, where they managed finances, served as magistrates, and administered the law. Other Greeks settled in military colonies and supplied the monarchy with fighting men. But in the second century B.C., Greeks and native Egyptians began to intermarry and mingle their cultures. The language of the native population influenced Greek, and many Greeks adopted Egyptian religion and ways of life. Simultaneously, natives adopted Greek customs and language and began to play a role in the administration of the kingdom and even to serve in the army. While many Greeks and Egyptians remained aloof from each other, the overall result was the evolution of a widespread Greco-Egyptian culture.

Meanwhile the Seleucid kings established many cities and military colonies in western Asia Minor and along the banks of the Tigris and Euphrates rivers in order to nurture a vigorous and large Greek population. Especially important to the Seleucids were the military colonies, for they needed Greeks to defend the kingdom. The Seleucids had no elaborate plan for Hellenizing the native population, but the arrival of so many Greeks was bound to have an impact. Seleucid military colonies were generally founded near native villages, thus exposing Easterners to all aspects of Greek life. Many Easterners found Greek political and cultural forms attractive and imitated them. In Asia Minor and Syria, for instance, numerous native villages and towns developed along Greek lines, and some of them became Hellenized cities. Farther east, the Greek kings who replaced the Seleucids in the third century B.C. spread Greek culture to their neighbors, even into the Indian subcontinent.

For Easterners the prime advantage of Greek culture was its very pervasiveness. The Greek language became the common speech of the East. A common dialect called *koine* even influenced the speech of peninsular Greece itself. Greek became the speech of the royal court, bureaucracy, and army. It was also the speech of commerce: any Easterner who wanted to compete in business had to learn it. As early as the third century B.C., some Greek cities were giving citizenship to Hellenized natives.

The vast majority of Hellenized Easterners, however, took only the externals of Greek culture while retaining the essentials of their own way of life. Though Greeks and Easterners adapted to each other's ways, there was never a true fusion of cultures. Nonetheless, each found useful things in the civilization of the other, and the two fertilized each other. This fertilization, this mingling of Greek and Eastern elements, is what makes Hellenistic culture unique and distinctive.

Hellenism and the Jews

A prime illustration of how the East took what it wanted from Hellenism while remaining true to itself is the impact of Greek culture on the Jews. At first, Jews in Hellenistic cities were treated as resident aliens. As they grew more numerous, they received permission to form a political corporation, a *politeuma,* which gave them a great deal of autonomy. The politeuma allowed Jews to attend to their religious and internal affairs without interference from the Greek municipal government. The Jewish politeuma had its own officials, the leaders of the synagogue. In time the Jewish politeuma gained the special right to be judged by its own law and its own officials, thus becoming in effect a Jewish city within a Hellenistic city.

The Jewish politeuma, like the Hellenistic city, obeyed the king's commands, but there was virtually no royal interference with the Jewish religion. Indeed, the Greeks were always reluctant to tamper with anyone's religion. Only the Seleucid king Antiochus Epiphanes (175–ca 164 B.C.) tried to suppress the Jewish religion in Judaea. He did so not because he hated the Jews (who were a small part of his kingdom), but because he was trying to unify his realm culturally to meet the threat of Rome. To the Jews he extended the same policy that he applied to all subjects. Apart from this instance, Hellenistic Jews suffered no official religious persecution. Some Jews were given the right to become full citizens of Hellenistic cities, but few exercised that right. Citizenship would have allowed them to vote in the assembly and serve as magistrates, but it would also have obliged them to worship the gods of the city—a practice few Jews chose to follow.

Jews living in Hellenistic cities often embraced a good deal of Hellenism. So many Jews learned Greek, especially in Alexandria, that the Old Testament was translated into Greek, and services in the synagogue came to be conducted in Greek. Jews often took Greek names, used Greek political forms, adopted Greek practice by forming their own trade associations, put inscriptions on graves as the Greeks did, and much else. Yet no matter how much of Greek culture or its externals Jews borrowed, they normally remained attached to their religion. Thus, in spite of Hellenistic trappings, Hellenized Jews remained Jews at heart. Their ideas and those of the Greeks were different. The exceptions were some Jews in Asia Minor and Syria who incorporated Greek or local Eastern cults into their worship. To some degree this development was due to the growing belief among Greeks and Easterners that all peoples, despite differences in cult and ritual, actually worshiped the same gods.

THE ECONOMIC SCOPE OF THE HELLENISTIC WORLD

Alexander's conquest of the Persian Empire not only changed the political face of the ancient world but also brought the East fully into the sphere of Greek economics. Yet the Hellenistic period did not see a revolution in the way people lived and worked. The material demands of Hellenistic society remained as simple as those of Athenian society in the fifth century B.C. Clothes and furniture were essentially unchanged, as were household goods, tools, and jewelry. The real achievement of Alexander and his successors was linking East and West in a broad commercial network. The spread of Greeks throughout the East created new markets and stimulated trade. The economic unity of the Hellenistic world, like its cultural bonds, would later prove valuable to the Romans.

Commerce

Alexander's conquest of the Persian Empire had immediate effects on trade. In the Persian capitals Alexander had found vast sums of gold, silver, and other treasure. This wealth financed the creation of new cities, the building of roads, and the development of harbors. Most of the great monarchies coined their money on the Attic standard, which meant that much of the money used in Hellenistic kingdoms had the same value. Traders were less in need of moneychangers than in the days when each major power coined money on a different standard. As a result of Alexander's conquests, geographical knowledge of the East increased dramatically, making the East far better known to the Greeks than previously. The Greeks spread their law and methods of transacting business throughout the East. Whole new fields lay open to Greek merchants, who eagerly took advantage of the new opportunities. Commerce itself was a leading area where Greeks and Easterners met on grounds of common interest. In bazaars, ports, and trading centers Greeks learned of Eastern customs and traditions while spreading knowledge of their own culture.

The Seleucid and Ptolemaic dynasties traded as far afield as India, Arabia, and sub-Saharan Africa. Overland trade with India and Arabia was conducted by caravan and was largely in the hands of Easterners. The caravan trade never dealt in bulk items or essential commodities; only luxury goods could be transported in this very expensive fashion. Once the goods reached the Hellenistic monarchies, Greek merchants took a hand in the trade.

In the early Hellenistic period, the Seleucids and Ptolemies ensured that the caravan trade proceeded efficiently. Later in the period—a time of increased war and confusion—they left the caravans unprotected. Taking advantage of this situation, Palmyra in the Syrian desert and Nabataean Petra in Arabia arose as caravan states. Such states protected the caravans from bandits and marauders and served as dispersal areas for caravan goods.

The Ptolemies discovered how to use monsoon winds to establish direct contact with India. One hardy merchant has left a firsthand account of sailing this important maritime route:

Hippalos, the pilot, observing the position of the ports and the conditions of the sea, first discovered how to sail across the ocean. Concerning the winds of the ocean in this region, when with us the Etesian winds begin, in India a wind between southwest and south, named for Hippalos, sets in from the open sea. From then until now some mariners set forth from Kanes and some from the Cape of Spices. Those sailing to Dimurikes [in southern India] throw the bow of the ship farther out to sea. Those bound for Barygaza and the realm of the Sakas [in northern India] hold to the land no more than three days; and if the wind remains favorable, they hold the same course through the outer sea, and they sail along past the previously mentioned gulfs.[4]

Although this sea route never replaced overland caravan traffic, it kept direct relations between East and West alive, stimulating the exchange of ideas as well as goods.

More economically important than this exotic trade were commercial dealings in essential commodities like raw materials, grain, and industrial products. The Hellenistic monarchies usually raised enough grain for their own needs as well as a surplus for export. For the cities of Greece and the Aegean this trade in grain was essential, because many of them could not grow enough. Fortunately for them, abundant wheat supplies were available nearby in Egypt and in the Crimea in southern Russia.

The large-scale wars of the Hellenistic period often interrupted both the production and the distribution of grain. This was especially true when Alexander's successors were trying to carve out kingdoms. In addition, natural calamities, such as excessive rain or drought, frequently damaged harvests. Throughout the Hellenistic period, famine or severe food shortage remained a grim possibility.

Most trade in bulk commodities was seaborne, and the Hellenistic merchant ship was the workhorse of the day. The merchant ship had a broad beam and relied on sails for propulsion. It was far more seaworthy than the contemporary warship, which was long, narrow, and built for speed. A small crew of experienced sailors could handle the merchant vessel easily. Maritime trade provided opportunities for workers in other industries and trades: sailors, shipbuilders, dock workers, accountants, teamsters, and pirates. Piracy was always a factor in the Hellenistic world and remained so until Rome extended its power throughout the East.

The Greek cities paid for their grain by exporting olive oil and wine. When agriculture and oil production developed in Syria, Greek products began to encounter competition from the Seleucid monarchy. Later in the Hellenistic period, Greek oil and wine found a lucrative market in Italy. Another significant commodity was fish, which for export was either salted, pickled, or dried. This trade was doubly important because fish provided poor people with an essential element of their diet. Salt, too, was often imported, and there was some very slight trade in salted meat, which was a luxury item. Far more important was the trade in honey, dried fruit, nuts, and vegetables. Of raw materials, wood was high in demand, but little trade occurred in manufactured goods.

Slaves were a staple of Hellenistic trade. The wars provided prisoners for the slave market; to a lesser extent, so did kidnaping and capture by pirates. The number of slaves involved cannot be estimated, but there is no doubt that slavery flourished. Both old Greek states and new Hellenistic kingdoms were ready slave markets, as was Rome when it emerged triumphant from the Second Punic War (see Chapter 5).

Throughout the Mediterranean world slaves were almost always in demand. Only the Ptolemies discouraged both the trade and slavery itself, and they did so only for economic reasons. Their system had no room for slaves, who would only have competed with free labor. Otherwise, slave labor was to be found in the cities and temples of the Hellenistic world, in the factories and fields, and in the homes of wealthier people. In Italy and some parts of the East, slaves performed manual labor for large estates and worked the mines. They were vitally important to the Hellenistic economy.

Industry

Although demand for goods increased during the Hellenistic period, no new techniques of production appear to have developed. The discoveries of Hellenistic mathematicians and thinkers failed to produce any significant corresponding technological development. Manual labor, not machinery, continued to turn out the raw materials and few manufactured goods the Hellenistic world used. Human labor was so cheap and so abundant that kings had no incentive to encourage the invention and manufacture of labor-saving machinery.

Perhaps only one noteworthy technological innovation dates to the Hellenistic period—the Archimedean screw, a device used to pump water into irrigation ditches and out of mines. At Thoricus in Attica miners dug ore by hand and hauled it from the mines for processing. This was grueling work; invariably miners were slaves, criminals, or forced laborers. The conditions under which they worked were frightful. The Ptolemies ran their gold mines along the same harsh lines. One historian gave a grim picture of the miners' lives:

The kings of Egypt condemn [to the mines] those found guilty of wrong-doing and those taken prisoner in war, those who are victims of false accusations and were put into jail because of royal anger. . . . The condemned—and they are very many—all of them are put in chains, and they work persistently and continually, both by day and throughout the night, getting no rest, and carefully cut off from escape.[5]

✦ **Harbor and Warehouses of Delos** During the Hellenistic period Delos became a thriving trading center. Shown here is the row of warehouses at water's edge. From Delos cargoes were shipped to virtually every part of the Mediterranean. *(Source: Adam Woolfitt/Woodfin Camp)*

The Ptolemies even condemned women and children to work in the mines. The strongest men lived and died swinging iron sledgehammers to break up the gold-bearing quartz rock. Others worked underground following the seams of quartz; laboring with lamps bound to their foreheads, they were whipped by overseers if they slacked off. Once the diggers had cut out blocks of quartz, young boys gathered up the blocks and carried them outside. All of them—men, women, and boys—worked until they died.

Apart from gold and silver, which were used primarily for coins and jewelry, iron was the most important metal and saw the most varied use. Even so, the method of its production never became very sophisticated. The Hellenistic Greeks did

❖ **Mendicant Musicians** Street musicians are not a modern novelty, as this Hellenistic mosaic proves. Here musicians play several different instruments for the same reasons that street players do today: for the fun of the music, to entertain passersby, and to earn a few coins. *(Source: National Museum, Naples)*

manage to produce a low-grade steel by adding carbon to iron.

Pottery remained an important commodity, and most of it was made locally. The pottery used in the kitchen, the coarse ware, did not change at all. Fancier pots and bowls, decorated with a shiny black glaze, came into use during the Hellenistic period. This ware originated in Athens, but potters in other places began to imitate its style, heavily cutting into the Athenian market. In the second century B.C. a red-glazed ware, often called Samian, burst on the market and soon dominated it. Athens still held its own, however, in the production of fine pottery. Despite the change in pottery styles, the method of production of all pottery, whether plain or fine, remained essentially unchanged.

Although new techniques of production and wider use of machinery did not develop, the volume of goods produced increased in the Hellenistic period. Small manufacturing establishments existed in nearly all parts of the Hellenistic world.

Agriculture

Hellenistic kings paid special attention to agriculture. Much of their revenue was derived from the produce of royal lands, rents paid by the tenants of royal land, and taxation of agricultural land. Some Hellenistic kings even sought out and supported agricultural experts. The Ptolemies, for instance, sponsored experiments on seed grain, selecting seeds that seemed hardy and productive and trying to improve their characteristics. Hellenistic authors wrote handbooks discussing how farms and large estates could most profitably be run. These handbooks described soil types, covered the proper times for planting and reaping, and discussed care of farm animals. Whether these efforts had any impact on the average farmer is difficult to determine.

The Ptolemies made the greatest strides in agriculture, and the reason for their success was largely political. Egypt had a strong tradition of central authority dating back to the pharaohs, which the

Ptolemies inherited and tightened. They could decree what crops Egyptian farmers would plant and what animals would be raised, and they had the power to carry out their commands. The Ptolemies recognized the need for well-planned and constant irrigation, and much native labor went into the digging and maintenance of canals and ditches. The Ptolemies also reclaimed a great deal of land from the desert, including the Fayum, a dried lake bed near the Nile.

The centralized authority of the Ptolemies explains how agricultural advances occurred at the local level in Egypt. But such progress was not possible in any other Hellenistic monarchy. Despite royal interest in agriculture and a more studied approach to it in the Hellenistic period, there is no evidence that agricultural productivity increased. Whether Hellenistic agricultural methods had any influence on Eastern practices is unknown.

✤ RELIGION IN THE HELLENISTIC WORLD

In religion Hellenism gave Easterners far less than the East gave the Greeks. At first the Hellenistic period saw the spread of Greek religious cults throughout the East. When Hellenistic kings founded cities, they also built temples and established new cults and priesthoods for the old Olympian gods. The new cults enjoyed the prestige of being the religion of the conquerors, and they were supported by public money. The most attractive aspects of the Greek cults were their rituals and festivities. Greek cults sponsored literary, musical, and athletic contests, which were staged in beautiful surroundings among impressive Greek buildings. In short, the cults offered bright and lively entertainment, both intellectual and physical. They fostered Greek culture and traditional sports and thus were a splendid means of displaying Greek civilization in the East.

Despite various advantages, Greek cults suffered from some severe shortcomings. They were primarily concerned with ritual. Participation in the civic cults did not even require belief (see Chapter 3). On the whole, the civic cults neither appealed to religious emotions nor embraced matters such as sin and redemption. Greek mystery religions helped fill this gap, but the centers of these religions were in old Greece. Although the new civic cults were lavish in pomp and display, they could not satisfy deep religious feelings or spiritual yearnings.

Even though the Greeks participated in the new cults for cultural reasons, they felt little genuine religious attachment to them. In comparison with the emotional and sometimes passionate religions of the East, the Greek cults seemed sterile. Greeks increasingly sought solace from other sources. Educated and thoughtful people turned to philosophy as a guide to life, while others turned to superstition, magic, or astrology. Still others might shrug and speak of *Tyche,* which meant "Fate" or "Chance" or "Doom"—a capricious and sometimes malevolent force.

In view of the spiritual decline of Greek religion, it is surprising that Eastern religions did not make more immediate headway among the Greeks. Although Hellenistic Greeks clung to their own cults as expressions of their Greekness rather than for any ethical principles, they did not rush to embrace native religions. Only in the second century B.C., after a century of exposure to Eastern religions, did Greeks begin to adopt them.

Nor did Hellenistic kings make any effort to spread Greek religion among their Eastern subjects. The Greeks always considered religion a matter best left to the individual. Greek cults were attractive only to those socially aspiring Easterners who adopted Greek culture for personal advancement. Otherwise, Easterners were little affected by Greek religion. Nor did native religions suffer from the arrival of the Greeks. Some Hellenistic kings limited the power of native priesthoods, but they also subsidized some Eastern cults with public money. Alexander the Great actually reinstated several Eastern cults that the Persians had suppressed.

The only significant junction of Greek and Eastern religious traditions was the growth and spread of new "mystery religions," so called because they featured a body of ritual not to be divulged to anyone not initiated into the cult. These new mystery cults incorporated aspects of both Greek and Eastern religions and had broad appeal for both Greeks and Easterners who yearned for personal immortality. Since the Greeks were already familiar with old mystery cults, such as the Eleusinian mysteries in Attica, the new cults did not strike them as alien or barbarian. Familiar, too, was the concept of preparation for an initiation. Devotees of the Eleusinian mysteries and other such cults had to prepare themselves mentally and physically before entering the gods' presence. Thus the mystery cults fit well with Greek usage.

The new religions enjoyed one tremendous advantage over the old Greek mystery cults. Whereas old Greek mysteries were tied to particular places, such as Eleusis, the new religions spread throughout the Hellenistic world. People did not have to undertake long and expensive pilgrimages just to become members of the religion. In that sense the mystery religions came to the people, for temples of the new deities sprang up wherever Greeks lived.

The mystery religions all claimed to save their adherents from the worst that fate could do and promised life for the soul after death. They all had a single concept in common: the belief that by the rites of initiation devotees became united with the god, who had himself died and risen from the dead.

The sacrifice of the god and his victory over death saved the devotee from eternal death. Similarly, all mystery religions demanded a period of preparation in which the convert strove to become holy, that is, to live by the religion's precepts. Once aspirants had prepared themselves, they went through an initiation in which they learned the secrets of the religion. The initiation was usually a ritual of great emotional intensity, symbolizing the entry into a new life.

The Eastern mystery religions that took the Hellenistic world by storm were the Egyptian cults of Serapis and Isis. Serapis, who was invented by King Ptolemy, combined elements of the Egyptian god Osiris with aspects of the Greek gods Zeus, Pluto (the prince of the underworld), and Asclepius. Serapis was believed to be the judge of souls, who rewarded virtuous and righteous people with eter-

❖ **Religious Syncretism**   This relief was found at the Greek outpost of Dura-Europus, located on the Euphrates. In the center sits Zeus Olympius-Baalshamin, a combination of a Greek god and a Semitic god. The Eastern priest at the right is burning incense on an altar, while the figure on the left in Macedonian dress crowns the god. Both the religious sentiments and the style of art show the meeting of East and West. *(Source: Yale University Art Gallery, Dura-Europos Collection)*

nal life. Like Asclepius, he was a god of healing. Serapis became an international god, and many Hellenistic Greeks thought of him as Zeus. Associated with Isis and Serapis was Anubis, the old Egyptian god who, like Charon in the Greek pantheon, guided the souls of initiates to the realm of eternal life.

The cult of Isis enjoyed even wider appeal than that of Serapis. Isis, wife of Osiris, claimed to have conquered Tyche and promised to save any mortal who came to her. She became the most important goddess of the Hellenistic world, and her worship was very popular among women. Her priests claimed that she had bestowed on humanity the gift of civilization and founded law and literature. She was the goddess of marriage, conception, and childbirth; and like Serapis she promised to save the souls of her believers.

There was neither conflict between Greek and Eastern religions nor wholesale acceptance of one or the other. Nonetheless, Greeks and Easterners noticed similarities among their respective deities and assumed that they were worshiping the same gods in different garb. These tendencies toward religious universalism and the desire for personal immortality would prove significant when the Hellenistic world came under the sway of Rome, for Hellenistic developments paved the way for the spread of Christianity.

✤ PHILOSOPHY AND THE PEOPLE

Philosophy during the Hellenic period was the exclusive province of the wealthy, for only they had leisure enough to pursue philosophical studies. During the Hellenistic period, however, philosophy reached out to touch the lives of more men and women than ever before. The reasons for this development were several. Since the ideal of the polis had declined, politics no longer offered people an intellectual outlet. Moreover, much of Hellenistic life, especially in the new cities of the East, seemed unstable and without venerable traditions. Greeks were far more mobile than they had ever been before, but their very mobility left them feeling uprooted. Many people in search of something permanent, something unchanging in a changing world, turned to philosophy. Another reason for the increased influence of philosophy was the decline of traditional religion and a growing belief in

✤ **Tyche** This statue depicts Tyche as the city-goddess of Antioch, a new Hellenistic foundation of the Seleucid king Antiochus. Some Hellenistic Greeks worshiped Tyche in the hope that she would be kind to them. Philosophers tried to free people from her whimsies. Antiochus tried to win her favor by honoring her. *(Source: Photo Vatican Museums)*

Tyche. To protect against the worst that Tyche could do, many Greeks looked to philosophy.

Philosophers themselves became much more numerous, and several new schools of philosophical thought emerged. The Cynics preached the joy of a simple life. The Epicureans taught that pleasure is the chief good. The Stoics emphasized the importance of deeds well done. There was a good deal of rivalry as philosophers tried to demonstrate the superiority of their views, but in spite of their differences the major branches of philosophy agreed on the necessity of making people self-sufficient. They all recognized the need to equip men and women to deal successfully with Tyche. The major schools of Hellenistic philosophy all taught that people could be truly happy only when they had turned their backs on the world and focused full attention on one enduring thing. They differed chiefly on what that enduring thing was.

Cynics

Undoubtedly the most unusual of the new philosophers were the Cynics, who urged a return to nature. They advised men and women to discard traditional customs and conventions (which were in decline anyway) and live simply. The Cynics believed that by rejecting material things people would become free and that nature would provide all necessities.

The founder of the Cynics was Antisthenes (b. ca 440 B.C.), but it was Diogenes of Sinope (ca 412–323 B.C.), one of the most colorful men of the period, who spread the philosophy. Diogenes came to Athens to study philosophy and soon evolved his own ideas on the ideal life. He hit on the solution that happiness was possible only by living according to nature and forgoing luxuries. He attacked social conventions because he considered them contrary to nature. Throughout Greece he gained fame for the rigorous way in which he put his beliefs into practice.

Diogenes' disdain for luxury and social pretense became legendary. Once, when he was living at Corinth, he was supposedly visited by Alexander the Great: "While Diogenes was sunning himself . . . Alexander stood over him and said: 'Ask me whatever gift you like.' In answer Diogenes said to him: 'Get out of my sunlight.'"[6] The story underlines the essence of Diogenes' teachings: even a great, powerful, and wealthy conqueror such as Alexander could give people nothing of any real value. Nature had already provided them with everything essential.

Diogenes did not establish a philosophical school in the manner of Plato and Aristotle. Instead, he and his followers took their teaching to the streets and marketplaces. More than any other philosophical group, they tried to reach the common people. As part of their return to nature, they often did without warm clothing, sufficient food, or adequate housing, which they considered un-

necessary. The Cynics also tried to break down political barriers by declaring that people owed no allegiance to any city or monarchy. They said, all people are cosmopolitan—that is, citizens of the world. The Cynics reached across political boundaries to create a community of people, all sharing their humanity and living as close to nature as humanly possible. The Cynics set a striking example of how people could turn away from materialism. Although comparatively few men and women could follow such rigorous precepts, the Cynics influenced all the other major schools of philosophy.

Epicureans

Epicurus (340–270 B.C.), who founded his own school of philosophy at Athens, based his view of life on scientific theories. Accepting Democritus's theory that the universe is composed of indestructible particles, Epicurus put forward a naturalistic theory of the universe. Although he did not deny the existence of the gods, he taught that they had no effect on human life. The essence of Epicurus's belief was that the principal good of human life is pleasure, which he defined as the absence of pain. He was not advocating drunken revels or sexual dissipation, which he thought actually caused pain. Instead, Epicurus concluded that any violent emotion is undesirable. Drawing on the teachings of the Cynics, he advocated mild self-discipline. Even poverty he considered good, as long as people had enough food, clothing, and shelter. Epicurus also taught that individuals can most easily attain peace and serenity by ignoring the outside world and looking into their personal feelings and reactions. Thus Epicureanism led to quietism.

Epicureanism taught its followers to ignore politics and issues, for politics led to tumult, which would disturb the soul. Although the Epicureans thought that the state originated through a social contract among individuals, they did not care about the political structure of the state. They were content to live in a democracy, oligarchy, monarchy, or any other form of government, and they never speculated about the ideal state. Their ideals stood outside all political forms.

Stoics

Opposed to the passivity of the Epicureans, Zeno (335–262 B.C.), a philosopher from Citium in Cyprus, advanced a different concept of human beings and the universe. When Zeno first came to Athens, he listened avidly to the Cynics. Concluding, however, that the Cynics were extreme, he stayed in Athens to form his own school, the Stoa, named after the building where he preferred to teach.

Stoicism became the most popular Hellenistic philosophy and the one that later captured the mind of Rome. Zeno and his followers considered nature an expression of divine will; in their view, people could be happy only when living in accordance with nature. They stressed the unity of man and the universe, stating that all men were brothers and obliged to help one another. Stoicism's science was derived from Heraclitus, but its broad and warm humanity was the work of Zeno and his followers.

Unlike the Epicureans, the Stoics taught that people should participate in politics and worldly affairs. Yet this idea never led to the belief that individuals should try to change the order of things. Time and again, the Stoics used the image of an actor in a play: the Stoic plays an assigned part but never tries to change the play. To the Stoics the important question was not whether they achieved anything, but whether they lived virtuous lives. In that way they could triumph over Tyche, for Tyche could destroy achievements but not the nobility of their lives.

Though the Stoics evolved the concept of a world order, they thought of it strictly in terms of the individual. Like the Epicureans, they were indifferent to specific political forms. They believed that people should do their duty to the state in which they found themselves. The universal state they preached about was ethical, not political. The Stoics' most significant practical achievement was the creation of the concept of natural law. The Stoics concluded that as all men were brothers, partook of divine reason, and were in harmony with the universe, one law—a part of the natural order of life—governed them all.

The Stoic concept of a universal state governed by natural law is one of the finest heirlooms the Hellenistic world passed on to Rome. The Stoic concept of natural law, of one law for all people, became a valuable tool when the Romans began to deal with many different peoples with different laws. The ideal of the universal state gave the Romans a rationale for extending their empire to the farthest reaches of the world. The duty of individuals to their fellows served the citizens of the Roman

Empire as the philosophical justification for doing their duty. In this respect, too, the real fruit of Hellenism was to ripen only under the cultivation of Rome.

✛ HELLENISTIC SCIENCE

The area in which Hellenistic culture achieved its greatest triumphs was science. Here, too, the ancient Near East made contributions to Greek thought. The patient observations of the Babylonians, who for generations had scanned the skies, had provided the raw materials for Thales' speculations, which were the foundation of Hellenistic astronomy. The most notable of the Hellenistic

❖ **Tower of the Four Winds** This remarkable building, which still stands in Athens, was built by an astronomer to serve as a sundial, water-clock, and weather vane. It is one of the few examples of the application of Hellenistic science to daily life. (*Source: Ekdotike Athenon*)

astronomers was Aristarchus of Samos (ca 310–230 B.C.), who was educated in Aristotle's school. Aristarchus concluded that the sun is far larger than the earth and that the stars are enormously distant from the earth. He argued against Aristotle's view that the earth is the center of the universe. Instead, Aristarchus propounded the *heliocentric theory*—that the earth and planets revolve around the sun. His work is all the more impressive because he lacked even a rudimentary telescope. Aristarchus had only the human eye and brain, but they were more than enough.

Unfortunately Aristarchus's theories did not persuade the ancient world. In the second century A.D. Claudius Ptolemy, a mathematician and astronomer in Alexandria, accepted Aristotle's theory of the earth as the center of the universe, and their view prevailed for 1,400 years. Aristarchus's heliocentric theory lay dormant until resurrected in the sixteenth century by the brilliant Polish astronomer Nicolaus Copernicus.

In geometry Hellenistic thinkers discovered little that was new, but Euclid (ca 300 B.C.), a mathematician who lived in Alexandria, compiled a valuable textbook of existing knowledge. His book *The Elements of Geometry* has exerted immense influence on Western civilization, for it rapidly became the standard introduction to geometry. Generations of students, from the Hellenistic period to the present, have learned the essentials of geometry from it.

The greatest thinker of the Hellenistic period was Archimedes (ca 287–212 B.C.), who was a clever inventor as well. He lived in Syracuse in Sicily and watched Rome emerge as a power in the Mediterranean. When the Romans laid siege to Syracuse in the Second Punic War, Archimedes invented a number of machines to thwart the armed forces. His catapults threw rocks large enough to sink ships and disrupt battle lines. His grappling devices lifted ships out of the water. Archimedes built such machines out of necessity, but they were of little real interest to him. In a more peaceful vein, he invented the Archimedean screw and the compound pulley. Plutarch described Archimedes' dramatic demonstration of how easily his pulley could move huge weights with little effort:

A three-masted merchant ship of the royal fleet had been hauled on land by hard work and many hands.

Archimedes put aboard her many men and the usual freight. He sat far away from her; without haste, but gently working a compound pulley with his hand, he drew her towards him smoothly and without faltering, just as though she were running on the surface of the sea.[7]

Archimedes was far more interested in pure mathematics than in practical inventions. His mathematical research, covering many fields, was his greatest contribution to Western thought. In his book *On Plane Equilibriums* Archimedes dealt for the first time with the basic principles of mechanics, including the principle of the lever. He once said that if he were given a lever and a suitable place to stand, he could move the world. With his treatise *On Floating Bodies* Archimedes founded the science of hydrostatics. He concluded that whenever a solid floats in a liquid, the weight of the solid is equal to the weight of liquid displaced. The way he made his discovery has become famous:

When he was devoting his attention to this problem, he happened to go to a public bath. When he climbed down into the bathtub there, he noticed that water in the tub equal to the bulk of his body flowed out. Thus, when he observed this method of solving the problem, he did not wait. Instead, moved with joy, he sprang out of the tub, and rushing home naked he kept indicating in a loud voice that he had indeed discovered what he was seeking. For while running he was shouting repeatedly in Greek, "eureka, eureka" ("I have found it, I have found it.").[8]

Archimedes was willing to share his work with others, among them Eratosthenes (285–ca 204 B.C.), a man of almost universal interests. From his native Cyrene in North Africa, Eratosthenes traveled to Athens, where he studied philosophy and mathematics. He refused to join any of the philosophical schools, for he was interested in too many things to follow any particular dogma. Around 245 B.C. King Ptolemy invited Eratosthenes to Alexandria. The Ptolemies had done much to make Alexandria an intellectual, cultural, and scientific center. Eratosthenes came to Alexandria to become librarian of the royal library, a position of great prestige. While there, he continued his mathematical work and by letter struck up his friendship with Archimedes.

Unlike his friend Archimedes, Eratosthenes did not devote his life entirely to mathematics, although he never lost interest in it. He used mathematics to further the geographical studies for which he is most famous. He calculated the circumference of the earth geometrically, estimating it as about 24,675 miles. He was not wrong by much: the earth is actually 24,860 miles in circumference. Eratosthenes also concluded that the earth is a spherical globe, that the land mass is roughly four-sided, and that the land is surrounded by ocean. He discussed the shapes and sizes of land and ocean and the irregularities of the earth's surface. He drew a map of the earth and used his own system of explaining the divisions of the earth's land mass.

Using geographical information gained by Alexander the Great's scientists, Eratosthenes tried to fit the East into Greek geographical knowledge. Although for some reason he ignored the western Mediterranean and Europe, he declared that a ship could sail from Spain either around Africa to India or directly westward to India. Not until the great days of Western exploration did sailors such as Vasco da Gama and Magellan actually prove Eratosthenes' theories. Like Eratosthenes, other Greek geographers also turned their attention southward to Africa. During this period the people of the Mediterranean learned of the climate and customs of Ethiopia and gleaned some scant information about equatorial Africa.

In his life and work Eratosthenes exemplifies the range and vitality of Hellenistic science. His varied interests included the cultural and humanistic as well as the purely scientific. Although his chief interest was in the realm of speculative thought, he did not ignore the practical. He was quite willing to deal with old problems and to break new ground.

In the Hellenistic period the scientific study of botany had its origin. Aristotle's pupil Theophrastus (ca 372–288 B.C.), who became head of the Lyceum, the school established by Aristotle, studied the botanical information made available by Alexander's penetration of the East. Aristotle had devoted a good deal of his attention to zoology, and Theophrastus extended his work to plants. He wrote two books on the subject, *History of Plants* and *Causes of Plants*. He carefully observed phenomena and based his conclusions on what he had actually seen. Theophrastus classified plants and

The Celestial Globe In Greek mythology the god Atlas held the world on his strong shoulders, thereby preventing it from falling. Hellenistic scientists formed a very accurate idea of the shape and dimension of the earth. Here Atlas holds the globe, which rests on its axis and displays the skies, with figures representing constellations as well as the equator, tropics, and polar circles *(Source: National Museum, Naples/Alinari/Art Resource)*

vented such machines as the air gun, the water organ, and even the steam engine, they never used their discoveries as labor-saving devices. No one has satisfactorily explained why these scientists were so impractical, but one answer is quite possible: they and the rest of society saw no real need for machines. Slave labor was especially abundant, a fact that made the use of labor-saving machinery superfluous. Science was applied only to war. Even though Hellenistic science did not lead the ancient world to an industrial revolution, later Hellenistic thinkers preserved the knowledge of machines and the principles behind them. In so doing, they saved the discoveries of Hellenistic science for the modern age.

 ## HELLENISTIC MEDICINE

The study of medicine flourished during the Hellenistic period, and Hellenistic physicians carried the work of Hippocrates into new areas. Herophilus, who lived in the first half of the third century B.C., worked at Alexandria and studied the writings of Hippocrates. He accepted Hippocrates' theory of the four humors and approached the study of medicine in a systematic, scientific fashion. He dissected dead bodies and measured what he observed. He discovered the nervous system and concluded that two types of nerves, motor and sensory, exist. Herophilus also studied the brain, which he considered the center of intelligence, and discerned the cerebrum and cerebellum. His other work dealt with the liver, lungs, and uterus. His younger contemporary, Erasistratus, also conducted research on the brain and nervous system and improved on Herophilus's work. He, too, followed in the tradition of Hippocrates and preferred to let the body heal itself by means of diet and air.

Both Herophilus and Erasistratus were members of the Dogmatic school of medicine at Alexandria. In this school speculation played an important part in research. So, too, did the study of anatomy. To learn more about human anatomy, Herophilus and Erasistratus dissected corpses and even vivisected criminals whom King Ptolemy contributed for the purpose. The practice of vivisection seems to have been short-lived, although dissection continued. Better knowledge of anatomy led to improvements

An Unsuccessful Delivery This funeral stele depicts a mother who has perhaps lost her own life as well as her baby's. Maternal and infant mortality were quite common in antiquity. A similar stele elsewhere bears the heartbreaking words attributed to the mother by her grieving family: "All my labor could not bring the child forth; he lies in my womb, among the dead." *(Source: National Museum, Athens)*

accurately described their parts. He detected the process of germination and realized the importance of climate and soil to plants. Some of Theophrastus's work found its way into agricultural handbooks, but for the most part Hellenistic science did not carry the study of botany further.

Despite its undeniable brilliance, Hellenistic science suffered from a remarkable weakness almost impossible for practical-minded Americans to understand. Although scientists of this period in-

in surgery. These advances enabled the Dogmatists to invent new surgical instruments and techniques.

In about 280 B.C. Philinus and Serapion, pupils of Herophilus, led a reaction against the Dogmatists. Believing that the Dogmatists had become too speculative, they founded the Empiric school of medicine at Alexandria. Claiming that the Dogmatists' emphasis on anatomy and physiology was misplaced, they concentrated instead on the observation and cure of illnesses. They also laid heavier stress on the use of drugs and medicine to treat illnesses. Heraclides of Tarentum (perhaps first century B.C.) carried on the Empirical tradition and dedicated himself to observation and use of medicines. He discovered the benefits of opium and worked with other drugs that relieved pain. He also steadfastly rejected the relevance of magic to drugs and medicines.

Hellenistic medicine had its dark side, for many physicians were moneygrubbers, fools, and quacks. One of the angriest complaints comes from the days of the Roman Empire:

Of all men only a physician can kill a man with total impunity. Oh no, on the contrary, censure goes to him who dies and he is guilty of excess, and furthermore he is blamed. . . . Let me not accuse their [physicians'] avarice, their greedy deals with those whose fate hangs in the balance, their setting a price on pain, and their demands for down payment in case of death, and their secret doctrines.[9]

Abuses such as these existed already in the Hellenistic period. As is true today, many Hellenistic physicians did not take the Hippocratic oath very seriously.

Besides incompetent and greedy physicians, the Hellenistic world was plagued by people who claimed to cure illnesses through incantations and magic. Their potions included such concoctions as blood from the ear of an ass mixed with water to cure fever, or the liver of a cat killed when the moon was waning and preserved in salt. Broken bones could be cured by applying the ashes of a pig's jawbone to the break. The dung of a goat mixed with old wine was good for healing broken ribs. One charlatan claimed that he could cure epilepsy by making the patient drink spring water, drawn at night, from the skull of a man who had been killed but not cremated. These quacks even claimed that they could cure mental illness. The treatment for a person suffering from melancholy was calf dung boiled in wine. No doubt the patient became too sick to be depressed.

Quacks who prescribed such treatments were very popular but did untold harm to the sick and injured. They and greedy physicians also damaged the reputation of dedicated doctors who honestly and intelligently tried to heal and alleviate pain. The medical abuses that arose in the Hellenistic period were so flagrant that the Romans, who later entered the Hellenistic world, developed an intense dislike and distrust of physicians. The Romans considered the study of Hellenistic medicine beneath the dignity of a Roman; and even as late as the time of the Roman Empire, few Romans undertook the study of Greek medicine. Nonetheless, the work of men like Herophilus and Serapion made valuable contributions to the knowledge of medicine, and the fruits of their work were preserved and handed on to the West.

SUMMARY

It can safely be said that Philip and Alexander broadened Greek and Macedonian horizons, but not in ways that they had intended. Although Alexander established Macedonian and Greek colonies across western and central Asia for military reasons, they resulted in the spread of Hellenism as a side effect. In the Aegean and Near East the fusion of Greek and Eastern cultures laid the social, intellectual, and cultural foundations on which the Romans would later build. In the heart of the old Persian Empire, Hellenism was only another new influence that was absorbed by older ways of thought and life. Yet overall, in the exchange of ideas and the opportunity for different cultures to learn about one another, a new cosmopolitan society evolved. That society in turn made possible such diverse advances as a wider extent of trade and agriculture, the creation of religious and philosophical ideas that paved the way for Christianity, and greater freedom for women. People of the Hellenistic period also made remarkable advances in science and medicine. They not only built on the achievements of their predecessors, but they also produced one of the most creative intellectual eras of classical antiquity.

NOTES

1. H. Bengtson, *Philipp und Alexander der Grosse* (Munich: Callwey, 1985), p. 7. John Buckler is the translator of all uncited quotations from a foreign language in Chapters 1–6.
2. Plutarch, *Moralia* 328E.
3. Quoted in W. W. Tarn and G. T. Griffith, *Hellenistic Civilizations,* 3d ed. (Cleveland and New York: Meridian Books, 1961), p. 199.
4. *Periplous of the Erythraian Sea* 57.
5. Diodorus 3.12.2–3.
6. Diogenes, *Laertius* 6.38.
7. Ibid., 14.13.
8. Vitruvius, *On Architecture* 9 Preface, 10.
9. Pliny the Elder, *Natural History* 29.8.18, 21.

SUGGESTED READING

General treatments of Hellenistic political, social, and economic history can be found in F. W. Walbank et al., *The Cambridge Ancient History,* 2d ed., vol. 7, pt. 1 (1984). Shorter is F. W. Walbank, *The Hellenistic World* (1981), a fresh appraisal by one of the foremost scholars in the field. The undisputed classic in this area is M. Rostovtzeff, *The Social and Economic History of the Hellenistic World,* 3 vols. (1941). R. M. Errington, *A History of Macedonia,* (English trans., 1990), places Macedonia clearly within a much broader Hellenistic context. Good selections of primary sources in accurate and readable translation can be found in M. M. Austin, *The Hellenistic World from Alexander to the Roman Conquest* (1981), and S. M. Burstein, *The Hellenistic Age from the Battle of Ipsos to the Death of Kleopatra III* (1985).

Each year brings a new crop of biographies of Alexander the Great. Still the best, however, is J. R. Hamilton, *Alexander the Great* (1973). Old but still useful is U. Wilcken, *Alexander the Great* (English trans., 1967), which has had a considerable impact on scholars and students alike. Although many historians have idealized Alexander the Great, recent scholarship has provided a more realistic and unflattering view of him. The foremost expert on Alexander is E. Badian, who has reinterpreted Alexander's career in a variety of journal articles: *Historia* 7 (1958): 425–444; *Classical Quarterly* 52 (1958): 144–157; *Journal of Hellenic Studies* 81 (1961): 16–43; and *Greece and Rome* 12 (1965): 166–182. Badian's analysis of Alexander also appears in *The Cambridge History of Iran,* vol. 2 (1985), chap. 8. Recent political studies of the Hellenistic period include A. B. Bosworth, *Conquest and*

Empire (1988), which sets Alexander's career in a broad context, and F. L. Holt, *Alexander the Great and Bactria* (1988), which discusses the formation of a Greco-Macedonian frontier in central Asia.

A. K. Bowman, *Egypt After the Pharaohs* (1986), is a readable account of the impact of the Greeks and Macedonians on Egyptian society. A major scholar in the field, in his *Greeks in Ptolemaic Egypt* (1986); and a brief, new study comes from the pen of another major scholar, A. E. Samuel, *The Shifting Sands of History: Interpretations of Ptolemaic Egypt* (1989), which deals with history and historiography. W. Heckel, *The Marshals of Alexander's Empire* (1992), treats the careers of the more than 130 men who were not actually Alexander's chief officers but nonetheless substantially shaped Hellenistic political history. S. Sherwin-White and A. Kuhrt, *From Samarkand to Sardis* (1992), offer a new study of the Seleucid Empire that puts it in an Asian rather than Greek perspective. J. D. Grainger, *Seleukos Nikator* (1990), examines how the Hellenistic king created his empire. R. A. Billows, *Antigone the One-Eyed and the Creation of the Hellenistic State* (1990), examines the career of the one man who most nearly reunited Alexander's empire. E. V. Hansen, *The Attalids of Pergamon,* 2d ed. (1971), though dated, is still the best treatment of that kingdom. B. Bar-Kochva, *Judas Maccabaeus* (1988), treats the Jewish struggle against the Seleucids and Hellenistic influences. A good portrait of one of the busiest ports in the Hellenistic world can be found in R. Garland, *Piraeus* (1987).

Much new work has focused on the spread of Hellenism throughout the Near East. Very extensive is A. Kuhrt and S. Sherwin-White, eds., *Hellenism in the East* (1988), which touches on a broad range of topics, including biblical studies, Christianity, and Islam. A. E. Samuel, *The Promise of the West* (1988), studies the connections among Greek, Roman, and Jewish culture and thought and their significance for Western history. P. McKechnie, *Outsiders in the Greek Cities of the Fourth Century* (1989), provides an interesting study of the social dislocation of the Greeks in the time of Philip II and Alexander the Great.

No specific treatment of women in the Hellenistic world yet exists, but two recent studies shed light on certain aspects of the topic. N. L. Goodrich, *Priestesses* (1989), examines the importance of priestesses in cults from the Near East to Ireland. S. B. Pomeroy, *Women in Hellenistic Egypt* (1984), studies women in the kingdom from which the most ancient evidence has survived.

Two general studies of religion in the Hellenistic world are F. Grant, *Hellenistic Religion: The Age of Syncretism* (1953), and H. J. Rose, *Religion in Greece and Rome* (1959). L. H. Feldman, *Jew and Gentile in the Ancient World* (1993), argues that the pagan response to Judaism within the Graeco-Roman period was not as negative as often thought. R. van den Broek et al., eds., *Knowledge of God in the Graeco-Roman World* (1988), is a difficult but rewarding collection of essays that points out how similarly pagans, Hellenistic Jews, and Christians thought about human attempts to know God. R. E. Witt, *Isis in the Graeco-Roman World* (1971), an illustrated volume, studies the origins and growth of the Isis cult; and more specifically, S. K. Heyob, *The Cult of Isis Among Women in the Graeco-Roman World* (1975), explores its popularity among women. The cult of Isis's consort Osiris is the subject of J. G. Griffiths, *The Origins of Osiris and His Cult* (1980); and for the mystery cults in general, see W. Burkert, *Ancient Mystery Cults* (1987), written by one of the finest scholars in the field.

Hellenistic philosophy and science have attracted the attention of a number of scholars, and the various philosophical schools are especially well covered. A general treatment can be recommended because it deals with the broader question of the role of the intellectual in the Classical and Hellenistic worlds: F. L. Vatai, *Intellectuals in Politics in the Greek World from Early Times to the Hellenistic Age* (1984). Broader is S. Blundell's *The Origin of Civilization in Greek and Roman Thought* (1986), a survey of classical political and social theories through a period of ten centuries, from Aristotle to the Stoics and their Roman successors. A convenient survey of Hellenistic philosophy is A. A. Long, *Hellenistic Philosophy* (1974). F. Sayre, *The Greek Cynics* (1948), focuses on Diogenes' thought and manners. H. Jones, *The Epicurean Tradition* (1989), covers Epicurean philosophy from its inception to late Roman times. Three treatments of Stoicism are J. Rist, *Stoic Philosophy* (1969); F. H. Sandbach, *The Stoics* (1975); and M. L. Colish, *The Stoic Tradition from Antiquity to the Early Middle Ages,* 2 vols. (1985), which devotes a great deal of attention to the impact of Stoicism on Christianity. A good survey of Hellenistic science is G. E. R. Lloyd, *Greek Science After Aristotle* (1963), and specific studies of major figures can be found in T. L. Heath's solid work, *Aristarchos of Samos* (1920), still unsurpassed, and E. J. Dijksterhuis, *Archimedes,* rev. ed. (1987).

A Queen's Sacrifice for Her Society

During the Hellenistic period, women in the eastern Mediterranean became prominent in society and more obvious in their public roles. In this respect, Hellenistic queens became important in ways they had not since the epic period of Greek history. They became role models for ordinary women. Nevertheless, even Hellenistic queens received criticism from men who felt that they had no business in public life, and they were often portrayed as vicious and vindictive. No one could ever say that of Queen Mother Cratesicleia of Sparta.

As described by the great Greek biographer Plutarch, the political situation of Sparta at the time of this episode (ca 226 B.C.) was one of extreme danger. Shorn of its previous might first by the Thebans and later by the Macedonians, Sparta was simply too weak to compete successfully in the power struggles of the period. As a result, Sparta had to choose sides, and the cost of that choice could be high. When Cleomenes, king of Sparta, asked the help of the Egyptian king Ptolemy against the Macedonians, the cost was dear:

Now, Ptolemy the king of Egypt promised him [Cleomenes] aid and assistance, but demanded his mother and his children as hostages. For a long time, therefore, he was ashamed to tell his mother, and though he often went to her and was at the very point of letting her know, he held his peace, so that she on her part became suspicious and enquired of his friends whether there was not something that he wished to tell her but hesitated to do so. Finally, when Cleomenes plucked up courage to speak of the matter, his mother burst into a hearty laugh and said: "Was this the thing that you were often of a mind to tell me but lost your courage? Make haste, put me on board a ship, and send this frail body wheresoever you think it will be of most use to Sparta, before old age destroys it sitting idly here."

Accordingly, when all things were ready, they came to Taenarus [a Spartan port] by land, while the army escorted them with the might of heavy-armed troops. And as Cratesicleia was about to embark, she drew Cleomenes aside by himself into the temple of Poseidon, and after embracing and kissing him in his anguish and deep trouble, said: "Come, O king of the Spartans, when we go forth let no one see us weeping or doing anything unworthy of Sparta. For this lies in our power, and this alone; but as for the issues of fortune, we shall have what the god may grant." After saying this, she composed her countenance and proceeded to the ship with her little grandson, and bade the captain put to sea with all speed.

When she arrived in Egypt, she learned that Sparta's enemies intended to use her and her grandson to pressure Cleomenes into surrender. Hostage though she was, she sent her son a message.

She sent word to him that he must do what was fitting and advantageous for Sparta, and not, because of one old woman and a little boy, be ever in fear of Ptolemy.

When Cleomenes was killed in a major battle, the alliance between Sparta and Ptolemy dissolved.

Cleomenes' death sealed Cratesicleia's fate. Ptolemy ordered her execution. She was not at all dismayed, and refused to grieve for herself. The words of Plutarch are a fitting tribute to her and other Spartan women.

So, then, Sparta, bringing her women's tragedy into emulous competition with that of her men, showed the world that in the last extremity Virtue cannot be outraged by Fortune.

Questions for Analysis

1. What does this episode tell us about the Spartan concept of duty and how it applies to men and women?

2. What does this episode convey about the importance of Cratesicleia, who held no actual political power?

3. What can be said of Plutarch's literary and historical portrayal of this incident? In the words he gave Cratesicleia, Sparta would not suffer from the death of one old woman. What sort of model was she setting for others?

Source: Slightly adapted and abbreviated from B. Perrin, trans., *Plutarch's Lives,* vol. 10 (Cambridge, Mass: Harvard University Press, 1921), pp. 99–141.

Coin depicting Queen Arsinoe II, wife of Ptolemy II, 265–246 B.C. *(Source: Ancient Art & Architecture Collection)*

5

The Rise of Rome

✥ "Who is so thoughtless and lazy that he does not want to know in what way and with what kind of government the Romans in less than 53 years conquered nearly the entire inhabited world and brought it under their rule—an achievement previously unheard of ?"[1] This question was first asked by Polybius, a Greek historian who lived in the second century B.C. With keen awareness Polybius realized that the Romans were achieving something unique in world history.

What was that achievement? Was it simply the creation of a huge empire? Hardly. The Persians had done the same thing. For that matter, Alexander the Great had conquered vast territories in a shorter time. Was it the creation of a superior culture? Even the Romans admitted that in matters of art, literature, philosophy, and culture they learned from the Greeks. Rome's achievement lay in the ability of the Romans not only to conquer peoples but to incorporate them into the Roman system. Rome succeeded where the Greek polis had failed. Unlike the Greeks, who refused to share citizenship, the Romans extended their citizenship first to the Italians and later to the peoples of the provinces. With that citizenship went Roman government and law. Rome created a world state that embraced the entire Mediterranean area and extended northward.

Nor was Rome's achievement limited to the ancient world. Rome's law, language, and administrative practices were a precious heritage to medieval and modern Europe. London, Paris, Vienna, and many other modern European cities began as Roman colonies or military camps. When the Founding Fathers created the American republic, they looked to Rome as a model. On the darker side, Napoleon and Mussolini paid their own tribute to Rome by aping its forms. Whether Founding Father or modern autocrat, all were acknowledging admiration for the Roman achievement.

Roman history is usually divided into two periods: the republic, the age

✥ ✥ ✥ ✥ ✥ ✥ ✥ ✥ ✥

Etruscan soldiers carrying a slain comrade, from the lid of a fourth-century B.C. bronze container. *(Source: Scala/Art Resource, NY)*

empire, the period when the republican constitution gave way to constitutional monarchy.

- How did Rome rise to greatness?
- What effects did the conquest of the Mediterranean have on the Romans themselves?
- Finally, why did the republic collapse?

These are the questions we will attempt to answer in this chapter.

✠ THE LAND AND THE SEA

To the west of Greece the boot-shaped peninsula of Italy, with Sicily at its toe, occupies the center of the Mediterranean basin. As Map 5.1 shows, Italy and Sicily thrust southward toward Africa: the distance between southwestern Sicily and the northern African coast is at one point only about a hundred miles. Italy and Sicily literally divide the Mediterranean into two basins and form the focal point between the halves.

Like Greece and other Mediterranean lands, Italy enjoys a genial, almost subtropical climate. The winters are rainy, but the summer months are dry. Because of the climate the rivers of Italy usually carry little water during the summer, and some go entirely dry. The low water level of the Arno, one of the principal rivers of Italy, once led Mark Twain to describe it as "a great historical creek with four feet in the channel and some scows floating around. It would be a very plausible river if they would pump some water into it."[2] The Arno at least is navigable. Most of Italy's other rivers are not. Clearly these small rivers were unsuitable for regular, large-scale shipping. Italian rivers, unlike Twain's beloved Mississippi, never became major thoroughfares for commerce and communications.

Geography encouraged Italy to look to the Mediterranean. In the north, Italy is protected by the Apennine Mountains, which break off from the Alps and form a natural barrier. The Apennines hindered but did not prevent peoples from penetrating Italy from the north. Throughout history, in modern times as well as ancient, various invaders have entered Italy by this route. North of the Apennines lies the Po valley, an important part of modern Italy. In antiquity this valley did not become Roman territory until late in the history of the republic. From the north the Apennines run southward the entire length of the Italian boot; they virtually cut off access to the Adriatic Sea, a feature that further induced Italy to look west to Spain and Carthage rather than east to Greece.

Even though most of the land is mountainous, the hill country is not as inhospitable as are the Greek highlands. In antiquity the general fertility of the soil provided the basis for a large population. Nor did the mountains of Italy so carve up the land as to prevent the development of political unity. Geography proved kinder to Italy than to Greece.

In their southward course the Apennines leave two broad and fertile plains, those of Latium and Campania. These plains attracted settlers and invaders from the time when peoples began to move into Italy. Among these peoples were the Romans, who established their city on the Tiber River in Latium.

This site enjoyed several advantages. The Tiber provided Rome with a constant source of water. Located at an easy crossing point on the Tiber, Rome stood astride the main avenue of communications between northern and southern Italy. The famous seven hills of Rome were defensible and safe from the floods of the Tiber. Rome was in an excellent position to develop the resources of Latium and maintain contact with the rest of Italy.

✠ THE ETRUSCANS AND ROME (750–509 B.C.)

In recent years archaeologists have found traces of numerous early peoples in Italy. The origins of these cultures and their precise relations with one another are not yet well understood. In fact, no clear account of the prehistory of Italy is yet possible. Of the period before the appearance of the Etruscans (1200–750 B.C.), one fundamental fact is indisputable: peoples speaking Indo-European languages were moving into Italy from the north, probably in small groups. They were part of the

✠ **MAP 5.1 Italy and the City of Rome** The geographical configuration of the Italian peninsula shows how Rome stood astride north-south communications and how the state that united Italy stood poised to move into Sicily and northern Africa.

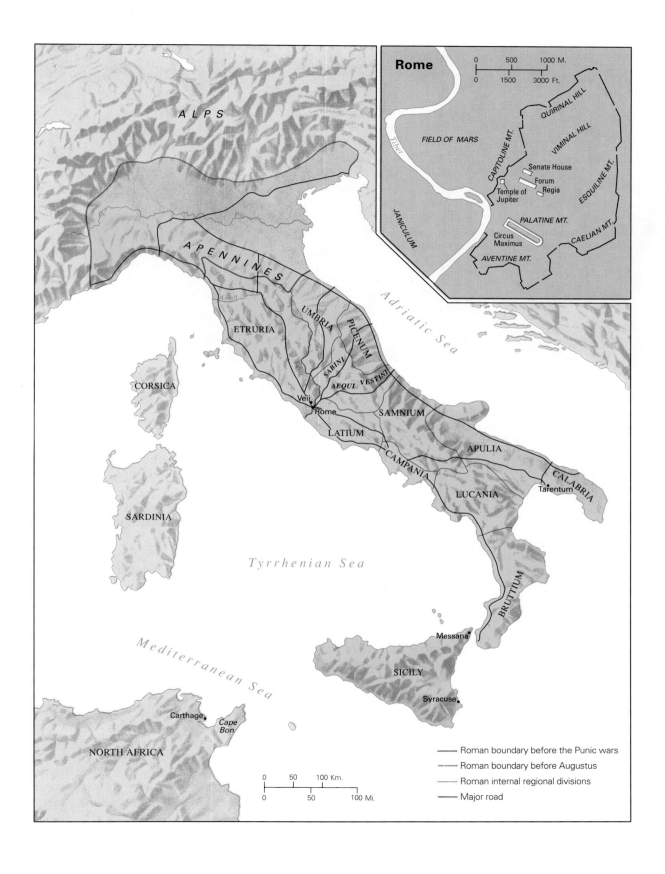

Rome

0	500	1000 M.
0	1500	3000 Ft.

Tiber

FIELD OF MARS

JANICULUM

QUIRINAL HILL

VIMINAL HILL

CAPITOLINE MT.

Senate House

Forum

Temple of Jupiter

Regia

ESQUILINE MT.

PALATINE MT.

CAELIAN MT.

Circus Maximus

AVENTINE MT.

ALPS

Po

A P E N N I N E S

Arno

UMBRIA

ETRURIA

PICENUM

Adriatic Sea

CORSICA

SABINI

AEQUI VESTINI

Veii

Rome

SAMNIUM

LATIUM

APULIA

CAMPANIA

CALABRIA

Tarentum

LUCANIA

SARDINIA

Tyrrhenian Sea

BRUTTIUM

Messana

Mediterranean Sea

SICILY

Syracuse

Carthage

Cape Bon

NORTH AFRICA

0	50	100 Km.
0	50	100 Mi.

— Roman boundary before the Punic wars
— Roman boundary before Augustus
— Roman internal regional divisions
— Major road

❖ **Sarcophagus of Lartie Seianti** The woman portrayed on this lavish sarcophagus
is the noble Etruscan Lartie Seianti. Although the sarcophagus is her place of burial, she is portrayed as in life, comfortable and at rest. The influence of Greek art
on Etruscan is apparent on almost every feature of the sarcophagus. *(Source: Archaeological Museum, Florence/Nimatallah/Art Resource, NY)*

awesome but imperfectly understood movement of
peoples that spread the Indo-European family of
languages from Spain to India.

Only with the coming of the Greeks does Italy
enter the light of history. A great wave of Greek
immigration swept into southern Italy and Sicily
during the eighth century B.C., as described on
pages 71–72. The Greeks brought urban life to
these regions, spreading cultural influence far beyond their city-states.

In the north the Greeks encountered the Etruscans, one of the truly mysterious peoples of antiquity. Who the Etruscans were and where they came
from are unknown. Nonetheless, this fascinating
people was to leave an indelible mark on the Romans. Skillful metalworkers, the Etruscans amassed
extensive wealth by trading their manufactured
goods in Italy and beyond. The strength of their
political and military institutions enabled them to
form a loosely organized league of cities whose
dominion extended as far north as the Po valley
and as far south as Latium and Campania (see Map
5.1). In Latium they founded cities and took over

control of Rome. Like the Greeks, the Etruscans
promoted urban life, and one of the places that
benefited from Etruscan influence was Rome.

The Etruscans found the Romans settled on
three of Rome's seven hills. The site of the future
Forum Romanum, the famous public square and
center of political life, was originally the cemetery
of the small community. According to Roman legend, Romulus and Remus had founded Rome in
753 B.C. Romulus built his settlement on the Palatine Hill, while Remus chose the Aventine (see
inset, Map 5.1). Jealous of his brother's work,
Remus ridiculed it by jumping over Romulus's
unfinished wall. In a rage, Romulus killed his
brother and vowed, "So will die whoever else shall
leap over my walls." In this instance, legend preserves some facts. Archaeological investigation has
confirmed that the earliest settlement at Rome was
situated on the Palatine Hill and that it dates to
the first half of the eighth century B.C. The legend
also shows traces of Etruscan influence on Roman
customs. The inviolability of Romulus's walls re-
calls the Etruscan concept of the *pomerium,* a sa-

cred boundary intended to keep out anything evil or unclean.

During the years 753 to 509 B.C., the Romans embraced many Etruscan customs. They adopted the Etruscan alphabet, which the Etruscans themselves had adopted from the Greeks. The Romans later handed on this alphabet to medieval Europe and thence to the modern Western world. The Romans also adopted symbols of political authority from the Etruscans. The symbol of the Etruscan king's right to execute or scourge his subjects was a bundle of rods and an ax, called in Latin the *fasces,* which the king's retainer carried before him on official occasions. When the Romans expelled the Etruscan kings, they created special attendants called "lictors" to carry the fasces before their new magistrates, the consuls. Even the *toga,* the white woolen robe worn by citizens, came from the Etruscans. In engineering and architecture the Romans adopted from the Etruscans the vault and the arch. Above all, it was thanks to the Etruscans that the Romans truly became urban dwellers.

Etruscan power and influence at Rome were so strong that Roman traditions preserved the memory of Etruscan kings who ruled the city. Under the Etruscans, Rome enjoyed contacts with the larger Mediterranean world, and the city began to grow. In the years 575 to 550 B.C., temples and public buildings began to grace the city. The Capitoline Hill became the religious center of the city when the temple of Jupiter Optimus Maximus (Jupiter the Best and Greatest) was built there. The Forum ceased to be a cemetery and began its history as a public meeting place, a development parallel to that of the Greek agora. Trade in metalwork became common, and the wealthier Roman classes began to import large numbers of fine Greek vases. The Etruscans had found Rome a collection of villages and made it a city.

✦ THE ROMAN CONQUEST OF ITALY (509–290 B.C.)

Early Roman history is an uneven mixture of fact and legend. Roman traditions often contain an important kernel of truth, but that does not make them history. In many cases they are significant because they illustrate the ethics, morals, and ideals that Roman society considered valuable. Rome's early history also presents the historian with another problem. Historical writing did not begin among the Romans until the third century B.C., hundreds of years after the founding of Rome. Much later still, around the time of Jesus, the historian Livy (59 B.C.–A.D. 17) gave final form to Roman legends.

How much genuine information about the early years did Romans such as Livy have? Did they simply take what they knew and try to make of it an intelligible story? Livy gave his own answer to these questions: "Events before Rome was born or thought of have come down to us in old tales with more of the charm of poetry than of sound historical record, and such traditions I propose neither to affirm nor refute."[3] Livy also admitted that these legends and tales depicted men and women not necessarily as they were, but as Romans should be. For him the story of early Rome was an impressive moral tale. Today historians would say that Livy took these legends and made of them a sweeping epic. But they would also admit that the epic preserved the broad outlines of the Roman conquest of Italy and the development of Rome's internal affairs. Both parts of the epic—legend and fact—are worth examining for what they say about the Romans.

According to Roman tradition, the Romans expelled the Etruscan king Tarquin the Proud from Rome in 509 B.C. and founded the republic. In the years that followed, the Romans fought numerous wars with their neighbors on the Italian peninsula. They became soldiers, and the grim fighting bred tenacity, a prominent Roman trait. War also involved diplomacy, at which the Romans became masters. At an early date they learned the value of alliances and how to provide leadership for their allies. Alliances with the Latin towns around them provided them with a large reservoir of manpower. Their alliances involved the Romans in still other wars and took them farther afield in the Italian peninsula.

One of the earliest wars was with two nearby peoples, the Aequi and the Volsci. From this contest arose the legend of Cincinnatus. At one point, when the Aequi had launched a serious invasion, the Romans called on Cincinnatus to assume the office of dictator. In this period the Roman dictator, unlike modern dictators, was a legitimate magistrate given ultimate powers for a specified period of time. The Roman officials found Cincinnatus working his three-acre farm. Wiping the sweat from himself, he listened to the appeal of his countrymen and accepted the office. Fifteen days later, after he had defeated the Aequi, he returned to his farm. Cincinnatus personified the ideal Roman citizen—a man of simplicity, who put his duty to Rome before any consideration of personal interest or wealth.

The growth of Roman power was slow but steady. Not until roughly a century after the founding of the republic did the Romans try to drive the Etruscans entirely out of Latium. In 405 B.C. they laid siege to Veii, the last neighboring Etruscan city. Ten years later they captured it. The story of the siege of Veii is in some ways the Roman equivalent of the Greek siege of Troy. But once again tradition preserves a kernel of truth, confirmed now by archaeological exploration of Veii. This was an important Roman victory, for the land of Veii went to the Romans and provided additional resources for Rome's growing population. Rome's concentrated landholdings formed a strong, unified core in central Italy. After the destruction of Veii, Rome overshadowed its Latin allies and enemies alike. Yet around 390 B.C. the Romans suffered a major setback when a new people, the Celts—or "Gauls," as the Romans called them—swept aside a Roman army and sacked Rome. More intent on loot than land, they agreed to abandon Rome in return for a thousand pounds of gold.

During the century from 390 B.C. to 290 B.C., Romans rebuilt their city and recouped their losses. They also reorganized their army to create the mobile legion, a flexible unit capable of fighting on either broken or open terrain. The Romans finally brought Latium and their Latin allies fully under their control and conquered Etruria. In 343 B.C. they grappled with the Samnites in a series of bitter wars for the possession of Campania and southern Italy. The Samnites were a formidable enemy and inflicted serious losses on the Romans. But the superior organization, institutions, and manpower of the Romans won out in the end. Although Rome had yet to subdue the whole peninsula, for the first time in history the city stood unchallenged in Italy.

Rome's success in diplomacy and politics was as important as its military victories. Unlike the Greeks, the Romans did not simply conquer and dominate. Instead, they shared with other Italians both political power and degrees of Roman citizenship. The Romans did not start out to build a system. They were always a practical people—that was one of their greatest strengths. When they

found a treaty or a political arrangement that worked, they used it wherever possible. When it did not, they turned to something else. Consequently, Rome had a network of alliances and treaties with other peoples and states. With many of their oldest allies, such as the Latin cities, they shared full Roman citizenship. In other instances they granted citizenship without the franchise (*civitas sine suffragio*). Allies who held this status enjoyed all the rights of Roman citizenship except that they could not vote or hold Roman offices. They were subject to Roman taxes and calls for military service but ran their own local affairs. The Latin allies were able to acquire full Roman citizenship by moving to Rome.

By their willingness to extend their citizenship, the Romans took Italy into partnership. Here the political genius of Rome triumphed where Greece had failed. Rome proved itself superior to the Greek polis because it both conquered and shared the fruits of conquest with the conquered. Rome could consolidate where Greece could only dominate. The unwillingness of the Greek polis to share its citizenship condemned it to a limited horizon. Not so with Rome. The extension of Roman citizenship strengthened the state, gave it additional manpower and wealth, and laid the foundation of the Roman Empire.

✤ THE ROMAN STATE

The Romans summed up their political existence in a single phrase: *senatus populusque Romanus,* "the Roman senate and the people." The real genius of the Romans lay in the fields of politics and law. Unlike the Greeks, they did not often speculate on the ideal state or on political forms. Instead, they realistically met actual challenges and created institutions, magistracies, and legal concepts to deal with practical problems. Change was consequently commonplace in Roman political life, and the constitution of 509 B.C. was far simpler than that of 27 B.C. Moreover, the Roman constitution, unlike the American, was not a single written document. Rather, it was a set of traditional beliefs, customs, and laws.

In the early republic, social divisions determined the shape of politics. Political power was in the hands of the aristocracy—the *patricians,* who were wealthy landowners. Patrician families formed clans, as did aristocrats in early Greece. They domi-

✦ **The Roman Forum** The forum was the center of Roman political life. From simple beginnings it developed into the very symbol of Rome's imperial majesty. *(Source: Josephine Powell, Rome)*

nated the affairs of state, provided military leadership in time of war, and monopolized knowledge of law and legal procedure. The common people of Rome, the *plebeians,* had few of the patricians' advantages. Some plebeians formed their own clans and rivaled the patricians in wealth. Many plebeian merchants increased their wealth in the course of Roman expansion, but most plebeians were poor. They were the artisans, small farmers, and landless urban dwellers. The plebeians, rich and poor alike, were free citizens with a voice in politics. Nonetheless, they were overshadowed by the patricians.

Historians today still argue about the origins of these two groups and how they functioned both socially and politically within the state. The question of how the distinction between patrician and plebeian arose can probably never be answered definitely. No one now knows whether it existed before the coming of the Etruscans, whether the

Etruscans introduced it in Rome, or whether it occurred at the creation of the republic. Despite all the contemporary research on the topic, only speculation is the result. In this area, as in many others, historians must possess the intelligence, the learning, and the humility to admit that they just do not know the answer. It is perfectly clear, however, that these two social groups determined the shape of Roman politics.

Perhaps the greatest institution of the republic was the senate, which had originated under the Etruscans as a council of noble elders who advised the king. During the republic the senate advised the consuls and other magistrates. Because the senate sat year after year, while magistrates changed annually, it provided stability and continuity. It also served as a reservoir of experience and knowledge. Technically, the senate could not pass legislation; it could only offer its advice. But increasingly, because of the senate's prestige, its advice came to have the force of law.

The Romans created several assemblies through which the people elected magistrates and passed legislation. The earliest was the *comitia curiata,* which had religious, political, and military functions. According to Roman tradition, King Servius Tullius (578–535 B.C.), who reorganized the state into 193 *centuries* for military purposes, created the *comitia centuriata* as a political body to decide Roman policy. The comitia centuriata voted in centuries, which in this instance means political blocs. The patricians possessed the majority of centuries because they shouldered most of the burden of defense. Thus they could easily outvote the plebeians. In 471 B.C. the plebeians won the right to meet in an assembly of their own, the *concilium plebis,* and to pass ordinances. In 287 B.C. the bills passed in the concilium plebis were recognized as binding on the entire population.

The chief magistrates of the republic were the two consuls, elected for one-year terms. At first the consulship was open only to patricians. The consuls commanded the army in battle, administered state business, convened the comitia centuriata, and supervised financial affairs. In effect, they and the senate ran the state. The consuls appointed *quaestors* to assist them in their duties, and in 421 B.C. the quaestorship became an elective office open to plebeians. The quaestors took charge of the public treasury and prosecuted criminals in the popular courts.

In 366 B.C. the Romans created a new office, that of *praetor,* and in 227 B.C. the number of praetors was increased to four. When the consuls were away from Rome, the praetors could act in their place. The praetors dealt primarily with the administration of justice. When he took office, a praetor issued a proclamation declaring the principles by which he would interpret the law. These proclamations became very important because they usually covered areas where the law was vague and thus helped clarify the law.

Other officials included the powerful *censors,* created in 443 B.C., who had many responsibilities, the most important being supervision of public morals, the power to determine who lawfully could sit in the senate, the registration of citizens, and the leasing of public contracts. Later officials were the *aediles,* four in number, who supervised the streets and markets and presided over public festivals.

After the age of overseas conquest (see pages 141–145), the Romans divided the Mediterranean area into provinces governed by ex-consuls and ex-praetors. Because of their experience in Roman politics, they were well suited to administer the affairs of the provincials and to fit Roman law and custom into new contexts.

One of the most splendid achievements of the Romans was their development of law. Roman law began as a set of rules that regulated the lives and relations of citizens. This civil law, or *ius civile,* consisted of statutes, customs, and forms of procedure. Roman assemblies added to the body of law, and praetors interpreted it. The spirit of the law aimed at protecting the property, lives, and reputations of citizens, redressing wrongs, and giving satisfaction to victims of injustice.

As the Romans came into more frequent contact with foreigners, they had to devise laws to deal with disputes between Romans and foreigners and between foreigners under Roman jurisdiction. In these instances, where there was no precedent to guide the Romans, the legal decisions of the praetors proved of immense importance. The praetors adopted aspects of other legal systems and resorted to the law of equity—what they thought was right and just to all parties. Free, in effect, to determine law, the praetors enjoyed a great deal of flexibility. This situation illustrates the practicality and the genius of the Romans. By addressing specific, actual circumstances the praetors developed a body of law, the *ius gentium,* "the law of peoples," that applied to Romans and foreigners and that laid the foundation for a universal conception of law. By the time of the late republic, Roman jurists were reaching decisions on the basis of the Stoic concept of *ius naturale,* "natural law," a universal law that could be applied to all societies.

✤ SOCIAL CONFLICT IN ROME

Another important aspect of early Roman history was a great social conflict, usually known as the Struggle of the Orders, which developed between patricians and plebeians. What the plebeians wanted was real political representation and safeguards against patrician domination. The plebeians' efforts to obtain recognition of their rights is the crux of the Struggle of the Orders.

Rome's early wars gave the plebeians the leverage they needed: Rome's survival depended on the army, and the army needed the plebeians. The first showdown between plebeians and patricians came, according to tradition, in 494 B.C. To force the patricians to grant concessions, the plebeians seceded from the state; they literally walked out of Rome and refused to serve in the army. The plebeians' general strike worked. Because of it the patricians made important concessions. One of these was social. In 445 B.C. the patricians passed a law, the *lex Canuleia,* which for the first time allowed patricians and plebeians to marry one another. Furthermore, the patricians recognized the right of plebeians to elect their own officials, the *tribunes.* The tribunes in turn had the right to protect the plebeians from the arbitrary conduct of patrician magistrates. The tribunes brought plebeian grievances to the senate for resolution. The plebeians were not bent on undermining the state. Rather, they used their gains only to win full equality under the law.

The law itself was the plebeians' next target. Only the patricians knew what the law was, and only they could argue cases in court. All too often they had used the law for their own benefit. The plebeians wanted the law codified and published. The result of their agitation was the Law of the Twelve Tables, so called because the laws, which covered civil and criminal matters, were inscribed on twelve large bronze plaques. Later still, the plebeians forced the patricians to publish legal procedures as well. The plebeians had broken the patricians' legal monopoly and henceforth enjoyed full protection under the law.

The decisive plebeian victory came with the passage of the Licinian-Sextian rogations (or laws) in 367 B.C. Licinius and Sextus were plebeian tribunes who led a ten-year fight for further reform. Rich plebeians, such as Licinius and Sextus themselves, joined the poor to mount a sweeping assault on patrician privilege. Wealthy plebeians wanted the opportunity to provide political leadership for the state. They demanded that the patricians allow them access to all the magistracies of the state. If they could hold the consulship, they could also sit in the senate and advise the senate on policy. The two tribunes won approval from the senate for a law that stipulated that one of the two annual consuls had to be a plebeian. Though decisive, the Licinian-Sextian rogations did not automatically end the Struggle of the Orders. That happened only in 287 B.C. with the passage of a law, the *lex Hortensia,* that gave the resolutions of the concilium plebis the force of law for patricians and plebeians alike.

The Struggle of the Orders resulted in a Rome stronger and better united than before. It could have led to anarchy, but again certain Roman traits triumphed. The values fostered by their social structure predisposed the Romans to compromise, especially in the face of common danger. Resistance and confrontation in Rome never exploded into class warfare. Instead, both sides resorted to compromises to hammer out a realistic solution. Important, too, were Roman patience, tenacity, and a healthy sense of the practical. These qualities enabled both sides to keep working until they had resolved the crisis. The Struggle of the Orders ended in 287 B.C. with a new concept of Roman citizenship. All citizens shared equally under the law. Theoretically, all could aspire to the highest political offices. Patrician or plebeian, rich or poor, Roman citizenship was equal for all.

✥ THE AGE OF OVERSEAS CONQUEST (282–146 B.C.)

In 282 B.C. Rome embarked on a series of wars that left it the ruler of the Mediterranean world. There was nothing ideological about these wars. Unlike Napoleon or Hitler, the Romans did not map out grandiose strategies for world conquest. They had no idea of what lay before them. If they could have looked into the future, they would have stood amazed. In many instances the Romans did not even initiate action; they simply responded to situations as they arose. Nineteenth-century Englishmen were fond of saying, "We got our empire in a fit of absence of mind." The Romans could not go quite that far. Though they sometimes declared war reluctantly, they nonetheless felt the need to dominate, to eliminate any state that could threaten them.

Rome was imperialistic, and its imperialism took two forms. In the barbarian West, the home of fierce tribes, Rome resorted to bald aggression to conquer new territory. In areas such as Spain and later Gaul, the fighting was fierce and savage, and gains came slowly. In the civilized East, the world of Hellenistic states, Rome tried to avoid annexing territory. The East was already heavily populated, and those people would have become Rome's responsibility. New responsibilities meant new problems, and such headaches the Romans shunned. In

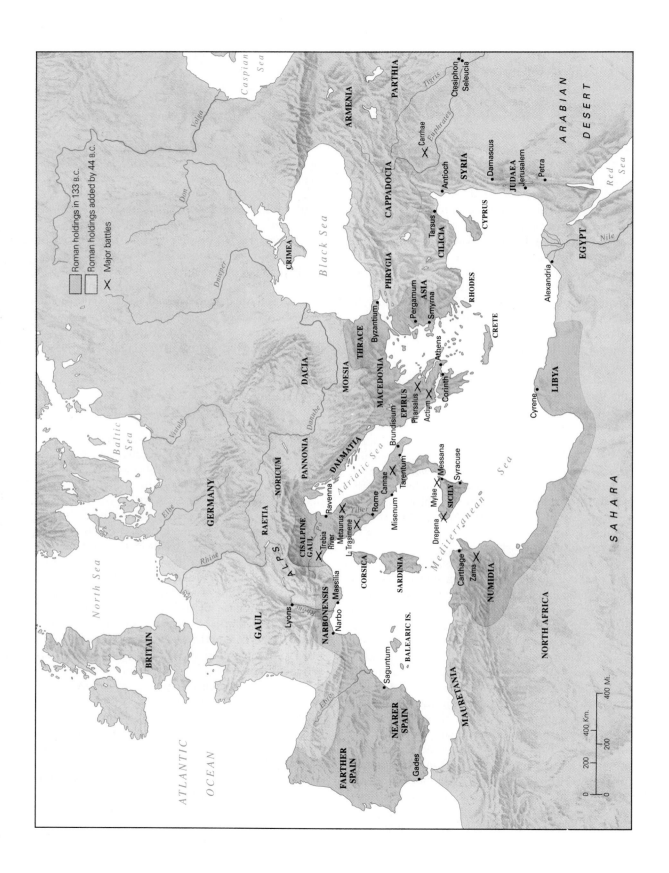

Roman holdings in 133 B.C.
Roman holdings added by 44 B.C.
X Major battles

ATLANTIC OCEAN

BRITAIN

North Sea

GERMANY

Baltic Sea

Elbe

Rhine

Vistula

Don

Volga

Caspian Sea

GAUL

Lyons

NARBONENSIS
Narbo

Massilia

ALPS

RAETIA

NORICUM

PANNONIA

DACIA

MOESIA

THRACE
Byzantium

Black Sea

CRIMEA

Dnieper

Danube

ARMENIA

PARTHIA

Tigris

Ctesiphon
Seleucia

Euphrates

Carrhae X

CAPPADOCIA

PHRYGIA
Pergamum
ASIA
Smyrna

Tarsus
CILICIA

SYRIA
Antioch
Damascus

JUDAEA
Jerusalem
Petra

ARABIAN DESERT

Red Sea

CYPRUS

RHODES

CRETE

EGYPT

Nile

Alexandria

CISALPINE GAUL

Po River
Trebia X
Metaurus X
Trasimene X

Ravenna

Rome
Cannae

Tiber

Misenum

CORSICA

SARDINIA

BALEARIC IS.

Saguntum

NEARER SPAIN

FARTHER SPAIN

Gades

Ebro

MAURETANIA

Carthage
Zama X
NUMIDIA

NORTH AFRICA

SAHARA

Mediterranean Sea

Drepena
Mylae X
Messana
Syracuse
SICILY

Tarentum

Brundisium

DALMATIA

Adriatic Sea

MACEDONIA

EPIRUS
Pharsalus X
Actium X
Corinth

Athens

Cyrene

LIBYA

400 Mi.

400 Km.

0   200   400

0   200

MASSILIA

the East the Romans preferred to be patrons rather than masters. Only when that policy failed did they directly annex land. But in 282 B.C. all this lay in the future.

The Samnite wars had drawn the Romans into the political world of southern Italy. In 282 B.C., alarmed by the powerful newcomer, the Greek city of Tarentum in southern Italy called for help from Pyrrhus, king of Epirus in western Greece. A relative of Alexander the Great and an excellent general, Pyrrhus won two furious battles but suffered heavy casualties—thus the phrase "Pyrrhic victory" for a victory involving severe losses. Roman bravery and tenacity led him to comment: "If we win one more battle with the Romans, we'll be completely washed up." Against Pyrrhus's army the Romans threw new legions, and in the end manpower proved decisive. In 275 B.C. the Romans drove Pyrrhus from Italy and extended their sway over southern Italy. Once they did, the island of Sicily became a key for them to block Carthaginian expansion northward.

Pyrrhus once described Sicily as a future "wrestling ground for the Carthaginians and Romans." The Phoenician city of Carthage in North Africa (Map 5.2) had for centuries dominated the western Mediterranean. Sicily had long been a Carthaginian target. Since Sicily is the steppingstone to Italy, the Romans could not let it fall to an enemy. In 264 B.C., Carthage and Rome came to blows over the city of Messana, which commanded the strait between Sicily and Italy.

This conflict, the First Punic War, lasted for twenty-three years (264–241 B.C.). The Romans quickly learned that they could not conquer Sicily unless they controlled the sea. Yet they lacked a fleet and hated the sea as fervently as cats hate water. Nevertheless, with grim resolution the Romans built a navy and challenged the Carthaginians at sea. The Romans fought seven major naval battles with the Carthaginians and won six. Twice their fleet went down in gales. But finally the Romans wore down the Carthaginians. In 241 B.C. the Romans defeated their rivals and took posses-

❖ **Coin of Hannibal** This Carthaginian coin bears one of the few profiles of Hannibal. The style of the profile is Roman, but the artist has captured the actual likeness of the archenemy of Rome. *(Source: Courtesy of the Trustees of the British Museum)*

sion of Sicily, which became their first real province. Once again Rome's resources, manpower, and determination proved decisive.

The peace treaty between the two powers brought no peace, in part because in 238 B.C. the Romans took advantage of Carthaginian weakness to seize Sardinia and Corsica. Although unable to resist, many Carthaginians concluded that genuine peace between Carthage and Rome was impossible. One such man was Hamilcar Barca, a Carthaginian commander who had come close to victory in Sicily. The only way Carthage could recoup its fortune was by success in Spain, where the Carthaginians already enjoyed a firm foothold. In 237 B.C. Hamilcar led an army to Spain in order to turn it into Carthaginian territory. With him he took his nineteen-year-old son, Hannibal, but not before he had led Hannibal to an altar and made him swear ever to be an enemy to Rome. In the following years Hamilcar and his son-in-law Hasdrubal subjugated much of southern Spain and in the process rebuilt Carthaginian power. Rome responded in two ways: first, the Romans made a treaty with Hasdrubal in which the Ebro River formed the boundary between Carthaginian and Roman interests, and second, the Romans began to extend their own influence in Spain.

❖ **MAP 5.2 Roman Expansion During the Republic** The main spurt of Roman expansion occurred between 264 and 133 B.C., when most of the Mediterranean fell to Rome, followed by the conquest of Gaul and the eastern Mediterranean by 44 B.C.

In 221 B.C. the young Hannibal became Carthaginian commander in Spain, and soon Roman and Carthaginian policies clashed at the city of Saguntum. When Hannibal laid siege to Saguntum, which lay within the sphere of Carthaginian interest, the Romans declared war, claiming that Carthage had attacked a friendly city. So began the Second Punic War, one of the most desperate wars ever fought by Rome. In 218 B.C. Hannibal struck first by marching more than a thousand miles over the Alps into Italy. Once there, he defeated one Roman army at the Battle of Trebia and later another at the Battle of Lake Trasimene in 217 B.C. In the following year, Hannibal won his greatest victory at the Battle of Cannae, in which he inflicted some forty thousand casualties on the Romans. He then spread devastation throughout Italy, and a number of cities in central and southern Italy rebelled against Rome. Syracuse, Rome's ally during the First Punic War, also went over to the Carthaginians. Yet Hannibal failed to crush Rome's iron circle of Latium, Etruria, and Samnium. The wisdom of Rome's political policy of extending rights and citizenship to its allies showed itself in these dark hours. And Rome fought back.

In 210 B.C. Rome found its answer to Hannibal in the young commander Scipio, later better known as Scipio Africanus. Scipio copied Hannibal's methods of mobile warfare, streamlining the legions by making their components capable of independent action and introducing new weapons. In the following years, Scipio operated in Spain, which in 207 B.C. he wrested from the Carthaginians. Also in 207 B.C. the Romans sealed Hannibal's

fate in Italy. At the Battle of Metaurus, the Romans destroyed a major Carthaginian army coming to reinforce Hannibal. With Hannibal now bottled up in southern Italy, Scipio in 204 B.C. struck directly at Carthage itself. A Roman fleet landed his legions in North Africa, which prompted the Carthaginians to recall Hannibal from Italy to defend the homeland.

In 202 B.C., near the town of Zama (see Map 5.2), Scipio defeated Hannibal in one of the world's truly decisive battles. Scipio's victory meant that the world of the western Mediterranean would henceforth be Roman. Roman language, law, and culture, fertilized by Greek influences, would in time permeate this entire region. The victory at Zama meant that Rome's heritage would be passed on to the Western world.

The Second Punic War contained the seeds of still other wars. Unabated fear of Carthage led to the Third Punic War, a needless, unjust, and savage conflict that ended in 146 B.C. when Scipio Aemilianus, grandson of Scipio Africanus, destroyed the old hated rival. As the Roman conqueror watched the death pangs of that great city, he turned to his friend Polybius with the words: "I fear and foresee that someday someone will give the same order about my fatherland." It would, however, be centuries before an invader would stand before the gates of Rome.

During the war with Hannibal, the Romans had invaded Spain, a peninsula rich in material resources and the home of fierce warriors. When the Roman legions tried to reduce Spanish tribes, they met with bloody and determined resistance. Not

✤ **Bronze Punic Armor** This armor is a breast and backplate found in a third-century B.C. tomb near Carthage. The ornamentation suggests an Italo-Greek origin. *(Source: Musée National du Bardo)*

until 133 B.C., after years of brutal and ruthless warfare, did Scipio Aemilianus finally conquer Spain.

During the dark days of the Second Punic War, the king of Macedonia made an alliance with Hannibal against Rome. Even while engaged in the West, the Romans turned east to settle accounts. When the Romans intervened in the Hellenistic East, they went from triumph to triumph. The kingdom of Macedonia fell to the Roman legions, as did Greece and the Seleucid monarchy. By 146 B.C. the Romans stood unchallenged in the eastern Mediterranean and had turned many states and kingdoms into provinces. In 133 B.C. the king of Pergamum in Asia Minor left his kingdom to the Romans in his will. The Ptolemies of Egypt meekly obeyed Roman wishes. The following years would bring the Romans new victories, and they would establish their system of provincial administration. But by 133 B.C. the work of conquest was largely done: the Mediterranean had become *mare nostrum,* "our sea."

✤ OLD VALUES AND GREEK CULTURE

Rome had conquered the Mediterranean world, but some Romans considered that victory a misfortune. The historian Sallust (86–34 B.C.), writing from hindsight, complained that the acquisition of an empire was the beginning of Rome's troubles:

But when through labor and justice our Republic grew powerful, great kings defeated in war, fierce nations and mighty peoples subdued by force, when Carthage the rival of the Roman people was wiped out root and branch, all the seas and lands lay open, then fortune began to be harsh and to throw everything into confusion. The Romans had easily borne labor, danger, uncertainty, and hardship. To them leisure, riches— otherwise desirable—proved to be burdens and torments. So at first money, then desire for power grew great. These things were a sort of cause of all evils.[4]

Sallust was not alone in his feelings. At the time, some senators had opposed the destruction of Carthage on the grounds that fear of their old rival would keep the Romans in check. In the second century B.C., Romans learned that they could not return to what they fondly considered a simple life. They were world rulers. The responsibilities they faced were complex and awesome. They had to change their institutions, social patterns, and way of thinking to meet the new era. They were in fact building the foundations of a great imperial system. It was an awesome challenge, and there were failures along the way. Roman generals and politicians would destroy each other. Even the republican constitution would eventually be discarded. But in the end Rome triumphed here just as it had on the battlefield, for out of the turmoil would come the *pax Romana*—"Roman peace."

How did the Romans of the day meet these challenges? How did they lead their lives and cope with these momentous changes? Obviously there are as many answers to these questions as there were Romans. Yet two men represent the major trends of the second century B.C. Cato the Elder shared the mentality of those who longed for the good old days and idealized the traditional agrarian way of life. Scipio Aemilianus led those who embraced the new urban life, with its eager acceptance of Greek culture. Forty-nine years older than Scipio, Cato was a product of an earlier generation, one that confronted a rapidly changing world. Cato and Scipio were both aristocrats and neither of them was typical, even of the aristocracy. But they do exemplify opposing sets of attitudes that marked Roman society and politics in the age of conquest.

Cato and the Traditional Ideal

Marcus Cato (234–149 B.C.) was born a plebeian, but his talent and energy carried him to Rome's highest offices. He cherished the old virtues and consistently imitated the old ways. In Roman society ties within the family were very strong. In this sense Cato and his family were typical. Cato was *paterfamilias,* a term that meant far more than merely "father." The paterfamilias was the oldest dominant male of the family. He held nearly absolute power over the lives of his wife and children as long as he lived. He could legally kill his wife for adultery or divorce her at will. He could kill his children or sell them into slavery. He could force them to marry against their will. Until the paterfamilias died, his sons could not legally own property. At his death, the wife and children of the paterfamilias inherited his property.

Despite his immense power, the paterfamilias did not necessarily act alone or arbitrarily. To deal with important family matters he usually called a

❖ **Scene of the Life of a Child** This scene depicts the life of Marcus Cornelius from his infancy to his playing with his ponies to his death. The entire scene suggests a pleasant and loving, if brief, childhood. *(Source: Louvre/Bildarchiv Foto Marburg/Art Resource, NY)*

council of the adult males. In this way the leading members of the family aired their views. They had the opportunity to give their support to the paterfamilias or to dissuade him from harsh decisions. In these councils the women of the family had no formal part, but it can safely be assumed that they played an important role behind the scenes. Although the possibility of serious conflicts between a paterfamilias and his grown sons is obvious, no one in ancient Rome ever complained about the institution. Perhaps in practice the paterfamilias preferred to be lenient rather than absolute.

Like most Romans, Cato and his family began the day early in the morning. The Romans divided the period of daylight into twelve hours and the darkness into another twelve. The day might begin as early as half past four in summer, as late as half past seven in winter. Because Mediterranean summers are invariably hot, the farmer and his wife liked to take every advantage of the cool mornings. Cato and his family, like modern Italians, ordinarily started the morning with a light breakfast, usually nothing more than some bread and cheese. After breakfast the family went about its work.

Because of his political aspirations, Cato often used the mornings to plead law cases. He walked to the marketplace of the nearby town and defended anyone who wished his help. He received no fees for these services but did put his neighbors in his debt. In matters of law and politics Roman custom was very strong. It demanded that Cato's clients give him their political support or their votes in repayment whenever he asked for them.

These clients knew and accepted their obligations to Cato for his help.

Cato's wife (whose name is unknown) was the matron of the family, a position of authority and respect. The virtues expected of a Roman matron were fidelity, chastity, modesty, and dedication to the family. Cato's wife also followed the old ways. While he was in town, she ran the household. She spent the morning spinning and weaving wool for the clothes the family wore. She supervised the domestic slaves, planned the meals, and devoted a good deal of attention to her son. In wealthy homes during this period, the matron had begun to employ a slave as a wet nurse. Cato's wife refused to delegate maternal duties. Like most ordinary Roman women, she nursed her son herself and bathed and swaddled him daily. Later the boy was allowed to play with toys and terra-cotta dolls. Roman children, like children everywhere, kept pets. Dogs were especially popular and valuable as house guards. Children played all sorts of games, and games of chance were very popular. Until the age of seven the child was under the matron's care. During this time the mother began to educate her daughter in the management of the household. After the age of seven, the son—and in many wealthy households the daughter, too—began to undertake formal education.

In the country, Romans like Cato continued to take their main meal at midday. This meal included either coarse bread made from the entire husk of wheat or porridge made with milk or water; it also included turnips, cabbage, olives, and beans. When

Romans ate meat, they preferred pork. Unless they lived by the sea, the average farm family did not eat fish, an expensive delicacy. Cato once complained that Rome was a place where a fish could cost more than a cow. With the midday meal the family drank ordinary wine mixed with water. Afterward, any Roman who could took a nap. This was especially true in the summer, when the Mediterranean heat can be fierce. Slaves, artisans, and hired laborers, however, continued their work. In the evening, Romans ate a light meal and went to bed at nightfall.

The agricultural year followed the sun and the stars—the farmer's calendar. Like Hesiod in Boeotia, the Roman farmer looked to the sky to determine when to plant, weed, shear sheep, and perform other chores. Spring was the season for plowing. Roman farmers plowed their land at least twice and preferably three times. The third plowing was to cover the sown seed in ridges and to use the furrows to drain off excess water. The Romans used a variety of plows. Some had detachable shares. Some were heavy for thick soil, others light for thin, crumbly soil. Farmers used oxen and donkeys to pull the plow, collecting the dung of the animals for fertilizer. Besides spreading manure, some farmers fertilized their fields by planting lupines and beans; when they began to pod, farmers plowed them under. The main money crops, at least for rich soils, were wheat and flax. Forage crops included clover, vetch, and alfalfa. Prosperous farmers like Cato raised olive trees chiefly for the oil. They also raised grapevines for the production of wine. Cato and his neighbors harvested their cereal crops in summer and their grapes in autumn. Harvests varied depending on the soil, but farmers could usually expect yields of $5\frac{1}{2}$ bushels of wheat or $10\frac{1}{2}$ bushels of barley per acre.

An influx of slaves resulted from Rome's wars and conquests. Prisoners from Spain, Africa, and the Hellenistic East and even some blacks and other prisoners from Hannibal's army came to Rome as the spoils of war. The Roman attitude toward slaves and slavery had little in common with modern views. To the Romans slavery was a misfortune that befell some people, but it did not entail any racial theories. Races were not enslaved because the Romans thought them inferior. The black African slave was treated no worse—and no better—than the Spaniard. Indeed, some slaves were valued because of their physical distinctiveness: black Africans and blond Germans were particular favorites. For the talented slave, the Romans always held out the hope of eventual freedom. *Manumission*—the freeing of individual slaves by their masters—became so common that it had to be limited by law. Not even Christians questioned the institution of slavery. It was just a fact of life.

Slaves were entirely their master's property and might be treated with great cruelty. Many Romans

Vase Portrait of an Ethiopian Woman This vase, dating to ca. 100 B.C., is typical of Roman curiosity about different peoples. It is realistic and not exaggerated. A silver inlay was used for the whites of the eyes, indicating that this was an expensive vase. *(Source: Courtesy of the Trustees of the British Museum)*

were practical enough to realize that they got more out of their slaves by kindness than by severity. Yet in Sicily slaveowners treated their slaves viciously. They bought slaves in huge numbers, branded them for identification, put them in irons, and often made them go without food and clothing. In 135 B.C. these conditions gave rise to a major slave revolt, during which many of the most brutal masters died at their slaves' hands. Italy, too, had trouble with slave unrest, but conditions there were generally better than in Sicily.

For Cato and most other Romans, religion played an important part in life. Originally the Romans thought of the gods as invisible, shapeless natural forces. Only through Etruscan and Greek influence did Roman deities take on human form. Jupiter, the sky-god, and his wife, Juno, became equivalent to the Greek Zeus and Hera. Mars was the god of war but also guaranteed the fertility of the farm and protected it from danger. The gods of the Romans were not loving and personal. They were stern, powerful, and aloof. But as long as the Romans honored the cults of their gods, they could expect divine favor.

Along with the great gods the Romans believed in spirits who haunted fields, forests, crossroads, and even the home itself (see Listening to the Past). Some of these deities were hostile; only magic could ward them off. The spirits of the dead, like ghosts in modern horror films, frequented places where they had lived. They, too, had to be placated but were ordinarily benign. As the poet Ovid (43 B.C.–A.D. 17) put it:

The spirits of the dead ask for little.
They are more grateful for piety than for an expen-
sive gift—
Not greedy are the gods who haunt the Styx below.
A rooftile covered with a sacrificial crown,
Scattered kernels, a few grains of salt,
Bread dipped in wine, and loose violets—
These are enough.
Put them in a potsherd and leave them in the middle
of the road.[5]

A good deal of Roman religion consisted of rituals such as those Ovid describes. These practices lived on long after the Romans had lost interest in the great gods. Even Christianity could not entirely wipe them out. Instead, Christianity was to incorporate many of these rituals into its own style of worship.

SCIPIO AEMILIANUS: GREEK CULTURE AND URBAN LIFE

The old-fashioned ideals that Cato represented came into conflict with a new spirit of wealth and leisure. The conquest of the Mediterranean world and the spoils of war made Rome a great city. Roman life, especially in the cities, was changing and becoming less austere. The spoils of war went to build baths, theaters, and other places of amusement. Romans and Italian townspeople began to spend more of their time in leisure pursuits. Simultaneously, the new responsibilities of governing the world produced in Rome a sophisticated society. Romans developed new tastes and a liking for Greek culture and literature. They began to learn the Greek language. It became common for an educated Roman to speak both Latin and Greek. Hellenism dominated the cultural life of Rome. Even diehards like Cato found a knowledge of Greek essential for political and diplomatic affairs. The poet Horace (64–8 B.C.) summed it up well: "Captive Greece captured her rough conqueror and introduced the arts into rustic Latium."

One of the most avid devotees of Hellenism and the new was Scipio Aemilianus, the destroyer of Carthage. Scipio realized that broad and worldly views had to replace the old Roman narrowness. The new situation called for new ways. Rome was no longer a small city on the Tiber; it was the capital of the world, and Romans had to adapt themselves to that fact. Scipio was ready to become an innovator in both politics and culture. He broke with the past in the conduct of his political career, choosing a more personal style of politics, one that reflected his own views and one that looked unflinchingly at the broader problems that the success of Rome brought to its people. He embraced Hellenism wholeheartedly. Perhaps more than anyone else of his day, Scipio represented the new Roman—imperial, cultured, and independent.

In his education and interests, too, Scipio broke with the past. As a boy he had received the traditional Roman training, learning to read and write Latin and becoming acquainted with the law. He mastered the fundamentals of rhetoric and learned how to throw the javelin, fight in armor, and ride a horse. But later Scipio also learned Greek and became a fervent Hellenist. As a young man he formed a lasting friendship with the historian Polybius, who actively encouraged him in his study of

Greek culture and in his intellectual pursuits. In later life Scipio's love of Greek learning, rhetoric, and philosophy became legendary. Scipio also promoted the spread of Hellenism in Roman society. He became the center of the Scipionic Circle, a small group of Greek and Roman artists, philosophers, historians, and poets. Conservatives like Cato tried to stem the rising tide of Hellenism, but men like Scipio carried the day and helped make the heritage of Greece an abiding factor in Roman life.

The new Hellenism profoundly stimulated the growth and development of Roman art and literature. The Roman conquest of the Hellenistic East resulted in wholesale confiscation of Greek paintings and sculpture to grace Roman temples, public buildings, and private homes. Roman artists copied many aspects of Greek art, but their emphasis on realistic portraiture carried on a native tradition.

Fabius Pictor (second half of the third century B.C.), a senator, wrote the first *History of Rome* in Greek. Other Romans translated Greek classics into Latin. Still others, such as the poet Ennius (239–169 B.C.), the father of Latin poetry, studied Greek philosophy, wrote comedies in Latin, and adapted many of Euripides' tragedies for the Roman stage. Ennius also wrote a history of Rome in Latin verse. Plautus (ca 254–184 B.C.) specialized in rough humor. He, too, decked out Greek plays in Roman dress but was no mere imitator. Indeed, his play *Amphitruo* was itself copied eighteen hundred years later by the French playwright Molière and the English poet John Dryden. The Roman dramatist Terence (ca 195–159 B.C.), a member of the Scipionic Circle, wrote comedies of refinement and grace that owed their essentials to Greek models. His plays lacked the energy and the slapstick of Plautus's rowdy plays. All of early Roman literature was derived from the Greeks, but it managed in time to speak in its own voice and to flourish because it had something of its own to say.

The conquest of the Mediterranean world brought the Romans leisure, and Hellenism influenced how they spent their free time. During the second century B.C. the Greek custom of bathing became a Roman passion and an important part of the day. In the early republic Romans had bathed infrequently, especially in the winter. Now large buildings containing pools and exercise rooms went up in great numbers, and the baths became an essential part of the Roman city. Archi-

Roman Baths Once introduced into the Roman world, social bathing became a passion. These baths, which date to the Roman Empire, are located in Bath, England, to which they gave their name. A triumph of sophisticated engineering, they also demonstrate how Roman culture and institutions influenced life even on the perimeters of the Roman Empire. *(Source: Michael Holford)*

tects built intricate systems of aqueducts to supply the bathing establishments with water. Conservatives railed at this Greek custom, calling it a waste of time and an encouragement to idleness. They were correct in that bathing establishments were more than just places to take a bath. They included gymnasia, where men exercised and played ball. Women had places of their own to bathe, generally sections of the same baths used by men; for some reason, women's facilities lacked gymnasia. The baths contained hot-air rooms to induce a good sweat and pools of hot and cold water to finish the actual bathing. They also contained snack bars and halls where people chatted and read. The baths were socially important places where men and women went to see and be seen. Social climbers tried to talk to "the right people" and wangle invitations to dinner; politicians took advantage of the occasion to discuss the affairs of the day. Despite the protests of conservatives and moralists, the baths at least provided people—rich and poor—with places for clean and healthy relaxation.

This period also saw a change in the eating habits of urban dwellers. The main meal of the day shifted from midday to evening. Dinner became a more elaborate meal, and dinner parties became fashionable. Although Scipio Aemilianus detested fat people, more and more Romans began to eat excessively. Rich men and women displayed their wealth by serving exotic dishes and gourmet foods. After a course of vegetables and olives came the main course of meat, fish, or fowl. Pig was a favorite dish, and a whole suckling pig might be stuffed with sausage. A lucky guest might even dine on peacock and ostrich, each served with rich sauces. Dessert, as in Italy today, usually consisted of fruit. With the meal the Romans served wine, and during this period vintage wines became very popular.

Although the wealthy gorged themselves whenever they could, poor artisans and workers could rarely afford rich meals. Their dinners resembled Cato's. Yet they, too, occasionally spent generously on food, especially during major festivals. The Roman calendar was crowded with religious festivals, occasions not of dreary piety but of cheerful celebration. One was the festival of Anna Perenna, a festival of fertility, longevity, and prosperity. It was an occasion for fun and exuberant but harmless excess. The poet Ovid caught all the joy and charm of the event:

♦ **Roman Table Manners** This mosaic is a floor that can never be swept clean. It whimsically suggests what a dining room floor looked like after a lavish dinner and also tells something about the menu: a chicken head, a wishbone, remains of various seafood, vegetables, and fruit are easily recognizable. *(Source: Museo Gregoria-Profano/ Scala/Art Resource)*

The ordinary people come [to the banks of the Tiber];
And scattering themselves over the green grass,
They drink and lie down, each man with his woman.
Some remain under the open sky, a few put up tents,
Others build leafy huts of twigs.
Some set up reeds instead of unbending columns,
Over which they spread their togas.
Yet they grow warm with sun and wine, and pray
For as many years as cups of wine they take, and they drink that many.

. . . .

There also they sing the songs they have heard in the theaters,
And they beat time to the words with lively hands.
Putting down the bowl, they join in rough ring dances,
And the trim girlfriend dances with her hair flying.
As they return home, they stagger and are a spectacle to the vulgar.
When meeting them, the crowd calls them blessed.
The procession came my way recently (a worthy sight in my opinion):
A drunk woman dragged along a drunk old man.[6]

Did Hellenism and new social customs corrupt the Romans? Perhaps the best answer is this: the Roman state and the empire it ruled continued to exist for six more centuries. Rome did not collapse;

the state continued to prosper. The golden age of literature was still before it. The high tide of its prosperity still lay in the future. The Romans did not like change but took it in stride. That was part of their practical turn of mind and their strength.

✣ THE LATE REPUBLIC (133–31 B.C.)

The wars of conquest created serious problems for the Romans, some of the most pressing of which were political. The republican constitution had suited the needs of a simple city-state but was inadequate to meet the requirements of Rome's new position in international affairs (see Map 5.2). Sweeping changes and reforms were necessary to make it serve the demands of empire. A system of provincial administration had to be established. Officials had to be appointed to govern the provinces and administer the law. These officials and administrative organs had to find places in the constitution. Armies had to be provided for defense, and a system of tax collection had to be created.

Other political problems were equally serious. During the wars Roman generals commanded huge numbers of troops for long periods of time. Men such as Scipio Aemilianus were on the point of becoming too mighty for the state to control. Although Rome's Italian allies had borne much of the burden of the fighting, they received fewer rewards than did Roman officers and soldiers. Italians began to agitate for full Roman citizenship and a voice in politics.

Unrest in Rome and Italy

There were serious economic problems, too. Hannibal's operations and the warfare in Italy had left the countryside a shambles. The movements of numerous armies had disrupted agriculture. The prolonged fighting had also drawn untold numbers of Roman and Italian men away from their farms for long periods. The families of these soldiers could not keep the land under full cultivation. The people who defended Rome and conquered the world for Rome became impoverished for having done their duty.

These problems, complex and explosive, largely account for the turmoil of the closing years of the republic. The late republic was one of the most dramatic eras in Roman history. It produced some

of Rome's most famous figures: the Gracchi, Marius, Sulla, Cicero, Pompey, and Julius Caesar, among others. In one way or another, each of these men attempted to solve Rome's problems. Yet they were also striving for the glory and honor that were the supreme goals of the senatorial aristocracy. Personal ambition often clashed with patriotism to create political tension throughout the period.

When the legionaries returned to their farms in Italy, they encountered an appalling situation. All too often their farms looked like the farms of people they had conquered. Two courses of action were open to them. They could rebuild as their forefathers had done. Or they could take advantage of an alternative not open to their ancestors and sell their holdings. The wars of conquest had made some men astoundingly rich. These men wanted to invest their wealth in land. They bought up small farms to create huge estates, which the Romans called *latifundia*.

The purchase offers of the rich landowners appealed to the veterans for a variety of reasons. Many veterans had seen service in the East, where they had tasted the rich city life of the Hellenistic states. They were reluctant to return home and settle down to a dull life on the farm. Often their farms were so badly damaged that rebuilding hardly seemed worthwhile. Besides, it was hard to make big profits from small farms. Nor could the veterans supplement their income by working on the latifundia. Although the owners of the latifundia occasionally hired free men as day laborers, they preferred to use slaves. Slaves could not strike or be drafted into the army. Confronted by these conditions, veterans and their families opted to sell their land. They took what they could get for their broken farms and tried their luck elsewhere.

Most veterans migrated to the cities, especially to Rome. Although some found work, most did not. Industry and small manufacturing were generally in the hands of slaves. Even when there was work, slave labor kept the wages of free men low. Instead of a new start, veterans and their families encountered slum conditions that matched those of modern American cities.

This trend held ominous consequences for the strength of Rome's armies. The Romans had always believed that only landowners should serve in the army, for only they had something to fight for. Landless men, even if they were Romans and lived in Rome, could not be conscripted into the army.

✥ **The Town of Terracina** The Romans founded numerous colonies, first in Italy and later throughout the Mediterranean. Roman colonies, which often grew into cities, were intended to be self-sufficient. This ancient drawing shows the colonia Axumas, now Terracina, with its walls and towers for protection of the population sitting astride the Appian Way, the famous road to Rome. The lines to the left show how Roman surveyors had marked out the land for cultivation. *(Source: Bibliotheca Apostolica Vaticana)*

These landless men may have been veterans of major battles and numerous campaigns; they may have won distinction on the battlefield. But once they sold their land they became ineligible for further military service. A large pool of experienced manpower was going to waste. The landless ex-legionaries wanted a new start, and they were willing to support any leader who would provide it.

One man who recognized the plight of Rome's peasant farmers and urban poor was an aristocrat, Tiberius Gracchus (163–133 B.C.). Appalled by what he saw, Tiberius warned his countrymen that the legionaries were losing their land while fighting Rome's wars:

The wild beasts that roam over Italy have every one of them a cave or lair to lurk in. But the men who fight and die for Italy enjoy the common air and light, indeed, but nothing else. Houseless and homeless they wander about with their wives and children. And it is with lying lips that their generals exhort the soldiers in their battles to defend sepulchres and shrines from the enemy, for not a man of them has an hereditary altar, not one of all these many Romans an ancestral tomb, but they fight and die to support others in luxury, and though they are styled masters of the world, they have not a single clod of earth that is their own.[7]

Until his death Tiberius Gracchus sought a solution to the problems of the veterans and the urban poor.

After his election as tribune of the people in 133 B.C., Tiberius proposed that public land be given to the poor in small lots. Although his reform enjoyed the support of some very distinguished and popular aristocrats, he immediately ran into trouble for a number of reasons. First, his reform bill angered many wealthy aristocrats who had usurped large tracts of public land for their own use. They had no desire to give any of it back, so they bitterly resisted Tiberius's efforts. This was to be expected, yet he unquestionably made additional problems for himself. He introduced his land bill in the concilium plebis without consulting the senate. When King Attalus III left the kingdom of Pergamum to the Romans in his will, Tiberius had the money appropriated to finance his reforms—another slap at the senate. As tribune he acted totally within his rights. Yet the way in which he proceeded was unprecedented. Many powerful Romans became suspicious of Tiberius's growing influence with the people, some even thinking that he aimed at tyranny. Others opposed him because of his unparalleled methods. After all, there were proper ways to do things in Rome, and he had not followed them. As a result, violence broke out when a large body of senators, led by the *pontifex maximus* (the chief priest), killed Tiberius in cold blood. It was a black day in Roman history. The very people who directed the affairs of state and administered the law had taken the law into their own hands. The death of Tiberius was the beginning of an era of political violence. In the end that violence would bring down the republic.

Although Tiberius was dead, his land bill became law. Furthermore, Tiberius's brother Gaius Gracchus (153–121 B.C.) took up the cause of reform. Gaius was a veteran soldier with an enviable record, but this fiery orator made his mark in the political arena. Gaius also became tribune and demanded even more extensive reform than his brother. To help the urban poor, Gaius pushed legislation to provide them with cheap grain for bread. He defended his brother's land law and suggested other measures for helping the landless. He proposed that Rome send many of its poor and propertyless people out to form colonies in southern Italy. The poor would have a new start and lead productive lives. The city would immediately benefit because excess, nonproductive families would leave for new opportunities abroad. Rome would be less crowded, sordid, and dangerous.

Gaius went a step further and urged that all Italians be granted full rights of Roman citizenship. This measure provoked a storm of opposition, and it was not passed in Gaius's lifetime. Yet in the long run he proved wiser than his opponents. In 91 B.C. many Italians revolted against Rome over the issue of full citizenship, thus triggering the Social War, so named from the Latin word *socius*, or "ally." After a brief but hard-fought war (91–88 B.C.), the senate gave Roman citizenship to all Italians. Had the senate listened to Gaius earlier, it could have prevented a great deal of bloodshed. Yet Gaius himself was also at fault. Like his brother Tiberius, Gaius aroused a great deal of personal and factional opposition. To many he seemed too radical and too hasty to change things. Many political opponents considered him belligerent and headstrong. When Gaius failed in 121 B.C. to win the tribunate

for the third time, he feared for his life. In desperation he armed his staunchest supporters, whereupon the senate ordered the consul Opimius to restore order. He did so by having Gaius killed, along with three thousand of Gaius's supporters who opposed the senate's order. Once again the cause of reform had met with violence.

The death of Gaius brought little peace, and trouble came from two sources: the outbreak of new wars in the Mediterranean basin and further political unrest in Rome. In 112 B.C. Rome declared war against the rebellious Jugurtha, king of Numidia in North Africa. Numidia had been one of Rome's *client kingdoms,* kingdoms still ruled by their own kings but subject to Rome. The Roman legions made little headway against Jugurtha until 107 B.C., when Gaius Marius, an Italian *new man* (a politician not from the traditional Roman aristocracy), became consul. Marius's values were those of the military camp. A man of fierce vigor and courage, Marius saw the army as the tool of his ambition. He took the unusual but not wholly unprecedented step of recruiting an army by permitting landless men to serve in the legions. Marius thus tapped Rome's vast reservoir of idle manpower. His volunteer army was a professional force, not a body of draftees. In 106 B.C. Marius and his new army handily defeated Jugurtha.

An unexpected war broke out in the following year when two German peoples, the Cimbri and Teutones, moved into Gaul and later into northern Italy. After the Germans had defeated Roman armies sent to repel them, Marius was again elected consul, even though he was legally ineligible. From 104 to 100 B.C., Marius annually held the consulship. Despite the military necessity, Marius's many consulships meant that a Roman commander repeatedly held unprecedented military power in his hands. This would later translate into a political problem that the Roman republic never solved.

Before engaging the Cimbri and Teutones, Marius reformed the Roman army. There was, however, a disturbing side to his reforms, one that would henceforth haunt the republic. To encourage enlistments, Marius promised land to his volunteers after the war. Poor and landless veterans flocked to him, and together they conquered the Germans by 101 B.C. When Marius proposed a bill to grant land to his veterans, the senate refused to act, in effect turning its back on the soldiers of Rome. It was a disastrous mistake. Henceforth the legionaries expected the commanders—not the senate or the state—to protect their interests. Through Marius's reforms the Roman army became an almost professional force, but it owed little allegiance to the state. By failing to reward the loyalty of Rome's troops, the senate set the stage for military rebellion and political anarchy.

Civil War

Marius's innovations had a huge impact on Roman soldiers and on the nature of the army. Until then, Roman soldiers, like classical Greek hoplites, were citizen-soldiers with their roots in the land. They were essentially amateurs, a situation that changed during the Second Punic War and the wars of expansion. Having served long in the field, they became very proficient veteran troops. Marius gave them the opportunity to serve longer, even if they owned no property. What he and his successors Pompey and Caesar did was simply to create private armies that owed only nominal loyalty to

The Roman Eagle The eagle symbolized the majesty of Rome, just as it has for other nations, including the United States. The onyx relief above, dating to ca 100 B.C., depicts an eagle in all its grandeur. Images of eagles became attached to Roman legionary standards. *(Source: Kunsthistorisches Museum, Vienna)*

Rome. This process was the predecessor of the creation of the professional armies of the empire.

The Social War brought Marius into conflict with Sulla, who was consul in 88 B.C. First Marius and later Sulla defeated the Italian rebels. In the final stages of the war, while putting down the last of the rebels, Sulla was deposed from his consulship because of factional chaos in Rome. He immediately marched on Rome and restored order, but it was an ominous sign of the deterioration of Roman politics and political ideals. With some semblance of order restored, Sulla in 88 B.C. led an army to the East, where King Mithridates of Pontus in Asia Minor challenged Roman rule. In Sulla's absence, rioting and political violence again exploded in Rome. Marius and his supporters marched on Rome and launched a reign of terror.

Although Marius died peacefully in 86 B.C., his supporters continued to hold Rome. Once Sulla had defeated Mithridates, he once again, this time in 82 B.C., marched on Rome. After a brief but intense civil war, Sulla entered Rome and ordered a ruthless butchery of his opponents. He also proclaimed himself dictator. He launched many political and judicial reforms, including strengthening the senate while weakening the tribunate; increasing the number of magistrates in order to administer Rome's provinces better; and restoring the courts.

In 79 B.C. Sulla voluntarily abdicated his dictatorship and permitted the republican constitution to function normally once again. Yet his dictatorship cast a long shadow over the late republic. Sulla the political reformer proved far less influential than Sulla the successful general and dictator. Civil war was to be the constant lot of Rome for the next fifty years, until the republican constitution gave way to the empire of Augustus in 27 B.C. The history of the late republic is the story of the power struggles of some of Rome's most famous figures: Julius Caesar and Pompey, Augustus and Marc Antony. One figure who stands apart is Cicero (106–43 B.C.), a practical politician whose greatest legacy to the Roman world and to Western civilization is his mass of political and oratorical writings.

Pompous, vain, and sometimes silly, Cicero was nonetheless one of the few men of the period to urge peace and public order. As consul in 63 B.C. he put down a conspiracy against the republic but refused to use force to win political power. Instead, he developed the idea of "concord of the orders," an idealistic, probably unattainable balance among the elements that constituted the Roman state. A truly brilliant master of Latin prose and undoubtedly Rome's finest orator, Cicero used his vast literary ability to promote political and social reforms and explore the underlying principles of statecraft. Cicero also wrote many letters to his political friends in which he commented on the events of the day, and these letters are an invaluable source of information to modern historians. Yet Cicero commanded no legions, and only legions commanded respect.

In the late republic the Romans were grappling with the simple and inescapable fact that their old city-state constitution was unequal to the demands of overseas possessions and the governing of provinces. Thus even Sulla's efforts to put the constitution back together proved hollow. Once the senate and other institutions of the Roman state had failed to come to grips with the needs of empire, once the authorities had lost control of their own generals and soldiers, and once the armies put their faith in commanders instead of in Rome, the republic was doomed.

Sulla's real political heirs were Pompey and Julius Caesar, with at least Caesar realizing that the days of the old republican constitution were numbered. Pompey, a man of boundless ambition, began his career as one of Sulla's lieutenants. After his army put down a rebellion in Spain, he himself threatened to rebel unless the senate allowed him to run for consul. He and another ambitious politician, Crassus, pooled political resources, and both won the consulship. They dominated Roman politics until the rise of Julius Caesar, who became consul in 59 B.C. Together the three concluded a political alliance, the First Triumvirate, in which they agreed to advance one another's interests.

The man who cast the longest shadow over these troubled years was Julius Caesar (100–44 B.C.). More than a mere soldier, Caesar was a cultivated man. Born of a noble family, he received an excellent education, which he furthered by studying in Greece with some of the most eminent teachers of the day. He had serious intellectual interests, and his literary ability was immense. Caesar was a superb orator, and his affable personality and wit made him popular. He was also a shrewd politician of unbridled ambition. Since military service was an effective steppingstone to politics, Caesar launched his military career in Spain, where his courage won the respect and affection of his troops. Personally brave and tireless, Caesar was a

✤ **Julius Caesar** This realistic bust of Caesar captures all of the power, intensity, and brilliance of the man. It is a study of determination and an excellent example of Roman portraiture. *(Source: National Archaeological Museum, Naples/Alinari/Art Resource, NY)*

military genius who knew how to win battles and turn victories into permanent gains.

In 58 B.C. Caesar became governor of Cisalpine Gaul, or modern northern Italy. By 50 B.C. he had conquered all of Gaul, or modern France. Caesar's account of his operations, his *Commentaries* on the Gallic wars, became a classic in Western literature and most schoolchildren's introduction to Latin. By 49 B.C. the First Triumvirate had fallen apart. Crassus had died in battle, and Caesar and Pompey, each suspecting the other of treachery, came to blows. The result was a long and bloody civil war that raged from Spain to Greece and across northern Africa to Egypt. Although Pompey enjoyed the official support of the government, Caesar finally defeated Pompey's forces in 45 B.C. He had overthrown the republic and made himself dictator.

Julius Caesar was not merely another victorious general. Politically brilliant, he was determined to make basic reforms, even at the expense of the old constitution. He took the first long step to break down the barriers between Italy and the provinces, extending citizenship to many of the provincials who had supported him. Caesar also took measures to cope with Rome's burgeoning population. By Caesar's day perhaps 750,000 people lived in Rome. Caesar drew up plans to send his veterans and some 80,000 of the poor and unemployed to colonies throughout the Mediterranean. He founded at least twenty colonies, most of which were located in Gaul, Spain, and North Africa. These colonies were important agents in spreading Roman culture in the western Mediterranean. A Roman empire composed of citizens, not subjects, was the result.

In 44 B.C. a group of conspirators assassinated Caesar and set off another round of civil war. Caesar had named his eighteen-year-old grandnephew, Octavian as his heir. Octavian joined forces with two of Caesar's lieutenants, Marc Antony and Lepidus, in a pact known as the Second Triumvirate, and together they hunted down and defeated Caesar's murderers. In the process, however, Octavian and Antony came into conflict. Antony, "boastful, arrogant, and full of empty exultation and capricious ambition," proved to be the major threat to Octavian's designs.[8] In 33 B.C., Octavian branded Antony a traitor and rebel. Octavian painted lurid pictures of Antony lingering in the eastern Mediterranean, a romantic and foolish captive of the seductive Cleopatra, queen of Egypt and bitter enemy of Rome. In 31 B.C., with the might of Rome at his back, Octavian met and defeated the army and navy of Antony and Cleopatra at the Battle of Actium in Greece. Octavian's victory put an end to an age of civil war that had lasted since the days of Sulla. In 27 B.C. the senate voted Octavian the name *Augustus* for his success in having ended the civil war. Ever since that day he has been known to history as Augustus.

SUMMARY

The rise of Rome to greatness resulted from many factors. At the outset the geographical position of Rome put it on good, natural lines of communication within Italy. The Italian peninsula itself was generally fertile, and the mountains did not prevent political unification. The Etruscans transformed the Roman settlements into a city. Once free of the Etruscans, the Romans used their political organization, their prosperity, and their population to conquer their neighbors. Yet instead of enslaving them, the Romans extended citizenship to the conquered. Having united Italy under them, the Romans became a major power that looked to the broader Mediterranean world. In a succession of wars with Carthage, in Spain, and in the Hellenistic East, Rome won an empire. These conquests not only prompted the Romans to invent a system to administer the empire but also brought them into the mainstream of Hellenistic civilization. The wealth derived from the empire meant that life for many Romans became richer. But there was also a dark side to these developments. Personal ambition, as well as defects in the Roman system of government, led some ambitious leaders to seize unprecedented power. Others resisted, throwing the republic into a series of civil wars. Finally, Caesar and his grandnephew Octavian restored order, but in the process the Roman republic had become a monarchy.

NOTES

1. Polybius, *The Histories* 1.1.5. John Buckler is the translator of all uncited quotations from a foreign language in Chapters 1–6.
2. Mark Twain, *The Innocents Abroad* (New York: Signet Classics, 1966), p. 176.
3. Livy, *History of Rome* Preface 6.
4. Sallust, *War with Catiline* 10.1–3.
5. Ovid, *Fasti* 2.535–539.
6. Ibid., 3.525–542.
7. Plutarch, *Life of Tiberius Gracchus* 9.5–6.
8. Plutarch, *Life of Antony* 2.8.

SUGGESTED READING

H. H. Scullard covers much of Roman history in a series of books: *The Etruscan Cities and Rome* (1967), *A History of the Roman World, 753–146 B.C.,* 4th ed. (1993), and *From the Gracchi to Nero,* 5th ed. (1982). R. T. Ridley, *The History of Rome* (1989), is an undogmatic history of Rome, firmly based in the sources. A. E. Astin, ed., *The Cambridge Ancient History,* 2d ed., vol. 7 (1988), discusses the rise of Rome and its relations with other Mediterranean powers. The Etruscans have inspired a great deal of work, most notably M. Pallottino, *A History of Earliest Italy* (1991), which treats the entire period of early relations among peoples; and R. M. Ogilvie, *Early Rome and the Etruscans* (1976), an excellent account of Rome's early relations with those people from the north. K. Christ, *The Romans* (English trans., 1984), is a general treatment by one of Germany's finest historians. E. Gabba, *Dionysius and the History of Archaic Rome* (1991), is the study by an eminent scholar of the origins of Rome. J. E. Stambaugh, *The Ancient Roman City* (1988), gives a full account of the topography of Rome and its institutions. E. T. Salmon, *The Making of Roman Italy* (1982), analyzes Roman expansion and its implications for Italy. Roman expansion is also the subject of J. Heurgon, *The Rise of Rome to 264 B.C.* (English trans., 1973); R. M. Errington, *The Dawn of Empire* (1971); and W. V. Harris, *War and Imperialism in Republican Rome 327–70 B.C.* (1979). J. F. Lazenby, *Hannibal's War: A Military History of the Second Punic War* (1978), is a detailed treatment of one of Rome's greatest struggles. More general and encompassing is E. Gabba, *Republican Rome, the Army, and the Allies* (English trans., 1976). One of the best studies of Rome's political evolution is the classic by A. N. Sherwin-White, *The Roman Citizenship,* 2d ed. (1973), a work of enduring value. J. F. Gardner, *Being a Roman Citizen* (1993), is a broad work that includes material on ex-slaves, the lower classes, and much else. While S. L. Dyson, *The Creation of the Roman Frontier* (1985), deals with the process by which the Romans established their frontiers, two other works concentrate on Rome's penetration of the Hellenistic East: A. N. Sherwin-White, *Roman Foreign Policy in the Near East* (1984), and the far better but longer book by E. S. Gruen, *The Hellenistic World and the Coming of Rome,* 2 vols. (1984). A. Keaveney, *Rome and the Unification of Italy* (1988), treats the way in which the Romans put down the revolt of their Italian allies and then integrated them into the Roman political system. See also E. S. Gruen, *Culture and National Identity in Republican Rome* (1992).

The great figures and events of the late republic have been the object of much work. E. S. Gruen, *The Last Generation of the Roman Republic* (1974), treats the period as a whole. Very important are the studies of E. Badian, *Roman Imperialism in the Late Republic* (1968) and *Publicans and Sinners* (1972). R. Syme, *The Roman Revolution,* rev. ed. (1952), is a classic. Valuable also are P. A. Brunt, *Social Conflicts in the Roman Republic* (1971); A. W. Lintott, *Violence in the*

Roman Republic (1968); and J. K. Evans, *War, Women and Children in Ancient Rome* (1991).

Many works deal with individual Romans who left their mark on this period. H. C. Boren, *The Gracchi* (1968), treats the work of the two brothers, and A. M. Eckstein's *Senate and Generals* (1987) discusses how the decisions of individual generals affected both the senate and Roman foreign relations. A. Keaveney, *Sulla: The Last Republican* (1983), is a study of a man who thought of himself as a reformer. A. E. Astin has produced two works that are far more extensive than their titles indicate: *Scipio Aemilianus* (1967) and *Cato the Censor* (1978). J. Leach, *Pompey the Great* (1978), surveys the career of this politician, and B. Rawson, *The Politics of Friendship: Pompey and Cicero* (1978), treats both figures in their political environment. M. Gelzer, *Caesar, Politician and Statesman* (English trans., 1968), is easily the best study of one of history's most significant figures. N. Wood, *Cicero's Social and Political Thought* (1991), is an original study of Cicero's thought about the Rome of his day. E. G. Huzar, *Marc Antony* (1987), offers a new assessment of the career of the man who challenged Octavian for control of the Roman world. Caesar's one-time colleague Marcus Crassus is studied in B. A. Marshall, *Crassus: A Political Biography* (1976), and A. Ward, *Marcus Crassus and the Late Roman Republic* (1977). R. S. Weigel, *Lepidus* (1992), covers the career of the third of the Second Triumvirs.

K. D. White, *Roman Farming* (1970), deals with agriculture. Greek cultural influence on Roman life is the subject of A. Wardman, *Rome's Debt to Greece* (1976). F. Schulz, *Classical Roman Law* (1951), is a useful introduction to an important topic. H. H. Scullard, *Festivals and Ceremonies of the Roman Republic* (1981), gives a fresh look at religious practices. Work on Roman social history has advanced in several areas. G. Alfoeldy, a major scholar, has written *The Social History of Rome* (1985), an ambitious undertaking. D. S. Levene, *Religion in Livy* (1993), traces the influence of religion on the foremost historian of Rome. S. Dixon, *The Roman Mother* (1988), focuses specifically on women's role as mothers within the Roman family. A wealth of other research on the Roman family and related topics has recently appeared, including K. R. Bradley, *Discovering the Roman Family* (1990), a series of essays on Roman social history; S. Dixon, *The Roman Family* (1992); S. Treggiari, *Roman Marriage* (1991); and R. A. Baumann, *Women and Politics in Ancient Rome* (1992). A novel work is E. Eyben, *Restless Youth in Ancient Rome* (1993), which explores the mores of youth of the upper class.

Popular Roman Views of Religion and Magic

Magic and enchantment have been constant factors wherever people have lived. Rome was no exception. A common aspect of Roman popular culture was the curse tablet. When people were particularly angry with others, they often went to professional sorcerers, who listened to their clients' complaints. Then they wrote the clients' curses on thin lead tablets and wrapped them around nails. The curses were considered binding, and the various gods invoked were expected to carry them out. In return, the gods received payment for having inflicted the curse.

Often people called down the wrath of the gods on troublesome neighbors or commercial rivals. Many other tablets involved love gone wrong. The first of the following three examples is one of them. For reasons that are left unstated, a woman calls down all sorts of catastrophes on her husband or lover, Plotius. The aggrieved party in this case makes it dramatically clear what she expects from Proserpina, the wife of Pluto, both gods of the underworld. The woman includes in her curse Cerberus, the hound that guarded the gates of Hades. We do not know the fate of her lover.

O wife of Pluto, good and beautiful Proserpina (unless I ought to call you Salvia), pray tear away from Plotius health, body, complexion, strength, faculties. Consign him to Pluto your husband. May he be unable to avoid this by devices of his. Consign that man to the fourth-day, the third-day, the every-day fever [malaria]. May they wrestle and wrestle it out with him, overcome and overwhelm him unceasingly until they tear away his life. So I consign him as victim to you Proserpina, unless, O Proserpina, unless I ought to call you Goddess of the Lower World. Send, I pray,

someone to call up the three-headed dog [Cerberus] with request that he may tear out Plotius' heart. Promise Cerberus that you will give him three offerings—dates, dried figs, and a black pig—if he has fulfilled his task before the month of March. All these, Proserpina Salvia, will I give you when you have made me master of my wish. I give you the head of Plotius, slave of Avonia. O Proserpina Salvia, I give you Plotius' forehead, Proserpina Salvia, I give you Plotius' eyebrows, Proserpina Salvia, I give you Plotius' eyelids. Proserpina Salvia, I give you Plotius' eye-pupils. Proserpina Salvia, I give you Plotius' nostrils, his ears, nose, and his tongue and teeth so that Plotius may not be able to utter what it is that gives him pain; his neck, shoulders, arms, fingers, so that he may not be able to help himself at all; his chest, liver, heart, lungs, so that he may not be able to feel what gives him pain; his abdomen, belly, navel, sides, so that he may not be able to sleep; his shoulder-blades, so that he may not be able to sleep well; his sacred part, so that he may not be able to make water; his buttocks, vent, thighs, knees, legs, shins, feet, ankles, soles, toes, nails, that he may not be able to stand by his own aid. Should there so exist any written curse, great or small—in what manner Plotius has, according to the laws of magic, composed any curse and entrusted it to writing, in such manner I consign, hand over to you, so that you may consign and hand over that fellow, in the month of February. Blast him! damn him! blast him utterly! Hand him over, consign him, that he may not be able to behold, see, and contemplate any month further!

Curses and enchantments were not limited to love affairs. The following one concerns the next day's chariot race in Rome. The person invoking the curse was certainly not betting on Eucherius the charioteer and his horses.

I conjure you up, holy beings and holy names; join in aiding this spell, and bind, enchant, thwart, strike, overturn, conspire against, destroy, kill, break, Eucherius, the charioteer, and all his horses tomorrow in the circus at Rome. May he not leave the barriers well; may he not be quick in the contest; may he not outstrip anyone; may he not make the turns well; may he not win any prizes; and if he has pressed someone hard, may he not come off the victor; and if he follows someone from behind, may he not overtake him; but may he meet with an accident; may he be bound; may he be broken; may he be dragged along by your power, in the morning and afternoon races. Now! Now! Quickly! Quickly!

The next curse is that of an outraged person who was the victim of a thief. The person calls on Hermes and other deities to catch the thief. The text is filled with many unintelligible words—"mumbo jumbo"—which supposedly have magical powers.

I call you, Hermes, immortal god, who cuts a furrow down Olympus, and who [presides over] the sacred boat, O light-bringer Iao, the great ever-living, terrible to behold and terrible to hear, give up the thief whom I seek. Aberamentho oulerthe xenax sonelueothenemareba. This spell is to be said twice at the purification. The spell of bread and cheese. Come to me, lisson maternamau, erte, preptektioun, intiki, ous, olokotous, periklusai, bring to me that which is lost, and make the thief manifest on this very day. And I invoke Hermes, the discoverer of thieves, and the sun and the eye-pupils of the sun, the two bringers-to-light of unlawful deeds, and Justice, and Errinys, and Ammon, and Parammon, to seize the throat of the thief and to manifest him this very day, at the present hour. The ceremony: the same spell [as that] pronounced at the purification. Take a flush-green vessel and put water in it and myrrh, and the herb cynocephalium, and dipping in it a branch of laurel, sprinkling each person with the water, take a tripod and place it upon an altar of earth. . . . Offer myrrh and frankincense and a frog's tongue, and taking some unsalted winter wheat and goat's cheese, give

✣ Curse tablet from the Roman temple at Uley in Gloucestershire, England. *(Source: Courtesy of the Trustees of the British Museum)*

these to each, pronouncing the spell at length. "Lord Iao, light-bearer, give up the thief whom I seek." And if any of them does not swallow what was given him, that one is the thief.

Questions for Analysis

1. Given the many forms of curses and the common use of these tablets, what social functions did such curse tablets serve in Roman society?

2. Since Romans resorted to these curses, does it mean that they considered magic more powerful than formal religion? Why or why not?

3. What do the tablets tell us about the common culture of the Romans?

Source: Slightly adapted from N. Lewis and M. Reinhold, *Roman Civilization,* 2 vols. (New York: Harper and Row, 1966), vol. 1, pp. 479–480; vol. 2, pp. 569–570.

6

The Pax Romana

✤✤ Had the Romans conquered the entire Mediterranean world only to turn it into their battlefield? Would they, like the Greeks before them, become their own worst enemies, destroying one another and wasting their strength until they perished? At Julius Caesar's death in 44 B.C. it must have seemed so to many. Yet finally, in 31 B.C., Augustus restored peace to a tortured world, and with peace came prosperity, new hope, and a new vision of Rome's destiny. The Roman poet Virgil expressed this vision most nobly:

You, Roman, remember—these are your arts:
To rule nations, and to impose the ways of peace,
To spare the humble and to war down the proud.[1]

In place of the republic, Augustus established what can be called a constitutional monarchy. He attempted to achieve lasting cooperation in government and balance among the people, magistrates, senate, and army. His efforts were not always successful. His settlement of Roman affairs did not permanently end civil war. Yet he carried on Caesar's work. It was Augustus who created the structure that the modern world calls the "Roman Empire." He did his work so well and his successors so capably added to it that Rome realized Virgil's hope. For the first and second centuries A.D. the lot of the Mediterranean world was the Roman peace—the *pax Romana,* a period of security, order, harmony, flourishing culture, and expanding economy. It was a period that saw the wilds of Gaul, Spain, Germany, and eastern Europe introduced to Greco-Roman culture. By the third century A.D., when the empire began to give way to the medieval world, the greatness of Rome and its culture had left an indelible mark on the ages to come.

❖ ❖ ❖ ❖ ❖ ❖ ❖ ❖

A Roman road in Timgad, ca. A.D. 100. *(Source: Adam Woolfitt/ Robert Harding Picture Library)*

• How did the Roman emperors govern the empire, and how did they spread Roman influence into northern Europe?

161

- What were the fruits of the pax Romana?

- Why did Christianity, originally a minor local religion, sweep across the Roman world to change it fundamentally?

- Finally, how did the Roman Empire meet the grim challenge of barbarian invasion and subsequent economic decline?

These are the main questions we will consider in this chapter.

✦ AUGUSTUS'S SETTLEMENT (31 B.C.–A.D. 14)

When Augustus put an end to the civil wars that had raged since 83 B.C., he faced monumental problems of reconstruction. Sole ruler of the entire Mediterranean world as no Roman had ever been before, he had a rare opportunity to shape the future. But how?

Augustus could easily have declared himself dictator, as Caesar had, but the thought was repugnant to him. Augustus was neither an autocrat nor a revolutionary. His solution, as he put it, was to restore the republic. But was that possible? Some eighteen years of anarchy and civil war had shattered the republican constitution. It could not be rebuilt in a day. Augustus recognized these problems but did not let them stop him. From 29 to 23 B.C., he toiled to heal Rome's wounds. The first problem facing him was to rebuild the constitution and the organs of government. Next he had to demobilize much of the army and care for the welfare of the provinces. Then he had to meet the danger of barbarians at Rome's European frontiers. Augustus was highly successful in meeting these challenges. His gift of peace to a war-torn world sowed the seeds of a literary flowering that produced some of the finest fruits of the Roman mind.

The Principate and the Restored Republic

Augustus claimed that in restoring constitutional government he was also restoring the republic. Typically Roman, he preferred not to create anything new; he intended instead to modify republican forms and offices to meet new circumstances. Augustus planned for the senate to take on a serious burden of duty and responsibility. He expected it to administer some of the provinces, continue to be the chief deliberative body of the state, and act as a court of law. Yet he did not give the senate enough power to become his partner in government. As a result, the senate could not live up to the responsibilities that Augustus assigned. Many of its prerogatives shifted to Augustus and his successors by default.

Augustus's own position in the restored republic was something of an anomaly. He could not simply surrender the reins of power, for someone else would only have seized them. But how was he to fit into a republican constitution? Again Augustus had his own answer. He became *princeps civitatis,* the "First Citizen of the State." This prestigious title carried no power; it indicated only that Augustus was the most distinguished of all Roman citizens. In effect, it designated Augustus as the first among equals, a little "more equal" than anyone else in the state. His real power resided in the magistracies he held, in the powers granted him by the senate, and above all in his control of the army, which he turned into a permanent, standing organization. Clearly, much of the *principate,* as the position of First Citizen is known, was a legal fiction. Yet that need not imply that Augustus, like a modern dictator, tried to clothe himself with constitutional legitimacy. In an inscription known as *Res Gestae (The Deeds of Augustus),* Augustus described his constitutional position:

In my sixth and seventh consulships [28–27 B.C.], I had ended the civil war, having obtained through universal consent total control of affairs. I transferred the Republic from my power to the authority of the Roman people and the senate. . . . After that time I stood before all in rank, but I had power no greater than those who were my colleagues in any magistracy.[2]

What is to be made of Augustus's constitutional settlement? Despite his claims to the contrary, Augustus had not restored the republic. Augustus had created a constitutional monarchy, something completely new in Roman history. The title *princeps,* First Citizen, came to mean in Rome, as it does today, "prince" in the sense of a sovereign ruler.

Augustus was not exactly being a hypocrite, but he carefully kept his real military power in the background. As consul he had no more constitutional and legal power than his fellow consul. Yet in addition to the consulship Augustus held many other magistracies, which his fellow consul did not. Constitutionally, his ascendancy within the state stemmed from the number of magistracies he held and the power granted him by the senate. At first he held the consulship annually; then the senate voted him proconsular power on a regular basis. The senate also voted him *tribunicia potestas*—the "full power of the tribunes." Tribunician power gave Augustus the right to call the senate into session, present legislation to the people, and defend their rights. He held either high office or the powers of chief magistrate year in and year out. No other magistrate could do the same. In 12 B.C. he became pontifex maximus, the chief priest of the state. By assuming this position of great honor, Augustus became chief religious official in the state. Without specifically saying so, he had created the office of emperor, which included many traditional powers separated from their traditional offices.

The main source of Augustus's power was his position as commander of the Roman army. His title *imperator,* with which Rome customarily honored a general after a major victory, came to mean "emperor" in the modern sense of the term. Augustus governed the provinces where troops were needed for defense. The frontiers were his special concern. There, Roman legionaries held the German barbarians at arm's length. The frontiers were also areas where fighting could be expected to break out. Augustus made sure that Rome went to war only at his command. He controlled deployment of the Roman army and paid its wages. He granted it bonuses and gave veterans retirement benefits. Thus he avoided the problems with the army that the old senate had created for itself. Augustus never shared control of the army, and no Roman found it easy to defy him militarily.

Augustus made a momentous change in the army by making it a permanent, professional force. This was Rome's first standing army. Soldiers received regular and standard training under career officers who advanced in rank according to experience, ability, valor, and length of service. Legions were transfered from place to place, as the need arose. They had no regular barracks. In that respect they were like American army divisions. In later years soldiers could live with their families in the camps themselves. By making the army professional, Augustus forged a reliable tool for the defense of the empire. The army could also act against the central authority, much as Marius's army had earlier. Yet the mere fact that men could make a career of the army meant that the army

❖ **Augustus as Imperator** Here Augustus, dressed in breastplate and uniform, emphasizes the imperial majesty of Rome and his role as *imperator.* The figures on his breastplate represent the restoration of peace, one of Augustus's greatest accomplishments and certainly one that he frequently stressed. (*Source: Alinari/Art Resource, NY*)

became a recognized institution of government and that its soldiers had the opportunity to achieve a military effectiveness superior to that of most of its enemies.

The very size of the army was a special problem for Augustus. Rome's legions numbered thousands of men, far more than were necessary to maintain peace. What was Augustus to do with so many soldiers? This sort of problem had constantly plagued the late republic, whose leaders never found a solution. Augustus gave his own answer in the *Res Gestae:* "I founded colonies of soldiers in

Africa, Sicily, Macedonia, Spain, Achaea, Gaul, and Pisidia. Moreover, Italy has 28 colonies under my auspices."[3] At least forty new colonies arose, most of them in the western Mediterranean. Augustus's veterans took abroad with them their Roman language and culture. His colonies, like Julius Caesar's, were a significant tool in the spread of Roman culture throughout the West.

Roman colonies were very different from earlier Greek colonies. Greek colonies were independent. Once founded, they went their own way. Roman colonies were part of a system—the Roman Empire—that linked East with West in a mighty political, social, and economic network. The glory of the Roman Empire was its great success in uniting the Mediterranean world and spreading Greco-Roman culture throughout it. Roman colonies played a crucial part in that process, and Augustus deservedly boasted of the colonies he founded.

Augustus, however, also failed to solve a momentous problem. He never found a way to institutionalize his position with the army. The ties between the princeps and the army were always personal. The army was loyal to the princeps but not necessarily to the state. The Augustan principate worked well at first, but by the third century A.D. the army would make and break emperors at will. Nonetheless, it is a measure of Augustus's success that his settlement survived as long and as well as it did.

Augustus's Administration of the Provinces

To gain an accurate idea of the total population of the empire, Augustus ordered a census to be taken in 28 B.C. In Augustus's day the population of the Roman Empire was between 70 and 100 million people, fully 75 percent of whom lived in the provinces. In the areas under his immediate jurisdiction, Augustus put provincial administration on an ordered basis and improved its functioning. Believing that the cities of the empire should look after their own affairs, he encouraged local self-government and urbanism. Augustus respected local customs and ordered his governors to do the same.

As a spiritual bond between the provinces and Rome, Augustus encouraged the cult of Roma, goddess and guardian of the state. In the Hellenistic East, where king-worship was an established custom, the cult of *Roma et Augustus* grew and spread rapidly. Augustus then introduced it in the West. By the time of his death in A.D. 14, nearly every province in the empire could boast an altar or shrine to *Roma et Augustus*. In the West it was not the person of the emperor who was worshiped but his *genius*—his guardian spirit. In praying for

❖ **The Gemma Augustea** This cameo represents Augustus being crowned by the gods. Next to him sits Roma, who looks on approvingly. To Roma's right stands a soldier, who symbolizes the army's defense of the empire. At the far left is a triumphal chariot to celebrate Augustus's achievement of bringing peace to the empire. (*Source: Kunsthistorisches Museum, Vienna*)

the good health and welfare of the emperor, Romans and provincials were praying for the empire itself. The cult became a symbol of Roman unity.

Roman Expansion into Northern and Western Europe

For the history of Western civilization one of the most momentous aspects of Augustus's reign was Roman expansion into the wilderness of northern and western Europe (Map 6.1). In this respect Augustus was following in Julius Caesar's footsteps. Carrying on Ceasar's work, Augustus pushed Rome's frontier into the region of modern Germany.

Augustus began his work in the west and north by completing the conquest of Spain. In Gaul, apart from minor campaigns, most of his work was peaceful. He founded twelve new towns, and the Roman road system linked new settlements with one another and with Italy. But the German frontier, along the Rhine River, was the scene of hard fighting. In 12 B.C. Augustus ordered a major invasion of Germany beyond the Rhine. Roman legions advanced to the Elbe River, and a Roman fleet explored the North Sea and Jutland. The area north of the Main River and west of the Elbe was on the point of becoming Roman. But in 9 A.D. Augustus's general Varus lost some twenty thousand troops at the Battle of the Teutoburger Forest. Thereafter the Rhine remained the Roman frontier.

Meanwhile, more successful generals extended the Roman standards as far as the Danube. Roman legions penetrated the area of modern Austria, southern Bavaria, and western Hungary. The regions of modern Serbia, Bulgaria, and Romania fell. Within this area the legionaries built fortified camps. Roads linked these camps with one another, and settlements grew up around the camps. Traders began to frequent the frontier and to traffic with the barbarians. Thus Roman culture—the rough-and-ready kind found in military camps—gradually spread into the northern wilderness.

One excellent example of this process comes from the modern French city of Lyons. The site was originally the capital of a native tribe; and after his conquest of Gaul, Caesar made it a Roman military settlement. Augustus took an important step toward romanization and conciliation in 12 B.C., when he made it a political and religious center, with responsibilities for administering the

❖ **Bronze Cock** This realistic statuette of a common barnyard bird was found in the waters of the Rhone river, near modern Lyons, France. It shows at a glance how well the Romanized Gauls had mastered Roman artistic techniques. *(Source: Erich Lessing/Art Resource, NY)*

area and for honoring the gods of the Romans and Gauls. Physical symbols of this fusion of two cultures can still be seen today. For instance, the extensive remains of the amphitheater and other buildings at Lyons testify to the fact that the Gallo-Roman city was prosperous enough to afford expensive Roman buildings and the style of life that they represented. Second, the buildings show that the local population appreciated Roman culture and did not find it alien. At Lyons, as at many other of these new cities, there emerged a culture that was both Roman and native.

Although Lyons is typical of the success of romanization in new areas, the arrival of the Romans often provoked resistance from barbarian tribes that simply wanted to be left alone. In other cases, the prosperity and wealth of the new Roman towns lured barbarians eager for plunder. The Romans maintained peaceful relations with the barbarians whenever possible, but Roman legions remained

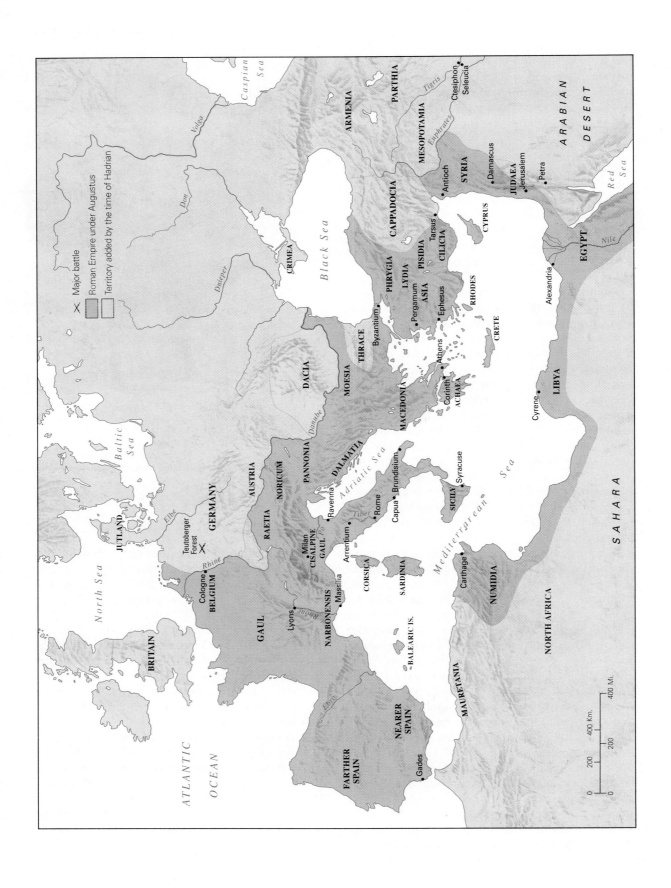

Caspian Sea

Volga

Don

Dnieper

Black Sea

CRIMEA

ARMENIA

PARTHIA

Tigris

MESOPOTAMIA

Ctesiphon
Seleucia

Euphrates

CAPPADOCIA

SYRIA
Antioch
Damascus

ARABIAN DESERT

JUDAEA
Jerusalem
Petra

Red Sea

Tarsus
CILICIA
PISIDIA
LYDIA
ASIA
Ephesus
Pergamum
PHRYGIA

CYPRUS

RHODES

EGYPT

Nile

Alexandria

THRACE
Byzantium

CRETE

LIBYA

Cyrene

DACIA

MOESIA

MACEDONIA

Athens
Corinth
ACHAEA

AUSTRIA

PANNONIA

NORICUM

DALMATIA

Adriatic Sea

Ravenna

RAETIA

GERMANY

Elbe

Teutoberger Forest ✗

JUTLAND

Baltic Sea

North Sea

Rhine

Cologne
BELGIUM

Milan
CISALPINE
GAUL
Po

Rome
Tiber

Arrentium

Capua
Brundisium

Syracuse
SICILY

Mediterranean Sea

Carthage

NUMIDIA

NORTH AFRICA

SAHARA

CORSICA

SARDINIA

Massilia
NARBONENSIS

GAUL

Lyons
Rhône

Saône

BRITAIN

ATLANTIC OCEAN

BALEARIC IS.

MAURETANIA

FARTHER SPAIN

NEARER SPAIN

Ebro

Gades

Major battle ✗
Roman Empire under Augustus
Territory added by the time of Hadrian

400 Mi.
400 Km.
200
200
0
0

on the frontier to repel hostile barbarians. The result was the evolution of a consistent, systematic frontier policy.

Literary Flowering

The Augustan settlement's gift of peace inspired a literary flowering unparalleled in Roman history. With good reason this period is known as the golden age of Latin literature. Augustus and many of his friends actively encouraged poets and writers. Horace, one of Rome's finest poets, offered his own opinion of Augustus and his era:

With Caesar [Augustus] the guardian of the state
Not civil rage nor violence shall drive out peace,
Nor wrath which forges swords
And turns unhappy cities against each other.[4]

These lines are not empty flattery, despite Augustus's support of many contemporary Latin writers. To a generation that had known only vicious civil war, Augustus's settlement was an unbelievable blessing.

The tone and ideal of Roman literature, like that of the Greeks, was humanistic and worldly. Roman poets and prose writers celebrated the dignity of humanity and the range of its accomplishments. They stressed the physical and emotional joys of a comfortable, peaceful life. Their works were highly polished, elegant in style, and intellectual in conception. Roman poets referred to the gods often and treated mythological themes, but always the core of their work was human, not divine.

Virgil (70–19 B.C.), Rome's greatest poet, celebrated the new age in the *Georgics,* a poetic work on agriculture in four books. Virgil delighted in his own farm, and his poems sing of the pleasures of peaceful farm life. The poet also tells how to keep bees, grow grapes and olives, plow, and manage a farm. Throughout the *Georgics* Virgil wrote about things he himself had seen, rather than drawing from the writings of others. Virgil could be vivid

❖ **Virgil and** *The Aeneid*   Virgil's great epic poem, *The Aeneid,* became a literary classic immediately on its appearance and has lost none of its power since. The Roman world honored Virgil for his poetic genius not only by treasuring his work but also by portraying him in art. Here two muses, who inspired artists, flank the poet while he writes his epic poem. *(Source: C. M. Dixon)*

and graphic as well as pastoral. Even a small event could be a drama for him. The death of a bull while plowing is hardly epic material, yet Virgil captures the sadness of the event in the image of the farmer unyoking the remaining animal:

Look, the bull, shining under the rough plough,
falls to the ground
and vomits from his mouth blood mixed with foam,
and releases his dying groan.
Sadly moves the ploughman, unharnessing the
young steer grieving for the death of his brother
and leaves in the middle of the job
the plough stuck fast.[5]

Virgil's poetry is robust yet graceful. A sensitive man who delighted in simple things, Virgil left in his *Georgics* a charming picture of life in the Italian countryside during a period of peace.

Virgil's masterpiece is the *Aeneid,* an epic poem that is the Latin equivalent of the Greek *Iliad* and

❖ **MAP 6.1 Roman Expansion Under the Empire**   Following Roman expansion during the Republic, Augustus added vast tracts of Europe to the Roman Empire, which the emperor Hadrian later enlarged by assuming control over parts of central Europe, the Near East, and North Africa.

Odyssey. In the *Aeneid* Virgil expressed his admiration for Augustus's work by celebrating the shining ideal of a world blessed by the pax Romana. Virgil's account of the founding of Rome and the early years of the city gave final form to the legend of Aeneas, the Trojan hero who escaped to Italy at the fall of Troy. The principal Roman tradition held that Romulus was the founder of Rome, but the legend of Aeneas was known as early as the fifth century B.C. Virgil linked the legends of Aeneas and Romulus and preserved them both; in so doing, he connected Rome with Greece's heroic past. He also mythologized later aspects of Roman history. Recounting the story of Aeneas and Dido, the queen of Carthage, Virgil made their ill-fated love affair the cause of the Punic wars. But, above all, the *Aeneid* is the expression of Virgil's passionate belief in Rome's greatness. It is a vision of Rome as the protector of the good and noble against the forces of darkness and disruption.

The poet Ovid shared Virgil's views of the simple pleasures of life and also celebrated the popular culture of the day. In his *Fasti* (ca A.D. 8) he takes a personal approach to discuss and explain the ordinary festivals of the Roman year, festivals that most Romans took for granted. Without his work the modern world would be much the poorer in its knowledge of the popular religion of imperial Rome. For instance, he tells his readers that on a journey to Rome he encountered a white-robed crowd in the middle of the road. A priest and farmers were performing an annual festival. Ovid stopped to ask the priest what was happening. The priest explained that they were sacrificing to Mildew, not a farmer's favorite goddess. By burning the offerings the priest and his friends asked the goddess to be so content with them that she would not attack the crops. He further asked her not to attack the farmer's tools but to be satisfied with swords and other weapons of iron. He reminded her that "there is no need for them; the world lives in peace."[6] In his poetry Ovid, like Virgil, celebrated the pax Romana, while giving a rare glimpse of ordinary Roman life.

In its own way Livy's history of Rome, entitled simply *Ab Urbe Condita (From the Founding of the City),* is the prose counterpart of the *Aeneid.* Livy (59 B.C.–A.D. 17) received training in Greek and Latin literature, rhetoric, and philosophy. He even urged the future emperor Claudius to write history. Livy loved and admired the heroes and great deeds of the republic, but he was also a friend of Augustus and a supporter of the principate. He especially approved of Augustus's efforts to restore republican virtues. Livy's history began with the legend of Aeneas and ended with the reign of Augustus. His theme of the republic's greatness fitted admirably with Augustus's program of restoring the republic. Livy's history was colossal, consisting of 142 books, and only a quarter of it still exists. Livy was a sensitive writer and something of a moralist. Like Thucydides, he felt that history should be applied to the present. His history later became one of Rome's legacies to the modern world. During the Renaissance *Ab Urbe Condita* found a warm admirer in the poet Petrarch and left its mark on Machiavelli, who read it avidly.

The poet Horace (65–8 B.C.) rose from humble beginnings to friendship with Augustus. The son of an ex-slave and tax collector, Horace nonetheless received an excellent education. He loved Greek literature and finished his education in Athens. After Augustus's victory he returned to Rome and became Virgil's friend. Horace happily turned his pen to celebrating Rome's newly won peace and prosperity. One of his finest odes commemorates Augustus's victory over Cleopatra at Actium in 31 B.C. Cleopatra is depicted as a frenzied queen, drunk with desire to destroy Rome. Horace saw in Augustus's victory the triumph of West over East, of simplicity over Oriental excess. One of the truly moving aspects of Horace's poetry, like Virgil's and Ovid's, is his deep and abiding gratitude for the pax Romana.

For Rome, Augustus's age was one of hope and new beginnings. Augustus had put the empire on a new foundation. Constitutional monarchy was firmly established, and government was to all appearances a partnership between princeps and senate. The Augustan settlement was a delicate structure, and parts of it would in time be discarded. Nevertheless, it worked, and by building on it later emperors would carry on Augustus's work.

The solidity of Augustus's work became obvious at his death in A.D. 14. Since the principate was not technically an office, Augustus could not legally hand it to a successor. Augustus had recognized this problem and long before his death had found a way to solve it. He shared his consular and tribunician powers with his adopted son, Tiberius, thus grooming him for the principate. In his will Augustus left most of his vast fortune to Tiberius,

✤ **Ara Pacis** This scene from the Ara Pacis, the Altar of Peace, celebrates Augustus's restoration of peace and the fruits of peace. Here Mother Earth is depicted with her children. The cow and the sheep under the goddess represent the prosperity brought by peace, especially the agricultural prosperity so highly cherished by Virgil. *(Source: Art Resource, NY)*

and the senate formally requested Tiberius to assume the burdens of the principate. Formalities apart, Augustus had succeeded in creating a dynasty.

✤ THE COMING OF CHRISTIANITY

During the reign of the emperor Tiberius (A.D. 14–37), perhaps in A.D. 29, Pontius Pilate, prefect of Judaea, the Roman province created out of the Jewish kingdom of Judah, condemned Jesus of Nazareth to death. At the time a minor event, this has become one of the best-known moments in history. How did these two men come to their historic meeting? The question is not idle, for Rome was as important as Judaea to Christianity. Jesus was born in a troubled time, when Roman rule aroused hatred and unrest among the Jews. This climate of hostility affected the lives of all who

lived in Judaea, Roman and Jew alike. It formed the backdrop of Jesus' life, and it had a fundamental impact on his ministry. Without an understanding of this age of anxiety in Judaea, Jesus and his followers cannot fully be appreciated.

Unrest in Judaea

The entry of Rome into Jewish affairs was anything but peaceful. The civil wars that destroyed the republic wasted the prosperity of Judaea and the entire eastern Mediterranean world. Jewish leaders took sides in the fighting, and Judaea suffered its share of ravages and military confiscations. Peace brought little satisfaction to the Jews. Although Augustus treated Judaea generously, the Romans won no popularity by making Herod king of Judaea (ca 73–4 B.C.). King Herod gave Judaea prosperity and security, but the Jews hated his acceptance of Greek culture. He was also a bloodthirsty prince who murdered his own wife and sons. At his death the Jews broke out in revolt. For the next ten years Herod's successor waged almost constant war against the rebels. Added to the horrors of civil war were years of crop failure, which caused famine and plague. Men calling themselves prophets proclaimed the end of the world and the coming of the Messiah, the savior of Israel.

At length the Romans intervened to restore order. Augustus put Judaea under the charge of a prefect answerable directly to the emperor. Religious matters and local affairs became the responsibility of the *Sanhedrin,* the highest Jewish judicial body. Although many prefects tried to perform their duties scrupulously and conscientiously, many others were rapacious and indifferent to Jewish culture. Often acting from fear rather than cruelty, some prefects fiercely stamped out any signs of popular discontent. Pontius Pilate, prefect from A.D. 26 to 36, is typical of such incompetent officials. Although eventually relieved of his duties in disgrace, Pilate brutally put down even innocent demonstrations. Especially hated were the Roman tax collectors, called "publicans," many of whom pitilessly gouged the Jews. *Publicans* and *sinners*— the words became synonymous. Clashes between Roman troops and Jewish guerrillas inflamed the anger of both sides.

In A.D. 40 the emperor Caligula undid part of Augustus's good work by ordering his statue erected in the temple at Jerusalem. The order, though never carried out, further intensified Jewish resentment. Thus the Jews became embittered by Roman rule because of taxes, sometimes unduly harsh enforcement of the law, and misguided religious interference.

Among the Jews two movements spread. First was the rise of the Zealots, extremists who worked and fought to rid Judaea of the Romans. Resolute in their worship of Yahweh, they refused to pay any but the tax levied by the Jewish temple. Their battles with the Roman legionaries were marked by savagery on both sides. As usual, the innocent caught in the middle suffered grievously. As Roman policy grew tougher, even moderate Jews began to hate the conquerors. Judaea came more and more to resemble a tinderbox, ready to burst into flames at a single spark.

The second movement was the growth of militant apocalyptic sentiment—the belief that the coming of the Messiah was near. This belief was an old one among the Jews. But by the first century A.D. it had become more widespread and fervent than ever before. Typical was the Apocalypse of Baruch, which foretold the destruction of the Roman Empire. First would come a period of great tribulation, misery, and injustice. At the worst of the suffering, the Messiah would appear. The Messiah would destroy the Roman legions and all the kingdoms that had ruled Israel. Then the Messiah would inaugurate a period of happiness and plenty for the Jews.

This was no abstract notion among the Jews. As the ravages of war became widespread and conditions worsened, more and more people prophesied the imminent coming of the Messiah. One such was John the Baptist, "the voice of one crying in the wilderness, Prepare ye the way of the lord."[7] Many Jews did just that. The sect described in the Dead Sea Scrolls readied itself for the end of the world. Its members were probably Essenes, and their social organization closely resembled that of early Christians. Members of this group shared possessions, precisely as John the Baptist urged people to do. Yet this sect, unlike the Christians, also made military preparations for the day of the Messiah.

Jewish religious aspirations were only one part of the story. What can be said of the pagan world of Rome and its empire, into which Christianity was shortly to be born? To answer that question one must first explore the spiritual environment of the pagans, many of whom would soon be caught up in the new Christian religion. The term *pagans* refers to all those who believed in the Greco-Roman gods. Paganism at the time of Jesus' birth can be broadly divided into three spheres: the official state religion of Rome, the traditional Roman cults of hearth and countryside, and the new mystery religions that flowed from the Hellenistic East. The official state religion and its cults honored the traditional deities: Jupiter, Juno, Mars, and such newcomers as Isis (see Chapter 4). This very formal religion was conducted on an official level by socially prominent state priests. It was above all a religion of ritual and grand spectacle, but it provided little emotional or spiritual comfort for the people. The state cults were a bond between the gods and the people, a religious contract to ensure the well-being of Rome. Most Romans felt that the official cults must be maintained, despite their lack of spiritual content, simply for the welfare of the state. After all, observance of the traditional official religion had brought Rome victory, empire, security, and wealth.

For emotional and spiritual satisfaction, many Romans observed the old cults of home and countryside, the same cults that had earlier delighted Cato the Elder (see Chapter 5). These traditional cults brought the Romans back in touch with nature and with something elemental to Roman life. Particularly popular were rustic shrines—often a small building or a sacred tree in an enclosure—to honor the native spirit of the locality. Though familiar and simple, even this traditional religion was not enough for many. They wanted something more personal and immediate. Many common people believed in a supernatural world seen dimly through dreams, magic, miracles, and spells. They wanted some sort of revelation about this supernatural world and security in it after death. Some people turned to astrology in the belief that they could read their destiny in the stars. But that was cold comfort, since they could not change what the stars foretold.

Many people in the Roman Empire found the answer to their need for emotionally satisfying religion and spiritual security in the various Hellenistic mystery cults. Such cults generally provided their adherents with an emotional outlet. For example, the cult of Bacchus was marked by wine drinking and often by drunken frenzy. The cult of the Great Mother, Cybele, was celebrated with emotional and even overwrought processions, and it offered its worshipers the promise of immortality. The appeal of the mystery religions was not simply that they provided emotional release. They gave their adherents what neither the traditional cults nor philosophy could—above all, security. Yet the mystery religions were by nature exclusive, and none was truly international, open to everyone.

The Life and Teachings of Jesus

Into this climate of Roman religious yearning, political severity, fanatical Zealotry, and messianic hope came Jesus of Nazareth (ca 5 B.C.–A.D. 29). He was raised in Galilee, stronghold of the Zealots. Yet Jesus himself was a man of peace. Jesus urged his listeners to love God as their father and one another as God's children. The kingdom that he preached was no earthly one, but one of eternal happiness in a life after death. Jesus' teachings are strikingly similar to those of Hillel (30 B.C.–A.D. 9), a rabbi and interpreter of the Scriptures who had also spread the message of devotion to God and love of other people.

Jesus' teachings were Jewish. He declared that he would change not one jot of the Jewish law. His orthodoxy enabled him to preach in the synagogue and the temple. His major deviation from orthodoxy was his insistence that he taught in his own name, not in the name of Yahweh. Was he then the Messiah? A small band of followers thought so, and Jesus claimed that he was. Yet Jesus had his own conception of the Messiah. Unlike the Messiah of the Apocalypse of Baruch, Jesus would not destroy the Roman Empire. He told his disciples flatly that they were to "render unto Caesar the things that are Caesar's." Jesus would establish a spiritual kingdom, not an earthly one. Repeatedly he told his disciples that his kingdom was "not of this world."

It is probably impossible to reconstruct the life of the historical Jesus. Much recent work has emphasized his human side and denied his divinity. This line of research studies him as a Jewish peasant in the Mediterranean context of the Roman Empire. Other scholars insist on the elements of mythology that surround his life. Still others go so far as to deny his very existence. There is, however, enough non-Christian evidence to indicate that Jesus lived, which to that extent supports the testimony of the Christian gospels, the accounts of Jesus' life and teachings found in the New Testament.

Of Jesus' life and teachings the prefect Pontius Pilate knew little and cared even less. All that concerned him was the maintenance of peace and order. The crowds following Jesus at the time of the Passover, a highly emotional time in the Jewish year, alarmed Pilate, who faced a volatile situation. Some Jews believed that Jesus was the long-awaited Messiah. Others were disappointed because he refused to preach rebellion against Rome. Still others who hated and feared Jesus wanted to be rid of him. The last thing Pilate wanted was a riot on his hands. Christian tradition has made much of Pontius Pilate. In the medieval West he was considered a monster. In the Ethiopian church he is considered a saint. Neither monster nor saint, Pilate was simply a hard-bitten Roman official who did his duty, at times harshly. In Judaea his duty was to enforce the law and keep the peace. These were the problems on his mind when Jesus stood before him. Jesus as king of the Jews did not worry him. The popular agitation surrounding Jesus did. To avert riot and bloodshed, Pilate condemned Jesus to death. It is a bitter historical irony that

❖ **Pontius Pilate and Jesus** This Byzantine mosaic from Ravenna illustrates a dramatic moment in Jesus' trial and crucifixion. Jesus stands accused before Pilate, but Pilate symbolically washes his hands of the whole affair. *(Source: Scala/Art Re- source, NY)*

such a gentle man died such a cruel death. After being scourged, he was hung from a cross until he died in the sight of family, friends, enemies, and the merely curious.

Once Pilate's soldiers had carried out the sentence, the entire matter seemed to be closed. Yet on the third day after Jesus' crucifixion, an odd rumor began to circulate in Jerusalem. Some of Jesus' followers were saying he had risen from the dead, while others accused them of having stolen his body. For the earliest Christians and for generations to come, the resurrection of Jesus became a central element of faith—and more than that, a promise: Jesus had triumphed over death, and his resurrection promised all Christians immortality. In Jerusalem, meanwhile, the tumult subsided. Jesus' followers lived quietly and peacefully, unmolested by Roman or Jew. Pilate had no quarrel with them, and Judaism already had many minor sects. Peter

(d. A.D. 67?), the first of Jesus' followers, became the head of the sect, which continued to observe Jewish law and religious customs. Peter, a man of traditional Jewish beliefs, felt that Jesus' teachings were meant exclusively for the Jews. Only in their practices of baptism and the Lord's Supper (the Eucharist) did the sect differ from normal Jewish custom. Meanwhile, they awaited the return of Jesus.

Christianity might have remained a purely Jewish sect had it not been for Paul of Tarsus (A.D. 5?–67?). The conversion of Hellenized Jews and of Gentiles (non-Jews) to Christianity caused the sect grave problems. Were the Gentiles subject to the law of Moses? If not, was Christianity to have two sets of laws? The answer to these questions was Paul's momentous contribution to Christianity. Paul was unlike Jesus or Peter. Born in a thriving, busy city filled with Romans, Greeks, Jews, Syrians, and others, he was at home in the world of Greco-Roman culture. After his conversion to Christianity, he taught that his native Judaism was the preparation for the Messiah and that Jesus by his death and resurrection had fulfilled the prophecy of Judaism and initiated a new age. Paul taught that Jesus was the son of God, the giver of a new law, and preached that Jesus' teachings were to be proclaimed to all, whether Jew or Gentile. Paul thus made a significant break with Judaism, Christianity's parent religion, for Judaism was exclusive and did not usually seek converts.

Paul's influence was far greater than that of any other early Christian. He traveled the length and breadth of the eastern Roman world, spreading his doctrine and preaching of Jesus. To little assemblies of believers in cities as distant as Rome and Corinth, he taught that Jesus had died to save all people. Paul's vision of Christianity won out over Peter's traditionalism. Christianity broke with Judaism and embarked on its own course.

The nature of that form of Christianity is preserved in the gospels. Yet they are not the only testimony about Jesus and early Christianity. Archaeological exploration in Egypt during the late nineteenth and the twentieth centuries has brought to light numerous other writings of the earliest Christian period. Among them are many fragments of what have come to be called the "Apocryphal Gospels," so named because some early Christians did not consider them authentic accounts of Jesus' life. A collection of Jesus' sayings, commonly called "The Book of Q," presents an account of Jesus' sayings that differs in many ways from that found in the gospels of the New Testament. What all of these documents prove is that Christianity was evolving religiously and intellectually during this early period.

What was Christianity's appeal to the Roman world? What did this obscure sect give people that other religions did not? Christianity possessed many different attractions. One of its appeals was its willingness to embrace both men and women, slaves and nobles. Many of the Eastern mystery religions with which Christianity competed were exclusive in one way or another. Mithraism, a mystery religion descended from Zoroastrianism, spread throughout the entire empire. Mithras the sun-god embodied good and warred against evil. Like Christianity, Mithraism offered elaborate and moving rituals including a form of baptism, a code of moral conduct, and the promise of life after death. Unlike Christianity, however, Mithraism permitted only men to become devotees.

Indeed, Christianity shared many of the features of mystery religions. It possessed a set of beliefs, such as the divinity of Jesus, and a literary history. Once people had prepared themselves for conversion by learning of Jesus' message and committing themselves to live by it, they were baptized. Like initiates in mystery religions, they entered the community of believers. The Christian community of believers was strengthened by the sacrament of the Eucharist, the communal celebration of the Lord's Supper. Christianity also had more than a priesthood to officiate at rituals; it developed an ecclesiastical administration that helped to ensure continuity within the new church.

Christianity appealed to common people and to the poor. Its communal celebration of the Lord's Supper gave men and women a sense of belonging. Christianity also offered its adherents the promise of salvation. Christians believed that Jesus on the cross had defeated evil and that he would reward his followers with eternal life after death. Christianity also offered the possibility of forgiveness. Human nature was weak, and even the best Christians would fall into sin. But Jesus loved sinners and forgave those who repented. In its doctrine of salvation and forgiveness alone, Christianity had a powerful ability to give solace and strength to believers.

Christianity was attractive to many because it gave the Roman world a cause. Hellenistic philosophy had attempted to make men and women self-sufficient: people who became indifferent to the outside world could no longer be hurt by it. That goal alone ruled out any cause except the attainment of serenity. The Romans, never innovators in philosophy, merely elaborated this lonely and austere message. Instead of passivity, Christianity stressed the ideal of striving for a goal. Every Christian, no matter how poor or humble, supposedly worked to realize the triumph of Christianity on earth. This was God's will, a sacred duty for every Christian. By spreading the word of Christ, Christians played their part in God's plan. No matter how small, the part each Christian played was important. Since this duty was God's will, Christians believed that the goal would be achieved. The Christian was not discouraged by temporary setbacks, believing Christianity to be invincible.

Christianity gave its devotees a sense of community. No Christian was alone. All members of the

Christian community strove toward the same goal of fulfilling God's plan. Each individual community was in turn a member of a greater community. And that community, the Church General, was indestructible. After all, Jesus himself had reportedly promised, "Thou art Peter, and upon this rock I will build my church; and the gates of hell shall not prevail against it."[8]

So Christianity's attractions were many, from forgiveness of sin to an exalted purpose for each individual. Its insistence on the individual's importance gave solace and encouragement, especially to the poor and meek. Its claim to divine protection fed hope in the eventual success of the Christian community. Christianity made participation in the universal possible for everyone. The ultimate reward promised by Christianity was eternal bliss after death.

✥ THE JULIO-CLAUDIANS AND THE FLAVIANS (27 B.C.–A.D. 96)

For fifty years after Augustus's death the dynasty that he established—known as the Julio-Claudians because they were all members of the Julian and Claudian clans—provided the emperors of Rome. Some of the Julio-Claudians, such as Tiberius and Claudius, were sound rulers and able administrators. Others, including Caligula and Nero, were weak and frivolous men who exercised their power stupidly and brought misery to the empire. Writers such as the biting and brilliant historian Tacitus (ca A.D. 55–ca 116) and the gossipy Suetonius (ca A.D. 75–150) have left unforgettable—and generally hostile—portraits of these emperors. Yet the venom of Tacitus and Suetonius cannot obscure the fact that Julio-Claudians were responsible for some notable achievements. During their reigns the empire largely prospered.

One of the most momentous achievements of the Julio-Claudians was Claudius's creation of an imperial bureaucracy composed of professional administrators. Even the most energetic emperor could not run the empire alone. The numerous duties and immense responsibilities of the emperor prompted Claudius to delegate power. He began by giving the freedmen of his household official duties, especially in finances. It was a simple, workable system. Claudius knew his ex-slaves well and could discipline them at will. The effect of

Claudius's innovations was to enable the emperor to rule the empire more easily and efficiently.

One of the worst defects of Augustus's settlement—the army's ability to interfere in politics—became obvious during the Julio-Claudian period. Augustus had created a special standing force, the Praetorian Guard, as an imperial bodyguard. In A.D. 41 one of the praetorians murdered Caligula while others hailed Claudius as the emperor. Under the threat of violence, the senate ratified the praetorians' choice. It was a story repeated frequently. During the first three centuries of the empire, the Praetorian Guard all too often murdered emperors they were supposed to protect and saluted emperors of their own choosing.

In A.D. 68 Nero's inept rule led to military rebellion and his death, thus opening the way to widespread disruption. In A.D. 69, the "Year of the Four Emperors," four men claimed the position of emperor. Roman armies in Gaul, on the Rhine, and in the East marched on Rome to make their commanders emperor. The man who emerged triumphant was Vespasian, commander of the eastern armies, who entered Rome in 70 and restored order. Nonetheless, the Year of the Four Emperors proved the Augustan settlement had failed to end civil war.

Not a brilliant politician, Vespasian did not institute sweeping reforms, as had Augustus, or solve the problem of the army in politics. To prevent usurpers from claiming the throne, Vespasian designated his sons Titus and Domitian as his successors. By establishing the Flavian dynasty (named after his clan), Vespasian turned the principate into an open and admitted monarchy. He also expanded the emperor's power by increasing the size of the budding bureaucracy Claudius had created.

One of Vespasian's first tasks was to suppress rebellions that had erupted at the end of Nero's reign. The most famous had taken place in Judaea, which still seethed long after Jesus' crucifixion. Long-standing popular unrest and atrocities committed by Jews and Romans alike sparked a massive revolt in A.D. 66. Four years later, a Roman army reconquered Judaea and reduced Jerusalem by siege. The Jewish survivors were enslaved, their state destroyed. The mismanagement of Judaea was one of the few—and worst—failures of Roman imperial administration.

The Flavians carried on Augustus's work on the frontiers. Domitian, the last of the Flavians, won

✦ **Triumph of Titus** After Titus, the son of Vespasian and later himself emperor, conquered Jerusalem, he ordered his soldiers to carry off as spoils of war the sacred objects of the rebellious Jews, most notably in this scene the seven-branched candlestick. *(Source: Art Resource)*

additional territory in Germany and consolidated it in two new provinces. He defeated barbarian tribes on the Danube frontier and strengthened that area as well. Even so, Domitian was one of the most hated of Roman emperors because of his cruelty, and he fell victim to an assassin's dagger. Nevertheless, the Flavians had given the Roman world peace and had kept the legions in line. Their work paved the way for the era of the "five good emperors," the golden age of the empire.

✤ THE AGE OF THE "FIVE GOOD EMPERORS" (A.D. 96–180)

In the second century of the Christian era, the Empire of Rome comprehended the fairest part of the earth, and the most civilised portion of mankind. The frontiers of that extensive monarchy were guarded by ancient renown and disciplined valor. The gentle but powerful influence of laws and manners had gradually cemented the union of the provinces. Their peaceful inhabitants enjoyed and abused the advantages of wealth and luxury. The image of a free constitution was preserved with decent reverence: the Roman senate appeared to possess the sovereign authority, and devolved on the emperors all the executive powers of government. During a happy period [A.D. 96–180] of more than fourscore years, the public administration was conducted by the virtue and abilities of Nerva, Trajan, Hadrian, and the two Antonines.[9]

Thus Edward Gibbon (1737–1794) began his monumental *History of the Decline and Fall of the Roman Empire*. Gibbon saw the era of Nerva, Trajan, Hadrian, Antoninus Pius, and Marcus Aurelius—the "five good emperors"—as the happiest in human history, a last burst of summer before an autumn of failure and barbarism. Gibbon recognized a great truth: the age of the Antonines, as the five good emperors are often called, was one of almost unparalleled prosperity for the empire. Wars were generally victorious and confined to the frontiers. Even the serenity of Augustus's day seemed to pale in comparison. These emperors were among the noblest, most dedicated, ablest men in Roman history. Yet fundamental political and military changes had taken place since the time of Augustus's rule.

The Antonine Monarchy

Augustus had claimed that his influence arose from the collection of offices the senate had bestowed on him. However, there was in law no such office as emperor. Augustus was merely the First Citizen. Under the Flavians the principate became a full-blown monarchy, and by the time of the Antonines the principate was an office with definite rights, powers, and prerogatives. In the years between Augustus and the Antonines, the emperor had become an indispensable part of the imperial machinery. In short, without the emperor the empire would quickly fall to pieces. Augustus had been

monarch in fact but not in theory; during their reigns, the Antonines were monarchs in both.

The five good emperors were not power-hungry autocrats. The concentration of power was the result of empire. The easiest and most efficient way to run the Roman Empire was to invest the emperor with vast powers. Furthermore, Roman emperors on the whole proved to be effective rulers and administrators. As capable and efficient emperors took on new tasks and functions, the emperor's hand was felt in more areas of life and government. Increasingly the emperors became the source of all authority and guidance in the empire. The five good emperors were benevolent and exercised their power intelligently, but they were absolute kings all the same. Lesser men would later throw off the façade of constitutionality and use this same power in a despotic fashion.

❖ **Scene from Trajan's Column** From 101 to 107 Trajan fought the barbarian tribes along the Danube. With remarkable realism, a feature of Roman art, this scene portrays Roman soldiers building field-works outside of a city. *(Source: Ancient Art & Architecture Collection)*

Typical of the five good emperors is the career of Hadrian, who became emperor in A.D. 117. He was born in Spain, a fact that illustrates the importance of the provinces in Roman politics. Hadrian received his education at Rome and became an ardent admirer of Greek culture. He caught the attention of his elder cousin Trajan, the future emperor, who started him on a military career. At age nineteen Hadrian served on the Danube frontier, where he learned the details of how the Roman army lived and fought and saw for himself the problems of defending the frontiers. When Trajan became emperor in A.D. 98, Hadrian was given important positions in which he learned how to defend and run the empire. At Trajan's death in 117, Hadrian assumed power.

Roman government had changed since Augustus's day. One of the most significant changes was the enormous growth of the imperial bureaucracy created by Claudius. Hadrian reformed this system by putting the bureaucracy on an organized, official basis. He established imperial administrative departments to handle the work formerly done by imperial freedmen. Hadrian also separated civil service from military service. Men with little talent or taste for the army could instead serve the state as administrators. Hadrian's bureaucracy demanded professionalism from its members. Administrators made a career of the civil service. These innovations made for more efficient running of the empire and increased the authority of the emperor—the ruling power of the bureaucracy.

Changes in the Army

The Roman army had also changed since Augustus's time. The Roman legion had once been a mobile unit, but its duties under the empire no longer called for mobility. The successors of Augustus generally called a halt to further conquests. The army was expected to defend what had already been won. Under the Flavian emperors (A.D. 69–96), the frontiers became firmly fixed. Forts and watch stations guarded the borders. Behind the forts the Romans built a system of roads that allowed the forts to be quickly supplied and reinforced in times of trouble. The army had evolved into a garrison force, with legions guarding specific areas for long periods.

The personnel of the legions was changing, too. Italy could no longer supply all the recruits needed

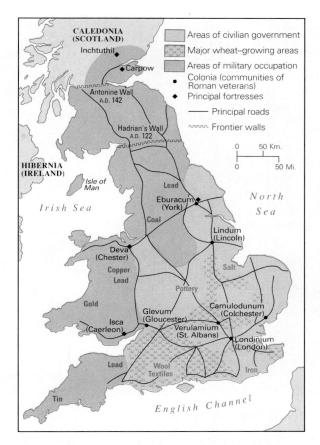

❖ **MAP 6.2 Roman Britain** Though the modern state of Great Britain plays a major role in modern international affairs, it was a peripheral part of the Roman Empire, a valuable area but nonetheless definitely on the frontier.

for the army. Increasingly, only the officers came from Italy and from the more romanized provinces. The legionaries were mostly drawn from the less civilized provinces, especially the ones closest to the frontiers. A major trend was already obvious in Hadrian's day: fewer and fewer Roman soldiers were really Roman. In the third century A.D. the barbarization of the army would result in an army indifferent to Rome and its traditions. In the age of the five good emperors however, the army was still a source of economic stability and a romanizing agent (Map 6.2). Men from the provinces and even barbarians joined the army to learn a trade and to gain Roman citizenship. Even so, the signs were ominous. Veterans from Julius Caesar's campaigns would hardly have recognized Hadrian's troops as Roman legionaries.

✦ **Apartment houses at Ostia**   At heavily populated places such as Rome and Ostia, which was the port of Rome, apartment buildings housed urban dwellers. The brick construction of this building is a good example of solid Roman work. In Rome some apartment buildings were notoriously shoddy and unsafe. *(Source: Art Resource)*

✢ LIFE IN THE "GOLDEN AGE"

Many people, both ancient and modern, have considered these years one of the happiest epochs in Western history. But popular accounts have also portrayed Rome as already decadent by the time of the five good emperors. If Rome was decadent, who kept the empire running? For that matter, can life in Rome itself be taken as representative of life in other parts of the empire? Rome was unique and must be seen as such. Surely, Rome no more resembled a provincial city like Cologne than New York could possibly resemble Keokuk, Iowa. Only when the uniqueness of Rome is understood in its own right can one turn to the provinces to obtain a full and reasonable picture of the empire under the Antonines.

Imperial Rome

Rome was truly an extraordinary city, especially by ancient standards. It was also enormous, with a population somewhere between 500,000 and 750,000. Although it could boast of stately palaces, noble buildings, and beautiful residential areas, most people lived in jerrybuilt apartment houses. Fire and crime were perennial problems, even after Augustus created fire and urban police forces. Streets were narrow and drainage inadequate. During the republic, sanitation had been a common problem. Numerous inscriptions record prohibitions against dumping human refuse and even cadavers on the grounds of sanctuaries and cemeteries. Under the empire this situation improved. By comparison with medieval and early modern European cities, Rome was a healthy enough place to live.

Rome was such a huge city that the surrounding countryside could not feed it. Because of the danger of starvation, the emperor, following republican practice, provided the citizen population with free grain for bread and, later, oil and wine. By feeding the citizenry the emperor prevented bread riots caused by shortages and high prices. For the rest of the urban population who did not enjoy the rights of citizenship, the emperor provided grain at low prices. This measure was designed to prevent speculators from forcing up grain prices in times of crisis. By maintaining the grain supply the emperor kept the favor of the people and ensured that Rome's poor and idle did not starve.

The emperor also entertained the Roman populace, often at vast expense. The most popular forms of public entertainment were gladiatorial contests and chariot racing. Gladiatorial fighting was originally an Etruscan funerary custom, a blood sacrifice for the dead. Even a humane man like Hadrian staged extravagant contests. In A.D. 126 he sponsored six days of such combats, during which 1,835 pairs of gladiators dueled, usually with swords and shields. Many gladiators were

criminals, some of whom were sentenced to be slaughtered in the arena. These convicts were given no defensive weapons and stood little real chance of survival. Other criminals were sentenced to fight in the arena as fully armed gladiators. Some gladiators were the slaves of gladiatorial trainers; others were prisoners of war. Still others were free men who volunteered for the arena. Even women at times engaged in gladiatorial combat. What drove these men and women? Some obviously had no other choice. For a criminal condemned to die, the arena was preferable to the imperial mines, where convicts worked digging ore and died under wretched conditions. At least in the arena the gladiator might fight well enough to win freedom. Others no doubt fought for the love of danger or for fame. Although some Romans protested gladiatorial fighting, most delighted in it—one of their least attractive sides. Not until the fifth century did Christianity put a stop to it.

The Romans were even more addicted to chariot racing than to gladiatorial shows. Under the empire, four permanent teams competed against one another. Each had its own color—red, white, green, or blue. Some Romans claimed that people cared more about their favorite team than about

Chariot Racing This brilliant mosaic found near Lyons, France gives in almost a snapshot view a typical chariot race. In the center around which the chariots raced was a decorative pond with gushing water, dolphins, and egg-shaped spheres. (*Source: Cliché Musée de la Civilisation Gallo-romaine de Lyon*)

the race itself. Two-horse and four-horse chariots ran a course of seven laps, about five miles. A successful driver could be the hero of the hour. One charioteer, Gaius Appuleius Diocles, raced for twenty-four years. During that time he drove 4,257 starts and won 1,462 of them. His admirers honored him with an inscription that proclaimed him champion of all charioteers.

But people like the charioteer Diocles were no more typical of the common Roman than Babe Ruth is of the average American. Ordinary Romans left their mark in the inscriptions that grace their graves. They were proud of their work and accomplishments, affectionate toward their families and friends, and eager to be remembered after death. Typical Romans did not spend their entire lives in idleness, watching gladiators or chariot races; instead, they had to make a living. They dealt with everyday problems and rejoiced over small pleasures. An impression of them and their cares can be gained from their epitaphs. The funerary inscription of Paprius Vitalis to his wife is particularly engaging: "If there is anything good in the lower regions—I, however, finish a poor life without you—be happy there too, sweetest Thalassia . . . married to me for 40 years."[10]

Even the personal philosophies of typical Romans have come down from antiquity. Marcus Antonius Encolpus erected a funerary inscription to his wife that reads in part:

Do not pass by my epitaph, traveler.
But having stopped, listen and learn, then go your
 way.
There is no boat in Hades, no ferryman Charon,
no caretaker Aiakos, no dog Cerberus.
All we who are dead below
have become bones and ashes, but nothing else.
I have spoken to you honestly, go on, traveler,
lest even while dead I seem loquacious to you.[11]

Others put it more simply: "I was, I am not, I don't care." "To each his own tombstone." These Romans went about their lives as people have always done.

The Provinces

In the provinces and even on the frontiers, the age of the five good emperors was one of extensive prosperity, especially in western Europe. The Roman army had beaten back the barbarians and exposed them to the civilizing effects of Roman traders. The resulting peace and security opened Britain, Gaul, Germany, and the lands of the Danube to immigration (see Listening to the Past). Agriculture flourished as large tracts of land came under cultivation. Most of this land was in the hands of free tenant farmers. From the time of Augustus slavery had declined in the empire, as had the growth of latifundia (see page 151). Augustus and his successors encouraged the rise of free farmers. Under the five good emperors this trend continued, and the holders of small parcels of land throve as never before. The emperors provided loans on easy terms to farmers, enabling them to rent land previously worked by slaves. They also permitted them to cultivate the new lands that were being opened up. Consequently, the small tenant farmer was becoming the backbone of Roman agriculture.

In continental Europe the army was largely responsible for the new burst of expansion. The areas where legions were stationed readily became romanized. When legionaries retired from the army, they often settled where they had served. Since they had usually learned a trade in the army, they brought essential skills to areas that badly needed trained men. These veterans took their retirement pay and used it to set themselves up in business.

The eastern part of the empire also participated in the boom. The Roman navy had swept the sea of pirates, and Eastern merchants traded throughout the Mediterranean. The flow of goods and produce in the East matched that of the West. Venerable cities like Corinth, Antioch, and Ephesus flourished. The cities of the East built extensively, bedecking themselves with new amphitheaters, temples, fountains, and public buildings. For the East this age was the heyday of the city. Life there grew ever richer and more comfortable.

Trade among the provinces increased dramatically. Britain and Belgium became prime grain producers, much of their harvests going to the armies of the Rhine. Britain's famous wool industry probably got its start under the Romans. Italy and southern Gaul produced wine in huge quantities. The wines of Italy went principally to Rome and the Danube, while Gallic wines were shipped to Britain and the Rhineland. Roman colonists had introduced the olive to southern Spain and northern Africa, an experiment so successful that these regions produced most of the oil consumed in the Western empire. In the East, Syrian farmers continued to cultivate the olive, and oil production reached an all-time high. Egypt was the prime grain producer of the East, and tons of Egyptian wheat went to feed the Roman populace. The Roman army in Mesopotamia consumed a high percentage of the raw materials and manufactured products of Syria and Asia Minor. The spread of trade meant the end of isolated and self-contained economies. By the time of the five good emperors, the empire had become an economic as well as a political reality (Map 6.3).

One of the most striking features of this period was the growth of industry in the provinces. Cities in Gaul and Germany eclipsed the old Mediterranean manufacturing centers. Italian cities were particularly hard-hit by this development. Cities like Arretium and Capua had dominated the production of glass, pottery, and bronze ware. Yet in the second century A.D., Gaul and Germany took over the pottery market. Lyons in Gaul became the new center of the glassmaking industry. The technique of glass blowing spread to Britain and Germany, and later in the second century Cologne replaced Lyons in glass production. The cities of Gaul were nearly unrivaled in the manufacture of bronze and brass. Gallic craftsmen invented a new technique of tin-plating and decorated their work with Celtic designs. Their wares soon drove Italian products out of the northern European market. For the first time in history, northern Europe was able to rival the Mediterranean as a producer of manufactured goods. Europe had entered fully into the economic and cultural life of the Mediterranean world.

The age of these emperors was generally one of peace, progress, and prosperity. The work of the Romans in northern and western Europe was a permanent contribution to the history of Western society. This period was also one of consolidation. Roads and secure sea-lanes linked the empire in one vast web. The empire had become a commonwealth of cities, and urban life was its hallmark.

Rome and the East

Their march to empire and their growing interest in foreign peoples brought the Romans into contact with a world much larger than Europe and the Mediterranean. As early as the late republic, Roman commanders in the East encountered peoples who created order out of the chaos left by Alexander the Great and his Hellenistic successors.

This meeting of West and East had two immediate effects, the first being a long military confrontation between the Romans and their Iranian neighbors. Second, Roman military expansion to the east coincided with Chinese expansion to the west, and the surprising result was a period when the major ancient civilizations of the world were in touch with one another. For the first time in history, peoples from the Greco-Roman civilization of the Mediterranean and from central Asia, India, and China met each other and observed one another's cultures at first hand. This was an era of human exploration, and key figures in the process were the peoples of cental Asia, especially the Parthians and Sassanids of Iran.

 ## CIVIL WARS AND INVASIONS IN THE THIRD CENTURY

The age of the five good emperors gave way to a period of chaos and stress. During the third century A.D. the empire was stunned by civil wars and barbarian invasions. By the time peace was restored, the economy was shattered, cities had shrunk in size, and agriculture was becoming manorial (see page 186). In the disruption of the third century and the reconstruction of the fourth, the medieval world had its origins.

After the death of Marcus Aurelius, the last of the five good emperors, his son Commodus, a man totally unsuited to govern the empire, came to the throne. His misrule led to his murder and a renewal of civil war. After a brief but intense spasm of fighting, the African general Septimius Severus defeated other rival commanders and established the Severan dynasty (A.D. 193–235). Although Septimius Severus was able to stabilize the empire, his successors proved incapable of disciplining the legions. When the last of the Severi was killed by one of his own soldiers, the empire plunged into still another grim, destructive, and this time prolonged round of civil war.

Over twenty different emperors ascended the throne in the forty-nine years between 235 and 284, and many rebels died in the attempt to seize power. At various times, parts of the empire were

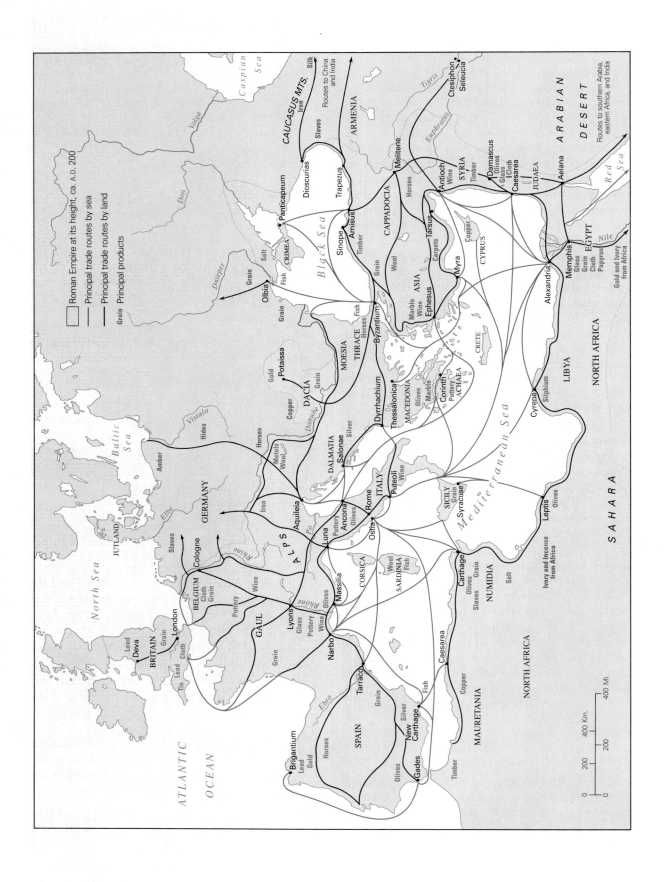

Roman Empire at its height, ca. A.D. 200
Principal trade routes by sea
Principal trade routes by land
Grain Principal products

ATLANTIC OCEAN

North Sea

Baltic Sea

JUTLAND

Amber

Hides

Elbe

Vistula

Volga

Don

Caspian Sea

Dnieper

GERMANY

Horses

Metals
Wool

Iron

Slaves

Cologne

BELGIUM
Cloth
Grain

Wine

Pottery

GAUL

Rhône

Lyons
Glass
Pottery
Wine Olives

Narbo

Massilia

Rhine

ALPS

Aquileia

Po

Luna

Pottery
Ancona
Olives

Rome
Ostia

ITALY

Puteoli
Wine

Grain

London

Deva

BRITAIN
Grain
Cloth

Lead

Tin Lead Cloth

Brigantium
Lead
Gold

Horses

Grain

SPAIN

Silver

New
Carthage

Gades

Olives

Ebro

Tarraco

Grain

Caesarea

Fish

MAURETANIA

Copper

Timber

NORTH AFRICA

NUMIDIA

Carthage
Olives
Slaves Grain

Salt

Leptis
Olives

SICILY
Grain
Syracuse

CORSICA

SARDINIA
Wool Fish

Mediterranean Sea

DALMATIA
Salonae

Silver

MOESIA

DACIA

Potaissa

Gold

Copper

Grain

Danube

THRACE
Horses

Byzantium

Fish

Dyrrhachium

Thessalonica

MACEDONIA

Marble

Corinth
Pottery
ACHAEA
Olives

Marble

CRETE

Silphium

Cyrene

LIBYA

Ivory and Incense
from Africa

SAHARA

Black Sea

Olbia

Grain

Fish

Grain

Panticapeum

CRIMEA

Salt

Dioscurias

Slaves

Trapezus

CAUCASUS MTS.
Iron

Silk

Routes to China
and India

ARMENIA

Tigris

Euphrates

Ctesiphon
Seleucia

Sinope

Amisus
Timber

Wool

CAPPADOCIA

Horses

Melitene

Carpets

Tarsus

Copper

Myra

CYPRUS

Marble
Wine
Ephesus

ASIA

Antioch
Wine

SYRIA
Timber

Damascus
Olives
Glass Cloth
Caesarea

JUDAEA

Aelana

Red Sea

ARABIAN DESERT

Routes to southern Arabia,
eastern Africa, and India

Memphis
Glass
Grain
Cloth
Papyrus

Alexandria

EGYPT

Nile

Gold and Ivory
from Africa

NORTH AFRICA

0 200 400 Km.
0 200 400 Mi.

lost to rebel generals, one of whom, Postumus, set up his own empire in Gaul for about ten years (A.D. 259–269). Yet other men, like the iron-willed Aurelian (A.D. 270–275), dedicated their energies to restoring order. So many military commanders seized rule that the middle of the third century has become known as the age of the "barracks emperors." The Augustan principate had become a military monarchy, and that monarchy was nakedly autocratic.

Barbarians on the Frontiers

The first and most disastrous result of the civil wars was trouble on the frontiers. It was Rome's misfortune that this era of anarchy coincided with immense movements of barbarian peoples. Historians still dispute the precise reason for these migrations, though their immediate cause was pressure from tribes moving westward across Asia. In the sixth century A.D., Jordanes, a Christianized Goth, preserved the memory of innumerable wars among the barbarians in his *History of the Goths.* Goths fought Vandals, Huns fought Goths. Steadily the defeated and displaced tribes moved toward the Roman frontiers. Finally, like "a swarm of bees"—to use Jordanes's image—the Goths, one such people, burst into Europe in A.D. 258.

When the barbarians reached the Rhine and Danube frontiers, they often found huge gaps in the Roman defenses. Typical is the case of Decius, a general who guarded the Danube frontier in Dacia (modern Romania). In A.D. 249 he revolted and invaded Italy in an effort to become emperor. Decius left the frontier deserted, and the Goths easily poured through, looking for new homes. During much of the third century A.D., bands of Goths devastated the Balkans as far south as Greece. They even penetrated Asia Minor. The Alamanni, a German people, swept across the Danube. At one point they entered Italy and reached Milan before they were beaten back. Meanwhile the Franks, still another German folk,

hit the Rhine frontier. The Franks then invaded eastern and central Gaul and northeastern Spain. Saxons from Scandinavia sailed into the English Channel in search of loot. In the East the Sassanids overran Mesopotamia. If the army had been guarding the borders instead of creating and destroying emperors, none of these invasions would have been possible. The barracks emperors should be credited with one accomplishment, however: they fought barbarians when they were not fighting each other. Only that kept the empire from total ruin.

Turmoil in Farm and Village Life

How did the ordinary people cope with this period of iron and blood? What did it mean to the lives of men and women on farms and in villages? How did local officials continue to serve their emperor and neighbors? Some people became outlaws. Others lived more prosaically. Some voiced their grievances to the emperor, thereby leaving a record of the problems they faced.

In a surprising number of cases, barbarians were less of a problem than lawless soldiers, imperial officials, and local agents. For many ordinary people, official corruption was the tangible and immediate result of the breakdown of central authority. In one instance, some tenant farmers in Lydia (modern Turkey) complained to the emperor about arbitrary arrest and the killing of prisoners. They claimed that police agents had threatened them and prevented them from cultivating the land. Tenant farmers in Phrygia (also in modern Turkey) voiced similar complaints. They suffered extortion at the hands of public officials. Military commanders, soldiers, and imperial agents requisitioned their livestock and compelled the farmers to forced labor. The farmers were becoming impoverished, and many people deserted the land to seek safety elsewhere. The inhabitants of an entire village in Thrace (modern Bulgaria) complained that they were being driven from their homes. From imperial and local officials they suffered insolence and violence. Soldiers demanded to be quartered and given supplies. Many villagers had already abandoned their homes to escape. The remaining villagers warned the emperor that, unless order was restored, they too would flee.

Local officials were sometimes unsympathetic or violent toward farmers and villagers because of their own plight. They were responsible for the

◆ **MAP 6.3 The Economic Aspect of the Roman Peace** The Roman Empire was not merely a political and military organization but also an intricate economic network through which goods from Armenia and Syria were traded for Western products from as far away as Spain and Britain.

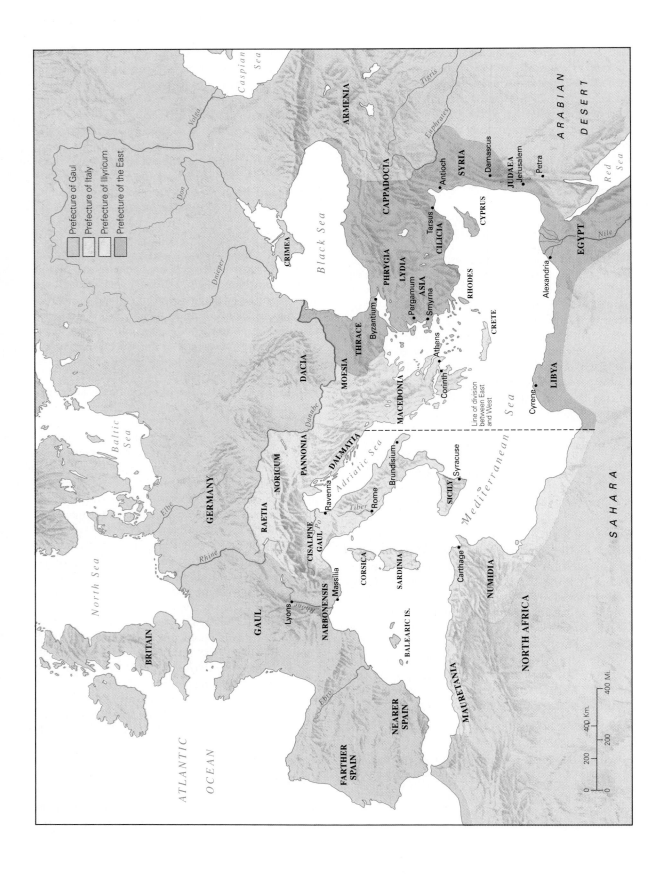

Prefecture of Gaul
Prefecture of Italy
Prefecture of Illyricum
Prefecture of the East

Caspian Sea

Volga

ARMENIA

Tigris

Don

Euphrates

ARABIAN

DESERT

CAPPADOCIA

SYRIA

Damascus

Antioch

JUDAEA

Jerusalem

Petra

Red Sea

CRIMEA

Dnieper

Black Sea

CYPRUS

PHRYGIA

LYDIA

Tarsus

CILICIA

EGYPT

Nile

ASIA

Pergamum

Smyrna

RHODES

Alexandria

Byzantium

THRACE

CRETE

DACIA

MOESIA

Athens

Danube

MACEDONIA

Corinth

LIBYA

Cyrene

Mediterranean Sea

Line of division between East and West

Baltic Sea

Elbe

GERMANY

PANNONIA

NORICUM

DALMATIA

Adriatic Sea

Brundisium

Syracuse

RAETIA

Ravenna

SICILY

North Sea

CISALPINE GAUL

Po

Rome

Tiber

Rhine

CORSICA

SARDINIA

Carthage

NUMIDIA

GAUL

NARBONENSIS

Massilia

Lyons

Saône

Rhône

BALEARIC IS.

NORTH AFRICA

SAHARA

BRITAIN

MAURETANIA

ATLANTIC OCEAN

Ebro

NEARER SPAIN

FARTHER SPAIN

0   200   400 Mi.

0   200   400 Km.

collection of imperial revenues. If their area could not meet its tax quota, they paid the deficit from their own pockets. Because the local officials were themselves so hard-pressed, they squeezed whatever they could from the villagers and farmers.

RECONSTRUCTION UNDER DIOCLETIAN AND CONSTANTINE (A.D. 284–337)

At the close of the third century A.D., the emperor Diocletian (r. 284–305) put an end to the period of turmoil. Repairing the damage done in the third century was the major work of the emperor Constantine (r. 306–337) in the fourth. But the price was high.

Under Diocletian, Augustus's polite fiction of the emperor as first among equals gave way to the emperor as absolute autocrat. The princeps became *dominus*—"lord." The emperor claimed that he was "the elect of God"—that he ruled because of God's favor. Constantine even claimed to be the equal of Jesus' first twelve followers. To underline the emperor's exalted position, Diocletian and Constantine adopted the gaudy court ceremonies and trappings of the Persian Empire. People entering the emperor's presence prostrated themselves before him and kissed the hem of his robes. Constantine went so far as to import Persian eunuchs to run the palace. The Roman emperor had become an Oriental monarch.

No mere soldier, but rather an adroit administrator, Diocletian gave serious thought to the empire's ailments. He recognized that the empire and its difficulties had become too great for one man to handle. He also realized that during the third century provincial governors had frequently used their positions to foment or participate in rebellions. To solve the first of these problems, Diocletian divided the empire into a western and an eastern half (Map 6.4). Diocletian assumed direct control of the eastern part; he gave the rule of the western part to a colleague, along with the title

Diocletian's Tetrarchy The emperor Diocletian's attempt to reform the Roman Empire by dividing rule among four men is represented in this piece of sculpture, which in many features illustrates the transition from ancient to medieval art. Here the four tetrarchs demonstrate their solidarity by clasping one another on the shoulder. Nonetheless each man has his other hand on his sword—a gesture that proved prophetic when Diocletian's reign ended and another struggle for power began. *(Source: Alinari/Art Resource)*

augustus, which had become synonymous with emperor. Diocletian and his fellow augustus further delegated power by appointing two men to assist them. Each man was given the title of *caesar* to indicate his exalted rank. Although this system is known as the *Tetrarchy* because four men ruled the empire, Diocletian was clearly the senior partner and final source of authority.

Each half of the empire was further split into two prefectures, each governed by a prefect responsible to an augustus. Diocletian reduced the power of the old provincial governors by dividing

MAP 6.4 The Roman World Divided Under Diocletian, the Roman Empire was first divided into a western and an eastern half, a development that foreshadowed the medieval division between the Latin West and the Byzantine East.

provinces into smaller units. He organized the prefectures into small administrative units called *dioceses,* which were in turn subdivided into small provinces. Provincial governors were also deprived of their military power, leaving them only civil and administrative duties.

Diocletian's political reforms were a momentous step. The Tetrarchy soon failed, but Diocletian's division of the empire into two parts became permanent. Constantine and later emperors tried hard but unsuccessfully to keep the empire together. Throughout the fourth century A.D., the eastern and the western sections drifted apart. In later centuries the western part witnessed the fall of Roman government and the rise of barbarian kingdoms, while the eastern empire evolved into the majestic Byzantine Empire.

The most serious immediate matters confronting Diocletian and Constantine were economic, social, and religious. They needed additional revenues to support the army and the imperial court. Yet the wars and the barbarian invasions had caused widespread destruction and poverty. The fighting had struck a serious blow to Roman agriculture, which the emperors tried to revive. Christianity had become too strong either to ignore or to crush. The responses to these problems by Diocletian, Constantine, and their successors helped create the economic and social patterns that medieval Europe inherited.

Inflation and Taxes

The barracks emperors had dealt with economic hardship by depreciating the currency, cutting the silver content of coins until money was virtually worthless. As a result, the entire monetary system fell into ruin. In Egypt, governors had to order bankers to accept imperial money. The immediate result was crippling inflation throughout the empire.

The empire was less capable of recovery than in earlier times. Wars and invasions had disrupted normal commerce and the means of production. Mines were exhausted in the attempt to supply much-needed ores, especially gold and silver. The turmoil had hit the cities especially hard. Markets were disrupted, and travel became dangerous. Craftsmen, artisans, and traders rapidly left devastated regions. The prosperous industry and commerce of Gaul and the Rhineland declined mark-

edly. Those who owed their prosperity to commerce and the needs of urban life likewise suffered. Cities were no longer places where trade and industry thrived. The devastation of the countryside increased the difficulty of feeding and supplying the cities. The destruction was so extensive that many wondered whether the ravages could be repaired at all.

The response of Diocletian and Constantine to these problems was marked by compulsion, rigidity, and loss of individual freedom. Diocletian's attempt to curb inflation illustrates the methods of absolute monarchy. In a move unprecedented in Roman history, he issued an edict that fixed maximum prices and wages throughout the empire. The measure proved a failure because it was unrealistic as well as unenforceable.

The emperors dealt with the tax system just as strictly and inflexibly. As in the past, local officials bore the responsibility of collecting imperial taxes. Constantine made these officials into a hereditary class; son followed father whether he wanted to or not. In this period of severe depression, many localities could not pay their taxes. In such cases these local officials had to make up the difference from their own funds. This system soon wiped out a whole class of moderately wealthy people.

With the monetary system in ruins, most imperial taxes became payable in kind—that is, in goods or produce instead of money. The major drawback of payment in kind is its demands on transportation. Goods have to be moved from where they are grown or manufactured to where they are needed. Accordingly, the emperors locked into their occupations all those involved in the growing, preparation, and transportation of food and essential commodities. A baker or shipper could not go into any other business, and his son took up the trade at his death. The late Roman Empire had a place for everyone, and everyone had a place.

The Decline of Small Farms

The late Roman heritage to the medieval world is most obvious in agriculture. Because of worsening conditions, free tenant farmers were reduced to serfdom. During the third century A.D., many were killed, fled the land to escape the barbarians, or abandoned farms ravaged in the fighting. Consequently, large tracts of land lay deserted. Great landlords with ample resources began at once to reclaim as much of this land as they could. The huge estates that resulted were the forerunners of medieval manors. Like manors, these villas were self-sufficient. Because they often produced more than they consumed, they successfully competed with the declining cities by selling their surplus in the countryside. They became islands of stability in an unsettled world.

While the villas were growing, the small farmers who remained on the land barely held their own. They were too poor and powerless to stand against the tide of chaos. They were exposed to the raids of barbarians or brigands and to the tyranny of imperial officials. For relief they turned to the great landlords. After all, the landowners were men of considerable resources, lords in their own right. They were wealthy and had many people working their land. They were independent and capable of defending themselves. If need be, they could—and at times did—field a small force of their own. Already influential, the landowning class united in protest against the demands of imperial officials.

In return for the protection and security landlords could offer, the small landholders gave over their lands. Free men and their families became clients of the landlords and lost much of their freedom. To guarantee a steady supply of labor, the landlords bound them to the soil. They could no longer decide to move elsewhere. Henceforth they and their families worked their patrons' land, not their own. Free men and women were in effect becoming serfs.

The Acceptance of Christianity

In religious affairs Constantine took the decisive step of recognizing Christianity as a legitimate religion. No longer would Christians suffer persecution for their beliefs as they had occasionally experienced earlier. Constantine himself died a Christian in 337. Why had the pagans persecuted Christians in the first place? Polytheism is by nature tolerant of new gods and accommodating in religious matters. Why was Christianity singled out for violence? Such questions as these are still matters of scholarly debate to which some broad answers can be given.

A splendid approach to these problems has recently come from the eminent Italian scholar Marta Sordi. Confronting a very complicated topic, she distinguishes among many different phases in the relationship between Christianity and official Roman acceptance of it. The Christians exaggerated the degree of pagan hostility to them, and most of the gory stories about the martyrs are fictitious. There were indeed some cases of pagan persecution of the Christians, but with few exceptions they were local and sporadic in nature. Even Nero's notorious persecution was temporary and limited to Rome. No constant persecution of Christians occurred. Instead, pagans and Christians alike enjoyed long periods of tolerance and even friendship. Nonetheless, some pagans thought that Christians were atheists because they scorned the traditional pagan gods. Christians in fact either denied the existence of pagan gods or called them evil spirits. They went so far as to urge people not to worship pagan gods. In turn, pagans, who believed in their gods as fervently as the Christians theirs, feared that the gods would withdraw their favor from the Roman Empire because of Christian blasphemy.

At first many pagans genuinely misunderstood Christian practices and rites. Even educated and cultured people like the historian Tacitus opposed Christianity because they saw it as a bizarre new sect. Tacitus believed that Christians hated the whole human race. As a rule, early Christians kept to themselves. Romans distrusted and feared their exclusiveness, which seemed unsociable and even subversive. They thought that such secret rites as the Lord's Supper, at which Christians said that they ate and drank the body and blood of Jesus, were an act of cannibalism. Pagans also thought that Christians indulged in immoral and indecent rituals. They considered Christianity one of the worst of the Oriental mystery cults, for one of the hallmarks of many of those cults was disgusting rituals.

Another source of misunderstanding was that the pagans did not demand that Christians *believe* in pagan gods. Greek and Roman religion was never a matter of belief or ethics. It was purely a religion of ritual. One of the clearest statements of pagan theological attitudes comes from the Roman senator Symmachus in the later fourth century A.D.:

We watch the same stars; heaven is the same for us all; the same universe envelops us: what importance is it in what way anyone looks for truth? It is impossible to arrive by one route at such a great secret.[12]

Yet Roman religion was inseparable from the state. An attack on one was an attack on the other. The Romans were being no more fanatical or intolerant than the eighteenth-century English judge who declared the Christian religion part of the law of the land. All the pagans expected was performance of the ritual act, a small token of sacrifice. Those Christians who sacrificed went free, no matter what they personally believed.

As time went on, pagan hostility decreased. Pagans realized that Christians were not working to overthrow the state and that Jesus was no rival of Caesar. The emperor Trajan forbade his governors to hunt down Christians. Trajan admitted that he thought Christianity an abomination, but he preferred to leave Christians in peace.

The stress of the third century, however, seemed to some emperors the punishment of the gods. What else could account for such anarchy? With the empire threatened on every side, a few emperors thought that one way to appease the gods was by offering them the proper sacrifices. Such sacrifices would be a sign of loyalty to the empire, a show of Roman solidarity and religious piety. Consequently, a new wave of persecutions began out of desperation. Although the Christians depicted the emperor Diocletian as a fiend, he persecuted them in the hope that the gods would restore their blessings on Rome. Yet even these persecutions were never very widespread or long-lived; most pagans were not greatly sympathetic to the new round of persecutions. By the late third century, pagans had become used to Christianity. Constantine's acceptance of Christianity can be seen as the pagans' alliance with the strongest god of them all. Pagan and Christian alike must have been relieved when Constantine legalized the Christian religion.

In time the Christian triumph would be complete. In 380 the emperor Theodosius made Christianity the official religion of the Roman Empire. At that point Christians began to persecute the pagans for their beliefs. History had come full circle.

The Construction of Constantinople

The triumph of Christianity was not the only event that made Constantine's reign a turning point in Roman history. Constantine took the bold step of building a new capital for the empire. Constantinople, the New Rome, was constructed on the site of Byzantium, an old Greek city on the Bosporus.

Throughout the third century, emperors had found Rome and the West hard to defend. The eastern part of the empire was more easily defensible and escaped the worst of the barbarian devastation. It was wealthy and its urban life still vibrant. Moreover, Christianity was more widespread in the East than in the West, and the city of Constantinople was intended to be a Christian center.

✛ TRANSFORMATION OF THE CLASSICAL WORLD

Great historical movements will always be the subject of interpretation and speculation. The "fall" of the Roman Empire is a classic example, and it demonstrates excellently how historians try to understand complex historical developments and make them understandable to others. Sometimes, as in the case of Rome, the process has a simple beginning. For instance, on the evening of October 15, 1764, Edward Gibbon, a young Englishman, sat in Rome among the ruins of the Capitol listening to the chanting of some monks. As the voices of the Christian present echoed against the stones of the pagan past, Gibbon wondered how the Roman Empire had given way to the medieval world. His curiosity aroused, he dedicated himself to the study of what he considered the greatest problem in history. Twelve years later, in 1776, Gibbon published *The History of the Decline and Fall of the Roman Empire,* one of the monuments of English literature, a brilliant work fashioned with wit, learning, humor, and elegance.

Gibbon's thesis is, as his title indicates, that the Roman Empire, after the first two centuries of existence, declined in strength, vitality, and prosperity, then fell into ruin. His concept of Rome's "decline and fall," a process that he called "the awful revolution," has dominated historical thought for over two hundred years. Even those who disagree with Gibbon over details have usually accepted his concept of decline and fall, yet one can nonetheless ask whether Gibbon's concept is valid, and whether it is the only way (or even the best way) to explore this historical phenomenon.

There may never be a satisfactory solution to this problem because of its very complexity. Nor is any one answer entirely convincing. Gibbon himself put the blame for the empire's decline largely on the spread of Christianity, which emphasized the

✦ **The Arch of Constantine** To celebrate the victory that made him emperor, Constantine built this triumphal arch in Rome. Rather than decorate the arch with the inferior work of his own day, Constantine plundered other Roman monuments, including those of Trajan and Marcus Aurelius. *(Source: C. M. Dixon)*

virtues of humility, piety, and the belief in an afterlife that was far more important than life here on earth. These qualities, in Gibbon's view, were entirely inadequate for the maintenance of a proud and vigorous empire.

Despite the value of Gibbon's work, Christianity cannot reasonably be made the villain of the piece. True, many very able minds and forceful characters devoted their lives and energies primarily to the Christian church and not to the empire. Yet the numbers involved in these pursuits were small in proportion to the total population. Furthermore, the Byzantine Empire, which evolved from the eastern part of the Roman Empire, demonstrated that Christians could handle the sword as well as the cross.

Ultimately, Gibbon begged his own question, as when he wrote that "instead of inquiring *why* the Roman Empire was destroyed, we should rather be surprised that it had subsisted for so long."[13] Yet once Gibbon raised the question of the causes for

Rome's fall, other historians were quick to answer it. Some of their answers are nonsensical, others useful; but all demonstrate the very many ways in which people view history and their own relation to it.

To explain the fall of the Roman Empire, some scholars have resorted to pseudoscientific theories. These efforts are in effect an abuse of science. For instance, some writers have looked at historical developments in biological terms. According to them, states and empires develop like living organisms, progressing through periods of birth and growth to maturity and consolidation, followed by decrepitude, decline, and collapse. This argument is simply false analogy, unsupported by any scientific evidence.

Others blame the "collapse" on ridiculous racial theories. They speculate that the Roman people became "mongrelized" when the physically strong, moral, and intelligent Romans intermingled with inferior Asian and African peoples, causing the Ro-

ROMAN HISTORY AFTER AUGUSTUS

Period	Important Emperors	Significant Events
Julio-Claudians 27 B.C.–A.D. 68	Augustus 27 B.C.–A.D. 14 Tiberius, 14–37 Caligula, 37–41 Claudius, 41–54 Nero, 54–68	Augustan settlement Beginning of the principate Birth and death of Jesus Expansion into northern and western Europe Creation of the imperial bureaucracy
Year of the Four Emperors	Nero Galba Otho Vitellius	Civil war Major breakdown of the concept of the principate
Flavians 69–96	Vespasian, 69–79 Titus, 79–81 Domitian, 81–96	Growing trend toward the concept of Monarchy Defense and further consolidation of the European frontiers
Antonines 96–192	Nerva, 96–98 Trajan, 98–117 Hadrian, 117–138 Antonius Pius, 138–161 Marcus Aurelius, 161–180 Commodus, 180–192	The "golden age"—the era of the "five good emperors" Economic prosperity Trade and growth of cities in northern Europe Beginning of barbarian menace on the frontiers
Severi 193–235	Septimius Severus, 193–211 Caracalla, 211–217 Elagabalus, 218–222 Severus Alexander, 222–235	Military monarchy All free men within the empire given Roman citizenship
"Barracks Emperors" 235–284	Twenty-two emperors in forty-nine years	Civil war Breakdown of the empire Barbarian invasions Severe economic decline
Tetrarchy 284–337	Diocletian, 284–305 Constantine, 306–337	Political recovery Autocracy Legalization of Christianity Transition to the Middle Ages in the West Birth of the Byzantine Empire in the East

mans to lose their physical and moral fiber. This theory, too, can be readily refuted: the eastern, supposedly inferior half of the empire survived a thousand years longer than the "superior" western half. One of the more amusing explanations appeared in the *New England Journal of Medicine* in 1983, when an author speculated that lead poison-

ing contributed to the fall of the empire. According to this view, the use of lead cooking pots, lead cups, and lead water pipes caused widespread gout and lead poisoning in Roman society. Yet skeletal remains of Romans show no excessive amounts of lead. All of these pseudoscientific explanations suffer from one basic error: they assume that conditions in Rome and Italy were general throughout the Roman Empire. They ignore the simple fact that people lived differently in different parts of the empire, just as Americans in New Mexico live differently from those in Alaska. The government and culture may be essentially the same over a large area, whether in the empire or in the United States, but local circumstances differ widely. Conditions in the city of Rome should not be taken as typical of the empire in general.

Others have offered an economic explanation of the awful revolution—a solution especially popular among Marxist historians. In their view, the Roman economy declined primarily because of its dependence on slave labor. At the same time, Roman expansion in northern Europe led to the growth of new centers of production there. Roman assimilation of barbarian peoples on the European fringe of the empire, combined with the economic development of the area, resulted in economic competition in which Rome's Mediterranean markets declined and economic stagnation set in. This interpretation suffers from two major weaknesses. First, slavery was hardly a significant factor in these events and certainly not the cause of them. In late antiquity slavery was itself in decline and manumission widespread. In fact, these are the very years in which the agricultural slave increasingly gave way to the free tenant farmer, even though the farmer himself was in an economically disadvantaged situation.

The second flaw in the economic view is its overestimation of the competition from northern Europe. It is true that the widespread settlement of retired Roman legionaries on the frontier and the demands of their barbarian customers led to the rise of new economic centers, but this process had existed from the days of Julius Caesar. No one would argue that most of what was produced along the frontier was consumed there. Moreover, this is the very region that was hardest hit by the barbarian invasions and civil wars. Meanwhile, in the core of the Roman Empire, the Mediterranean basin, a sturdy commerce continued over the traditional sea-lanes. The later Roman Empire indeed suffered from significant economic problems, but the origins of those difficulties stemmed neither from slavery nor from competition from the European fringe.

Over the years, political explanations for the empire's decline have won the widest acceptance. The Roman imperial government never solved the problem of succession: it never devised a peaceful and regular way to pass on the imperial power when an emperor died. The legions enjoyed too much power, often creating and destroying civil governments at will and in the process gradually destroying the state. The assassinations of emperors and frequent changes of government produced chronic instability, weakening the state's ability to solve its problems.

From the late third century on, successive approaches to Rome's economic difficulties proved disastrous. Emperors depreciated the coinage. The middle classes carried an increasingly heavy tax burden, and the imperial bureaucracy grew bigger, though not more efficient. These factors combined to destroy the ordinary citizen's confidence in the state. Consequently, according to the explanation of political historians, with the economy and society so undermined, the Roman Empire was destroyed by internal difficulties. In this way, most of the economic problems of Rome's decline can be traced to political causes.

Yet there is no real reason even to accept Gibbon's concept of a "fall" or "decline" of the Roman Empire. No one in the late Roman Empire woke up one morning and said, "Oh, I see that the empire has fallen, classical antiquity has ended, and the Middle Ages have begun." Rather, the concept of change and development, instead of decline, has much to recommend it, particularly since so many aspects of the Roman world survived. Both barbarians and popes eagerly embraced Roman political forms and ideas, and a great many aspects of the Roman world survived to influence the medieval and eventually the modern world. Roman law left its traces on the legal and political systems of most European countries. Roman roads, aqueducts, bridges, and buildings remained in use, not as museum pieces but rather as constant practical reminders of the Roman past that became a part of the growing present. The Latin language lay at the root of many of the modern languages of western Europe. It also served as a major cultural link. For almost two thousand years, Latin language and literature remained at the core of Western education. Those who used the old Roman roads or who studied Latin came to some degree under the spell of Rome. Especially in the intellectual realm, Roman attitudes and patterns of thought fertilized the lives and manner of thinking of generation after generation of Europeans. Slowly, almost imperceptibly, the Roman Empire gave way to the medieval world.

SUMMARY

The Roman emperors expanded the provincial system established during the republic. They gave it more definite organization, both militarily to defend it and bureaucratically to administer it. The result was the pax Romana, a period of peace and prosperity for the empire. Into this climate came Christianity, which was able to spread throughout the Roman world because peace and security made communications within the empire safe and easy. Christianity satisfied people's emotional and spiritual needs in ways that traditional pagan religions did not. Although other mystery religions existed, they were normally exclusive in one way or another. Christianity was open to all, rich and poor, men and women. Paul of Tarsus was the first of many talented Christians to spread the new religion throughout a receptive world. But that world was disrupted in the third century by a combination of barbarian invasions, civil war, and economic decline. The bonds that held the empire together weakened, and only the herculean efforts of the emperors Diocletian and Constantine restored order. Those emperors repulsed the barbarians, defeated rebellious generals, and reformed the economy in a restrictive way. The result was an empire very changed from the time of the Augustan peace, but one that left an enduring legacy for later generations.

NOTES

1. Virgil, *Aeneid* 6.851–853. John Buckler is the translator of all uncited quotations from a foreign language in Chapters 1–6.
2. Augustus, *Res Gestae* 6.34.
3. Ibid., 5.28.
4. Horace, *Odes* 4.15.
5. Virgil, *Georgics* 3.515–519.
6. Ovid, *Fasti* 4.925.
7. Matthew 3:3.
8. Matthew 16:18.
9. Edward Gibbon, *The History of the Decline and Fall of the Roman Empire* (New York: Modern Library, n.d.), 1.1.
10. *Corpus Inscriptionum Latinarum,* vol. 6 (Berlin: G. Reimer, 1882), no. 9792.
11. Ibid., vol. 6, no. 14672.
12. Symmachus, *Relations* 3.10.
13. Gibbon, 2.438.

SUGGESTED READING

Some good general treatments of the empire include P. Garnsey and R. Saller, *The Roman Empire* (1987), and J. Wacher, ed., *The Roman World,* 2 vols. (1987), which attempts a comprehensive survey of the world of the Roman Empire. The role of the emperor is superbly treated by F. Millar, *The Emperor in the Roman World* (1977).

Favorable to Augustus is M. Hammond, *The Augustan Principate* (1933). C. M. Wells, *The German Policy of Augustus* (1972), uses archaeological findings to illustrate Roman expansion into northern Europe. H. Schutz, *The Romans in Central Europe* (1985), treats Roman expansion, its problems, and its successes in a vital area of the empire. In *The Augustan Aristocracy* (1985), one of the great Roman historians of this century, R. Syme, studies the new order that Augustus created to help him administer the empire. Rather than study the Augustan poets individually, one can now turn to D. A. West and A. J. Woodman, *Poetry and Politics in the Age of Augustus* (1984).

Even though Augustus himself still remains an enigma, F. Millar and E. Segal, eds., *Caesar Augustus: Seven Aspects* (1984), is an interesting volume of essays that attempts, not always successfully, to penetrate the official façade of the emperor. Several books examine the reigns of some supposedly unpopular emperors. D. Shotter, *Tiberius Caesar* (1993), presents the most recent biography of this controversial emperor, while A. Ferrill, *Caligula, Emperor of Rome* (1992), does the same for his subject. B. W. Jones, *The Emperor Domitian* (1992), attempts to understand this often hated emperor. N. Hannestad, *Roman Art and Imperial Policy* (1988), examines the way in which the emperors used art as a means of furthering imperial policy. M. Hammond, *The Antonine Monarchy* (1959), is a classic study of the evolution of the monarchy under the five good emperors.

Work on the Roman army includes M. Speidel, *Roman Army Studies,* vol. 1 (1984), and L. Keppie, *The Making of the Roman Army from Republic to Empire* (1984). The army that carried out the emperor's strategy is the subject of G. Webster, *The Roman Imperial Army* (1969). R. MacMullen, *Enemies of the Roman Order* (1993), treats the ways in which the Romans dealt with alien and sometime hostile behavior within the empire. More specific is V. Rudich, *Political Dissidence under Nero* (1993), which provides an unorthodox treatment of the subject that examines the reasons behind some popular rejections of official policy. D. J. Breeze and B. Dobson, *Roman Officers and Frontiers* (1993), analyze the careers of officers and how they defended the frontiers.

The commercial life of the empire is the subject of an interesting book by K. Greene, *The Archaeology of the Roman Economy* (1986), which offers an intriguing way in which to picture the Roman economy through physical remains. The classic treatment, which ranges across the empire, is M. Rostovtzeff, *The Economic and Social History of the Roman Empire* (1957). P. W. de Neeve, *Colonies: Private Farm-Tenancy in Roman Italy* (1983), covers agriculture and the styles of landholding from the republic to the early empire. J. Rich, *The City in Late Antiquity* (1992), traces the influence of late Roman cities on their medieval successors. J. D. Deiss, *Herculaneum* (1989), describes one of the most important sites in Italy and reconstructs the lives of its people.

Social aspects of the empire are the subject of R. MacMullen, *Roman Social Relations, 50 B.C. to A.D. 284* (1981), and a recent contribution is L. A. Thompson, *Romans and Blacks* (1989). An important feature of Roman history is treated by R. P. Saller, *Personal Patronage Under the Early Empire* (1982). J. Humphrey, *Roman Circuses and Chariot Racing* (1985), treats a topic very dear to the hearts of ancient Romans. C. A. Barton, *The Sorrows of the Ancient Romans* (1993), is an intriguing and daring attempt to understand the Roman fascination for gladitorial games. K. R. Bradley, *Slaves and Masters in the Roman Empire* (1988), discusses social controls in a slaveholding society. Lastly, B. Cunliffe, *Greeks, Romans and Barbarians* (1988), uses archaeological and literary evidence to discuss the introduction of Greco-Roman culture into western Europe.

Christianity, paganism, Judaism, and the ways in which they all met have received much recent attention. K. Wengst, *Pax Romana and the Peace of Jesus Christ* (English trans., 1987), is an interesting study of the social atmosphere of the lower classes at the time when Christianity was spreading. More recent is A. Chester, *The Social Context of Early Christianity*

(1989). The life of Jesus and the history of early Christianity are the subjects of much recent scholarship. In general, see M. Sordi, *The Christians and the Roman Empire* (English trans., 1986), and J. T. Burtchaell, *From Synagogue to Church* (1992); related is J. Lieu, ed., *The Jews among Pagans and Christians* (1992), which expores relations among all three sets of beliefs. P. Fredriksen, *From Jesus to Christ* (1988), re-examines the New Testament images of Jesus. More dramatic perhaps are J. D. Crossan, *The Historical Jesus* (1991); J. Meier, *A Marginal Jew* (1992); and two studies of the roots of early Christianity: B. Mack, *A Myth of Innocence* (1989) and *The Lost Gospel* (1993), which studies "The Book of Q" and its relation to Christian origins. F. R. Trombley, *Hellenic Religion and Christianization, c. 370–529,* 2 vols. (1993), is an excellent examination of how Greek religion influenced the development of Christianity in the eastern parts of the later Roman Empire.

Convenient surveys of Roman literature are J. W. Duff's, *Literary History of Rome from the Origins to the Close of the Golden Age* (1953) and *Literary History of Rome in the Silver Age,* 3d ed. (1964). New treatments of two of the most important Augustan poets are C. Kallendorf, ed., *Virgil* (1993), and W. S. Anderson, ed., *Ovid* (1993).

Ever since Gibbon's *History of the Decline and Fall of the Roman Empire,* one of the masterpieces of English literature, the decline of the empire has been a fertile field of investigation. S. Perowne, *Hadrian* (1987), is an assessment of the emperor who attempted to limit Roman expansion. Broader are A. M. H. Jones, *The Decline of the Ancient World* (1966), and F. W. Walbank, *The Awful Revolution* (1969). S. N. C. Lieu and M. Dodgeon, *Rome's Eastern Frontier, A.D. 226–363* (1988), rely primarily on documents to trace Rome's policy in the East during this difficult period. Two studies analyze the attempts at recovery from the breakdown of the barracks emperors: T. D. Barnes, *The New Empire of Diocletian and Constantine* (1982), which, as its title indicates, concerns itself with the necessary innovations made by the two emperors; and, more narrowly, S. Williams, *Diocletian and the Roman Recovery* (1985). A. Ferrill, *The Fall of the Roman Empire* (1986), with plans and illustrations, offers a military explanation for the "fall." R. MacMullen, *Constantine* (1988), written by a leading scholar in the field, provides a broad and lucid interpretation of Constantine and the significance of his reign.

Rome Extends Its Citizenship

One of the most dramatic achievements of the pax Romana was the extension of citizenship throughout the Roman Empire. People who had never visited Rome, and perhaps had never even seen a provincial governor, became members, not subjects, of their government. By granting citizenship to most people in the empire, the Roman government in effect took them into partnership.

Yet various emperors went even further by viewing Rome not only as a territorial but also as a political concept. In their eyes Rome was a place and an idea. Not every Roman agreed with these cosmopolitan views. Emperor Claudius (41–54) took the first major step in this direction by allowing romanized Gauls to sit in the senate. He was roundly criticized by some Romans, but in the damaged stone inscription that follows he presents his own defense.

Surely both my great-uncle, the deified Augustus, and my uncle, Tiberius Caesar, were following a new practice when they desired that all the flower of the colonies and the municipalities everywhere—that is, the better class and the wealthy men—should sit in this senate house. You ask me: Is not an Italian senator preferable to a provincial? I shall reveal to you in detail my views on this matter when I come to obtain approval for this part of my censorship [a magistracy that determined who was eligible for citizenship and public offices]. But I think that not even provincials ought to be excluded, provided that they can add distinction to this senate house.

Look at that most distinguished and most flourishing colony of Vienna [the modern Vienne in France], how long a time already it is that it has furnished senators to this house! From that colony comes that ornament of the equestrian order—and there are few to equal him—Lucius Vestinus, whom I cherish most intimately and whom at this very time I em-

ploy in my affairs. And it is my desire that his children may enjoy the first step in the priesthoods, so as to advance afterwards, as they grow older, to further honors in their rank. . . . I can say the same of his brother, who because of this wretched and most shameful circumstance cannot be a useful senator for you.

The time has now come, Tiberius Caesar Germanicus [Claudius himself], now that you have reached the farthest boundaries of Narbonese Gaul, for you to unveil to the members of the senate the import of your address. All these distinguished youths whom I gaze upon will no more give us cause for regret if they become senators than does my friend Persicus, a man of most noble ancestry, have cause for regret when he reads among the portraits of his ancestors the name Allobrogicus. But if you agree that these things are so, what more do you want, when I point out to you this single fact, that the territory beyond the boundaries of Narbonese Gaul already sends you senators, since we have men of our order from Lyons and have no cause for regret. It is indeed with hesitation, members of the senate, that I have gone outside the borders of the provinces with which you are accustomed and familiar, but I must now plead openly the cause of Gallia Comata [a region in modern France]. And if anyone, in this connection, has in mind that these people engaged the deified Julius in war for ten years, let him set against that the unshakable loyalty and obedience of a hundred years, tested to the full in many of our crises. When my father Drusus was subduing Germany, it was they who by their tranquility afforded him a safe and securely peaceful rear, even at a time when he had been summoned away to the war from the task of organizing the census which was still new and unaccustomed to the Gauls.

How difficult such an operation is for us at this precise moment we are learning all too well from experience, even though the survey is aimed at nothing more than an official record of our resources. [The rest of the inscription is lost.]

Only later in A.D. 212 did the emperor Caracalla (198–217) extend Roman citizenship to all free-born men with the exception of those called dediticii, whose identity remains a source of controversy. Caracalla claimed that he made this proclamation because the gods had saved him from a plot on his life. Some modern scholars, however, have suggested that he wanted more citizens to tax. Whatever the truth, Caracalla continued the work of Augustus (27 B.C.–A.D. 14) and Claudius. The Romans succeeded where the Greeks had failed: they built an empire of citizens. The following is a damaged copy of Caracalla's edict.

The Emperor Caesar Marcus Aurelius Severus Antoninus Augustus [Caracalla] declares: . . . I may show my gratitude to the immortal gods for preserving me in such [circumstances?]. Therefore I consider that in this way I can . . . rend proper service to their majesty . . . by bringing with me to the worship [?] of the gods all who enter into the number of my people. Accordingly, I grant Roman citizenship to all aliens, throughout the world, with no one remaining outside the citizen bodies except the *dediticii*. For it is proper that the multitude should not only help carry [?] all the burdens but should also now be included in my victory.

Citizenship was often granted to soldiers who had fought in the Roman army. The usual reasons were conspicuous bravery or wounds suffered in the course of duty. The emperor Trajan (98–117) made such a grant of citizenship in 106 to British soldiers who had served in the campaign in Dacia, a southern region of the former Yugoslavia. These men were also honored for their valor with an early discharge.

The Emperor Trajan . . . has granted Roman citizenship before completion of military service to the infantrymen and cavalrymen whose names appear below, serving in the First British Thousand-Man Ulpian Decorated Loyal Fortunate Cohort composed of Roman citizens, which is on duty in Dacia under

Provocatio, the right of appeal, was considered a fundamental element of Roman citizenship. *(Source: Courtesy of the Trustees of the British Museum)*

Decimus Terentius Scaurianus, for having dutifully and faithfully discharged the Dacian campaign.

Questions for Analysis

1. What was the basic justification underlying Claudius's decision to allow Gallic nobles to sit in the senate? Did he see them as debasing the quality of the senate?

2. What do his words tell us about the changing nature of the Roman empire?

3. What was the significance of Caracalla's extension of Roman citizenship to all free-born men?

4. Notice that the Roman government did not extend citizenship to women. Speculate about the practical and ideological reasons for women's exclusion from political power.

Source: Slightly adapted and abbreviated from N. Lewis and M. Reinhold, *Roman Civilization*, vol. 2 (New York: Harper and Row, 1966), pp. 133–134, 427–428, 525.

7

The Making of Europe

The centuries between approximately 400 and 900 present a paradox. On the one hand, they witnessed the disintegration of the western Roman Empire, which had been one of humanity's great political and cultural achievements. On the other hand, these five centuries were a creative and seminal period, during which Europeans laid the foundations for medieval and modern Europe. It is not too much to say that this period saw the making of Europe.

The basic ingredients that went into the making of a distinctly European civilization were the cultural legacy of Greece and Rome, the customs and traditions of the Germanic peoples, and the Christian faith. The most important of these was Christianity, because it absorbed and assimilated the other two. It reinterpreted the classics in a Christian sense. It instructed the Germanic peoples and gave them new ideals of living and social behavior. Christianity became the cement that held European society together.

During this period the Byzantine Empire, centered at Constantinople, served as a protective buffer between Europe and peoples to the east. The Byzantine Greeks preserved the philosophical and scientific texts of the ancient world, which later formed the basis for study in science and medicine, and produced a great synthesis of Roman law, the Justinian Code. In the urbane and sophisticated life led at Constantinople, the Greeks set a standard far above the primitive existence of the West.

In the seventh and eighth centuries, Arabic culture spread around the southern fringes of Europe—to Spain, Sicily, and North Africa, and to Syria, Palestine, and Egypt. The Arabs translated the works of such Greek thinkers as Euclid, Hippocrates, and Galen and made important contributions in mathematics, astronomy, and physics. In Arabic translation, Greek texts trickled to the West, and most later European scientific study rested on the Arabic work.

Interior (view from the apse) of the Byzantine church San Vitale, Ravenna, 526–7 A.D. (*Source: Scala/Art Resource, NY*)

197

The civilization later described as European resulted from the fusion of the Greco-Roman heritage, Germanic traditions, the Christian faith, and significant elements of Islamic culture.

- How did these components act on one another?
- How did they lead to the making of Europe?
- What influence did the Byzantine and Islamic cultures have on the making of Europe?

This chapter will focus on these questions.

✤ THE GROWTH OF THE CHRISTIAN CHURCH

Christianity was a *syncretic* faith, absorbing and adapting many of the religious ideas of the eastern Mediterranean world. From Judaism came the concept, unique in the ancient world, of monotheism, belief in one God, together with the rich ethical and moral precepts of the Old Testament Scriptures. From Orphism, a set of sixth-century B.C. religious ideas, came the belief that the body is the prison of the soul. From Hellenistic thought derived the notion of the superiority of spirit over matter. Likewise, scholars have noticed the similarity between the career of Jesus and that of the gods of eastern mystery cults such as Mithra who died, rose from the dead, and whose followers had a ceremony of communion in which the god's flesh was symbolically eaten. All of these ideas played a part in the formulation of Christian doctrine and in attracting people to it.

While many elements of the Roman Empire disintegrated, then, the Christian church survived and grew. What is the church? Scriptural scholars tell us that the earliest use of the word *church* (in Greek, *ekklesia*) in the New Testament appears in Saint Paul's Letter to the Christians of Thessalonica in northern Greece, written about A.D. 51. By *ekklesia* Paul meant the local community of Christian believers. In Paul's later letters, the term *church* refers to the entire Mediterranean-wide assembly of Jesus' followers. After the legalization of Christianity by the emperor Constantine (see page 187) and the growth of institutional offices and officials, the word *church* was sometimes applied to those officials—much as we use the terms *the college* or *the university* when referring to academic administrators. Then the bishops of Rome—known as "popes" from the Latin word *papa,* meaning "father"—claimed to speak and act as the source of unity for all Christians. The popes claimed to be the successors of Saint Peter and heirs to his authority as chief of the apostles, on the basis of Jesus' words:

You are Peter, and on this rock I will build my church, and the jaws of death shall not prevail against it. I will entrust to you the keys of the kingdom of heaven. Whatever you declare bound on earth shall be bound in heaven; whatever you declare loosed on earth shall be loosed in heaven.[1]

Roman bishops used this text, known as the Petrine Doctrine, to support their assertions of authority over other bishops in the church. Thus the popes maintained that they represented "the church." The word *church,* therefore, has several connotations. Although modern Catholic theology frequently defines the church as "the people of God" and identifies it with local and international Christian communities, in the Middle Ages the institutional and monarchial interpretations tended to be stressed.

Having gained the support of the fourth-century emperors, the church gradually adopted the Roman system of organization. Christianity had a dynamic missionary policy, and the church slowly succeeded in *assimilating*—that is, adapting—pagan peoples, both Germans and Romans, to Christian teaching. Moreover, the church possessed able administrators and leaders and highly literate and creative thinkers. These factors help to explain the survival and growth of the Christian church in the face of repeated Germanic invasions.

The Church and the Roman Emperors

The church benefited considerably from the emperors' support. In return, the emperors expected the support of the Christian church in maintaining order and unity. Constantine had legalized the practice of Christianity within the empire in 312. Although he was not baptized until he was on his deathbed, Constantine encouraged Christianity throughout his reign. He freed the clergy from imperial taxation. At the churchmen's request, he helped settle theological disputes and thus preserve doctrinal unity within the church. Constantine generously endowed the building of Christian churches, and one of his gifts—the Lateran Palace in Rome—remained the official residence of the popes until the fourteenth century. Constantine also declared Sunday a public holiday, a day of rest for the service of God. As the result of its favored position in the empire, Christianity slowly became the leading religion.

In 380 the emperor Theodosius went further than Constantine and made Christianity the official religion of the empire. Theodosius stripped Roman pagan temples of statues, made the practice of the old Roman state religion a treasonable offense, and persecuted Christians who dissented from ortho-dox doctrine. Most significant, he allowed the church to establish its own courts. Church courts began to develop their own body of law, called "canon law." These courts, not the Roman gov-ernment, had jurisdiction over the clergy and ec-clesiastical disputes. At the death of Theodosius, the Christian church was considerably independent of the Roman state. The foundation for the me-dieval church's power had been laid.

What was to be the church's relationship to secular powers? How was the Christian to render unto Caesar the things that were Caesar's while returning to God what was due to God? This problem had troubled the earliest disciples of Christ. The toleration of Christianity and the com-ing to power of Christian emperors in the fourth century did not make it any easier.

In the fourth century, theological disputes fre-quently and sharply divided the Christian commu-nity. Some disagreements had to do with the na-ture of Christ. For example, Arianism, which originated with Arius (ca 250–336), a priest of Alexandria, denied that Christ was divine and coeternal with God the Father—two propositions of orthodox Christian belief. Arius held that God the Father was by definition uncreated and un-changeable. Jesus, however, was born of Mary, grew in wisdom, and suffered punishment and death. Therefore, Arius reasoned, Jesus the Son must be less or inferior to the Unbegotten Father, who is incapable of suffering and did not die. Jesus was created by the will of the Father and thus was not coeternal with the Father. This argument im-plies that Jesus must be somewhere between God the Creator and humanity in need of redemption. Orthodox theologians branded Arius's position a *heresy*—denial of a basic doctrine of faith.

Arianism enjoyed such popularity and provoked such controversy that Constantine, to whom relig-ious disagreement meant civil disorder, interceded. He summoned a council of church leaders to Ni-caea in Asia Minor and presided over it personally. The council produced the Nicene Creed, which defined the orthodox position that Christ is "eter-nally begotten of the Father" and of the same substance as the Father. Arius and those who re-fused to accept the creed were banished, the first case of civil punishment for heresy. This participa-tion of the emperor in a theological dispute within the church paved the way for later emperors to claim that they could do the same.

So active was the emperor Theodosius's partici-pation in church matters that he eventually came to loggerheads with Bishop Ambrose of Milan (339–397). Theodosius ordered Ambrose to hand over his cathedral church to the emperor. Am-brose's response had important consequences for the future:

At length came the command, "Deliver up the Basil-ica"; I reply, "It is not lawful for us to deliver it up, nor for your Majesty to receive it. By no law can you violate the house of a private man, and do you think that the house of God may be taken away? It is as-serted that all things are lawful to the Emperor, that all things are his. But do not burden your conscience with the thought that you have any right as Emperor over sacred things. Exalt not yourself, but if you would reign the longer, be subject to God. It is written, God's to God and Caesar's to Caesar. The palace is the Emperor's, the Churches are the Bishop's. To you is committed jurisdiction over public, not over sacred buildings." [2]

Ambrose's statement was to serve as the corner-stone of the ecclesiastical theory of state-church relations throughout the Middle Ages. Ambrose insisted that the church was independent of the state's jurisdiction and that, in matters relating to the faith or the church, the bishops were to be the judges of emperors, not the other way around. In a Christian society, harmony and peace depended on agreement between the bishop and the secular ruler. But if disagreement developed, the church was ultimately the superior power because the church was responsible for the salvation of all (in-cluding the emperor). In later centuries, theologi-ans, canonists, and propagandists repeatedly cited

Ambrose's position as the basis of relations between the two powers.

Inspired Leadership

The early Christian church benefited from the brilliant administrative abilities of some church leaders and from identification of the authority and dignity of the bishop of Rome with the imperial traditions of the city. Some highly able Roman citizens accepted baptism and applied their intellectual powers and administrative skills to the service of the church rather than the empire. With the empire in decay, educated people joined and worked for the church in the belief that it was the one institution able to provide leadership. Bishop Ambrose, for example, the son of the Roman prefect of Gaul, was a trained lawyer and governor of a province. He is typical of those Roman aristocrats who held high public office, were converted to Christianity, and subsequently became bishops. Such men later provided social continuity from Roman to Germanic rule. As bishop of Milan, Ambrose himself exercised responsibility in the temporal as well as the ecclesiastical affairs of northern Italy.

During the reign of Diocletian (284–305), the Roman Empire had been divided for administrative purposes into geographical units called dioceses. Gradually the church made use of this organizational structure. Christian bishops—the leaders of early Christian communities elected by the Christian people—established their headquarters, or *sees,* in the urban centers of the old Roman dioceses. Their jurisdiction extended throughout all parts of the diocese. The center of the bishop's authority was his cathedral (the word derives from the Latin *cathedra,* meaning "chair"). Thus church leaders capitalized on the Roman imperial method of organization and adapted it to ecclesiastical purposes.

After the removal of the capital and the emperor to Constantinople (see page 188), the bishop of Rome exercised considerable influence in the West because he had no real competitor there. The bishops of Rome stressed that Rome had been the capital of a worldwide empire and emphasized the special importance of Rome in the framework of that empire. Successive bishops of Rome reminded Christians in other parts of the world that Rome was the burial place of Saint Peter and Saint Paul. Moreover, according to tradition, Saint Peter, the chief of Christ's first twelve followers, had lived and been executed in Rome. No other city in the world could make such claims. Hence the bishop of Rome was called "Patriarch of the West." In the East the bishops of Antioch, Alexandria, Jerusalem, and Constantinople, because of the special dignity of their sees, also gained the title of *patriarch.* Their jurisdictions extended over lands adjoining their sees; they consecrated bishops, investigated heresy, and heard judicial appeals.

In the fifth century the bishops of Rome began to stress their supremacy over other Christian communities and to urge other churches to appeal to Rome for the resolution of disputed doctrinal issues. Thus Pope Innocent I (401–417) wrote to the bishops of Africa:

We approve your action in following the principle that nothing which was done even in the most remote and distant provinces should be taken as finally settled unless it came to the notice of this See, that any just pronouncement might be confirmed by all the authority of this See, and that the other churches might from thence gather what they should teach.[3]

The prestige of Rome and the church as a whole was also enhanced by the courage and leadership of the Roman bishops. According to tradition, Pope Leo I (440–461) met the advancing army of Attila the Hun in 452 and, through his power of persuasion, saved Rome from destruction. Three years later, according to legend, Leo persuaded the Vandal leader Gaiseric not to burn the city, though the pope could not prevent a terrible sacking.

By the time Gregory I (590–604) became pope, there was no civic authority left to handle the problems pressing the city. Flood, famine, plague, and invasion by the Lombards made for an almost disastrous situation. Pope Gregory concluded a peace with the Lombards, organized relief services that provided water and food for the citizens, and established hospitals for the sick and dying. The fact that it was Christian leaders, rather than imperial administrators who responded to the city's dire needs could not help but increase the prestige and influence of the church.

Although Innocent I and Leo I strongly asserted the primacy of the Roman papacy, it would be inaccurate to think those assertions were universally accepted. Local Christian communities and their leaders often exercised decisive authority over their churches. Particular social and political conditions determined the actual power of the bishop of Rome in a given circumstance. The importance of arguments for the Roman primacy rests in the fact that they served as precedents for later appeals.

Missionary Activity

The word *catholic* derives from a Greek word meaning "general," "universal," or "worldwide." Christ had said that his teaching was for all peoples, and Christians sought to make their faith catholic—that is, believed everywhere. This could be accomplished only through missionary activity. As Saint Paul had written to the Christian community at Colossae in Asia Minor:

. . . there is no room for distinction between Greek and Jew, between the circumcised or the uncircumcised, or between barbarian or Scythian, slave and free man. There is only Christ; he is everything and he is in everything.[4]

Paul urged Christians to bring the "good news" of Christ to all peoples. The Mediterranean served as the highway over which Christianity spread to the cities of the empire.

During the Roman occupation, Christian communities were scattered throughout Gaul and Britain. The effective beginnings of Christianity in Gaul can be traced to Saint Martin of Tours (ca 316–397), a Roman soldier who, after giving away half his cloak to a naked beggar, had a vision of Christ and was baptized. Martin founded the monastery of Ligugé, the first in Gaul, which became a center for the evangelization of the country districts. In 372 he became bishop of Tours and introduced a rudimentary parish system.

Tradition identifies the conversion of Ireland with Saint Patrick (ca 385–461). Born in western England to a Christian family of Roman citizenship, Patrick was captured and enslaved by Irish raiders and taken to Ireland, where he worked for six years as a herdsman. He escaped and returned to England, where a vision urged him to Christianize Ireland. In preparation, Patrick studied in Gaul and in 432 was consecrated a bishop. He landed in Ireland, and at Tara in present-day County Meath—seat of the high kings of Ireland—he made his first converts. Patrick's missionary activities followed the existing social pattern: he converted the Irish, tribe by tribe, having first baptized

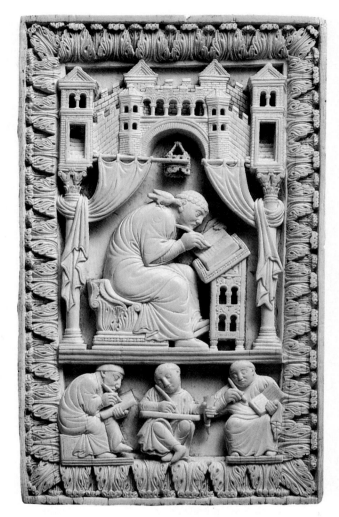

❖ **Pope Gregory I (590–604) and Scribes** One of the four "Doctors" (or Learned Fathers) of the Latin Church, Gregory is shown in this tenth-century ivory book cover writing at his desk while the Holy Spirit in the form of a dove whispers in his ear. Below, scribes copy Gregory's works. *(Source: Kunsthistorisches Museum, Vienna)*

the king. In 445, with the approval of Pope Leo I, Patrick established his see in Armagh. The ecclesiastical organization that Patrick set up, however, differed in a fundamental way from church structure on the Continent: Armagh was a monastery, and the monastery, rather than the diocese, served as the center of ecclesiastical organization. Local tribes and the monastery were interdependent, with the clan supporting the monastery economically and the monastery providing religious and

MAP 7.1 Anglo-Saxon England The seven kingdoms of the Heptarchy—Northumbria, Mercia, East Anglia, Essex, Kent, Sussex, and Wessex—dominated but did not subsume Britain. Scotland remained a Pict stronghold while the Celts resisted invasion of their native Wales by Germanic tribes.

educational services for the tribe. Patrick also introduced the Roman alphabet and supported the codification of traditional laws. By the time of his death, the majority of the Irish people had received Christian baptism.

A strong missionary fervor characterized Irish Christianity. Perhaps the best representative of Irish-Celtic zeal was Saint Columba (ca 521–597), who established the monastery of Iona on an island in the Inner Hebrides off the west coast of Scotland. Iona served as a base for converting the pagan Picts of Scotland. Columba's proselytizing efforts won him the title "Apostle of Scotland," and his disciples carried the Christian Gospel to the European continent.

The Christianization of the English really began in 597, when Pope Gregory I sent a delegation of monks under the Roman Augustine to Britain to convert the English. Augustine's approach, like Patrick's, was to concentrate on converting the king. When he succeeded in converting Ethelbert, king of Kent, the baptism of Ethelbert's people took place as a matter of course. Augustine established his headquarters, or see, at Canterbury, the capital of Kent. Kings who converted, such as Ethelbert and the Frankish chieftain Clovis (see page 217), sometimes had Christian wives. Besides the personal influence a Christian wife exerted on her husband, conversion may have indicated that barbarian kings wanted to enjoy the cultural advantages that Christianity brought, such as literate assistants and an ideological basis for their rule.

In the course of the seventh century, two Christian forces competed for the conversion of the pagan Anglo-Saxons: Roman-oriented missionaries traveling north from Canterbury and Celtic monks from Ireland and northwestern Britain. Monasteries were established at Iona, Lindisfarne, Jarrow, and Whitby (Map 7.1).

The Roman and Celtic traditions differed completely in their forms of church organization, types of monastic life, and methods of arriving at the date of the central feast of the Christian calendar, Easter. At the Synod (ecclesiastical council) of Whitby in 664, the Roman tradition was completely victorious. The conversion of the English and the close attachment of the English church to Rome had far-reaching consequences because Britain later served as a base for the Christianization of the Continent (Map 7.2).

Between the fifth and tenth centuries, the great majority of peoples living on the European continent and the nearby islands accepted the Christian religion—that is, they received baptism, though baptism in itself did not automatically transform people into Christians.

Religion influenced all aspects of tribal life. Religion was not a private or individual matter; it was a social affair and the religion of the chieftain or king determined the religion of the people. Thus missionaries concentrated their initial efforts not on the people but on kings or tribal chieftains. According to custom, tribal chiefs negotiated with all foreign powers, including the gods. Because the Christian missionaries represented a "foreign" power (the Christian God), the king dealt with them. Germanic kings accepted Christianity because they believed the Christian God was more powerful than pagan ones and the Christian God

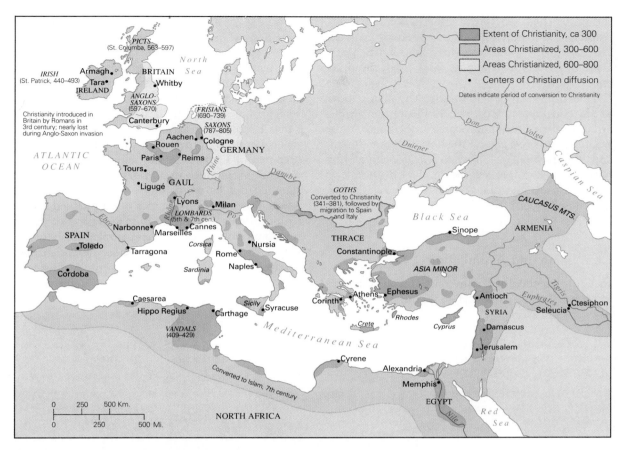

MAP 7.2 The Spread of Christianity Originating in Judaea, the southern part of modern Israel and Jordan, Christianity spread throughout the Roman world. Roman sea lanes and Roman roads facilitated the expansion.

would deliver victory in battle; or because Christianity taught obedience to (kingly) authority; or because Christian priests possessed a knowledge and a charisma that could be associated with kingly power.

Once a ruler had marched his people to the waters of baptism, however, the work of Christianization had only begun. Baptism meant either sprinkling the head or immersing the body in water. Conversion meant mental and heartfelt acceptance of the beliefs of Christianity. What does it mean to be a Christian? This question has troubled sincere people from the time of Saint Paul to the present. The problem rests in part in the basic teaching of Jesus in the Gospel:

Then fixing his eyes on his disciples he said: "How happy are you who are poor: yours is the kingdom of God. Happy you who are hungry now: you shall be satisfied. Happy you who weep now: you shall laugh.

"Happy are you when people hate you, drive you out, abuse you, denounce your name as criminal, on account of the Son of Man. Rejoice when that day comes and dance for joy, then your reward will be great in heaven.

"But I say this to you who are listening: Love your enemies, do good to those who hate you, bless those who curse you, pray for those who treat you badly . . . Treat others as you would like them to treat you."[5]

These ideas are among the most radical and revolutionary the world has heard.

The German peoples were warriors who idealized the military virtues of physical strength, ferocity in battle, and loyalty to the leader. Victors in battle enjoyed the spoils of success and plundered the vanquished. The greater the fighter, the more trophies and material goods he collected. Thus the Germans had trouble accepting the Christian precepts of "love your enemies" and "turn the other cheek."

The Germanic tribes found the Christian notions of sin and repentance virtually incomprehensible. Sin in Christian thought meant disobedience to the will of God as revealed in the Ten Commandments and the teaching of Christ. Good or "moral" behavior to the barbarians meant the observance of tribal customs and practices. Dishonorable behavior caused social ostracism. The inculcation of Christian ideals took a very long time.

Conversion and Assimilation

In Christian theology, conversion involves a turning toward God—that is, a conscious effort to live according to the Gospel message. How did missionaries and priests get masses of pagan and illiterate peoples to understand and live by Christian ideals and teachings? Through preaching, through assimilation, and through the penitential system. Preaching aimed at instruction and edification. Instruction presented the basic teachings of Christianity. Edification was intended to strengthen the newly baptized in their faith through stories about the lives of Christ and the saints. But deeply ingrained pagan customs and practices could not be stamped out by words alone or even by imperial edicts. Christian missionaries often pursued a policy of assimilation, easing the conversion of pagan men and women by stressing similarities between their customs and beliefs and those of Christianity. A letter from Pope Gregory I beautifully illustrates this policy. Sent to Augustine of Canterbury in Britain in 601, it expresses the pope's intention

❖ **The Pantheon (Interior)** Originally a temple for the gods, the Pantheon later served as a Christian church. As such, it symbolizes the adaptation of pagan elements to Christian purposes. *(Source: Alinari/Art Resource)*

that pagan buildings and practices be given a Christian significance:

To our well beloved son Abbot Mellitus: Gregory servant of the servants of God. . . . Therefore, when by God's help you reach our most reverent brother, Bishop Augustine, we wish you to inform him that we have been giving careful thought to the affairs of the English, and have come to the conclusion that the temples of the idols among that people should on no account be destroyed. The idols are to be destroyed, but the temples themselves are to be aspersed with holy water, altars set up in them, and relics deposited there. For if these temples are well-built, they must be purified from the worship of demons and dedicated to the service of the true God. In this way, we hope that the people, seeing that their temples are not destroyed, may abandon their error and, flocking more readily to their accustomed resorts, may come to know and adore the true God. . . .[6]

How assimilation works is perhaps best appreciated through the example of a festival familiar to all Americans, Saint Valentine's Day. There were two Romans named Valentine. Both were Christian priests, and both were martyred for their beliefs around the middle of February in the third century. Since about 150 B.C. the Romans had celebrated the festival of Lupercalia, at which they asked the gods for fertility for themselves, their fields, and their flocks. This celebration occurred in mid-February, shortly before the Roman New Year and the arrival of spring. Thus the early church "converted" the old festival of Lupercalia into Saint Valentine's Day. (Nothing in the lives of the two Christian martyrs connects them with lovers or the exchange of messages and gifts. That practice began in the later Middle Ages.) The fourteenth of February was still celebrated as a festival, but it had taken on Christian meaning.

A process that had an equally profound, if gradual, impact on the conversion of the pagan masses was the rite of reconciliation in which the sinner revealed his or her sins in order to receive God's forgiveness. In the early Church "confession" meant that the sinner *publicly* acknowledged charges laid against him or her and publicly carried out the penitential works prescribed by the priest or bishop. For example, the adulterer might have to stand outside the church before services wearing a sign naming his or her sin and asking the prayers of everyone who entered.

Beginning in the late sixth century, however, Irish and English missionaries brought the more private penitential system to continental Europe. *Penitentials* were manuals for the examination of conscience. The penitent knelt before the priest, who questioned the penitent about the sins he or she might have committed. A penance was then imposed. Penance usually meant fasting for a period of time on bread and water, which was intended as a medicine for the soul. Here is a section of the penitential prepared by Archbishop Theodore of Canterbury (668–690) which circulated widely at the time:

If anyone commits fornication with a virgin he shall do penance for one year. If with a married woman, he shall do penance for four years.

A male who commits fornication with a male shall do penance for three years.

If a woman practices vice with a woman, she shall do penance for three years.

Whoever has often committed theft, seven years is his penance, or such a sentence as his priest shall determine, that is, according to what can be arranged with those whom he has wronged. . . .

Women who commit abortion before [the fetus] has life, shall do penance for one year or for the three forty-day periods or for forty days, according to the nature of the offense; and if later, that is, more than forty days after conception, they shall do penance as murderesses.

If a poor woman slays her child, she shall do penance for seven years. In the canon it is said that if it is a case of homicide, she shall do penance for ten years.[7]

As this sample suggests, writers of penitentials were preoccupied with sexual transgressions. Penitentials are much more akin to the Jewish law of the Old Testament than to the spirit of the New Testament. They provide an enormous amount of information about the ascetic ideals of early Christianity and about the crime-ridden realities of Celtic and Germanic societies. Penitentials also reveal the ecclesiastical foundations of some modern attitudes toward sex, birth control, and abortion. Unlike the earlier public penances, Celtic forms permitted the repeated reconciliation of the same sinner in a *private* situation involving only the priest and penitent. We do not know whether these severe penances were actually enforced; some scholars believe they were not. In any case, the penitential system contributed to the growth of a different attitude toward religion: formerly public, corporate, and social, religious observances became private, personal, and individual.[8]

CHRISTIAN ATTITUDES TOWARD CLASSICAL CULTURE

Probably the major dilemma the early Christian church faced concerned Greco-Roman culture. The Roman Empire as a social, political, and economic force gradually disintegrated. Its culture, however, survived. In Greek philosophy, art, and architecture, in Roman law, literature, education, and engineering, the legacy of a great civilization continued. The Christian religion had begun and spread within this intellectual and psychological milieu. What was to be the attitude of Christians to the Greco-Roman world of ideas?

Adjustment

Christians in the first and second centuries believed that the end of the world was near. Christ had promised to return, and Christians expected to witness that return. Therefore, they considered knowledge useless and learning a waste of time. The important duty of the Christian was to prepare for the Second Coming of the Lord. Good Christians who sought the Kingdom of Heaven through the imitation of Christ believed they had to disassociate themselves from the "filth" that Roman culture embodied.

As Saint Paul wrote, "The wisdom of the world is foolishness, we preach Christ crucified." Tertullian (ca 160–220), an influential African Church Father and writer, condemned all secular literature as foolishness in the eyes of God. He called the Greek philosophers, such as Aristotle, "hucksters of eloquence" and compared them to "animals of self-glorification." "What has Athens to do with Jerusalem," he demanded, "the Academy with the Church? We have no need for curiosity since Jesus Christ, nor for inquiry since the gospel." Tertullian insisted that Christians would find in the Bible all the wisdom they needed.

On the other hand, Christianity encouraged adjustment to the ideas and institutions of the Roman world. Some biblical texts clearly urged Christians to accept the existing social, economic, and political establishment. Specifically addressing

Christians living among non-Christians in the hostile environment of Rome, the author of the First Letter of Peter had written about the obligations of Christians:

Toward Pagans

Always behave honorably among pagans, so that they can see your good works for themselves and, when the day of reckoning comes, give thanks to God for the things which now make them denounce you as criminals.

Toward Civil Authority

For the sake of the Lord, accept the authority of every social institution: the emperor, as the supreme authority, and the governors as commissioned by him to punish criminals and praise good citizenship. God wants you to be good citizens. . . . Have respect for everyone and love for your community; fear God and honour the emperor.[9]

Christians really had little choice. Christianity did not emerge in a social or intellectual vacuum; Jewish and Roman cultures were the only cultures Christians knew. Many early Christians had grown up as pagans, been educated as pagans, and been converted only as adults.

Even had early Christians wanted to give up Greco-Roman ideas and patterns of thought, they would have had great difficulty doing so. Therefore, they had to adapt their Roman education to their Christian beliefs. Saint Paul himself believed there was a good deal of truth in pagan thought, as long as it was correctly interpreted and understood.

The result was a compromise. Christians gradually came to terms with Greco-Roman culture. Saint Jerome (340–419), a distinguished theologian and linguist, remains famous for his translation of the Old and New Testaments from Hebrew and Greek into vernacular Latin. Called the "Vulgate," his edition of the Bible served as the official translation until the sixteenth century; even today, scholars rely on it. Familiar with the writings of classical authors, St. Jerome also believed that Christians should study the best of ancient thought because it would direct their minds to God. Jerome maintained that the best ancient literature should be interpreted in light of the Christian faith.

Christian attitudes toward women and toward homosexuality illustrate the ways early Christians adopted the views of their contemporary world.

Jesus, whom Christians accept as the Messiah, considered women the equal of men in his plan of salvation. He attributed no disreputable qualities to women, made no comment on the wiles of women, no reference to them as inferior creatures. On the contrary, women were among his earliest and most faithful converts. He discussed his mission with them (John 4:21–25); he accepted the ministrations of a reformed prostitute; and women were the first persons to whom he revealed himself after his resurrection (Matthew 28:9–10). Jewish and Christian writers, however, not Jesus, had the greater influence on the formation of medieval (and modern) attitudes toward women.

Jesus' message emphasized love for God and one's fellow human beings; later writers tended to stress Christianity as a religion of renunciation and asceticism. Their views derive from Platonic-Hellenistic ideas of the contemporary Mediterranean world. The Hellenistic Jewish philosopher Philo of Alexandria (ca 20 B.C.–ca 50 A.D.), for example, held that since the female represented sense perception and the male the higher, rational soul, the female was inferior to the male. Philo accepted the biblical command to increase and multiply but argued that the only good of marriage was the production of children for the continuation of the race. Female beauty may come from God, who created everything, the African Church Father Tertullian wrote, but it should be feared. Women should wear veils or men will be endangered by the sight of them. While early Christian writers repeated such statements, perhaps the most revolting image of women comes from St. John Chrysostom (347–407), patriarch of Constantinople, a ruthless critic of contemporary morals. Commenting on female beauty, he wrote that "if a man consider what is stored up inside those beautiful eyes and that straight nose, and the mouth and the cheeks, you will affirm the well-shaped body to be nothing else than a white sepulchre; the parts within are full of so much uncleanliness. Moreover, when you see a rag with any of these things on it, such as phlegm or spittle, you cannot bear to touch it, with even the tips of your fingers, nay you cannot even endure looking at it; yet you are in a flutter of excitement about the storehouses and depositories [women] of these things."[10]

The church fathers acknowledged that God had established marriage for the generation of children, but they believed it was a concession to weak souls who could not bear celibacy. God had clearly sanc-

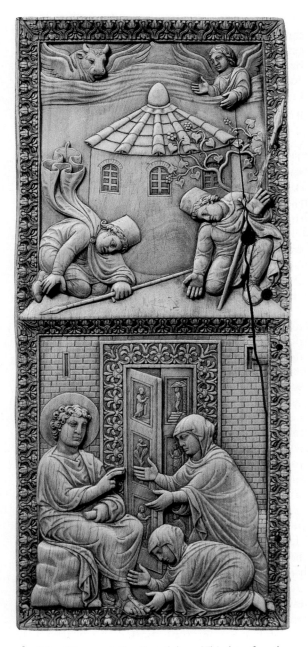

❖ **The Marys at the Sepulcher** This late fourth-century ivory panel tells the story (Matthew 28:1–6) of Mary Magdalene and another Mary (lower) who went to Jesus' tomb to discover the stone at the entrance rolled away; that an angel had descended from heaven; and in shock the guards assigned (upper) to watch the tomb "trembled and became like dead men." The angel told the women that Jesus had risen. The blend of Roman artistic style—in spacing, drapery, men's hair fashion—and Christian subject matter shows the assimilation of classical form and Christian teaching. (*Source: Castello Sforzesco/Scala/Art Resource, NY*)

tioned marriage, and coitus was theoretically good since it was created by God. But in daily life every act of intercourse was evil, the child was conceived by a sinful act and came into the world tainted with "original sin" (see page 209). Celibacy was the highest good; intercourse little more than animal lust.

Because women were considered incapable of writing on the subject, we have none of their views. The church fathers, by definition, were all males. Since many of them became aware of their physical desires when in the presence of women, *misogyny* (hatred of women) entered Christian thought. Although early Christian writers believed women the spiritual equals of men, and although some women, such as Saints Melania and Scholastica (see page 213) exercised influence as teachers and charismatic leaders, Christianity became a male-centered and sex-negative religion. "The Church Fathers regarded sex as at best something to be tolerated, an evil whose only good was procreation."[11] Until perhaps very recently, this attitude dominated Western thinking on human sexuality.

Toward homosexuality, according to a controversial study, Christians of the first three or four centuries simply imbibed the attitude of the world in which they lived. Like the Greeks, many Romans indulged in homosexual activity, and contemporaries did not consider such behavior (or inclinations to it) immoral, bizarre, or harmful. Several emperors were openly homosexual, and homosexuals participated freely in all aspects of Roman life and culture. Early Christians, too, considered homosexuality a conventional expression of physical desire and were no more susceptible to anti-homosexual prejudices than pagans were. Some prominent Christians experienced loving same-gender relationships that probably had a sexual element. What eventually led to a change in public and Christian attitudes toward sexual behavior was the shift from the sophisticated urban culture of the Greco-Roman world to the rural culture of medieval Europe.[12]

Synthesis: Saint Augustine

The finest representative of the blending of classical and Christian ideas, and indeed one of the most brilliant thinkers in the history of the Western world, was Saint Augustine of Hippo (354–430). Saint Augustine was born into an urban family in what is now Algeria in North Africa. His father was a pagan; his mother, Monica, a devout Christian. Because his family was poor—his father was a minor civil servant—the only avenue to success in a highly competitive world was a classical education.

Augustine's mother believed that a good classical education, though pagan, would make her son a better Christian, so Augustine's father scraped together the money to educate him. The child received his basic education in the local school. By modern and even medieval standards, that education was extremely narrow: textual study of the writings of the poet Virgil, the orator-politician Cicero, the historian Sallust, and the playwright Terence. At that time, learning meant memorization. Education in the late Roman world aimed at appreciation of words, particularly those of renowned and eloquent orators.

At the age of seventeen, Augustine went to nearby Carthage to continue his education. There he took a mistress with whom he lived for fifteen years. At Carthage, Augustine entered a difficult psychological phase and began an intellectual and spiritual pilgrimage that led him through experiments with several philosophies and heretical Christian sects. In 383 he traveled to Rome, where he endured not only illness but also disappointment in his teaching: his students fled when their bills were due.

Finally, in Milan in 387, through the insights he gained from reading Saint Paul's Letter to the Romans, Augustine received Christian baptism. He later became bishop of the seacoast city of Hippo Regius in his native North Africa. He was a renowned preacher to Christians there, a vigorous defender of orthodox Christianity, and the author of over ninety-three books and treatises.

Augustine's autobiography, *The Confessions,* is a literary masterpiece and one of the most influential books in the history of Europe. Written in the form of a prayer, *The Confessions* describes Augustine's moral struggle, the conflict between his spiritual and intellectual aspirations and his sensual and material self.

Great are thou, O Lord, and exceedingly to be praised: great is thy power and of thy wisdom there is no reckoning. And man, indeed, one part of thy creation, has the will to praise thee: yea, man, though he bears his mortality about with him . . . even man, a small portion of thy creation, has the will to praise thee. Thou dost stir him up, that it may delight him to praise thee, for thou hast made us for thyself, and our hearts are restless till they find repose in thee.[13]

The Confessions reveals the change and development of a human mind and personality steeped in the philosophy and culture of the ancient world. Many Greek and Roman philosophers had taught that knowledge and virtue are the same: a person who really knows what is right will do what is right. Augustine rejected this idea. He believed that a person may know what is right but fail to act righteously because of the innate weakness of the human will. People do not always act on the basis of rational knowledge. Here Augustine made a profound contribution to the understanding of human nature: he demonstrated that a learned person can also be corrupt and evil. *The Confessions,* written in the rhetorical style and language of late Roman antiquity, marks the synthesis of Greco-Roman forms and Christian thought.

Augustine's ideas on sin, grace, and redemption became the foundation of all subsequent Christian theology, Protestant as well as Catholic. He wrote that the basic or dynamic force in any individual is the *will,* which he defined as "the power of the soul to hold on to or to obtain an object without constraint." The end or goal of the will determines the moral character of the individual. When Adam ate the fruit forbidden by God in the garden of Eden (Genesis 3:6), he committed the "original sin" and corrupted the will; by concupiscence or sexual desire, which all humans have, Adam's sin was passed on by hereditary transmission through the flesh to all humanity. Original sin thus became a common social stain. Because Adam disobeyed God and fell, so all human beings have an innate tendency to sin: their will is weak. But according to Augustine, God restores the strength of the will through grace, which is transmitted through the sacraments.

Augustine also contributed to the discussion on the nature of the church sparked by the Donatist heretical movement. Promoted by the North African bishop of Carthage, Donatus (313–347), Donatism denied the value of sacraments administered by priests or bishops who had denied their faith under persecution or had committed grave sin. For the Donatists, the holiness of the minister was as important as the sacred rites he performed. Donatists viewed themselves as a separate "chosen people" that had preserved its purity and identity in a corrupt world. The true church, therefore, consisted of a small spiritual elite that was an alternative to society. Augustine responded with extensive preaching and the treatise *On Baptism and Against the Donatists* (A.D. 400). He argued that, through God's action, the rites of the church have an objective and permanent validity, regardless of the priest's spiritual condition. Being a Christian and a member of the church, Augustine maintained, meant striving for holiness; rather than seeing themselves as apart from society, Christians must live in and transform society. The notion of the church as a special spiritual elite, distinct from and superior to the rest of society, recurred many times in the Middle Ages. Each time it was branded a heresy, and Augustine's arguments were marshaled against it.

When the Visigothic chieftain Alaric conquered Rome in 410, horrified pagans blamed the disaster on the Christians. In response, Augustine wrote *City of God.* This profoundly original work contrasts Christianity with the secular society in which it existed. *City of God* presents a moral interpretation of the Roman government—in fact, of all history. Filled with references to ancient history and mythology, it remained for centuries the standard statement of the Christian philosophy of history.

According to Augustine, history is the account of God acting in time. Human history reveals that there are two kinds of people: those who live according to the flesh in the City of Babylon and those who live according to the spirit in the City of God. The former will endure eternal hellfire; the latter enjoy eternal bliss.

Augustine maintained that states came into existence as the result of Adam's fall and people's inclination to sin. The state is a necessary evil, but it can work for the good by providing the peace, justice, and order that Christians need in order to pursue their pilgrimage to the City of God. The particular form of government—whether monarchy, aristocracy, or democracy—is basically irrelevant. Any civil government that fails to provide justice is no more than a band of gangsters.

Although the state results from moral lapse—from sin—neither is the church (the Christian community) entirely free from sin. The church is certainly not equivalent to the City of God. But the church, which is concerned with salvation, is responsible for everyone, including Christian rulers. Churches in the Middle Ages used Augustine's theory to defend their belief in the ultimate supe-riority of the spiritual power over the temporal. This remained the dominant political theory until the late thirteenth century.

Writing about a century after Augustine, the Roman consul Boethius (480–524) also had a pro-found influence on the synthesis of classical and Christian thought. An official under the Ostro-gothic king Theodoric (see page 217) Boethius was falsely accused of treason. While awaiting exe-cution, he wrote *The Consolation of Philosophy,* a defense of Christianity through the use of Platonic philosophy. *The Consolation* became one of the most widely read books of the Middle Ages.

✤ CHRISTIAN MONASTICISM

Christianity began and spread as a city religion. Since the first century, however, some especially pious Christians had felt that the only alternative to the decadence of urban life was complete sepa-ration from the world. All-consuming pursuit of material things, gross sexual promiscuity, and gen-eral political corruption disgusted them. They be-lieved that the Christian life as set forth in the Gospel could not be lived in the midst of such immorality. They rejected the values of Roman so-ciety and were the first real nonconformists in the church.

The fourth century witnessed a significant change in the relationship of Christianity and the broader society. Until Constantine's legalization of Christianity, Christians were a persecuted minority. People were tortured and killed for their faith. Christians greatly revered these *martyrs,* the men and women who, like Jesus, suffered and died for their faith. The martyrs were the great heroes of the early church. When Christianity was legalized and the persecutions ended, a new problem arose. Where Christians had been a suffering minority, now they came to be identified with the state: non-Christians could not advance in the imperial service. And if Christianity had triumphed, so had "the world," since secular attitudes and values per-vaded the church. The church of martyrs no longer existed, and some scholars believe the monasteries provided a way of life for those Christians who wanted to make a total response to Christ's teach-ings, people who wanted more than a lukewarm Christianity. The monks became the new martyrs.

Saint Anthony of Egypt (d. 356), the first monk for whom there is concrete evidence and the per-son later considered the father of monasticism, went to Alexandria during the last persecution in the hope of gaining martyrdom. Christians be-lieved that monks, like the martyrs before them, could speak to God and that their prayers had special influence with him.

Western Monasticism

Monasticism began in Egypt in the third century. At first individuals and small groups withdrew from cities and organized society to seek God through prayer in caves and shelters in the desert or moun-tains. Gradually large colonies of monks emerged in the deserts of upper Egypt. They were called hermits from the Greek word *eremos,* meaning desert. Many devout women also were attracted to the monastic life. We have no way of knowing how many hermits there were in the fourth and fifth centuries because their conscious aim was a hidden life known only to God. Although monks (and nuns) led isolated lives and the monastic move-ment represented the antithesis of the ancient ideal of an urban social existence, ordinary people soon recognized the monks and nuns as holy people and sought them as spiritual guides.

When monasticism spread to western Europe, several factors worked against the continuation of the eremitical form. The cold, snow, ice, and fog that covered much of northern Europe for many months of the year discouraged isolated living. Dense forests filled with wild animals and wander-ing Germanic tribes presented obvious dangers. Also, church leaders did not really approve of ere-mitical life. Hermits sometimes claimed to have mystical experiences, direct communications with God. No one could verify these experiences. If hermits could communicate directly with the Lord, what need had they for the priest and the institu-tional church? Saint Basil (329?–379), the scholarly bishop of Caesarea in Cappadocia in Asia Minor, opposed the eremitical life on other grounds: the impossibility of material self-sufficiency; the danger of excessive concern with the self; and, he argued, the eremitical life did not provide the opportunity for the exercise of charity, the first virtue of any Christian. The Egyptian ascetic Pachomius (290–346?) had organized communities of men and women at his coenobitic monastery at Tabennisi on the Upper Nile drawing thousands of recruits. Saint Basil and the church hierarchy encouraged instead *coenobitic monasticism,* communal living in monasteries. Communal living, they felt, provided an environment for training the aspirant in the virtues of charity, poverty, and freedom from self-deception.

In the fourth, fifth, and sixth centuries, many experiments in communal monasticism were made in Gaul, Italy, Spain, Anglo-Saxon England, and Ireland. While at Rome, Saint Jerome attracted a group of aristocratic women, whom he instructed in the Scriptures and the ideals of ascetic life. After studying both eremitical and coenobitic monasticism in Egypt and Syria, John Cassian established two monasteries near Marseilles in Gaul around 415. One of Cassian's books, *Conferences,* based on conversations he had had with holy men in the East, discussed the dangers of the isolated hermit's life. The abbey of Lérins on the Mediterranean Sea near Cannes (ca 410) also had significant contacts with monastic centers in western Asia and North Africa. Lérins encouraged the severely penitential and extremely ascetic behavior common in the East, such as long hours of prayer, fasting, and self-flagellation. It was this tradition of harsh self-mortification that the Roman-British monk Saint Patrick carried from Lérins to Ireland in the fifth century.

Around 540 the Roman senator Cassiodorus retired from public service and established a monastery, the Vivarium, on his estate in Italy. Cassiodorus wanted the Vivarium to become an educational and cultural center and enlisted highly educated and sophisticated men for it. He set the monks to copying both sacred and secular manuscripts, intending this to be their sole occupation. Cassiodorus started the association of monasticism with scholarship and learning. That developed into a great tradition in the medieval and modern worlds. But Cassiodorus's experiment did not become the most influential form of monasticism in European society. The fifth and sixth centuries witnessed the appearance of many other monastic lifestyles.

The Rule of Saint Benedict

In 529 Benedict of Nursia (480–543), who had experimented with both the eremitical and the communal forms of monastic life, wrote a brief set of regulations for the monks who had gathered around him at Monte Cassino between Rome and Naples. Recent research has shown that Benedict's *Rule* derives from a longer, repetitious, and sometimes turgid document called *The Rule of the Master.* Benedict's guide for monastic life proved more adaptable and slowly replaced all others. *The Rule of Saint Benedict* has influenced all forms of organized religious life in the Roman church.

Saint Benedict conceived of his *Rule* as a simple code for ordinary men. It outlined a monastic life of regularity, discipline, and moderation. Each monk had ample food and adequate sleep. Self-destructive acts of mortification were forbidden. In an atmosphere of silence, the monk spent part of the day in formal prayer, which Benedict called the "Work of God." This consisted of chanting psalms and other prayers from the Bible in that part of the monastery church called the "choir." The rest of the day was passed in study and manual labor. After a year of probation, the monk made three vows.

First, the monk vowed stability: he promised to live his entire life in the monastery of his profession. The vow of stability was Saint Benedict's major contribution to Western monasticism; his object was to prevent the wandering so common in his day. Second, the monk vowed conversion of manners—that is, to strive to improve himself and to come closer to God. Third, he promised obedience, the most difficult vow because it meant the complete surrender of his will to the *abbot,* or head of the monastery.

The Rule of Saint Benedict expresses the assimilation of the Roman spirit into Western monasticism. It reveals the logical mind of its creator and the Roman concern for order, organization, and respect for law. Its spirit of moderation and flexibility is reflected in the patience, wisdom, and understanding with which the abbot is to govern and, indeed, with which life is to be led. The *Rule* could be used in vastly different physical and geographical circumstances, in damp and cold Germany as well as in warm and sunny Italy. The *Rule* was quickly adapted for women, and many convents of nuns were established in the early Middle Ages.

Saint Benedict's *Rule* implies that a person who wants to become a monk or nun need have no previous ascetic experience or even a particularly strong bent toward the religious life. Thus it allowed for the admission of newcomers with different backgrounds and personalities. From Chapter 59, "The Offering of Sons by Nobles or by the

❖ **St. Benedict** Holding his *Rule* in his left hand, the seated and cowled Patriarch of Western Monasticism blesses a monk with his right hand. His monastery, Monte Cassino, is in the background. *(Source: Biblioteca Apostolica Vaticana)*

Poor," and from Benedict's advice to the abbot— "The abbot should avoid all favoritism in the monastery. . . . A man born free is not to be given higher rank than a slave who becomes a monk" (Chapter 2)—we know that men of different social classes belonged to his monastery. This flexibility helps to explain the attractiveness of Benedictine monasticism throughout the centuries.

At the same time, the *Rule* no more provides a picture of actual life in a Benedictine abbey of the seventh or eighth (or twentieth) century than the American Constitution of 1789 describes living conditions in the United States today. A code of laws cannot do that. Monasteries were composed of individuals, and human beings defy strict classification according to rules, laws, or statistics. *The Rule of Saint Benedict* had one fundamental purpose. The exercises of the monastic life were designed to draw the individual slowly but steadily away from attachment to the world and love of self and toward the love of God.

Why did the Benedictine form of monasticism eventually replace other forms of Western monas-

ticism? The answer lies partly in its spirit of flexibility and moderation and partly in the balanced life it provided. Early Benedictine monks and nuns spent part of the day in prayer, part in study or some other form of intellectual activity, and part in manual labor. The monastic life as conceived by Saint Benedict did not lean too heavily in any one direction; it struck a balance between asceticism and idleness. It thus provided opportunities for persons of entirely different abilities and talents— from mechanics to gardeners to literary scholars. Benedict's *Rule* contrasts sharply with Cassiodorus's narrow concept of the monastery as a place for aristocratic scholars and bibliophiles.

Benedictine monasticism also suited the social circumstances of early medieval society. The German invasions had fragmented European life: the self-sufficient rural estate replaced the city as the basic unit of civilization. A monastery, too, had to be economically self-sufficient. It was supposed to produce from its lands and properties all that was needed for food, clothing, shelter, and liturgical service of the altar. The monastery fitted in—indeed, represented—the trend toward localism. The Benedictine form of religious life also proved congenial to women. Five miles from Monte Cassino at Plombariola, Benedict's twin sister Scholastica (480–543) adapted the *Rule* for the use of her community of nuns. The adoption of Benedict's *Rule* by houses of women paralleled that in houses of men.

Benedictine monasticism also succeeded partly because it was so materially successful. In the seventh and eighth centuries, monasteries pushed back forest and wasteland, drained swamps, and experimented with crop rotation. For example, the abbey of Saint Wandrille, founded in 645 near Rouen in northwestern Gaul, sent squads of monks to clear the forests that surrounded it. Within seventy-five years the abbey was immensely wealthy. Such Benedictine houses made a significant contribution to the agricultural development of Europe. The communal nature of their organization, whereby property was held in common and profits pooled and reinvested, made this contribution possible.

Finally, monasteries conducted schools for local young people. Some learned about prescriptions and herbal remedies and went on to provide medical treatment for their localities. A few copied manuscripts and wrote books. This training did not go unappreciated in a society desperately in need of it. Local and royal governments drew on the services of the literate men and able administrators the monasteries produced. This was not what Saint Benedict had intended, but the effectiveness of the institution he designed made it perhaps inevitable.

Eastern Monasticism

From Egypt, Christian monasticism also spread to the Greek provinces of Syria and Palestine and to Byzantium itself. Saint Basil (see page 210) composed a set of regulations that considerably influenced Eastern monasticism. Called the *Long Rules,* Basil's regulations recommended communities of economically self-sufficient monks (or nuns) who lived lives of moderation. Basil discouraged the severe asceticism that was so common in Egypt and also supported the establishment of urban monasteries.

With financial assistance from the emperor Justinian I (527–565) and from wealthy noble men

and women, monasteries soon spread throughout the empire, with 70 abbeys erected in Constantinople alone. Justinian granted the monks the right to inherit property from private citizens and the right to receive *solemnia*, or annual gifts from the imperial treasury or from the taxes of certain provinces, and he prohibited lay confiscation of monastic estates. Beginning in the tenth century, the monasteries acquired fields, pastures, livestock, mills, salt works, and urban rental properties, as well as cash and precious liturgical vessels. The exemption of Byzantine monasteries from state taxes also served to increase monastic wealth.

What did the monasteries do with their revenues? Did the Greek monasteries have an impact on the broader society? Implementing Saint Basil's belief that *philanthropia,* active love for humankind, was a central part of the monastic vocation, monasteries performed important social services: they distributed food, clothing, and money to the poor and needy. Many monasteries contained within their compounds hospitals for the sick (see pages 226, 319); homes for the destitute elderly staffed by monks or nuns; and inns for travelers where the food and lodging were free. Orphans, handicapped, the mentally ill, and battered women also found temporary or permanent refuges in the monasteries of monks or nuns. The great Byzantine scholar Norman Baynes has written, "The Byzantine in his hour of need turned instinctively to the ascete (monk) in the full assurance of his sympathy and succor." A few monks undertook evangelical work. For example, Saint Nikon (c. 930–1000) reconverted the peoples of Crete after the Muslim occupation and preached among the pagan Slavs of the Peloponnesus. The Christian East, however, never regarded missionary or charitable work as the primary work of monasticism.

The main duty of monks or nuns was to pray. They served the world not so much by what they *did* as by what they *were:* people of prayer. The monastery was the scene of the daily and continuous ritual of the divine office; the monks and nuns spent heavily on the sacred vestments and vessels used in their liturgies, which in the course of the centuries became famous for their elaborateness and splendor. The holy and charismatic *elder* (or *starets* in Slavonic) became a characteristic figure in Orthodox monasticism: he or she was the spiritually mature physician capable of guiding others and healing their souls. Thus, Saint Melania (383–

439), abbess of a community of nuns at the Mount of Olives in Jerusalem, guided Evagrius of Pontus (ca 345–ca 399), a Syrian who later served as the spiritual father of many of the Egyptian monks at Nitria and Kellia in Upper Egypt.

Monasticism in the Greek Orthodox world differed in fundamental ways from the monasticism that evolved in western Europe. First, while the *Rule of Saint Benedict* gradually became the universal guide or constitution for all western European monasteries, each individual house in the Byzantine world developed its own *typikon,* or set of rules for organization and behavior. The *typika* contain regulations about novitiate, diet, clothing, liturgical functions, commemorative services for benefactors, and the election of officials, such as the *hegoumenos,* or superior of the house. Second, while stability in the monastery eventually characterized Western monasticism, many Orthodox monks, especially those with a reputation for holiness, "moved frequently from one monastery to another or alternated between a coenobitic monastery and a hermit's kellion"[14] (cell). Finally, unlike the West, where monasteries often established schools for the education of the youth of the neighborhood, education never became a central feature of the Greek houses. Monks and nuns had to be literate, to perform the services of the choir, and children destined for the monastic life were taught to read and write. In the monasteries where monks or nuns devoted themselves to study and writing, their communities sometimes played important roles in the development of theology and in the intellectual life of the empire. But those houses were very few, and no monastery assumed responsibility for the general training of the local young. Since bishops and patriarchs of the Greek church were recruited only from the monasteries, Greek houses did, however, exercise a cultural influence.

✣ THE MIGRATION OF THE GERMANIC PEOPLES

The migration of peoples from one area to another has been a dominant and continuing feature of Western history. Mass movements of Europeans occurred in the fourth through sixth centuries, in the ninth and tenth centuries, and in the twelfth and thirteenth centuries. From the sixteenth century to the present, such movements have been almost continuous, involving not just the European continent but the entire world. The causes of early migrations varied and are not thoroughly understood by scholars. But there is no question that they profoundly affected both the regions to which peoples moved and the ones they left behind.

The *Völkerwanderungen,* or migrations of the Germanic peoples, were important in the decline of the western Roman Empire and in the making of European civilization. Many twentieth-century scholars have tried to explain who the Germans were and why they migrated, but historians and sociologists are only beginning to provide satisfactory explanations. The present consensus, based on the study of linguistic and archaeological evidence, seems to be that there were not one but many Germanic peoples with very different cultural traditions. Archaeological remains—bone fossils, cooking utensils, jewelry, weapons of war, and other artifacts—combined with linguistic data suggest three broad groupings of Germanic peoples. One group lived along the North and Baltic seas in the regions of present-day northern Germany, southern Sweden, and Denmark. A second band inhabited the area between the Elbe and Oder rivers. A third group lived along the Rhine and Weser rivers, closest to the Roman frontier. Although these groupings sometimes showed cultural affiliation, they were very fluid and did not possess political, social, or ethnic solidarity.

Since about 150, Germanic tribes had pressed along the Rhine-Danube frontier of the Roman Empire. Some tribes, such as the Visigoths and Ostrogoths, led a settled existence, engaged in agriculture and trade, and accepted Arian Christianity. Tribes such as the Anglo-Saxons and Huns led a nomadic life unaffected by Roman influences. Scholars do not know exactly when the Mongolian tribe called the Huns began to move westward from China, but about 376 they pressured the Goths along the Rhine-Danube frontier.

Why did the Germans migrate? We do not know. As an authority on the Ostrogoths recently wrote, "Despite a century of keen historical investigation and archaeological excavation, the cause and nature of the *Völkerwanderung* challenge the inquirer as much as ever." Perhaps overpopulation and the resulting food shortages caused migration. Perhaps victorious tribes forced the vanquished to move southward. Probably "the primary stimulus for this gradual migration was the Roman frontier, which increasingly offered service in the army and work for pay around the camps."[15]

Romanization and Barbarization

The Roman Empire, it should be remembered, centered around the Mediterranean. Italy, Spain, and North Africa were the areas most vital to it. Aside from Rome, obviously, Alexandria, Antioch, Ephesus, and later Constantinople represented the great economic, cultural, and population centers. North of Italy, in Gaul, Germany, and Britain, Celtic and Germanic peoples had long predominated. The Roman army had spread a veneer of Roman culture in the territories it controlled, but from the third to the sixth century, as Roman influence declined, native Germanic traditions reasserted themselves.

The Roman army had been the chief means of romanization throughout the empire (see Chapter 6). But from the third century, the army became the chief agent of barbarization. How? In the third and fourth centuries, increasing pressures on the frontiers from the east and north placed greater demands on military manpower, which plague and a declining birthrate had reduced. Therefore, Roman generals recruited barbarians to fill the ranks. They bribed Germanic chiefs with treaties and gold, the masses with grain. By the late third century, a large percentage of military recruits came from the Germanic peoples.

Besides army recruits, several types of barbarian peoples entered the empire and became affiliated with Roman government. The *laeti,* refugees or prisoners of war, were settled with their families in areas of Gaul and Italy under the supervision of Roman prefects and landowners. Generally isolated from the local Roman population, the laeti farmed regions depopulated by plague. The men had to serve in the Roman army. Free barbarian units called *foederati,* stationed near major provincial cities, represented a second type of affiliated barbarian group. Recent research has suggested that rather than giving them land, the Romans assigned the foederati shares of the tax revenues from the region.[16] Living in close proximity to Roman communities, the foederati quickly assimilated into Roman culture. In fact, in the fourth century, some foederati rose to the highest ranks of the army and moved in the most cultured and aristocratic circles. Third, the arrival of the Huns in the west in 376 precipitated the entry of entire peoples, the *gentes,* into the Roman empire. Pressured by defeat in battle, starvation, or the movement of other peoples, tribes such as the Ostrogoths and Visigoths entered in large numbers, perhaps as many as

❖ **Helmet of King Agiluf** German chieftains wanted to be portrayed as Roman-style rulers, so that the representation would convey Roman ideals of power. On this plaque for the helmet of Lombard king Agiluf the king sits enthroned in majesty flanked by bodyguards, while subject cities bring tribute. *(Source: Scala/Art Resource, NY)*

twenty thousand men, women, and children.[17] Under the pro-Roman general Fritigern, the Visigoths petitioned the emperor Valens to admit them to the empire. Seeing in the hordes of warriors the solution to his manpower problem, Valens agreed. Once the Visigoths were inside the empire, Roman authorities exploited their hunger by forcing them to sell their own people in exchange for dogflesh: "the going rate was one dog for one Goth." The bitterness of those enslaved was aggravated by the arrival of the Ostrogoths. A huge rebellion erupted, and when Valens attempted to put it down, the Goths crushed the Roman army at Adrianople on August 9, 378.[18] This date marks the beginning of massive German invasions into the empire (Map 7.3).

Except for the Lombards, whose conquests of Italy persisted into the mid-eighth century, the movements of Germanic peoples on the Continent ended about 600. Between 450 and 565 the Germans established a number of kingdoms, but none except the Frankish kingdom lasted very long. Since the German kingdoms did not have definite geographical boundaries, their locations are approximate. The Visigoths overran much of southwestern Gaul. Establishing their headquarters at Toulouse, they exercised a weak domination over Spain until a great Muslim victory at Guadalete in 711 ended Visigothic rule. The Vandals, whose destructive ways are commemorated in the word *vandal,* settled in North Africa. In northern and western Europe in the sixth century, the Burgundi-

✤ **MAP 7.3 The Germanic Migrations** The Germanic tribes infiltrated and settled in all parts of western Europe. The Huns, who were not German ethnically, originated in central Asia. The Huns' victory over the Ostrogoths led the emperor to allow the Visigoths to settle within the empire, a decision that proved disastrous for Rome.

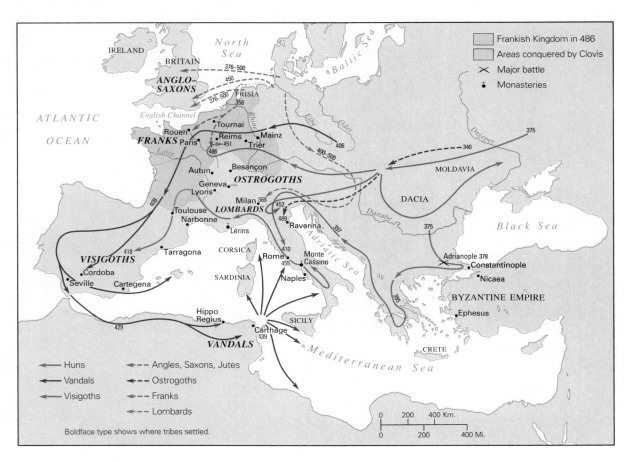

❖ **Baptism of Clovis** (A.D. 496) In this ninth-century ivory carving, St. Remi, bishop of Reims, baptizes the Frankish chieftain by immersing him in a pool of water. Legend holds that on this occasion a dove brought a vial of holy oil from heaven, later used in the coronations of French kings. *(Source: Musée Condé, Chantilly/Laurie Platt Winfrey, Inc.)*

ans established rule over lands roughly circumscribed by the old Roman army camps at Lyons, Besançon, Geneva, and Autun.

In northern Italy the Ostrogothic king Theodoric (r. 471–526) established his capital at Ravenna and gradually won control of all Italy, Sicily, and the territory north and east of the upper Adriatic. Although attached to the customs of his people, Theodoric pursued a policy of assimilation between Germans and Romans. He maintained close relations with the emperor at Constantinople and attracted to his administration able scholars such as Cassiodorus (see page 211). Theodoric's accomplishments were not insignificant, but after his death his administration fell apart.

The most enduring Germanic kingdom was established by the Frankish chieftain Clovis (r. 481–511). Originally only a petty chieftain with headquarters in the region of Tournai in northwestern Gaul (modern Belgium), Clovis began to expand his territories in 486. His Catholic wife Clothilde worked to convert her husband and supported the founding of churches and monasteries. Clothilde (and Bertha, who as the wife of Ethelbert of Kent in sixth-century England exercised a similar influence) is representative of the role women played in the Christianization and romanization of the Germanic kingdoms. Clovis's conversion to orthodox Christianity in 496 won him the crucial support of the papacy and the bishops of Gaul. As the defender of Roman Catholicism against heretical German tribes, he went on to conquer the Visigoths, extending his domain as far as the Pyrenees and making Paris his headquarters. Because he was descended from the half-legendary chieftain Merovech, the dynasty Clovis founded has been called "Merovingian." Clovis's sons subjugated the Burgundians in eastern Gaul and the Ostrogothic tribes living north of the Alps (see Listening to the Past).

 ## GERMANIC SOCIETY

Germanic society had originated with Iron Age peoples (800–500 B.C.) in the northern parts of central Europe and the southern regions of Scandinavia. After the Germans replaced the Romans, re-establishing their rule over most of the European continent, German customs and traditions formed the basis of European society for centuries. What patterns of social, political, and economic life characterized the Germans?

Scholars are hampered in answering such questions because the Germans did not write and thus kept no written records before their conversion to Christianity. The earliest information about them comes from moralistic accounts by such Romans as the historian Tacitus, who was acquainted only with the tribes living closest to the borders of the empire. Furthermore, Tacitus imposed Greco-Roman categories of tribes and nations on the German peoples he described, ethnographic classifications that have dominated scholarly writing until very recently. Only in the past few decades have anthropologists begun to study early German society on its own terms.

Kinship, Custom, and Class

The Germans had no notion of the state as we in the twentieth century use the term; they thought in social, not political, terms. The basic Germanic social unit was the tribe, or *folk*. Members of the folk believed that they were all descended from a common ancestor. Blood united them. Kinship protected them. Law was custom—unwritten, preserved in the minds of the elders of the tribe, and handed down by word of mouth from generation to generation. Custom regulated everything. Every tribe had its customs, and every member of the tribe knew what they were. Members were subject to their tribe's customary law wherever they went, and friendly tribes respected one another's laws.

In the second and third centuries, Germanic peoples experienced continued stress and pressures from other peoples. A radical restructuring of tribes occurred as tribal groups splintered, some disappeared, and new tribes were formed. What bound a tribe, at least temporarily, was a shared peace—peace among those peoples who considered themselves part of a tribe.

Germanic tribes were led by kings, or tribal chieftains. The chief was that member of the folk recognized as the strongest and bravest in battle, elected from among the male members of the strongest family. He led the tribe in war, settled disputes among its members, conducted negotiations with outside powers, and offered sacrifices to the gods. The period of migrations and conquests of the western Roman Empire witnessed the strengthening of kingship among the Germanic tribes. Tribes that did not migrate did not develop kings.

Closely associated with the king in some southern tribes was the *comitatus,* or "war band." Writing at the end of the first century, Tacitus described the war band as the bravest young men in the tribe. They swore loyalty to the chief, fought with him in battle, and were not supposed to leave the battlefield without him; to do so implied cowardice, disloyalty, and social disgrace. A social egalitarianism existed among members of the war band.

During the Völkerwanderungen of the third and fourth centuries, however, and as a result of constant warfare, the war band was transformed into a system of stratified ranks. For example, among the Ostrogoths a warrior-nobility and several other nobilities evolved. Contact with the Romans, who produced such goods as armbands for trade with the barbarians, stimulated demand for armbands. Thus armbands, especially the gold ones reserved for the "royal families," promoted the development of hierarchical ranks within war bands. During the Ostrogothic conquest of Italy under Theodoric, warrior-nobles also sought to acquire land, both as a mark of prestige and as a means to power. As land and wealth came into the hands of a small elite class, social inequalities emerged and gradually grew stronger.[19] These inequalities help to explain the origins of the European noble class (see pages 221, 240).

Law

As long as custom determined all behavior, the early Germans had no need for written law. Beginning in the late sixth century, however, German tribal chieftains began to collect, write, and publish lists of their customs. Why then? The Christian missionaries who were slowly converting the Germans to Christianity wanted to know the tribal customs, and encouraged German rulers to set down their customs in written form. Churchmen wanted to read about German ways in order to assimilate the tribes to Christianity. Augustine of Canterbury, for example, persuaded King Ethelbert of Kent to have his folk laws written down: these *Dooms of Ethelbert* date from between 601 and 604, roughly five years after Augustine's arrival in Britain. Moreover, by the sixth century the German kings needed regulations for the Romans under their jurisdiction as well as for their own people.

Today, if a person holds up a bank, American law maintains that the robber attacks both the bank and the state in which it exists—a sophisticated notion involving the abstract idea of the state. In early German law, all crimes were regarded as crimes against a person.

According to the code of the Salian Franks, every person had a particular monetary value to the tribe. This value was called the *wergeld,* which literally means "man-money" or "money to buy off the spear." Men of fighting age had the highest wergeld, then women of child-bearing age, then children, and finally the aged. Everyone's value reflected his or her potential military worthiness. If a person accused of a crime agreed to pay the wergeld and if the victim and his or her family accepted the payment, there was peace (hence the expression "money to buy off the spear"). If the accused refused to pay the wergeld or if the victim's family refused to accept it, a blood feud ensued. Individuals depended on their kin for protection, and kinship served as a force of social control.

Historians and sociologists have difficulty interpreting the early law codes, partly because they are patchwork affairs studded with additions made in later centuries. Yet much historical information can be gleaned from these codes. For example, the Salic Law—the law code of the Salian Franks issued by Clovis—offers a general picture of Germanic life and problems in the early Middle Ages and is typi-

❖ **King Lhodari of the Alemanni** The Alemanni occupied territory in southwestern Germany and Switzerland in the fifth century but didn't accept Christianity until the late seventh or early eighth century. King Lhodari had Alemanni law (hitherto transmitted orally) written down in Latin. (In French speech the name Allemands came to signify all Germans.) Here the ninth-century artist portrays Lhodari in Roman military garb. (*Source: Bibliothèque Nationale, Paris*)

cal of the law codes of other tribes, such as the Visigoths, Burgundians, Lombards, and Anglo-Saxons.

The Salic Law lists the money fines to be paid to the victim or the family for such injuries as theft, rape, assault, arson, and murder:

✤ **Vandal Landowner** The adoption of Roman dress—short tunic, cloak, and sandals—reflects the way the Germanic tribes accepted Roman lifestyles. Likewise both the mosaic art form and the man's stylized appearance show the Germans' assimilation of Roman influences. (Notice that the rider has a saddle but not stirrups.) *(Source: Courtesy of the Trustees of the British Museum)*

If any person strike another on the head so that the brain appears, and the three bones which lie above the brain shall project, he shall be sentenced to 1200 denars, which make 300 shillings. . . .

If any one have killed a free woman after she has begun bearing children, he shall be sentenced to 2400 denars, which make 600 shillings. . . .

If any one shall have drawn a harrow through another's harvest after it has sprouted, or shall have gone through it with a wagon where there was no road, he shall be sentenced to 120 denars, which make 30 shillings. . . .[20]

This is not really a code of law at all, but a list of tariffs or fines for particular offenses. German law aimed at the prevention or reduction of violence. It was not concerned with abstract justice.

At first, Romans had been subject to Roman law and Germans to Germanic custom. As German kings accepted Christianity and as Romans and Germans increasingly intermarried, the distinction between the two laws blurred and, in the course of the seventh and eighth centuries, disappeared. The result would be the new feudal law, to which Romans and Germans were subject alike.

German Life

The Germans usually resided in small villages where climate and geography determined the basic patterns of agricultural and pastoral life. In the flat or open coastal regions, German males engaged in animal husbandry, especially cattle raising. They also domesticated pigs, sheep, goats, horses, chickens, and geese. Many tribes lived in small settlements on the edges of clearings where they raised barley, wheat, oats, peas, and beans. They tilled their fields with a simple wooden scratch plow and harvested their grains with a small iron sickle. The kernels of grain were ground with a grindstone, and the resulting flour made into a dough that was baked on clay trays into flat cakes. Much of the grain was fermented into a strong, thick beer. Women performed the heavy work of raising, grinding, and preserving cereals, a mark, some scholars believe, of their low status in a male-dominated society. Women also had responsibility for weaving and spinning the thread that went into the manufacture of clothing and all textiles.

Within the small villages, there were great differences in wealth and status. Free men constituted the largest class. The number of cattle a man possessed indicated his wealth and determined his social status. "Cattle were so much the quintessential indicator of wealth in traditional society that the modern English term 'fee' (meaning cost of goods or services), which developed from the medieval term 'fief,' had its origin in the Germanic term *fihu* . . . , meaning cattle, chattels, and hence, in general, wealth."[21] Free men also shared in tribal warfare. Slaves (prisoners of war) worked as farm laborers, herdsmen, or household servants.

German society was patriarchal: within each household the father had authority over his wives, children, and slaves. The Germans practiced polygamy, and men who could afford them had more than one wife.

Did the Germans produce goods for trade and exchange? Ironworking represented the most advanced craft of the Germanic peoples. Much of northern Europe had iron deposits at or near the earth's surface, and the dense forests provided wood for charcoal. Most villages had an oven and smiths who produced agricultural tools and instruments of war—one-edged swords, arrowheads, and shields. In the first two centuries A.D., the quantity and quality of German goods increased dramatically, and the first steel swords were superior to the weapons of Roman troops. But German goods were produced for war and the subsistence economy, not for trade. Goods were also used for gift giving, a major social custom. Gift giving conferred status on the giver who, in giving, showed his higher (economic) status, cemented friendship, and placed the receiver in the giver's debt.[22] Goods that could not be produced in the village were

acquired by raiding and warfare rather than by commercial exchanges. Warfare constituted the main characteristic of Germanic society. Raids between tribes brought the victors booty; the cattle and slaves captured were traded or given as gifts. Warfare determined the economy and the individual's status within the Germanic society.

What was the position of women in Germanic society? The law codes provide the best evidence. The codes show societies that regarded women as family property. The marriageable daughter went to the highest bidder. A woman of child-bearing years had a very high wergeld. The codes also protected the virtue of women. For example, the Salic Law of the Franks fined a man the large amount of 15 solidi (from *solidus,* a coin originally minted by Constantine and later the basis of much European currency, such as the English shilling) if he pressed the hand of a woman, 35 if he touched her above the elbow. On the other hand, heavy fines did not stop injury, rape, or abduction. Widows were sometimes seized on the battlefields where their dead husbands lay and forced to marry the victors. The sixth-century queen Radegund was forced to marry Chlotar I, the murderer of several of her relatives. Radegund later escaped her polygamous union and lived out her life in a convent.

A few slaves and peasant women used their beauty and their intelligence to advance their positions. The slave Fredegunda, for whom King Chilperic murdered his Visigothic wife, became a queen and held her position after her husband's death. Another slave, Balthilda, became the wife of Clovis II. During her sons' minority she worked to alleviate the evils of the slave trade.[23]

Anglo-Saxon England

The island of Britain, conquered by Rome during the reign of Claudius, shared fully in the life of the Roman Empire during the first four centuries of the Christian era. A military aristocracy governed, and the official religion was the cult of the emperor. Towns were planned in the Roman fashion, with temples, public baths, theaters, and amphitheaters. In the countryside, large manors controlled the surrounding lands. Roman merchants brought Eastern luxury goods and Eastern religions—including Christianity—into Britain. The native Britons, a peaceful Celtic people, had become thoroughly romanized. Their language was Latin. Their lifestyle was Roman.

But an event in the distant eastern province of Thrace changed all this. In 378 the Visigothic defeat of the emperor Valens at Adrianople (see page 216) forced Rome to retrench. Roman troops were withdrawn from Britain, leaving it unprotected. The savage Picts from Scotland continued to harass the north. Teutonic tribes from modern-day Norway, Sweden, and Denmark—the Angles, Saxons, and Jutes—stepped up their assaults, attacking in a hit-and-run fashion. Their goal was plunder, and at first their invasions led to no permanent settlements. As more Germans arrived, however, they took over the best lands and humbled the Britons. Increasingly, the Britons fled to Wales in the west and across the English Channel to Brittany. The sporadic raids continued for over a century and led to Germanic control of most of Britain. Historians have labeled the period 500 to 1066, the year of the Norman conquest, "Anglo-Saxon."

Except for the Jutes, who probably came from Jutland (modern Denmark), the Teutonic tribes came from the least romanized and the least civilized parts of Europe. The Germans destroyed Roman culture in Britain. Tribal custom superseded Roman law.

The Anglo-Saxon invasion gave rise to a rich body of Celtic mythology, based on the writings of the ninth-century Welsh scholar Nennius; the mythology became known as the Arthurian legends. When Arthur, the illegitimate son of the king of Britain, successfully drew a sword from a stone, Merlin, the court magician, revealed Arthur's royal parentage. Arthur won recognition as king, and the mysterious Lady of the Lake gave him the invincible sword Excalibur with which he fought many battles against the Saxon invaders. Arthur held his court at Camelot with his knights seated at a Round Table (to avoid quarrels over precedence). Those knights—including Sir Tristan, Sir Lancelot, Sir Galahad, and Sir Percival (Parsifal), who came to represent the ideal of medieval knightly chivalry—played a large role in later medieval and modern literature.

The Arthurian legends represent Celtic hostility to the Anglo-Saxon invaders. The beginnings of the Germanic kingdoms in Britain are very obscure, but scholars suspect they came into being in the seventh and eighth centuries. Writing in the eighth century, the scholar Bede described seven kingdoms: the Jutish kingdom of Kent; the Saxon kingdoms of the East Saxons (Essex), South Sax-

ons (Sussex), and West Saxons (Wessex); and the kingdoms of the Angles, Mercians, and Northumbrians (see Map 7.1). The names imply that these peoples thought of themselves in tribal rather than geographical terms. They referred to the kingdom of the West Saxons, for example, rather than simply to Wessex. Because of Bede's categorization, scholars often refer to the Heptarchy, or seven kingdoms, of Anglo-Saxon Britain. The suggestion of total Anglo-Saxon domination, however, is not entirely accurate. Germanic tribes never subdued Scotland, where the Picts remained strong, or Wales, where the Celts and native Britons continued to put up stubborn resistance.

Thus Anglo-Saxon England was divided along racial and political lines. The Teutonic kingdoms in the south, east, and center were opposed by the Britons in the west, who wanted to get rid of the invaders. The Anglo-Saxon kingdoms also fought among themselves, causing boundaries to shift constantly. Finally, in the ninth century, under pressure of the Danish, or Viking, invasions, the Britons and the Germanic peoples were molded together under the leadership of King Alfred of Wessex (r. 871–899).

✠ THE BYZANTINE EAST (CA 400–788)

Constantine had tried to maintain the unity of the Roman Empire, but during the fifth and sixth centuries the western and eastern halves drifted apart. Later emperors worked to hold the empire together. Justinian (r. 527–565) waged long and hard-fought wars against the Ostrogoths and temporarily regained Italy and North Africa. But his conquests had disastrous consequences. Justinian's wars exhausted the resources of the Byzantine state, destroyed Italy's economy, and killed a large part of Italy's population. The wars paved the way for the easy conquest of Italy by another Germanic tribe, the Lombards, shortly after Justinian's death. In the late sixth century, the territory of the western Roman Empire came under Germanic sway, while in the East the Byzantine Empire continued the traditions and institutions of the caesars.

Latin Christian culture was only one legacy the Roman Empire bequeathed to the Western world. The Byzantine culture centered at Constantinople—Constantine's "new Rome"—was another.

The Byzantine Empire maintained a high standard of living, and for centuries the Greeks were the most civilized people in the Western world. Most important, however, is the role of Byzantium as preserver of the wisdom of the ancient world. Byzantium protected and then handed on to the West the intellectual heritage of Greco-Roman civilization.

Byzantine East and Germanic West

As imperial authority disintegrated in the West during the fifth century, civic functions were performed first by church leaders and then by German chieftains. Meanwhile, in the East, the Byzantines preserved the forms and traditions of the old Roman Empire and even called themselves Romans. Byzantine emperors traced their lines back past Constantine to Augustus. The senate that sat in Constantinople carried on the traditions and preserved the glory of the old Roman senate. The army that defended the empire was the direct descendant of the old Roman legions. Even the chariot factions of the Roman Empire lived on under the Byzantines, who cheered their favorites as enthusiastically as had the Romans of Hadrian's day.

The position of the church differed considerably in the Byzantine East and the Germanic West. The fourth-century emperors Constantine and Theodosius had wanted the church to act as a unifying force within the empire, but the Germanic invasions made that impossible. The bishops of Rome repeatedly called on the emperors at Constantinople for military support against the invaders, but rarely could the emperors send it. The church in the West steadily grew away from the empire and became involved in the social and political affairs of Italy and the West. Nevertheless, until the eighth century, the popes, who were often selected by the clergy of Rome, continued to send announcements of their elections to the emperors at Constantinople—a sign that the Roman popes long thought of themselves as bishops of the Roman Empire. Most church theology in the West came from the East, and the overwhelming majority of popes were themselves of Eastern origin.

Tensions occasionally developed between church officials and secular authorities in the West. The dispute between Bishop Ambrose of Milan and the emperor Theodosius (see page 199) is a good example. A century later, Pope Gelasius I (492–496) insisted that bishops, not civil authorities, were responsible for the administration of the church. Gelasius maintained that two powers governed the world: the sacred authority of popes and the royal power of kings. Because priests had to answer to God even for the actions of kings, the sacred power was the greater.

Such an assertion was virtually unheard of in the East, where the emperor's jurisdiction over the church was fully acknowledged. The emperor in Constantinople nominated the patriarch, as the highest prelate of the Eastern church was called. The emperor looked on religion as a branch of state. Religion was such a vital aspect of the social life of the people that the emperor devoted considerable attention to it, considering it his duty to protect the faith, not only against heathen enemies, but also against heretics within the empire. In case of doctrinal disputes, the emperor, following Constantine's example at Nicaea, summoned councils of bishops and theologians to settle problems.

The steady separation of the Byzantine East and the Germanic West rests partly on the ways Christianity and classical culture were received in the two parts of the Roman Empire. In the West, Christians initially constituted a small, alien minority within the broad Roman culture; they kept apart from the rest of society. Roman society and classical culture were condemned, avoided, and demystified. In Byzantium, by contrast, most Greeks were Christian. *Apologists,* or defenders, of Christianity insisted on harmony between Christianity and classical culture: they used Greek philosophy to buttress Christian tenets. Politically, as we have seen, emperors beginning with Constantine worked for the unanimity of church and state.

The expansion of the Arabs in the Mediterranean in the seventh and eighth centuries furthered the separation of the Western and Eastern churches by dividing the two parts of Christendom. Separation bred isolation. Isolation, combined with prejudice on both sides, bred hostility. Finally, in 1054, a theological disagreement led the bishop of Rome and the patriarch of Constantinople to excommunicate each other. The outcome was a permanent *schism,* or split, between the Roman Catholic and the Greek Orthodox churches. The Byzantine church claimed to be *orthodox,* that is, that it always possessed right doctrine.

Despite religious differences, the Byzantine Empire served as a bulwark for the West, protecting it

✥ **The Empress Theodora and Her Attendants** This mosaic detail is composed of thousands of tiny cubes of colored glass or stone called tessarae set in plaster against a blazing golden background. A halo, symbol of power in eastern art, surrounds the empress's head. An attempt has been made at naturalistic portraiture. *(Source: Scala/Art Resource, NY)*

against invasions from the East. The Greeks stopped the Persians in the seventh century. They blunted—though they could not stop—Arab attacks in the seventh and eighth centuries, and they fought courageously against Turkish invaders until the fifteenth century, when they were finally overwhelmed. Byzantine Greeks slowed the impetus of Slavic incursions in the Balkans and held the Russians at arm's length.

Turning from war to peace, the Byzantines set about civilizing the Slavs, both in the Balkans and in Russia. Byzantine missionaries spread the word of Christ, and one of their triumphs was the conversion of the Russians in the tenth century. The Byzantine missionary Cyril invented a Slavic alphabet using Greek characters, and this script (called the "Cyrillic alphabet") is still in use today. Cyrillic script made possible the birth of Russian literature. Similarly, Byzantine art and architecture became

the basis and inspiration of Russian forms. The Byzantines were so successful that the Russians claimed to be the successors of the Byzantine Empire. For a time, Moscow was even known as the "Third Rome" (the second Rome being Constantinople).

The Law Code of Justinian

One of the most splendid achievements of the Byzantine emperors was the preservation of Roman law for the medieval and modern worlds. Roman law had developed from many sources—decisions by judges, edicts of the emperors, legislation passed by the senate, and the opinions of jurists expert in the theory and practice of law. By the fourth century, Roman law had become a huge, bewildering mass. Its sheer bulk made it almost unusable. Some laws had become outdated; some repeated or contradicted others.

Sweeping and systematic codification took place under the emperor Justinian. He appointed a committee of eminent jurists to sort through and organize the laws. The result was the *Code,* which distilled the legal genius of the Romans into a coherent whole, eliminated outmoded laws and contradictions, and clarified the law itself. Not content with the *Code,* Justinian set about bringing order to the equally huge body of Roman *jurisprudence,* the science or philosophy of law.

During the second and third centuries, the foremost Roman jurists, at the request of the emperors, had expressed learned opinions on complex legal problems, but often these opinions differed from one another. To harmonize this body of knowledge, Justinian directed his jurists to clear up disputed points and to issue definitive rulings. Accordingly, in 533 his lawyers published the *Digest,* which codified Roman legal thought. Finally, Justinian's lawyers compiled a handbook of civil law, the *Institutes.* These three works—the *Code, Digest,* and *Institutes*—are the backbone of the *corpus juris civilis,* the "body of civil law," which is the foundation of law for nearly every modern European nation.

The following excerpts from the Corpus Juris Civilis on marriage and adultery provide valuable information on the status of women in Roman and Byzantine law:

—*Roman citizens unite in legal marriage when they are joined according to the precepts of the law, and males have attained the age of puberty and the females are capable of childbirth . . . [they must] if the latter have also the consent of the relatives under whose authority they may be, for this should be obtained and both civil and natural law require that it should be secured.*

—*The lex Julia ("Julian law," dating from 18 B.C.) declares that wives have no right to bring criminal accusations for adultery against their husbands, even though they may desire to complain of the violation of the marriage vow, for while the law grants this privilege to men it does not concede it to women . . .*

—*. . . A husband cannot accuse his wife of adultery if he continues to retain her in marriage . . . Under the new law, however, he can do so, and if the accusation is proved to be true, he can then repudiate her, and he should file a written accusation against her . . .*

—*The right is granted to the father to kill a man who commits adultery with his daughter while she is under his control.*[24]

Byzantine Intellectual Life

Among the Byzantines, education was highly prized, and because of them many masterpieces of ancient Greek literature survived to influence the intellectual life of the modern world. The literature of the Byzantine Empire was predominantly Greek, although Latin was long spoken among top politi-

❖ **Woman Carrying Pitcher** This detail from a floor mosaic in the Great Palace at Constantinople shows a woman balancing a huge water ewer on her shoulder, which suggests part of her daily work. Notice the large earrings and the coiffured hair. *(Source: Scala/Art Resource, NY)*

cians, scholars, and lawyers. Indeed, Justinian's *Code* was first written in Latin. Among the large reading public, history was a favorite subject. Generations of Byzantines read the historical works of Herodotus, Thucydides, and others. Some Byzantine historians abbreviated long histories, such as those of Polybius, while others wrote detailed narratives of their own days.

The most remarkable Byzantine historian was Procopius (ca 500–ca 562), who left a rousing account praising Justinian's reconquest of North Africa and Italy. Proof that the wit and venom of ancient writers like Archilochus and Aristophanes lived on in the Byzantine era can be found in Procopius's *Secret History,* a vicious and uproarious attack on Justinian and his wife, the empress Theodora. Witness Procopius's description of Justinian's character:

For he was at once villainous and amenable; as people say colloquially, a moron. He was never truthful with anyone, but always guileful in what he said and did, yet easily hoodwinked by any who wanted to deceive him. His nature was an unnatural mixture of folly and wickedness.[25]

How much of this is true, how much the hostility of a sanctimonious hypocrite relishing the gossip he spreads, we will never know. Certainly *The Secret History* is robust reading.

Later Byzantine historians chronicled the victories of their emperors and the progress of their barbarian foes. Like Herodotus before them, they were curious about foreigners and left striking descriptions of the Turks, who eventually overwhelmed Byzantium. They sometimes painted unflattering pictures of the uncouth and grasping princes of France and England, whom they encountered on the Crusades.

In mathematics and geometry the Byzantines discovered little that was new. Yet they were exceptionally important as catalysts, for they passed Greco-Roman learning on to the Arabs, who assimilated it and made remarkable advances with it. The Byzantines were equally uncreative in astronomy and natural science, but at least they faithfully learned what the ancients had to teach.

Only when science could be put to military use did the Byzantines make advances. For example, the best known Byzantine scientific discovery was chemical—"Greek fire" or "liquid fire," an explosive compound made of crude oil mixed with resin

and sulphur, which was heated and propelled by a pump through a bronze tube. As the liquid jet left the tube it was ignited—somewhat like a modern flame thrower. "Greek fire" saved Constantinople from Arab assault in 678. In mechanics the Byzantines continued the work of Hellenistic and Roman inventors of artillery and siege machinery. Just as Archimedes had devised machines to stop the Romans, so Byzantine scientists improved and modified devices for defending their empire.

The Byzantines devoted a great deal of attention to medicine, and the general level of medical competence was far higher in the Byzantine Empire than it was in the medieval West. The Byzantines assimilated the discoveries of Hellenic and Hellenistic medicine but added very few of their own. The basis of their medical theory was Hippocrates' concept of the four humors (see page 93). Byzantine physicians emphasized the importance of diet and rest and relied heavily on herbal drugs. Perhaps their chief weakness was excessive use of bleeding and burning, which often succeeded only in further weakening an already feeble patient.

Greek medical science could not, however, cope with the terrible disease, often called the "Justinian plague," that swept through the Byzantine Empire, Italy, southern France, Iberia, and the Rhine valley between 541 and about 700. Probably originating in northwestern India and carried to the Mediterranean region by ships, the disease followed the syndrome of modern forms of the bubonic plague. Characterized by high fevers, chills, delirium, and enlarged lymph nodes (the buboes that gave the disease its name), or by inflammation of the lungs that caused hemorrhages of black blood, the "Justinian plague" carried off tens of thousands of people.

The epidemic had profound political as well as social consequences. It weakened Justinian's military resources, thus hampering his efforts to restore unity to the Mediterranean world. Demographic disasters resulting from the plague also prevented the Byzantine and Persian forces from offering more than token opposition to the Muslim armies when the Arabs swarmed out of Arabia in 634[26] (see page 230).

Still, by the ninth or tenth century, most major Greek cities had hospitals for the care of the sick. The hospital operated by the Pantokrator monastery in Constantinople possessed fifty beds divided into five wards for different illnesses; a female gynecologist practiced in the women's ward. The hospital staff also included an ophthalmologist (specialist in the functions and diseases of the eye), a surgeon who performed hernia repairs, two general practitioners, two surgeons who worked an outpatient clinic, and an attendant responsible for keeping instruments clean. The imperial Byzantine government bore the costs of this and other hospitals.

✤ THE ARABS AND ISLAM

In the seventh century C.E., two empires dominated the area today called the Middle East: the Byzantine-Greek-Christian empire and the Sasanian-Persian-Zoroastrian empire. The Arabian peninsula lay between the two. The Sasanian dynasty, which descended from Persian-speaking people of (present-day) southern Iran, maintained political control over very diverse peoples through governmental officials and by requiring loyalty to the ancient religion of Iran, Zoroastrianism (see page 55). The Sasanian capital of Ctesiphon in what is now central Iran had become a center for Jewish religious learning and a refuge for pagan philosophers and medical scientists from the Greek cities of the Mediterranean world. The cosmopolitan culture thus created became the source for much classical Greek philosophical and medical knowledge that later came to the European world through the channel of Arabic translations.

Around 610, in the important commercial city of Mecca in what is now Saudi Arabia, a merchant called Muhammad began to have religious visions. By the time he died in 632, all Arabia had accepted his creed. A century later, his followers controlled Syria, Palestine, Egypt, North Africa, Spain, and part of France. This Arabic expansion profoundly affected the development of Western civilization. Through centers at Salerno in southern Italy and Toledo in central Spain, Arabic and Greek learning reached the West.

The Arabs

In Muhammad's time, Arabia was inhabited by various tribes, most of them Bedouins. These nomadic peoples grazed goats and sheep on the sparse patches of grass that dotted the vast, semiarid peninsula. Other Arabs lived in the southern valleys and coastal towns along the Red Sea—in Yemen, Mecca, Medina, and in the northwestern region called "Hejaz." The Hejazi led a more sophisticated life and supported themselves by agriculture and trade. Their caravan routes crisscrossed Arabia and carried goods to Byzantium, Persia, and Syria. The Hejazi had wide commercial dealings but avoided cultural contacts with their Jewish, Christian, and Persian neighbors. The wealth produced by their business transactions led to luxurious and extravagant living in the towns.

Although the nomadic Bedouins condemned the urbanized lifestyle of the Hejazi as immoral and corrupt, Arabs of both types respected one another's local tribal customs. They had no political unity beyond their tribal bonds. Tribal custom regulated their lives. Custom demanded the rigid observance of family obligations and the performance of religious rituals. Custom insisted that an Arab be proud, generous, and swift to take revenge. Custom required courage in public and avoidance of behavior that could bring social disgrace.

Although the various tribes differed markedly, they did have certain religious rules in common. For example, all Arabs kept three months of the year as sacred; during that time, fighting stopped so that everyone could attend holy ceremonies in peace. The city of Mecca was the religious center of the Arab world, and fighting was never tolerated there. All Arabs prayed at the Kaaba, the sanctuary in Mecca. Within the Kaaba was a sacred black stone that Arabs revered because they believed it had fallen from heaven.

What eventually molded the diverse Arab tribes into a powerful political and social unity was the religion founded by Muhammad.

Muhammad and the Faith of Islam

Except for a few vague autobiographical remarks in the Qur'an, the sacred book of Islam, Muhammad (ca 571–632) left no account of his life. Arab tradition accepts as historically true some of the sacred legends that developed about him, but those legends were not written down until about a century after his death. (Similarly, the earliest accounts of the life of Jesus, the Christian gospels, were not written until forty or fifty years after his death.) Orphaned at the age of six, Muhammad was brought up by his grandfather. As a young man he became a merchant in the caravan trade. Later he entered the service of a wealthy widow, and their subsequent marriage brought him financial independence. The Qur'an reveals him as an extremely devout man, ascetic, self-disciplined, literate but not educated.

Since childhood Muhammad had been subject to seizures during which he completely lost consciousness and had visions. After 610 these attacks and the accompanying visions apparently became more frequent. Unsure for a time what he should do, Muhammad discovered his mission after a vision in which the angel Gabriel instructed him to preach. Muhammad described his visions in verse form and used these verses as his *Qur'an,* or "prayer recitation." During Muhammad's lifetime his secretary jotted down these revelations haphazardly. After Muhammad's death, scribes organized the revelations into chapters, and in 651 Muhammad's third successor as religious leader, Othman, arranged to have an official version of them published.

The religion Muhammad founded is called "Islam"; a believer in that faith is called a "Muslim." Muhammad's religion eventually attracted great numbers of people, partly because of the straightforward nature of its doctrines. The subtle and complex reasoning Christianity had acquired by the seventh century was absent from early Islam.

The strictly monotheistic theology outlined in the Qur'an has only a few tenets. Allah, the Muslim God, is all-powerful and all-knowing. Muhammad, Allah's prophet, preached his word and carried his message. Muhammad described himself as the successor both of the Jewish patriarch Abraham and of Christ, and he claimed that his teachings replaced theirs. Muhammad invited and won converts from Judaism and Christianity.

Because Allah is all-powerful, believers must submit themselves to him. (*Islam* literally means "submission to the word of God.") This Islamic belief is closely related to the central feature of Muslim doctrine, the coming Day of Judgment. Muslims need not be concerned about *when* judgment will occur, but they must believe with absolute and total conviction that the Day of Judg-

Jonah and the Whale   The story of Jonah in the Old Testament describes a prophet who tried to avoid his responsibilities and is swallowed up by a whale; it is a parable of divine mercy, urging people to repent and seek forgiveness. The Chinese artist who executed this superb painting had never seen a whale but he possessed imagination, delicacy, and mastery of movement. *(Source: Edinburgh University Library)*

ment *will* come. Consequently, all of a Muslim's thoughts and actions should be oriented toward the Last Judgment and the rewards of heaven.

In order for a person to merit the rewards of heaven, Muhammad prescribed a strict code of moral behavior. The Muslim must recite a profession of faith in God and in Muhammad as God's prophet: "There is no god but Allah and Muhammad is his prophet." The believer must pray five times a day, fast and pray during the sacred month of Ramadan, make a pilgrimage to the holy city of Mecca once during his or her lifetime, and give alms to the poor. The Qur'an forbids alcoholic beverages and gambling. It condemns business *usury*—that is, lending money at interest rates or taking advantage of market demand for products by charging high prices for them. A number of foods, such as pork, are also forbidden, a dietary regulation adopted from the Mosaic law of the Hebrews.

By earlier Arab standards, the Qur'an sets forth an austere sexual morality. Muslim jurisprudence condemned licentious behavior on the part of men as well as women, which enhanced the status of women in Muslim society. About marriage, illicit intercourse, and inheritance, the Qur'an states:

[Of] women who seem good in your eyes, marry but two, three, or four; and if ye still fear that ye shall not act equitably, then only one. . . . The whore and the fornicator: whip each of them a hundred times. . . .

The fornicator shall not marry other than a whore; and the whore shall not marry other than a fornicator. . . .

Men who die and leave wives behind shall bequeath to them a year's maintenance.

And your wives shall have a fourth part of what you leave, if you have no issue; but if you have issue, then they shall have an eighth part. . . .

With regard to your children, God commands you to give the male the portion of two females; . . .

By contrast, Western law has tended to punish prostitutes but not their clients. Westerners tend to think polygamy degrading to women, but in a military society where there were apt to be many widows, polygamy provided women a measure of security. With respect to matters of property, Muslim women were more emancipated than Western women. For example, a Muslim woman retained complete jurisdiction over one-third of her property when she married and could dispose of it in any way she wished. Most women in the Germanic West lacked such power in the early Middle Ages.[27]

The Muslim who faithfully observed the laws of the Qur'an could hope for salvation. According to the Qur'an, salvation is by God's grace and choice alone. Technically a Muslim cannot "win" salvation as a reward for good behavior. Because God is all-knowing and all-powerful, he knows from the moment of a person's conception whether or not that person will be saved. Although later Muslim scholars held a number of positions on the topic of predestination, from complete fatalism to a strong belief in human free will, Muhammad maintained that predestination gave believers the will and courage to try to achieve the impossible. Devout Muslims came to believe that the performance of the faith's basic rules would automatically gain them salvation. Moreover, the believer who suffered and died for his faith in battle was immediately ensured the rewards of the Muslim heaven.

Historians and ecumenically minded theologians have pointed out many similarities among Islam, Christianity, and Judaism. All three religions are monotheistic; all worship the same God. Like Jews, Muslims customarily worshiped together at sundown on Fridays, and no assembly or organized church was essential. Muslims call Jews and Christians *dhimmis,* or "protected people," because they were people of the book, the Hebrew Scriptures.

Islam transcended the public and corporate aspects of tribal religion. Every Muslim hoped that by following the requirements of Islam he or she could achieve salvation. For the believer, the petty disputes and conflicts of tribal society paled before the simple teachings of Allah. On this basis, Muhammad united the nomads of the desert and the merchants of the cities. The doctrines of Islam, instead of the ties of local custom, bound all Arabs.

Nevertheless, a schism soon developed within the Islamic faith. In 661 the caliph Ali was assassinated. The title *caliph,* which meant "successor" to the Prophet, combined the ideas of spiritual and political leader of the *umma,* or Muslim community. Ali had claimed the caliphate on the basis of family ties: he was Muhammad's cousin and son-in-law. When Ali was murdered, his followers argued that he had been the Prophet's prescribed successor. These supporters of Ali were called *Shi'ites* or *Shi'a,* Arabic terms meaning "supporters" or "partisans" of Ali. In succeeding generations, Shi'ites emphasized the blood descent from Ali and claimed to have divine knowledge that

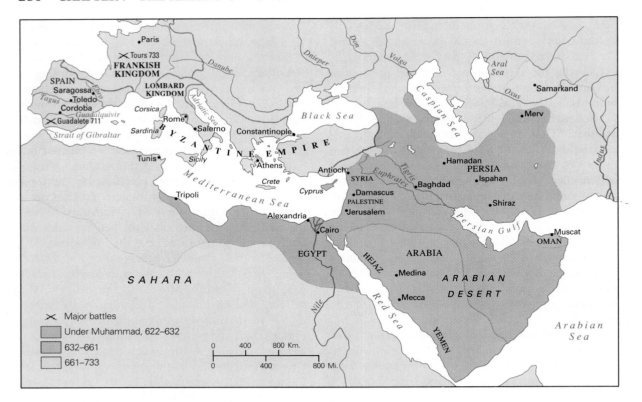

❖   **MAP 7.4 The Expansion of Islam to 733**   Political weaknesses in the territories they conquered, as well as superior fighting skills, help explain the speed with which the Muslims expanded.

Muhammad had given to them as his heirs. Other Muslims adhered to the practice and beliefs of the Islamic community, based on the precedents of the Prophet; they were called *Sunnis,* a term derived from the Arabic *Sunna,* the account of Muhammad's sayings and conduct in particular situations. When an issue arose for which the Qur'an offered no solution, Muslim scholars searched for a precedent in the Sunna, which gained an authority comparable to the Qur'an itself. Sunnis identified themselves with religious orthodoxy; they considered the Shi'ites, who claimed special religious knowledge deriving from Ali, heretical. The Shi'ites were always a minority within Islam, but a potentially dangerous one.

Despite this division within Islam, the faith of Allah united the Arabs sufficiently to redirect their energies. Hostilities were launched outward. By the time Muhammad died in 632, he had welded together all the Bedouin tribes. The crescent of Islam, the Muslim symbol, prevailed throughout the Arabian peninsula. During the next century,

between 632 and 733, one rich province of the old Roman Empire after another came under Muslim domination—first Syria, then Egypt, and then all of North Africa (Map 7.4). The governmental headquarters of this vast new empire was established at Damascus in Syria by the ruling Umayyad family. A contemporary proverb speaks of the Mediterranean as a Muslim lake. (This is an exaggeration, because Muslim control of the Mediterranean began only during the late ninth and early tenth centuries; and the Byzantines at Constantinople always contested that control.)

In 711 a Muslim force crossed the Strait of Gibraltar and at Guadalete in southern Spain easily defeated the weak Visigothic kingdom in Spain. A few Christian princes supported by the Frankish rulers held out in northern mountain fortresses, but the Muslims controlled most of Spain until the twelfth century. Between the tenth and fourteenth centuries, these northern Christian kingdoms, propelled by population growth, land hunger, nobles' demands for estates, advances in military technology and the appetites of transhumant sheep (moving from one grazing ground to another), pushed southward. In the fourteenth century clerical propagandists labeled this movement the *reconquista* (reconquest): a sacred patriotic crusading struggle to wrest the country from "alien" Muslim hands and to restore Christian control. This religious myth subsequently became part of Spanish political history and of Spanish "national" psychology.[28]

Muslim expansion was not confined to northern Africa and southern Europe. From the Arabian peninsula, Muslims carried their faith deep into Africa and across Asia all the way to India. In the West, however, Arab political influence was felt almost exclusively in Spain. A member of the Umayyad dynasty, Abd al-Rahman (r. 756–788), established a kingdom in Spain with its capital at Cordoba. In the eleventh century the Umayyad caliphate splintered into a number of small kingdoms. With Muslim rule thus divided, the small northern Christian kingdoms expanded southward. In the meantime, Jews in Muslim Spain were generally well treated and Christians tolerated so long as they paid a small tax.

In Spain as elsewhere in the Arab world the Muslims had an enormous impact on agricultural development. They began the cultivation of rice, sugar cane, oranges, lemons, grapefruit, dates, figs, eggplant, carrots, and, after the eleventh century, cotton. These crops, together with new methods of field irrigation, led to what one scholar has called "a green revolution." Andalusian (southern) Spain developed "a complex and varied agricultural system, whereby a greater variety of soil types were put to efficient use; where fields that had been yielding one crop at most prior to the Islamic invasion were now capable of yielding three or more crops, in rotation; and where agricultural production responded to the demands of an increasingly sophisticated and cosmopolitan urban population by providing the towns with a variety of products unknown in northern Europe."[29]

In the urban areas Muslims made significant advances in thought. Toledo, for example, became an important center of learning, through which Arab intellectual achievements entered and influenced western Europe. Arabic knowledge of science and mathematics, derived from the Chinese, Greeks, and Hindus, was highly sophisticated. The Muslim mathematician al-Khwarizmi (d. 830) wrote the important treatise *Algebra,* the first work in which the word *algebra* is used mathematically. Al-

Khwarizmi adopted the Hindu system of numbers (1, 2, 3, 4 etc.), used it in his *Algebra,* and applied mathematics to problems of physics and astronomy. Scholars at Baghdad translated Euclid's *Elements,* the basic text for plane and solid geometry. Muslims also instructed Westerners in the use of the zero, which permitted the execution of complicated problems of multiplication and long division. Use of the zero represented an enormous advance over clumsy Roman numerals. (Since our system of numbers is actually Hindu in origin, the term "Arabic numerals" is a misnomer, coined about 1847).

❖ **Harvesting Dates** This detail from an ivory casket given to a Cordoban prince reflects the importance of fruit cultivation in the Muslim-inspired agricultural expansion in southern Europe in the ninth and tenth centuries. *(Source: Louvre © Photo R.MN.)*

Muslim medical knowledge far surpassed that of the West. By the ninth century, Arab physicians had translated most of the treatises of Hippocrates. The Baghdad physician al-Razi (865–925) produced an encyclopedic treatise on medicine that was translated into Latin and circulated widely in the West. Al-Razi was the first physician to make the clinical distinction between measles and smallpox. The great surgeon of Cordoba, al-Zahrawi (d. 1013), produced an important work in which he discussed the cauterization of wounds (searing with a branding iron) and the crushing of stones in the bladder. In ibn-Sina of Bukhara (980–1037), known in the West as Avicenna, a physician, philologist, philosopher, poet, and scientist, Arabic science reached its peak. His al-Qanun codified all Greco-Arabic medical thought, described the contagious nature of tuberculosis and the spreading of diseases, and listed 760 pharmaceutical drugs.

Unfortunately, many of these treatises came to the West as translations from Greek to Arabic to Latin and inevitably lost a great deal in translation. Nevertheless, in the ninth and tenth centuries, Arabic knowledge and experience in anatomy and pharmaceutical prescriptions much enriched Western knowledge. Later, Greek philosophical thought passed to the West by way of Arabic translation.

Muslim-Christian Relations

Europeans and Muslims of the Middle East were geographical neighbors. They shared a common cultural heritage from the Judeo-Christian past. But mutual animosities restricted contact between them. The Muslim assault on Christian Europe in the eighth and ninth centuries—with villages burned, monasteries sacked, and Christians sold into slavery, left a legacy of bitter hostility. Europeans' fierce intolerance helped form a barrier between the two peoples. Christians felt threatened by a faith that acknowledged God as creator of the universe but denied the doctrine of the Trinity; that accepted Christ as a prophet but denied his divinity; that believed in the Last Judgment but seemed to make sex heaven's greatest reward. Popes preached against the Muslims, theologians penned tracts against them, and church councils condemned them. Europeans' perception of Islam as a menace helped to inspire the Crusades of the eleventh through thirteenth centuries (see pages 281–286).

During the Crusades Europeans imposed Christianity on any lands they conquered from Islam, and they compelled Muslims to choose among conversion, exile, and death.

By the thirteenth century, Western literature portrayed the Muslims as the most dreadful of Europe's enemies, guilty of every kind of crime. In his Inferno, the great Florentine poet Dante placed the Muslim philosophers Avicenna and Averroes with other virtuous "heathens," among them Socrates and Aristotle, in the first circle of hell, where they endured only moderate punishment. Muhammad, however, Dante consigned to the ninth circle, near Satan himself, where he was condemned as a spreader of discord and scandal. His punishment was to be continually torn apart from his chin to his anus.

Muslims had a strong aversion to travel in Europe. They were quite willing to trade with Europeans, but they rejected European culture. Medieval Europe had no resident Muslim communities where a traveler could find the mosques, food, or other things desirable for the Muslim way of life. Muslims generally had a horror of going among those they perceived as infidels, and when compelled to make diplomatic or business contacts, they preferred to send Jewish or Christian intermediaries, the dhimmis. Commercially, from the Muslim perspective, Europe had very little to offer. Apart from woolens from the Frisian islands in the Northern Sea, which the Muslims admired, there was only a trickle of slaves from central and southeastern Europe. Muslims felt that the only thing Europeans had to sell was their own people.

Did Western culture have any impact on Islam—which could be expected, given the geographical proximity of Europe and the Middle East? Muslims looked on Christianity as a flawed religion that Islam had superseded. One distinguished historian has written, "For the Muslim, Christ was a precursor, for the Christian Muhammad was an impostor. For the Muslim, Christianity was an early, incomplete, and obsolete form of the true religion." Religion dominated the Islamic perception of Europe. Muslims understood Europe not as Western, or European, or white, but as Christian. And the fact that European culture was Christian immediately discredited it in Muslim eyes. Christians were presumed to be hostile to Islam and thought to be culturally inferior. Therefore, Muslims had little interest in them or in European culture. For example, an enormous quantity of Muslim historical writing survives from the period between about 800 and 1600. Although the material reflects some knowledge of European geography, it shows an almost total lack of interest among Muslim scholars in European languages, life, and culture. Before the nineteenth century, not a single grammar book or dictionary of any Western language existed in the Muslim world. (By contrast, Western scholarship on the Islamic world steadily advanced. By the early seventeenth century, curious European students could find an extensive literature on the history, religion, and culture of the Muslim peoples.[30]

A few of the words that came into English from Arabic suggest the extent of Arabic influence: *admiral, alcohol, algebra, almanac, candy, cipher, coffee, damask, lemon, orange, sherbet,* and *zero.* Muslim expansion meant that Mediterranean civilization would be divided into three spheres of influence: the Byzantine, the Arabic, and the Western.

SUMMARY

The civilization that emerged in eighth-century Europe represented a fusion of classical, Christian, and Germanic elements. Latin was the language of educated people, and through the medium of Latin Christian thinkers expressed both their own ideals and religious doctrines and the laws and customs of the Germanic peoples. Christian missionaries preached the Gospel to the Germanic peoples, instructed them in the basic tenets of the Christian faith, and used penitentials to give them a sense of right moral behavior. Monasteries provided a model of Christian living, a pattern of agricultural development, and a place for education and learning. Christianity, because it energetically and creatively fashioned the Germanic and classical legacies, proved the most powerful agent in the making of Europe.

Islam and Byzantium also made contributions. As the ancient world declined, religious faith, rather than imperial rule, became the core of social identity. Each area came to define its world in religious terms. Christians called their world *ecumenical,* meaning universal. Muslims divided the world into two fundamental sections: the House of Islam, which consisted of all those regions where the law of Islam prevailed, and the House of War, which was the rest of the world. "As there is one God in heaven, so there can be only one

❖ **Mosque of Cordoba** Ordered by Abd al-Rahman (756–768), founder of the independent Ummayad dynasty in Spain, the mosque at the market city and river port of Cordoba is located on the site of a Roman temple and Visigothic church. The vaulting is supported by twelve aisles of columns rhythmically repeated in every direction. Some architectural historians consider this mosque the most spectacular Islamic building in the world. *(Source: MAS, Barcelona)*

ruler on earth." By the logic of Islamic law, no political entity outside of Islam could exist permanently. Islam and Christianity thus each fused the social and political aspects of culture into a self-contained system.

Byzantium could not confine Islam to Arabia, but it thwarted the Muslim challenge to Christianity by restricting Arab expansion. This Byzantine check permitted a separate medieval Christendom to rise in the West. In the eighth century, spiritual loyalty to Rome enabled the papacy to develop into a supranational authority virtually independent of a secular power. The goals and energy of the bishops of Rome, combined with the military strength of the Frankish rulers, built a strong Christian faith in the Latin West.[31]

NOTES

1. Matthew 16:18–19.
2. R. C. Petry, ed., *A History of Christianity: Readings in the History of Early and Medieval Christianity* (Englewood Cliffs, N.J.: Prentice-Hall, 1962), p. 70.
3. H. Bettenson, ed., *Documents of the Christian Church* (Oxford: Oxford University Press, 1947), p. 113.
4. Colossians 3:9–11.
5. Luke 6:20–31.
6. L. Sherley-Price, trans., *Bede: A History of the English Church and People* (Baltimore: Penguin Books, 1962), pp. 86–87.
7. J. T. McNeill and H. Gamer, trans., *Medieval Handbooks of Penance* (New York: Octagon Books, 1965), pp. 184–197.
8. L. White, "The Life of the Silent Majority," in R. S. Hoyt, ed., *Life and Thought in the Early Middle Ages* (Minneapolis: University of Minnesota Press, 1967), p. 100.
9. 1 Peter 2:11–20.
10. V. L. Bullough, *The Subordinate Sex: A History of Attitudes Toward Women* (Urbana: University of Illinois Press, 1973), pp. 118–119.
11. Ibid., pp. 118–119.
12. See J. Boswell, *Christianity, Social Tolerance, and Homosexuality: Gay People in Western Europe from the Beginning of the Christian Era to the Fourteenth Century* (Chicago: University of Chicago Press, 1980), chaps. 3 and 5, esp. pp. 87, 127–131.
13. F. J. Sheed, trans., *The Confessions of St. Augustine* (New York: Sheed & Ward, 1953), bk. 1, pt. 3.
14. Talbot, "Monasteries," in A. Kazhdan, ed., *The Oxford Dictionary of Byzantium,* vol. 2 (New York: Oxford University Press, 1991), p. 1393.
15. T. Burns, *A History of the Ostrogoths* (Bloomington: Indiana University Press, 1984), pp. 18, 21.
16. See W. Goffart, *Barbarians and Romans: The Techniques of Accommodation* (Princeton, N.J.: Princeton University Press, 1980), chap. 3, and esp. Conclusion, pp. 211–230.
17. See P. J. Geary, *Before France and Germany: The Creation and Transformation of the Merovingian World* (New York: Oxford University Press, 1988), pp. 18–25.
18. Ibid., p. 24.
19. Ibid., pp. 108–112.
20. E. F. Henderson, ed., *Select Historical Documents of the Middle Ages* (London: G. Bell & Sons, 1912), pp. 176–189.
21. Geary, p. 46.
22. Ibid., p. 50.
23. See S. F. Wemple, "Sanctity and Power: The Dual Pursuit of Early Medieval Women," in R. Bridenthal et al., ed., *Becoming Visible: Women in European History,* 2d ed. (Boston: Houghton Mifflin, 1987), pp. 133–136.
24. Quoted in J. B. Bury, *History of the Later Roman Empire,* vol. 1 (New York: Dover, 1958), pp. 233–234.
25. R. Atwater, trans., *Procopius: The Secret History* (Ann Arbor: University of Michigan Press, 1963), bk. 8.
26. W. H. McNeill, *Plagues and Peoples* (New York: Doubleday, 1976), pp. 127–128.
27. J. O'Faolain and L. Martines, eds., *Not in God's Image: Women in History from the Greeks to the Victorians* (New York: Harper & Row, 1973), pp. 108–115.
28. See R. Fletcher, *Moorish Spain* (New York: Henry Holt and Co., 1992), pp. 6–7.
29. T. F. Glick, *Islamic and Christian Spain in the Early Middle Ages* (Princeton, N.J.: Princeton University Press, 1979), pp. 77–78.
30. See B. Lewis, *The Muslim Discovery of Europe* (Norton: New York, 1982), pp. 296–297.
31. See J. Herrin, *The Formation of Christendom* (Princeton, N.J.: Princeton University Press, 1987), pp. 7–8, 477, et passim.

SUGGESTED READING

Students seeking information on the early Christian church will find sound material in the following reference works: Angelo Di Berardino, ed., *Encyclopedia of the Early Church,* A. Walford, trans., 2 vols. (1992),

J. F. Kelly, *The Concise Dictionary of Early Christianity* (1992), J. McManners, ed., *The Oxford Illustrated History of Christianity* (1990), and A. Kazhdan, ed., *The Oxford Dictionary of Byzantium* (1991).

J. Herrin's *The Formation of Christendom* (1987) is the best recent synthesis of the history of the early Middle Ages; it also contains an excellent discussion of Byzantine, Muslim, and Western art. In addition to the other studies listed in the Notes, students may consult the following works for a more detailed treatment of the early Middle Ages. Both M. Grant, *The Dawn of the Middle Ages* (1981), which emphasizes innovation and development, and P. Brown, *The World of Late Antiquity, A.D. 150–750,* rev. ed. (1989), which stresses social and cultural change, are lavishly illustrated and lucidly written introductions to the entire period. J. Pelikan, *The Excellent Empire: The Fall of Rome and the Triumph of the Church* (1987), describes how interpretations of the fall of Rome have influenced our understanding of Western culture.

J. Pelikan, *Jesus Through the Centuries: His Place in the History of Culture* (1985), discusses the image of Jesus held by various cultures over the centuries and its function in the development of these cultures. F. Oakley, *The Medieval Experience: Foundations of Western Cultural Singularity* (1974), emphasizes the Christian roots of Western cultural uniqueness. W. Meeks, *The First Urban Christians: The Social World of the Apostle Paul* (1983), shows that the early Christians came from all social classes. For a solid appreciation of Christian life in a non-Christian society, see M. Mullin, *Called to Be Saints: Christian Living in First Century Rome* (1992). J. Richards, *Consul of God: The Life and Times of Gregory the Great* (1980), is the first significant study in seventy years of this watershed pontificate. P. Brown, *The Cult of the Saints: Its Rise and Function in Latin Christianity* (1982), describes the significance of the saints in popular religion. Students seeking to understand early Christian attitudes on sexuality and how they replaced Roman ones should consult the magisterial work of P. Brown, *The Body and Society: Men, Women, and Sexual Renunciation in Early Christianity* (1988).

For the synthesis of classical and Christian cultures, see C. N. Cochrane, *Christianity and Classical Culture* (1957), a deeply learned monograph. The best biography of Saint Augustine is P. Brown, *Augustine of Hippo* (1967), which treats him as a symbol of change. J. B. Russell, *Dissent and Order in the Middle Ages: The Search for Legitimate Authority* (1992), offers a provocative discussion of religious orthodoxy and heresy in the church.

For the Germans see P. J. Heather, *Goths and Romans A.D. 332–489* (1992), and A. Lewis, *Emerging Europe, A.D. 400–1000* (1967), both of which describe German customs and society and the Germanic impact on the Roman Empire. A rich but difficult study is H. Wolfram, *History of the Goths,* T. J. Dunlop, trans. (1988), which explores German tribal formation and places Gothic history within the context of late Roman society and institutions. F. Lot, *The End of the Ancient World* (1965), emphasizes the economic and social causes of Rome's decline.

The phenomenon of monasticism has attracted interest throughout the centuries. The best modern edition of the document is T. Fry et al., eds., *RB 1980: The Rule of St. Benedict in Latin and English with Notes* (1981), which contains a history of Western monasticism and a scholarly commentary on the *Rule.* L. Eberle, trans., *The Rule of the Master* (1977), offers the text of and a commentary on Benedict's major source. Two beautifully illustrated syntheses by leading authorities are D. Knowles, *Christian Monasticism* (1969), which sketches monastic history through the middle of the twentieth century, and G. Zarnecki, *The Monastic Achievement* (1972), which focuses on the medieval centuries. For women in monastic life, see S. F. Wemple, *Women in Frankish Society: Marriage and the Cloister, 500–900* (1981), an important book with a good bibliography.

For Byzantium and the Arabs, see J. J. Norwich, *Byzantium: The Early Centuries* (1989), an elegantly written sketch; E. Patlagean, "Byzantium in the Tenth and Eleventh Centuries," in *A History of Private Life,* vol. I: *From Pagan Rome to Byzantium* (1987); J. Hussey, *The Byzantine World* (1961); S. Runciman, *Byzantine Civilization* (1956); and A. Bridge, *Theodora: Portrait in a Byzantine Landscape* (1984), a romantic and amusing biography of the courtesan who became empress. A. Harvey, *Economic Expansion in the Byzantine Empire, 900–1200* (1989), should prove useful for research on social and economic change. J. L. Esposito, *Islam: The Straight Path* (1988), is an informed and balanced work based on the best modern scholarship, while the older study of M. Rodinson, *Mohammed* (1974) is still useful. R. Collins, *The Arab Conquest of Spain, 710–797* (1994) assesses the cultural impact of Arab rule, and D. J. Wasserstein, *The Caliphate in the West. An Islamic Political Institution in the Iberian Peninsula* (1993) studies the major policial institution. L. Ahmed, *Women and Gender in Islam. Historical Roots of a Modern Debate* (1992), is a most important contribution and the starting point for all research on Islam and gender, while N. R. Keddie and B. Brown, eds., *Women in Middle Eastern History. Shifting Boundaries in Sex and Gender* (1992), provides a variety of perspectives on women's roles.

The Conversion of Clovis

Modern Christian doctrine holds that conversion is a process, the gradual turning toward Jesus and the teachings of the Christian gospels. But in the early medieval world, conversion was perceived more as a onetime event determined by the tribal chieftain. If he accepted baptism, the mass conversion of his people followed. The selection here about the Frankish king Clovis is from the History of the Franks *by Gregory, bishop of Tours (ca. 540–594), written about a century after the events it describes.*

The first child which Clotild bore for Clovis was a son. She wanted to have her baby baptized, and she kept urging her husband to agree to this. "The gods whom you worship are no good," she would say. "They haven't even been able to help themselves, let alone others. . . . Take your Saturn, for example, who ran away from his own son to avoid being exiled from his kingdom, or so they say; and Jupiter, that obscene perpetrator of all sorts of mucky deeds, who couldn't keep his hands off other men, who had his fun with all his female relatives and couldn't even refrain from intercourse with his own sister. . . .

"You ought instead to worship Him who created at a word and out of nothing heaven, and earth, the sea and all that therein is, who made the sun to shine, who lit the sky with stars, who peopled the water with fish, the earth with beasts, the sky with flying creatures, by whose hand the race of man was made, by whose gift all creation is constrained to serve in deference and devotion the man He made." However often the Queen said this, the King came no nearer to belief. . . .

The Queen, who was true to her faith, brought her son to be baptized. . . . The child was baptized; he was given the name Ingomer; but no sooner had he received baptism that he died in his white robes. Clovis was extremely angry. He began immediately to reproach his Queen. "If he had been dedicated in the name of my gods," he said, "he would have lived without question; but now that he has been baptized in the name of your God he has not been able to live a single day!" "I give thanks to Almighty God," replied Clotild, "the Creator of all things who has not found me completely unworthy, for He has deigned to welcome into his Kingdom a child conceived in my womb. . . ."

Some time later Clotild bore a second son. He was baptized Chlodomer. He began to ail and Clovis said, "What else do you expect? It will happen to him as it happened to his brother: no sooner is he baptized in the name of your Christ than he will die!" Clotild prayed to the Lord and at His commands the baby recovered.

Queen Clotild continued to pray that her husband might recognize the true God and give up his idol-worship. Nothing could persuade him to accept Christianity. Finally war broke out against the Alammani and in this conflict he was forced by necessity to accept what he had refused of his own free will. It so turned out that when the two armies met on the battlefield there was a great slaughter and the troops of Clovis were rapidly being annihilated. He raised his eyes to heaven when he saw this, felt compunction in his heart and was moved to tears. "Jesus Christ," he said, "you who Clotild maintains to be the Son of the living God, you who deign to give help to those in travail and victory to those who trust in you, in faith I beg the glory of your help. If you will give me victory over my enemies, and if I may have evidence to that miraculous power which the people dedicated to your name say that they have experienced, then I will believe in you and I will be baptized in your name. I have called upon my own gods, but, as I see only too clearly, they have no intention of helping me. I therefore cannot believe that they possess any power for they do not come to the assistance of those who trust them. I now call upon you. I want to believe in you, but I must first be saved from my enemies." Even as he said this the Alamanni turned their backs and began to run away. As soon as they saw that their King was killed, they submitted to Clovis. "We beg you," they said, "to put an end to this slaughter. We are prepared to obey you." Clovis stopped the war. He made a speech in which he called for peace. Then he went home. He told the Queen how he had won a victory by calling on the name of Christ. This happened in the fifteenth year of his reign (496).

The Queen then ordered Saint Remigius, Bishop of the town of Rheims, to be summoned in secret. She begged him to impart the word of salvation to the King. The Bishop asked Clovis to meet him in private and began to urge him to believe in the true God, Maker of heaven and earth, and to forsake his idols, which were powerless to help him or anyone else. The King replied: "I have listened to you willingly, holy father. There remains one obstacle. The people under my command will not agree to forsake their gods. I will go and put to them what you have just said to me." He arranged a meeting with this people, but God in his power had preceded him, and before he could say a word all those present shouted in unison: "We will give up worshipping our mortal gods, pious King, and we are prepared to follow the immortal God about whom Remigius preaches." This news was reported to the Bishop. He was greatly pleased and he ordered the baptismal pool to be made ready. . . . The baptistry was prepared, sticks of incense gave off clouds of perfume, sweet-smelling candles gleamed bright and the holy place of baptism was filled with divine fragrance. God filled the hearts of all present with such grace that they imagined themselves to have been transported to some perfumed paradise. King Clovis asked that he might be baptized first by the Bishop. Like some new Constantine he stepped forward to the baptismal pool, ready to wash away the sores of his old leprosy and to be cleansed in flowing water from the sordid stains which he had borne so long.

King Clovis confessed his belief in God Almighty, three in one. He was baptized in the name of the Father, the Son and the Holy Ghost, and marked in holy chrism [an anoint-

❖ Ninth-century ivory carving showing Clovis being baptized by St. Remi. *(Source: Musee Condé, Cahntilly/Laurie Platt Winfrey, Inc.)*

ing oil] with the sign of the Cross of Christ. More than three thousand of his army were baptized at the same time.

Questions for Analysis

1. Who took the initiative in urging Clovis's conversion? What can we deduce from that?

2. According to this account, why did Clovis ultimately accept Christianity?

3. For the Salian Franks, what was the best proof of divine power?

4. On the basis of this selection, do you consider the *History of the Franks* reliable history? Why or why not?

Sources: L. Thorpe, trans., *The History of the Franks by Gregory of Tours* (Harmondsworth: Penguin, 1974), pp. 159; P. J. Geary, ed., *Readings in Medieval History* (Peterborough, Ontario: Broadview Press, 1991), pp. 165–166.

8

The Carolingian World: Europe in the Early Middle Ages

Cover of *Codex Aureus* of St. Emmeram, ca. 870 A.D. *(Source: Staatsbibliothek)*

✠ The Frankish chieftain Charles Martel defeated Muslim invaders in 733 at the Battle of Tours in central France.[1] Muslims and Christians have interpreted the battle differently. To the Muslims, it was only a minor skirmish, won by the Franks because of Muslim difficulties in maintaining supply lines over long distances and the distraction of ethnic conflicts and unrest in Islamic Spain. For Christians, the Frankish victory has been perceived as one of the great battles of history: it halted Muslim expansion in Europe. A century after this victory, in 843, Charles Martel's three great-great-grandsons concluded the Treaty of Verdun, which divided the European continent among themselves.

Between 733 and 843, a distinctly European society emerged. A new kind of social and political organization, later called "feudalism," appeared. And for the first time since the collapse of the Roman Empire, most of western Europe was united under one government. That government reached the peak of its development under Charles Martel's grandson, Charlemagne. Christian missionary activity among the Germanic peoples continued, and strong ties were forged with the Roman papacy. A revival of study and learning, sometimes styled the "Carolingian Renaissance," occurred under Charlemagne.

- How did Charlemagne acquire and govern his vast empire?
- What was the significance of the relations between Carolingian rulers and the church?
- The culture of the Carolingian Empire has been described as the "first European civilization." What does this mean?

239

- What factors contributed to the disintegration of the Carolingian Empire?
- In a society wracked with constant war and violence, what medical care was available?
- What was feudalism, and how did it come about?
- How did Viking expansion lead to the establishment of the Kievan principality?

These are the questions this chapter will explore.

✥ THE FRANKISH ARISTOCRACY AND THE RISE OF THE CAROLINGIAN DYNASTY

Through a series of remarkable victories over other Germanic tribes, the Franks under Clovis had emerged as the most powerful people in Europe by the early sixth century (see page 218). The Frankish kingdom included most of what is now France and a large section of southwestern Germany. Clovis's baptism into orthodox Christianity won him church support against other Germanic tribes, most of them Arian Christians. By selecting as his "capital" Paris—legendary scene of the martyrdom of Saint Denis, thought to be a disciple of Saint Paul—Clovis identified himself with the cult of Saint Denis and used it to strengthen his rule. Clovis died in 511, and the Merovingian dynasty went on to rule for the next two centuries.

Rule is, of course, too strong a verb. Conquering the vast territories proved easier for the Merovingians than governing them, given their inadequate political institutions. When he died, Clovis divided his kingdom among his four sons, according to Frankish custom; because of its vast size the division also made sense. Practically, however, Clovis's decision was disastrous, because it led to incessant civil war. The Merovingians bitterly hated each other, and each king fought to deprive his relatives of their portions of the kingdom. Violence and assassination ceased only when one man had killed off all his rivals. Thus in 558 Clovis's youngest son, Lothair, acquired the whole kingdom after he had murdered two nephews and eliminated one rebellious son by burning him and his family alive. After Lothair died, the other sons continued the civil war until one king survived.

In this domestic violence the remarkable Queen Brunhilda (d. 631), wife of King Sigebert of the East Frankish kingdom, played an important role. Her sister Galswintha was murdered by her husband Chilperic, ruler of the West Frankish kingdom, so that he could marry his mistress Fredegunda (see page 221). Brunhilda thereupon instigated war between the two kingdoms. Hatred of Fredegunda led her to continue the war even after the deaths of kings Sigebert and Chilperic. During the reigns of her son and grandson, Brunhilda actually ruled the East Frankish kingdom as well as Burgundy, which was united to the East Frankish kingdom through her astute plans. Brunhilda displayed considerable political skill, and her merciless use of violence in pursuit of her goals was fully characteristic of the times.

The long period of civil war in the Frankish kingdom may have provided the opportunity for the emergence of a distinct aristocratic class. Recent research in Frankish family history has revealed that a noble ruling class existed before the mid-sixth century. Members of this class belonged to families of high reputation, who gradually intermarried with members of the old Gallo-Roman senatorial class. They possessed wealth and great villas where they led an aristocratic lifestyle. They exercised rights of lordship over their lands and tenants, dispensing local customary, not royal, law. These families provided almost all the bishops of the church. Because they had a self-conscious awareness of their social, economic, and political distinction from the rest of society, they constituted a noble class.[2]

In the seventh century the central government of the Merovingians could not control these nobles. Primitive and disorganized, the government consisted of a few household officials, the most important of whom was the mayor of the palace. He was in charge of administration and acted as the king's deputy; he also represented the interests of the nobility. Since the Frankish kingdom was divided into East Frankland, West Frankland, and Burgundy, each with its own ruler, and since some territories such as Bavaria were virtually independent, the Merovingian kingdom slowly disintegrated.

Reconstruction of the Frankish kingdom began with the efforts of Pippin of Landen, a member of one aristocratic family. In the early seventh century, he was mayor of the palace in East Frankland. His grandson, Pippin II (d. 714), after a military victory in 687, gained the position of mayor of the palace because of royal weakness, the most power-

✦ **Merovingian Army** This sixth- or seventh-century ivory depicts a nobleman in civilian dress followed by seven warriors. Note that the mounted men do not have
stirrups and that they seem to have fought with spears and bows and arrows. The
power of the Frankish aristocracy rested on these private armies. *(Source: Landesmuseum, Trier)*

ful person in East Frankland) in both East and
West Frankland. It was this Pippin's son Charles
Martel, who defeated the Muslims at Tours and
thus checked Arab expansion into Europe.
Charles's wars against the Burgundians and
Frisians broke those weakening forces. His victory
over the Muslims and his successful campaigns
within the Frankish kingdom added to his family's
prestige a reputation for great military strength.
From 714 until his death in 741, Charles Martel
thus held the real power in the Frankish kingdom;
the Merovingians were kings in name only.

The rise of the Carolingian dynasty—whose
name derives from the Latin *Carolus,* for
Charles—rested partly on papal support. In the
early eighth century, missionaries supported Charles Martel and his son Pippin III as they attempted
to bring the various Germanic tribes under their
jurisdiction. The most important was the Anglo-
Saxon missionary Wynfrith, or Boniface (680–
754), as he was later called. Given the barbarian
peoples with whom he was dealing, Boniface's
achievements were remarkable. He helped shape
the structure of the German church. He established the *Rule of Saint Benedict* in all the monas-

teries he founded or reformed, thus promoting
monastic unity. And with the support of Pippin III,
he held councils to reform the Frankish church.

Saint Boniface preached throughout Germany
against divorce, polygamous unions, and incest.
On these matters German custom and ecclesiastical
law completely disagreed. The Germans allowed
divorce simply by the man's repudiation of his
wife; divorce did not require her consent. The
Germanic peoples also practiced polygamy and *incest*—sexual relations between brothers and sisters
or parents and children—on a wide scale. Church
councils and theologians stressed that marriage,
validly entered into, that is—freely consented to—
could not be ended.

Boniface's preaching was not without impact,
for in 802 Charles Martel's grandson Charlemagne
prohibited incest and decreed that a husband
might separate from an adulterous wife. The
woman could be punished, and the man could not
remarry in her lifetime. Charlemagne also encouraged severe punishment for adulterous men. The
publication of laws does not usually or instantly
end deeply rooted social practices, but in attempting to abolish incest and to check divorce by a

man's simple verbal repudiation of his wife, Charlemagne contributed to the dignity of marriage and of women.

Charles Martel and Pippin III protected Boniface, and he preached Christian obedience to rulers. Because of his staunch adherence to Roman ideas and the Roman pope, the romanization of Europe accompanied its Christianization.

Charles Martel had been king of the Franks in fact but not in title. His son Pippin III (r. 751–768) made himself king in title as well as in fact. In Germanic custom—and custom was law—the kingship had to pass to someone of royal blood. Pippin did not want to murder the ineffectual Merovingian king, but he did want the kingship. Because the missionary activity of Boniface had spread Christian ideas and enhanced papal influence in the Frankish kingdom, Pippin decided to consult the pope. Accordingly, Pippin sent envoys to Rome to ask the pope whether the man with the power was entitled to be king. Pope Zacharias, guided by the Augustinian principle that the real test of kingship is whether it provides for order and justice, responded in 751 that he who has the power should also have the title. This answer, which tacitly supported the deposition of the last Merovingian king, constituted recognition of the Carolingians. The Merovingian ruler was removed and forced to become a monk.

Just as the emperors Constantine and Theodosius had taken actions in the fourth century that would later be cited as precedents in church-state relations (see pages 198–199), so Pippin III in the mid-eighth century took papal confirmation as official approval of his title. In 751 Pippin III was formally elected king of the Franks by the great lords, or magnates, of the Frankish territory. Two years later, the pope—who needed Pippin's protection from the Lombards—came to Gaul and personally anointed Pippin (marked his forehead and hands with sacred oil) king at Paris.

Thus an important alliance was struck between the papacy and the Frankish ruler. In 754 Pope Stephen gave Pippin the title of protector of the Roman church. Pippin in turn agreed to restore to the papacy territories in northern Italy recently seized by the Lombards; he promptly marched into Italy and defeated the Lombards. The papal alliance with the Franks implicitly represented a break with the Byzantine court at Constantinople. Preoccupied with Muslim assaults, iconoclasm (the bitter theological disputes between 730 and 843 over the veneration of icons), and with fiscal difficulties, the Byzantine government was unable to help the papacy. Then, when Pippin III's son Charles came to Rome in 800, Pope Leo III showed him the signs of respect due only to the emperor. When the pope crowned Charles as Holy Roman Emperor on Christmas Day (below), the pope performed the Greek proskynesis (obeisance), a rite traditionally given only to the emperor. The Carolingian family thus received official recognition from the leading spiritual power in Europe, and the papacy gained a military protector. The Greeks regarded the papal acts as rebellious and Charlemagne as a usurper. The imperial coronation marks a decisive break between Rome and Constantinople.

On a second successful campaign in Italy in 756, Pippin made a large donation to the papacy. The gift consisted of estates in central Italy that technically belonged to the Byzantine emperor. Known as the Papal States, they existed on paper, but not in political reality, until the pontificate of Innocent III in the thirteenth century.

Because of his anointment, Pippin's kingship took on a special spiritual and moral character. Before Pippin, only priests and bishops had received anointment. Pippin became the first to be anointed with the sacred oils and acknowledged as *rex et sacerdos* ("king and priest"). Anointment, rather than royal blood, set the Christian king apart. Pippin also cleverly eliminated possible threats to the Frankish throne, and the pope promised him support in the future. When Pippin died, his son Charlemagne succeeded him.

✣ THE EMPIRE OF CHARLEMAGNE

Charles the Great (r. 768–814), generally known as Charlemagne, built on the military and diplomatic foundations of his ancestors. Charles's secretary and biographer, Einhard, wrote a lengthy idealization of this warrior-ruler. It has serious flaws, partly because it is modeled directly on the Roman author Suetonius's *Life of the Emperor Augustus*. Still, it is the earliest medieval biography of a layman, and historians consider it generally accurate:

Charles was large and strong, and of lofty stature, though not disproportionately tall . . . the upper part of his head was round, his eyes very large and ani-

*mated, nose a little long, hair fair, and face laughing
and merry. Thus his appearance was always stately
and dignified . . . although his neck was thick and
somewhat short, and his belly rather prominent; but
the symmetry of the rest of his body concealed these
defects. His gait was firm, his whole carriage manly,
and his voice clear, but not so strong as his size led
one to expect. His health was excellent, except during
the four years preceding his death. . . .*

*Even in those years he consulted rather his own
inclinations than the advice of physicians, who were
almost hateful to him, because they wanted him to give
up roasts, to which he was accustomed, and to eat
boiled meat instead. In accordance with the national
custom, he took frequent exercise on horseback and
in the chase, accomplishments in which scarcely any
people in the world can equal the Franks. He enjoyed
the exhalations from natural warm springs, and often
practiced swimming, in which he was such an adept
that none could surpass him; and hence it was that
he built his palace at Aix-la-Chapelle [Aachen], and
lived there constantly during his latter years until his
death. He used not only to invite his sons to his bath,
but his nobles and friends, and now and then a troop
of his retinue or bodyguard.*[3]

Though crude and brutal, Charlemagne was a
man of enormous intelligence. He appreciated
good literature, such as Saint Augustine's *City of
God,* and Einhard considered him an unusually
effective speaker. Recent scholarship disputes Einhard's claim that Charlemagne could not write.

The security and continuation of his dynasty and
the need for diplomatic alliances governed Charlemagne's complicated marriage pattern. The high
rate of infant mortality required many sons. Married first to the daughter of Desiderius, king of the
Lombards, Charlemagne divorced her on grounds
of sterility. His second wife, Hildegard, produced
nine children in twelve years. When she died,
Charlemagne married Fastrada, daughter of an
East Frankish count whose support Charles needed
in his campaign against the Saxons. Charlemagne
had a total of four legal wives and six concubines,
and even after the age of sixty-five continued to
sire children. Though three sons reached adulthood, only one outlived him. Four surviving
grandsons, however, ensured perpetuation of the
family. The most striking feature of Charlemagne's
character was his phenomenal energy, which helps
to explain his great military achievements.[4]

❖ **Charlemagne in the Twelfth Century** The image of a stern, slender Charles in classical Roman
garb reflects twelfth-century physical and political
ideals, not the squat, pot-bellied ruler described
by his contemporary Einhard. Charles wears a
crown or helmet, symbol of his duty to protect
and defend his people. In his right hand he carries an orb surmounted by a cross, representing
universal power and his obligation to give justice
under God; his left hand bears the scepter, em-
blem of authority. The statue shows the fusion of
legend and history in early medieval culture.
(Source: Ann Münchow, Aachen)

Territorial Expansion

Continuing the expansionist policies of his ancestors, Charlemagne fought more than fifty campaigns and became the greatest warrior of the early Middle Ages. He subdued all of the north of modern France. In the south, the lords of the mountainous ranges of Aquitaine—what is now called "Basque country"—fought off his efforts at total conquest. The Muslims in northeastern Spain were checked by the establishment of strongly fortified areas known as *marches*.

Charlemagne's greatest successes were in today's Germany. There his concerns were basically defensive. In the course of a thirty-year war against the semibarbaric Saxons, he added most of the northwestern German tribes to the Frankish kingdom. Because of their repeated rebellions, Charlemagne ordered, according to Einhard, more than four thousand Saxons slaughtered in one day.

To the south, he also achieved spectacular results. In 773 to 774 the Lombards in northern Italy again threatened the papacy. Charlemagne marched south, overran fortresses at Pavia and Spoleto, and incorporated Lombardy into the Frankish kingdom. To his title as king of the Franks he added king of the Lombards. Charlemagne also ended Bavarian independence and defeated the nomadic Avars, opening the Danubian plain for later settlement. He successfully fought the Byzantine Empire for Venetia (excluding the city of Venice itself), Istria, and Dalmatia and temporarily annexed those areas to his kingdom.

Charlemagne also tried to occupy Basque territory in northwestern Spain. When his long siege of Saragossa proved unsuccessful and the Saxons on his northeastern borders rebelled, Charlemagne decided to withdraw, but the Basques annihilated his rear guard under Count Roland at Roncesvalles (778). This attack represented Charlemagne's only defeat, and he forbade people to talk about it. However, the expedition inspired the great medieval epic *The Song of Roland*. Based on legend and written down about 1100 at the beginning of the European crusading movement, the poem portrays Roland as the ideal chivalric knight and Charlemagne as exercising a sacred kind of kingship. Although many of the epic's details differ from the historical evidence, *The Song of Roland* is important because it reveals the popular image of Charlemagne in later centuries.

By around 805, the Frankish kingdom included all of continental Europe except Spain, Scandinavia, southern Italy, and the Slavic fringes of the East (Map 8.1). Not since the third century A.D. had any ruler controlled so much of the Western world.

The Government of the Carolingian Empire

Charlemagne ruled a vast rural world dotted with isolated estates and characterized by constant petty violence. His empire was definitely not a state as people today understand that term; it was a collection of primitive peoples and semibarbaric tribes. Apart from a small class of warrior-aristocrats and clergy, almost everyone engaged in agriculture. Trade and commerce played only a small part in the economy. Cities served as the headquarters of bishops and as ecclesiastical centers.

By constant travel, personal appearances, and the sheer force of his personality, Charlemagne sought to awe conquered peoples with his fierce presence and terrible justice. By confiscating the estates of great territorial magnates, he acquired lands and goods with which to gain the support of lesser lords, further expanding the territory under his control.

The political power of the Carolingians rested on the cooperation of the dominant social class, the Frankish aristocracy. By the seventh century, through mutual cooperation and frequent marriage alliances, these families exercised great power that did not derive from the Merovingian kings. The Carolingians themselves had emerged from this aristocracy, and the military and political success that Carolingians such as Pippin II achieved depended on the support of the nobility. The lands and booty with which Charles Martel and Charlemagne rewarded their followers in these noble families enabled the nobles to improve their economic position; but it was only with noble help that the Carolingians were able to wage wars of expansion and suppress rebellions. In short, Carolingian success was a matter of reciprocal help and reward.[5]

Two or three hundred counts from this imperial aristocracy governed at the local level. They had full military and judicial power and held their offices for life but could be removed for misconduct. As a link between local authorities and the central government, Charlemagne appointed

Monasteries

Frankish Kingdom, 768

Areas conquered by Charlemagne

Tributary peoples

Byzantine Empire

❖ **MAP 8.1 The Carolingian World** The extent of Charlemagne's nominal jurisdiction was extraordinary: it was not equalled until the nineteenth century.

officials called *missi dominici,* "agents of the lord king." The empire was divided into visitorial districts. Each year, beginning in 802, two missi, usually a count and a bishop or abbot, visited assigned districts. They held courts and investigated the district's judicial, financial, and clerical activities. They held commissions to regulate crime, moral conduct, the clergy, education, the poor, and many other matters. The missi checked up on the counts and worked to prevent their positions from becoming hereditary: strong counts with hereditary estates would have weakened Charlemagne's power. In the "marches" or "marks" (especially unstable areas) officials called "margraves" had extensive powers to govern their dangerous localities.

A modern state has institutions of government, such as a civil service, courts of law, financial agencies for collecting and apportioning taxes, and police and military powers with which to maintain order internally and defend against foreign attack. These simply did not exist in Charlemagne's empire. Instead, society was held together by dependent relationships cemented by oaths promising faith and loyalty.

Although the empire lacked viable institutions, some Carolingians involved in governing did have vigorous political ideas. The abbots and bishops who served as Charlemagne's advisers worked out what was for their time a sophisticated political ideology. In letters and treatises, they set before their ruler high ideals of behavior and of government. They wrote that a ruler may hold power from God but is responsible to the law. Just as all subjects of the empire were required to obey him, so he, too, was obliged to respect the law. They envisioned a unified Christian society presided over by a king who was responsible for maintaining peace, law, and order and doing justice, without which neither the ruler nor the kingdom had any justification. These views derived largely from Saint Augustine's theories of kingship. Inevitably, they could not be realized in an illiterate, preindustrial society. But they were the seeds from which medieval and even modern ideas of government were to develop.

The Imperial Coronation of Charlemagne

In the autumn of the year 800, Charlemagne paid a momentous visit to Rome. Einhard gave his account of what happened:

His last journey there [to Rome] was due to another factor, namely that the Romans, having inflicted many injuries on Pope Leo—plucking out his eyes and tearing out his tongue, he had been compelled to beg the assistance of the king. Accordingly, coming to Rome in order that he might set in order those things which had exceedingly disturbed the condition of the Church, he remained there the whole winter. It was at the time that he accepted the name of Emperor and

Augustus. At first he was so much opposed to this that he insisted that although that day was a great [Christian] feast, he would not have entered the Church if he had known beforehand the pope's intention. But he bore very patiently the jealousy of the Roman Emperors [that is, the Byzantine rulers] who were indignant when he received these titles. He overcame their arrogant haughtiness with magnanimity, a virtue in which he was considerably superior to them, by sending frequent ambassadors to them and in his letters addressing them as brothers.[6]

For centuries scholars have debated the significance of the imperial coronation of Charlemagne. Did Charles plan the ceremony in Saint Peter's on Christmas Day, or did he merely accept the title of emperor? What did he have to gain from it? If, as Einhard implied, the coronation displeased Charlemagne, did that displeasure rest on Pope Leo's role in the ceremony which, on the principle that he who gives can also take away, placed the pope in a higher position that the emperor? Did Pope Leo III arrange the coronation in order to identify the Frankish monarchy with the papacy and papal policy?

Though final answers will probably never be found, several things seem certain. First, Charlemagne gained the imperial title of Holy Roman emperor and considered himself a Christian king ruling a Christian people. His motto, *Renovatio romani imperi* ("Revival of the Roman Empire"), "implied a revival of the Western Empire in the image of Augustinian political philosophy."[7] Charles was consciously perpetuating old Roman imperial notions, while at the same time identifying with the new Rome of the Christian church. Charlemagne and his government represented a combination of Frankish practices and Christian ideals, the two basic elements of medieval European society. Second, later German rulers were anxious to gain the imperial title and to associate themselves with the legends of Charlemagne and ancient Rome. They wanted to use the ideology of imperial Rome to strengthen their positions. Finally, ecclesiastical authorities continually cited the event as proof that the dignity of the imperial crown could be granted only by the pope. The imperial coronation of Charlemagne, whether planned by the Carolingian court or by the papacy, was to have a profound effect on the course of German history and on the later history of Europe.

THE CAROLINGIAN INTELLECTUAL REVIVAL

It is ironic that Charlemagne's most enduring legacy was the stimulus he gave to scholarship and learning. Barely literate himself, preoccupied with the control of vast territories, much more a warrior than a thinker, he nevertheless set in motion a cultural revival that had widespread and long-lasting consequences. The revival of learning associated with Charlemagne and his court at Aachen drew its greatest inspiration from seventh- and eighth-century intellectual developments in the Anglo-saxon kingdom of Northumbria, situated at the northernmost tip of the old Roman world.

Northumbrian Culture

Despite the victory of the Roman forms of Christian liturgy at the Synod of Whitby in 664 (see page 202), Irish-Celtic culture permeated the Roman church in Britain and resulted in a flowering of artistic and scholarly activity. Northumbrian creativity owes a great deal to the intellectual curiosity and collecting zeal of Saint Benet Biscop (ca 628–689). A strong supporter of Benedictine monasticism, Benet Biscop introduced the Roman ceremonial form into new religious houses he founded and encouraged it in older ones. Benet Biscop made five dangerous trips to Italy, raided libraries, and brought back to Northumbria manuscripts, relics, paintings, and other treasures that formed the libraries on which much later study was based.

Northumbrian monasteries produced scores of books: *missals* (used for the celebration of the mass), *psalters* (which contained the 150 psalms and other prayers used by the monks in their devotions), commentaries on the Scriptures, illuminated manuscripts, law codes, and collections of letters and sermons. The finest product of Northumbrian art is probably the Gospel book produced at Lindisfarne around 700. The incredible expense involved in the publication of such a book—for vellum (calfskin or lambskin specially prepared for writing), coloring, and gold leaf—represents in part an aristocratic display of wealth. The script, *uncial,* is a Celtic version of contemporary Greek and Roman handwriting. The illustrations have a strong Eastern quality, combining the abstract, nonrepresentational style of the Christian Middle East and the narrative (story-telling) approach of classical Roman art. Likewise, the use of geometrical decorative designs shows the influence of Syrian art. Many scribes, artists, and illuminators must have participated in the book's preparation.

In Gaul and Anglo-Saxon England, women shared with men in the work of evangelization and in the new Christian learning. Kings and nobles, seeking suitable occupations for daughters who did not or would not marry, founded monasteries for nuns, some of which were *double monasteries*. A double monastery housed both men and women in two adjoining establishments and was governed by one superior, an *abbess.* Double monasteries

❖ **Lindisfarne Gospels** "In the beginning was the Word" (John 1:1), and the crucial texts for the preservation and spread of the Christian faith were the gospels. Bishop Eadfrith of Lindisfarne c. 690 produced this carpet, or cover page, for a gospel book, reflecting the Celtic tradition of interlaced ornaments and figurative imagery. As a superb example of Northumbrian culture, the style became celebrated throughout Christian Europe. (*Source: British Library*)

✤ **St. Hilda** The superior of a mixed monastery of men and women at Whitby in Northumbria, St. Hilda (614–680) here receives a copy of the scholar Aldhelm's treatise *In Praise of Holy Virgins.* The simple drapery of the nuns' clothing with its nervous quality is characteristic of the eleventh-century Anglo-Saxon scriptoria. *(Source: His Grace the Archbishop of Canterbury and the Trustees of Lambeth Palace Library)*

provided women of the ruling class with something to rule. Nuns and monks worked together. Nuns looked after the children given to the monastery as *oblates* ("offerings"), the elderly who retired at the monastery, and travelers who needed hospitality. Monks provided protection, since in a violent age an isolated house of women invited attack; the monks also did the heavy work on the land. Perhaps the most famous abbess of the Anglo-Saxon period was Saint Hilda (d. 680). A noblewoman of considerable learning and administrative ability, she ruled the double monastery of Whitby on the Northumbrian coast, advised kings and princes, hosted the famous synod of 664, and encouraged scholars and poets. "She compelled those under her direction to devote time to the study of the Holy Scriptures, and to exercise themselves in works of justice," with the result that five monks from Whitby became bishops. Several generations after Hilda, Saint Boniface (see page 241) wrote many letters to Whitby and other houses of

nuns, pleading for copies of books; these attest to the nuns' intellectual reputations.[8]

The finest representative of Northumbrian and indeed all Anglo-Saxon scholarship is the Venerable Bede (ca 673–735). At the age of seven he was given by his parents as an oblate to Benet Biscop's monastery at Wearmouth. Later he was sent to the new monastery at Jarrow five miles away, where, surrounded by the books Benet Biscop had brought from Italy, Bede spent the rest of his life.

The author of learned commentaries on the Scriptures, Bede also devoted himself to other scholarly fields. Modern scholars praise him for his *Ecclesiastical History of the English Nation.* Broader in scope than the title suggests, the work is the chief source of information about early Britain. Bede searched far and wide for his information, discussed the validity of his evidence, compared various sources, and exercised a rare critical judgment. For these reasons, he has been called "the first scientific intellect among the Germanic peoples of Europe."[9]

Bede was probably the greatest master of chronology in the Middle Ages. He also popularized the system of dating events from the birth of Christ, rather than from the foundation of the city of Rome, as the Romans had done, or from the regnal years of kings, as the Germans did. Bede introduced the term *anno Domini,* "in the year of the Lord," abbreviated A.D. He fit the entire history of the world into this new dating method. (The reverse dating system of B.C., "before Christ," does not seem to have been widely used before 1700.) Saint Boniface introduced this system of reckoning time throughout the Frankish empire of Charlemagne.

At about the time that monks at Lindisfarne were producing their Gospel book and Bede at Jarrow was writing his *History,* another Northumbrian monk was at work on a nonreligious epic poem that provides considerable information about the society that produced it. In contrast to the works of Bede, which were written in Latin, the poem *Beowulf* was written in the vernacular Anglo-Saxon. Although Beowulf is the only native English heroic epic, all the events of the tale take place in Denmark and Sweden, suggesting the close relationship between England and the Continent in the eighth century. Scholars have hailed it as a masterpiece of Western literature.

In the epic the great hall of the Danish king Hrothgar has been ravaged by a monster called Grendel. Beowulf, a relative of the Swedish royal house, hears of Grendel's murderous destruction. With a bodyguard of trusted warriors, Beowulf sails to Denmark and destroys Grendel in a brutal battle. Hrothgar and his queen, Wealhtheow, give a great banquet for Beowulf and his followers. Afterward, Grendel's mother enters the hall and carries off one of Hrothgar's closest advisers to avenge her son's death. Beowulf ultimately catches and destroys her. This victory is followed by more feasting, and Beowulf returns home to Sweden laden with rich gifts.

Beowulf later becomes king of a Swedish tribe. When his country is ravaged by a terrible dragon, the aged Beowulf challenges him. In the ensuing battle, Beowulf defeats the dragon but is wounded and dies.[10]

The story resembles ordinary Norse legends but is actually permeated with classical, Germanic, and Christian elements. Though the poem was written in England, all the action takes place in Scandinavia. This reflects the "international" quality of the age's culture, or at least the close ties between England and the Continent in the eighth century.

Beowulf 's values are military and aristocratic: the central institution in the poem is the *gesith,* the Germanic band of warriors, united to fight with Beowulf. The highest virtue is loyalty to him, and loyalty is maintained by giving gifts. Yet the author was a Christian monk, and the basic theme of the poem is the conflict between good and evil. Beowulf, however, does not exhibit any Christian humility. Never one to hide his light under a bushel, he boasts of his exploits unashamedly. In this he embodies the classical idea of fame: the notion that fame is the greatest achievement because it is all a person leaves behind.

Pagan and Germanic symbols and practices suffuse *Beowulf.* Fighting, feasting, and drinking preoccupy its warrior-heroes. There is no glimpse of those who raised and prepared the food they consume; the author did not think peasants deserved mention. In a famous scene, Hrothgar's beautiful queen, Wealhtheow, enters the great hall, dispensing grace and gifts. The scene suggests that upper-class women served as peacemakers. But Wealhtheow may have been handing out presents to the warriors because she had custody of and responsibility for her husband's treasure.

In another scene, the body of a dead king, along with considerable treasure, is put on a ship and floated out to sea. That this was a typical method of burial for Scandinavian kings is known from the ship burial uncovered in 1939 at Sutton Hoo in England. Such customs are a far cry from traditional Christian burial. A monk may have composed *Beowulf,* but the persistence of this burial practice indicates that conversion was still imperfect in much of Europe.

The physical circumstances of life in the seventh and eighth centuries make Northumbrian cultural achievements like the Lindisfarne Gospelbook and *Beowulf* all the more remarkable. Learning was pursued under terribly difficult conditions. Monasteries such as Jarrow and Lindisfarne stood on the very fringes of the European world. The barbarian Picts, just an afternoon's walk from Jarrow, were likely to attack at any time.

Food was not the greatest problem. The North Sea and nearby rivers, the Tweed and the Tyne, yielded abundant salmon and other fish, which could be salted or smoked for winter, a nutritious if monotonous diet. Climate was another matter. Winter could be extremely harsh. In 664, for example, deep snow was hardened by frost from early winter until mid-spring. When it melted away, many animals, trees, and plants were found dead. To make matters worse, disease could take terrible tolls. Bede described events in the year 664:

❖ **St. Luke from the Ada Gospels** (late 8th/early 9th century) After the cross, the most famous early Christian symbols were representations of the four evangelists: Matthew (man), Mark (lion), Luke (a winged ox), and John (eagle), based on the text in Revelations 4:7. The "Ada School" of painting was attached to the court of Charlemagne, and gets its name from Ada, a sister of Charlemagne who commissioned some of the school's work. In this lavishly illuminated painting, a statuesque St. Luke sits enthroned, his draperies falling in nervous folds reminiscent of Byzantine art, and surrounded by an elaborate architectural framework. A splendid example of Carolingian Renaissance art. *(Source: Municipal Library, Trier)*

In the same year of our Lord 664 there was an eclipse of the sun on the third day of May at about four o'clock in the afternoon. Also in that year a sudden pestilence first depopulated the southern parts of Britain and then attacked the kingdom of the Northumbrians as well. Raging far and wide for a long time with cruel devastation it struck down a great multitude of men. . . . This same plague oppressed the island of Ireland with equal destruction.[11]

Damp cold with bitter winds blowing across the North Sea must have pierced everything, even stone monasteries. Inside, only one room, the *calefactory* or "warming room," had a fire. Scribes in the *scriptorium,* or "writing room," had to stop frequently to rub circulation back into their numb hands. These monk-artists and monk-writers paid a high physical price for what they gave to posterity.

Had they remained entirely insular, Northumbrian cultural achievements would have been of slight significance. As it happened, an Englishman from Northumbria played a decisive role in the transmission of English learning to the Carolingian Empire and continental Europe.

The Carolingian Renaissance

Charlemagne's empire disintegrated shortly after his death in 814. But the support he gave to education and learning preserved the writings of the ancients and laid the foundations for all subsequent medieval culture. Charlemagne promoted a revival that scholars have named the "Carolingian Renaissance."

At his court at Aachen, Charlemagne assembled learned men from all over Europe. The most important scholar and the leader of the palace school was the Northumbrian Alcuin (ca 735–804). From 781 until his death, Alcuin was the emperor's chief adviser on religious and educational matters. An unusually prolific scholar, Alcuin prepared some of the emperor's official documents and wrote many moral *exempla,* or "models," which set high standards for royal behavior and constitute a treatise on kingship. Alcuin's letters to Charlemagne set forth political theories on the authority, power, and responsibilities of a Christian ruler.

Aside from Alcuin's literary efforts, what did the scholars at Charlemagne's court do? They copied books and manuscripts and built up libraries. They used the beautifully clear handwriting known as

"Carolingian minuscule," from which modern Roman type is derived. (This script is called "minuscule" because it has both lower case and capital letters; the Romans had only capitals.) Carolingian minuscule meant that a sheet of vellum (calfskin or lambskin) could contain more words and thus be used more efficiently; with the materials at hand, many more manuscripts could be copied.

Carolingian minuscule illustrates the way a seemingly small technological change had broad cultural consequences. The scholars at Aachen established schools all across Europe, attaching them to monasteries and cathedrals. They placed great emphasis on the education of priests, trying to make all priests at least able to read, write, and do simple arithmetic. Their greatest contribution was not so much the originality of their ideas as their hard work of salvaging and preserving the thought and writings of the ancients. Thus the Carolingian Renaissance was a rebirth of interest in, study of, and preservation of the ideas and achievements of classical Greece and Rome.

The revival of learning inspired by Charlemagne and directed by Alcuin helped to limit the dangers of illiteracy on the European continent. Although hardly widespread by later standards, basic literacy was established among the clergy and even among some of the nobility. The small group of scholars at Aachen preserved Latin culture from total extinction in the West.

Although the scholars worked with Latin, the common people spoke their local or vernacular languages. The Bretons, for example, retained their local dialect; and the Saxons and Bavarians could not understand each other (see Map 8.1). Communication among the diverse peoples of the Carolingian Empire was possible only through the medium of Latin.

Once basic literacy was established, monastic and other scholars went on to more difficult work. By the middle years of the ninth century, there was a great outpouring of more sophisticated books. Ecclesiastical writers, imbued with the legal ideas of ancient Rome and the theocratic ideals of Saint Augustine, instructed the semibarbaric rulers of the West. And it is no accident that medical study in the West began, at Salerno in southern Italy, in the late ninth century, *after* the Carolingian Renaissance.

Alcuin completed the work of his countryman Boniface—the Christianization of northern Europe. Latin Christian attitudes penetrated deeply

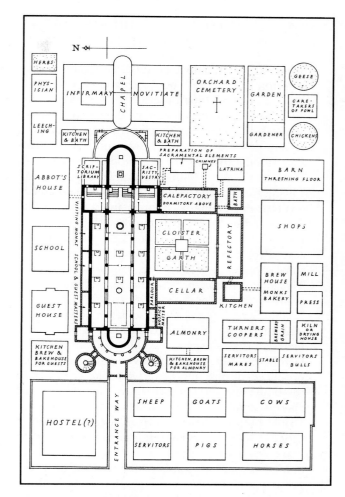

❖ **Plan for an Ideal Monastery** This is a ninth-century architectural design for a self-supporting monastic community of two hundred and seventy members. The monks' lives mainly focused on the church and the cloister, which appropriately appear in the center of the plan. Note the herb garden close to the physician's quarters. The western entrance for visitors was surrounded by the hostel for poor guests and pens for farm animals—with all the inevitable smells. *(Source: Kenneth John Conant,* Carolingian and Romanesque Architecture, 800–1200. *Pelican History of Art, 2nd rev. ed. New York: Pelican, 1978, p. 57)*

into the consciousness of European peoples. By the tenth century, the patterns of thought and lifestyles of educated western Europeans were those of Rome and Latin Christianity. Even the violence and destruction of the great invasions of the late ninth and tenth centuries could not destroy the strong foundations laid by Alcuin and his colleagues.

HEALTH AND MEDICAL CARE IN THE EARLY MIDDLE AGES

Scholars' examination of medical treatises, prescription (or herbal) books, manuscript illustrations, and archaeological evidence has recently revealed a surprising amount of information about medical treatment in the early Middle Ages. In a society devoted to fighting, warriors and civilians alike stood a strong chance of wounds from sword, spear, battle-ax, or blunt instrument. Trying to eke a living from poor soil with poor tools, perpetually involved in pushing back forest and wasteland, the farmer and his family daily ran the risk of accidents. Poor diet weakened everyone's resistance to disease. People bathed rarely. Low standards of personal hygiene increased the danger of infection. This being the case, what medical attention was available to medieval people?

The Germanic peoples had no rational understanding of the causes and cures of disease. They believed that sickness was due to one of three factors: elf-shot, in which elves hurled darts that produced disease and pain; wormlike creatures in the body; and the number 9. Treatments included charms, amulets, priestly incantations, and potions. Drinks prepared from mistletoe, for example, were thought to serve as an antidote to poison and to make women fertile.

Medical practice consisted primarily of drug and prescription therapy. Through the monks' efforts and recovery of Greek and Arabic manuscripts, a large body of the ancients' prescriptions was preserved and passed on. For almost any ailment, several recipes were likely to exist in the prescription lists. Balsam was recommended for coughs. For asthma, an ointment combining chicken, wormwood, laurel berries, and oil of roses was to be rubbed on the chest. The scores of prescriptions to rid the body of lice, fleas, and other filth reflect frightful standards of personal hygiene. The large number of prescriptions for eye troubles suggests that they, too, must have been common. This is understandable, given the widespread practice of locating the fireplace in the center of the room. A lot of smoke and soot filtered into the room, rather than going up the chimney. One remedy calls for bathing the eyes in a solution of herbs mixed with honey, balsam, rainwater, saltwater, or wine.

Poor diet caused frequent stomach disorders and related ailments such as dysentery, constipation, and diarrhea. The value of dieting and avoiding greasy foods was recognized. For poor circulation, a potion of meadow wort, oak rind, and lustmock was recommended. Pregnant women were advised to abstain from eating the flesh of almost all male animals, because such meat might deform the child. Men with unusually strong sexual appetites were advised to fast and to drink at night the juice of agrimony (an herb of the rose family) boiled in ale. If a man suffered from lack of drive, the same plant boiled in milk gave him "courage."

Because of the need for agricultural laborers in the peasant classes and for male heirs in all classes, early medieval people placed a high priority on procreation. The Franks, as we have seen (p. 220), laid a high fine on anyone who molested a woman of childbearing years. Pregnancy and childbirth, however, posed grave threats of infection for both mother and child. Also, heavy field work could cause miscarriages. Some recent scholars have argued that midwives possessed a store of pharmaceutical information deriving from the Romans about fertility, contraception, pregnancy, and childbirth. (Men had no experience in these matters, because modesty forbade their presence at a baby's birth; thus, everything associated with childbirth was entirely in the female domain.) The weight of present evidence on pre- and postnatal matters, however, is that midwives and matrons actually knew very little about drugs to increase contractions, episiotomy (surgical incision of the perineum to allow birth), or the use of forceps (a seventeenth-century invention) during childbirth. The result was a staggeringly high death rate for mothers and the newborn. Recent research on the village of Frénouville in Normandy for the fifth to eighth centuries reveals a 45 percent infant mortality rate; in addition, many mothers died of puerperal fever, an illness resulting from postpartum infection. However, some parts of the Carolingian Empire, such as the estates of the abbey of Saint Victor near Marseilles, show surges in the birthrate, with 38 percent of the population composed of young unmarried people.[12]

Physicians, or "leeches," as they were known in Anglo-Saxon England, were not concerned with the treatment of specific illnesses. They did not examine patients but treated only what they could see or deduce from obvious symptoms. Physicians knew little about the pathology of disease or physiological functions, of internal medicine. They had no accurate standards of weights and measures. Prescriptions called for "a pinch of" or "a handful" or "an eggshell full."

All wounds and open injuries invited infection, and infection invited gangrene. Several remedies were known for wounds. Physicians appreciated the antiseptic properties of honey, and prescriptions recommended that wounds be cleaned with it. When an area or limb had become gangrenous, a good technique of amputation existed. The physician was instructed to cut above the diseased flesh—that is, to cut away some healthy tissue and bone—in order to hasten cure. The juice of white poppy plants—the source of heroin—could be added to wine and drunk as an anesthetic. White poppies, however, grew only in southern Europe and North Africa. If a heavy slug of wine was not enough to dull the patient, he or she had to be held down forcibly while the physician cut. Egg whites, which have a soothing effect, were prescribed for burns.

Teeth survive long periods of burial and give reasonably good information about disease. Evidence from early medieval England shows that the incidence of tooth decay was very low. In the adult population, the rate of cavities was only one-sixth that of today. Cavities below the gum line, however, were very common, because of the prevalence of carbohydrates in the diet. The result was abscesses of the gums. These and other forms of periodontal disease were widespread after the age of thirty.[13]

The spread of Christianity in the Carolingian era had a beneficial effect on medical knowledge and treatment. Several of the church fathers expressed serious interest in medicine. Some of them even knew something about it. The church was deeply concerned about human suffering, whether physical or mental. Christian teaching vigorously supported concern for the poor, sick, downtrodden, and miserable. Churchmen taught that, while all knowledge came from God, he had supplied it so that people could use it for their own benefit.

In the period of the bloodiest violence, the sixth and seventh centuries, medical treatment was provided by monasteries. No other places offered the calm, quiet atmosphere necessary for treatment and recuperation. Monks took care of the sick. They collected and translated the ancient medical treatises. They cultivated herb gardens from which medicines were prepared.

Trotula Famous for her treatise on obstetrics, Trotula was also the most renowned woman teacher at the medical school at Salerno. In this illustration for a twelfth-century manuscript, she holds an orb in her left hand, suggesting that she is "empress" of midwives, while instructing with her right hand and pointed finger. *(Source: Courtesy, Wellcome Institute)*

The foundation of a school at Salerno in southern Italy sometime in the ninth century gave a tremendous impetus to medical study by lay people. The school's location attracted Arabic, Greek, and Jewish physicians from all over the Mediterranean region. Students flocked there from northern Europe. The Jewish physician Shabbathai Ben Abraham (931–982) left behind pharmacological notes that were widely studied in later centuries.

Bone-setting of Jaw Byzantine physicians relied on classical medical treatises, especially those of Hippocrates and Galen; they did not simply parrot their sources, but rearranged and supplemented them with contemporary experimentation. A ninth-century Greek physician added this illustration to this commentary on a first-century manuscript. With the patient sitting on a stool and an assistant holding his head, the doctor takes the dislocated jaw between his fingers and puts it back into place. By medieval standards, Byzantine practical medicine was on a high level. *(Source: Biblioteca Medicea Laurenziana, Florence/ Scandigli, photographer)*

By the eleventh century, the medical school at Salerno enjoyed international fame. Its most distinguished professor then was Constantine the African, a native of Carthage who had studied medicine throughout western Asia. Because of his thorough knowledge of Oriental languages, he served as an important transmitter of Arabic culture to the West. Constantine taught and practiced medicine at Salerno for some years before becoming a monk at Monte Cassino.

How available was medical treatment? Most people lived on isolated rural estates and had to take such advice and help as was available locally. Physicians were few in the early Middle Ages. They charged a fee that only the rich could afford. Apparently, most illnesses simply took their course. People had to develop a stoical attitude. Death came early. A person of forty was considered old. People's vulnerability to ailments for which there was no probable cure contributed to a fatalistic acceptance of death at an early age. Early medical literature shows that attempts to relieve pain were crude; still, attempts *were* made.

✤ DIVISION AND DISINTEGRATION OF THE CAROLINGIAN EMPIRE (814–987)

Charlemagne left his vast empire to his only surviving son, Louis the Pious (814–840), who had actually been crowned emperor in his father's lifetime. Deeply religious Louis was, and well educated, but he was no soldier. Thus he could not retain the respect and loyalty of the warrior-aristocracy on whom he depended for troops and for administration of his territories. The disintegration that had begun in Charlemagne's last years accelerated as soon as he died.

The basic reason for the collapse of the Carolingian Empire is simply that it was too big. Bad roads swarming with thugs and rivers infested with pirates made communication within the empire very difficult. In Charlemagne's lifetime the empire was held together by the sheer force of his personality and driving energy. After his death, it began to fall apart. The empire lacked a bureaucracy like that of the Roman Empire—the administrative machinery necessary for strong and enduring government. It was a collection of tribes held together at the pleasure of warrior-aristocrats, men most interested in strengthening their own local positions and ensuring that they could pass on to their sons the offices and estates they had amassed. Counts, abbots, bishops—both lay and ecclesiastical magnates needed estates to support themselves and reward their followers. In their localities, they simply assumed judicial, military, and financial functions. Why should they obey an unimpressive distant ruler who represented a centralizing power that threatened their local interests? What counted was strength in one's own region and the preservation of family holdings.

The Frankish custom of dividing estates among all male heirs hastened the empire's disintegration. Between 817 and his death in 840, Louis the Pious made several divisions of the empire. Dissatisfied with their portions and anxious to gain the imperial title, Louis's sons—Lothair, Louis the German, and Charles the Bald—fought bitterly among themselves. Finally, in the Treaty of Verdun of 843, the brothers agreed to partition the empire (Map 8.2).

Lothair, the eldest, received the title of emperor, still a source of prestige, and the "middle kingdom," which included Italy and the territories bordered by the Meuse, Saône, and Rhône rivers in the west and the Rhine in the east. Almost immediately, this kingdom broke up into many petty principalities extending diagonally across Europe from Flanders to Lombardy. From the tenth to the twelfth and thirteenth centuries, when French and German monarchs were trying to build strong central governments, this area was constantly contested among them. Even in modern times, the "middle kingdom" of Lothair has been blood-soaked.

The eastern and most Germanic part of the Carolingian Empire passed to Louis the German. The western kingdom went to Charles the Bald; it included the provinces of Aquitaine and Gascony and formed the basis of medieval and modern France. The descendants of Charles the Bald held on in the west until 987, when the leading magnates elected Hugh Capet as king. The heirs of Louis the German ruled the eastern kingdom until 911, but real power was in the hands of local chieftains. Everywhere in the tenth century, fratricidal warfare among the descendants of Charlemagne accelerated the spread of feudalism.

✤ FEUDALISM

The adjective *feudal* is often used disparagingly today to describe something antiquated and barbaric. It is similarly commonplace to think of medieval feudalism as a system that let a small group of lazy military leaders exploit the producing class, the tillers of the soil. This is not a very useful

✤ **MAP 8.2 Division of the Carolingian Empires, 843** The treaty of Verdun (843), which divided the empire among Charlemagne's grandsons, is frequently taken as the start of the separate development of Germany, France, and Italy. The "Middle Kingdom" of Lothair, however, lacking defensive borders and any political or linguistic unity, quickly broke up into numerous small territories.

approach. Preindustrial societies from ancient Greece to the American South before the Civil War to some twentieth-century Latin American countries have been characterized by sharp divisions between "exploiters" and "exploited." To call all such societies "feudal" strips the term of significant meaning and distorts our understanding of medieval feudalism. Many twentieth-century scholars have demonstrated that, when feudalism developed, it served the needs of medieval society (see Listening to the Past).

The Two Levels of Feudalism

Webster's *Third New International Dictionary* defines *government* as "the officials collectively comprising the governing body of a political unit and constituting the organization as an active agency." Feudalism, which emerged in western Europe in the ninth century, was a type of government "in which political power was treated as a private possession and was divided among a large number of lords."[14] This kind of government characterized most parts of western Europe from about 900 to 1300. Feudalism actually existed at two social levels: first, at the level of armed retainers who became knights; and second, at the level of royal officials, such as counts, who ruled great feudal principalities. A wide and deep gap in social standing and political function separated these social levels.

Scholars have debated two theories about the origins of feudalism. According to the older explanation, in the early eighth century, the Carolingian kings and other powerful men needed bodyguards and retainers, armed men who could fight effectively on horseback. The arrival in western Europe around this time of a Chinese technological invention, the stirrup, revolutionized warfare. By making the rider's seat secure and human energy bolstered with animal power, the stirrup welded horse and rider into a powerful fighting unit. While an unstirruped horseman could seldom impale an adversary, a rider in stirrups could utilize the galloping animal's force to strike and damage his enemy. Charles Martel recognized the potential of an effective cavalry; thus the availability of stirrups and the invention increased his need for large numbers of retainers. Horses and armor were terribly expensive, and few could afford them. It also took considerable time to train an experienced cavalryman. The value of retainers increased. Therefore, Charles and other powerful men bound their retainers by oaths of loyalty and ceremonies of homage.

The other, more recent theory of the origin feudalism does not give much importance to the stirrup. According to this interpretation, the stirrup did not lead to the wide use of mounted troops, since most warfare in the Carolingian pe-

Commendation and Initiation Just as the spiritual power of priests is bequeathed by the laying of the priests' hands on the candidate's head at ordination, so the military virtues of strength and loyalty were conveyed to the warrior by the act of commendation when he placed his clasped hands between the hands of his lord. A kiss, symbolizing peace, often concluded the ceremony. *(Source: Universitätsbibliothek, Heidelberg)*

riod was siege warfare conducted by infantry. Rather, Charles Martel, using techniques common among his Merovingian predecessors, purchased the support and loyalty of his followers with grants of land or estates taken from churchmen or laymen, or moveable wealth such as weapons or jewelry, captured in battle.[15] Charles and other powerful men bound their retainers by oaths of loyalty and ceremonies of homage. Personal ties of loyalty cemented the relationship between lord and retainer; in exchange for the promise of service and loyalty, the lord distributed land or some other means of material support, such as cash.

These retainers became known as *vassals,* from a Celtic term meaning "servant." Since knights were not involved in any governmental activity, and since only men who exercised political power were considered noble, knights were not part of the noble class. Down to the eleventh century, political power was concentrated in a small group of counts.

Counts, descended from the old Frankish aristocracy (see page 240), constituted the second level of feudalism. Under Charles Martel and his heirs, counts monopolized the high offices in the Carolingian Empire. At the local level, they had full judicial, military, and financial power. They held courts that dispensed justice, collected taxes, and waged wars. For most ordinary people, the counts were the government. Charlemagne regularly sent missi to inspect the activities of the counts, but there was slight chance of a corrupt or wicked count being removed from office.

While countships were not hereditary in the eighth century, they tended to remain within the same family. In the eighth and early ninth centuries, regional concentrations of power depended on family connections and political influence at the king's court. The disintegration of the Carolingian Empire, however, served to increase the power of regional authorities. Civil wars weakened the power and prestige of kings, because there was little they could do about domestic violence. Likewise, the great invasions of the ninth century, especially the Viking invasions (see pages 258–260), weakened royal authority. The West Frankish kings could do little to halt the invaders, and the aristocracy had to assume responsibility for defense. Common people turned for protection to the strongest local power, the counts, whom they considered their rightful rulers. Thus, in the ninth and tenth centuries, great aristocratic families increased

their authority in the regions of their vested interests. They governed virtually independent territories in which distant and weak kings could not interfere. "Political power had become a private, heritable property for great counts and lords."[16] This is what is meant by feudalism as a form of government.

Because feudal society was a military society, men held the dominant positions in it. A high premium was put on physical strength, fighting skill, and bravery. The legal and social position of women was not as insignificant as might be expected, however. Charters recording gifts to the church indicate that women held land in many areas. Women frequently endowed monasteries, churches, and other religious establishments. The possession of land obviously meant economic power. Moreover, women inherited fiefs, or landed estates. In southern France and Catalonia in Spain, women inherited feudal property as early as the tenth century. Other kinds of evidence attest to women's status. In parts of northern France, children sometimes identified themselves in legal documents by their mother's name rather than their father's, indicating that the mother's social position in the community was higher than the father's.

In a treatise he wrote in 822 on the organization of the royal household, Archbishop Hincmar of Reims placed the queen directly above the treasurer. She was responsible for giving the knights their annual salaries. She supervised the manorial accounts. Thus, in the management of large households with many knights to oversee and complicated manorial records to supervise, the lady of the manor had highly important responsibilities. With such responsibility went power and influence.[17]

Manorialism

Feudalism concerned the rights, powers, and lifestyle of the military elite; *manorialism* involved the services and obligations of the peasant classes. The economic power of the warring class rested on landed estates, which were worked by peasants. Hence feudalism and manorialism were inextricably linked. Peasants needed protection, and lords demanded something in return for that protection. Free peasants surrendered themselves and their lands to the lord's jurisdiction. The land was given back, but the peasants became tied to the land by various kinds of payments and services. In France, England, Germany, and Italy, local custom determined precisely what those services were, but certain practices became common everywhere. The peasant was obliged to turn over to the lord a percentage of the annual harvest, usually in produce, sometimes in cash. The peasant paid a fee to marry someone from outside the lord's estate. To inherit property the peasant paid a fine, often the best beast the person owned. Above all, the peasant became part of the lord's permanent labor force. With vast stretches of uncultivated virgin land and a tiny labor population, lords encouraged population growth and immigration. The most profitable form of capital was not land but laborers.

❖ **Animal Headpost from Viking Ship** Skilled woodcarvers produced ornamental headposts for ships, sledges, wagons, and bedsteads; the fearsome quality of many carvings suggests they were intended to ward off evil spirits. This highly sculpted tenth-century carving, showing the Viking appreciation for fine detail, was discovered in a burial ship at Oseberg, along the Oslo Fjord, Norway, in 1903. *(Source: Viking Ship Museum, Bygdoy/Werner Forman/Art Resource, NY)*

In entering into a relationship with a feudal lord, free farmers lost status. Their position became servile, and they became *serfs*. That is, they were bound to the land and could not leave it without the lord's permission. They were also subject to the jurisdiction of the lord's court in any dispute over property and in any case of suspected criminal behavior.

The transition from freedom to serfdom was slow; its speed was closely related to the degree of political order in a given region. Even in the late eighth century, there were still many free peasants. And within the legal category of serfdom there were many economic levels, ranging from the highly prosperous to the desperately poor. Nevertheless, a social and legal revolution was taking place. By the year 800, perhaps 60 percent of the population of western Europe—completely free a century before—had been reduced to serfdom. The ninth-century Viking assaults on Europe created extremely unstable conditions and individual insecurity, leading to additional loss of personal freedom. Chapter 10 will detail the lives of the peasants. As it will show, the later Middle Ages witnessed considerable upward social mobility.

❖ GREAT INVASIONS OF THE NINTH CENTURY

After the Treaty of Verdun and the division of Charlemagne's empire among his grandsons, continental Europe presented an easy target for foreign invaders. All three kingdoms were torn by domestic dissension and disorder. No European political power was strong enough to put up effective resistance to external attacks. The frontier and coastal defenses erected by Charlemagne and maintained by Louis the Pious were completely neglected. Three groups attacked Europe: Vikings from Scandinavia, representing the final wave of Germanic migrants; Muslims from the Mediterranean; and Magyars, Asiatic nomads forced westward by other peoples (Map 8.3). The combination of their assaults hastened the collapse of the Carolingian empire.

Assaults on Western Europe

From the moors of Scotland to the mountains of Sicily, there arose in the ninth century the prayer, "Save us, O God, from the violence of the North-

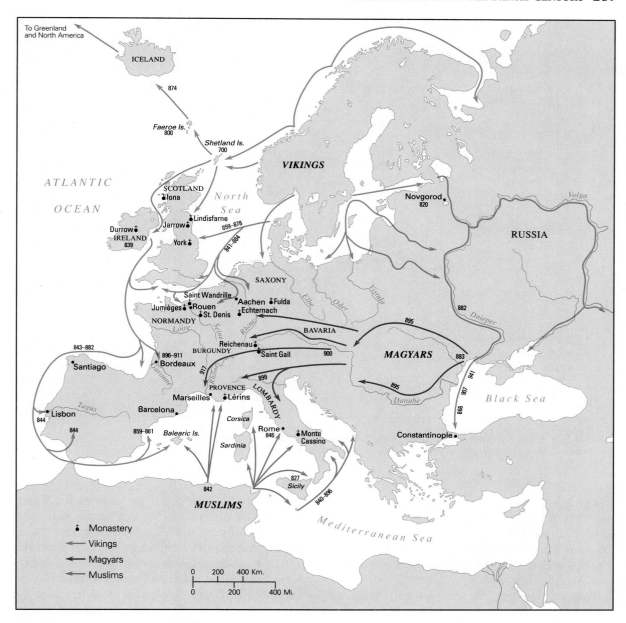

ICELAND

874

Faeroe Is.
800

Shetland Is.
700

VIKINGS

*North
Sea*

ATLANTIC

OCEAN

SCOTLAND
Iona

Novgorod
820

Lindisfarne
859–878

Durrow
IRELAND
839

Jarrow

841–884

York

RUSSIA

882

Volga

SAXONY

Saint Wandrille
Aachen Fulda
Jumièges Rouen Echternach
St. Denis

NORMANDY

Elbe *Oder*

Rhine

BAVARIA

895

Vistula

Dnieper

843–882

Reichenau
BURGUNDY
Saint Gall

896–911
Bordeaux

900

MAGYARS

883

941

907

866

Garonne

917

899

PROVENCE
Marseilles Lérins

LOMBARDY

895

Danube

Santiago

*Black
Sea*

Barcelona

Lisbon
844

844

859–861 *Balearic Is.*

Tagus

Corsica

Sardinia

Rome
846

Monte
Cassino

Constantinople

842

827
Sicily

840–896

MUSLIMS

Mediterranean Sea

Monastery
Vikings
Magyars
Muslims

0   200   400 Km.

0   200   400 Mi.

❖ **MAP 8.3 The Great Invasions of the Ninth Century** Note the Viking penetration of eastern Europe and their probable expeditions to North America. What impact did their various invasions have on European society?

men." The Northmen, also known as Normans or Vikings, were Germanic peoples from Norway, Sweden, and Denmark who had remained beyond the sway of the Christianizing and civilizing influences of the Carolingian Empire. Some scholars believe that the name *Viking* derives from the Old Norse word *vik,* meaning "creek." A Viking,

then, was a pirate who waited in a creek or bay to attack passing vessels.

Charlemagne had established marches, fortresses, and watchtowers along his northern coasts to defend his territory against Viking raids. Their assaults began around 787, and by the mid-tenth century they had brought large chunks of conti-

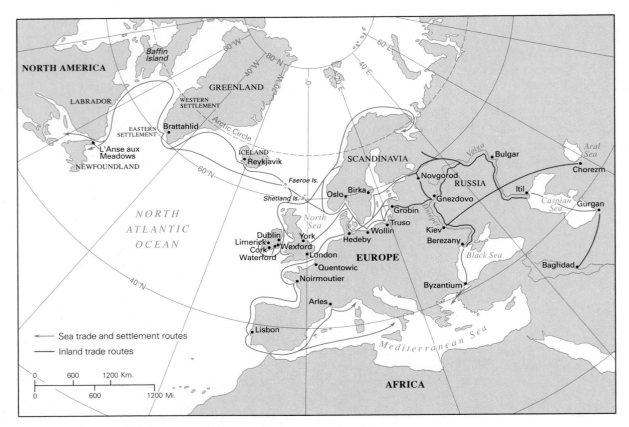

❖ MAP 8.4 Viking Settlement and Trade Routes Viking trade and settlements extended from Newfoundland and Greenland to deep in Russia.

nental Europe and Britain under their sway. In the east they pierced the rivers of Russia as far as the Black Sea (see Map 8.3). In the west they sailed as far as Iceland, Greenland, and even the coast of North America, perhaps as far south as Long Island Sound, New York.

The Vikings were superb seamen. Their advanced methods of boat building gave them great speed and maneuverability. Propelled either by oars or by sails, deckless, about sixty-five feet long, a Viking ship could carry between forty and sixty men—quite enough to harass an isolated monastery or village. These ships, navigated by thoroughly experienced and utterly fearless sailors, moved through the most complicated rivers, estuaries, and waterways in Europe. The Carolingian Empire, with no navy and no notion of the importance of sea power, was helpless. The Vikings moved swiftly, attacked, and escaped to return again.

Scholars disagree about the reasons for Viking attacks and migrations. Some maintain that overpopulation forced the Vikings to emigrate. Others argue that climatic conditions and crop failures forced migration. Still others insist that the Vikings were looking for trade and new commercial contacts. What better targets for plunder than the mercantile centers of northern France and Frisia?

Plunder they did. Viking attacks were bitterly savage. At first they attacked and sailed off laden with booty. Later, on returning, they settled down and colonized the areas they had conquered (Map 8.4). Between 876 and 954, Viking control extended from Dublin across the Irish Sea to Britain, across northern Britain between the Dee and the Solway, and then across the North Sea to the Vikings' Scandinavian homelands. These invaders also overran a large part of northwestern France and called the territory "Norsemanland," from which the word *Normandy* derives.

Scarcely had the savagery of the Viking assaults begun to subside when Europe was hit from the east and south. Beginning about 890, Magyar tribes crossed the Danube and pushed steadily westward. (Since people thought of them as returning Huns, the Magyars came to be known as "Hungarians.") They subdued northern Italy, compelled Bavaria and Saxony to pay tribute, and penetrated even into the Rhineland and Burgundy. These roving bandits attacked isolated villages and monasteries, taking prisoners and selling them in the Eastern slave markets. The Magyars were not colonizers; their sole object was booty and plunder.

The Vikings and Magyars depended on fear. In their initial attacks on isolated settlements, many people were put to the sword. The Vikings also seized thousands of captives as slaves from all the countries where their power reached. From the British Isles and territories along the Baltic, the Vikings took *thralls* (slaves) for the markets of Magdeburg on the Elbe River and Regensburg in Bavaria on the Danube, for the fairs of Lyons on the Rhône River, and to supply the huge demand for slaves in the Muslim world. The slave trade represented an important part of Viking commerce. The Icelander Hoskuld Dala-Kolsson of Laxardal paid three marks of silver, three times the price of a common concubine, for a pretty Irish girl; she was one of twelve offered by a Viking trader. No wonder many communities bought peace by paying tribute.

From the south the Muslims also began new encroachments, concentrating on the two southern peninsulas, Italy and Spain. Seventh- and early eighth-century Islamic movements (see pages 230–231) had been for purposes of conquest and colonization, but the goal of ninth and tenth century incursions was plunder; these later raids were essentially piratical attacks. In Italy the monks of Monte Cassino were forced to flee. The Muslims drove northward and sacked Rome in 846. Expert seamen, they sailed around the Iberian Peninsula, braved the notoriously dangerous shoals and winds of the Atlantic coast, and also attacked the Mediterranean settlements along the coast of Provence. But Muslim attacks on the European continent in the ninth and tenth centuries were less destructive than the Viking and Magyar assaults. Compared to the rich, sophisticated culture of the Arab capitals, northern Europe was primitive, backward, and offered little.

❖ **Vikings Invade Britain** In this twelfth-century representation of the Viking invasions, warriors appear to be armed with helmets, spears, and shields. Crossing the rough North Sea and English Channel in open, oar-propelled boats, they had great courage. *(Source: The Pierpont Morgan Library)*

What was the effect of these invasions on the structure of European society? Viking, Magyar, and Muslim attacks accelerated the development of feudalism. Lords capable of rallying fighting men, supporting them, and putting up resistance to the invaders did so. They also assumed political power in their territories. Weak and defenseless people sought the protection of local strongmen. Free peasants sank to the level of serfs. Consequently, European society became further fragmented. Public power became increasingly decentralized.

The ninth-century invaders also left significant traces of their own cultures. As discussed in Chapter 7, the Muslims made an important contribution to European agriculture, primarily through their influence in Spain (see page 231). The Vikings, too, made positive contributions to the areas they settled. They carried everywhere their unrivaled knowledge of shipbuilding and seamanship. The northeastern and central parts of England where the Vikings settled became known as the *Danelaw* because Danish law and customs, not English, prevailed there. Scholars believe that some legal institutions, such as the ancestor of the modern grand jury, originated in the Danelaw. York in northern England, once a Roman army camp and then an Anglo-Saxon town, became a thriving center of Viking trade with Scandinavia. At Dublin on the east coast of Ireland, Viking iron and steel workers and comb makers established a center for trade with the Hebrides, Iceland, and Norway. The Irish cities of Limerick, Cork, Wexford, and Waterford trace their origins to Viking trading centers.

The Vikings and the Kievan Principality

In antiquity the Slavs lived as a single people in central Europe. With the start of the mass migrations of the late Roman Empire, the Slavs moved in different directions and split into three groups. Between the fifth and ninth centuries, the eastern Slavs, from whom the Ukrainians, the Russians, and the White Russians descend, moved into the vast and practically uninhabited area of present-day European Russia and the Ukraine.

This enormous area consisted of an immense virgin forest to the north, where most of the eastern Slavs settled, and an endless prairie grassland to the south. Probably organized as tribal communities, the eastern Slavs, like many North American pioneers much later, lived off the great abundance of wild game and a crude "slash and burn" agriculture. After clearing a piece of the forest to build log cabins, they burned the stumps and brush. The ashes left a rich deposit of potash and lime, and the land gave several good crops before it was exhausted. The people then moved on to another untouched area and repeated the process.

In the ninth century, the Vikings, those fearless warriors from Scandinavia, appeared in the lands of the eastern Slavs. Called "Varangians" in the old Russian chronicles, the Vikings were interested pri-

marily in international trade, and the opportunities were good, since the Muslim conquests of the eighth century had greatly reduced Christian trade in the Mediterranean. Moving up and down the rivers, the Vikings soon linked Scandinavia and northern Europe to the Black Sea and to the Byzantine Empire with its capital at Constantinople. They built a few strategic forts along the rivers, from which they raided the neighboring Slavic tribes and collected tribute. Slaves were the most important article of tribute, and *Slav* even became the word for "slave" in several European languages.

In order to increase and protect their international commerce, the Vikings declared themselves the rulers of the eastern Slavs. According to tradition, the semilegendary chieftain Ruirik founded the princely dynasty about 860. In any event, the Varangian ruler Oleg (r. 878–912) established his residence at Kiev. He and his successors ruled over a loosely united confederation of Slavic territories—the Kievan state—until 1054. The Viking prince and his clansmen quickly became assimilated into the Slavic population, taking local wives and emerging as the noble class.

Assimilation was accelerated by the conversion of the Vikings and local Slavs to Eastern Orthodox Christianity by missionaries of the Byzantine Empire. The written language of these missionaries, an early form of Slavic now known as Old Church Slavonic, was subsequently used in all religious and nonreligious documents in the Kievan principality. Thus the rapidly Slavified Vikings left two important legacies for the future. They created a loose unification of Slavic territories under a single ruling prince and a single ruling dynasty. And they imposed a basic religious unity by accepting Orthodox Christianity, as opposed to Roman Catholicism, for themselves and the eastern Slavs.

Even at its height under Great Prince Iaroslav the Wise (r. 1019–1054), the unity of the Kievan principality was extremely tenuous. Trade, rather than government, was the main concern of the rulers. Moreover, the Slavified Vikings failed to find a way of peacefully transferring power from one generation to the next. In medieval western Europe this fundamental problem of government was increasingly resolved by resort to the principle of primogeniture: the king's eldest son received the crown as his rightful inheritance when his father died. Civil war was thus averted; order was preserved. In early Kiev, however, there were apparently no fixed rules, and much strife accompanied each succession.

Possibly to avoid such chaos, Great Prince Iaroslav before his death in 1054 divided the Kievan principality among his five sons, who in turn divided their properties when they died. Between 1054 and 1237, Kiev disintegrated into more and more competing units, each ruled by a prince claiming to be a descendant of Ruirik. Even when only one prince was claiming to be the great prince, the whole situation was very unsettled.

The princes divided their land like private property because they thought of it as private property. A given prince owned a certain number of farms or landed estates and had them worked directly by his people, mainly slaves, called *kholops* in Russian. Outside of these estates, which constituted the princely domain, the prince exercised only very limited authority in his principality. Excluding the clergy, two kinds of people lived there: the noble *boyars* and the commoner peasants.

The boyars were the descendants of the original Viking warriors, and they also held their lands as free and clear private property. Although the boyars normally fought in princely armies, the customary law declared that they could serve any prince they wished. The ordinary peasants were also truly free. They could move at will wherever opportunities were greatest. In the touching phrase of the times, theirs was "a clean road, without boundaries."[18] In short, fragmented princely power, private property, and personal freedom all went together.

SUMMARY

Building on the military and diplomatic foundations of his ancestors, Charlemagne waged constant warfare to expand his kingdom. His wars with the Saxons in northwestern Germany and with the Lombards in northern Italy proved successful, and his kingdom ultimately included most of continental Europe. He governed this vast territory through a military elite, the Frankish counts who exercised political, economic, and judicial authority at the local level.

The culture that emerged in Europe between 733 and 843 has justifiably been called the "first" European civilization. That civilization had definite characteristics: it was Christian, feudal, and infused with Latin ideas and models. Almost all people were baptized Christians. Latin was the common language—written as well as spoken—of educated people everywhere. This culture resulted from the mutual cooperation of civil and ecclesiastical authorities. Kings and church leaders supported each others' goals and utilized each others' prestige and power. Kings encouraged preaching and publicized church doctrines, such as the stress on monogamous marriage. In return, church officials urged obedience to royal authority. The support that Charlemagne gave to education and learning, the intellectual movement known as the Carolingian Renaissance, proved his most enduring legacy.

The enormous size of Charlemagne's empire, its lack of viable administrative institutions, the domestic squabbles among his descendants, and the invasions of the Vikings, Magyars, and Muslims—these factors all contributed to the empire's disintegration. As the empire broke down, a new form of decentralized government, later known as feudalism, emerged. In a feudal society public and political power was held by a small group of military leaders. No civil or religious authority could maintain stable government over a very wide area. Local strongmen provided what little security existed. Commerce and long-distance trade were drastically reduced. Because of their agricultural and commercial impact, the Viking and Muslim invaders represent the most dynamic and creative forces of the period. By the twelfth century, the Kievan Principality, Slavic in ethnicity, Greek Orthodox in religion, and the center of considerable trade with the Chinese and Muslim worlds, constituted a loose collection of territories without strong central government.

NOTES

1. For the date of this battle, October 17, 733, see L. White, *Medieval Technology and Social Change* (Oxford: Clarendon Press, 1962), pp. 3 n. 3, 12.
2. See F. Irsigler, "On the Aristocratic Character of Early Frankish Society," in T. Reuter, ed. and trans., *The Medieval Nobility: Studies on the Ruling Class of France and Germany from the Sixth to the Twelfth Century,* (New York: North-Holland, 1978), pp. 105–136, esp. p. 123.

3. Einhard, *The Life of Charlemagne,* with a fore-word by S. Painter (Ann Arbor: University of Michigan Press, 1960), pp. 50–51.

4. P. Stafford, *Queens, Concubines, and Dowagers: The King's Wife in the Early Middle Ages* (Athens: University of Georgia Press, 1983), pp. 60–62.

5. See K. F. Werner, "Important Noble Families in the Kingdom of Charlemagne," in Reuter, pp. 174–184.

6. B. D. Hill, ed., *Church and State in the Middle Ages* (New York: John Wiley & Sons, 1970), pp. 46–47.

7. P. Geary, "Carolingians and the Carolingian Empire," in J. R. Strayer, ed., *Dictionary of the Middle Ages,* vol. 3, (New York: Charles Scribner's Sons, 1983), p. 110.

8. J. Nicholson, "Feminae Gloriosae: Women in the Age of Bede," in D. Baker, ed., *Medieval Women,* (Oxford: Basil Blackwell, 1978), pp. 15–31, esp. p. 19, and C. Fell, *Women in Anglo-Saxon England and the Impact of 1066* (Bloomington: Indiana University Press, 1984), p. 109.

9. R. W. Southern, *Medieval Humanism and Other Studies* (Oxford: Basil Blackwell, 1970), p. 3.

10. D. Wright, trans., *Beowulf* (Baltimore: Penguin Books, 1957), pp. 9–19.

11. L. Sherley-Price, trans., *Bede: A History of the English Church and People* (Baltimore: Penguin Books, 1962), bk. 3, chap. 27, p. 191.

12. C. Klapisch-Zuber, ed., *A History of Women,* Vol. 2: *Silences of the Middle Ages* (Cambridge, Mass.: Harvard University Press, 1992), pp. 289–290.

13. See S. Rubin, *Medieval English Medicine* (New York: Barnes & Noble, 1974).

14. J. R. Strayer, "The Two Levels of Feudalism," in *Medieval Statecraft and the Perspectives of History* (Princeton, N.J.: Princeton University Press, 1971), p. 63. This section leans heavily on this seminal study.

15. See B. S. Bachrach, "Charles Martel, Mounted Shock Combat, the Stirrup, and Feudalism," in *Studies in Medieval and Renaissance History,* vol. VII (1970), pp. 49–75, esp. pp. 66–75.

16. Strayer, "The Two Levels," pp. 65–76, esp. p. 71.

17. See D. Herlihy, "Land, Family, and Women in Continental Europe, 701–1200," in S. M. Stuard, ed., *Women in Medieval Society,* (Philadelphia: University of Pennsylvania Press, 1976), pp. 13–45.

18. Quoted in R. Pipes, *Russia Under the Old Regime* (New York: Charles Scribner's Sons, 1974), p. 48.

SUGGESTED READING

The best general treatment of the material discussed in this chapter is R. McKitterick, *The Frankish Kingdom under the Carolingians, 751–987* (1983). The same author's *The Carolingians and the Written Word* (1989) will prove essential for many aspects of the Carolingian Renaissance, as will *The Uses of Literacy in Early Medieval Europe* (1990), for which she served as editor, which includes articles on Ireland, Anglo-Saxon England, Merovingian Gaul, Muslim Spain, and Byzantium. R. Hodges and D. Whitehouse, *Mohammed, Charlemagne & the Origins of Europe: Archeology and the Pirenne Thesis* (1983), approaches some of the problems treated in the chapter from the perspective of archaeology.

Einhard's *Life of Charlemagne,* cited in the Notes, is a good starting point for study of the great chieftain. The best general biography of Charlemagne is D. Bullough, *The Age of Charlemagne* (1965). P. Riche, *Daily Life in the World of Charlemagne,* J. McNamara, trans. (1978), is a richly detailed study of many facets of Carolingian society by a distinguished authority. The same scholar's *Education and Culture in the Barbarian West: From the Sixth Through the Eighth Century* (trans. J. J. Contreni, 1976) provides an excellent, if technical, treatment of Carolingian intellectual activity. Both volumes contain solid bibliographies. For agricultural and economic life, G. Duby, *The Early Growth of the European Economy: Warriors and Peasants from the Seventh to the Twelfth Century* (1978), relates economic behavior to other aspects of human experience in a thoroughly readable style. The importance of technological developments in the Carolingian period is described by L. White, *Medieval Technology and Social Change* (1962), now a classic work. For the meaning of war to the Merovingian and Carolingian kings, see J. M. Wallace-Hadrill, "War and Peace in the Early Middle Ages," in *Early Medieval History* (1975). As the title implies, G. Barraclough, *The Crucible of Europe: The Ninth and Tenth Centuries in European History* (1976), sees those centuries as crucial in the formation of European civilization. E. James, *The Origins of France: From Clovis to the Capetians, 500–1000* (1982), is a solid introductory survey of early French history, with emphasis on family relationships.

In addition to the references to Bede and *Beowulf* in the Notes, D. L. Sayers, trans., *The Song of Roland* (1957), provides an excellent key, in epic form, to the values and lifestyles of the feudal classes, while the evocation by P. H. Blair, *Northumbria in the Days of Bede* (1976) is highly recommended.

For the development of the Christian church as an institution and its impact on pagan Germanic peoples, see the monumental work of F. Kempf et al., *The Church in the Age of Feudalism,* A. Biggs, trans. (1980), vol. 3 of the *History of the Church* series edited by H. Jedin and J. Dolan. Important aspects of Christian spirituality are traced in B. McGinn and J. Meyendorff, eds., *Christian Spirituality: From the Apostolic Fathers to the Twelfth Century* (1985). The scope of G. Tellenbach, *The Church in Western Europe from the Tenth to the Early Twelfth Century,* T. Reuter, trans. (1993), is indicated by its title. F. Paxton, *Christianizing Death: The Creation of Ritual Process in Early Medieval Europe* (1990), and T. Head, *Hagiography and the Cult of the Saints* (1990), are valuable books dealing with specialized topics.

Those interested in women and children in early medieval society should see the titles by Klapisch-Zuber and Herlihy cited in the Notes and S. F. Wemple, *Women in Frankish Society: Marriage and the Cloister, 500 to 900* (1981), a fundamental work.

The following studies are also important and useful: J. McNamara, "A Legacy of Miracles: Hagiography and Nunneries in Merovingian Gaul," in J. Kirshner and S. Wemple, eds., *Women of the Medieval World: Essays in Honor of John H. Mundy* (1985); A. Warren, *Anchorites and Their Patrons in Medieval England* (1985); P. Stafford, *Queens, Concubines, and Dowagers: The King's Wife in the Early Middle Ages* (1983); and the book by C. Fell cited in the Notes.

For health and medical treatment, the curious student should consult W. H. McNeill, *Plagues and Peoples* (1976); A. Castiglioni, *A History of Medicine* (E. B. Krumbhaar, trans., 1941); S. Rubin's book cited in the Notes, esp. pp. 97–149; and the important article by J. M. Riddle, "Theory and Practice in Medieval Medicine," *Viator* 5 (1974): 157–184. Richer than the title might imply, J. C. Russell, *The Control of Late Ancient and Medieval Population* (1985), discusses diet, disease, and demography.

For feudalism and manorialism see, in addition to the references given in the Notes, F. L. Ganshof, *Feudalism* (1961), and J. R. Strayer, "Feudalism in Western Europe," in R. Coulborn, ed., *Feudalism in History* (1956). M. Bloch, *Feudal Society,* L. A. Manyon, trans., (1961), remains important. The more recent treatments of G. Duby, in the book mentioned earlier, and P. Anderson, *Passages from Antiquity to Feudalism* (1978), stress the evolution of social structures and mental attitudes. For the significance of the ceremony of vassalage, see J. Le Goff, "The Symbolic Ritual of Vassalage," in his *Time, Work, and Culture in the Middle Ages,* A. Goldhammer, trans., (1982), a collection of provocative but difficult essays that includes "The Peasants and the Rural World in the Literature of the Early Middle Ages." The best broad treatment of peasant life and conditions is G. Duby, *Rural Economy and Country Life in the Medieval West,* C. Postan, trans., (1968).

J. Brondsted, *The Vikings* (1960), is an excellently illustrated study of many facets of Viking culture. G. Jones, *A History of the Vikings,* rev. ed. (1984), provides a comprehensive survey of the Viking world based on the latest archaeological findings and numismatic evidence, while P.H. Sawyer, *Kings and Vikings: Scandinavia and Europe, A.D. 700–1100* (1983), relies heavily on the literary evidence.

Feudal Homage and Fealty

Feudalism was a social and political system held together by bonds of kinship, homage, and fealty and by grants of benefices—lands or estates given by king, lay lord, or ecclesiastical (bishop or abbot) officer to another member of the nobility or to a knight. In return for the benefice, or fief, the recipient became the vassal of the lord and agreed to perform certain services, usually military ones. Feudalism developed in the ninth century during the disintegration of the Carolingian empire because rulers needed fighting men and officials. In a society that lacked an adequate government bureaucracy, a sophisticated method of taxation, or even the beginnings of national consciousness, personal ties provided some degree of cohesiveness.

In the first document, a charter dated 876, the emperor Charles the Bald (r. 843–877), Charlemagne's grandson, grants a benefice. In the second document, dated 1127, the Flemish notary Galbert of Bruges describes homage and fealty before Count Charles the Good of Flanders (r. 1119–1127). The ceremony consists of three parts: the act of homage; the oath of fealty, intended to reinforce the act; and the investiture (apparently with property). Because all three parts are present, historians consider this evidence of a fully mature feudal system.

In the name of the holy and undivided Trinity. Charles by the mercy of Almighty God august emperor . . . let it be known to all the faithful of the holy church of God and to our now, present and to come, that one of our faithful subjects, by name of Hildebertus, has ap-

proached our throne and has beseeched our serenity that through this command of our authority we grant to him for all the days of his life and to his son after him, in right of usufruct and benefice, certain estates which are . . . called Cavaliacus, in the county of Limoges. Giving assent to his prayers for reason of his meritorious service, we have ordered this charter to be written, through which we grant to him the estates already mentioned, in all their entirety, with lands, vineyards, forests, meadows, pastures, and with the men living upon them, so that, without causing any damage through exchanges or diminishing or lessening the land, he for all the days of his life and his son after him, as we have said, may hold and possess them in right of benefice and usufruct. . . .

Done of the sixteenth kalends of August [July 15th] the thirty-seventh year of the reign of Charles most glorious emperor in France . . . at Ponthion in the palace of the emperor. In the name of God, happily. Amen.

On Thursday, the seventh of the ides of April [April 7, 1127], acts of homage were again made to the count, which were brought to a conclusion through this method of giving faith and assurance. First, they performed homage in this fashion: the count inquired if [the prospective vassal] wished completely to become his man. He replied, "I do wish it," and with his hands joined and covered by the hands of the count, the two who were united by a kiss. Second, he who had done the homage gave faith to the representative of the count in these words: "I promise in my faith that I shall henceforth be faithful to Count William, and I shall fully observe the homage owed him against all men, in good faith and without deceit." Third, he took an oath on the relics of the saints. Then the count, with the rod which he had in his right hand, gave investiture to all those who by this promise had given assurance and due homage to the count, and had taken the oath.

Questions for Analysis

1. Why was the charter drawn up? Why did Charles grant the benefice?

2. Who were the "men living on it," and what economic functions did they perform?

3. What did the joined hands of the prospective vassal and the kiss symbolize?

4. In the oath of fealty, what was meant by the phrase "in my faith"? Why did the vassal swear on relics of the saints? What were these, and why were they used?

5. What does this ceremony tell us about the society that used it?

Source: THE HISTORY OF FEUDALISM *by* D. Herliny, ed. Copyright © 1970 by Harper and Row.

❖ Charles the Bald with Roman attributes of rule, from a Bible, ca. 846 A.D. (*Source: Bibliothèque Nationale, Paris*)

Revival, Recovery, and Reform

 By the last quarter of the tenth century, after a long and bitter winter of discontent, the first hints of European spring were appearing. The European springtime lasted from the middle of the eleventh century to the end of the thirteenth. This period from about 1050 to 1300 has often been called the "High Middle Ages." The term designates a time of crucial growth and remarkable cultural achievement between two eras of economic, political, and social crisis.

- What were the ingredients of revival, and how did they come about?
- How did political revival affect the reform of the church? How, in turn, did religious reform influence secular developments?
- How did the reform of the Christian church affect relations between the church and civil authorities?
- What were the Crusades, and how did they manifest the influence of the church and the ideals of medieval society?

These are the questions that will frame discussion in this chapter.

Rievaulx Abbey in York-shire, England, was com-pleted in 1175 A.D.
(Source: Bruce Coleman Ltd.)

POLITICAL REVIVAL

The eleventh century witnessed the beginnings of political stability in western Europe. Foreign invasions gradually declined, and domestic disorder subsided. This development gave people security in their persons and property. Political order and security provided the foundation for economic recovery and contributed to a slow increase in population.

The Decline of Invasion and Civil Disorder

In the tenth century, Charlemagne's descendants continued to hold the royal title in the West Frankish kingdom, but they exercised no effective control over the great feudal lords. Recent research on medieval France has focused on regions and principalities, emphasizing the diversity of languages and cultures, the differences of social structures, and the division of public authority. Northern French society, for example, had strong feudal elements, but the fief and vassalage were almost unknown in the south. The southern territories used Roman law, while the northern counties and duchies relied on unwritten customary law that was not codified until the thirteenth century. The kings of France in the eleventh century were kings in name—petty barons in fact; no ruler exercised wide jurisdiction. Broad generalizations about France are therefore very dangerous.[1]

Five counties dominated northern France: Anjou, Blois-Chartres, Brittany, Flanders, and Normandy. In the early eleventh century all five experienced considerable internal disorder and all were aggressively expansionist. But Normandy gradually emerged as the strongest territory with the greatest relative level of peace.

The territory that we call Normandy takes its name from the Northmen, or Vikings, who settled there in the tenth century. In 911 the West Frankish ruler Charles the Simple, unable to oust the Vikings, officially recognized their leader Rollo and later invested him with more lands; in return, Rollo gave allegiance and agreed to hold the region as a barrier against future Viking attacks. Rollo and his men were baptized as Christians and supported the West Frankish ruler when he needed their help. Although additional Northmen arrived, they were easily pacified. The late tenth and early eleventh centuries saw the assimilation of Norman and French, and major assaults on France had ended.

During the minority of Rollo's descendant Duke William I (r. 1035–1089), however, rebellious lords ignored ducal authority, built private castles, and engaged in private warfare—with general instability the result. The alliance of Count Geoffrey Martel of Anjou and King Henry I of France posed a dire threat to ducal authority until 1054, when William defeated them. This victory turned the tide. Beginning in 1060, William united the Norman nobility under threat of external aggression and defended his frontier with a circle of castles.

William also made feudalism work as a system of government. He insisted on the homage of his vassals, attached specific quotas of knight service to the lands he distributed, swiftly executed vassals who defaulted on their obligations, limited private warfare, and forbade the construction of private castles, always the symbol of feudal independence. The duke controlled the currency and supervised the church by participating in the selection of all bishops and abbots. By 1066 the Norman frontiers were stable, and the duchy possessed a feudal hierarchy. By the standards of the time, Normandy was an orderly and well-controlled principality.

Following the death of the last Carolingian ruler in 987, an assembly of nobles met to choose a successor. Accepting the argument of the archbishop of Reims that the French monarchy was elective, the nobles selected Hugh Capet, dux Francorum, duke of "France," from which the country got its name, and head of a powerful clan in the West Frankish kingdom. The Capetian kings (so called from the "cope," or cloak, Hugh wore as abbot of Saint-Denis) subsequently saved France from further division. But this was hardly apparent in 987. Compared with the duke of Normandy, the first Capetians were weak; but by hanging on to what they had, they laid the foundations for later political stability.

Recovery followed a different pattern in Anglo-Saxon England. The Vikings had made a concerted effort to conquer and rule the whole island, and probably no part of Europe suffered more. Before the Viking invasions, England had never been united under a single ruler, and in 877 only parts of the kingdom of Wessex survived. The victory of the remarkable Alfred, king of the West Saxons (or Wessex), over Guthrun the Dane at Edington in 878 inaugurated a great political revival. Alfred and his immediate successors built a system of local defenses and slowly extended royal rule beyond Wessex to other Anglo-Saxon peoples until one law, royal law, replaced local custom. Alfred and his successors also laid the foundations for an efficient system of local government responsible directly to the king. Under the pressure of the Vikings England was gradually united under one ruler.

In 1013 the Danish ruler Swen Forkbeard invaded England: his son Canute completed the subjugation of the island. King of England (1016–1035) and after 1030 king of Norway as well, Canute made England the center of his empire.

Canute promoted a policy of assimilation and reconciliation between Anglo-Saxons and Vikings. Slowly the two peoples were molded together. The assimilation of Anglo-Saxon and Viking was personified by King Edward the Confessor (r. 1042–1066), the son of an Anglo-Saxon father and a Norman mother who had taken Canute as her second husband.

In the East, the German king Otto I (r. 936–973) inflicted a crushing defeat on the Hungarians at the banks of the Lech River in 955. This battle halted the Magyars' westward expansion and threat to Germany and made Otto a great hero to the Germans. It also signified the revival of the German monarchy and demonstrated that Otto was a worthy successor to Charlemagne.

When chosen king, Otto had selected Aachen as the site of his coronation to symbolize his intention to continue the tradition of Charlemagne. The basis of his power was alliance with and control of the church. Otto asserted the right to control ecclesiastical appointments. Before receiving religious consecration, bishops and abbots had to perform feudal homage for the lands that accompanied the church office. (This practice, later known "investiture," was to create a grave crisis in the eleventh century [see pages 278–280].)

Otto realized that he had to use the financial and military resources of the church to halt feudal anarchy. He used the higher clergy extensively in his administration, and the bulk of his army came from monastic and other church lands. Between 936 and 955 Otto succeeded in breaking the territorial power of the great German dukes.

Some of our knowledge of Otto derives from *The Deeds of Otto,* a history of his reign in heroic verse written by a nun, Hrotswitha of Gandersheim (ca 935–ca 1003). A learned poet, she also produced six verse plays, and she is considered the first dramatist after the fall of the ancient classical theater. Hrotswitha's literary productions give her an important place in the mainstream of tenth-century civilization.

Otto's coronation by the pope in 962 revived the imperial dignity and laid the foundation for what was later called the Holy Roman Empire. Further, the coronation showed that Otto had the support of the church in Germany and Italy. The uniting of the kingship with the imperial crown advanced German interests. Otto filled a power vacuum in northern Italy and brought peace among the great aristocratic families. The level of order there improved for the first time in over a century.

Peace and political stability in turn promoted the revival of northern Italian cities. Although plague, climatic deterioration that reduced agricultural productivity, and invasions had drastically reduced population throughout Italy, most of the northern city states had survived the disorders of the early Middle Ages. By the ninth century, some of these cities showed considerable economic dynamism, in particular Venice, which won privileged access to Byzantine markets and imported silk, textiles, cosmetics, and Crimean slaves to sell to Padua and other cities. By the eleventh century Venetian commerce had stimulated economic growth in Milan and Cremona, with those cities and Sicily supplying Venice with food in exchange for luxury goods from the East. The rising economic importance of Venice and later of Genoa, Pisa, and other Italian

❖ **Christ Enthroned with Saints and the Emperor Otto I** (tenth century) Between 933 and 973, Emperor Otto I founded the church of St. Mauritius in Magdeburg. As a memorial to the event, Otto commissioned the production of this ivory plaque showing Christ accepting a model of the church from the emperor. Ivory was a favorite medium of Ottonian artists, and squat figures in a simple geometrical pattern characterize their work. *(Source: The Metropolitan Museum of Art, Bequest of George Blumenthal, 1941 (41.100.157))*

cities became a central factor in the struggle between the papacy and the German empire.

Population, Climate, and Mechanization

A steady growth of population also contributed to Europe's general recovery. The decline of foreign invasions and internal civil disorder reduced the number of people killed and maimed. Feudal armies in the eleventh through thirteenth centuries continued their destruction, but they were very small by modern standards and fought few pitched battles. Most medieval conflicts consisted of sieges directed at castles or fortifications. As few as twelve men could defend a castle. With sufficient food and an adequate water supply, they could hold out for a long time. Monastic chroniclers, frequently bored and almost always writing from hearsay evidence, tended to romanticize medieval warfare (as long as it was not in their own neighborhoods). Most conflicts were petty skirmishes with slight loss of life. The survival of more young people—those most often involved in war and usually the most sexually active—meant a population rise.

Nor was there any "natural," or biological, hindrance to population expansion. Between the tenth and fourteenth centuries, Europe was not hit by any major plague or other medical scourge, though leprosy and malaria did strike down some people. Leprosy, caused by a virus, was not very contagious, and it worked slowly. Lepers presented a frightful appearance: the victim's arms and legs rotted away, and gangrenous sores emitted a horrible smell. Physicians had no cure. For these reasons, and because of the command in the thirteenth chapter of Leviticus that lepers be isolated, medieval lepers were eventually segregated in hospitals called "leprosaria."

Malaria, spread by protozoa-carrying mosquitoes that infested swampy areas, caused problems primarily in Italy. Malaria is characterized by alternate chills and fevers and leaves the afflicted person extremely weak. Peter the Venerable, ninth abbot of Cluny (1122–1156), suffered in his later years from recurring bouts of malaria contracted on a youthful trip to Rome. Still, relatively few people caught malaria or leprosy. Crop failure and the ever-present danger of starvation were much more pressing threats.

The weather cooperated with the revival. Meteorologists believe that a slow but steady retreat of polar ice occurred between the ninth and eleventh centuries. A significant warming trend continued until about 1200. The century between 1080 and 1180 witnessed exceptionally clement weather in England, France, and Germany, with mild winters and dry summers. Good weather helps to explain advances in population growth, land reclamation, and agricultural yield. Increased agricultural output had a profound impact on society: it affected Europeans' health, commerce, industry, and general lifestyle. A better diet had an enormous impact on women's lives: it meant increased body fat, which increased fertility; also, more iron in the diet meant that women were less anemic and less subject to opportunistic diseases. Some researchers believe that it was in the high Middle Ages that Western women began to outlive men.

The tenth and eleventh centuries also witnessed a remarkable spurt in mechanization, especially in the use of energy. The increase in the number of water mills was spectacular. The Romans had devised a vertical water wheel fitted with blades, "which drove the upper millstone through 90 degree gearing. The gearing permitted a much higher speed of rotation in the stones than in the wheels."[2] An ancient water mill unearthed near Monte Cassino could grind about 1.5 tons of grain in 10 hours, a quantity that would formerly have required the exertions of 40 slaves. The abundance of slave labor in the ancient world had retarded the development of mills, but by the mid-ninth century, on the lands of the abbey of Saint-Germain-des-Prés near Paris, there were 59 water mills. Succeeding generations saw a continued increase. Thus, on the Robec River near Rouen, there were 2 mills in the tenth century, 4 in the eleventh century, 10 in the thirteenth, and 12 in the fourteenth century. *Domesday Book,* William the Conqueror's great survey of English economic resources in the late eleventh century (see page 329), recorded 5,624 water mills. Of the 9,250 manors in England at that time, 3,463 had at least one mill. One scholar has calculated that on average each mill supplied 50 households. Besides grinding wheat or other grains to produce flour, water mills became essential in fulling, the process of scouring, cleansing, and thickening cloth. Rather than men or women trampling cloth in a trough, wooden hammers were raised and dropped on the cloth by means of a revolving drum connected to the spindle of a water wheel. Water mills revolutionized the means of grinding and fulling by using natural, rather than human, energy.

✦ **Arabic Water Mill** Land irrigation, essential to the growth of an agricultural economy, was greatly advanced by Arab inventions such as this *noria*, or water wheel,
which harnessed the power of moving water. *(Source: Biblioteca Apostolica Vaticana)*

Successful at adapting waterpower to human needs, medieval engineers soon harnessed wind-power. They replaced the wheels driven by water with sails. But while water always flows in the same direction, wind can blow from many directions. Windmill engineers solved this problem very ingeniously by mounting the framed wooden body, which contained the machinery and carried the sails, on a massive upright post free to turn with the wind.[3]

✦ REVIVAL AND REFORM IN THE CHRISTIAN CHURCH

The eleventh century also witnessed the beginnings of a remarkable religious revival. Monasteries, always the leaders in ecclesiastical reform, remodeled themselves under the leadership of the Burgundian abbey of Cluny. Subsequently, new religious orders, such as the Cistercians, were founded and became a broad spiritual movement.

The papacy itself, after a century of corruption and decadence, was cleaned up. The popes worked to clarify church doctrine and codify church law. They and their officials sought to communicate with all the clergy and peoples of Europe through a clearly defined, obedient hierarchy of bishops. The popes wanted the basic loyalty of all members of the clergy. Pope Gregory VII's strong assertion of papal power led to profound changes and serious conflict with secular authorities. The revival of the church was manifested in the twelfth and thirteenth centuries by a flowering of popular piety, reflected in the building of magnificent cathedrals.

Monastic Revival

In the early Middle Ages, the best Benedictine monasteries had been citadels of good Christian living and centers of learning. Between the seventh and ninth centuries, religious houses such as Bobbio in northern Italy, Luxeuil in France, and Jarrow in England copied and preserved manuscripts,

✦ **Mont St.-Michel** At the summit of a 250-foot cone of rock rising out of the sea and accessible only at low tide, Mont St.-Michel combined fortified castle and monastery. Thirteenth-century monarchs considered it crucial to their power in northwestern France, and it played a decisive role in French defenses against the English during the Hundred Years' War. The abbots so planned the architecture that monastic life went on undisturbed by military activity. *(Source: Giraudon/Art Resource)*

maintained schools, and set high standards of monastic observance. Charlemagne had encouraged and supported these monastic activities, and the collapse of the Carolingian Empire had disastrous effects.

The Viking, Magyar, and Muslim invaders attacked and ransacked many monasteries across Europe. Some communities fled and dispersed. In the period of political disorder that followed the disintegration of the Carolingian Empire, many religious houses fell under the control and domination of local feudal lords. Powerful laymen appointed themselves or their relatives as abbots, while keeping their wives or mistresses. They took for themselves the lands and goods of monasteries, spending monastic revenues and selling monastic offices. Temporal powers all over Europe dominated the monasteries. The level of spiritual observance and intellectual activity declined.

In the eleventh and twelfth centuries monasteries became inextricably involved in the feudal order. Since the time of Charlemagne, secular powers had selected church officials and compelled them to become their vassals. Abbots, bishops, and archbishops thus had military responsibilities that required them to fight with their lords, or at least to send contingents of soldiers when called on to do so. Church law forbade clerics to shed blood, but many prelates found the excitement of battle too great to resist. In the ninth century, abbot Lupus of Ferriéres wrote his friend abbot Odo of Corbie,

I am often most anxious about you, recalling your habit of heedlessly throwing yourself, all unarmed, into the thick of battle whenever your youthful energy is overcome with the greedy desire to conquer . . . I, as you know, have never learned how to strike an enemy or to avoid his blows. Nor do I know how to execute all the other obligations of military service on foot or horseback.

Lupus preferred the quiet of his scriptorium to the noise of the battlefield.[4] But as late as the twelfth and thirteenth centuries, ecclesiastical barons owed heavy contingents of knight service. For example, in twelfth-century England, the abbot of Peterborough owed the king the service of 60 knights, the abbot of Bury St. Edmund's 40 knights, and the archbishop of Canterbury the huge service of 500 knights, though after 1166 the service was usually commuted into a cash payment.[5] As feudal lords, ecclesiastical officials also had judicial authority over the knights, whose cases prelates tried in their feudal courts, and peasants, whose disputes they resolved in the manorial courts. For some prelates the conflict between their religious duties on the one hand, and their judicial and military obligations on the other, posed a serious dilemma.

In 909 William the Pious, duke of Aquitaine, established the abbey of Cluny near Macon in Burgundy. This was to be a very important event. In his charter of endowment, Duke William declared that Cluny was to enjoy complete independence from all feudal (or secular) and episcopal lordship. The new monastery was to be subordinate only to the authority of Saints Peter and Paul as represented by the pope. The duke then renounced his own possession of and influence over Cluny.

This monastery and its foundation charter came to exert vast religious influence. The first two abbots of Cluny, Berno (910–927) and Odo (927–942), set very high standards of religious behavior. They stressed strict observance of the *Rule of Saint Benedict,* the development of a personal spiritual life by the individual monk, and the importance of the liturgy. Cluny gradually came to stand for clerical celibacy and the suppression of *simony* (the sale of church offices). In the eleventh century, Cluny

❖ **Consecration of the Church of Cluny** Pope Urban II surrounded by mitred bishops appears on the left, Abbot Hugh of Cluny with cowled monks on the right. A French nobleman who had been a monk of Cluny, Urban coined the term *curia* as the official designation of the central government of the church. *(Source: Bibliothèque Nationale, Paris)*

was fortunate in having a series of highly able abbots who ruled for a long time. These abbots paid careful attention to sound economic management. In a disorderly world, Cluny gradually came to represent religious and political stability. Therefore, laypersons placed lands under its custody and monastic priories under its jurisdiction for reform. Benefactors wanted to be associated with Cluniac piety. Moreover, properties and monasteries under Cluny's jurisdiction enjoyed special protection, at least theoretically, from violence.[6] In this way hundreds of monasteries, primarily in France and Spain, came under Cluny's authority.

Cluny was not the only center of monastic reform. The abbey of Gorze in Lotharingia (modern Lorraine) exercised a correcting influence on German religious houses. With royal support and through such abbeys as Saint Emmeran at Regensburg, Gorze directed a massive reform of monasteries in central Europe. Recent scholarship has shown that Gorze and Cluny represented two different monastic traditions. Gorze became a center of literary culture, Cluny of liturgical ceremony. Gorze personified the simple lifestyle, Cluny the elaborate. Gorze accepted lay authority over monasteries, Cluny did not. Gorze served the empire, Cluny the Gregorian reformers (see pages 278–280). In some ways, Gorze stood for the German East, Cluny for the French West.[7]

Deeply impressed lay people showered gifts on monasteries with high reputations. Jewelry, rich vestments, elaborately carved sacred vessels, even lands and properties poured into some houses. But with this wealth came lay influence. As the monasteries became richer, the lifestyle of the monks grew increasingly luxurious. Monastic observance and spiritual fervor declined. Soon fresh demands for reform were heard, and the result was the founding of new religious orders in the late eleventh and early twelfth centuries. The best representatives of the new reforming spirit were the Cistercians.

In 1098 a group of monks left the rich abbey of Molesmes in Burgundy and founded a new house in the swampy forest of Cîteaux. They had specific goals and high ideals. They planned to avoid all involvement with secular feudal society. They decided to accept only uncultivated lands far from regular habitation. They intended to refuse all gifts of mills, serfs, tithes, ovens—the traditional manorial sources of income. The early Cistercians determined to avoid elaborate liturgy and ceremony and to keep their chant simple. Finally, they refused to allow the presence of powerful lay people in their monasteries, because they knew that such influence was usually harmful to careful observance.

The first monks at Cîteaux experienced sickness, a dearth of recruits, and terrible privations. But

❖ **Fountains Abbey,** which takes its name from the springs (fontes) on the surrounding slopes, was founded in 1132. Wealth from sheep farming not only supported a large community of monks and lay-brothers, but also enabled Fountains before 1152 to send out 91 monks to found six new monasteries in England and one in Norway, and permitted in the thirteenth century enormous architectural expansion. Perhaps the finest monastic ruins in England today, Fountains Abbey attests to the deep piety and economic innovation of the Cistercians in the twelfth century. *(Source: Cambridge University Collection of Air Photographs; copyright reserved)*

their obvious sincerity and high idealism eventually attracted attention. In 1112 a twenty-three-year-old nobleman called Bernard joined the community at Cîteaux, together with thirty of his aristocratic companions. Thereafter, this reforming movement gained impetus. Cîteaux founded 525 new monasteries in the course of the twelfth century, and its influence on European society was profound. Unavoidably, however, Cistercian success brought wealth, and wealth brought power. By the later twelfth century, economic prosperity and political power had begun to compromise the primitive Cistercian ideals.

Reform of the Papacy

Some scholars believe that the monastic revival spreading from Cluny influenced reform of the Roman papacy and eventually of the entire Christian church. Certainly Abbot Odilo of Cluny (994–1048) was a close friend of the German emperor Henry III, who promoted reform throughout the empire. Pope Gregory VII, who carried the ideals of reform to extreme lengths, had spent some time at Cluny. And the man who consolidated the reform movement and strengthened the medieval papal monarchy, Pope Urban II (1088–1099), had been a monk and prior at Cluny. The precise degree of Cluny's impact on the reform movement cannot be measured. But the broad goals of the Cluniac movement and those of the Roman papacy were the same.

The papacy provided little leadership to the Christian peoples of Western Europe in the tenth century. Factions in Rome sought to control the papacy for their own material gain. Popes were appointed to advance the political ambitions of their families—the great aristocratic families of the city—and not because of special spiritual qualifications. The office of pope, including its spiritual powers and influence, was frequently bought and sold, though the grave crime of simony had been condemned by Saint Peter. The licentiousness and debauchery of the papal court weakened the pope's religious prestige and moral authority. According to a contemporary chronicler, for example, Pope John XII (955–963), who had secured the papal office at the age of eighteen, wore himself out with sexual excesses before he was twenty-eight.

At the local parish level there were many married priests. Taking Christ as the model for the priestly life, the Roman church had always encouraged clerical celibacy, and it had been an obligation for ordination since the fourth century. But in the tenth and eleventh centuries, probably a majority of European priests were married or living with a woman. Such priests were called "Nicolaites" from a reference in the Book of Revelation to early Christians who advocated a return to pagan sexual practices.

Serious efforts at reform began under Pope Leo IX (1049–1054). Not only was Leo related to Emperor Henry III but, as bishop of Toul and a German, he was also an outsider who owed nothing to any Roman faction. Leo traveled widely and held councils at Pavia, Reims, and Mainz that issued decrees against simony, Nicolaism, and violence. Leo's representatives held church councils across Europe, pressing for moral reform. They urged those who could not secure justice at home to appeal to the pope, ultimate source of justice.

By his character and actions, Leo set high moral standards for the West. But the reform of the papacy had legal as well as moral aspects. During Leo's pontificate a new collection of ecclesiastical law was prepared, the *Collection of 74 Titles,* which laid great emphasis on papal authority. In substance the collection stressed the rights, legal position, and supreme spiritual prerogatives of the bishop of Rome as successor of Saint Peter.

Papal reform continued after Leo IX. During the short reign of Nicholas II (1058–1061), a council held in the ancient church of Saint John Lateran in 1059 reached a momentous decision. To remove the influence of Roman artistocratic factions from papal elections, a new method of electing the pope was devised. Since the eighth century, the priests of the major churches in and around Rome had constituted a special group, called a "college," that advised the pope when he summoned them to meetings. These chief priests were called "cardinals" from the Latin *cardo,* meaning "hinge." The cardinals were the hinges on which the church turned. The Lateran Synod of 1059 decreed that the authority and power to elect the pope rested solely in this college of cardinals. The college retains that power today.

When the office of pope was vacant, the cardinals were responsible for governing the church. (In the Middle Ages the college of cardinals numbered around twenty-five or thirty, most of them from Italy. In 1586 the figure was set at seventy. In the 1960s Pope Paul VI virtually doubled that number, appointing men from all parts of the globe to reflect the international character of the church.) By 1073 the progress of reform in the Christian church was well advanced. The election of Cardinal Hildebrand as Pope Gregory VII changed the direction of reform from a moral to a political one.

✣ THE GREGORIAN REVOLUTION

The papal reform movement of the eleventh century is frequently called the Gregorian reform movement, after Pope Gregory VII (1073–1085). The label is not accurate, in that reform began long before Gregory's pontificate and continued after it. Gregory's reign did, however, inaugurate a radical or revolutionary phase that had important political and social consequences.

Pope Gregory VII's Ideas

Cardinal Hildebrand had received a good education at Rome and spent some time at Cluny, where his strict views of clerical life were strengthened. He had served in the papal secretariat under Leo IX and after 1065 was probably the chief influence there. Hildebrand was dogmatic, inflexible, and unalterably convinced of the truth of his own views. He believed that the pope, as the successor of Saint Peter, was the Vicar of God on earth and that papal orders were the orders of God.

Once Hildebrand became pope, the reform of the papacy took on a new dimension. Its goal was not just the moral regeneration of the clergy and centralization of the church under papal authority. Gregory and his assistants began to insist on the "freedom of the church." By this they meant the freedom of churchmen to obey canon law and freedom from control and interference by lay people.

"Freedom of the church" pointed to the end of *lay investiture*—the selection and appointment of church officials by secular authority. Bishops and abbots were invested with the staff representing pastoral jurisdiction and the ring signifying union with the diocese or monastic community. When laymen gave these symbols, they appeared to be distributing spiritual authority. Ecclesiastical opposition to lay investiture was not new in the eleventh century. It, too, had been part of church theory for centuries. But Gregory's attempt to put theory into practice was a radical departure from tradition. Since feudal monarchs depended on churchmen

for the operation of their governments, Gregory's program seemed to spell disaster for stable royal administration. It provoked a terrible crisis.

The Controversy over Lay Investiture

In February 1075 Pope Gregory held a council at Rome. It published decrees not only against Nicolaism and simony but also against lay investiture:

If anyone henceforth shall receive a bishopric or abbey from the hands of a lay person, he shall not be considered as among the number of bishops and abbots. . . . if any emperor, king . . . or any one at all of the secular powers, shall presume to perform investiture with bishoprics or with any other ecclesiastical dignity . . . he shall feel the divine displeasure as well with regard to his body as to his other belongings.[8]

In short, clerics who accepted investiture from laymen were to be deposed, and laymen who invested clerics were to be *excommunicated* (cut off from the sacraments and all Christian worship).

The church's penalty of excommunication relied for its effectiveness on public opinion. Gregory believed the strong support he enjoyed for his *moral* reform would carry over to his political ones; he thought that excommunication would compel rulers to abide by his changes. Immediately, however, Henry IV in the empire, William the Conqueror in England, and Philip I in France protested.

The strongest reaction came from Germany. Henry IV had supported the moral aspects of church reform within the empire. In fact, they would not have had much success without him. Most eleventh-century rulers depended on churchmen for their governments; they could not survive without the literacy and administrative knowledge of bishops and abbots. Naturally, then, kings selected and invested most of them. In this respect, as recent research has shown, German kings scarcely varied from other rulers. In two basic ways, however, the relationship of the German kings to the papacy differed from that of other monarchs: the pope crowned the German emperor, and both the empire and the papal states claimed northern Italy. Since the time of Charlemagne (see page 244), the emperor had controlled some territory and bishops in Italy.

In addition to the subject of lay investiture, a more fundamental issue was at stake. Gregory's decree raised the question of the proper role of the monarch in a Christian society. Did a king have ultimate jurisdiction over all his subjects, including the clergy? For centuries, tradition had answered this question in favor of the ruler; so it is no wonder that Henry protested the papal assertions about investiture. Indirectly, they undermined imperial power and sought to make papal authority supreme.

An increasingly bitter exchange of letters ensued. Gregory accused Henry of lack of respect for the papacy and insisted that disobedience to the pope was disobedience to God. Henry protested in a now-famous letter beginning, "Henry King not by usurpation, but by the pious ordination of God, to Hildebrand, now not Pope, but false monk."

Within the empire, those who had most to gain from the dispute quickly took advantage of it. In January 1076 the German bishops who had been invested by Henry withdrew their allegiance from the pope. Gregory replied by excommunicating them and suspending Henry from the kingship. The lay nobility delighted in the bind the emperor had been put in: with Henry IV excommunicated and cast outside the Christian fold, they did not have to obey him and could advance their own interests. Gregory hastened to support them. The Christmas season of 1076 witnessed an ironic situation in Germany: the clergy supported the emperor, while the great nobility favored the pope.

Henry outwitted Gregory. Crossing the Alps in January 1077, he approached the pope's residence at Canossa in northern Italy. According to legend, Henry stood for three days in the snow seeking forgiveness. As a priest, Pope Gregory was obliged to grant absolution and to readmit the emperor to the Christian community. Henry's trip to Canossa is often described as the most dramatic incident in the High Middle Ages. Some historians claim that it marked the peak of papal power because the most powerful ruler in Europe, the emperor, had bowed before the pope. Actually, Henry scored a temporary victory. When the sentence of excommunication was lifted, Henry regained the kingship and authority over his rebellious subjects. But in the long run, in Germany and elsewhere, secular rulers were reluctant to pose a serious challenge to the papacy for the next two hundred years.

For Germany the incident at Canossa settled nothing. The controversy over lay investiture and the position of the king in Christian society continued. In 1080 Gregory VII again excommunicated and deposed the emperor; in return, Henry invaded Italy, captured Rome, and controlled the

✤ **The Countess Matilda** mediates. A staunch supporter of the reforming ideals of the papacy, the Countess Matilda of Tuscany (c. 1046–1115) arranged the dramatic meeting of the pope and emperor at her castle at Canossa near Reggio Emilia in the Appenines. The arrangement of the figures—with Henry IV kneeling, Gregory lecturing, and Matilda persuading—suggests contemporary understanding of the scene where Henry received absolution. Matilda's vast estates in northern Italy and her political contacts in Rome made her a powerful figure in the late eleventh century. *(Source: Biblioteca Apostolica Vaticana)*

city when Gregory died in 1085. But Henry won no lasting victory. Gregory's successors encouraged Henry's sons to revolt against their father. With lay investiture the ostensible issue, the conflict between the papacy and the successor of Henry IV continued into the twelfth century.

Finally, in 1122, at a conference held at Worms, the issue was settled by compromise. Bishops were to be chosen according to canon law—that is, by the clergy—in the presence of the emperor or his delegate. The emperor surrendered the right of investing bishops with the ring and staff. But since lay rulers were permitted to be present at ecclesiastical elections and to accept or refuse feudal homage from the new prelates, they still possessed an effective veto over ecclesiastical appointments. At the same time, the papacy achieved technical success, because rulers could no longer invest. Papal power was enhanced, and neither side won a clear victory.

William the Conqueror of England and Philip I of France were just as guilty of lay investiture as the German emperor, and both quarreled openly with Gregory. However, Rome's conflict with the western rulers never reached the proportions of the dispute with the German emperor. Gregory VII and his successors had the diplomatic sense to avoid creating three enemies at once.

The long controversy had tremendous social and political consequences in Germany. For half a century, between 1075 and 1125, civil war was chronic in the empire. Preoccupied with Italy and the quarrel with the papacy, emperors could do little about it. The lengthy struggle between papacy and emperor allowed emerging noble dynasties, such as the Zähringer of Swabia, to enhance their position. As recent research has revealed, by the eleventh century these great German families had achieved a definite sense of themselves as noble.[9] To control their lands, the great lords built castles, symbolizing their increased power and growing independence. (In no European country do more castles survive today.) The castles were both military strongholds and centers of administration for the surrounding territories. The German aristocracy subordinated the knights and reinforced their dependency with strong feudal ties. They reduced free men and serfs to an extremely servile position. Henry IV and Henry V were compelled to surrender rights and privileges to the nobility. When the papal-imperial conflict ended in 1122, the nobility held the balance of power in Germany, and later German kings, such as Frederick Barbarossa (see page 332), would fail in their efforts to strengthen the monarchy against the princely families. For these reasons, particularism, localism, and feudal independence characterized the Holy Roman Empire in the High Middle Ages. The investiture controversy had a catastrophic effect there, severely retarding development of a strong centralized monarchy.

The Papacy in the High Middle Ages

In the late eleventh century and throughout the twelfth, the papacy pressed Gregory's campaign for reform of the church. Pope Urban II laid the foundations for the papal monarchy by reorganizing the central government of the Roman church, the papal writing office (the chancery), and papal finances. He recognized the college of cardinals as a definite consultative body. These agencies, together with the papal chapel, constituted the papal court, or *curia Romana*—the papacy's administrative bureaucracy and its court of law. The papal curia, although not fully developed until the mid-twelfth century, was the first well-organized institution of monarchial authority in medieval Europe.

The Roman curia had its greatest impact as a court of law. As the highest ecclesiastical tribunal, it formulated canon law for all of Christendom. It was the instrument with which the popes pressed the goals of reform and centralized the church. The curia sent legates to hold councils in various parts of Europe. Councils published decrees and sought to enforce the law. When individuals in any part of Christian Europe felt they were being denied justice in their local church courts, they could appeal to Rome. Slowly but surely, in the High Middle Ages the papal curia developed into the court of final appeal for all of Christian Europe.

What kinds of appeals came to the Roman curia? The majority of cases related to disputes over church property or ecclesiastical elections and above all to questions of marriage and annulment. Since the fourth century Christian values had influenced the administration of the law, and bishops frequently sat in courts that heard marriage cases. Beginning in the tenth and eleventh centuries, church officials began to claim that they had exclusive jurisdiction over marriage. Appeals to an ecclesiastical tribunal, rather than to a civil court, or appeals from a civil court to a church court, implied the acceptance of the latter's jurisdiction. Moreover, most of the popes in the twelfth and thirteenth centuries were canon lawyers who pressed the authority of church courts. The most famous of them, the man whose pontificate represented the height of medieval papal power, was Innocent III (1198–1216).

Innocent judged a vast number of cases. He compelled King Philip Augustus of France to take back his wife, Ingeborg of Denmark. He arbitrated the rival claims of two disputants to the imperial crown of Germany. He forced King John of England to accept as archbishop of Canterbury a man John did not really want.

By the early thirteenth century, papal efforts at reform begun more than a century before had attained phenomenal success. The popes themselves were men of high principles and strict moral behavior. The frequency of clerical marriage and the level of violence had declined considerably. The practice of simony was much more the exception than the rule.

Yet the seeds of future difficulties were being planted. As the volume of appeals to Rome multiplied, so did the size of the papal bureaucracy. As the number of lawyers increased, so did concern for legal niceties and technicalities, fees, and church offices. As early as the mid-twelfth century, John of Salisbury, an Englishman working in the papal curia, had written that the people condemned the curia for its greed and indifference to human suffering. Nevertheless, the power of the curia continued to grow, as did its bureaucracy.

Thirteenth-century popes devoted their attention to the bureaucracy and their conflicts with the German emperor Frederick II. Some, like Gregory IX (1227–1241), abused their prerogatives to such an extent that their moral impact was seriously weakened. Even worse, Innocent IV (1243–1254) used secular weapons, including military force, to maintain his leadership. These popes badly damaged papal prestige and influence. By the early fourteenth century, the seeds of disorder would grow into a vast and sprawling tree, and once again cries for reform would be heard.

THE CRUSADES

The Crusades of the eleventh and twelfth centuries were the most obvious manifestation of the papal claim to the leadership of Christian society. The enormous popular response to papal calls for crusading reveals the influence of the reformed papacy. The Crusades also reflect the church's new understanding of the noble warrior class. As a distinguished scholar of the Crusades wrote:

At around the turn of the millennium [the year 1000], the attitude of the church toward the military class underwent a significant change. The contrast between militia Christi [war for Christ] and militia saecularis [war for worldly purposes] was overcome and just as rulership earlier had been Christianized . . . , so now was the military profession; it acquired a direct ecclesiastical purpose, for war in the service of the church or for the weak came to be regarded as holy and was declared to be a religious duty not only for the king but also for every individual knight.[10]

Crusades in the late eleventh and early twelfth centuries were holy wars sponsored by the papacy for the recovery of the Holy Land from the Muslim Arabs or the Turks. They grew out of the long conflict between Christians and Muslims in Spain,

◆ **The Siege of Antioch** The author of the *Deeds of the Franks,* a chronicle of the First Crusade, described eleventh-century Antioch (northern Syria) as a "city extremely beautiful, distinguished, and delightful." It withstood siege for eight months, before falling to the Crusaders on June 3, 1093. Here the Seljuk Turks, who had taken the city from Byzantium in 1085, defend the walls with bows and arrows. *(Source: Bibliothèque Nationale, Paris)*

whereby about 1250 Christian kings had regained roughly 90 percent of the peninsula. Throughout this period, Christian pilgrims alone and in groups left Europe in a steady trickle for the Middle East. Although people of all ages and classes participated in the Crusades, so many knights did so that crusading became a distinctive feature of the upper-class lifestyle. In an aristocratic, military society, men coveted reputations as Crusaders; the Christian knight who had been to the Holy Land enjoyed great prestige. The Crusades manifested the religious and chivalric ideals—as well as the tremendous vitality—of medieval society.

The Roman papacy supported the holy war in Spain and by the late eleventh century had strong reasons for wanting to launch an expedition against Muslim infidels in the East as well. The papacy had been involved in the bitter struggle over investiture with the German emperors. If the pope could muster a large army against the enemies of Christianity, his claim to be leader of Christian society in the West would be strengthened. Moreover, in 1054 a serious theological disagreement had split the Greek church of Byzantium and the Roman church of the West. The pope believed that a crusade would lead to strong Roman influence in Greek territories and eventually the reunion of the two churches.

In 1071 at Manzikert in eastern Anatolia, Turkish soldiers in the pay of the Arabs defeated a Greek army and occupied much of Asia Minor. The emperor at Constantinople appealed to the West for support. Shortly afterward, the holy city of Jerusalem, the scene of Christ's preaching and burial, fell to the Turks. Pilgrimages to holy places in the Middle East became very dangerous, and the papacy claimed to be outraged that the holy city was in the hands of unbelievers. Since the Muslims had held Palestine since the eighth century, the papacy actually feared that the Seljuk Turks would be less accomodating to Christian pilgrims than the Muslims had been.

In 1095 Pope Urban II journeyed to Clermont in France and called for a great Christian holy war against the infidels. Urban's appeal at Clermont represents his policy of *rapprochement,* or reconciliation with Byzantium, with church union his ultimate goal. (Mutual ill will, quarrels, and the plundering of Byzantine property by undisciplined westerners were to frustrate this hope.) He stressed the sufferings and persecution of Christians in Jerusalem. He urged Christian knights who had been

fighting one another to direct their energies against the true enemies of God, the Muslims. Urban proclaimed an *indulgence,* or remission of the temporal penalties imposed by the church for sin, to those who would fight for and regain the holy city of Jerusalem. Few speeches in history have had such a dramatic effect as Urban's call at Clermont for the First Crusade.

The response to Urban's call at Clermont was enthusiastic. Godfrey of Bouillon, Geoffrey of Lorraine, and other great lords from northern France immediately had the cross of the Crusader sewn on their tunics. Encouraged by popular preachers like Peter the Hermit and by papal legates in Germany, Italy, and England, thousands of people of all classes joined the crusade. Although most of the Crusaders were French, pilgrims from many regions streamed southward from the Rhineland, through Germany and the Balkans. Of all of the developments of the High Middle Ages, none better reveals Europeans' religious and emotional fervor and the influence of the reformed papacy than the extraordinary outpouring of support for the First Crusade (see Listening to the Past).

Religious convictions inspired many, but mundane motives were also involved. For the curious and the adventurous, the crusade offered foreign travel and excitement. It provided kings, who were trying to establish order and build states, the perfect opportunity to get rid of troublemaking knights. It gave land-hungry younger sons a chance to acquire fiefs in the Middle East. Even some members of the middle class who stayed at home profited from the crusade. Nobles often had to borrow money from the burghers to pay for their expeditions, and they put up part of their land as security. If a noble did not return home or could not pay the interest on the loan, the middle-class creditor took over the land.

The Crusades also brought to the surface latent Christian prejudice against the Jews. Between the sixth and tenth centuries, descendants of Sephardic (from the modern Hebrew word *Separaddi,* meaning Spanish or Portuguese) Jews had settled along the trade routes of western Europe; in the eleventh century, they played a major role in the international trade between the Muslim Middle East and the West. Jews also lent money to peasants, townspeople, and nobles. Because the Jews performed these useful economic services, kings and lords protected them. When the First Crusade was launched, many poor knights had to borrow from

❖ **The Capture of Jerusalem in 1099** As engines hurl stones to breach the walls, Crusaders enter on scaling ladders. Scenes from Christ's passion (above) identify the city as Jerusalem. *(Source: Bibliothèque Nationale, Paris)*

Jews to equip themselves for the expedition. Debt bred resentment. Further, Christian preachers often focused their remarks on Jerusalem, the scene of Jesus's crucifixion. (Preachers conveniently ignored the fact that Jesus had forgiven all his executioners—Luke 22:34.) With the atmosphere thus poisoned, crusading armies passing through the Rhineland in 1096 directed assaults on Jewish communities in Speyer, Worms, Mainz, Cologne, Trier, and Metz, resulting in terrible massacres. These pogroms testify to the general ig-

norance, bigotry, and lack of concentrated strategy that characterized the entire crusading movement.

Nonetheless, the First Crusade was successful, mostly because of the dynamic enthusiasm of the participants. The Crusaders had little more than religious zeal. They knew nothing about the geography or climate of the Middle East. Although there were several counts with military experience among the host, the Crusaders could never agree on a leader, and the entire expedition was marked by disputes among the great lords. Lines of supply were never set up. Starvation and disease wracked the army, and the Turks slaughtered hundreds of noncombatants. Nevertheless, convinced that "God wills it"—the war cry of the Crusaders—the army pressed on and in 1099 captured Jerusalem. Although the Crusaders fought bravely, Arab disunity was a chief reason for their victory. At Jerusalem, Edessa, Tripoli, and Antioch, Crusader kingdoms were founded on the Western feudal model (Map 9.1).

Between 1096 and 1270, the crusading ideal was expressed in eight papally approved expeditions to the East. Despite the success of the First Crusade, none of the later ones accomplished very much. The Third Crusade (1189–1192) was precipitated by the recapture of Jerusalem by the sultan Saladin in 1187. Frederick Barbarossa of the Holy Roman Empire, Richard (Lion-Heart) of England, and Philip Augustus of France participated, and the Third Crusade was better financed than previous ones. But disputes among the leaders and strategic problems prevented any lasting results. In 1208, in one of the most memorable episodes, two expeditions of children set out on a crusade to the Holy Land. One contingent turned back; the other was captured and sold into slavery.

During the Fourth Crusade (1202–1204), careless preparation and inadequate financing had disastrous consequences for Latin-Byzantine relations. When the Crusaders could not pay the Venetians the money promised for transport to the Holy Land, the Venetians agreed to postpone the debt in return for a Crusader attack on the Christian city of Zara on the Dalmatian coast, the Dalmatian forests being the source of the oak used for Venetian ships. The Crusaders took Zara on November 24, 1202. While at Zara, the crusaders met with envoys from the dethroned Byzantine emperor Isaac II and his son Alexius, who promised reunification of the Greek and Latin churches, large payments to the Venetians, and Byzantine support for the expedition to the Holy Land. Thus in April 1204, the Crusaders and Venetians stormed Constantinople, sacked the city destroying its magnificent library—and grabbed thousands of relics, which were later sold in Europe. From this destruction the Byzantine Empire as a political unit never recovered. Although the Crusader Baldwin IX of Flanders was chosen emperor, the empire splintered into three parts and soon consisted of little more than the city of Constantinople. Moreover, the assault of one Christian people on another—when one of the goals of the crusade was reunion of Greek and Latin churches—made the split between the Greek and Latin churches permanent. It also helped to discredit the entire crusading movement. Two later crusades against the Muslims, undertaken by King Louis IX of France, added to his prestige as a pious ruler. The last of the official crusades accomplished nothing at all.

Crusades were also mounted against groups perceived as Christian Europe's social enemies. In 1208, Pope Innocent III proclaimed a crusade against the Albigensians, a heretical sect. The Albigensians, whose name derived from the southern French town of Albi where they were concentrated, rejected orthodox doctrine on the relationship of God and man, the sacraments, and clerical hierarchy. Fearing that religious division would lead to civil disorder, the French monarchy joined the crusade against the Albigensians. Under Count Simon de Montfort, the French inflicted a savage defeat on the Albigensians at Muret in 1213; the county of Toulouse passed to the authority of the French crown. Fearful of encirclement by imperial territories, the popes also promoted crusades against Emperor Frederick II in 1227 and 1239. This use of force backfired, damaging papal credibility as the sponsor of peace.

What impact did the Crusades have on women? That is a difficult question. Fewer women than men directly participated, since the Crusades were primarily military expeditions and all societies have perceived war as a masculine enterprise. Given the aristocratic bias of the chroniclers, we have more information about royal and noble ladies who went to the Holy Land than about middle-class and peasant women, though the latter groups contributed the greater numbers. Eleanor of Aquitaine (1122?–1204) accompanied her husband, King Louis VII, on the Second Crusade (1147–1149), and the thirteenth-century English chronicler Matthew Paris says that large numbers of women went on the Seventh Crusade (1248–1254) so that they could obtain the crusading indulgence. The Crusades illustrate that women in feudal society exercised considerable power. Women who stayed home assumed their husband's responsibilities in the management of estates, the dispensation of justice to vassals and serfs, and the protection of property from attack. Since Crusaders frequently could finance the expedition only by borrowing, it fell to their wives to repay the loans. These heavy responsibilities brought women a degree of power.

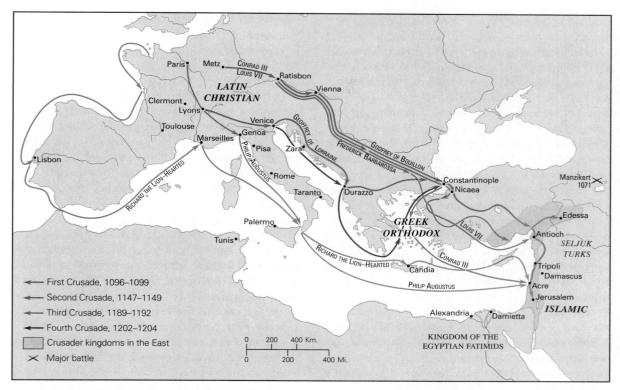

❖ **MAP 9.1 The Routes of the Crusades** The Crusades led to a major cultural encounter between Muslim and Christian values. What significant intellectual and economic effects resulted?

The many women who operated inns and shops in the towns through which crusading armies passed profited from the rental of lodgings and the sale of foodstuffs, clothing, arms, and fodder for animals. For prostitutes, also, crusading armies offered business opportunities.

The Crusades introduced some Europeans to Eastern luxury goods, but their overall cultural impact on the West remains debatable. By the late eleventh century, strong economic and intellectual ties with the East had already been made. The Crusades testify to the religious enthusiasm of the High Middle Ages. But, as Steven Runciman, a distinguished scholar of the Crusades, concluded in his three-volume history:

The triumphs of the Crusade were the triumphs of faith. But faith without wisdom is a dangerous thing. . . . In the long sequence of interaction and fusion between Orient and Occident out of which our civilization has grown, the Crusades were a tragic and destructive episode. . . . High ideals were besmirched by cruelty and greed, enterprise and endurance by a

blind and narrow self-righteousness; and the Holy War itself was nothing more than a long act of intolerance in the name of God, which is the sin against the Holy Ghost.[11]

Along the Syrian and Palestinian coasts, the Crusaders set up a string of feudal states that managed to survive for about two centuries before the Muslims reconquered them. The Crusaders left two more permanent legacies in the Middle East, however, that continue to affect us today. First, the long struggle between Islam and Christendom and the example of persecution set by Christian kings and prelates left an inheritance of deep bitterness; relations between Muslims and their Christian and Jewish subjects worsened. Here is a funny twelfth-century account of a Muslim's impression of primitive European medical practice:

The Lord of Munaytira (a Crusading Baron) wrote to my uncle asking him to send a physician to treat one of his companions who was sick. He sent him a physician called Thabit. He had hardly been away for ten days, when he returned, and we said to him: "How quickly you have healed the sick!" and he replied, "They brought me two patients, a knight with an abscess on his leg, and a woman afflicted with a mental disorder. I made the knight a poultice, and the abscess burst and he felt better. I put the woman on a diet and kept her humour moist. Then a Frankish physician came to them and said to them: 'This man knows nothing about how to treat them!' Then he said to the knight: 'Which do you prefer, to live with one leg or to die with two?' and the knight said: 'To live with one.' Then the physician said: 'Bring me a strong knight and an ax,' and they brought them. Meanwhile I stood by. Then he put the sick man's leg on a wooden block and said to the knight: 'Strike his leg with the ax and cut it off with one blow!' Then, while I watched, he struck one blow, but the leg was not severed; then he struck a second blow, and the marrow of the leg spurted out, and the man died at once.

"The physician then turned to the woman, and said: 'This woman has a devil in her head who has fallen in love with her. Shave her hair off.' So they shaved her head, and she began once again to eat their usual diet, with garlic and mustard and such like. Her disorder got worse, and he said:

"'The devil has entered her head.' Then he took a razor, incised a cross on her head and pulled off the skin in the middle until the bone of the skull appeared; this he rubbed with salt, and the woman died forthwith.

"Then I said to them: 'Have you any further need of me?' and they said no and so I came home, having learned things about their medical practice which I did not know before.[12]*"*

Second, European merchants, primarily Italians, had established communities in the Crusader states. After those kingdoms collapsed, Muslim rulers still encouraged trade with European businessmen. Commerce with the West benefited both Muslims and Europeans, and it continued to flourish.[13]

SUMMARY

The end of the great invasions signaled the beginning of profound changes in European society—social, political, and ecclesiastical. In the year 1000, having enough to eat was the rare privilege of a few nobles, priests, and monks. By the eleventh century, however, manorial communities were slowly improving their agricultural output through increased mechanization, especially the use of waterpower and windpower; these advances, aided by warmer weather, meant more food and increasing population.

In the eleventh century also, rulers and local authorities gradually imposed some degree of order within their territories. Peace and domestic security contributed to the rise in population, bringing larger crops for the peasants and improving trading conditions for the townspeople. The church overthrew the domination of lay influences, and the spread of the Cluniac and Cistercian orders marked the ascendancy of monasticism. The Gregorian reform movement, with its stress on "the freedom of the church" led to a grave conflict with kings over lay investiture. The papacy achieved a technical success on the religious issue, but in Germany the greatly increased power of the nobility, at the expense of the emperor, represents the significant social consequence. Having put its own house in order, the Roman papacy in the twelfth and thirteenth centuries built the first strong government bureaucracy. In the High Middle Ages, the church exercised general leadership of European society. The Crusades exhibit that leadership, though their consequences for Byzantine-Western and for Christian-Muslim relations proved disastrous.

NOTES

1. See E. M. Hallam, *Capetian France, 987–1328* (Longman: New York, 1980), pp. 12–43.
2. J. Gimpel, *The Medieval Machine: The Industrial Revolution of the Middle Ages* (New York: Penguin Books, 1976), p. 7.
3. Ibid., pp. 10–15.
4. Cited in P. Riche, *Daily Life in the World of Charlemagne,* trans. JoAnn McNamara (Philadelphia: University of Pennsylvania Press, 1978), p. 86.
5. See D. Knowles, *The Monastic Order in England,* rev. ed. (Cambridge: Cambridge University Press, 1950), p. 712.
6. See B. Rosenwein, *Rhinoceros Bound: Cluny in the Tenth Century* (Philadelphia: University of Pennsylvania Press, 1982), chap. 2.
7. See K. Hallinger, *Gorze-Kluny: Studien zu den monastichen Lebensformen und Gegensätzen im Hochmittelalter,* Studia Anselmiana xxii–v (Rome: Herder, 1950–1951), esp. p. 40.

8. B. D. Hill, ed., *Church and State in the Middle Ages* (New York: John Wiley & Sons, 1970), p. 68.

9. See J. B. Freed, *The Counts of Falkenstein: Noble Selfconsciousness in Twelfth-century Germany,* Transactions of the American Philosophical Society, vol. 74, pt. 6 (Philadelphia, 1984), pp. 9–11.

10. C. Erdmann, *The Origin of the Idea of the Crusade,* trans. M. Baldwin and W. Goffart (Princeton, N.J.: Princeton University Press, 1977), p. 57.

11. S. Runciman, *A History of the Crusades,* vol. 3, *The Kingdom of Acre* (Cambridge: Cambridge University Press, 1955), p. 480.

12. Cited in B. Lewis, *The Muslim Discovery of Europe* (New York: W. W. Norton, 1982), pp. 222.

13. Cited in *Ibid.,* pp. 23–25.

SUGGESTED READING

Two broad surveys, D. Nicholas, *The Evolution of the Medieval World. Society, Government and Thought in Europe, 312–1500* (1992), and G. Holmes, ed., *The Oxford History of Medieval Europe* (1992), contain useful, up-to-date material. G. Barraclough, *The Crucible of Europe: The Ninth and Tenth Centuries in European History* (1976), surveys the entire period and emphasizes the transformation from a time of anarchy to one of great creativity. His *The Origins of Modern Germany* (1963) is essential for central and eastern Europe. Two studies by G. M. Spiegel—"The Cult of Saint Denis and Capetian Kingship," *Journal of Medieval History* 1 (April 1975): 43–69, and *The Chronicle Tradition of Saint-Denis* (1978)—treat the close relationship between the Capetian dynasty and the royal abbey of Saint-Denis. D. Bates, *Normandy before 1066* (1982), traces the history of the region from the earliest Viking settlement to the time of ducal government, with important material on social history. For Spain, R. Fletcher, *The Quest for El Cid* (1990), provides an excellent introduction to Spanish social and political conditions through a study of Rodrigo Dias, the eleventh-century soldier of fortune who became the Spanish national hero. Fletcher's *Moorish Spain* (1992) provides a highly readable sketch of the history of Islamic Spain from the eighth to the seventeenth century. For the developing social and economic importance of the Flemish towns, see D. Nicholas, *Medieval Flanders* (1992).

For monastic reform, the papacy, and ecclesiastical developments, see B. Rosenwein, *To Be The Neighbor of Saint Peter. The Social Meaning of Cluny's Property, 909–1049* (1989), and the same scholar's earlier study, *Rhinoceros Bound: Cluny in the Tenth Century* (1982), which offer the most up-to-date interpretations of Cluny; while C. B. Bouchard, *Sword, Miter, and Cloister: Nobility and the Church in Burgundy* (1987) and her *Holy Entrepreneurs: Cistercians, Knights, and Economic Exchange in Twelfth-Century Burgundy* (1991) are basic for study of the Cistercians. C. H. Berman, *Medieval Agriculture, the Southern French Countryside, and the Early Cistercians: A Study of Forty-three Monasteries* (1986), presents an important revisionist interpretation of some French Cistercian houses. For the legal, social, and liturgical significance of property gifts to monasteries, see S. D. White, *Custom, Kinship, and Gifts to Saints: The Laudatio Parentum in Western France, 1050–1150* (1988). The relationship of the monks to the ecclesiastical crisis of the late eleventh century is discussed by N. F. Cantor, "The Crisis of Western Monasticism," *American Historical Review* 66 (1960), but see also the essential analysis of J. Van Engen, "The 'Crisis of Cenobitism' Reconsidered: Benedictine Monasticism in the Years 1050–1150," *Speculum* 61 (1986): 269–304. I. S. Robinson, *The Papacy, 1073–1198: Continuity and Innovation* (1990), explores the changing role of the papacy in the eleventh and twelfth centuries and the development of the new model of papal government. G. Tellenbach, *Church, State, and Christian Society at the Time of the Investiture Contest* (1959), emphasizes the revolutionary aspects of the Gregorian reform program. Using the insights of modern anthropological theory, J. Lynch, *Godparents and Kinship in Early Medieval Europe* (1986), explores the relationships created by the baptismal sponsorship of children and adults.

There are excellent articles on many facets of the Crusades, including "The Children's Crusade," "Crusade Propaganda," "Crusader Art and Architecture," and "The Political Crusades"—all written by authorities and based on the latest research—in J. R. Strayer, ed., *The Dictionary of the Middle Ages,* vol. 4 (1984). These articles contain up-to-date bibliographies. For the Fourth Crusade, see the excellent study of D. E. Queller, *The Fourth Crusade. The Capture of Constantinople* (1977), which gives an important revisionist interpretation. C. M. Brand, *Byzantium Confronts the West, 1180–1204* (1968), provides the Greek perspective on the Crusades, while B. Lewis, *The Muslim Discovery of Europe* (1982), gives the Muslim point of view. Serious students will eventually want to consult the multivolume work of K. M. Setton, gen. ed., *A History of the Crusades* (1955–1977). C. Tyerman, *England and the Crusades, 1095–1588* (1988), discusses the financial, political, and social implications of the Crusades.

An Arab View of the Crusades

The Crusades helped shape the understanding that Arabs and Europeans had of each other and all subsequent relations between the Christian West and the Arab world. To medieval Christians, the crusades were papally approved military expeditions for the recovery of holy places in Palestine; to the Arabs, these campaigns were "Frankish wars" or "Frankish invasions" for the acquisition of territory.

Early in the thirteenth century, Ibn Al-Athir (1160–1223), a native of Mosul, an important economic and cultural center in northern Mesopotamia (modern Iraq), wrote a history of the First Crusade. He relied on Arab sources for the events he described. Here is his account of the Crusaders' capture of Antioch:

The power of the Franks first became apparent when in the year 478/1085–86[1] they invaded the territories of Islam and took Toledo and other parts of Andalusia. Then in 484/1091 they attacked and conquered the island of Sicily and turned their attention to the African coast. Certain of their conquests there were won back again but they had other successes, as you will see.

In 490/1097 the Franks attacked Syria. This is how it all began: Baldwin, their King, a kinsman of Roger the Frank who had conquered Sicily, assembled a great army and sent word to Roger saying: "I have assembled a great army and now I am on my way to you, to use your bases for my conquest of the African coast. Thus you and I shall become neighbors."

Roger called together his companions and consulted them about these proposals. "This will be a fine thing for them and for us!" they declared, "for by this means these lands will be converted to the Faith!" At this Roger raised one leg and farted loudly, and swore that it was of more use than their advice. "Why?" "Because if this army comes here it will need quantities of provisions and fleets of ships to transport it to Africa, as well as reinforcements from my own troops. Then, if the Franks succeed in conquering this territory they will take it over and will need provisioning from Sicily. This will cost me my annual profit from the harvest. If they fail they will return here and be an embarrassment to me here in my own domain." . . .

He summoned Baldwin's messenger and said to him: "If you have decided to make war on the Muslims your best course will be to free Jerusalem from their rule and thereby win great honor. I am bound by certain promises and treaties of allegiance with the ruler of Africa." So the Franks made ready to set out to attack Syria.

Another story is that the Fatimids of Egypt were afraid when they saw the Seljuqids extending their empire through Syria as far as Gaza, until they reached the Egyptian border and Atsiz invaded Egypt itself. They therefore sent to invite the Franks to invade Syria and so protect Egypt from the Muslims.[2] But God knows best.

When the Franks decided to attack Syria they marched east to Constantinople, so that they could cross the straits and advance into Muslim territory by the easier, land route. When they reached Constantinople, the Emperor of the East refused them permission to pass through his domains. He said: "Unless you first promise me Antioch, I shall not allow you to cross into the Muslim empire." His real intention was to incite them to attack the Muslims, for he was convinced that the Turks, whose invincible control over Asia Minor he had observed, would exterminate every one of them. They accepted his conditions and in 490/1097 they crossed the Bosphorus at

Constantinople. . . . They . . . reached Antioch, which they besieged.

When Yaghi Siyan, the ruler of Antioch, heard of their approach, he was not sure how the Christian people of the city would react, so he made the Muslims go outside the city on their own to dig trenches, and the next day sent the Christians out alone to continue the task. When they were ready to return home at the end of the day he refused to allow them. "Antioch is yours," he said, "but you will have to leave it to me until I see what happens between us and the Franks." "Who will protect our children and our wives?" they said. "I shall look after them for you." So they resigned themselves, to their fate, and lived in the Frankish camp for nine months, while the city was under siege.

Yaghi Siyan showed unparalleled courage and wisdom, strength and judgment. If all the Franks who died had survived they would have overrun all the lands of Islam. He protected the families of the Christians in Antioch and would not allow a hair of their heads to be touched.

After the siege had been going on for a long time the Franks made a deal with . . . a cuirass-maker called Ruzbih whom they bribed with a fortune in money and lands. He worked in the tower that stood over the river-bed, where the river flowed out of the city into the valley. The Franks sealed their pact with the cuirass-maker, God damn him! and made their way to the water-gate. They opened it and entered the city. Another gang of them climbed the tower with their ropes. At dawn, when more than 500 of them were in the city and the defenders were worn out after the night watch, they sounded their trumpets. . . . Panic seized Yaghi Siyan and he opened the city gates and fled in terror, with an escort of thirty pages. His army commander arrived, but when he discovered on enquiry that Yaghi Siyan had fled, he made his escape by another gate. This was of great help to the Franks, for if he had stood firm for an hour, they would have been wiped out. They entered the city by the gates and sacked it, slaughtering all the Muslims they found there. This happened in jumada I (491/April/May 1098). . . .

It was the discord between the Muslim princes . . . that enabled the Franks to overrun the country.

✦ Miniature showing heavily-armored knights fighting lightly-clad Muslims. (Source: *Bibliothèque Nationale, Paris*)

Questions for Analysis

1. From the Arab perspective, when did the Crusade begin?

2. How did Ibn Al-Athir explain the Crusaders' expedition to Syria?

3. Why did Antioch fall to the Crusaders?

4. The use of dialogue in historical narrative is a very old device dating from the Greek historian Thucydides (fifth century B.C.). Assess the value of Ibn Al-Athir's dialogues for the modern historian.

1. Muslims traditionally date events from Muhammad's hegira, or emigration, to Medina which occurred in 622 according to the Christian calendar. 2. Although Muslims, Fatimids were related doctrinally to the Shi'ites, and the dominant Sunni Muslims therefore considered the Fatimids heretics.

Sources: P. J. Geary, ed., *Readings in Medieval History* (Peterborough, Ontario: Broadview Press, 1991), pp. 443–444; E. J. Costello, trans., *Arab Historians of the Crusades* (Berkeley and Los Angeles: University of California Press, 1969).

10

Life in Christian Europe in the High Middle Ages

In one of the writings produced at the court of the late-ninth-century Anglo-Saxon king Alfred, Christian society is described as composed of those who pray (the monks), those who fight (the nobles), and those who work (the peasants). Close links existed between educated circles on both sides of the English Channel; in France, Bishop Adalbero of Laon used the same device in a poem written about 1028. This image of the structure of society, in which function determined social classification,[1] gained wide circulation in the High Middle Ages. These social divisions, however, do not exactly reflect reality: in the eleventh and twelfth centuries, most clerics and monks descended from the noble class and as monks retained aristocratic attitudes and values; the lay brothers who did most of the actual agricultural labor on monastic estates derived from the peasant classes. The division of society into fighters, monks, and peasants also presents too static a view of world in which there was considerable social mobility. Moreover, such a social scheme does not take into consideration townspeople and the emerging commercial classes (see Chapter 11). Traders and other city dwellers were not typical of medieval society, however. Medieval people were usually contemptuous (at least officially) of profit-making activities, and even after the appearance of urban commercial groups, the ideological view of medieval Christian society remained the one formulated in the ninth century. The most representative figures of Christian society in the High Middle Ages were peasants, nobles, and monks. The use of these sociological divisions provides insight into the medieval mind.

- How did these people actually live?
- What were their preoccupations and lifestyles?
- To what extent was social mobility possible for them?

Allegorical harvesting scenes from a German manuscript *Speculum Virginum,* ca. 1190. *(Source: Rheinisches Landesmuseum, Bonn)*

These are among the questions that this chapter will explore.

✛ THOSE WHO WORK

The largest and economically most productive group in medieval European society was the peasants. "Peasants were rural dwellers who possess (if they do not own) the means of agricultural production." Some peasants worked continuously on the land, others supplemented their ordinary work as brewers, carpenters, tailors, or housemaids with wage labor in the field. In either case, all peasants supported lords, clergy, townspeople, as well as themselves.[2] The men and women who worked the land in the twelfth and thirteenth centuries made up the overwhelming majority of the population, probably more than 90 percent. Yet it is difficult to form a coherent picture of them. The records that serve as historical sources were written by and for the aristocratic classes. Since peasants did not perform what were considered "noble" deeds, the aristocratic monks and clerics did not waste time or precious writing materials on them. When peasants were mentioned, it was usually with contempt or in terms of the services and obligations they owed.

Usually—but not always. In the early twelfth century, Honorius, a monk and teacher at Autun, wrote: "What do you say about the agricultural classes? Most of them will be saved because they live simply and feed God's people by means of their sweat."[3] This sentiment circulated widely. Honorius's comment suggests that peasant workers may have been appreciated and in a sense respected more than is generally believed.

In the past twenty-five years, historians have made remarkable advances in their knowledge of the medieval European peasantry. They have been able to do so by bringing fresh and different questions to old documents, by paying greater attention to such natural factors as geography and climate, and by studying demographic changes. Nevertheless, this new information raises additional questions, and a good deal remains unknown.

In 1932 a distinguished economic historian wrote, "The student of medieval social and economic history who commits himself to a generalization is digging a pit into which he will later assuredly fall and nowhere does the pit yawn deeper than in the realm of rural history."[4] This remark is as true today as when it was written. It is therefore important to remember that peasants' conditions varied widely across Europe, that geographical and climatic features as much as human initiative and local custom determined the peculiar quality of rural life. The problems that faced the farmer in Yorkshire, England, where the soil was rocky and the climate rainy, were very different from those of the Italian peasant in the sun-drenched Po valley.

Another difficulty has been historians' tendency to group all peasants into one social class. That is a serious mistake. It is true that medieval theologians lumped everyone who worked the land into the category of "those who work." In fact, however, there were many levels of peasants, ranging from complete slaves to free and very rich farmers. The period from 1050 to 1250 was one of considerable fluidity with significant social mobility. The status of the peasantry fluctuated widely all across Europe.

Slavery, Serfdom, and Upward Mobility

Slaves were found in western Europe in the High Middle Ages, but in steadily declining numbers. That the word *slave* derives from "Slav" attests to the widespread trade in men and women from the Slavic areas in the early Middle Ages. Around the year 1200, there were in aristocratic and upper-middle-class households in Provence, Catalonia, Italy, and Germany a few slaves—blond Slavs from the Baltic, olive-skinned Syrians, and blacks from Africa.

Since ancient times, it had been a universally accepted practice to enslave conquered peoples. The church had long taught that all baptized Christians were brothers in Christ and that all Christians belonged to one "international" community. Although the church never issued a blanket condemnation of slavery, it vigorously opposed the enslaving of Christians. In attacking the enslavement of Christians and in criticizing the reduction of pagans and infidels to slavery, the church made a contribution to the development of human liberty.

In western Europe during the Middle Ages, legal language differed considerably from place to place, and the distinction between slave and serf was not always clear. Both lacked freedom—the power to do as one wished—and both were subject

The Three Classes
Medieval people believed that their society was divided among warriors, clerics, and workers, here represented by a monk, a knight, and a peasant. The new commercial class had no recognized place in the agrarian military world. *(Source: The British Library)*

to the arbitrary will of one person, the lord. A serf, however, could not be bought and sold like an animal or an inanimate object, as the slave could.

The serf was required to perform labor services on the lord's land. The number of workdays varied, but it was usually three days a week except in the planting or harvest seasons, when it would be more. Serfs frequently had to pay arbitrary levies. When a man married, he had to pay his lord a fee. When he died, his son or heir had to pay an inheritance tax to inherit his parcels of land. The precise amounts of tax paid to the lord on these important occasions depended on local custom and tradition. Every manor had its particular obligations. A free person had to do none of these things. For his or her landholding, rent had to be paid to the lord, and that was often the sole obligation. A free person could move and live as he or she wished.

Serfs were tied to the land, and serfdom was a hereditary condition. A person born a serf was

likely to die a serf, though many did secure their freedom. About 1187 Glanvill, an official of King Henry II and an expert on English law, described how *villeins* (literally, "inhabitants of small villages")—as English serfs were called—could be made free:

A person of villein status can be made free in several ways. For example, his lord, wishing him to achieve freedom from the villeinage by which he is subject to him, may quit-claim [release] him from himself and his heirs; or he may give or sell him to another with intent to free him. It should be noted, however, that no person of villein status can seek his freedom with his own money, for in such a case he could, according to the law and custom of the realm, be recalled to villeinage by his lord, because all the chattels of a villein are deemed to such an extent the property of his lord that he cannot redeem himself from villeinage with his own money, as against his lord. If, however, a third party provides the money and buys the villein in order to free him, then he can maintain himself for ever in a state of freedom as against his lord who sold him. . . . If any villein stays peaceably for a year and a day in a privileged town and is admitted as a citizen into their commune, that is to say, their gild, he is thereby freed from villeinage.[5]

Many energetic and hard-working serfs acquired their freedom in the High Middle Ages. More than anything else, the economic revival that began in the eleventh century (see pages 342–351) advanced the cause of individual liberty. The revival saw the rise of towns, increased land productivity, the growth of long-distance trade, and the development of a money economy. With the advent of a money economy, serfs could save money and, through a third-person intermediary, buy their freedom.

Another opportunity for increased personal freedom, or at least for a reduction in traditional manorial obligations and dues, was provided by the reclamation of waste and forest land in the eleventh and twelfth centuries. Resettlement on newly cleared land offered unusual possibilities for younger sons and for those living in areas of acute land shortage or on overworked, exhausted soil. Historians still do not know very much about this movement: how the new frontier territory was advertised, how men were recruited, how they and their households were transported, and how the new lands were distributed. It is certain, however, that there was significant migration and that only a lord with considerable authority over a wide territory could sponsor such a movement. Great lords supported the fight against the marshes of northern and eastern Germany and against the sea in the Low Countries. For example, in the twelfth century the invitation of German and Slavic rulers led to peasant settlements in "the territory between the Saale and the upper Elbe" rivers.[6] The thirteenth century witnessed German peasant migrations into Brandenburg, Pomerania, Prussia, and the Baltic states.

In the thirteenth century, the noble class frequently needed money to finance crusading, building, or other projects. For example, in 1240 when Geoffrey de Montigny became abbot of Saint-Pierre-le-Vif in the Senonais region of France, he found the abbey church in bad disrepair. Geoffrey also discovered that the descendants of families who had once owed the abbey servile obligations now refused to recognize their bondage. Some of

these peasants had grown wealthy. When the abbot determined to reclaim these peasants in order to get the revenues to rebuild his church, a legal struggle ensued. In 1257 a compromise was worked out whereby Geoffrey manumitted 366 persons who in turn agreed to pay him 500 pounds a year over a twelve-year period.[7]

As land long considered poor was brought under cultivation, there was a steady nibbling away at the wasteland on the edges of old villages. Clearings were made in forests. Marshes and fens were drained and slowly made arable. This type of agricultural advancement frequently improved the peasants' social and legal condition. A serf could clear a patch of fen or forest land, make it productive, and, through prudent saving, buy more land and eventually purchase freedom. In the thirteenth century there were many free tenants on the lands of the bishop of Ely in eastern England, tenants who had moved into the area in the twelfth century and drained the fens. Likewise, settlers on the lowlands of the abbey of Bourbourg in Flanders, who had erected dikes and extended the arable lands, possessed hereditary tenures by 1159. They secured personal liberty and owed their overlord only small payments.

Peasants who remained in the villages of their birth often benefited because landlords, threatened with the loss of serfs, relaxed ancient obligations and duties. While it would be unwise to exaggerate the social impact of the settling of new territories, frontier lands in the Middle Ages did provide opportunities for upward mobility.

The Manor

In the High Middle Ages, most European peasants, free and unfree, lived on estates called "manors." The word *manor* derives from a Latin term meaning "dwelling," "residence," or "homestead." In the twelfth century it meant the estate of a lord and his dependent tenants.

The manor was the basic unit of medieval rural organization and the center of rural life. All other generalizations about manors and manorial life have to be limited by variations in the quality of the soil, local climatic conditions, and methods of cultivation. Manors varied from several thousand to as little as 120 acres. Recent archaeological evidence suggests that a manor might include several villages, a village whose produce was divided among several lords, or an isolated homestead.

The arable land of the manor was divided into two sections. The *demesne,* or home farm, was cultivated for the lord. The other part was held by the peasantry. Usually the peasants' portion was larger, held on condition that they cultivate the lord's demesne. All the arable land, both the lord's and the peasants', was divided into strips, and the strips belonging to any given individual were scattered throughout the manor. All peasants cooperated in the cultivation of the land, working it as a group. This meant that all shared in any disaster as well as any large harvest.

A manor usually held pasture or meadowland for the grazing of cattle, sheep, and sometimes goats. Often the manor had some forest land as well. Forests had enormous economic importance. They were the source of wood for building and resin for lighting; ash for candles, and ash and lime for fertilizers and all sorts of sterilizing products; wood for fuel and bark for the manufacture of rope. From the forests came wood for the construction of barrels, vats, and all sorts of storage containers. Last but hardly least, the forests were used for feeding pigs, cattle, and domestic animals on nuts, roots, and wild berries. If the manor was intersected by a river, it had a welcome source of fish and eels.

Agricultural Methods

The fundamental objective of all medieval agriculture was the production of an adequate food supply. According to the method historians have called the "open-field system," the arable land of a manor was divided into two or three fields without hedges or fences to mark the individual holdings of the lord, serfs, and freemen. On the premise that all should share in the poor as well as the good soil, the holdings of individual peasants were scattered in strips throughout the fields. If one strip yielded little, other strips (of better soil) might be more bountiful. Beginning in the eleventh century in those parts of France, England, and Germany where the quality of the soil permitted intensive cultivation, peasants divided all the arable land into three large fields, two of which in any one year were cultivated, while the third lay fallow. One part of the land was sown with winter cereals such as rye and wheat, the other with spring crops, such as peas, beans, and barley. What was planted in a particular field varied each year when the crops were rotated.

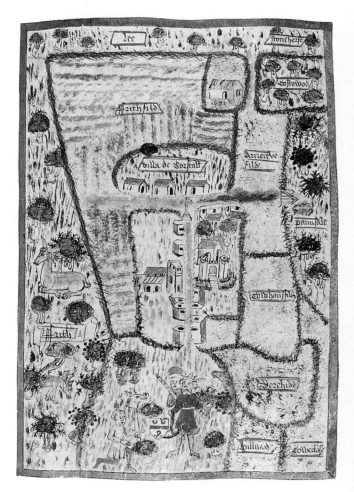

❖ **Boarstall Manor, Buckinghamshire** In 1440, Edmund Rede, lord of this estate, had a map made showing his ancestor receiving the title from King Edward I (lower field). Note the manor house, church, peasants' cottages along the central road. In the common fields, divided by hedges, peasants cultivated on a three-year rotation cycle winter wheat, spring oats, a year fallow. Peasants' pigs grazed freely in the woods, indicated by trees; we don't know whether they could hunt the deer. *(Source: Buckinghamshire Record Office, Aylesbury)*

Local needs, the fertility of the soil, and dietary customs determined what was planted and the method of crop rotation. Where one or several manors belonged to a great aristocratic establishment, such as the abbey of Cluny, which needed large quantities of oats for horses, more of the arable land would be planted in oats than in other cereals. Where the land was extremely fertile, such as in the Alsace region of Germany, a biennial cycle was used: one crop of wheat was sown and harvested every other year, and in alternate years all the land lay fallow. The author of an English agricultural treatise advised his readers to stick to a two-field method of cultivation and insisted that a rich harvest every second year was preferable to two mediocre ones every three years.

Farmers knew the value of animal fertilizers. Chicken manure, because of its high nitrogen content, was the richest but was limited in quantity. Sheep manure was also valuable. Gifts to English Cistercian monasteries were frequently given on condition that the monks' sheep be allowed to graze at certain periods on the benefactor's demesne. Because cattle were fed on the common pasture and were rarely stabled, gathering their manure was laborious and time-consuming. Nevertheless, whenever possible, animal manure was gathered and thinly spread. So also was house garbage—eggshells, fruit cores, onion skins—that had disintegrated in a compost heap.

Tools and farm implements are often shown in medieval manuscripts. But accepting such representations at face value is misleading. Rather than going out into a field to look at a tool, medieval artists simply copied drawings from classical and other treatises. Thus a plow or harrow pictured in a book written in the Ile-de-France may actually have been used in England or Italy a half-century before.

In the early twelfth century, the production of iron increased greatly. There is considerable evidence for the manufacture of iron plowshares (the part of the plow that cuts the furrow and grinds up the earth). In the thirteenth century, the wooden plow continued to be the basic instrument of agricultural production, but its edge was strengthened with iron. Only after the start of the fourteenth century, when lists of manorial equipment began to be kept, is there evidence for pitchforks, spades, axes, and harrows. The harrow, a cultivating instrument with heavy teeth, broke up and smoothed the soil. While the modern harrow has steel teeth (or disks), medieval ones were wooden and weighed down with stones to force a deep cut in the earth.

❖ **Late Medieval Wheelless Plow** This plow has a sharp-pointed colter, which cut the earth while the attached mold-board lifted, turned, and pulverized the soil. As the man steers the plow, his wife prods the oxen. The caption reads, "God speed the plow, and send us corn (wheat) enough." *(Source: Trinity College Library, Cambridge)*

Plow and harrow were increasingly drawn by horses. The development of the padded horse collar, resting on the horse's shoulders and attached to the load by shafts, led to an agricultural revolution. The horse collar meant that the animal could put its entire weight into the task of pulling. The use of horses, rather than oxen, spread in the twelfth century, because horses' greater strength brought greater efficiency to farming and reduced the amount of human labor involved. The quality of the soil and the level of rainfall in the area seem to have determined whether peasants shifted from ox teams to horses. Horses worked best on light, dry, and easily worked soil, but they had difficulties plowing through clay soils and in places where heavy moisture caused earth to cling to the plow. Oxen, on the other hand, worked well on heavy, muddy, or clay soil, but they slipped and suffered hoof damage on dry, stony land. At the same time, horses were an enormous investment, perhaps comparable to a modern tractor. They had to be shod (another indication of increased iron production), and the oats they ate were costly. Although horses represent a crucial element in the improvement of husbandry, students of medieval agriculture remain uncertain as to whether the greater use of horses increased crop yields.

The thirteenth century, did however, witness a tremendous spurt in the use of horses to haul carts to market. Large and small farmers increasingly relied on horses to pull wagons because they could travel much faster than oxen. Consequently, goods reached market faster, and the number of markets to which the peasant had access increased. The opportunities and temptations for consumer spending on nonagricultural goods multiplied.[8]

Agricultural yields varied widely from place to place and from year to year. Even with good iron tools, horsepower, and careful use of seed and fertilizer, medieval peasants were at the mercy of the weather. Even today, lack of rain or too much rain can cause terrible financial loss and extreme hardship. How much more vulnerable was the medieval peasant with his primitive tools! By twentieth-century standards, medieval agricultural yields were very low. Inadequate soil preparation, poor seed selection, lack of manure—all made this virtually inevitable.

Yet there was striking improvement over time. Between the ninth and early thirteenth centuries, it appears that yields of cereals approximately doubled, and on the best-managed estates, for every bushel of seed planted, the farmer harvested five bushels of grain. This is a tentative conclusion. Because of the scarcity of manorial inventories before the thirteenth century, the student of medieval agriculture has great difficulty determining how much the land produced. The author of a treatise on land husbandry, Walter of Henley, who lived in the mid-thirteenth century, wrote that the land should yield three times its seed; that amount was necessary for sheer survival. The surplus would be sold to grain merchants in the nearest town. Townspeople were wholly dependent on the surrounding countryside for food, which could not be shipped a long distance. A poor harvest meant that both town and rural people suffered.

Grain yields were probably greatest on large manorial estates, where there was more professional management. For example, the estates of Battle Abbey in Sussex, England, enjoyed a very high yield of wheat, rye, and oats in the century and a half between 1350 and 1499. This was due to heavy seeding, good crop rotation, and the use of manure from the monastery's sheep flocks. Battle Abbey's yields seem to have been double those of smaller, less efficiently run farms. A modern Illinois farmer expects to get 40 bushels of soybeans, 150 bushels of corn, and 50 bushels of wheat for every bushel of seeds planted. Of course, modern costs of production in labor, seed, and fertilizer are quite high, but this yield is at least ten times that of the farmer's medieval ancestor. While some manors may have achieved a yield of 12 or even 15 to 1, the *average* manor probably got a yield of only 5 to 1 in the thirteenth century.[9] As low as that may seem by current standards, it marked a rise in productivity equal to that of the years just before the great agricultural revolution of the eighteenth century.

Life on the Manor

Life for most people in medieval Europe meant country life. A person's horizons were largely restricted to the manor on which he or she was born. True, peasants who colonized such sparsely settled regions as eastern Germany must have traveled long distances. But most people rarely traveled more than 25 miles beyond their villages. Everyone's world was small, narrow, and provincial in the original sense of the word: limited by the boundaries of the province. This way of life did not have entirely unfortunate results. A farmer had a strong sense of family and the certainty of its support and help in time of trouble. People knew what their life's work would be—the same as their mother's or father's. They had a sense of place, and pride in that place was reflected in adornment of the village church. Religion and the village gave people a sure sense of identity and with it psychological peace. Modern people—urban, isolated, industrialized, rootless, and thoroughly secularized—have lost many of these reinforcements.

On the other hand, even aside from the unending physical labor, life on the manor was dull. Medieval men and women must have had a crushing sense of frustration. Often they sought escape in heavy drinking. English judicial records of the thirteenth century reveal a surprisingly large number of "accidental" deaths. Strong, robust, commonsensical farmers do not ordinarily fall on their knives and stab themselves, or slip out of boats and drown, or get lost in the woods on a winter's night, or fall from horses and get trampled. They were probably drunk. Many of these accidents occurred, as the court records say, "coming from an ale." Brawls and violent fights were frequent at taverns.

Scholars have recently spent much energy investigating the structure of medieval peasant households. Because little concrete evidence survives, conclusions are very tentative. It appears, however, that a peasant household consisted of a simple nuclear family: a married couple alone, a couple with children, or widows or widowers with children. Peasant households were *not* extended families containing grandparents or married sons and daughters and their children. The simple family predominated in thirteenth-century England, in northern France in the fourteenth century, and in fifteenth-century Tuscany. Before the first appearance of the Black Death, perhaps 94 percent of peasant farmers married, and bride and groom were both in their early twenties. The typical household numbered about five people, the parents and three children.[10]

Women played a significant role in the agricultural life of medieval Europe. This obvious fact is often overlooked by historians. Women worked with men in wheat and grain cultivation, in the vineyards, and in the harvest and preparation of crops needed by the textile industry—flax and plants used for dyeing cloth, such as madder (which produces shades of red) and woad (which yields blue dye). Especially at harvest time women

shared with their fathers and husbands the backbreaking labor in the fields, work that was probably more difficult for them because of weaker muscular development and frequent pregnancies. Lords of great estates commonly hired female day laborers to shear sheep, pick hops (used in the manufacture of beer and ale), tend gardens, and do household chores such as cleaning, laundry, and baking; servant girls in the country considered their hired status as temporary, until they married. Thrifty farm wives contributed to the family income by selling for cash the produce of their gardens or kitchen: butter, cheese, eggs, fruit, soap, mustard, cucumbers. The adage from the Book of Proverbs—"Houses and riches are the inheritance of fathers; but a prudent wife is from the Lord"—was seldom more true than in an age when careful management was often all that separated a household from starvation in a year of crisis. And starvation was a very real danger to the peasantry down to the eighteenth century.

Women managed the house. The size and quality of peasants' houses varied according to their relative prosperity, and that prosperity usually depended on the amount of land held. Poorer peasants lived in windowless cottages built of wood and clay or wattle and thatched with straw. These cottages consisted of one large room that served as the kitchen and living quarters for all. Everyone slept there. The house had an earthen floor and a fireplace. The lack of windows meant that the room was very sooty. A trestle table, several stools, one or two beds, and a chest for storing clothes constituted the furniture. A shed attached to the house provided storage for tools and shelter for animals. Prosperous peasants added rooms and furniture as they could be afforded, and some wealthy peasants in the early fourteenth century had two-story houses with separate bedrooms for parents and children.

Every house had a small garden and an outbuilding. Onions, garlic, turnips, and carrots were grown and stored through the winter in the main room of the dwelling or in the shed attached to it. Cabbage was raised almost everywhere and, after being shredded, salted, and packed in vats in hot water, was turned into kraut. Peasants ate vegetables not because they appreciated their importance for good health but because there was usually little else. Some manors had fruit trees—apple, cherry, and pear in northern Europe; lemon, lime, and olive in the south. But because of the high price of sugar, when it was available, fruit could not be preserved. Preserving and storing other foods were the basic responsibility of the women and children.

Women dominated in the production of ale for the community market. This industry required an initial investment in large vessels and knowledge of the correct proportions of barley, water, yeast, and hops. Women found brewing hard and dangerous work: it involved carrying 12-gallon vats of hot liquid. Records of the English coroners' courts reveal that 5 percent of women who died lost their lives in brewing accidents, by falling into the vats of boiling liquid.[11] Ale was the universal drink of the common people in northern Europe. By modern American standards the rate of consumption was heroic. Each monk of Abingdon Abbey in twelfth-century England was allotted 3 gallons a day, and a man working in the fields for ten hours probably drank much more.[12]

The mainstay of the diet for peasants everywhere—and for all other classes—was bread. It was a hard, black substance made of barley, millet, and oats, rarely of expensive wheat flour. The housewife usually baked the household supply once a week. Where sheep, cows, or goats were raised, she also made cheese. In places like the Bavarian Alps of southern Germany, where hundreds of sheep grazed on the mountainsides,[13] or at Cheddar in southwestern England, cheese was a staple.

The diet of those living in an area with access to a river, lake, or stream would be supplemented with fish, which could be preserved by salting; people living close to the sea could gather shellfish such as oysters, mussels, and whelks. In many places there were severe laws against hunting and trapping in the forests. Deer, wild boars, and other game were strictly reserved for the king and nobility. These laws were flagrantly violated, however, and stolen rabbits and wild game often found their way to the peasants' tables. Woods and forests also provided nuts, which housewives and small children would gather in the fall.

Lists of peasant obligations and services to the lord, such as the following from Battle Abbey, commonly included the payment of chickens and eggs: "John of Coyworth holds a house and thirty acres of land, and owes yearly 2 p at Easter and Michaelmas; and he owes a cock and two hens at Christmas, of the value of 4 d."[14] Chickens and eggs must have been highly valued in the prudently managed household. Except for the rare chicken or illegally caught wild game, meat appeared on

✤ **Woman's Work** Carrying a heavy sack of grain to the mill was part of this medieval woman's everyday work. *(Source: The Pierpont Morgan Library)*

the table only on the great feast days of the Christian year: Christmas, Easter, and Pentecost. Then the meat was likely to be pork from the pig slaughtered in the fall and salted for the rest of the year. Some scholars believe that, by the mid-thirteenth century, there was an increase in the consumption of meat generally. If so, this improvement in diet is further evidence of an improved standard of living.

Breakfast, eaten at dawn before people departed for their farmwork, might well consist of bread, an onion (easily stored through the winter months), and a piece of cheese, washed down with milk or ale. Farmers, then as now, ate their main meal around noon. This was often soup—a thick *potage* of boiled cabbage, onions, turnips, and peas, seasoned with a bone or perhaps a sliver of meat. The evening meal, taken at sunset, consisted of leftovers from the noon meal, perhaps with bread, cheese, milk, or ale.

Once children were able to walk, they helped their parents in the hundreds of chores that had to be done. Small children were set to collecting eggs, if the family had chickens, or gathering twigs and sticks for firewood. As they grew older, children had more responsible tasks, such as weeding the family vegetable garden, milking the cows, shearing the sheep, cutting wood for fires, helping with the planting or harvesting, and assisting their mothers in the endless tasks of baking, cooking, and preserving. Because of poor diet, terrible sanitation, and lack of medical care, the death rate among children was phenomenally high.

Health Care

What of health care? What medical attention was available to the sick person in western Europe from the mid-eleventh century to the beginning of the fourteenth? Scholars are only beginning to explore these questions, and there are many aspects of public health that we know little about. The steady rise in population in these centuries, usually attributed to the beginnings of political stability and the reduction of violence and to the great expansion of land put under cultivation and thus the increased food supply, may also be ascribed partly to better health care. Survival to adulthood probably meant a tough people. A recent study of skeletal remains in the village of Brandes in Burgundy showed that peasants enjoyed very good health: they were well built, had excellent teeth, and their bones revealed no signs of chronic disease. Obviously we cannot generalize about the health of all people on the basis of evidence of one village, but preliminary research confirms the picture in romantic literature: in the prime of life the average person had a raw vitality that enabled him or her to eat, drink, and make love with great gusto.[15]

In recent years scholars have produced some exciting information relating to the natural processes of pregnancy and childbirth. But the acquisition of information has not been easy, because, since modesty forbade the presence of men at the birth of a child, very few men could write about it; and because of the general illiteracy of women. One woman who wrote extensively, the twelfth century physician Trotula of Salerno tended to explain gynecological and obstetrical problems in terms of the relative degree of heat and cold, of moisture and dryness within the female body. Thus on the potential difficulty of parturition, she wrote

A Cesarean Birth, unlike a normal one, was a surgical procedure; as such, male physicians in the fourteenth century gradually marginalized women in the field of obstetrics, which they had always dominated. Here the midwife (identifiable from her head-dress) lifts a male child from the abdominal opening in the mother's dead body. Her helper prepares the tub of water to bathe the child. Since few infants survived the procedure, midwives needed witnesses to assert that they had not bungled the birth nor deliberately killed the infant. *(Source: British Library)*

There are, however, certain women so narrow in the function of childbearing that scarcely ever or never do they succeed. This is wont to happen for various reasons. Sometimes external heat comes up around the internal organs and they are straightened in the act of giving birth. Sometimes the exit from the womb is too small, the woman is too fat, or the foetus is dead, not helping nature by its own movements. This often happens to a woman giving birth in winter. If she has by nature a tight opening of the womb, the coldness of the season constricts the womb still more. Sometimes the heat all goes out of the woman herself and she is left without strength to help herself in childbearing.

Trotula believed that sneezing, which forced the woman to push her inner organs downward, should be induced.[16] Her general knowledge cannot be called scientific.

Midwives learned their work through a practical apprenticeship, not through any sort of professional study. Most could not read, and even if they could few medical texts existed. The first pregnancy of many women ended fatally, and thus women of all social classes had a great fear of childbirth. Trotula, Hildegard of Bingen and other writers on obstetrics urged pregnant women to pray that Christ would grant them a safe childbed. Given the possibility of complications and the limited information midwives had, this advice seems appropriate.[17]

In the thirteenth century midwives began the practice of delivery by cesarean section, birth by an incision through the abdominal wall and uterus, so-called from the traditional belief that the Roman statesman Julius Caesar had been born by this operation. Cesarean sections were performed only if the mother had died in labor; the purpose of the operation was the baptism of the child (the theological premise being that the baptism assured its salvation). But the cesareans posed serious ethical problems: who was to decide if the mother was dead? (The stethoscope or instrument for measuring sounds within the body, such as heartbeat, was not invented until 1819.) Who could decide if the fetus was alive after the mother's death? In a very difficult birth should the life of the mother be sacrificed for the sake of the child? A translation of Trotula's advice to midwives states that "when the woman is feeble and the child may not come out, then it is better that the child is slain than that the mother of the child also die." The greatest theo-

logian of the age, Saint Thomas Aquinas (see chapter 11) in his treatise on baptism is also explicit: "Evil should not be done that good may come. Therefore one should not kill the mother in order to baptize the child; if, however, the child be still alive in the womb after the mother has died, the mother should be opened in order to baptize the child."[18] Since cesareans were performed only after the mother was dead, the choice of the mother's life or the child's never arose.[19] About 1400, male surgeons, motivated by professional, scientific, and probably financial interests, began to perform cesarean sections. Thus, through cesarean births men entered the field of obstetrics.[20]

Childhood diseases, poor hygiene, tooth decay, wounds received in fighting, and the myriad ailments and afflictions for which even modern medical science has no cure, from cancer to the common cold, must have caused considerable suffering. One student of medieval medicine estimates that in the mid-twelfth century one person in 200 suffered from leprosy.[21] What care existed for the sick?

As in the past, the sick everywhere depended above all on the private nursing care of relatives and friends. For public health English sources provide the largest evidence to date. In the British Isles, however, the twelfth century witnessed a momentous breakthrough in the establishment of institutional care in "hospitals, that is professional centers with physicians, laboratories, medicines, operations and convalescing patients." In addition to the infirmaries run by monks and nuns, there were at least 113 hospitals in England with possibly as many as 3,494 beds, or one bed for every 600 to 1,000 persons. (In 1982 the ratio in England was 1:108 persons.) The organization of hospitals followed the structure and routine of monastic communities. Patients were segregated according to sex, wore a common uniform, and were required to keep periods of silence and to attend devotions in the hospital chapel. We have no information about rates of recovery. Medieval hospitals were built by the royal family, the clergy, barons, and ordinary people to alleviate the suffering of the sick, not just to house them. Hospitals attracted considerable popular support, and women played an especially strong role in the endowment of hospitals.[22]

As in the developed modern world, persons living in or near a town or city had a better chance of receiving some form of professional attention

effectus · gaudiũ nobiſ lęticiamq; suscitauit non modicam · [CAPT · XI · ∞∞:]

✤ **St. Maurus, Healing** A rich body of legends developed around Maurus, the no-bleman's son given as an oblate to St. Benedict. In the eleventh century, Maurus had the reputation, unsupported by evidence, of medical knowledge and curative powers. Here he is depicted giving a patient some kind of pharmaceutical prepara-tion. *(Source: Bibliothèque municipale de Troyes)*

than did those in remote rural areas. English docu-ments label at least 90 practitioners as *medicus,* meaning physician, surgeon, or medical man, but that is a pitifully small number in a population of perhaps 2 million people. With so few doctors, only the largest cities, such as London, York, Win-chester, and Canterbury, which all catered to pil-grims and travelers, had resident physicians; at other hospitals physician consultants were brought in as the occasion required. Most people, of course, did not live in or near large towns. They relied for assistance on the chance medical lore of local people—a monk or nun with herb and phar-maceutical knowledge who could prescribe therapy for particular ailments, a local person skilled in setting broken bones, the wise woman or man of the village experienced in treating diseases.

The Latin words *matronae* and *obstetrices* appear occasionally to refer to midwives. Since public mo-rality and ancient tradition forbade the examina-tion of female patients by men, obstetrics and gy-necology were the only branches of medicine that women could practice.[23] Although women played active roles as healers and in the general care of the sick, male doctors jealously guarded their status and admitted very few women to university medi-cal schools when they were founded; Francesca Romano, who was licensed as a surgeon in 1321 by Duke Carl of Calabria is the exception that proves the rule. The medical faculty at the Univer-sity of Paris in the fourteenth century penalized women who practiced medicine because they lacked a degree—which they were not allowed to get.

Popular Religion

Apart from the land, the weather, and the peculiar conditions that existed on each manor, the Chris-tian religion had the greatest impact on the daily lives of ordinary people in the High Middle Ages. Religious practices varied widely from country to country and even from province to province. But nowhere was religion a one-hour-on-Sunday or High Holy Days affair. Christian practices and at-titudes permeated virtually all aspects of everyday life.

In the ancient world, participation in religious rituals was a public and social duty. As the Ger-manic and Celtic peoples were Christianized, their new religion became a fusion of Jewish, pagan, Roman, and Christian practices. By the High Middle Ages, religious rituals and practices represented a synthesis of many elements, and all people shared as a natural and public duty in the religious life of the community.

The village church was the center of community life—social, political, and economic as well as religious. Most of the important events in a person's life took place in or around the church. A person was baptized there, within hours of birth. Men and women confessed their sins to the village priest there and received, usually at Easter and Christmas, the sacrament of the Eucharist. In front of the church, the bishop reached down from his horse and confirmed a person as a Christian by placing his hands over the candidate's head and making the sign of the cross on the forehead. (Bishops Thomas Becket of Canterbury and Hugh of Lincoln were considered especially holy men because they got down from their horses to confirm.) Young people courted in the churchyard and, so the sermons of the priests complained, made love in the church cemetery. Priests urged couples to

marry publicly in the church, but many married privately, without witnesses (see page 389).

In the church, women and men could pray to the Virgin and the local saints. The stone in the church altar contained relics of the saints, often a local saint to whom the church itself had been dedicated. The saints had once lived on earth and thus could well understand human problems. They could be helpful intercessors with Christ or God the Father. The cult of the saints had begun in the East (chapter 7), and it gained enormous popularity in the West in the eleventh and twelfth centuries. People believed the saints possessed supernatural powers that enabled them to perform miracles, and the saint became the special property of the locality where his or her relics rested. Thus to secure the saint's support and to guarantee the region's prosperity, a busy traffic in relics developed—bones, articles of clothing, the saint's tears, saliva, even the dust from the saint's tomb. The understanding that existed between the saint and the peasants rested on the customary medieval relationship of mutual fidelity and aid: peasants would offer the saint prayers, loyalty, and gifts to

The Eucharist The Fourth Lateran Council of 1215 encouraged all Christians to receive the eucharist at least once a year, after confession and penance. Here a priest places the consecrated host on peoples' tongues. *(Source: Biblioteca Apostolica Vaticana)*

the shrine or church under his or her patronage, in return for the saint's healing and support. Sometimes when they failed to receive the attention they felt they deserved, saints took offense and were vindictive. An English knight whose broken arm was healed by Saint James forgot to thank him at his shrine at Reading, whereupon the saint punished him by breaking his other arm.

In the later Middle Ages, popular hagiographies (biographies of saints based on myths, legends, and popular stories) attributed specialized functions to the saints. Saint Elmo (ca. 300), who supposedly had preached unharmed during a thunder and lightning storm, became the patron of sailors. Saint Agatha (third century), whose breasts were torn with shears because she rejected the attentions of a powerful suitor, became the patron of wet nurses, of women with breast difficulties, and of bellringers (because of the resemblance of breasts to bells). Saint Jude the Apostle, whom no one invoked because his name resembled that of Jesus' betrayer, Judas, became the patron of lost causes; Saint Gertrude was reputed to guard houses against the entry of mice.

How were saints chosen and what was the official Church's position on them? What had been their social background when alive? "The initiative in creating a cult (of a saint) always belonged to believers"[24] (ordinary people). Since the early days of Christianity, individuals whose exemplary virtue was proved by miracles at their tomb had been venerated by lay people. Although, as part of the general centralization of papal power in the twelfth and thirteenth centuries, the Roman authorities insisted that they had the exclusive right to examine the lives and activities of candidates for sainthood in a formal "trial," popular opinion still continued to declare people saints. Between 1185 and 1431, only seventy official investigations were held at Rome, but hundreds of new persons across Europe were venerated as saints. Church officials and educated clergy evaluated candidates according to the "heroic virtue" of their lives, but lay people judged solely by the saint's miracles. Some clergy preached against the veneration of relics and called it idolatry, but their appeals had little effect.

Current research suggests that a connection exists between the models of holiness and the character of the social structure in different parts of Europe. Northern and southern Europeans chose saints of different social backgrounds or classes. In Italy and Mediterranean lands, saints tended to be *popolani*—non-nobles—non-aristocrats, whereas in France and Germany, primarily men and women of the nobility became saints. The cult of the saints which developed in a rural and uneducated environment represents a central feature of popular culture in the Middle Ages.[25]

According to official church doctrine, the center of the Christian religious life was the Mass, the re-enactment of Christ's sacrifice on the cross. Every Sunday and on holy days, the villagers stood at Mass or squatted on the floor (there were no chairs), breaking the painful routine of work. At the end of their lives, people wanted to be buried in the church cemetery, close to the holy place and the saints believed to reside there.

The feasts that accompanied baptisms, weddings, funerals, and other celebrations were commonly held in the churchyard. Medieval drama originated within the church. Mystery plays, based on biblical episodes, were performed first in the sanctuary, then on the church porch, and finally in the village square, which was often in front of the west door.

From the church porch the priest read to his parishioners orders and messages from royal and ecclesiastical authorities. Royal judges traveling on circuit opened their courts on the church porch. The west front of the church, with its scenes of the Last Judgment, was the background against which the justices disposed of civil and criminal cases. Farmers from outlying districts pushed their carts to the marketplace in the village square near the west front. In busy mercantile centers such as London, business agreements and commercial exchanges were made in the aisles of the church itself, as at Saint Paul's.

Popular religion consisted largely of rituals heavy with symbolism. Before slicing a loaf of bread, the good wife tapped the sign of the cross on it with her knife. Before the planting, the village priest customarily went out and sprinkled the fields with water, symbolizing refreshment and life. Shortly after a woman had successfully delivered a child, she was "churched." This was a ceremony of thanksgiving, based on the Jewish rite of purification. When a child was baptized, a few grains of salt were dropped on its tongue. Salt had been the symbol of purity, strength, and incorruptibility for the ancient Hebrews, and the Romans had used it in their sacrifices. It was used in Christian baptism to drive away demons and to strengthen the infant in its new faith.

The entire calendar was designed with reference to Christmas, Easter, and Pentecost. Saints' days were legion. Everyone participated in village processions. The colored vestments the priests wore at Mass gave the villagers a sense of the changing seasons of the church's liturgical year. The signs and symbols of Christianity were visible everywhere.

Was popular religion largely a matter of rituals and ceremonies? What did people actually *believe*? It is difficult to say, partly because medieval peasants left few written records of their thoughts, partly because in any age there is often a great disparity between what people profess to believe and their conduct or the ways they act on their beliefs. Recent research has shown, however, that in the High Middle Ages a new religious understanding emerged. "Whereas early Christianity looked to holy men and women and early medieval society turned to saints to effect the connection between God and humankind through prayers of intercession," in the twelfth century a sacramental system developed; the seven sacraments, or signs (baptism, penance, eucharist, confirmation, marriage, holy orders, extreme unction), brought grace, the divine assistance or help needed to lead a good Christian life and to merit salvation. Sermons and homilies taught that at the center of the sacramental system stood the Eucharist, the small piece of bread, that through the words of priestly consecration at the Mass became the living body of Christ and, when worthily consumed, became a channel of Christ's grace. The ritual of consecration, repeated at every altar of Christendom, became a unifying symbol in a complex world.[26]

The Mass was in Latin, but the priest delivered sermons on the Gospel in the vernacular. Or he was supposed to. An almost universal criticism of the parish clergy in the twelfth and thirteenth centuries was that they were incapable of explaining basic Christian teaching to their parishioners. The growth of the universities (see page 352) did not improve the situation, because few diocesan clerics attended them, and those who did and won degrees secured administrative positions with prelates or lay governments. The only parish priest to be canonized in the entire Middle Ages, the Breton lawyer and priest Saint Yves (d. 1303), had resigned a position as a diocesan judge to serve rural parishioners. At the trial for his canonization, lay people stressed that not only had he led a simple and frugal life but he had put his forensic skills to the service of preaching the Christian gospels. He

represents a great exception to the prevailing inability of the medieval parish clergy to preach in a rural milieu. Parish priests celebrated the liturgy and administered the sacraments, but they had other shortcomings. A thirteenth century Alsatian chronicler said that the peasants of the region did not complain that their pastors lived in concubinage, because that made them less fearful for the virtue of their daughters.[27]

Nevertheless, people grasped the meaning of biblical stories and church doctrines from the paintings on the village church wall. If their parish was wealthy, the scenes depicted in the church's stained-glass windows instructed them. Illiterate and uneducated, they certainly could not reason out the increasingly sophisticated propositions of clever theologians. Still, scriptural references and proverbs dotted everyone's language. The English "good-bye," the French "adieu," and the Spanish "adios" all derive from words meaning "God be with you." Christianity was a basic element in the common people's culture; indeed, it was the foundation of their culture.

Christians had long had special reverence and affection for the Virgin Mary, as the Mother of Christ. In the eleventh century, theologians began to emphasize the depiction of Mary at the crucifixion in the Gospel of John:

But standing by the cross of Jesus were his mother, and his mother's sister, Mary the wife of Clopas, and Mary Magdalene. When Jesus saw his mother and the disciple whom he loved standing near, he said to his mother, "Woman, behold, your son!" Then he said to the disciple, "Behold, your mother!"[28]

Medieval scholars interpreted this passage as expressing Christ's compassionate concern for all humanity and Mary's spiritual motherhood of all Christians. The huge outpouring of popular devotions to Mary concentrated on her role as Queen of Heaven and, because of her special relationship to Christ, as all-powerful intercessor with him. Masses on Saturdays specially commemorated her, sermons focused on her unique influence with Christ, and hymns and prayers to her multiplied. The most famous prayer, "Salve Regina," perfectly expresses medieval people's confidence in Mary, their advocate with Christ:

Hail, holy Queen, Mother of Mercy! Our life, our sweetness, and our hope. To thee we cry, poor ban-

ished children of Eve; to thee we send up our sighs, mourning and weeping in this valley of tears. Turn, then, most gracious advocate, thy merciful eyes upon us; and after this our exile show us the blessed fruit of thy womb, Jesus. O merciful, O loving, O sweet Virgin Mary!

Peasants had a strong sense of the universal presence of God. They believed that God intervened directly in human affairs and could reward the virtuous with peace, health, and material prosperity. They believed that God punished men and women for their sins with disease, poor harvests, and the destructions of war. Sin was caused by the Devil, who lurked everywhere. The Devil constantly incited people to evil deeds and sin, especially sins of the flesh. Sin frequently took place in the dark. Thus evil and the Devil were connected in the peasant's mind with darkness or blackness. In some medieval literature the Devil is portrayed as black, an identification that has had a profound and sorry impact on Western racial attitudes.

For peasants, life was not only hard but short. Few lived beyond the age of forty. They had a great fear of nature: storms, thunder, and lightning terrified them. They had a terror of hell, whose geography and awful tortures they knew from sermons. And they certainly saw that the virtuous were not always rewarded but sometimes suffered considerably on earth. These things, which they could not explain, bred a deep pessimism.

Belief in an afterlife where the dead were rewarded or punished according to how they had lived on earth was a central principle of medieval people's faith. The clergy taught the immortality of the soul after the death of the body. The deceased, however, did not go immediately to heaven or hell. Rather, people believed the recently deceased returned to the places they had frequented during their lives and either sought the prayers of the living or settled accounts with them. Hence the widespread belief in ghosts who haunted their former houses and frightened relatives and friends. Late in the twelfth century, to free houses and people of the haunting presence of the dead, the church affirmed the existence of *purgatory,* a temporary place where distressed souls made amends for their earthly sins before being assigned one of the eternal places, hell or heaven.[29] Prayers and masses helped those in purgatory. So did *indulgences,* statements bearing the pope's name that released the souls from purgatory. (Indulgences, it

was believed, also relieved the living of those penalties imposed by the priest in confession for serious sins.) Indulgences could be secured for a small fee. Unfortunately, people came to believe that indulgences and pilgrimages to the shrines of saints "promised" salvation. Vast numbers embarked on pilgrimages to the shrines of Saint James at Compostella in Spain, Saint Thomas Becket at Canterbury, Saint-Gilles de Provence, and Saints Peter and Paul at Rome.

 ## THOSE WHO FIGHT

The nobility, though a small fraction of the total population, strongly influenced all aspects of medieval culture—political, economic, religious, educational, and artistic. For that reason, European society in the twelfth and thirteenth centuries may be termed aristocratic. Despite political, scientific, and industrial revolutions, the nobility continued to hold real political and social power in Europe down to the nineteenth century. In order to account for this continuing influence, it is important to understand its development in the High Middle Ages.

During the past twenty years, historians have discovered a great deal about the origins and status of the medieval European nobility. We now know, for example, that ecclesiastical writers in the tenth and eleventh centuries frequently used the term *nobilitas* in reference to the upper classes but did not define it. Clerical writers, however, had no trouble distinguishing who was and was not noble. By the thirteenth century, nobles were broadly described as "those who fight"—those who had the profession of arms. What was a noble? How did the social status and lifestyle of the nobility in the twelfth and thirteenth centuries differ from their tenth-century forms? What political and economic role did the nobility play?

First, in the tenth and eleventh centuries, the social structure in different parts of Europe varied considerably. There were distinct regional customs and social patterns. Broad generalizations about the legal and social status of the nobility, therefore, are dangerous, because they are not universally applicable. For example, in Germany until about 1200, approximately one thousand families, descended from the Carolingian imperial aristocracy and perhaps from the original German tribal nobility, formed the ruling social group. Its members intermarried and held most of the important positions in church and state.[30] Rigid distinctions existed between free and nonfree individuals, preventing the absorption of those of servile birth into the ranks of the nobility. Likewise, in the region around Paris from the tenth century on, a group of great families held public authority, was self-conscious about its ancestry and honorable status, was bound to the royal house, and was closed to the self-made man. From this aristocracy descended the upper nobility of the High Middle Ages.[31] To the west, however, in the provinces of Anjou and Maine, men of fortune who gained wealth and power became part of the closely related web of noble families by marrying into those families; in these regions, considerable upward mobility existed. Some scholars argue that before the thirteenth century the French nobility was an open caste.[32] Across the English Channel, the English nobility in the High Middle Ages derived from the Norman, Breton, French, and Flemish warriors who helped Duke William of Normandy defeat the Anglo-Saxons at the Battle of Hastings in 1066. In most places, for a son or daughter to be considered a noble, both parents had to be noble. Non-noble women could not usually enter the nobility through marriage, though evidence from Germany shows that some women were ennobled because they had married nobles. There is no evidence of French or English women being raised to the nobility.

Members of the nobility enjoyed a special legal status. A nobleman was free personally and in his possessions. He had immunity from almost all outside authorities. He was limited only by his military obligation to king, duke, or prince. As the result of his liberty, he had certain rights and responsibilities. He raised troops and commanded them in the field. He held courts that dispensed a sort of justice. Sometimes he coined money for use within his territories. He conducted relations with outside powers. He was the political, military, and judicial lord of the people who settled on his lands. He made political decisions affecting them, resolved disputes among them, and protected them in time of attack. The liberty of the noble and the privileges that went with his liberty were inheritable, perpetuated by blood and not by wealth alone.

The nobleman was a professional fighter. His social function, as churchmen described it, was to protect the weak, the poor, and the churches by arms. He possessed a horse and a sword. These,

and the leisure time in which to learn how to use them in combat, were the visible signs of his nobility. He was encouraged to display chivalric virtues. Chivalry was a code of conduct originally devised by the clergy to transform the crude and brutal behavior of the knightly class. A knight was supposed to be brave, anxious to win praise, courteous, loyal to his commander, generous, and gracious. The medieval nobility developed independently of knighthood and preceded it; all nobles were knights, but not all knights were noble.[33]

During the eleventh century, the term *chevalier,* meaning "horseman" or "knight," gained wide currency in France. Non-French people gradually adopted it to refer to the nobility, "who sat up high on their war-horses, looking down on the poor masses and terrorizing the monks."[34] In France and England by the twelfth century, the noble frequently used the Latin term *miles,* or "knight." By this time the word connoted moral values, a consciousness of family, and participation in a superior hereditary caste. Those who aspired to the aristocracy desired a castle, the symbol of feudal independence and military lifestyle. Through military valor, a fortunate marriage, or outstanding service to king or lord, poor knights could and did achieve positions in the upper nobility of France and England. Not so in Germany, where a large class of unfree knights, or *ministerials,* existed. Recruited from the servile dependents of great lords, ministerials fought as warriors or served as stewards who managed nobles' estates or households. In the twelfth century, ministerials sometimes acquired fiefs and wealth. The most important ministerials served the German kings and had significant responsibilities. Legally, however, they remained of servile status: they were not noble.[35] Consequently, in southeastern Germany the term *knight* applied to the servile position of a ministerial.

Infancy and Childhood

Very exciting research has been done on childbirth in the Middle Ages. Most of the information comes from manuscript illuminations, which depict the birth process from the moment of coitus through pregnancy to delivery. An interesting thirteenth-century German miniature from Vienna shows a woman in labor. She is sitting on a chair or stool surrounded by four other women, who are present to help her in the delivery. They could be relatives or neighbors. If they are midwives, the woman in labor is probably noble or rich, since midwives charged a fee. Two midwives seem to be shaking the mother up and down to hasten delivery. One of the women is holding a coriander seed near the mother's vagina. Coriander is an herb of the carrot family, and its seeds were used for cleaning purposes. They were thought to be helpful for expelling gas from the alimentary canal—hence their purported value in speeding up delivery.

The rate of infant mortality (the number of babies who would die before their first birthday) in the High Middle Ages must have been staggering. Such practices as jolting the pregnant woman up and down and inserting coriander seeds into her to speed delivery surely contributed to the death rate of both the newborn and the mother. Natural causes—disease and poor or insufficient food—also resulted in many deaths. Infanticide, however,

which was common in the ancient world, seems to have declined in the High Middle Ages. Ecclesiastical pressure worked steadily against it. Infanticide in medieval Europe is another indication of the slow and very imperfect Christianization of European peoples.

On the other hand, the abandonment of infant children seems to have been the most favored form of family limitation, widely practiced throughout the entire Middle Ages. Abandonment was "the voluntary relinquishing of control over children by their natal parents or guardians, whether by leaving them somewhere, selling them, or legally consigning authority to some other person or institution."[36] Why did parents do this? What became of the children? What was the rate of abandonment? What attitudes did medieval society have toward this practice?

Poverty or local natural disaster led some parents to abandon their children because they could not support them. Before the eleventh century, food was so scarce few parents could feed themselves, let alone children. Thus Saint Patrick wrote that, in times of famine, fathers would sell their sons and daughters so that the children could be fed. Parents sometimes gave children away because they were illegitimate or the result of incestuous unions. An eighth-century penitential collection describes the proper treatment for a woman who exposes her unwanted child—that is, leaves it in the open to die—because she has been raped by an enemy or is unable to nourish it. She is not to be blamed, but she should do penance.[37]

Sometimes parents believed that someone of greater means or status might find the child and bring it up in better circumstances than the natal parents could provide. Disappointment in the sex of the child, or its physical weakness or deformity, might also lead parents to abandon it. Finally, some parents were indifferent—they "simply could not be bothered" with the responsibilities of parenthood.[38]

The Christian Middle Ages witnessed a significant development in the disposal of superfluous children: they were given to monasteries as *oblates*. The word *oblate* derives from the Latin *oblatio*, meaning "offering." Boys and girls were given to monasteries or convents as permanent gifts. Saint Benedict (see pages 211–212), in the fifty-ninth chapter of his *Rule*, takes oblation as a normal method for entrance into the monastic life. By the seventh century, church councils and civil codes

❖ **Midwives Hastening Delivery** Women had exclusive control over all aspects of childbirth, until the 15th century when all-male medical school faculties and urban administrators began to exclude them. A seated position for delivery was universal worldwide: it allowed the mother to push. *(Source: Österreichische Nationalbibliothek)*

had defined the practice: "Parents of any social status could donate a child, of either sex, at least up to the age of ten." Contemporaries considered oblation a religious act, since the child was offered to God often in recompense for parental sin. But oblation also served social and economic functions. The monastery nurtured and educated the child in a familial atmosphere, and it provided career opportunities for the mature monk or nun despite his or her humble origins. Oblation has justifiably been described as "in many ways the most humane form of abandonment ever devised in the West."[39]

The fragmentary medieval evidence prevents the modern student from gaining precise figures on the rate of abandonment. Recent research suggests, however, that abandonment was very common until about the year 1000. The next two hundred years, which saw great agricultural change and relative prosperity, witnessed a low point in abandonment. On the other hand, in the twelfth and thirteenth centuries, the incidence of noble parents giving their younger sons and daughters to religious houses increased dramatically; nobles wanted to preserve the estate intact for the eldest son. Consequently, oblates composed a high percentage of monastic populations. At Winchester in England, for example, 85 percent of the new monks between 1030 and 1070 were oblates. In the early thirteenth century, the bishop of Paris observed that children were ". . . cast into the cloister by parents and relatives just as if they were kittens or piglets whom their mothers could not nourish; so that they may die to the world not spiritually but . . . civilly, that is—so that they may be deprived of their hereditary position and that it may devolve on those who remain in the world." The abandonment of children remained a socially acceptable institution. Ecclesiastical and civil authorities never legislated against it.[40]

In addition to abandonment, nobles used other family-planning strategies to preserve family estates, but scholars disagree about the nature of these methods. According to one authority, "The struggle to preserve family holdings intact led them to primogeniture [the exclusive right of the first-born son to inherit] . . . [41] Another student has argued persuasively that nobles deliberately married late or limited the number of their children who could marry by placing them in the church or forbidding them to marry while still laypersons. Nobles may also have practiced birth control. The counts of Falkenstein, who held lord-

✦ **Children Given to Creditors** Ecclesiastical laws against lending money at interest were widely flouted, and many nobles, having borrowed beyond their ability to repay, fell heavily into debt. As illustrated here, the selling or giving of children to creditors was one solution to indebtedness. *(Source: The Bodleian Library, Oxford)*

ships in Upper Bavaria and Lower Austria, adopted the strategy of late marriages and few children. This custom plus a violent lifestyle ultimately backfired and extinguished the dynasty.[42] Another student, using evidence from tenth-century Saxony, maintains that parents during their lifetimes commonly endowed their sons with estates. This practice allowed sons to marry at a young age and to demonstrate their military prowess.[43] Until we know more about family size and local customs in the High Middle Ages, we cannot generalize about universal practices.

For children of aristocratic birth, the years from infancy to around the age of seven or eight were primarily years of play. Infants had their rattles, as the twelfth-century monk Guibert of Nogent reports, and young children their special toys. Of course, then as now, children would play with anything handy—balls, rings, pretty stones, horns, any small household object. Gerald of Wales, who later became a courtier of King Henry II, describes how as a child he built monasteries and churches in the sand while his brothers were making castles and palaces. Vincent of Beauvais, who composed a great encyclopedia around 1250, recommended that children be bathed twice a day, fed well, and given ample playtime.

Guibert of Nogent speaks in several places in his autobiography of "the tender years of childhood"—the years from six to twelve. Describing the severity of the tutor whom his mother assigned to him, Guibert wrote:

Placed under him, I was taught with such purity and checked with such honesty from the vices which commonly spring up in youth that I was kept from ordinary games and never allowed to leave my master's company, or to eat anywhere else than at home, or to accept gifts from anyone without his leave; in everything I had to show self-control in word, look, and deed, so that he seemed to require of me the conduct of a monk rather than a clerk. While others of my age wandered everywhere at will and were unchecked in the indulgence of such inclinations as were natural at their age, I, hedged in with constant restraints and dressed in my clerical garb, would sit and look at the troops of players like a beast awaiting sacrifice. Even on Sundays and saints' days I had to submit to the severity of school exercises.[44]

Guibert's mother had intended him for the church. Other boys and girls had more playtime and freedom.

At about the age of seven, a boy of the noble class who was not intended for the church was placed in the household of one of his father's friends or relatives. There he became a servant to the lord and received his formal training in arms. He was expected to serve the lord at the table, to assist him as a private valet when called on to do so, and, as he gained experience, to care for the lord's horses and equipment. The boy might have a great deal of work to do, depending on the size of the household and the personality of the lord. The work children did, medieval people believed, gave them experience and preparation for later life.

Training was in the arts of war. The boy learned to ride and to manage a horse. He had to acquire skill in wielding a sword, which sometimes weighed as much as 25 pounds. He had to be able to hurl a lance, shoot with a bow and arrow, and care for armor and other equipment. Increasingly, in the eleventh and twelfth centuries, noble youths learned to read and write some Latin. Still, on

thousands of charters from that period, nobles signed with a cross (+) or some other mark. Literacy for the nobility became more common in the thirteenth century. Formal training was concluded around the age of twenty-one with the ceremony of knighthood. The custom of knighting, though never universal, seems to have been widespread in France and England but not in Germany. The ceremony of knighthood was one of the most important in a man's life. Once knighted, a young man was supposed to be courteous, generous, and, if possible, handsome and rich. Above all, he was to be loyal to his lord and brave in battle. In a society lacking strong institutions of government, loyalty was the cement that held aristocratic society together. That is why the greatest crime was called a "felony," which meant treachery to one's lord.

Youth

Knighthood did not necessarily mean adulthood, power, and responsibility. Sons were completely dependent on their fathers for support. Unless a young man's father was dead, he was still considered a youth. He remained a youth until he was in a financial position to marry—that is, until his father died. That might not happen until he was in his late thirties, and marriage at forty was not uncommon. A famous English soldier of fortune, William Marshal, had to wait until he was forty-five to take a wife. One factor—the inheritance of land and the division of properties—determined the lifestyle of the aristocratic nobility. The result was tension, frustration, and sometimes violence.

Once knighted, the young man traveled. His father selected a group of friends to accompany, guide, and protect him. The band's chief pursuit was fighting. They meddled in local conflicts, sometimes departed on crusades, hunted, and did the tournament circuit. The *tournament,* in which a number of men competed from horseback (in contrast to the *joust,* which involved only two competitors), gave the bachelor knight experience in pitched battle. Since the horses and equipment of the vanquished were forfeited to the victors, the knight could also gain a reputation and a profit. Young knights took great delight in spending money on horses, armor, gambling, drinking, and women. Everywhere they went they stirred up trouble. It is no wonder that kings supported the Crusades to rid their countries of the violence caused by bands of footloose young knights.

✤ **A Knightly Tournament or the Battle of the Sexes** The lid of this exquisitely carved French ivory casket shows ladies and gentlemen on a balcony watching a tournament among mounted knights, while men storm the castle of love (left) and a lady and knight tilt with branches of flowers (right). *(Source: Walters Art Gallery, Baltimore)*

The period of traveling lasted two or three years. Although some young men met violent death and others were maimed or injured, many returned home, still totally dependent on their fathers for support. Serious trouble frequently developed at this stage, for the father was determined to preserve intact the properties of the lordship and to maintain his power and position in the family.

Parents often wanted to settle daughters' futures as soon as possible. Men, even older men, tended to prefer young brides. A woman in her late twenties or thirties would have fewer years of married fertility, limiting the number of children she could produce and thus threatening the family's survival. Therefore, aristocratic girls in the High Middle Ages were married at around the age of sixteen.

The future of many young women was not enviable. For a girl of sixteen, marriage to a man in his thirties was not the most attractive prospect, and marriage to a widower in his forties and fifties was even less so. If there were a large number of marriageable young girls in a particular locality, their "market value" was reduced. In the early

Middle Ages, it had been the custom for the groom to present a dowry to the bride and her family, but by the late twelfth century the process was reversed. Thereafter, the size of the marriage portions offered by brides and their families rose higher and higher.

Within noble families and medieval society as a whole, paternal control of the family property and wealth led to serious difficulties. Because marriage was long delayed for men, a considerable age difference existed between husbands and wives and between fathers and sons. Because of this generation gap, as one scholar has written: "The father became an older, distant, but still powerful figure. He could do favors for his sons, but his very presence, once his sons had reached maturity, blocked them in the attainment and enjoyment of property and in the possession of a wife."[45] Consequently, disputes between the generations were common in the twelfth and thirteenth centuries. Older men held on to property and power. Younger sons wanted a "piece of the action." The conflicts and rebellions in the years 1173 to 1189 involving

Henry II of England and his sons Henry, Geoffrey, and John were quite typical.

The relationship between the mother and her sons was also affected. Closer in years to her children than her husband, she seemed better able to understand their needs and frustrations. She often served as a mediator between conflicting male generations. One authority on French epic poetry has written, "In extreme need, the heroes betake themselves to their mother, with whom they always find love, counsel and help. She takes them under her protection, even against their father."[46]

When society included so many married young women and unmarried young men, sexual tensions also arose. The young male noble, unable to marry for a long time, could satisfy his lust with peasant girls or prostitutes. But what was a young woman unhappily married to a much older man to do? The literature of courtly love is filled with stories of young bachelors in love with young married women. How hopeless their love was is not known. The cuckolded husband is also a stock figure in such masterpieces as *The Romance of Tristan and Isolde,* Chaucer's *The Merchant's Tale,* and Boccaccio's *Fiammetta's Tale.*

In the High Middle Ages, for economic reasons, a man might remain a bachelor knight—a "youth"—for a very long time. The identification of bachelorhood with youth has survived into modern times, and the social attitude persists that marriage makes a man mature—an adult. Marriage, however, is no guarantee of that.

Power and Responsibility

A male member of the nobility became an adult when he came into the possession of his property. He then acquired vast authority over lands and people. With it went responsibility. In the words of Honorius of Autun:

Soldiers: You are the arm of the Church, because you should defend it against its enemies. Your duty is to aid the oppressed, to restrain yourself from rapine and fornication, to repress those who impugn the Church with evil acts, and to resist those who are rebels against priests. Performing such a service, you will obtain the most splendid of benefices from the greatest of Kings.[47]

Nobles rarely lived up to this ideal, and there are countless examples of nobles attacking the church.

In the early thirteenth century, Peter of Dreux, count of Brittany, spent so much of his time attacking the church that he was known as the "Scourge of the Clergy."

The nobles' conception of rewards and gratification did not involve the kind of postponement envisioned by the clergy. They wanted rewards immediately. Since by definition a military class is devoted to war, those rewards came through the pursuit of arms. When nobles were not involved in local squabbles with neighbors—usually disputes over property or over real or imagined slights—they participated in tournaments.

Complete jurisdiction over properties allowed the noble, at long last, to gratify his desire for display and lavish living. Since his status in medieval society depended on the size of his household, he would be anxious to increase the number of his household retainers. The elegance of his clothes, the variety and richness of his table, the number of his horses and followers, the freedom with which he spent money—all were public indications of his social standing. The aristocratic lifestyle was luxurious and extravagant. To maintain it, nobles often borrowed from financiers or wealthy monasteries.

At the same time, nobles had a great deal of work to do. The responsibilities of a noble in the High Middle Ages depended on the size and extent of his estates, the number of his dependents, and his position in his territory relative to others of his class and to the king. As a vassal he was required to fight for his lord or for the king when called on to do so. By the mid-twelfth century, this service was limited in most parts of western Europe to forty days a year. The noble might have to perform guard duty at his lord's castle for a certain number of days a year. He was obliged to attend his lord's court on important occasions when the lord wanted to put on great displays, such as at Easter, Pentecost, and Christmas. When the lord knighted his eldest son or married off his eldest daughter, he called his vassals to his court. They were expected to attend and to present a contribution known as a "gracious aid."

Throughout the year, a noble had to look after his own estates. He had to appoint prudent and honest overseers and make sure that they paid him the customary revenues and services. Since a great lord's estates were usually widely scattered, he had to travel frequently.

Until the late thirteenth century, when royal authority intervened, a noble in France or England had great power over the knights and peasants on his estates. He maintained order among them and dispensed justice to them. Holding the manorial court, which punished criminal acts and settled disputes, was one of his gravest obligations. The quality of justice varied widely: some lords were vicious tyrants who exploited and persecuted their peasants; others were reasonable and evenhanded. In any case, the quality of life on the manor and its productivity were related in no small way to the temperament and decency of the lord—and his lady.

Women played a large and important role in the functioning of the estate (see Listening to the Past). They were responsible for the practical management of the household's "inner economy"—cooking, brewing, spinning, weaving, caring for yard animals. The lifestyle of the medieval warrior-nobles required constant travel, both for purposes of war and for the supervision of distant properties. When the lord was away for long periods, the women frequently managed the herds, barns, granaries, and outlying fields as well.

Frequent pregnancies and the reluctance to expose women to hostile conditions kept the lady at home and therefore able to assume supervision of the family's fixed properties. When a husband went away on crusade—and this could last anywhere from two to five years, if he returned at all—his wife often became the sole manager of the family properties. When her husband went to the Holy Land between 1060 and 1080, the lady Hersendis was the sole manager of her family's properties in northern France.

Nor were women's activities confined to managing households and estates in their husbands' absence. Medieval warfare was largely a matter of brief skirmishes, and few men were killed in any single encounter. But altogether the number slain ran high, and there were many widows. Aristocratic widows frequently controlled family properties and fortunes and exercised great authority. Although the evidence is scattered and sketchy, there are indications that women performed many of the functions of men. In Spain, France, and Germany they bought, sold, and otherwise transferred property. Gertrude, labeled "Saxony's almighty widow" by the chronicler Ekkehard of Aura, took a leading role in conspiracies against the emperor Henry V. And Eilika Billung, widow of Count Otto of Ballenstedt, built a castle at Burgwerben on the Saale River and, as advocate of the monastery of Goseck,

removed one abbot and selected his successor. From her castle at Bernburg, the countess Eilika was also reputed to ravage the countryside.

Throughout the High Middle Ages, fighting remained the dominant feature of the noble lifestyle. The church's preachings and condemnations reduced but did not stop violence. Lateness of inheritance, depriving the nobility of constructive outlets for their energy, together with the military ethos of their culture, encouraged petty warfare and disorder. The nobility thus represented a constant source of trouble for the monarchy. In the thirteenth century, kings drew on the financial support of the middle classes to build the administrative machinery that gradually laid the foundations for strong royal government. The Crusades relieved the rulers of France, England, and the Ger-

Women Defending Castle As in virtually every other kind of activity, women shared with men the difficulties and dangers of defending castles. Armed with rocks, bows, and arrows, even a finger poked through the chain mail helmet into the eye of a knight scaling the walls on a ladder, these noble ladies try to fight off attackers. *(Source: Bibliothèque royale Albert 1er, Brussels)*

man Empire of some of their most dangerous elements. Complete royal control of the nobility, however, came only in modern times.

✤ THOSE WHO PRAY

Medieval people believed that monks performed an important social service, prayer. In the Middle Ages, prayer was looked on as a vital service, one as crucial as the labor of peasants and the military might of nobles. Just as the knights protected and defended society with the sword and the peasants provided sustenance through their toil, so the monks with their prayers and chants worked to secure God's blessing for society.

Monasticism represented some of the finest aspirations of medieval civilization. The monasteries were devoted to prayer, and their standards of Christian behavior influenced the entire church. The monasteries produced the educated elite that was continually drawn into the administrative service of kings and great lords. Monks kept alive the remains of classical culture and experimented with new styles of architecture and art. They introduced new techniques of estate management and land reclamation. Although relatively few in number in the High Middle Ages, the monks played a significant role in medieval society.

Recruitment

Toward the end of his *Ecclesiastical History of England and Normandy,* when he was well into his sixties, Orderic Vitalis, a monk of the Norman abbey of Saint Evroul, interrupted his narrative to explain movingly how he happened to become a monk:

And so, O glorious God, you didst inspire my father Odeleric to renounce me utterly and submit me in all things to thy governance. So, weeping, he gave me, a weeping child, into the care of the monk Reginald, and sent me away into exile for love of thee, and never saw me again. And I, a mere boy, did not presume to oppose my father's wishes, but obeyed him in all things, for he promised me for his part that if I became a monk I should taste of the joys of Heaven with the Innocents after my death. . . . And so, a boy of ten, I crossed the English channel and came into Normandy as an exile, unknown to all, knowing no one. Like Joseph in Egypt I heard a language which I could not

understand. But thou didst suffer me through thy grace to find nothing but kindness among strangers. I was received as an oblate in the abbey of St. Evroul by the venerable abbot Mainier in the eleventh year of my life. . . . The name of Vitalis was given me in place of my English name, which sounded harsh to the Normans.[48]

Orderic Vitalis (ca 1075–ca 1140) was one of the leading scholars of his time. As such, he is not a representative figure or even a typical monk. Intellectuals, those who earn their living or spend most of their time working with ideas, are never typical figures of their times. In one respect, however, Orderic was quite representative of the monks of the High Middle Ages: although he had no doubt that God wanted him to be a monk, the decision was actually made by his parents, who gave him to a monastery as a child-oblate. Orderic was the third son of a knight who fought for William the Conqueror at the Battle of Hastings (1066). For his participation in the Norman conquest of England, he was rewarded with lands in western England. Concern for the provision of his two older sons probably led him to give his youngest to the monastery.

Medieval monasteries were religious institutions whose organization and structure fulfilled the social needs of the feudal nobility. The monasteries provided noble children with both an honorable and aristocratic life and opportunities for ecclesiastical careers.[49]

Until well into modern times, and certainly in the Middle Ages, almost everyone believed in the thorough subjection of children to their parents. This belief was the logical consequence of the fact that young noblemen were not expected to work and were therefore totally dependent on their fathers. Some men did become monks as adults, apparently for a wide variety of reasons: belief in a direct call from God, disgust with the materialism and violence of the secular world, the encouragement and inspiration of others, economic failure or lack of opportunity, poverty, sickness, fear of hell. However, most men who became monks, until about the early thirteenth century, seem to have been given as child-oblates by their parents.

In the thirteenth century, the older Benedictine and Cistercian orders had to compete with new orders of friars—the Franciscans and Dominicans. More monks had to be recruited from the middle class, that is, from small landholders or traders in the district near the abbey. As medieval society changed economically, and as European society ever so slowly developed middle-class traits, the monasteries almost inevitably drew their manpower, when they were able, from the middle classes. Until that time, they were preserves of the aristocratic nobility.

The Nuns

Throughout the Middle Ages, social class also defined the kinds of religious life open to women. Kings and nobles usually established convents for their daughters, sisters, aunts, or aging mothers. Entrance was restricted to women of the founder's class. Since a well-born lady could not honorably be apprenticed to a tradesperson, and since her dignity did not permit her to do any kind of manual labor, the sole alternative to life at home was the religious life.

The founder's endowment and support greatly influenced the later social, economic, and political status of the convent. Social and religious bonds between benefactors and communities of nuns frequently continued over many generations. A few convents received large endowments and could accept many women. Amesbury Priory in Wiltshire, England, for example, received a handsome endowment from King Henry II in 1177, and his successors Henry III and Edward I also made lavish gifts. In 1256 Amesbury supported a prioress and 76 nuns, 7 priests, and 16 lay brothers. It owned 200 oxen, 23 horses, 7 cows, 4 calves, 300 pigs, and 4,800 sheep. The convent raised 100 pounds in annual rents and 40 pounds from the wool clip, very large sums at the time. The entrance of such highborn ladies as the dowager queen Eleanor (widow of Henry III), Edward I's daughter Mary, and his niece Isabella of Lancaster stimulated the gift of additional lands and privileges. By 1317 Amesbury had 177 nuns.[50] Most houses of women, however, possessed limited resources and remained small in numbers.

The office of abbess or prioress, the house's superior, customarily went to a nun of considerable social standing. Thus William the Conqueror's daughter Cecelia became abbess of her mother's foundation, Holy Trinity Abbey in Caen, and Henry II's daughter became abbess of Barking. Since an abbess or prioress had responsibility for governing her community and for representing it in any business with the outside world, she was a woman of local power and importance. Sometimes her position brought national prominence. In 1306 Edward I of England summoned several abbesses to Parliament; he wanted their financial support for the expenses connected with knighting his eldest son.

What kind of life did the nuns lead? Religious duties held prime importance. Then there were business responsibilities connected with lands, properties, and rents that preoccupied those women of administrative ability. Sewing, embroidery, and fine needlework were considered the special pursuits of gentlewomen. Nuns in houses with an intellectual tradition copied manuscripts. Although the level of intellectual life in the women's houses varied widely, the careers of two nuns—Hildegard of Bingen and Isabella of Lancaster—suggest the activities of some nuns in the High Middle Ages.

The tenth child of a lesser noble family, Hildegard (1098–1179) was given when eight years old as an oblate to an abbey in the Rhineland, where she learned Latin and received a good education. Obviously possessed of leadership and administrative talents, Hildegard went in 1147 to found the convent of Rupertsberg near Bingen. There she produced a body of writings including the *Scivias (Know the Ways)*, a record of her mystical visions that incorporates vast theological learning; the *Physica (On the Physical Elements)*, a classification of the natural elements, such as plants, animals, metals, and the movements of the heavenly bodies; a mystery play; and a medical work that led a distinguished twentieth-century historian of science to describe Hildegard as "one of the most original writers of the Latin West in the twelfth century." At the same time, she carried on a vast correspondence with scholars, prelates, and ordinary people and had such a reputation for wisdom that a recent writer has called her "the Dear Abby of the twelfth century to whom everyone came or wrote for advice or comfort."[51] An exceptionally gifted person, Hildegard represents the Benedictine ideal of great learning combined with a devoted monastic life.

As with monks, however, intellectual nuns were not typical of the era. The life of the English nun Isabella of Lancaster better exemplifies the careers of highborn women who became nuns. The niece of King Edward I, she was placed at Amesbury Priory in early childhood, grew up there, made her profession of commitment to the convent life, and

❖ **Synagogue** Hildegard of Bingen, the first major German mystic, developed a rich theology on the basis of visions she received. Here Synagogue is portrayed as a tall woman commanded by God to prepare humanity for the coming of Christ. In her arms Moses holds up the stone tablets of the commandments, in her lap the patriarchs and prophets who foretold the birth of Christ. The headband symbolizes the Virgin Mary: because Mary gave the world the savior, Hildegard makes Synagogue the Mother of the Incarnation. *(Source: Rheinische Bildarchiv)*

became abbess in 1343. Isabella seems to have been a conventional but not devout nun. She traveled widely, spent long periods at the royal court, and with the support of her wealthy relations maintained a residence apart from the priory. She was, however, an able administrator who handled the community finances with prudent skill. Amesbury lacked the intellectual and spiritual standards of Bingen. Isabella's interests were secular and her own literary production was a book of romances.

Prayer and Other Work

In medieval Europe the monasteries of men greatly outnumbered those of women. The pattern of life within individual monasteries varied widely from house to house and from region to region. Each monastic community was shaped by the circumstances of its foundation and endowment, by tradition, by the interests of its abbots and members, and by local conditions. It would therefore be a mistake to think that Christian monasticism in the High Middle Ages was everywhere the same. One central activity, however—the work of God—was performed everywhere. Daily life centered around the liturgy.

Seven times a day and once during the night, the monks went to choir to chant the psalms and other prayers prescribed by Saint Benedict. Prayers were offered for peace, rain, good harvests, the civil authorities, the monks' families, and their benefactors. Monastic patrons in turn lavished gifts on the monasteries, which often became very wealthy. Through their prayers the monks performed a valuable service for the rest of society.

Prayer justified the monks' spending a large percentage of their income on splendid objects to enhance the liturgy; monks praised God, they believed, not only in prayer but in everything connected with prayer. They sought to accumulate priestly vestments of the finest silks, velvets, and embroideries, as well as sacred vessels of embossed silver and gold. Thuribles containing sweet-smelling incense brought at great expense from the Orient were used at the altars, following ancient Jewish ritual. The pages of Gospel books were richly decorated with gold leaf, and the books' bindings were ornamented and bejeweled. Every monastery tried to acquire the relics of its patron saint, which necessitated the production of a beautiful reliquary to house the relics. The liturgy, then, inspired a great deal of art, and the monasteries became the crucibles of art in Western Christendom.

The monks fulfilled their social responsibility by praying. It was generally agreed that they could best carry out this duty if they were not distracted by worldly needs. Thus great and lesser lords gave the monasteries lands that would supply the community with necessities. Each manorial unit was responsible for provisioning the abbey for a definite period of time.

The administration of the abbey's estates and properties consumed considerable time. The operation of a large establishment, such as Cluny in Burgundy or Bury Saint Edmunds in England, which by 1150 had several hundred monks, involved planning, prudence, and wise management. Although the abbot or prior had absolute authority in making assignments, common sense advised that tasks be allotted according to the talents of individual monks.

The usual method of economic organization was the manor. Many monastic manors were small enough and close enough to the abbey to be supervised directly by the abbot. But if a monastery held and farmed vast estates, the properties were divided into administrative units under the supervision of one of the monks of the house. The lands of the German abbey of Saint Emmeran at Regensburg, for example, were divided into thirty-three manorial centers.

Because the *choir monks* were aristocrats, they did not till the land themselves. In each house one monk, the *cellarer,* or general financial manager, was responsible for supervising the peasants or lay brothers who did the actual agricultural labor. *Lay brothers* were vowed religious drawn from the servile classes, with simpler religious and intellectual obligations than those of the choir monks. The cellarer had to see to it that the estates of the monastery produced enough income to cover its expenses. Another monk, the *almoner,* was responsible for feeding and caring for the poor of the neighborhood. At the French abbey of Saint-Requier in the eleventh century, 110 persons were

❖ **Richard of Wallingford, abbot and astronomer** In the thirteenth century, some monasteries, such as St. Alban's just north of London, were great intellectual centers. The monastic community there included artist Walter of Colchester and historian Matthew Paris. The abbot of St. Alban's, Richard of Wallingford (c. 1292–1336) here shown with the crozier symbol of his authority under his left arm, had scientific interests. Using a compass and square, he constructs an instrument, probably as astrolabe which was used to calculate the position of the sun or other celestial bodies before the invention (1628) of the sextant. *(Source: British Library)*

fed every day. At Corbie, fifty loaves of bread were distributed daily to the poor.

The *precentor* or *cantor* was responsible for the library and the careful preservation of books. The *sacristan* of the abbey had in his charge all the materials and objects connected with the liturgy—vestments, candles, incense, sacred vessels, altar cloths, and hangings. The *novice master* was responsible for the training of recruits, instructing them in the *Rule,* the chant, the Scriptures, and the history and traditions of the house. For some monks, work was some form of intellectual activity, such as the copying of books and manuscripts, the preparation of manuals, and the writing of letters.

Although several orders forbade monks to study law and medicine, that rule was often ignored. In the twelfth and thirteenth centuries, many monks gained considerable reputations for their knowledge and experience in the practice of both the canon law of the church and the civil law of their countries. For example, the Norman monk Lanfranc, because of his legal knowledge and administrative ability, became the chief adviser of William the Conqueror.

Although knowledge of medicine was primitive by twentieth-century standards, monastic practitioners were less ignorant than one would suspect. Long before 1066, a rich medical literature had been produced in England. The most important of these treatises was *The Leech Book of Bald* (*leech* means "medical"). This work exhibits a wide knowledge of herbal prescriptions, ancient authorities, and empirical practice. Bald discusses diseases of the lungs and stomach together with their remedies and demonstrates his acquaintance with surgery. Medical knowledge was sometimes rewarded. King Henry I of England enriched several of his physicians, and Henry II made his medical adviser, the monk Robert de Veneys, abbot of Malmesbury.

The religious houses of medieval Europe usually took full advantage of whatever resources and opportunities their location offered. For example, the raising of horses could produce income in a world that depended on horses for travel and for warfare. Some monasteries, such as the Cistercian abbey of Jervaulx in Yorkshire, became famous for and quite wealthy from their production of prime breeds. In the eleventh and twelfth centuries, a period of considerable monastic expansion, large tracts of swamp, fen, forest, and wasteland were brought under cultivation—principally by the Cistercians (Map 10.1).

The Cistercians, whose constitution insisted that they accept lands far from human habitation and forbade them to be involved in the traditional feudal-manorial structure, were ideally suited to the agricultural needs and trends of their times. In the Low Countries (present-day Holland, Belgium, and French Flanders) they built dikes to hold back the sea, and the reclaimed land was put to the production of cereals. In the eastern parts of Germany—Silesia, Mecklenburg, and Pomerania—they took the lead in draining swamps and cultivating wasteland. Because of a labor shortage, they advertised widely across Europe for monks and brothers. As a result of their efforts, the rich, rolling land of French Burgundy was turned into lush vineyards. In northern and central England, the rocky soil and damp downs of Lincolnshire, poorly suited to agriculture, were turned into sheep runs. By the third quarter of the twelfth century, the Cistercians were raising sheep and playing a large role in the production of England's staple crop, wool.

Some monasteries got involved in iron and lead mining. In 1291 the Cistercian abbey of Furness operated at least forty forges. The German abbeys of Königsbronn, Waldsassen, and Saabergen also mined iron in the thirteenth century. The monks entered this industry first to fill their own needs, but in an expanding economy they soon discovered a large market. Iron had hundreds of uses. Nails, hammers, plows, armor, spears, axes, stirrups, horseshoes, and many weapons of war were all made from this basic metal. When King Richard of England was preparing to depart on crusade in 1189, he wanted to take fifty thousand horseshoes with him. Lead also had a great variety of uses. It could be used for roofing; as an alloy for strengthening silver coinage; for framing pane-glass windows in parish, monastery, and cathedral churches; even for lavatory drainpipes.

Some monasteries lent their surplus revenues to the local nobility and peasantry. In the twelfth century the abbey of Savigny in Normandy, for example, acted as a banking house, providing loans at interest to many noble families of Normandy and Brittany. Although church law opposed usury, or lending at interest, one reliable scholar has recently written that "it was clerics and ecclesiastical institutions (monasteries and nunneries) that constituted the main providers of credit."[52]

Whatever work particular monks did and whatever economic activities individual monasteries

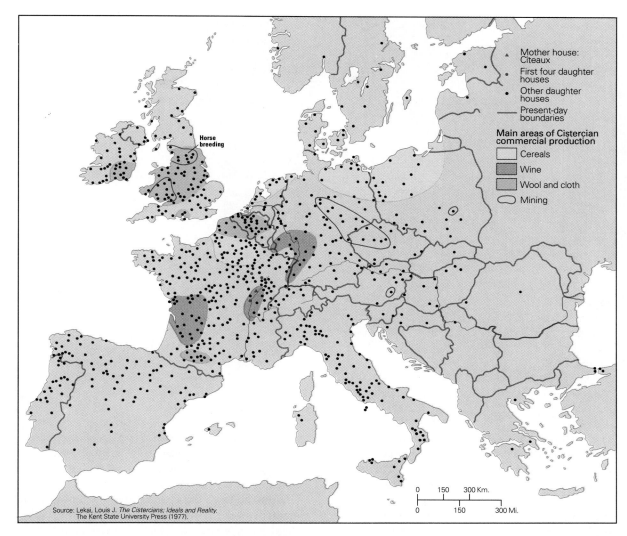

Horse
breeding

Mother house:
Cîteaux
First four daughter
houses
Other daughter
houses
Present-day
boundaries

Main areas of Cistercian
commercial production

Cereals

Wine

Wool and cloth

Mining

0   150   300 Km.

0   150   300 Mi.

Source: Lekai, Louis J. *The Cistercians; Ideals and Reality.*
The Kent State University Press (1977).

❖ **MAP 10.1 Cistercian Expansion** The rapid expansion of the Cistercian Order in
the twelfth century reflects the spiritual piety of the age and its enormous economic vitality. The White Monks (so-called because of their white robes) took advantage of whatever economic opportunities their locales offered: coal, iron, and silver mining, sheep farming, cereal growing, wine producing, and horse breeding.

were involved in, monks also performed social
services and exerted an influence for the good.
Monasteries often ran schools that gave primary
education to young boys. Abbeys like Saint Albans,
situated north of London on a busy thoroughfare,
served as hotels and resting places for travelers.
Monasteries frequently operated "hospitals" and
leprosaria, which provided care and attention to
the sick, the aged, and the afflicted—primitive care,
it is true, but often all that was available. In short,
monasteries performed a variety of social services

in an age when there was no "state" and no conception of social welfare as a public responsibility.

Economic Difficulties

In the twelfth century, expenses in the older Benedictine monastic houses increased more rapidly
than did income, leading to a steadily worsening
economic situation. Cluny is a good example. Life
at Cluny was lavish and extravagant. There were
large quantities of rich food. The monks' habits

✤ **Bee Keeping at Monte Cassino** Because of the scarcity and expense of sugar, honey was the usual sweetener for pastries and liquids throughout the Middle Ages. This illustrator had never actually seen the process: without veils, nets, and gloves, the bee keepers would be badly stung. (*Source: Biblioteca Apostolica Vaticana*)

were made of the best cloth available. Cluny's abbots and priors traveled with sizable retinues, as great lords were required to do. The abbots worked to make the liturgy ever more magnificent, and large sums were spent on elaborate vestments and jeweled vessels. Hugh, the sixth abbot (1049–1109), embarked on an extraordinarily expensive building program. He rebuilt the abbey church, and when Pope Urban II consecrated it in 1095, it was the largest church in Christendom. The monks lived like lords, which in a sense they were.

Revenue came from the hundreds of monasteries scattered across France, Italy, Spain, and England that Cluny had reformed in the eleventh century; each year they paid Cluny a cash sum. Novices were expected to make a gift of land or cash when they entered. For reasons of security, knights departing on crusade often placed their estates under Cluny's authority. Still this income was not enough. The management of Cluny's manors across Europe was entrusted to bailiffs or wardens who were not monks and were given lifetime contracts. Frequently these bailiffs were poor managers and produced no profits. But they could not be removed and replaced. In order to meet expenses,

Cluny had to rely on cash reserves. For example, Cluny's estates produced only a small percentage of needed food supplies; the rest had to be paid for from cash reserves.

Cluny had two basic alternatives—improve management to cut costs or borrow money. The abbey could have placed the monastic manors under the jurisdiction of monks, rather than hiring bailiffs who would grow rich as middlemen. It could have awarded annual rather than lifetime contracts, supervised all revenues, and tried to cut costs within the monastery. But Cluny chose the second alternative—borrowing. The abbey spent hoarded reserves of cash and fell into debt.

In contrast to the abbot of Cluny, Suger, the superior of the royal abbey of Saint-Denis near Paris from 1122 to 1151, was a shrewd manager. Though he, too, spared no expense to enhance the beauty of his monastery and church, Suger kept an eye on costs and made sure that his properties were soundly managed. But the management of Saint-Denis was unusual. Far more typical was the economic mismanagement at Cluny. By the later twelfth century, small and great monasteries were facing comparable financial difficulties.

SUMMARY

Generalizations about peasant life in the High Middle Ages must always be qualified according to manorial customs, the weather and geography, and the personalities of local lords. Everywhere, however, the performance of agricultural services and the payment of rents preoccupied peasants. Though peasants led hard lives, the reclamation of waste and forest lands, migration to frontier territory, or flight to a town (see Chapter 11) offered means of social mobility. The Christian faith, though perhaps not understood at an intellectual level, provided a strong emotional and spiritual solace.

By 1100 the knightly class was united in its ability to fight on horseback, its insistence that each member was descended from a valorous ancestor, its privileges, and its position at the top of the social hierarchy. The nobility possessed a strong class consciousness. Aristocratic values and attitudes shaded all aspects of medieval culture. Trained for war, nobles often devoted considerable time to fighting, and intergenerational squabbles were common. Yet a noble might have shouldered heavy judicial, political, and economic responsibilities, depending on the size of his estates.

The monks and nuns exercised a profound influence on matters of the spirit. In their prayers, monks and nuns battled for the Lord, just as the chivalrous knights did on the battlefield. In their chant and rich ceremonial, in their architecture and literary productions, and in the example of many monks' lives, the monasteries inspired Christian peoples to an incalculable degree. As the crucibles of sacred art, the monasteries became the cultural centers of Christian Europe.

NOTES

1. G. Duby, *The Chivalrous Society,* C. Postan, trans. (Berkeley: University of California Press, 1977), pp. 90–93.
2. B. A. Hanawalt, *The Ties That Bound: Peasant Families in Medieval England* (New York: Oxford University Press, 1986), p. 5.
3. Honorius of Autun, "Elucidarium sive Dialogus de Summa Totius Christianae Theologiae," in *Patrologia Latina,* J. P. Migne, ed. (Paris: Garnier Brothers, 1854), vol. 172, col. 1149.
4. E. Power, "Peasant Life and Rural Conditions," in J. R. Tanner et al., *The Cambridge Medieval History,* vol. 7 (Cambridge: Cambridge University Press, 1958), p. 716.
5. Glanvill, "De Legibus Angliae," bk. 5, chap. 5, in *Social Life in Britain from the Conquest to the Reformation,* G. G. Coulton, ed. (London: Cambridge University Press, 1956), pp. 338–339.
6. J. B. Freed, *The Friars and German Society in the Thirteenth Century* (Cambridge, Mass.: Medieval Academy of America, 1977), p. 55.
7. See W. C. Jordan, *From Servitude to Freedom: Manumission in the Senonais in the Thirteenth Century* (Philadelphia: University of Pennsylvania Press, 1986), esp. chap. 3, pp. 37–58.
8. See J. L. Langdon, *Horses, Oxen, and Technological Innovation: The Use of Draught Animals in English Farming, 1066–1500* (New York: Cambridge University Press, 1986), esp. pp. 254–270.
9. G. Duby, *The Early Growth of the European Economy: Warriors and Peasants from the Seventh to the Twelfth Century* (Ithaca, N.Y.: Cornell University Press, 1978), pp. 213–219.
10. Hanawalt, pp. 90–100.
11. Ibid., p. 149.
12. On this quantity and medieval measurements, see D. Knowles, "The Measures of Monastic Beverages," in *The Monastic Order in England* (Cambridge: Cambridge University Press, 1962), p. 717.
13. G. Duby, *Rural Economy and Country Life in the Medieval West,* C. Postan, trans. (London: Edward Arnold, 1968), pp. 146–147.
14. S. R. Scargill-Bird, ed., *Custumals of Battle Abbey in the Reigns of Edward I and Edward II* (London: Camden Society, 1887), pp. 213–219.
15. G. Duby, ed., *A History of Private Life.* Col. II: *Revelations of the Middle Ages* (Cambridge, Mass.: Harvard University Press, 1988), p. 585.
16. Cited in E. Amt, ed., *Women's Lives in the Middle Ages: A Sourcebook.* (New York: Routledge, 1992), pp. 103–104.
17. See C. Klapisch-Zuber ed., *A History of Women.* vol. II: *Silences of the Middle Ages* (Cambridge, Mass.: Harvard University Press, 1992), p. 289 et seq.
18. See R. Blumenfeld-Kosinski, *Not of Woman Born: Representations of Caesarian Birth in Medieval and Renaissance Culture* (Ithaca, N.Y.: Cornell University Press, 1990), p. 27.
19. *Ibid.*
20. *Ibid.* p. 47.
21. E. J. Kealey, *Medieval Medicus: A Social History of Anglo-Norman Medicine* (Baltimore: The Johns Hopkins University Press, 1981), p. 102.
22. Ibid. pp. 88–97.
23. Klapisch-Zuber, *Op. cit.,* p. 299.

24. See A. Gurevich, *Medieval Popular Culture. Problems of Belief and Perception,* J. M. Bak and P. A. Hollingsworth, trans. (New York: Cambridge University Press, 1990), chap. 2, pp. 39–77, esp. p. 76.

25. Ibid.

26. See M. Rubin, *Corpus Christi: The Eucharist in Late Medieval Culture* (New York: Cambridge University Press, 1992), p. 13 et. seq.

27. A. Vauchez, *The Laity in the Middle Ages: Religious Beliefs and Devotional Practices,* D. E. Bornstein, ed., M. J. Schneider, trans. (Notre Dame, Ind.: University of Notre Dame Press, 1993), pp. 99–102.

28. John 19:25–27.

29. Vauchez, pp. 85–87

30. J. B. Freed, "The Origins of the European Nobility: The Problem of the Ministerials," *Viator* 7 (1976): 213.

31. Duby, *The Chivalrous Society,* pp. 104–105.

32. See C. Bouchard, "The Origins of the French Nobility," *The American Historical Review* 86 (1981): 501–532.

33. Duby, *The Chivalrous Society,* p. 98.

34. G. Duby, *The Age of the Cathedrals: Art and Society 980–1420,* E. Levieux and B. Thompson, trans. (Chicago: University of Chicago Press, 1981), p. 38.

35. Freed, "The Origins of the European Nobility," p. 214.

36. J. Boswell, *The Kindness of Strangers: The Abandonment of Children in Western Europe from Late Antiquity to the Renaissance* (New York: Pantheon Books, 1989), p. 24. This section relies heavily on this important work.

37. Ibid., pp. 214, 223.

38. Ibid., pp. 428–429.

39. Ibid., pp. 238–239.

40. Ibid., pp. 297, 299, and the Conclusion.

41. J. C. Russell, *Late Ancient and Medieval Population Control* (Philadelphia: American Philosophical Society, 1985), p. 180.

42. See J. B. Freed, *The Counts of Falkenstein: Noble Self-Consciousness in Twelfth-Century Germany,* Transactions of the American Philosophical Society, vol. 74, pt. 6 (Philadelphia, 1984), pp. 163–167.

43. R. J. Leyser, *Rule and Conflict in an Early Medieval Society: Ottonian Saxony* (Bloomington: Indiana University Press, 1979), pp. 49, 59.

44. J. F. Benton, ed. and trans., *Self and Society in Medieval France: The Memoirs of Abbot Guibert of Nogent* (New York: Harper & Row, 1970), p. 46.

45. D. Herlihy, "The Generation Gap in Medieval History," *Viator* 5 (1974): 360.

46. Quoted in ibid., p. 361.

47. Honorius of Autun, in *Patrologia Latina,* vol. 172, col. 1148.

48. M. Chibnall, ed. and trans., *The Ecclesiastical History of Orderic Vitalis* (Oxford: Oxford University Press, 1972), 2.xiii.

49. R. W. Southern, *Western Society and the Church in the Middle Ages* (Baltimore: Penguin Books, 1970), pp. 224–230, esp. p. 228.

50. See M. W. Labarge, *A Small Sound of the Trumpet: Women in Medieval Life* (Boston: Beacon Press, 1986), pp. 104–105.

51. J. M. Ferrante, "The Education of Women in the Middle Ages in Theory, Fact, and Fantasy," in *Beyond Their Sex: Learned Women of the European Past,* P. H. Labalme, ed. (New York: New York University Press, 1980), pp. 22–24.

52. W. C. Jordan, *Women and Credit in Pre-Industrial and Developing Societies* (Philadelphia: University of Pennsylvania Press, 1993), p. 61.

SUGGESTED READING

Students seeking further elaboration of the material of this chapter will find the titles by Amt, Boswell, Duby, Hanawalt, Jordan, Landon, and Vauchez especially valuable. For a broad general treatment of cultural change, see the fine work of R. Bartlett, *The Making of Europe: Conquest, Colonization and Cultural Change, 950–1350* (1993).

The student interested in aspects of medieval slavery, serfdom, or the peasantry should begin with M. Bloch, "How Ancient Slavery Came to an End" and "Personal Liberty and Servitude in the Middle Ages, Particularly in France," in *Slavery and Serfdom in the Middle Ages: Selected Essays* (W. R. Beer, trans., 1975) but see also P. Bonnassie, *From Slavery to Feudalism* (1991), and P. Freedman, *The Origins of Peasant Servitude in Medieval Catalonia* (1991). There is an excellent discussion of these problems in the magisterial work of G. Duby, *Rural Economy and Country Life in the Medieval West* (C. Postan, trans., 1968). G. C. Homans, *English Villagers of the Thirteenth Century* (1975) has a good combination of sociological and historical scholarship. E. L. Ladurie, *Montaillou: Cathars and Catholics in a French Village, 1294–1324* (B. Bray, trans., 1978), is a fascinating glimpse of village life. G. Duby, *The Early Growth of the European Economy,* cited in the Notes, is a superb synthesis by a leading authority. Advanced students should see the same author's *The Three Orders: Feudal Society Imagined* (1980), a brilliant but difficult book.

For the religion of the people, in addition to the works by Vauchez and Gurevich cited in the Notes, two studies are recommended: R. and C. Brooke,

Popular Religion in the Middle Ages (1984), a readable synthesis, and T. J. Heffernan, *Sacred Biography: Saints and Their Biographers in the Middle Ages* (1992), a most important study of the goals, assumptions, and audiences of saints' lives, an important and scholarly study. For the development of lay literacy, see M. T. Clanchy, *From Memory to Written Record: England, 1066–1307* (1979).

For the origins and status of the nobility in the High Middle Ages, students are strongly urged to see the studies by Bouchard, Duby, and Freed cited in the Notes. See, in addition, L. Genicot, "The Nobility in Medieval Francia: Continuity, Break, or Evolution?"; A. Borst, "Knighthood in the High Middle Ages: Ideal and Reality"; and two studies by G. Duby, "The Nobility in Eleventh and Twelfth Century Maconnais" and "Northwestern France: The 'Youth' in Twelfth Century Aristocratic Society." All these articles appear in F. L. Cheyette, ed., *Lordship and Community in Medieval Europe: Selected Readings* (1968). C. A. Newman, *The Anglo-Norman Nobility in the Reign of Henry I* (1988) examines the economic, political, and religious network of noble relationships in twelfth century England, while P. R. Coss, *Lordship, Knighthood and Locality. A study in English Society, c. 1180–1280* (1991), also focuses on English social conditions. Social mobility among both aristocracy and peasantry is discussed in T. Evergates, *Feudal Society in the Bailliage of Troyes Under the Counts of Champagne, 1152–1284* (1976). K. F. Bosl, "Kingdom and Principality in Twelfth-Century France," and the same author's "'Noble Unfreedom': The Rise of the Ministerials in Germany," in T. Reuter, ed., *The Medieval Nobility: Studies on the Ruling Classes of France and Germany from the Sixth to the Twelfth Century* (1978), are also useful. The older study of M. Bloch, *Feudal Society* (1966), is now somewhat dated. The career of the man described by contemporaries as "the greatest of knights" is celebrated in G. Duby, *William Marshal: The Flowering of Chivalry* (R. Howard, trans., 1985), a remarkable rags-to-riches story.

There is no dearth of good material on the monks in medieval society. The titles listed in the Suggested Reading for Chapter 7 represent a good starting point for study. B. D. Hill's articles, "Benedictines" and "Cistercian Order," in J. R. Strayer, ed., *Dictionary of the Middle Ages,* vols. 2 and 3 (1982 and 1983), provide broad surveys of the premier monastic orders and contain useful bibliographies. B. Harvey, *Living and Dying in England: The Monastic Experience, 1100–1540* (1993) has valuable material on monastic diet, clothing, routine, sickness, and death. L. J. Lekai, *The Cistercians: Ideals and Reality* (1977), synthesizes research on the white monks and carries their story down to the twentieth century. P. D. Johnson, *Prayer, Patronage, and Power: The Abbey of La Trinité, Vend-*

come, 1032–1187 (1981), examines one important French monastery in its social environment; this book is a valuable contribution to medieval local history. T. Verdon, ed., *Monasticism and the Arts* (1984), is a rich compilation of papers on various aspects of monastic culture, some of them written by leading scholars. B. P. McGuire, *Friendship and Community: The Monastic Experience, 350–1250* (1988) explores monastic friendships within the context of religious communities. Both W. Braunfels, *Monasteries of Western Europe: The Architecture of the Orders* (1972), and C. Brooke, *The Monastic World* (1974), have splendid illustrations and good bibliographies. The best study of medieval English Cistercian architecture is P. Fergusson, *Architecture of Solitude: Cistercian Abbeys in Twelfth Century England* (1984).

For women and children, in addition to the titles by Labarge and Boswell cited in the Notes, see Hanawalt, *Growing Up in Medieval London: The Experience of Childhood in History* (1993), which has exciting material on class and gender, apprenticeship, and the culture of matrimony; D. Herlihy, *Medieval Households* (1985), which treats marriage patterns, family size, sexual relations, and emotional life; and C. Brooke, *The Medieval Idea of Marriage* (1991), which draws on a wide variety of evidence to answer his question, "What is marriage and what sets it apart from other human relationships?" J. M. Bennett, *Women in the Medieval English Countryside* (1987) is an important and pioneering study of women in rural, preindustrial society. Also useful are A. Macfarlane, *Marriage and Love in England, 1300–1840* (1987); J. McNamara and S. F. Wemple, "Sanctity and Power: The Dual Pursuit of Medieval Women," in R. Bridenthal and C. Koonz, eds., *Becoming Visible: Women in European History* (1987); B. Hanawalt, ed., *Women and Work in Preindustrial Europe* (1986), which describes the activities of women as ale-wives, midwives, businesswomen, nurses, and servants; and D. Baker, ed., *Medieval Women* (1978), which contains articles on many facets of women's history.

For further treatment of nuns, see, in addition to the titles by Lekai and Brooke cited earlier, B. Newman, *Sister of Wisdom: St. Hildegard's Theology of the Feminine* (1987), a learned and lucidly written study; S. Elkins, *Holy Women in Twelfth-Century England* (1985); C. Bynum, *Jesus as Mother: Studies in the Spirituality of the High Middle Ages* (1984), which contains valuable articles on facets of women's religious history and an excellent contrast of the differing spirituality of monks and nuns; and C. Bynum's *Holy Feast and Holy Fast* (1987), which treats the significance of food for nuns and others in medieval society. For health and medical care, B. Rowland, *Medieval Woman's Guide to Health* (1981), makes very interesting reading.

A Medieval Noblewoman

In 1115 Guibert (c. 1064?–1124), descendent of a noble family and abbot of Noyon in Picardy, wrote an autobiography, one of the rare examples in the Middle Ages of this literary genre. Cast in the form of a prayer to God, like St. Augustine's Confessions *on which it was modeled, Guibert's autobiography includes a sketch of his mother's life. Guibert deeply loved his mother, was dependent on her, and seems to have concentrated on her virtues. He thus gives us an informed, if perhaps idealized, picture of a twelfth-century French noblewoman.*

First and above all, therefore, I render thanks to Thee for that Thou didst bestow on me a mother fair, yet chaste, modest and most devout. . . .

Almost the whole of Good Friday had my mother passed in excessive pain of travail. . . . Racked, therefore, by pains long-endured, and her tortures increasing as her hour drew near, when she thought I had at last in a natural course come to the birth, instead I was returned within the womb. By this time my father, friends, and kinsfolk were crushed with dismal sorrowing for both of us, for whilst the child was hastening the death of the mother, and she her child's in denying him deliverance, all had reason for compassion. . . . So they ask[ed] counsel in their need and [fled] for help to the altar of the Lady Mary, and to her . . . this vow was made and in the place of an offering this gift laid upon the Gracious Lady's altar: that should a male child come to the birth, he should be given up to the service of God and of herself in the ministry, but if one of the weaker sex, she should be handed over to the corresponding calling. At once was born a weak little being, almost an abortion, and at that timely birth there was rejoicing only for my mother's deliverance, the child

being such as miserable object. . . . On that same day . . . I was put into the cleansing water [baptized, for fear of death]. . . .

Once I had been beaten in school—the school being no other than the dining-hall in our house, for he had given up the charge of others to take me alone, my mother having wisely required him to do this for a higher emolument and a better position. When, therefore, at a certain hour in the evening, my studies, such as they were, had come to an end, I went to my mother's knees after a more severe beating than I had deserved. And when she, as she was wont, began to ask me repeatedly whether I had been whipped that day, I, not to appear a tell-tale, entirely denied it. Then she, whether I liked it or not, threw off the inner garments which they call a vest or shirt, and saw my little arms blackened and the skin of my back everywhere puffed up with the cuts from the twigs. And being grieved to the heart by the very savage punishment inflicted on my tender body, troubled, agitated and weeping with sorrow, she said: "You shall never become a clerk, nor any more suffer so much to get learning." At that I, looking at her with what reproach I could, replied: "If I had to die on the spot, I would not give up learning my book and becoming a clerk." Now she had promised that if I wished to become a knight, when reached the age for it, she would give me the arms and equipment.

She, when hardly of marriageable age, was given to my father, a mere youth, by provision of my grandfather. . . . Now it so happened that at the very beginning of that lawful union conjugal intercourse was made ineffective through the bewitchments of certain persons. For it was said that their marriage drew upon them the envy of a step-mother, who, having nieces of great beauty and nobility, was plotting to entangle one of them with my father. Meeting with no success in her designs, she is said to have used magical arts to prevent entirely the consummation of the marriage. His wife's virginity thus remaining intact for three years, during which he endured his great misfortune in silence, at last, driven to it by his kinsfolk, my father was the first to reveal the facts. Imagine how my kinsmen tried hard in every way to bring about a divorce, and their constant pressure upon my father, young and raw, to become a monk. . . . This, however, was not done for his soul's good, but with the purpose of getting possession of his property. But when their suggestion produced no effect, they began to hound the girl herself, far away as she was from her kinsfolk and harassed by the violence of strangers, into voluntary flight out of sheer exhaustion under their insults, and without waiting for divorce. Meanwhile she endured all this, bearing with calmness the abuse that was aimed at her, and, if out of this rose any strife, pretending ignorance of it. Besides certain rich men perceiving that she was not in fact a wife, began to assail the heart of the young girl; but Thou, O lord, the builder of inward chastity, didst inspire her with purity stronger than her nature or her youth. . . .

In plainness of living there was nothing that she could do, for her delicacy and her sumptuous rearing did not admit of a meagre diet. In other matters no one knew what self-denial she practised. With these eyes I have seen and made certain by touch that whereas over all she wore garments of rich material, next to her skin she was covered with the roughest haircloth, which she wore not only in the daytime, but, what was a great hardship for a delicate body, she even slept in it at night.

The night offices she hardly ever missed, being as regular at the services attended by all God's people in holy seasons; in such fashion that scarcely ever in her house was there rest from the singing of God's praises by her chaplains. . . . A few years before her death she conceived a strong desire to take the sacred veil. When I tried to dissuade her, putting forward as authority the passage where it is written, "Let no prelate attempt to veil widows," saying that her most chaste life would be sufficient without the external veil . . . yet so much more was she inflamed and by no

◆ Medieval noblewoman at work, from a 15th-century manuscript. *(Source: British Library)*

reasoning could be driven from her resolve. So she prevailed, and when taking the veil in the presence of John, the Abbot of that place, gave satisfactory reasons for this act, and in the end she proved that . . . her consecration was invited by signs from heaven.

Questions for Analysis

1. What values shaped Guibert's representation of his mother?

2. How did her marriage come about, and how would you describe her married life?

3. What is the value of this picture of a noblelady for a present-day historian?

Sources: C. C. Swinton Bland, trans., *The Autobiography of Guibert of Nogentsous-Coucy* (New York: 1925), E. Amt, ed., *Women's Lives in Medieval Europe* (New York: Routledge, 1993), pp. 142–149.

11

The Creativity and Vitality of the High Middle Ages

The cathedral towers over the rooftops of the medieval city of Strasbourg. *(Source: Jean Dieuzaide, Toulouse)*

✠ The High Middle Ages witnessed some of the most remarkable achievements in the entire history of Western society. Europeans displayed tremendous creativity and vitality in many facets of culture. Political rulers tried to establish contact with all their peoples, developed new legal and financial institutions, and slowly consolidated power in the hands of the monarchy. The kings of France and England succeeded in laying the foundations of modern national states. The European economy underwent a remarkable recovery, as evidenced by the growth and development of towns and the revival of long-distance trade. Some towns and urbanized areas saw the growth of heretical movements. The university, a uniquely Western contribution to civilization and a superb expression of medieval creativity, came into being at the same time. The Gothic cathedral manifested medieval people's deep Christian faith and their appreciation for the worlds of nature, humanity, and God.

- How did medieval rulers in England, France, and Germany work to solve their problems of government, thereby laying the foundations of the modern state?
- How did medieval towns originate, and how do they reveal the beginnings of radical change in medieval society?
- Why did towns become the center of religious heresy, and what was the church's response?
- How did universities evolve, and what needs of medieval society did they serve?
- What do the Gothic cathedral and troubadour poetry reveal about the ideals, attitudes, and interests of medieval people?

327

This chapter will focus on these questions.

MEDIEVAL ORIGINS OF THE MODERN STATE

Rome's great legacy to Western civilization had been the concepts of the state and the law; but for almost five hundred years after the disintegration of the Roman Empire in the West, the state as a reality did not exist. Political authority was completely decentralized. Power was spread among many feudal lords, who gave their localities such protection and security as their strength allowed. The fiefdoms, kingdoms, and territories that covered the continent of Europe did not have the characteristics or provide the services of a modern state. They did not have jurisdiction over many people, and their laws affected a relative few. In the mid-eleventh century, there existed many frequently overlapping layers of authority—earls, counts, barons, knights—between a king and the ordinary people.

In these circumstances, medieval rulers had common goals. The rulers of England, France, and Germany wanted to strengthen and extend royal authority within their territories. They wanted to establish an effective means of communication with all peoples, in order to increase public order. They wanted more revenue and efficient bureaucracies. The solutions they found to these problems laid the foundations for modern national states.

The modern state is an organized territory with definite geographical boundaries that are recognized by other states. It has a body of law and institutions of government. If the state claims to govern according to law, it is guided in its actions by the law. The modern national state counts on the loyalty of its citizens, or at least of a majority of them. In return, it provides order so that citizens can go about their daily work and other activities. It protects its citizens in their persons and property. The state tries to prevent violence and to apprehend and punish those who commit it. It supplies a currency or medium of exchange that permits financial and commercial transactions. The state conducts relations with foreign governments. In order to accomplish even these minimal functions, the state must have officials, bureaucracies, laws, courts of law, soldiers, information, and money. States with these attributes are relatively recent developments.

Unification and Communication

Political developments in England, France, and Germany provide good examples of the beginnings of the national state in the High Middle Ages. Under the pressure of the Danish (or Viking) invasions of the ninth and tenth centuries, the seven kingdoms of Anglo-Saxon England united under one king (see page 270). At the same time, for reasons historians still cannot fully explain, England was divided into local units called "shires," or counties, each under the jurisdiction of a sheriff appointed by the king. The Danish king Canute (r. 1016–1035) and his successor, Edward the Confessor (r. 1042–1066), exercised broader authority than any contemporary ruler on the Continent. All the English *thegns,* or local chieftains, recognized the central authority of the kingship. The kingdom of England, therefore, had a political head start on the rest of Europe.

When Edward the Confessor died, his cousin Duke William of Normandy—known in English history as William the Conqueror—claimed the English throne and in 1066 defeated the Anglo-Saxon claimant on the battlefield of Hastings. As William subdued the rest of the country, he distributed lands to his Norman followers and assigned specific military quotas to each estate. He also required all feudal lords to swear an oath of allegiance to him as king.

William the Conqueror (r. 1066–1087) preserved the Anglo-Saxon institution of sheriffs representing the king at the local level but replaced Anglo-Saxon sheriffs with Normans. A sheriff had heavy duties. He maintained order in the shire. He caught criminals and had them tried in the hundred court, over which his deputy, the undersheriff, presided. He collected taxes and, when the king ordered him to do so, raised an army of foot soldiers. The sheriff also organized adult males in groups of ten, with each member liable for the good behavior of the others. The Conqueror thus made local people responsible for order in their communities. For all his efforts, the sheriff received no pay. This system, whereby unpaid officials governed the county, served as the basic pattern of English local government for many centuries. It cost the Crown nothing, but it restricted opportunities for public service to the well-to-do.

William also retained another Anglo-Saxon device, the *writ.* This brief administrative order, written in the vernacular (Anglo-Saxon) by a govern-

❖ **The Bayeux Tapestry** Measuring 231 feet by 19 1/2 inches, the Bayeux Tapestry gives a narrative description of the events surrounding the Norman Conquest of England. The tapestry provides an important historical source for the clothing, armor, and lifestyles of the Norman and Anglo-Saxon warrior class. *(Source: Tapisserie de Bayeux et avec autorisation spéciale de la Ville de Bayeux)*

ment clerk, was the means by which the central government communicated with people at the local level. Sheriffs were empowered to issue writs relating to matters in their counties.

The Conqueror introduced into England a major innovation, the Norman inquest. At his Christmas court in 1085, William discussed the state of the kingdom with his vassals and decided to conduct a systematic investigation of the entire country. The survey was to be made by means of *inquests,* or general inquiries, held throughout England. William wanted to determine how much wealth there was in his new kingdom, who held what land, and what lands had been disputed among his vassals since the conquest of 1066. Groups of royal officials or judges were sent to every part of the country. In every village and farm, the priest and six local people were put under oath to answer the questions of the king's commissioners truthfully. In the words of a contemporary chronicler:

He sent his men over all England into every shire and had them find out how many hundred hides there were
in the shire [a hide was a measure of land large enough to support one family], or what land and cattle the king himself had, or what dues he ought to have in twelve months from the shire. Also . . . what or how much everybody had who was occupying land in England, in land or cattle, and how much money it was worth. So very narrowly did he have it investigated, that there was no single hide nor yard of land, nor indeed . . . one ox nor one cow nor one pig was there left out, and not put down in his record: and all these records were brought to him afterwards.[1]

The resulting record, called *Domesday Book* from the Anglo-Saxon word *doom* meaning "judgment," still survives. It is an invaluable source of social and economic information about medieval England (Map 11.1).

The Conqueror's scribes compiled *Domesday Book* in less than a year. *Domesday Book,* a unique document, provided William and his descendants with information vital for the exploitation and government of the country. Knowing the amount of wealth every area possessed, the king could tax accordingly. Knowing the amount of land his vas-

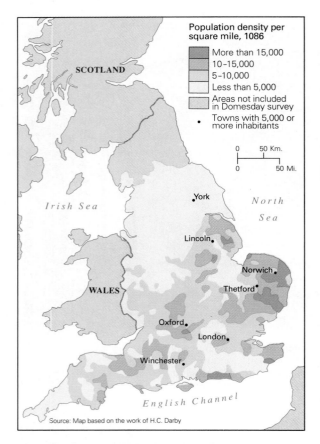
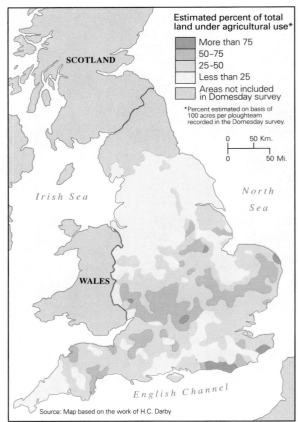

❖ **MAP 11.1 Domesday Population and Agriculture, 1086** The incomparably
rich evidence of *Domesday Book* enables modern demographers and historians to
calculate the English population and land under cultivation in the eleventh century.

sals had, he could allot knight service fairly. The
inclusion of material covering England helped
English kings to regard their country as one unit.

In 1128 the Conqueror's granddaughter Matilda was married to Geoffrey of Anjou. Their son,
who became Henry II of England and inaugurated
the Angevin (from Anjou, his father's county) dynasty, inherited the French provinces of Normandy,
Anjou, Maine, and Touraine in northwestern
France. When Henry married the great heiress
Eleanor of Aquitaine in 1152, he claimed lordships
over Aquitaine, Poitou, and Gascony in southwestern France. The territory some scholars call the
"Angevin empire" included most of the British
Isles and half of France (Map 11.2). The histories
of England and France in the High Middle Ages
were thus closely intertwined.

In the early twelfth century, France consisted of
a number of virtually independent provinces. Each

was governed by its local ruler; each had its own
laws and customs; each had its own coinage; each
had its own dialect. Unlike the king of England,
the king of France had jurisdiction over a very
small area. Chroniclers called King Louis VI
(r. 1108–1137) *roi de Saint-Denis,* king of Saint-
Denis, because the territory he controlled was limited to Paris and the Saint-Denis area surrounding
the city. This region, called the *Île-de-France,* or
royal domain, became the nucleus of the French
state. The clear goal of the medieval French king
was to increase the royal domain and extend his
authority (see Map 11.2).

The term *Saint-Denis* had political and religious
charisma, which the Crown exploited. Following
the precedent of the Frankish chieftain Clovis (see
page 217), Louis VI and his Capetian successors
strongly supported and identified with the cult of
Saint Denis, a deeply revered saint whom the

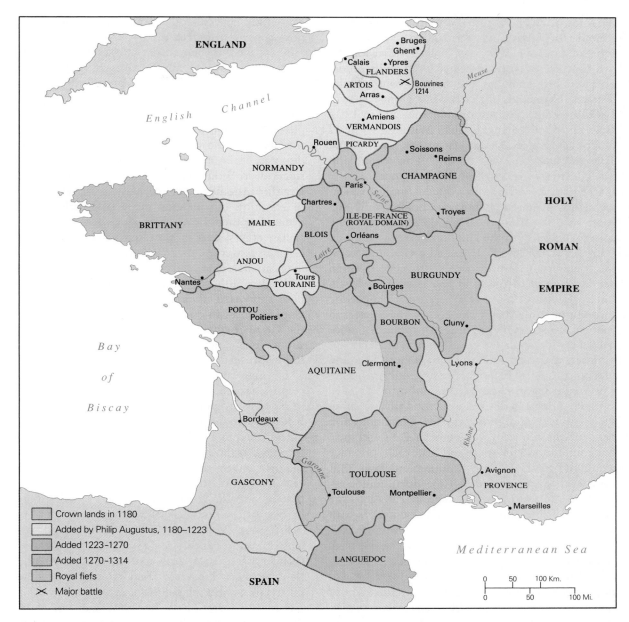

❖ **MAP 11.2 The Growth of the Kingdom of France** Some scholars believe that
Philip II received the title "Augustus" (from a Latin word meaning "to increase")
because he vastly expanded the territories of the kingdom of France.

French believed protected the country from danger. Under Saint Denis's banner, the oriflamme,
French kings fought their battles and claimed their
victories. The oriflamme rested in the abbey of
Saint-Denis, which was richly endowed by the
Crown and served as the burial place of the French
kings. The Capetian kings identified themselves
with the cult of Saint Denis in order to tap "popu-

lar" devotion to him and tie that devotion and
loyalty to the monarchy.[2]

The work of unifying France began under Louis
VI's grandson Philip II (r. 1180–1223). Rigord,
Philip's biographer, gave him the title "Augustus"
(from a Latin word meaning "to increase") because he vastly enlarged the territory of the kingdom of France. By defeating a baronial plot against

the Crown, Philip Augustus acquired the northern counties of Artois and Vermandois. When King John of England, who was Philip's vassal for the rich province of Normandy, defaulted on his feudal obligation to come to the French court, Philip declared Normandy forfeit to the French crown. He enforced his declaration militarily, and in 1204 Normandy fell to the French. Within two years Philip also gained the farmlands of Maine, Touraine, and Anjou. By the end of his reign Philip was effectively master of northern France.

In the thirteenth century, Philip Augustus's descendants acquired important holdings in the south. Louis VIII (r. 1223–1226) added the county of Poitou to the kingdom of France by war. Louis IX (r. 1226–1270) gained a vital interest in the Mediterranean province of Provence through his marriage to Margaret of Provence. Louis's son Philip III (r. 1270–1285) secured Languedoc through inheritance. By the end of the thirteenth century, most of the provinces of modern France had been added to the royal domain through diplomacy, marriage, war, and inheritance. The king of France was stronger than any group of nobles who might try to challenge his authority.

Philip Augustus devised a method of governing the provinces and providing for communication between the central government in Paris and local communities. Philip decided that each province would retain its own institutions and laws. But royal agents, called *baillis* in the north and *seneschals* in the south, were sent from Paris into the provinces as the king's official representatives with authority to act for him. Often middle-class lawyers, these men possessed full judicial, financial, and military jurisdiction in their districts. The baillis and seneschals were appointed by, paid by, and responsible to the king. Unlike the English sheriffs, they were never natives of the provinces to which they were assigned, and they could not own land there. This policy reflected the fundamental principle of French administration that royal interests superseded local interests.

The political problems of Germany differed considerably from those of France and England. The eleventh-century investiture controversy between the German emperor and the Roman papacy had left Germany shattered and divided (see pages 279–280). In the twelfth and thirteenth centuries, Germany was split into hundreds of independent provinces, principalities, bishoprics, duchies, and free cities. Princes, dukes, and local rulers held power over small areas.

There were several barriers to the development of a central government. The German rulers lacked a strong royal domain, like that of the French kings, to use as a source of revenue and a base from which to expand royal power. No accepted principle of succession to the throne existed; as a result, the death of the emperor was often followed by disputes, civil war, and anarchy. Moreover, German rulers were continually attracted south by the wealth of the northern Italian cities or by dreams of restoring the imperial glory of Charlemagne. Time after time the German kings got involved in Italian affairs, and in turn the papacy, fearful of German power in northern Italy, interfered in German affairs. German princes took bribes from whichever authority—the emperor or the pope—best supported their own particular ambitions. Consequently, in contrast to France and England, the German empire witnessed little royal centralization; in medieval Germany power remained in the hands of the numerous princes.

Through most of the first half of the twelfth century, civil war wracked Germany as the emperors tried to strengthen their position by playing off baronial factions against one another. When Conrad III died in 1152, the resulting anarchy was so terrible that the *electors*—the seven princes responsible for choosing the emperor—decided that the only alternative to continued chaos was the selection of a strong ruler. They chose Frederick Barbarossa of the house of Hohenstaufen.

Frederick Barbarossa (r. 1152–1190) tried valiantly to unify the empire. Just as the French rulers branched out from their compact domain in the Île-de-France, Frederick tried to use his family duchy of Swabia in southwestern Germany as a power base (Map 11.3). Just as William the Conqueror had done, Frederick required all vassals in Swabia to take an oath of allegiance to him as emperor, no matter who their immediate lord might be. He appointed ministerials (see page 307) to exercise the full imperial authority over administrative districts of Swabia. Ministerials linked the emperor and local communities.

❖ **MAP 11.3 The Holy Roman Empire, ca 1200** Frederick Barbarossa tried to use the feudal bond to tie the different provinces to the imperial monarchy.

Lübeck
HOLSTEIN
POMERANIA
Bremen
BRANDENBURG
FRISIA
SAXONY
Brandenburg
POLAND
Goslar
LUSATIA
LOWER
LORRAINE
Cologne
THURINGIA
MEISSEN
Aix-la-Chapelle
Prague
FRANCONIA
BOHEMIA
Mainz
Trier
MORAVIA
Worms
Verdun
UPPER
LORRAINE
Toul
Augsburg
BAVARIA
AUSTRIA
Salzburg
FRANCE
SWABIA
STYRIA
Besançon
CARINTHIA
HUNGARY
CARNIOLA
BURGUNDY-
ARLES
VERONA
Legnano 1176
Venice
LOMBARDY
Milan
Pavia
Roncaglia
REPUBLIC OF VENICE
Avignon
Arles
Florence
Marseilles
PAPAL
STATES
TUSCANY
CORSICA
Rome
Capua
APULIA
Naples
Salerno
SARDINIA
KINGDOM OF SICILY
Messina
✕ Major battle
Palermo
Holy Roman Empire, ca 1200
Kingdom of Sicily
SICILY
Republic of Venice

0 100 200 300 Km.
0 100 200 300 Mi.

Outside of Swabia, Frederick tried to make feudalism work as a system of government. Throughout the empire princes exercised tremendous power, and Frederick tried to subordinate them to the authority of the royal government. He made alliances with the great lay princes in which they acknowledged that their lands were fiefs of the emperor, and he in turn recognized their military and political jurisdiction over their territories. Frederick also compelled the great churchmen to become his vassals, so that when they died he could control their estates. Frederick solved the problem of chronic violence by making the princes responsible for the establishment of peace within their territories. In 1158 he forbade private warfare and ordered severe penalties for violations of the peace.

❖ **Frederick Barbarossa** A thirteenth-century chronicler portrayed the German emperor in classical Roman garb, but with the sign of the Crusader on his chest and shield. His left hand holds an orb, symbol of his (theoretically) universal sovereignty, while a tonsured monk holds up the scriptures. *(Source: Biblioteca Apostolica Vaticana)*

Unfortunately, Frederick Barbarossa did not concentrate his efforts and resources in one area. He, too, became embroiled in the affairs of Italy. He, too, wanted to restore the Holy Roman Empire, joining Germany and Italy. In the eleventh and twelfth centuries, the northern Italian cities had grown rich on trade, and Frederick believed that if he could gain the imperial crown, he could cash in on Italian wealth. Frederick saw that, although the Italian cities were populous and militarily strong, they lacked stable governments and were often involved in struggles with one another.

Between 1154 and 1188, Frederick made six expeditions into Italy. His scorched-earth policy was successful at first, making for significant conquests in the north. The brutality of his methods, however, provoked revolts, and the Italian cities formed an alliance with the papacy. In 1176 Frederick suffered a defeat at Legnano (see Map 11.3). This battle marked the first time a feudal cavalry of armed knights was decisively defeated by bourgeois infantrymen. Frederick was forced to recognize the municipal autonomy of the northern Italian cities. Germany and Italy remained separate and followed separate courses of development.

Frederick Barbarossa's Italian ventures contributed nothing to the unification of the German states. Because the empire lacked a stable bureaucratic system of government, his presence was essential for the maintenance of peace. In Frederick's absences, the fires of independence and disorder spread. The princes and magnates consolidated their power, and the unsupervised royal ministerials gained considerable independence. By 1187 Frederick had to accept again the reality of private warfare. The power of the princes cost the growth of a centralized monarchy.

Finance

As medieval rulers expanded territories and extended authority, they required more officials, larger armies, and more money. Officials and armies had to be paid, and kings had to find ways to raise revenue.

In England, William the Conqueror's son Henry I (r. 1100–1135) established a bureau of finance called the "Exchequer" (for the checkered cloth at which his officials collected and audited royal accounts). Henry's income came from a variety of sources: from taxes paid by peasants living on the king's estates; from the *Danegeld,* an old tax originally levied to pay tribute to the Danes; from the *dona,* an annual gift from the church; from money paid to the Crown for settling disputes; and from fines paid by people found guilty of crimes. Henry also received income because of his position as feudal lord. If, for example, one of his vassals died and the son wished to inherit the father's properties, the heir had to pay Henry a tax called *relief.* From the knights Henry took *scutage,* money paid in lieu of the performance of military service. With the scutage collected, Henry could hire mercenary troops. The sheriff in each county was responsible for collecting all these sums and paying them twice a year to the king's Exchequer. Henry, like other medieval kings, made no distinction between his private income and state revenues.

An accurate record of expenditures and income is needed to ensure a state's solvency. Henry assigned a few of the barons and bishops at his court to keep careful records of the monies paid into and out of the royal treasury. These financial officials, called "barons of the Exchequer," gradually developed a professional organization with its own rules, procedures, and esprit de corps. The Exchequer, which by 1170 sat at Westminster, became the first institution of the governmental bureaucracy of England. Because of its work, an almost-complete series of financial records for England dating back to 1130 survives; after 1154 the series is complete.

The development of royal financial agencies in most continental countries lagged behind the English Exchequer. Twelfth-century French rulers derived their income from their royal estates in the Île-de-France. As Philip Augustus and his successors added provinces to the royal domain, the need for money became increasingly acute. Philip made the baillis and seneschals responsible for collecting taxes in their districts. This income came primarily from fines and confiscations imposed by the courts. Three times a year the baillis and seneschals reported to the king's court with the money they had collected.

In the thirteenth century, French rulers found additional sources of revenue. They acquired some income from the church and some from people living in the towns. Townspeople paid *tallage* or the *taille*—a tax arbitrarily laid by the king. In all parts of the country, feudal vassals owed military service to the king when he called for it. Louis IX converted this military obligation into a cash payment, called "host tallage," and thus increased his

❖ **The Pipe Rolls** Twice yearly English medieval sheriffs appeared before the Barons of the Exchequer to account for the monies they had collected from the royal estates and from fines for civil and criminal offenses. Clerks recorded these revenues and royal expenditures on the pipe rolls whose name derives from the pipelike form of the rolled parchments. A roll exists for 1129–1130, then continuously from 1156 to 1832, representing the largest series of English public records. *(Source: Public Record office, London)*

revenues. Moreover, pervasive anti-semitism allowed Philip Augustus, Louis VIII, and Louis IX to tax their Jewish subjects mercilessly.

Medieval people believed that a good king lived on the income of his own land and taxed only in time of a grave emergency—that is, a just war. Because the church, and not the state, performed

✦ **The Chancellery at Palermo** Reflecting the fact that Vandals, Ostrogoths, Greeks, Muslims, and Normans had left their imprint on Sicily, the imperial court bureaucracy kept official records in Greek, Arabic, and Latin, as this manuscript illustration shows. *(Source: Burgerbibliothek Bern)*

what twentieth-century people call social services, such as education and care of the sick, the aged, and orphaned children, there was no ordinary need for the government to tax. Taxation meant war financing. The French monarchy could not continually justify taxing the people on the grounds of the needs of war. Thus the French kings were slow to develop an efficient bureau of finance. French localism—in contrast to England's early unification—also retarded the growth of a central financial agency. Not until the fourteenth century, as a result of the Hundred Years' War, did a state financial bureau emerge—the Chamber of Accounts.

In the twelfth century, in finance, law, and bureaucratic development, the papal curia represented the most advanced government. The one secular government other than England that developed a financial bureaucracy was the kingdom of Sicily. Sicily is a good example of how strong government could be built on a feudal base by determined rulers.

Like England, Sicily had come under Norman domination. Between 1061 and 1091, a bold Norman knight, Roger de Hauteville, with a small band of mercenaries had defeated the Muslims and Greeks who controlled the island. Like William the Conqueror in England, Roger introduced Norman feudalism in Sicily and made it work as a system of government. Roger distributed scattered fiefs to his followers, so that no vassal had a centralized power base. He took an inquest of royal properties and rights, and he forbade private warfare. Roger adapted his Norman experience to Arabic and Greek governmental practices. Thus he retained the Muslims' main financial agency, the *diwan,* a sophisticated bureau for record keeping.

His son and heir, Count Roger II (r. 1130–1154), continued the process of state building. He subdued the province of Apulia in southern Italy, united it with his Sicilian lands, and had himself crowned king of Sicily. Roger II organized the economy in the interests of the state; for example, the Crown secured a monopoly on the sale of salt and lumber. With the revenues thus acquired, Roger hired mercenary troops. His judiciary welcomed appeals from local communities. The army, the judiciary, and the diwan were staffed by Greeks and Muslims as well as Normans.

Under Frederick II Hohenstaufen (r. 1212–1250), grandson of Roger II, Sicily underwent remarkable development. Frederick, also the grandson and heir of Frederick Barbarossa, was a brilliant legislator and administrator, and he constructed the most advanced bureaucratic state in medieval Europe. The institutions of the kingdom of Sicily were harnessed in the service of the state as represented by the king.

Frederick banned private warfare and placed all castles and towers under royal administration. Frederick also replaced town officials with royal governors. In 1231 he published the *Constitutions of Melfi,* a collection of laws that vastly enhanced royal authority. Both feudal and ecclesiastical courts were subordinated to the king's courts. Each year, royal judges visited all parts of the kingdom, and the supreme court at Capua heard appeals from all lesser courts. Thus churchmen accused of crimes were tried in the royal courts. Royal control of the nobility, of the towns, and of the judicial system added up to great centralization, which required a professional bureaucracy and sound state financing.

In 1224 Frederick founded the University of Naples to train clerks and officials for his bureaucracy. University-educated administrators and lawyers emphasized the stiff principles of Roman law, such as the Justinian maxim that "what pleases the prince has the force of law." Frederick's financial experts regulated agriculture, public works, even business. His customs service supervised all imports and exports, collecting taxes for the Crown on all products, increasing royal revenues. Moreover, Frederick strictly regulated the currency and forbade the export of gold and silver bullion.

Finally, Frederick secured the tacit consent of his people to regular taxation. This was a noteworthy achievement when most people believed that taxes should be levied only in time of grave emergency. Frederick defined emergency broadly. For much of his reign he was involved in a bitter dispute with the papacy. Churchmen hardly considered the emperor's wars with the popes as just, but Frederick's position was so strong that he could ignore criticism and levy taxes.

Frederick's contemporaries called him the "Wonder of the World." He certainly transformed the kingdom of Sicily, creating a state that was in many ways modern. But Frederick was highly ambitious: he wanted to control the entire peninsula of Italy. The popes, fearful of being encircled, waged a long conflict to prevent that. The kingdom of Sicily required constant attention, and Frederick's absences took their toll. Shortly after he died, the unsupervised bureaucracy he had built fell to pieces. The pope, as the feudal overlord of Sicily, called in a French prince to rule.

Frederick showed little interest in Germany. He concentrated his attention on Sicily rather than on the historic Hohenstaufen stronghold in Swabia, and the focus of imperial concerns shifted southward. When he visited the empire, in the expectation of securing German support for his Italian policy, he made sweeping concessions to the princes, bishops, duchies, and free cities. In 1220, for example, he exempted German churchmen from taxation and from the jurisdiction of imperial authorities. In 1231 he gave lay princes the same exemptions and even threw in the right to coin money. Frederick gave away so much that imperial authority was seriously weakened. In the later Middle Ages, lay and ecclesiastical princes held sway in the Holy Roman Empire. The centralizing efforts of Frederick Barbarossa were destroyed by his grandson Frederick II.

Law and Justice

Throughout Europe, the form and application of laws depended on local and provincial custom and practice. In the twelfth and thirteenth centuries, the law was a hodgepodge of Germanic customs, feudal rights, and provincial practices. Kings wanted to blend these elements into a uniform system of rules acceptable and applicable to all their peoples. In France and England, kings successfully contributed to the development of national states through the administration of their laws. Legal developments in continental countries like France were strongly influenced by Roman law, while England slowly built up a unique, unwritten common law.

The French king Louis IX (r. 1226–1270) was famous in his time for his concern for justice. Each French province, even after being made part of the kingdom of France, retained its unique laws and procedures, but Louis IX created a royal judicial system. He established the Parlement of Paris, a kind of supreme court that welcomed appeals from local administrators and from the courts of feudal lords throughout France. By the very act of appealing the decisions of feudal courts to the Parlement of Paris, French people in far-flung provinces were recognizing the superiority of royal justice.

Louis sent royal judges to all parts of the country to check up on the work of the baillis and seneschals and to hear complaints of injustice. He was the first French monarch to publish laws for the entire kingdom. The Parlement of Paris registered (or announced) these laws, which forbade private warfare, judicial duels, gambling, blaspheming, and prostitution. Louis sought to identify justice with the kingship, and gradually royal justice touched all parts of the kingdom.

Under Henry II (r. 1154–1189), England developed and extended a *common law,* a law common

Anointing of Philip II Having sworn to preserve the peace, to forbid iniquity, and to enforce justice and mercy, the young Philip is anointed by his uncle, the archbishop of Reims. The contemporary chronicler, Rigord of Saint-Denis who described the scene, gave Philip the name "Augustus," because he had been born in the month of August and because he had greatly "augmented" the French kingdom. Tradition held that the oil (used at the consecration of all French kings) had originally been sent from heaven to St. Remi for the baptism of Clovis. *(Source: The Walters Art Gallery, Baltimore)*

to and accepted by the entire country. No other country in medieval Europe did so. Henry I had occasionally sent out *circuit judges* (royal officials who traveled a given circuit or district) to hear civil and criminal cases. Henry II made this way of extending royal justice an annual practice. Every year, royal judges left London and set up court in the counties. Wherever the king's judges sat, there sat the king's court. Slowly, the king's court gained jurisdiction over all property disputes and criminal actions.

Henry also improved procedure in criminal justice. In 1166 he instructed the sheriffs to summon local juries to conduct inquests and draw up lists of known or suspected criminals. These lists, sworn to by the juries, were to be presented to the royal judges when they arrived in the community. This accusing jury is the ancestor of the modern grand jury.

An accused person formally charged with a crime did *not* undergo trial by jury. He or she was tried by ordeal. The accused was tied hand and foot and dropped in a lake or river. People believed that water was a pure substance and would reject anything foul or unclean. Thus a person who sank was considered innocent, and a person who floated was considered guilty. Trial by ordeal was a ritual that appealed to the supernatural for judgment. God determined innocence or guilt, and thus a priest had to be present to bless the water.

Henry II and others considered this ancient Germanic method irrational and, since the community decided whether the accused sank or floated, disliked community control of the process. But Henry had no alternative. In 1215 the Fourth Lateran Council of the church forbade the presence of priests at trials by ordeal and thus effectively abolished them. Gradually, in the course of the thirteenth century, the king's judges adopted the practice of calling on twelve people (other than the accusing jury) to consider the question of innocence or guilt. This became the jury of trial, but it was very slowly accepted because medieval people had more confidence in the judgment of God than in that of twelve ordinary people.

One aspect of Henry's judicial reforms encountered stiff resistance from an unexpected source: a friend and former chief adviser whom Henry had made archbishop of Canterbury—Thomas Becket. Henry selected Becket as archbishop in 1162 because he believed he could depend on Becket's support. But when Henry wanted to bring all per-

Limoges Casket The principal city of the Limousin in west central France, Limoges was famous for the superb work of its enamelers and goldsmiths. This casket, or chest, showing Thomas Becket's execution (lower panel) and burial (upper panel) was used to preserve his relics. The two scenes are done on gilded copper plaques nailed over wood. *(Source: British Rail Pension Fund)*

sons in the kingdom under the jurisdiction of the royal courts, Thomas Becket's opposition led to another dramatic conflict between temporal and spiritual powers.

In the 1160s many literate people accused of crimes claimed "benefit of clergy," even though they were not clerics and often had no intention of being ordained. Benefit of clergy gave the accused the right to be tried in church courts, which meted out mild punishments. A person found guilty in the king's court might suffer mutilation—loss of a hand, foot, castration—or even death. Ecclesiastical punishments tended to be an obligation to say certain prayers or to make a pilgrimage. In 1164 Henry II insisted that everyone, including clerics, be subject to the royal courts. Becket vigorously protested that church law required clerics to be subject to church courts. When he proceeded to excommunicate one of the king's vassals, the issue became more complicated. Because no one was supposed to have any contact with an excommunicated person, it appeared that the church could arbitrarily deprive the king of necessary military forces. The disagreement between Henry II and Becket dragged on for years. The king grew increasingly bitter that his appointment of Becket

had proved to be such a mistake. Late in December 1170, in a fit of rage, Henry expressed the wish that Becket be destroyed. Four knights took the king at his word, went to Canterbury, and killed the archbishop in his cathedral as he was leaving evening services.

What Thomas Becket could not achieve in life, he gained in death. The assassination of an archbishop in his own church during the Christmas season turned public opinion in England and throughout western Europe against the king. Within months, miracles were recorded at Becket's tomb, and in a short time Canterbury Cathedral became a major pilgrimage and tourist site. Henry had to back down. He did public penance for the murder and gave up his attempts to bring clerics under the authority of the royal court.

Henry II's sons Richard I, known as Lion-Heart (r. 1189–1199), and John (r. 1199–1216) lacked their father's interest in the work of government. Richard looked on England as a source of revenue for his military enterprises. Soon after his accession, he departed on crusade to the Holy Land. During his reign he spent only six months in England, and the government was run by ministers trained under Henry II.

Unlike Richard, King John was incompetent as a soldier and unnecessarily suspicious that the barons were plotting against him. His basic problems, however, were financial. King John inherited a heavy debt from his father and brother. The country had paid dearly for Richard's crusading zeal. While returning from the Holy Land, Richard had been captured, and England had paid an enormous ransom to secure his release. Further, during the entire period 1180–1220, England experienced a severe inflation, which drove prices up. In 1204 John lost the rich province of Normandy to Philip Augustus of France and then spent the rest of his reign trying to get it back. To finance that war, he got in deeper and deeper trouble with his barons. John squeezed as much money as possible from his position as feudal lord. He took scutage, and each time increased the amount due. He forced widows to pay exorbitant fines to avoid unwanted marriages. He sold young girls who were his feudal wards to the highest bidder. These actions antagonized the nobility.

John also alienated the church and the English townspeople. He rejected Pope Innocent III's nominee to the see of Canterbury. And he infuriated the burghers of the towns by extorting money from them and threatening to revoke their charters of self-government.

All the money John raised did not bring him success. In July 1214, John's coalition of Flemish, German, and English cavalry suffered a severe defeat at the hands of Philip Augustus of France at Bouvines in Flanders. This battle ended English hopes for the recovery of territories from France and also strengthened the barons' opposition to John. On top of his heavy taxation, his ineptitude as a soldier in a society that idealized military glory was the final straw. Rebellion begun by northern barons eventually grew to involve many of the English nobility, including the archbishop of Canterbury and the earl of Pembroke, the leading ecclesiastical and lay peers. After lengthy negotiations, John met the barons at Runnymede, a meadow along the Thames River. There he was forced to approve and to attach his seal to the treaty called "Magna Carta," which became the cornerstone of English justice and law.

Magna Carta signifies the principle that the king and the government shall be under the law, that everyone—including the king—must obey the law. It defends the interests of widows, orphans, townspeople, free men, and the church. Some clauses contain the germ of the ideas of due process of law and the right to a fair and speedy trial. Every English king in the Middle Ages reissued Magna Carta as evidence of his promise to observe the law. Because it was reissued frequently and because later generations appealed to Magna Carta as a written statement of English liberties, it acquired an almost sacred importance as a guarantee of law and justice.

In the thirteenth century, the judicial precedents set under Henry II slowly evolved into permanent institutions. The king's judges asserted the royal authority and applied the same principles everywhere in the country. English people found the king's justice more rational and evenhanded than the justice meted out in the baronial courts. Respect for the king's law and courts promoted loyalty to the Crown. By the time of Henry's great-grandson Edward I (r. 1272–1307), one law, the common law, operated all over England.

In the later Middle Ages, the English common law developed features that differed strikingly from the system of Roman law operative in continental Europe. The common law relied on precedents: a decision in an important case served as an authority for deciding similar cases. By contrast, continental judges, trained in Roman law, used the fixed legal maxims of the Justinian *Code* (see page 225) to decide their cases. Thus the common-law system evolved according to the changing experience of the people, while the Roman-law tradition tended toward an absolutist approach. In countries influenced by the common law, such as Canada and the United States, the court is open to the public; in countries with Roman-law traditions, such as France and the Latin American nations, courts need not be public. Under the common law, people accused in criminal cases have a right to access to the evidence against them; under the other system, they need not. The common law urges judges to be impartial; in the Roman-law system, judges interfere freely in activities in their courtrooms. Finally, whereas torture is foreign to the common-law tradition, it was once widely used in the Roman legal system.

The extension of law and justice led to a phenomenal amount of legal codification all over Europe. The English judge Henry of Bracton (d. 1268) wrote the *Treatise on the Laws and Customs of England;* the French jurist Philippe de Beaumanoir (1250–1296) produced the *Customs of Beaumanoir;* the German scholar Eike von Repgow compiled the *Sachsenspiegel* (ca 1225); and Pope Gregory IX (1227–1241) published a codification of ecclesiastical law, the *Liber extra,* the main source of canon law until 1917. Legal texts and encyclopedias exalted royal authority, consolidated royal power, and emphasized political and social uniformity. The pressure for social conformity in turn contributed to a rising hostility toward minorities, Jews, and homosexuals.

By the late eleventh century, many towns in western Europe had small Jewish populations. Jews had emigrated in post-Roman times from the large cities of the Mediterranean region to France, the Rhineland, and Britain. During the Carolingian period, Jews had the reputation of being richer and more learned than the semibarbaric peoples among whom they lived. They typically earned their livelihoods in the lesser trades or by lending money at interest, and Jews engaged in trade had to be literate to keep records. The laws of most countries forbade Jews to own land, though they could hold land pledged to them for debts. By the twelfth century, many Jews were usurers: they lent to consumers but primarily to new or growing business enterprises. New towns and underdeveloped areas where cash was scarce welcomed Jewish settlers. Like other business people, the Jews preferred to live near their work; they also settled close to their synagogue or school. Thus originated the Jews' street or quarter or ghetto. Such neighborhoods gradually became legally defined sections where Jews were required to live.

Jews had been generally tolerated and had become important parts of the urban economies through trade and finance. Some Jews had risen to positions of power and prominence. Through the twelfth century, for example, Jews managed the papal household. The later twelfth and entire thirteenth centuries, however, witnessed increasingly ugly anti-Semitism. Why? Present scholarship does not provide completely satisfactory answers, but we have some clues. Shifting agricultural and economic patterns aggravated social tensions. The indebtedness of peasants and nobles to Jews in an increasingly cash-based economy; the xenophobia that accompanied and followed the Crusades; Christian merchants' and financiers' resentment of Jewish business competition; the spread of vicious accusations of ritual murders or sacrileges against Christian property and persons; royal and papal legislation aimed at social conformity—these factors all contributed to rising anti-Semitism. Thus,

from 1180 to 1182, Philip Augustus of France used hostility to Jews as an excuse to imprison them and then to demand heavy ransom for their release. The Fourth Lateran Council of 1215 forbade Jews to hold public office, restricted their financial activities, and required them to wear distinctive clothing. In 1290, Edward I of England capitalized on mercantile and other resentment of Jews to expel them from the country in return for a large parliamentary grant. In 1302, Philip IV of France followed suit by expelling the Jews from his kingdom and confiscating their property. Fear, ignorance, greed, stupidity, and the pressure for social conformity all played a part in the anti-Semitism of the High Middle Ages.

Early Christians, as we have seen (page 208), displayed no special prejudice against homosexuals. While some of the church fathers, such as Saint

❖ **A Jewish Expulsion** Subject to ancient and irrational prejudices and lacking legal rights, Jewish people lived and worked in an area, according to the pleasure of kings and lords. The increasing anti-Semitism of the thirteenth century led to their expulsion from many places. Here an entire family with domestic animals is forced to move. Artists commonly used conical caps to identify Jews. *(Source: Zentralbibliothek Zürich)*

John Chrysostom (347–407), preached against them, a general indifference to homosexual activity prevailed throughout the early Middle Ages. In the early twelfth century, a large homosexual literature circulated. Publicly known homosexuals such as Ralph, archbishop of Tours (1087–1118), and King Richard I of England held high ecclesiastical and political positions.

Beginning in the late twelfth century, however, a profound change occurred in public attitudes toward homosexual behavior. Why did this happen, if prejudice against homosexuals cannot be traced to early Christianity? Scholars have only begun to investigate this question, and the root cause of intolerance rarely yields to easy analysis. In the thirteenth century, a fear of foreigners, especially Muslims, became associated with the crusading movement. Heretics were the most despised minority in an age that stressed religious and social uniformity. The notion spread that both Muslims and heretics, the great foreign and domestic menaces to the security of Christian Europe, were inclined to homosexual relations. Finally, the systematization of law and the rising strength of the state made any religious or sexual distinctiveness increasingly unacceptable. Whatever the precise cause, by 1300 homosexuality became illegal in most of Europe—and the most common penalty for conviction was death.[3] Most of these laws remained on statute books until the twentieth century. Anti-Semitism and hostility to homosexuals reflect a dark and evil side of high medieval culture, not the general creativity and vitality of the period.

❖ ECONOMIC REVIVAL

A salient manifestation of Europe's recovery after the tenth-century disorders and of the vitality of the High Middle Ages was the rise of towns and the development of a new business and commercial class. This development was to lay the foundations for Europe's transformation, centuries later, from a rural agricultural society into an industrial urban society—a change with global implications.

Why did these developments occur when they did? What is known of town life in the High Middle Ages? What relevance did towns have for medieval culture? Part of the answer to at least one of these questions has already been given. Without increased agricultural output, there would not have been an adequate food supply for new town dwellers. Without a rise in population, there would have been no one to people the towns. Without a minimum of peace and political stability, merchants could not have transported and sold goods.

The Rise of Towns

Early medieval society was traditional, agricultural, and rural. The emergence of a new class that was none of these constituted a social revolution. The new class—artisans and merchants—came from the peasantry. They were landless younger sons of large families, driven away by land shortage. Or they were forced by war and famine to seek new possibilities. Or they were unusually enterprising and adventurous, curious and willing to take a chance.

Historians have proposed three basic theories to explain the origins of European towns. Some scholars believe towns began as *boroughs*—that is, as fortifications erected during the ninth-century Viking invasions. According to this view, towns were at first places of defense, into which farmers from the surrounding countryside moved when their area was attacked. Later, merchants were attracted to the fortifications because they had something to sell and wanted to be where customers were. But most residents of early towns made their living by farming outside the town.

Belgian historian Henri Pirenne maintained that towns sprang up when merchants who engaged in long-distance trade gravitated toward attractive or favorable spots, such as a fort. Usually traders settled just outside the walls, in the *faubourgs* or *suburbs*—both of which mean "outside" or "in the shelter of the walls." As their markets prospered and as their number outside the walls grew, the merchants built a new wall around themselves, every century or so. According to Pirenne, a medieval town consisted architecturally of a number of concentric walls, and the chief economic pursuit of its residents was trade and commerce.

A third explanation focuses on the great cathedrals and monasteries, which represented a demand for goods and services. Cathedrals such as Notre Dame in Paris conducted schools, which drew students from far and wide. Consequently, traders and merchants settled near religious establishments to cater to the residents' economic needs. Concentrations of people accumulated, and towns came into being.

All three theories have validity, though none of them explains the origins of *all* medieval towns.

Few towns of the tenth and eleventh centuries were "new" in the sense that American towns and cities were new in the seventeenth and eighteenth centuries, carved out of forest and wilderness. Some medieval towns that had become flourishing centers of trade by the mid-twelfth century had originally been Roman army camps. York in northern England, Bordeaux in west central France, and Cologne in west central Germany are good examples of ancient towns that underwent revitalization in the eleventh century. Some Italian seaport cities, such as Venice, Pisa, and Genoa, had been centers of shipping and commerce in earlier times. Muslim attacks and domestic squabbles had cut their populations and drastically reduced the volume of their trade in the early Middle Ages, but trade with Constantinople and the East had never stopped entirely. The restoration of order and political stability promoted rebirth and new development. Pirenne's interpretation accurately describes the Flemish towns of Ghent, Bruges and Ypres. It does not fit the course of development in the Italian cities or in such centers as London. Nor does the Pirenne thesis take into account the significance of local trade and markets in the growth of towns. Moreover, the twelfth century witnessed the foundation of completely new towns, such as Lübeck, Berlin, and Munich.

Whether evolving from a newly fortified place or an old Roman army camp, from a cathedral site or a river junction or a place where several overland routes met, medieval towns had a few common characteristics. Walls enclosed the town. (The terms *burgher* and *bourgeois* derive from the Old English and Old German words *burg, burgh, borg,* and *borough* for "a walled or fortified place." Thus a burgher or bourgeois was originally a person who lived or worked inside the walls.) The town had a marketplace. It often had a mint for the coining of money and a court to settle disputes.

In each town, many people inhabited a small, cramped area. As population increased, towns

❖ **Hammering Cobblestones** into place on a roadbed made of loose earth, laborers pave the highways leading from the walled city of Bavay in France. Upkeep of the roads and walls were often a town's greatest expenses. *(Source: Bibliothèque royale Albert 1ᵉʳ, Brussels)*

rebuilt their walls, expanding the living space to accommodate growing numbers. Through an archaeological investigation of the amount of land gradually enclosed by walls, historians have gained a rough estimate of medieval town populations. For example, the walled area of the German city of Cologne equaled 100 hectares in the tenth century (1 hectare = 2.471 acres), about 185 hectares in 1106, about 320 in 1180, and 397 hectares in the fourteenth century. In 1180 Cologne's population was at least 32,000; in the mid-fourteenth century, perhaps 40,000.[4] The concentration of the textile industry in the Low Countries brought into being the most populous cluster of cities in western Europe: Ghent with about 56,000 people, Bruges with 27,000, Tournai and Brussels each with perhaps 20,000.[5] Paris, together with Milan, Venice, and Florence, each with about 80,000, led all Europe in population (Map 11.4).

In their backgrounds and abilities, townspeople represented diversity and change. They constituted an entirely new element in medieval society. They fit into none of the traditional categories. Their occupations, their preoccupations, were different from those of the feudal nobility and the laboring peasantry.

The aristocratic nobility glanced down with contempt and derision at the moneygrubbing townspeople but were not above borrowing from them. The rural peasantry peered up with suspicion and fear at the town dwellers. Though some fled to the towns seeking wealth and freedom, what was the point, most farmers wondered, of making money? Only land had real permanence. Nor did the new commercial class make much sense initially to churchmen. The immediate goal of the middle class was obviously not salvation. It was to be a long while before churchmen developed a theological justification for the new class.

Town Liberties

In the words of the Greek poet Alcaeus, "Not houses finely roofed or well built walls, nor canals or dockyards make a city, but men able to use their opportunity."[6] People and opportunity. That is fundamentally what medieval towns meant—concentrations of people and varieties of chances. No matter where groups of traders congregated, they settled on someone's land and had to secure from king or count, abbot or bishop, permission to live and trade. Aristocratic nobles and churchmen were

suspicious of and hostile to the middle class. They soon realized, however, that profits and benefits flowed to them and their territories from the markets set up on their land.

The history of towns in the eleventh through thirteenth centuries consists largely of merchants' efforts to acquire liberties. In the Middle Ages, *liberties* meant special privileges. For the town dweller, liberties included the privilege of living and trading on the lord's land. The most important privilege a medieval townsperson could gain was personal freedom. It gradually developed that an individual who lived in a town for a year and a day, and was accepted by the townspeople, was free of servile obligations and status. More than anything else, perhaps, the liberty of personal freedom that came with residence in a town contributed to the emancipation of the serfs in the High Middle Ages. Liberty meant citizenship, and citizenship in a town implied the right to buy and sell goods there. Unlike foreigners and outsiders of any kind, the full citizen did not have to pay taxes and tolls in the market. Obviously, this increased profits.

In the twelfth and thirteenth centuries, towns fought for, and slowly gained, legal and political rights. Since the tenth century, some English boroughs had held courts with jurisdiction over members of the town in civil and criminal matters. In the twelfth century, such English towns as London and Norwich developed courts that applied a special kind of law, called "law merchant." It dealt with commercial transactions, debt, bankruptcy, proof of sales, and contracts. Law merchant was especially suitable to the needs of the new bourgeoisie. Gradually, towns across Europe acquired the right to hold municipal courts that alone could judge members of the town. In effect, this right gave them judicial independence.[7]

In the acquisition of full rights of self-government, the *merchant guilds* played a large role. Medieval people were long accustomed to communal enterprises. In the late tenth and early eleventh centuries, those who were engaged in foreign trade joined together in merchant guilds; united enterprise provided them greater security and less risk of losses than did individual action. At about the same time, the artisans and craftsmen of particular trades formed their own guilds. Members of the *craft guilds* determined the quality, quantity, and price of the goods produced and the number of apprentices and journeymen affiliated with the guild.

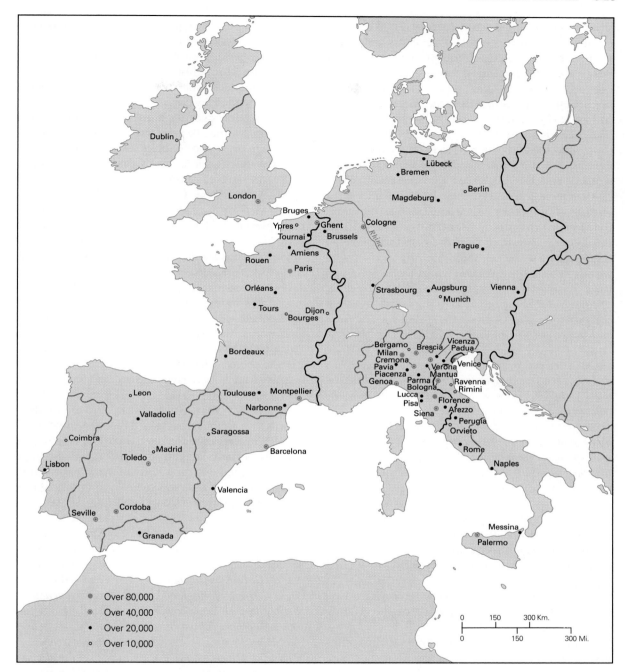

❖ MAP 11.4 Population of European Urban Areas, ca Late Thirteenth Century Though there were scores of urban centers in the thirteenth century, the Italian and Flemish towns had the largest concentrations of people. By modern standards, Paris was Europe's only real city.

Recent research indicates that, by the fifteenth century, women composed the majority of the adult urban population. Many women were heads of households.[8] They engaged in every kind of

urban commercial activity, both as helpmates to their husbands and independently. In many manufacturing trades women predominated, and in some places women were a large percentage of the labor force. In fourteenth-century Frankfurt, for example, about 33 percent of the crafts and trades were entirely female, about 40 percent wholly male, and the remaining crafts roughly divided between the sexes. Craft guilds provided greater opportunity for women than did merchant guilds. In late-twelfth-century Cologne, women and men had equal rights in the turners' guild (the guild for those who made wooden objects on a lathe). Most members of the Paris silk and woolen trades were women, and some achieved the mastership. Widows frequently followed their late husbands' professions, but if they remarried outside the craft, they lost the mastership. Between 1254 and 1271, the chief magistrate of Paris drew up the following regulations for the silk industry: Any woman who wishes to be a silk spinster [woman who spins] on large spindles in the city of Paris—i.e., reeling, spinning, doubling and re-twisting—may freely do so, provided she observe the following customs and usages of the crafts:

No spinster on large spindles may have more than three apprentices, unless they be her own or her husband's children born in true wedlock; nor may she contract with them for an apprenticeship of less than seven years or for a fee of less than 20 Parisian sols to be paid to her, their mistress. . . . If a working woman comes from outside Paris and wishes to practice the said craft in the city, she must swear before the guardians of the craft that she will practice it well and loyally and conform to its customs and usages. . . . No man of this craft who is without a wife may have more than one apprentice; . . . if, however, both husband and wife practice the craft, they may have two apprentices and as many journeymen as they wish.[9]

Guild records show that women received lower wages than men for the same work, on the grounds that they needed less income.

Recent research also demonstrates that women with ready access to cash, such as female innkeepers, alewives, and women in trade, "extended credit on purchases, gave cash advances to good customers or accepted articles on pawn . . . and many widows supplemented their earnings from their late husbands' businesses or homesteads by putting out cash at interest." Likewise, Christian noblewomen, nuns, and Jewish businesswomen participated in money lending. In every part of Europe that Jews lived, Jewish women were active moneylenders: England, Flanders, northern France (where in the thirteenth century Jewish women constituted one-third of all Jewish lenders), the German-speaking parts of Europe, Navarre, Catalonia, and throughout Italy. Loans made by all women tended to be very small (in comparison to those extended by men), for domestic consumption (to "tide over" a household in some emergency, in contrast to productive loans such as those to repair or replace a piece of farm equipment), and for short terms (a few weeks or a month).[10]

By the late eleventh century, especially in the towns of the Low Countries and northern Italy, the leaders of the merchant guilds were quite rich and powerful. They constituted an oligarchy in their towns, controlling economic life and bargaining with kings and lords for political independence. Full rights of self-government included the right to hold a town court, the right to select the mayor and other municipal officials, and the right to tax and collect taxes. Kings often levied on their serfs and unfree townspeople the arbitrary tax, tallage. Such a tax (also known as "customs") called attention to the fact that men were not free. Citizens of a town much preferred to levy and collect their own taxes.

A charter that King Henry II of England granted to the merchants of Lincoln around 1157 nicely illustrates the town's rights. The emphasized passages clearly suggest that the merchant guild had been the governing body in the city for almost a century and that anyone who lived in Lincoln for a year and a day was considered free:

Henry, by the grace of God, etc. . . . Know that I have granted to my citizens of Lincoln all their liberties and customs and laws which they had in the time of Edward [King Edward the Confessor] and William and Henry, kings of England. And I have granted them their gild-merchant, comprising men of the city and other merchants of the shire, as well and freely as they had it in the time of our aforesaid predecessors, . . . And all the men who live within the four divisions of the city and attend the market, shall stand in relation to gelds [taxes] and customs and the assizes [ordinances or laws] of the city as well as ever they stood in the time of Edward, William and Henry, kings of England. I also confirm to them that if anyone has lived in Lincoln for a year and a day without dispute from any claimant, and has paid the customs, and if the citizens can show by the laws and customs of the city that the claimant has remained in England during that period and has made no claim, then let the de-

fendant remain in peace in my city of Lincoln as my citizen, without [having to defend his] right.[11]

Kings and lords were reluctant to grant towns self-government, fearing loss of authority and revenue if they gave the merchant guilds full independence. But the lords discovered that towns attracted increasing numbers of people to an area—people whom the lords could tax. Moreover, when burghers bargained for a town's political independence, they offered sizable amounts of ready cash. Consequently, feudal lords ultimately agreed to self-government.

Town Life

Protective walls surrounded almost all medieval towns and cities. The valuable goods inside a town were too much of a temptation to marauding bands for the town to be without the security of bricks and mortar. Gates pierced the walls, and visitors waited at the gates to gain entrance to the town. When the gates were opened early in the morning, guards inspected the quantity and quality of the goods brought in and collected the customary taxes. Part of the taxes went to the lord on whose land the town stood, part to the town council for civic purposes. Constant repair of the walls was usually the town's greatest expense.

Peasants coming from the countryside and merchants traveling from afar set up their carts as stalls just inside the gates. The result was that the road nearest the gate was the widest thoroughfare. It was the ideal place for a market, because everyone coming in or going out used it. Most streets in a medieval town were marketplaces as much as passages for transit.

Medieval cities served, above all else, as markets. In some respects the entire city was a marketplace. The place where a product was made and sold was also typically the merchant's residence. Usually the ground floor was the scene of production. A window or door opened from the main workroom directly onto the street. The window displayed the finished product, and passersby could look in and see the goods being produced. The merchant's family lived above the business on the second or third floor. As the business and the family expanded, the merchant built additional stories on top of the house.

Because space within the town walls was limited, expansion occurred upward. Second and third sto-

ries were built jutting out over the ground floor and thus over the street. Neighbors on the opposite side did the same. Since the streets were narrow to begin with, houses lacked fresh air and light. Initially, houses were made of wood and thatched with straw. Fire represented a constant danger, and because houses were built so close together, fires spread rapidly. Municipal governments consequently urged construction in stone or brick.

Most medieval cities developed haphazardly. There was little town planning. As the population increased, space became more and more limited. Air and water pollution presented serious problems. Many families raised pigs for household consumption in sties next to the house. Horses and oxen, the chief means of transportation and power, dropped tons of dung on the streets every year. It was universal practice in the early towns to dump household waste, both animal and human, into the road in front of one's house. The stench must have been abominable. In 1298 the burgesses of the town of Boutham in Yorkshire, England, received the following order (one long, vivid sentence):

To the bailiffs of the abbot of St. Mary's York, at Boutham. Whereas it is sufficiently evident that the pavement of the said town of Boutham is so very greatly broken up . . . ., and in addition the air is so corrupted and infected by the pigsties situated in the king's highways and in the lanes of that town and by the swine feeding and frequently wandering about . . . and by dung and dunghills and many other foul things placed in the streets and lanes, that great repugnance overtakes the king's ministers staying in that town and also others there dwelling and passing through, the advantage of more wholesome air is impeded, the state of men is grievously injured, and other unbearable inconveniences . . . ., to the nuisance of the king's ministers aforesaid and of others there dwelling and passing through, and to the peril of their lives . . . : the king, being unwilling longer to tolerate such great and unbearable defects there, orders the bailiffs to cause the pavement to be suitably repaired within their liberty before All Saints next, and to cause the pigsties, aforesaid streets and lanes to be cleansed from all dung . . . and to cause them to be kept thus cleansed hereafter.[12]

A great deal of traffic passed through Boutham in 1298 because of the movement of English troops to battlefronts in Scotland. Conditions there were

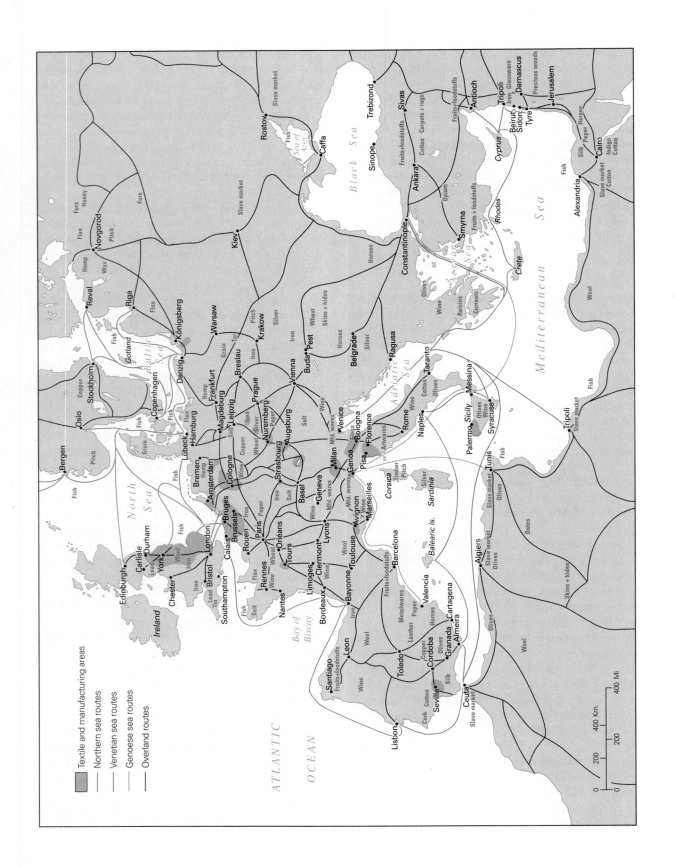

Textile and manufacturing areas

Northern sea routes

Venetian sea routes

Genoese sea routes

Overland routes

ATLANTIC OCEAN

North Sea

Baltic Sea

Black Sea

Sea of Azov

Mediterranean Sea

Adriatic Sea

Aegean Sea

Bay of Biscay

Ireland

Gotland

Cyprus

Crete

Rhodes

Corsica

Sardinia

Balearic Is.

Sicily

Bergen — Fish, Pitch
Oslo — Fish
Edinburgh
Carlisle
Durham
York — Wool, Iron
Chester
Lead
Tin
Bristol — Iron
Southampton — Fish, Salt
London
Calais
Rouen
Nantes
Rennes
Bordeaux
Bayonne
Toulouse
Clermont
Limoges
Tours
Orléans
Paris
Brussels
Bruges
Amsterdam
Bremen
Hamburg
Lübeck
Cologne
Magdeburg
Leipzig
Frankfurt
Nuremberg
Augsburg
Strasbourg
Basel
Geneva
Lyons
Avignon
Marseilles
Barcelona
Valencia
Cartagena
Almeira
Granada
Cordoba
Seville
Ceuta
Lisbon
Santiago
Leon
Toledo

Stockholm — Copper
Copenhagen
Reval
Riga
Königsberg
Danzig
Warsaw
Breslau
Prague
Vienna
Buda
Pest
Krakow
Kiev
Novgorod
Rostov
Caffa
Sinope
Trebizond
Sivas
Ankara
Smyrna
Constantinople
Belgrade
Ragusa
Venice
Milan
Genoa
Pisa
Florence
Bologna
Rome
Naples
Taranto
Messina
Palermo
Syracuse
Tunis
Tripoli
Algiers

Antioch
Tripoli
Beirut
Sidon
Tyre
Damascus
Jerusalem
Cairo
Alexandria

Furs
Honey
Flax
Hemp
Wax
Pitch
Furs
Copper
Fish
Fish
Flax
Flax
Pitch
Tar
Silver
Wheat
Iron
Iron
Silver
Iron
Horses
Horses
Skins + hides
Horses
Silver
Wine
Grain
Hemp
Flax
Fish
Salt
Copper
Wheat
Salt
Iron
Wheat
Silver
Paper
Salt
Wine
Iron
Paper
Wine
Wine
Wool
Wool
Wool
Flax
Wine
Wheat
Iron
Leather
Metalwares
Copper
Olives
Silk
Cork
Cotton
Cotton
Olives
Olives
Olives
Olives
Dates
Skins + hides
Wool
Fruits + foodstuffs
Fruits + foodstuffs
Fruits + foodstuffs
Mfd. wares
Mfd. wares
Glass
Artwares
Wine
Olives
Raisins
Currants
Fruits + foodstuffs
Opium
Cotton
Carpets + rugs
Fruits + foodstuffs
Iron
Glassware
Precious woods
Silk
Paper
Horses
Slave market
Cotton
Indigo
Cotton
Fish
Fish
Timber
Pitch
Silver
Slave market
Olives
Slave market
Slave market
Slave market
Slave market

400 Mi
400 Km.
200
0

probably not typical. Still, this document suggests that space, air pollution, and sanitation problems bedeviled urban people in medieval times, as they do today.

People wanted to get into medieval cities because they represented a means of economic advancement, social mobility, and improvement in legal status. For the adventurous, the ambitious, and the shrewd, cities offered tremendous opportunities (see Listening to the Past).

The Revival of Long-Distance Trade

The eleventh century witnessed a remarkable revival of trade, as artisans and craftsmen manufactured goods for local and foreign consumption (Map 11.5). Most trade centered in towns and was controlled by professional traders. Because long-distance trade was risky and required large investments of capital, it could be practiced only by professionals. The transportation of goods involved serious risks. Shipwrecks were common. Pirates infested the sea lanes, and robbers and thieves roamed virtually all of the land routes. Since the risks were so great, merchants preferred to share them. A group of people would thus pool some of their capital to finance an expedition to a distant place. When the ship or caravan returned and the goods brought back were sold, the investors would share the profits. If disaster struck the caravan, an investor's loss was limited to the amount of that individual's investment.

What goods were exchanged? What towns took the lead in medieval "international" trade? In the late eleventh century, the Italian cities, especially Venice, led the West in trade in general and completely dominated the Oriental market. Ships carried salt from the Venetian lagoon, pepper and other spices from North Africa, and silks and purple textiles from the East to northern and western Europe. In the thirteenth century, Venetian caravans brought slaves from the Crimea and Chinese silks from Mongolia to the West. Lombard and Tuscan merchants exchanged those goods at the town markets and regional fairs of France, Flan-

▲ **MAP 11.5 Trade and Manufacturing in Medieval Europe** Note the number of cities and the sources of silver, iron, copper, lead, paper, wool, carpets and rugs, and slaves.

ders, and England. (Fairs were periodic gatherings that attracted buyers, sellers, and goods from all over Europe.) Flanders controlled the cloth industry. The towns of Bruges, Ghent, and Ypres built up a vast industry in the manufacture of cloth. Italian merchants exchanged their products for Flemish tapestries, fine broadcloth, and various other textiles.

Two circumstances help to explain the lead Venice and the Flemish towns gained in long-distance trade. Both enjoyed a high degree of peace and political stability. Geographical factors were equally, if not more, important. Venice was ideally located at the northwestern end of the Adriatic Sea, with easy access to the transalpine land routes as well as the Adriatic and Mediterranean sea lanes. The markets of North Africa, Byzantium, and Russia and the great fairs of Ghent in Flanders and Champagne in France provided commercial opportunities that Venice quickly seized. The geographical situation of Flanders also offered unusual possibilities. Just across the Channel from England, Flanders had easy access to English wool. Indeed, Flanders and England developed a very close economic relationship.

Sheep had been raised for their wool in England since Roman times. The rocky soil and damp climate of Yorkshire and Lincolnshire, though poorly suited for agriculture, were excellent for sheep farming. Beginning in the early twelfth century, but especially after the arrival of Cistercian monks around 1130, the size of the English flocks doubled and then tripled. Scholars have estimated that, by the end of the twelfth century, roughly six million sheep grazed on the English moors and downs. They produced fifty thousand sacks of wool a year.[13] Originally, a "sack" of wool was the burden one packhorse could carry, an amount eventually fixed at 364 pounds; fifty thousand sacks, then, represented huge production.

Wool was the cornerstone of the English medieval economy. Population growth in the twelfth century and the success of the Flemish and Italian textile industries created foreign demand for English wool. The production of English wool stimulated Flemish manufacturing, and the expansion of the Flemish cloth industry in turn spurred the production of English wool. The availability of raw wool also encouraged the development of domestic cloth manufacture within England. The towns of Lincoln, York, Leicester, Northampton, Winchester, and Exeter became important cloth-producing towns. The port cities of London, Hull, Boston, and Bristol thrived on the wool trade. In the thirteenth century, commercial families in these towns grew fabulously rich.

The Commercial Revolution

A steadily expanding volume of international trade from the late eleventh through the thirteenth centuries was a sign of the great economic surge, but it was not the only one. In cities all across Europe, trading and transportation firms opened branch offices. Credit was widely extended, considerably facilitating exchange. Merchants devised the letter of credit, which made unnecessary the slow and dangerous shipment of coin for payment.

◆ **Hanseatic League Merchants at Hamburg** In the thirteenth century, the merchants of Hamburg and other cities in northern Germany formed an association for the suppression of piracy and the acquisition of commercial privileges in foreign countries. Members of the Hansa traded in furs, fish, wax, and oriental luxury goods. *(Source: Staatsarchiv Hamburg)*

A new capitalistic spirit developed. Professional merchants were always on the lookout for new markets and opportunities. They invested surplus capital in new enterprises. They diversified their interests and got involved in a wide variety of operations. The typical prosperous merchant in the later thirteenth century might well be involved in buying and selling, shipping, lending some capital at interest, and other types of banking. Medieval merchants were fiercely competitive.

Some scholars consider capitalism a modern phenomenon, beginning in the fifteenth or sixteenth century. But in their use of capital to make more money, in their speculative pursuits and willingness to gamble, in their competitive spirit, and in the variety of their interests and operations, medieval businessmen showed traits of capitalists.

The ventures of the German Hanseatic League illustrate these impulses. The Hanseatic League was a mercantile association of towns. Though scholars trace the league's origin to the foundation of the city of Lübeck in 1159, the mutual protection treaty later signed between Lübeck and Hamburg marks the league's actual expansion. Lübeck and Hamburg wanted mutual security, exclusive trading rights, and, where possible, a monopoly. During the next century, perhaps two hundred cities from Holland to Poland, including Cologne, Brunswick, Dortmund, Danzig, and Riga, joined the league, but Lübeck always remained the dominant member. From the thirteenth to the sixteenth century, the Hanseatic League controlled trade over an axis of Novgorod-Reval-Lübeck-Hamburg-Bruges-London, that is, the trade of northern Europe (see Map 11.5). In the fourteenth century, the Hanseatics branched out into southern Germany and Italy by land and into French, Spanish, and Portuguese ports by sea.

Across regular, well-defined trade routes along the Baltic and North seas, the ships of league cities carried furs, wax, copper, fish, grain, timber, and wine. These goods were exchanged for finished products, mainly cloth and salt, from Western cities. At cities such as Bruges and London, Hanseatic merchants secured special trading concessions exempting them from all tolls and allowing them to trade at local fairs. Hanseatic merchants established foreign trading centers, called "factories," the most famous of which was the London Steelyard, a walled community with warehouses, offices, a church, and residential quarters for company representatives.[14]

By the late thirteenth century, Hanseatic merchants had developed an important business technique, the business register. Merchants publicly recorded their debts and contracts and received a league guarantee for them. This device proved a decisive factor in the later development of credit and commerce in northern Europe.[15] These activities required capital, risk-taking, and aggressive pursuit of opportunities—the essential ingredients of capitalism. They also yielded fat profits.

These developments added up to what one modern scholar has called "a commercial revolution, . . . probably the greatest turning point in the history of our civilization."[16] This is not a wildly extravagant statement. In the long run, the commercial revolution of the High Middle Ages brought about radical change in European society. One remarkable aspect of this change is that the commercial classes constituted a small part of the total population—never more than 10 percent. They exercised an influence far in excess of their numbers.

The commercial revolution created a great deal of new wealth. Wealth meant a higher standard of living. The new availability of something as simple as spices, for example, allowed for variety in food. Dietary habits gradually changed. Tastes became more sophisticated. Contact with Eastern civilizations introduced Europeans to eating utensils and table manners improved. Nobles learned to eat with forks and knives, instead of tearing the meat from a roast with their hands. They began to use napkins, instead of wiping their greasy fingers on the dogs lying under the table.

The existence of wealth did not escape the attention of kings and other rulers. Wealth could be taxed, and through taxation kings could create strong and centralized states. In the years to come, alliances with the middle classes were to enable kings to defeat feudal powers and aristocratic interests and to build the states that came to be called "modern."

The commercial revolution also provided the opportunity for thousands of serfs to improve their social position. The slow but steady transformation of European society from almost completely rural and isolated to relatively more sophisticated constituted the greatest effect of the commercial revolution that began in the eleventh century.

Even so, merchants and business people did not run medieval communities, except in central and northern Italy and in the county of Flanders. Most towns remained small. The castle, the manorial village, and the monastery dominated the landscape. The feudal nobility and churchmen determined the preponderant social attitudes, values, and patterns of thought and behavior. The commercial changes of the eleventh through thirteenth centuries did, however, lay the economic foundations for the development of urban life and culture.

MEDIEVAL UNIVERSITIES

Just as the first strong secular states emerged in the thirteenth century, so did the first universities. This was no coincidence. The new bureaucratic states and the church needed educated administrators, and universities were a response to this need. The word *university* derives from the Latin *universitas,* meaning "corporation" or "guild." Medieval universities were educational guilds that produced educated and trained individuals. They were also an expression of the tremendous vitality and creativity of the High Middle Ages. Their organization, methods of instruction, and goals continue to influence institutionalized learning in the Western world.

Origins

In the early Middle Ages, anyone who received education got it from a priest. Priests instructed the clever boys on the manor in the Latin words of the Mass and taught them the rudiments of reading and writing. Few boys acquired elementary literacy, however, and peasant girls did not obtain even that. The peasant who wished to send his son to school had to secure the permission of his lord, because the result of formal schooling tended to be a career in the church or some trade. If a young man were to pursue either, he would have to leave the manor and gain free status. Because the lord stood to lose the services of educated peasants, he limited the number of serfs sent to school.

Few schools were available anyway. Society was organized for war and defense and gave slight support to education. By the late eleventh century, however, social conditions had markedly improved. There was greater political stability, and favorable economic conditions had advanced many people beyond the level of bare subsistence. The curious and able felt the lack of schools and teachers.

Since the time of the Carolingian Empire, monasteries and cathedral schools had offered the only formal instruction. The monasteries were geared to religious concerns, and the monastic curriculum consisted of studying the Scriptures and the writings of the church fathers. Monasteries wished to maintain an atmosphere of seclusion and silence and were unwilling to accept large numbers of noisy lay students. In contrast, schools attached to cathedrals and run by the bishop and his clergy were frequently situated in bustling cities, and in the eleventh century in Italian cities like Bologna, wealthy businessmen had established municipal schools. Cities inhabited by peoples of many backgrounds and "nationalities" stimulated the growth and exchange of ideas. In the course of the twelfth century, cathedral schools in France and municipal schools in Italy developed into universities (Map 11.6).

The school at Chartres Cathedral in France became famous for its studies of the Latin classics and for the broad literary interests it fostered in its students. The most famous graduate of Chartres was the Englishman John of Salisbury (d. 1180), who wrote *The Statesman's Book,* an important treatise on the corrupting effects of political power. But Chartres, situated in the center of rich farmland, remote from the currents of commercial traffic and intellectual ideas, did not develop into a university. The first European universities appeared in Italy, at Bologna and Salerno.

The growth of the University of Bologna coincided with a revival of interest in Roman law. The study of Roman law as embodied in the Justinian *Code* had never completely died out in the West, but this sudden burst of interest seems to have been inspired by Irnerius (d. 1125), a great teacher at Bologna. His fame attracted students from all over Europe. Irnerius not only explained the Roman law of the Justinian *Code,* he applied it to difficult practical situations. An important school of civil law was founded at Montpellier in France, but Bologna remained the greatest law school throughout the Middle Ages.

At Salerno, interest in medicine had persisted for centuries. Greek and Muslim physicians there had studied the use of herbs as cures and experimented with surgery. The twelfth century ushered in a new interest in Greek medical texts and in the work of Arab and Greek doctors. Students of medicine poured into Salerno and soon attracted royal attention. In 1140, when King Roger II of Sicily took the practice of medicine under royal control, his ordinance stated:

Who, from now on, wishes to practice medicine, has to present himself before our officials and examiners, in order to pass their judgment. Should he be bold enough to disregard this, he will be punished by imprisonment and confiscation of his entire property. In this way we are taking care that our subjects are not endangered by the inexperience of the physicians.[17]

In the first decades of the twelfth century, students converged on Paris. They crowded into the cathedral school of Notre Dame and spilled over into the area later called the "Latin Quarter"— whose name probably reflects the Italian origin of many of the students attracted to Paris by the surge of interest in the classics, logic, and theology. The cathedral school's international reputation had already drawn to Paris scholars from all over Europe, one of whom was Peter Abelard.

The son of a minor Breton knight, Peter Abelard (1079–1142) studied in Paris, quickly absorbed a large amount of material, and set himself up as a teacher. Abelard was fascinated by logic, which he believed could be used to solve most problems. He had a brilliant mind and, although orthodox in his philosophical teaching, appeared to challenge ecclesiastical authorities. His book *Sic et Non (Yes and No)* was a list of apparently contradictory propositions drawn from the Bible and the writings of the church fathers. One such proposition, for example, stated that sin is pleasing to God and is not pleasing to God. Abelard used a method of systematic doubting in his writing and teaching. As he put it in the preface of *Sic et Non,* "By doubting we come to questioning, and by questioning we perceive the truth." While other scholars merely asserted theological principles, Abelard discussed and analyzed them. Through reasoning he even tried to describe the attributes of the three persons of the Trinity, the central mystery of the Christian faith. Abelard was severely censured by a church council, but his cleverness, boldness, and imagination made him a highly popular figure among students.

❖ **MAP 11.6 Intellectual Centers of Medieval Europe** Universities obviously provided more sophisticated instruction than did monastic and cathedral schools. What other factors distinguish the three kinds of intellectual centers?

SCOTLAND

St. Andrews

Glasgow

North Sea

DENMARK

Copenhagen

Baltic Sea

Uppsala

IRELAND

Durham
Jarrow
Rievaulx
York

ENGLAND

Petersborough
Cambridge
Bury St. Edmunds
Oxford
Canterbury
Salisbury
Winchester

Magdeburg
Berlin

Leipzig

HOLY

Cologne
Louvain
Ypres
Brussels
Amiens
Fulda
Mainz
Prague
Cracow

ROMAN

ATLANTIC OCEAN

Jumièges
Bec
Laon
Reims
Heidelberg
Regensburg
Bamberg

Mont St. Michel
Notre Dame
St.-Denis
Paris
Hirsau
Lorch
Vienna
Savigny
Chartres
Beauvais
Orléans
Fleury
Clairvaux
Munich
Tours
Bourges
Cîteaux
Basel
St.-Gall

EMPIRE

Poitiers
Cluny

FRANCE

Bordeaux
Padua
Cahors
Grenoble
Pavia
Piacenza

Santiago de Compostela
Leon
Toulouse
Montpellier
Avignon
Bologna
Florence
Vallombrosa

Valladolid
Perugia

Coimbra
Salamanca
Avila
SPAIN
Rome
Monte Cassino
Toledo
Naples
Salerno

Valencia

Corsica

Sardinia

Barcelona

Seville

Mediterranean Sea

Palermo

Sicily

◆ University

■ Monastery school

⛫ Cathedral school

0   100   200   300 Km.

0   100   200   300 Mi.

The influx of students eager for learning, together with dedicated and imaginative teachers, created the atmosphere in which universities grew. In northern Europe—at Paris and later at Oxford and Cambridge in England—associations or guilds of professors organized universities. They established the curriculum, set the length of time for study, and determined the form and content of examinations.

Instruction and Curriculum

University faculties grouped themselves according to academic disciplines, called "schools"—law, medicine, arts, and theology. The professors, known as "schoolmen" or "Scholastics," developed a method of thinking, reasoning, and writing in which questions were raised and authorities cited on both sides of the question. The goal of the Scholastic method was to arrive at definitive answers and to provide a rational explanation for what was believed on faith. Schoolmen held that reason and faith constitute two harmonious realms whose truths complement each other.

The Scholastic approach rested on the recovery of classical philosophical texts. Ancient Greek and Arabic texts had entered Europe in the early twelfth century, primarily through Toledo in Muslim Spain. Thirteenth-century philosophers relied on Latin translations of these texts, especially translations of Aristotle, who had stressed direct observation of nature, as well as the principles that theory must follow fact and that knowledge of a thing requires an explanation of its causes. The schoolmen reinterpreted Aristotelian texts in a Christian sense.

In exploration of the natural world, Aristotle's axioms were not precisely followed. Medieval scientists argued from authority, such as the Bible, the Justinian *Code,* or an ancient scientific treatise, rather than from direct observation and experimentation, as modern scientists do. Thus the conclusions of medieval scientists were often wrong. Nevertheless, natural science gradually emerged as a discipline distinct from philosophy. Scholastics made important contributions to the advancement of knowledge. They preserved the Greek and Arabic texts that contained the body of ancient scientific knowledge, which would otherwise have been lost. And, in asking questions about nature and the universe, Scholastics laid the foundations for later scientific work.

Many of the problems that Scholastic philosophers raised dealt with theological issues. For example, they addressed the question that interested all Christians, educated and uneducated: how is a person saved? Saint Augustine's thesis—that, as a result of Adam's fall, human beings have a propensity to sin—had become a central feature of medieval church doctrine. The church taught that it possessed the means to forgive the sinful: grace conveyed through the sacraments. However, although grace provided a predisposition to salvation, the Scholastics held that one must also *decide* to use the grace received. In other words, a person must use his or her reason to advance to God.

Thirteenth-century Scholastics devoted an enormous amount of time to collecting and organizing knowledge on all topics. These collections were published as *summa,* or reference books. There were summa on law, philosophy, vegetation, animal life, and theology. Saint Thomas Aquinas (1225–1274), a professor at Paris, produced the most famous collection, the *Summa Theologica,* which deals with a vast number of theological questions.

Aquinas drew an important distinction between faith and reason. He maintained that, although reason can demonstrate many basic Christian principles such as the existence of God, other fundamental teachings such as the Trinity and original sin cannot be proved by logic. That reason cannot establish them does not, however, mean they are contrary to reason. Rather, people understand such doctrines through revelation embodied in Scripture. Scripture cannot contradict reason, nor reason Scripture:

The light of faith that is freely infused into us does not destroy the light of natural knowledge [reason] implanted in us naturally. For although the natural light of the human mind is insufficient to show us these things made manifest by faith, it is nevertheless impossible that these things which the divine principle gives us by faith are contrary to these implanted in us by nature [reason]. Indeed, were that the case, one or the other would have to be false, and, since both are given to us by God, God would have to be the author of untruth, which is impossible. . . . [I]t is impossible that those things which are of philosophy can be contrary to those things which are of faith.[18]

Aquinas also investigated the branch of philosophy called *epistemology,* which is concerned with how a person knows something. Aquinas stated that one knows, first, through sensory perception of the physical world—seeing, hearing, touching, and so on. He maintained that there can be nothing in the mind that is not first in the senses. Second, knowledge comes through reason, the mind exercising its natural abilities. Aquinas stressed the power of human reason to know, even to know God. Proofs of the existence of God exemplify the Scholastic method of knowing.

Aquinas began with the things of the natural world—earth, air, trees, water, birds. Then he inquired about their original source or cause: the mover, creator, planner who started it all. Everything, Aquinas maintained, has an ultimate and essential explanation, a reason for existing. Here he was following Aristotle. Aquinas went further and identified the reason for existing, or first mover, with God. Thomas Aquinas and all medieval intellectuals held that the end of both faith and reason was the knowledge of, and union with, God. His work later became the fundamental text of Roman Catholic doctrine.

At all universities, the standard method of teaching was the *lecture*—that is, a reading. The professor read a passage from the Bible, the Justinian *Code,* or one of Aristotle's treatises. He then explained and interpreted the passage; his interpretation was called a *gloss*. Students wrote down everything. Texts and glosses were sometimes collected and reproduced as textbooks. For example, the Italian Peter Lombard (d. 1160), a professor at Paris, wrote what became the standard textbook in theology, *Sententiae (The Sentences),* a compilation of basic theological principles.

Because books had to be copied by hand, they were extremely expensive, and few students could afford them. Students therefore depended for study on their own or friends' notes accumulated over a period of years. The choice of subjects was narrow. The syllabus at all universities consisted of a core of ancient texts that all students studied and, if they wanted to get ahead, mastered.

There were no examinations at the end of a series of lectures. Examinations were given after three, four, or five years of study, when the student applied for a degree. The professors determined the amount of material students had to know for each degree, and students frequently insisted that the professors specify precisely what that material was. When the candidate for a degree believed himself prepared, he presented himself to a committee of professors for examination.

Examinations were oral and very difficult. If the candidate passed, he was awarded the first, or bachelor's, degree. Further study, about as long, arduous, and expensive as it is today, enabled the graduate to try for the master's and doctor's degrees. All degrees certified competence in a given subject, and degrees were technically licenses to teach. Most students, however, did not become teachers. They staffed the expanding royal and papal administrations.

✤ GOTHIC ART

Medieval churches stand as the most spectacular manifestations of medieval vitality and creativity. It is difficult for twentieth-century people to appreciate the extraordinary amounts of energy, imagination, and money involved in building them. Between 1180 and 1270 in France alone, eighty cathedrals, about five hundred abbey churches, and tens of thousands of parish churches were constructed. This construction represents a remarkable investment for a country of scarcely eighteen million people. More stone was quarried for churches in medieval France than had been mined in ancient Egypt, where the Great Pyramid alone consumed 40.5 million cubic feet of stone. All these churches displayed a new architectural style. Fifteenth-century critics called the new style "Gothic" because they mistakenly believed the fifth-century Goths had invented it. It actually developed partly in reaction to the earlier "Romanesque" style, which resembled ancient Roman architecture.

Gothic cathedrals were built in towns and reflect both bourgeois wealth and enormous civic pride. The manner in which a society spends its wealth expresses its values. Cathedrals, abbeys, and village churches testify to the deep religious faith and piety of medieval people. If the dominant aspect of medieval culture had not been the Christian faith, the builder's imagination and the merchant's money would have been used in other ways.

From Romanesque Gloom to "Uninterrupted Light"

The relative political stability and increase of ecclesiastical wealth in the eleventh century encouraged the arts of peace. In the ninth and tenth centuries, the Vikings and Magyars had burned hundreds of wooden churches. In the eleventh century, the abbots wanted to rebuild in a more permanent fashion, and after the year 1000, church building increased on a wide scale. Because fireproofing was essential, ceilings had to be made of stone. Therefore, builders replaced wooden roofs with arched stone ceilings called "vaults." The stone ceilings were heavy; only thick walls would support them. Because the walls were so thick, the windows were small, allowing little light into the interior of the church. The basic features of such Romanesque architecture are stone vaults in the ceiling, a rounded arch over the nave (the central part of the

❖ **Interior of La Sainte Chapelle, Paris** The central features of the Gothic style: the pointed arch, ribbed vaulting, and flying buttress made possible the construction of churches higher than ever before and the use of stained glass to replace stone walls. King Louis IX built this church to house the crown of thorns and other relics that he brought back from the crusades. The result is a building of breathtaking beauty, a jewelled reliquary. *(Source: Art Resource, NY)*

church), and thick, heavy walls. In northern Europe, twin bell towers often crowned Romanesque churches, giving them a powerful, fortresslike appearance. Built primarily by monasteries, Romanesque churches reflect the quasi-military, aristocratic, and pre-urban society that built them.

The inspiration for the Gothic style originated in the brain of one monk, Suger, abbot of Saint-Denis (1122–1151). When Suger became abbot, he decided to reconstruct the old Carolingian abbey church at Saint-Denis. Work began in 1137. On June 11, 1144, King Louis VII and a large crowd of bishops, dignitaries, and common people witnessed the solemn consecration of the first Gothic church in France.

The basic features of Gothic architecture—the pointed arch, the ribbed vault, and the flying buttress—were not unknown before 1137. What was without precedent was the interior lightness they made possible. Since the ceiling of a Gothic church weighed less than that of a Romanesque church, the walls could be thinner. Stained-glass windows were cut into the stone, flooding the church with light. The bright interior was astounding. Suger, describing his achievement, exulted:

Moreover, it was cunningly provided that . . . the central nave of the old nave should be equalized, by means of geometrical and arithmetical instruments, with the central nave of the new addition; and, likewise, that the dimensions of the old side-aisles should be equalized with the new dimensions of the new side-aisles, except for that elegant and praiseworthy extension, in [the form of] a circular string of chapels, by virtue of which the whole [church] would shine with the wonderful and uninterrupted light of most sacred windows, pervading the interior beauty.[19]

Begun in the Île-de-France, Gothic architecture spread throughout France with the expansion of royal power. French architects were soon invited to design and supervise the construction of churches in other parts of Europe. For example, William of Sens was commissioned to rebuild Canterbury Cathedral after a disastrous fire in 1174. The distinguished scholar John of Salisbury was then in Canterbury and observed William's work. After John became bishop of Chartres, he wanted William of Sens to assist in the renovation of Chartres Cathedral. Through such contacts the new style traveled rapidly over Europe.

The Creative Outburst

The construction of a Gothic cathedral represented a gigantic investment of time, money, and corporate effort. It was the bishop and the clergy of the cathedral who made the decision to build, but they depended on the support of all the social classes. Bishops raised revenue from contributions by people in their dioceses, and the clergy appealed to the king and the nobility. Since Suger deliberately utilized the Gothic to glorify the French monarchy, the Gothic was called "French royal style" from its inception. Thus the French kings were generous patrons of many cathedrals. Louis IX endowed churches in the Île-de-France—most notably, Sainte-Chapelle, a small chapel to house the crown of thorns. Noble families often gave contributions in order to have their crests in the stained-glass windows. Above all, the church relied on the financial help of those with the greatest amount of ready cash, the commercial classes.

Money was not the only need. A great number of craftsmen had to be assembled: quarrymen, sculptors, stonecutters, masons, mortar makers, carpenters, blacksmiths, glassmakers, roofers. Each master craftsman had apprentices, and unskilled laborers had to be recruited for the heavy work. The construction of a large cathedral was rarely completed in a lifetime; many were never finished at all. Because generation after generation added to the building, many Gothic churches show the architectural influences of two or even three centuries.

Since cathedrals were symbols of civic pride, towns competed to build the largest and most splendid church. In northern France in the late twelfth and early thirteenth centuries, cathedrals grew progressively taller. In 1163 the citizens of Paris began Notre Dame Cathedral, intending it to reach the height of 114 feet. When reconstruction on Chartres Cathedral was begun in 1194, it was to be 119 feet. The people of Beauvais exceeded everyone: their church, started in 1247, reached 157 feet. Unfortunately, the weight imposed on the vaults was too great, and the building collapsed in 1284. Medieval people built cathedrals to glorify God—and if mortals were impressed, so much the better.[20]

Cathedrals served secular as well as religious purposes. The sanctuary containing the altar and the bishop's chair belonged to the clergy, but the rest of the church belonged to the people. In addition to marriages, baptisms, and funerals, there were scores of feast days on which the entire town gathered in the cathedral for festivities. Amiens Cathedral could hold the entire town population. Local guilds, which fulfilled the economic, fraternal, and charitable functions of modern labor unions, met in the cathedrals to arrange business deals and plan recreational events and the support of disabled members. Magistrates and municipal officials held political meetings there. Some towns never built town halls, because all civic functions took place in the cathedral. Pilgrims slept there, lovers courted there, traveling actors staged plays there. The cathedral belonged to all.

First and foremost, however, the cathedral was intended to teach the people the doctrines of Christian faith through visual images. Architecture became the servant of theology. The main altar was at the east end, pointing toward Jerusalem, the city of peace. The west front of the cathedral faced the setting sun, and its wall was usually devoted to the scenes of the Last Judgment. The north side, which received the least sunlight, displayed events from the Old Testament. The south side, washed in warm sunshine for much of the day, depicted scenes from the New Testament. This symbolism implied that the Jewish people of the Old Testament lived in darkness and that the Gospel brought by Christ illuminated the world. Every piece of sculpture, furniture, and stained glass had some religious or social significance.

Stained glass beautifully reflects the creative energy of the High Middle Ages. It is both an integral part of Gothic architecture and a distinct form of painting. The glassmaker "painted" the picture with small fragments of glass held together with strips of lead. As Gothic churches became more skeletal and had more windows, stained glass replaced manuscript illumination as the leading kind of painting.

Contributors to the cathedral and workers left their imprints on it. Stonecutters cut their individual marks on each block of stone, partly so that they would be paid. At Chartres the craft and merchant guilds—drapers, furriers, haberdashers, tanners, butchers, bakers, fishmongers, and wine merchants—donated money and are memorialized in stained-glass windows. Thousands of scenes in the cathedral celebrate nature, country life, and the activities of ordinary people. All members of medieval society had a place in the City of God, which the Gothic cathedral represented. No one, from king to peasant, was excluded.

Tapestry making also came into its own in the fourteenth century. Heavy woolen tapestries were first made in the monasteries and convents as wall hangings for churches. Because they could be moved and lent an atmosphere of warmth, they subsequently replaced mural paintings. Early tapestries depicted religious scenes, but later hangings produced for the knightly class bore secular designs, especially romantic forests and hunting spectacles.

The drama, derived from the church's liturgy, emerged as a distinct art form during the same period. For centuries, skits based on Christ's Nativity and Resurrection had been performed in monasteries and cathedrals. Beginning in the thirteenth century, plays based on these and other biblical themes and on the lives of the saints were performed in the towns. Guilds financed these "mystery plays," so called because they were based on the mysteries of the Christian faith. Performed first at the cathedral altar, then in the church square, and later in the town marketplace, mystery plays enjoyed great popularity. By combining comical farce based on ordinary life with serious religious scenes, they allowed the common people to understand and identify with religious figures and the mysteries of their faith. While provoking the individual conscience to reform, mystery plays were also an artistic manifestation of local civic pride.

This period also witnessed several creative developments in music. The *organum* style of singing

West Front of Notre Dame Cathedral In this powerful vision of the Last Judgment, Christ sits in judgment surrounded by angels, the Virgin, and Saint John. Scenes of paradise fill the arches on Christ's right, scenes of hell on the left. In the lower lintel, the dead arise incorruptible, and in the upper lintel (below Christ's feet), the saved move off to heaven, while devils push the damned to hell. Below, the twelve apostles line the doorway. *(Source: Alinari/ Scala/Art Resource)*

Fifteenth-Century Flemish Tapestry The weavers of Tournai (in present-day Belgium) spent twenty-five years (1450–1475) producing this magnificent tapestry, which is based on the Old Testament story of Jehu, Jezebel, and the sons of Ahab (2 Kings, 9–10). *(Source: Isabella Stewart Gardner Museum, Boston)*

began: a second voice, carrying a parallel melody of four or five tones above or below, accompanied the principal melody sung by a tenor. *Counterpoint,* the harmonizing of two or more distinct melodies, was introduced in the thirteenth century. The system of musical *notation*—using square notes and other symbols on a four-line staff to express quantities—evolved. New instruments appeared or came into widespread use: stringed instruments, such as the lute, virginal, and clavichord; reed instruments, such as the shawm; and brass instruments, such as trumpets and various horns. Not only great cathedrals but parish churches sought to acquire pipe organs. Monks in their choirs, workers in the fields, spinsters at their looms, and cobblers at their benches sang. Like stained glass windows, song touched people's hearts and lifted their spirits.

Troubadour Poetry

In the twelfth and thirteenth centuries a remarkable literary culture blossomed in southern France. The word *troubadour* comes from the Provençal word *trobar,* which in turn derives from the Arabic *taraba,* meaning "to sing" or "to sing poetry." A troubadour was a poet of Provençal who wrote lyric verse in his or her native language and sang it at one of the noble courts. Troubadour songs had

a great variety of themes: "courtly love," the pure love a knight felt for his lady whom he sought to win by military prowess and patience; or the love he felt for the wife of his feudal lord; or carnal desires seeking satisfaction. Women troubadours (*trobairitz*) focused on their emotions or their experiences with men. Some poems exalted the married state, others idealized adulterous relationships; some were earthy and bawdy, others advised young girls to remain chaste in preparation for marriage. Many poems celebrate the beauties of nature; a few speak of the sexual frustrations of nuns. The married Countess Beatrice of Dia (1150–1200?) expresses the hurt she feels after being jilted by a young knight:

I've suffered great distress
From a knight whom I once owned.
Now, for all time, be it known:
I loved him-yes, to excess.
His jilting I've regretted,
Yet his love I never really returned.
Now for my sin I can only burn:
Dressed, or in my bed.

O if I had that knight to caress
Naked all night in my arms,
He'd be ravished by the charm
Of using, for cushion, my breast.

His love I more deeply prize
Than Floris did Blancheflor's
Take that love, my core,
*   My sense, my life, my eyes!*

Lovely lover, gracious, kind,
When will I overcome your fight?
O if I could lie with you one night!
Feel those loving lips on mine!
*   Listen, one thing sets me afire:*
Here in my husband's place I want you,
If you'll just keep your promise true:
*   Give me everything I desire.*[21]

Because of its varied and contradictory themes, courtly love has been one of the most hotly debated topics in all medieval studies. One scholar concludes that it was at once "a literary movement, an ideology, an ethical system, an expression of the play element in culture, which arose in an aristocratic Christian environment exposed to Hispano-Arabic influences."[22] Another scholar insists there is no evidence for the practice of courtly love. If, however, the knight's love represented the respect of a vassal for his lady, a respect that inspired him to noble deeds, then perhaps courtly love contributed to an improvement in the status of women.

Hispano-Arabic influences troubadours certainly felt. In the eleventh century Christians of southern France were in intimate contact with the Arabized world of Andalusia, where reverence for the lady in a "courtly" tradition had long existed. In 1064 the Provençal lord Guillaume de Montreuil captured Barbastro and, according to legend, took 1,000 slave girls from Andalusia in southern Spain back to Provence. Even if this figure is an exaggeration, those women who came to southern France would have been familiar with the Arabic tradition of sung poetry and continued it in their new land. Troubadour poetry thus represents another facet of the strong Muslim influence on European culture and life.[23] Troubadour lyric poetry enjoyed the patronage of many of the great lords of southern France, including William IX, duke of Aquitaine, himself a famed author, and Richard Lion-Heart of England.

The romantic motifs of the troubadours also influenced the northern French *trouvères* who wrote adventure-romances in the form of epic poems. Trouvères wrote in their native language, which we call Old French. At the court of his patron Marie of Champagne, Chrétien de Troyes (ca 1135–1183) used the legends of the fifth century British king Arthur (see page 222) to discuss contemporary chivalric ideals and their moral implications. Such poems as *Lancelot*, *Percival and the Holy Grail*, and *Tristan and Isolde* reveal Chrétien as the founding father of the Western romantic genre and as the most innovative figure in the twelfth century vernacular literature. The theme of these romances centers on the knight errant seeking adventures who, when faced with crises usually precipitated by love, acquires new values and grows in stature.

Since the songs of the troubadours and trouvères were widely imitated in Italy, England, and Germany, they spurred the development of the nascent vernacular languages. In the thirteenth century, for example, German Minnesängers (love singers) such as Walther von der Wogelweide (1170–1220) wrote stylized verses on a variety of topics. Most of the troubadours and trouvères came from and wrote for the aristocratic classes, and their poetry suggests the interests and values of noble culture in the High Middle Ages. This genre also illustrates the cultural creativity of the period.

✠ HERESY AND THE FRIARS

As the commercial revolution of the High Middle Ages fostered urban development, the towns experienced an enormous growth of heresy. In fact, in the twelfth and thirteenth centuries, "the most economically advanced and urbanized areas: northern Italy, southern France, Flanders-Brabant, and the lower Rhine Valley" witnessed the strongest heretical movements.[24] Why did heresy flourish in such places? The bishops, usually drawn from the feudal nobility, did not understand urban culture and were suspicious of it. Christian theology, formulated for an earlier, rural age, did not address the problems of the more sophisticated mercantile society. The new monastic orders of the twelfth century, deliberately situated in remote, isolated areas, had little relevance to the towns.[25] Finally, townspeople wanted a pious clergy, capable of preaching the Gospel in a manner that satisfied their spiritual needs. They disapproved of clerical ignorance and luxurious living. Critical of the clergy, neglected, and spiritually unfulfilled, townspeople turned to heretical sects.

The term *heresy,* which derives from the Greek *hairesis,* meaning "individual choosing," is older than Christianity. At the end of the fourth century, when Christianity became the official religion of the Roman Empire, religious issues took on a legal dimension. Theologians and kings defined the Roman Empire as a Christian society. Since religion was thought to bind society in a fundamental way, religious unity was essential for social cohesion. A heretic, therefore, threatened not only the religious part of the community, but the community itself. As described in Chapter 7, civil authority could (and did) punish heresy. In the early Middle Ages, the term *heresy* came to be applied to the position of a Christian who chose and stubbornly held to doctrinal error in defiance of church authority.[26]

Ironically, the eleventh-century Gregorian reform movement, which had worked to purify the church of disorder, led to some twelfth and thirteenth-century heretical movements. Papal efforts to improve the sexual morality of the clergy, for example, had largely succeeded. When Gregory VII forbade married priests to celebrate church ceremonies, he expected public opinion to force priests to put aside their wives and concubines. But Gregory did not foresee the consequences of this order. Laypersons assumed they could remove immoral priests. Critics and heretics could accuse clergymen of immorality and thus weaken their influence. Moreover, by forbidding sinful priests to administer the sacraments, Gregory unwittingly revived the old Donatist heresy, which held that sacraments given by an immoral priest were useless; thus Donatist beliefs spread. The clergy's inability to provide adequate instruction weakened its position.

In northern Italian towns, Arnold of Brescia, a vigorous advocate of strict clerical poverty, denounced clerical wealth. In France, Peter Waldo, a rich merchant of Lyons, gave his money to the poor and preached that only prayers, not sacraments, were needed for salvation. The "Waldensians"—as Peter's followers were called—bitterly attacked the sacraments and church hierarchy, and they carried these ideas across Europe. Another group, known either as the Cathars (from the Greek *katharos,* meaning "pure") or as the Albigensians (from the town of Albi in southern France), rejected not only the hierarchical organization and the sacraments of the church, but the Roman church itself. The Cathars' primary tenet was the dualist belief that God had created spiritual things and the Devil had created material things; thus the soul was good and the body evil. Forces of good and evil battled constantly, and leading a perfect life meant being stripped of all physical and material things. Thus sexual intercourse was evil because it led to the creation of more physical bodies. To free oneself from the power of evil, a person had to lead a life of extreme asceticism, avoiding all material things. Albigensians were divided into the "perfect," who followed the principles of Catharism, and the "believers," who led ordinary lives until their deaths, when they repented and were saved.

The Albigensian heresy won many adherents in southern France. Townspeople admired the virtuous lives of the "perfect," which contrasted very favorably with the luxurious living of the Roman clergy. Women were attracted because the Albigensians treated them as men's equals, and nobles were drawn because they coveted the wealth of the clergy. Faced with widespread defection in southern France, in 1208 Pope Innocent III proclaimed a crusade against the Albigensian heretics. When the papal legate was murdered by a follower of Count Raymond of Toulouse, the greatest lord in southern France and a suspected heretic, the crusade took on a political character; heretical beliefs became fused with feudal rebellion against the French crown. Northern French lords joined the crusade and inflicted severe defeats on the towns of the province of Languedoc. The Albigensian crusade, however, was a political rather than a religious success, and the heresy went underground.

In its continuing struggle against heresy, the church gained the support of two remarkable men, Saint Dominic and Saint Francis, and of the orders they founded. Born in Castile, the province of Spain famous for its zealous Christianity and militant opposition to Islam, Domingo de Gúzman (1170?–1221) received a sound education and was ordained a priest. In 1206 he accompanied his bishop on a mission to preach to the Albigensian heretics in Languedoc. Although the austere simplicity in which they traveled contrasted favorably with the pomp and display of the papal legate in the area, Dominic's efforts had little practical success. Determined to win the heretics back with ardent preaching, Dominic subsequently returned to France with a few followers. In 1216 the group—known as the "Preaching Friars"—won papal recognition as a new religious order. Their name indicates their goal; they were to preach, and in order to preach effectively, they had to study. Dominic sent his recruits to the universities for training in theology.

Francesco di Bernardone (1181–1226), son of a wealthy cloth merchant from the northern Italian town of Assisi, was an extravagant wastrel until he had a sudden conversion. Then he determined to devote himself entirely to living the Gospel. Directed by a vision to rebuild the dilapidated chapel of Saint Damiano in Assisi, Francis sold some of his father's cloth to finance the reconstruction. His enraged father insisted that he return the money and enlisted the support of the bishop. When the bishop told Francis to obey his father, Francis took off all his clothes and returned them to his father. Thereafter he promised to obey only his Father in heaven. Francis was particularly inspired by two biblical texts: "If you seek perfection, go, sell your possessions, and give to the poor. You will have treasure in heaven. Afterward, come back and follow me" (Matthew 19:21); and Jesus' advice to his disciples as they went out to preach, "Take nothing for the journey, neither walking staff nor travelling bag, no bread, no money" (Luke 9:3). Over the centuries, these words have stimulated countless young people. With Francis, however, there was a radical difference: he intended to observe them literally and without compromise. He set out to live and preach the Gospel in absolute poverty.

The simplicity, humility, and joyful devotion with which Francis carried out his mission soon attracted companions. Although he resisted pressure to establish an Order, his followers became so numerous that he was obliged to develop some formal structure. In 1221 the papacy approved the "Rule of the Little Brothers of Saint Francis," as the Franciscans were known.

The new Dominican and Franciscan orders differed significantly from older monastic orders such as the Benedictines and the Cistercians. (So also did the Beguines, laywomen who wished to live a religious life without becoming cloistered nuns; they lived in or near cities in northwestern Europe, led prayerful lives, and supported themselves through manual labor, teaching or writing.) First, the Dominicans and Franciscans were friars, not monks. Their lives and work centered in the cities and university towns, the busy centers of commercial and intellectual life, not the secluded and cloistered world of monks. Second, the friars stressed apostolic poverty, a life based on the Gospel's

teachings, in which they would own no property and depend on Christian people for their material needs. Hence they were called *mendicants*, begging friars. Benedictine and Cistercian abbeys, on the other hand, held land—not infrequently great tracts of land. Finally, the friars drew their members largely from the burgher class, from small property owners and shopkeepers. The monastic orders, by contrast, gathered their members (at least until the thirteenth century) overwhelmingly from the nobility.[27]

The friars represented a response to the spiritual and intellectual needs of the thirteenth century. Research on the German friars has shown that, while the Franciscans initially accepted uneducated men, the Dominicans always showed a marked preference for university graduates.[28] A more urban and sophisticated society required a highly educated clergy. The Dominicans soon held professorial chairs at leading universities, and they count Thomas Aquinas, probably the greatest medieval philosopher in Europe, as their most famous member. But the Franciscans followed suit at the universities and also produced intellectual leaders. The Franciscans' mission to the towns and the poor, their ideal of poverty, and their compassion for the human condition made them vastly popular. The friars interpreted Christian doctrine for the new urban classes. By living Christianity as well as by preaching it, they won the respect of the medieval bourgeoisie.

Dominic started his order to combat heresy. Francis's followers were motivated by the ideal of absolute poverty. Beginning in 1233, the papacy used the friars to staff a new ecclesiastical court, the Inquisition. Popes selected the friars to direct the Inquisition because bishops proved unreliable and because special theological training was needed. *Inquisition* means "investigation," and the Franciscans and Dominicans developed expert methods of rooting out unorthodox thought. Modern Americans consider the procedures of the Inquisition exceedingly unjust, and there was substantial criticism of it in the Middle Ages. The accused did not learn the evidence against them or see their accusers; they were subjected to lengthy interrogations often designed to trap them; and torture could be used to extract confessions. Medieval people, however, believed that heretics destroyed the souls of their neighbors. By attacking religion, it was also thought, heretics destroyed the very bonds of society. By the mid-thirteenth century secular governments steadily pressed for social conformity, and they had the resources to search out and to punish heretics. So successful was the Inquisition as a tool of royal power, that within a century heresy had been virtually extinguished.

⟡ A CHALLENGE TO RELIGIOUS AUTHORITY

Societies, like individuals, cannot maintain a high level of energy indefinitely. In the later years of the thirteenth century, Europeans seemed to run out of steam. The crusading movement gradually fizzled out. Few new cathedrals were constructed, and if a cathedral had not been completed by 1300, the chances were high that it never would be. The strong rulers of England and France, building on the foundations of their predecessors, increased their authority and gained the loyalty of all their subjects. The vigor of those kings, however, did not pass to their immediate descendants. Meanwhile, the church, which for two centuries had guided Christian society, began to face grave difficulties. A violent dispute between the papacy and the kings of England and France badly damaged the prestige of the pope.

In 1294, King Edward I of England and Philip the Fair of France declared war on each other. To finance this war, both kings laid taxes on the clergy. Kings had been taxing the church for decades. Pope Boniface VIII (1294–1303), arguing from precedent, insisted that kings gain papal consent for taxation of the clergy and forbade churchmen to pay the taxes. But Edward and Philip refused to accept this decree, partly because it hurt royal finances and partly because the papal order threatened royal authority within their countries. Edward immediately denied the clergy the protection of the law, an action that meant its members could be attacked with impunity. Philip halted the shipment of all ecclesiastical revenue to Rome. Boniface had to back down.

Philip the Fair and his ministers continued their attack on all powers in France outside royal authority. Philip arrested a French bishop who was also the papal legate. When Boniface defended the ecclesiastical status and diplomatic immunity of the bishop, Philip replied with the trumped-charge that the pope was a heretic. The papacy and the French monarchy waged a bitter war of propaganda. Finally, in 1302, in a letter entitled *Unam Sanctam* (because its opening sentence spoke of one holy Catholic church), Boniface insisted that all Christians are subject to the pope. Although the letter made no specific reference to Philip, it held

⟡ **St. Dominic and the Inquisition** The fifteenth-century court painter to the Spanish rulers Ferdinand and Isabella, Pedro Berruguete here portrays an event from the life of St. Dominic: Dominic presides at the trial of Count Raymond of Toulouse who had supported the Albigensian heretics. Raymond, helmeted and on horseback, repented and was pardoned; his companions, who would not repent, were burned. Smoke from the fire has put one of the judges to sleep, and other officials, impervious to the human tragedy, chat among themselves. (*Source: Museo del Prado, Madrid*)

that kings should submit to papal authority. Philip's university-trained advisers responded with an argument drawn from Roman law. They maintained that the king of France was completely sovereign in his kingdom and responsible to God alone. French mercenary troops went to Italy and arrested the aged pope at Anagni. Although Boniface was soon freed, he died shortly afterward. The confrontation at Anagni foreshadowed serious difficulties within the Christian church, but religious struggle was only one of the crises that would face Western society in the fourteenth century.

SUMMARY

The High Middle Ages represent one of the most creative periods in the history of Western society. Advances were made in the evolution of strong government and urban life, economic development, architectural design, and education. Through the instruments of justice and finance, the kings of England and France attacked feudal rights and provincial practices, built centralized bureaucracies, and gradually came in contract with all their subjects. In so doing these rulers laid the foundations for modern national states. The German emperors, preoccupied with Italian affairs and with a quest for the imperial crown, allowed feudal and local interests to triumph.

Medieval cities—whether beginning around the sites of cathedrals, fortifications, or market towns—recruited people from the countryside and brought into being a new social class, the middle class. Cities provided economic opportunity, which, together with the revival of long-distance trade and a new capitalistic spirit, led to greater wealth, a higher standard of living, and upward social mobility. The soaring Gothic cathedrals that medieval towns erected demonstrate civic pride, deep religious faith, and economic vitality. Universities, institutions of higher learning unique to the West, emerged from cathedral and municipal schools and provided trained officials for the new government bureaucracies. While the church exercised leadership of Christian society in the High Middle Ages, the clash between the papacy and the kings of France and England at the end of the thirteenth century seriously challenged papal power.

NOTES

1. D. C. Douglas and G. E. Greenaway, eds., *English Historical Documents*, vol. 2 (London: Eyre & Spottiswoode, 1961), p. 853.
2. See G. M. Spiegel, "The Cult of Saint Denis and Capetian Kingship," *Journal of Medieval History 1* (April 1975): 43–65, esp. 56–64.
3. J. Boswell, *Christianity, Social Tolerance, and Homosexuality: Gay People in Western Europe from the Beginning of the Christian Era to the Fourteenth Century* (Chicago: University of Chicago Press, 1980), pp. 270–293; the quotation is from p. 293. For alternative interpretations, see K. Thomas, "Rescuing Homosexual History," *New York Review of Books,* Dec. 4, 1980, 26ff.; and J. DuQ. Adams, *Speculum* 56 (April 1981): 350ff. For the French monarchy's persecution of the Jews, see J. W. Baldwin, *The Government of Philip Augustus: Foundations of French Royal Power in the Middle Ages* (Berkeley: University of California Press, 1986), pp. 51–52, and W. C. Jordan, *The French Monarchy and the Jews* (Philadelphia: University of Pennsylvania Press, 1989).
4. J. C. Russell, *Medieval Regions and Their Cities* (Bloomington: University of Indiana Press, 1972), p. 91.
5. Ibid., pp. 113–117.
6. Quoted in R. S. Lopez, "Of Towns and Trade," in *Life and Thought in the Early Middle Ages,* R. S. Hoyt, ed. (Minneapolis: University of Minnesota Press, 1967), p. 33.
7. H. Pirenne, *Economic and Social History of Medieval Europe* (New York: Harcourt Brace, 1956), p. 53.
8. See D. Herlihy, *Medieval and Renaissance Pistoia: The Social History of an Italian Town, 1200–1430* (New Haven: Yale University Press, 1967), p. 257.
9. Quoted in J. O'Faolain and L. Martines, eds., *Not in God's Image: Women in History from the Greeks to the Victorians* (New York: Harper & Row, 1973), pp. 155–156.
10. W. C. Jordan, *Women and Credit in Pre-Industrial and Developing Societies* (Philadelphia: University of Pennsylvania Press, 1993), pp. 20 et seq.
11. Douglas and Greenaway, pp. 969–970.
12. H. Rothwell, ed., *English Historical Documents*, vol. 3 (London: Eyre & Spottiswoode, 1975), p. 854.
13. M. M. Postan, *The Medieval Economy and Society: An Economic History of Britain in the Middle Ages* (Baltimore: Penguin Books, 1975), pp. 213–214.

14. See P. Dollinger, *The German Hansa,* D. S. Ault and S. H. Steinberg, trans. and ed. (Stanford, Calif.: Stanford University Press, 1970).

15. C. M. Cipolla, *Before the Industrial Revolution: European Society and Economy, 1000–1700,* 2d ed. (New York: W. W. Norton, 1980), p. 197.

16. R. S. Lopez, "The Trade of Medieval Europe: The South," in *The Cambridge Economic History of Europe,* vol. 2, M. M. Postan and E. E. Rich, ed. (Cambridge: Cambridge University Press, 1952), p. 289.

17. Quoted in H. E. Sigerist, *Civilization and Disease* (Chicago: University of Chicago Press, 1943), p. 102.

18. Quoted in J. H. Mundy, *Europe in the High Middle Ages, 1150–1309* (New York: Basic Books, 1973), pp. 474–475.

19. E. Panofsky, trans. and ed., *Abbot Suger on the Abbey Church of St. Denis and Its Art Treasures* (Princeton, N.J.: Princeton University Press, 1946), p. 101.

20. See J. Gimpel, *The Cathedral Builders* (New York: Grove Press, 1961), pp. 42–49.

21. Quoted in J. J. Wilhelm ed., *Lyrics of the Middle Ages: An Anthology* (New York: Garland Publishers, 1993), pp. 83–84.

22. Quoted from R. Boase, *The Origin and Meaning of Courtly Love* (Manchester, 1977), pp. 129–130.

23. I have leaned on the very persuasive interpretation of M. R. Menocal, *The Arabic Role in Medieval Literary History* (Philadelphia: University of Pennsylvania Press, 1990), pp. ix–xv and 27–33.

24. J. B. Freed, *The Friars and German Society in the Thirteenth Century* (Cambridge, Mass.: Medieval Academy of America, 1977), p. 8.

25. Ibid., p. 9.

26. See F. Oakley, *The Western Church in the Later Middle Ages* (Ithaca, N.Y.: Cornell University Press, 1979), p. 175.

27. See Freed, pp. 119–128.

28. Ibid., esp. p. 125.

SUGGESTED READING

The curious student will have no difficulty finding exciting material on the points raised in this chapter. Three general surveys of the period 1050 to 1300 are especially recommended: D. Nicholas, *The Evolution of the Medieval World* (1992), explores the major themes of the age in depth; G. Holmes, ed., *The Oxford History of Medieval Europe* (1992), discusses the creativity of the period in a series of essays; and J. R. Strayer, *Western Europe in the Middle Ages* (1955), is a masterful synthesis.

R. A. Brown, *The Normans* (1983), revitalizes the old thesis that the conquerors of England and Sicily were an exceptionally creative force in the eleventh and twelfth centuries. D. Howarth, *1066: The Year of the Conquest* (1981), is a lively and cleverly written account, from Norman, Scandinavian, and English perspectives, of the Norman conquest of England. G. O. Sayles, *The Medieval Foundations of England* (1961), traces political and social conditions to the end of the twelfth century, while H. G. Richardson and G. O. Sayles, *The Governance of Medieval England from the Conquest to Magna Carta* (1963), focuses on administrative developments.

Students interested in crime, society, and legal developments will find the following works useful and sound: J. S. Cockburn and T. A. Green, *Twelve Good Men and True: The Criminal Trial Jury in England, 1200–1800* (1988); J. B. Given, *Society and Homicide in Thirteenth-Century England* (1977); R. C. Palmer, *The County Courts of Medieval England, 1150–1350* (1982). E. M. Hallam, *Domesday Book Through Nine Centuries* (1986), is an excellent appreciation of that important document, while J. R. Strayer, *On the Medieval Origins of the Modern State* (1970), is a fine synthesis of political, legal, and administrative developments.

For the Becket controversy, see F. Barlow, *Thomas Becket* (1986), the best recent study; D. Knowles *Thomas Becket* (1970); and B. Smalley, *The Becket Controversy and the Schools: A Study of Intellectuals in Politics in the Twelfth Century* (1973). J. C. Holt, *Magna Carta* (1969), remains the best modern treatment of the document.

For France, both E. Hallam, *The Capetian Kings of France, 987–1328* (1980), and R. Fawtier, *The Capetian Kings of France* (1962), are readable introductions. Advanced students of medieval French administrative history should see J. Baldwin, *The Government of Philip Augustus: Foundations of French Royal Power in the Middle Ages* (1986); W. C. Jordan, *Louis IX and the Crusade* (1979); and J. R. Strayer, *The Reign of Philip the Fair* (1980). On Germany, A. Haverkamp, *Medieval Germany 1056–1273,* trans. H. Braun and R. Mortimer (1992) gives a comprehensive picture, H. Furhman, *Germany in the High Middle Ages,* T. Reuther, trans. (1986), and G. Barraclough, *The Origins of Modern Germany* (1963), is a fine example of the Marxist interpretation of medieval history. M. Pacaut, *Frederick Barbarossa,* A. J. Pomerans, trans. (1980), is perhaps the best one-volume treatment of that important ruler, but P. Munz, *Frederick Barbarossa* (1979), is also useful.

LISTENING TO THE
PAST

London in the Late Twelfth Century

As a background to his Life of Thomas Becket *(ca 1175), the chronicler William fitz-Stephen provided a lengthy description of London, which is excerpted here. The author clearly knew London well, and his account represents a superb example of civic pride and patriotism.*

Among the noble and celebrated cities of the world that of London, the capital of the kingdom of the English, is one which extends its glory farther than all the others and sends its wealth and merchandise more widely into distant lands. . . . It is happy in the healthiness of its air; in its observance of Christian practice; in the strength of its fortifications; in its natural situation; in the honour of its citizens; and in the modesty of its matrons. It is cheerful in its sports, and the fruitful mother of noble men. . . . The citizens of London are regarded as conspicuous above all others for their polished manners, for their dress and for the good tables, which they keep. . . .

In London the three principal churches have famous schools by special privilege and by virtue of their ancient dignity. But through the favour of some magnate, or through the presence of teachers who are notable or famous in philosophy, there are also other schools. On feast-days the masters hold meetings for their pupils in the church whose festival it is. The scholars dispute, some with oratory and some with argument. . . .

Those engaged in business of various kinds, sellers of merchandise, hirers of labour, are distributed every morning into their several localities according to their trade. Besides, there is in London on the river bank among the wines for sale in ships and in the cellars of the vintners a public cook-shop. There daily you may find food according to the season, dishes of meat, roast, fried and boiled, large and small fish, coarser meats for the poor and more delicate for the rich, such as venison and big and small birds. If any of the citizens should unexpectedly receive visitors, weary from their journey, who would fain not wait until fresh food is bought and cooked, or until the servants have brought bread or water for washing, they hasten to the river bank and there find all they need. . . .

Immediately outside one of the gates there is a field [Smithfield] which is smooth both in fact and in name. On every sixth day of the week, unless it be a major feast-day, there takes place there a famous exhibition of fine horses for sale. Earls, barons and knights, who are in the town, and many citizens some out to see or to buy. It is pleasant to see the high-stepping palfreys with their gleaming coats, as they go through their paces, putting down their feet alternately on one side together. . . .

By themselves in another part of the field stand the goods and animals of the country-folk: implements of husbandry, swine with long flanks, cows with full udders, oxen of immense size, and woolly sheep. There also stand the mares fit for plough, some big with foal, and others with brisk young colts closely following them.

To this city from every nation under heaven merchants delight to bring their trade by sea. The Arabian sends gold; the Sabaean spice and incense. The Scythian brings arms, and from the rich, fat lands of Babylon comes oil of palms. The Nile sends precious stones; the men of Norway and Russia, furs and sables; nor is China absent with pure silk. The Gauls come with their wines.

I do not think there is a city with a better record for church-going, doing honour to God's ordinances, keeping feast-days, giving alms and hospitality to strangers, confirming betrothals, contracting marriages, celebrating weddings, providing feasts, entertaining guests, and also, it may be added, in care for funerals and for the burial of the dead. The only plagues of London are the immoderate drinking of fools and the frequency of fires.

Instead of shows in the theatre and stage-plays, London provides plays of a more sacred character, wherein are presented the miracles worked by saintly confessors or the sufferings which made illustrious the constancy of martyrs. Furthermore, every year on the day called Carnival—to begin with the sports of boys (for we were all boys once)—scholars from the different schools bring fighting-cocks to their masters, and the whole morning is set apart to watch their cocks do battle in the schools, for the boys are given a holiday that day. After dinner all the young men of the town go out into the fields in the suburbs to play ball. The scholars of the various schools have their own ball, and almost all the followers of each occupation have theirs also. The seniors and the fathers and the wealthy magnates of the city come on horseback to watch the contests of the younger generation, and in their turn recover their lost youth. . . .

Every Sunday in Lent after dinner a fresh swarm of young men goes forth into the fields on war-horses, steeds foremost in the contest, each of which is skilled and schooled to run in circles. . . . They make a pretence at war, carry out field-exercises and indulge in mimic combats. Thither too come many courtiers, when the king is in town, and from the households of bishops, earls and barons come youths and adolescents, not yet girt with the belt of knighthood, for the pleasure of engaging in combat with one another. Each is inflamed with the hope of victory.

❖ The first-known view of London, from a road map, 1252. *(Source: British Library)*

Questions for Analysis

1. What educational, commercial, religious, and recreational opportunities did late-twelfth-century London offer? Which of these did the author consider most important? Why?

2. According to fitz-Stephen, what were London's disadvantages?

3. A modern scholar would welcome more contemporary information about London's government and business activity. Why, in your judgment, did fitz-Stephen fail to give more detail on these topics?

Source: "Life of Thomas Beckett" by William fitz Stephen from *English Historical Documents II*, by D. C. Douglas and G. E. Greenaway, eds. Copyright © 1961 by Eyre and Spottiswoode.

D. Abulafia, *Frederick II: A Medieval Emperor* (1992) is a beautifully written revisionist study.

For the economic revival of Europe, see in addition to the titles by Dollinger, Herlihy, Postan, and Russell given in the Notes, D. Nicholas, *Medieval Flanders* (1992) and T. H. Lloyd, *England and the German Hanse, 1157–1611: A Study in Their Trade and Commercial Diplomacy* (1992). The effect of climate on population and economic growth is discussed in the remarkable work of E. L. Ladurie, *Times of Feast, Times of Famine: A History of Climate Since the Year 1000*, B. Bray, trans. (1971). A masterful account of agricultural changes and their sociological implications is to be found in G. Duby, *The Early Growth of the European Economy: Warriors and Peasants from the Seventh to the Twelfth Century* (1978).

For women, see C. Klapisch-Zuber ed., *A History of Women*, vol. II: *Silences of the Middle Ages* (1992), which contains useful essays on many aspects of women's lives and status, and S. Shahar, *The Fourth Estate: Women in the Middle Ages* (1983), a provocative work. J. M. Bennett, *Women in the Medieval English Countryside: Gender and Household in Brigstock before the Plague* (1987), is a fascinating case study, while E. Amt, ed., *Women's Lives in Medieval Europe: A Sourcebook* (1993), has fresh primary material on many aspects of women's lives.

Students interested in the origins of medieval towns and cities will learn how historians use the evidence of coins, archaeology, tax records, geography, and laws in J. F. Benton, ed., *Town Origins: The Evidence of Medieval England* (1968). S. Reynolds, *An Introduction to the History of English Medieval Towns* (1982), explores the social structure, political organization and economic livelihood of English towns, while R. H. Hilton, *English and French Towns in Feudal Society* (1992), is an exciting comparative study. R. Muir, *The English Village* (1980), offers a survey of many aspects of ordinary people's daily lives. For readability, few works surpass J. and F. Gies, *Life in a Medieval City* (1973).

For the new currents of thought in the High Middle Ages, see D. W. Robertson, Jr., *Abélard and Héloise* (1972), which is highly readable, commonsensical, and probably the best study of Abelard and the love affair he supposedly had; C. H. Haskins, *The Renaissance of the Twelfth Century* (1971), a classic; and C. W. Hollister, ed., *The Twelfth Century Renaissance* (1969), a well-constructed anthology with source materials on many aspects of twelfth-century culture. N. Orme, *Education and Society in Medieval and Renaissance England* (1989), focuses on early education, schools, and literacy in English medieval society, while J. Leclercq, *The Love of Learning and the Desire of God* (1974), discusses monastic literary culture. For the development of literacy among lay people and the formation of a literate mentality, the advanced student should see M. T. Clanchy, *From Memory to Written Record: England, 1066–1307* (1979). Written by outstanding scholars in a variety of fields, R. L. Benson and G. Constable with C. D. Lanham, eds., *Renaissance and Renewal in the Twelfth Century* (1982), contains an invaluable collection of articles.

On the medieval universities, H. De Ridder-Symoens, ed., *A History of the University in Europe*, vol. I: *Universities in the Middle Ages* (1991), offers up-to-date interpretations by leading scholars, while H. Rashdall, *The Universities of Europe in the Middle Ages* (1936), is the standard scholarly work. G. Leff, *Paris and Oxford Universities in the Thirteenth and Fourteenth Centuries* (1968), gives a fascinating sketch and includes a useful bibliography. For the beginnings of scholasticism and humanism, see the essential R. W. Southern, *Scholastic Humanism and the Unification of Western Europe*, vol. I, (1994).

F. and J. Gies, *Cathedral, Forge, and Waterwheel* (1993), provides an exciting and illustrated survey of medieval technological achievements. The following studies are all valuable for the evolution and development of the Gothic style: J. Harvey, *The Gothic World* (1969); the same author's *The Master Builders* (1971); P. Frankl, *The Gothic* (1960); and J. Bony, *French Gothic Architecture of the 12th and 13th Centuries* (1983). D. Grivot and G. Zarnecki, *Gislebertus, Sculptor of Autun* (1961), is the finest appreciation of Romanesque architecture written in English. For the actual work of building, see D. Macaulay, *Cathedral: The Story of Its Construction* (1961), which explores the engineering problems involved in cathedral building and places the subject within its social context. Advanced students will enjoy E. Male, *The Gothic Image: Religious Art in France in the Thirteenth Century* (1958), which contains a wealth of fascinating and useful detail. For the most important cathedrals in France, architecturally and politically, see A. Temko, *Notre Dame of Paris: The Biography of a Cathedral* (1968); G. Henderson, *Chartres* (1968); and A. Katzenellengoben, *The Sculptural Programs of Chartres Cathedral* (1959). E. Panofsky, *Abbot Suger on the Abbey Church of St.-Denis and Its Art Treasures* (1946), provides a contemporary background account of the first Gothic building, while C. A. Bruzelius, *The Thirteenth-Century Church at St. Denis* (1985), traces later reconstruction. J. Gimpel, *The Medieval Machine: The Industrial Revolution of the Middle Ages* (1977), an extremely useful book, discusses the mechanical and scientific problems involved in early industrialization and shows how construction affected the medieval environment.

On troubadour poetry see, in addition to the titles by R. Boase and J. J. Wilhelm cited in the Notes, M. Bogin, *The Women Troubadours* (1980).

12

The Crisis of the Later
Middle Ages

❖❖ During the later Middle Ages, the last book of the New Testament, the Book of Revelation, inspired thousands of sermons and hundreds of religious tracts. The Book of Revelation deals with visions of the end of the world, with disease, war, famine, and death. It is no wonder this part of the Bible was so popular. Between 1300 and 1450, Europeans experienced a frightful series of shocks: economic dislocation, plague, war, social upheaval, and increased crime and violence. Death and preoccupation with death make the fourteenth century one of the most wrenching periods of Western civilization. Yet, in spite of the pessimism and crises, important institutions and ideas, such as representative assemblies and national literatures, emerged.

The miseries and disasters of the later Middle Ages bring to mind a number of questions.

- What economic difficulties did Europe experience?
- What were the social and psychological effects of repeated attacks of plague and disease?
- Some scholars maintain that war is often the catalyst for political, economic, and social change. Does this theory have validity for the fourteenth century?
- What provoked schism in the church, and what impact did it have on the lives of ordinary people?
- What political and social developments do new national literatures express?

This chapter will focus on these questions.

❖ ❖ ❖ ❖ ❖ ❖ ❖ ❖

Miniature of King Charles VII presiding at the trial of the Duc d'Alençon. *(Source: Bayerische Staatsbibliothek, Munich)*

PRELUDE TO DISASTER

Economic difficulties originating in the later thirteenth century were fully manifest by the start of the fourteenth. In the first decade, the countries of northern Europe experienced a considerable price inflation. The cost of grain, livestock, and dairy products rose sharply. Severe weather, which historical geographers label "The Little Ice Age," made a serious situation frightful. An unusual number of storms brought torrential rains, ruining the wheat, oat, and hay crops on which people and animals depended almost everywhere. Since long-distance transportation of food was expensive and difficult, most urban areas depended for bread and meat on areas no more than a day's journey away. Poor harvests—and one in four was likely to be poor—led to scarcity and starvation. Almost all of northern Europe suffered a terrible famine in the years 1315 to 1317.

Hardly had western Europe begun to recover from this disaster when another struck. An epidemic of typhoid fever carried away thousands. In 1316, 10 percent of the population of the city of Ypres may have died between May and October alone. Then in 1318 disease hit cattle and sheep, drastically reducing the herds and flocks. Another bad harvest in 1321 brought famine and death.

The province of Languedoc in France presents a classic example of agrarian crisis. For over 150 years Languedoc had enjoyed continual land reclamation, steady agricultural expansion, and enormous population growth. Then the fourteenth century opened with four years of bad harvests. Torrential rains in 1310 ruined the harvest and brought on terrible famine. Harvests failed again in 1322 and 1329. In 1332 desperate peasants survived the winter on raw herbs. In the half-century from 1302 to 1348, poor harvests occurred twenty times. The undernourished population was ripe for the Grim Reaper, who appeared in 1348 in the form of the Black Death.

These catastrophes had grave social consequences. Population had steadily increased in the twelfth and thirteenth centuries, and large amounts of land had been put under cultivation. The amount of food yielded, however, did not match the level of population growth. Bad weather had disastrous results. Poor harvests meant that marriages had to be postponed. Later marriages and the deaths caused by famine and disease meant a reduction in population. Meanwhile, the international character of trade and commerce meant that a disaster in one country had serious implications elsewhere. For example, the infection that attacked English sheep in 1318 caused a sharp decline in wool exports in the following years. Without wool, Flemish weavers could not work, and thousands were laid off. Without woolen cloth, the businesses of Flemish, Hanseatic, and Italian merchants suffered. Unemployment encouraged people to turn to crime.

To none of these problems did governments have any solutions. In fact, they even lacked policies. After the death of Edward I in 1307, England was governed by the incompetent and weak Edward II (r. 1307–1327), whose reign was dominated by a series of baronial conflicts. In France the three sons of Philip the Fair, who followed their father to the French throne between 1314 and 1328, took no interest in the increasing economic difficulties. In Germany power drifted into the hands of local rulers. The only actions the governments took tended to be in response to the demands of the upper classes. Economic and social problems were aggravated by the appearance in western Europe of a frightful disease.

 THE BLACK DEATH

In 1291 Genoese sailors had opened the Strait of Gibraltar to Italian shipping by defeating the Moroccans. Then, shortly after 1300, important advances were made in the design of Italian merchant ships. A square rig was added to the mainmast, and ships began to carry three masts instead of just one. Additional sails better utilized wind power to propel the ship. The improved design permitted year-round shipping for the first time, and Venetian and Genoese merchant ships could sail the dangerous Atlantic coast even in the winter months. With ships continually at sea, their rats too were constantly on the move, and thus any rat-transmitted disease could spread rapidly.

Scholars dispute the origins of the bubonic plague, often known as the Black Death. Some students hold that it broke out in China or central Asia around 1331, and during the next fifteen years merchants and soldiers carried it over the caravan routes until in 1346 it reached the Crimea in southern Russia. Other scholars believe the plague was endemic in southern Russia. In either case, from the Crimea the plague had easy access to Mediterranean lands and western Europe.

In October 1347, Genoese ships brought the plague to Messina, from where it spread across Sicily. Venice and Genoa were hit in January 1348, and from the port of Pisa the disease spread south to Rome and east to Florence and all Tuscany. By late spring, southern Germany was attacked. Frightened French authorities chased a galley bearing the disease from the port of Marseilles, but not before plague had infected the city, from where it spread to Languedoc and Spain. In June 1348 two ships entered the Bristol Channel and introduced it into England. All Europe felt the scourge of this horrible disease (Map 12.1).

Pathology and Care

Modern understanding of the bubonic plague rests on the research of two bacteriologists, one French and one Japanese, who in 1894 independently identified the bacillus that causes the plague, *Pasteurella pestis* (so labeled after the French scientist's teacher, Louis Pasteur). The bacillus liked to live in the bloodstream of an animal or, ideally, in the stomach of a flea. The flea in turn resided in the hair of a rodent, sometimes a squirrel but preferably the hardy, nimble, and vagabond black rat. Why the host black rat moved so much, scientists still do not know, but it often traveled by ship. There the black rat could feast for months on a cargo of grain or live snugly among bales of cloth. Fleas bearing the bacillus also had no trouble nesting in saddlebags.[1] Comfortable, well fed, and often having greatly multiplied, the black rats ended their ocean voyage and descended on the great cities of Europe.

The plague took two forms—bubonic and pneumonic. In the bubonic form, the rat was the vector, or transmitter, of the disease. In the pneumonic form, the plague was communicated directly from one person to another.

Although by the fourteenth century urban authorities from London to Paris to Rome had begun to try to achieve a primitive level of sanitation, urban conditions remained ideal for the spread of disease. Narrow streets filled with mud, refuse, and human excrement were as much cesspools as thoroughfares. Dead animals and sore-covered beggars greeted the traveler. Houses whose upper stories projected over the lower ones eliminated light and air. And extreme overcrowd-

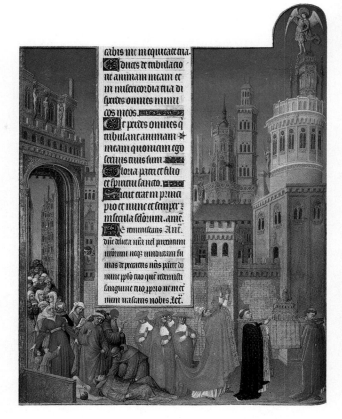

✦ **Procession of Saint Gregory** According to the *Golden Legend,* a thirteenth-century collection of saints' lives, in 590 when plague ravaged Rome (p. 200), Pope Gregory I ordered a procession around the city to beg heaven to end the epidemic. As the people circle the walls, a deacon falls victim, and Pope Gregory sees an angel on top of Hadrian's tomb (thereafter called Castel Sant'Angelo), which Gregory interprets to mean the plague is ending. (*Source: Musée Condé, Chantilly/The Bridgeman Art Library, London*)

ing was commonplace. When all members of an aristocratic family lived and slept in one room, it should not be surprising that six or eight persons in a middle-class or poor household slept in one bed—if they had one. Closeness, after all, provided warmth. Houses were beginning to be constructed of brick, but many remained of wood, clay, and mud. A determined rat had little trouble entering such a house.

Standards of personal hygiene remained frightfully low. True, most large cities had public bathhouses, but we have no way of knowing how frequently ordinary people used them. Lack of personal cleanliness, combined with any number of

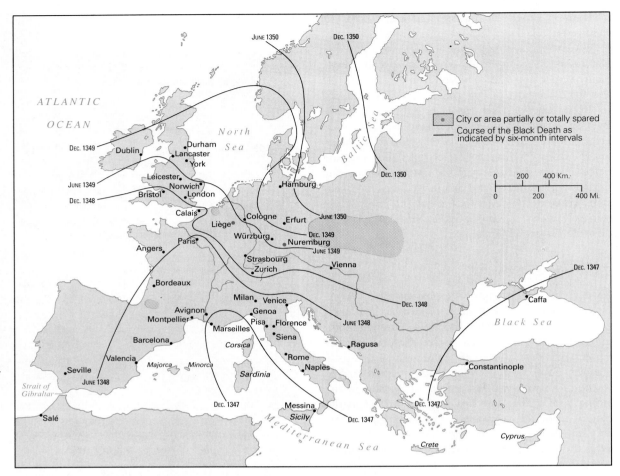

❖ **MAP 12.1 The Course of the Black Death in Fourteenth-Century Europe**
Note the routes that the bubonic plague took across Europe. How do you account
for the fact that several regions were spared the "dreadful death"?

temporary ailments such as diarrhea and the common cold, weakened the body's resistance to serious disease. Fleas and body lice were universal
afflictions: everyone from peasants to archbishops
had them. One more bite did not cause much
alarm. But if that nibble came from a bacillus-bear-
ing flea, an entire household or area was doomed.

The symptoms of the bubonic plague started
with a growth the size of a nut or an apple in the
armpit, in the groin, or on the neck. This was the
boil, or *buba,* that gave the disease its name and
caused agonizing pain. If the buba was lanced and
the pus thoroughly drained, the victim had a
chance of recovery. The secondary stage was the
appearance of black spots or blotches caused by
bleeding under the skin. (This syndrome did not

give the disease its common name; contemporaries
did not call the plague the Black Death. Sometime
in the fifteenth century, the Latin phrase *atra mors,*
meaning "dreadful death," was translated "black
death," and the phrase stuck.) Finally, the victim
began to cough violently and spit blood. This
stage, indicating the presence of millions of bacilli
in the bloodstream, signaled the end, and death
followed in two or three days. Rather than evoking
compassion for the victim, a French scientist has
written, everything about the bubonic plague provoked horror and disgust: "All the matter which
exuded from their bodies let off an unbearable
stench; sweat, excrement, spittle, breath, so fetid
as to be overpowering; urine turbid, thick, black
or red."[2]

Medieval people had no rational explanation for the disease nor any effective medical treatment for it. Fourteenth-century medical literature indicates that physicians could sometimes ease the pain, but they had no cure. Most people—lay, scholarly, and medical—believed that the Black Death was caused by some "vicious property in the air" that carried the disease from place to place. When ignorance was joined to fear and ancient bigotry, savage cruelty sometimes resulted. Many people believed that the Jews had poisoned the wells of Christian communities and thereby infected the drinking water. This charge led to the murder of thousands of Jews across Europe. According to one chronicler, sixteen thousand were killed at the imperial city of Strasbourg alone in 1349. Though sixteen thousand is probably a typically medieval numerical exaggeration, the horror of the massacre is not lessened. Scholars have yet to explain the economic impact that the loss of such a productive people had on Strasbourg and other cities.

The Italian writer Giovanni Boccaccio (1313–1375), describing the course of the disease in Florence in the preface to his book of tales, *The Decameron,* pinpointed the cause of the spread:

Moreover, the virulence of the pest was the greater by reason that intercourse was apt to convey it from the sick to the whole, just as fire devours things dry or greasy when they are brought close to it. Nay, the evil went yet further, for not merely by speech or associa-tion with the sick was the malady communicated to the healthy with consequent peril of common death, but any that touched the clothes of the sick or aught else that had been touched or used by them, seemed thereby to contract the disease.[3]

The highly infectious nature of the plague, especially in areas of high population density, was recognized by a few sophisticated Arabs. When the disease struck the town of Salé in Morocco, Ibu Abu Madyan shut in his household with sufficient food and water and allowed no one to enter or leave until the plague had passed. Madyan was entirely successful. The rat that carried the disease-bearing flea avoided travel outside the cities. Thus the countryside was relatively safe. City dwellers who could afford to move fled to the country.

If fourteenth and fifteenth century medical science had no effective treatment for the disease, how could victims' suffering be eased? Perhaps in hospitals. What was the geographical distribution of hospitals, and, although our estimates of medieval populations remain rough, what was the hospital-to-population ratio? How many patients could a hospital serve? Where earlier, the feudal lord had made philanthropic foundations, beginning in the thirteenth century individual merchants—out of compassion, generosity, the custom of giving to parish collections, and in the belief that the sick would be prayerful intercessors with God for the donors sins—endowed hospitals. Business people

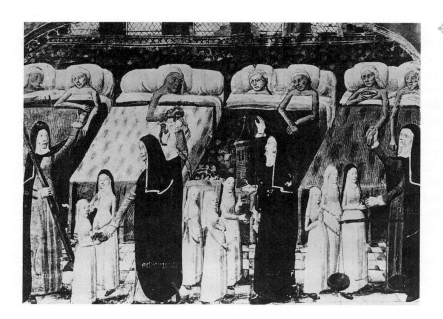

✣ **Patients in a Hospital Ward, 15th Century** In many cities hospitals could not cope with the large numbers of plague victims. The practice of putting two or more adults in the same bed, as shown here, contributed to the spread of the disease. At the Hôtel-Dieu, in Paris, nurses complained of being forced to put eight to ten children in a single bed in which a patient had recently died. *(Source: Musée de l'Assistance Publique, Paris)*

established hospitals in the towns and cities of northern France and Flanders; Milan, Genoa, and Venice were well served, and the 30 hospitals in Florence provided 1,000 beds in 1339. Sixty hospitals served the French capital city of Paris in 1328—but probably not enough for its population of 200,000. The many hospitals in southern France and the Iberian Peninsula continued the Muslim tradition of care for the poor and ill. Merchants in the larger towns of the German empire, in Poland, and in Hungary also founded hospitals in the fourteenth century, generally later than those in western Europe. In addition, guild fraternities set up hospitals for their members: for example, in Brussels, Ghent, and Venice the weavers, fullers, and shearers each had their hospices, as did the ironsmiths at Liège. Sailors, long viewed as potential carriers of disease, benefited from hospitals reserved for them; and in 1300 the Venetian government appointed and paid a surgeon to care for sick sailors. At the time the plague erupted, therefore, most towns and cities had hospital facilities.

When trying to determine the number of people a hospital could accommodate, the modern researcher considers the number of beds, the size of the staff, and the building's physical layout. Since each hospital bed might serve two or more patients, we cannot calculate the number of patients on the basis of the beds alone. We do know that rural hospices usually had 12 to 15 beds, and city hospitals, as at Lisbon, Narbonne, and Genoa had on average 25 to 30 beds, but these figures do not tell us how many patients were accommodated. Nor does the size of the staff. When archbishop Eudes of Rouen visited all the medical houses of his Norman archdiocese between 1261 and 1267, he found a staff of 42 (priests, nursing sisters, servants) attached to all the hospitals in Rouen. Rouen was a sizable town and the number of what we call health care workers small in proportion to the population. Only the very rare document listing the number of wrapping sheets and coffins for the dead purchased in a given period provides the modern scholar with precise information on the number of patients a hospital had.

Hospitals actually provided shelter for the sick, homeless, and the poor more than medical care. The typical hospital diet of salted meat, bread, and wine, though intended to compensate for years of malnutrition, was not only lacking in vitamins but was hardly beneficial to people wracked with fever (up to 107 degrees), delirium, and hemorrhage.

Financially limited hospitals could hardly afford the foods recommended by the University of Paris medical faculty to avoid the plague: good wheat bread, white meat, young lamb, and the avoidance of vegetables, especially leeks, onions, and turnips, "which cause flatulence." Hospitals could only offer shelter, compassion, and care for the dying.[4]

Mortality rates cannot be specified, because population figures for the period before the arrival of the plague do not exist for most countries and cities. The largest amount of material survives for England, but it is difficult to use; after enormous scholarly controversy, only educated guesses can be made. Of a total English population of perhaps 4.2 million, probably 1.4 million died of the Black Death in its several visits.[5] Densely populated Italian cities endured incredible losses. Florence lost between half and two-thirds of its 1347 population of 85,000 when the plague visited in 1348. The disease recurred intermittently in the 1360s and 1370s and reappeared many times down to 1700. Population losses in Bohemia and Poland seem to have been much less. Historians of medicine have recently postulated that people with blood type O are immune to the bubonic disease; since this blood type predominated in Hungary, that region would have been slightly affected. No estimates of population losses have ever been attempted for Russia and the Balkans.

Social and Psychological Consequences

Economic historians and demographers sharply dispute the impact of the plague on the economy in the late fourteenth century. The traditional view that the plague had a disastrous effect has been greatly modified. The clearest evidence comes from England, where the agrarian economy showed remarkable resilience. While the severity of the disease varied from region to region, it appears that by about 1375 most landlords enjoyed revenues near those of the pre-plague years. By the early fifteenth century seigneurial prosperity reached a medieval peak. Why? The answer appears to lie in the fact that England and many parts of Europe suffered from overpopulation in the early fourteenth century. Population losses caused by the Black Death "led to increased productivity by restoring a more efficient balance between labour, land, and capital."[6] Population decline meant a sharp increase in per capita wealth. Increased demand for labor meant greater mobility among peasant and working classes. Wages rose, providing better distribution of income. The shortage of labor and steady requests for higher wages put landlords on the defensive. They retaliated with such measures as the English Statute of Laborers (1351), which attempted to freeze salaries and wages at pre-1347 levels. The statute could not be enforced and therefore was largely unsuccessful. Some places, such as Florence, experienced economic prosperity as a long-term consequence of the plague.

Even more significant than the social effects were the psychological consequences. The knowledge that the disease meant almost certain death provoked the most profound pessimism. Imagine an entire society in the grip of the belief that it was at the mercy of a frightful affliction about which nothing could be done, a disgusting disease from which family and friends would flee, leaving one to die alone and in agony. It is not surprising that some sought release in orgies and gross sensuality while others turned to the severest forms of asceticism and frenzied religious fervor. Some extremists joined groups of *flagellants,* who whipped and scourged themselves as penance for their and society's sins, in the belief that the Black Death was God's punishment for humanity's wickedness.

The literature and art of the fourteenth century reveal a terribly morbid concern with death. One highly popular artistic motif, the Dance of Death, depicted a dancing skeleton leading away a living person. No wonder survivors experienced a sort of shell shock and a terrible crisis of faith. Lack of confidence in the leaders of society, lack of hope for the future, defeatism, and malaise wreaked enormous anguish and contributed to the decline of the Middle Ages. A long international war added further misery to the frightful disasters of the plague.

✢ THE HUNDRED YEARS' WAR (CA 1337–1453)

In January 1327, Queen Isabella of England, her lover Mortimer, and a group of barons, having deposed and murdered Isabella's incompetent husband, King Edward II, proclaimed his fifteen-year-old son king as Edward III. Isabella and Mortimer, however, held real power until 1330, when Edward seized the reins of government. In 1328, Charles IV of France, the last surviving son of the French king Philip the Fair, died childless. With him ended the Capetian dynasty. An assembly of French barons, meaning to exclude Isabella—who was Charles's sister and the daughter of Philip the Fair—and her son Edward III from the French throne, proclaimed that "no woman nor her son could succeed to the [French] monarchy." The French barons rested their position on the Salic Law, a Germanic law code that forbade females or those descended in the female line to succeed to offices. The barons passed the crown to Philip VI of Valois (r. 1328–1350), a nephew of Philip the Fair. In these actions lie the origins of another phase of the centuries-old struggle between the English and French monarchies, one that was fought intermittently from 1337 to 1453.

Causes

The Hundred Years' War had both distant and immediate causes. In 1259 France and England signed the Treaty of Paris, in which the English king agreed to become—for himself and his successors—vassal of the French crown for the duchy of Aquitaine. The English claimed Aquitaine as an ancient inheritance. French policy, however, was strongly expansionist, and the French kings resolved to absorb the duchy into the kingdom of France. In 1329, Edward III paid homage to Philip VI for Aquitaine. In 1337 Philip, determined to exercise full jurisdiction there, confiscated the duchy. This action was the immediate cause of the war. Edward III maintained that the only way he could exercise his rightful sovereignty over Aquitaine was by assuming the title of king of France.[7] As the eldest surviving male descendant of Philip the Fair, he believed he could rightfully make this claim. Moreover, the dynastic argument had feudal implications: in order to increase their independent power, French vassals of Philip VI used the excuse that they had to transfer their loyalty to a more legitimate overlord, Edward III. One reason the war lasted so long was that it became a French civil war, with French barons supporting English monarchs in order to thwart the centralizing goals of the French crown.

Economic factors involving the wool trade and the control of Flemish towns had served as justifications for war between France and England for centuries. The causes of the conflicts known as the Hundred Years' War were thus dynastic, feudal, political, and economic. Recent historians have stressed economic factors. The wool trade between England and Flanders served as the cornerstone of both countries' economies; they were closely interdependent. Flanders was a fief of the French crown, and the Flemish aristocracy was highly sympathetic to the monarchy in Paris. But the wealth of Flemish merchants and cloth manufacturers depended on English wool, and Flemish burghers strongly supported the claims of Edward III. The disruption of commerce with England threatened their prosperity.

The Popular Response

The governments of both England and France manipulated public opinion to support the war. Whatever significance modern scholars ascribe to the economic factor, public opinion in fourteenth-century England held that the war was waged for one reason: to secure for King Edward the French crown he had been denied.[8] Edward III issued letters to the sheriffs describing in graphic terms the evil deeds of the French and listing royal needs. Kings in both countries instructed the clergy to deliver sermons filled with patriotic sentiment. Frequent assemblies of Parliament—which in the fourteenth century were meetings of representatives of the nobility, clergy, counties, and towns, as well as royal officials summoned by the king to provide information or revenue or to do justice—spread royal propaganda for the war. The royal courts sensationalized the wickedness of the other side and stressed the great fortunes to be made from the war. Philip VI sent agents to warn communities about the dangers of invasion and to stress the French crown's revenue needs to meet the attack.

The royal campaign to rally public opinion was highly successful, at least in the early stage of the war. Edward III gained widespread support in the 1340s and 1350s. The English developed a deep hatred of the French and feared that King Philip intended "to have seized and slaughtered the entire realm of England." As England was successful in the field, pride in the country's military proficiency increased.

Most important of all, the Hundred Years' War was popular because it presented unusual opportunities for wealth and advancement. Poor knights and knights who were unemployed were promised regular wages. Criminals who enlisted were granted pardons. The great nobles expected to be rewarded with estates. Royal exhortations to the

troops before battles repeatedly stressed that, if victorious, the men might keep whatever they seized. The French chronicler Jean Froissart wrote that, at the time of Edward III's expedition of 1359, men of all ranks flocked to the English king's banner. Some came to acquire honor, but many came in order "to loot and pillage the fair and plenteous land of France."[9]

The Indian Summer of Medieval Chivalry

The period of the Hundred Years' War witnessed the final flowering of the aristocratic code of medieval chivalry. Indeed, the enthusiastic participation of the nobility in both France and England was in response primarily to the opportunity the war provided to display chivalric behavior. What better place to display chivalric qualities than on the field of battle?

War was considered an ennobling experience; there was something elevating, manly, fine, and beautiful about it. When Shakespeare in the sixteenth century wrote of "the pomp and circumstance of glorious war," he was echoing the fourteenth- and fifteenth-century chroniclers who had glorified the trappings of war. Describing the French army before the Battle of Poitiers (1356), a contemporary said: "Then you might see banners and pennons unfurled to the wind, whereon fine gold and azure shone, purple, gules and ermine. Trumpets, horns and clarions—you might hear sounding through the camp; the Dauphin's [title borne by the eldest son of the king of France] great battle made the earth ring."[10]

At Poitiers it was marvelous and terrifying to hear the thundering of the horses' hooves, the cries of the wounded, the sound of the trumpets and clarions, and the shouting of war cries. The tumult was heard at a distance of more than 9 miles. And it was a great grief to behold the flower of all the nobility and chivalry of the world go thus to destruction, death, and martyrdom.

This romantic view of war holds little appeal for modern men and women, who are more conscious of the slaughter, brutality, dirt, and blood that war inevitably involves. Also, modern thinkers are usually conscious of the broad mass of people, while the chivalric code applied only to the aristocratic military elite. Chivalry had no reference to those outside the knightly class.

The knight was supposed to show courtesy, graciousness, and generosity to his social equals, but

The Battle of Crécy, 1346 Pitched battles were unusual in the Hundred Years' War. At Crécy, the English (on the right with lions on their royal standard) scored a spectacular victory. The longbow proved a more effective weapon over the French crossbow, but characteristically the artist concentrated on the aristocratic knights. *(Source: Bibliotheque Nationale, Paris)*

certainly not to his social inferiors. When English knights fought French ones, they were social equals fighting according to a mutually accepted code of behavior. The infantry troops were looked on as inferior beings. When a peasant force at Longueil destroyed a contingent of English knights, their comrades mourned them because "it was too much that so many good fighters had been killed by mere peasants."[11]

The Course of the War to 1419

The war was fought almost entirely in France and the Low Countries (Map 12.2). It consisted mainly of a series of random sieges and cavalry raids. In 1335 the French began supporting Scottish incursions into northern England, ravaging the countryside in Aquitaine, and sacking and burning English coastal towns, such as Southampton. Naturally such tactics lent weight to Edward III's propaganda campaign. In fact, royal propaganda on both sides fostered a kind of early nationalism.

During the war's early stages, England was highly successful. At Crécy in northern France in 1346, English longbowmen scored a great victory over French knights and crossbowmen. Although the fire of the longbow was not very accurate, it allowed for rapid reloading, and English archers could send off three arrows to the French crossbowmen's one. The result was a blinding shower of arrows that unhorsed the French knights and caused mass confusion. The firing of cannon—probably the first use of artillery in the West—created further panic. Thereupon the English horsemen charged and butchered the French.

This was not war according to the chivalric rules that Edward III would have preferred. The English victory at Crécy rested on the skill and swiftness of the yeomen archers, who had nothing at all to do with the chivalric ideals for which the war was being fought. Ten years later, Edward the Black Prince, using the same tactics as at Crécy, smashed the French at Poitiers, captured the French king, and held him for ransom. Again, at Agincourt near Arras in 1415, the chivalric English soldier-king Henry V (r. 1413–1422) gained the field over vastly superior numbers. Henry followed up his triumph at Agincourt with the reconquest of Nor-

ENGLAND

Southampton

English Channel

Calais
FLANDERS

NORMANDY
Paris
Seine
CHAMPAGNE

BRITTANY
ANJOU
Loire
BLOIS
BURGUNDY

HOLY
ROMAN
EMPIRE

POITOU

AQUITAINE

Bordeaux
Garonne

Rhône

GASCONY
TOULOUSE

SPAIN

*Mediterranean
Sea*

0   100 Km.
0   100 Mi.

1337
(before the Battle of Crécy)

Held by the kings
of England

ENGLAND

English Channel

Calais
FLANDERS
✕ Crécy
1346
Rouen

NORMANDY
Paris
Seine
CHAMPAGNE

BRITTANY
ANJOU
Loire
BLOIS

HOLY
ROMAN
EMPIRE

Poitiers
1356 ✕
POITOU
BURGUNDY

AQUITAINE

Bordeaux
Garonne

Rhône

GASCONY
TOULOUSE

SPAIN

*Mediterranean
Sea*

0   100 Km.
0   100 Mi.

1360
(after the Battle of Poitiers)

Held by the kings
of England
✕   Major battles

ENGLAND

Calais
FLANDERS
Agincourt
1415

English Channel

Rouen
Reims
NORMANDY
CHAMPAGNE
Paris
Domrémy
Seine

BRITTANY
ANJOU
Orléans
Loire
BLOIS

HOLY
ROMAN
EMPIRE

BURGUNDY

POITOU

AQUITAINE

Bordeaux
Garonne

Rhône

GASCONY
TOULOUSE

SPAIN

*Mediterranean
Sea*

0   100 Km.
0   100 Mi.

ca 1429
(after the siege of Orléans)

Held by the kings
of England
✕   Major battle

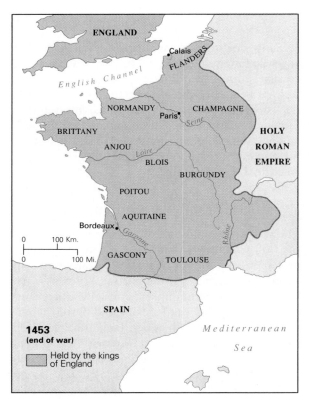

ENGLAND

Calais
FLANDERS

English Channel

NORMANDY
Paris
Seine
CHAMPAGNE

BRITTANY
ANJOU
Loire
BLOIS

HOLY
ROMAN
EMPIRE

BURGUNDY

POITOU

AQUITAINE

Bordeaux
Garonne

Rhône

GASCONY
TOULOUSE

SPAIN

*Mediterranean
Sea*

0   100 Km.
0   100 Mi.

1453
(end of war)

Held by the kings
of England

mandy. By 1419 the English had advanced to the walls of Paris (see Map 12.2). But the French cause was not lost. Though England had scored the initial victories, France won the war.

Joan of Arc and France's Victory

The ultimate French success rests heavily on the actions of an obscure French peasant girl, Joan of Arc, whose vision and work revived French fortunes and led to victory. A great deal of pious and popular legend surrounds Joan the Maid, because of her peculiar appearance on the scene, her astonishing success, her martyrdom, and her canonization by the Catholic church. The historical fact is that she saved the French monarchy, which was the embodiment of France.

Born in 1412 to well-to-do peasants in the village of Domremy in Champagne, Joan of Arc grew up in a religious household. During adolescence she began to hear voices, which she later said belonged to Saint Michael, Saint Catherine, and Saint Margaret. In 1428 these voices spoke to her with great urgency, telling her that the dauphin (the uncrowned King Charles VII) had to be crowned and the English expelled from France. Joan went to the French court, persuaded the king to reject the rumor that he was illegitimate, and secured his support for her relief of the besieged city of Orléans.

The astonishing thing is not that Joan the Maid overcame serious obstacles to see the dauphin, not even that Charles and his advisers listened to her. What is amazing is the swiftness with which they were convinced. French fortunes had been so low for so long that the court believed only a miracle could save the country. Because Joan cut her hair short and dressed like a man, she scandalized the court. But hoping she would provide the miracle, Charles allowed her to accompany the army that was preparing to raise the English siege of Orléans.

In the meantime Joan, herself illiterate, dictated this letter calling on the English to withdraw:

Joan of Arc This is how the court scribe who made this sketch in 1429, the year Joan raised the siege of Orléans, imagined her. He had never seen her. *(Source: Archives Nationales, Paris)*

Jhesus Maria
King of England, and you Duke of Bedford, calling yourself regent of France, you William Pole, Count of Suffolk . . . , do right in the King of Heaven's sight. Surrender to The Maid *sent hither by God the King of Heaven, the keys of all the good towns you have taken and laid waste in France. She comes in God's name to establish the Blood Royal, ready to make peace if you agree to abandon France and repay what you have taken. And you, archers, comrades in arms, gentles and others, who are before the town of Orléans, retire in God's name to your own country. . . .*[12]

Joan arrived before Orléans on April 28, 1429. Seventeen years old, she knew little of warfare and believed that if she could keep the French troops

MAP 12.2 English Holdings in France During the Hundred Years' War The year 1429 marked the greatest extent of English holdings in France. Why was it unlikely that England could have held these territories permanently?

from swearing and frequenting brothels, victory would be theirs. On May 8 the English, weakened by disease and lack of supplies, withdrew from Orléans. Ten days later, Charles VII was crowned king at Reims. These two events marked the turning point in the war.

In 1430 England's allies, the Burgundians, captured Joan and sold her to the English. When the English handed her over to the ecclesiastical authorities for trial, the French court did not intervene. While the English wanted Joan eliminated for obvious political reasons, sorcery (witchcraft) was the ostensible charge at her trial. Witch persecution was increasing in the fifteenth century, and Joan's wearing of men's clothes appeared not only aberrant but indicative of contact with the devil. In 1431 the court condemned her as a heretic— her claim of direct inspiration from God, thereby denying the authority of church officials, constituted heresy—and burned her at the stake in the marketplace at Rouen. A new trial in 1456 rehabilitated her name. In 1920 she was canonized and declared a holy maiden, and today she is revered as the second patron saint of France. The nineteenth-century French historian Jules Michelet extolled Joan of Arc as a symbol of the vitality and strength of the French peasant classes.

The relief of Orléans stimulated French pride and rallied French resources. As the war dragged on, loss of life mounted, and money appeared to be flowing into a bottomless pit, demands for an end increased in England. The clergy and intellectuals pressed for peace. Parliamentary opposition to additional war grants stiffened. Slowly the French reconquered Normandy and, finally, ejected the English from Aquitaine. At the war's end in 1453, only the town of Calais remained in English hands.

Costs and Consequences

For both France and England, the war proved a disaster. In France the English had slaughtered thousands of soldiers and civilians. In the years after the sweep of the Black Death, this additional killing meant a grave loss of population. The English had laid waste to hundreds of thousands of acres of rich farmland, leaving the rural economy of many parts of France a shambles. The war had disrupted trade and the great fairs, resulting in the drastic reduction of French participation in international commerce. Defeat in battle and heavy taxation contributed to widespread dissatisfaction and aggravated peasant grievances.

In England only the southern coastal ports experienced much destruction, and the demographic effects of the Black Death actually worked to restore the land-labor balance (see page 376). The costs of the war, however, were tremendous. England spent over £5 million on the war effort, a huge sum in the fourteenth and fifteenth centuries. Manpower losses had greater social consequences. The knights who ordinarily handled the work of local government as sheriffs, coroners, jurymen, and justices of the peace were abroad, and their absence contributed to the breakdown of order at the local level. The English government attempted to finance the war effort by raising taxes on the wool crop. Because of steadily increasing costs, the Flemish and Italian buyers could not afford English wool. Consequently, raw wool exports slumped drastically between 1350 and 1450.

Many men of all social classes had volunteered for service in France in the hope of acquiring booty and becoming rich. The chronicler Walsingham, describing the period of Crécy, tells of the tremendous prosperity and abundance resulting from the spoils of war: "For the woman was of no account who did not possess something from the spoils of . . . cities overseas in clothing, furs, quilts, and utensils . . . tablecloths and jewels, bowls of murra [semiprecious stone] and silver, linen and linen cloths."[13] Walsingham is referring to 1348, in the first generation of war. As time went on, most fortunes seem to have been squandered as fast as they were made.

If English troops returned with cash, they did not invest it in land. In the fifteenth century, returning soldiers were commonly described as beggars and vagabonds, roaming about making mischief. Even the large sums of money received from the ransom of the great—such as the £250,000 paid to Edward III for the freedom of King John of France—and the money paid as indemnities by captured towns and castles did not begin to equal the more than £5 million spent. England suffered a serious net loss.[14]

The long war also had a profound impact on the political and cultural lives of the two countries. Most notably, it stimulated the development of the English Parliament. Between 1250 and 1450, representative assemblies from several classes of society flourished in many European countries. In the English Parliament, French Estates, German diets, and Spanish Cortes, deliberative practices developed that laid the foundations for the representative institutions of modern liberal-democratic nations. While representative assemblies declined in most countries after the fifteenth century, the English Parliament endured. Edward III's constant need for money to pay for the war compelled him to summon not only the great barons and bishops, but knights of the shires and burgesses from the towns as well. Between the outbreak of the war in 1337 and the king's death in 1377, parliamentary assemblies met twenty-seven times. Parliament met in thirty-seven of the fifty years of Edward's reign.[15]

The frequency of the meetings is significant. Representative assemblies were becoming a habit. Knights and burgesses—or the "Commons," as they came to be called—recognized their mutual interests and began to meet apart from the great lords. The Commons gradually realized that they held the country's purse strings, and a parliamentary statute of 1341 required that all nonfeudal levies have parliamentary approval. When Edward III signed the law, he acknowledged that the king of England could not tax without Parliament's consent. Increasingly, during the course of the war, money grants were tied to royal redress of grievances: if the government was to raise money, it had to correct the wrongs its subjects protested.

In England theoretical consent to taxation and legislation was given in one assembly for the entire country. France had no such single assembly; instead, there were many regional or provincial assemblies. Why did a national representative assembly fail to develop in France? The initiative for convening assemblies rested with the king, who needed revenue almost as much as the English ruler. But the French monarchy found the idea of representative assemblies thoroughly distasteful. Large gatherings of the nobility potentially or actually threatened the king's power. The advice of a counselor to King Charles VI (r. 1380–1422), "above all things be sure that no great assemblies of nobles or of *communes* take place in your kingdom," was accepted.[16] Charles VII (r. 1422–1461) even threatened to punish those proposing a national assembly.

No one in France wanted a national assembly. Linguistic, geographic, economic, legal, and political differences were very strong. People tended to think of themselves as Breton, Norman, Burgundian, or whatever, rather than French. Through much of the fourteenth and early fifteenth centuries, weak monarchs lacked the power to call a national assembly. Provincial assemblies, highly jealous of their independence, did not want a national assembly. The costs of sending delegates to it would be high, and the result was likely to be increased taxation. Finally, the Hundred Years' War itself hindered the growth of a representative body of government. Possible violence on dangerous roads discouraged people from travel.

In both countries, however, the war did promote the growth of *nationalism*—the feeling of unity and identity that binds together a people who speak the same language, have a common ancestry and customs, and live in the same area. In the fourteenth century, nationalism largely took the form of hostility toward foreigners. Both Philip VI and Edward III drummed up support for the war by portraying the enemy as an alien, evil people. Edward III sought to justify his personal dynastic quarrel by linking it with England's national interests. As the Parliament Roll of 1348 states:

"The Knights of the shires and the others of the Commons were told that they should withdraw together and take good counsel as to how, for withstanding the malice of the said enemy and for the salvation of our said lord the King and his Kingdom of England . . . the King could be aided."[17]

After victories, each country experienced a surge of pride in its military strength. Just as English patriotism ran strong after Crécy and Poitiers, so French national confidence rose after Orléans. French national feeling demanded the expulsion of the enemy not merely from Normandy and Aquitaine but from French soil. Perhaps no one expressed this national consciousness better than Joan of Arc, when she exulted that the enemy had been "driven out of *France*."

✠ THE DECLINE OF THE CHURCH'S PRESTIGE

In times of crisis or disaster, people of all faiths have sought the consolation of religion. In the fourteenth century, however, the official Christian church offered very little solace. In fact, the leaders of the church added to the sorrow and misery of the times.

The Babylonian Captivity

From 1309 to 1376, the popes lived in Avignon in southeastern France. In order to control the church and its policies, Philip the Fair of France pressured Pope Clement V to settle in Avignon (see page 364). Clement, critically ill with cancer, lacked the will to resist Philip. This period in church history is often called the Babylonian Captivity (referring to the seventy years the ancient Hebrews were held captive in Mesopotamian Babylon).

The Babylonian Captivity badly damaged papal prestige. The Avignon papacy reformed its financial administration and centralized its government. But the seven popes at Avignon concentrated on bureaucratic matters to the exclusion of spiritual objectives. Though some of the popes led austere lives there, the general atmosphere was one of luxury and extravagance. The leadership of the church was cut off from its historic roots and the source of its ancient authority, the city of Rome. In the absence of the papacy, the Papal States in Italy lacked stability and good government. The economy of Rome had long been based on the presence of the papal court and the rich tourist trade the papacy attracted. The Babylonian Captivity left Rome poverty-stricken.

Many devout Christians urged the popes to return to Rome. The Dominican mystic Catherine of Siena (1347–1380), for example, made a special trip to Avignon to plead with the pope to return. Public opinion credited her influence as decisive. Catherine later supported Urban VI against the Avignonese antipope, and she died in Urban's service. Her 350 letters and compositions describing her mystical experiences, dictated because she could not write, survive. Catherine was canonized by the Sienese Pope Pius II and is revered as one of the patron saints of Italy.

In 1377, Pope Gregory XI brought the papal court back to Rome. Unfortunately, he died shortly after the return. At Gregory's death, Roman citizens demanded an Italian pope who would remain in Rome. Determined to influence the papal conclave (the assembly of cardinals who chose the new pope) to elect an Italian, a Roman mob surrounded Saint Peter's Basilica, blocked the roads leading out of the city, and seized all boats on the Tiber River. Between the time of Gregory's death and the opening of the conclave, great pressure was put on the cardinals to elect an Italian. At the time, none of them protested this pressure.

Sixteen cardinals—eleven Frenchmen, four Italians, and one Spaniard—entered the conclave on April 7, 1378. After two ballots they unanimously chose a distinguished administrator, the archbishop of Bari, Bartolomeo Prignano, who took the name Urban VI. Each of the cardinals swore that Urban had been elected "sincerely, freely, genuinely, and canonically."

Urban VI (1378–1389) had excellent intentions for church reform. He wanted to abolish simony, *pluralism* (holding several church offices at the same time), absenteeism, clerical extravagance, and ostentation. These were the very abuses being increasingly criticized by Christian people across Europe. Unfortunately, Pope Urban went about the work of reform in a tactless, arrogant, and bullheaded manner. The day after his coronation he delivered a blistering attack on cardinals who lived in Rome while drawing their income from benefices elsewhere. His criticism was well founded but ill timed and provoked opposition among the hierarchy before Urban had consolidated his authority.

In the weeks that followed, Urban stepped up attacks on clerical luxury, denouncing individual cardinals by name. He threatened to strike the cardinal archbishop of Amiens. Urban even threatened to excommunicate certain cardinals, and when he was advised that such excommunications would not be lawful unless the guilty had been warned three times, he shouted, "I can do anything, if it be my will and judgment."[18] Urban's quick temper and irrational behavior have led scholars to question his sanity. Whether he was medically insane or just drunk with power is a moot point. In any case, Urban's actions brought on disaster.

In groups of two and three, the cardinals slipped away from Rome and met at Anagni. They declared Urban's election invalid because it had come about under threats from the Roman mob, and they asserted that Urban himself was excommunicated. The cardinals then proceeded to the city of Fondi between Rome and Naples and elected Cardinal Robert of Geneva, the cousin of King Charles V of France, as pope. Cardinal Robert took the name Clement VII. There were thus two popes—Urban at Rome and the antipope Clement VII (1378–1394), who set himself up at Avignon in opposition to the legally elected Urban. So began the Great Schism, which divided Western Christendom until 1417.

The Great Schism

The powers of Europe aligned themselves with Urban or Clement along strictly political lines. France naturally recognized the French antipope, Clement. England, France's historic enemy, recognized Pope Urban. Scotland, whose attacks on England were subsidized by France, followed the French and supported Clement. Aragon, Castile, and Portugal hesitated before deciding for Clement at Avignon. The emperor, who bore ancient hostility to France, recognized Urban VI. At first the Italian city-states recognized Urban; when he alienated them, they opted for Clement.

John of Spoleto, a professor at the law school at Bologna, eloquently summed up intellectual opinion of the schism: *"The longer this schism lasts, the more it appears to be costing, and the more harm it does; scandal, massacres, ruination, agitations, troubles and disturbances . . ."*[19] The scandal "rent the seamless garment of Christ," as the church was called, and provoked horror and vigorous cries for reform. The common people, wracked by inflation, wars, and plague, were thoroughly confused about which pope was legitimate. The schism weakened the religious faith of many Christians and gave rise to instability and religious excesses. It brought the church leadership into serious disrepute. At a time when ordinary Christians needed the consolation of religion and confidence in religious leaders, church officials were fighting among themselves for power.

The Conciliar Movement

Calls for church reform were not new. A half-century before the Great Schism, in 1324, Marsiglio of Padua, then rector of the University of Paris, had published *Defensor Pacis (The Defender of the Peace)*. Dealing as it did with the authority of state and church, *Defensor Pacis* proved to be one of the most controversial works written in the Middle Ages.

Marsiglio argued that the state was the great unifying power in society and that the church was subordinate to the state. He put forth the revolutionary ideas that the church had no inherent jurisdiction and should own no property. Authority in the Christian church, according to Marsiglio, should rest in a general council, made up of laymen as well as priests and superior to the pope. These ideas directly contradicted the medieval notion of a society governed by the church and the state, with the church supreme. *Defensor Pacis* was condemned by the pope, and Marsiglio was excommunicated.

Even more earthshaking than the theories of Marsiglio of Padua were the ideas of the English scholar and theologian John Wyclif (1329–1384). Wyclif wrote that papal claims of temporal power

❖ **The Holy Roman Emperor Sigismund** (1410–1437), persuaded to take the initiative in summoning the Council of Constance, is here shown in procession at the council. When the Bohemian reformer John Hus declared that sin vitiates a clerical or civil office, Hus lost the emperor's support, was tried, condemned, and burned at the stake. Sigismund thereby kindled Bohemian nationalism, which led to the Hussite wars. *(Source: Rosgarten Museum, Konstanz)*

had no foundation in the Scriptures, and that the Scriptures alone should be the standard of Christian belief and practice. He urged the abolition of such practices as the veneration of saints, pilgrimages, pluralism, and absenteeism. Sincere Christians, according to Wyclif, should read the Bible for themselves. In response to that idea, the first English translation of the Bible was produced and circulated. Wyclif's views had broad social and economic significance. He urged that the church be stripped of its property. His idea that every Christian free of mortal sin possessed lordship was seized on by peasants in England during a revolt in 1381 and used to justify their goals.

In advancing these views, Wyclif struck at the roots of medieval church structure and religious practices. Consequently, he has been hailed as the precursor of the Reformation of the sixteenth century. Although Wyclif's ideas were vigorously condemned by ecclesiastical authorities, they were widely disseminated by humble clerics and enjoyed great popularity in the early fifteenth century. Wyclif's followers were called "Lollards." The term, which means "mumblers of prayers and psalms," refers to what they criticized. Lollard teaching allowed women to preach and to consecrate the Eucharist. Women, some well educated, played a significant role in the movement. After Anne, sister of Wenceslaus, king of Germany and Bohemia, married Richard II of England, members of her household carried Lollard principles back to Bohemia, where they were spread by John Hus, rector of the University of Prague.

In response to continued calls throughout Europe for a council, the two colleges of cardinals—one at Rome, the other at Avignon—summoned a council at Pisa in 1409. A distinguished gathering of prelates and theologians deposed both popes and selected another. Neither the Avignon pope nor the Roman pope would resign, however, and the appalling result was the creation of a threefold schism.

Finally, because of the pressure of the German emperor Sigismund, a great council met at the imperial city of Constance (1414–1418). It had three objectives: to end the schism, to reform the church "in head and members" (from top to bottom), and to wipe out heresy. The council condemned the Lollard ideas of John Hus, and he was burned at the stake. The council eventually deposed both the Roman pope and the successor of the pope chosen at Pisa, and it isolated the Avignon antipope. A conclave elected a new leader, the Roman cardinal Colonna, who took the name Martin V (1417–1431).

Martin proceeded to dissolve the council. Nothing was done about reform. The schism was over, and though councils subsequently met at Basel and at Ferrara-Florence, in 1450 the papacy held a jubilee, celebrating its triumph over the conciliar movement. In the later fifteenth century, the papacy concentrated on Italian problems to the exclusion of universal Christian interests. But the schism and the conciliar movement had exposed the crying need for ecclesiastical reform, thus laying the foundations for the great reform efforts of the sixteenth century.

 THE LIFE OF THE PEOPLE

In the fourteenth century, economic and political difficulties, disease, and war profoundly affected the lives of European peoples. Decades of slaughter and destruction, punctuated by the decimating visits of the Black Death, made a grave economic situation virtually disastrous. In many parts of France and the Low Countries, fields lay in ruin or untilled for lack of labor power. In England, as taxes increased, criticisms of government policy and mismanagement multiplied. Crime, aggravated economic troubles, and throughout Europe the frustrations of the common people erupted into widespread revolts. But for most people, marriage and the local parish church continued to be the center of their lives.

Marriage

Marriage and the family provided such peace and satisfaction as most people attained. What do we know about peasant marriages in the later Middle Ages? Scholars long believed that because peasants were illiterate and left very few statements about their marriages, generalizations could not be made about them. Recent research in English manorial, ecclesiastical, and coroners' records, however, has uncovered fascinating material. Evidence abounds of teenage flirtations, and many young people had sexual contacts—some leading to conception. Premarital pregnancy may have been deliberate: because children were economically important, the couple wanted to be sure of fertility before entering marriage.

"Whether rich or poor, male or female, the most important rite de passage for peasant youth was marriage."[20] Did they select their own spouses? or accept parents' choices? Church law stressed that for a marriage to be valid both parents must freely consent to it. Nevertheless, the evidence over-whelmingly shows, above all where land or prop-erty accompanied the union, that parents took the lead in arranging their children's marriages; if the parents were dead the responsibility fell to the in-heriting son. Marriage determined not only the life partner, and the economic circumstances in which the couple would live, but also the son-in-law who might take over the family land, or the daughter-in-law who might care for her elderly in-laws. These kinds of interests required careful planning.

Most marriages were between men and women of the same village; where the name and residence of a husband is known, perhaps 41 percent were outsiders. Once the prospective bride or groom had been decided on, parents paid the *merchet* (fine to the lord for a woman's marriage—since he stood to lose a worker). Parents saw that the parish priest published on three successive Sundays the *banns,* public announcements that the couple planned to marry, to allow for objections to the union. And parents made the financial settlement. The couple then proceeded to the church door, where they made the vows, rings were blessed and exchanged, and the ceremony concluded with some kind of festivity. The church strongly discouraged the sol-emnization of marriage during the holy seasons of Lent, Advent, and on the rogation days (prescribed days of fasting and prayer for the harvest). There-fore, most marriages (and conceptions) took place in the summer months, during the harvest season (October, November), or in January.[21]

Although most peasants were illiterate, the gen-try could write. The letters exchanged between Margaret and John Paston, who lived in Norfolk, England, in the fifteenth century provide impor-tant evidence for the experience of one couple. John and Margaret Paston were married about 1439, after an arrangement concluded entirely by their parents. John spent most of his time in Lon-don fighting through the law courts to increase his family properties and business interests; Margaret remained in Norfolk to supervise the family lands. Her enormous responsibilities involved managing the Paston estates, hiring workers, collecting rents, ordering supplies for the large household, hearing complaints and settling disputes among tenants,

and marketing her crops. In these duties she proved herself a remarkably shrewd businessper-son. Moreover, when an army of over a thousand men led by the aristocratic thug Lord Moleyns attacked her house, she successfully withstood the siege. When the Black Death entered her area, Margaret moved her family to safety.

Margaret Paston did all this on top of raising eight children (there were probably other children who did not survive childhood). Her husband died before she was forty-three, and she later conducted the negotiations for the children's marriages. Her children's futures, like her estate management, were planned with an eye toward economic and social advancement. When one daughter secretly married the estate bailiff, an alliance considered beneath her, the girl was cut off from the family as if she were dead.[22]

The many letters surviving between Margaret and John reveal slight tenderness toward their chil-dren. They seem to have reserved their love for each other, and during many of his frequent ab-sences they wrote to express mutual affection and devotion. How typical the Paston relationship was modern historians cannot say, but the marriage of John and Margaret, although completely arranged by their parents, was based on respect, responsibil-ity, and love.[23]

At what age did people usually marry? The larg-est amount of evidence on age at first marriage survives from Italy, and a comparable pattern prob-ably existed in northern Europe. For girls, popu-lation surveys at Prato place the age at 16.3 years in 1372 and 21.1 in 1470. Chaucer's Wife of Bath says that she married first in her twelfth year. Among the German nobility recent research has indicated that in the Hohenzollern family in the later Middle Ages "five brides were between 12 and 13; five about 14, and five about 15."

Men were older. An Italian chronicler writing about 1354 says that men did not marry before the age of 30. At Prato in 1371, the average age of men at first marriage was 24 years, very young for Italian men, but these data may represent an attempt to regain population losses due to the recent attack of the plague. In England Chaucer's Wife of Bath describes her first three husbands as "goode men, and rich, and old." Among seventeen males in the noble Hohenzollern family, eleven were over 20 years when married, five between 18 and 19, one 16. The general pattern in late medie-val Europe was marriage between men in their middle or late twenties and women under twenty.[24] Poor peasants and wage laborers did not marry until their mid or late twenties.

With marriage for men postponed, was there any socially accepted sexual outlet? Recent research on the southern French province of Languedoc in the fourteenth and fifteenth centuries has revealed the establishment of legal houses of prostitution. Prostitution involves "a socially definable group of women [who] earn their living primarily or exclusively from the commerce of their bodies."[25] Municipal authorities in Toulouse, Montpellier, Albi, and other towns set up houses or red-light districts either outside the city walls or away from respectable neighborhoods. For example, authorities in Montpellier set aside Hot Street for prostitution, required public women to live there, and forbade anyone to molest them. Prostitution thus passed from being a private concern to a social matter requiring public supervision.[26] Publicly owned brothels were more easily policed and supervised

Prostitute Invites a Traveling Merchant Poverty and male violence drove women into prostitution, which, though denounced by moralists, was accepted as a normal part of the medieval social fabric. In the cities and larger towns where prostitution flourished, public officials passed laws requiring prostitutes to wear a special mark on their clothing, regulated hours of business, forbade women to drag men into their houses, and denied business to women with the "burning sickness," gonorrhea. (*Source: The Bodleian Library, Oxford*)

than privately run ones. Prostitution was an urban phenomenon, because only populous towns had large numbers of unmarried young men, communities of transient merchants, and a culture accustomed to a cash exchange. Although the risk of disease limited the number of years a woman could practice this profession, many women prospered. Some acquired sizable incomes. In 1361, Françoise of Florence, a prostitute working in a brothel in Marseilles, made a will in which she made legacies to various charities and left a large sum as a dowry for a poor girl to marry. Archives in several cities show expensive properties bought by women who named their occupation as prostitution.

The towns of Languedoc were not unique. Public authorities in Amiens, Dijon, Paris, Venice, Genoa, London, Florence, Rome, most of the larger German towns, and in the English port of Sandwich set up brothels. Legalized prostitution suggests that public officials believed the prostitute could make a positive contribution to the society; it does not mean the prostitute was respected. Rather, she was scorned and distrusted. Legalized brothels also reflect a greater tolerance for male than for female sexuality.[27]

In the later Middle Ages, as earlier—indeed, until the late nineteenth century—economic factors, rather than romantic love or physical attraction, determined whom and when a person married. The young agricultural laborer on the manor had to wait until he had sufficient land. Thus most men had to wait until their fathers died or yielded the holding. The age of marriage was late, and this in turn affected the number of children a couple had. The journeyman craftsman in the urban guild faced the same material difficulties. Once a couple married, the union ended only with the death of one partner.

Deep emotional bonds knit members of medieval families. Most parents delighted in their children, and the church encouraged a cult of paternal care. The church stressed its right to govern and sanctify marriage, and it emphasized monogamy. Tighter moral and emotional unity within marriages resulted.

Divorce did not exist in the Middle Ages. The church held that a marriage validly entered into could not be dissolved. A valid marriage consisted of the mutual oral consent or promise of two parties. Church theologians of the day urged that the couple's union be celebrated and witnessed in a church ceremony and blessed by a priest.

A great number of couples did not observe the church's regulations. Some treated marriage as a private act—they made the promise and spoke the words of marriage to each other without witnesses and then proceeded to enjoy the sexual pleasures of marriage. This practice led to a great number of disputes, because one of the two parties could later deny having made a marriage agreement. The records of the ecclesiastical courts reveal many cases arising from privately made contracts. Evidence survives of marriages contracted in a garden, in a blacksmith's shop, at a tavern, and, predictably, in a bed. The records of church courts that relate to marriage reveal that, rather than suing for divorce, the great majority of petitions asked the court to enforce the marriage contract that one of the parties believed she or he had validly made. Annulments were granted in extraordinary circumstances, such as male impotence, on the grounds that a lawful marriage had never existed.[28]

Life in the Parish

In the later Middle Ages, the land and the parish remained the focus of life for the European peasantry. Work on the land continued to be performed collectively. Both men and women cooperated in the annual tasks of planting and harvesting. The close association of the cycle of agriculture and the liturgy of the Christian calendar endured. The parish priest blessed the fields before the annual planting, offering prayers on behalf of the people for a good crop. If the harvest was rich, the priest led the processions and celebrations of thanksgiving.

How did the common people feel about their work? Since the vast majority were illiterate and inarticulate, it is difficult to say. It is known that the peasants hated the ancient services and obligations on the lords' lands and tried to get them commuted for money rents. When lords attempted to reimpose service duties, the peasants revolted.

In the thirteenth century, the craft guilds provided the small minority of men and women living in towns and cities with the psychological satisfaction of involvement in the manufacture of a superior product. The guild member also had economic security. The craft guilds set high standards for their merchandise. The guilds looked after the sick, the poor, the widowed, and the orphaned. Masters and employees worked side by side.

In the fourteenth century, those ideal conditions began to change. The fundamental objective of the craft guild was to maintain a monopoly on its product, and to do so recruitment and promotion were carefully restricted. Some guilds required a high entrance fee for apprentices; others admitted only relatives of members. Apprenticeship increasingly lasted a long time, seven years. Even after a young man had satisfied all the tests for full membership in the guild and had attained the rank of master, other hurdles had to be passed, such as finding the funds to open his own business or special connections just to get in a guild. Restrictions limited the number of apprentices and journeymen to match the anticipated openings for masters. Women experienced the same exclusion. A careful study of the records of forty-two craft guilds in Cologne shows that in the fifteenth century all but six became virtual male preserves, either greatly restricting women's participation or allowing so few female members that they cannot be considered mixed guilds.[29] The larger a particular business was, the greater was the likelihood that the master did not know his employees. The separation of master and journeyman and the decreasing number of openings for master craftsmen created serious frustrations. Strikes and riots occurred in the Flemish towns, in France, and in England.

The recreation of all classes reflected the fact that late medieval society was organized for war and that violence was common. The aristocracy engaged in tournaments or jousts; archery and wrestling had great popularity among ordinary people. Everyone enjoyed the cruel sports of bullbaiting and bearbaiting. The hangings and mutilations of criminals were exciting and well-attended events, with all the festivity of a university town before a Saturday football game. Chroniclers exulted in describing executions, murders, and massacres. Here a monk gleefully describes the gory execution of William Wallace in 1305:

Wilielmus Waleis, a robber given to sacrilege, arson and homicide . . . was condemned to most cruel but justly deserved death. He was drawn through the streets of London at the tails of horses, until he reached a gallows of unusual height, there he was suspended by a halter; but taken down while yet alive, he was mutilated, his bowels torn out and burned in a fire, his head then cut off, his body divided into four, and his quarters transmitted to four principal parts of Scotland.[30]

Violence was as English as roast beef and plum pudding, as French as bread, cheese, and *potage*.

❖ **SHEPHERDS DANCING** As in all ages, young people (and some not so young) enjoyed dancing, and the marriage or baptismal feast, or harvest celebration, provided the occasion, perhaps accompanied by singing or the music of someone talented on the harmonica or as here (lower right) on a bagpipe. *(Source: Bibliothèque National, Paris)*

If violent entertainment was not enough to dispel life's cares, alcohol was also available. Beer or ale commonly provided solace to the poor, and the frequency of drunkenness reflects their terrible frustrations.

During the fourteenth and fifteenth centuries, the laity began to exercise increasing control over parish affairs. Churchmen were criticized. The constant quarrels of the mendicant orders (the Franciscans and Dominicans), the mercenary and grasp-ing attitude of the parish clergy, the scandal of the Great Schism and a divided Christendom—all these did much to weaken the spiritual mystique of the clergy in the popular mind. The laity steadily took responsibility for the management of parish lands. Lay people organized associations to vote on and purchase furnishings for the church. And ordinary lay people secured jurisdiction over the structure of the church building, its vestments, books, and furnishings. These new responsibilities of the laity reflect the increased dignity of parishioners in the late Middle Ages.[31]

Fur-Collar Crime

The Hundred Years' War had provided employment and opportunity for thousands of idle and fortune-seeking knights. But during periods of truce and after the war finally ended, many nobles once again had little to do. Inflation also hurt them. Although many were living on fixed incomes, their chivalric code demanded lavish generosity and an aristocratic lifestyle. Many nobles turned to crime as a way of raising money. The fourteenth and fifteenth centuries witnessed a great deal of "fur-collar crime," so called for the miniver fur the nobility alone were allowed to wear on their collars. England provides a good case study of upper-class crime (see Listening to the Past).

Fur-collar crime rarely involved such felonies as homicide, robbery, rape, and arson. Instead, nobles used their superior social status to rob and extort from the weak and then to corrupt the judicial process. Groups of noble brigands roamed the English countryside stealing from both rich and poor. Sir John de Colseby and Sir William Bussy led a gang of thirty-eight knights who stole goods worth £3,000 in various robberies. Operating like modern urban racketeers, knightly gangs demanded that peasants pay "protection money" or else have their hovels burned and their fields destroyed. Members of the household of a certain Lord Robert of Payn beat up a victim and then demanded money for protection from future attack.

Attacks on the rich often took the form of kidnaping and extortion. Individuals were grabbed in their homes, and wealthy travelers were seized on the highways and held for ransom. In northern England a gang of gentry led by Sir Gilbert de Middleton abducted Sir Henry Beaumont; his brother, the bishop-elect of Durham; and two Roman cardinals in England on a peacemaking visit. Only after a ransom was paid were the victims released.[32]

Fur-collar criminals were terrorists, but like some twentieth-century white-collar criminals who commit nonviolent crimes, medieval aristocratic criminals got away with their outrages. When accused of wrongdoing, fur-collar criminals intimidated witnesses. They threatened jurors. They used "pull" or cash to bribe judges. As a fourteenth-century English judge wrote to a young nobleman, "For the love of your father I have hindered charges being brought against you and have prevented execution of indictment actually made."[33]

The ballads of Robin Hood, a collection of folk legends from late medieval England, describe the adventures of the outlaw hero and his band of followers, who lived in Sherwood Forest and attacked and punished those who violated the social system and the law. Most of the villains in these simple tales are fur-collar criminals—grasping landlords, wicked sheriffs such as the famous sheriff of Nottingham, and mercenary churchmen. Robin and his merry men performed a sort of retributive justice. Robin Hood was a popular figure, because he symbolized the deep resentment of aristocratic corruption and abuse; he represented the struggle against tyranny and oppression.

Criminal activity by nobles continued decade after decade because governments were too weak to stop it. Then, too, much of the crime was directed against a lord's own serfs, and the line between a noble's legal jurisdiction over his peasants and criminal behavior was a fine one indeed. Persecution by lords, on top of war, disease, and natural disaster, eventually drove long-suffering and oppressed peasants all across Europe to revolt.

Peasant Revolts

Peasant revolts occurred often in the Middle Ages. Early in the thirteenth century, the French preacher Jacques de Vitry asked rhetorically, "How many serfs have killed their lords or burnt their castles?"[34] And in the fourteenth and fifteenth centuries, social and economic conditions caused a great increase in peasant uprisings (Map 12.3).

In 1358, when French taxation for the Hundred Years' War fell heavily on the poor, the frustrations of the French peasantry exploded in a massive uprising called the *Jacquerie*, after a supposedly happy agricultural laborer, Jacques Bonhomme (Good Fellow). Two years earlier, the English had captured the French king John and many nobles and held them for ransom. The peasants resented paying for their lords' release. Recently hit by plague, experiencing famine in some areas, and harassed by fur collar criminals, the peasants in Picardy, Champagne, and the Île de France (the area around Paris) erupted in anger and frustration. Crowds swept through the countryside slashing the throats of nobles, burning their castles, raping their wives and daughters, killing or maiming their horses and cattle. Peasants blamed the nobility for oppressive taxes, for the criminal brigandage of the countryside, for defeat in war, and for the general misery. Artisans, small merchants, and parish priests joined the peasants. Urban and rural groups committed terrible destruction, and for several weeks the nobles were on the defensive. Then the upper class united to repress the revolt with merciless ferocity. Thousands of the "Jacques," innocent as well as guilty, were cut down.

This forcible suppression of social rebellion, without some effort to alleviate its underlying causes, served to drive protest underground. Between 1363 and 1484, serious peasant revolts swept the Auvergne; in 1380 uprisings occurred in the Midi; and in 1420 they erupted in the Lyonnais region of France.

The Peasants' Revolt in England in 1381, involving perhaps a hundred thousand people, was probably the largest single uprising of the entire Middle Ages (see Map 12.3). The causes of the rebellion were complex and varied from place to place. In general, though, the thirteenth century had witnessed the steady commutation of labor services for cash rents, and the Black Death had drastically cut the labor supply. As a result, peasants demanded higher wages and fewer manorial obligations. Thirty years earlier the parliamentary Statute of Laborers of 1351 (see page 377) had declared: "Whereas to curb the malice of servants who after the pestilence were idle and unwilling to serve without securing excessive wages, it was recently ordained . . . that such servants, both men and women, shall be bound to serve in return for salaries and wages that were customary . . . five or six years earlier."[35]

This attempt by landlords to freeze wages and social mobility could not be enforced. As a matter of fact, the condition of the English peasantry steadily improved in the course of the fourteenth

❖ **MAP 12.3 Fourteenth-Century Peasant Revolts** In the later Middle Ages and early modern times, peasant and urban uprisings were endemic, as common as factory strikes in the industrial world. The threat of insurrection served to check unlimited exploitation.

century. Some scholars believe that the peasantry in most places was better off in the period 1350 to 1450 than it had been for centuries before or was to be for four centuries after.

Why then was the outburst in 1381 so serious? It was provoked by a crisis of rising expectations. The relative prosperity of the laboring classes led to demands that the upper classes were unwilling to grant. Unable to climb higher, the peasants found release for their economic frustrations in revolt. But economic grievances combined with other factors. The south of England, where the revolt broke out, had been subjected to frequent and destructive French raids. The English government did little to protect the south, and villages grew increasingly scared and insecure. This fear erupted into revolt. Moreover, decades of aristocratic violence, much of it perpetrated against the weak peasantry, had bred hostility and bitterness. In France frustration over the lack of permanent victory increased. In England the social and religious agitation of the popular preacher John Ball fanned the embers of discontent. Such sayings as Ball's famous couplet *"When Adam delved and Eve span; Who was then the gentleman?"* reflect real revolutionary sentiment.

The straw that broke the camel's back in England was the reimposition of a head tax on all adult males. Although the tax met widespread opposition in 1380, the royal council ordered the sheriffs to collect it again in 1381 on penalty of a huge fine. Beginning with assaults on the tax collectors, the uprising in England followed much the same course as had the Jacquerie in France. Castles and manors were sacked; manorial records were destroyed. Many nobles, including the archbishop of Canterbury, who had ordered the collection of the tax, were murdered.

Although the center of the revolt lay in the highly populated and economically advanced south and east, sections of the north and the Midlands also witnessed rebellions. Violence took different forms in different places. The townspeople of Cambridge expressed their hostility toward the university by sacking one of the colleges and building a bonfire of academic property. In towns containing skilled Flemish craftsmen, fear of competition led to their being attacked and murdered. Urban discontent merged with rural violence. Apprentices and journeymen, frustrated because the highest positions in the guilds were closed to them, rioted.

The boy-king Richard II (r. 1377–1399) met the leaders of the revolt, agreed to charters ensuring peasants' freedom, tricked them with false promises, and then proceeded to crush the uprising with terrible ferocity. Although the nobility tried to restore ancient duties of serfdom, virtually a century of freedom had elapsed, and the commutation of manorial services continued. Rural serfdom had disappeared in England by 1550.

Conditions in England and France were not unique. In Florence in 1378, the *ciompi,* the poor propertyless workers, revolted. Serious social trouble occurred in Lübeck, Brunswick, and other German cities. In Spain in 1391, aristocratic attempts to impose new forms of serfdom, combined with demands for tax relief, led to massive

John Ball, a priest of Kent, often preached his radical egalitarianism out of doors after Mass: ". . . matters goeth not well . . . in England nor shall (they) till everything be common and . . . there by no villains (serfs) nor gentlemen . . . What have we deserved, or why should we be kept thus in servage (servitude)?" All contemporary writers blamed Ball for fomenting the rebellion of 1381. But the evidence of peasant demands shows that they were limited and local: hunting rights in the woods, freedom from miscellaneous payments, exemption from special work on the lord's bridges or parks. *(Source: From a private collection)*

working-class and peasant uprisings in Seville and Barcelona. These took the form of vicious attacks on Jewish communities. Rebellions and uprisings everywhere reveal deep peasant and working-class frustration and the general socioeconomic crisis of the time.

✥ VERNACULAR LITERATURE

Few developments expressed the development of national consciousness more vividly than the emergence of national literatures. Across Europe people spoke the language and dialect of their particular locality and class. In England, for example, the common people spoke regional English dialects, while the upper classes conversed in French. Official documents and works of literature were written in Latin or French. Beginning in the fourteenth century, however, national languages—the vernacular—came into widespread use not only in verbal communication but in literature as well. Three masterpieces of European culture, Dante's *Divine Comedy* (1310–1320), Chaucer's *Canterbury Tales* (1387–1400), and Villon's *Grand Testament* (1461), brilliantly manifest this new national pride.

Dante Alighieri (1265–1321) descended from an aristocratic family in Florence, where he held several positions in the city government. Dante called his work a "comedy" because he wrote it in Italian and in a different style from the "tragic" Latin; a later generation added the adjective "divine," referring both to its sacred subject and to Dante's artistry. The *Divine Comedy* is an allegorical trilogy of one hundred cantos (verses) whose three equal parts (1 + 33 + 33 + 33) each describe one of the realms of the next world, Hell, Purgatory, and Paradise. Dante recounts his imaginary journey through these regions toward God. The Roman poet Virgil, representing reason, leads Dante through Hell, where he observes the torments of the damned and denounces the disorders of his own time, especially ecclesiastical ambition and corruption. Passing up into Purgatory, Virgil shows the poet how souls are purified of their disordered inclinations. From Purgatory, Beatrice, a woman Dante once loved and the symbol of divine revelation in the poem, leads him to Paradise. In Paradise, home of the angels and saints, Saint Bernard—representing mystic contemplation—leads Dante to the Virgin Mary. Through her intercession he at last attains a vision of God.

The *Divine Comedy* portrays contemporary and historical figures, comments on secular and ecclesiastical affairs, and draws on Scholastic philosophy. Within the framework of a symbolic pilgrimage to the City of God, the *Divine Comedy* embodies the psychological tensions of the age. A profoundly Christian poem, it also contains bitter criticism of some church authorities. In its symmetrical structure and use of figures from the ancient world, such as Virgil, the poem perpetuates the classical tradition, but as the first major work of literature in the Italian vernacular, it is distinctly modern.

Geoffrey Chaucer (1340–1400), the son of a London wine merchant, was an official in the administrations of the English kings Edward III and Richard II and wrote poetry as an avocation. Chaucer's *Canterbury Tales* is a collection of stories in lengthy, rhymed narrative. On a pilgrimage to the shrine of Saint Thomas Becket at Canterbury (see page 339), thirty people of various social backgrounds each tell a tale. The Prologue sets the scene and describes the pilgrims, whose characters are further revealed in the story each one tells. For example, the gentle Christian Knight relates a chivalric romance; the gross Miller tells a vulgar story about a deceived husband; the earthy Wife of Bath, who has buried five husbands, sketches a fable about the selection of a spouse; and the elegant Prioress, who violates her vows by wearing jewelry, delivers a homily on the Virgin. In depicting the interests and behavior of all types of people, Chaucer presents a rich panorama of English social life in the fourteenth century. Like the *Divine Comedy, Canterbury Tales* reflects the cultural tensions of the times. Ostensibly Christian, many of the pilgrims are also materialistic, sensual, and worldly, suggesting the ambivalence of the broader society's concern for the next world and frank enjoyment of this one.

Our knowledge of François Villon (1431–1463), probably the greatest poet of late medieval France, derives from Paris police records and his own poetry. Born to poor parents in the year of Joan of Arc's execution, Villon was sent by his guardian to the University of Paris, where he earned the master of arts degree. A rowdy and free-spirited student, he disliked the stuffiness of academic life. In 1455 Villon killed a man in a street brawl; banished from Paris, he joined one of the bands of wandering thieves that harassed the countryside after the Hundred Years' War. For his fellow bandits he composed ballads in thieves' jargon.

Villon's *Lais* (1456), a pun on the word *legs* ("legacy"), is a series of farcical bequests to friends and enemies. "Ballade des Pendus" ("Ballad of the Hanged") was written while contemplating that fate in prison. (His execution was commuted.) Villon's greatest and most self-revealing work, the *Grand Testament,* contains another string of bequests, including a legacy to a prostitute, and describes his unshakable faith in the beauty of life on earth. The *Grand Testament* possesses elements of social rebellion, bawdy humor, and rare emotional depth. While the themes of Dante's and Chaucer's poetry are distinctly medieval, Villon's celebration of the human condition brands him as definitely modern. Although he used medieval forms of versification, Villon's language was the despised vernacular of the poor and the criminal.

Perhaps the most versatile and prolific French writer of the later Middle Ages was Christine de Pisan (1363?–1434?). The daughter of a professor of astrology at Bologna whose international reputation won him a post at the French royal court where she received her excellent education, Christine had a broad knowledge of Greek, Latin, French, and Italian literature. The deaths of her father and husband left her with three small children and her mother to support, and she resolved to earn her living with her pen. In addition to poems and books on love, religion, and morality, Christine produced the *Livre de la mutacion de fortune,* a major historical work; a biography of King Charles V; the *Ditié,* celebrating Joan of Arc's victory; and many letters. *The City of Ladies* lists the great women of history and their contributions to society, and *The Book of Three Virtues* provides prudent and practical advice on household management for women of all social classes and at all stages of life. Christine de Pisan's wisdom and wit are illustrated in her autobiographical *Avison-Christine.* She records that a man told her an educated woman is unattractive, since there are so few, to which she responded that an ignorant man was even less attractive, since there are so many.

From the fifth through the thirteenth century, the overwhelming majority of people who could read and write were priests, monks, and nuns. Beginning in the fourteenth century, a variety of evidence attests to the increasing literacy of laypeople. Wills and inventories reveal that many people, not just nobles, possessed books, mainly devotional, but also romances, manuals on manners and etiquette, histories, sometimes legal and philosophical

The Wife of Bath The fame of medieval England's greatest poet, Geoffrey Chaucer, rests on *The Canterbury Tales,* consisting of a Prologue and the stories of 24 pilgrims on their way to Canterbury. The earthy, vivacious Wife of Bath, having had five husbands "not counting other company in youth," is very blunt about her charms and her power:

In wyfhode I wol use myn instrument
As freely as my Maker hath it sent.

Faithful to Chaucer's description, the artist shows her with wide-brimmed hat, hair in a net, and riding astride, not sidesaddle as ladies were expected to do. *(Source: Reproduced by permission of The Huntington Library, San Marino, California)*

texts. In England, as one scholar has recently shown, the number of schools in the diocese of York quadrupled between 1350 and 1500. Information from Flemish and German towns is similar: children were sent to schools and received the fundamentals of reading, writing, and arithmetic. Laymen increasingly served as managers or stewards of estates and as clerks to guilds and town governments; such positions obviously required that they be able to keep administrative and financial records.

vou jm su toll almum is ug wer re wiu oulge vur jmmwerlug ge
fellen frouwen und junchfrouwen wer fin bedarff der kum har jn der
wirt druwlich gelert um em zimlichen lon · aber die junge knabe
und meitliu noch deu fronualten wie gewonheit ift · ı 5 ı 6 ·

Schoolmaster and His Wife Teaching Ambrosius Holbein, elder brother of the more famous Hans Holbein, produced this signboard for the Swiss educator Myconius; it is an excellent example of what we would call commercial art—art used to advertise, in this case Myconius's profession. The German script above promised that all who enrolled would learn to read and write. By modern standards the classroom seems bleak: the windows have glass panes but they don't admit much light, and the schoolmaster is prepared to use the sticks if the boy makes a mistake. (*Source: Öffentliche Kunstsammlung Basel/Martin Bühler, photographer*)

The penetration of laymen into the higher positions of governmental administration, long the preserve of clerics, also illustrates rising lay literacy. For example, in 1400 beneficed clerics held most of the posts in the English Exchequer; by 1430, clerics were the exception. With growing frequency the upper classes sent their daughters to convent schools, where, in addition to instruction in singing, religion, needlework, deportment, and household management, girls gained the rudiments of reading and sometimes writing. Reading and writing represent two kinds of literacy. Scholars estimate that many more people, especially women, possessed the first literacy, but not the second. The spread of literacy represents a response to the needs of an increasingly complex society. Trade, commerce, and expanding governmental bureaucracies required more and more literate people. Late medieval culture remained an oral culture in which most people received information by word of mouth. But by the mid-fifteenth century, even before the printing press was turning out large quantities of reading materials, the evolution toward a literary culture is already perceptible.[36]

SUMMARY

Late medieval preachers likened the crises of their times to the Four Horsemen of the Apocalypse in the Book of Revelation, who brought famine, war, disease, and death. The crises of the fourteenth and fifteenth centuries were acids that burned deeply into the fabric of traditional medieval European society. Bad weather brought poor harvests, which contributed to the international economic depression. Disease, over which people also had little control, fostered widespread depression and dissatisfaction. Population losses caused by the Black Death and the Hundred Years' War encouraged the working classes to try to profit from the labor shortage by selling their services higher: they wanted to move up the economic ladder. The ideas of thinkers like John Wyclif, John Hus, and John

Ball fanned the flames of social discontent. When peasant frustrations exploded in uprisings, the frightened nobility and upper middle class joined to crush the revolts and condemn heretical preachers as agitators of social rebellion. But the war had heightened social consciousness among the poor.

The Hundred Years' War served as a catalyst for the development of representative government in England. In France, on the other hand, the war stiffened opposition to national assemblies.

The war also stimulated technological experimentation, especially with artillery. Cannon revolutionized warfare, because the stone castle was no longer impregnable against them. Because only central governments, and not private nobles, could afford cannon, they strengthened the military power of national states.

Religion held society together. European culture was a Christian culture. But the Great Schism weakened the prestige of the church and people's faith in papal authority. The conciliar movement, by denying the church's universal sovereignty, strengthened the claims of secular government to jurisdiction over all their peoples. The later Middle Ages witnessed a steady shift of basic loyalty from the church to the emerging national states.

The increasing number of schools leading to the growth of lay literacy represents another positive achievement of the later Middle Ages. So also does the development of national literatures. The first sign of a literary culture appeared.

NOTES

1. W. H. McNeill, *Plagues and Peoples* (New York: Doubleday, 1976), pp. 151–168.
2. Quoted in P. Ziegler, *The Black Death* (Harmondsworth, Eng.: Pelican Books, 1969), p. 20.
3. J. M. Rigg, trans., *The Decameron of Giovanni Boccaccio* (London: J. M. Dent & Sons, 1903), p. 6.
4. M. Mollatt, *The Poor in the Middle Ages: An Essay in Social History,* A. Goldhammer, trans. (New Haven: Yale University Press, 1986), pp. 146–153, 193–197.
5. Ziegler, pp. 232–239.
6. J. Hatcher, *Plague, Population and the English Economy, 1348–1530* (London: Macmillan Education, 1986), p. 33.
7. See G. P. Cuttino, "Historical Revision: The Causes of the Hundred Years' War," *Speculum* 31 (July 1956): 463–472.
8. J. Barnie, *War in Medieval English Society: Social Values and the Hundred Years' War* (Ithaca, N.Y.: Cornell University Press, 1974), p. 6.
9. Quoted in Barnie, p. 34.
10. Ibid., p. 73.
11. Ibid., pp. 72–73.
12. W. P. Barrett, trans., *The Trial of Jeanne d'Arc* (London: George Routledge, 1931), pp. 165–166.
13. Quoted in Barnie, pp. 36–37.
14. M. M. Postan, "The Costs of the Hundred Years' War," *Past and Present* 27 (April 1964): 34–53.
15. See G. O. Sayles, *The King's Parliament of England* (New York: W. W. Norton, 1974), app., pp. 137–141.
16. Quoted in P. S. Lewis, "The Failure of the Medieval French Estates," *Past and Present* 23 (November 1962): 6.
17. C. Stephenson and G. F. Marcham, eds., *Sources of English Constitutional History,* rev. ed. (New York: Harper & Row, 1972), p. 217.
18. Quoted in J. H. Smith, *The Great Schism 1378: The Disintegration of the Medieval Papacy* (New York: Weybright & Talley, 1970), p. 141.
19. Ibid., p. 15.
20. B. A. Hanawalt, *The Ties That Bound. Peasant Families in Medieval England* (New York: Oxford University Press, 1986), p. 197. This section leans heavily on Hanawalt's work.
21. Ibid., pp. 194–204.
22. A. S. Haskell, "The Paston Women on Marriage in Fifteenth Century England," *Viator* 4 (1973): 459–469.
23. Ibid., p. 471.
24. See D. Herlihy, *Medieval Households* (Cambridge, Mass.: Harvard University Press, 1985), pp. 103–111.
25. L. L. Otis, *Prostitution in Medieval Society: The History of an Urban Institution in Languedoc* (Chicago: University of Chicago Press, 1987), p. 2.
26. Ibid., pp. 25–27, 64–66, 100–106.
27. Ibid., pp. 118–130.
28. See R. H. Helmholz, *Marriage Litigation in Medieval England* (Cambridge: Cambridge University Press, 1974), pp. 28–29, et passim.
29. See M. C. Howell, *Women, Production, and Patriarchy in Late Medieval Cities* (Chicago: University of Chicago Press, 1986), pp. 134–135.
30. A. F. Scott, ed., *Everyone a Witness: The Plantagenet Age* (New York: Thomas Y. Crowell, 1976), p. 263.
31. See E. Mason, "The Role of the English Parish-

LISTENING TO THE
PAST

A Crime Wave

Crime tells us a great deal about a society. From the late thirteenth through much of the fourteenth century, England experienced a great increase in all kinds of crime and on all social levels. Over-population, a stagnant economy, and lack of op-portunity seem to have led many people into lives of crime. The English government responded with plans for reducing crime and violence: it passed laws that defined criminal action more precisely; it appointed new officials, keepers of the peace, to assist sheriffs in arresting criminals and holding them for trial; and it revived the general eyre (journey). On a general eyre royal judges traveled a specific circuit with broad com-missions not only to hear civil and criminal cases but also to check up on local officials (e.g., sher-iffs, coroners), who themselves sometimes failed to do their jobs and engaged in graft and cor-ruption. From November 6, 1329, to June 22, 1330, apart from brief holidays at Christmas and Easter, judges sat in small Northamptonshire in central England six days a week hearing and resolving cases. Here is a tiny sample of the criminal cases they heard. The section on "Law and Justice" in Chapter 11 provides a useful background to this material.

Robert of Coleworth attacked Richard le Por-ter of Aynho in the fields of Brackley and struck him through to the heart with a lance, so that he immediately died. The aforesaid Robert fled immediately after the deed. After-wards he was arrested and held in the gaol of Northampton castle. The aforesaid John Druel was sheriff at that time. Therefore he or his heirs or the holders of the lands that belonged to him are to answer what became of Robert. Robert's chattels[1] are confiscated for flight; his chattels are worth *6s. 7d.,* and the sheriff is charged with that sum.

Afterwards the jurors state that John Bryan, John Knotte, and Thomas of Marche were present when the aforesaid felony was com-mitted and that they are living in the county. Let them be *arrested.* And because the afore-said John Bryan fled, his chattels are confis-cated for flight. His chattels are worth *6d.,* and the sheriff is charged with that sum.

Afterwards the aforesaid John Brayn and Thomas of Marche appear, brought into court by the sheriff. The jurors do in no way suspect John Brayn of being guilty of the aforesaid killing. But because he was present and did not raise the hue[2] or arrest the perpetrators of the deed, he is remanded to gaol. Later he made fine with the king for the aforesaid tres-pass, by 20d.; William Riche is his pledge[3] for payment.

Because the aforesaid Thomas fled and ren-dered himself suspect of the aforesaid killing, he is asked how he wishes to clear himself. He denies the killing, everything, and all that is against the peace, and to establish that he is not guilty he puts himself for better or worse upon the country.[4] The jurors of the township of Brackley say upon oath that the aforesaid Thomas is not guilty of the aforesaid killing. Thomas is therefore acquitted. But because he was present and did not arrest the perpetrator of the deed, he is in mercy.[5]

No one answers for the aforesaid John as to what became of the aforesaid Robert of Cole-worth, nor does it appear from the rolls of the coroners that Robert died in gaol. Therefore an escape by the same Robert is adjudged against the holders of the lands that belonged to the same John.

On 1 June 1329, before Simon of Keyl-mersh, coroner, Geoffrey of Wodhull became an approver[6] and confessed that he was guilty of several thefts and appealed Simon of Wendlyngburgh of Rothewell, charging that Simon was with him and that together they stole, in the fields of Rushton about Michael-mas 1327, 22 sheep worth 35s. and a horse worth 5s., whence Geoffrey the approver took 12d. as his share of the proceeds. And now the aforesaid approver appears in court, and Simon likewise. The approver is asked if he wishes to prosecute his aforesaid appeal. He says that he is a cleric and cannot answer in this matter without his ordinary.[7] Thereupon the master of the hospital of St John of Northampton comes forward, representing the bishop of Lincoln according to the bishop's letter enrolled above, and asks that the approver be delivered to him as a cleric. *He is delivered to him,* to be guarded upon due peril. He had no chattels.

The aforesaid Simon, being asked . . . how he wishes to clear himself of the aforesaid felony, denies all felony etc. and everything that is against the peace etc. and puts himself for better or worse upon the country. The jurors of Rothwell hundred say upon their oath that the aforesaid Simon is not guilty of the aforesaid thefts with which he was charged. Therefore he is *acquitted.*

A certain Robert le Barkere of Brackele died unexpectedly in the fields of Whitfield on account of weakness. No one is suspected of any guilt. Judgment, *misadventure.*[8] No action is to be taken concerning the first-finder, because he has died. The township of Syresham buried the body without its having been viewed by the coroner; the township is therefore in *mercy.* And the township of Whitfield is in *mercy* because it did not come to the coroner's inquest.[9]

A man was arraigned of felony. A jury was called from the hundred where the felony was said to have been committed, and he refused it. Another jury was called, from a neighbouring hundred, and he also refused that. Scrope said that if he should refuse the third hundred-jury he would be put to the *peine forte et dure*[10] on the same day.

A man and his wife were arraigned of robbery upon an indictment. They pleaded Not guilty. They were found guilty. The justices did not inquire whether the woman committed the robbery in the company of her husband, nor whether her husband forced her to do it, but condemned them to be hanged. Because the woman was pregnant the constable was commanded to hold her in safe custody until she should be delivered; and it was commanded that she should then be hanged. It was not commanded that she should receive any wages on which to live.

Source: D. W. Sutherland, ed., *The Eyre of Northamptonshire, 3-4 Edward III, A.D., 1329–1330,* vol. 1 (London: Selden Society, 1983), pp. 152, 162, 179, and 199.

Medieval miniature of a guilty man being taken to prison. (*Source; Bibliothèque Nationale, Paris*)

Questions for Analysis

1. Who was responsible for the apprehension of criminals? How did the judges enforce that responsibility?

2. In addition to the reduction of crime and violence, what other advantages accrued to the Crown as result of the general eyre?

3. How do the actions of a medieval approver and a modern plea bargainer help the cause of law, order, and justice?

4. When a criminal suspect claimed to be a cleric, what happened to him? What does this suggest about the nature of royal authority in late medieval England?

1. Chattels are movable property. 2. When a crime was committed, all persons in the area were to raise the hue and cry, shout out, chase, and try to stop the suspect. 3. A pledge acted as security for the debt. 4. To "put oneself on the country" meant to accept trial by jury. 5. In mercy meant liable for a fine: all fines and confiscated property were forfeited to the king. 6. An approver was an accomplice in crime who accused others of the same offense and admitted his guilt in order to save himself or to secure a light sentence; this was an early form of a plea bargain, which does the same thing. 7. An ordinary was a bishop; clerics were subject to his court. 8. Misadventure is accidental death. 9. It was (and is) the coroner's duty to examine dead bodies in suspicious circumstances in order to determine the cause of death. Because the coroner had not done his job and the community had buried the dead, the community was fined. 10. If the accused repeatedly refused trial by jury, the judges applied peine forte et dure: the accused was tied down, and heavy stones were placed on his chest until he accepted the jury or his rib cage was crushed. By 1300 trial by jury was almost, but obviously not completely, universal. Sir Geoffrey Scrope was the chief justice of the eyre.

ioner, 1000–1500," *Journal of Ecclesiastical History* 27 (January 1976): 17–29.

32. B. A. Hanawalt, "Fur Collar Crime: The Pattern of Crime Among the Fourteenth-Century English Nobility," *Journal of Social History* 8 (Spring 1975): 1–14.

33. Ibid., p. 7.

34. Quoted in M. Bloch, *French Rural History,* J. Sondeimer, trans. (Berkeley: University of California Press, 1966), p. 169.

35. Stephenson and Marcham, p. 225.

36. See M. Keen, *English Society in the Later Middle Ages, 1348–1500* (New York: Penguin Books, 1990), pp. 219–239.

SUGGESTED READING

For the Black Death, see the classic work of P. Ziegler, *The Black Death* (1969), a fascinating and highly readable study. For the social implications of disease, see L. Poos, *A Rural Society after the Black Death: Essex, 1350–1525* (1991); W. H. McNeill, *Plagues and Peoples* (1976). For the economic effects of the plague, see J. Hatcher, *Plague, Population, and the English Economy, 1348–1550* (1977).

The standard study of the long military conflicts of the fourteenth and fifteenth centuries remains that of E. Perroy, *The Hundred Years' War* (1959), but see also C. Allmand, *The Hundred Years War: England and France at War, ca 1300–1450* (1988), while the broad survey of J. Keegan, *A History of Warfare* (1993), contains a useful summary of significant changes in military technology during the war. The main ruler of the age has found his biographer in W. M. Ormrod, *The Reign of Edward III. Crown and Political Society in England, 1327–1377* (1990). J. Henneman, *Royal Taxation in Fourteenth Century France: The Development of War Financing, 1322–1356* (1971), is an important technical work by a distinguished historian. J. Keegan, *The Face of Battle* (1977), chap. 2, "Agincourt," describes what war meant to the ordinary soldier. B. Tuchman, *A Distant Mirror: The Calamitous Fourteenth Century* (1980), gives a vivid picture of many facets of fourteenth-century life, while concentrating on the war. For strategy, tactics, armaments, and costumes of war, see H. W. Koch, *Medieval Warfare* (1978), a beautifully illustrated book. R. Barber, *The Knight and Chivalry* (1982), and M. Keen, *Chivalry* (1984), give fresh interpretations of the cultural importance of chivalry.

For political and social conditions in the fourteenth and fifteenth centuries, see the works by Lewis, Sayles, Bloch, and especially Hanawalt and Helmholz, cited in the Notes. C. Dyer, *Standards of Living in the Later*

Middle Ages (1989), contains much valuable social history. The papers in R. H. Hilton and T. H. Aston, eds., *The English Rising of 1381* (1984), stress the importance of urban, as well as rural, participation in the movement, but see also R. Hilton, *Bond Men Made Free: Medieval Peasant Movements and the English Rising of 1381* (1973), a comparative study; M. Keen, *The Outlaws of Medieval Legend* (1961); and P. Wolff, "The 1391 Pogrom in Spain: Social Crisis or Not?" *Past and Present* 50 (February 1971): 4–18. P. C. Maddern, *Violence and Social Order, East Anglia 1422–1442* (1992) and I. M. W. Harvey, *Jack Cade's Rebellion of 1450* (1991) are important works in local history. Students are especially encouraged to consult the brilliant work of E. L. Ladurie, *The Peasants of Languedoc* J. Day, trans. (1976). J. C. Holt, *Robin Hood* (1982), is a soundly researched and highly readable study of the famous outlaw. For the Pastons, see R. Barber, ed., *The Pastons: Letters of a Family in the Wars of the Roses* (1984).

For women's economic status in the late medieval period, see the titles by M. C. Howell and B. Hanawalt cited in the Notes. D. Nicholas, *The Domestic Life of a Medieval City: Women, Children, and the Family in Fourteenth-Century Ghent* (1985), focuses on an urban society. P. J. P. Goldberg, *Women, Work, and Life Cycle in a Medieval Economy. Women in York and Yorkshire, c 1300–1520* (1992) explores the relationship between economic opportunity and marriage.

The poetry of Dante, Chaucer, and Villon may be read in the following editions: D. Sayers, trans., *Dante: The Divine Comedy,* 3 vols. (1963); N. Coghill, trans., *Chaucer's Canterbury Tales* (1977); P. Dale, trans., *The Poems of Villon* (1973). The social setting of *Canterbury Tales* is brilliantly evoked in D. W. Robertson, Jr., *Chaucer's London* (1968). Students interested in further study of Christine de Pisan should consult A. J. Kennedy, *Christine de Pisan: A Bibliographical Guide* (1984); and C. C. Willard, *Christine de Pisan: Her Life and Works* (1984).

For the religious history of the period, F. Oakley, *The Western Church in the Later Middle Ages* (1979), is an excellent introduction, while R. N. Swanson, *Church and Society in Late Medieval England* (1989), provides a good synthesis of English conditions. S. Ozment, *The Age of Reform, 1250–1550* (1980), discusses the Great Schism and the conciliar movement in the intellectual context of the ecclesiopolitical tradition of the Middle Ages. For great detail consult H. Beck et al., *From the High Middle Ages to the Eve of the Reformation,* A. Biggs, trans., vol. 14 in the History of the Church series edited by H. Jedin and J. Dolan (1980). J. Bossy, "The Mass as a Social Institution, 1200–1700," *Past and Present* 100 (August 1983): 29–61, provides a technical study of the central public ritual of the Latin church.

13

European Society in the Age of the Renaissance

While the Four Horsemen of the Apocalypse were carrying war, plague, famine, and death across the Continent, a new culture was emerging in southern Europe. The fourteenth century witnessed the beginnings of remarkable changes in many aspects of Italian society. In the fifteenth century, these phenomena spread beyond Italy and gradually influenced society in northern Europe. These cultural changes have been collectively labeled the "Renaissance."

- What does the term *Renaissance* mean?
- How was the Renaissance manifested in politics, government, and social organization?
- What were the intellectual and artistic hallmarks of the Renaissance?
- Did the Renaissance involve shifts in religious attitudes?
- What developments occurred in the evolution of the nation-state?

This chapter will concentrate on these questions.

Michelangelo painted the entire Sistine Chapel ceiling by himself, 1508–1512. *(Source: Nippon Television Network Corporation, Tokyo, 1994)*

THE EVOLUTION OF THE ITALIAN RENAISSANCE

Economic growth laid the material basis for the Italian Renaissance. The period extending roughly from 1050 to 1300 witnessed phenomenal commercial and financial development, the growing political power of self-governing cities, and great population expansion. Then the period from the late thirteenth to the late sixteenth century was characterized by an incredible efflorescence of artistic energies.[1] Scholars commonly use the term *Renaissance* to describe the cultural achievements of the fourteenth through sixteenth centuries; those achievements rest on the economic and political developments of earlier centuries.

In the great commercial revival of the eleventh century, northern Italian cities led the way. By the middle of the twelfth century, Venice, supported by a huge merchant marine, had grown enormously rich through overseas trade. It profited tremendously from the diversion of the Fourth Crusade to Constantinople (see page 284). Genoa and Milan also enjoyed the benefits of a large volume of trade with the Middle East and northern Europe. These cities fully exploited their geographical positions as natural crossroads for mercantile exchange between the East and West. Furthermore, in the early fourteenth century Genoa and Venice made important strides in shipbuilding that allowed their ships for the first time to sail all year long. Advances in ship construction greatly increased the volume of goods that could be transported; improvements in the mechanics of sailing accelerated speed. Most goods were purchased directly from the producers and sold a good distance away. For example, Italian merchants bought fine English wool directly from the Cistercian abbeys of Yorkshire in northern England. The wool was transported to the bazaars of North Africa either overland or by ship through the Strait of Gibraltar. The risks in such an operation were great, but the profits were enormous. These profits were continually reinvested to earn more.

Scholars tend to agree that the first artistic and literary manifestations of the Italian Renaissance appeared in Florence, which possessed enormous wealth despite geographical constraints: it was an inland city without easy access to water transportation. But toward the end of the thirteenth century, Florentine merchants and bankers acquired control of papal banking. From their position as tax collectors for the papacy, Florentine mercantile families began to dominate European banking on both sides of the Alps. These families had offices in Paris, London, Bruges, Barcelona, Marseilles, Tunis and other North African ports, and, of course, Naples and Rome. The profits from loans, investments, and money exchanges that poured back to Florence were pumped into urban industries. Such profits contributed to the city's economic vitality.

The Florentine wool industry, however, was the major factor in the city's financial expansion and population increase. Florence purchased the best-quality wool from England and Spain, developed remarkable techniques for its manufacture into cloth, and employed thousands of workers in the manufacturing process. Florentine weavers produced immense quantities of superb woolen cloth, which brought the highest prices in the fairs, markets, and bazaars of Europe, Asia, and Africa.

By the first quarter of the fourteenth century, the economic foundations of Florence were so strong that even severe crises could not destroy the city. In 1344 King Edward III of England repudiated his huge debts to Florentine bankers and forced some of them into bankruptcy. Florence suffered frightfully from the Black Death, losing at least half of its population. Serious labor unrest, such as the ciompi revolts of 1378 (see page 393), shook the political establishment. Nevertheless, the basic Florentine economic structure remained stable. Driving enterprise, technical know-how, and competitive spirit saw Florence through the difficult economic period of the late fourteenth century.

Communes and Republics

The northern Italian cities were *communes,* sworn associations of free men seeking complete political and economic independence from local nobles. The merchant guilds that formed the communes built and maintained the city walls, regulated trade, raised taxes, and kept civil order. In the course of the twelfth century, communes at Milan, Florence, Genoa, Siena, and Pisa fought for and won their independence from surrounding feudal nobles. The nobles, attracted by the opportunities of long-distance and maritime trade, the rising value of urban real estate, the new public offices available in the expanding communes, and the chances for advantageous marriages into rich commercial families, frequently settled within the cities. Marriage vows often sealed business contracts between the rural nobility and the mercantile aristocracy. This merger of the northern Italian feudal nobility and the commercial aristocracy constituted the formation of a new social class, an urban nobility. Within this nobility, groups tied by blood, economic interests, and social connections formed tightly knit alliances to defend and expand their rights.

This new class made citizenship in the communes dependent on a property qualification, years of residence within the city, and social connections. Only a tiny percentage of the male population

❖ **A Bank Scene, Florence** Originally a "bank" was just a counter; if covered with a carpet like this Ottoman geometric rug with a kufic border, it became a bank of distinction. Money-changers who sat behind the counter became "bankers," exchanging different currencies and holding deposits for merchants and businesspeople. *(Source: Prato, San Francesco/Scala/Art Resource, NY)*

possessed these qualifications and thus could hold office in the commune's political councils. A new force, called the *popolo,* disenfranchised and heavily taxed, bitterly resented their exclusion from power. The popolo wanted places in the communal government and equality of taxation. Throughout most of the thirteenth century, in city after city, the popolo used armed forces and violence to take over the city governments. Republican governments were established in Bologna, Siena, Parma, Florence, Genoa, and other cities. The victory of the popolo, however, proved temporary. Because they practiced the same sort of political exclusivity as had the noble communes—denying influence to the classes below them, whether the poor, the unskilled, or new immigrants—the popolo never won the support of other groups. Moreover, the popolo

could not establish civil order within their cities. Consequently, these movements for republican government failed. By 1300 *signori* (despots, or one-man rulers) or *oligarchies* (the rule of merchant aristocracies) had triumphed everywhere.[2]

For the next two centuries, the Italian city-states were ruled by signori or by constitutional oligarchies. In the signories, despots pretended to observe the law while actually manipulating it to conceal their basic illegality. Oligarchic regimes possessed constitutions, but through a variety of schemes a small, restricted class of wealthy merchants exercised the judicial, executive, and legislative functions of government. Thus in 1422 Venice had a population of 84,000, but 200 men held all power; Florence had about 40,000 people, but 600 men ruled. Oligarchic regimes maintained only a façade of republican government, in which political power theoretically resides in the people and is exercised by its chosen representatives. The Renaissance nostalgia for the Roman form of government, combined with calculating shrewdness, prompted the leaders of Venice, Milan, and Florence to use the old forms.

In the fifteenth century, political power and elite culture centered at the princely courts of despots and oligarchs. "A court was the space and personnel around a prince as he made laws, received ambassadors, made appointments, took his meals, and proceeded through the streets."[3] The princely court afforded the despot or oligarch the opportunity to display and assert his wealth and power. He flaunted his patronage of learning and the arts by munificent gifts to writers, philosophers, and artists. He used ceremonies connected with family births, baptisms, marriages, funerals, or triumphant entrances into the city as occasions for magnificent pageantry and elaborate ritual.

The Balance of Power Among the Italian City-States

Renaissance Italians had a passionate attachment to their individual city-states: political loyalty and feeling centered on the local city. This intensity of local feeling perpetuated the dozens of small states and hindered the development of one unified state. Italy, consequently, was completely disunited.

In the fifteenth century, five powers dominated the Italian peninsula: Venice, Milan, Florence, the Papal States, and the kingdom of Naples (Map 13.1). The rulers of the city-states—whether despots in Milan, patrician elitists in Florence, or oligarchs in Venice—governed as monarchs. They crushed urban revolts, levied taxes, killed their enemies, and used massive building programs to employ, and the arts to overawe, the masses.

Venice, with its enormous trade and vast colonial empire, ranked as an international power. Though Venice had a sophisticated constitution and was a republic in name, an oligarchy of merchant aristocrats actually ran the city. Milan was also called a republic, but despots of the Sforza family ruled harshly and dominated the smaller cities of the north. Likewise in Florence the form of government was republican, with authority vested in several councils of state. In reality, between 1434 and 1494, power in Florence was held by the great Medici banking family. Though not public officers,

Cosimo (1434–1464) and Lorenzo (1469–1492) ruled from behind the scenes.

Central Italy consisted mainly of the Papal States, which during the Babylonian Captivity had come under the sway of important Roman families. Pope Alexander VI (1492–1503), aided militarily and politically by his son Cesare Borgia, reasserted papal authority in the papal lands. Cesare Borgia became the hero of Machiavelli's *The Prince* because he began the work of uniting the peninsula by ruthlessly conquering and exacting total obedience from the principalities making up the Papal States.

South of the Papal States was the kingdom of Naples, consisting of virtually all of southern Italy and, at times, Sicily. The kingdom of Naples had long been disputed by the Aragonese and by the French. In 1435 it passed to Aragon.

The major Italian city-states controlled the smaller ones, such as Siena, Mantua, Ferrara, and Modena, and competed furiously among themselves for territory. The large cities used diplomacy, spies, paid informers, and any other available means to get information that could be used to advance their ambitions. While the states of northern Europe were moving toward centralization and consolidation, the world of Italian politics resembled a jungle where the powerful dominated the weak.

In one significant respect, however, the Italian city-states anticipated future relations among competing European states after 1500. Whenever one Italian state appeared to gain a predominant position within the peninsula, other states combined to establish a balance of power against the major threat. In 1450, for example, Venice went to war against Milan in protest against Francesco Sforza's acquisition of the title of duke of Milan. Cosimo de' Medici of Florence, a long-time supporter of a Florentine-Venetian alliance, switched his position and aided Milan. Florence and Naples combined with Milan against powerful Venice and the papacy. In the peace treaty signed at Lodi in 1454, Venice received territories in return for recognizing Sforza's right to the duchy. This pattern of shifting alliances continued until 1494. In the formation of these alliances, Renaissance Italians invented the machinery of modern diplomacy: permanent embassies with resident ambassadors in capitals where political relations and commercial ties needed continual monitoring. The resident ambassador was one of the great achievements of the Italian Renaissance.

❖ **MAP 13.1 The Italian City-Stages, ca 1494** In the fifteenth century the Italian city-states represented great wealth and cultural sophistication. The political divisions of the peninsula invited foreign intervention.

At the end of the fifteenth century, Venice, Florence, Milan, and the papacy possessed great wealth and represented high cultural achievement. However, their imperialistic ambitions at one another's expense and their resulting inability to form a common alliance against potential foreign enemies made Italy an inviting target for invasion. When Florence and Naples entered into an agree-

ment to acquire Milanese territories, Milan called on France for support.

At Florence the French invasion had been predicted by Dominican friar Girolamo Savonarola (1452–1498). In a number of fiery sermons between 1491 and 1494, Savonarola attacked what he considered the paganism and moral vice of the city, the undemocratic government of Lorenzo de'

Medici, and the corruption of Pope Alexander VI. For a time Savonarola enjoyed popular support among the ordinary people; he became the religious leader of Florence and as such contributed to the fall of the Medici. Eventually, however, people wearied of his moral denunciations, and he was excommunicated by the pope and executed. Savonarola stands as proof that the common people did not share the worldly outlook of the commercial and intellectual elite. His career also illustrates the internal instability of Italian cities such as Florence, an instability that invited foreign invasion.

The invasion of Italy in 1494 by the French king Charles VIII (r. 1483–1498) inaugurated a new period in Italian and European power politics. Italy became the focus of international ambitions and the battleground of foreign armies. Charles swept

✢ **Palazzo Vecchio, Florence** Built during the late thirteenth and early fourteenth centuries as a fortress of defense against both popular uprising and foreign attack, the building housed the *podesta,* the city's highest magistrate, and all the offices of the government. *(Source: Scala/Art Resource NY)*

down the peninsula with little opposition, and Florence, Rome, and Naples soon bowed before him. When Piero de' Medici, Lorenzo's son, went to the French camp seeking peace, the Florentines exiled the Medicis and restored republican government.

Charles's success simply whetted French appetites. In 1508 his cousin and heir, Louis XII, formed the League of Cambrai with the pope and the German emperor Maximilian for the purpose of stripping rich Venice of its mainland possessions. Pope Leo X (1513–1521) soon found the French a dangerous friend and in a new alliance called on the Spanish and Germans to expel the French from Italy. This anti-French combination was temporarily successful. In 1519 Charles V succeeded his grandfather Maximilian (1493–1519) as Holy Roman emperor. When the French returned to Italy in 1522, a series of conflicts called the Habsburg-Valois Wars (named for the German and French dynasties) began, whose battlefield was often Italy.

In the sixteenth century, the political and social life of Italy was upset by the relentless competition for dominance between France and the empire. The Italian cities suffered severely from continual warfare, especially in the frightful sack of Rome in 1527 by imperial forces under Charles V. Thus the failure of the city-states to form some federal system, consolidate, or at least establish a common foreign policy led to the continuation of the centuries-old subjection of the peninsula by outside invaders. Italy was not to achieve unification until 1870.

✥ INTELLECTUAL HALLMARKS OF THE RENAISSANCE

The Renaissance was characterized by self-conscious awareness among fourteenth- and fifteenth-century Italians that they were living in a new era. The realization that something new and unique was happening first came to men of letters in the fourteenth century, especially to the poet and humanist Francesco Petrarch (1304–1374). Petrarch thought that he was living at the start of a new age, a period of light following a long night of Gothic gloom. He considered the first two centuries of the Roman Empire to represent the peak in the development of human civilization. Medieval people had believed that they were continuing the glories that had been ancient Rome and had recognized no cultural division between the world of the emperors and their own times. But for Petrarch, the Germanic invasions had caused a sharp cultural break with the glories of Rome and inaugurated what he called the "Dark Ages." He believed, with many of his contemporaries, that the thousand-year period between the fourth and the fourteenth centuries constituted a barbarian, Gothic, or "middle" age. The sculptors, painters, and writers of the Renaissance spoke contemptuously of their medieval predecessors and identified themselves with the thinkers and artists of Greco-Roman civilization. Petrarch believed that he was witnessing a new golden age of intellectual achievement—a rebirth or, to use the French word that came into English, a renaissance. The division of historical time into periods is often arbitrary and done for the convenience of historians. In terms of the way most people lived and thought, no sharp division exists between the Middle Ages and the Renaissance. Some important poets, writers, and artists, however, believed they were living in a new golden age.

The Renaissance also manifested itself in a new attitude toward men, women, and the world—an attitude that may be described as individualism. A humanism characterized by a deep interest in the Latin classics and a deliberate attempt to revive antique lifestyles emerged, as did a bold new secular spirit.

Individualism

Though the Middle Ages had seen the appearance of remarkable individuals, recognition of such persons was limited. The examples of Saint Augustine in the fifth century and Peter Abelard and Guibert of Nogent in the twelfth—men who perceived themselves as unique and produced autobiographical statements—stand out for that very reason: Christian humility discouraged self-absorption. In the fourteenth and fifteenth centuries, moreover, such characteristically medieval and corporate attachments as the guild and the parish continued to provide strong support for the individual and to exercise great social influence. Yet in the Renaissance intellectuals, unlike their counterparts in the Middle Ages, developed a new sense of historical distance from earlier periods. A large literature specifically concerned with the nature of individuality emerged. This literature represented the flowering of a distinctly Renaissance individualism.

The Renaissance witnessed the emergence of many distinctive personalities who gloried in their uniqueness. Italians of unusual abilities were self-consciously aware of their singularity and unafraid to be unlike their neighbors; they had enormous confidence in their ability to achieve great things. Leon Battista Alberti (1404–1474), a writer, architect, and mathematician, remarked, "Men can do all things if they will."[4] Florentine goldsmith and sculptor Benvenuto Cellini (1500–1574) prefaced his *Autobiography* with a sonnet that declares:

My cruel fate hath warr'd with me in vain:
Life, glory, worth, and all unmeasur'd skill,
Beauty and grace, themselves in me fulfill
That many I surpass, and to the best attain.[5]

Cellini, certain of his genius, wrote so that the whole world might appreciate it.

Individualism stressed personality, uniqueness, genius, and the fullest development of capabilities and talents. Artist, athlete, painter, scholar, sculptor, whatever—a person's abilities should be stretched until fully realized. Thirst for fame, a driving ambition, and a burning desire for success drove such people to the complete achievement of their potential. The quest for glory was a central component of Renaissance individualism.

Humanism

In the cities of Italy, especially Rome, civic leaders and the wealthy populace showed phenomenal archeological zeal for the recovery of manuscripts, statues, and monuments. Pope Nicholas V (1447–1455), a distinguished scholar, planned the Vatican Library for the nine thousand manuscripts he had collected. Pope Sixtus IV (1471–1484) built that library, which remains one of the richest repositories of ancient and medieval documents.

Patrician Italians consciously copied the lifestyle of the ancients and even searched out pedigrees dating back to ancient Rome. Aeneas Silvius Piccolomini, a native of Siena who became Pope Pius II (1458–1464), once pretentiously declared, "Rome is as much my home as Siena, for my House, the Piccolomini, came in early times from the capital to Siena, as is proved by the constant use of the names Aeneas and Silvius in my family."[6]

The revival of antiquity also took the form of profound interest in and study of the Latin classics. This feature of the Renaissance became known as the "new learning," or simply "humanism," the term of Florentine rhetorician and historian Leonardo Bruni (1370–1444). The words *humanism* and *humanist* derived ultimately from the Latin *humanitas,* which Cicero used to mean the literary culture needed by anyone who would be considered educated and civilized. Humanists studied the Latin classics to learn what they reveal about human nature. Humanism emphasized human beings, their achievements, interests, and capabilities. Although churchmen supported the new learning, by the later fifteenth century Italian humanism was increasingly a lay phenomenon.

Appreciation for the literary culture of the Romans had never died in the West. Bede and John of Salisbury, for example, had studied and imitated the writings of the ancients. Medieval writers, however, had studied the ancients in order to come to know God. Medieval scholars had interpreted the classics in a Christian sense and had invested the ancients' poems and histories with Christian meaning.

Renaissance humanists, although deeply Christian, approached the classics differently. Where medieval writers accepted pagan and classical authors uncritically, Renaissance humanists were skeptical of their authority, conscious of the historical distance separating themselves from the ancients, and fully aware that classical writers often disagreed among themselves. Where medieval writers looked to the classics to reveal God, Renaissance humanists studied the classics to understand human nature, and while they fully grasped the moral thought of pagan antiquity, Renaissance humanists viewed humanity from a strongly Christian perspective: men and women were made in the image and likeness of God. For example, in a remarkable essay, *On the Dignity of Man,* the Florentine writer Pico della Mirandola stressed that man possesses great dignity because he was made as Adam in the image of God before the Fall and as Christ after the Resurrection. According to Pico, man's place in the universe is somewhere between the beasts and the angels, but because of the divine image planted in him, there are no limits to what he can accomplish. Humanists rejected classical ideas that were opposed to Christianity. Or they sought through reinterpretation an underlying harmony between the pagan and secular and the Christian faith. The fundamental difference between Renaissance humanists and medieval ones is that the former were more self-conscious about what they

were doing, and they stressed the realization of human potential.[7]

The fourteenth- and fifteenth-century humanists loved the language of the classics and considered it superior to the corrupt Latin of the medieval schoolmen. Renaissance writers were very excited by the purity of ancient Latin. They eventually became concerned more about form than about content, more about the way an idea was expressed than about the significance and validity of the idea. Literary humanists of the fourteenth century wrote each other highly stylized letters imitating ancient authors, and they held witty philosophical dialogues in conscious imitation of the Platonic Academy of the fourth century B.C. Whenever they could, Renaissance humanists heaped scorn on the "barbaric" Latin style of the medievalists. The leading humanists of the early Renaissance were rhetoricians, seeking effective and eloquent communication, both oral and written.

Secular Spirit

Secularism involves a basic concern with the material world instead of with the eternal world of spirit. A secular way of thinking tends to find the ultimate explanation of everything and the final end of human beings within the limits of what the senses can discover. Even though medieval business people ruthlessly pursued profits and medieval monks fought fiercely over property, the dominant ideals focused on the otherworldly, on life after death. Renaissance people often held strong and deep spiritual interests, but in their increasingly secular society, attention was concentrated on the here and now, often on the acquisition of material things. The fourteenth and fifteenth centuries witnessed the slow but steady growth of such secularism in Italy.

The economic changes and rising prosperity of the Italian cities in the thirteenth century worked a fundamental change in social and intellectual attitudes and values. Worries about shifting rates of interest, shipping routes, personnel costs, and employee relations did not leave much time for thoughts about penance and purgatory. The busy bankers and merchants of the Italian cities calculated ways of making and increasing their money. Such wealth allowed greater material pleasures, a more comfortable life, the leisure time to appreciate and patronize the arts. Money could buy many sensual gratifications, and the rich, social-climbing patricians of Venice, Florence, Genoa, and Rome came to see life as an opportunity to be enjoyed than as a painful pilgrimage to the City of God.

In *On Pleasure,* humanist Lorenzo Valla (1406–1457) defended the pleasures of the senses as the highest good. Scholars praise Valla as a father of modern historical criticism. His study *On the False Donation of Constantine* (1444) demonstrated by careful textual examination that an anonymous eighth-century document supposedly giving the papacy jurisdiction over vast territories in western Europe was a forgery. Medieval people had accepted the Donation of Constantine as a reality, and the proof that it was an invention weakened the foundations of papal claims to temporal authority. Lorenzo Valla's work exemplifies the application of critical scholarship to old and almost-sacred writings as well as the new secular spirit of the Renaissance.

The tales in the *Decameron* by the Florentine Giovanni Boccaccio (1313–1375), which describe ambitious merchants, lecherous friars, and cuck-olded husbands, portray a frankly acquisitive, sensual, and worldly society. Although Boccaccio's figures were stock literary characters, the *Decameron* contains none of the "contempt of the world" theme so pervasive in medieval literature. Renaissance writers justified the accumulation and enjoyment of wealth with references to ancient authors.

Nor did church leaders do much to combat the new secular spirit. In the fifteenth and early sixteenth centuries, the papal court and the households of the cardinals were just as worldly as those of great urban patricians. Of course, most of the popes and higher church officials had come from the bourgeois aristocracy. Renaissance popes beautified the city of Rome, patronized artists and men of letters, and expended enormous enthusiasm and huge sums of money. A new papal chancellery, begun in 1483 and finished in 1511, stands as one of the architectural masterpieces of the High Renaissance. Pope Julius II (1503–1513) tore down the old Saint Peter's Basilica and began work on the present structure in 1506. Michelangelo's dome for Saint Peter's is still considered his greatest work. Papal interests, far removed from spiritual concerns, fostered, rather than discouraged, the new worldly attitude.

The broad mass of the people and the intellectuals and leaders of society remained faithful to the Christian church. Few people questioned the basic

 **Jan Massys (1509–1575): The Usurers** At a desk heaped with coins, pawned goods, jewelry, and a sandbox (for sprinkling sand on an inky page to dry it), one man records the day's receipts in his ledger (his wealth indicated by his ring, fur collar, and pearl brooch on his hat), while his partner casts a sneering, grasping eye on the viewer, no doubt calculating his worth. *(Source: Staatliche Museen zu Berlin/Preussischer Kulturbesitz)*

tenets of the Christian religion. Italian humanists and their aristocratic patrons were anti-ascetic, anti-Scholastic, and ambivalent, but they were not agnostics or skeptics. The thousands of pious paintings, sculptures, processions, and pilgrimages of the Renaissance period prove that strong religious feeling persisted.

ART AND THE ARTIST

No feature of the Renaissance evokes greater admiration than its artistic masterpieces. The 1400s (*quattrocento*) and 1500s (*cinquecento*) bore witness to a dazzling creativity in painting, architecture, and sculpture. In all the arts, the city of Florence led the way. According to Renaissance art historian Giorgio Vasari (1511–1574), the painter

❖ **Ghiberti: The Creation of Adam** (left) **and Eve** (right) After completing 28 scenes from the life of Christ for the doors of the Baptistery of Florence, the sculptor and goldsmith Lorenzo Ghiberti (1378–1455) was commissioned to produce 10 large panels with scenes from the old Testament in perspective relief for a second pair of bronze doors; their fame rests on Michelangelo's observation that "these doors were worthy to form the gates of paradise." Notice the tree of knowledge and the snake. *(Source: Alinari/Art Resource, NY)*

Perugino once asked why it was in Florence and not elsewhere that men achieved perfection in the arts. The first answer he received was, "There were so many good critics there, for the air of the city makes men quick and perceptive and impatient of mediocrity."[8] But Florence was not the only artistic center. In the period art historians describe as the "High Renaissance" (1500–1527), Rome took the lead. The main characteristics of High Renaissance art—classical balance, harmony, and restraint—are revealed in the masterpieces of Leonardo da Vinci (1452–1519), Raphael (1483–1520), and Michelangelo (1475–1564), all of whom worked in Rome.

Art and Power

In early Renaissance Italy, art manifested corporate power. Powerful urban groups such as guilds or religious confraternities commissioned works of art. The Florentine cloth merchants, for example, delegated Filippo Brunelleschi to build the magnificent dome on the cathedral of Florence and selected Lorenzo Ghiberti to design the bronze doors of the Baptistry. These works represented the merchants' dominant influence in the community. Corporate patronage was also reflected in the Florentine government's decision to hire Michelangelo to create the sculpture of David, the great Hebrew hero and king. The subject matter of art through the early fifteenth century, as in the Middle Ages, remained overwhelmingly religious. Religious themes appeared in all media—wood carvings, painted frescoes, stone sculptures, paintings. As in the Middle Ages, art served an educational purpose. A religious picture or statue was intended to spread a particular doctrine, act as a profession of faith, or recall sinners to a moral way of living.

Increasingly in the later fifteenth century, individuals and oligarchs, rather than corporate groups, sponsored works of art. Patrician merchants and bankers, popes and princes supported the arts as a means of glorifying themselves and their families. Vast sums were spent on family chapels, frescoes, religious panels, and tombs. Writing about 1470, Florentine oligarch Lorenzo de' Medici declared that over the previous thirty-five years his family had spent the astronomical sum of 663,755 gold florins for artistic and architectural commissions. Yet "I think it casts a brilliant light on our estate [public reputation] and it seems to me that the monies were well spent and I am very pleased with this." Powerful men wanted to exalt themselves, their families, and their offices. A magnificent style of living, enriched by works of art, served to prove the greatness and the power of the despot or oligarch.[9]

As the fifteenth century advanced, the subject matter of art became steadily more secular. The study of classical texts brought deeper understanding of ancient ideas. Classical themes and motifs, such as the lives and loves of pagan gods and goddesses, figured increasingly in painting and sculpture. Religious topics, such as the Annunciation of the Virgin and the Nativity, remained popular among both patrons and artists, but frequently the patron had himself and his family portrayed. People were conscious of their physical uniqueness and wanted their individuality immortalized. Paintings were also means of displaying wealth.

The content and style of Renaissance art were decidedly different from those of the Middle Ages.

The individual portrait emerged as a distinct artistic genre. In the fifteenth century, members of the newly rich middle class often had themselves painted in a scene of romantic chivalry or courtly society. Rather than reflecting a spiritual ideal, as medieval painting and sculpture tended to do, Renaissance portraits mirrored reality. The Florentine painter Giotto (1276–1337) led the way in the use of realism; his treatment of the human body and face replaced the formal stiffness and artificiality that had for so long characterized representation of the human body. The sculptor Donatello (1386–1466) probably exerted the greatest influence of any Florentine artist before Michelangelo. His many statues express an appreciation of the incredible variety of human nature. Whereas medieval artists had depicted the nude human body only in a spiritualized and moralizing context, Donatello revived the classical figure, with its balance and self-awareness. The short-lived Florentine Masaccio (1401–1428), sometimes called the father of modern painting, inspired a new style characterized by great realism, narrative power, and remarkably effective use of light and dark. As important as realism was the new "international style," so called because of the wandering careers of influential artists, the close communications and rivalry of princely courts, and the increased trade in works of art. Rich color, decorative detail, curvilinear rhythms, and swaying forms characterized the international style. As the term *international* implies, this style was European, not merely Italian.

Narrative artists depicted the body in a more scientific and natural manner. The female figure is voluptuous and sensual. The male body, as in Michelangelo's *David* and *The Last Judgment,* is strong and heroic. Renaissance glorification of the human body revealed the secular spirit of the age. Filippo Brunelleschi (1377–1446) and Piero della Francesca (1420–1492) seem to have pioneered *perspective* in painting, the linear representation of distance and space on a flat surface. *The Last Supper* by Leonardo da Vinci, with its stress on the tension between Christ and the disciples, is an incredibly subtle psychological interpretation.

The Status of the Artist

In the Renaissance the social status of the artist improved. Whereas the lower-middle-class medieval master mason had been viewed in the same

❖ **Michelangelo: David** In 1501 the new republican government of Florence commissioned the twenty-six-year-old Michelangelo to carve David as a symbol of civic independence and resistance to oligarchial tyranny. Tensed in anticipation of action but certain of victory over his unseen enemy Goliath (1 Samuel 17), this male nude represents the ideal of youthful physical perfection. *(Source: Scala/Art Resource, NY)*

light as a mechanic, the Renaissance artist was considered a free intellectual worker. Artists did not produce unsolicited pictures or statues for the general public; that could mean loss of status. They usually worked on commission from a powerful prince. The artist's reputation depended on the support of powerful patrons, and through them some artists and architects achieved not only economic security but also very great wealth. All aspiring artists received a practical (not theoretical) education in a recognized master's workshop. For example, Michelangelo (1475–1564) was apprenticed at age thirteen to the artist Ghirlandaio (1449–1494), although he later denied that fact to make it appear he never had any formal training. The more famous the artist, the more he attracted assistants or apprentices. Lorenzo Ghiberti (1378–1455) had twenty assistants during the period when he was working on the bronze doors of the Baptistry in Florence, his most famous achievement.

Ghiberti's salary of 200 florins a year compared very favorably with that of the head of the city government, who earned 500 florins. Moreover, at a time when a person could live in a princely fashion on 300 ducats a year, Leonardo da Vinci was making 2,000 annually. Michelangelo was paid 3,000 ducats for painting the ceiling of the Sistine Chapel. When he agreed to work on Saint Peter's Basilica, he refused a salary; he was already a wealthy man.[10]

Renaissance society respected and rewarded the distinguished artist. In 1537 the prolific letter writer, humanist, and satirizer of princes Pietro Aretino (1492–1556) wrote to Michelangelo while he was painting the Sistine Chapel:

To the Divine Michelangelo:

Sir, just as it is disgraceful and sinful to be unmindful of God so it is reprehensible and dishonourable for any man of discerning judgement not to honour you as a brilliant and venerable artist whom the very stars use as a target at which to shoot the rival arrows of their favour. You are so accomplished, therefore, that hidden in your hands lives the idea of a new king of creation. . . . It is surely my duty to honour you with this salutation, since the world has many kings but only one Michelangelo.[11]

When Holy Roman Emperor Charles V (r. 1519–1556) visited the workshop of the great Titian (1477–1576) and stooped to pick up the artist's dropped paintbrush, the emperor was demonstrating that the patron himself was honored in the act of honoring the artist. The social status of the artist of genius was immortally secured.

Renaissance artists were not only aware of their creative power; they also boasted about it. Describing his victory over five others, including Brunelleschi, in the competition to design the bronze doors of Florence's Baptistry, Ghiberti exulted, "The palm of victory was conceded to me by all the experts and by all my fellow-competitors. By universal consent and without a single exception the glory was conceded to me."[12] Some medieval painters and sculptors had signed their works; Renaissance artists almost universally did so, and many of them incorporated self-portraits, usually as bystanders, in their paintings.

The Renaissance, in fact, witnessed the birth of the concept of the artist as genius. In the Middle Ages, people believed that only God created, albeit through individuals; the medieval conception recognized no particular value in artistic originality.

❖ **Benozzo Gozzoli: Journey of the Magi** Few Renaissance paintings better illustrate art in the service of the princely court, in this case the Medici. Commissioned by Piero de' Medici to adorn his palace chapel, everything in this fresco—the large crowd, the feathers and diamonds adorning many of the personages, the black servant in front—serve to flaunt the power and wealth of the House of Medici. There is nothing especially religious about it; the painting could more appropriately be called "Journey of the Medici." The artist has discreetly placed himself in the crowd, the name Benozzo embroidered on his cap. *(Source: Scala/Art Resource, NY)*

Renaissance artists and humanists came to think that a work of art was the deliberate creation of a unique personality, of an individual who transcended traditions, rules, and theories. A genius had a peculiar gift, which ordinary laws should not inhibit. Cosimo de' Medici described a painter, because of his genius, as "divine," implying that the artist shared in the powers of God. The word *divine* was widely applied to Michelangelo.

But the student must guard against interpreting Italian Renaissance culture in twentieth-century democratic terms. The culture of the Renaissance was that of a small mercantile elite, a business patriciate with aristocratic pretensions. Renaissance culture did not directly affect the broad middle classes, let alone the vast urban proletariat. A small, highly educated minority of literary humanists and artists created the culture of and for an exclusive elite. They cared little for ordinary people. Renaissance humanists were a smaller and narrower group than the medieval clergy had ever been. High churchmen had commissioned the construction of the Gothic cathedrals, but once finished, the buildings were for all to enjoy. The modern visitor can still see the deep ruts in the stone floors of Chartres and Canterbury where the poor pilgrims slept at night. Nothing comparable was built in the Renaissance. Insecure, social-climbing merchant princes were hardly egalitarian.[13] The Renaissance maintained a gulf between the learned minority and the uneducated multitude that has survived for many centuries.

✤ SOCIAL CHANGE

The Renaissance changed many aspects of Italian, and subsequently European, society. The new developments brought about real breaks with the medieval past. What impact did the Renaissance have on educational theory and practice, on political thought? How did printing, the era's most stunning technological discovery, affect fifteenth- and sixteenth-century society? How did Renaissance culture affect the experience of women? What roles did blacks play in Renaissance society?

Education and Political Thought

One of the central preoccupations of the humanists was education and moral behavior. Humanists poured out treatises, often in the form of letters, on the structure and goals of education and the training of rulers. In one of the earliest systematic programs for the young, Peter Paul Vergerio (1370–1444) wrote Ubertinus, the ruler of Carrara:

For the education of children is a matter of more than private interest; it concerns the State, which indeed regards the right training of the young as, in certain aspects, within its proper sphere. . . . Tutors and comrades alike should be chosen from amongst those likely to bring out the best qualities, to attract by good example, and to repress the first signs of evil. . . . Above all, respect for Divine ordinances is of the deepest importance; it should be inculcated from the earliest years. Reverence towards elders and parents is an obligation closely akin.

We call those studies liberal *which are worthy of a free man; those studies by which we attain and practice virtue and wisdom; that education which calls forth, trains and develops those highest gifts of body and of mind which ennoble men, and which are rightly judged to rank next in dignity to virtue only.*[14]

Part of Vergerio's treatise specifies subjects for the instruction of young men in public life: history teaches virtue by examples from the past, ethics focuses on virtue itself, and rhetoric or public speaking trains for eloquence.

No book on education had broader influence than Baldassare Castiglione's *The Courtier* (1528). This treatise sought to train, discipline, and fashion the young man into the courtly ideal, the gentleman. According to Castiglione, the educated man of the upper class should have a broad background in many academic subjects, and his spiritual and physical as well as intellectual capabilities should be trained. The courtier should have easy familiarity with dance, music, and the arts. Castiglione envisioned a man who could compose a sonnet, wrestle, sing a song and accompany himself on an instrument, ride expertly, solve difficult mathematical problems, and, above all, speak and write eloquently (see Listening to the Past).

In the sixteenth and seventeenth centuries, *The Courtier* was widely read. It influenced the social mores and patterns of conduct of elite groups in Renaissance and early modern Europe. The courtier became the model of the European gentleman.

No Renaissance book on any topic, however, has been more widely read and studied in all the centuries since its publication (1513) than the short political treatise *The Prince,* by Niccolò Machiavelli (1469–1527). Some political scientists maintain that Machiavelli was describing the actual competitive framework of the Italian states with which he was familiar. Others praise *The Prince* because it revolutionized political theory and destroyed medieval views of the nature of the state. Still other scholars consider this work a classic because it deals with eternal problems of government and society.

Born to a modestly wealthy Tuscan family, Machiavelli received a good education in the Latin classics. He entered the civil service of the Florentine government and served on thirty diplomatic missions. When the exiled Medicis returned to power in the city in 1512, they expelled Machiavelli from his position as an officer of the city government. In exile he wrote *The Prince.*

The subject of *The Prince* is political power: how the ruler should gain, maintain, and increase it. Machiavelli implicitly addressed the question of the citizen's relationship to the state. As a good humanist, he explored the problems of human nature and concluded that human beings are selfish and out to advance their own interests. This pessimistic view of humanity led him to maintain that the prince may have to manipulate the people in any way he finds necessary:

For a man who, in all respects, will carry out only his professions of good, will be apt to be ruined amongst so many who are evil. A prince therefore who desires to maintain himself must learn to be not always good, but to be so or not as necessity may require.[15]

The prince should combine the cunning of a fox with the ferocity of a lion to achieve his goals. Asking rhetorically whether it is better for a ruler to be loved or feared, Machiavelli wrote:

It will naturally be answered that it would be desirable to be both the one and the other; but as it is difficult to be both at the same time, it is much more safe to be feared than to be loved, when you have to choose between the two. For it may be said of men in general that they are ungrateful and fickle, dissemblers, avoiders of danger, and greedy of gain. So long as you shower benefits upon them, they are all yours.[16]

Medieval political theory had derived ultimately from Saint Augustine's view that the state arose as a consequence of Adam's fall and people's propensity to sin. The test of good government was whether it provided justice, law, and order. Political theorists and theologians from Alcuin to Marsiglio of Padua had stressed the way government *ought* to be; they had set high moral and Christian standards for the ruler's conduct.

Machiavelli maintained that the ruler should be concerned not with the way things ought to be but with the way things actually are. The sole test of a "good" government is whether it is effective, whether the ruler increases his power. Machiavelli did not advocate amoral behavior, but he believed that political action cannot be restricted by moral, considerations. While amoral action might be the most effective approach in a given situation, he did not argue for generally amoral, rather than moral behavior. In the *Discourses of the Ten Books of Titus Livy,* Machiavelli even showed his strong commitment to republican government. Nevertheless, on the basis of a crude interpretation of *The Prince,* the word *Machiavellian* entered the language as a synonym for the politically devious, corrupt, and crafty, indicating actions in which the end justifies the means. The ultimate significance of Machiavelli rests on two ideas: first, that one permanent social order reflecting God's will cannot be established and, second, that politics has its own laws and ought to be a science.[17]

The Printed Word

Sometime in the thirteenth century, paper money and playing cards from China reached the West. They were *block-printed*—that is, Chinese characters or pictures were carved into a wooden block, inked, and the words or illustrations transferred to paper. Since each word, phrase, or picture was on a separate block, this method of reproduction was extraordinarily expensive and time consuming.

Around 1455, probably through the combined efforts of three men—Johann Gutenberg, Johann Fust, and Peter Schöffer, all experimenting at Mainz—movable type came into being. The mirror image of each letter (rather than entire words or phrases) was carved in relief on a small block. Individual letters, easily movable, were put together to form words; words separated by blank spaces formed lines of type; and lines of type were brought together to make up a page. Since letters could be arranged into any format, an infinite variety of texts could be printed by reusing and rearranging pieces of type.

✦ The Print Shop Sixteenth-century printing involved a division of labor. Two persons (left) at separate benches set the pieces of type. Another (center, rear) inks the chase [or locked plate containing the set type]. Another (right) operates the press, which prints the sheets. The boy removes the printed pages and sets them to dry. Meanwhile, a man carries in fresh paper on his head. *(Source: Bettmann/Hulton)*

By the middle of the fifteenth century, paper was no problem. The knowledge of paper manufacture had originated in China, and the Arabs introduced it to the West in the twelfth century. Europeans quickly learned that durable paper was far less expensive than the vellum (calfskin) and parchment (sheepskin) on which medieval scribes had relied for centuries.

The effects of the invention of movable-type printing were not felt overnight. Nevertheless, within a half-century of the publication of Gutenberg's Bible of 1456, movable type had brought about radical changes. Printing transformed both the private and the public lives of Europeans (Map 13.2). Governments that "had employed the cumbersome methods of manuscripts to communicate with their subjects switched quickly to print to announce declarations of war, publish battle accounts, promulgate treaties or argue disputed points in pamphlet form. Theirs was an effort 'to

win the psychological war.'" Printing made propaganda possible, emphasizing differences between opposing groups, such as Crown and nobility, church and state. These differences laid the basis for the formation of distinct political parties. Printed materials reached an invisible public, allowing silent individuals to join causes and groups of individuals widely separated by geography to form a common identity; this new group consciousness could compete with older, localized loyalties.

Printing also stimulated the literacy of lay people and eventually came to have a deep effect on their private lives. Although most of the earliest books and pamphlets dealt with religious subjects, students, housewives, businessmen, and upper- and middle-class people sought books on all subjects. Printers responded with moralizing, medical, practical, and travel manuals. Pornography as well as piety assumed new forms. For example, satirist Pietro Aretino (1492–1556) used the shock of sex

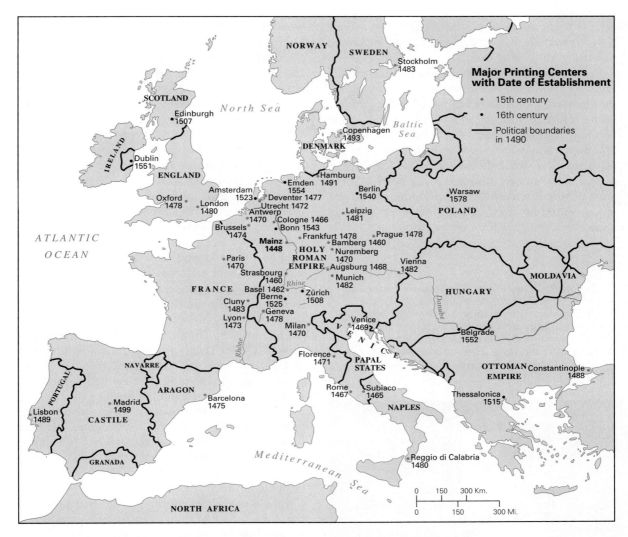

❖ **MAP 13.2 The Growth of Printing in Europe** Although many commercial and academic centers developed printing technology, the press at Venice, employing between 400 and 500 people and producing one-eighth of all printed books, was by far the largest in Europe.

in pornography as a vehicle to criticize: his *Sonnetti Lussuriosi* (1527) and *Ragionamenti* (1534–1536), sonnets accompanying sixteen engravings of as many sexual positions, attacked princely court life, humanist education, and false clerical piety.[18] Broadsides and flysheets allowed great public festivals, religious ceremonies, and political events to be experienced vicariously by the stay-at-home. Since books and other printed materials were read aloud to illiterate listeners, print bridged the gap between written and oral cultures.[19]

Women in Renaissance Society

Did women have a Renaissance? Did women participate in the intellectual and artistic changes of the period? How did the status of women in the fourteenth to sixteenth centuries compare with that of the eleventh to thirteenth centuries?

During the Renaissance the status of upper-class women declined. In terms of the kind of work they performed, their access to property and political power, and their role in shaping the outlook of their society, women in the Renaissance ruling classes generally had less power than comparable women in the feudal age.

In the cities of Renaissance Italy, well-to-do girls received an education similar to boys'. Young ladies learned their letters and studied the classics. Many read Greek as well as Latin, knew the poetry of Ovid and Virgil, and could speak one or two "modern" languages, such as French or Spanish. In this respect, Renaissance humanism represented a real educational advance for women. Some women, though a small minority among humanists, acquired great learning and fame. In the later sixteenth century, at least twenty-five women pub-

Sofonisba Anguissola: The Artist's Sister Minerva A nobleman's daughter and one of the first Italian women to become a recognized artist, Sofonisba did portraits of her five sisters and of prominent people. The coiffure, elegant gown, necklaces, and rings depict aristocratic dress in the mid-sixteenth century. *(Source: Milwaukee Art Museum)*

lished books in Italy, Sofonisba Anguissola (1530–1625) and Artemisia Gentileschi (1593–1653) achieved international renown for their paintings, and Isabella Andreini (1562–1604) enjoyed a reputation as the greatest actress of her day.

Laura Cereta (1469–1499) illustrates the successes and failures of educated Renaissance women. Educated by her father, who was a member of the governing elite of Brescia in Lombardy, she learned languages, philosophy, theology, and mathematics. She also gained self-confidence and a healthy respect for her own potential. By the age of fifteen, when she married, her literary career was already launched, as her letters to several cardinals attest. For Laura Cereta, however, as for all educated women of the period, the question of marriage forced the issue: she could choose a husband, family, and full participation in social life or else study and withdrawal from the world. Marriage brought domestic responsibilities and usually prevented women from fulfilling their scholarly potential. Although Cereta chose marriage, she was widowed at eighteen, and she spent the remaining twelve years of her life in study. But she had to bear the envy of other women and the hostility of men who felt threatened. In response, Cereta condemned "empty women, who strive for no good but exist to adorn themselves. . . . These women of majestic pride, fantastic coiffures, outlandish ornament, and necks bound with gold or pearls bear the glittering symbols of their captivity to men." For Laura Cereta, women's inferiority was derived not from the divine order of things but from women themselves: "For knowledge is not given as a gift, but through study. . . . The free mind, not afraid of labor, presses on to attain the good."[20] Despite Cereta's faith in women's potential, men frequently believed that in becoming learned, a woman violated nature and thus ceased to be a woman. Brilliant women such as Laura Cereta were severely attacked by men who feared threats to male dominance in the intellectual realm.

Laura Cereta was a prodigy. Ordinary girls of the urban upper middle class, in addition to a classical education, received some training in painting, music, and dance. What were they to do with this training? They were to be gracious, affable, charming—in short, decorative. So although Renaissance women were better educated than their medieval counterparts, their education prepared them for the social functions of the home. An educated woman was supposed to know how to attract artists and literati to her husband's court and how to grace her husband's household, whereas an educated man was supposed to know how to rule and participate in public affairs.

Whatever the practical reality, a striking difference also existed between the medieval literature of courtly love, the etiquette books and romances, and the widely studied Renaissance manual on courtesy and good behavior, Castiglione's *The Courtier.* In the medieval books, manners shaped the man to please the woman; in *The Courtier* the woman was to make herself pleasing to the man. With respect to love and sex, the Renaissance witnessed a downward shift in women's status. In contrast to the medieval tradition of relative sexual equality, Renaissance humanists laid the foundations for the bourgeois double standard. Men, and men alone, operated in the public sphere; women belonged in the home. Castiglione, the foremost spokesman of Renaissance love and manners, completely separated love from sexuality. For women, sex was restricted entirely to marriage. Women were bound to chastity and then to the roles of wife and mother in a politically arranged marriage. Men, however, could pursue sensual indulgence outside marriage.[21]

Did the Renaissance impact the lives of ordinary women? Women, of course, continued to perform economic functions: rural women assisted husbands and fathers in agricultural tasks; urban women helped in the shops and were heavily involved in the Florentine textile industry weaving cloth, reeling, and winding silk; and in the Venetian Arsenal, the state-controlled dock and ship construction area—the largest single industrial plant in Europe—women made the ships' sails. Across Europe tens of thousands of women worked as midwives, maids, household servants, cooks, laundresses. Widows frequently ran their husbands' businesses, and in Italy and France some became full members of guilds. Educational opportunities being severely limited, few girls received an education. And education was the great social divide. Women may have taken civic pride in the new monuments and art works in their localities, as far as they could understand them. But apart from that, the literary and art works of the Renaissance had no effect on ordinary women—or men. Many scholars believe the Renaissance witnessed the establishment of an irreversible divide

between an educated elite that participated in a "high culture" of art, music, literature, and learning and a broad mass whose "popular culture" involved tools, houses, the human-made environment, and beliefs.[22]

Official attitudes toward rape provide another index of the status of women in the Renaissance. According to a careful study of the legal evidence from Venice in the years 1338 to 1358 (the Venetian shipping and merchant elite held economic and political power and made the laws), rape was not considered a particularly serious crime against either the victim or society. Noble youths committed a higher percentage of rapes than their small numbers in Venetian society would imply. The rape of a young girl of marriageable age or a child under twelve was considered a graver crime than the rape of a married woman. Nevertheless, the punishment for rape of a noble, marriageable girl was only a fine or about six months' imprisonment. In an age when theft and robbery were punished by mutilation, and forgery and sodomy by burning, this penalty was very mild indeed. When a youth of the upper class was convicted of the rape of a non-noble girl, his punishment was even lighter. By contrast, the sexual assault of a noblewoman by a man of working-class origin, which was extraordinarily rare, resulted in severe penalization because the crime had social and political overtones.

In the eleventh century, William the Conqueror had decreed that rapists be castrated, implicitly according women protection and a modicum of respect. But in the early Renaissance, Venetian laws and their enforcement show that the governing oligarchy believed that rape damaged, but only slightly, men's property—women.[23]

Evidence from Florence in the fifteenth century also sheds light on infanticide, which historians are only now beginning to study in the Middle Ages and the Renaissance. Early medieval penitentials and church councils had legislated against abortion and infanticide, though it is known that Pope Innocent III (1198–1216) was moved to establish an orphanage "because so many women were throwing their children into the Tiber."[24] In the fourteenth and early fifteenth centuries, a considerable number of children died in Florence under suspicious circumstances. Some were simply abandoned outdoors. Some were said to have been crushed to death while sleeping in the same bed with their parents. Some died from "crib death," or suffocation. These deaths occurred too frequently to have all been accidental. And far more girls than boys died, thus reflecting societal discrimination against girl children as inferior and less useful than boys. The dire poverty of parents led them to do away with unwanted children.

The gravity of the problem of infanticide, which violated both the canon law of the church and the civil law of the state, forced the Florentine government to build the Foundling Hospital. Supporters of the institution maintained that without public responsibility, "many children would soon be found dead in the rivers, sewers, and ditches, unbaptized."[25] The large size of the hospital suggests that great numbers of children were abandoned.

Blacks in Renaissance Society

Ever since the time of the Roman republic, a few black people had lived in western Europe. They had come, along with white slaves, as the spoils of war. Even after the collapse of the Roman Empire, Muslim and Christian merchants continued to import them. The evidence of medieval art attests to the presence of Africans in the West and to Europeans' awareness of them. In the twelfth and thirteenth centuries, a large cult surrounded Saint Maurice, martyred in the fourth century for refusing to renounce his Christian faith, who was portrayed as a black knight. Saint Maurice received the special veneration of the nobility. The numbers of blacks, however, had always been small.

But beginning in the fifteenth century, sizable numbers of black slaves entered Europe. Portuguese explorers imported perhaps a thousand a year and sold them at the markets of Seville, Barcelona, Marseilles, and Genoa. By the mid-sixteenth century, blacks, slave and free, constituted about 10 percent of the populations of the Portuguese cities of Lisbon and Évora; other cities had smaller percentages. In all, blacks made up roughly 3 percent of the Portuguese population. The Venetians specialized in the import of white slaves, but blacks were so greatly in demand at the Renaissance courts of northern Italy that the Venetians defied papal threats of excommunication to secure them. What roles did blacks play in Renaissance society? What image did Europeans have of Africans?

The medieval interest in curiosities, the exotic, and the marvelous continued into the Renaissance. Black servants, because of their rarity, were highly prized and much sought after. In the late fifteenth century, Isabella, the wife of Gian Galazzo Sforza, took pride in the fact that she had ten blacks, seven of them females; a black lady's-maid was both a curiosity and a symbol of wealth. In 1491 Isabella of Este, duchess of Mantua, instructed her agent to secure a black girl between four and eight years old, "shapely and as black as possible." The duchess saw the child as a source of entertainment: "We shall make her very happy and shall have great fun with her." She hoped that the little girl would become "the best buffoon in the world."[26] The cruel ancient tradition of a noble household retaining a professional "fool" for the family's amusement persisted through the Renaissance—and even down to the twentieth century.

Adult black slaves filled a variety of positions. Many served as maids, valets, and domestic servants. Italian aristocrats such as Marchesa Elena Grimaldi had their portraits painted with their black page boys to indicate their wealth. The Venetians employed blacks—slave and free—as gondoliers and stevedores on the docks. In Portugal kings, nobles, laborers, religious institutions such as monasteries and convents, and prostitutes owned slaves. They supplemented the labor force in virtually all occupations—as agricultural laborers, craftsmen, herdsmen, grape pickers, workers in the manufacture of olive oil, and seamen on ships going to Lisbon and Africa.[27] Tradition, stretching back at least as far as the thirteenth century, connected blacks with music and dance. In Renaissance Spain and Italy, blacks performed as dancers, as actors and actresses in courtly dramas, and as musicians, sometimes making up full orchestras.[28] Slavery during the Renaissance foreshadowed the American, especially the later Brazilian, pattern.

Before the sixteenth-century "discoveries" of the non-European world, Europeans had little concrete knowledge of Africans and their cultures. What Europeans did know was based on biblical accounts. The European attitude toward Africans was ambivalent. On the one hand, Europeans perceived Africa as a remote place, the home of strange people isolated by heresy and Islam from superior European civilization. Africans' contact even as slaves with Christian Europeans could only "improve" the blacks. Most Europeans' knowledge of the black as a racial type was based entirely on theological speculation. Theologians taught that God was light. Blackness, the opposite of light, therefore represented the hostile forces of the un-

✦ **Carpaccio: Black Laborers on the Venetian Docks** Slave and free blacks, besides working as gondoliers on the Venetian canals, served on the docks: here seven black men (background) careen—clean, caulk, and repair—a ship. Carpaccio's reputation as one of Venice's outstanding painters rests on his eye for details of everyday life. *(Source: Gallerie dell'Accademia, Venice/Art Resource, NY)*

derworld: evil, sin, and the devil. Thus the devil was commonly represented as a black man in medieval and early Renaissance art. On the other hand, blackness possessed certain positive qualities. It symbolized the emptiness of worldly goods, the humility of the monastic way of life. Black clothes permitted a conservative and discreet display of wealth. Black vestments and funeral trappings indicated grief, and Christ had said that those who mourn are blessed. Until the exploration and observation of the sixteenth, seventeenth, and nineteenth centuries allowed, ever so slowly, for the development of more scientific knowledge, the Western conception of black people remained bound up with religious notions.[29] In Renaissance society, blacks, like women, were signs of wealth; both were used for display.

✦ THE RENAISSANCE IN THE NORTH

In the last quarter of the fifteenth century, Italian Renaissance thought and ideals penetrated northern Europe. Students from the Low Countries, France, Germany, and England flocked to Italy, imbibed the "new learning," and carried it back to their countries. Northern humanists interpreted Italian ideas about and attitudes toward classical antiquity, individualism, and humanism in terms of their own traditions. The cultural traditions of northern Europe tended to remain more distinctly Christian, or at least pietistic, than those of Italy. Italian humanists certainly were strongly Christian, as the example of Pico della Mirandola shows. But in Italy secular and pagan themes and Greco-Roman motifs received more humanistic attention. North of the Alps, the Renaissance had a distinctly religious character, and humanists stressed biblical and early Christian themes. What fundamentally distinguished Italian humanists from northern ones is that the latter had a program for broad social reform based on Christian ideals.

Christian humanists were interested in the development of an ethical way of life. To achieve it, they believed that the best elements of classical and Christian cultures should be combined. For example, the classical ideals of calmness, stoical patience, and broad-mindedness should be joined in human conduct with the Christian virtues of love, faith, and hope. Northern humanists also stressed the use of reason, rather than acceptance of dogma, as the foundation for an ethical way of life. Like the Italians, they were impatient with Scholastic philosophy. Christian humanists had a profound faith in the power of human intellect to bring about moral and institutional reform. They believed that, although human nature had been corrupted by sin, it was fundamentally good and capable of improvement through education, which would lead to piety and an ethical way of life.

The work of French priest Jacques Lefèvre d'Étaples (ca 1455–1536) was one of the early attempts to apply humanistic learning to religious problems. A brilliant thinker and able scholar, he believed that more accurate texts of the Bible would lead people to live better lives. According to Lefèvre, a solid education in the Scriptures would increase piety and raise the level of behavior in Christian society. Lefèvre produced an edition of the Psalms and a commentary on Saint Paul's epistles. In 1516, when Martin Luther lectured to his students at Wittenberg on Paul's *Letter to the Romans*, he relied on Lefèvre's texts.

Englishman Thomas More (1478–1535) towered above other figures in sixteenth-century English social and intellectual history. More's political stance later, at the time of the Reformation (see page 461), a position that in part flowed from his humanist beliefs, cost him his life, and has tended to obscure his contribution to Christian humanism.

The early career of Thomas More presents a number of paradoxes that reveal the marvelous complexity of the man. Trained as a lawyer, More lived as a student in the London Charterhouse, a Carthusian monastery. He subsequently married and practiced law but became deeply interested in the classics; his household served as a model of warm Christian family life and as a mecca for foreign and English humanists. In the career pattern of such Italian humanists as Petrarch, More entered government service under Henry VIII and was sent as ambassador to Flanders. There More found the time to write *Utopia* (1516), which presented a revolutionary view of society.

Utopia, which means "nowhere," describes an ideal socialistic community on an island somewhere off the mainland of the New World. All its children receive a good education, primarily in the Greco-Roman classics, and learning does not cease with maturity, for the goal of all education is to develop rational faculties. Adults divide their days equally between manual labor or business pursuits and various intellectual activities.

Because the profits from business and property are held strictly in common, there is absolute social equality. The Utopians use gold and silver both to make chamber pots and to prevent wars by buying off their enemies. By this casual use of precious metals, More meant to suggest that the basic problems in society were caused by greed. Utopian law exalts mercy above justice. Citizens of Utopia lead an ideal, nearly perfect existence because they live by reason; their institutions are perfect. More punned on the word *utopia,* which he termed "a good place. A good place which is no place."

More's ideas were profoundly original in the sixteenth century. Contrary to the long-prevailing view that vice and violence existed because women and men were basically corrupt, More maintained that acquisitiveness and private property promoted all sorts of vices and civil disorders. Since society protected private property, *society's* flawed institutions were responsible for corruption and war. Today this view is so much taken for granted that it is difficult to appreciate how radical More's approach was in the sixteenth century. According to More, the key to improvement and reform of the individual was reform of the social institutions that molded the individual.

Better known by contemporaries than Thomas More was the Dutch humanist Desiderius Erasmus (1466?–1536) of Rotterdam. Orphaned as a small boy, Erasmus was forced to enter a monastery. Although he intensely disliked the monastic life, he developed there an excellent knowledge of the Latin language and a deep appreciation for the Latin classics. During a visit to England in 1499, Erasmus met John Colet, who decisively influenced his life's work: the application of the best humanistic learning to the study and explanation of the Bible. As a mature scholar with an international reputation stretching from Cracow to London, a fame that rested largely on his exceptional knowledge of Greek, Erasmus could boast with truth, "I brought it about that humanism, which among the Italians . . . savored of nothing but pure paganism, began nobly to celebrate Christ."[30]

Erasmus's long list of publications includes *The Adages* (1500), a list of Greek and Latin precepts on ethical behavior; *The Education of a Christian Prince* (1504), a book combining idealistic and practical suggestions for the formation of a ruler's character through the careful study of Plutarch, Aristotle, Cicero, and Plato; *The Praise of Folly* (1509), a satire of worldly wisdom and a plea for the simple and spontaneous Christian faith of children; and, most important of all, a critical edition of the Greek New Testament (1516). In the preface to the New Testament, Erasmus explained the purpose of his great work:

Only bring a pious and open heart, imbued above all things with a pure and simple faith. . . . For I utterly dissent from those who are unwilling that the sacred Scriptures should be read by the unlearned translated into their vulgar tongue, as though Christ had taught such subtleties that they can scarcely be understood even by a few theologians. . . . Christ wished his mysteries to be published as openly as possible. I wish that even the weakest woman should read the Gospel—should read the epistles of Paul. And I wish these were translated into all languages, so that they might be read and understood, not only by Scots and Irishmen, but also by Turks and Saracens. . . . Why do we prefer to study the wisdom of Christ in men's writings rather than in the writing of Christ himself?[31]

Two fundamental themes run through all of Erasmus's scholarly work. First, education is the means to reform, the key to moral and intellectual improvement. The core of education ought to be study of the Bible and the classics. Second, the essence of Erasmus's thought is, in his own phrase, "the philosophy of Christ." By this Erasmus meant that Christianity is an inner attitude of the heart or spirit. Christianity is not formalism, special ceremonies, or law; Christianity is Christ—his life and what he said and did, not what theologians have written. The Sermon on the Mount, for Erasmus, expresses the heart of the Christian message.

Whereas the writings of Colet, Erasmus, and More have strong Christian themes and have drawn the attention primarily of scholars, the stories of French humanist François Rabelais (1490?–1553) possess a distinctly secular flavor and have attracted broad readership among the literate public. Rabelais's *Gargantua* and *Pantagruel* (serialized between 1532 and 1552) belong among the great comic masterpieces of world literature. These stories' gross and robust humor introduced the adjective *Rabelaisian* into the language.

Gargantua and *Pantagruel* can be read on several levels: as comic romances about the adventures of the giant Gargantua and his son, Pantagruel; as a spoof on contemporary French society; as a program for educational reform; or as illustrations of Rabelais's prodigious learning. The reader enters a world of Renaissance vitality, ribald joviality, and intellectual curiosity. On his travels Gargantua meets various absurd characters, and within their hilarious exchanges occur serious discussions on religion, politics, philosophy, and education. Rabelais had received an excellent humanistic education in a monastery, and Gargantua discusses the disorders of contemporary religious and secular life. Like More and Erasmus, Rabelais did not denounce institutions directly. Like Erasmus, Rabelais satirized hypocritical monks, pedantic academics, and pompous lawyers. But where Erasmus employed intellectual cleverness and sophisticated wit, Rabelais would apply wild and gross humor. Like Thomas More, Rabelais believed that institutions molded individuals and that education was indeed the key to a moral and healthy life. Whereas the middle-class inhabitants of More's Utopia lived lives of restrained moderation, the aristocratic residents of Rabelais's Thélèma lived for the full gratification of their physical instincts and rational curiosity.

Thélèma, the abbey Gargantua establishes, parodies traditional religion and other social institutions. Thélèma, whose motto is "Do as Thou Wilt," admits women *and* men; allows all to eat, drink, sleep, and work when they choose; provides excellent facilities for swimming, tennis, and football; and encourages sexual experimentation and marriage. Rabelais believed profoundly in the basic goodness of human beings and the rightness of instinct.

The most roguishly entertaining Renaissance writer, Rabelais was convinced that "laughter is the essence of manhood." A believer in the Roman Catholic faith, he included in Gargantua's education an appreciation for simple and reasonable prayer. Rabelais combined the Renaissance zest for life and enjoyment of pleasure with a classical insistence on the cultivation of the body and the mind.

The distinctly religious orientation of the literary works of the Renaissance in the north also characterized northern art and architecture. Some Flemish painters, notably Rogier van der Weyden (1399/1400–1464) and Jan van Eyck (1366–1441), were considered the artistic equals of Italian painters, were much admired in Italy, and worked a generation before Leonardo and Michelangelo. Van Eyck, one of the earliest artists to use oil-based paints successfully, shows the Flemish love for detail in paintings such as *Ghent Altarpiece* and the portrait of *Giovanni Arnolfini and His Bride*; the

 Jan van Eyck: Madonna of Chancellor Rodin The tough and shrewd chancellor who ordered this rich painting visits the Virgin and Christ-Child (though they seem to be visiting him). An angel holds the crown of heaven over the Virgin's head while Jesus, the proclaimed savior of the world, holds it in his left hand and raises his right hand in blessing. Through the colonnade, sculpted with scenes from Genesis, is the city of Bruges. Van Eyck's achievement in portraiture is extraordinary; his treatment of space and figures and his ability to capture the infinitely small and very large prompted the art historian Erwin Panofsky to write that "his eye was at one and the same time a microscope and a telescope." *(Source: Louvre/Cliché des Musées Nationaux, Paris)*

effect is great realism and remarkable attention to human personality.

Another Flemish painter, Jerome Bosch (1450?–1516), frequently used religious themes, but in combination with grotesque fantasies, colorful imagery, and peasant folk legends. Many of Bosch's paintings reflect the confusion and anguish often associated with the end of the Middle Ages. In *Death and the Miser,* Bosch's dramatic treatment of the Dance of Death theme, the miser's gold, increased by usury, is ultimately controlled by diabolical rats and toads, while his guardian angel urges him to choose the crucifix.

A quasi-spiritual aura likewise infuses architectural monuments in the north. The city halls of wealthy Flemish towns such as Bruges, Brussels, Louvain, and Ghent strike the viewer more as shrines to house the bones of saints than as settings for the mundane decisions of politicians and business people. Northern architecture was little influenced by the classical revival so obvious in Renaissance Rome and Florence.

POLITICS AND THE STATE IN THE RENAISSANCE (CA 1450–1521)

The High Middle Ages had witnessed the origins of many of the basic institutions of the modern state. Sheriffs, inquests, juries, circuit judges, professional bureaucracies, and representative assemblies all trace their origins to the twelfth and thirteenth centuries (see page 388). The linchpin for the development of states, however, was strong monarchy, and during the period of the Hundred Years' War, no ruler in western Europe was able to provide effective leadership. The resurgent power of feudal nobilities weakened the centralizing work begun earlier.

Beginning in the fifteenth century, rulers utilized the aggressive methods implied by Renaissance political ideas to rebuild their governments. First in Italy, then in France, England, and Spain, rulers began the work of reducing violence, curbing unruly nobles and troublesome elements, and establishing domestic order. Within the Holy Roman

Empire of Germany, lack of centralization helps account for the later German distrust of the Roman papacy. Divided into scores of independent principalities, Germany could not deal with the Roman church as an equal.

The dictators and oligarchs of the Italian city-states, together with Louis XI of France, Henry VII of England, and Ferdinand of Aragon, were tough, cynical, calculating rulers. In their ruthless push for power and strong governments, they subordinated morality to hard results. They preferred to be secure, if feared, rather than loved. They could not have read Machiavelli's *The Prince*, but they acted as though they understood its ideas.

Some historians have called Louis XI, Henry VII, and Ferdinand and Isabella in Spain "new monarchs." The term is only partly appropriate. These monarchs were new in that they invested kingship with a strong sense of royal authority and national purpose. They stressed that monarchy was the one institution that linked all classes and peoples within definite territorial boundaries. These rulers emphasized royal majesty and royal sovereignty and insisted on the respect and loyalty of all subjects. These monarchs ruthlessly suppressed opposition and rebellion, especially from the nobility. They loved the business of kingship and worked hard at it.

In other respects, however, the methods of these rulers, which varied from country to country, were not so new. They reasserted long-standing ideas and practices of strong monarchs in the Middle Ages. They seized on the maxim of the Justinian Code, "What pleases the prince has the force of law," to advance their authority. Some medieval rulers, such as Henry I of England, had depended heavily on middle-class officials. Renaissance rulers, too, tended to rely on middle-class civil servants. With tax revenues, medieval rulers had built armies to crush feudal anarchy. Renaissance townspeople with commercial and business interests naturally

❖ **Jerome Bosch: Death and the Miser** Netherlandish painters frequently used symbolism, and Bosch (ca 1450–1516) is considered the master artist of symbolism and fantasy. Here rats, which because of their destructiveness symbolize evil, control the miser's gold. Bosch's imagery appealed strongly to twentieth-century surrealist painters. (*Source: National Gallery of Art, Washington, D.C., Samuel H. Kress Collection*)

wanted a reduction of violence, and usually they were willing to pay taxes in order to achieve it.

France

The Hundred Years' War left France badly divided, drastically depopulated, commercially ruined, and agriculturally weak. Nonetheless, the ruler whom Joan of Arc had seen crowned at Reims, Charles VII (r. 1422–1461), revived the monarchy and France. He seemed an unlikely person to do so. Frail, indecisive, and burdened with questions about his paternity (his father had been deranged; his mother, notoriously promiscuous), Charles VII nevertheless began France's long recovery.

Charles reconciled the Burgundians and Armagnacs, who had been waging civil war for thirty years. By 1453 French armies had expelled the English from French soil except in Calais. Charles reorganized the royal council, giving increased influence to the middle-class men, and strengthened royal finances through such taxes as the *gabelle* (on salt) and the taille land tax. These taxes remained the Crown's chief sources of state income until the Revolution of 1789.

Charles also reformed the justice system and remodeled the army. By establishing regular companies of cavalry and archers—recruited, paid, and inspected by the state—Charles created the first permanent royal army. (In the victory over the English in 1453, however, French artillery played the decisive role.) In 1438 Charles published the Pragmatic Sanction of Bourges, asserting the superiority of a general council over the papacy, giving the French crown major control over the appointment of bishops, and depriving the pope of French ecclesiastical revenues. The Pragmatic Sanction established the Gallican (or French) liberties because it affirmed the special rights of the French crown over the French church. Greater control over the church, the army, and justice helped consolidate the authority of the French crown.

Charles's son Louis XI (r. 1461–1483), called the "Spider King" by his subjects because of his treacherous and cruel character, was very much a Renaissance prince. Facing the perpetual French problems of unification of the realm and reduction of feudal disorder, he saw money as the answer. Louis promoted new industries, such as silk weaving at Lyons and Tours. He welcomed tradesmen and foreign craftsmen, and he entered into commercial treaties with England, Portugal, and the towns of the Hanseatic League (see page 350). He used the revenues raised through these economic activities and severe taxation to improve the army. With the army Louis stopped aristocratic brigandage and slowly cut into urban independence.

Luck favored his goal of expanding royal authority and unifying the kingdom. On the timely death of Charles the Bold, duke of Burgundy, in 1477, Louis invaded Burgundy and gained some territories. Three years later, the extinction of the house of Anjou brought Louis the counties of Anjou, Bar, Maine, and Provence.

Some scholars have credited Louis XI with laying the foundations for later French royal absolutism. Indeed, he worked tirelessly to remodel the government following the disorders of the fourteenth and fifteenth centuries. In his reliance on finances supplied by the middle classes to fight the feudal nobility, Louis was thought to be typical of the new monarchs.

Two further developments strengthened the French monarchy. The marriage of Louis XII (r. 1498–1515) and Anne of Brittany added the large western duchy of Brittany to the state. Then the French king Francis I and Pope Leo X reached a mutually satisfactory agreement in 1516. The new treaty, the Concordat of Bologna, rescinded the Pragmatic Sanction's assertion of the superiority of a general council over the papacy and approved the pope's right to receive the first year's income of new bishops and abbots. In return, Leo X recognized the French ruler's right to select French bishops and abbots. French kings thereafter effectively controlled the appointment and thus the policies of church officials within the kingdom.

England

English society suffered severely from the disorders of the fifteenth century. The aristocracy dominated the government of Henry IV (r. 1399–1413) and indulged in mischievous violence at the local level. Population, decimated by the Black Death, continued to decline. Even though Henry V (r. 1413–1422) gained chivalric prestige for his military exploits in France, he was totally dependent on the feudal magnates who controlled the royal council and Parliament. Henry V's death, leaving a nine-month-old son, the future Henry VI (r. 1422–1461), gave the barons a perfect opportunity to entrench their power. Between 1455 and 1471,

❖ **van Schwanenburgh: The Spinners** In the late 16th century, the prosperity of Leyden in Holland rested on the textile industry, which in turn depended on the import of merino wool from Spain. In this lush scene three large spinning wheels are operated simultaneously. Although women composed 30 percent of the work force, they earned much less than men. (*Source: Stedelijk Museum, "De Lakenhal," Leiden, Holland*)

adherents of the ducal houses of York and Lancaster waged civil war, commonly called the Wars of the Roses because the symbol of the Yorkists was a white rose and that of the Lancastrians a red one. Although only a small minority of the nobility participated, the chronic disorder hurt trade, agriculture, and domestic industry. Under the pious but mentally disturbed Henry VI, the authority of the monarchy sank lower than it had been in centuries.

Edward IV (r. 1461–1483) began establishing domestic tranquility. He succeeded in defeating the Lancastrian forces and after 1471 began to reconstruct the monarchy and consolidate royal power. Edward, his brother Richard III (r. 1483–1485), and Henry VII (r. 1485–1509) of the Welsh house of Tudor worked to restore royal prestige, to crush the power of the nobility, and to establish order and law at the local level. All three rulers used methods that Machiavelli himself would have praised—ruthlessness, efficiency, and secrecy.

The Hundred Years' War had cost the nation dearly, and the money to finance it had been raised by Parliament. Dominated by various baronial factions, Parliament had been the arena where the nobility exerted its power. As long as the monarchy was dependent on the Lords and the Commons for revenue, the king had to call Parliament. Thus Edward IV revived the medieval ideal that he would "live of his own," meaning on his own financial resources. He reluctantly established a policy the monarchy was to follow with rare exceptions down to 1603. Edward, and subsequently the Tudors, excepting Henry VIII, conducted foreign policy on the basis of diplomacy, avoiding expensive wars. Thus the English monarchy did not depend on Parliament for money, and the Crown undercut that source of aristocratic influence.

Henry VII did, however, summon several meetings of Parliament in the early years of his reign. He used these assemblies primarily to confirm laws. Parliament remained the highest court in the land, and a statute registered (approved) there by the lords, bishops, and Commons gave the appearance of broad national support plus thorough judicial authority.

The center of royal authority was the royal council, which governed at the national level. There Henry VII revealed his distrust of the nobility: though not completely excluded, very few great lords were among the king's closest advisers. Regular representatives on the council numbered between twelve and fifteen men, and while many gained high ecclesiastical rank (the means, as it happened, by which the Crown paid them), their origins were in the lesser landowning class, and their education was in law. They were, in a sense, middle class.

The royal council handled any business the king put before it—executive, legislative, judicial. For example, the council conducted negotiations with foreign governments and secured international recognition of the Tudor dynasty through the marriage in 1501 of Henry VII's eldest son, Arthur, to Catherine of Aragon, the daughter of Ferdinand and Isabella of Spain. The council prepared laws for parliamentary ratification. The council dealt with real or potential aristocratic threats through a judicial offshoot, the court of Star Chamber, so called because of the stars painted on the ceiling of the room.

Henry set up the court of Star Chamber to prevent aristocratic interference in the administration of justice and to combat fur-collar criminal activity (see pages 390–391). The court applied principles of Roman law, and its methods were sometimes terrifying: accused persons were not entitled to see evidence against them, sessions were secret, torture could be applied to extract confessions, and juries were not called. These procedures ran directly counter to English common-law precedents, but they effectively reduced aristocratic troublemaking.

Unlike the continental countries of Spain and France, England had no standing army or professional civil service bureaucracy. The Tudors relied

on the support of unpaid local officials, the justices of the peace. These influential landowners in the shires handled all the work of local government. They apprehended and punished criminals, enforced parliamentary statutes, supervised conditions of service, fixed wages and prices, maintained proper standards of weights and measures, and even checked up on moral behavior.

The Tudors won the support of the influential upper middle class because the Crown linked government policy with the interests of that class. A commercial or agricultural upper class fears and dislikes few things more than disorder and violence. If the Wars of the Roses served any useful purpose, it was killing off dangerous nobles and thus making the Tudors' work easier. The Tudors promoted peace and social order, and the gentry did not object to arbitrary methods, like those of the court of Star Chamber, because the government had halted the long period of anarchy.

Grave, secretive, cautious, and always thrifty, Henry VII rebuilt the monarchy. He encouraged the cloth industry and built up the English merchant marine. Both English exports of wool and the royal export tax on that wool steadily increased. Henry crushed an invasion from Ireland and secured peace with Scotland through the marriage of his daughter Margaret to the Scottish king. When Henry VII died in 1509, he left a country at peace both domestically and internationally, a substantially augmented treasury, and the dignity and role of the royal majesty much enhanced.

Spain

Political development in Spain followed a pattern different from that of France and England. The central theme in the history of medieval Spain—or, more accurately, of the separate kingdoms Spain comprised—was disunity and plurality. The various peoples who lived in the Iberian Peninsula lacked a common cultural tradition. Different languages, laws, and religious communities made for a rich diversity. Complementing the legacy of Hispanic, Roman, and Visigothic peoples, Muslims and Jews had significantly affected the course of Spanish society.

The centuries-long *reconquista*—the attempts of the northern Christian kingdoms to control the entire peninsula—had both military and religious objectives: expulsion or conversion of the Arabs and Jews and political control of the south. By the middle of the fifteenth century, the kingdoms of Castile and Aragon dominated the weaker Navarre, Granada, and Portugal, and with the exception of Granada, the Iberian Peninsula had been won for Christianity. The wedding in 1469 of the dynamic and aggressive Isabella, heiress of Castile, and the crafty and persistent Ferdinand, heir of Aragon, was the final major step in the unification and Christianization of Spain. This marriage, however, constituted a dynastic union of two royal houses, not the political union of two peoples. Although Ferdinand and Isabella (r. 1474–1516) pursued a common foreign policy, Spain under their rule remained a loose confederation of separate states. Each kingdom continued to maintain its own *cortes* (parliament), laws, courts, and systems of coinage and taxation.

Isabella and Ferdinand determined to strengthen royal authority. To curb rebellious and warring aristocracy, they revived an old medieval institution: the *hermandades,* or "brotherhoods," which were popular groups in the towns given the authority to act both as local police forces and as judicial tribunals. Local communities were made responsible for raising troops and apprehending and punishing criminals. The hermandades repressed violence with such savage punishments that by 1498 they could be disbanded.

The decisive step Ferdinand and Isabella took to curb aristocratic power was the restructuring of the royal council. Aristocrats and great territorial magnates were rigorously excluded; thus the influence of the nobility on state policy was greatly reduced. Ferdinand and Isabella intended the council to be the cornerstone of their government system, with full executive, judicial, and legislative power under the monarchy. The council was also to be responsible for the supervision of local authorities. The king and queen therefore appointed to the council only people of middle-class background. The council and various government boards recruited men trained in Roman law, a system that exalted the power of the Crown as the embodiment of the state.

In the extension of royal authority and the consolidation of the territories of Spain, the church was the linchpin. The major issue confronting Isabella and Ferdinand was the appointment of bishops. If the Spanish crown could select the higher clergy, then the monarchy could influence ecclesiastical policy, wealth, and military resources. Through a diplomatic alliance with the Spanish

pope Alexander VI, the Spanish monarchs secured the right to appoint bishops in Spain and in the Hispanic territories in America. This power enabled the "Catholic Kings of Spain," a title granted Ferdinand and Isabella by the papacy, to establish, in effect, a national church.[32]

Revenues from ecclesiastical estates provided the means to raise an army to continue the reconquista. The victorious entry of Ferdinand and Isabella into Granada on January 6, 1492, signaled the culmination of eight centuries of Spanish struggle against the Arabs in southern Spain and the conclusion of the reconquista (Map 13.3). Granada in the south was incorporated into the Spanish kingdom, and in 1512 Ferdinand conquered Navarre in the north.

Although the Arabs had been defeated, there still remained a sizable and, in the view of the Catholic sovereigns, potentially dangerous minority, the Jews. Since ancient times, Christian governments had seldom tolerated religious pluralism; religious faiths that differed from the official state religion were considered politically dangerous. Medieval writers quoted fourth-century Byzantine theologian Saint John Chrysostom, who had asked rhetorically, "Why are the Jews degenerate? Because of their odious assassination of Christ." John Chrysostom and his admirers in the Middle Ages chose to ignore two facts: that it was the Romans who had killed Christ (because they considered him a *political* troublemaker) and that Christ had forgiven his executioners from the cross. France and England had expelled their Jewish populations in the Middle Ages, but in Spain Jews had been tolerated. In fact, Jews had played a decisive role in the economic and intellectual life of the several Spanish kingdoms.

Anti-Semitic riots and pogroms in the late fourteenth century had led many Jews to convert; they were called *conversos.* By the middle of the fifteenth century, many conversos held high positions in Spanish society as financiers, physicians, merchants, tax collectors, and even officials of the church hierarchy. Numbering perhaps 200,000 in a total population of about 7.5 million, Jews exercised an influence quite disproportionate to their numbers. Aristocratic grandees who borrowed heavily from Jews resented their financial dependence, and churchmen questioned the sincerity of Jewish conversions. At first, Isabella and Ferdinand continued the policy of royal toleration—Ferdinand himself had inherited Jewish blood from his

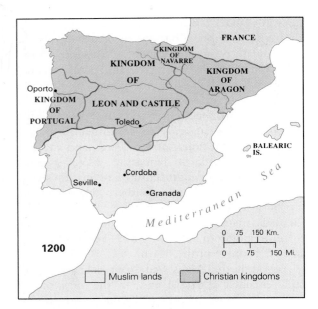

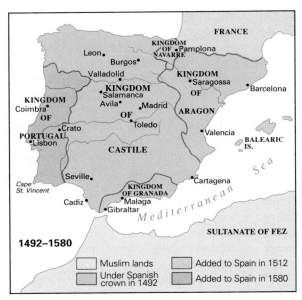

 MAP 13.3 The Christianization and Unification of Spain The political unification of Spain was inextricably tied up with conversion or expulsion of the Muslims
and the Jews. Why?

mother. But many conversos apparently reverted to
the faith of their ancestors, prompting Ferdinand
and Isabella to secure Rome's permission to revive
the Inquisition, a medieval judicial procedure for
the punishment of heretics.

Although the Inquisition was a religious institution established to ensure the Catholic faith, it was
controlled by the Crown and served primarily as a
politically unifying force in Spain. Because the
Spanish Inquisition commonly applied torture to
extract confessions, first from lapsed conversos,
then from Muslims, and later from Protestants, it
gained a notorious reputation. Thus the word *inquisition,* meaning "any judicial inquiry conducted
with ruthless severity," came into the English language. The methods of the Spanish Inquisition
were cruel, though not as cruel as the investigative
methods of some twentieth-century governments.
In 1478 the deeply pious Ferdinand and Isabella
introduced the Inquisition into their kingdoms to
handle the problem of backsliding conversos. They
solved the problem in a dire and drastic manner.
Shortly after the reduction of the Moorish stronghold at Granada in 1492, Isabella and Ferdinand
issued an edict expelling all practicing Jews from
Spain. Of the community of perhaps 200,000
Jews, 150,000 fled. (Efforts were made, through
last-minute conversions, to retain good Jewish

physicians.) Absolute religious orthodoxy and purity of blood (untainted by Jews or Muslims)
served as the theoretical foundation of the Spanish
national state.

The diplomacy of the Catholic rulers of Spain
achieved a success they never anticipated. Partly
out of hatred for the French and partly out of a
desire to gain international recognition for their
new dynasty, Ferdinand and Isabella in 1496 married their second daughter, Joanna, heiress to
Castile, to the archduke Philip, heir through his
mother to the Burgundian Netherlands and
through his father to the Holy Roman Empire.
Philip and Joanna's son, Charles V (r. 1519–1556),
thus succeeded to a vast patrimony on two continents. When Charles's son Philip II united Portugal to the Spanish crown in 1580, the Iberian
Peninsula was at last politically united.

SUMMARY

The Italian Renaissance rested on the phenomenal
economic growth of the High Middle Ages. In the
period from about 1050 to 1300, a new economy
emerged based on Venetian and Genoese shipping
and long-distance trade and on Florentine banking

and cloth manufacture. These commercial activities, combined with the struggle of urban communes for political independence from surrounding feudal lords, led to the appearance of a new wealthy aristocratic class. The centuries extending roughly from 1300 to 1600 witnessed a remarkable intellectual flowering. Based on a strong interest in the ancient world, the Renaissance had a classicizing influence on many facets of culture: law, literature, government, education, religion, and art. In the city-states of fifteenth- and sixteenth-century Italy, oligarchic or despotic powers governed; Renaissance culture was manipulated to enhance the power of those rulers.

Expanding outside Italy, the intellectual features of this movement affected the culture of all Europe. The intellectual characteristics of the Renaissance were a secular attitude toward life, a belief in individual potential, and a serious interest in the Latin classics. The printing press revolutionized communication. Meanwhile, the status of women in society declined, and black people entered Europe in sizable numbers for the first time since the collapse of the Roman Empire. In northern Europe, city merchants and rural gentry allied with rising monarchies. With taxes provided by business people, kings established greater peace and order, both essential for trade. In Spain, France, and England, rulers also emphasized royal dignity and authority, and they utilized Machiavellian ideas to ensure the preservation and continuation of their governments. Feudal monarchies gradually evolved in the direction of nation-states.

❖ **A Barcelona Seder** On the northeastern coast of Spain, Barcelona had a vibrant Jewish community in the fourteenth and fifteenth centuries, as this scene suggests. The seven days of Passover, commemorating the exodus of the Jews from Egypt after 430 years of servitude (Exodus 22), begin with a simple meal, or seder, on the evening of the first day. Special food, including unleavened bread or matzo symbolizing Jewish hardships under the Egyptians, is eaten, and the Haggadah [narrative of the exodus] is read. Here the celebrant removes a napkin from the basket of matzo fancifully placed on the boy's head and recites, "This is the bread of affliction." Note the Middle Eastern designs on the wall hanging, the Hebrew lettering, and copies of the Haggadah on the table. *(Source: The British Library)*

NOTES

1. See L. Martines, *Power and Imagination: City-States in Renaissance Italy* (New York: Vintage Books, 1980), esp. pp. 332–333.
2. Ibid., pp. 22–61.
3. Ibid., p. 221.
4. Quoted in J. Burckhardt, *The Civilization of the Renaissance in Italy* (London: Phaidon Books, 1951), p. 89.
5. *Memoirs of Benvenuto Cellini; A Florentine Artist; Written by Himself* (London: J. M. Dent & Sons, 1927), p. 2.
6. Quoted in Burckhardt, p. 111.
7. See C. Trinkaus, *In Our Image and Likeness: Humanity and Divinity in Italian Humanist Thought,* vol. 2 (London: Constable, 1970), pp. 505–529.
8. B. Burroughs, ed., *Vasari's Lives of the Artists* (New York: Simon & Schuster, 1946), pp. 164–165.
9. See Martines, chap. 13, esp. pp. 241, 243.
10. See A. Hauser, *The Social History of Art,* vol. 2 (New York: Vintage Books, 1959), chap. 3, esp. pp. 60, 68.

11. G. Bull, trans., *Aretino: Selected Letters* (Baltimore: Penguin Books, 1976), p. 109.

12. Quoted in P. and L. Murray, *A Dictionary of Art and Artists* (Baltimore: Penguin Books, 1963), p. 125.

13. Hauser, pp. 48–49.

14. Quoted in W. H. Woodward, *Vittorino da Feltre and Other Humanist Educators* (Cambridge: Cambridge University Press, 1897), pp. 96–97.

15. C. E. Detmold, trans., *The Historical, Political and Diplomatic Writings of Niccolo Machiavelli* (Boston: J. R. Osgood, 1882), pp. 51–52.

16. Ibid., pp. 54–55.

17. See F. Gilbert, *Machiavelli and Guicciardini: Politics and History in Sixteenth Century Florence* (New York: W. W. Norton, 1984), pp. 197–200.

18. See L. Hunt, *The Invention of Pornography: Obscenity and the Origins of Modernity, 1500–1800* (New York: Zone Books, 1993), pp. 10, 93–95.

19. E. L. Eisenstein, *The Printing Press as an Agent of Change: Communications and Cultural Transformations in Early Modern Europe,* vol. 1 (New York: Cambridge University Press, 1979), p. 135; for an overall discussion, see pp. 126–159.

20. M. L. King, "Book-Lined Cells: Women and Humanism in the Early Italian Renaissance," in *Beyond Their Sex: Learned Women of the European Past,* ed. P. H. Labalme (New York: New York University Press, 1980), pp. 66–81, esp. p. 73.

21. This account rests on J. Kelly-Gadol, "Did Women Have a Renaissance?" in *Becoming Visible: Women in European History,* ed. R. Bridenthal and C. Koontz (Boston: Houghton Mifflin, 1977), pp. 137–161, esp. p. 161.

22. See Peter Burke, "What Is the History of Popular Culture?" in *What Is History Today?*, ed. J. Gardiner (Atlantic Highlands, N.J.: Humanities Press, 1989), pp. 121–123.

23. G. Ruggerio, "Sexual Criminality in Early Renaissance Venice, 1338–1358," *Journal of Social History* 8 (Spring 1975): 18–31.

24. Quoted in R. C. Trexler, "Infanticide in Florence: New Sources and First Results," *History of Childhood Quarterly* 1 (Summer 1973): 99.

25. Ibid., p. 100.

26. J. Devisse and M. Mollat, *The Image of the Black in Western Art,* trans. W. G. Ryan, vol. 2 (New York: William Morrow, 1979), pt. 2, pp. 187–188.

27. See A. C. DE. C. M. Saunders, *A Social History of Black Slaves and Freedmen in Portugal, 1441–1555* (New York: Cambridge University Press, 1982), pp. 59, 62–88, 176–179.

28. Ibid., pp. 190–194.

29. Ibid., pp. 255–258.

30. Quoted in E. H. Harbison, *The Christian Scholar and His Calling in the Age of the Reformation* (New York: Charles Scribner's Sons, 1956), p. 109.

31. Quoted in F. Seebohm, *The Oxford Reformers* (London: J. M. Dent & Sons, 1867), p. 256.

32. See J. H. Elliott, *Imperial Spain, 1469–1716* (New York: Mentor Books, 1963), esp. pp. 75, 97–108.

SUGGESTED READING

There are scores of exciting studies available on virtually all aspects of the Renaissance. In addition to the titles given in the Notes, the curious student should see P. Burke, *The Italian Renaissance: Culture and Society in Italy* (1986), an important sociological interpretation relating culture and society, and J. H. Plumb, *The Italian Renaissance* (1965), a superbly written book. P. Burke, *The Historical Anthropology of Early Modern Italy* (1987), contains many useful essays on Italian cultural history in a comparative European framework, while G. Holmes, ed., *Art and Politics in Renaissance Italy* (1993) treats the art of Florence and Rome against the political background. J. R. Hale, *Renaissance Europe: The Individual and Society, 1480–1520* (1978), is an excellent treatment of individualism by a distinguished authority. For Renaissance humanism and education, see P. F. Grendler, *Schooling in Renaissance Italy: Literacy and Learning, 1300–1600* (1989); J. H. Moran, *The Growth of English Schooling, 1340–1548: Learning, Literacy, and Laicization in Pre-Reformation York Diocese* (1985); and J. F. D'Amico, *Renaissance Humanism in Papal Rome: Humanists and Churchmen on the Eve of the Reformation* (1983), which are all highly readable works of outstanding scholarship. The older study of M. P. Gilmore, *The World of Humanism* (1962), has not been superseded on many subjects. For the city where much of the Renaissance originated, G. A. Brucker, *Renaissance Florence* (1969), gives a good description of Florentine economic, political, social, and cultural history. Learned, provocative, beautifully written, and the work on which this chapter leans heavily, L. Martines, listed in the Notes, is probably the best broad appreciation of the period produced in several decades. For the Renaissance court, see the splendid achievement of G. Lubkin, *A Renaissance Court: Milan Under Galeazzo Maria Sforza* (1994).

J. R. Hale, *Machiavelli and Renaissance Italy* (1966), is a sound short biography, but advanced students may want to consult the sophisticated intellectual biography by S. de Grazia, *Machiavelli in Hell* (1989), which is based on Machiavelli's literary as well as political writing. F. Gilbert, mentioned in the Notes, places Machiavelli and Guicciardini in their intellectual and social context. C. Singleton, trans., *The Courtier* (1959), presents an excellent picture of Renaissance court life.

The best introduction to the Renaissance in northern Europe and a book that has greatly influenced twentieth-century scholarship is J. Huizinga, *The Waning of the Middle Ages: A Study of the Forms of Life, Thought, and Art in France and the Netherlands in the Dawn of the Renaissance* (1954). This book challenges the whole idea of a Renaissance. R. J. Knecht, *Renaissance Warrior and Patron: The Reign of Francis I* (1994), is the standard study of that important French ruler, whereas L. Febvre, *Life in Renaissance France* (1977), is a brilliant evocation of French Renaissance civilization. W. Blockman and W. Prevenier, *The Burgundian Netherlands* (1986), is essential for the culture of Burgundy. The leading northern humanist is sensitively treated in M. M. Phillips, *Erasmus and the Northern Renaissance* (1956), and J. Huizinga, *Erasmus of Rotterdam* (1952). R. Marius, *Thomas More: A Biography* (1984), is an original study of the great English humanist and statesman, but the student may also want to consult E. E. Reynolds, *Thomas More* (1962), and R. W. Chambers, *Thomas More* (1935). J. Leclercq, trans., *The Complete Works of Rabelais* (1963), is easily available.

The following titles should prove useful for various aspects of Renaissance social history: E. L. Eisenstein, *The Printing Press as an Agent of Change: Communications and Cultural Transformations in Early Modern Europe*, 2 vols. (1979), a fundamental work; G. Ruggerio, *Violence in Early Renaissance Venice* (1980), a pioneering study of crime and punishment in a stable society; D. Weinstein and R. M. Bell, *Saints and Society: The Two Worlds of Christendom, 1000–1700* (1982), an essential book for an understanding of the perception of holiness and of the social origins of saints in early modern Europe; J. C. Brown, *Immodest Acts: The Life of a Lesbian Nun in Renaissance Italy* (1985), which is helpful for an understanding of the role and status of women; and I. Maclean, *The Renaissance Notion of Women* (1980). The student who wishes to study blacks in medieval and early modern European society should see the rich and original achievement of J. Devisse and M. Mollat cited in the Notes.

Renaissance art has understandably inspired vast researches. In addition to Vasari's volume of biographical sketches on the great masters referred to in the Notes, M. Baxandall, *Painting and Experience in Fif-* *teenth Century Italy* (1988), is essential; A. Martindale, *The Rise of the Artist in the Middle Ages and Early Renaissance* (1972), is a splendidly illustrated introduction. B. Berenson, *Italian Painters of the Renaissance* (1957), the work of an American expatriate who was an internationally famous art historian, has become a classic. One of the finest appreciations of Renaissance art, written by one of the greatest art historians of this century, is E. Panofsky, *Meaning in the Visual Arts* (1955). Both Italian painting and northern painting are treated in the brilliant study by M. Meiss, *The Painter's Choice: Problems in the Interpretation of Renaissance Art* (1976), a collection of essays dealing with Renaissance style, form, and meaning. L. Steinberg, *The Sexuality of Christ in Renaissance Art and in Modern Oblivion* (1983), is a brilliant work that relates Christ's sexuality to incarnational theology. J. M. Saslow, *Ganymede in the Renaissance* (1986), which uses images of Ganymede as a metaphor for emotional and sexual relations between men and youths, provides information on social attitudes toward homosexuality in this period. R. Jones and N. Penny, *Raphael* (1983), celebrates the achievements of that great master.

Students interested in the city of Rome might consult P. Partner, *Renaissance Rome, 1500–1559: A Portrait of a Society* (1979), and the elegantly illustrated study by C. Hibbert, *Rome: The Biography of a City* (1985). Da Vinci's scientific and naturalist ideas and drawings are available in I. A. Richter, ed., *The Notebooks of Leonardo da Vinci* (1985). The magisterial achievement by J. Pope-Hennessy, *Cellini* (1985), is a superb evocation of that artist's life and work.

The following works not only are useful for the political and economic history of the Renaissance but also contain valuable bibliographical information: A. J. Slavin, ed., *The "New Monarchies" and Representative Assemblies* (1965), a collection of interpretations, and R. Lockyer, *Henry VII* (1972), a biography with documents illustrative of the king's reign. For Spain, see P. Liss, *Isabel the Queen: Life and Times* (1992); N. Rubin, *Isabella of Castile: The First Renaissance Queen* (1991); J. S. Gerber, *The Jews of Spain: A History of the Sephardic Experience* (1992); H. Kamen, *Inquisition and Society in Spain in the Sixteenth and Seventeenth Centuries* (1985); B. Bennasar, *The Spanish Character: Attitudes and Mentalities from the Sixteenth to the Nineteenth Century* (1979); and J. H. Elliott, *Imperial Spain: 1469–1716* (1966). For the Florentine business classes, see I. Origo, *The Merchant of Prato* (1957); G. Brucker, *Two Memoirs of Renaissance Florence: The Diaries of Buonaccorso Pitti and Gregorio Dati* (1967); and Paul Grendler, ed., *An Italian Renaissance Reader* (1987).

A Universal Man

Some people of the Renaissance believed in the ideal of universality, the achievement of distinction in many different skills and branches of knowledge. As one humanist put it, "A man is able to learn many things and make himself universal in many excellent arts." (Not everyone thought this: while Michelangelo was painting the Sistine Chapel, he complained to his father that "painting is not my profession.") Leon Battista Alberti (1404–1474), the illegitimate son of a family exiled from Florence, strongly believed he could be a universal man. A scholar-humanist, mathematician, and musician, he wrote treatises on domestic morality, the physical remains of antiquity, painting, and architecture. Here is a section of Alberti's autobiography.

And finally he embraced with zeal and forethought everything which pertained to fame. To omit the rest, he strove so hard to attain a name in modelling and painting that he wished to neglect nothing by which he might gain the approbation of good men. His genius was so versatile that you might almost judge all the fine arts to be his. . . .

He played ball, hurled the javelin, ran, leaped, wrestled, and above all delighted in the steep ascent of mountains; he applied himself to all these things for the sake of health rather than sport or pleasure. As a youth he excelled in warlike games. With his feet together, he could leap over the shoulders of men standing by; he had almost no equal among those hurling the lance. An arrow shot by his hand from his chest could pierce the strongest iron breastplate. . . . On horseback, holding in his hand one end of a long wand, while the other was firmly fixed to his foot, he could ride his horse violently in all directions for hours at a time as he wished, and the wand would remain completely immobile. Strange and marvellous! that the most spirited horses and those most impatient of riders would, when he first mounted them, tremble

violently and shudder as if in great fear. He learned music without teachers, and his compositions were approved by learned musicians. He sang throughout his whole life, but in private, or alone. . . . He delighted in the organ and was considered an expert among the leading musicians.

When he had begun to mature in years, neglecting everything else, he devoted himself entirely to the study of letters, and spent some years of labour on canon and civil law. Finally after so many nightly vigils and such great constancy, he fell gravely ill from the exertion of his studies. Since his relatives were neither kind nor humane to him in his illness, by way of consoling himself between his convalescence and cure he wrote the play *Philodoxeos,* putting aside his legal studies—this when he was only twenty years old. And as soon as his health permitted, he resumed his studies, intending to complete the law, but again he was seized by a grave illness. . . .

At length, on the orders of his doctors, he desisted from those studies which were most fatiguing to the memory, just when they were about to flourish. But in truth, because he could not live without letters, at the age of twenty-four he turned to physics and the mathematical arts. . . .

Although he was affable, gentle, and harmful to no one, nevertheless he felt the animosity of many evil men, and hidden enmities, both annoying and very burdensome; in particular the harsh injuries and intolerable insults from his own relatives. He lived among the envious and malevolent with such modesty and equanimity that none of his detractors or rivals, although very hostile towards him, dared to utter a word about him in the presence of good and worthy men unless it was full of praise and admiration. . . .

When he heard that a learned man of any kind had arrived, he would at once work his way into a position of familiarity with him and thus from any source whatsoever he began to learn what he was ignorant of. From craftsmen, architects, shipbuilders, and even from cobblers he sought information to see if by chance they preserved anything rare or unusual or special in their arts; and he would then communicate such things to those citizens who wished to know them. He pretended to be ignorant in many things so that he might observe the talents and habits and skill of others. And so he was a zealous observer of whatsoever pertained to inborn talent or the arts.

He wholly despised the pursuit of material gain. He gave his money and goods to his friends to take care of and to enjoy. Among those by whom he believed himself loved, he was not only outgoing about his affairs and his habits but even about his secrets. He never betrayed the secrets of another but remained silent forever. . . .

He was by nature prone to wrath and bitter in spirit, but he could repress his rising indignation immediately by taking thought. Sometimes he deliberately fled from the verbose and the headstrong because with them he could not subdue his wrath. At other times he voluntarily submitted to the bold, in order to grow in patience. . . .

He wrote some books entitled *On Painting,* and in this very art of painting he created works unheard of and unbelievable to those who saw them, . . .

He had within himself a ray by which he could sense the good or evil intentions of men towards himself. Simply by looking at them, he could discover most of the defects of anyone in his presence. He used all kinds of reasoning and great effort, but in vain, to make more gentle towards himself those whom he had learned at one glance would be inimical. . . .

He could endure pain and cold and heat. When, not yet fifteen, he received a serious wound in the foot, and the physician, according to his custom and skill, drew together the broken parts of the foot and sewed them through the skin with a needle, he scarcely uttered a sound of pain. With his own hands, though in such great pain, he even aided the ministering doctor and treated his own wound though he was burning with fever. . . . By some defect in his nature he loathed garlic and also honey, and the mere sight of them, if by chance they were offered to him, brought on vomiting. But he conquered himself by force

Bronze medallion of Leon Battista Alberti, by Matteo di Andrea de' Pasti. *(Source: Alinari/Art Resource, NY)*

of looking at and handling the disagreeable objects, so that they came to offend him less, thus showing by example that men can do anything with themselves if they will.

He took extraordinary and peculiar pleasure in looking at things in which there was any mark of beauty or adornment. He never ceased to wonder at old men who were endowed with dignity of countenance, and unimpaired and vigorous, and he proclaimed that he honoured them as "delights of nature." He declared that quadrupeds, birds, and other living things of outstanding beauty were worthy of benevolence because by the very distinction of their nature they deserved favour. When his favourite dog died he wrote a funeral oration for him.

Questions for Analysis

1. What distinctively Renaissance traits did Alberti show?

2. According to his assessment, what personal or human qualities did Alberti possess?

3. Did Alberti appear to have any psychological complexes or difficulties? How would you explain them?

Source: "Self-Portrait of a Universal Man" by Leon Battista Alberti from *The Portable Renaissance Reader,* edited by J. B. Ross and M. M. McLaughlin. Copyright 1968 by Penguin USA.

14

Reform and Renewal in the Christian Church

❖ The idea of reform is as old as Christianity itself. In his letter to the Christians at Rome, Saint Paul exhorted, "Do not model yourselves on the behavior of the world around you, but let your behavior change, reformed by your new mind. That is the only way to discover the will of God and know what is good, what it is that God wants, what is the perfect thing to do."[1] In the early fifth century, Saint Augustine of Hippo, describing the final stage of world history, wrote, "In the sixth age of the world our reformation becomes manifest, in newness of mind, according to the image of Him who created us." In the middle of the twelfth century, Saint Bernard of Clairvaux complained about the church of his day: "There is as much difference between us and the men of the primitive Church as there is between muck and gold." The Christian humanists of the late fifteenth and early sixteenth centuries—More, Erasmus, Colet, and Lefèvre d'Etaples—urged reform of the church on the pattern of the early church, primarily through educational and social change.

The need for reform of the individual Christian and of the institutional church is central to the Christian faith. Men and women of every period believed the early Christian church represented a golden age, and critics in every period called for reform. Thus sixteenth-century cries for reformation were hardly new. What was new, however, were the criticisms of educated lay people whose religious needs were not being met. Many scholars interpret the sixteenth-century Reformation against the background of reforming trends begun in the fourteenth century.

- What late medieval religious developments paved the way for the adoption and spread of Protestant thought?
- What role did political and social factors play in the several reformations?

- What were the consequences of religious division?
- Why did the theological ideas of Martin Luther trigger political, social, and economic reactions?
- What response did the Catholic church make to the movements for reform?

This chapter will explore these questions.

✠ THE CONDITION OF THE CHURCH (CA 1400–1517)

The papal conflict with the German emperor Frederick II in the thirteenth century, followed by the Babylonian Captivity and then the Great Schism, badly damaged the prestige of church leaders. In the fourteenth and fifteenth centuries, leaders of the conciliar movement reflected educated public opinion when they called for the reform of the church "in head and members." The humanists of Italy and the Christian humanists of the north denounced corruption in the church. As Machiavelli put it, "We Italians are irreligious and corrupt above others, because the Church and her representatives set us the worst example."[2] In *The Praise of Folly,* Erasmus condemned the absurd superstitions of the parish clergy and the excessive rituals of the monks. The records of episcopal visitations of parishes, civil court records, and even such literary masterpieces as Chaucer's *Canterbury Tales* and Boccaccio's *Decameron* tended to confirm the sarcasms of the humanists.

Signs of Disorder

The religious life of most people in early-sixteenth-century Europe took place at the village or local level. At this parish level, priests were peasants, and they were poor. All too frequently, the spiritual quality of their lives was not much better than that of the people to whom they ministered. The clergy identified religion with life; that is, they injected religious symbols and practices into everyday living. Some historians have therefore accused the clergy of vulgarizing religion. But even if the level of belief and practice was vulgarized, the lives of rural, isolated, and semipagan people were still spiritualized.

In the early sixteenth century, critics of the church concentrated their attacks on three disorders: clerical immorality, clerical ignorance, and clerical pluralism, with the related problem of absenteeism. There was little pressure for doctrinal change; the emphasis was on moral and administrative reform.

Since the fourth century, church law had required that candidates for the priesthood accept absolute celibacy. That requirement had always been difficult to enforce. Many priests, especially those ministering to country people, had concubines, and reports of neglect of the rule of celibacy were common. Immorality of course included more than sexual transgressions. Clerical drunkenness, gambling, and indulgence in fancy dress were frequent charges. There is no way of knowing how many priests were guilty of such behavior. But because such conduct was so much at odds with the church's rules and moral standards, it scandalized the educated faithful.

The bishops only casually enforced regulations regarding the education of priests. As a result, standards for ordination were shockingly low. When Saint Antonio, archbishop of Florence, conducted a visitation of his metropolitan see in the late fifteenth century, he found churches and service books in a deplorable state and many priests barely able to read and write. The evidence points consistently to the low quality of the Italian clergy, although in northern Europe—in England, for example—recent research shows an improvement in clerical educational standards in the early sixteenth century. Nevertheless, parish priests throughout Europe were not as educated as the educated laity. Predictably, Christian humanists, with their concern for learning, condemned the ignorance or low educational level of the clergy. Many priests could barely read and write, and critics laughed at the illiterate priest mumbling Latin words to the mass that he could not understand.

In regard to absenteeism and pluralism, many clerics, especially higher ecclesiastics, held several *benefices* (or offices) simultaneously but seldom visited their benefices, let alone performed the spiritual responsibilities those offices entailed. Instead, they collected revenues from all of them and hired a poor priest, paying him just a fraction of the income to fulfill the spiritual duties of a particular local church.

Many Italian officials in the papal curia held benefices in England, Spain, and Germany. Revenues from those countries paid the Italian priests' salaries, provoking not only charges of absenteeism but also nationalistic resentment. King Henry VIII's chancellor Thomas Wolsey was archbishop of York for fifteen years before he set foot in his diocese. The French king Louis XII's famous diplomat Antoine du Prat was perhaps the most notorious example of absenteeism: as archbishop of Sens, the first time he entered his cathedral was in his own funeral procession. Critics condemned pluralism, absenteeism, and the way money seemed to change hands when a bishop entered into his office.

Although royal governments strengthened their positions and consolidated their territories in the fifteenth and sixteenth centuries, rulers lacked sufficient revenues to pay and reward able civil servants. The Christian church, with its dioceses and abbeys, possessed a large proportion of the wealth of the countries of Europe. What better way to reward government officials, who were usually clerics in any case, than with high church offices? After all, the practice was sanctioned by centuries of tradition. Thus in Spain, France, England, and

❖ **Hawking Indulgences** With the papal arms prominently displayed to legitimize the proceedings, the Dominican friar Johann Tetzel preaches, while an ignorant man comes forward to drop a coin in the money chest. Cheaply produced woodcuts rapidly spread Luther's criticism of the entire penitential system.

the Holy Roman Empire—in fact, all over Europe—because church officials served their monarchs, those officials were allowed to govern the church. Churchmen served as royal councilors, diplomats, treasury officials, chancellors, viceroys, and judges. These positions had nothing whatsoever to do with spiritual matters. Bishops worked for their respective states as well as for the church, and they were paid by the church for their services to the state. It is astonishing that so many conscientiously tried to carry out their religious duties on top of their public burdens.

In most countries except England, members of the nobility occupied the highest church positions. The sixteenth century was definitely not a democratic age. The spectacle of proud, aristocratic prelates living in magnificent splendor contrasted very unfavorably with the simple fishermen who had been Christ's disciples. Nor did the popes of the period 1450 to 1550 set much of an example. They lived like secular Renaissance princes. Pius II (1458–1464), although deeply learned and a tireless worker, enjoyed a reputation as a clever writer of love stories and Latin poetry. Sixtus IV (1471–1484) beautified the city of Rome, built the famous Sistine Chapel, and generously supported several artists. Innocent VIII (1484–1492) made the papal court a model of luxury and scandal. All three popes used papal power and wealth to advance the material interests of their own families.

The court of the Spanish Pope, Alexander VI (1492–1503), who publicly acknowledged his mistress and children, reached new heights of impropriety. Because of the prevalence of intrigue, sexual promiscuity, and supposed poisonings, the name Borgia became a synonym for moral corruption. Julius II (1503–1513), the nephew of Sixtus IV, donned military armor and personally led papal troops against the French invaders of Italy in 1506. After him, Giovanni de' Medici, the son of Lorenzo de' Medici, carried on as Pope Leo X (1513–1521) the Medicean tradition of being a great patron of the arts.

Signs of Vitality

Calls for reform testify to the spiritual vitality of the church as well as to its numerous problems. In the late fifteenth and early sixteenth centuries, both individuals and groups within the church were working actively for reform. In Spain, for example, Cardinal Francisco Jiménez (1436–1517) visited religious houses, encouraged the monks and friars to uphold their rules and constitutions, and set high standards for the training of the diocesan clergy.

In Holland beginning in the late fourteenth century, a group of pious lay people called the "Brethren of the Common Life" lived in stark simplicity while daily carrying out the Gospel teaching of feeding the hungry, clothing the naked, and visiting the sick. The Brethren also taught in local schools with the goal of preparing devout candidates for the priesthood and the monastic life. Through prayer, meditation, and careful study of the Scriptures, the Brethren sought to make religion a personal, inner experience. The spirituality of the Brethren of the Common Life found its finest expression in the classic *The Imitation of Christ* by Thomas à Kempis. Though written in Latin for monks and nuns, *The Imitation* gained wide appeal among lay people. It urges Christians to take Christ as their model and seek perfection in a simple way of life. Like later Protestants, the Brethren stressed the centrality of the Scriptures in spiritual life.[3] In the mid-fifteenth century, the movement had founded houses in the Netherlands, in central Germany, and in the Rhineland; it was a true religious revival.

So, too, were the activities of the Oratories of Divine Love in Italy. The oratories were groups of priests living in communities who worked to revive the church through prayer and preaching. They did not withdraw from the world as medieval monks had done but devoted themselves to pastoral and charitable activities such as founding hospitals and orphanages. Oratorians served God in an active ministry.

If external religious observances are a measure of depth of heartfelt conviction, Europeans in the early sixteenth century remained deeply pious and loyal to the Roman Catholic church. Villagers participated in processions honoring the local saints. Middle-class people made pilgrimages to the great shrines, such as Saint Peter's in Rome. The upper classes continued to remember the church in their wills. In England, for example, between 1480 and 1490 almost 30,000 pounds, a prodigious sum in those days, was bequeathed to religious foundations. People of all social classes devoted an enormous amount of their time and income to religious causes and foundations.

The papacy also expressed concern for reform. Pope Julius II summoned an ecumenical (universal) council, which met in the church of Saint John Lateran in Rome from 1512 to 1517. Since most of the bishops were Italian and did not represent a broad cross-section of international opinion, the term *ecumenical* is not really appropriate to describe their meetings. Nevertheless, the bishops and theologians present strove earnestly to reform the church. The council recommended higher standards for education of the clergy and instruction of the common people. The bishops placed the responsibility for eliminating bureaucratic corruption squarely on the papacy and suggested significant doctrinal reforms. But many obstacles stood in the way of ecclesiastical change. Nor did the actions of an obscure German friar immediately force the issue.

MARTIN LUTHER AND THE BIRTH OF PROTESTANTISM

As the result of a personal religious struggle, a German Augustinian friar, Martin Luther (1483–1546), launched the Protestant Reformation of the sixteenth century. Luther was not a typical person of his time; miners' sons who become professors of theology are never typical. But Luther was representative of his time in the sense that he articulated the widespread desire for reform of the Christian church and a deep yearning for salvation. In the sense that concern for salvation was an important motivating force for Luther and other reformers, the sixteenth-century Reformation was in part a continuation of the medieval religious search.

Luther's Early Years

Martin Luther was born at Eisleben in Saxony, the second son of a copper miner and, later, mine owner. At considerable sacrifice, his father sent him to school and then to the University of Erfurt, where he earned a master's degree with distinction at the young age of twenty-one. Hans Luther intended his son to proceed to the study of law and a legal career, which for centuries had been the

steppingstone to public office and material success. Badly frightened during a thunderstorm, however, Martin Luther vowed to become a friar. Without consulting his father, he entered the monastery of the Augustinian friars at Erfurt in 1505. Luther was ordained a priest in 1507 and after additional study earned a doctorate of theology. From 1512 until his death in 1546, he served as professor of the Scriptures at the new University of Wittenberg.

Martin Luther was exceedingly scrupulous in his monastic observances and devoted to prayer, penances, and fasting; nevertheless, the young friar's conscience troubled him constantly. The doubts and conflicts felt by any sensitive young person who has just taken a grave step were especially intense in young Luther. He had terrible anxieties about sin and worried continually about his salvation. Luther intensified his monastic observances but still found no peace of mind.

A psychological interpretation of Luther's early life suggests that he underwent a severe inner crisis in the years 1505 to 1515. Luther had disobeyed his father, thus violating one of the Ten Commandments, and serious conflict persisted between them. The religious life seemed to provide no answers to Luther's mental and spiritual difficulties. Three fits that he suffered in the monastic choir during those years may have been outward signs of his struggle.[4] Luther was grappling, as had thousands of medieval people before him, with the problem of salvation and thus the meaning of life. He was also searching for his life's work.

Luther's wise and kindly confessor, John Staupitz, directed him to the study of Saint Paul's letters. Gradually, Luther arrived at a new understanding of the Pauline letters and of all Christian doctrine. He came to believe that salvation comes not through external observances and penances but through a simple faith in Christ. Faith is the means by which God sends humanity his grace, and faith is a free gift that cannot be earned. Thus Martin Luther discovered himself, God's work for him, and the centrality of faith in the Christian life.

The Ninety-five Theses

An incident illustrative of the condition of the church in the early sixteenth century propelled Martin Luther onto the stage of history and brought about the Reformation in Germany. The

❖ **Lucas Cranach the Younger: Luther and the Wittenberg Reformers** The massive figure of John Frederick, Elector of Saxony, who protected and supported Luther, dominates this group portrait. Luther is on the far left, his associate Philip Melancthon in the front row on the right. Luther's face shows a quiet determination. *(Source: The Toledo Museum of Art, Toledo, Ohio; Gift of Edward Drummond Libbey)*

University of Wittenberg lay within the ecclesiastical jurisdiction of the archdiocese of Magdeburg. The twenty-seven-year-old archbishop of Magdeburg, Albert, was also administrator of the see of Halberstadt and had been appointed archbishop of Mainz. To hold all three offices simultaneously—blatant pluralism—required papal dispensation. At

that moment, Pope Leo X was eager to continue the construction of Saint Peter's Basilica but was hard pressed for funds. Archbishop Albert borrowed money from the Fuggers, a wealthy banking family of Augsburg, to pay for the papal dispensation allowing him to hold the several episcopal benefices. Only a few powerful financiers and churchmen knew the details of the arrangement, but Leo X authorized Archbishop Albert to sell indulgences in Germany to repay the Fuggers.

Wittenberg was in the political jurisdiction of Frederick of Saxony, one of the seven electors of the Holy Roman Empire. When Frederick forbade the sale of indulgences within his duchy, people of Wittenberg, including some of Professor Luther's students, streamed across the border from Saxony into Jütenborg in Thuringia to buy indulgences.

What exactly was an *indulgence?* According to Catholic theology, individuals who sin alienate themselves from God and his love. In order to be reconciled to God, the sinner must confess his or her sins to a priest and do the penance assigned. For example, a person who steals must first return the stolen goods and then perform the penance given by the priest, usually certain prayers or good works. This is known as the temporal (or earthly) penance since no one knows what penance God will ultimately require.

The doctrine of indulgence rested on three principles. First, God is merciful, but he is also just. Second, Christ and the saints, through their infinite virtue, established a "treasury of merits" on which the church, through its special relationship with Christ and the saints, can draw. Third, the church has the authority to grant sinners the spiritual benefits of those merits. Originally an indulgence was a remission of the temporal (priest-imposed) penalties for sin. Beginning in the twelfth century, the papacy and bishops had given Crusaders such indulgences. By the later Middle Ages, people widely believed that an indulgence secured total remission of penalties for sin—on earth or in purgatory—and ensured swift entry into heaven.

Archbishop Albert hired Dominican friar John Tetzel to sell the indulgences. Tetzel mounted an advertising blitz (see page 441). One of his slogans—"As soon as coin in coffer rings, the soul from purgatory springs"—brought phenomenal success. Men and women could buy indulgences not only for themselves but also for deceased parents, relatives, or friends. Tetzel even drew up a chart with specific prices for the forgiveness of particular sins.

Luther was severely troubled that ignorant people believed they had no further need for repentance once they had purchased an indulgence. Thus, according to historical tradition, in the academic fashion of the times, on the eve of All Saints' Day, October 31, 1517, he attached to the door of the church at Wittenberg Castle a list of ninety-five theses (or propositions) on indulgences. By this act Luther intended only to start a theological discussion of the subject and to defend the theses publicly.

Luther firmly rejected the notion that salvation could be achieved by good works, such as indulgences. Some of his theses challenged the pope's power to grant indulgences, and others criticized papal wealth: "Why does not the Pope, whose riches are at this day more ample than those of the wealthiest of the wealthy, build the one Basilica of St. Peter's with his own money, rather than with that of poor believers . . .?"[5]

The theses were soon translated from Latin into German, printed, and read throughout the empire. Immediately, broad theological issues were raised. When questioned, Luther rested his fundamental

✥ **Jerome Bosch: Christ before Pilate.** Pilate (right) grasps the pitcher of water as he prepares to wash his hands. The peasant faces around Christ are vicious, grotesque, even bestial, perhaps signifying humanity's stupidity and blindness. Notice the duncecap on one man, Christ's embroidered undergarment, the nose and lip rings on some faces.

argument on the principle that there was no biblical basis for indulgences. But, replied Luther's opponents, to deny the legality of indulgences was to deny the authority of the pope who had authorized them. The issue was drawn: where did authority lie in the Christian church?

Through 1518 and 1519 Luther studied the history of the papacy. In 1519 in a large public disputation with Catholic debater John Eck at Leipzig, Luther denied both the authority of the pope and the infallibility of a general council. The Council of Constance, he said, had erred when it condemned John Hus (see page 386).

The papacy responded with a letter condemning some of Luther's propositions, ordering that his books be burned, and giving him two months to recant or be excommunicated. Luther retaliated by publicly burning the letter. By January 3, 1521, when the excommunication was supposed to become final, the controversy involved more than theological issues. The papal legate wrote, "All Germany is in revolution. Nine-tenths shout 'Luther' as their war cry; and the other tenth cares nothing about Luther, and cries 'Death to the court of Rome.'"[6]

In this highly charged atmosphere the twenty-one-year-old emperor Charles V held his first diet (assembly of the Estates of the empire) at Worms and summoned Luther to appear before it. When ordered to recant, Luther replied in language that rang all over Europe:

Unless I am convinced by the evidence of Scripture or by plain reason—for I do not accept the authority of the Pope or the councils alone, since it is established that they have often erred and contradicted themselves—I am bound by the Scriptures I have cited and my conscience is captive to the Word of God. I cannot and will not recant anything, for it is neither safe nor right to go against conscience. God help me. Amen.[7]

Though Luther was declared an outlaw of the empire and denied legal protection, Duke Frederick of Saxony protected him.

Protestant Thought

Between 1520 and 1530, Luther worked out the basic theological tenets that became the articles of faith for his new church and subsequently for all Protestant groups. The word *Protestant* derives from the protest drawn up by a small group of reforming German princes at the Diet of Speyer in 1529. The princes "protested" the decisions of the Catholic majority. At first Protestant meant "Lutheran," but with the appearance of many protesting sects, it became a general term applied to all non-Catholic Christians. Lutheran Protestant thought was officially formulated in the Confession of Augsburg in 1530.

Ernst Troeltsch, a German student of the sociology of religion, has defined Protestantism as a "modification of Catholicism, in which the Catholic formulation of questions was retained, while a different answer was given to them." Luther provided new answers to four old, basic theological issues.

First, how is a person to be saved? Traditional Catholic teaching held that salvation is achieved by both faith and good works. Luther held that salvation comes by faith alone. Women and men are saved, said Luther, by the arbitrary decision of God, irrespective of good works or the sacraments. God, not people, initiates salvation.

Second, where does religious authority reside? Christian doctrine had long maintained that authority rests both in the Bible and in the traditional teaching of the church. Luther maintained that authority rests in the Word of God as revealed in the Bible alone and as interpreted by an individual's conscience. He urged that each person read and reflect on the Scriptures.

Third, what is the church? Luther re-emphasized the Catholic teaching that the church consists of the entire community of Christian believers. Medieval churchmen, however, had tended to identify the church with the clergy.

Fourth, what is the highest form of Christian life? The medieval church had stressed the superiority of the monastic and religious life over the secular. Luther argued that all vocations have equal merit, whether ecclesiastical or secular, and that every person should serve God in his or her individual calling.[8] Protestantism, in sum, represented a reformulation of the Christian heritage.

As Protestant thought developed, it differed from Roman Catholic teaching on several other fundamental issues. Whereas Catholic doctrine held that there are seven sacraments (see Chapter 10), Luther believed that the Scriptures support

✤ **Hans Holbein the Younger, CHRIST AS THE MAN OF SORROWS** The scriptural foundation for this concept rests on Isaiah 53: 3–5: "He was pierced for our offenses, crushed by our sins. Upon him was the chastisement that makes us whole, by his stripes we were healed." Using a theme characteristic of early sixteenth century German piety, and placing the subject within a Renaissance architectural structure, Holdbein produced this devotional painting in 1520 for the private use of the donor. *(Source: Öffentliche Kunstsammlung Basel)*

only three sacraments—baptism, penance, and the eucharist, or Lord's Supper. Protestant sects, as they emerged, developed a theology of the eucharist, because it is an important source of grace. Catholics hold the dogma of *transubstantiation*: by the consecrating words of the priest during the mass, the bread and wine become the actual body and blood of Christ, who is then fully present in the bread and wine. In opposition, Luther defined *consubstantiation*, the belief that after consecration the bread and wine undergo a spiritual change whereby Christ is really present (the Real Presence) but the bread and wine are not transformed. Swiss reformer Ulrich Zwingli affirmed that the Lord's Supper is a *memorial* of the Last Supper and that no change whatever occurs in the elements. For John Calvin, the body and blood of Christ are spiritually but not physically present in the bread and wine, and they are consumed spiritually. Catholics and Protestants agreed that the sacrament must be received worthily and that it is a source of grace.

❖ **The Folly of Indulgences** In this woodcut the Church's sale of indulgences is viciously satirized. With one claw in the holy water symbolizing the rite of purification (Psalm 50), and the other claw resting on the coins paid for indulgences, the Church in the form of a rapacious eagle with its right hand stretched out for offerings, writes out an indulgence with excrement—which represents its worth. Fools, in a false security, sit in the animal's gaping mouth, representing hell, to which a devil delivers the pope in a three-tiered crown and holding the keys to heaven originally given to St. Peter. *(Source: Kunstsammlungen der Veste Coburg)*

The Social Impact of Luther's Beliefs

As early as 1521, Luther had a vast following. Every encounter he had with ecclesiastical or political authorities attracted attention. Pulpits and printing presses spread his message all over Germany. By the time of his death, people of all social classes had become Lutheran. What was the immense appeal of Luther's religious ideas?

Recent historical research on the German towns has shown that two significant late medieval developments prepared the way for Luther's ideas. First, since the fifteenth century, city governments had expressed resentment at clerical privileges and immunities. Priests, monks, and nuns paid no taxes and were exempt from civic responsibilities, such as defending the city. Yet religious orders frequently held large amounts of urban property. At Zurich in 1467, for example, religious orders held one-third of the city's taxable property. City governments were determined to integrate the clergy into civic life by reducing their privileges and giving them public responsibilities. Accordingly, the Zurich magistracy subjected the religious to taxes, inspected wills so that legacies to the church and legacies left by churchmen could be controlled, and placed priests and monks under the jurisdiction of the civil courts.

Second, critics of the late medieval church, especially informed and intelligent townspeople, condemned the irregularity and poor quality of sermons. As a result, prosperous burghers in many towns established preacherships. Preachers were men of superior education who were required to deliver about a hundred sermons a year, each lasting about forty-five minutes. Endowed preacherships had important consequences after 1517. Luther's ideas attracted many preachers, and in such towns as Stuttgart, Reutlingen, Eisenach, and Jena, preachers became Protestant leaders. Preacherships also encouraged the Protestant form of worship, in which the sermon, not the eucharist, was the central part of the service.[9]

In the countryside the attraction of the German peasants to Lutheran beliefs was predictable. Luther himself came from a peasant background, and he admired the peasants' ceaseless toil. For their part, peasants respected Luther's defiance of church authority. Moreover, they thrilled to the words Luther used in his treatise *On Christian Liberty* (1520): "A Christian man is the most free lord of all and subject to none." Taken by themselves, these words easily contributed to social unrest.

Fifteenth-century Germany had witnessed several peasant revolts (see Listening to the Past). In the early sixteenth century, the economic condition of the peasantry varied from place to place but was generally worse than it had been in the fifteenth century and was deteriorating. Crop failures in 1523 and 1524 aggravated an explosive situation. In 1525 representatives of the Swabian peasants met at the city of Memmingen and drew up the Twelve Articles, which expressed their grievances. The Twelve Articles condemn lay and ecclesiastical lords and summarized the agrarian crisis of the early sixteenth century. The articles complained that nobles had seized village common lands, which traditionally had been used by all; that they had imposed new rents on manorial properties and new services on the peasants working those properties; and that they had forced the poor to pay unjust death duties in the form of the peasants' best horses or cows. Wealthy, socially mobile peasants especially resented these burdens, which they emphasized as new.[10] The peasants believed their demands conformed to the Scriptures and cited Luther as a theologian who could prove that they did.

Luther wanted to prevent rebellion. Initially he sided with the peasants, and in his tract *An Admonition to Peace* (1525) he blasted the lords:

We have no one on earth to thank for this mischievous rebellion, except you lords and princes, especially you blind bishops and mad priests and monks. . . . In your government you do nothing but flay and rob your subjects in order that you may lead a life of splendor and pride, until the poor common folk can bear it no longer.[11]

But, he warned, nothing justified the use of armed force: "The fact that rulers are unjust and wicked does no excuse tumult and rebellion; to punish wickedness does not belong to everybody, but to the worldly rulers who bear the sword." As for biblical support for the peasants' demands, he maintained that Scripture had nothing to do with earthly justice or material gain.[12]

Massive revolts first broke out near the Swiss frontier and then swept through Swabia, Thuringia, the Rhineland, and Saxony. The crowds' slogans came directly from Luther's writings. "God's righteousness" and the "Word of God" were invoked in an effort to secure social and economic justice. The peasants who expected Luther's support were soon disillusioned. He had written of the "freedom" of the Christian, but he had meant the freedom to obey the Word of God, for in sin men and women lose their freedom and break their relationship with God. Freedom for Luther meant independence from the authority of the Roman church; it did *not* mean opposition to legally established secular powers. Firmly convinced that rebellion hastened the end of civilized society, he wrote a tract *Against the Murderous, Thieving Hordes of the Peasants:* "Let everyone who can smite, slay, and stab [the peasants], secretly and openly, remembering that nothing can be more poisonous, hurtful or devilish than a rebel."[13] The nobility ferociously crushed the revolt. Historians estimate that over 75,000 peasants were killed in 1525.

Luther took literally these words of Saint Paul's Letter to the Romans: "Let every soul be subject to the higher powers. For there is no power but of God: the powers that be are established by God. Whosoever resists the power, resists the ordinance

❖ **Peasants Sack the Abbey of Weissenau** Convinced that the monks lived idle, luxurious lives on money squeezed from the poor, peasants sacked the abbeys during the great revolt of 1525. *(Source: Château de Waldburg, Archives/Schneiders/Artephot)*

of God: and they that resist shall receive to themselves damnation."[14] As Lutheran theology developed, it exalted the state, subordinated the church to the state, and everywhere championed "the powers that be." The consequences for German society were profound and have redounded into the twentieth century. The revolt of 1525 strengthened the authority of lay rulers. Peasant economic conditions, however, moderately improved. For example, in many parts of Germany, enclosed fields, meadows, and forests were returned to common use.

Scholars in many disciplines have attributed Luther's fame and success to the invention of the printing press, which rapidly reproduced and made known his ideas. Equally important was Luther's incredible skill with language. Some thinkers have lavished praise on the Wittenberg reformer; others have bitterly condemned him. But in the words of psychologist Erik Erikson:

The one matter on which professor and priest, psychiatrist and sociologist, agree is Luther's immense gift for language: his receptivity for the written word; his memory for the significant phrase; and his range of verbal expression (lyrical, biblical, satirical, and vulgar) which in English is paralleled only by Shakespeare.[15]

Language proved to be the weapon with which this peasant's son changed the world.

Like the peasants, educated people and humanists were much attracted by Luther's words. He advocated a simpler, personal religion based on faith, a return to the spirit of the early church, the centrality of the Scriptures in the liturgy and in Christian life, the abolition of elaborate ceremonies—precisely the reforms the northern humanists had been calling for. Ulrich Zwingli (1484–1531), for example, a humanist of Zurich, was strongly influenced by Luther's bold stand; it stimulated

Zwingli's reforms in the Swiss city of Zurich and later in Bern. Nobleman Ulrich von Hutten (1488–1523), who had published several humanistic tracts, in 1519 dedicated his life to the advancement of Luther's Reformation. And Frenchman John Calvin (1509–1564), often called the organizer of Protestantism, owed a great deal to Luther's thought.

Luther's linguistic skill, together with his translation of the New Testament into German in 1523, led to the acceptance of his dialect of German as the standard version of German. His insistence that everyone should read and reflect on the Scriptures attracted the literate and thoughtful middle classes partly because Luther appealed to their intelligence. Moreover, the business classes, preoccupied with making money, envied the church's wealth, disapproved of the luxurious lifestyle of some churchmen, and resented tithes and ecclesiastical taxation. Luther's doctrines of salvation by faith and the priesthood of all believers not only raised the religious status of the commercial classes but also protected their pocketbooks.

Hymns, psalms, and Luther's two catechisms (1529), compendiums of basic religious knowledge, also show the power of language in spreading the ideals of the Reformation. The reformers knew "that rhyme, meter, and melodies could forcefully impress minds and affect sensibilities." Such hymns as the famous "A Mighty Fortress Is Our God" expressed deep human feelings, were easily remembered, and imprinted on the mind central points of doctrine. Luther's *Larger Catechism* contained brief sermons on the main articles of faith, whereas the *Shorter Catechism* gave concise explanations of doctrine in question-and-answer form. Both catechisms stressed the importance of the Ten Commandments, the Lord's Prayer, the Apostle's Creed, and the sacraments for the believing Christian. Although originally intended for the instruction of pastors, these catechisms became powerful techniques for the indoctrination of men and women of all ages, especially the young.[16]

What appeal did Luther's message have for women? Luther's argument that all vocations have equal merit in the sight of God gave dignity to those who performed ordinary, routine, domestic tasks. The abolition of monasticism in Protestant territories led to the exaltation of the home, which Luther and other reformers stressed as the special domain of the wife. The Christian home, in contrast to the place of business, became the place for the exercise of the gentler virtues—love, tenderness, reconciliation, the carrying of one another's burdens. The Protestant abolition of private confession to a priest freed women from embarrassing explorations of their sexual lives and activities. Protestants established schools where girls as well as boys became literate in the catechism and the Bible. Finally, the reformers stressed marriage as the cure for clerical concupiscence. Protestantism thus proved attractive to the many women who had been priests' concubines and mistresses: now they became legal and honorable wives.[17]

For his time, Luther held enlightened views on matters of sexuality and marriage. He wrote a letter to a young man, "Dear lad, be not ashamed that you desire a girl, nor you my maid, the boy. Just let it lead you into matrimony and not into promiscuity, and it is no more cause for shame than eating and drinking."[18] Luther was confident that God took delight in the sexual act and denied that original sin affected the goodness of creation. He believed, however, that marriage was a woman's career. A student recorded Luther as saying early in his public ministry, "Let them bear children until they are dead of it; that is what they are for." A happy marriage to ex-nun Katharine von Bora mellowed him, and another student later quoted him as saying, "Next to God's Word there is no more precious treasure than holy matrimony. God's highest gift on earth is a pious, cheerful, God-fearing, home-keeping wife, with whom you may live peacefully, to whom you may entrust your goods, and body and life."[19] Though Luther deeply loved his "dear Katie," he believed that women's concerns revolved exclusively around the children, the kitchen, and the church. A happy woman was a patient wife, an efficient manager, and a good mother. Kate was an excellent financial manager (which Luther—much inclined to give money and goods away—was not). Himself a stern, if often indulgent, father, Luther held that the father should rule the household, while the wife controlled its economy. With many relatives and constant visitors, Luther's home was a large and happy household, certainly a model for Protestants, if an abomination for Catholics. The wives of other reformers, though they exercised no leadership role in the reform, shared their husbands' work and concerns.

GERMANY AND THE PROTESTANT REFORMATION

The history of the Holy Roman Empire in the later Middle Ages is a story of dissension, disintegration, and debility. Unlike Spain, France, and England, the empire lacked a strong central power. The Golden Bull of 1356 legalized what had long existed—government by an aristocratic federation. Each of seven electors—the archbishops of Mainz, Trier, and Cologne, the margrave of Brandenburg, the duke of Saxony, the count palatine of the Rhine, and the king of Bohemia—gained virtual sovereignty in his own territory. The agreement ended disputed elections in the empire; it also reduced the central authority of the emperor. Germany was characterized by weak borders, localism, and chronic disorder. The nobility strengthened its territories, while imperial power declined.

Against this background of decentralization and strong local power, Martin Luther had launched a movement to reform the church. Two years after Luther posted the Ninety-five Theses, the electors chose as emperor a nineteen-year-old Habsburg prince who ruled as Charles V. Luther's interests and motives were primarily religious, but many people responded to his teachings for political, social, or economic reasons. How did the goals and interests of the emperor influence the course of the Reformation in Germany? What impact did the upheaval in the Christian church have on the political condition in Germany?

The Rise of the Habsburg Dynasty

The marriage in 1477 of Maximilian I of the house of Habsburg and Mary of Burgundy was a decisive event in early modern European history. Burgundy consisted of two parts: the French duchy, with its capital at Dijon, and the Burgundian Netherlands, with its capital at Brussels. Through this union with the rich and powerful duchy of Burgundy, the Austrian house of Habsburg, already the strongest ruling family in the empire, became an international power.

THE HERITAGE OF CHARLES V

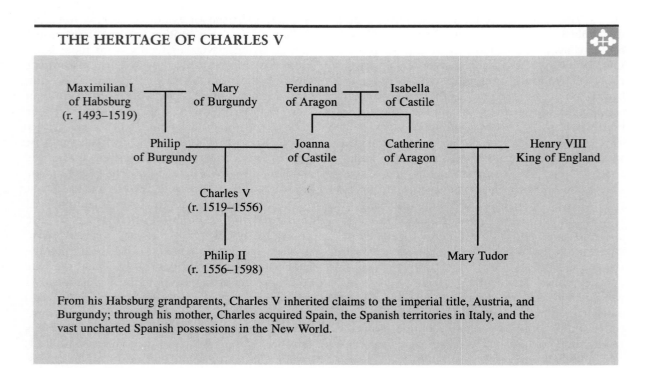

From his Habsburg grandparents, Charles V inherited claims to the imperial title, Austria, and Burgundy; through his mother, Charles acquired Spain, the Spanish territories in Italy, and the vast uncharted Spanish possessions in the New World.

In the fifteenth and sixteenth centuries, as in the Middle Ages, relations among states continued to be greatly affected by the connections of royal families. Marriage often determined the diplomatic status of states. The Habsburg-Burgundian marriage angered the French, who considered Burgundy part of French territory and had lusted after the Burgundian Netherlands (Flanders) for centuries. Louis XI of France repeatedly ravaged parts of the Burgundian Netherlands until he was able to force Maximilian to accept French terms: the Treaty of Arras (1482) declared French Burgundy a part of the kingdom of France. The Habsburgs, however, never really renounced their claim to Burgundy, and intermittent warfare over it continued between France and Maximilian. Louis could not claim that the Salic law (which denied that a woman could succeed to the crown) applied in the Burgundian Netherlands because it had had women rulers. Nor could Louis conquer them. They remained outside French control (see Chapters 15 and 16). Within the empire, German principalities that resented Austria's pre-eminence began to see that they shared interests with France. The marriage of Maximilian and Mary inaugurated centuries of conflict between the Austrian house of Habsburg and the kings of France. And Germany was to be the chief arena of the struggle.

"Other nations wage war; you, Austria, marry." Historians dispute the origins of this adage, but no one questions its accuracy. The heir of Mary and Maximilian, Philip of Burgundy, married Joanna of Castile, daughter of Ferdinand and Isabella of Spain. Philip and Joanna's son Charles V (1500–1558) fell heir to a vast conglomeration of territories. Through a series of accidents and unexpected deaths, Charles inherited Spain from his mother, together with her possessions in the New World and the Spanish dominions in Italy, Sicily, Sardinia, and Naples. From his father he inherited the Habsburg lands in Austria, southern Germany, the Low Countries, and Franche-Comté in east-central France.

Charles's inheritance was an incredibly diverse collection of states and peoples, each governed in a different manner and held together only by the person of the emperor (Map 14.1). Charles's Italian adviser, the grand chancellor Gattinara, told the young ruler, "God has set you on the path toward world monarchy." Charles not only believed this, he was also convinced that it was his duty to maintain the political and religious unity of Western Christendom. In this respect Charles V was the last medieval emperor.

Charles needed and in 1519 secured the imperial title. Forward-thinking Germans proposed governmental reforms. They urged placing the administration in the hands of an imperial council whose president, the emperor's appointee, would have ultimate executive power. Reforms of the imperial finances, the army, and the judiciary were also recommended. Such ideas did not interest the young emperor at all. When he finally arrived in Germany from Spain and opened his first diet at Worms in January 1521, he naively announced that "the empire from of old has had not many masters, but one, and it is our intention to be that one." Charles went on to say that he was to be treated as of greater account than his predecessors because he was more powerful than they had been. In view of the long history of aristocratic power, Charles's notions were pure fantasy.

Charles continued the Burgundian policy of his grandfather Maximilian. That is, German revenues and German troops were subordinated to the needs of other parts of the empire, first Burgundy and then Spain. Habsburg international interests came before the need for reform in Germany.

The Political Impact of Luther's Beliefs

In the sixteenth century, the practice of religion remained a public matter. Everyone participated in the religious life of the community, just as almost everyone shared in the local agricultural work. Whatever spiritual convictions individuals held in the privacy of their consciences, the emperor, king, prince, magistrate, or other civil authority determined the official form of religious practice within his jurisdiction. Almost everyone believed that the presence of a faith different from that of the majority represented a political threat to the security of the state. Only a tiny minority, and certainly none of the princes, believed in religious liberty.

Against this background, the religious storm launched by Martin Luther swept across Germany. Several elements in his religious reformation stirred patriotic feelings. Anti-Roman sentiment ran high.

MAP 14.1 The European Empire of Charles V Charles V exercised theoretical jurisdiction over more territory than anyone since Charlemagne. This map does not show his Latin American and Asian possessions.

Humanists lent eloquent intellectual support. And Luther's translation of the New Testament evoked national pride.

For decades devout lay people and churchmen had called on the German princes to reform the church. In 1520 Luther took up the cry in his *Appeal to the Christian Nobility of the German Nation.* Unless the princes destroyed papal power in Germany, Luther argued, reform was impossible. He urged the princes to confiscate ecclesiastical wealth and to abolish indulgences, dispensations, pardons, and clerical celibacy. He told them that it was their public duty to bring about the moral reform of the church. Luther based his argument in part on the papacy's financial exploitation of Germany:

> *How comes it that we Germans must put up with such robbery and such extortion of our property at the hands of the pope? If the Kingdom of France has prevented it, why do we Germans let them make such fools and apes of us? It would all be more bearable if in this way they only stole our property; but they lay waste the churches and rob Christ's sheep of their pious shepherds, and destroy the worship and the Word of God. As it is they do nothing for the good of Christendom; they only wrangle about the incomes of bishoprics and prelacies, and that any robber could do.*[20]

These words fell on welcome ears and itchy fingers. Luther's appeal to German patriotism gained him strong support, and national feeling influenced many princes otherwise confused by or indifferent to the complexities of the religious issues.

The church in Germany possessed great wealth. And unlike other countries, Germany had no strong central government to check the flow of gold to Rome. Rejection of Roman Catholicism and adoption of Protestantism would mean the legal confiscation of lush farmlands, rich monasteries, and wealthy shrines. Some German princes, such as the prince-archbishop of Cologne, Hermann von Wied, were sincerely attracted to Lutheranism, but many civil authorities realized that they had a great deal to gain by embracing the new faith. A steady stream of duchies, margraviates, free cities, and bishoprics secularized church property, accepted Lutheran theological doctrines, and adopted simpler services conducted in Ger-

man. The decision reached at Worms in 1521 to condemn Luther and his teaching was not enforced because the German princes did not want to enforce it.

Charles V was a vigorous defender of Catholicism, and contemporary social and political theory denied the possibility of two religions coexisting peacefully in one territory. Thus many princes used the religious issue to extend their financial and political independence. When doctrinal differences became linked to political ambitions and financial receipts, the results were unfortunate for the improvement of German government. The Protestant movement ultimately proved a political disaster for Germany.

Charles V must share blame with the German princes for the disintegration of imperial authority in the empire. He neither understood nor took an interest in the constitutional problems of Germany, and he lacked the material resources to oppose Protestantism effectively there. Throughout his reign he was preoccupied with his Flemish, Spanish, Italian, and American territories. Moreover, the Turkish threat prevented him from acting effectively against the Protestants; Charles's brother, Ferdinand, needed Protestant support against the Turks who besieged Vienna in 1529.

Five times between 1521 and 1555, Charles V went to war with the Valois kings of France. The issue each time was the Habsburg lands acquired by the marriage of Maximilian and Mary of Burgundy. Much of the fighting occurred in Germany. The cornerstone of French foreign policy in the sixteenth and seventeenth centuries was the desire to keep the German states divided. Thus Europe witnessed the paradox of the Catholic king of France supporting the Lutheran princes in their challenge to his fellow Catholic, Charles V. French foreign policy contributed to the continuing division of Germany. The long dynastic struggle commonly called the Habsburg-Valois Wars advanced the cause of Protestantism and promoted the political fragmentation of the German empire.

Finally, in 1555 Charles agreed to the Peace of Augsburg, which, in accepting the status quo, officially recognized Lutheranism. Each prince was permitted to determine the religion of his territory. Most of northern and central Germany became Lutheran, while the south remained Roman Catholic. There was no freedom of religion, how-

❖ **Fresco of Pope Clement VII and the Emperor Charles V** by Giorgio Vasari. Since Vasari's *Lives of the Most Eminent Italian Painters, Architects, Painters, and Sculptors* (rev. ed. 1568), still the basic historical source for Renaissance art and culture, held that "art is the imitation of nature," we may assume that these are faithful likenesses of the Medici pope and the Holy Roman Emperor. *(Source: Alinari/Art Resource, NY)*

ever. Princes or town councils established state churches to which all subjects of the area had to belong. Dissidents, whether Lutheran or Catholic, had to convert or leave. The political difficulties Germany inherited from the Middle Ages had been compounded by the religious crisis of the sixteenth century.

❖ THE GROWTH OF THE PROTESTANT REFORMATION

By 1555 much of northern Europe had broken with the Roman Catholic church. All of Scandinavia, England (except under Mary Tudor), Scotland, and such self-governing cities as Geneva and Zurich in Switzerland and Strasbourg in Germany had rejected the religious authority of Rome and adopted new faiths. Because a common religious faith had been the one element uniting all of Europe for almost a thousand years, the fragmentation of belief led to profound changes in European life and society. The most significant new form of Protestantism was Calvinism, of which the Peace of Augsburg had made no mention at all.

Calvinism

In 1509 while Luther was studying for a doctorate at Wittenberg, John Calvin (1509–1564) was being born in Noyon in northwestern France. Luther inadvertently launched the Protestant Reformation. Calvin, however, had the greater impact on future generations. His theological writings profoundly influenced the social thought and attitudes of Europeans and English-speaking peoples all over the world, especially in Canada and the United States. Although he had originally intended to have an ecclesiastical career, Calvin studied law, which had a decisive impact on his mind and later thought. In 1533 he experienced a religious crisis, as a result of which he converted to Protestantism.

Convinced that God selects certain people to do his work, Calvin believed that God had specifically called him to reform the church. Accordingly, he accepted an invitation to assist in the reformation of the city of Geneva. There, beginning in 1541, Calvin worked assiduously to establish a Christian society ruled by God through civil magistrates and reformed ministers. Geneva, "a city that was a Church," became the model of a Christian community for sixteenth-century Protestant reformers.

To understand Calvin's Geneva, it is necessary to understand Calvin's ideas. These he embodied in *The Institutes of the Christian Religion,* first published in 1536 and definitively issued in 1559. The cornerstone of Calvin's theology was his belief in the absolute sovereignty and omnipotence of God and the total weakness of humanity. Before the infinite power of God, he asserted, men and women are as insignificant as grains of sand.

Calvin did not ascribe free will to human beings because that would detract from the sovereignty of God. Men and women cannot actively work to achieve salvation; rather, God in his infinite wisdom decided at the beginning of time who would be saved and who damned. This viewpoint constitutes the theological principle called *predestination:*

Predestination we call the eternal decree of God, by which he has determined in himself, what he would have become of every individual of mankind. For they are not all created with a similar destiny; but eternal life is foreordained for some, and eternal damnation for others. . . . In conformity, therefore, to the clear doctrine of the Scripture, we assert, that by an eternal and immutable counsel, God has once for all determined, both whom he would admit to salvation, and whom he would condemn to destruction. We affirm that this counsel, as far as concerns the elect, is founded on his gratuitous mercy, totally irrespective of human merit; but that to those whom he devotes to

condemnation, the gate of life is closed by a just and irreprehensible, but incomprehensible, judgment. How exceedingly presumptuous it is only to inquire into the causes of the Divine will; which is in fact, and is justly entitled to be, the cause of everything that exists. . . . For the will of God is the highest justice; so that what he wills must be considered just, for this very reason, because he wills it.[21]

Many people have found the doctrine of predestination, which dates back to Saint Augustine and Saint Paul, a pessimistic view of the nature of God, who, they feel, revealed himself in the Old and New Testaments as merciful as well as just. But

❖ **John Calvin** The lean, ascetic face with the strong jaw reflects the iron will and determination of the organizer of Protestantism. The fur collar represents his training in law. *(Source: Bibliothèque Nationale/Snark/Art Resource)*

"this terrible decree," as even Calvin called it, did not lead to pessimism or fatalism. Rather, the Calvinist believed in the redemptive work of Christ and was confident that God had elected (saved) him or her. Predestination served as an energizing dynamic, forcing a person to undergo hardships in the constant struggle against evil.

Calvin aroused Genevans to a high standard of morality. He had two remarkable assets: complete mastery of the Scriptures and exceptional fluency in French. Through his sermons and a program of religious education, God's laws and man's were enforced in Geneva. Calvin's powerful sermons delivered the Word of God and thereby monopolized the strongest contemporary means of communication: preaching. Through his *Genevan Catechism,* published in 1541, children and adults memorized set questions and answers and acquired a summary of their faith and a guide for daily living. Calvin's sermons and his *Catechism* gave a whole generation of Genevans thorough instruction in the reformed religion.[22]

In the reformation of the city, the Genevan Consistory also exercised a powerful role. This body consisted of twelve laymen plus the Company of Pastors, of which Calvin was the permanent moderator (presider). The duties of the Consistory were "to keep watch over every man's life [and] to admonish amiably those whom they see leading a disorderly life." Even though Calvin emphasized that the Consistory's activities should be thorough and "its eyes may be everywhere," corrections were considered only "medicine to turn sinners to the Lord."[23]

Although all municipal governments in early modern Europe regulated citizens' conduct, none did so with the severity of Geneva's Consistory under Calvin's leadership. Nor did it make any distinction between what we would consider crimes against society and simple un-Christian conduct. Absence from sermons, criticism of ministers, dancing, card playing, family quarrels, and heavy drinking were all investigated and punished by the Consistory. Serious crimes and heresy were handled by the civil authorities, which, with the Consistory's approval, sometimes used torture to extract confessions. Between 1542 and 1546 alone, seventy-six persons were banished from Geneva and fifty-eight executed for heresy, adultery, blasphemy, and witchcraft.

Calvin reserved his harshest condemnation for religious dissenters, declaring them "dogs and swine":

God makes plain that the false prophet is to be stoned without mercy. We are to crush beneath our heel all affections of nature when His honor is concerned. The father should not spare his child, nor brother his brother, nor husband his own wife or the friend who is dearer to him than life. No human relationship is more than animal unless it be grounded in God.[24]

Calvin translated his words into action. In the 1550s Spanish humanist Michael Servetus had gained international notoriety for his publications denying the Christian dogma of the Trinity, which holds that God is three divine persons, Father, Son, and Holy Spirit. Servetus had been arrested by the Inquisition but escaped to Geneva, where he hoped for support. He was promptly rearrested. At his trial he not only held to his belief that there is no scriptural basis for the Trinity but also rejected child baptism and insisted that a person under twenty cannot commit a mortal sin. The city fathers considered this last idea dangerous to public morality, "especially in these days when the young are so corrupted." Though Servetus begged that he be punished by banishment, Calvin and the town council maintained that the denial of child baptism and the Trinity amounted to a threat to all society. Whispering "Jesus, Son of the eternal God, have pity on me," Servetus was burned at the stake.

To many sixteenth-century Europeans, Calvin's Geneva seemed "the most perfect school of Christ since the days of the Apostles." Religious refugees from France, England, Spain, Scotland, and Italy visited the city. Subsequently, the Reformed church of Calvin served as the model for the Presbyterian church in Scotland, the Huguenot church in France, and the Puritan churches in England and New England. For women, the Calvinist provision for congregational participation and vernacular liturgy helped satisfy their desire to belong to and participate in a meaningful church organization.

Calvinism became the compelling force in international Protestantism. The Calvinist ethic of the "calling" dignified all work with a religious aspect. Hard work, well done, was pleasing to God. This doctrine encouraged an aggressive, vigorous activ-

❖ **Calvinist Worship** A converted house in Lyons, France, serves as a church for the simple Calvinist service. Although Calvin's followers believed in equality and elected officials administered the church, here men and women are segregated, and some people sit on hard benches while others sit in upholstered pews. Beside the pulpit an hourglass hangs to time the preacher's sermon. (Could the dog sit still for that long?) *(Source: Bibliothèque publique et universitaire, Geneva)*

ism. In the *Institutes* Calvin provided a systematic theology for Protestantism. The Reformed church of Calvin had a strong and well-organized machinery of government. These factors, together with the social and economic applications of Calvin's theology, made Calvinism the most dynamic force in sixteenth- and seventeenth-century Protestantism.

The Anabaptists

The name *Anabaptist* derives from a Greek word meaning "to baptize again." The Anabaptists, sometimes described as the "left wing of the Ref-

ormation," believed that only adults could make a free choice about religious faith, baptism, and entry into the Christian community. Thus they considered the practice of baptizing infants and children preposterous and claimed there was no scriptural basis for it. They wanted to rebaptize believers who had been baptized as children. Anabaptists took the Gospel and, at first, Luther's teachings absolutely literally and favored a return to the kind of church that had existed among the earliest Christians—a voluntary association of believers who had experienced an inner light.

Anabaptists maintained that only a few people would receive the inner light. This position meant

460 CHAPTER 14 REFORM AND RENEWAL IN THE CHRISTIAN CHURCH

that the Christian community and the Christian state were not identical. In other words, Anabaptists believed in the separation of church and state and in religious tolerance. They almost never tried to force their values on others. In an age that believed in the necessity of state-established churches, Anabaptist views on religious liberty were thought to undermine that concept.

Each Anabaptist community or church was entirely independent; it selected its own ministers and ran its own affairs. In 1534 the community at Münster in Germany, for example, established a legal code that decreed the death penalty for insubordinate wives. Moreover, the Münster community also practiced polygamy and forced all women under a certain age to marry or face expulsion or execution.

Anabaptists admitted women to the ministry. They shared goods as the early Christians had done, refused all public offices, and would not serve in the armed forces. In fact, they laid great stress on pacifism. A favorite Anabaptist scriptural quotation was "By their fruits you shall know them," suggesting that if Christianity was a religion of peace, then the Christian should not fight. Good deeds were the sign of Christian faith, and to be a Christian meant to imitate the meekness and mercy of Christ. With such beliefs Anabaptists were inevitably a minority. Anabaptism later attracted the poor, the unemployed, the uneducated. Geographically, Anabaptists drew their members from depressed urban areas—from among the followers of Zwingli in Zurich and from Basel, Augsburg, and Nuremberg.

Ideas such as absolute pacifism and the distinction between the Christian community and the state brought down on these unfortunate people fanatical hatred and bitter persecution. Zwingli, Luther, Calvin, and Catholics all saw—quite correctly—the separation of church and state as leading ultimately to the complete secularization of society. The powerful rulers of Swiss and German society immediately saw the connection between religious heresy and economic dislocation. Civil authorities feared that the combination of religious differences and economic grievances would lead to civil disturbances. In Saxony, in Strasbourg, and in the Swiss cities, Anabaptists were either banished or cruelly executed by burning, beating, or drowning. Their community spirit and the edifying ex-

ample of their lives, however, contributed to the survival of Anabaptist ideas. Later, the Quakers, with their gentle pacifism; the Baptists, with their emphasis on an inner spiritual light; the Congregationalists, with their democratic church organization; and, in 1787, the authors of the U.S. Constitution, with their concern for the separation of church and state would all trace their origins, in part, to the Anabaptists of the sixteenth century.

The English Reformation

As on the Continent, the Reformation in England had social and economic causes as well as religious ones. As elsewhere, too, Christian humanists had for decades been calling for the purification of the church. When the personal matter of the divorce of King Henry VIII (r. 1509–1547) became enmeshed with political issues, a complete break with Rome resulted.

Demands for ecclesiastical reform dated back at least to the fourteenth century. The Lollards (see page 386) had been driven underground in the fifteenth century but survived in parts of southern England and the Midlands. Working-class people, especially cloth workers, were attracted to their ideas. The Lollards stressed the individual's reading and interpretation of the Bible, which they considered the only standard of Christian faith and holiness. Consequently, they put no stock in the value of the sacraments and were vigorously anticlerical. Lollards opposed ecclesiastical wealth, the veneration of the saints, prayers for the dead, and all war. Although they had no notion of justification by faith, like Luther they insisted on the individual soul's direct responsibility to God.

The work of English humanist William Tyndale (1494?–1536) stimulated cries for reform. Tyndale visited Luther at Wittenberg in 1524 and a year later at Antwerp began printing an English translation of the New Testament. From Antwerp, merchants carried the New Testament into England, where it was distributed by Lollards. Fortified with copies of Tyndale's English Bible and some of Luther's ideas, the Lollards represented the ideal of "a personal, scriptural, non-sacramental, and lay-dominated religion."[25] In this manner, doctrines that would later be called Protestant flourished underground in England before any official or state-approved changes. The Lollards, however, represented a very small group.

Recent scholarship on the condition of the English church in the early sixteenth century indicates that it was in a very healthy condition. Traditional Catholicism exerted an enormously strong, diverse, and vigorous hold over the imagination and loyalty of the people. The teachings of Christianity were graphically represented in the liturgy, reiterated in sermons, enacted in plays, carved and printed on walls, screens, and the windows of churches. A zealous clergy, increasingly better educated, engaged in a "massive catechetical enterprise." No substantial gulf existed between the religion of the clergy and educated elite and the broad mass of the English people.[26] The Reformation in England was an act of state initiated by the king's emotional life.

In 1527, having fallen in love with Anne Boleyn, Henry wanted his marriage to Catherine of Aragon annulled. When Henry had married Catherine, he had secured a dispensation from Pope Julius II eliminating all legal technicalities about Catherine's previous union with Henry's late brother, Arthur (see page 430). Henry claimed that a disputed succession and the anarchy of the Wars of the Roses would be repeated if a woman, the princess Mary, sole surviving child of his marriage to Catherine, inherited the throne. Accordingly, Henry petitioned Pope Clement VII for an annulment, stating that a valid marriage to Catherine had never existed. The pope was an indecisive man whose attention at the time was focused on the Lutheran revolt in Germany and the Habsburg-Valois struggle for control of Italy. But there is a stronger reason Clement could not grant Henry's petition. Henry argued that Pope Julius's dispensation had contradicted the law of God—that a man may not marry his brother's widow. The English king's request reached Rome at the very time that Luther was widely publishing tracts condemning the papacy as the core of wickedness. Had Clement granted Henry's annulment and thereby admitted that his recent predecessor, Julius II, had erred, Clement would have given support to the Lutheran assertion that popes substituted their own evil judgments for the law of God. This Clement could not do, so he delayed acting on Henry's request.[27] The capture and sack of Rome in 1527 by the emperor Charles V, Queen Catherine's nephew, thoroughly tied the pope's hands.

Since Rome appeared to be thwarting Henry's matrimonial plans, he decided to remove the English church from papal jurisdiction. Henry used Parliament to legalize the Reformation in England. The Act in Restraint of Appeals (1533) declared the king to be the supreme sovereign in England and forbade judicial appeals to the papacy, thus establishing the Crown as the highest legal authority in the land. The Act for the Submission of the Clergy (1534) required churchmen to submit to the king and forbade the publication of ecclesiastical laws without royal permission. The Supremacy Act (1534) declared the king the supreme head of the Church of England. Both the Act in Restraint of Appeals and the Supremacy Act led to heated debate in the House of Commons. An authority on the Reformation Parliament has written that probably only a small number of those who voted for the Restraint of Appeals actually knew they were voting for a permanent break with Rome.[28] Some opposed the king. John Fisher, the bishop of Rochester, a distinguished scholar, and a humanist, lashed the clergy with scorn for its cowardice. Another humanist, Thomas More, resigned the chancellorship: he could not take the oath required by the Supremacy Act because it rejected papal authority and made the king head of the English church. Fisher, More, and other dissenters were beheaded.

When Anne Boleyn failed twice to produce a male child, Henry VIII charged her with adulterous incest and in 1536 had her beheaded. Parliament promptly proclaimed the princess Elizabeth illegitimate and, with the royal succession thoroughly confused, left the throne to whomever Henry chose. His third wife, Jane Seymour, gave Henry the desired son, Edward, but died in childbirth. Henry went on to three more wives. Before he passed to his reward in 1547, he got Parliament to reverse the decision of 1536, relegitimating Mary and Elizabeth and fixing the succession first in his son and then in his daughters.

Between 1535 and 1539, under the influence of his chief minister, Thomas Cromwell, Henry decided to dissolve the English monasteries because he wanted their wealth. The king ended nine hundred years of English monastic life, dispersed the monks and nuns, and confiscated their lands. Hundreds of properties were sold to the middle and upper classes and the proceeds spent on war. The

✦ **Allegorical Painting,** c. 1548 Henry VIII on his deathbed points to his heir Edward, surrounded by Protestant worthies, as the wave of the future. The pope collapses, monks flee, through the window iconoclasts knock down statues, symbolizing error and superstition; stressing Protestantism's focus on Scripture, the Bible is open to 1 Peter 1:24: "The word of the Lord endures forever." Since the new order lacked broad popular support, propagandistic paintings like this and the printing press had to be mobilized to sway public opinion. *(Source: By courtesy of the National Portrait Gallery, London)*

dissolution of the monasteries did not achieve a more equitable distribution of land and wealth. Rather, the "bare ruined choirs where late the sweet birds sang"—as Shakespeare described in Sonnet 73 the desolate religious houses—testified to the loss of a valuable cultural force in English life. The redistribution of land strengthened the upper classes and tied them to the Tudor dynasty.

Did the religious changes accompanying this political upheaval have broad popular support? Recent scholarship has emphasized that the English Reformation came from above. The surviving evidence does not allow us to gauge the degree of opposition to (or support for) Henry's break with Rome. Certainly, many lay people wrote to the king begging him to spare the monasteries. "Most laypeople acquiesced in the Reformation because they hardly knew what was going on, were understandably reluctant to jeopardise life or limb, a career or the family's good name."[29] But all did not quietly acquiesce. In 1536 popular opposition in the north to the religious changes led to the Pilgrimage of Grace, a massive multiclass rebellion that proved the largest in English history. In 1546 serious rebellions in East Anglia and in the west, despite possessing economic and Protestant components, reflected considerable public opposition to the state-ordered religious changes.[30]

Henry's motives combined personal, political, social, and economic elements. Theologically he retained such traditional Catholic practices and doctrines as auricular confession, clerical celibacy, and transubstantiation. Meanwhile, Protestant literature circulated, and Henry approved the selection of men of Protestant sympathies as tutors for his son.

The nationalization of the church and the dissolution of the monasteries led to important changes in government administration. Vast tracts of formerly monastic land came temporarily under the Crown's jurisdiction, and new bureaucratic machinery had to be developed to manage those properties. Cromwell reformed and centralized the king's household, the council, the secretariats, and the Exchequer. New departments of state were set up. Surplus funds from all departments went into a liquid fund to be applied to areas where there were deficits. This balancing resulted in greater efficiency and economy. Henry VIII's reign saw the growth of the modern centralized bureaucratic state.

After Henry's death, the English church shifted left and right. In the short reign of Henry's sickly son, Edward VI (r. 1547–1553), strongly Protestant ideas exerted a significant influence on the religious life of the country. Archbishop Thomas Cranmer simplified the liturgy, invited Protestant theologians to England, and prepared the first *Book of Common Prayer* (1549). In stately and dignified English, the *Book of Common Prayer* included, together with the Psalter, the order for all services of the Church of England.

The equally brief reign of Mary Tudor (r. 1553–1558) witnessed a sharp move back to Catholicism. The devoutly Catholic daughter of Catherine of Aragon, Mary rescinded the Reformation legislation of her father's reign and fully restored Roman Catholicism. Mary's marriage to her cousin Philip of Spain, son of the emperor Charles V, proved highly unpopular in England, and her persecution and execution of several hundred Protestants further alienated her subjects. During her reign, many Protestants fled to the Continent. Mary's death raised to the throne her sister Elizabeth (r. 1558–1603) and inaugurated the beginnings of religious stability.

Elizabeth had been raised a Protestant, but at the start of her reign sharp differences existed in England. On the one hand, Catholics wanted a Roman Catholic ruler. On the other hand, a vocal number of returning exiles wanted all Catholic elements in the Church of England eliminated. The latter, because they wanted to "purify" the church, were called "Puritans." Probably one of the shrewdest politicians in English history, Elizabeth chose a middle course between Catholic and Puritan extremes. She insisted on dignity in church services and political order in the land. She did not care what people believed as long as they kept quiet about it. Avoiding precise doctrinal definitions, Elizabeth had herself styled "Supreme Governor of the Church of England, Etc.," and left it to her subjects to decide what the "Etc." meant.

The parliamentary legislation of the early years of Elizabeth's reign—laws sometimes labeled the "Elizabethan Settlement"—required outward conformity to the Church of England and uniformity in all ceremonies. Everyone had to attend Church of England services; those who refused were fined. In 1563 a convocation of bishops approved the Thirty-nine Articles, a summary in thirty-nine short statements of the basic tenets of the Church of England. During Elizabeth's reign, the Anglican church (from the Latin *Ecclesia Anglicana*), as the Church of England was called, moved in a moderately Protestant direction. Services were conducted in English, monasteries were not re-established, and clergymen were allowed to marry. But the bishops remained as church officials, and apart from language, the services were quite traditional.

The Establishment of the Church of Scotland

Reform of the church in Scotland did not follow the English model. In the early sixteenth century, the church in Scotland presented an extreme case of clerical abuse and corruption, and Lutheranism initially attracted sympathetic support. In Scotland as elsewhere, political authority was the decisive influence in reform. The monarchy was weak, and factions of virtually independent nobles competed for power. King James V and his daughter, Mary, Queen of Scots (r. 1560–1567), staunch Catholics and close allies of Catholic France, opposed reform. The Scottish nobles supported it. One man, John Knox (1505?–1572), dominated the movement for reform in Scotland.

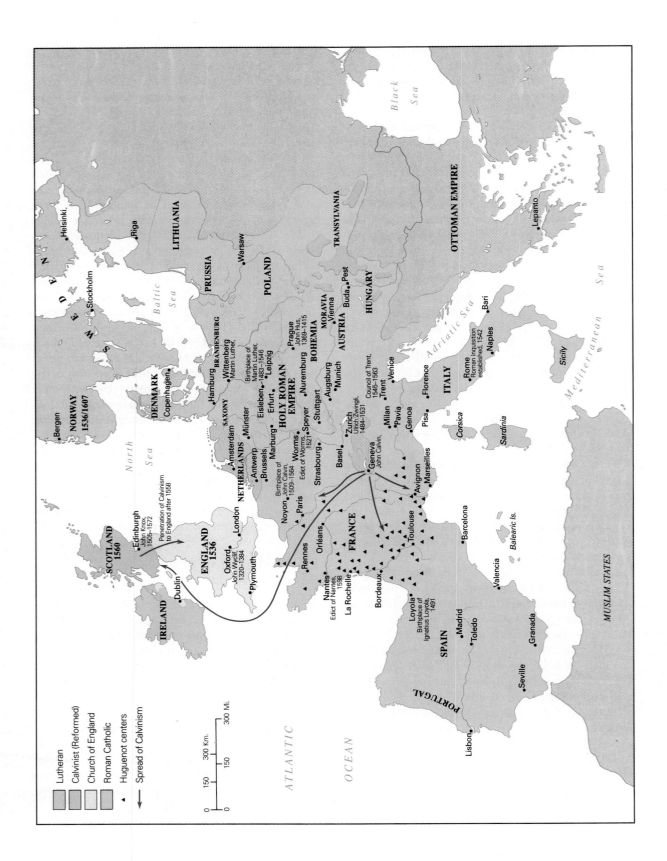

Lutheran

Calvinist (Reformed)

Church of England

Roman Catholic

▲ Huguenot centers

→ Spread of Calvinism

BERGEN

NORWAY 1536/1607

Stockholm

SWEDEN

Helsinki

Riga

LITHUANIA

Warsaw

PRUSSIA

POLAND

TRANSYLVANIA

Buda Pest

HUNGARY

MORAVIA

Vienna

AUSTRIA

BOHEMIA

Prague
John Hus,
1369–1415

Nuremburg

BRANDENBURG

Wittenberg
Martin Luther,
Birthplace of
Martin Luther,
1483–1546 Leipzig

Hamburg

DENMARK

Copenhagen

Saxony

Münster

Eisleben Erfurt

HOLY ROMAN
EMPIRE

Speyer

Stuttgart

Augsburg Munich

Zurich
Ulrich Zwingli,
1484–1531

Council of Trent,
1545–1563

Trent Venice

Milan

Pavia

Genoa

Pisa Florence

ITALY

Rome
Roman Inquisition
established, 1542

Naples

Bari

Sicily

Adriatic Sea

Mediterranean Sea

Corsica

Sardinia

Balearic Is.

MUSLIM STATES

Lepanto

Black Sea

OTTOMAN EMPIRE

Amsterdam

Antwerp

Brussels

NETHERLANDS

Birthplace of
John Calvin,
1509–1564

Noyon Paris

Marburg

Worms
Edict of Worms,
1521

Strasbourg

Basel

Geneva
John Calvin,

Marseilles

Avignon

Toulouse

FRANCE

Orléans

Rennes

Nantes
Edict of Nantes,
1598

La Rochelle

Bordeaux

Loyola
Birthplace of
Ignatius Loyola,
1491

SPAIN

Madrid

Toledo

Granada

Seville

Barcelona

Valencia

PORTUGAL

Lisbon

Bergen

NORTH
Sea

Baltic
Sea

Edinburgh
John Knox,
1505–1572

Penetration of Calvinism
to England after 1558

SCOTLAND
1560

ENGLAND 1536

Oxford,
John Wyclif,
1320–1384

London

Plymouth

Dublin

IRELAND

ATLANTIC

OCEAN

0   150   300 Mi.

0   150   300 Km.

In 1559 Knox, a dour, narrow-minded, and fear-less man with a reputation as a passionate preacher, set to work reforming the church. He had studied and worked with Calvin in Geneva and was determined to structure the Scottish church after the model of Calvin's Geneva. In 1560 Knox persuaded the Scottish parliament, which was dominated by reform-minded barons, to enact legislation ending papal authority. The mass was abolished and attendance at it forbidden under penalty of death. Knox then established the Presbyterian Church of Scotland, so named because *presbyters,* or ministers, not bishops, governed it. The Church of Scotland was strictly Calvinist in doctrine, adopted a simple and dignified service of worship, and laid great emphasis on preaching. Knox's *Book of Common Order* (1564) became the liturgical directory for the church. The Presbyterian Church of Scotland was a national, or state, church, and many of its members maintained close relations with English Puritans.

Protestantism in Ireland

To the ancient Irish hatred of English political and commercial exploitation, the Reformation added the bitter antagonism of religion. Henry VIII wanted to "reduce that realm to the knowledge of God and obedience to us." English rulers in the sixteenth century regarded the Irish as barbarians, and a policy of complete extermination was rejected only because "to enterprise [attempt] the whole extirpation and total destruction of all the Irishmen in the land would be a marvelous sumptious charge and great difficulty."[31] In other words, it would have cost too much.

In 1536 on orders from London, the Irish parliament, which represented only the English landlords and the people of the Pale (the area around Dublin), approved the English laws severing the church from Rome and making the English king sovereign over ecclesiastical organization and practice. The Church of Ireland was established on the English pattern, and the (English) ruling class

♦ **MAP 14.2 The Protestant and the Catholic Reformations** The reformations shattered the religious unity of Western Christendom. What common cultural traits predominated in regions where a particular branch of the Christian faith was maintained or took root?

adopted the new reformed faith. Most of the Irish, probably for political reasons, defiantly remained Roman Catholic. Monasteries were secularized. Catholic property was confiscated and sold and the profits shipped to England. With the Roman church driven underground, Catholic churchmen acted as national as well as religious leaders.

Lutheranism in Sweden, Norway, and Denmark

In Sweden, Norway, and Denmark, the monarchy took the initiative in the religious Reformation. The resulting institutions were Lutheran state churches. Since the late fourteenth century, the Danish kings had ruled Sweden and Norway as well as Denmark. In 1520 Swedish nobleman Gustavus Vasa (r. 1523–1560) led a successful revolt against Denmark, and Sweden became independent. As king, Gustavus Vasa seized church lands and required the bishops' loyalty to the Swedish crown. Wittenberg-educated Swedish reformer Olaus Petri (1493–1552) translated the New Testament into Swedish and, with the full support of Gustavus Vasa, organized the church along strict Lutheran lines. This consolidation of the Swedish monarchy in the sixteenth century was to profoundly affect the development of Germany in the seventeenth century.

Christian III, king of Denmark (r. 1503–1559) and of Norway (r. 1534–1559), secularized church property and set up a Lutheran church. Norway, which was governed by Denmark until 1814, adopted Lutheranism as its state religion under Danish influence.

♦ THE CATHOLIC AND THE COUNTER-REFORMATIONS

Between 1517 and 1547, the reformed versions of Christianity known as Protestantism made remarkable advances. All of England, Scandinavia, much of Scotland and Germany, and sizable parts of France and Switzerland adopted the creeds of Luther, Calvin, and other reformers. Nevertheless, the Roman Catholic church made a significant comeback. After about 1540, no new large areas of Europe, except for the Netherlands, accepted Protestant beliefs (Map 14.2).

Historians distinguish between two types of reform within the Catholic church in the sixteenth and seventeenth centuries. The Catholic Reformation began before 1517 and sought renewal basically through the stimulation of a new spiritual fervor. The Counter-Reformation started in the 1540s as a reaction to the rise and spread of Protestantism. The Counter-Reformation involved Catholic efforts to convince or coerce dissidents or heretics to return to the church lest they corrupt the entire community of Catholic believers. Fear of the "infection" of all Christian society by the religious dissident was a standard sixteenth-century attitude. If the heretic could not be persuaded to reconvert, counter-reformers believed it necessary to call on temporal authorities to defend Christian society by expelling or eliminating the dissident. The Catholic Reformation and the Counter-Reformation were not mutually exclusive; in fact, after about 1540 they progressed simultaneously.

The Slowness of Institutional Reform

The Renaissance princes who sat on the throne of Saint Peter were not blind to the evils that existed. Modest reform efforts had begun with the Lateran Council called in 1512 by Pope Julius II. The Dutch pope Adrian VI (1522–1523) instructed his legate in Germany to

say that we frankly confess that God permits this [Lutheran] persecution of his church on account of the sins of men, especially those of the priests and prelates. . . . We know that in this Holy See now for some years there have been many abominations, abuses in spiritual things, excesses in things commanded, in short that all has become perverted. . . . We have all turned aside in our ways, nor was there, for a long time, any who did right—no, not one.[32]

Adrian VI tried desperately to reform the church and to check the spread of Protestantism. His reign lasted only thirteen months, however, and the austerity of his life and his Dutch nationality provoked the hostility of pleasure-loving Italian curial bureaucrats.

Overall, why did the popes, spiritual leaders of the Western church, move so slowly? The answers lie in the personalities of the popes themselves, their preoccupation with political affairs in Italy, and the awesome difficulty of reforming so complicated a bureaucracy as the Roman curia.

Clement VII (r. 1523–1534), a true Medici, was far more interested in elegant tapestries and Michelangelo's painting of the Last Judgment than in theological disputes in barbaric Germany. Indecisive and vacillating, Pope Clement must bear much of the responsibility for the great spread of Protestantism. While Emperor Charles V and the French king Francis I competed for the domination of divided Italy, the papacy worried about the security of the Papal States. Clement tried to follow a middle course, backing first the emperor and then the French ruler. At the Battle of Pavia in 1525, Francis I suffered a severe defeat and was captured. In a reshuffling of diplomatic alliances, the pope switched from Charles and the Spanish to Francis I. The emperor was victorious once again, however, and in 1527 his Spanish and German mercenaries sacked and looted Rome and captured the pope. Obviously, papal concern about Italian affairs and the Papal States diverted attention from reform.

The idea of reform was closely linked to the idea of a general council representing the entire church. A strong contingent of countries beyond the Alps—Spain, Germany, and France—wanted to reform the vast bureaucracy of Latin officials, reducing offices, men, and revenues. Popes from Julius II to Clement VII, remembering fifteenth-century conciliar attempts to limit papal authority, resisted calls for a council. The papal bureaucrats who were the popes' intimates warned the popes against a council, fearing loss of power, revenue, and prestige. Five centuries before, Saint Bernard of Clairvaux had anticipated the situation: "The most grievous danger of any Pope lies in the fact that, encompassed as he is by flatterers, he never hears the truth about his own person and ends by not wishing to hear it."

The Council of Trent

In the papal conclave that followed the death of Clement VII, Cardinal Alexander Farnese promised two German cardinals that if he was elected pope, he would summon a council. He won the election and ruled as Pope Paul III (1534–1549). This Roman aristocrat, humanist, and astrologer, who immediately made his teen-age grandsons cardinals, seemed an unlikely person to undertake serious reform. Yet Paul III appointed as cardinals several learned and reform-minded men, such as Gian Pietro Caraffa (later Pope Paul IV); established the Inquisition in the Papal States; and—true to his word—called a council, which finally met at Trent, an imperial city close to Italy.

The Council of Trent met intermittently from 1545 to 1563. It was called not only to reform the church but also to secure reconciliation with the Protestants. Lutherans and Calvinists were invited to participate, but their insistence that the Scriptures be the sole basis for discussion made reconciliation impossible. International politics repeatedly cast a shadow over the theological debates. Charles V opposed discussions on any matter that might further alienate his Lutheran subjects, fearing the loss of additional imperial territory to Lutheran princes. Meanwhile, the French kings worked against the reconciliation of Roman Catholicism and Lutheranism. As long as religious issues divided the German states, the empire would be weakened, and a weak and divided empire meant a stronger France. Portugal, Poland, Hungary, and Ireland sent representatives, but very few German bishops attended.

Another problem was the persistence of the conciliar theory of church government. Some bishops wanted a concrete statement asserting the supremacy of a church council over the papacy. The adoption of the conciliar principle could have led to a divided church. The bishops had a provincial and national outlook; only the papacy possessed an international religious perspective. The centralizing tenet was established that all acts of the council required papal approval.

In spite of the obstacles, the achievements of the Council of Trent were impressive. It dealt with both doctrinal and disciplinary matters. The council gave equal validity to the Scriptures and to tradition as sources of religious truth and authority. It reaffirmed the seven sacraments and the traditional Catholic teaching on transubstantiation. Thus it rejected Lutheran and Calvinist positions.

The council tackled the problems arising from ancient abuses by strengthening ecclesiastical discipline. Tridentine (from *Tridentum,* the Latin word for Trent) decrees required bishops to reside in their own dioceses, suppressed pluralism and simony, and forbade the sale of indulgences. Clerics who kept concubines were to give them up. The jurisdiction of bishops over all the clergy of their dioceses was made almost absolute, and bishops were ordered to visit every religious house within the diocese at least once every two years. In a highly original canon, the council required every diocese to establish a seminary for the education and training of the clergy; the council even prescribed the curriculum and insisted that preference for admission be given to sons of the poor. Seminary professors were to determine if candidates for ordination had *vocations,* genuine callings as determined by purity of life, detachment from the broader secular culture, and a steady inclination

❖ **Raphael: Pope Leo X and His Cousins**   In this dynastic portrait of the Medici family, so suggested by the Medici ball on the back of the chair, the pope sits clothed in velvet and damask, while his cousins Cardinals Guilio de' Medici (later Pope Clement VII) and Luigi de Rossi stand. A fine humanist and musician, Cardinal Guilio was one of the most handsome men ever elected pope. The book on the table is opened to the beginning of St. John's Gospel, indicating Leo's namesake, Giovanni or John; weak eyesight forced him to use an eyeglass to read. *(Source: Alinari/Art Resource)*

toward the priesthood. This was a novel idea since from the time of the early church, parents had determined their sons' (and daughters') religious careers (see page 314). Finally, great emphasis was laid on preaching and instructing the laity, especially the uneducated.

One decision had especially important social consequences for lay people. Since the time of the Roman Empire, many couples had treated marriage as a completely personal matter, exchanged vows privately without witnesses, and thus formed what were called clandestine (secret) unions. This widespread practice frequently led later to denials by one party, conflicts over property, and disputes in the ecclesiastical courts that had jurisdiction over marriage once it became a sacrament (which occurred in the twelfth century). The Tridentine decree Tametsi (November 1563) stipulated that for a marriage to be valid, consent (the essence of marriage) as given in the vows had to be made publicly before witnesses, one of whom had to be the parish priest. Trent thereby ended secret marriages in Catholic countries. (They remained a problem for civil and church courts in England until the Hardwicke Act of 1753 abolished them.)

The Council of Trent did not meet everyone's expectations. Reconciliation with Protestantism was not achieved, nor was reform brought about immediately. Nevertheless, the Tridentine decrees laid a solid basis for the spiritual renewal of the church and for the enforcement of correction. For four centuries, the doctrinal and disciplinary legislation of Trent served as the basis for Roman Catholic faith, organization, and practice.

❖ **School of Titian: The Council of Trent** Since the early sessions were sparsely attended, this well-attended meeting seems to be a later session. Few bishops from northern Europe, however, ever attended. The Swiss guards (forefront) of the Vatican were founded by Pope Julius II in 1505 to defend the papacy. (*Source: Louvre © R.M.N.*)

New Religious Orders

The establishment of new religious orders within the church reveals a central feature of the Catholic Reformation. These new orders developed in response to one crying need: to raise the moral and intellectual level of the clergy and people. Education was a major goal of them all.

The Ursuline order of nuns, founded by Angela Merici (1474–1540), attained enormous prestige for the education of women. The daughter of a country gentleman, Angela Merici worked for many years among the poor, sick, and uneducated around her native Brescia in northern Italy. In 1535 she established the Ursuline order to combat heresy through Christian education. The first women's religious order concentrating exclusively on teaching young girls, the Ursulines sought to re-Christianize society by training future wives and mothers. Approved as a religious community by Paul III in 1544, the Ursulines rapidly grew and spread to France and the New World. Their schools in North America, stretching from Quebec to New Orleans, provided superior education for young women and inculcated the spiritual ideals of the Catholic Reformation.

The Society of Jesus, founded by Ignatius Loyola (1491–1556), a former Spanish soldier, played a powerful international role in resisting the spread of Protestantism, converting Asians and Latin American Indians to Catholicism, and spreading Christian education all over Europe. While recuperating from a severe battle wound in his legs, Loyola studied a life of Christ and other religious books and decided to give up his military career and become a soldier of Christ. During a year spent in seclusion, prayer, and personal mortification, he gained the religious insights that went into his great classic, *Spiritual Exercises* (1548). This work, intended for study during a four-week period of retreat, directed the individual imagination and will to the reform of life and a new spiritual piety.

Loyola was apparently a man of considerable personal magnetism. After study at universities in Salamanca and Paris, he gathered a group of six companions and in 1540 secured papal approval of the new Society of Jesus, whose members were called "Jesuits." The first Jesuits, recruited primarily from the wealthy merchant and professional classes, saw the Reformation as a pastoral problem, its causes and cures related not to doctrinal issues but to people's spiritual condition. Reform of the church, as Luther and Calvin understood that term, played no role in the future the Jesuits planned for themselves. Their goal was "to help souls." Loyola also possessed a gift for leadership that consisted in spotting talent and in seeing "how at a given juncture change is more consistent with one's scope than staying the course."[33]

The Society of Jesus developed into a highly centralized, tightly knit organization. Candidates underwent a two-year novitiate, in contrast to the usual one-year probation. In addition to the traditional vows of poverty, chastity, and obedience, professed members vowed "special obedience to the sovereign pontiff regarding missions."[34] Thus as stability—the promise to live his life in the monastery—was what made a monk, so mobility—the commitment to go anywhere for the help of souls—was the defining characteristic of a Jesuit. Flexibility and the willingness to respond to the needs of time and circumstance formed the Jesuit tradition. In this respect Jesuits were very modern; and they attracted many recruits.

They achieved phenomenal success for the papacy and the reformed Catholic church. Jesuit schools adopted the modern humanist curricula and methods, and even though they first concentrated on the children of the poor, they were soon educating the sons of the nobility. As confessors and spiritual directors to kings, Jesuits exerted great political influence. Operating on the principle that the end sometimes justifies the means, they were not above spying. Indifferent to physical comfort and personal safety, they carried Christianity to India and Japan before 1550, to Brazil, North America, and the Congo in the seventeenth century. Within Europe the Jesuits brought southern Germany and much of eastern Europe back to Catholicism.

The Sacred Congregation of the Holy Office

In 1542 Pope Paul III established the Sacred Congregation of the Holy Office, with jurisdiction over the Roman Inquisition, a powerful instrument of the Counter-Reformation. The Inquisition was a committee of six cardinals with judicial authority over all Catholics and the power to arrest, imprison, and execute. Under the fanatical Cardinal Caraffa, it vigorously attacked heresy.

❖ **Juan de Valdes Leal: Pope Paul III Approves the Jesuit Constitutions** Although Paul III devoted considerable energy to advancing the interests of his (Farnese) family, he also tried to meet the challenge of Protestantism—through the Council of Trent and new religious Orders. When the Jesuit constitutions were read to him, Paul III supposedly murmured, "There is the finger of God." The portrait of Ignatius Loyola is a reasonable likeness, that of the pope an idealization: in 1540 he was a very old man.

The Roman Inquisition operated under the principles of Roman law. It accepted hearsay evidence, was not obliged to inform the accused of charges against them, and sometimes applied torture. Echoing one of Calvin's remarks about heresy, Cardinal Caraffa wrote, "No man is to lower himself by showing toleration towards any sort of heretic, least of all a Calvinist."[35] The Holy Office published the *Index of Prohibited Books,* a catalogue of forbidden reading.

Within the Papal States, the Inquisition effectively destroyed heresy (and some heretics). Outside the papal territories, however, its influence was slight. Governments had their own judicial systems for the suppression of treasonable activities, as religious heresy was then considered. The republic of Venice is a good case in point.

In the sixteenth century, Venice was one of the great publishing centers of Europe. The Inquisition and the *Index* could have badly damaged the Venetian book trade, but authorities there cooperated with the Holy Office only when heresy became a great threat to the security of the republic. The *Index* had no influence on scholarly research in nonreligious areas such as law, classical literature, and mathematics. As a result of the Inquisition, Venetians and Italians were *not* cut off from the main currents of European learning.[36]

SUMMARY

Demands for reform of the Christian church is a continuing theme in European history. In the fifteenth and early sixteenth centuries, movements such as the Brethren of the Common Life, Lollardy, the Oratories of Divine Love, and the efforts of the Roman papacy itself paved the way for institutional reform. Martin Luther's strictly religious call for reform, rapidly spread by preaching, hymns, and the printing press, soon became enmeshed in social, economic, and political issues. The German peasants interpreted Luther's ideas in an economic sense: Christian liberty for them meant the end of harsh manorial burdens. Princes used the cloak of the new religious ideas both to acquire the material wealth of the church and to thwart the centralizing goals of the emperor. In England the political issue of the royal succession triggered that country's break with Rome, and in Switzerland and France the political and social ethos of Calvinism attracted many people. The Protestant doctrine that all callings have equal merit in God's sight and its stress on the home as the special domain of women drew women to Protestantism. The reformulation of Roman Catholic doctrine at the Council of Trent, the new religious orders such as the Jesuits and the Ursulines, and the Roman Inquisition all represented the Catholic response to the demands for reform.

The age of the Reformation presents very real paradoxes. The break with Rome and the rise of Lutheran, Anglican, Calvinist, and other faiths destroyed the unity of Europe as an organic Christian society. Saint Paul's exhortation "There should be no schism in the body [of the church]. . . . You are all one in Christ,"[37] was widely ignored. Yet religious belief remained tremendously strong. In fact, the strength of religious convictions caused political fragmentation. In the later sixteenth century and through most of the seventeenth, religion and religious issues continued to play a major role in the lives of individuals and in the policies and actions of governments. Religion, whether Protestant or Catholic, decisively influenced the growth of national states.

Scholars have maintained that the sixteenth century witnessed the beginnings of the modern world. They are both right and wrong. Although most of the church reformers rejected the idea of religious toleration, they helped pave the way for

it. They also paved the way for the eighteenth-century revolt against the Christian God, one of the strongest supports of life in Western culture. In this respect, the Reformation marked the beginning of the modern world, with its secularism and rootlessness. At the same time, it can equally be argued that the sixteenth century represented the culmination of the Middle Ages. Martin Luther's anxieties about salvation showed him to be very much a medieval man. His concerns had deeply troubled serious individuals since the time of Saint Augustine. In modern times, such concerns have tended to take different forms.

NOTES

1. Romans 12:2–3.
2. Quoted in J. Burckhardt, *The Civilization of the Renaissance in Italy* (London: Phaidon Books, 1951), p. 262.
3. See R. R. Post, *The Modern Devotion: Confrontation with Reformation and Humanism* (Leiden: E. J. Brill, 1968), esp. pp. 237–238, 255, 323–348.
4. E. Erikson, *Young Man Luther: A Study in Psychoanalysis and History* (New York: W. W. Norton, 1962).
5. Quoted in T. C. Mendenhall et al., eds., *Ideas and Institutions in European History: 800–1715* (New York: Henry Holt, 1948), p. 220.
6. Quoted in O. Chadwick, *The Reformation* (Baltimore: Penguin Books, 1976), p. 55.
7. Quoted in E. H. Harbison, *The Age of Reformation* (Ithaca, N.Y.: Cornell University Press, 1963), p. 52.
8. This passage is based heavily on ibid., pp. 52–55.
9. See S. E. Ozment, *The Reformation in the Cities: The Appeal of Protestantism to Sixteenth-Century Germany and Switzerland* (New Haven: Yale University Press, 1975), pp. 32–45.
10. See S. E. Ozment, *The Age of Reform, 1250–1550: An Intellectual and Religious History of Late Medieval and Reformation Europe* (New Haven: Yale University Press, 1980), pp. 273–279.
11. Quoted in ibid., p. 280.
12. Ibid., p. 281.
13. Ibid., p. 284.
14. Romans 13:1–2.
15. Erikson, p. 47.
16. G. Strauss, *Luther's House of Learning: Indoctrination of the Young in the German Reformation*

(Baltimore: Johns Hopkins University Press, 1978), esp. pp. 159–162, 231–233.

17. See R. H. Bainton, *Women of the Reformation in Germany and Italy* (Minneapolis: Augsburg, 1971), pp. 9–10; and Ozment, *The Reformation in the Cities,* pp. 53–54, 171–172.

18. Quoted in H. G. Haile, *Luther: An Experiment in Biography* (Garden City, N.Y.: Doubleday, 1980), p. 272.

19. Quoted in J. Atkinson, *Martin Luther and the Birth of Protestantism* (Baltimore: Penguin Books, 1968), pp. 247–248.

20. *Martin Luther: Three Treatises* (Philadelphia: Muhlenberg Press, 1947), pp. 28–31.

21. J. Allen, trans., *John Calvin: The Institutes of the Christian Religion* (Philadelphia: Westminster Press, 1930), bk. 3, chap. 21, paras. 5, 7.

22. E. W. Monter, *Calvin's Geneva* (New York: John Wiley & Sons, 1967), pp. 98–108.

23. Ibid., p. 137.

24. Quoted in Bainton, pp. 69–70.

25. A. G. Dickens, *The English Reformation* (New York: Schocken Books, 1964), p. 36.

26. E. Duffy, *The Stripping of the Altars: Traditional Religion in England, 1400–1580* (New Haven: Yale University Press, 1992), pp. 2–6.

27. See R. Marius, *Thomas More: A Biography* (New York: Alfred A. Knopf, 1984), pp. 215–216.

28. See S. E. Lehmberg, *The Reformation Parliament, 1529–1536* (Cambridge: Cambridge University Press, 1970), pp. 174–176, 204–205.

29. J. J. Scarisbrick, *The Reformation and the English People* (Oxford: Basil Blackwell, 1984), p. 81.

30. Ibid.

31. Quoted in P. Smith, *The Age of the Reformation,* rev. ed. (New York: Henry Holt, 1951), p. 346.

32. Ibid., p. 84.

33. See J. W. O'Malley, *The First Jesuits* (Cambridge, Mass.: Harvard University Press, 1993), p. 376

34. Ibid., p. 298.

35. Quoted in Chadwick, p. 270.

36. See P. Grendler, *The Roman Inquisition and the Venetian Press, 1540–1605* (Princeton, N.J.: Princeton University Press, 1977).

37. 1 Corinthians 1:25, 27.

SUGGESTED READING

There are many easily accessible and lucidly written general studies of the reformations of the sixteenth century. P. Chaunu, ed., *The Reformation* (1989), is a lavishly illustrated anthology of articles by an interna-tional team of scholars, a fine appreciation of both theological and historical developments, with an up-to-date bibliography. E. Cameron, *The European Ref-ormation* (1991), provides a comprehensive survey based on recent research; A. Pettegree, ed., *The Early Reformation in Europe* (1992), explores the reforma-tion as an international movement and compares de-velopments in different parts of Europe, and the books by Chadwick and Harbison listed in the Notes are good general introductions. L. W. Spitz, *The Prot-estant Reformation, 1517–1559* (1985), provides a comprehensive survey that incorporates the latest scholarly research. For the recent trend in scholarship interpreting the Reformation against the background of fifteenth-century reforming developments, see the excellent study of J. F. D'Amico, *Renaissance Human-ism in Papal Rome: Humanists and Churchmen on the Eve of the Reformation* (1983), and J. H. Overfield, *Humanism and Scholasticism in Late Medieval Germany* (1984), which portrays the intellectual life of the German universities, the milieu from which the Prot-estant Reformation emerged. Older studies include R. R. Post, *The Modern Devotion* (1968); G. Strauss, ed., *Manifestations of Discontent in Germany on the Eve of the Reformation* (1971), a useful and exciting col-lection of documents; and S. Ozment, *The Age of Reform, 1250–1550: An Intellectual and Religious His-tory of Late Medieval and Reformation Europe* (1980), which combines intellectual and social history. For the condition of the church in the late fifteenth and early sixteenth centuries, see D. Hay, *The Church in Italy in the Fifteenth Century* (1977), and P. Heath, *The Eng-lish Parish Clergy on the Eve of the Reformation* (1969); J. Moran, *The Growth of English Schooling, 1340–1548* (1985), also contains useful material.

For the central figure of the early Reformation, Martin Luther, students should see the works by At-kinson, Erikson, and Haile mentioned in the Notes; G. Brendler, *Martin Luther: Theology and Revolution* (1991), a response to the Marxist interpretation of Luther as a tool of the aristocracy who sold out the peasantry; and H. Boehmer, *Martin Luther: Road to Reformation* (1960), a well-balanced work treating Luther's formative years. Students may expect thor-ough and sound treatments of Luther's theology in the following distinguished works: H. Bornkamm, *Luther in Mid-Career, 1521–1530* (1983); A. E. McGrath, *Luther's Theology of the Cross: Martin Luther on Justification* (1985); M. Brecht, *Martin Luther: His Road to Reformation* (1985), which includes an explo-ration of Luther's background and youth; and J. Peli-kan, *Reformation of Church and Dogma, 1300–1700* (1986).

The best study of John Calvin is W. J. Bouwsma, *John Calvin: A Sixteenth-Century Portrait* (1988), an authoritative study that situates Calvin within Renaissance culture. See also F. Wendel, *Calvin: The Origins and Development of His Thought* (1963). W. E. Monter, *Calvin's Geneva* (1967), is an excellent account of the effect of Calvin's reforms on the social life of that Swiss city. R. T. Kendall, *Calvinism and English Calvinism to 1649* (1981), presents English conditions, whereas R. M. Mitchell, *Calvin and the Puritan's View of the Protestant Ethic* (1979), interprets the socioeconomic implications of Calvin's thought. Students interested in the left wing of the Reformation should see the profound, though difficult, work of G. H. Williams, *The Radical Reformers* (1962). For reform in other parts of Switzerland, see T. Brady, *Turning Swiss,* and L. P. Wendel, *Always Among Us: Images of the Poor in Zwingli's Zurich* (1990).

For various aspects of the social history of the period, see, in addition to the titles by Bainton and Ozment cited in the Notes, S. Ozment, *Magdalena and Balthasar* (1987), which reveals many features of social life through the letters of a Nuremburg couple; L. P. Buck and J. W. Zophy, eds., *The Social History of the Reformation* (1972); and K. von Greyerz, ed., *Religion and Society in Early Modern Europe, 1500–1800* (1984), both of which contain interesting essays on religion, society, and popular culture. Two books listed in the Notes make important contributions to social history: Ozment, *The Reformation in the Cities,* and Strauss, which describes how plain people were imbued with Reformation ideals and patterns of behavior. R. L. De Molen, *Leaders of the Reformation* (1984), contains provocative portraits of several figures, including Zwingli, Loyola, Cromwell, and Calvin. For women, see M. E. Wiesner, *Women and Gender in Early Modern Europe* (1993); L. Roper, *The Holy Household: Women and Morals in Reformation Augsburg* (1991), an important study in local, religious history as well as the history of gender; M. Wiesner, *Women in the Sixteenth Century: A Bibliography* (1983), a useful reference tool; and S. M. Wyntjes, "Women in the Reformation Era," in R. Bridenthal and C. Koonz, eds., *Becoming Visible: Women in European History* (1977), an interesting general survey. The best recent treatment of marriage and the family is S. Ozment, *When Fathers Ruled: Family Life in Reformation Europe* (1983). Ozment's edition of *Reformation Europe: A Guide to Research* (1982), contains not only helpful references but also valuable articles on such topics as "The German Peasants," "The Anabaptists," and "The Confessional Age: The Late Reformation in Germany." For

Servetus, see R. H. Bainton, *Hunted Heretic: The Life and Death of Michael Servetus* (1953), which remains valuable.

For England, in addition to the fundamental works by Duffy and Dickens cited in the Notes, K. Thomas, *Religion and the Decline of Magic* (1971), provides a useful treatment of pre-Reformation popular religion, as does Scarisbrick, also mentioned in the Notes, and S. T. Bindoff, *Tudor England* (1959), a good short synthesis. S. J. Gunn and P. G. Lindley, eds., *Cardinal Wolsey: Church, State and Art* (1991), is a useful study of that important prelate. The marital trials of Henry VIII are treated in both the sympathetic study by G. Mattingly, *Catherine of Aragon* (1949), and A. Fraser, *The Wives of Henry VIII* (1992). The legal implications of Henry VIII's divorces have been thoroughly analyzed in J. J. Scarisbrick, *Henry VIII* (1968), an almost definitive biography. On the dissolution of the English monasteries, see D. Knowles, *The Religious Orders in England,* vol. 3 (1959), one of the finest examples of historical prose in English written in the twentieth century. D. Knowles, *Bare Ruined Choirs* (1976), is an attractively illustrated abridgment of *The Religious Orders.* G. R. Elton, *The Tudor Revolution in Government* (1959), discusses the modernization of English government under Thomas Cromwell, whereas the same author's *Reform and Reformation: England, 1509–1558* (1977), combines political and social history in a broad study. Many aspects of English social history are discussed in J. Youings, *Sixteenth Century England* (1984), a beautifully written work, which is highly recommended. The biography of Thomas More by Marius, listed in the Notes, provides a thorough and perceptive study of the great humanist, lord chancellor, and saint.

P. Janelle, *The Catholic Reformation* (1951), is a comprehensive treatment of the Catholic Reformation from a Catholic point of view, and A. G. Dickens, *The Counter Reformation* (1969), gives the Protestant standpoint in a beautifully illustrated book. The definitive study of the Council of Trent was written by H. Jedin, *A History of the Council of Trent,* 3 vols. (1957–1961). For the Jesuits, see W. W. Meissner, *Ignatius of Loyola: The Psychology of a Saint* (1993), and J. W. O'Malley, *The First Jesuits* (1963). These books are basic not only for the beginnings of the society but also for the refutation of many myths. Perhaps the best recent work on the Spanish Inquisition is W. Monter, *Frontiers of Heresy: The Spanish Inquisition from the Basque Lands to Sicily* (1990).

LISTENING TO THE
PAST

Grievances of the Peasants of Stühlingen and Lupfen

When Count Sigismund von Lupfen inherited estates in the county of Stühlingen in southwestern Germany, he found himself in dire financial trouble: his late father had been very extravagant. The count determined to squeeze as much revenue as possible from his peasants. In June 1524 he ordered the peasants to stop harvest work to collect strawberries for a banquet and snail shells on which the ladies of the manor wound thread. Strawberries proved to be the proverbial straws that broke the camel's back.

Rebellion and disorder erupted among the rural population. When attempts at negotiation failed, the peasants sought the support of Duke Ulrich of Wurttemburg, and the revolt soon spread to about a third of Germany. Ultimately, peasant demands were drawn up and presented to the justices of the Imperial Chamber Court, an extraterritorial "national" tribunal. The articles that follow provide a detailed statement of peasant grievances and a picture of peasant conditions in early modern times.

The counts of Stühlingen and Lupfen should not imprison any resident involved in a civil action.

In the old days it was the custom and usage in the above-mentioned county to imprison no one against whom a civil action was pending, as long as the man held some property in the county and was willing to furnish surety for the matter or sum being asked of him. In recent times, however, our lords have ignored our village courts, where, according to our laws and customs, they should bring action. If they think that a man owes them something or if they suspect that someone has committed an offense, they order the bailiff to take the accused to prison and let him lie there until he has made his peace with them according to their bidding. . . .

What happens when a marriage partner dies and the deceased is claimed by the lord as a bondsman?

Marriage is an institution sanctioned by divine and Christian laws and is, moreover, free, so that in case of death nothing should be taken away from either of the partners. But when a man or a woman of the county takes for wife or husband a person not from the county and not bonded to the count, and the man dies and is claimed by the count as his bondsman, the count's officials come and take the best head of cattle. If the woman dies, they take her best frocks, even her wedding garments, and sometimes also a bed. In some places they also take clothes when the husband has died. It is our request that in future such exactions cease and we be no longer compelled to surrender cattle, clothes, beds, or anything else in case of death.

Our lords and their bailiffs and retainers do their hawking and hunting on our fields without showing consideration for the condition of the crops.

We till our fields and meadows with great effort, cost, and work so as to be able to fulfill our obligations to our lords and to nourish our wives and children. In return for this our lords and their bailiffs ought to guard us and our property and protect us from harm. Instead, they ride and tramp over our meadows and fields in pursuit of the pleasure of hunting, hawking, and the chase. They do this without giving a thought to the harm and grief that come to us as we see our crops so brutally destroyed. It is our plea that our lords be made to realize that they should refrain from this destructive sport, but if they persist and we continue to suffer the ruin of our crops, they should be held accountable for the damage.

The penalty for assault used to be three or five shillings, but now this offense is treated as a felony.

The old customs hold that when a man strikes another on the face and is convicted of it, he forfeits a fine not to exceed five shillings and is tried before his own sub-bailiff or bailiff. But nowadays our lords have begun to treat the offense as a felony and transferred jurisdiction over it from our sub-bailiffs to their own officials. We ask that the old custom be restored and the offense in question be treated as nothing more than a misdemeanor and not as a felony. . . .

Wild game ought to be altogether free.

We perform long and hard labor on our fields in order to raise crops (of which we are obliged to give a portion to our lords) and to make a living for ourselves and our wives and children. But much of our work is brought to nothing by the profusion in our land of wild game, which is ruinous to our crops. Though God and the common law decree that wild game, having been created to supply the common needs of mankind, may be trapped and hunted by everyone, our lords have proclaimed injunctions and heavy penalties against the snaring, trapping, hunting and catching of game. If a man violates these prohibitions and is caught, they gouge out his eye or torture him in other ways according to the counts' or their bailiffs' pleasure. It is our plea that by the authority of divine and common law, we be henceforth permitted to hunt, shoot, and trap all game found on our fields and properties and use it to fill our requirements. . . .

Concerning bondage and serfdom.

Although by rights every man is born free and neither we nor our ancestors have been guilty of anything that should have made serfs of us, our lords claim that we are and ought to be their bondsmen and that we are obliged to do whatever they command us to do as though we were born slaves—and it may well happen in time that we will be sold like slaves. It is our strong plea and request that the counts be made to recognize that they ought to release us from serfdom and should never press another man into bondage. Apart from this plea, we pledge ourselves to act as loyal subjects, and we promise faithfully to perform all duties we owe to our lords according to custom and tradition.

❖ Peasants fighting at the Battle of Gaisbeuren during the Peasants' War, 1525. *(Source: Siegfried Lauterwasser)*

Questions for Analysis

1. What were the peasants' grievances?

2. On what basis did the peasants justify those grievances? (Bear in mind that in many parts of Europe law was custom embedded in folk memory and community knowledge.)

3. How do you account for the fact that there were no religious issues involved?

Source: G. Strauss, ed. and trans., *Manifestations of Discontent in Germany on the Eve of the Reformation* Copyright © 1971 by Indiana University Press.

15

The Age of European Expansion and Religious Wars

Between 1560 and 1648 two developments dramatically altered the world in which Europeans lived: overseas expansion and the reformations of the Christian churches. Overseas expansion broadened the geographical horizons of Europeans and brought them into confrontation with ancient civilizations in Africa, Asia, and the Americas. These confrontations led first to conquest, then to exploitation, and finally to profound social changes in both Europe and the conquered territories. Likewise, the Renaissance and the reformations drastically changed cultural, political, religious, and social life in Europe and inspired magnificent literary, artistic, and musical achievements. War and religious issues dominated politics and were intertwined: religion was commonly used to rationalize wars, which were fought for power and territorial expansion. Meanwhile, Europeans carried their political, religious, and social attitudes to their newly acquired territories.

- How and why, in the sixteenth and seventeenth centuries, did a relatively small group living on the edge of the Eurasian landmass gain control of the major sea-lanes of the world and establish political and economic hegemony on distant continents?

- What immediate effect did overseas expansion have on Europe and on the conquered societies?

- What were the causes and consequences of the religious wars in France, the Netherlands, and Germany?

- How did the religious crises of this period affect religious faith, literary and artistic developments, and the status of women?

A detail from an early 16th-century Flemish painting depicting maps, illustrated travel books, a globe, a compass, and an astrolabe. *(Source: Reproduced by courtesy of the Trustees, The National Gallery, London)*

- How and why did slave labor become the dominant form of labor organization in the New World?

This chapter will address these questions.

✥ DISCOVERY, RECONNAISSANCE, AND EXPANSION

Historians have variously called the period from 1450 to 1650 the "Age of Discovery," the "Age of Reconnaissance," and the "Age of Expansion." All three labels are appropriate. The Age of Discovery refers to the era's phenomenal advances in geographical knowledge and technology, often achieved through trial and error. In 1350 it took as long to sail from the eastern end of the Mediterranean to the western end as it had taken a thousand years earlier. Even in the fifteenth century, Europeans knew little more about the earth's surface than the Romans had. By 1650, however, Europeans had made an extensive reconnaissance—or preliminary exploration—and had sketched fairly accurately the physical outline of the whole earth. Much of the geographical information they had gathered was tentative and not fully understood—hence the appropriateness of the term the Age of Reconnaissance.

The designation of the era as the Age of Expansion refers to the migration of Europeans to other parts of the world. This colonization resulted in political control of much of South and North America; coastal regions of Africa, India, China, and Japan; and many Pacific islands. This political hegemony was accompanied by economic exploitation, religious domination, and the introduction of European patterns of social and intellectual life. Indeed, the sixteenth-century expansion of European society launched a new age in world history.

Overseas Exploration and Conquest

The outward expansion of Europe began with the Viking voyages across the Atlantic in the ninth and tenth centuries. Under Eric the Red and Leif Ericson, the Vikings discovered Greenland and the eastern coast of North America. The Vikings also made permanent settlements in, and a legal imprint on, Iceland, Ireland, England, Normandy, and Sicily (see pages 259–260). The Crusades of the eleventh through thirteenth centuries were another phase in Europe's attempt to explore and exploit peoples on the periphery of the Continent. But the lack of a strong territorial base, superior Muslim military strength, and sheer misrule combined to make the Crusader kingdoms short-lived. In the mid-fifteenth century, Europe seemed ill-prepared for further international ventures, and by 1450 a grave new threat had appeared in the East—the Ottoman Turks.

Combining excellent military strategy with efficient administration of their conquered territories, the Turks had subdued most of Asia Minor and begun to settle on the western side of the Bosporus. The Muslim Ottoman Turks under Sultan Mohammed II (r. 1451–1481) captured Constantinople in 1453, pressed northwest into the Balkans, and by the early sixteenth century controlled the eastern Mediterranean. The Turkish menace badly frightened Europeans. In France in the fifteenth and sixteenth centuries, twice as many books were printed about the Turkish threat as about the American discoveries. Yet the fifteenth and sixteenth centuries witnessed a fantastic continuation, on a global scale, of European expansion.

Political centralization in Spain, France, and England helps explain those countries' outward push. In the fifteenth century, Isabella and Ferdinand had consolidated their several kingdoms to achieve a more united Spain. The Catholic rulers revamped the Spanish bureaucracy and humbled the Muslims and the Jews. The Spanish monarchy was stronger than ever before and in a position to support foreign ventures; it could bear the costs and dangers of exploration. But Portugal, situated on the extreme southwestern edge of the European continent, got the start on the rest of Europe. Still insignificant as a European land power despite its recently secured frontiers, Portugal sought greatness in the unknown world overseas.

Portugal's taking of Ceuta, an Arab city in northern Morocco, in 1415 marked the beginning of European exploration and control of overseas territory. The objectives of Portuguese policy included the historic Iberian crusade to Christianize Muslims and to find gold, an overseas route to the spice markets of India, and the mythical Christian ruler of Ethiopia, Prester John.

In the early phases of Portuguese exploration, Prince Henry (1394–1460), called "the Naviga-

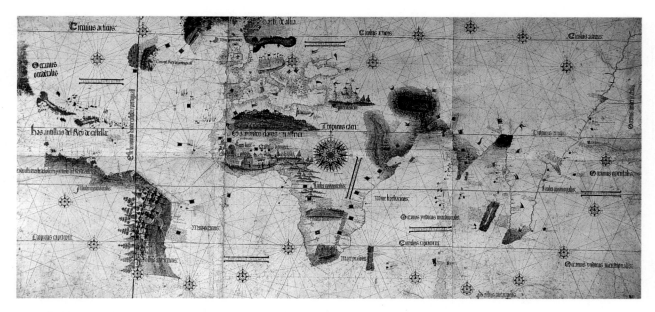

❖ **The Cantino Map** (1502), named for the agent secretly commissioned to design it in Lisbon for the Duke of Ferrara, an avid Italian map collector, reveals such a good knowledge of the African continent, of the islands of the West Indies, and of the shoreline of present-day Venezuela, Guiana, and Brazil in South America that modern scholars suspect there may have been clandestine voyages to the Americas shortly after Columbus's. *(Source: Biblioteca Estense Universitaria, Modena)*

tor" because of the annual expeditions he sent down the western coast of Africa, played the leading role. In the fifteenth century, most of the gold that reached Europe came from the Sudan in West Africa and from the Akan peoples living near the area of present-day Ghana. Muslim caravans brought the gold from the African cities of Niani and Timbuktu and carried it north across the Sahara to Mediterranean ports. Then the Portuguese muscled in on this commerce in gold. Prince Henry's carefully planned expeditions succeeded in reaching Guinea, and under King John II (r. 1481–1495) the Portuguese established trading posts and forts on the Guinea coast and penetrated into the continent all the way to Timbuktu (Map 15.1). Portuguese ships transported gold to Lisbon, and by 1500 Portugal controlled the flow of gold to Europe. The golden century of Portuguese prosperity had begun.

Still the Portuguese pushed farther south down the west coast of Africa. In 1487 Bartholomew Diaz rounded the Cape of Good Hope at the southern tip, but storms and a threatened mutiny forced him to turn back. On a later expedition (1497–1499), the Portuguese mariner Vasco da Gama reached India and returned to Lisbon loaded with samples of Indian wares. King Manuel (r. 1495–1521) promptly dispatched thirteen ships under the command of Pedro Alvares Cabral, assisted by Diaz, to set up trading posts in India. On April 22, 1500, the coast of Brazil in South America was sighted and claimed for the crown of Portugal. Cabral then proceeded south and east around the Cape of Good Hope and reached India. Half the fleet was lost on the return voyage, but the six spice-laden vessels that dropped anchor in Lisbon harbor in July 1501 more than paid for the entire expedition. Thereafter, convoys were sent out every March. Lisbon became the entrance port for Asian goods into Europe—but this was not accomplished without a fight.

For centuries the Muslims had controlled the rich spice trade of the Indian Ocean, and they did not surrender it willingly. Portuguese commercial activities were accompanied by the destruction or seizure of strategic Muslim coastal forts, which

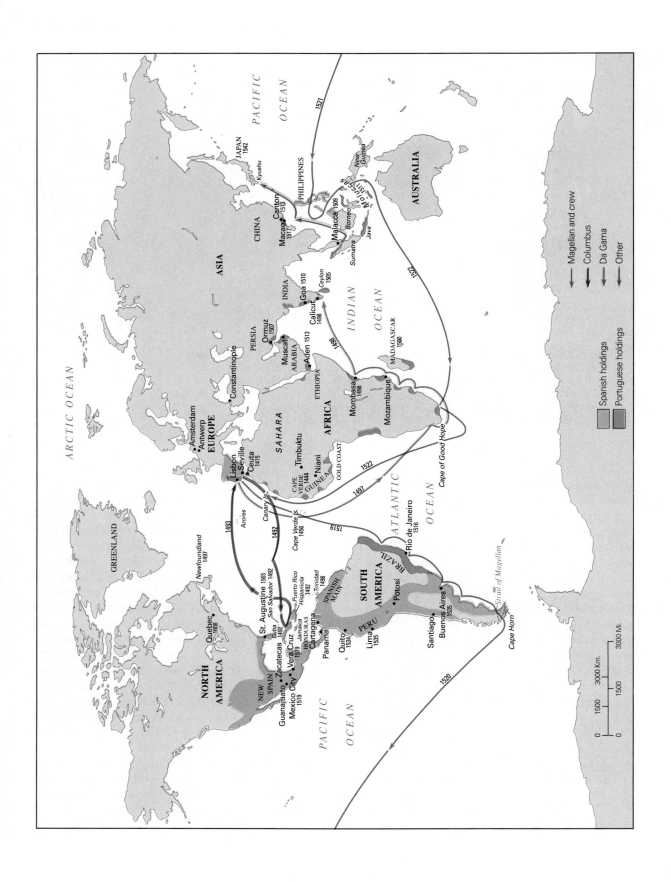

later served Portugal as both trading posts and military bases. Alfonso de Albuquerque, whom the Portuguese crown appointed as governor of India (1509–1515), decided that these bases, not inland territories, should control the Indian Ocean. Accordingly, his cannon blasted open the ports of Calicut, Ormuz, Goa, and Malacca, the vital centers of Arab domination of south Asian trade. This bombardment laid the foundation for Portuguese imperialism in the sixteenth and seventeenth centuries: a strange way to bring Christianity to "those who were in darkness." As one scholar wrote about the opening of China to the West, "while Buddha came to China on white elephants, Christ was borne on cannon balls."[1]

In March 1493, between the voyages of Diaz and da Gama, Spanish ships entered Lisbon harbor bearing a triumphant Italian explorer in the service of the Spanish monarchy. Christopher Columbus (1451–1506), a Genoese mariner, had secured Spanish support for an expedition to the East (see Listening to the Past). He had sailed from Palos, Spain, to the Canary Islands and crossed the Atlantic to the Bahamas, landing in October 1492 on an island that he named "San Salvador" and believed to be the coast of India.

Technological Stimuli to Exploration

Technological developments were the key to Europe's remarkable outreach. By 1350 *cannon*— iron or bronze guns that fired iron or stone balls— had been fully developed in western Europe. These pieces of artillery emitted frightening noises and great flashes of fire and could batter down fortresses and even city walls. Sultan Mohammed II's siege of Constantinople in 1453 provides a classic illustration of the effectiveness of cannon fire.

Constantinople had very strong walled fortifications. The sultan secured the services of a Western technician who built fifty-six small cannon and a gigantic gun that could hurl stone balls weighing about 800 pounds. The gun could be moved only by several hundred oxen and loaded and fired only by about a hundred men working together. Re-

◆ **MAP 15.1 Overseas Exploration and Conquest, Fifteenth and Sixteenth Centuries** The voyages of discovery marked another phase in the centuries-old migrations of European peoples. Consider the major contemporary significance of each of the three voyages depicted on the map.

loading took two hours. This awkward but powerful weapon breached the walls of Constantinople, which cracked on the second day of the bombardment. Lesser cannon finished the job.

Early cannon posed serious technical difficulties. Iron cannon were cheaper than bronze to construct, but they were difficult to cast effectively and were liable to crack and injure artillerymen. Bronze guns, made of copper and tin, were less subject than iron to corrosion, but they were very expensive. All cannon were extraordinarily difficult to move, required considerable time for reloading, and were highly inaccurate. They thus proved inefficient for land warfare. However, they could be used at sea.

The mounting of cannon on ships and improved techniques of shipbuilding gave impetus to European expansion. Since ancient times, most seagoing vessels had been narrow, open boats called *galleys,* propelled largely by manpower. Slaves or convicts who had been sentenced to the galleys manned the oars of the ships that sailed the Mediterranean, and both cargo ships and warships carried soldiers for defense. Though well suited to the placid and thoroughly explored waters of the Mediterranean, galleys could not withstand the rough winds and uncharted shoals of the Atlantic. The need for sturdier craft as well as population losses caused by the Black Death forced the development of a new style of ship that would not require soldiers for defense or much manpower to sail.

In the course of the fifteenth century, the Portuguese developed the *caravel,* a small, light, three-masted sailing ship. Though somewhat slower than the galley, the caravel held more cargo and was highly maneuverable. When fitted with cannon, it could dominate larger vessels, such as the round ships commonly used as merchantmen. The substitution of windpower for manpower, and artillery fire for soldiers, signaled a great technological advance and gave Europeans navigational and fighting ascendancy over the rest of the world.[2]

Other fifteenth-century developments in navigation helped make possible the conquest of the Atlantic. The magnetic compass enabled sailors to determine their direction and position at sea. The *astrolabe,* an instrument developed by Muslim navigators in the twelfth century and used to determine the altitude of the sun and other celestial bodies, permitted mariners to plot their *latitude,* or position north or south of the equator. Steadily

❖ **Nocturnal** An instrument for determining the hour of night at sea by finding the progress of certain stars around the polestar (center aperture). *(Source: National Maritime Museum, London)*

improved maps and sea charts provided information about distance, sea depths, and general geography.

The Explorers' Motives

The expansion of Europe was not motivated by demographic pressures. The Black Death had caused serious population losses from which Europe had not recovered in 1500. Few Europeans emigrated to North or South America in the sixteenth century. Half of those who did sail to begin a new life in America died en route; half of those who reached the New World eventually returned to their homeland. Why, then, did explorers brave the Atlantic and Pacific oceans, risking their lives to discover new continents and spread European culture?

The reasons are varied and complex. People of the sixteenth century were still basically medieval in the sense that their attitudes and values were shaped by religion and expressed in religious terms. In the late fifteenth century, crusading fervor remained a basic part of the Portuguese and Spanish national ideal. The desire to Christianize

Muslims and pagan peoples played a central role in European expansion. Queen Isabella of Spain, for example, showed a fanatical zeal for converting the Muslims to Christianity, and she concentrated her efforts on the Muslims in Granada. After the abortive crusading attempts of the thirteenth century, Isabella and other rulers realized full well that they lacked the material resources to mount the full-scale assault on Islam necessary for victory. Crusading impulses thus shifted from the Muslims to the pagan peoples of Africa and the Americas.

Moreover, after the reconquista, enterprising young men of the Spanish upper classes found their economic and political opportunities severely limited. As a recent study of the Castilian city of Ciudad Real shows, the ancient aristocracy controlled the best agricultural land and monopolized urban administrative posts. Great merchants and a few nobles (surprisingly, since Spanish law forbade noble participation in commercial ventures) dominated the textile and leather-glove manufacturing industries. Consequently, many ambitious men immigrated to the Americas to seek their fortunes.[3]

Government sponsorship and encouragement of exploration also accounted for the results of the various voyages. Mariners and explorers could not as private individuals afford the massive sums needed to explore mysterious oceans and control remote continents. The strong financial support of Prince Henry the Navigator led to Portugal's phenomenal success in the spice trade. Even the grudging and modest assistance of Isabella and Ferdinand eventually brought untold riches—and complicated problems—to Spain. The Dutch in the seventeenth century, through such government-sponsored trading companies as the Dutch East India Company, reaped enormous wealth, and although the Netherlands was a small country in size, it dominated the European economy in 1650. In England, by contrast, Henry VII's lack of interest in exploration delayed English expansion for a century.

Scholars have frequently described the European discoveries as a manifestation of Renaissance curiosity about the physical universe, the desire to know more about the geography and peoples of the world. There is truth to this explanation. Cosmography, natural history, and geography aroused enormous interest among educated people in the fifteenth and sixteenth centuries. Just as science fiction and speculation about life on other planets excite readers today, quasi-scientific literature about Africa, Asia, and the Americas captured the imaginations of literate Europeans. Fernández de Oviedo's *General History of the Indies* (1547), a detailed eyewitness account of plants, animals, and peoples, was widely read.

Spices were another important incentive to voyages of discovery. Introduced into western Europe

❖ **Pepper Harvest** To break the monotony of a bland diet, Europeans had a passion for pepper which—along with cinnamon, cloves, nutmeg, and ginger—was the main object of the Asian trade. Since one kilo of pepper cost two grams of silver at the place of production in the East Indies, 10 to 14 grams of silver in Alexandria, Egypt, 14 to 18 grams in Venice, and 20 to 30 grams at the markets of northern Europe, we can appreciate the 15th-century expression "As dear as pepper." Here natives fill vats, while the dealer tastes a pepper corn for pungency. *(Source: Bibliothèque Nationale, Paris)*

by the Crusaders in the twelfth century, nutmeg, mace, ginger, cinnamon, and pepper added flavor and variety to the monotonous diet of Europeans. Spices were also used in the preparation of medicinal drugs and incense for religious ceremonies. In the late thirteenth century, Venetian Marco Polo (1254?–1324?), the greatest of medieval travelers, had visited the court of the Chinese emperor. The widely publicized account of his travels in the *Book of Various Experiences* (c. 1298) stimulated the trade in spices between Asia and Italy. The Venetians came to hold a monopoly of that trade in western Europe.

Spices were grown in India and China, shipped across the Indian Ocean to ports on the Persian Gulf, and then transported by Arabs across the Arabian Desert to Mediterranean ports. But the rise of the Ming Dynasty in China in the late fourteenth century resulted in the expulsion of foreigners. And the steady penetration of the Ottoman Turks into the eastern Mediterranean and of Muslims across North Africa forced Europeans to seek a new route to the Asian spice markets.

The basic reason for European exploration and expansion, however, was the quest for material profit. Mariners and explorers frankly admitted this. As Bartholomew Diaz put the matter, his motives were "to serve God and His Majesty, to give light to those who were in darkness and to grow rich as all men desire to do." When Vasco da Gama reached the port of Calicut, India, in 1498, a native asked what the Portuguese wanted. Da Gama replied, "Christians and spices."[4] The bluntest of the Spanish conquistadors, Hernando Cortez, announced as he prepared to conquer Mexico, "I have come to win gold, not to plow the fields like a peasant."[5]

Spanish and Portuguese explorers carried the fervent Catholicism and missionary zeal of the Iberian Peninsula to the New World, and once in America they urged home governments to send clerics. At bottom, however, wealth was the driving motivation. A sixteenth-century diplomat, Ogier Gheselin de Busbecq, summed up this paradoxical attitude well: in expeditions to the Indies and the Antipodes, he said, "religion supplies the pretext and gold the motive."[6]

The Problem of Christopher Columbus

The year 1992, which marked the quincentenary of Columbus's first voyages to the Americas,

spawned an enormous amount of discussion about the significance of his voyages. Journalists, scholars, amateurs, and polemicists debated Columbus's accomplishments and failures. Until the 1980s, however, most writers would have generally agreed with Harvard historian Samuel Eliot Morison in his 1942 biography of the explorer:

The whole history of the Americas stems from the Four Voyages of Columbus; and as the Greek city-states looked back to the deathless gods as their founders, so today a score of independent nations and dominions unite in homage to Columbus, the stout-hearted son of Genoa, who carried Christian civilization across the Ocean Sea.[7]

In 1942, we must remember, the Western Powers believed they were engaged in a life and death struggle to defend "Christian civilization" against the evil forces of fascism.

In contrast to this lavish praise, Columbus has recently undergone severe criticism. He enslaved and sometimes killed the Indians he encountered. He was a cruel and ineffective governor of Spain's Caribbean colony. Moreover, he did not discover the continents: others—Africans and European—had been there before him. And not only did he not discover the continents; he also misunderstood what he had found. In short, he was a fool who did not know what was going on around him. Some have criticized him because he abandoned the mother of his illegitimate son. Other writers have faulted Columbus as an opportunistic adventurer who loved the trappings of grand titles. Some claim he was the originator of European exploitation of the non-European world; he destroyed the paradise that had been the New World.[8] Because these judgments rest on social and ethical standards that did not exist in Columbus's world, responsible scholars consider them ahistorical.

Using the evidence of his journal (sea log) and letters, let us ask three basic questions. First, what kind of man was Columbus, and what forces or influences shaped him? Second, in sailing westward from Europe, what were his goals? Third, did he achieve his goals, and what did he make of his discoveries?

The central feature in the character of Christopher Columbus is that he was a deeply religious man. He began the *Journal* of his voyage to the Americas in the form of a letter to Ferdinand and Isabella of Spain:

On 2 January in the year 1492, when your Highnesses had concluded their war with the Moors who reigned in Europe, I saw your Highnesses banners victoriously raised on the towers of the Alhambra, the citadel of the city, and the Moorish king come out of the city gates and kiss the hands of your Highnesses and the prince, My Lord. And later in that same month, on the grounds of information I had given your Highnesses concerning the lands of India . . . your Highnesses decided to send me, Christopher Columbus, to see these parts of India and the princes and peoples of those lands and consider the best means for their conversion.[9]

Thus he had witnessed the Spanish reconquest of Granada and shared fully in the religious and nationalistic fervor surrounding that event. Just seven months separated Isabella and Ferdinand's entry into Granada on January 2 and Columbus's departure westward on August 3, 1492. In his mind, the two events were clearly linked. Long after Europeans knew something of Columbus's discoveries in the Caribbean, they nevertheless considered the restoration of Muslim Granada to Christian hands as Ferdinand and Isabella's greatest achievement; for the reconquest the Spanish pope Alexander VI rewarded them in 1494 with the title "Most Catholic Kings." Like the Spanish rulers and most Europeans of his age, Columbus understood Christianity as a missionary religion that should be carried to places and peoples where it did not exist. Although Columbus certainly had material and secular goals, first and foremost, as he wrote in 1498, he believed he was a divine agent:

God made me the messenger of the new heaven and the new earth of which he spoke in the Apocalypse of St. John after having spoken of it through the mouth of the prophet Isaiah; and he showed me the post where to find it.[10]

Columbus was also very knowledgeable about the sea. He was familiar with such fifteenth-century Portuguese navigational developments as portolans—written description of the courses along which ships sailed showing bays, coves, capes, ports, and the distances between these places—and the use of the magnetic needle as a nautical instrument. Columbus had spent years consulting geographers, mapmakers, and navigators. And, as he implied in his *Journal,* he had acquired not only theoretical but also practical experience: "I have spent twenty-three years at sea and have not left it for any length of time worth mentioning, and I have seen everything from east to west [meaning he had been to England] and I have been to Guinea [north and west Africa]."[11] Although some of Columbus's geographical theories, such as his measurement of the distance from Portugal to Japan at 2,760 miles, when it is actually 12,000, proved inaccurate, his successful thirty-three-day voyage to the Caribbean owed a great deal to his seamanship and his knowledge of accurate use of instruments.

What was the object of this first voyage? What did Columbus set out to do? He gave the answer in the very title of the expedition, "The Enterprise of the Indies." He wanted to find a direct ocean route to Asia that would provide the opportunity for a greatly expanded trade in which the European economy, and especially Spain, would participate. Two recent scholars have written, "If Columbus had not sailed westward in search of Asia, someone else would have done so. The time was right for such a bold undertaking." Someone else might have done so, but the fact remains that Columbus, displaying a characteristic Renaissance curiosity and restless drive, actually did it.

How did Columbus interpret what he had found, and in his mind did he achieve what he had set out to do? His mind had been formed by the Bible and the geographical writings of classical authors, as had the minds of most educated people of his times. Thus as people have often done in every age, Columbus ignored the evidence of his eyes and described what he saw in the Caribbean as an idyllic paradise, a peaceful garden of Eden. When accounts of his travels were published, Europeans' immediate fascination with this image of the New World meant that Columbus's propaganda created an instant myth. But having sensed that he had not found the spice markets and bazaars of Asia, his goal shifted from establishing trade with the (East) Indians and Chinese to establishing the kind of trade the Portuguese then conducted with Africa and with the Atlantic islands. That meant setting up some form of government in the islands, and Columbus had little interest in or capacity for governing. In 1496 he had forcibly subjugated the island of Hispaniola, enslaved the Indians, and laid the basis for a system of land grants tied to the Indians' labor service. Borrowing practices and institutions from reconquest Spain and the Canary Islands, Columbus laid the foundation for Spanish imperial administration. In all of this, Columbus was very much a man of his times. He never understood, however, that the scale of his discoveries created problems of trade, settlers, relations with the Indians, and, above all, government bureaucracy.[12]

LATER EXPLORERS

News of Columbus's first voyage rapidly spread across Europe. On April 1, 1493, a printer in Barcelona published in Spanish Columbus's letter describing what he believed he had found. By the end of that month the letter had been translated into Latin and published in Rome as *De Insulis Inventis* (On the Discoveries of the Islands). Within a year, printers in Paris, Basel, Antwerp, and Venice had brought out six more Latin editions, which were soon followed by translations in German and Tuscan, the dialect of the Florentines. In a 1503 letter Florentine navigator Amerigo Vespucci (1454–1512), in whose honor America was named, wrote, "Those new regions which we found and explored with the fleet . . . we may rightly call a New World." This letter, titled *Mundus Novus* (The New World), was the first document to describe America as a continent separate from Asia. Some scholars today try to avoid the terms *discovery* and *New World,* lest they be considered Eurocentric, but the use of those words rests on a tradition begun by the early explorers themselves.

The Caribbean islands—the West Indies—represented to zealous Spanish missionaries millions of Indian natives for conversion to Christianity. Hispaniola, Cuba, and Puerto Rico also offered, they thought, gold. Forced labor and starvation in the Spaniards' gold mines rapidly killed off the Indians. Even more, diseases brought by Europeans, against which the long-isolated Indians had no immunity, had a devastating effect on the native people. When Columbus arrived in 1492, the population of Hispaniola stood at approximately 100,000; in 1570, 300 people survived. Indian slaves from the Bahamas and black Africans from Guinea were then imported to do the mining.

The search for precious metals determined the direction of Spanish exploration and expansion into South America. When it became apparent that placer mining (in which ore is separated from soil by panning) in the Caribbean islands was slow and the rewards slim, new routes to the East and new sources of gold and silver were sought.

In 1519 Spanish ruler Charles V commissioned Ferdinand Magellan (1480–1521) to find a direct route to the Moluccan Islands off the southeast coast of Asia. Magellan sailed southwest across the Atlantic to Brazil and proceeded south around Cape Horn into the Pacific Ocean (see Map 15.1). He crossed the Pacific, sailing west, to the Malay Archipelago, which he called the "Western Isles." (Some of these islands were conquered in the 1560s and named the "Philippines" for Philip II of Spain.)

Though Magellan was killed, the expedition continued, returning to Spain in 1522 from the east by way of the Indian Ocean, the Cape of Good Hope, and the Atlantic. Terrible storms, mutiny, starvation, and disease haunted this voyage. Nevertheless, it verified the theory that the earth was round and brought information about the vastness of the Pacific. Magellan also proved that the earth was much larger than Columbus had estimated.

In the West Indies, the slow recovery of gold, the shortage of a healthy labor force, and sheer restlessness speeded up Spain's search for wealth. In 1519, the year Magellan departed on his worldwide expedition, a brash and determined Spanish adventurer, Hernando Cortez (1485–1547), crossed from Hispaniola to mainland Mexico with six hundred men, seventeen horses, and ten cannon. Within three years, Cortez had conquered the fabulously rich Aztec Empire, taken captive the Aztec emperor Montezuma, and founded Mexico City as the capital of New Spain. The subjugation of northern Mexico took longer, but between 1531 and 1550 the Spanish gained control of Zacatecas and Guanajuato, where rich silver veins were soon tapped.

Another Spanish conquistador, Francisco Pizarro (1470–1541), repeated Cortez's feat in Peru. Between 1531 and 1536, with even fewer resources, Pizarro crushed the Inca Empire in western South America and established the Spanish viceroyalty of Peru, with its center at Lima. In 1545 the Spanish opened at Potosí in the Peruvian highlands what became the richest silver mines in the New World.

Between 1525 and 1575, the riches of the Americas poured into the Spanish port of Seville and the Portuguese capital of Lisbon. For all their new wealth, however, Lisbon and Seville did not become important trading centers. It was the Flemish city of Antwerp, controlled by the Spanish Habsburgs, that developed into the great entrepôt for overseas bullion and Portuguese spices and served as the commercial and financial capital of the entire European world.

Since the time of the great medieval fairs, cities of the Low Countries (so called because much of the land lies below sea level) had been important sites for the exchange of products from the Baltic and Italy. Antwerp, ideally situated on the Scheldt River at the intersection of many trading routes, steadily expanded as the chief intermediary for international commerce and finance. English woolens; Baltic wheat, fur, and timber; Portuguese spices; German iron and copper; Spanish fruit; French wines and dyestuffs; Italian silks, marbles, and mirrors; and vast amounts of cash—all were exchanged at Antwerp. The city's harbor could dock twenty-five hundred vessels at once, and five thousand merchants from many nations gathered daily in the *bourse* (or exchange). Spanish silver was drained to the Netherlands to pay for food and luxury goods. Even so, the desire for economic independence from Spain was to play a major role in the revolt of the Netherlands in the late sixteenth century.

By the end of the sixteenth century, Amsterdam had overtaken Antwerp as the financial capital of Europe. The Dutch had also embarked on foreign exploration and conquest. The Dutch East India Company, founded in 1602, became the major organ of Dutch imperialism and within a few decades expelled the Portuguese from Ceylon and other East Indian islands. By 1650 the Dutch West India Company had successfully intruded on the Spanish possessions in the Americas, in the process gaining control of much of the African and American trade.

English and French explorations lacked the immediate, sensational results of those of the Spanish and Portuguese. In 1497 John Cabot, a Genoese merchant living in London, sailed for Brazil but discovered Newfoundland. The next year he returned and explored the New England coast and perhaps as far south as Delaware. Since these expeditions found no spices or gold, King Henry VII lost interest in exploration. Between 1534 and 1541, Frenchman Jacques Cartier made several voyages and explored the Saint Lawrence region of

Canada, but the first permanent French settlement, at Quebec, was not founded until 1608.

The Economic Effects of Spain's Discoveries in the New World

The sixteenth century has often been called the "Golden Century" of Spain. The influence of Spanish armies, Spanish Catholicism, and Spanish wealth was felt all over Europe. This greatness rested largely on the influx of precious metals from the New World. The mines at Zacatecas and Guanajuato in Mexico and Potosí in Peru poured out huge quantities of precious metals. To protect this treasure from French and English pirates, armed convoys transported it each year to Spain. Between 1503 and 1650, 16 million kilograms of silver and 185,000 kilograms of gold entered the port of Seville.

Meanwhile, Spain was experiencing a steady population increase, creating a sharp rise in the demand for food and goods. Spanish colonies in the Americas also represented a demand for products. Because Spain had expelled some of its best farmers and business people, the Jews in 1492 and the Muslims in the sixteenth and seventeenth centuries, the Spanish economy suffered and could not meet the new demands. Prices rose and with them, the costs of manufacturing cloth and other goods. As a result, Spanish products could not compete in the international market with cheaper products made elsewhere. The textile industry was badly hurt. Prices spiraled upward faster than the government could levy taxes to dampen the economy. (Higher taxes would have cut the public's buying power; with fewer goods sold, prices would have come down.)

Did the flood of American silver bullion *cause* the inflation? Scholars have long debated this question. Prices rose most steeply before 1565, but bullion imports reached their peak between 1580 and 1620. Thus there is no direct correlation between silver imports and the inflation rate. Did the substantial population growth accelerate the inflation rate? Perhaps: when the population pressure declined after 1600, prices gradually stabilized. One fact is certain: the price revolution severely strained government budgets. Several times between 1557 and 1647, Philip II and his successors were forced to repudiate the state debt, which in turn undermined confidence in the government.

❖ **Indians Panning for Gold** The Flemish engraver Theodore de Bry (1528–1598) produced many scenes of American life based on geographers' accounts; he was not an eyewitness of what he illustrated. Here Native Americans working in a stream on Hispaniola dredge up and sift alluvial sand for gold dust and nuggets. The island had very little. *(Source: By permission of the Houghton Library, Harvard University)*

By the seventeenth century, the economy was a shambles, and Spanish predominance was over.

As Philip II paid his armies and foreign debts with silver bullion, the Spanish inflation was transmitted to the rest of Europe. Between 1560 and 1600, much of Europe experienced large price increases. Prices doubled and in some cases quadrupled, and wages did not keep pace with prices. Spain suffered most severely, but all European countries were affected. People who lived on fixed incomes, such as the continental nobles, were badly hurt because their money bought less. Those who owed fixed sums of money, such as the middle class, prospered: in a time of rising prices, debts had less value each year. Food costs rose most sharply, and the poor fared worst of all.

Colonial Administration

Columbus, Cortez, and Pizarro claimed the lands they had "discovered" for the crown of Spain. How were these lands to be governed? According to the Spanish theory of absolutism, the Crown was entitled to exercise full authority over all imperial lands. In the sixteenth century, the Crown divided its New World territories into four viceroyalties, or administrative divisions: New Spain, which consisted of Mexico, Central America, and present-day California, Arizona, New Mexico, and Texas, with the capital at Mexico City; Peru, originally all the lands in continental South America, later reduced to the territory of modern Peru, Chile, Bolivia, and Ecuador, with the viceregal seat at Lima; New Granada, including present-day Venezuela, Colombia, Panama, and, after 1739, Ecuador, with Bogotá as its administrative center; and La Plata, consisting of Argentina, Uruguay, and Paraguay, with Buenos Aires as the capital. Within each territory, the viceroy, or imperial governor, exercised broad military and civil authority as the direct representative of the sovereign in Madrid. The viceroy presided over the *audiencia,* a board of twelve to fifteen judges that served as his advisory council and the highest judicial body. The enlightened Spanish king Charles III (r. 1759–1788) introduced the system of *intendants.* These royal officials possessed broad military, administrative, and financial authority within their intendancy and were responsible not to the viceroy but to the monarchy in Madrid.

From the early sixteenth century to the beginning of the nineteenth, the Spanish monarchy acted on the mercantilist principle that the colonies existed for the financial benefit of the home country. The mining of gold and silver was always the most important industry in the colonies. The Crown claimed the *quinto,* one-fifth of all precious metals mined in South America. Gold and silver yielded the Spanish monarchy 25 percent of its total income. In return, it shipped manufactured goods to the Americas and discouraged the development of native industries.

The Portuguese governed their colony of Brazil in a similar manner. After the union of the crowns of Portugal and Spain in 1580, Spanish administrative forms were introduced. Local officials called *corregidores* held judicial and military powers. Mercantilist policies placed severe restrictions on Brazilian industries that might compete with those of Portugal. In the seventeenth century, the use of black slave labor made possible the cultivation of coffee and cotton, and in the eighteenth century Brazil led the world in the production of sugar. The unique feature of colonial Brazil's culture and society was its thoroughgoing intermixture of Indians, whites, and blacks.

POLITICS, RELIGION, AND WAR

In 1559 France and Spain signed the Treaty of Cateau-Cambrésis, which ended the long conflict known as the Habsburg-Valois Wars. This event marked a watershed in early modern European history. Spain was the victor. France, exhausted by the struggle, had to acknowledge Spanish dominance in Italy, where much of the war had been fought. Spanish governors ruled in Sicily, Naples, and Milan, and Spanish influence was strong in the Papal States and Tuscany.

Emperor Charles V had divided his attention between the Holy Roman Empire and Spain. Under his son Philip II (r. 1556–1598), however, the center of the Habsburg Empire and the political center of gravity for all of Europe shifted westward to Spain. Before 1559 Spain and France had fought bitterly for control of Italy; after 1559 the two Catholic powers aimed their guns at Protestantism. The Treaty of Cateau-Cambrésis ended an era of strictly dynastic wars and initiated a period of conflicts in which politics and religion played the dominant roles.

Because a variety of issues were stewing, it is not easy to generalize about the wars of the late sixteenth century. Some were continuations of struggles between the centralizing goals of monarchies and the feudal reactions of nobilities. Some were crusading battles between Catholics and Protestants. Some were struggles for national independence or for international expansion.

These wars differed considerably from earlier wars. Sixteenth- and seventeenth-century armies were bigger than medieval ones; some forces numbered as many as fifty thousand men. Because large armies were expensive, governments had to reorganize their administrations to finance these armies. The use of gunpowder altered both the nature of war and popular attitudes toward it. Guns and cannon killed and wounded from a distance, indiscriminately. Writers scorned gunpowder as a coward's weapon that allowed a common soldier to kill a gentleman. Italian poet Ariosto lamented:

Through thee is martial glory lost, through
Thee the trade of arms becomes a worthless art:
And at such ebb are worth and chivalry that
The base often plays the better part.[13]

Gunpowder weakened the notion, common during the Hundred Years' War, that warfare was an ennobling experience. At the same time, governments utilized propaganda, pulpits, and the printing press to arouse public opinion to support war.[14]

Late-sixteenth-century conflicts fundamentally tested the medieval ideal of a unified Christian society governed by one political ruler, the emperor, to whom all rulers were theoretically subordinate, and one church, to which all people belonged. The Protestant Reformation had killed this ideal, but few people recognized it as dead. Catholics continued to believe that Calvinists and Lutherans could be reconverted; Protestants persisted in thinking that the Roman church should be destroyed. Most people believed that a state could survive only if its members shared the same faith. Catholics and Protestants alike feared people of the other faith living in their midst. The settlement finally achieved in 1648, known as the Peace of Westphalia, signaled the end of the medieval ideal.

The Origins of Difficulties in France (1515–1559)

In the first half of the sixteenth century, France continued the recovery begun under Louis XI (see page 428). The population losses caused by the plague and the disorders accompanying the Hundred Years' War had created such a labor shortage that serfdom virtually disappeared. Cash rents replaced feudal rents and servile obligations. This development clearly benefited the peasantry. Meanwhile, the declining buying power of money hurt the nobility. The increase in France's population in the late fifteenth and sixteenth centuries brought new lands under cultivation, but the division of property among sons meant that most peasant holdings were very small. Domestic and foreign trade picked up, mercantile centers such as Rouen and Lyons expanded, and in 1517 a new port city was founded at Le Havre.

The charming and cultivated Francis I (r. 1515–1547) and his athletic, emotional son, Henry II (r. 1547–1559) governed through a small, efficient council. Great nobles held titular authority in the provinces as governors, but Paris-appointed baillis and seneschals continued to exercise actual fiscal and judicial responsibility (see page 332). In 1539 Francis issued an ordinance that placed the whole of France under the jurisdiction of the royal law courts and made French the language of those courts. This act had a powerful centralizing impact. The *taille,* a tax on land, provided what strength the monarchy had and supported a strong standing army. Unfortunately, the tax base was too narrow for France's extravagant promotion of the arts and ambitious foreign policy.

Deliberately imitating the Italian Renaissance princes, the Valois monarchs lavished money on a magnificent court, a vast building program, and Italian artists. Francis I commissioned Paris architect Pierre Lescot to rebuild the palace of the Louvre. Francis secured the services of Michelangelo's star pupil, Il Rosso, who decorated the wing of the Fontainebleau chateau, subsequently called the Gallery Francis I, with rich scenes from classical and mythological literature. After acquiring Leonardo da Vinci's *Mona Lisa,* Francis brought Leonardo himself to France. Henry II built a castle at Dreux for his mistress, Diana de Poitiers, and a palace in Paris, the Tuileries, for his wife, Catherine de' Medici. Art historians credit Francis I and Henry II with importing Italian Renaissance art and architecture to France. But whatever praise these monarchs deserve for their cultural achievement, they spent far more than they could afford.

The Habsburg-Valois Wars, waged intermittently through the first half of the sixteenth century, also cost more than the government could afford. Financing the war posed problems. In addition to the time-honored practices of increasing taxes and engaging in heavy borrowing, Francis I tried two new devices to raise revenue: the sale of public offices and a treaty with the papacy. The former proved to be only a temporary source of money. The offices sold tended to become hereditary within a family, and once a man bought an office, he and his heirs were tax exempt. The sale of public offices thus created a tax-exempt class called the "nobility of the robe," which held positions beyond the jurisdiction of the Crown.

The treaty with the papacy was the Concordat of Bologna (see page 428), in which Francis agreed

❖ **Rossi and Primaticcio: The Gallery of Francis I** Flat paintings alternating with rich sculpture provide a rhythm that directs the eye down the long gallery at Fontainebleau, constructed between 1530 and 1540. Francis I sought to re-create in France the elegant Renaissance lifestyle found in Italy. *(Source: Art Resource NY)*

to recognize the supremacy of the papacy over a universal council. In return, the French crown gained the right to appoint all French bishops and abbots. This understanding gave the monarchy a rich supplement of money and offices and a power over the church that lasted until the Revolution of 1789. The Concordat of Bologna helps explain why France did not later become Protestant: in effect, it established Catholicism as the state religion. Because French rulers possessed control over appointments and had a vested financial interest in Catholicism, they had no need to revolt from Rome.

However, the Concordat of Bologna perpetuated disorders within the French church. Ecclesiastical offices were used primarily to pay and re-ward civil servants. Churchmen in France, as elsewhere, were promoted to the hierarchy not because they possessed any special spiritual qualifications but because they had rendered services to the state. Such bishops were unlikely to work to elevate the intellectual and moral standards of the parish clergy. Few of the many priests in France devoted scrupulous attention to the needs of their parishioners. Thus the teachings of Luther and Calvin, as the presses disseminated them, found a receptive audience.

Luther's tracts first appeared in France in 1518, and his ideas attracted some attention. After the publication of Calvin's *Institutes* in 1536, sizable numbers of French people were attracted to the "reformed religion," as Calvinism was called. Be-

✦ **Triple Profile Portrait** The portrait from the late sixteenth century exemplifies the very high finish and mannered sophistication of the School of Fontainebleau. These courtiers served Henry III, one of the weak sons of Henry II. *(Source: Milwaukee Art Museum, Gift of Women's Exchange)*

cause Calvin wrote in French rather than Latin, his ideas gained wide circulation. Initially, Calvinism drew converts from among reform-minded members of the Catholic clergy, the industrious middle classes, and artisan groups. Most Calvinists lived in major cities, such as Paris, Lyons, Meaux, and Grenoble.

In spite of condemnation by the universities, government bans, and massive burnings at the stake, the numbers of Protestants grew steadily. When Henry II died in 1559, there were 40 well-organized Protestant churches and 2,150 mission stations in France. Perhaps one-tenth of the population had become Calvinist.

Religious Riots and Civil War in France (1559–1589)

For thirty years, from 1559 to 1589, violence and civil war divided and shattered France. The feebleness of the monarchy was the seed from which

the weeds of civil violence sprang. The three weak sons of Henry II who occupied the throne could not provide the necessary leadership. Francis II (r. 1559–1560) died after seventeen months. Charles IX (r. 1560–1574) succeeded at the age of ten and was thoroughly dominated by his opportunistic mother, Catherine de' Medici, who would support any party or position to maintain her influence. The intelligent and cultivated Henry III (r. 1574–1589) divided his attention between debaucheries with his male lovers and frantic acts of repentance.

The French nobility took advantage of this monarchial weakness. In the second half of the sixteenth century, between two-fifths and one-half of the nobility at one time or another became Calvinist. Just as German princes in the Holy Roman Empire had adopted Lutheranism as a means of opposition to Emperor Charles V, so French nobles frequently adopted the reformed religion as a religious cloak for their independence. No one believed that peoples of different faiths could coexist peacefully within the same territory. The Reformation thus led to a resurgence of feudal disorder. Armed clashes between Catholic royalist lords and Calvinist antimonarchial lords occurred in many parts of France.

Among the upper classes the Catholic-Calvinist conflict was the surface issue, but the fundamental object of the struggle was power. At lower social levels, however, religious concerns were paramount. Working-class crowds composed of skilled craftsmen and the poor wreaked terrible violence on other people and property. Both Calvinists and Catholics believed that the others' books, services, and ministers polluted the community. Preachers incited violence, and ceremonies such as baptisms, marriages, and funerals triggered it. Protestant pastors encouraged their followers to destroy statues and liturgical objects in Catholic churches. Catholic priests urged their flocks to shed the blood of the Calvinist heretics.

In 1561 in the Paris church of Saint-Médard, a Protestant crowd cornered a baker guarding a box containing the consecrated eucharistic bread. Taunting "Does your God of paste protect you now from the pains of death?" the mob proceeded to kill the poor man.[15] Calvinists believed that the Catholic emphasis on symbols in religious ritual desecrated what was truly sacred and promoted the worship of images. In scores of attacks on Catholic churches, religious statues were knocked down, stained-glass windows were smashed, and sacred vestments, vessels, and eucharistic elements were defiled. In 1561 a Catholic crowd charged a group of just-released Protestant prisoners, killed them, and burned their bodies in the street. Hundreds of Huguenots, as French Calvinists were called, were tortured, had their tongues cut out or throats slit, were maimed or murdered.

In the fourteenth and fifteenth centuries, crowd action—attacks on great nobles and rich prelates— had expressed economic grievances. In contrast, religious rioters of the sixteenth century believed that they could assume the power of public magistrates and rid the community of corruption. Municipal officials criticized the crowds' actions, but the participation of pastors and priests in these riots lent them some legitimacy.[16]

A savage Catholic attack on Calvinists in Paris on August 24, 1572 (Saint Bartholomew's Day), followed the usual pattern. The occasion was a religious ceremony, the marriage of the king's sister Margaret of Valois to the Protestant Henry of Navarre, which was intended to help reconcile Catholics and Huguenots. Among the many Calvinists present for the wedding festivities was Admiral Gaspard de Coligny, head of one of the great noble families of France and leader of the Huguenot party. Coligny had recently replaced Catherine de' Medici in influence over the young king Charles IX. When, the night before the wedding, the leader of the Catholic aristocracy, Henry of Guise, had Coligny attacked, rioting and slaughter followed. The Huguenot gentry in Paris were massacred, and religious violence spread to the provinces. Between August 25 and October 3, perhaps twelve thousand Huguenots perished at Meaux, Lyons, Orléans, and Paris. The contradictory orders of the unstable Charles IX worsened the situation.

The Saint Bartholomew's Day massacre led to fighting that launched the War of the Three Henrys, a civil conflict among factions led by the Catholic Henry of Guise, the Protestant Henry of Navarre, and King Henry III, who succeeded the tubercular Charles IX. Though King Henry remained Catholic, he realized that the Catholic Guise group represented his greatest danger. The Guises wanted, through an alliance of Catholic nobles called the "Holy League," not only to destroy Calvinism but also to replace Henry III with a member of the Guise family. France suffered fifteen more years of religious rioting and domestic anarchy. Agriculture in many areas was destroyed; commercial life declined severely; starvation and death haunted the land.

What ultimately saved France was a small group of Catholic moderates called *politiques* who believed that only the restoration of strong monarchy could reverse the trend toward collapse. No religious creed was worth the incessant disorder and destruction. Therefore, the politiques favored accepting the Huguenots as an officially recognized and organized pressure group. (But religious toleration, the full acceptance of peoples of different religious persuasions within a pluralistic society, with minorities having the same civil liberties as the majority, developed only in the eighteenth century.) The death of Catherine de' Medici, followed by the assassinations of Henry of Guise and King Henry III, paved the way for the accession of Henry of Navarre, a politique who became Henry IV (r. 1589–1610).

This glamorous prince, "who knew how to fight, to make love, and to drink," as a contemporary remarked, wanted above all a strong and united France. He knew, too, that the majority of the French were Roman Catholics. Declaring "Paris is worth a Mass," Henry knelt before the archbishop of Bourges and was received into the Roman Catholic church. Henry's willingness to sacrifice religious principles to political necessity saved France. The Edict of Nantes, which Henry published in 1598, granted to Huguenots liberty of conscience and liberty of public worship in two hundred fortified towns, such as La Rochelle. The reign of Henry IV and the Edict of Nantes prepared the way for French absolutism in the seventeenth century by helping restore internal peace in France.

The Netherlands Under Charles V

In the last quarter of the sixteenth century, the political stability of England, the international prestige of Spain, and the moral influence of the Roman papacy all became mixed up with the religious crisis in the Low Countries. The Netherlands was the pivot around which European money, diplomacy, and war revolved. What began as a movement for the reformation of the church developed into a struggle for Dutch independence.

Emperor Charles V (r. 1519–1556) had inherited the seventeen provinces that compose present-day Belgium and Holland (see page 453). Ideally situated for commerce between the Rhine and Scheldt rivers, the great towns of Bruges, Ghent, Brussels, Arras, and Amsterdam made their living by trade and industry. The French-speaking southern towns produced fine linens and woolens, while the wealth of the Dutch-speaking northern cities rested on fishing, shipping, and international banking. The city of Antwerp was the largest port and the greatest money market in Europe. In the cities of the Low Countries, trade and commerce had produced a vibrant cosmopolitan atmosphere, as personified by the urbane Erasmus of Rotterdam.

Each of the seventeen provinces of the Netherlands possessed historical liberties: each was self-governing and enjoyed the right to make its own laws and collect its own taxes. In addition to important economic connections, only the recognition of a common ruler in the person of Emperor Charles V united the provinces. Delegates from the various provinces met together in the Estates General, but important decisions had to be referred back to each province for approval. In the middle of the sixteenth century, the provinces of the Netherlands had a limited sense of federation.

In the Low Countries as elsewhere, corruption in the Roman church and the critical spirit of the Renaissance provoked pressure for reform. Lutheran tracts and Dutch translations of the Bible flooded the seventeen provinces in the 1520s and 1530s, attracting many people to Protestantism. Charles V's government responded with condemnation and mild repression. This policy was not particularly effective, however, because ideas circulated freely in the cosmopolitan atmosphere of the commercial centers. But Charles's Flemish loyalty checked the spread of Lutheranism. Charles had been born in Ghent and raised in the Netherlands; he was Flemish in language and culture. He identified with the Flemish and they with him.

In 1556, however, Charles V abdicated, dividing his territories between his brother, Ferdinand, who received Austria and the Holy Roman Empire, and his son Philip, who inherited Spain, the Low Countries, Milan and the kingdom of Sicily, and the Spanish possessions in the Americas. Charles delivered his abdication speech before the Estates General at Brussels. The emperor was then fifty-five years old, white haired, and so crippled in the legs that he had to lean for support on the young Prince William of Orange. According to one contemporary account of the emperor's appearance:

His under lip, a Burgundian inheritance, as faithfully transmitted as the duchy and county, was heavy and hanging, the lower jaw protruding so far beyond the upper that it was impossible for him to bring together the few fragments of teeth which still remained, or to speak a whole sentence in an intelligible voice.[17]

Charles spoke in Flemish. Philip responded in Spanish; he could speak neither French nor Flemish. Netherlanders had always felt that Charles was one of their own. They were never to forget that Philip was Spanish.

The Revolt of the Netherlands (1566–1587)

Lutheranism had posed no serious threat to Spanish rule; it was the spread of Calvinism that upset the apple cart. By the 1560s, there was a strong, militant minority of Calvinists in most of the cities of the Netherlands. The seventeen provinces possessed a large middle-class population, and the reformed religion, as a contemporary remarked, had a powerful appeal "to those who had grown rich by trade and were therefore ready for revolution."[18] Calvinism appealed to the middle classes because of its intellectual seriousness, moral gravity, and emphasis on any form of labor well done. It took deep root among the merchants and financiers in Amsterdam and the northern provinces. Working-class people were also converted, partly because their employers would hire only other Calvinists. Well organized and backed by rich merchants, Calvinists quickly gained a wide following. Whereas Lutherans taught respect for the powers that be, Calvinist reformed religion in the 1570s tended to encourage opposition to "illegal" civil authorities.

In 1559 Philip II appointed his half-sister Margaret as regent of the Netherlands (r. 1559–1567). A proud, energetic, and strong-willed woman, who once had Ignatius Loyola as her confessor, Margaret pushed Philip's orders to wipe out Protestantism. She introduced the Inquisition. Her more immediate problem, however, was revenue to finance the government of the provinces. Charles V had steadily increased taxes in the Low Countries. When Margaret appealed to the Estates General, it claimed that the Low Countries were more heavily taxed than Spain. Nevertheless, Margaret raised taxes and succeeded in uniting the opposition to the government's fiscal policy with the opposition to official repression of Calvinism.

In August 1566, a year of very high grain prices, fanatical Calvinists, primarily of the poorest classes, embarked on a rampage of frightful destruction. As in France, Calvinist destruction in the Low Countries was incited by popular preaching, and attacks were aimed at religious images as symbols of false doctrines, not at people. The cathedral of Notre Dame at Antwerp was the first target.

Begun in 1124 and finished only in 1518, this church stood as a monument to the commercial prosperity of Flanders, the piety of the business classes, and the artistic genius of centuries. On six successive summer evenings, crowds swept through the nave. While the town harlots held tapers to the greatest concentration of art works in northern Europe, people armed with axes and sledgehammers smashed altars, paintings, books, tombs, ecclesiastical vestments, missals, manuscripts, ornaments, stained-glass windows, and sculptures. Before the havoc was over, thirty more churches had been sacked and irreplaceable libraries burned. From Antwerp the destruction spread

To Purify the Church The destruction of pictures and statues representing biblical events, Christian doctrine, or sacred figures was a central feature of the Protestant Reformation. Here Dutch Protestant soldiers destroy what they consider idols in the belief that they are purifying the church. *(Source: Fotomas Index)*

MAP 15.2 The Netherlands, 1578–1609
Though small in geographical size, the Netherlands held a strategic position in the religious struggles of the sixteenth century. Why?

Protestants and between the seventeen provinces and Spain. A series of Spanish generals could not halt the fighting. In 1576 the seventeen provinces united under the leadership of Prince William of Orange, called "the Silent" because of his remarkable discretion. In 1578 Philip II sent his nephew Alexander Farnese, duke of Parma, to crush the revolt once and for all. A general with a superb sense of timing, an excellent knowledge of the geography of the Low Countries, and a perfect plan, Farnese arrived with an army of German mercenaries. Avoiding pitched battles, he fought by patient sieges. One by one the cities of the south fell—Maastricht, Tournai, Bruges, Ghent, and, finally, the financial capital of northern Europe, Antwerp. Calvinism was forbidden in these territories, and Protestants were compelled to convert or leave. The collapse of Antwerp marked the farthest extent of Spanish jurisdiction and ultimately the religious division of the Netherlands.

The ten southern provinces, the Spanish Netherlands (the future Belgium), remained under the control of the Spanish Habsburgs. The seven northern provinces, led by Holland, formed the Union of Utrecht and in 1581 declared their independence from Spain. Thus was born the United Provinces of the Netherlands (Map 15.2).

Geography and sociopolitical structure differentiated the two countries. The northern provinces were ribboned with sluices and canals and therefore were highly defensible. Several times the Dutch had broken the dikes and flooded the countryside to halt the advancing Farnese. In the southern provinces the Ardennes Mountains interrupted the otherwise flat terrain. In the north the commercial aristocracy possessed the predominant power; in the south the landed nobility had the greater influence. The north was Protestant; the south remained Catholic.

Philip II and Alexander Farnese did not accept this geographical division, and the struggle continued after 1581. The United Provinces repeatedly asked the Protestant queen of England, Elizabeth, for assistance.

The crown on the head of Elizabeth I (see page 463) did not rest easily. She had steered a moderately Protestant course between the Puritans, who sought the total elimination of Roman Catholic elements in the English church, and the Roman Catholics, who wanted full restoration of the old

to Brussels and Ghent and north to the provinces of Holland and Zeeland.

From Madrid, Philip II sent twenty thousand Spanish troops under the duke of Alva to pacify the Low Countries. Alva interpreted "pacification" to mean the ruthless extermination of religious and political dissidents. On top of the Inquisition he opened his own tribunal, soon called the "Council of Blood." On March 3, 1568, fifteen hundred men were executed. Even Margaret was sickened and resigned her regency. Alva resolved the financial crisis by levying a 10 percent sales tax on every transaction, which in a commercial society caused widespread hardship and confusion.

For ten years, between 1568 and 1578, civil war raged in the Netherlands between Catholics and religion. Elizabeth survived a massive uprising by the Catholic north in 1569 to 1570. She survived two serious plots against her life. In the 1570s the presence in England of Mary, Queen of Scots, a Roman Catholic and the legal heir to the English throne, produced a very embarrassing situation. Mary was the rallying point of all opposition to Elizabeth, yet the English sovereign hesitated to set the terrible example of regicide by ordering Mary executed.

Elizabeth faced a grave dilemma. If she responded favorably to Dutch pleas for military support against the Spanish, she would antagonize Philip II. The Spanish king had the steady flow of silver from the Americas at his disposal, and Elizabeth, lacking such treasure, wanted to avoid war. But if she did not help the Protestant Netherlands and it was crushed by Farnese, the likelihood was that the Spanish would invade England.

Three developments forced Elizabeth's hand. First, the wars in the Low Countries—the chief market for English woolens—badly hurt the English economy. When wool was not exported, the Crown lost valuable customs revenues. Second, the murder of William the Silent in July 1584 eliminated not only a great Protestant leader but also the chief military check on the Farnese advance. Third, the collapse of Antwerp appeared to signal a Catholic sweep through the Netherlands. The next step, the English feared, would be a Spanish invasion of their island. For these reasons, Elizabeth pumped 250,000 pounds and two thousand troops into the Protestant cause in the Low Countries between 1585 and 1587. Increasingly fearful of the plots of Mary, Queen of Scots, Elizabeth finally signed her death warrant. Mary was beheaded on February 18, 1587. Sometime between March 24 and 30, the news of Mary's death reached Philip II.

Philip II and the Spanish Armada

Philip pondered the Dutch and English developments at the Escorial northwest of Madrid. Begun in 1563 and completed under the king's personal supervision in 1584, the monastery of Saint Lawrence of the Escorial served as a residence for Jeromite monks, a tomb for the king's Habsburg ancestors, and a royal palace for Philip and his family. The vast buildings resemble a gridiron, the instrument on which Saint Lawrence (d. 258) had supposedly been roasted alive. The royal apartments were in the center of the Italian Renaissance building complex. King Philip's tiny bedchamber possessed a concealed sliding window that opened directly onto the high altar of the monastery church so that he could watch the services and pray along with the monks. In this somber atmosphere, surrounded by a community of monks and close to the bones of his ancestors, the Catholic ruler of Spain and much of the globe passed his days.

Philip of Spain considered himself the international defender of Catholicism and the heir to the medieval imperial power. Hoping to keep England within the Catholic church when his wife, Mary Tudor, died, Philip had asked Elizabeth to marry him; she had refused. Several popes had urged him to move against England. When Pope Sixtus V (1585–1590) heard of the death of Mary, he promised to pay Philip 1 million gold ducats the moment Spanish troops landed in England. Alexander Farnese had repeatedly warned that to subdue the Dutch, he would have to conquer England and cut off the source of Dutch support. Philip also worried that the vast amounts of South American silver he was pouring into the conquest of the Netherlands seemed to be going down a bottomless pit. Two plans for an expedition were considered. Philip's naval adviser recommended that a fleet of 150 ships sail from Lisbon, attack the English navy in the Channel, and invade England. Another proposal had been to assemble a collection of barges and troops in Flanders to stage a cross-Channel assault. With the expected support of English Catholics, Spain would achieve a great victory. Farnese opposed this plan as militarily unsound.

Philip compromised. He prepared a vast fleet to sail from Lisbon to Flanders, fight off Elizabeth's navy *if* it attacked, rendezvous with Farnese, and escort his barges across the English Channel. The expedition's purpose was to transport the Flemish army.

On May 9, 1588, *la felicissima armada*—"the most fortunate fleet," as it was ironically called in official documents—sailed from Lisbon harbor. The Spanish fleet of 130 vessels carried 123,790 cannonballs and perhaps thirty thousand men, every one of whom had confessed his sins and received the eucharist. An English fleet of about

✦ **The Battle of Lepanto,** October 7, 1571. The fleet of the Holy League (Spain, Venice, the Papacy), under Don Juan of Austria, met the Ottoman Turkish navy at a bay in the mouth of the Gulf of Patros off Lepanto in western Greece. Since most of the Ottoman sailors had been sent home for winter, the Turkish fleet was hardly prepared. Superior European numbers and command prevailed and the Ottomans were routed. The battle broke the spell of complete Turkish supremacy in the Mediterranean, Europe celebrated a great victory, and the Christian galleys gained a huge crop of prisoners to man the oars. But the Turks quickly rebuilt their navy and regained effective control of the Mediterranean. *(Source: National Maritime Museum, London)*

150 ships met the Spanish in the Channel. The English fleet was composed of smaller, faster, more maneuverable ships, many of which had greater firing power than their Spanish counterparts. A combination of storms and squalls, spoiled food and rank water, inadequate Spanish ammunition, and, to a lesser extent, English fire ships that caused the Spanish to scatter gave England the victory. Many Spanish ships went down on the journey home around Ireland; perhaps 65 managed to reach home ports.

The battle in the Channel has frequently been described as one of the decisive battles in the history of the world. In fact, it had mixed consequences. Spain soon rebuilt its navy, and after 1588

the quality of the Spanish fleet improved. The destruction of the Armada did not halt the flow of silver from the New World. More silver reached Spain between 1588 and 1603 than in any other fifteen-year period. The war between England and Spain dragged on for years.

The defeat of the Spanish Armada was decisive, however, in the sense that it prevented Philip II from reimposing unity on western Europe by force. He did not conquer England, and Elizabeth continued her financial and military support of the Dutch. In the Netherlands neither side gained significant territory. The borders of 1581 tended to become permanent. In 1609 Philip III of Spain (r. 1598–1621) agreed to a truce, in effect recogniz-

THE HABSBURG SUCCESSION, 1493–1637

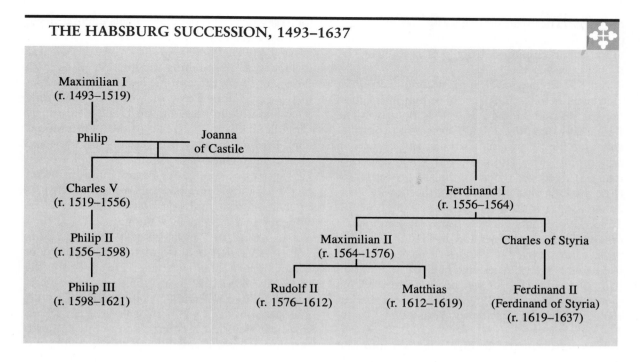

ing the independence of the United Provinces. In seventeenth-century Spain memory of the defeat of the Armada contributed to a spirit of defeatism. In England the victory contributed to a David and Goliath legend that enhanced English national sentiment.

The Thirty Years' War (1618–1648)

While Philip II dreamed of building a second armada and Henry IV began the reconstruction of France, the political-religious situation in central Europe deteriorated. An uneasy truce had prevailed in the Holy Roman Empire since the Peace of Augsburg of 1555 (see page 455). The Augsburg settlement, in recognizing the independent power of the German princes, further undermined any authority of the central government. The Habsburg ruler in Vienna enjoyed the title of "emperor" but had no imperial power.

According to the Augsburg settlement, the faith of the prince determined the religion of his subjects. Later in the century, however, Catholics grew alarmed because Lutherans, in violation of the Peace of Augsburg, were steadily acquiring German bishoprics. The spread of Calvinism further confused the issue. The Augsburg settlement had pertained only to Lutheranism and Catholicism, so Calvinists ignored it and converted several princes. Lutherans feared that the Augsburg principles would be totally undermined by Catholic and Calvinist gains. Also, the militantly active Jesuits had reconverted several Lutheran princes to Catholicism. In an increasingly tense situation, Lutheran princes formed the Protestant Union (1608), and Catholics retaliated with the Catholic League (1609). Each alliance was determined that the other should make no religious (that is, territorial) advance. The empire was composed of two armed camps.

Dynastic interests were also involved in the German situation. When Charles V abdicated in 1556, he had divided his possessions between his son, Philip II, and his brother Ferdinand I. This partition began the Austrian and Spanish branches of the Habsburg family. Ferdinand inherited the imperial title and the Habsburg lands in central Europe, including Austria. Ferdinand's grandson Matthias had no direct heirs and promoted the candidacy of his fiercely Catholic cousin, Ferdinand of Styria. The Spanish Habsburgs strongly supported the goals of their Austrian relatives: the unity of the empire and the preservation of Catholicism within it.

In 1617 Ferdinand of Styria secured election as king of Bohemia, a title that gave him jurisdiction over Silesia and Moravia as well as Bohemia. The Bohemians were Czech and German in nationality and Lutheran, Calvinist, Catholic, and Hussite in religion; all these faiths enjoyed a fair degree of religious freedom. When Ferdinand proceeded to close some Protestant churches, the heavily Protestant Estates of Bohemia protested. On May 23, 1618, Protestants hurled two of Ferdinand's officials from a castle window in Prague. They fell 70 feet but survived: Catholics claimed that angels had caught them; Protestants said that the officials had fallen on a heap of soft horse manure. Called the "defenestration of Prague," this event marked the beginning of the Thirty Years' War (1618–1648).

Historians traditionally divide the war into four phases. The first, or Bohemian, phase (1618–1625) was characterized by civil war in Bohemia between the Catholic League, led by Ferdinand, and the Protestant Union, headed by Prince Frederick of the Palatinate. The Bohemians fought for religious liberty and independence from Habsburg rule. In 1618 the Bohemian Estates deposed Ferdinand and gave the crown of Bohemia to Frederick, thus uniting the interests of German Protestants with those of the international enemies of the Habsburgs. Frederick wore his crown only a few months. In 1620 he was totally defeated by Catholic forces at the Battle of the White Mountain. Ferdinand, who had recently been elected Holy Roman emperor as Ferdinand II, followed up his victories by wiping out Protestantism in Bohemia through forcible conversions and the activities of militant Jesuit missionaries. Within ten years, Bohemia was completely Catholic.

The second, or Danish, phase of the war (1625–1629)—so called because of the participation of King Christian IV of Denmark (r. 1588–1648), the ineffective leader of the Protestant cause—witnessed additional Catholic victories. The Catholic imperial army led by Albert of Wallenstein scored smashing victories. It swept through Silesia, north through Schleswig and Jutland to the Baltic, and east into Pomerania. Wallenstein who had made himself indispensable to the emperor Ferdinand, was an unscrupulous opportunist who used his vast riches to build an army loyal only to himself. The general seemed interested more in carving out an

❖ **The Horrors of War** Following Richelieu's invasion of Lorraine in 1633, the French engraver Jacques Callot (1592/3–1635) produced a series of etchings collectively titled *The Great Miseries of War,* depicting the theft, rape, and brutality for which soldiers of the Thirty Years' War gained an enduring reputation. *(Source: Courtesy of the Trustees of the British Museum)*

❖ **Soldiers Pillage a Farmhouse** Billeting troops on civilian populations caused untold hardships. In this late seventeenth-century Dutch illustration, brawling soldiers
take over a peasant's home, eat his food, steal his possessions, and insult his family.
Peasant retaliation sometimes proved swift and bloody. *(Source: Rijksmuseum, Amsterdam)*

empire for himself than in aiding the Catholic
cause. He quarreled with the Catholic League, and
soon the Catholic forces were divided. Religion
was eclipsed as a basic issue of the war.

The year 1629 marked the peak of Habsburg
power. The Jesuits persuaded the emperor to issue
the Edict of Restitution, whereby all Catholic
properties lost to Protestantism since 1552 were to
be restored and only Catholics and Lutherans (*not*
Calvinists, Hussites, or other sects) were to be
allowed to practice their faiths. Ferdinand appeared
to be embarked on a policy to unify the empire.
When Wallenstein began ruthless enforcement of
the edict, Protestants throughout Europe feared
collapse of the balance of power in north-central
Europe.

The third, or Swedish, phase of the war (1630–
1635) began with the arrival in Germany of the

Swedish king Gustavus Adolphus (r. 1594–1632).
The ablest administrator of his day and a devout
Lutheran, Gustavus Adolphus intervened to support the oppressed Protestants within the empire
and to assist his relatives, the exiled dukes of Mecklenburg. Cardinal Richelieu, the chief minister of
King Louis XIII of France (r. 1610–1643), subsidized the Swedes, hoping to weaken Habsburg
power in Europe. In 1631 with a small but well-
disciplined army equipped with superior muskets
and warm uniforms, Gustavus Adolphus won a
brilliant victory at Breitenfeld. Again in 1632 he
was victorious at Lützen, though he was fatally
wounded in the battle.

The participation of the Swedes in the Thirty
Years' War proved decisive for the future of Protestantism and later German history. When Gustavus Adolphus landed on German soil, he had

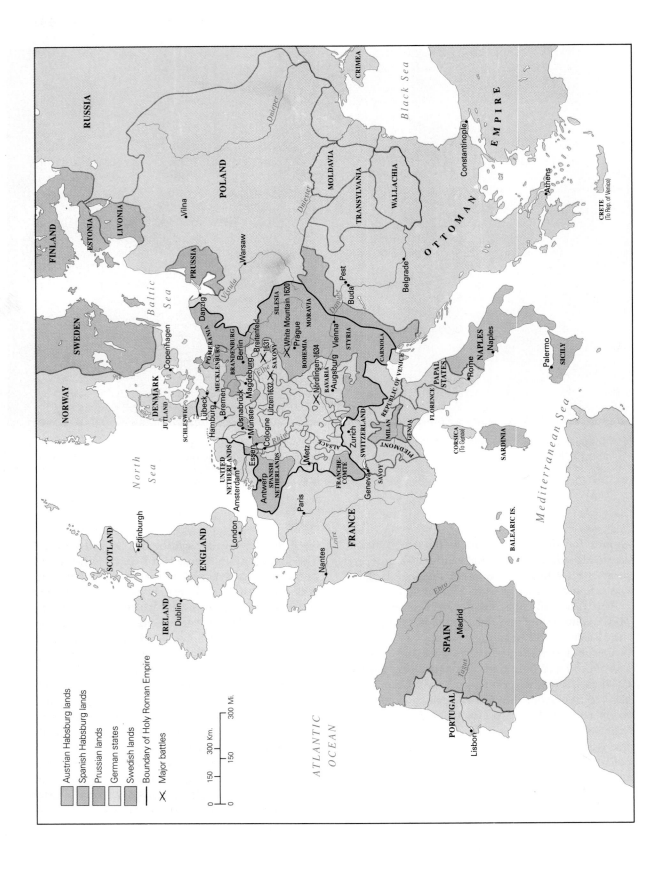

RUSSIA

FINLAND

ESTONIA

LIVONIA

•Vilna

Baltic Sea

SWEDEN

CRIMEA

Black Sea

POLAND

Dnieper

MOLDAVIA

TRANSYLVANIA

WALLACHIA

OTTOMAN EMPIRE

Constantinople •

Athens •

CRETE
[To Rep. of Venice]

NORWAY

Copenhagen •

DENMARK

JUTLAND

SCHLESWIG

Dniester

PRUSSIA

Danzig

Warsaw •

Vistula

Pest •

Buda •

Belgrade •

Danube

North Sea

Edinburgh •

SCOTLAND

ENGLAND

London •

IRELAND

Dublin •

Lübeck

Hamburg •

Bremen

MECKLENBURG

POMERANIA

BRANDENBURG

Berlin •

Breitenfeld

✕1631

SAXONY

Elbe

Magdeburg •

Lützen 1632 ✕

Osnabrück •

Münster •

Essen •

Cologne •

Rhine

UNITED NETHERLANDS

Amsterdam •

SPANISH NETHERLANDS

Antwerp •

Paris •

FRANCE

Loire

Nantes •

SILESIA

White Mountain 1620 ✕

Prague •

BOHEMIA

MORAVIA

Nördlingen 1634 ✕

BAVARIA

Augsburg •

Vienna •

STYRIA

CARNIOLA

REPUBLIC OF VENICE

NAPLES

Rome •

PAPAL STATES

FLORENCE

Naples •

Palermo •

SICILY

Metz •

ALSACE

FRANCHE-COMTÉ

Geneva •

Zurich •

SWITZERLAND

SAVOY

PIEDMONT

MILAN

GENOA

CORSICA
[To Genoa]

SARDINIA

BALEARIC IS.

Mediterranean Sea

Ebro

SPAIN

Madrid •

Tagus

PORTUGAL

Lisbon •

ATLANTIC OCEAN

Austrian Habsburg lands

Spanish Habsburg lands

Prussian lands

German states

Swedish lands

Boundary of Holy Roman Empire

✕ Major battles

0   150   300 Mi.

0   150   300 Km.

already brought Denmark, Poland, Finland, and the smaller Baltic states under Swedish influence. The Swedish victories ended the Habsburg ambition of uniting all the German states under imperial authority.

The death of Gustavus Adolphus, followed by the defeat of the Swedes at the Battle of Nördlingen in 1634, prompted the French to enter the war on the side of the Protestants. Thus began the French, or international, phase of the Thirty Years' War (1635–1648). For almost a century, French foreign policy had been based on opposition to the Habsburgs because a weak empire divided into scores of independent principalities enhanced France's international stature. In 1622 when the Dutch had resumed the war against Spain, the French had supported Holland. Now in 1635 Cardinal Richelieu declared war on Spain and again sent financial and military assistance to the Swedes and the German Protestant princes. The war dragged on. French, Dutch, and Swedes, supported by Scots, Finns, and German mercenaries, burned, looted, and destroyed German agriculture and commerce. The Thirty Years' War lasted so long because neither side had the resources to win a quick, decisive victory. Finally in October 1648, peace was achieved.

The treaties signed at Münster and Osnabrück, commonly called the "Peace of Westphalia," marked a turning point in European political, religious, and social history. The treaties recognized the sovereign, independent authority of the German princes. Each ruler could govern his particular territory and make war and peace as well. With power in the hands of more than three hundred princes, with no central government, courts, or means of controlling unruly rulers, the Holy Roman Empire as a real state was effectively destroyed (Map 15.3).

The independence of the United Provinces of the Netherlands was acknowledged. The international stature of France and Sweden was also greatly improved. The political divisions within the empire, the weak German frontiers, and the acquisition of the province of Alsace increased France's size and prestige. The treaties allowed France to

❖ **MAP 15.3 Europe in 1648** Which country emerged from the Thirty Years' War as the strongest European power? What dynastic house was that country's major rival in the early modern period?

intervene at will in German affairs. Sweden received a large cash indemnity and jurisdiction over German territories along the Baltic Sea. The powerful Swedish presence in northeastern Germany subsequently posed a major threat to the future kingdom of Brandenburg-Prussia. The treaties also denied the papacy the right to participate in German religious affairs—a restriction symbolizing the reduced role of the church in European politics.

In religion, the Westphalian treaties stipulated that the Augsburg agreement of 1555 should stand permanently. The sole modification was that Calvinism, along with Catholicism and Lutheranism, would become a legally permissible creed. In practice, the north German states remained Protestant; the south German states, Catholic. The war settled little.

Germany After the Thirty Years' War

The Thirty Years' War was a disaster for the German economy and society, probably the most destructive event in German history before the twentieth century. Population losses were frightful. Perhaps one-third of the urban residents and two-fifths of the inhabitants of rural areas died. Entire areas of Germany were depopulated, partly by military actions, partly by disease—typhus, dysentery, bubonic plague, and syphilis accompanied the movements of armies—and partly by the thousands of refugees who fled to safer areas.

In the late sixteenth and early seventeenth centuries, all Europe experienced an economic crisis primarily caused by the influx of silver from South America. Because the Thirty Years' War was fought on German soil, these economic difficulties were badly aggravated in the empire. Scholars still cannot estimate the value of losses in agricultural land and livestock, in trade and commerce. The trade of southern cities such as Augsburg, already hard hit by the shift in transportation routes from the Mediterranean to the Atlantic, was virtually destroyed by the fighting in the south. Meanwhile, towns such as Lübeck, Hamburg, and Bremen in the north and Essen in the Ruhr area actually prospered because of the many refugees they attracted. The destruction of land and foodstuffs, compounded by the flood of Spanish silver, brought on a severe price rise. During and after the war, inflation was worse in Germany than anywhere else in Europe.

Agricultural areas suffered catastrophically. The population decline caused a rise in the value of labor, and owners of great estates had to pay more for agricultural workers. Farmers who needed only small amounts of capital to restore their lands started over again. Many small farmers, however, lacked the revenue to rework their holdings and had to become day laborers. Nobles and landlords bought up many small holdings and acquired great estates. In some parts of Germany, especially east of the Elbe River in areas such as Mecklenburg and Pomerania, peasants' loss of land led to the rise of a new serfdom.[19] Thus the Thirty Years' War contributed to the legal and economic decline of the largest segment of German society.

✣ CHANGING ATTITUDES

What were the cultural consequences of the religious wars and of the worldwide discoveries? What impact did the discoveries and wars have on Europeans' attitudes? The clash of traditional religious and geographical beliefs with the new knowledge provided by explorers—combined with decades of devastation and disorder within Europe—bred confusion, uncertainty, and insecurity. Geographical evidence based on verifiably scientific proofs contradicted the evidence of the Scriptures and of the classical authors.

The age of religious wars was one of extreme and violent contrasts. It was a deeply religious period in which people fought passionately for their beliefs; 70 percent of the books printed dealt with religious subjects. Yet the times saw the beginnings of religious skepticism. Europeans explored new continents, partly with the missionary aim of Christianizing the peoples they encountered. Yet the Spanish, Portuguese, Dutch, and English proceeded to dominate and enslave the Indians and blacks they found. While Europeans indulged in gross sensuality, the social status of women declined. The exploration of new continents reflected deep curiosity and broad intelligence, yet Europeans believed in witches and burned thousands at the stake. Sexism, racism, and skepticism had all originated in ancient times. But late in the sixteenth century, they began to take on their familiar modern forms.

The Status of Women

Did new ideas about women appear in this period? Theological and popular literature on marriage in Reformation Europe helps answer this question. These manuals emphasized the qualities expected of each partner. A husband was obliged to provide for the material welfare of his wife and children. He was directed to protect his family while remaining steady and self-controlled. Especially was a husband and father to rule his household firmly but justly. But he was not to behave as a tyrant, a guideline counselors repeated frequently. A wife should be a mature person, a good household manager, and a subservient and faithful spouse. The husband also owed fidelity, and both Protestant and Catholic moralists rejected the double standard of sexual morality as a threat to family unity. Counselors believed that marriage should be based on mutual respect and trust. While they discouraged impersonal unions arranged by parents, they did not think romantic attachments—based on physical attraction and emotional love—a sound basis for an enduring relationship.

Moralists held that the household was a woman's first priority. She might assist in her own or her husband's business and do charitable work. Involvement in social or public activities, however, was inappropriate because it distracted the wife from her primary responsibility, her household. If women suffered under their husbands' yoke, writers explained that submission was the punishment they had inherited from Eve, penance for man's fall, like the pain of childbearing. Moreover, they said, a woman's lot was no worse than a man's: he had to earn the family's bread by the sweat of his brow.[20]

Catholics viewed marriage as a sacramental union, which, validly entered into, could not be dissolved. Protestants saw marriage as a contract, whereby each partner promised the other support, companionship, and the sharing of mutual goods. Protestants recognized a mutual right to divorce and remarriage for various reasons, including adultery and irreparable breakdown.[21] Society in the early modern period was patriarchal. While women neither lost their identity nor lacked meaningful work, the all-pervasive assumption was that men ruled. Leading students of the Lutherans, Catholics, French Calvinists, and English Puritans tend to concur that there was no amelioration in women's definitely subordinate status.

There were some remarkable success stories, however. Elizabeth Hardwick, the orphaned daughter of an obscure English country squire, made four careful marriages, each of which brought her more property and carried her higher up the social ladder. She managed her estates, amounting to more than 100,000 acres, with a degree of business sense rare in any age. The two great mansions she built, Chatsworth and Hardwick, stand today as monuments to her acumen. Having established several aristocratic dynasties, she died in 1608, past her eightieth year, one of the richest people in England.[22]

Artists' drawings of plump, voluptuous women and massive, muscular men revealed the contemporary standards of physical beauty. It was a sensual age that gloried in the delights of the flesh. Some people, such as humanist poet Aretino, found sexual satisfaction with both sexes. Reformers and public officials simultaneously condemned and condoned sexual "sins." The oldest profession had many practitioners, and when in 1566 Pope Pius IV expelled all the prostitutes from Rome, so many people left and the city suffered such a loss of revenue that in less than a month the pope was forced to rescind the order. Scholars debated Saint Augustine's notion that whores serve a useful social function by preventing worse sins. Prostitution was common because desperate poverty forced women and young men into it. Since the later Middle Ages, licensed houses of prostitution had been common in urban centers (see page 388). The general public took the matter for granted. Consequently, civil authorities in both Catholic and Protestant countries licensed houses of public prostitution. These establishments were intended, however, for the convenience of single men, and some Protestant cities, such as Geneva and Zurich, installed officials in the brothels with the express purpose of preventing married men from patronizing them.

Moralists naturally railed against prostitution. For example, Melchior Ambach, the Lutheran editor of many tracts against adultery and whoring, wrote in 1543 that if "houses of women" for single and married men were allowed, why not provide a "house of boys" for women who lacked husbands to service them? "Would whoring be any worse for the poor, needy female sex?"[23] Ambach, of course, was not being serious: by treating infidelity from the perspective of female, rather than male, customers, he was still insisting that prostitution destroyed the family and society.

Single women of the middle and working classes in the sixteenth and seventeenth centuries worked in many occupations and professions—as butchers, shopkeepers, nurses, goldsmiths, midwives, and workers in the weaving and printing industries. Women who were married normally assisted in their husbands' businesses. And what became of the thousands of women who left convents and nunneries during the Reformation? This question concerns primarily women of the upper classes, who formed the dominant social group in the religious houses of late medieval Europe.

Luther and the Protestant reformers believed that celibacy had no scriptural basis, that young girls were forced by their parents into convents, and that once there they were bullied by men into staying. Therefore, reformers favored the suppression of women's religious houses and encouraged ex-nuns to marry. Marriage, the reformers maintained, not only gave women emotional and sexual satisfaction; it also freed them from clerical domination, cultural deprivation, and sexual repression.[24] Consequently, these women apparently passed from clerical domination to subservience to husbands.

If some nuns in the Middle Ages lacked a genuine religious vocation and if some religious houses witnessed financial mismanagement and moral laxness, convents nevertheless provided women of the upper classes with scope for their literary, artistic, medical, or administrative talents if they could not or would not marry. With the closing of convents, marriage became virtually the only occupation for upper-class Protestant women. This helps explain why Anglicans, Calvinists, and Lutherans established communities of religious women, such as the Lutheran one at Kaiserwerth in the Rhineland, in the eighteenth and nineteenth centuries.[25]

The Great European Witch-hunt

The great European witch scare reveals something about contemporary attitudes toward women. The period of the religious wars witnessed a startling increase in the phenomenon of witch-hunting,

❖ **Witches Worshiping the Devil** In medieval Christian art, a goat symbolizes the damned at the Last Judgment, following Christ's statement that the Son of Man would separate believers from nonbelievers, as a shepherd separates the sheep from the goats (Matthew 25:31–32). In this manuscript illustration, a witch arrives at a sabbat and prepares to venerate the devil in the shape of a goat by kissing its anus. *(Source: Bodleian Library, Oxford)*

whose prior history was long but sporadic. "A witch," according to Chief Justice Coke of England, "was a person who hath conference with the Devil to consult with him or to do some act." This definition by the highest legal authority in England demonstrates that educated as well as ignorant people believed in witches. Witches were thought to be individuals who could mysteriously injure other people or animals—by causing a person to become blind or impotent, for instance, or by preventing a cow from giving milk. Belief in witches predated Christianity. For centuries, tales had circulated about old women who made nocturnal travels on greased broomsticks to *sabbats,* or assemblies of witches, where they participated in sex-

ual orgies and feasted on the flesh of infants. In the popular imagination witches had definite characteristics. The vast majority were married women or widows between fifty and seventy years old, crippled or bent with age, with pockmarked skin. They often practiced midwifery or folk medicine, and most had sharp tongues and were quick to scold.

Religious reformers' extreme notions of the devil's powers and the insecurity created by the religious wars contributed to the growth of belief in witches. The idea developed that witches made pacts with the devil in return for the power to work mischief on their enemies. Since pacts with the devil meant the renunciation of God, witchcraft was considered heresy. Although persecution for witchcraft had actually begun in the later fourteenth century when witchcraft was declared heresy, persecution reached its most virulent stage in the late sixteenth and seventeenth centuries.

Fear of witches took a terrible toll of innocent lives in parts of Europe. In southwestern Germany, 3,229 witches were executed between 1561 and 1670, most by burning. The communities of the Swiss Confederation tried 8,888 persons between 1470 and 1700 and executed 5,417 of them as witches. In all the centuries before 1500, witches in England had been suspected of causing perhaps "three deaths, a broken leg, several destructive storms and some bewitched genitals." Yet between 1559 and 1736, witches were thought to have caused thousands of deaths, and in that period almost 1,000 witches were executed in England.[26]

Historians and anthropologists have offered a variety of explanations for the great European witch-hunt. Some scholars maintain that charges of witchcraft were a means of accounting for inexplicable misfortunes. Just as the English in the fifteenth century had blamed their military failures in France on Joan of Arc's witchcraft, so in the seventeenth century the English Royal College of Physicians attributed undiagnosable illnesses to witchcraft. Some scholars hold that in small communities, which typically insisted on strict social conformity, charges of witchcraft were a means of attacking and eliminating the nonconformist; witches, in other words, served the collective need for scapegoats. The evidence of witches' trials, some writers suggest, shows that women were not accused because they harmed or threatened their neighbors; rather, their communities believed such women worshiped the devil, engaged in wild sexual activities with him, and ate infants. Other scholars argue the exact opposite: that people were tried and executed as witches because their neighbors feared their evil powers. Finally, there is the theory that the unbridled sexuality attributed to witches was a psychological projection on the part of their accusers resulting from Christianity's repression of sexuality.

Though these different hypotheses exist, scholars still cannot fully understand the phenomenon. The exact reasons for the persecution of women as witches probably varied from place to place. Nevertheless, given the broad strand of misogyny (hatred of women) in Western religion, the long-held belief in the susceptibility of women (so-called weaker vessels) to the devil's allurements, and the pervasive seventeenth-century belief about women's multiple and demanding orgasms and thus their sexual insatiability, it is not difficult to understand why women were accused of all sorts of mischief and witchcraft. Charges of witchcraft provided a legal basis for the execution of tens of thousands of women. As the most important capital crime for women in early modern times, witchcraft has considerable significance for the history and status of women.[27]

European Slavery and the Origins of American Racism

Almost all peoples in the world have engaged in the enslavement of other human beings at some time in their histories. Since ancient times, victors in battle have enslaved conquered peoples. In the later Middle Ages slavery was deeply entrenched in southern Italy, Sicily, Crete, and Mediterranean Spain. The bubonic plague, famines, and other epidemics created a severe shortage of agricultural and domestic workers throughout Europe, encouraging Italian merchants to buy slaves from the Balkans, Thrace, southern Russia, and central Anatolia for sale in the West. In 1364 the Florentine government allowed the unlimited importation of slaves so long as they were not Catholics. Between 1414 and 1423, at least ten thousand slaves were sold in Venice alone. The slave trade represented one aspect of Italian business enterprise during the Renaissance: where profits were lucrative, papal

threats of excommunication completely failed to stop Genoese slave traders. The Genoese set up colonial stations in the Crimea and along the Black Sea, and according to an international authority on slavery, these outposts were "virtual laboratories" for the development of slave plantation agriculture in the New World.[28] This form of slavery had nothing to do with race; almost all slaves were

✤ **African Slave and Indian Woman** A black slave approaches an Indian prostitute. Unable to explain what he wants, he points with his finger; she eagerly grasps for the coin. The Spanish caption above moralizes on the black man using stolen money—yet the Spaniards ruthlessly expropriated all South American mineral wealth. (*Source: New York Public Library*)

white. How, then, did black African slavery enter the European picture and take root in the New World?

In 1453 the Ottoman capture of Constantinople halted the flow of white slaves from the Black Sea region and the Balkans. Mediterranean Europe, cut off from its traditional source of slaves, had no alternative source for slave labor but sub-Saharan Africa. The centuries-old trans-Saharan trade was greatly stimulated by the existence of a ready market in the vineyards and sugar plantations of Sicily and Majorca. By the later fifteenth century, the Mediterranean had developed an "American" form of slavery before the discovery of America.

Meanwhile, the Genoese and other Italians had colonized the Canary Islands in the western Atlantic. Prince Henry the Navigator's sailors (see pages 478–479) discovered the Madeira Islands and made settlements there. In this stage of European expansion, "the history of slavery became inextricably tied up with the history of sugar." Though it was an expensive luxury that only the affluent could afford, population increases and monetary expansion in the fifteenth century led to an increasing demand for sugar. Resourceful Italians provided the capital, cane, and technology for sugar cultivation on plantations in southern Portugal, Madeira, and the Canary Islands. Meanwhile, in the period 1490 to 1530, the port of Lisbon saw between three hundred and two thousand black slaves arrive annually (Map 15.4). From Lisbon, where African slaves performed most of the manual labor and constituted 10 percent of the city's population, slaves were transported to the sugar plantations of Madeira, the Azores, the Cape Verde Islands, and then Brazil. Sugar and the small Atlantic islands gave New World slavery its distinctive shape. Columbus himself, who spent a decade in Madeira, took sugar plants on his voyages to "the Indies."[29]

As already discussed, European expansion across the Atlantic led to the economic exploitation of the Americas. In the New World the major problem settlers faced was a shortage of labor. As early as 1495, the Spanish solved the problem by enslaving the native Indians. In the next two centuries, the Portuguese, Dutch, and English followed suit.

Unaccustomed to any form of forced labor, certainly not to panning gold for more than twelve hours a day in the broiling sun, the Indians died "like fish in a bucket," as one Spanish settler reported.[30] In 1515 a Spanish missionary, Bartolomé de las Casas (1474–1566), who had seen the evils of Indian slavery, urged the future emperor Charles V to end Indian slavery in his American dominions. Las Casas recommended the importation of blacks from Africa, both because church law did not strictly forbid black slavery and because he thought blacks could better survive under South American conditions. Charles agreed, and in 1518 the African slave trade began. (When the blacks arrived, Las Casas immediately regretted his suggestion.) Columbus's introduction of sugar plants, moreover, stimulated the need for black slaves; and the experience and model of plantation slavery in Portugal and the Atlantic islands encouraged the establishment of a similar agricultural pattern in the New World.

Several European nations participated in the African slave trade. Portugal brought the first slaves to Brazil; by 1600, 4,000 were being imported annually. After its founding in 1621, the Dutch West India Company, with the full support of the government of the United Provinces, transported thousands of Africans to Brazil and the Caribbean. Only in the late seventeenth century, with the chartering of the Royal African Company, did the English get involved. Thereafter, large numbers of African blacks poured into the West Indies and North America. In 1790 there were 757,181 blacks in a total U.S. population of 3,929,625. When the first census was taken in Brazil in 1798, blacks numbered about 2 million in a total population of 3.25 million.

Settlers brought to the Americas the racial attitudes they had absorbed in Europe. Settlers' beliefs and attitudes toward blacks derived from two basic sources: Christian theological speculation (see page 422) and Muslim ideas. In the sixteenth and seventeenth centuries, the English, for example, were extremely curious about Africans' lives and customs, and slavers' accounts were extraordinarily popular. Travel literature depicted Africans as savages because of their eating habits, morals, clothing, and social customs; as barbarians because of their language and methods of war; and as heathens because they were not Christian. English people saw similarities between apes and Africans; thus the terms *bestial* and *beastly* were frequently applied to Africans. Africans were believed to pos-

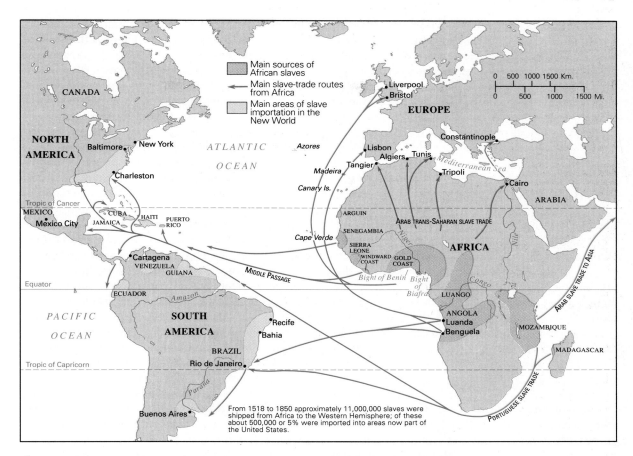

Main sources of
African slaves

Main slave-trade routes
from Africa

Main areas of slave
importation in the
New World

0 500 1000 1500 Km.
0 500 1000 1500 Mi.

From 1518 to 1850 approximately 11,000,000 slaves were
shipped from Africa to the Western Hemisphere; of these
about 500,000 or 5% were imported into areas now part of
the United States.

❖ **MAP 15.4 The African Slave Trade** Decades before the discovery of America,
Greek, Russian, Bulgarian, Armenian, and then black slaves worked the plantation
economies of southern Italy, Sicily, Portugal, and Mediterranean Spain—thereby
serving as models for the American form of slavery.

sess a potent sexuality. One seventeenth-century
observer considered Africans "very lustful and im-
pudent, . . . (for a Negroes hiding his members,
their extraordinary greatness) is a token of their
lust." African women were considered sexually aggressive, with a "temper hot and lascivious."[31]

"At the time when Columbus sailed to the New
World, Islam was the largest world religion, and
the only world religion that showed itself capable
of expanding rapidly in areas as far apart and as
different from each other as Senegal [in northwest
Africa], Bosnia [in the Balkans], Java, and the Philippines."[32] Medieval Arabic literature emphasized
blacks' physical repulsiveness, mental inferiority,
and primitivism. In contrast to civilized peoples
from the Mediterranean to China, some Muslim

writers claimed, sub-Saharan blacks were the only
peoples who had produced no sciences or stable
states. Fourteenth-century Arab historian ibn-
Khaldun wrote that "the only people who accept
slavery are the Negroes, owing to their low degree
of humanity and their proximity to the animal
stage." Though black kings, Khaldun alleged, sold
their subjects without even a pretext of crime or
war, the victims bore no resentment because they
gave no thought to the future and had "by nature
few cares and worries; dancing and rhythm are for
them inborn."[33] It is easy to see how such absurd
images developed into the classic stereotypes used
to justify black slavery in South and North America
in the seventeenth, eighteenth, and nineteenth
centuries. Medieval Christians and Muslims had

similar notions of blacks as inferior and primitive people ideally suited to enslavement. Perhaps centuries of commercial contacts between Muslim and Mediterranean peoples had familiarized the latter with Muslim racial attitudes. The racial beliefs that the Portuguese, Spanish, Dutch, and English brought to the New World, however, derived primarily from Christian theological speculation.

✤ LITERATURE AND ART

The age of religious wars and overseas expansion also experienced an extraordinary degree of intellectual and artistic ferment. This effervescence can be seen in the development of the essay as a distinct literary genre; in other prose, poetry, and drama; in art; and in music. In many ways, literature, the visual arts, music, and the drama of the period mirrored the social and cultural conditions that gave rise to them.

The Essay: Michel de Montaigne

Decades of religious fanaticism, bringing famine, civil anarchy, and death, led both Catholics and Protestants to doubt that any one faith contained absolute truth. The late sixteenth and seventeenth centuries witnessed the beginning of modern skepticism. *Skepticism* is a school of thought founded on doubt that total certainty or definitive knowledge is ever attainable. The skeptic is cautious and critical and suspends judgment. Perhaps the finest representative of early modern skepticism is Frenchman Michel de Montaigne (1533–1592).

Montaigne came from a bourgeois family that had made a fortune selling salted herring and wine and in 1477 had purchased the title and property of Montaigne in Gascony; his mother descended from a Jewish family that had been forced to flee Spain. Montaigne received a classical education before studying law and securing a judicial appointment in 1554. Though a member of the nobility, in embarking on a judicial career, he identified with the new nobility of the robe. He condemned the ancient nobility of the sword for being more concerned with war and sports than with the cultivation of the mind.

At the age of thirty-eight, Montaigne resigned his judicial post, retired to his estate, and devoted the rest of his life to study, contemplation, and an effort to understand himself. His wealth provided him with the leisure time to do so. A humanist, he believed that the object of life was to "know thyself," for self-knowledge teaches men and women how to live in accordance with nature and God. Montaigne developed a new literary genre, the essay—from the French *essayer*, meaning "to test or try"—to express his thoughts and ideas.

Montaigne's *Essays* provide insight into the mind of a remarkably humane, tolerant, and civilized man. From the ancient authors, especially the Roman Stoic Seneca, Montaigne acquired a sense of calm, inner peace, and patience. The ancient authors also inculcated in him tolerance and broadmindedness. Montaigne had grown up during the French civil wars, perhaps the worst kind of war. Religious ideology had set family against family, even brother against brother. He wrote:

In this controversy . . . France is at present agitated by civil wars, the best and soundest side is undoubtedly that which maintains both the old religion and the old government of the country. However, among the good men who follow that side . . . we see many whom passion drives outside the bounds of reason, and makes them sometimes adopt unjust, violent, and even reckless courses.[34]

Though he remained a Catholic, Montaigne possessed a detachment, an independence, an openness of mind, and a willingness to look at all sides of a question. As he wrote, "I listen with attention to the judgment of all men; but so far as I can remember, I have followed none but my own. Though I set little value upon my own opinion, I set no more on the opinions of others."

In a violent and cruel age, Montaigne was a gentle and sensitive man. In his famous essay "On Cruelty," he stated:

Among other vices I cruelly hate cruelty, both by nature and by judgment, as the extreme of all vices. . . .

I live in a time when we abound in incredible examples of this vice, through the license of our civil wars; and we see in the ancient histories nothing more extreme than what we experience of this every day. But that has not reconciled me to it at all.[35]

In the book-lined tower where Montaigne passed his days, he became a deeply learned man.

Yet he was not ignorant of worldly affairs, and he criticized scholars and bookworms who ignored the life around them. Montaigne's essay "On Cannibals" reflects the impact of overseas discoveries on Europeans' consciousness. His tolerant mind rejected the notion that one culture is superior to another:

I long had a man in my house that lived ten or twelve years in the New World, discovered in these latter days, and in that part of it where Villegaignon landed [Brazil]. . . .

I find that there is nothing barbarous and savage in [that] nation, by anything that I can gather, excepting, that every one gives the title of barbarism to everything that is not in use in his own country. As, indeed, we have no other level of truth and reason, than the example and idea of the opinions and customs of the place wherein we live.[36]

In his belief in the nobility of human beings in the state of nature, uncorrupted by organized society, and in his cosmopolitan attitude toward different civilizations, Montaigne anticipated many eighteenth-century thinkers.

The thought of Michel de Montaigne marked a sharp break with the past. Faith and religious certainty had characterized the intellectual attitudes of Western society for a millennium. Montaigne's rejection of any kind of dogmatism, his secularism, and his skepticism thus represented a basic change. In his own time and throughout the seventeenth century, few would have agreed with him. The publication of his ideas, however, anticipated a basic shift in attitudes. Montaigne inaugurated an era of doubt. "Wonder," he said, "is the foundation of all philosophy, research is the means of all learning, and ignorance is the end."[37]

✥ ELIZABETHAN AND JACOBEAN LITERATURE

In addition to the essay as a literary genre, the period fostered remarkable creativity in other branches of literature. England, especially in the latter part of Elizabeth's reign and in the first years of her successor, James I (r. 1603–1625), witnessed remarkable literary expression. The terms *Elizabethan* and *Jacobean* (referring to the reign of James) are used to designate the English music, poetry, prose, and drama of this period. The poetry of Sir Philip Sidney (1554–1586), such as *Astrophel and Stella,* strongly influenced later poetic writing. *The Faerie Queene* of Edmund Spenser (1552–1599) endures as one of the greatest moral epics in any language. The rare poetic beauty of the plays of Christopher Marlowe (1564–1593), such as *Tamburlaine* and *The Jew of Malta,* paved the way for the work of Shakespeare. Above all, the immortal dramas of William Shakespeare (1564–1616) and the stately prose of the Authorized, or King James, Bible marked the Elizabethan and Jacobean periods as the golden age of English literature.

William Shakespeare, the son of a successful glove manufacturer who rose to the highest municipal office in the Warwickshire town of Stratford-on-Avon, chose a career on the London stage. By 1592 he had gained recognition as an actor and playwright. Between 1599 and 1603, Shakespeare performed in the Lord Chamberlain's Company and became co-owner of the Globe Theatre, which after 1603 presented his plays.

Shakespeare's genius lies in the originality of his characterizations, the diversity of his plots, his understanding of human psychology, and his unexcelled gift for language. Shakespeare was a Renaissance man in his deep appreciation for classical culture, individualism, and humanism. Such plays as *Julius Caesar, Pericles,* and *Antony and Cleopatra* deal with classical subjects and figures. Several of his comedies have Italian Renaissance settings. The nine history plays, including *Richard II, Richard III,* and *Henry IV,* enjoyed the greatest popularity among Shakespeare's contemporaries. Written during the decade after the defeat of the Spanish Armada, the history plays express English national consciousness. Lines such as these from *Richard II* reflect this sense of national greatness with unparalleled eloquence:

This royal Throne of Kings, this sceptre'd Isle,
This earth of Majesty, this seat of Mars,
This other Eden, demi-paradise,
This fortress built by Nature for herself,
Against infection and the hand of war:
This happy breed of men, this little world,
This precious stone, set in the silver sea,
Which serves it in the office of a wall,
Or as a moat defensive to a house,
Against the envy of less happier Lands,
This blessed plot, this earth, this Realm, this England.

Shakespeare's later plays, above all the tragedies *Hamlet, Othello,* and *Macbeth,* explore an enormous range of human problems and are open to an almost infinite variety of interpretations. *Othello,* which nineteenth-century historian Thomas Macaulay called "perhaps the greatest work in the world," portrays an honorable man destroyed by a flaw in his own character and the satanic evil of his supposed friend Iago. *Macbeth's* central theme is exorbitant ambition. Shakespeare analyzes the psychology of sin in the figures of Macbeth and Lady Macbeth, whose mutual love under the pressure of ambition leads to their destruction. The central figure in *Hamlet,* a play suffused with individuality, wrestles with moral problems connected with re-

venge and with the human being's relationship to life and death. The soliloquy in which Hamlet debates suicide is perhaps the most widely quoted passage in English literature:

To be, or not to be: that is the question:
Whether 'tis nobler in the mind to suffer
The slings and arrows of outrageous fortune,
Or to take arms against a sea of troubles,
And by opposing end them?

Hamlet's sad cry "There is nothing either good or bad but thinking makes it so" expresses the anguish and uncertainty of modern life. *Hamlet* has always enjoyed great popularity because in his

❖ **Titus Andronicus** With classical allusions, fifteen murders and executions, a Gothic queen who takes a black lover, and incredible violence, this early Shakespearean tragedy (1594) was a melodramatic thriller that enjoyed enormous popularity with the London audience. Modern critics believe that it foreshadowed King Lear with its emphasis on suffering and madness.

many-faceted personality people have seen an aspect of themselves.

Shakespeare's dynamic language bespeaks his extreme sensitivity to the sounds and meanings of words. Perhaps no phrase better summarizes the reason for his immortality than this line from *Antony and Cleopatra*: "Age cannot wither [him], nor custom stale/ [his] infinite variety."

In 1929, in lectures at Oxford University, English novelist Virginia Woolf created an imaginary situation: what would have happened had Shakespeare had a wonderfully gifted sister who wanted to be an actress and to write poetry or plays? Unlike her brother, she would not have been sent to grammar school, and if on her own she had learned to read and write and occasionally picked up a book, her parents would soon have interrupted and told her to mend the stockings or mind the stew. Before she was out of her teens, her parents, loving though they were, would have selected a husband for her, and if the force of her gift for learning and the stage had been strong enough, she would have had the choice of obeying her parents or leaving their home. If she had succeeded in getting to London, she would have discovered that the theater did not hire women. Dependent on the kindness of strangers even for food, she would soon have found herself pregnant. And then "who shall measure the heat and violence of the poet's heart when caught and tangled in a woman's body?—she kills herself." Woolf concluded her story:

This may be true or it may be false—who can say?— but what is true in it, so it seemed to me, reviewing the story of Shakespeare's sister as I have made it, is that any woman born with a great gift in the sixteenth century would certainly have gone crazed, shot herself, or ended her days in some lonely cottage outside the village, half witch, half wizard, feared and mocked at. For it needs little skill in psychology to be sure that a highly gifted girl who had tried to use her gift for poetry would have been so thwarted and hindered by other people, so tortured and pulled asunder by her own contrary instincts, that she must lose her health and sanity to a certainty.[38]

Unlike Montaigne, Shakespeare's sister would not have had "a room of her own"—that is, the financial means to study and to write—even apart from the social and cultural barriers against a woman doing so.

Another great masterpiece of the Jacobean period was the Authorized Bible. At a theological conference in 1604, a group of Puritans urged James I to support a new translation of the Bible. The king in turn assigned the task to a committee of scholars, who published their efforts in 1611. Based on the best scriptural research of the time and divided into chapters and verses, the Authorized Version is actually a revision of earlier Bibles more than an original work. Yet it provides a superb expression of the mature English vernacular in the early seventeenth century. Consider Psalm 37:

Fret not thy selfe because of evill doers, neither bee thou envious against the workers of iniquitie.
For they shall soone be cut downe like the grasse; and wither as the greene herbe.
Trust in the Lord, and do good, so shalt thou dwell in the land, and verely thou shalt be fed.
Delight thy selfe also in the Lord; and he shall give thee the desires of thine heart.
Commit thy way unto the Lord: trust also in him, and he shall bring it to passe.
And he shall bring forth thy righteousness as the light, and thy judgement as the noone day.

The Authorized Version, so called because it was produced under royal sponsorship—it had no official ecclesiastical endorsement—represented the Anglican and Puritan desire to encourage lay people to read the Scriptures. It quickly achieved great popularity and displaced all earlier versions. British settlers carried this Bible to the North American colonies, where it became known as the King James Bible. For centuries the King James Bible has had a profound influence on the language and lives of English-speaking peoples.

✦ BAROQUE ART AND MUSIC

Throughout European history, the cultural tastes of one age have often seemed quite unsatisfactory to the next. So it was with the baroque. The term *baroque* itself may have come from the Portuguese word for an "odd-shaped, imperfect pearl" and was commonly used by late-eighteenth-century art critics as an expression of scorn for what they considered an overblown, unbalanced style. The hostility of these critics, who also scorned the Gothic style of medieval cathedrals in favor of a classicism inspired by antiquity and the Renaissance, has long since passed. Specialists now agree that the triumphs of the baroque marked one of the high points in the history of Western culture.

The early development of the baroque is complex, but most scholars stress the influence of Rome and the revitalized Catholic church of the later sixteenth century. The papacy and the Jesuits encouraged the growth of an intensely emotional, exuberant art. These patrons wanted artists to go beyond the Renaissance focus on pleasing a small, wealthy, cultural elite. They wanted artists to appeal to the senses and thereby touch the souls and kindle the faith of ordinary churchgoers while proclaiming the power and confidence of the reformed Catholic church. In addition to this underlying religious emotionalism, the baroque drew its sense of drama, motion, and ceaseless striving from the Catholic Reformation. The interior of the famous Jesuit Church of Jesus in Rome—the Gesù—combined all these characteristics in its lavish, shimmering, wildly active decorations and frescoes.

Taking definite shape in Italy after 1600, the baroque style in the visual arts developed with exceptional vigor in Catholic countries—in Spain and Latin America, Austria, southern Germany, and Poland. Yet baroque art was more than just "Catholic art" in the seventeenth century and the first half of the eighteenth. True, neither Protestant England nor the Netherlands ever came fully under the spell of the baroque, but neither did Catholic France. And Protestants accounted for some of the finest examples of baroque style, especially in music. The baroque style spread partly because its tension and bombast spoke to an agitated age, which was experiencing great violence and controversy in politics and religion.

In painting, the baroque reached maturity early with Peter Paul Rubens (1577–1640), the most outstanding and representative of baroque painters. Studying in his native Flanders and in Italy, where he was influenced by masters of the High Renaissance such as Michelangelo, Rubens developed his own rich, sensuous, colorful style, which was characterized by animated figures, melodramatic contrasts, and monumental size. Although Rubens excelled in glorifying monarchs such as Queen Mother Marie de' Medici of France, he was

❖ **Veronese: Feast in the House of Levi** Using the story in Mark 2:15, which says that many tax collectors and sinners joined Jesus at dinner, the Venetian painter celebrated patrician wealth and luxury in Venice's golden age. The black servants, dwarfs, and colonnades all contribute to the sumptuous setting. *(Source: Gallerie dell'Accademia/Archivio Cameraphoto Venezia/Art Resource, NY)*

also a devout Catholic. Nearly half of his pictures treat Christian subjects. Yet one of Rubens's trademarks was fleshy, sensual nudes, who populate his canvases as Roman goddesses, water nymphs, and remarkably voluptuous saints and angels.

Rubens was enormously successful. To meet the demand for his work, he established a large studio and hired many assistants to execute his rough sketches and gigantic murals. Sometimes the master artist added only the finishing touches. Rubens's wealth and position—on occasion he was given special diplomatic assignments by the Habsburgs—affirmed that distinguished artists continued to enjoy the high social status they had won in the Renaissance.

In music, the baroque style reached its culmination almost a century later in the dynamic, soaring lines of the endlessly inventive Johann Sebastian Bach (1685–1750), one of the greatest composers the Western world has ever produced. Organist and choirmaster of several Lutheran churches across Germany, Bach was equally at home writing secular concertos and sublime religious cantatas. Bach's organ music, the greatest ever written, combined the baroque spirit of invention, tension, and emotion in an unforgettable striving toward the infinite. Unlike Rubens, Bach was not fully appreciated in his lifetime, but since the early nineteenth century his reputation has grown steadily.

❖ **Velázquez: Juan de Pareja** This portrait (1650) of the Spanish painter Velázquez's one-time assistant, a black man of obvious intellectual and sensual power and himself a renowned religious painter, suggests the integration of some blacks in seventeenth-century society. The elegant lace collar attests to his middle-class status. *(Source: The Metropolitan Museum of Art)*

SUMMARY

In the sixteenth and seventeenth centuries, Europeans for the first time gained access to large parts of the globe. European peoples had the intellectual curiosity, driving ambition, and scientific technology to attempt feats that were as difficult and expensive then as going to the moon is today. Exploration and exploitation contributed to a more sophisticated standard of living, in the form of spices and Asian luxury goods, and to a terrible international inflation resulting from the influx of South American silver and gold. Governments, the upper classes, and the peasantry were badly hurt by the resulting inflation. Meanwhile, the middle class of bankers, shippers, financiers, and manufacturers prospered for much of the seventeenth century.

European expansion and colonization took place against a background of religious conflict and rising national consciousness. The seventeenth century was by no means a secular period. Though the medieval religious framework had broken down, people still thought largely in religious terms. Europeans explained what they did politically and economically in terms of religious doctrine. Religious ideology served as a justification for a variety of goals, such as the French nobles' opposition to the Crown and the Dutch struggle for political and economic independence from Spain. In Germany, religious hatreds and foreign ambitions led to the Thirty Years' War. After 1648 the divisions between Protestant and Catholic tended to become permanent. Religious skepticism and racial attitudes were harbingers of developments to come.

The essays of Montaigne, the plays of Marlowe and Shakespeare, the King James Bible, and the splendors of baroque art remain classic achievements of Western cultural heritage.

NOTES

1. Quoted in C. M. Cipolla, *Guns, Sails, and Empires: Technological Innovation and the Early Phases of European Expansion, 1400–1700* (New York: Minerva Press, 1965), pp. 115–116.
2. J. H. Parry, *The Age of Reconnaissance* (New York: Mentor Books, 1963), chaps. 3 and 5.
3. See C. R. Phillips, *Ciudad Real, 1500–1750: Growth, Crisis, and Readjustment in the Spanish Economy* (Cambridge, Mass.: Harvard University Press, 1979), pp. 103–104, 115.
4. Quoted in Cipolla, p. 132.
5. Quoted in F. H. Littell, *The Macmillan Atlas History of Christianity* (New York: Macmillan, 1976), p. 75.
6. Quoted in Cipolla, p. 133.
7. Quoted in S. E. Morison, *Admiral of the Ocean Sea: A Life of Christopher Columbus* (Boston: Little, Brown, 1946), p. 339.
8. Quoted in T. K. Rabb, "Columbus: Villain or Hero," *The Princeton Alumni Weekly* (October 14, 1992): 13.
9. J. M. Cohen, ed. and trans., *The Four Voyages of Christopher Columbus* (New York: Penguin Books, 1969), p. 37.
10. Quoted in R. L. Kagan, "The Spain of Ferdinand and Isabella," in *Circa 1492: Art in the Age of Exploration*, ed. J. A. Levinson (Washington, D.C.: National Gallery of Art, 1991), p. 60.
11. Quoted in F. Maddison, "Tradition and Innovation: Columbus' First Voyage and Portuguese Navigation in the Fifteenth Century," in ibid., p. 69.
12. See W. D. Phillips and C. R. Phillips, *The Worlds of Christopher Columbus* (Cambridge: Cambridge University Press, 1992), p. 273.
13. Quoted in J. Hale, "War and Public Opinion in the Fifteenth and Sixteenth Centuries," *Past and Present* 22 (July 1962): 29.
14. See ibid., pp. 18–32.
15. Quoted in N. Z. Davis, "The Rites of Violence: Religious Riot in Sixteenth Century France," *Past and Present* 59 (May 1973): 59.
16. See ibid., pp. 51–91.
17. Quoted in J. L. Motley, *The Rise of the Dutch Republic* (Philadelphia: David McKay, 1898), 1.109.
18. Quoted in P. Smith, *The Age of the Reformation* (New York: Henry Holt, 1951), p. 248.
19. H. Kamen, "The Economic and Social Consequences of the Thirty Years' War," *Past and Present* 39 (April 1968): 44–61.
20. This passage is based heavily on S. Ozment, *When Fathers Ruled: Family Life in Reformation Europe* (Cambridge, Mass.: Harvard University Press, 1983), pp. 50–99.
21. Ibid., pp. 85–92.
22. See D. Durant, *Bess of Hardwick: Portrait of an Elizabethan Dynast* (London: Weidenfeld & Nicolson, 1977).
23. Quoted in Ozment, p. 56.
24. Ibid. pp. 9–14.
25. See F. Biot, *The Rise of Protestant Monasticism* (Baltimore: Helicon Press, 1968), pp. 74–78.
26. N. Cohn, *Europe's Inner Demons: An Enquiry Inspired by the Great Witch-Hunt* (New York: Basic Books, 1975), pp. 253–254; K. Thomas, *Religion and the Decline of Magic* (New York: Charles Scribner's Sons, 1971), pp. 450–455.
27. See E. W. Monter, "The Pedestal and the Stake: Courtly Love and Witchcraft," in *Becoming Visible: Women in European History*, ed. R. Bridenthal and C. Koonz (Boston: Houghton Mifflin, 1977), pp. 132–135; and A. Fraser, *The Weaker Vessel* (New York: Random House, 1985), pp. 100–103.
28. C. Verlinden, *The Beginnings of Modern Colonization*, trans. Y. Freccero (Ithaca, N.Y.: Cornell University Press, 1970), pp. 5–6, 80–97.
29. This section leans heavily on D. B. Davis, *Slavery and Human Progress* (New York: Oxford University Press, 1984), pp. 54–62; the quotation is on p. 58.
30. Quoted in D. P. Mannix, with M. Cowley, *Black Cargoes: A History of the Atlantic Slave Trade* (New York: Viking Press, 1968), p. 5.
31. Ibid., p. 19.
32. See P. Brown, "Understanding Islam," *New York Review of Books*, February 22, 1979, pp. 30–33.
33. Davis, pp. 43–44.
34. D. M. Frame, trans., *The Complete Works of Montaigne* (Stanford, Calif.: Stanford University Press, 1958), pp. 175–176.
35. Ibid., p. 306.
36. C. Cotton, trans., *The Essays of Michel de Montaigne* (New York: A. L. Burt, 1893), pp. 207, 210.
37. Ibid., p. 523.
38. V. Woolf, *A Room of One's Own* (New York: Harcourt, Brace & World, 1957), p. 51.

SUGGESTED READING

Perhaps the best starting point for the study of European society in the age of exploration is Levenson, listed in the Notes, which treats geographical, nautical, political, and humanistic developments in a worldwide context. Parry, cited in the Notes, which treats the causes and consequences of the voyage of discovery, and J. H. Parry, *The Discovery of South America* (1979), which examines Europeans' reactions to the maritime discoveries and the whole concept of discovery, are still valuable. The urbane studies of C. M. Cipolla, that listed in the Notes; *Clocks and Culture, 1300–1700* (1967); *Cristofano and the Plague: A Study in the History of Public Health in the Age of Galileo* (1973); and *Public Health and the Medical Profession in the Renaissance* (1976), present fascinating material on technological and sociological developments written in a lucid style. Morison's work, cited in the Notes, is the standard biography of Columbus, but the recent work of W. D. Phillips and C. R. Phillips, *The Worlds of Christopher Columbus* (1991), is strongly recommended. The advanced student should consult F. Braudel, *Civilization and Capitalism, Fifteenth–Eighteenth Century,* vol. 1, *The Structures of Everyday Life* (1981); vol. 2, *The Wheels of Commerce* (1982); and vol. 3, *The Perspective of the World* (1984). These three fat volumes combine vast erudition, a global perspective, and remarkable illustrations.

For the religious wars, in addition to the references in the Suggested Reading for Chapter 14 and the Notes to this chapter, see H. Kamen, *The Iron Century: Social Change in Europe, 1550–1660* (1971), a fundamental work, and G. Huppert, *After the Black Death: A Social History of Early Modern Europe* (1986), a lucidly written and highly recommended work for students. J. H. M. Salmon, *Society in Crisis: France in the Sixteenth Century* (1975), traces the fate of French institutions during the civil wars. A. N. Galpern, *The Religions of the People in Sixteenth-Century Champagne* (1976), is a useful case study in religious anthropology, and W. A. Christian, Jr., *Local Religion in Sixteenth-Century Spain* (1981), traces the attitudes and practices of ordinary Spanish people.

A cleverly illustrated introduction to the Low Countries is K. H. D. Kaley, *The Dutch in the Seventeenth Century* (1972). For Spanish military operations in the Low Countries, see G. Parker, *The Army of Flanders and the Spanish Road, 1567–1659: The Logistics of Spanish Victory and Defeat in the Low Countries' Wars* (1972), and the more recent R. A. Stradling, *The Armada of Flanders: Spanish Maritime Policy and European War, 1568–1668* (1992). Parker's *Spain and the Netherlands, 1559–1659: Ten Studies* (1979), contains useful essays, of which students may especially want to consult "Why Did the Dutch Revolt Last So Long?" For the later phases of the Dutch-Spanish conflict, see J. I. Israel, *The Dutch Republic and the Hispanic World, 1606–1661* (1982), which treats the struggle in global perspective.

The starting point for the study of England's great ruler is W. MacCaffrey, *Elizabeth I* (1993); N. Jones, *The Birth of the Elizabethan Age* (1993), brings to life the concerns of the English people. MacCaffrey's *Queen Elizabeth and the Making of Policy* (1981) focuses on the political and religious problems of the reign and Elizabeth's solutions to them. C. Erickson, *The First Elizabeth* (1983), gives a psychologically resonant portrait, and the studies of C. Haight, *Elizabeth I* (1988); J. E. Neale, *Queen Elizabeth I* (1957); and L. B. Smith, *Elizabeth Tudor: Portrait of a Queen* (1980), remain helpful.

Nineteenth- and early-twentieth-century historians described the defeat of the Spanish Armada as a great victory for Protestantism, democracy, and capitalism, which those scholars tended to link together. Recent historians have treated the event in terms of its contemporary significance. For a sympathetic but judicious portrait of the man who launched the Armada, see G. Parker, *Philip II* (1978); A. W. Lovett, *Early Habsburg Spain, 1517–1598* (1986), discusses many facets of Spanish culture as well as giving a provocative portrait of Philip II. D. Howarth, *The Voyage of the Armada* (1982), discusses the expedition largely in terms of the individuals involved, whereas G. Mattingly, *The Armada* (1959), gives the diplomatic and political background; both Howarth and Mattingly tell very exciting tales. M. Lewis, *The Spanish Armada* (1972), also tells a good story, but strictly from the English perspective. The best recent account of the Armada is G. Parker and C. Martin, *The Spanish Armada* (1988). Significant aspects of Portuguese culture are treated in A. Hower and R. Preto-Rodas, eds., *Empire in Transition: The Portuguese World in the Time of Camões* (1985).

C. V. Wedgwood, *The Thirty Years' War* (1961), must be qualified in light of recent research on the social and economic effects of the war. G. Parker, *The Thirty Years' War* (1984), is an important but densely written work. A variety of opinions on the causes and results of the war are given in T. K. Rabb's anthology, *The Thirty Years' War* (1981). Several articles in the scholarly journal *Past and Present* provide some of the latest important findings. Two of these articles, by Kamen and Hale, respectively, are mentioned in the Notes; the others are J. V. Polisensky, "The Thirty Years' War and the Crises and Revolutions of Sixteenth Century Europe," 39 (1968), and M. Roberts, "Queen Christina and the General Crisis of the Seventeenth

Columbus Describes His First Voyage

On his return voyage to Spain in January 1493, Christopher Columbus composed a letter intended for wide circulation and had copies of it sent ahead to Isabella and Ferdinand and others when the ship docked at Lisbon. Because the letter sums up Columbus's understanding of his achievements, it is considered the most important document of his first voyage. Remember that his knowledge of Asia rested heavily on Marco Polo's Travels, *published around 1298.*

Since I know that you will be pleased at the great success with which the Lord has crowned my voyage, I write to inform you how in thirty-three days I crossed from the Canary Islands to the Indies, with the fleet which our most illustrious sovereigns gave me. I found very many islands with large populations and took possession of them all for their Highnesses; this I did by proclamation and unfurled the royal standard. No opposition was offered.

I named the first island that I found 'San Salvador,' in honour of our Lord and Saviour who has granted me this miracle. . . . When I reached Cuba, I followed its north coast westwards, and found it so extensive that I thought this must be the mainland, the province of Cathay.[1] . . . From there I saw another island eighteen leagues eastwards which I then named 'Hispaniola.'[2] . . .

Hispaniola is a wonder. The mountains and hills, the plains and meadow lands are both fertile and beautiful. They are most suitable for planting crops and for raising cattle of all kinds, and there are good sites for building towns and villages. The harbours are incredibly fine and there are many great rivers with broad channels and the majority contain gold.[3] The trees, fruits and plants are very different from those of Cuba. In Hispaniola there are many spices and large mines of gold and other metals. . . .[4]

The inhabitants of this island, and all the rest that I discovered or heard of, go naked, as their mothers bore them, men and women alike. A few of the women, however, cover a single place with a leaf of a plant or piece of cotton which they weave for the purpose. They have no iron or steel or arms and are not capable of using them, not because they are not strong and well built but because they are amazingly timid. All the weapons they have are canes cut at seeding time, at the end of which they fix a sharpened stick, but they have not the courage to make use of these, for very often when I have sent two or three men to a village to have conversation with them a great number of them have come out. But as soon as they saw my men all fled immediately, a father not even waiting for his son. And this is not because we have harmed any of them; on the contrary, wherever I have gone and been able to have conversation with them, I have given them some of the various things I had, a cloth and other articles, and received nothing in exchange. But they have still remained incurably timid. True, when they have been reassured and lost their fear, they are so ingenuous and so liberal with all their possessions that no one who has not seen them would believe it. If one asks for anything they have they never say no. On the contrary, they offer a share to anyone with demonstrations of heartfelt affection, and they are immediately content with any small thing, valuable or valueless, that is given them. I forbade the men to give them bits of broken crockery, fragments of glass or tags of laces, though if they could get them they fancied them the finest jewels in the world.

I hoped to win them to the love and service of their Highnesses and of the whole Spanish nation and to persuade them to collect and give us of the things which they possessed in abundance and which we needed. They have no religion and are not idolaters; but all believe that power and goodness dwell in the sky and they are firmly convinced that I have come from the sky with these ships and people. In this belief they gave me a good reception everywhere, once they had overcome their fear; and this is not because they are stupid—far from it, they are men of great intelligence, for they navigate all those seas, and give a marvellously good account of everything—but because they have never before seen men clothed or ships like these. . . .

In all these islands the men are seemingly content with one woman, but their chief or king is allowed more than twenty. The women appear to work more than the men and I have not been able to find out if they have private property. As far as I could see whatever a man had was shared among all the rest and this particularly applies to food. . . . In another island, which I am told is larger than Hispaniola, the people have no hair. Here there is a vast quantity of gold, and from here and the other islands I bring Indians as evidence.

In conclusion, to speak only of the results of this very hasty voyage, their Highnesses can see that I will give them as much gold as they require, if they will render me some very slight assistance; also I will give them all the spices and cotton they want . . . I will also bring them as much aloes as they ask and as many slaves, who will be taken from the idolaters. I believe also that I have found rhubarb and cinnamon and there will be countless other things in addition . . .

So all Christendom will be delighted that our Redeemer has given victory to our most illustrious King and Queen and their renowned kingdoms, in this great matter. They should hold great celebrations and render solemn thanks to the Holy Trinity with many solemn prayers, for the great triumph which they will have, by the conversion of so many peoples to our holy faith and for the temporal benefits which will follow, for not only Spain, but all Christendom will receive encouragement and profit.

This is a brief account of the facts.
Written in the caravel off the Canary Islands.[5]

15 February 1493

At your orders
THE ADMIRAL

German woodcut depicting Columbus' landing of San Salvador. *(Source: New York Public Library)*

Questions for Analysis

1. How did Columbus explain the success of his voyage?

2. What was Columbus's view of the native Americans he met?

3. Evaluate his statements that the Caribbean islands possessed gold, cotton, and spices.

4. Why did Columbus cling to the idea that he had reached Asia?

Source: J. M. Cohen, ed. and trans., *The Four Voyages of Christopher Columbus.* Copyright © 1969 Penguin Books Ltd.

1. [Cathay is the old name for China.] In the log-book and later in this letter Columbus accepts the native story that Cuba is an island which they can circumnavigate in something more than twenty-one days, yet he insists here and later, during the second voyage, that it is in fact part of the Asiatic mainland. 2. [Hispaniola is the second largest island of the West Indies; Haiti occupies the western third of the island, the Dominican Republic the rest.] 3. This did not prove to be true. 4. These statements are also inaccurate. 5. Actually Columbus was off Santa Maria in the Azores.

Century," 22 (1962), which treats the overall significance of Swedish participation.

As background to the intellectual changes instigated by the Reformation, D. C. Wilcox, *In Search of God and Self: Renaissance and Reformation Thought* (1975), contains a perceptive analysis, and T. Ashton, ed., *Crisis in Europe, 1560–1660* (1967), is fundamental. On witches and witchcraft, see, in addition to the titles by Cohn and Thomas in the Notes, J. B. Russell, *Witchcraft in the Middle Ages* (1976) and *Lucifer: The Devil in the Middle Ages* (1984); R. Kieckhefer, *European Witch Trials: Their Foundations in Popular and Learned Culture, 1300–1500* (1976), which places the subject within the social context; H. C. E. Midelfort, *Witch Hunting in Southwestern Germany: The Social and Intellectual Foundations* (1972), a sensitive and informed work; E. W. Monter, *Witchcraft in France and Switzerland* (1976), which discusses the subject with wit and wisdom; C. Ginzburg, *The Night Battle: Witchcraft and Agrarian Cults in the Sixteenth and Seventeenth Centuries* (1983), for small Italian communities; J. C. Baroja, *The World of Witches* (1964), for Spain; and the recent study of G. R. Quaife, *Godly Zeal and Furious Rage: The Witch in Early Modern Europe* (1987), an excellent and lucidly written synthesis.

For women, marriage, and the family, see L. Stone, *The Family, Sex, and Marriage in England, 1500–1800* (1977), a controversial work; D. Underdown, "The Taming of the Scold," and S. Amussen, "Gender, Family, and the Social Order," in A. Fletcher and J. Stevenson, eds., *Order and Disorder in Early Modern England* (1985); A. Macfarlane, *Marriage and Love in England: Modes of Reproduction, 1300–1848* (1986); C. R. Boxer, *Women in Iberian Expansion Overseas, 1415–1815* (1975), an invaluable study of women's role in overseas migration; S. M. Wyntjes, "Women in the Reformation Era," in R. Bridenthal and C. Koonz, eds., *Becoming Visible: Women in European History* (1977), a quick survey of conditions in different countries; A. Clark, *The Working Life of Women in the Seventeenth Century* (1968); K. M. Wilson, ed.,

Women Writers of the Renaissance and Reformation (1987); M. J. M. Ezell, *The Patriarch's Wife: Literary Evidence and the History of the Family* (1987); L. Pollock, *A Lasting Relationship: Parents and Children over Three Centuries* (1987); and L. Schwoerer, *Lady Russel: One of the Best Women* (1988). Ozment's work listed in the Notes is a seminal study concentrating on Germany and Switzerland. For the tragedies and triumphs of one remarkable Jewish businesswoman, see M. Lowenthal, ed. and trans., *The Memoirs of Glückel of Hamelin* (1977).

As background to slavery and racism in North and South America, students should see J. L. Watson, ed., *Asian and African Systems of Slavery* (1980), a valuable collection of essays, as well as the works by Davis and by Mannix and Cowley mentioned in the Notes: Davis shows how slavery was viewed as a progressive force in the expansion of the Western world; and Mannix and Cowley provide a hideously fascinating account of the slave trade. For North American conditions, interested students should consult W. D. Jordan, *The White Man's Burden: Historical Origins of Racism in the United States* (1974). The excellent essays in G. M. Frederickson, *The Arrogance of Race: Historical Perspectives on Slavery, Racism, and Social Inequality* (1988), stress the social and economic circumstances associated with the rise of plantation slavery. For Caribbean and South American developments, see F. P. Bowser, *The African Slave in Colonial Peru* (1974); J. S. Handler and F. W. Lange, *Plantation Slavery in Barbados: An Archeological and Historical Investigation* (1978); and R. E. Conrad, *Children of God's Fire: A Documentary History of Black Slavery in Brazil* (1983).

The leading authority on Montaigne is D. M. Frame. See his *Montaigne's Discovery of Man* (1955) and his translation, listed in the Notes. For baroque art, see V. L. Tapié, *The Age of Grandeur: Baroque Art and Architecture* (1961), a standard work, and J. Montagu, *Roman Baroque Sculpture: The Industry of Art* (1985), an original and entertaining recent study.

16

Absolutism and Constitutionalism in Western Europe (ca 1589–1715)

The Queen's staircase is among the grandest of the surviving parts of Louis XIV's Versailles. *(Source: © Photo R.M.N.)*

The seventeenth century was a period of revolutionary transformation. That century witnessed agricultural and manufacturing crises that had profound political consequences. A colder and wetter climate throughout most of the period meant a shorter farming season. Grain yields declined. In an age when cereals constituted the bulk of the diet for most people everywhere, smaller harvests led to food shortages and starvation. Food shortages in turn meant population decline or stagnation. Industry also suffered. While the evidence does not permit broad generalizations, it appears that the output of woolen textiles, one of the most important manufactures, declined sharply in the first half of the century. This economic crisis was not universal: it struck various sections of Europe at different times and to different degrees. In the middle decades of the century, Spain, France, Germany, and England all experienced great economic difficulties; but these years saw the golden age of the Netherlands.

Meanwhile, governments increased their spending, primarily for state armies; in the seventeenth century, armies grew larger than they had been since the time of the Roman Empire. To pay for these armies, governments taxed. The greatly increased burden of taxation, falling on a population already existing at a subsistence level, triggered revolts. All across Europe peasant revolts were extremely common, and everywhere the burden of new taxes or the increase of old ones contributed to almost every revolt of the period.[1]

Princes struggled to free themselves from the restrictions of custom, powerful social groups, or competing institutions. Spanish and French monarchs gained control of the major institution in their domains, the Roman Catholic church. Rulers of England and some of the German principalities, who could not completely regulate the church, set up national churches. In the German Empire, the Treaty of Westphalia placed territorial sovereignty in the princes' hands. The kings of France, England, and Spain claimed the basic loyalty of their subjects. Monarchs made laws, to which everyone within their borders was subject. These powers added up to something close to sovereignty.

A state may be termed *sovereign* when it possesses a monopoly over the instruments of justice and the use of force within clearly defined boundaries. In a sovereign state no system of courts, such as ecclesiastical tribunals, competes with state courts in the dispensation of justice; and private armies, such as those of feudal lords, present no threat to royal authority because the state's army is stronger. Royal law touches all persons within the country.

Sovereignty had been evolving during the late sixteenth century. Most seventeenth-century governments now needed to address the problem of *which* authority within the state would possess sovereignty—the Crown or privileged groups. In the period between roughly 1589 and 1715, two basic patterns of government emerged in Europe: absolute monarchy and the constitutional state. Almost all subsequent governments have been modeled on one of these patterns.

- How did these forms of government differ from the feudal and dynastic monarchies of earlier centuries?

- In what sense were these forms "modern"?

- What social and economic factors limited absolute monarchs?

- Which Western countries most clearly illustrate the new patterns of political organization?

- Why is the seventeenth century considered the "golden age of the Netherlands"?

This chapter will explore these questions.

✣ ABSOLUTISM

In the *absolutist* state, sovereignty is embodied in the person of the ruler. Absolute kings claimed to rule by divine right, meaning they were responsible to God alone. (Medieval kings governed "by the grace of God," but invariably they acknowledged that they had to respect and obey the law.) Absolute monarchs in the seventeenth and eighteenth centuries had to respect the fundamental laws of the land, though they claimed to rule by divine right.

Absolute rulers tried to control competing jurisdictions, institutions, or interest groups in their territories. They regulated religious sects. They abolished the liberties long held by certain areas, groups, or provinces. Absolute kings also secured the cooperation of the one class that historically had posed the greatest threat to monarchy, the nobility. Medieval governments, restrained by the church, the feudal nobility, and their own financial limitations, had been able to exert none of these controls.

In some respects, the key to the power and success of absolute monarchs lay in how they solved their financial problems. Medieval kings frequently had found temporary financial support through bargains with the nobility: the nobility agreed to an ad hoc grant of money in return for freedom from future taxation. In contrast, the absolutist solution was the creation of new state bureaucracies that directed the economic life of the country in the interests of the king, either forcing taxes ever higher or devising alternative methods of raising revenue.

Bureaucracies were composed of career officials appointed by and solely accountable to the king. The backgrounds of these civil servants varied. Absolute monarchs sometimes drew on the middle class, as in France, or utilized members of the nobility, as in Spain and eastern Europe. Where there was no middle class or an insignificant one, as in Austria, Prussia, Spain, and Russia, the government of the absolutist state consisted of an interlocking elite of monarchy, aristocracy, and bureaucracy.

Royal agents in medieval and Renaissance kingdoms had used their public offices and positions to benefit themselves and their families. In England, for example, Crown servants from Thomas Becket to Thomas Wolsey had treated their high offices as their private property and reaped considerable profit from them. The most striking difference between seventeenth-century bureaucracies and their predecessors was that seventeenth-century civil servants served the state as represented by the king. Bureaucrats recognized that the offices they held were public, or state, positions. The state paid them salaries to handle revenues that belonged to the Crown, and they were not supposed to use their positions for private gain. Bureaucrats gradually came to distinguish between public duties and private property.

Absolute monarchs also maintained permanent standing armies. Medieval armies had been raised by feudal lords for particular wars or campaigns, after which the troops were disbanded. In the seventeenth century, monarchs alone recruited and maintained armies—in peacetime as well as wartime. Kings deployed their troops both inside and outside the country in the interests of the monarchy. Armies became basic features of absolutist, and modern, states. Absolute rulers also invented new methods of compulsion. They concerned themselves with the private lives of potentially troublesome subjects, often through the use of secret police.

The rule of absolute monarchs was not all-embracing because they lacked the financial and military resources and the technology to make it so. Thus the absolutist state was not the same as a totalitarian state. *Totalitarianism* is a twentieth-century phenomenon; it seeks to direct all facets of a state's culture—art, education, religion, the economy, and politics—in the interests of the state. By definition totalitarian rule is *total* regulation. By twentieth-century standards, the ambitions of absolute monarchs were quite limited: each sought the exaltation of himself or herself as the embodiment of the state. Whether or not Louis XIV of France actually said, *"L'état, c'est moi!"* ("I am the state!"), the remark expresses his belief that he personified the French nation. Yet the absolutist state did foreshadow recent totalitarian regimes in two fundamental respects: in the glorification of the state over all other aspects of the culture and in the use of war and an expansionist foreign policy to divert attention from domestic ills. All of this is best illustrated by the experience of France, aptly known as the model of absolute monarchy.

The Foundations of French Absolutism: Sully and Richelieu

The ingenious Huguenot-turned-Catholic Henry IV (see page 493) ended the French religious wars with the Edict of Nantes (1598). The first of the Bourbon dynasty, and probably the first French ruler since Louis IX in the thirteenth century genuinely to care about the French people, Henry IV and his great minister Maximilian de Béthune, duke of Sully (1560–1641), laid the foundations

❖ **Luca Giordana: The Pasta Eater** In the 17th century, rich people carried a fork when they dined out, but its use spread very slowly from Italy and came into common use only about 1750. A German preacher damned the fork as a diabolical luxury: "God would not have given us fingers if he wanted us to use forks." So, if King Louis XIV could eat chicken stew with his fingers without spilling it, how can we fault this Neapolitan workingman for enjoying his spaghetti without a fork? *(Source: The Art Museum, Princeton University Museum purchase, John Maclean Magie and Gertrude Magie Fund)*

of later French absolutism. Henry denied influence on the royal council to the nobility, which had harassed the countryside for half a century. Maintaining that "if we are without compassion for the people, they must succumb and we all perish with them," Henry also lowered the severe taxes on the overburdened peasantry.

Sully proved himself a financial genius. He reduced the crushing royal debt accumulated during the era of religious conflict and began to build up the treasury. He revived an annual tax, the *paulette,* on people who had purchased judicial and financial offices and had consequently been exempt from taxation. The paulette provided a specific amount of revenue each year, and Sully assigned specific expenses against that revenue. One of the first French officials to appreciate the significance of overseas trade, Sully subsidized the Company for Trade with the Indies. He started a countrywide highway system and even dreamed of an international organization for the maintenance of peace.

In twelve short years, Henry IV and Sully restored public order in France and laid the foundations for economic prosperity. By the standards of the time, Henry IV's government was progressive and promising. His murder in 1610 by a crazed fanatic led to a severe crisis.

After the death of Henry IV, the queen-regent Marie de' Medici headed the government for the child-king Louis XIII (r. 1610–1643), but in fact feudal nobles and princes of the blood dominated the political scene. In 1624 Marie de' Medici secured the appointment of Armand Jean du Plessis—Cardinal Richelieu (1585–1642)—to the council of ministers. It was a remarkable appointment. The next year Richelieu became president of the council, and after 1628 he was first minister of the French crown. Richelieu used his strong influence over King Louis XIII to exalt the French monarchy as the embodiment of the French state. One of the greatest servants of that state, Richelieu set in place the cornerstone of French absolutism, and his work served as the basis for France's cultural hegemony of Europe in the later seventeenth century.

Richelieu's policy was the total subordination of all groups and institutions to the French monarchy. The French nobility, with its selfish and independent interests, had long constituted the foremost threat to the centralizing goals of the Crown and to a strong national state. Therefore, Richelieu tried to break the power of the nobility. He leveled castles, long the symbol of feudal independence. He crushed aristocratic conspiracies with quick executions. For example, when the duke of Montmorency, the first peer of France and the godson of Henry IV, became involved in a revolt in 1632, he was summarily put to death.

The constructive genius of Cardinal Richelieu is best reflected in the administrative system he established. He extended the use of the royal commissioners called intendants. France was divided into thirty-two *généralités* ("districts"), in each of which a royal intendant had extensive responsibility for justice, police, and finances. The intendants were authorized "to decide, order and execute all that they see good to do." Usually members of the upper middle class or minor nobility, the intendants were appointed directly by the monarch, to whom they were solely responsible. They could not be natives of the districts where they held authority; thus they had no vested interest in their localities. The intendants recruited men for the army, supervised the collection of taxes, presided over the administration of local law, checked up on the local nobility, and regulated economic activities—commerce, trade, the guilds, marketplaces—in their districts. They were to use their power for two related purposes: to enforce royal orders in the *généralités* of their jurisdiction and to weaken the power and influence of the regional nobility. The system of government by intendants derived from Philip Augustus's baillis and seneschals and ultimately from Charlemagne's missi dominici. As the intendants' power grew during Richelieu's administration, so did the power of the centralized state.

The cardinal perceived that Protestantism often served as a cloak for the political intrigues of ambitious lords. When the Huguenots revolted in 1625 under the duke of Rohan, Richelieu personally supervised the siege of their walled city, La Rochelle, and forced it to surrender. Thereafter, fortified cities were abolished. Huguenots were allowed to practice their faith, but they no longer possessed armed strongholds or the means to be an independent party in the state. Another aristocratic prop was knocked down.

French foreign policy under Richelieu was aimed at the destruction of the fence of Habsburg territories that surrounded France. Consequently, Richelieu supported the Habsburgs' enemies. In 1631 he signed a treaty with the Lutheran king Gustavus Adolphus promising French support against the Catholic Habsburgs in what has been called the Swedish phase of the Thirty Years' War (see page 501). French influence became an important factor in the political future of the German Empire. Richelieu acquired for France extensive rights in Alsace in the east and Arras in the north.

Richelieu's efforts at centralization extended even to literature. In 1635 he gave official recognition to a group of philologists who were interested in grammar and rhetoric. Thus was born the French Academy. With Richelieu's encouragement, the French Academy began the preparation of a dictionary to standardize the French language; it was completed in 1694. The French Academy survives as a prestigious society, and its membership now includes people outside the field of literature.

All of these new policies, especially war, cost money. In his *Political Testament,* Richelieu wrote, "I have always said that finances are the sinews of the state." He fully realized that revenues determine a government's ability to inaugurate and enforce policies and programs. A state secures its revenues through taxation. But the political and economic structure of France greatly limited the government's ability to tax. Seventeenth-century France remained "a collection of local economies and local societies dominated by local elites." The rights of some assemblies in some provinces, such as Brittany, to vote their own taxes; the hereditary exemption from taxation of many wealthy members of the nobility and the middle class; and the royal pension system drastically limited the government's power to tax.

Richelieu and, later, Louis XIV temporarily solved their financial problems by securing the cooperation of local elites. The central government shared the proceeds of tax revenue with local powers. It never gained all the income it needed. Because the French monarchy could not tax at will, it never completely controlled the financial system. In practice, therefore, French absolutism was strictly limited.[2]

In building the French state, Richelieu believed he had to resort to drastic measures against persons and groups within France and to conduct a tough anti-Habsburg foreign policy. He knew also that his approach sometimes seemed to contradict traditional Christian teaching. As a priest and bishop, how did he justify his policies? He developed his own *raison d'état* ("reason of state"): "What is done for the state is done for God, who is the basis and foundation of it." Richelieu had no doubt that "the French state was a Christian state . . . governed by a Christian monarch with the valuable aid of an enlightened Cardinal Minister." "Where the interests of the state are concerned," the cardinal himself wrote, "God absolves actions which, if privately committed, would be a crime."[3]

Richelieu persuaded Louis XIII to appoint protégé Jules Mazarin (1602–1661) as successor. An Italian diplomat of great charm, Mazarin had served on the council of state under Richelieu, acquiring considerable political experience. He became a cardinal in 1641 and a French citizen in 1643. When Louis XIII followed Richelieu to the grave in 1643 and a regency headed by Queen Anne of Austria governed for the child-king Louis XIV, Mazarin became the dominant power in the government. He continued Richelieu's centralizing policies, but his attempts to increase royal revenues led to the civil wars known as the "Fronde."

The word *fronde* means "slingshot" or "catapult," and a *frondeur* was originally a street urchin who threw mud at the passing carriages of the rich. The term came to be used for anyone who opposed the policies of the government. The policies of Richelieu and Mazarin had vastly increased the political power of the monarchy. By 1660 the state

❖ **Philippe de Champaigne: Cardinal Richelieu**
This portrait, with its penetrating eyes, expression of haughty and imperturable cynicism, and dramatic sweep of red robes, suggests the authority, grandeur, and power that Richelieu wished to convey as first minister of France. *(Source: Reproduced by courtesy of the Trustees, The National Gallery, London)*

bureaucracy included about sixty thousand office-holders, who represented a great expansion of the royal presence and a broad means of extracting the wealth of the working people. Naturally, these officeholders and state bureaucrats were the bitter targets of the exploited peasants and artisans. But these officials, who considered their positions the path to economic and social advancement, felt they were manipulated by the Crown and their interests ignored.[4] When in 1648 Mazarin proposed new methods of raising state income, bitter civil war ensued between the monarchy on the one side and the frondeurs (the nobility and middle class) on the other. Riots and public turmoil wracked Paris and the nation. Violence continued intermittently for the next twelve years.

The conflicts of the Fronde had three significant results for the future. First, it became apparent that the government would have to compromise with the bureaucrats and social elites that controlled local institutions and constituted the state bureaucracy. These groups were already largely exempt from taxation, and Louis XIV confirmed their privileged social status. Second, the French economy was badly disrupted and would take years to rebuild. Third, the Fronde had a traumatic effect on the young Louis XIV. The king and his mother were frequently threatened and sometimes treated as prisoners by aristocratic factions. On one occasion a mob broke into the royal bedchamber to make sure the king was actually there; it succeeded in giving him a bad fright. Louis never forgot such humiliations. The period of the Fronde formed the cornerstone of his political education and of his conviction that the sole alternative to anarchy was absolute monarchy. The personal rule of Louis XIV

The King Governs Personally, 1661 The central ceiling panel of the Hall of Mirrors at Versailles shows Louis in Roman armor but wearing the French royal mantle and guided by Minerva, goddess of wisdom. Putti, angelic boys, at his feast rejoice in the king's rule, but above, foreign enemies riding on clouds plot war. The portrait combines Louis' love of classical imagery and his devotion to war. *(Source: Giraudon/Art Resources, NY)*

represented the culmination of the process of centralization, but it also witnessed the institutionalization of procedures that would ultimately undermine the absolute monarchy.

The Absolute Monarchy of Louis XIV

According to the court theologian Bossuet, the clergy at the coronation of Louis XIV in Reims Cathedral asked God to cause the splendors of the French court to fill all who beheld it with awe. God subsequently granted that prayer. In the reign of Louis XIV (r. 1643–1715), the longest in European history, the French monarchy reached the peak of absolutist development. In the magnificence of his court, in his absolute power, in the brilliance of the culture that he presided over and that permeated all of Europe, and in his remarkably long life, the "Sun King" dominated his age. No wonder scholars have characterized the second half of the seventeenth century as the "Grand Century," the "Age of Magnificence," and, echoing the eighteenth-century philosopher Voltaire, the "Age of Louis XIV."

Who was this phenomenon of whom it was said that when Louis sneezed, all Europe caught cold? Born in 1638, king at the age of five, he entered into personal, or independent, rule in 1661. One of the first tales recorded about him gained wide circulation during his lifetime. Taken as a small child to his father's deathbed, he identified himself as *Louis Quatorze* ("Louis the fourteenth"). Since neither Louis nor his father referred to himself with numerals, the story is probably untrue. But it reveals the incredible sense of self that contemporaries, both French and foreign, believed that Louis possessed throughout his life.

In old age, Louis claimed that he had grown up learning very little, but recent historians think he was being modest. True, he knew little Latin and only the rudiments of arithmetic and thus by Renaissance standards was not well educated. Nevertheless, he learned to speak Italian and Spanish fluently, he spoke and wrote elegant French, and he knew some French history and more European geography than the ambassadors accredited to his court. He imbibed the devout Catholicism of his mother, Anne of Austria, and throughout his long life scrupulously performed his religious duties. (Beginning in 1661 Louis attended mass daily, but rather than paying attention to the liturgy, he said his rosary—to the scorn of his courtiers, who considered this practice "rustic.") Religion, Anne, and Mazarin all taught Louis that God had established kings as his rulers on earth. The royal coronation consecrated Louis to God's service, and he was certain—to use Shakespeare's phrase—that there was a divinity that doth hedge a king. Though kings were a race apart, they could not do as they pleased: they had to obey God's laws and rule for the good of the people.

Louis's education was more practical than formal. Under Mazarin's instruction, he studied state papers as they arrived, and he attended council meetings and sessions at which French ambassadors were dispatched abroad and foreign ambassadors received. He learned by direct experience and gained professional training in the work of government. Above all, the misery he suffered during the Fronde gave him an eternal distrust of the nobility and a profound sense of his own isolation. Accordingly, silence, caution, and secrecy became political tools for the achievement of his goals. His characteristic answer to requests of all kinds became the enigmatic *Je verrai* ("I shall see").

Louis grew up with an absolute sense of his royal dignity. Contemporaries considered him tall (he was actually 5 feet 5 inches) and distinguished in appearance but inclined to heaviness because of the gargantuan meals in which he indulged. A highly sensual man easily aroused by an attractive female face and figure, Louis nonetheless ruled without the political influence of either his wife, Queen Maria Theresa, whom he married as a result of a diplomatic agreement with Spain, or his mistresses. Anne-Marie-Louise, duchess of Montpensier, who was known as La Grande Mademoiselle, described him this way:

He has an elevated, distinguished, proud, intrepid, agreeable air . . . a face that is at the same time sweet and majestic. . . . His manner is cold; he speaks little except to people with whom he is familiar . . . [and then] he speaks well and effectively, and says what is apropos. . . . He has natural goodness, is charitable, liberal, and properly acts out the role of king.[5]

Louis XIV was a consummate actor, and his "terrifying majesty" awed all who saw him. He worked extremely hard and succeeded in being "every moment and every inch a king." Because he so relished the role of monarch, historians have had difficulty distinguishing the man from the monarch.

Historians have often said that Louis XIV introduced significant government innovations, the greatest of which was "the complete domestication of the nobility." By this phrase scholars meant that he exercised complete control over the powerful social class that historically had opposed the centralizing goals of the French monarchy. Recent research has demonstrated, however, that notions of "domestication" represent a gross exaggeration. What Louis XIV actually achieved was the cooperation or collaboration of the nobility. Throughout France the nobility agreed to participate in projects that both exalted the monarchy and reinforced the aristocrats' ancient prestige. Thus the relationship between the Crown and the nobility constituted collaboration rather than absolute control.

In the province of Languedoc, for example, Louis and his agents persuaded the notables to support the construction of the Canal des Deux Mers, a waterway linking the Mediterranean Sea and the Atlantic Ocean. Royal encouragement for the manufacture of luxury draperies in Languedocian towns likewise tied provincial business people to national goals, although French cloths subsequently proved unable to compete with cheaper Dutch ones. Above all, in the campaign for the repression of the Huguenots, the interests of the monarchy and nobility coincided. Aristocrats repeatedly petitioned Louis XIV to close Protestant churches and schools and to expel Huguenot ministers. In 1685 the king ultimately agreed. In each instance, through mutual collaboration, the nobility and the king achieved goals that neither could have won without the other. For his part, Louis won increased military taxation from the Estates of Languedoc. In return, Louis graciously granted the nobility and dignitaries privileged social status and increased access to his person, which meant access to the enormous patronage the king had to dispense. French government rested on the social and political structure of seventeenth-century France, a structure in which the nobility historically exercised great influence. In this respect, therefore, French absolutism was not so much modern as the last phase of a historical feudal society.[6]

Louis XIV installed his royal court at Versailles, a small town 10 miles from Paris. He required all the great nobility of France, at the peril of social, political, and sometimes economic disaster, to come live at Versailles for at least part of the year. Today Versailles stands as the best surviving museum of a vanished society on earth. In the seventeenth century, it became a model of rational order, the center of France, and the perfect symbol of the king's power (see Listening to the Past).

Louis XIII had begun Versailles as a hunting lodge, a retreat from a queen he did not like. His son's architects, Le Nôtre and Le Vau, turned what the duke of Saint-Simon called "the most dismal and thankless of sights" into a veritable paradise. Wings were added to the original building to make the palace U-shaped. Everywhere at Versailles the viewer had a sense of grandeur, vastness, and elegance. Enormous state rooms became display galleries for inlaid tables, Italian marble statuary, Gobelin tapestries woven at the state factory in Paris, silver ewers, and beautiful (if uncomfortable) furniture. If genius means attention to detail, Louis XIV and his designers had it: the decor was perfected down to the last doorknob and keyhole. In the gigantic Hall of Mirrors, later to reflect so much of German as well as French history, hundreds of candles illuminated the domed ceiling, where allegorical paintings celebrated the king's victories.

The art and architecture of Versailles served as fundamental tools of state policy under Louis XIV. The king used architecture to overawe his subjects and foreign visitors. Versailles was seen as a reflection of French genius. Thus the Russian tsar Peter the Great imitated Versailles in the construction of his palace, Peterhof, as did the Prussian emperor Frederick the Great in his palace at Potsdam outside Berlin.

As in architecture, so, too, in language. Beginning in the reign of Louis XIV, French became the language of polite society and the vehicle of diplomatic exchange. French also gradually replaced Latin as the language of international scholarship and learning. The wish of other kings to ape the courtly style of Louis XIV and the imitation of French intellectuals and artists spread the language all over Europe. The royal courts of Sweden, Russia, Poland, and Germany all spoke French. In the eighteenth century, the great Russian aristocrats were more fluent in French than in Russian. In England the first Hanoverian king, George I, spoke fluent French and only halting English. France inspired a cosmopolitan European culture in the late seventeenth century, and that culture was inspired by the king. The French today revere Louis XIV as one of their greatest national heroes because of the culture that he inspired and symbolized.

Against this background of magnificent splendor, so Saint-Simon describes him, Louis XIV

reduced everyone to subjection, and brought to his court those very persons he cared least about. Whoever was old enough to serve did not dare demur. It was still another device to ruin the nobles by accustoming them to equality and forcing them to mingle with everyone indiscriminately. . . .

Upon rising, at bedtime, during meals, in his apartments, in the gardens of Versailles, everywhere the courtiers had a right to follow, he would glance right and left to see who was there; he saw and noted everyone; he missed no one, even those who were hoping they would not be seen. . . .

Louis XIV took great pains to inform himself on what was happening everywhere, in public places, private homes, and even on the international scene. . . . Spies and informers of all kinds were numberless. . . .

But the King's most vicious method of securing information was opening letters.[7]

Though this passage was written by one of Louis's severest critics, all agree that the king used court ceremonials to undermine the power of the great nobility. By excluding the highest nobles from his councils, he weakened their ancient right to advise the king and to participate in government; they became mere instruments of royal policy. Operas, fetes, balls, gossip, and trivia occupied the nobles' time and attention. Through painstaking attention to detail and precisely calculated showmanship, Louis XIV reduced the major threat to his power. He separated power from status and grandeur: he secured the nobles' cooperation, and the nobles enjoyed the status and grandeur in which they lived.

Louis dominated the court, and in his scheme of things, the court was more significant than the government. In government Louis utilized several councils of state, which he personally attended, and the intendants, who acted for the councils throughout France. A stream of questions and instructions flowed between local districts and Versailles, and under Louis XIV a uniform and centralized administration was imposed on the country. In 1685 France was the strongest and most highly centralized state in Europe.

Councilors of state came from the recently ennobled or the upper middle class. Royal service provided a means of social mobility. These professional bureaucrats served the state in the person of

✧ **Hall of Mirrors, Versailles** The grandeur and elegance of the Sun King's reign are reflected in the Hall of Mirrors, where the king's victories were celebrated in paintings on the domed ceiling. Hundreds of candles lit up the dome. *(Source: Michael Holford)*

the king, but they did not share power with him. Louis stated that he chose bourgeois officials because he wanted "people to know by the rank of the men who served him that he had no intention of sharing power with them."[8] If great ones were the king's advisers, they would seem to share the royal authority; professional administrators from the middle class would not.

Throughout his long reign and despite increasing financial problems, he never called a meeting of the Estates General. The nobility therefore had no means of united expression or action. Nor did Louis have a first minister; he kept himself free from worry about the inordinate power of a Richelieu. Louis's use of spying and terror—a secret police force, a system of informers, and the practice of opening private letters—foreshadowed some of the devices of the modern state. French government remained highly structured, bureau-

The Spider and the Fly In reference to the insect symbolism (upper left), the caption on the lower left side of this illustration states, "The noble is the spider, the peasant the fly." The other caption (upper right) notes, "The more people have, the more they want. The poor man brings everything—wheat, fruit, money, vegetables. The greedy lord sitting there ready to take everything will not even give him the favor of a glance." This satirical print summarizes peasant grievances. (*Source: New York Public Library*)

cratic, centered at Versailles, and responsible to Louis XIV.

Financial and Economic Management Under Louis XIV: Colbert

Finance was the grave weakness of Louis XIV's absolutism. An expanding professional bureaucracy, the court of Versailles, and extensive military reforms (discussed later in this chapter) cost a great amount of money. The French method of collecting taxes consistently failed to produce enough revenue. Tax farmers, agents who purchased from the Crown the right to collect taxes in a particular district, pocketed the difference between what they raked in and what they handed over to the state.

Consequently, the tax farmers profited, while the government got far less than the people paid. In addition, by an old agreement between the Crown and the nobility, the king could freely tax the common people provided he did not tax the nobles. The nobility thereby relinquished a role in government: since nobles did not pay taxes, they could not legitimately claim a say in how taxes were spent. Louis, however, lost enormous potential revenue. The middle classes, moreover, secured many tax exemptions. With the rich and prosperous classes exempt, the tax burden fell heavily on those least able to pay, the poor peasants.

The king named Jean-Baptiste Colbert (1619–1683), the son of a wealthy merchant financier of Reims, as controller general of finances. Colbert came to manage the entire royal administration and proved himself a financial genius. Colbert's central principle was that the wealth and the economy of France should serve the state. He did not invent the system called "mercantilism," but he rigorously applied it to France.

Mercantilism is a collection of governmental policies for the regulation of economic activities, especially commercial activities, by and for the state. In seventeenth- and eighteenth-century economic theory, a nation's international power was thought to be based on its wealth, specifically its gold supply. Because, mercantilist theory held, resources were limited, state intervention was needed to secure the largest part of a limited resource. To accumulate gold, a country always had to sell more goods abroad than it bought. Colbert believed that a successful economic policy meant more than a favorable balance of trade, however. He insisted that the French sell abroad and buy *nothing* back. France should be self-sufficient, able to produce within its borders everything the subjects of the French king needed. Consequently, the outflow of gold would be halted, debtor states would pay in bullion, and with the wealth of the nation increased, its power and prestige would be enhanced.

Colbert attempted to accomplish self-sufficiency through state support for both old industries and newly created ones. He subsidized the established cloth industries at Abbeville, Saint-Quentin, and Carcassonne. He granted special royal privileges to the rug and tapestry industries at Paris, Gobelin, and Beauvais. New factories at Saint-Antoine in Paris manufactured mirrors to replace Venetian imports. Looms at Chantilly and Alençon competed with lacemaking at Bruges in the Spanish Netherlands, and foundries at Saint-Étienne made steel and firearms that reduced Swedish imports. To ensure a high-quality finished product, Colbert set up a system of state inspection and regulation. To ensure order within every industry, he compelled all craftsmen to organize into guilds, and within every guild he gave the masters absolute power over their workers. Colbert encouraged skilled foreign craftsmen and manufacturers to immigrate to France, and he gave them special privileges. To improve communications, he built roads and canals, the most famous linking the Mediterranean and the Bay of Biscay. To protect French goods, he abolished many domestic tariffs and enacted high foreign tariffs, which prevented foreign products from competing with French ones.

Colbert's most important work was the creation of a powerful merchant marine to transport French goods. He gave bonuses to French shipowners and shipbuilders and established a method of maritime conscription, arsenals, and academies for the training of sailors. In 1661 France possessed 18 unseaworthy vessels; by 1681 it had 276 frigates, galleys, and ships of the line. Colbert tried to organize and regulate the entire French economy for the glory of the French state as embodied in the king.

Colbert hoped to make Canada—rich in untapped minerals and some of the best agricultural land in the world—part of a vast French empire. He gathered four thousand peasants from western France and shipped them to Canada, where they peopled the province of Quebec. (In 1608, one year after the English arrived at Jamestown, Virginia, Sully had established the city of Quebec, which became the capital of French Canada.) Subsequently, the Jesuit Jacques Marquette and the merchant Louis Joliet sailed down the Mississippi River and took possession of the land on both sides as far south as present-day Arkansas. In 1684 the French explorer Robert La Salle continued down the Mississippi to its mouth and claimed vast territories and the rich delta for Louis XIV. The area was called, naturally, "Louisiana."

How successful were Colbert's policies? His achievement in the development of manufacturing was prodigious. The textile industry, especially in woolens, expanded enormously, and "France . . . had become in 1683 the leading nation of the world in industrial productivity."[9] The commercial classes prospered, and between 1660 and 1700 their position steadily improved. The national economy, however, rested on agriculture. Al-

though French peasants did not become serfs, as did the peasants of eastern Europe, they were mercilessly taxed. After 1685 other hardships afflicted them: poor harvests, continuing deflation of the currency, and fluctuation in the price of grain. Many peasants emigrated. With the decline in population and thus in the number of taxable people (the poorest), the state's resources fell. A totally inadequate tax base and heavy expenditure for war in the later years of the reign made Colbert's goals unattainable.

The Revocation of the Edict of Nantes

The absolutist state also attempted to control religion.

We now see with the proper gratitude what we owe to God . . . for the best and largest part of our subjects of the so-called reformed religion have embraced Catholicism, and now that, to the extent that the execution of the Edict of Nantes remains useless, we have judged that we can do nothing better to wipe out the memory of the troubles, of the confusion, of the evils that the progress of this false religion has caused our kingdom . . . than to revoke entirely the said Edict.[10]

Thus in 1685 Louis XIV revoked the Edict of Nantes, by which his grandfather Henry IV had granted liberty of conscience to French Huguenots. The new law ordered the destruction of churches, the closing of schools, the Catholic baptism of Huguenots, and the exile of Huguenot pastors who refused to renounce their faith. Why? There had been so many mass conversions during previous years (many of them forced) that Madame de Maintenon, Louis's second wife, could say that "nearly all the Huguenots were converted." Some Huguenots had emigrated. Richelieu had already deprived French Calvinists of political rights. Why, then, did Louis, by revoking the edict, persecute some of his most loyal and industrially skilled subjects, force others to flee abroad, and provoke the outrage of Protestant Europe?

Although recent scholarship has convincingly shown that Louis XIV was basically tolerant, he considered religious unity politically necessary to realize his goal of "one king, one law, one faith." He hated division within the realm and insisted that religious unity was essential to his royal dignity and to the security of the state. The seventeenth century, moreover, was generally not a tolerant one. While France in the early years of Louis's reign permitted religious liberty, it was not a popular policy. In fact, as mentioned earlier, aristocrats had petitioned Louis to crack down on Protestants. But the revocation was solely the king's decision, and it won him enormous praise. "If the flood of congratulation means anything, it . . . was probably the one act of his reign that, at the time, was popular with the majority of his subjects."[11]

While contemporaries applauded Louis XIV, scholars in the eighteenth century and later damned him for the adverse impact that revocation had on the economy and foreign affairs. Tens of thousands of Huguenot craftsmen, soldiers, and business people emigrated, depriving France of

their skills and tax revenues and carrying their bitterness to Holland, England, Prussia, and Capetown in South Africa. Modern scholarship has greatly modified this picture, however. While Huguenot settlers in northern Europe aggravated Protestant hatred for Louis, the revocation of the Edict of Nantes had only minor and scattered effects on French economic development.[12]

French Classicism

Scholars characterize the art and literature of the age of Louis XIV as "French classicism." By this they mean that the artists and writers of the late seventeenth century deliberately imitated the sub-

❖ **Poussin: The Rape of the Sabine Women** (ca 1636) Considered the greatest French painter of the seventeenth century, Poussin in this dramatic work shows his complete devotion to the ideals of classicism. The heroic figures are superb physical specimens, but hardly life-like. *(Source: The Metropolitan Museum of Art, New York, Harris Brisbane Dick Fund, 1946 (46.160))*

ject matter and style of classical antiquity, that their work resembled that of Renaissance Italy, and that French art possessed the classical qualities of discipline, balance, and restraint. Classicism was the official style of Louis's court. In painting, however, French classicism had already reached its peak before 1661, the beginning of the king's personal government.

Nicholas Poussin (1594–1665) is generally considered the finest example of French classicist painting. Poussin spent all but eighteen months of his creative life in Rome because he found the atmosphere in Paris uncongenial. Deeply attached to classical antiquity, he believed that the highest aim of painting was to represent noble actions in a logical and orderly, but not realistic, way. His masterpiece, *The Rape of the Sabine Women,* exhibits these qualities. Its subject is an incident in Roman history; the figures of people and horses are ideal representations, and the emotions expressed are studied, not spontaneous. Even the buildings are exact architectural models of ancient Roman structures.

Poussin, whose paintings still had individualistic features, did his work before 1661. After Louis's accession to power, the principles of absolutism molded the ideals of French classicism. Individualism was not allowed, and artists' efforts were directed to the glorification of the state as personified by the king. Precise rules governed all aspects of culture, with the goal of formal and restrained perfection.

Contemporaries said that Louis XIV never ceased playing the role of grand monarch on the stage of his court. If the king never fully relaxed from the pressures and intrigues of government, he did enjoy music and theater and used them as a backdrop for court ceremonials. Louis favored Jean-Baptiste Lully (1632–1687), whose orchestral works combined lively animation with the restrained austerity typical of French classicism. Lully also composed court ballets, and his operatic productions achieved a powerful influence throughout Europe. Louis supported François Couperin (1668–1733), whose harpsichord and organ works possessed the regal grandeur the king loved, and Marc-Antoine Charpentier (1634–1704), whose solemn religious music entertained him at meals. Charpentier received a pension for the *Te Deums,* hymns of thanksgiving, he composed to celebrate French military victories.

Louis XIV loved the stage, and in the plays of Molière and Racine his court witnessed the finest

❖ **Jean-Baptiste Poquelin or Molière** An elegant, sensuous, and romantic portrait of the playwright whose works set the moral tone of Louis' court. Louis basked in Molière's admiration, approved his social criticism, and amply rewarded him. *(Source: Musée de Versailles/Photographie Bulloz)*

achievements in the history of the French theater. When Jean-Baptiste Poquelin (1622–1673), the son of a prosperous tapestry maker, refused to join his father's business and entered the theater, he took the stage name "Molière." As playwright, stage manager, director, and actor, Molière produced comedies that exposed the hypocrisies and follies of society through brilliant caricature. *Tartuffe* satirized the religious hypocrite, *Le Bourgeois Gentilhomme* (The Bourgeois Gentleman) attacked the social parvenu, and *Les Femmes Savantes* (The Learned Women) mocked the fashionable pseudo-intellectuals of the day. In structure Molière's plays followed classical models, but they were based on careful social observation. Molière made the bourgeoisie the butt of his ridicule; he stopped short of criticizing the nobility, thus reflecting the policy of his royal patron.

While Molière dissected social mores, his contemporary Jean Racine (1639–1699) analyzed the power of love. Racine based his tragic dramas on Greek and Roman legends, and his persistent theme was the conflict of good and evil. Several plays—*Andromaque, Bérénice, Iphigénie,* and *Phèdre*—bore the names of women and dealt with the power of passion in women. Louis preferred *Mithridate* and *Britannicus* because of the "grandeur" of their themes. For simplicity of language, symmetrical structure, and calm restraint, the plays of Racine represent the finest examples of French classicism. His tragedies and Molière's comedies are still produced today.

Louis XIV's Wars

On his deathbed Louis XIV is reputed to have said, "I have gone to war too lightly and pursued it for vanity's sake." Perhaps he never actually said this. If he did, perhaps it was part of the confessional style of the time, which required that a penitent exaggerate his sins.[13] In any case, the course of Louis's reign suggests that he acted according to his observation that "the character of a conqueror is regarded as the noblest and highest of titles." In pursuit of the title of "conqueror," he kept France at war for thirty-three of the fifty-four years of his personal rule.

It is an axiom of history that war or the preparation for war is always a government's greatest expense. In 1635 when Richelieu became first minister of Louis XIII, the French army consisted of 25,000 men. At Richelieu's death in 1642 the army had 100,000 men. In 1659 at the time of the Peace of the Pyrenees, which ended the war with Spain, the army theoretically was composed of 250,000 men. These numbers represent a phenomenal expansion of the military and an enormous increase in costs to the state. In 1666 Louis appointed François le Tellier (later marquis de Louvois) secretary of state for war. Under the king's watchful eye, Louvois created a professional army that was modern in the sense that the French state, rather than private nobles, employed the soldiers. The king himself took command and directly supervised all aspects and details of military affairs.

Louis personally appointed not only the marshals of France (the highest rank) but also all officers down to the rank of colonel. Louvois utilized several methods in recruiting troops: by dragooning, in which press gangs seized men off the streets, often drunks, bums, and criminals (this method was not popular); conscription; and, after

1688, lottery. Louvois also recruited regiments of foreign mercenaries in Italy, Germany, England, Scotland, Ireland, and Switzerland. Under the strict direction of Jean Martinet (d. 1672), whose name became a byword in the French and English languages for absolute adherence to the rules, the foreign and native-born soldiers were turned into a tough, obedient, military machine. A commissariat was established to feed the troops, thereby taking the place of the ancient method of living off the countryside. An ambulance corps was designed to look after the wounded. Uniforms and weapons were standardized. A rational system of training and promotion was imposed. All this added up to a military revolution. A new military machine now existed that enabled one national state, France, to dominate the affairs of the Continent for the first time in European history.

Louis continued on a broader scale the expansionist policy begun by Cardinal Richelieu. In 1667, using a dynastic excuse, he invaded Flanders, part of the Spanish Netherlands, and Franche-Comté in the east. In consequence he acquired twelve towns, including the important commercial centers of Lille and Tournai (Map 16.1). Five years later, Louis personally led an army of over 100,000 men into Holland, and the Dutch ultimately saved themselves only by opening the dikes and flooding the countryside. This war, which lasted six years and eventually involved the Holy Roman Empire and Spain, was concluded by the Treaty of Nijmegen (1678). Louis gained additional Flemish towns and all of Franche-Comté.

Encouraged by his successes, by the weakness of the German Empire, and by divisions among the other European powers, Louis continued his aggression. In 1681 he seized the city of Strasbourg and three years later sent his armies into the province of Lorraine. At that moment the king seemed invincible. In fact, Louis had reached the limit of his expansion at Nijmegen. The wars of the 1680s and 1690s brought him no additional territories. In 1689 the Dutch prince William of Orange (r. 1689–1702), a bitter foe of Louis XIV, became king of England. William joined the League of Augsburg—which included the Habsburg emperor, the kings of Spain and Sweden, and the electors of Bavaria, Saxony, and the Palatinate. William was the unquestioned leader of the coalition, and he threw the weight of England and the Netherlands into the struggle. Neither the French nor

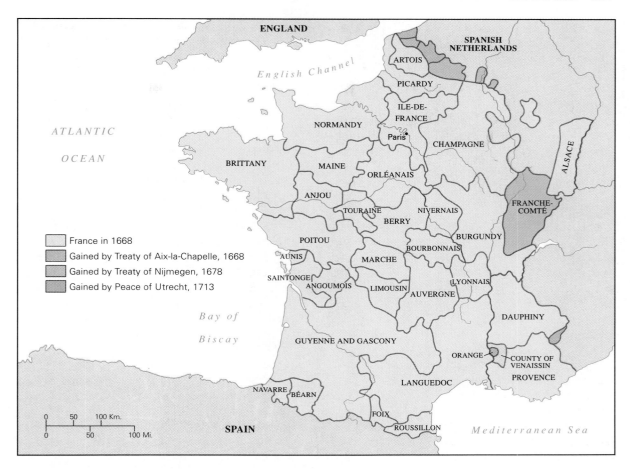

ENGLAND

English Channel

SPANISH
NETHERLANDS

ARTOIS

PICARDY

ILE-DE-
FRANCE

ATLANTIC

NORMANDY

Paris

CHAMPAGNE

ALSACE

OCEAN

BRITTANY

MAINE

ORLÉANAIS

ANJOU

TOURAINE

NIVERNAIS

BERRY

FRANCHE-
COMTÉ

POITOU

BURGUNDY

BOURBONNAIS

AUNIS

MARCHE

SAINTONGE

ANGOUMOIS

LIMOUSIN

LYONNAIS

AUVERGNE

Bay of

DAUPHINY

Biscay

GUYENNE AND GASCONY

ORANGE

COUNTY OF
VENAISSIN

PROVENCE

NAVARRE BÉARN

LANGUEDOC

FOIX

SPAIN

ROUSSILLON

Mediterranean Sea

☐ France in 1668
▨ Gained by Treaty of Aix-la-Chapelle, 1668
▨ Gained by Treaty of Nijmegen, 1678
▨ Gained by Peace of Utrecht, 1713

0   50   100 Km.
0   50   100 Mi.

✤ **MAP 16.1 The Acquisitions of Louis XIV, 1668–1713** The desire for glory and the weakness of his German neighbors encouraged Louis' expansionist policy. But he paid a high price for his acquisitions.

the league won any decisive victories. France lacked the means to win; it was financially exhausted.

Louis was attempting to support an army of 200,000 men, in several different theaters of war, against the great nations of Europe, the powerful Bank of Amsterdam, and (after 1694) the Bank of England. This task far exceeded French resources, given the very inequitable system of taxation. The military revolution involving the reform and great expansion of the army required funding that the state could not meet. Claude Le Peletier, Colbert's successor as minister of finance, resorted to the devaluation of the currency (which hurt those who hoarded coins) and the old device of selling offices, tax exemptions, and titles of nobility. To raise revenue for the war effort, on December 14, 1689, Louis published a declaration ordering that all the nation's silverware be handed over to the mint. Setting an example, Louis sent off the silver furniture of Versailles—cabinets, mirrors, tables, arm chairs, stools, chimney decorations, *guéridons* (pedestal tables), bowls, urns, vases, candelabra, saltcellars, trays, flowerpots, pails, and spittoons. The royal apartments and the Hall of Mirrors looked like a house repossessed by sheriffs.[14] This action did little good. None of these measures produced enough revenue. So the weight of taxation fell on the already overburdened peasants. They expressed their frustrations in widespread revolts that hit all parts of France in the 1690s.

A series of bad harvests between 1688 and 1694 brought catastrophe. Cold, wet summers reduced the harvests by an estimated one-third to two-thirds. The price of wheat skyrocketed. The result

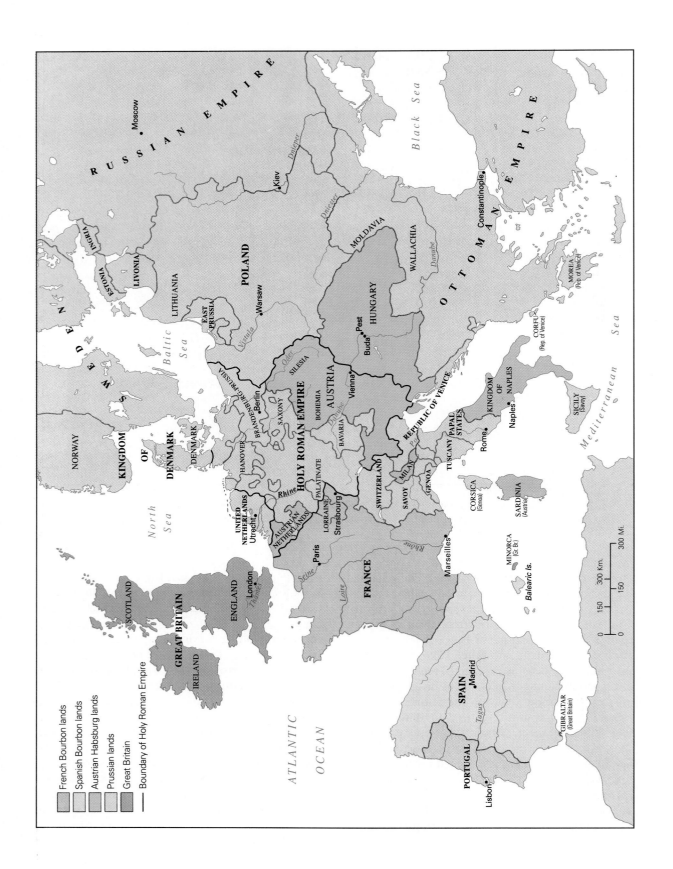

RUSSIAN EMPIRE

Moscow

Kiev

Dnieper

Dniester

POLAND

Warsaw

MOLDAVIA

WALLACHIA

Danube

Black Sea

OTTOMAN EMPIRE

Constantinople

SWEDEN

FINLAND

ESTONIA

LIVONIA

LITHUANIA

EAST PRUSSIA

Vistula

SILESIA

BOHEMIA

HUNGARY

Buda Pest

Vienna

AUSTRIA

Danube

Oder

BRANDENBURG-PRUSSIA

Berlin

SAXONY

BAVARIA

HOLY ROMAN EMPIRE

REPUBLIC OF VENICE

Po

MOREA
(Rep. of Venice)

CORFU
(Rep. of Venice)

Baltic Sea

NORWAY

KINGDOM OF DENMARK

DENMARK

HANOVER

Rhine

PALATINATE

SWITZERLAND

MILAN

SAVOY

GENOA

TUSCANY

PAPAL STATES

Rome

KINGDOM OF NAPLES

Naples

SICILY
(Savoy)

Mediterranean Sea

North Sea

UNITED NETHERLANDS

Utrecht

AUSTRIAN NETHERLANDS

LORRAINE

Strasbourg

Paris

Seine

Loire

FRANCE

Marseilles

Rhône

CORSICA
(Genoa)

SARDINIA
(Austria)

MINORCA
(Gr. Br.)

Balearic Is.

SCOTLAND

GREAT BRITAIN

IRELAND

ENGLAND

London

Thames

ATLANTIC OCEAN

SPAIN

Madrid

Tagus

GIBRALTAR
(Great Britain)

PORTUGAL

Lisbon

300 Mi.

300 Km.

150

150

0

0

French Bourbon lands
Spanish Bourbon lands
Austrian Habsburg lands
Prussian lands
Great Britain
Boundary of Holy Roman Empire

was widespread starvation, and in many provinces the death rate rose to several times the normal figure. Parish registers reveal that France buried at least one-tenth of its population in those years, perhaps 2 million in 1693 to 1694 alone. Rising grain prices, new taxes for war on top of old ones, a slump in manufacturing and thus in exports, and the constant nuisance of pillaging troops—all these meant great suffering for the French people. France wanted peace at any price. Louis XIV granted a respite for five years while he prepared for the conflict later known as the War of the Spanish Succession.

In 1694 the controller general of finance, Louis Pontchartrain (1643–1727), imposed the *capitation,* an annual poll tax. On the theory that the poor would pay more willingly if they knew that the rich also were taxed, the capitation fell on the entire civil population, including the nobility. Pontchartrain intended to associate the entire civil population in the war effort.

The War of the Spanish Succession (1701–1713), provoked by the territorial disputes of the previous century, also involved the dynastic question of the succession to the Spanish throne. It was an open secret in Europe that the king of Spain, Charles II (r. 1665–1700), was mentally defective and sexually impotent. In 1698 the European powers, including France, agreed by treaty to partition, or divide, the vast Spanish possessions between the king of France and the Holy Roman Emperor, who were Charles II's brothers-in-law. When Charles died in 1700, however, his will left the Spanish crown and the worldwide Spanish Empire to Philip of Anjou, Louis XIV's grandson. While the will specifically rejected union of the French and Spanish crowns, Louis was obviously

❖ **MAP 16.2 Europe in 1715** The series of treaties commonly called the Peace of Utrecht (April 1713–November 1715) ended the War of the Spanish Succession and redrew the map of Europe. A French Bourbon king succeeded to the Spanish throne on the understanding that the French not attempt to unite the French and Spanish crowns. France surrendered to Austria the Spanish Netherlands (later Belgium), then in French hands; and France recognized the Hohenzollern rulers of Prussia. Spain ceded Gibraltar to Great Britain, for which it has been a strategic naval station ever since. Spain also granted to Britain the *asiento,* the contract for supplying African slaves to America.

the power in France, not his seventeen-year-old grandson. Louis reneged on the treaty and accepted the will.

The Dutch and the English would not accept French acquisition of the Spanish Netherlands and of the rich trade with the Spanish colonies. The union of the Spanish and French crowns, moreover, would have totally upset the European balance of power. Claiming that he was following both Spanish national interests and French dynastic and national interests, Louis presented Philip of Anjou to the Spanish ambassador saying, "You may salute him as your king." After a mass of thanksgiving, the Spanish ambassador was heard to say, "What rapture! The Pyrenees no longer exist."[15] The possibility of achieving this goal provoked the long-anticipated crisis.

In 1701 the English, Dutch, Austrians, and Prussians formed the Grand Alliance against Louis XIV. They claimed that they were fighting to prevent France from becoming too strong in Europe, but during the previous half-century, overseas maritime rivalry among France, Holland, and England had created serious international tension. The secondary motive of the allied powers was to check France's expanding commercial power in North America, Asia, and Africa. In the ensuing series of conflicts, two great soldiers dominated the alliance against France: Eugene, prince of Savoy, representing the Holy Roman Empire, and Englishman John Churchill, subsequently duke of Marlborough. Eugene and Churchill inflicted a severe defeat on Louis in 1704 at Blenheim in Bavaria. Marlborough followed with another victory at Ramillies near Namur in Brabant.

The war was finally concluded at Utrecht in 1713, where the principle of partition was applied. Louis's grandson, Philip, remained the first Bourbon king of Spain on the understanding that the French and Spanish crowns would never be united. France surrendered Newfoundland, Nova Scotia, and the Hudson Bay territory to England, which also acquired Gibraltar, Minorca, and control of the African slave trade from Spain. The Dutch gained little because Austria received the former Spanish Netherlands (Map 16.2).

The Peace of Utrecht had important international consequences. It represented the balance-of-power principle in operation, setting limits on the extent to which any one power—in this case, France—could expand. The treaty completed the decline of Spain as a great power. It vastly expanded the British Empire. And it gave European powers experience in international cooperation, thus preparing them for the alliances against France at the end of the century.

The Peace of Utrecht marked the end of French expansionist policy. In Louis's thirty-five-year quest for military glory, his main territorial acquisition was Strasbourg. Even revisionist historians, who portray the aging monarch as responsible in negotiation and moderate in his demands, acknowledge "that the widespread misery in France during the period was in part due to royal policies, especially the incessant wars."[16] To raise revenue for the wars, forty thousand additional offices had been sold, thus increasing the number of families exempt from future taxation. In 1714 France hovered on the brink of financial bankruptcy. Louis had exhausted the country without much compensation. It is no wonder that when he died on September 1, 1715, Saint-Simon wrote, "Those . . . wearied by the heavy and oppressive rule of the King and his ministers, felt a delighted freedom. . . . Paris . . . found relief in the hope of liberation. . . . The provinces . . . quivered with delight . . . [and] the people, ruined, abused, despairing, now thanked God for a deliverance which answered their most ardent desires."[17]

The Decline of Absolutist Spain in the Seventeenth Century

Spanish absolutism and greatness had preceded those of the French. In the sixteenth century, Spain (or, more precisely, the kingdom of Castile) had developed the standard features of absolute monarchy: a permanent bureaucracy staffed by professionals employed in the various councils of state, a standing army, and national taxes, the *servicios,* which fell most heavily on the poor.

France depended on financial and administrative unification within its borders; Spain had developed an international absolutism on the basis of silver bullion from Peru. Spanish gold and silver, armies, and glory had dominated the Continent for most of the sixteenth century, but by the 1590s the seeds of disaster were sprouting. While France in the seventeenth century was representing the classic model of the modern absolute state, Spain was experiencing steady decline. The lack of a strong middle class, largely the result of the expulsion of the Jews and Moors (see page 432), the agricul-

tural crisis and population decline, the failure to invest in productive enterprises, the intellectual isolation and psychological malaise—all combined to reduce Spain, by 1715, to a second-rate power.

The fabulous and seemingly inexhaustible flow of silver from Mexico and Peru had led Philip II (see page 497) to assume the role of defender of Roman Catholicism in Europe. To humble the Dutch and to regain control of all the Low Countries, Philip believed that England, the Netherlands' greatest supporter, had to be crushed. He poured millions of Spanish ducats and all of Spanish hopes into the vast fleet that sailed in 1588. When the "Invincible Armada" went down, a century of Spanish pride and power went with it. After 1590 a spirit of defeatism and disillusionment crippled almost all efforts at reform.

Philip II's Catholic crusade had been financed by the revenues of the Spanish-Atlantic economy. These included, in addition to silver and gold bullion, the sale of cloth, grain, oil, and wine to the colonies. In the early seventeenth century, the Dutch and English began to trade with the Spanish colonies, cutting into the revenues that had gone to Spain. Mexico and Peru themselves developed local industries, further lessening their need to buy from Spain. Between 1610 and 1650, Spanish trade with the colonies fell 60 percent.

At the same time, the native Indians and African slaves who worked the South American silver mines under conditions that would have shamed the ancient Egyptian pharaohs suffered frightful epidemics of disease. Moreover, the lodes started to run dry. Consequently, the quantity of metal produced for Spain steadily declined. However, in Madrid royal expenditures constantly exceeded income. The remedies applied in the face of a mountainous state debt and declining revenues were devaluation of the coinage and declarations of bankruptcy. In 1596, 1607, 1627, 1647, and 1680, Spanish kings found no solution to the problem of an empty treasury other than to cancel the national debt. Given the frequency of cancellation, public confidence in the state naturally deteriorated.

Spain, in contrast to the other countries of western Europe, had only a tiny middle class. Disdain for money in a century of increasing commercialism and bourgeois attitudes was a significant facet of Spanish culture. Public opinion, taking its cue from the aristocracy, condemned moneymaking as vulgar and undignified. Those with influence or connections sought titles of nobility and social prestige. Thousands entered economically unproductive professions or became priests, monks, and nuns: there were said to be nine thousand monasteries in the province of Castile alone. The flood of gold and silver had produced severe inflation, pushing the costs of production in the textile industry higher and higher to the point that Castilian cloth could not compete in colonial and international markets. Many businessmen found so many obstacles in the way of profitable enterprise that they simply gave up.[18]

Spanish aristocrats, attempting to maintain an extravagant lifestyle they could no longer afford, increased the rents on their estates. High rents and heavy taxes in turn drove the peasants from the land. Agricultural production suffered, and the peasants departed for the large cities, where they swelled the ranks of unemployed beggars.

Their most Catholic majesties, the kings of Spain, had no solutions to these dire problems. If one can discern personality from pictures, the portraits of Philip III (r. 1598–1622), Philip IV (r. 1622–1665), and Charles II (r. 1665–1700) hanging in the Prado, the Spanish national museum in Madrid, reflect the increasing weakness of the dynasty. Their faces—the small, beady eyes; the long noses; the jutting Habsburg jaws; the pathetically stupid expressions—tell a story of excessive inbreeding and decaying monarchy. The Spanish kings all lacked force of character. Philip III, a pallid, melancholy, and deeply pious man "whose only virtue appeared to reside in a total absence of vice," handed the government over to the lazy duke of Lerma, who used it to advance his personal and familial wealth. Philip IV left the management of his several kingdoms to Gaspar de Guzmán, Count-Duke of Olivares.

Olivares was an able administrator. He did not lack energy and ideas; he devised new sources of revenue. But he clung to the grandiose belief that the solution to Spain's difficulties rested in a return to the imperial tradition. Unfortunately, the imperial tradition demanded the revival of war with the Dutch at the expiration of a twelve-year truce in 1622 and a long war with France over Mantua (1628–1659). Spain thus became embroiled in the Thirty Years' War. These conflicts, on top of an empty treasury, brought disaster.

❖ **Velazquez: The Forge of Vulcan** Primarily a portraitist, Velazquez (1599–1660) also did religious, classical, and mythological scenes. Influenced by the Venetian masters, especially Titian, Velazquez produced this picture, based on the Roman poet Ovid's *Metamorphoses:* Apollo comes to Vulcan's dusky, tool-littered forge (blacksmith's shop) to tell him of his wife Venus's infidelity with Mars. The refined technique, naturalism, and representation of emotion through expression and gesture gave Velazquz the reputation of being Spain's greatest painter. *(Source: Museo del Prado, Madrid)*

In 1640 Spain faced serious revolts in Catalonia and Portugal; in 1643 the French inflicted a crushing defeat on a Spanish army in Belgium. By the Treaty of the Pyrenees of 1659, which ended the French-Spanish wars, Spain was compelled to surrender extensive territories to France. This treaty marked the end of Spain as a great power.

Seventeenth-century Spain was the victim of its past. It could not forget the grandeur of the sixteenth century and look to the future. The bureaucratic councils of state continued to function as symbols of the absolute Spanish monarchy. But because those councils were staffed by aristocrats, it was the aristocracy that held the real power. Spanish absolutism had been built largely on slave-produced gold and silver. When the supply of bullion decreased, the power and standing of the Spanish state declined.

The most cherished Spanish ideals were military glory and strong Roman Catholic faith. In the seventeenth century, Spain lacked the finances and the manpower to fight the expensive wars in which it foolishly got involved. Spain also ignored the new mercantile ideas and scientific methods because they came from heretical nations, Holland and England. The incredible wealth of South America destroyed what remained of the Spanish middle class and created contempt for business and manual labor.

The decadence of the Habsburg dynasty and the lack of effective royal councilors also contributed to Spanish failure. Spanish leaders seemed to lack the will to reform. Pessimism and fatalism permeated national life. In the reign of Philip IV, a royal council was appointed to plan the construction of a canal linking the Tagus and Manzanares rivers in Spain. After interminable debate, the committee decided that "if God had intended the rivers to be navigable, He would have made them so."

In the brilliant novel *Don Quixote,* Spanish writer Miguel de Cervantes (1547–1616) produced one of the great masterpieces of world literature. *Don Quixote*—on which the modern play *Man of La Mancha* is based—delineates the whole fabric of sixteenth-century Spanish society. The main character, Don Quixote, lives in a world of dreams, traveling about the countryside seeking military glory. From the title of the book, the English language has borrowed the word *quixotic.* Meaning "idealistic but impractical," the term characterizes seventeenth-century Spain. As a leading scholar has written, "The Spaniard convinced himself that reality was what he felt, believed, imagined. He filled the world with heroic reverberations. Don Quixote was born and grew."[19]

CONSTITUTIONALISM

The seventeenth century, which witnessed the development of absolute monarchy, also saw the appearance of the constitutional state. While France and, later, Prussia, Russia, and Austria solved the question of sovereignty with the absolutist state, England and Holland evolved toward the constitutional state. What is constitutionalism? Is it identical to democracy?

Constitutionalism is the limitation of government by law. Constitutionalism also implies a balance between the authority and power of the government, on the one hand, and the rights and liberties of the subjects, on the other. The balance is often very delicate.

A nation's constitution may be written or unwritten. It may be embodied in one basic document, occasionally revised by amendment or judicial decision, like the Constitution of the United States. Or it may be partly written and partly unwritten and include parliamentary statutes, judicial decisions, and a body of traditional procedures and practices, like the English, Canadian, and Dutch constitutions. Whether written or unwritten, a constitution gets its binding force from the government's acknowledgment that it must respect that constitution—that is, that the state must govern according to the laws. Likewise, in a constitutional state, the people look on the laws and the constitution as the protectors of their rights, liberties, and property.

Modern constitutional governments may take either a republican or a monarchial form. In a constitutional republic, the sovereign power resides in the electorate and is exercised by the electorate's representatives. In a constitutional monarchy, a king or queen serves as the head of state and possesses some residual political authority, but again the ultimate, or sovereign, power rests in the electorate.

A constitutional government is not, however, quite the same as a democratic government. In a complete democracy, *all* the people have the right to participate either directly or indirectly (through their elected representatives) in the government of the state. Democratic government, therefore, is intimately tied up with the *franchise* (the vote). Most men could not vote until the late nineteenth century. Even then, women—probably the majority in Western societies—lacked the franchise; they gained the right to vote only in the twentieth century. Consequently, although constitutionalism developed in the seventeenth century, full democracy was achieved only in very recent times.

The Decline of Royal Absolutism in England (1603–1649)

In 1588 Queen Elizabeth I of England exercised very great personal power; by 1689 the English monarchy was severely circumscribed. Change in England was anything but orderly. Seventeenth-century England displayed little political stability. It executed one king, experienced a bloody civil war, experimented with military dictatorship, then restored the son of the murdered king, and finally, after a bloodless revolution, established constitutional monarchy. Political stability came only in the 1690s. How do we account for the fact that after such a violent and tumultuous century, England laid the foundations for constitutional monarchy? What combination of political, socioeconomic, and religious factors brought on a civil war in 1642 to 1649 and then the constitutional settlement of 1688 to 1689?

The extraordinary success of Elizabeth I had rested on her political shrewdness and flexibility, her careful management of finances, her wise selection of ministers, her clever manipulation of Parliament, and her sense of royal dignity and devotion to hard work. The aging queen had always refused to discuss the succession. After her Scottish cousin James Stuart succeeded her as James I (r. 1603–1625), Elizabeth's strengths seemed even greater than they actually had been.

King James was well educated, learned, and, with thirty-five years' experience as king of Scotland, politically shrewd. But he was not as interested in displaying the majesty and mystique of monarchy as Elizabeth had been. He also lacked the common touch. Urged to wave at the crowds who waited to greet their new ruler, James complained that he was tired and threatened to drop his breeches "so they can cheer at my arse." The new king failed to live up to the role expected of

him in England. Moreover, James's Scottish accent, in a society already hostile to the Scots and concerned about proper spoken English, proved another disadvantage.[20]

James was devoted to the theory of the divine right of kings. He expressed his ideas about divine right in his essay "The Trew Law of Free Monarchy." According to James I, a monarch has a divine (or God-given) right to his authority and is responsible only to God. Rebellion is the worst of political crimes. If a king orders something evil, the subject should respond with passive disobedience but should be prepared to accept any penalty for noncompliance.

He went so far as to lecture the House of Commons: "There are no privileges and immunities which can stand against a divinely appointed King." This notion, implying total royal jurisdiction over the liberties, persons, and properties of English men and women, formed the basis of the Stuart concept of absolutism. Such a view ran directly counter to the long-standing English idea that a person's property could not be taken away without due process of law. James's expression of such views before the English House of Commons constituted a grave political mistake.

The House of Commons guarded the state's pocketbook, and James and later Stuart kings badly needed to open that pocketbook. Elizabeth had bequeathed to James a sizable royal debt. Through prudent management the debt could have been gradually reduced, but James I looked on all revenues as a happy windfall to be squandered on a lavish court and favorite courtiers. In reality, the extravagance displayed in James's court as well as the public flaunting of his male lovers weakened respect for the monarchy.

Elizabeth had also left to her Stuart successors a House of Commons that appreciated its own financial strength and intended to use that strength to acquire a greater say in the government of the state. The knights and burgesses who sat at Westminster in the late sixteenth and early seventeenth centuries wanted to discuss royal expenditures, religious reform, and foreign affairs. In short, the Commons wanted what amounted to sovereignty.

Profound social changes had occurred since the sixteenth century. The English House of Commons during the reigns of James I and his son Charles I (r. 1625–1649) was very different from the assembly Henry VIII had manipulated into passing his Reformation legislation. A social revolution had brought about the change. The dissolution of the monasteries and the sale of monastic land had enriched many people. Agricultural techniques such as the draining of wasteland and the application of fertilizers had improved the land and its yield. In the seventeenth century old manorial common land was enclosed and turned into sheep runs, breeding was carefully supervised, and the size of the flocks increased. In these activities as well as in the renting and leasing of parcels of land, precise accounts were kept.

Many people invested in commercial ventures at home, such as the expanding cloth industry, and through partnerships and joint stock companies engaged in foreign enterprises. Many also made prudent marriages. All these developments led to a great deal of social mobility. Both in commerce and in agriculture, the English in the late sixteenth and early seventeenth centuries were capitalists, investing their profits to make more money. Though the international inflation of the period hit everywhere, in England commercial and agricultural income rose faster than prices. Wealthy country gentry, rich city merchants, and financiers invested abroad.

The typical pattern was for the commercially successful to set themselves up as country gentry, thus creating an elite group that possessed a far greater proportion of land and of the national wealth in 1640 than had been the case in 1540. Small wonder that in 1640 someone could declare in the House of Commons, probably accurately, "We could buy the House of Lords three times over." Increased wealth had also produced a better-educated and more articulate House of Commons. Many members had acquired at least a smattering of legal knowledge, and they used that knowledge to search for medieval precedents from which to argue against the king. The class that dominated the Commons wanted political power corresponding to its economic strength.

In England, unlike France, there was no social stigma attached to paying taxes. Members of the House of Commons were willing to tax themselves provided they had some say in the expenditure of those taxes and in the formulation of state policies. The Stuart kings, however, considered such ambitions intolerable presumption and a threat to their divine-right prerogative. Consequently, at every Parliament between 1603 and 1640, bitter squabbles erupted between the Crown and the wealthy, articulate, and legally minded Commons. Charles I's attempt to govern without Parliament (1629–1640), and to finance his government by arbitrary nonparliamentary levies, brought the country to a crisis.

An issue graver than royal extravagance and Parliament's desire to make law also disturbed the English and embittered relations between the king and the House of Commons. That problem was religion. In the early seventeenth century, increasing numbers of English people felt dissatisfied with the Church of England established by Henry VIII and reformed by Elizabeth. Many Puritans (see page 463) believed that the Reformation had not gone far enough. They wanted to "purify" the Anglican church of Roman Catholic elements— elaborate vestments and ceremonials, the position of the altar in the church, even the giving and wearing of wedding rings.

It is very difficult to establish what proportion of the English population was Puritan. According to the present scholarly consensus, the dominant religious groups in the early seventeenth century were Calvinist; their more zealous members were Puritans. It also seems clear that many English men and women were attracted by the socioeconomic implications of John Calvin's theology. Calvinism emphasized hard work, sobriety, thrift, competition, and postponement of pleasure, and it tended to link sin and poverty with weakness and moral corruption. These attitudes fit in precisely with the economic approaches and practices of many (successful) business people and farmers. These values have frequently been called the "Protestant ethic," "middle-class ethic," or "capitalist ethic." While it is hazardous to identify capitalism and progress with Protestantism—there were many successful Catholic capitalists, for example—the "Protestant virtues" represented the prevailing values of members of the House of Commons.

James I and Charles I both gave the impression of being highly sympathetic to Roman Catholicism. Charles supported the policies of William Laud (1573–1645), archbishop of Canterbury, who tried to impose elaborate ritual and rich ceremonials on all churches. Laud insisted on complete uniformity of church services and enforced that uniformity through an ecclesiastical court called the "Court of High Commission." People believed the country was being led back to Roman Catholicism. In 1637 Laud attempted to impose two new elements on the church organization in Scotland: a new prayer book, modeled on the Anglican *Book of Common Prayer,* and bishoprics, which the Presbyterian Scots firmly rejected. The Scots therefore revolted. To finance an army to put down the Scots, King Charles was compelled to summon Parliament in November 1640.

For eleven years Charles I had ruled without Parliament, financing his government through extraordinary stopgap levies considered illegal by most English people. For example, the king revived a medieval law requiring coastal districts to help pay the cost of ships for defense, but he levied the tax, called "ship money," on inland as well as coastal counties. When the issue was tested in the courts, the judges, having been suborned, decided in the king's favor.

Most members of Parliament believed that such taxation without consent amounted to arbitrary and absolute despotism. Consequently, they were not willing to trust the king with an army. Accordingly, this Parliament, commonly called the "Long Parliament" because it sat from 1640 to 1660, proceeded to enact legislation that limited the power of the monarch and made arbitrary government impossible.

In 1641 the Commons passed the Triennial Act, which compelled the king to summon Parliament every three years. The Commons impeached Archbishop Laud and abolished the Court of High Commission. It went further and threatened to abolish the institution of episcopacy. King Charles, fearful of a Scottish invasion—the original reason for summoning Parliament—accepted these measures. Understanding and peace were not achieved, however, partly because radical members of the Commons pushed increasingly revolutionary propositions, partly because Charles maneuvered to rescind those he had already approved. An uprising in Ireland precipitated civil war.

Ever since Henry II had conquered Ireland in 1171, English governors had mercilessly ruled the land, and English landlords had ruthlessly exploited the Irish people. The English Reformation had made a bad situation worse: because the Irish remained Catholic, religious differences became united with economic and political oppression. Without an army, Charles I could neither come to terms with the Scots nor put down the Irish rebellion, and the Long Parliament remained unwilling

to place an army under a king it did not trust. Charles thus instigated military action against parliamentary forces. He recruited an army drawn from the nobility and its cavalry staff, the rural gentry, and mercenaries. The parliamentary army was composed of the militia of the city of London, country squires with business connections, and men with a firm belief in the spiritual duty of serving.

The English civil war (1642–1649) tested whether sovereignty in England was to reside in the king or in Parliament. The civil war did not resolve that problem, however, although it ended in 1649 with the execution of King Charles on the charge of high treason—a severe blow to the theory of divine-right monarchy. The period between 1649 and 1660, called the "Interregnum" because it separated two monarchial periods, witnessed England's solitary experience of military dictatorship.

Puritanical Absolutism in England: Cromwell and the Protectorate

The problem of sovereignty was vigorously debated in the middle years of the seventeenth century. In *Leviathan,* English philosopher and political theorist Thomas Hobbes (1588–1679) maintained that sovereignty is ultimately derived from the people, who transfer it to the monarchy by implicit contract. The power of the ruler is absolute, but kings do not hold their power by divine right. This view pleased no one in the seventeenth century.

When Charles I was beheaded on January 30, 1649, the kingship was abolished. A *commonwealth,* or republican form of government, was proclaimed. Theoretically, legislative power rested in the surviving members of Parliament, and executive power was lodged in a council of state. In fact, the army that had defeated the royal forces controlled the government, and Oliver Cromwell controlled the army. Though called the "Protectorate," the rule of Cromwell (1653–1658) constituted military dictatorship.

Oliver Cromwell (1599–1658) came from the country gentry, the class that dominated the House of Commons in the early seventeenth century. He himself had sat in the Long Parliament. Cromwell rose in the parliamentary army and

Christ Church Coll: Ox: Canterbury Minster   Trinn: Colledge Camb:

MERCURIUS RUSTICUS

Countys of Rivers plundered pag: 31

St John Lucas house plundered pag: 5

THE COUNTRYS COMPLAINT Recounting the sad Events of the late unparalleld REBELLION

Sr Rich: Mynshall: hous plundered pag: 31

A Bonfire for the voting downe Episcopacy pag: 16:

Mr Jones a Min: carried on a Beare pag: 81

Edge hill   Battle

Warder Castle defended by a Lady. pag: 41:

❖ **Periodical Sheet on the Civil War** Single sheets or broadsides spread the positions of the opposing sides to the nonliterate public. *Mercurius Rusticus,* intended for country people, conveyed the royalist argument. *(Source: The British Library)*

achieved nationwide fame by infusing the army with his Puritan convictions and molding it into a highly effective military machine, called the "New Model Army," which defeated the royalist forces.

The army had prepared a constitution, the Instrument of Government (1653), that invested executive power in a lord protector (Cromwell) and a council of state. The instrument provided for triennial parliaments and gave Parliament the sole

power to raise taxes. But after repeated disputes, Cromwell tore the document up. He continued the standing army and proclaimed quasi-martial law. He divided England into twelve military districts, each governed by a major general. The major generals acted through the justices of the peace though sometimes overrode them. On the issue of religion, Cromwell favored broad toleration, and the Instrument of Government gave all Christians, except Roman Catholics, the right to practice their faith. Toleration meant state protection of many different Protestant sects, however, and most English people had no enthusiasm for such a notion; the idea was far ahead of its time. As for Irish Catholicism, Cromwell identified it with sedition. In 1649 he crushed rebellion in Ireland with merciless savagery, leaving a legacy of Irish hatred for England that has not yet subsided. The state rigorously censored the press, forbade sports, and kept the theaters closed in England.

Cromwell's regulation of the nation's economy had features typical of seventeenth-century absolutism. The lord protector's policies were mercantilist, similar to those Colbert established in France. Cromwell enforced a Navigation Act (1651) requiring that English goods be transported on English ships. The navigation act was a great boost to the development of an English merchant marine and brought about a short but successful war with the commercially threatened Dutch. Cromwell also welcomed the immigration of Jews because of their skills, and they began to return to England after four centuries of absence.

Absolute government collapsed when Cromwell died in 1658. Fed up with military rule, the English longed for a return to civilian government, restoration of the common law, and social stability. Moreover, the strain of creating a community of Puritanical saints proved too psychologically exhausting. Government by military dictatorship was an unfortunate experiment that the English never forgot or repeated. By 1660 they were ready to restore the monarchy.

The Restoration of the English Monarchy

The Restoration of 1660 re-established the monarchy in the person of Charles II (r. 1660–1685), eldest son of Charles I. At the same time, both houses of Parliament were restored, together with the established Anglican church, the courts of law, and the system of local government through justices of the peace. The Restoration failed to resolve two serious problems, however. What was to be the attitude of the state toward Puritans, Catholics, and dissenters from the established church? And what was to be the constitutional position of the king—that is, what was to be the relationship between the king and Parliament?

About the first of these issues, Charles II, a relaxed, easygoing, and sensual man, was basically indifferent. He was not interested in doctrinal issues. The new members of Parliament were, and they proceeded to enact a body of laws that sought to compel religious uniformity. Those who refused to receive the sacrament of the Church of England could not vote, hold public office, preach, teach, attend the universities, or even assemble for meetings, according to the Test Act of 1673. But these restrictions could not be enforced. When the Quaker William Penn held a meeting of his Friends and was arrested, the jury refused to convict him.

In politics, Charles II was determined "not to set out in his travels again," which meant that he intended to get along with Parliament. Charles II's solution to the problem of the relationship between the king and the House of Commons had profound importance for later constitutional development. Generally good rapport existed between the king and the strongly royalist Parliament that had restored him. This rapport was due largely to the king's appointment of a council of five men who served both as his major advisers and as members of Parliament, thus acting as liaison agents between the executive and the legislature. This body—known as the "Cabal" from the names of its five members (Clifford, Arlington, Buckingham, Ashley-Cooper, and Lauderdale)—was an ancestor of the later cabinet system (see page 548). It gradually came to be accepted that the Cabal was answerable in Parliament for the decisions of the king. This development gave rise to the concept of ministerial responsibility: royal ministers must answer to the Commons.

Harmony between the Crown and Parliament rested on the understanding that Charles would summon frequent parliaments and that Parliament would vote him sufficient revenues. However, although Parliament believed Charles had a virtual divine right to govern, it did not grant him an adequate income. Accordingly, in 1670 Charles entered into a secret agreement with Louis XIV.

The French king would give Charles 200,000 pounds annually, and in return Charles would relax the laws against Catholics, gradually re-Catholicize England, support French policy against the Dutch, and convert to Catholicism himself.

When the details of this secret treaty leaked out, a great wave of anti-Catholic fear swept England. This fear was compounded by a crucial fact: although Charles had produced several bastards, he had no legitimate children. It therefore appeared that his brother and heir, James, duke of York, who had publicly acknowledged his Catholicism, would inaugurate a Catholic dynasty. A combination of hatred for the French absolutism embodied in Louis XIV, hostility to Roman Catholicism, and fear of a permanent Catholic dynasty produced virtual hysteria. The Commons passed an exclusion bill denying the succession to a Roman Catholic, but Charles quickly dissolved Parliament, and the bill never became law.

James II (r. 1685–1688) did succeed his brother. Almost at once the worst English anti-Catholic fears, already aroused by Louis XIV's revocation of the Edict of Nantes, were realized. In direct violation of the Test Act, James appointed Roman Catholics to positions in the army, the universities, and local government. When these actions were tested in the courts, the judges, whom James had appointed, decided for the king. The king was suspending the law at will and appeared to be reviving the absolutism of his father and grandfather. He went further. Attempting to broaden his base of support with Protestant dissenters and nonconformists, James issued a declaration of indulgence granting religious freedom to all.

Two events gave the signals for revolution. First, seven bishops of the Church of England petitioned the king that they not be forced to read the declaration of indulgence because of their belief that it was an illegal act. They were imprisoned in the Tower of London but subsequently acquitted amid great public enthusiasm. Second, in June 1688 James's second wife produced a male heir. A Catholic dynasty seemed assured. The fear of a Roman Catholic monarchy supported by France and ruling outside the law prompted a group of eminent persons to offer the English throne to James's Protestant daughter, Mary, and her Dutch husband, Prince William of Orange. In December 1688 James II, his queen, and their infant son fled to France and became pensioners of Louis XIV.

Early in 1689, William and Mary were crowned king and queen of England.

The Triumph of England's Parliament: Constitutional Monarchy and Cabinet Government

The English call the events of 1688 to 1689 the "Glorious Revolution." The revolution was indeed glorious in the sense that it replaced one king with another with a minimum of bloodshed. It also represented the destruction, once and for all, of the idea of divine-right monarchy. William and Mary accepted the English throne from Parliament and in so doing explicitly recognized the supremacy of Parliament. The revolution of 1688 established the principle that sovereignty, the ultimate power in the state, was divided between king and Parliament and that the king ruled with the consent of the governed.

The men who brought about the revolution quickly framed their intentions in the Bill of Rights, the cornerstone of the modern British constitution. The basic principles of the Bill of Rights were formulated in direct response to Stuart absolutism. Law was to be made in Parliament; once made, it could not be suspended by the Crown. Parliament had to be called at least every three years. Both elections to and debate in Parliament were to be free in the sense that the Crown was not to interfere in them (this aspect of the bill was widely disregarded in the eighteenth century). Judges would hold their offices "during good behavior," a provision that assured the independence of the judiciary. No longer could the Crown get the judicial decisions it wanted by threats of removal. There was to be no standing army in peacetime—a limitation designed to prevent the repetition of either Stuart or Cromwellian military government. The Bill of Rights granted "that the subjects which are Protestants may have arms for their defense suitable to their conditions and as allowed by law,"[21] meaning that Catholics could not possess firearms because the Protestant majority feared them. Additional legislation granted freedom of worship to Protestant dissenters and nonconformists and required that the English monarch always be Protestant.

The Glorious Revolution found its best defense in political philosopher John Locke's *Second Treatise of Civil Government* (1690). Locke (1632–1704) maintained that people set up civil governments to protect life, liberty, and property. A government that oversteps its proper function—protecting the natural rights of life, liberty, and property—becomes a tyranny. (By "natural" rights, Locke meant rights basic to all men because all have the ability to reason.) Under a tyrannical government, the people have the natural right to rebellion. Such rebellion can be avoided if the government carefully respects the rights of citizens and if people zealously defend their liberty. Recognizing the close relationship between economic and political freedom, Locke linked economic liberty and private property with political freedom; his defense of property included a justification for a narrow franchise. Locke served as the great spokesman for the liberal English revolution of 1688 to 1689 and for representative government. His idea, inherited from ancient Greece and Rome (see Chapter 4), that there are natural or universal rights equally valid for all peoples and societies played a powerful role in eighteenth-century Enlightenment thought. His ideas on liberty and tyranny were especially popular in colonial America.

The events of 1688 to 1689 did not constitute a *democratic* revolution. The revolution placed sovereignty in Parliament, and Parliament represented the upper classes. The great majority of English people acquired no say in their government. The English revolution established a constitutional monarchy; it also inaugurated an age of aristocratic government, which lasted at least until 1832 and in many ways until 1914.

In the course of the eighteenth century, the cabinet system of government evolved. The term *cabinet* derives from the small private room in which English rulers consulted their chief ministers. In a cabinet system, the leading ministers, who must have seats in and the support of a majority of the House of Commons, formulate common policy and conduct the business of the country. During the administration of one royal minister, Sir Robert Walpole, who led the cabinet from 1721 to 1742, the idea developed that the cabinet was responsible to the House of Commons. The Hanoverian king George I (r. 1714–1727) normally presided at cabinet meetings throughout his reign, but his son and heir, George II (r. 1727–1760), discontinued the practice. The influence of the Crown in decision making accordingly declined. Walpole enjoyed the favor of the monarchy and of the House of Commons and came to be called the king's first, or "prime," minister. In the English cabinet system, both legislative power and executive power are held by the leading ministers, who form the government.

The Dutch Republic in the Seventeenth Century

In the late sixteenth century, the seven northern provinces of the Netherlands, of which Holland and Zeeland were the most prosperous, had succeeded in throwing off Spanish domination. This success was based on their geographical lines of defense, the wealth of their cities, the military strategy of William the Silent, the preoccupation of Philip II of Spain with so many additional concerns, and the northern provinces' vigorous Calvinism. In 1581 the seven provinces of the Union of Utrecht had formed the United Provinces (see page 496). Philip II continued trying to crush the Dutch, but in 1609 his son Philip III agreed to a truce that implicitly recognized the independence of the United Provinces. At the time neither side

expected the peace to be permanent. The Peace of Westphalia in 1648, however, confirmed the Dutch republic's independence.

The seventeenth century witnessed an unparalleled flowering of Dutch scientific, artistic, and literary achievement. In this period, often called the "golden age of the Netherlands," Dutch ideas and attitudes played a profound role in shaping a new and modern world-view. At the same time, the Republic of the United Provinces of the Netherlands was another model of the development of the modern constitutional state.

Within each province an oligarchy of wealthy merchants called "regents" handled domestic affairs in the local Estates. The provincial Estates held virtually all the power. A federal assembly, or States General, handled matters of foreign affairs, such as war. But the States General did not possess sovereign authority since all issues had to be referred back to the local Estates for approval. The States General appointed a representative, the *stadholder,* in each province. As the highest executive

❖ **Rembrandt: The Jewish Bride** Holland's greatest painter, Rembrandt (1606–1669) combined an expressive mastery of technique, emotional depth, psychological penetration, and enormous range—religious scenes, still lifes, portraits. The so-called Jewish Bride (c. 1665), perhaps a wedding portrait of two wealthy people, reveals the artist's unsurpassed handling of light, so characteristic of his later work. *(Source: Rijksmuseum-Stichting)*

there, the stadholder carried out ceremonial functions and was responsible for defense and good order. The sons of William the Silent, Maurice and William Louis, held the office of stadholder in all seven provinces. As members of the House of Orange, they were closely identified with Dutch patriotism. The regents in each province jealously guarded local independence and resisted efforts at centralization. Nevertheless, Holland, which had the largest navy and the most wealth, dominated the republic and the States General. Significantly, the Estates assembled at Holland's capital, The Hague.

The government of the United Provinces fit none of the standard categories of seventeenth-century political organization. The Dutch were not monarchial but fiercely republican. The government was controlled by wealthy merchants and financiers. Though rich, their values were not aristocratic but strongly middle class, emphasizing thrift, hard work, and simplicity in living. The Dutch republic was not a strong federation but a confederation—that is, a weak union of strong provinces. The provinces were a temptation to powerful neighbors, yet the Dutch resisted the long Spanish effort at reconquest and withstood both French and English attacks in the second half of the century. Louis XIV's hatred of the Dutch was proverbial. They represented all that he despised—middle-class values, religious toleration, and political independence.

The political success of the Dutch rested on the phenomenal commercial prosperity of the Netherlands. The moral and ethical bases of that commercial wealth were thrift, frugality, and religious toleration. John Calvin had written, "From where do the merchant's profits come except from his own diligence and industry?" This attitude undoubtedly encouraged a sturdy people who had waged a centuries-old struggle against the sea.

Alone of all European peoples in the seventeenth century, the Dutch practiced religious toleration. Peoples of all faiths were welcome within their borders. Although there is scattered evidence of anti-Semitism, Jews enjoyed a level of acceptance and absorption in Dutch business and general culture unique in early modern Europe. It is a testimony to the urbanity of Dutch society that in a century when patriotism was closely identified with religious uniformity, the Calvinist province of Holland under its highest official, Jan van Oldenbarneveldt, allowed Catholics to practice their faith. As long as business people conducted their religion in private, the government did not interfere with them.

Toleration also paid off: it attracted a great deal of foreign capital and investment. Deposits at the Bank of Amsterdam were guaranteed by the city council, and in the middle years of the century the bank became Europe's best source of cheap credit and commercial intelligence and the main clearing-house for bills of exchange. People of all races and creeds traded in Amsterdam, at whose docks on the Amstel River five thousand ships were berthed. Joost van den Vondel, the poet of Dutch imperialism, exulted:

God, God, the Lord of Amstel cried, hold every conscience free;
And Liberty ride, on Holland's tide, with billowing sails to sea,
And run our Amstel out and in; let freedom gird the bold,
And merchant in his counting house stand elbow deep in gold.[22]

The fishing industry was the cornerstone of the Dutch economy. For half the year, from June to December, fishing fleets combed the dangerous English coast and the North Sea and raked in tiny herring. Profits from herring stimulated shipbuilding, and even before 1600 the Dutch were offering the lowest shipping rates in Europe. The Dutch merchant marine was the largest in Europe. In 1650 contemporaries estimated that the Dutch had sixteen thousand merchant ships, half the European total. All the wood for these ships had to be imported: the Dutch bought whole forests from Norway. They also bought entire vineyards from French growers before the grapes were harvested. They controlled the Baltic grain trade, buying entire wheat and rye crops in Poland, east Prussia, and Swedish Pomerania. Because the Dutch dealt in bulk, nobody could undersell them. Foreign merchants coming to Amsterdam could buy anything from precision lenses for the microscope (recently invented by Dutchman Anton van Leeuwenhoek) to muskets for an army of five thousand. Although Dutch cities became famous for their exports—diamonds and linens from Haarlem, pottery from Delft—Dutch wealth depended less on exports than on transport.

In 1602 a group of the regents of Holland formed the Dutch East India Company, a joint

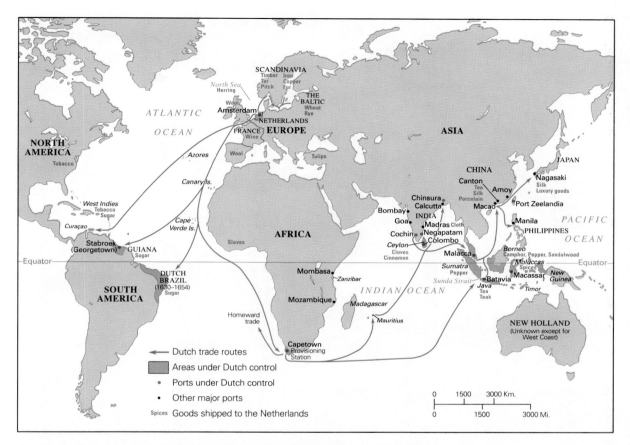

✣ **MAP 16.3 Seventeenth-century Dutch Commerce** Dutch wealth rested on commerce, and commerce depended on the huge Dutch merchant marine, manned by perhaps 48,000 sailors. The fleet carried goods from all parts of the globe to the port of Amsterdam.

stock company. The investors each received a percentage of the profits proportional to the amount of money they had put in. Within half a century, the Dutch East India Company had cut heavily into Portuguese trading in East Asia. The Dutch seized the Cape of Good Hope, Ceylon, and Malacca and established trading posts in each place. In the 1630s the Dutch East India Company was paying its investors about a 35 percent annual return on their investments. The Dutch West India Company, founded in 1621, traded extensively with Latin America and Africa (Map 16.3).

Trade and commerce brought the Dutch prodigious wealth. In the seventeenth century, the Dutch enjoyed the highest standard of living in Europe, perhaps in the world. Amsterdam and Rotterdam built massive granaries where the surplus of one year could be stored against possible

shortages the next. Thus, excepting the 1650s when bad harvests reduced supplies, food prices fluctuated very little. By the standards of Cologne, Paris, or London, salaries were high for all workers—except women, and even women's wages were high when compared with those of women in other parts of Europe. All classes of society, including unskilled laborers, ate well. The low price of bread meant that, compared to other places in Europe, a higher percentage of the worker's income could be spent on fish, cheese, butter, vegetables, even meat. A scholar recently described the Netherlands as "an island of plenty in a sea of want." Consequently, the Netherlands experienced very few of the food riots that characterized the rest of Europe.[23]

Although the initial purpose of the Dutch East and West India companies was commercial—the

Job Berckheyde: The Amsterdam Stock Exchange Small shareholders (through brokers) as well as rich capitalists could buy and sell and, by various combinations, speculate without having any money at all in the Amsterdam stock market. Shares in the Dutch East India Company were major objects of speculation. The volume, fluidity, and publicity of the Exchange were its new and distinctly modern features. *(Source: Museum Boymans-van Beuningen, Rotterdam)*

import of spices and silks to Europe—the Dutch found themselves involved in the imperialist exploitation of parts of East Asia and Latin America, with great success. In 1652 the Dutch founded Cape Town on the southern tip of Africa as a fueling station for ships planning to cross the Pacific. But war with France and England in the 1670s hurt the United Provinces. The long War of the Spanish Succession, in which the Dutch supported England against France, was a costly drain on Dutch labor and financial resources. The peace signed in 1715 to end the war marked the beginning of Dutch economic decline.

SUMMARY

According to Thomas Hobbes, the central drive in every human is "a perpetual and restless desire of Power, after Power, that ceaseth only in Death." The seventeenth century solved the problem of sovereign power in two fundamental ways: absolutism and constitutionalism. The France of Louis XIV witnessed the emergence of the fully absolutist state. The king commanded all the powers of the state: judicial, military, political, and, to a great extent, ecclesiastical. France developed a centralized bureaucracy, a professional army, and a state-directed economy, all of which Louis personally supervised. For the first time in history, all the institutions and powers of the national state were effectively controlled by a single person. The king saw himself as the representative of God on earth, and it has been said that "to the seventeenth century imagination God was a sort of image of Louis XIV."[24]

As Louis XIV personifies absolutism, so Stuart England exemplifies the evolution of the first modern constitutional state. The conflicts between Parliament and the first two Stuart rulers, James I and Charles I, tested where sovereign power would rest in the state. The resulting civil war did not solve the problem. The Instrument of Government, the document produced in 1653 by the victorious parliamentary army, provided for a balance of government authority and recognition of popular rights; as such, the instrument has been called the first modern constitution. Unfortunately, it lacked public support. James II's absolutist tendencies brought on the Glorious Revolution of 1688 to 1689, and the people who made that revolution settled three basic issues. Sovereign power was divided between king and Parliament, with Parliament enjoying the greater share. Government was to be based on the rule of law. And the liberties of English people were made explicit in written form in the Bill of Rights. The framers of the English constitution left to later generations the task of making constitutional government work.

The models of governmental power established by seventeenth-century England and France strongly influenced other states then and ever since. As American novelist William Faulkner wrote, "The past isn't dead; it's not even past."

NOTES

1. G. Parker and L. M. Smith, "Introduction," and N. Steensgaard, "The Seventeenth Century Crisis," in *The General Crisis of the Seventeenth Cen-*tury, ed. G. Parker and L. M. Smith (London: Routledge & Kegan Paul, 1985), pp. 1–53, esp. p. 12.

2. J. B. Collins, *Fiscal Limits of Absolutism: Direct Taxation in Early Seventeenth Century France* (Berkeley and Los Angeles: University of California Press, 1988), pp. 1, 3–4, 215–222.

3. Cited in J. H. Elliot, *Richelieu and Olivares* (Cambridge: Cambridge University Press, 1984), p. 135; and in W. F. Church, *Richelieu and Reason of State* (Princeton, N.J.: Princeton University Press, 1972), p. 507.

4. D. Parker, *The Making of French Absolutism* (New York: St. Martin's Press, 1983), pp. 146–148.

5. Quoted in J. Wolf, *Louis XIV* (New York: W. W. Norton, 1968), p. 115.

6. See W. Beik, *Absolutism and Society in Seventeenth Century France: State Power and Provincial Aristocracy in Languedoc* (Cambridge: Cambridge University Press, 1985), pp. 279–302.

7. S. de Gramont, ed., *The Age of Magnificence: Memoirs of the Court of Louis XIV by the Duc de Saint Simon* (New York: Capricorn Books, 1964), pp. 141–145.

8. Quoted in Wolf, p. 146.

9. Quoted in A. Trout, *Jean-Baptiste Colbert* (Boston: Twayne, 1978), p. 128.

10. Quoted in Wolf, p. 394.

11. Ibid.

12. See W. C. Scoville, *The Persecution of the Huguenots and French Economic Development: 1680–1720* (Berkeley and Los Angeles: University of California Press, 1960).

13. Cited in F. Bluche, *Louis XIV,* trans. M. Greengrass (Oxford: Basil Blackwell, 1990), p. 607.

14. Ibid., p. 458.

15. Quoted in Bluche, p. 519.

16. W. F. Church, *Louis XIV in Historical Thought: From Voltaire to the Annales School* (New York: W. W. Norton, 1976), p. 92.

17. Gramont, p. 183.

18. J. H. Elliott, *Imperial Spain, 1469–1716* (New York: Mentor Books, 1963), pp. 306–308.

19. B. Bennassar, *The Spanish Character: Attitudes and Mentalities from the Sixteenth to the Nineteenth Century,* trans. B. Keen (Berkeley and Los Angeles: University of California Press, 1979), p. 125.

20. For a revisionist interpretation, see J. Wormald, "James VI and I: Two Kings or One?" *History* 62 (June 1983): 187–209.

21. C. Stephenson and G. F. Marcham, *Sources of English Constitutional History* (New York: Harper & Row, 1937), p. 601.

22. Quoted in D. Maland, *Europe in the Seventeenth Century* (New York: Macmillan, 1967), pp. 198–199.

23. S. Schama, *The Embarrassment of Riches: An Interpretation of Dutch Culture in the Golden Age* (New York: Alfred A. Knopf, 1987), pp. 165–170; quotation is on p. 167.

24. Quoted in C. J. Friedrich and C. Blitzer, *The Age of Power* (Ithaca, N.Y.: Cornell University Press, 1957), p. 112.

Suggested Reading

Students who wish to explore the problems presented in this chapter in greater depth will easily find a rich and exciting literature, with many titles available in paperback editions. The following surveys all provide good background material: H. Kamen, *The Iron Century: Social Change in Europe, 1550–1660* (1971); G. Parker, *Europe in Crisis, 1598–1618* (1980), a sound introduction to the social, economic, and religious tensions of the period; R. S. Dunn, *The Age of Religious Wars, 1559–1715* (1979), which examines the period from the perspective of the confessional strife between Protestants and Catholics but contains material on absolutism and constitutionalism; and T. Aston, ed., *Crisis in Europe, 1560–1660* (1967). P. Anderson, *Lineages of the Absolutist State* (1974), is a Marxist interpretation of absolutism in western and eastern Europe. M. Beloff, *The Age of Absolutism* (1967), concentrates on the social forces that undergirded administrative change. H. Rosenberg, "Absolute Monarchy and Its Legacy," in N. F. Cantor and S. Werthman, eds., *Early Modern Europe, 1450–1650* (1967), is a seminal study. The classic treatment of constitutionalism remains that of C. H. McIlwain, *Constitutionalism: Ancient and Modern* (1940), written by a great scholar during the rise of German fascism.

Louis XIV and his age have predictably attracted the attention of many scholars. Bluche, although hagiographical, is an almost definitive study, though Wolf remains valuable; both are cited in the Notes. The excellent work of P. Burke, *The Fabrication of Louis XIV* (1992), explores the images or representations of the king in stone, bronze, paint, plays, operas, and rituals. Two works of W. H. Lewis, *The Splendid Century* (1957) and *The Sunset of the Splendid Century* (1963), make delightful light reading, especially for the beginning student. The advanced student will want to consult the excellent historiographical analysis by Church mentioned in the Notes. Perhaps the best works of the Annales school on the period are P. Goubert, *Louis XIV and Twenty Million Frenchmen* (1972), and his heavily detailed *The Ancien Régime: French Society, 1600–1750*, 2 vols. (1969–1973), which contains invaluable material on the lives and work of ordinary people. For the French economy and financial conditions, the old study of C. W. Cole, *Colbert and a Century of French Mercantilism*, 2 vols. (1939), is still valuable but should be supplemented by R. Bonney, *The King's Debts: Finance and Politics in France, 1589–1661* (1981), and by the works of Trout and Scoville listed in the Notes. Scoville's book is a significant contribution to revisionist history. For Louis XIV's foreign policy and wars, see P. Sonnino, *Louis XIV and the Origins of the Dutch Wars* (1988); H. Kamen, *The War of Succession in Spain, 1700–1715* (1969); R. Hatton, "Louis XIV: Recent Gains in Historical Knowledge," *Journal of Modern History* 45 (1973); and R. Hatton, ed., *Louis XIV and Europe* (1976), an important collection of essays. Hatton's *Europe in the Age of Louis XIV* (1979) is a splendidly illustrated survey of many aspects of seventeenth-century European culture. O. Ranum, *Paris in the Age of Absolutism* (1968), describes the geographical, political, economic, and architectural significance of the cultural capital of Europe, whereas V. L. Tapie, *The Age of Grandeur: Baroque Art and Architecture* (1960), emphasizes the relationship between art and politics and has excellent illustrations.

For Spain and Portugal, in addition to the works in the Notes, see H. Kamen, *Spain in the Later Seventeenth Century, 1665–1700* (1980); M. Defourneaux, *Daily Life in Spain in the Golden Age* (1976), highly useful for an understanding of ordinary people and of Spanish society; and C. R. Phillips, *Ciudad Real, 1500–1750: Growth, Crisis, and Readjustment in the Spanish Economy* (1979), a significant case study.

The following works all offer solid material on English political and social issues of the seventeenth century: M. Ashley, *England in the Seventeenth Century* (1980); and *The House of Stuart: Its Rise and Fall* (1980); C. Hill, *A Century of Revolution* (1961); J. P. Kenyon, *Stuart England* (1978); and K. Wrightson, *English Society, 1580–1680* (1982). Perhaps the most comprehensive treatments of Parliament are C. Russell's *Crisis of Parliaments, 1509–1660* (1971) and *Parliaments and English Politics, 1621–1629* (1979). On the background of the English civil war, L. Stone, *The Crisis of the Aristocracy* (1965) and *The Causes of the English Revolution* (1972), are standard works; both B. Manning, *The English People and the English Revolution* (1976), and D. Underdown, *Revel, Riot, and Rebellion* (1985), discuss the extent of popular involvement; Underdown's is the more sophisticated treatment. For English intellectual currents, see J. O. Appleby, *Economic Thought and Ideology in Seventeenth Century England* (1978); and C. Hill, *Intellectual Origins of the English Revolution* (1966) and

Society and Puritanism in Pre-revolutionary England (1964).

For the several shades of Protestant sentiment in the early seventeenth century, see P. Collinson, *The Religion of Protestants* (1982). C. M. Hibbard, *Charles I and the Popish Plot* (1983), treats Roman Catholic influence; like Collinson's work, it is an excellent, fundamental reference for religious issues, though the older work of W. Haller, *The Rise of Puritanism* (1957), is still valuable. For women, see R. Thompson, *Women in Stuart England and America* (1974), and A. Fraser, *The Weaker Vessel* (1985). For Cromwell and the Interregnum, C. Firth, *Oliver Cromwell and the Rule of the Puritans in England* (1956); C. Hill, *God's Englishman* (1972); and A. Fraser, *Cromwell, the Lord Protector* (1973), are all valuable. J. Morrill, *The Revolt of the Provinces,* (1980), is the best study of religious neutralism, whereas C. Hill, *The World Turned Upside Down* (1972), discusses radical thought during the period.

For the Restoration and the Glorious Revolution, see R. Hutton, *Charles II: King of England, Scotland and Ireland* (1989), and A. Fraser, *Royal Charles: Charles II and the Restoration* (1979), two highly readable biographies; R. Ollard, *The Image of the King: Charles I and Charles II* (1980), which examines the nature of monarchy; J. Miller, *James II: A Study in Kingship* (1977); J. Childs, *The Army, James II, and the Glorious Revolution* (1980); J. R. Jones, *The Revolution of 1688 in England* (1972); and L. G. Schwoerer, *The Declaration of Rights, 1689* (1981), a fine assessment of that fundamental document. The ideas of John Locke are analyzed by J. P. Kenyon, *Revolution Principles: The Politics of Party, 1689–1720* (1977). R. Hutton, *The Restoration, 1658–1667* (1985), is a thorough, if somewhat difficult, narrative.

On Holland, the starting point for serious study is Schama, mentioned in the Notes, a brilliant and beautifully illustrated achievement. K. H. D. Haley, *The Dutch Republic in the Seventeenth Century* (1972), is a splendidly illustrated appreciation of Dutch commercial and artistic achievements; J. L. Price, *Culture and Society in the Dutch Republic During the Seventeenth Century* (1974), is a sound scholarly work. R. Boxer, *The Dutch Seaborne Empire* (1980), and the appropriate chapters of the Maland work cited in the Notes are useful for Dutch overseas expansion and the reasons for Dutch prosperity. The following works focus on the economic and cultural life of the leading Dutch city: V. Barbour, *Capitalism in Amsterdam in the Seventeenth Century* (1950), and D. Regin, *Traders, Artists, Burghers: A Cultural History of Amsterdam in the Seventeenth Century* (1977). J. M. Montias, *Artists and Artisans in Delft: A Socio-economic Study of the Seventeenth Century* (1982), examines another major city. The leading statesmen of the period may be studied in these biographies: H. H. Rowen, *John de Witt, Grand Pensionary of Holland, 1625–1672* (1978); S. B. Baxter, *William the III and the Defense of European Liberty, 1650–1702* (1966); and J. den Tex, *Oldenbarnevelt,* 2 vols. (1973).

Many facets of the lives of ordinary French, Spanish, English, and Dutch people are discussed by P. Burke, *Popular Culture in Early Modern Europe* (1978), an important and provocative study.

LISTENING TO THE
PAST

The Court at Versailles

*Although a soldier, courtier, and diplomat, the
enduring reputation of the Duc de Saint-Simon
(1675–1755) rests on his* Memoirs *(1788), an
eyewitness account of the personality and court
of Louis XIV. A nobleman of ancient lineage,
Saint-Simon resented Louis's "domestication" of
the nobility and his promotion of the bourgeoisie.
The* Memoirs, *excerpted here, remains a monument of French literature and an indispensable
historical source, partly for its portrait of the
court at Versailles.*

Very early in the reign of Louis XIV the Court
was removed from Paris, never to return. The
troubles of the minority had given him a dislike to that city; his enforced and surreptitious
flight from it still rankled in his memory; he
did not consider himself safe there, and
thought cabals would be more easily detected
if the Court was in the country, where the
movements and temporary absences of any of
its members would be more easily noticed.
. . . No doubt that he was also influenced by
the feeling that he would be regarded with
greater awe and veneration when no longer
exposed every day to the gaze of the multitude.

His love-affair with Mademoiselle de la Val-
lière, which at first was covered as far as possible with a veil of mystery, was the cause of
frequent excursions to Versailles. . . . The visits
of Louis XIV becoming more frequent, he
enlarged the *château* by degrees till its immense buildings afforded better accommodation for the Court than was to be found at St.
Germain, where most of the courtiers had to
put up with uncomfortable lodgings in the
town. The Court was therefore removed to
Versailles in 1682, not long before the
Queen's death. The new building contained

an infinite number of rooms for courtiers, and
the King liked the grant of these rooms to be
regarded as a coveted privilege.

He availed himself of the frequent festivities
at Versailles, and his excursions to other
places, as a means of making the courtiers
assiduous in their attendance and anxious to
please him; for he nominated beforehand
those who were to take part in them, and
could thus gratify some and inflict a snub on
others. He was conscious that the substantial
favours he had to bestow were not nearly
sufficient to produce a continual effect; he had
therefore to invent imaginary ones, and no
one was so clever in devising petty distinctions
and preferences which aroused jealousy and
emulation. The visits to Marly later on were
very useful to him in this way; also those to
Trianon [Marly and Trianon were small country houses], where certain ladies, chosen beforehand, were admitted to his table. It was
another distinction to hold his candlestick at
his *coucher;* as soon as he had finished his
prayers he used to name the courtier to whom
it was to be handed, always choosing one of
the highest rank among those present. . . .

Not only did he expect all persons of distinction to be in continual attendance at
Court, but he was quick to notice the absence
of those of inferior degree; at his *lever* [formal
rising from bed in the morning], his *coucher*
[preparations for going to bed], his meals, in
the gardens of Versailles (the only place where
the courtiers in general were allowed to follow
him), he used to cast his eyes to right and left;
nothing escaped him, he saw everybody. If any
one habitually living at Court absented himself he insisted on knowing the reason; those
who came there only for flying visits had also
to give a satisfactory explanation; any one who
seldom or never appeared there was certain to
incur his displeasure. If asked to bestow a

favour on such persons he would reply haughtily: "I do not know him"; of such as rarely presented themselves he would say, "He is a man I never see"; and from these judgements there was no appeal.

He always took great pains to find out what was going on in public places, in society, in private houses, even family secrets, and maintained an immense number of spies and talebearers. These were of all sorts; some did not know that their reports were carried to him; others did know it; there were others, again, who used to write to him directly, through channels which he prescribed; others who were admitted by the backstairs and saw him in his private room. Many a man in all ranks of life was ruined by these methods, often very unjustly, without ever being able to discover the reason; and when the King had once taken a prejudice against a man, he hardly ever got over it. . . .

No one understood better than Louis XIV the art of enhancing the value of a favour by his manner of bestowing it; he knew how to make the most of a word, a smile, even of a glance. If he addressed any one, were it but to ask a trifling question or make some commonplace remark, all eyes were turned on the person so honored; it was a mark of favour which always gave rise to comment. . . .

He loved splendour, magnificence, and profusion in all things, and encouraged similar tastes in his Court; to spend money freely on equipages [the king's horse carriages] and buildings, on feasting and at cards, was a sure way to gain his favour, perhaps to obtain the honour of a word from him. Motives of policy had something to do with this; by making expensive habits the fashion, and, for people in a certain position, a necessity, he compelled his courtiers to live beyond their income, and gradually reduced them to depend on his bounty for the means of subsistence. This was a plague which, once introduced, became a scourge to the whole country, for it did not take long to spread to Paris, and thence to the armies and the provinces; so that a man of any position is now estimated entirely according to his expenditure on his table and other luxuries. This folly, sustained by pride and ostentation, has already produced widespread confusion; it threatens to end in nothing short of ruin and a general overthrow.

❖ Painting of Louis XIV by Mignard Pierre (1612–1695). *(Source: Galleria Sabauda, Turin/Scala/Art Resource, NY)*

Questions for Analysis

1. How would you define the French *court*? Why did Louis XIV move it to Versailles?

2. By what means did Louis control the nobility at Versailles? Why did he use those particular means?

3. Consider the role of ritual and ceremony in some modern governments, such as the American. How does it compare to Louis XIV's use of ceremony, as portrayed by Saint-Simon?

4. Saint-Simon faulted Louis for encouraging the nobles' extravagance. Is that a justifiable criticism?

Source: F. Arkwright, ed., *The Memoirs of the Duke de Saint-Simon* (New York: Brentano's, n.d.), vol. 5, pp. 271–274, 276–278.

17

Absolutism in Eastern Europe to 1740

The seventeenth century witnessed a struggle between constitutionalism and absolutism in eastern Europe. With the notable exception of the kingdom of Poland, monarchial absolutism was triumphant in eastern Europe; constitutionalism was decisively defeated. Absolute monarchies emerged in Austria, Prussia, and Russia. This was a development of great significance for at least two reasons. First, these three monarchies exercised enormous influence until 1918, and they created an authoritarian tradition that remains strong in eastern Europe. Second, the absolute monarchs of eastern Europe had a powerful impact on culture, encouraging a magnificent flowering of the baroque style in architecture and the arts.

Although the monarchs of eastern Europe were greatly impressed by Louis XIV and his model of royal absolutism, their states differed in several important ways from that of their French counterpart. Louis XIV built French absolutism on the foundation of a well-developed medieval monarchy and a strong royal bureaucracy. And when Louis XIV came to the throne, the powers of the nobility were already somewhat limited, the French middle class was relatively strong, and the peasants were generally free from serfdom. Eastern absolutism rested on a very different social reality: a powerful nobility, a weak middle class, and an oppressed peasantry composed of serfs.

These differences in social conditions raise three major questions:

- Why did the basic structure of society in eastern Europe move away from that of western Europe in the early modern period?

- How and why did the rulers of Austria, Prussia, and Russia, each in a different social environment, manage to build powerful absolute monarchies that proved more durable than that of Louis XIV?

A magnificent jewelled Orb of Power, commissioned about 1662 by Alexei Mikhailovich, the second Romanov Tsar. (*Source: David Douglas Duncan*)

- How did the absolute monarchs' interaction with artists and architects contribute to the splendid achievements of baroque culture?

These are the questions that this chapter will explore.

❖ LORDS AND PEASANTS IN EASTERN EUROPE

When absolute monarchy took shape in eastern Europe in the seventeenth century, it built on social and economic foundations laid between roughly 1400 and 1650. In those years, the princes and the landed nobility of eastern Europe rolled back the gains made by the peasantry during the High Middle Ages and reimposed a harsh serfdom on the rural masses. The nobility also reduced the importance of the towns and the middle classes. This process differed profoundly from developments in western Europe at the same time. In the west, peasants won greater freedom, and the urban capitalistic middle class continued its rise. Thus the east that emerged contrasted sharply with the west—another aspect of the shattered unity of medieval Latin Christendom.

The Medieval Background

Between roughly 1400 and 1650, nobles and rulers re-established serfdom in the eastern lands of Bohemia, Silesia, Hungary, eastern Germany, Poland, Lithuania, and Russia. The east—the land east of the Elbe River in Germany, which historians often call "East Elbia"—gained a certain social and economic unity in the process. But eastern peasants lost their rights and freedoms. They became bound first to the land they worked and then, by degrading obligations, to the lords they served.

This development was a tragic reversal of trends in the High Middle Ages. The period from roughly 1050 to 1300 had been a time of general economic expansion characterized by the growth of trade, towns, and population. Expansion also meant clearing the forests and colonizing the frontier beyond the Elbe River. Anxious to attract German settlers to sparsely populated lands, the rulers and nobles of eastern Europe had offered potential newcomers economic and legal incentives. Large numbers of incoming settlers obtained land on excellent terms and gained much greater personal freedom. These benefits were also gradually extended to the local Slavic populations, even those of central Russia. Thus by 1300 a very general improvement in peasant conditions had occurred in eastern Europe; serfdom had all but disappeared. Peasants bargained freely with their landlords and moved about as they pleased. Opportunities and improvements east of the Elbe had a positive impact on western Europe, where the weight of serfdom was also reduced between 1100 and 1300.

After about 1300, however, as Europe's population and economy both declined grievously, mainly because of the Black Death, the east and the west went in different directions. In both east and west, a many-sided landlord reaction occurred as lords sought to solve their tough economic problems by more heavily exploiting the peasantry. Yet this reaction generally failed in the west. In many western areas by 1500, almost all of the peasants were free, and in the rest of western Europe serf obligations had declined greatly. East of the Elbe, however, the landlords won. By 1500 eastern peasants were well on their way to becoming serfs again.

Throughout eastern Europe, as in western Europe, the drop in population and prices in the fourteenth and fifteenth centuries caused severe labor shortages and hard times for the nobles. Yet rather than offer better economic and legal terms to keep old peasants and attract new ones, eastern landlords used political and police power to turn the tables on peasants. They did this in two ways.

First, the lords made their kings and princes issue laws that restricted or eliminated the peasants' precious, time-honored right of free movement. Thus a peasant could no longer leave to take advantage of better opportunities elsewhere without the lord's permission, and the lord had no reason to make such concessions. In Prussian territories by 1500, the law required that runaway peasants be hunted down and returned to their lords; a runaway servant was to be nailed to a post by one ear and given a knife to cut himself loose. Until the middle of the fifteenth century, medieval Russian peasants had been free to move wherever they wished and seek the best landlord. Thereafter this freedom was gradually curtailed, so that by 1497 a Russian peasant had the right to move only during a two-week period after the fall harvest. Eastern peasants were losing their status as free and independent men and women.

Second, lords steadily took more and more of their peasants' land and imposed heavier and heav-

✣ **Punishing Serfs** This seventeenth-century illustration from Olearius's famous *Travels to Moscovy* suggests what eastern serfdom really meant. The scene is set in eastern Poland. There, according to Olearius, a common command of the lord was, "Beat him till the skin falls from the flesh." Selections from Olearius's graphic account are found in this chapter's Listening to the Past. *(Source: University of Illinois Library, Champaign)*

ier labor obligations. Instead of being independent farmers paying reasonable, freely negotiated rents, peasants tended to become forced laborers on the lords' estates. By the early 1500s, lords in many territories could command their peasants to work for them without pay as many as six days a week. A German writer of the mid-sixteenth century described peasants in eastern Prussia who "do not possess the heritage of their holdings and have to serve their master whenever he wants them."[1]

The gradual erosion of the peasantry's economic position was bound up with manipulation of the legal system. The local lord was also the local prosecutor, judge, and jailer. As a matter of course, he ruled in his own favor in disputes with his peasants. There were no independent royal officials to provide justice or uphold the common law.

The Consolidation of Serfdom

Between 1500 and 1650, the social, legal, and economic conditions of peasants in eastern Europe continued to decline. Free peasants lost their freedom and became serfs. In Poland, for example,

nobles gained complete control over their peasants in 1574, after which they could legally inflict the death penalty on their serfs whenever they wished. In Prussia a long series of oppressive measures reached their culmination in 1653. Not only were all the old privileges of the lords reaffirmed, but peasants were also assumed to be in "hereditary subjugation" to their lords unless they could prove the contrary in the lords' courts, which was practically impossible. Prussian peasants were serfs tied to their lords as well as to the land.

In Russia the right of peasants to move from a given estate was "temporarily" suspended in the 1590s and permanently abolished in 1603. In 1649 a new law code completed the process. At the insistence of the lower nobility, the Russian tsar lifted the nine-year time limit on the recovery of runaways. Henceforth runaway peasants were to be returned to their lords whenever they were caught. The last small hope of escaping serfdom was gone. Control of serfs was strictly the lords' own business, for the new law code set no limits on the lords' authority over their peasants. Although the political development of the various eastern states differed, the legal re-establishment of permanent hereditary serfdom had become the common fate of peasants in the east by the middle of the seventeenth century.

This consolidation of serfdom was accompanied by the growth of estate agriculture, particularly in Poland and eastern Germany. In the sixteenth century, European economic expansion and population growth resumed after the great declines of the late Middle Ages. Prices for agricultural commodities also rose sharply as gold and silver flowed in from the New World. Thus Polish and German lords had powerful economic incentives to increase the production of their estates. And they did.

Lords seized more and more peasant land for their own estates and then demanded and received ever-more unpaid serf labor on those enlarged estates. Even when the estates were inefficient and technically backward, as they generally were, the great Polish nobles and middle-rank German lords squeezed sizable, cheap, and thus very profitable surpluses out of their impoverished peasants. Surpluses in wheat and timber were easily sold to big foreign merchants, who exported them to the growing cities of the west. Thus the poor east helped feed the much wealthier west.

The re-emergence of serfdom in eastern Europe in the early modern period was clearly a momentous human development, and historians have advanced a variety of explanations for it. As always, some scholars have stressed the economic interpretation. Agricultural depression and population decline in the fourteenth and fifteenth centuries led to a severe labor shortage, they have argued, and thus eastern landlords naturally tied their precious peasants to the land. With the return of prosperity and the development of export markets in the sixteenth century, the landlords finished the job, grabbing the peasants' land and making them work as unpaid serfs on the resulting enlarged estates. This argument by itself is not very convincing, for almost identical economic developments "caused" the opposite result in the west. Indeed, some historians have maintained that labor shortage and subsequent expansion were key factors in the virtual disappearance of western serfdom.

It seems fairly clear, therefore, that political, rather than economic, factors were crucial in the simultaneous rise of serfdom in the east and decline of serfdom in the west. Specifically, eastern lords enjoyed much greater political power than their western counterparts. In the late Middle Ages, when much of eastern Europe experienced innumerable wars and general political chaos, the noble landlord class greatly increased its political power at the expense of the ruling monarchs. There were, for example, many disputed royal successions, so that weak kings were forced to grant political favors to win the support of the nobility. Thus while strong "new monarchs" were rising in Spain, France, and England and providing effective central government, kings were generally losing power in the east. Such weak kings could not resist the demands of the lords regarding their peasants.

Moreover, most eastern monarchs did not want to resist even if they could. The typical king was only first among equals in the noble class. He, too, thought mainly in private, rather than public, terms. He, too, wanted to squeeze as much as he could out of his peasants and enlarge his estates. The western concept and reality of sovereignty, as embodied in a king who protected the interests of all his people, was not well developed in eastern Europe before 1650.

The political power of the peasants was also weaker in eastern Europe and declined steadily after about 1400. Although there were occasional bloody peasant uprisings against the oppression of the landlords, they never succeeded. Nor did eastern peasants effectively resist day-by-day infringements on their liberties by their landlords. Part of the reason was that the lords, rather than the kings, ran the courts—one of the important concessions nobles extorted from weak monarchs. It has also been suggested that peasant solidarity was weaker in the east, possibly reflecting the lack of long-established village communities on the eastern frontier.

Finally, with the approval of weak kings, the landlords systematically undermined the medieval privileges of the towns and the power of the urban classes. Instead of selling products to local merchants in the towns, as required in the Middle Ages, the landlords sold directly to big foreign capitalists. For example, Dutch ships sailed up the rivers of Poland and eastern Germany to the loading docks of the great estates, completely short-circuiting the local towns. Moreover, "town air" no longer "made people free," for the eastern towns had lost their medieval right of refuge and were now compelled to return runaways to their lords. The population of the towns and the importance of the urban middle classes declined greatly. These developments both reflected and promoted the supremacy of noble landlords in most of eastern Europe in the sixteenth century.

✠ THE RISE OF AUSTRIA AND PRUSSIA

Despite the strength of the nobility and the weakness of many monarchs before 1600, strong kings did begin to emerge in many lands in the course of the seventeenth century. War and the threat of war aided rulers greatly in their attempts to build absolute monarchies. There was also an endless struggle for power, as eastern rulers not only fought each other but also battled with hordes of Asiatic invaders. In this atmosphere of continual wartime emergency, monarchs reduced the political power of the landlord nobility. Cautiously leaving the nobles the unchallenged masters of their peasants, the would-be absolutist monarchs of eastern Europe gradually gained and monopolized political power in three key areas. First, they imposed and collected permanent taxes without consent. Second, they maintained permanent standing armies, which policed the country in addition to fighting abroad. Third, they conducted relations with other states as they pleased.

As with all general historical developments, there were important variations on the absolutist theme in eastern Europe. The royal absolutism created in Prussia was stronger and more effective than that established in Austria. This advantage gave Prussia a thin edge over Austria in the struggle for power in east-central Europe in the eighteenth century. That edge had enormous long-term political significance, for it was a rising Prussia that unified the German people in the nineteenth century and imposed on them a fateful Prussian stamp.

Austria and the Ottoman Turks

Like all the other peoples and rulers of central Europe, the Habsburgs of Austria emerged from the Thirty Years' War impoverished and exhausted. Their efforts to root out Protestantism in the German lands and to turn the weak Holy Roman Empire into a real state had failed utterly. The Habsburgs did remain the hereditary emperors of the ancient Holy Roman Empire, which was inhabited mainly by German speakers and was more accurately called the German Empire. But the authority of the empire and its Habsburg emperors

had declined almost to the vanishing point. Real power in the German Empire lay in the hands of a bewildering variety of three hundred separate political jurisdictions, which included independent cities, small principalities, medium-sized states such as Bavaria and Saxony, and some (but not all) of the territories of Prussia and the Habsburgs.

Defeat in central Europe opened new vistas for the Habsburgs. They were forced to turn inward and eastward in an attempt to fuse their diverse holdings into a strong unified state. An important step in this direction had actually been taken in Bohemia during the Thirty Years' War. Protestantism had been strong among the Czechs, a Slavic people concentrated in Bohemia. Indeed, the lesser Czech nobility was largely Protestant in 1600 and had considerable political power because it dominated the Bohemian Estates—the representative body of the different legal orders in Bohemia. In 1618 the Bohemian Estates had risen up in defense of Protestant rights. This revolt was crushed in 1620 at the Battle of the White Mountain, a momentous turning point in Czech history. The victorious Habsburg king, Ferdinand II (r. 1619–1637), drastically reduced the power of the Bohemian Estates. Ferdinand also confiscated the landholdings of many Protestant nobles and gave them to a few great Catholic nobles who had remained loyal and to a motley band of aristocratic soldiers of fortune who had nothing in common with the Czech-speaking peasants. After 1650 a large portion of the Bohemian nobility was of recent foreign origin and owed everything to the Habsburgs.

With the help of this new nobility, the Habsburgs established strong direct rule over reconquered Bohemia. The condition of the enserfed peasantry worsened substantially: three days per week of unpaid labor—the *robot*—became the norm, and a quarter of the serfs worked for their lords every day but Sundays and religious holidays. Serfs also paid the taxes, which further strengthened the alliance between the Habsburg monarch and the Bohemian nobility. Protestantism was also stamped out, in the course of which a growing unity of religion was brought about. The reorganization of Bohemia was a giant step toward absolutism.

After the Thirty Years' War, Ferdinand III (r. 1637–1657) centralized the government in the hereditary German-speaking provinces, most notably Austria, Styria, and the Tyrol, which formed the second part of the Habsburg holdings. For the

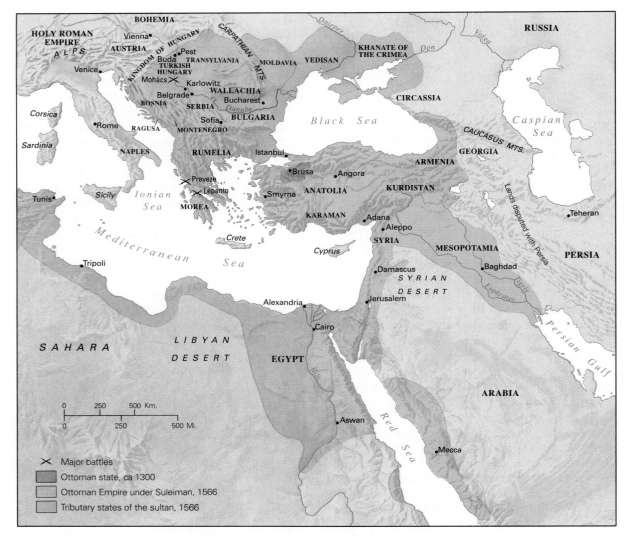

✦ **MAP 17.1 The Ottoman Empire at Its Height, 1566** The Ottomans, like their great rivals the Habsburgs, rose to rule a vast dynastic empire encompassing many different peoples and ethnic groups. The army and the bureaucracy served to unite the disparate territories into a single state.

first time, Ferdinand III's reign saw the creation of a permanent standing army ready to put down any internal opposition. The Habsburg monarchy was then ready to turn toward the vast plains of Hungary, which it claimed as the third and largest part of its dominion, in opposition to the Ottoman Turks.

The Ottomans had come out of Anatolia, in present-day Turkey, to create one of history's greatest military empires. At their peak in the middle of the sixteenth century under Suleiman the Magnificent (r. 1520–1566), they ruled the most

powerful empire in the world. Their possessions stretched from western Persia across North Africa and up into the heart of central Europe (Map 17.1). Apostles of Islam, the Ottoman Turks were old and determined foes of the Catholic Habsburgs. Their armies had almost captured Vienna in 1529, and for more than 150 years thereafter the Ottomans ruled the many different ethnic groups living in the Balkans, almost all of Hungary, and part of southern Russia.

The Ottoman Empire was originally built on a fascinating and very non-European conception of state and society. There was an almost complete absence of private landed property. All the agricultural land of the empire was the personal hereditary property of the sultan, who exploited the land as he saw fit according to Ottoman political theory. There was therefore no security of landholding and no hereditary nobility. Everyone was dependent on the sultan and virtually his slave.

Indeed, the top ranks of the bureaucracy were staffed by the sultan's slave corps. Every year the sultan levied a "tax" of one to three thousand male children on the conquered Christian populations in the Balkans. These and other slaves were raised in Turkey as Muslims and trained to fight and to administer. The most talented slaves rose to the top of the bureaucracy; the less fortunate formed the brave and skillful core of the sultan's army, the so-called janissary corps.

As long as the Ottoman Empire expanded, the system worked well. As the sultan won more territory, he could impose his slave tax on larger populations. Moreover, he could amply reward loyal and effective servants by letting them draw a carefully defined income from conquered Christian peasants on a strictly temporary basis. For a long time, Christian peasants in eastern Europe were economically exploited less by the Muslim Turks than by Christian nobles, and they were not forced to convert to Islam. After about 1570, however, the powerful, centralized Ottoman system slowly began to disintegrate as the Turks' western advance was stopped. Temporary Muslim landholders became hard-to-control permanent oppressors. Weak sultans left the glory of the battlefield for the delights of the harem, and the army lost its dedication and failed to keep up with European military advances.

Yet in the late seventeenth century, under vigorous reforming leadership, the Ottoman Empire succeeded in marshaling its forces for one last mighty blow at Christian Europe. After wresting territory from Poland, fighting a long inconclusive war with Russia, and establishing an alliance with Louis XIV of France, the Turks turned again on Austria. A huge Turkish army surrounded Vienna and laid siege to it in 1683. But after holding out against great odds for two months, the city was relieved at the last minute by a mixed force of Habsburg, Saxon, Bavarian, and Polish troops, and the Ottomans were forced to retreat. Soon the retreat became a rout. As Russian and Venetian allies attacked on other fronts, the Habsburgs conquered almost all of Hungary and Transylvania (part of present-day Romania) by 1699 (Map 17.2).

The Turkish wars and this great expansion strengthened the Habsburg army and promoted some sense of unity in the Habsburg lands. The Habsburgs moved to centralize their power and make it as absolute as possible. But these efforts to create a fully developed, highly centralized, absolutist state were only partly successful.

The Habsburg state was composed of three separate and distinct territories—the old "hereditary provinces" of Austria, the kingdom of Bohemia, and the kingdom of Hungary. These three parts were tied together primarily by their common ruler, the Habsburg monarch. Each part had its own laws and political life, for the three noble-dominated Estates continued to exist, though with reduced powers. The Habsburgs themselves were well aware of the fragility of the union they had forged. In 1713 Charles VI (r. 1711–1740) proclaimed the so-called Pragmatic Sanction, which stated that the Habsburg possessions were never to be divided and were always to be passed intact to a single heir, who might be female since Charles had no sons. Charles spent much of his reign trying to get this principle accepted by the various branches of the Habsburg family, by the three different Estates of the realm, and by the states of Europe. His fears turned out to be well founded.

The Hungarian nobility, despite its reduced strength, effectively thwarted the full development of Habsburg absolutism. Time and again throughout the seventeenth century, Hungarian nobles—the most numerous in Europe, making up 5 to 7 percent of the Hungarian population—rose in revolt against Vienna's attempts to impose absolute rule. They never triumphed decisively, but neither were they ever crushed, as the Czech nobility had been in 1620.

Hungarians resisted because many of them remained Protestants, especially in the area long ruled by the more tolerant Turks, and hated the heavy-handed attempts of the conquering Habsburgs to re-Catholicize everyone. Moreover, the lords of Hungary often found a powerful military ally in Turkey. Finally, the Hungarian nobility, and even part of the Hungarian peasantry, had become attached to a national ideal long before most of the other peoples of eastern Europe did so. Hungarian nobles were determined to maintain as much independence and local control as possible. Thus when

❖ **Siege of Vienna, 1683** A huge Turkish army surrounded the Austrian capital and then tried to tunnel under the city's massive, star-shaped fortifications, shown here, and blow them up with mines. The Turks penetrated the outer ring of defense, but at the last moment a relief army arrived and delivered a surprise attack that routed the Turks and saved Vienna. *(Source: Mansell Collection)*

the Habsburgs were bogged down in the War of the Spanish Succession (see page 539), the Hungarians rose in one last patriotic rebellion under Prince Francis Rákóczy in 1703. Rákóczy and his forces were eventually defeated, but this time the Habsburgs had to accept a definitive compromise. Charles VI restored many of the traditional privileges of the Hungarian aristocracy in return for Hungarian acceptance of hereditary Habsburg rule. Thus Hungary, unlike Austria or Bohemia, never came close to being fully integrated into a centralized, absolute Habsburg state.

Prussia in the Seventeenth Century

After 1400 the status of east German peasants declined steadily; their serfdom was formally spelled out in the early seventeenth century. While the local princes lost political power and influence, a revitalized landed nobility became the undisputed ruling class. The Hohenzollern family, which ruled through its senior and junior branches as the imperial electors of Brandenburg and the dukes of Prussia, had little real princely power. The Hohenzollern rulers of Brandenburg and Prussia were nothing more than the first among equals, the largest landowners in a landlord society.

Nothing suggested that the Hohenzollern family and its princely territories would ever play an important role in European or even German affairs. The elector of Brandenburg's right to help choose the Holy Roman emperor with six other electors was of little practical value, and the elector had no military strength whatsoever. Moreover, geography conspired against the Hohenzollerns. Brandenburg, their power base, was completely cut off from the sea (see Map 17.2). A tiny part of the vast north European plain that stretches from

France to Russia, Brandenburg lacked natural frontiers and lay open to attack from all directions. The land was poor, a combination of sand and swamp. Contemporaries contemptuously called Brandenburg the "sand-box of the Holy Roman Empire."[2]

Moreover, the territory of the elector's cousin, the duke of Prussia, was totally separated from Brandenburg and was part of Poland. Prussia had originally been conquered in the thirteenth century by the Germanic order of Teutonic Knights as part of a larger struggle between German settlers and the indigenous Slavic populations. However, by 1600 Prussia's German-speaking peasants had much in common with Polish peasants in other provinces, for both ethnic groups had seen most of their freedoms reduced or revoked by their noble landlords. (Poland's numerous lesser nobility

also dominated the Polish state, which was actually a republic headed by an elected king who had little real power.) In 1618 the junior branch of the Hohenzollern family died out and Prussia reverted to the elector of Brandenburg.

The elector of Brandenburg was a helpless spectator in the Thirty Years' War, his territories alternately ravaged by Swedish and Habsburg armies. Population fell drastically, and many villages disappeared. The power of the Hohenzollerns reached its lowest point. Yet the devastation of Brandenburg and Prussia prepared the way for Hohenzollern absolutism because foreign armies dramatically weakened the political power of the Estates—the representative assemblies of the realm. This weakening of the Estates helped the very talented young elector Frederick William (r. 1640–1688), later

❖ **MAP 17.2 The Growth of Austria and Brandenburg-Prussia to 1748** Austria expanded to the southwest into Hungary and Transylvania at the expense of the Ottoman Empire. It was unable to hold the rich Germane province of Silesia, however, which was conquered by Brandenburg-Prussia.

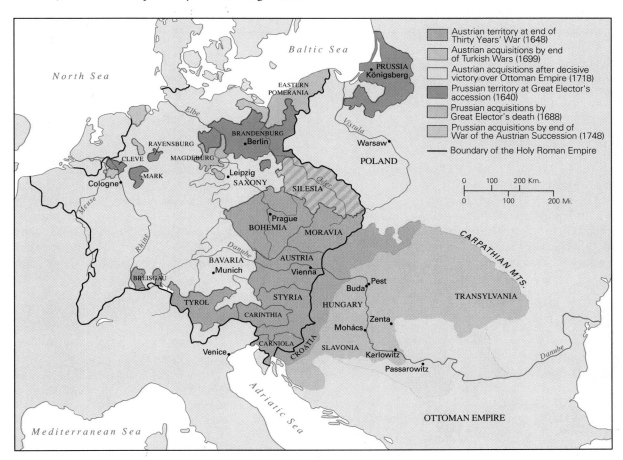

known as the "Great Elector," to ride roughshod over traditional parliamentary liberties and to take a giant step toward royal absolutism. This constitutional struggle, often unjustly neglected by historians, was the most crucial in Prussian history for hundreds of years, until that of the 1860s.

When he came to power in 1640, the twenty-year-old Great Elector was determined to unify his three quite separate provinces and add to them by diplomacy and war. These provinces were Brandenburg itself, the area around Berlin; Prussia, inherited in 1618 and legally a part of the Polish state; and completely separate, scattered holdings along the Rhine in western Germany, inherited in 1614 (see Map 17.2). Each of the three provinces was inhabited by Germans, but each had its own Estates, whose power had increased until about 1600 as the power of the rulers declined. Although the Estates had not met regularly during the chaotic Thirty Years' War, they still had the power of the purse in their respective provinces. Taxes could not be levied without their consent. The Estates of Brandenburg and Prussia were dominated by the nobility and the landowning classes, known as the "Junkers." But this was also the case in most European countries that had representative bodies, and it was certainly true of the English Parliament before and after the civil war. Had the Estates successfully resisted the absolutist demands of the Great Elector, they, too, might have evolved toward more broadly based constitutionalism.

The struggle between the Great Elector and the provincial Estates was long, complicated, and intense. After the Thirty Years' War, representatives

❖ **Molding the Prussian Spirit**   Discipline was strict and punishment brutal in the Prussian army. This scene, from an eighteenth-century book used to teach school children in Prussia, shows one soldier being flogged while another is being beaten with canes as he walks between rows of troops. The officer on horseback proudly commands. *(Source: University of Illinois Library, Champaign)*

of the nobility zealously reasserted the right of the Estates to vote taxes, a right the Swedish armies of occupation had simply ignored. Yet first in Brandenburg in 1653 and then in Prussia between 1661 and 1663, the Great Elector eventually had his way.

To pay for the permanent standing army he first established in 1660, Frederick William forced the Estates to accept the introduction of permanent taxation without consent. Moreover, the soldiers doubled as tax collectors and policemen, becoming the core of the rapidly expanding state bureaucracy. The power of the Estates declined rapidly thereafter, for the Great Elector had both financial independence and superior force. He turned the screws of taxation: the state's total revenue tripled during his reign. The size of the army leaped about tenfold. In 1688 a population of one million was supporting a peacetime standing army of thirty thousand. Many of the soldiers were French Huguenot immigrants, whom the Great Elector welcomed as the talented, hard-working citizens they were.

In accounting for the Great Elector's fateful triumph, two factors appear central. As in the formation of every absolutist state, war was a decisive factor. The ongoing struggle between Sweden and Poland for control of the Baltic after 1648 and the wars of Louis XIV in western Europe created an atmosphere of permanent crisis. The wild Tartars of southern Russia swept through Prussia in the winter of 1656 to 1657, killing and carrying off as slaves more than fifty thousand people, according to an old estimate. This invasion softened up the Estates and strengthened the urgency of the elector's demands for more money for more soldiers. It was no accident that, except for commercially minded Holland, constitutionalism won out only in England, the only major country to escape devastating foreign invasions in the seventeenth century.

Second, the nobility had long dominated the government through the Estates, but only for its own narrow self-interest. When the crunch came, Prussian nobles proved unwilling to join the representatives of the towns in a consistent common front against royal pretensions. The nobility was all too concerned with its own rights and privileges, especially its freedom from taxation and its unlimited control over the peasants. When, therefore, the Great Elector reconfirmed these privileges in 1653 and after, even while reducing the political power of the Estates, the nobility growled but did not bite. It accepted a compromise whereby the bulk of the new taxes fell on towns and royal authority stopped at the landlords' gates. The elector could and did use naked force to break the liberties of the towns. The main leader of the urban opposition in the key city of Königsberg, for example, was simply arrested and imprisoned for life without trial.

The Consolidation of Prussian Absolutism

By the time of his death in 1688, the Great Elector had created a single state out of scattered principalities. But his new creation was still small and fragile. All the leading states of Europe had many more people—France with twenty million was fully twenty times as populous—and strong monarchy was still a novelty. Moreover, the Great Elector's successor, Elector Frederick III, "the Ostentatious" (r. 1688–1713), was weak of body and mind, and he focused on imitating the style of Louis XIV. This imitation was largely confined to building an expensive palace and cultivating the arts, however, since his only real political accomplishment was to be crowned King Frederick I in 1701 as a reward for aiding the Holy Roman emperor in the War of the Spanish Succession.

This tendency toward luxury-loving, happy, and harmless petty tyranny was completely reversed by Frederick William I, "the Soldiers' King" (r. 1713–1740). A crude, dangerous psychoneurotic, Frederick William I was nevertheless the most talented reformer ever produced by the Hohenzollern family. It was he who truly established Prussian absolutism and gave it a unique character. It was he who created the best army in Europe, for its size, and who infused military values into a whole society. In the words of a leading historian of Prussia:

For a whole generation, the Hohenzollern subjects were victimized by a royal bully, imbued with an obsessive bent for military organization and military scales of value. This left a deep mark upon the institutions of Prussiandom and upon the molding of the "Prussian spirit."[3]

Frederick William's attachment to the army and military life was intensely emotional. He had, for example, a bizarre, almost pathological love for tall soldiers, whom he credited with superior strength and endurance. Austere and always faithful to his

❖ **A Prussian Giant Grenadier** Frederick William I wanted tall, handsome soldiers. He dressed them in tight bright uniforms to distinguish them from the peasant population from which most soldiers came. He also ordered several portraits of his favorites from his court painter, J. C. Merk. Grenadiers wore the distinctive mitre cap instead of an ordinary hat so that they could hurl their heavy hand grenades unimpeded by a broad brim. *(Source: Copyright reserved to Her Majesty Queen Elizabeth II)*

wife, he nevertheless confided to the French ambassador, "The most beautiful girl or woman in the world would be a matter of indifference to me, but tall soldiers—they are my weakness." Like some fanatical modern-day basketball coach in search of a championship team, he sent his agents throughout Prussia and all of Europe to trick, buy, and kidnap top recruits. Neighboring princes sent him their giants as gifts to win his gratitude. Prussian mothers told their sons, "Stop growing or the recruiting agents will get you."[4]

Profoundly military in temperament, Frederick William always wore an army uniform, and he lived the highly disciplined life of the professional soldier. He began his work by five or six in the morning; at ten he almost always went to the parade ground to drill or inspect his troops. A man of violent temper, Frederick William personally punished the most minor infractions on the spot: a missing button off a soldier's coat quickly provoked a savage beating with a heavy walking stick.

Frederick William's love of the army was also based on a hardheaded conception of the struggle for power and a dog-eat-dog view of international politics. Even before ascending the throne, he bitterly criticized his father's ministers: "They say that they will obtain land and power for the king with the pen; but I say it can be done only with the sword." Years later he summed up his life's philosophy in his instructions to his son: "A formidable army and a war chest large enough to make this army mobile in times of need can create great respect for you in the world, so that you can speak a word like the other powers."[5] This unshakable belief that the welfare of king and state depended on the army above all else reinforced Frederick William's passion for playing soldier.

The cult of military power provided the rationale for a great expansion of royal absolutism. As the ruthless king himself put it: "I must be served with life and limb, with house and wealth, with honour and conscience, everything must be committed except eternal salvation—that belongs to God, but all else is mine."[6] To make good these extraordinary demands, Frederick William created a strong centralized bureaucracy. More commoners probably rose to top positions in the civil government than at any other time in Prussia's history. Meanwhile the last traces of the parliamentary Estates and local self-government vanished.

The king's grab for power brought him into considerable conflict with the noble landowners, the Junkers. In his early years, he even threatened to destroy them; yet, in the end, the Prussian nobility was not destroyed but enlisted—into the army. Responding to a combination of threats and opportunities, the Junkers became the officer caste. By 1739 all but 5 of 245 officers with the rank of major or above were aristocrats, and most of them were native Prussians. A new compromise had been worked out whereby the proud nobility imperiously commanded the peasantry in the army as well as on the estates.

Coarse and crude, penny-pinching and hard working, Frederick William achieved results. Above all, he built a first-rate army on the basis of third-rate resources. The standing army increased from thirty-eight thousand to eighty-three thousand during his reign. Prussia, twelfth in Europe in population, had the fourth largest army by 1740. Only the much more populous states of France, Russia, and Austria had larger forces, and even France's army was only twice as large as Prussia's. Moreover, soldier for soldier, the Prussian army became the best in Europe, astonishing foreign observers with its precision, skill, and discipline. For the next two hundred years, Prussia and then Prussianized Germany would usually win the crucial military battles.

Frederick William and his ministers also built an exceptionally honest and conscientious bureaucracy, which not only administered the country but also tried with some success to develop the country economically. Finally, like the miser he was known to be, living very frugally off the income of his own landholdings, the king loved his "blue boys" so much that he hated to "spend" them. This most militaristic of kings was, paradoxically, almost always at peace.

Nevertheless, the Prussian people paid a heavy and lasting price for the obsessions of their royal drillmaster. Civil society became rigid and highly disciplined. Prussia became the "Sparta of the North"; unquestioning obedience was the highest virtue. As a Prussian minister later summed up, "To keep quiet is the first civic duty."[7] Thus the policies of Frederick William I combined with harsh peasant bondage and Junker tyranny to lay the foundations for probably the most militaristic country of modern times.

✛ THE DEVELOPMENT OF RUSSIA

One of the favorite parlor games of nineteenth-century Russian (and non-Russian) intellectuals was debating whether Russia was a Western, European or a non-Western, Asiatic society. This question was particularly fascinating because it was unanswerable. To this day Russia differs fundamentally from the West in some basic ways, though Russian history has paralleled that of the West in other aspects. A good case can be made for either position: thus the hypnotic attraction of Russian history.

Certainly Russian developments in the early medieval period had important parallels with those in the West. Both the conversion of the eastern Slavs to Christianity (of the Eastern Orthodox variety) and the loose but real political unification of the eastern Slavic territories under a single prince and a single dynasty in the eleventh century were in the mainstream of European medieval civilization. So, too, was the typical feudal division of the land-based society into a boyard nobility and a commoner peasantry. But after the death of Great Prince Iaroslav the Wise (r. 1019–1054), the Kievan principality disintegrated into competing political units, a process that continued until 1237. However, similar fragmentations of central authority occurred in many European kingdoms at various points in the Middle Ages, and one might have reasonably expected that a strong native ruler would eventually emerge from the contending descendants of Iaroslav the Wise and resume the centralizing work of earlier Kievan monarchs.

Such was not the case, however. From the mid-thirteenth century to the late seventeenth century, the lands of the eastern Slavs followed a unique path of European development. Brutally conquered and subjugated by a foreign invader, Russia created a system of rule that was virtually unknown in the West. Thus the differences between Russia and the West became striking and profound in the long period until 1700, when Russia's overall development again began to draw progressively closer to that of its Western neighbors. And when absolute monarchy finally and decisively triumphed under the rough guidance of Peter the Great in the early eighteenth century, it was a quite different type of absolute monarchy from that of France or even Prussia.

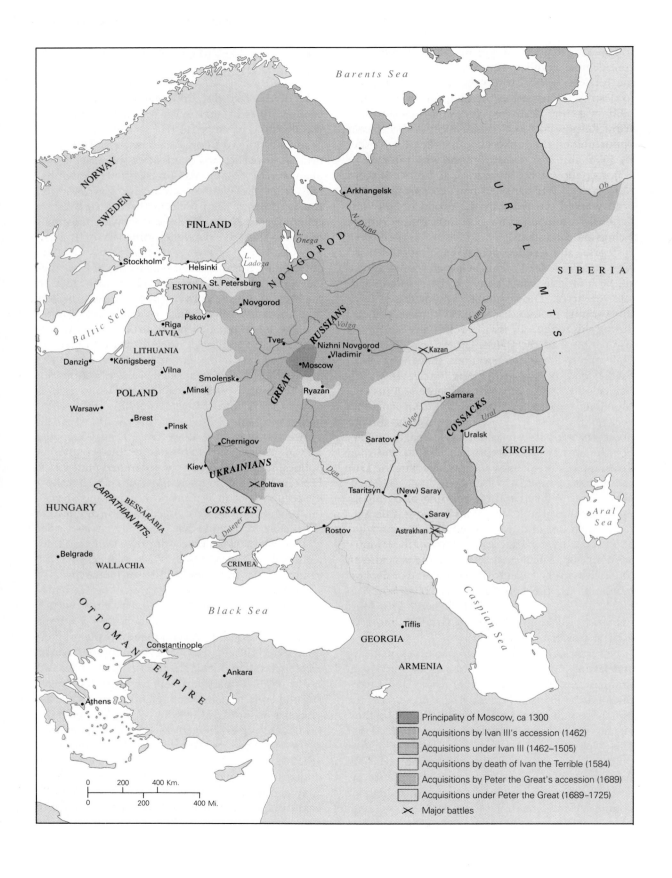

Barents Sea

NORWAY

SWEDEN

FINLAND

• Stockholm

• Helsinki

St. Petersburg •

L. Ladoga

L. Onega

• Arkhangelsk

N. Dvina

U R A L   M T S.

Ob

SIBERIA

ESTONIA

• Novgorod

Baltic Sea

• Riga

LATVIA

• Pskov

LITHUANIA

Danzig • • Königsberg

• Vilna

• Tver

RUSSIANS

Nizhni Novgorod

• Vladimir

✕ Kazan

Volga

Kama

NOVGOROD

• Smolensk

GREAT

• Moscow

POLAND

• Minsk

• Ryazan

• Samara

COSSACKS

Ural

Warsaw •

• Brest

• Pinsk

Saratov •

• Uralsk

KIRGHIZ

• Chernigov

Volga

Kiev •

UKRAINIANS

Don

CARPATHIAN MTS.

BESSARABIA

HUNGARY

COSSACKS

Dnieper

✕ Poltava

Tsaritsyn •

(New) Saray •

• Saray

Aral Sea

• Rostov

Astrakhan • ✕

• Belgrade

WALLACHIA

CRIMEA

O T T O M A N   E M P I R E

Black Sea

Constantinople •

• Ankara

Caspian Sea

• Tiflis

GEORGIA

ARMENIA

• Athens

	Principality of Moscow, ca 1300
	Acquisitions by Ivan III's accession (1462)
	Acquisitions under Ivan III (1462–1505)
	Acquisitions by death of Ivan the Terrible (1584)
	Acquisitions by Peter the Great's accession (1689)
	Acquisitions under Peter the Great (1689–1725)
✕	Major battles

0   200   400 Km.

0   200   400 Mi.

The Mongol Yoke and the Rise of Moscow

The eastern Slavs, like the Germans and the Italians, might have emerged from the Middle Ages weak and politically divided had it not been for a development of extraordinary importance—the Mongol conquest of the Kievan state. Nomadic, loosely confederated tribes from present-day Mongolia, the Mongols were temporarily unified in the thirteenth century by Jenghiz Khan (1162–1227), one of history's greatest conquerors. In five years his armies subdued all of China. His successors then turned westward, smashing everything in their path and reaching the plains of Hungary victorious before they pulled back in 1242 because of political uncertainties raised by the death of the Great Khan. The Mongol army—the Golden Horde—was savage in the extreme, often slaughtering entire populations of cities before burning them to the ground. En route to Mongolia in 1245, Archbishop John of Plano Carpini, the papal ambassador to Mongolia, passed through Kiev, which the Mongols had sacked in 1242, and wrote an unforgettable eyewitness account:

The Mongols went against Russia and enacted a great massacre in the Russian land. They destroyed towns and fortresses and killed people. They besieged Kiev, which had been the capital of Russia, and after a long siege they took it and killed the inhabitants of the city. For this reason, when we passed through that land, we found lying in the field countless heads and bones of dead people; for this city had been extremely large and very populous, whereas now it has been reduced to nothing: barely two hundred houses stand there, and those people are held in the harshest slavery.[8]

Having devastated and conquered, the Mongols ruled the eastern Slavs for more than two hundred years. They built their capital of Saray on the lower Volga (Map 17.3). They forced all the bickering Slavic princes to submit to their rule and to give them tribute and slaves. If the conquered peoples rebelled, the Mongols were quick to punish with

❖ **MAP 17.3 The Expansion of Russia to 1725** After the disintegration of the Kievan state and the Mongol conquest, the princes of Moscow and their descendants gradually extended their rule over an enormous territory. Ivan the Terrible acquired more territory than Peter the Great.

death and destruction. Thus the Mongols unified the eastern Slavs, for the Mongol khan was acknowledged by all as the supreme ruler.

The Mongol unification completely changed the internal political situation. Although the Mongols conquered, they were quite willing to use local princes as obedient servants and tax collectors. Therefore, they did not abolish the title of "great prince," bestowing it instead on the prince who served them best and paid them most handsomely.

Beginning with Alexander Nevsky in 1252, the previously insignificant princes of Moscow became particularly adept at serving the Mongols. They loyally put down popular uprisings and collected the khan's harsh taxes. By way of reward, the princes of Moscow emerged as hereditary great princes. Eventually the Muscovite princes were able to destroy their princely rivals and even replace the khan as supreme ruler. In this complex process, two princes of Moscow after Alexander Nevsky—Ivan I and Ivan III—were especially noteworthy.

Ivan I (r. 1328–1341) was popularly known as Ivan the Moneybag. A bit like Frederick William of Prussia, Ivan was extremely stingy and built up a large personal fortune. This enabled him to buy more property and to increase his influence by loaning money to less frugal princes to pay their Mongol taxes. Ivan's most serious rival was the prince of Tver, whom the Mongols at one point appointed as great prince.

In 1327 the population of Tver revolted against Mongol oppression, and the prince of Tver joined his people. Ivan immediately went to the Mongol capital of Saray, where he was appointed commander of a large Russian-Mongol army, which then laid waste to Tver and its lands. For this proof of devotion, the Mongols made Ivan the general tax collector for all the Slavic lands they had subjugated and named him great prince. Ivan also convinced the metropolitan of Kiev, the leading churchman of all eastern Slavs, to settle in Moscow. Ivan I thus gained greater prestige, and the church gained a powerful advocate before the khan.

In the next hundred-odd years, in the course of innumerable wars and intrigues, the great princes of Moscow significantly increased their holdings. Then in the reign of Ivan III (r. 1462–1505), the long process was largely completed. After purchasing Rostov, Ivan conquered and annexed other principalities, of which Novgorod, with its lands extending as far as the Baltic Sea, was the most

❖ **Collecting Taxes in Russia** Ivan I, known as Ivan the Moneybag and pictured here at the center, zealously served his Mongol masters. This work by an unknown artist shows the great prince's agents beating peasants into paying the heavy Mongol tax, a portion of which Ivan skimmed off to increase his own wealth and power. *(Source: Novosti)*

crucial (see Map 17.3). Thus more than four hundred years after Iaroslav the Wise had divided the embryonic Kievan state, the princes of Moscow defeated all the rival branches of the house of Ruirik to win complete princely authority.

Another dimension to princely power developed. Not only was the prince of Moscow the *unique* ruler. He was also the *absolute* ruler, the autocrat, the *tsar*—the Slavic contraction for "caesar," with all its connotations. This imperious conception of absolute power was expressed in a famous letter from the aging Ivan III to Holy Roman Emperor Frederick III (r. 1440–1493). Frederick had offered Ivan the title of king in conjunction with the marriage of a niece to Ivan's nephew. Ivan proudly refused: "We by the grace of God have been sovereigns over our domains from the beginning, from our first forebears, and our right we hold from God, as did our forebears. . . . As in the past we have never needed appointment from anyone, so now do we not desire it."[9]

The Muscovite idea of absolute authority was powerfully reinforced by two developments. First,

about 1480 Ivan III stopped acknowledging the khan as supreme ruler. There is good evidence to suggest that Ivan and his successors saw themselves as khans. Certainly they assimilated the Mongol concept of kingship as the exercise of unrestrained and unpredictable power.

Second, after the fall of Constantinople to the Turks in 1453, the tsars saw themselves as the heirs of both the caesars and Orthodox Christianity, the one true faith. All the other kings of Europe were heretics; only the tsars were rightful and holy rulers. This idea was promoted by Orthodox churchmen, who spoke of "holy Russia" as the "Third Rome." As the monk Pilotheus stated, "Two Romes have fallen, but the third stands, and a fourth there will not be."[10] Ivan's marriage to the daughter of the last Byzantine emperor further enhanced the aura of an imperial inheritance for Moscow. Worthy successor to the mighty khan and the true Christian emperor, the Muscovite tsar was a king above all others.

Tsar and People to 1689

By 1505 the great prince of Moscow, the tsar, had emerged as the single hereditary ruler of "all the Russias"—all the lands of the eastern Slavs—and he was claiming unrestricted power as his God-given right. In effect, the tsar was demanding the same kind of total authority over all his subjects that the princely descendants of Ruirik had long exercised over their slaves on their own landed estates. This was an extremely radical demand.

As peasants had begun losing their freedom of movement in the fifteenth century, the noble boyars begun losing power and influence. Ivan III pioneered in this regard, as in so many others. When Ivan conquered the principality of Novgorod in the 1480s, he confiscated fully 80 percent of the land, executing the previous owners or resettling them nearer Moscow. He then kept more than half of the confiscated land for himself and distributed the remainder to members of a newly emerging service nobility. The boyars had previously held their land as hereditary private property and been free to serve the prince of their choosing. The new service nobility held the tsar's land on the explicit condition that they serve in the tsar's army. Moreover, Ivan III began to require boyars outside of Novgorod to serve him if they wished to retain their lands. Since there were no competing princes left to turn to, the boyars had to yield.

✤ **St. Basil's Cathedral in Moscow,** with its sloping roofs and colorful onion-shaped domes, is a striking example of powerful Byzantine influences on Russian culture. According to tradition, an enchanted Ivan the Terrible blinded the cathedral's architects to ensure that they would never duplicate their fantastic achievement, which still dazzles the beholder in today's Red Square. *(Source: George Holton/Photo Researchers)*

The rise of the new service nobility accelerated under Ivan IV (r. 1533–1584), the famous Ivan the Terrible. Having ascended the throne at age three, Ivan suffered insults and neglect at the hands of the haughty boyars after his mother mysteriously died, possibly poisoned, when he was just eight. At age sixteen he suddenly pushed aside his hated boyar advisers. In an awe-inspiring ceremony complete with gold coins pouring down on his head, he majestically crowned himself and officially took the august title of tsar for the first time.

Selecting the beautiful and kind Anastasia of the popular Romanov family for his wife and queen, the young tsar soon declared war on the remnants of Mongol power. He defeated the faltering khanates of Kazan and Astrakhan between 1552 and 1556, adding vast new territories to Russia. In the course of these wars, Ivan virtually abolished the old distinction between hereditary boyar private property and land granted temporarily for service.

All nobles, old and new, had to serve the tsar in order to hold any land.

The process of transforming the entire nobility into a service nobility was completed in the second part of Ivan the Terrible's reign. In 1557 Ivan turned westward, and for the next twenty-five years Muscovy waged an exhausting, unsuccessful war primarily against the large Polish-Lithuanian state, which joined Poland with much of Ukraine in the sixteenth century. Quarreling with the boyars over the war and blaming them for the sudden death of his beloved Anastasia in 1560, the increasingly cruel and demented Ivan turned to strike down all who stood in his way.

Above all, he struck down the ancient Muscovite boyars with a reign of terror. Leading boyars, their relatives, and even their peasants and servants were executed en masse by a special corps of unquestioning servants. Dressed in black and riding black horses, they were forerunners of the modern dictator's secret police. Large estates were confiscated, broken up, and reapportioned to the lower service nobility. The great boyar families were severely reduced. The newer, poorer, more nearly equal service nobility, still less than 0.5 percent of the total population, was totally dependent on the autocrat.

Ivan also took giant strides toward making all commoners servants of the tsar. His endless wars and demonic purges left much of central Russia depopulated. It grew increasingly difficult for the lower service nobles to squeeze a living for themselves out of the peasants left on their landholdings. As the service nobles demanded more from the remaining peasants, more and more peasants fled toward the wild, recently conquered territories to the east and south. There they formed free groups and outlaw armies known as "Cossacks." The Cossacks maintained a precarious independence beyond the reach of the oppressive landholders and the tsar's hated officials. The solution to this problem was to complete the tying of the peasants to the land, making them serfs perpetually bound to serve the noble landholders, who were bound in turn to serve the tsar.

In the time of Ivan the Terrible, urban traders and artisans were also bound to their towns and jobs so that the tsar could tax them more heavily. Ivan assumed that the tsar owned Russia's trade and industry, just as he owned all the land. In the course of the sixteenth and seventeenth centuries, the tsars therefore took over the mines and industries and monopolized the country's important commercial activities. The urban classes had no security in their work or property, and even the wealthiest merchants were basically dependent agents of the tsar. If a new commercial activity became profitable, it was often taken over by the tsar and made a royal monopoly. This royal monopolization was in sharp contrast to developments in western Europe, where the capitalist middle classes were gaining strength and security in their private property. The tsar's service obligations checked the growth of the Russian middle classes, just as they led to the decline of the boyars, the rise of the lower nobility, and the final enserfment of the peasants.

Ivan the Terrible's system of autocracy and compulsory service struck foreign observers forcibly.

❖ **Ivan the Terrible** Ivan IV, the first to take the title Tsar of Russia, executed many Muscovite boyars and their peasants and servants. His ownership of all the land, trade, and industry restricted economic development, *(Source: National Museum, Copenhagen, Denmark)*

✤ **The Election of Michael Romanov** in 1613 reaffirmed tsarist autocracy and founded the Romanov dynasty, which ruled Russia until the revolution of 1917. Here the boy-tsar receives the homage of notables on the outskirts of Moscow. As this drawing suggests, seventeenth-century Moscow had wooden walls, wooden houses, and log streets. Fire periodically ravaged the city. *(Source: Novosti)*

Sigismund Herberstein, a German traveler to Russia, wrote in 1571; "All the people consider themselves to be *kholops,* that is, slaves of their Prince." At the same time, Jean Bodin, the French thinker who did so much to develop the modern concept of sovereignty, concluded that Russia's political system was fundamentally different from those of all other European monarchies and comparable only to that of the Turkish empire. In both Turkey and Russia, as in other parts of Asia and Africa, "the prince is become lord of the goods and persons of his subjects . . . governing them as a master of a family does his slaves."[11] The Mongol inheritance weighed heavily on Russia.

As has so often occurred in Russia, the death of an iron-fisted tyrant—in this case, Ivan the Terrible in 1584—ushered in an era of confusion and violent struggles for power. Events were particularly chaotic after Ivan's son, Theodore died, in 1598 without an heir. The years 1598 to 1613 were aptly called the "Time of Troubles."

The close relatives of the deceased tsar intrigued against and murdered each other, alternately fighting and welcoming the invading Swedes and Poles, who even occupied Moscow. Most serious for the cause of autocracy, there was a great social upheaval as Cossack bands marched northward, rallying peasants and slaughtering nobles and officials. The mass of Cossacks and peasants called for the "true tsar," who would restore their freedom of movement and allow them to farm for whomever they pleased, who would reduce their heavy taxes and lighten the yoke imposed by the landlords.

This social explosion from below, which combined with a belated surge of patriotic opposition to Polish invaders, brought the nobles, big and small, to their senses. In 1613 they elected Ivan's sixteen-year-old grandnephew, Michael Romanov, the new hereditary tsar. Then they rallied around him in the face of common internal and external threats. Michael's election was a real restoration, and his reign saw the gradual re-establishment of tsarist autocracy. Michael was understandably more kindly disposed toward the supportive nobility than toward the sullen peasants. Thus while peasants were completely enserfed in 1649, Ivan's heavy military obligations on the nobility were relaxed considerably. In the long reign of Michael's successor, the pious Alexis (r. 1645–1676), this asymmetry of obligations was accentuated. The nobility gained more exemptions from military service, while the peasants were further ground down.

The result was a second round of mass upheaval and protest. In the later seventeenth century, the unity of the Russian Orthodox church was torn apart by a great split. The initiating event was the religious reforms introduced in 1652 by the patriarch Nikon, a dogmatic purist who wished to bring "corrupted" Russian practices of worship into line with the Greek Orthodox model. The self-serving church hierarchy quickly went along, but the intensely religious common people resisted. They saw Nikon as the Anti-Christ, who was stripping them of the only thing they had—the true religion of "holy Russia."

Great numbers left the church and formed illegal communities of "Old Believers," who were hunted down and persecuted. As many as twenty thousand people burned themselves alive, singing the "hallelujah" in their chants three times rather than twice, as Nikon had demanded, and crossing themselves in the old style, with two rather than three fingers, as they went down in flames. After the great split, the Russian masses were alienated from the established church, which became totally dependent on the state for its authority.

Again the Cossacks revolted against the state, which was doggedly trying to catch up with them on the frontiers and reduce them to serfdom. Under Stenka Razin they moved up the Volga River in 1670 and 1671, attracting a great undisciplined army of peasants, murdering landlords and high church officials, and proclaiming freedom from oppression. This rebellion to overthrow the established order was finally defeated by the government. In response, the thoroughly scared upper classes tightened the screws of serfdom even further. Holding down the peasants, and thereby maintaining the tsar, became almost the principal obligation of the nobility until 1689.

The Reforms of Peter the Great

It is now possible to understand the reforms of Peter the Great (r. 1682–1725) and his kind of monarchial absolutism. Contrary to some historians' assertions, Peter was interested primarily in military power, not in some grandiose westernization plan. A giant for his time, at six feet seven inches, and possessing enormous energy and will power, Peter was determined to redress the defeats the tsar's armies had occasionally suffered in their wars with Poland and Sweden since the time of Ivan the Terrible.

To be sure, these western foes had never seriously threatened the existence of the tsar's vast kingdom, except perhaps when they had added to the confusion of civil war and domestic social upheaval in the Time of Troubles. Russia had even gained a large mass of Ukraine from weak and decentralized Poland in 1667 (see Map 17.3). And tsarist forces had completed the conquest of the primitive tribes of all Siberia in the seventeenth century. Muscovy, which had been as large as all the rest of Europe combined in 1600, was three times as large as the rest of Europe in 1682 and by far the largest kingdom on earth. But territorial expansion was the soul of tsardom. Therefore, it was natural that the seventeen-year-old Peter would seek further gains when he overturned the regency in 1689 and assumed personal rule. The thirty-six years of that rule knew only one year of peace.

When Peter took control in 1689, the heart of his army still consisted of cavalry made up of boyars and service nobility. Foot soldiers played a secondary role, and the whole army served on a part-time basis. The Russian army was lagging behind the professional standing armies being formed in Europe in the seventeenth century. The core of such armies was a highly disciplined infantry that fired and refired rifles as it fearlessly advanced, until it charged with bayonets fixed. Such a large, permanent army was enormously expensive and could be created only at the cost of great sacrifice. Given the desire to conquer more territory, Peter's military problem was serious.

Peter's solution was, in essence, to tighten up Muscovy's old service system and really make it work. He put the nobility back in harness with a vengeance. Every nobleman, great or small, was once again required to serve in the army or in the civil administration—for life. Since a more modern army and government required skilled technicians and experts, Peter created schools and even universities to produce them. One of his most hated reforms required five years of compulsory education away from home for every young nobleman. Peter established an interlocking military-civilian bureaucracy with fourteen ranks, and he decreed that all had to start at the bottom and work toward the top. Some people of non-noble origins rose to high positions in this embryonic meritocracy. Peter searched out talented foreigners—twice in his reign he went abroad to study and observe—and placed them in his service. These measures combined to make the army and government more powerful and efficient.

Peter also greatly increased the service requirements of the commoners. He established a regular standing army of more than 200,000 soldiers, made up mainly of peasants commanded by officers from the nobility. In addition, special forces of Cossacks and foreigners numbered more than 100,000. The departure of a drafted peasant boy was celebrated by his family and village almost like a funeral, as indeed it was, since the recruit was drafted for life. The peasantry also served with its taxes, which increased threefold during Peter's reign, as people—"souls"—replaced land as the primary unit of taxation. Serfs were also arbitrarily assigned to work in the growing number of factories and mines. Most of these industrial enterprises were directly or indirectly owned by the state, and they were worked almost exclusively for the military. In general, Russian serfdom became more oppressive under the reforming tsar.

The constant warfare of Peter's reign consumed 80 to 85 percent of all revenues but brought only modest territorial expansion. Yet the Great Northern War with Sweden, which lasted from 1700 to 1721, was crowned in the end by Russian victory. After initial losses, Peter's new war machine crushed the smaller army of Sweden's Charles XII in Ukraine at Poltava in 1709, one of the most significant battles in Russian history. Sweden never really regained the offensive, and Russia eventually annexed Estonia and much of present-day Latvia (see Map 17.3), lands that had never before been under Russian rule. Russia became the dominant power on the Baltic Sea and very much a European Great Power. If victory or defeat is the ultimate historical criterion, Peter's reforms were a success.

There were other important consequences of Peter's reign. Because of his feverish desire to use modern technology to strengthen the army, many Westerners and Western ideas flowed into Russia for the first time. A new class of educated Russians began to emerge. At the same time, vast numbers of Russians, especially among the poor and weak, hated Peter's massive changes. The split between the enserfed peasantry and the educated nobility thus widened, even though all were caught up in the endless demands of the sovereign.

A new idea of state interest, as distinct from the tsar's personal interests, began to take hold. Peter himself fostered this conception of the public interest by claiming time and again to be serving the common good. For the first time, a Russian tsar attached explanations to his decrees in an attempt to gain the confidence and enthusiastic support of the populace. Yet as before, the tsar alone decided what the common good was. Here was a source of future tension between tsar and people.

Thus Peter built on the service obligations of old Muscovy. His monarchial absolutism was truly the culmination of the long development of a unique Russian civilization. Yet the creation of a more modern army and state introduced much that was new and Western to that civilization. This development paved the way for Russia to move much closer to the European mainstream in its thought and institutions during the Enlightenment, especially under Catherine the Great.

Peter the Great This painting by Louis Karavack celebrates the power and determination of Russia's famous ruler. Most appropriately, it shows him imperiously leading his armies into battle. Peter waged war almost continually throughout his long reign and the desire to build a large modern army motivated many of his reforms. *(Source: Hermitage, Leningrad/Novosti)*

⚜ ABSOLUTISM AND THE BAROQUE

The rise of royal absolutism in eastern Europe had many consequences. Nobles served their powerful rulers in new ways, while the great inferiority of the urban middle classes and the peasants was reconfirmed. Armies became larger and more professional, while taxes rose and authoritarian traditions were strengthened. Nor was this all. Royal absolutism also interacted with baroque culture and art, baroque music and literature. Inspired in part by Louis XIV of France, the great and not-so-great rulers called on the artistic talent of the age to glorify their power and magnificence. This exaltation of despotic rule was particularly striking in the lavish masterpieces of architecture.

Palaces and Power

As soaring Gothic cathedrals expressed the idealized spirit of the High Middle Ages, so dramatic baroque palaces symbolized the age of absolutist power. By 1700 palace building had become a veritable obsession for the rulers of central and eastern Europe. Their baroque palaces were clearly intended to overawe the people with the monarch's strength. The great palaces were also visual declarations of equality with Louis XIV and were therefore modeled after Versailles to a greater or lesser extent. One such palace was Schönbrunn, an enormous Viennese Versailles begun in 1695 by Emperor Leopold to celebrate Austrian military victories and Habsburg might. Charles XI of Sweden, having reduced the power of the aristocracy,

⚜ **Würzburg, the Prince-Bishop's Palace** The baroque style brought architects, painters, and sculptors together in harmonious, even playful partnership. This magnificent monumental staircase, designed by Johann Balthasar Neumann in 1735, merges into the vibrant ceiling frescos by Giovanni Battista Tiepolo. A man is stepping out of the picture, and a painted dog resembles a marble statue. *(Source: Erich Lessing Culture and Fine Arts Archives)*

ordered the construction in 1693 of his Royal Palace, which dominates the center of Stockholm to this day. Frederick I of Prussia began his imposing new royal residence in Berlin in 1701, the same year he attained the title of king.

Petty princes in the German lands also contributed mightily to the palace-building mania. Frederick the Great of Prussia noted that every descendent of a princely family "imagines himself to be something like Louis XIV. He builds his Versailles, has his mistresses, and maintains his army."[12] The not-very-important elector-archbishop of Mainz, the ruling prince of that city, confessed apologetically that "building is a craze which costs much, but every fool likes his own hat."[13] The archbishop of Mainz's own "hat" was an architectural gem, like that of another churchly ruler, the prince-bishop of Würzburg.

In central and eastern Europe, the favorite noble servants of royalty became extremely rich and powerful, and they, too, built grandiose palaces in the capital cities. These palaces were in part an extension of the monarch, for they surpassed the buildings of less favored nobles and showed all the high road to fame and fortune. Take, for example, the palaces of Prince Eugene of Savoy. A French nobleman by birth and education, Prince Eugene entered the service of Emperor Leopold I with the relief of the besieged Vienna in 1683 and became Austria's most famous military hero. It was Eugene who led the Austrian army, smashed the Turks, fought Louis XIV to a standstill, and generally guided the triumph of absolutism in Austria. Rewarded with great wealth by his grateful royal employer, Eugene called on the leading architects of the day, J. B. Fischer von Erlach and Johann Lukas von Hildebrandt, to consecrate his glory in stone and fresco. Fischer built Eugene's Winter (or Town) Palace in Vienna, and he and Hildebrandt collaborated on the prince's Summer Palace on the city's outskirts.

The Summer Palace was actually two enormous buildings, the Lower Belvedere and the Upper Belvedere, completed in 1713 and 1722, respectively and joined by one of the most exquisite gardens in Europe. The Upper Belvedere, Hildebrandt's masterpiece, stood gracefully, even playfully, behind a great sheet of water. One entered through magnificent iron gates into a hall where sculptured giants crouched as pillars; then one moved on to a great staircase of dazzling whiteness and ornamentation. Even today, the emotional impact of this building is great: here art and beauty create a sense of immense power and wealth.

Palaces like the Upper Belvedere were magnificent examples of the baroque style. They expressed the baroque delight in bold, sweeping statements, which were intended to provide a dramatic emotional experience. To create this experience, baroque masters dissolved the traditional artistic frontiers: the architect permitted the painter and the artisan to cover a building's undulating surfaces with wildly colorful paintings, graceful sculptures, and fanciful carvings. Space was used in a highly original way to blend everything together in a total environment. These techniques shone in all their glory in the churches of southern Germany and in the colossal halls of royal palaces. Artistic achievement and political statement reinforced each other.

Royal Cities

Absolute monarchs and baroque architects were not content with fashioning ostentatious palaces. They remodeled existing capital cities, or even built new ones, to reflect royal magnificence and the centralization of political power. Karlsruhe, founded in 1715 as the capital city of a small German principality, is one extreme example. There, broad, straight avenues radiated out from the palace so that all roads—like all power—were focused on the ruler. More typically, the monarch's architects added new urban areas alongside the old city; these areas then became the real heart of the expanding capital.

The distinctive features of these new additions were their broad avenues, their imposing government buildings, and their rigorous mathematical layout. Along these major thoroughfares nobles built elaborate baroque townhouses; stables and servants' quarters were built on the alleys behind. Wide avenues also facilitated the rapid movement of soldiers through the city to quell any disturbance (the king's planners had the needs of the military constantly in mind). Under the arcades along the avenues appeared smart and very expensive shops, the first department stores, with plate-glass windows and fancy displays.

The new avenues brought reckless speed to the European city. Whereas everyone had walked through the narrow, twisting streets of the medieval town, the high and mighty raced down the broad boulevards in their elegant carriages. A social gap opened between the wealthy riders and the gaping, dodging pedestrians. "Mind the carriages!" wrote one eighteenth-century observer in Paris:

Here comes the black-coated physician in his chariot, the dancing master in his coach, the fencing master in his surrey—and the Prince behind six horses at the gallop as if he were in the open country. . . . The threatening wheels of the overbearing rich drive as rapidly as ever over stones stained with the blood of their unhappy victims.[14]

Speeding carriages on broad avenues, an endless parade of power and position: here were the symbols and substance of the baroque city.

The Growth of St. Petersburg

No city illustrated better than St. Petersburg the close ties among politics, architecture, and urban development in this period. In 1700 when the Great Northern War between Russia and Sweden began, the city did not exist. There was only a small Swedish fortress on one of the water-logged islands at the mouth of the Neva River, where it flows into the Baltic Sea. In 1702 Peter the Great's armies seized this desolate outpost. Within a year the reforming tsar had decided to build a new city there and to make it, rather than ancient Moscow, his capital.

Since the first step was to secure the Baltic coast, military construction was the main concern for the next eight years. A mighty fortress was built on Peter Island, and a port and shipyards were built across the river on the mainland as a Russian navy came into being. The land was swampy and uninhabited, the climate damp and unpleasant. But Peter cared not at all: for him, the inhospitable northern marshland was a future metropolis, gloriously bearing his name.

After the decisive Russian victory at Poltava in 1709 greatly reduced the threat of Swedish armies, Peter moved into high gear. In one imperious decree after another, he ordered his people to build a city that would equal any in the world. Such a city had to be Western and baroque, just as Peter's army had to be Western and permanent. From such a new city, his "window on Europe," Peter also believed it would be easier to reform the country militarily and administratively.

These general political goals matched Peter's architectural ideas, which had been influenced by his travels in western Europe. First, Peter wanted a comfortable, "modern" city. Modernity meant broad, straight, stone-paved avenues; houses built in a uniform line and not haphazardly set back from the street; large parks; canals for drainage; stone bridges; and street lighting. Second, all building had to conform strictly to detailed architectural regulations set down by the government. Finally, each social group—the nobility, the merchants, the artisans, and so on—was to live in a certain section of town. In short, the city and its population were to conform to a carefully defined urban plan of the baroque type.

Peter used the traditional but reinforced methods of Russian autocracy to build his modern capital. The creation of St. Petersburg was just one of the heavy obligations he dictatorially imposed on all social groups in Russia. The peasants bore the heaviest burdens. Just as the government drafted peasants for the army, it also drafted twenty-five to forty thousand men each summer to labor in St. Petersburg for three months without pay. Every ten to fifteen peasant households had to furnish one such worker each summer and then pay a special tax in order to feed that worker in St. Petersburg.

Peasants hated this forced labor in the capital, and each year one-fourth to one-third of those sent risked brutal punishment and ran away. Many peasant construction workers died each summer from hunger, sickness, and accidents. Many also died because peasant villages tended to elect old men or young boys to labor in St. Petersburg since strong and able-bodied men were desperately needed on the farm in the busy summer months. Thus beautiful St. Petersburg was built on the shoveling, carting, and paving of a mass of conscripted serfs.

Peter also drafted more privileged groups to his city, but on a permanent basis. Nobles were summarily ordered to build costly stone houses and palaces in St. Petersburg and to live in them most of the year. The more serfs a noble possessed, the bigger his dwelling had to be. Merchants and artisans were also commanded to settle and build in St. Petersburg. These nobles and merchants were then required to pay for the city's avenues, parks, canals, embankments, pilings, and bridges, all of which were very costly in terms of both money and lives because they were built on a swamp. The building of St. Petersburg was, in truth, an enormous direct tax levied on the wealthy, which in turn forced the peasantry to do most of the work.

❖ **St. Petersburg, ca 1760** Rastrelli's remodeled Winter Palace, which housed the royal family until the Russian Revolution of 1917, stands on the left along the Neva River. The Navy Office with its famous golden spire and other government office buildings are nearby and across the river. Russia became a naval power and St. Petersburg a great port. (*Source: Michael Holford*)

The only immediate beneficiaries were the foreign architects and urban planners. No wonder so many Russians hated Peter's new city.

Yet the tsar had his way. By the time of his death in 1725, there were at least six thousand houses and numerous impressive government buildings in St. Petersburg. Under the remarkable women who ruled Russia throughout most of the eighteenth century, St. Petersburg blossomed fully as a majestic and well-organized city, at least in its wealthy showpiece sections. Peter's youngest daughter, the quick-witted Elizabeth (r. 1741–1762), named as her chief architect Bartolomeo Rastrelli, who had come to Russia from Italy as a boy of fifteen in 1715. Combining Italian and Russian traditions into a unique, wildly colorful St. Petersburg style, Rastrelli built many palaces for the nobility and all the larger government buildings erected during Elizabeth's reign. He also rebuilt the Winter Palace as an enormous, aqua-colored royal residence, now the Hermitage Museum. There Elizabeth estab-

lished a flashy, luxury-loving, and slightly crude court, which Catherine the Great in turn made truly imperial. All the while St. Petersburg grew rapidly, and its almost 300,000 inhabitants in 1782 made it one of the world's largest cities. Peter and his successors had created out of nothing a magnificent and harmonious royal city, which unmistakably proclaimed the power of Russia's rulers and the creative potential of the absolutist state.

SUMMARY

From about 1400 to 1650, social and economic developments in eastern Europe increasingly diverged from those in western Europe. In the east, peasants and townspeople lost precious freedoms, while the nobility increased its power and prestige. It was within this framework of resurgent serfdom and entrenched nobility that Austrian and Prussian monarchs fashioned absolutist states in the seventeenth and early eighteenth centuries. These monarchs won absolutist control over standing armies, permanent taxes, and legislative bodies. But they did not question underlying social and economic relationships. Indeed, they enhanced the privileges of the nobility, which furnished the leading servitors for enlarged armies and growing state bureaucracies.

In Russia the social and economic trends were similar, but the timing of political absolutism was different. Mongol conquest and rule were a crucial experience, and a harsh, indigenous tsarist autocracy was firmly in place by the reign of Ivan the Terrible in the sixteenth century. More than a century later, Peter the Great succeeded in tightening up Russia's traditional absolutism and modernizing it by reforming the army, the bureaucracy, and the defense industry. In Russia and throughout eastern Europe, war and the needs of the state in time of war weighed heavily in the triumph of absolutism.

Triumphant absolutism interacted spectacularly with the arts. Baroque art, which had grown out of the Catholic Reformation's desire to move the faithful and exalt the true faith, admirably suited the secular aspirations of eastern European rulers. They built grandiose baroque palaces, monumental public squares, and even whole cities to glorify their power and majesty. Thus baroque art attained magnificent heights in eastern Europe, symbolizing the ideal and harmonizing with the reality of imperious royal absolutism.

NOTES

1. Quoted in F. L. Carsten, *The Origins of Prussia* (Oxford: Clarendon Press, 1954), p. 152.
2. Ibid., p. 175.
3. H. Rosenberg, *Bureaucracy, Aristocracy, and Autocracy: The Prussian Experience, 1660–1815* (Boston: Beacon Press, 1966), p. 38.
4. Quoted in R. Ergang, *The Potsdam Fuhrer: Frederick William I, Father of Prussian Militarism* (New York: Octagon Books, 1972), pp. 85, 87.
5. Ibid., pp. 6–7, 43.
6. Quoted in R. A. Dorwart, *The Administrative Reforms of Frederick William I of Prussia* (Cambridge, Mass.: Harvard University Press, 1953), p. 226.
7. Quoted in Rosenberg, p. 40.
8. Quoted in N. V. Riasanovsky, *A History of Russia* (New York: Oxford University Press, 1963), p. 79.
9. Quoted in I. Grey, *Ivan III and the Unification of Russia* (New York: Collier Books, 1967), p. 39.
10. Quoted in ibid., p. 42.
11. Both quoted in R. Pipes, *Russia Under the Old Regime* (New York: Charles Scribner's Sons, 1974), pp. 65, 85.
12. Quoted in Ergang, p. 13.
13. Quoted in J. Summerson, in *The Eighteenth Century: Europe in the Age of Enlightenment,* ed. A. Cobban (New York: McGraw-Hill, 1969), p. 80.
14. Quoted in L. Mumford, *The Culture of Cities* (New York: Harcourt Brace Jovanovich, 1938), p. 97.

SUGGESTED READING

All of the books cited in the Notes are recommended. Carsten's is the best study on early Prussian history, and Rosenberg's is a masterful analysis of the social context of Prussian absolutism. In addition to Ergang's work, an exciting and critical biography of ramrod Frederick William I, there is G. Ritter, *Frederick the Great* (1968), a more sympathetic study of the talented son by one of Germany's leading conservative historians. G. Craig, *The Politics of the Prussian Army, 1640–1945* (1964), expertly traces the great influence of the military on the Prussian state over three hundred years. J. Gagliardo, *Germany Under the Old Regime, 1600–1790* (1991), is an impressive recent survey of developments in all the German states and provides an excellent, up-to-date bibliography. M. Hughes, *Early Modern Germany, 1477–1802* (1992), is another recommended synthesis. R. J. Evans, *The Making of the Habsburg Empire, 1550–1700* (1979), is an impressive achievement. C. Ingrao, *The Habsburg Monarchy, 1618–1815* (1994), and R. A. Kann, *A History of the Habsburg Empire, 1526–1918* (1974), also analyze the development of absolutism in Austria, as does A. Wandruszka, *The House of Habsburg* (1964). J. Stoye, *The Siege of Vienna* (1964), is a fascinating account of the last great Ottoman offensive, which is also treated in the interesting study by P. Coles, *The Ottoman Impact on Europe, 1350–1699* (1968). The Austro-Ottoman conflict is also a theme of L. S. Stavrianos, *The Balkans Since 1453* (1958), and D. McKay's fine biography, *Prince Eugene of Savoy* (1978). A good general account is provided in D. McKay and H. Scott, *The Rise of the Great Powers, 1648–1815* (1983).

On eastern European peasants and serfdom, D. Chirot, ed., *The Origins of Backwardness in Eastern Europe: Economics and Politics from the Middle Ages Until the Twentieth Century* (1989), is a wide-ranging introduction, which may be compared with J. Blum, "The Rise of Serfdom in Eastern Europe," *American Historical Review* 62 (July 1957): 807–836. E. Levin, *Sex and Society in the World of the Orthodox Slavs, 900–1700* (1989), carries family history to eastern Europe; R. Mousnier, *Peasant Uprisings in Seventeenth-Century France, Russia, and China* (1970), is a fine comparative study. Another valuable comparative study, analyzing the political struggle between rulers and nobles in Poland, Hungary, Latvia, Moldavia, and Ukraine, is O. Subtelny, *Domination in Eastern Europe* (1986). J. Blum, *Lord and Peasant in Russia from the Ninth to the Nineteenth Century* (1961), provides a good look at conditions in rural Russia, and P. Avrich, *Russian Rebels, 1600–1800* (1972), treats some of the violent peasant upheavals those conditions produced. R. Hellie, *Enserfment and Military Change in Muscovy* (1971), is outstanding, as is A. Yanov's provocative *Origins of Autocracy: Ivan the Terrible in Russian History* (1981). In addition to the fine surveys by Pipes

and Riasanovsky cited in the Notes, J. Billington, *The Icon and the Axe* (1970), is a stimulating history of early Russian intellectual and cultural developments, such as the great split in the church. M. Raeff, *Origins of the Russian Intelligentsia* (1966), skillfully probes the mind of the Russian nobility in the eighteenth century. B. H. Sumner, *Peter the Great and the Emergence of Russia* (1962), is a fine brief introduction, which may be compared with the brilliant biography by Russia's greatest prerevolutionary historian, V. Klyuchevsky, *Peter the Great* (English trans., 1958), and with N. Riasanovsky, *The Image of Peter the Great in Russian History and Thought* (1985). G. Vernadsky and R. Fisher, eds., *A Source Book of Russian History from Early Times to 1917,* 3 vols. (1972), is an invaluable, highly recommended collection of documents and contemporary writings. S. Baron, ed., *The Travels of Olearius in Seventeenth-Century Russia* (1967), is also recommended.

Three good books on art and architecture are E. Hempel, *Baroque Art and Architecture in Central Europe* (1965); G. Hamilton, *The Art and Architecture of Russia* (1954); and N. Pevsner, *An Outline of European Architecture,* 6th ed. (1960).

LISTENING TO THE
PAST

A Foreign Traveler in Russia

Russia in the seventeenth century remained a remote and mysterious land for western and even central Europeans, who had few direct contacts with the tsar's dominion. Knowledge of Russia came mainly from occasional travelers who had visited Muscovy and sometimes wrote accounts of what they had seen.

The most famous of these accounts was by the German Adam Olearius (ca 1599–1671), who was sent to Moscow by the duke of Holstein on three diplomatic missions in the 1630s. These missions ultimately proved unsuccessful, but they provided Olearius with a rich store of information for his Travels in Moscovy, *from which the following excerpts are taken. Published in German in 1647 and soon translated into several languages (but not Russian), Olearius's unflattering but well-informed study played a major role in shaping European ideas about Russia.*

The government of the Russians is what political theorists call a "dominating and despotic monarchy," where the sovereign, that is, the tsar or the grand prince who has obtained the crown by right of succession, rules the entire land alone, and all the people are his subjects, and where the nobles and princes no less than the common folk—townspeople and peasants—are his serfs and slaves, whom he rules and treats as a master treats his servants. . . .

If the Russians be considered in respect to their character, customs, and way of life, they are justly to be counted among the barbarians. . . . The vice of drunkenness is so common in this nation, among people of every station, clergy and laity, high and low, men and women, old and young, that when they are seen now and then lying about in the streets, wallowing in the mud, no attention is paid to it, as something habitual. If a cart driver comes upon such a drunken pig whom he happens to know, he shoves him onto his

cart and drives him home, where he is paid his fare. No one ever refuses an opportunity to drink and to get drunk, at any time and in any place, and usually it is done with vodka. . . .

The Russians being naturally tough and born, as it were, for slavery, they must be kept under a harsh and strict yoke and must be driven to do their work with clubs and whips, which they suffer without impatience, because such is their station, and they are accustomed to it. Young and half-grown fellows sometimes come together
on certain days and train themselves in fisticuffs, to accustom themselves to receiving blows, and, since habit is second nature, this makes blows given as punishment easier to bear. Each and all, they are slaves and serfs. . . .

Because of slavery and their rough and hard life, the Russians accept war readily and are well suited to it. On certain occasions, if need be, they reveal themselves as courageous and daring soldiers. . . .

Although the Russians, especially the common populace, living as slaves under a harsh yoke, can bear and endure a great deal out of love for their masters, yet if the pressure is beyond measure, then it can be said of them: "Patience, often wounded, finally turned into fury." A dangerous indignation results, turned not so much against their sovereign as against the lower authorities, especially if the people have been much oppressed by them and by their supporters and have not been protected by the higher authorities. And once they are aroused and enraged, it is not easy to appease them. Then, disregarding all dangers that may ensue, they resort to every kind of violence and behave like madmen. . . .
They own little; most of them have no feather beds; they lie on cushions, straw, mats, or their clothes; they sleep on benches and, in winter,

like the non-Germans [i.e., natives] in Livonia, upon the oven, which serves them for cooking and is flat on the top; here husband, wife, children, servants, and maids huddle together. In some houses in the countryside we saw chickens and pigs under the benches and the ovens. . . .

Russians are not used to delicate food and dainties; their daily food consists of porridge, turnips, cabbage, and cucumbers, fresh and pickled, and in Moscow mostly of big salt fish which stink badly, because of the thrifty use of salt, yet are eaten with relish. . . .

The Russians can endure extreme heat. In the bathhouse they stretch out on benches and let themselves be beaten and rubbed with bunches of birch twigs and wisps of bast (which I could not stand); and when they are hot and red all over and so exhausted that they can bear it no longer in the bathhouse, men and women rush outdoors naked and pour cold water over their bodies; in winter they even wallow in the snow and rub their skin with it as if it were soap; then they go back into the hot bathhouse. And since bathhouses are usually near rivers and brooks, they can throw themselves straight from the hot into the cold bath. . . .

Generally noble families, even the small nobility, rear their daughters in secluded chambers, keeping them hidden from outsiders; and a bridegroom is not allowed to have a look at his bride until he receives her in the bridal chamber. Therefore some happen to be deceived, being given a misshapen and sickly one instead of a fair one, and sometimes a kinswoman or even a maidservant instead of a daughter; of which there have been examples even among the highborn. No wonder therefore that often they live together like cats and dogs and that wife-beating is so common among Russians. . . .

In the Kremlin and in the city there are a great many churches, chapels, and monasteries, both within and without the city walls, over two thousand in all. This is so because every nobleman who has some fortune has a chapel built for himself, and most of them are of stone. The stone churches are round and vaulted inside. . . . They allow neither organs nor any other musical instruments in their churches, saying: Instruments that have neither souls nor life cannot praise God. . . .

In their churches there hang many bells, sometimes five or six, the largest not over two

✧ V. Vasnetsou (1848–1926), Red Square in the late 17th Century. *(Source: Sovfoto/Eastfoto)*

hundredweights. They ring these bells to summon people to church, and also when the priest during mass raises the chalice. In Moscow, because of the multitude of churches and chapels, there are several thousand bells, which during the divine service create such a clang and din that one unaccustomed to it listens in amazement.

Questions for Analysis

1. In what ways were all social groups in Russia similar, according to Olearius?

2. How did Olearius characterize the Russians in general? What supporting evidence did he offer for his judgment?

3. Did Olearius find any positive or admirable traits in the Russian people? What were they?

4. On the basis of these representative passages, why do you think Olearius's book was so popular and influential in central and western Europe?

Source: G. Vernadsky and R. T. Fisher Jr., eds., *A Source Book for Russian History.* Copyright © 1972 by Yale University Press. Resprinted by permission.

A History of Western Society: A Brief Overview

	Government	Society and Economy
3200 B.C.	Dominance of Sumerian cities in Mesopotamia, ca 3200–2340 Unification of Egypt; Archaic Period, ca 3100–2660 Old Kingdom of Egypt, ca 2660–2180 Dominance of Akkadian empire in Mesopotamia, ca 2331–2200 Middle Kingdom in Egypt, ca 2080–1640	Neolithic Peoples rely on settled agriculture, while others pursue nomadic life, ca 7000–ca 3000 Development of wheeled transport in Mesopotamia, by ca 3200 Expansion of Mesopotamian trade and culture to the north into the south of modern Turkey, the west into the modern Middle East, and the east into modern Iran, ca 2600
2000 B.C.	Babylonian empire in Mesopotamia, ca 2000–1595 Hyksos "invasion" of Egypt, ca 1640–1570 Hittite empire in Asia Minor, ca 1600–1200 Kassites overthrow Babylonians, ca 1595 New Kingdom in Egypt, ca 1570–1075	First wave of Indo-European migrants, by 2000 Extended commerce in Egypt, by ca 2000 Horses introduced into western Asia, by ca 2000
1500 B.C.	Third Intermediate Period in Egypt, ca 1100–700 Unified Hebrew Kingdom under Saul, David, and Solomon, ca 1025–925	Use of iron increases in western Asia, by ca 1300–1100 Second wave of Indo-European migrants, by ca 1200
1000 B.C.	Hebrew Kingdom divided into Israel and Judah, 925 Rise and Fall of Assyrian empire, ca 900–612 Phoenicians found Carthage, 813 Kingdom of Kush conquers and reunifies Egypt, 8th c. Medes conquer Persia, 710 Cypselus becomes tyrant at Corinth, ca 650 Babylon wins independence from Assyria, 626 Dracon's laws on homicide at Athens, ca 621 Peisistratus becomes tyrant of Athens, ca 561 Cyrus the Great conquers Medes, founds Persian Empire, 550 Solon's reforms at Athens, ca 549 Persians complete conquest of ancient Near East, 521–464 Reforms of Cleisthenes in Athens, 508	Concentration of landed wealth in Greece, ca 750–600 Greek overseas expansion, ca 750–550 Beginning of coinage in western Asia, ca 640

Religion and Philosophy	Science and Technology	Arts and Letters
Growth of anthropomorphic religion in Mesopotamia, ca 3000–2000	Development of wheeled transport in Mesopotamia, by ca 3200	Sumerian cuneiform writing, ca 3200
Emergence of Egyptian polytheism and belief in personal immortality, ca 2660	Use of widespread irrigation in Mesopotamia and Egypt, ca 3000	Egyptian hieroglyphic writing, ca 3100
Spread of Mesopotamian and Egyptian religious ideas as far north as modern Anatolia and as far south as central Africa, ca 2600	Construction of the first pyramid in Egypt, ca 2600	
Emergence of Hebrew monotheism, ca 1700	Construction of the first ziggurats in Mesopotamia, ca 2000	Epic of Gilgamesh, ca 1900
Mixture of Hittite and Near Eastern religious beliefs, ca 1595	Widespread use of bronze in the ancient Near East, ca 1900	Code of Hammurabi, ca 1790
	Babylonian mathematical advances, ca 1800	
Exodus of the Hebrews from Egypt into Palestine, 13th c.	Hittites introduce iron technology, ca 1400	Phoenicians develop alphabet, ca 1400
Religious beliefs of Akhenaten, ca 1367		Naturalistic art in Egypt under Akhenaten, ca 1367
		Hymn to Aton, ca 1350
		Egyptian Book of the Dead, ca 1300
Era of the prophets in Israel, ca 1100-500	Babylonian astronomical advances, ca 750–400	Beginning of the Hebrew Bible, ca 9th c.
Intermixture of Etruscan and Roman religious cults, ca 753–509		Traditional beginning of the Olympic Games, 776
Growing popularity of local Greek religious cults, ca 700 B.C.–A.D. 337		Babylonian astronomical advances, ca 750-400
Babylonian captivity of the Hebrews, 586–539		Homer, traditional author of the *Iliad* and *Odyssey*, ca 700
		Hesiod, author of the *Theogony* and *Works and Days*, ca 700
		Archilochos, lyric poet, 648
		Aeschylus, first significant Athenian tragedian, 525/4–456

	Government	Society and Economy
500 B.C.	Ionian Revolt from Persia, 499–494 Battle of Marathon, 490 Xerxes' invasion of Greece, 480–479 Athenian establishment of the Delian Confederacy, 478/7 Publication of the Twelve Tables in Rome, 451/0 Valerio-Horatian laws in Rome, 449 Peloponnesian War, 431–404 Rome captures Veii, 396 Gauls sack Rome, 390 Roman expansion in Italy, 390–290 Theban hegemony in Greece, 371–362 Macedonian conquest of Greece, 338 Conquests of Alexander the Great, 334–323 Punic Wars, 264–146 Reforms of the Gracchi, 133–121	Building of the Via Appia begins in Italy, 312 Growth of Hellenistic trade and cities, ca 300–100 Roman overseas expansion, ca 282–146 Beginning of Roman silver coinage, 269 Growth of slavery, decline of small farmers in Rome, ca 250–100 Agrarian reforms of the Gracchi, 133–121
100 B.C.	Dictatorship of Sulla, 88–79 Civil war in Rome, 78–27 Dictatorship of Caesar, 45–44 Principate of Augustus, 31 B.C. – A.D. 14	Reform of the Roman calendar, 46
300	Constantine removes capital of Roman empire to Constantinople, ca 315 Visigoths defeat Roman army at Adrianople (378), signaling massive German invasions into the empire Bishop Ambrose refuses to yield cathedral church of Milan to Theodosius, thereby asserting church's independence from the state, 380 Death of emperor Romulus Augustus marks end of Roman empire in the West, 476 Clovis issues Salic law of the Franks, ca 490	Growth of Serfdom in Roman empire, ca 200–500 Economic contraction in Roman empire, 3rd c.
500	Law Code of Justinian, 529 Dooms of Ethelbert, king of Kent, ca 604 Spread of Islam across Arabia, the Mediterranean region, Spain, North Africa, and Asia as far as India, ca 630–733	Gallo-Roman aristocracy intermarries with Germanic chieftains Decline of towns and trade, ca 500–700 Agrarian economy predominates in the West, ca 500–1500
700	Charles Martel defeats Muslims at Tours, 733 Pippin III anointed king of the Franks, 754 Charlemagne secures Frankish crown, r. 768–814	Height of Muslim commercial activity, ca 700–1300

Religion and Philosophy	Science and Technology	Arts and Letters
Pre-Socratic philosophers, 5th c. Socrates and his emphasis on ethics, 469–399 Plato, founder of the Academy, 429–347 Diogenes, leading proponent of Cynicism, ca 412–323 Aristotle, founder the Peripatetic school, 384–322 Epicurus, founder of the school named after him, 340–270 Zeno, founder of Stoic philosophy, 335–262 Emergence of Mithraism, ca 300 Spread of Hellenistic mystery religions, 2nd c. Greek cults brought to Rome, ca 200	Hippocrates, formal founder of medicine ca 430 Aristotle, advances in political science, physics, and ethics, 384–322 Theophrastus, founder of botany, ca 372–288 Aristarchos of Samos, advances in astronomy, ca 310–230 Euclid codifies geometry, ca 300 Herophilus, discoveries in medicine, ca 300–250 Archimedes, works on physics and hydrologics, ca 287–212	Sophocles, tragedian who used his plays to explore moral and political problems, ca 496–406 Euripides, the most personal of the Athenian tragedians, ca 480–406 Thucydides, historian of the Peloponnesian War, ca 460–400 Aristophanes, the greatest writer of Old Comedy, ca 457–ca 385 Herodotus, the father of history, ca 450
Mithraism spreads to Rome, 27 B.C. –A.D. 270 Dedication of the Ara Pacis Augustae, 9 Traditional birth of Jesus, ca 3	Pliny the Elder, student of natural history, 23 B.C.–A.D. 79 Frontinus, engineering advances in Rome, 30 B.C.–A.D. 104	Virgil, author of the *Aeneid* and *Georgics*, 70–19 Livy, author of the great history of the Roman republic, ca 59 B.C.–A.D. 17 Ovid, elegant writer of elegiacs and Roman customs, 43 B.C.–A.D. 17
Constantine legalizes Christianity, 312 Theodosius declares Christianity the official state religion, 380 Donatist heretical movement at its height, ca 400 St. Augustine, *The City of God*, ca 425 Clovis adopts Roman Christianity, 496		St. Jerome publishes the Latin *Vulgate*, late 4th c. St. Augustine, *Confessions*, ca 390 Byzantines preserve Greco-Roman culture, ca 400–1000
Boethius, *The Consolation of Philosophy*, ca 520 *Rule of St. Benedict*, 529 Monasteries established in Anglo-Saxon England, 7th c. Muhammad preaches reform, ca 610 Publication of the Qu'ran, 651 Synod of Whitby, 664	Using watermills, Benedictine monks exploit energy of fast-flowing rivers and streams Heavy plow and improved harness facilitate use of multiple-ox teams; harrow widely used in northern Europe	Boethius, *The Consolation of Philosophy*, ca 520 Justinian constructs church of Santa Sophia, 532–537 Pope St. Gregory (the Great) publishes *Dialogues, Pastoral Care, Moralia*, 590–604
Missionary work of St. Boniface in Germany, ca 710–750 Iconoclastic controversy in Byzantine empire, 726–843 Pippin III donates Papal States to the papacy, 756	Byzantines successfully use "Greek fire" in naval combat against Arab fleets attacking Constantinople, 673, 717	Lindisfarne Gospel Book, ca 700 Bede, *Ecclesiastical History of the English Nation*, ca 700 *Beowulf*, ca 700 Carolingian Renaissance, ca 780–850

	Government	Society and Economy
800	Imperial coronation of Charlemagne, Christmas 800 Treaty of Verdun, 843 Viking, Magyar, and Muslim invasions complete disintegration of Carolingian empire; growth of feudalism, ca 845–900	Byzantine commerce and industry, ca 800–1000 Viking invasions and unstable conditions lead to vast increase of serfdom
1000	Seljuk Turks conquer Muslim Baghdad, 1055 Norman conquest of England, 1066 Penance of Henry IV at Canossa, 1077	Agrarian economy predominates in the West, 1000–1500 Height of Muslim commerce and industry, ca 900–1300 Decline of Byzantine free peasantry, ca 1025–1100 Growth of towns and trade in the West, ca 1050–1300 Domesday Book, 1086
1100	Henry I of England, r. 1100–1135 Louis VI of France, r. 1108–1137 Frederick I of Germany, r. 1152–1190 Henry II of England, r. 1154–1189 Thomas Becket murdered, December 1170 Philip Augustus of France, r. 1180–1223	Henry I of England establishes the Exchequer, 1130 Beginnings of the Hanseatic League, 1159
1200	Spanish victory over Muslims at Las Navas de Tolosa, 1212 Battle of Bouvines, July 1214 Frederick II of Germany and Sicily, r. 1212–1250 Magna Carta, 1215 Louis IX of France, r. 1226–1270 Mongols destroy Baghdad and end the Abbasid caliphate, 1258 Edward I of England, r. 1272–1307 Philip IV (the Fair) of France, r. 1285–1314 War opens between England and France, 1296	Economic revival, growth of towns, clearing of wasteland contribute to great growth of personal freedom, 13th c. Agricultural expansion leads to population growth, ca 1225–1300
1300	Philip IV orders arrest of Pope Boniface at Anagni, 1303 Hundred Years' War, 1337–1450 Political chaos in Germany, ca 1350–1450 Merchant oligarchies or despots rule Italian city-states	European economic depression, ca 1300–1450 Black Death begins ca 1347; returns intermittently until 18th c. Height of the Hanseatic League, 1350–1450 Peasant and working class revolts: Jacquerie (France, 1358), Ciompi (Florence, 1378), Peasants (England, 1381)
1400	Appearance of Joan of Arc, 1429–1431 Medici domination of Florence begins, 1434	Population decline, peasants' revolts, high labor costs contribute to decline of serfdom in Western Europe

Religion and Philosophy	Science and Technology	Arts and Letters
Foundation of abbey of Cluny, 909 Byzantine conversion of Russia, late 10th c.	Stirrup and nailed horseshoes become widespread in shock combat Paper, invented in China ca 2nd c., enters Europe through Muslim Spain in 10th c. Spain develops paper industry, 10th c.	Byzantines develop the Cyrillic script, late 10th c.
Avicenna, Arab translator of Greek science, medicine, mathematics, d. 1037 Beginning of reformed papacy, 1046 Schism between Roman and Greek Orthodox churches, 1054 Pope Gregory VII, 1073–1085 Peter Abelard, 1079–1142 St. Bernard of Clairvaux, 1090–1153 First Crusade, 1095–1099	Arab conquests bring new irrigation methods, cotton cultivation, and manufacture to Spain, Sicily, southern Italy	Romanesque style in architecture and art, ca 1000–1200 *Song of Roland*, ca 1095 Muslim musicians introduce stringed instruments, lute, rebec; ancestors of violin
Beginnings of universities, ca 1100–1300 Concordat of Worms ends investiture controversy, 1122 Height of Cistercian monasticism, 1125–1175 Aristotle's works translated into Latin, ca 1140–1260 Jerusalem falls to Muslims; start of the Third Crusade, 1187 Pope Innocent III, 1198–1216	In castle construction Europeans, copying Muslim and Byzantine models, erect rounded towers and crenelated walls Windmill invented, ca 1180 Some monasteries, such as Clairvaux and Canterbury Cathedral Priory, supplied by underground pipes with running water and indoor latrines; elsewhere these very rare until 19th c.	*Rubaiyat of Umar Khayyam*, ca 1120 Dedication of abbey church of Saint-Denis launches gothic style, June 1144 Hildegard of Bingen (1098–1179) produces theological treatises, ca 1150 Court of troubador poetry, especially that of Chretian de Troyes, circulates widely
Crusaders capture Constantinople (Fourth Crusade), 1204 Maimonides, 1204 Founding of Franciscan Order, 1210 Fourth Lateran Council, 1215 Founding of Dominican Order, 1216 Thomas Aquinas (1225–1274) marks height of Scholasticism Pope Boniface VIII, 1294–1303	*Notebooks* of Villard de Honnecourt, a master mason (architect) a major source for gothic engineering, ca 1250 Development of double-entry bookkeeping in Florence and Genoa, ca 1250–1340 Venetians purchase secrets of glass manufacture from Syria, 1277 Mechanical clock invented, ca 1290	*Parzifal, Roman de la Rose, King Arthur and the Round Table* celebrate virtues of knighthood Height of gothic style, ca 1225–1300
Babylonian Captivity of the papacy, 1307–1377 John Wyclif, ca 1330–1384 Great Schism in the papacy, 1377–1418	Edward III of England uses cannon in siege of Calais, 1346	Patrarch, 1304–1374 Paintings of Giotto, ca 1305–1337 Dante, *Divine Comedy*, ca 1310 Boccaccio, *The Decameron*, ca 1350 Jan van Eyck, 1366–1441 Brunelleschi, 1377–1446 Chaucer, *Canterbury Tales*, ca 1385–1400
Council of Constance, 1414–1418 Pragmatic Sanction of Bourges, 1438 Expulsion of Jews from Spain, 1492	Water-powered blast furnaces operative in Sweden, Austria, the Rhine Valley, Liège, ca 1400 Leonardo Fibonacci's *Liber Abaci* (1202) popularizes use of Hindu-	Masaccio, 1401–1428 Botticelli, 1444–1510 Leonardo da Vinci, 1452–1519 Albrecht Dürer, 1471–1528

	Government	Society and Economy
1400 (cont.)	Princes in Germany consolidate power, ca 1450–1500 Ottoman Turks under Mahomet II capture Constantinople, May 1453 Wars of the Roses in England, 1453–1471 Ferdinand and Isabella of Spain capture Granada, the last Muslim stronghold, January 1492 French invasion of Italy, 1494	Christopher Columbus reaches the Americas, October 1492 Portuguese gain control of East Indian spice trade, 1498–1511
1500	Charles V, Holy Roman Emperor, 1519–1556 Imperial sack of Rome, 1527 Philip II of Spain, r. 1556–1598 Revolt of the Netherlands, 1566–1609 St. Bartholemew's Day massacre, August 24, 1572 Defeat of the Spanish Armada, 1588 Henry IV of France issues Edict of Nantes, 1598	Balboa discovers the Pacific, 1513 Magellan's crew circumnavigates the earth, 1519–1522 Spain gains control of Central and South America, ca 1520–1550 Peasants' Revolt in Germany, 1524–1525 "Times of Troubles" in Russia, 1598–1613
1600	Thirty Years' War, 1618–1648 Richelieu dominates French government, 1624–1643 Frederick William, Elector of Brandenburg, r. 1640–1688 English Civil War, 1642–1649 Louis XIV, r. 1643–1715 Peace of Westphalia, 1648 The Fronde in France, 1648–1660	Chartering of British East India Company, 1600 Famine and oppressive taxation lead to widespread revolts in Western Europe, ca 1600–1650 Continuing decline of serfdom in Western Europe, ca 1600–1650 English Poor Law, 1601 Chartering of Dutch East India Company, 1602 Height of Dutch commercial activity, ca 1630–1665
1650	Protectorate in England, 1653–1658 Leopold I, Habsburg emperor, r. 1658–1705 Treaty of the Pyrenees, 1659 Restoration of English monarchy, 1660 Siege of Vienna, 1683 Revocation of Edict of Nantes, 1685 Glorious Revolution in England, 1688–1689 Peter the Great of Russia, r. 1689–1725	Height of mercantilism in Europe, ca 1650–1750 Principle of peasants' "hereditary subjugation" to their lords affirmed in Prussia, 1653 Colbert's economic reforms in France, ca 1663–1683 Cossack revolt in Russia, 1670–1671

Religion and Philosophy	Science and Technology	Arts and Letters
	Arabic numerals, "a major factor in the rise of science in the Western world" Paris and largest Italian cities paved streets, making cleaning possible Printing and movable type, ca 1450	Michelangelo, 1475–1564 Raphael, 1483–1520 Rabelais, ca 1490–1553
Lateran Council attempts reforms of church abuses, 1512–1517 Machiavelli, *The Prince*, 1513 Concordat of Bologna, 1516 Thomas More, *Utopia*, 1516 Martin Luther publishes the *Ninety-Five Theses*, 1517 Castiglione, *The Courtier*, 1528 Henry VIII of England breaks with Rome, 1532–1534 Anabaptists control Munster, 1534 Ignatius Loyola establishes the Society of Jesus, 1540 John Calvin establishes a theocracy in Geneva, 1541 Angela Merici establishes the Ursuline Order, first religious order for education of women, 1544 Council of Trent, 1545–1563 Peace of Augsburg, 1555 Thomas Hobbes, 1588–1679 René Descartes, 1596–1650	Copernicus, *On the Revolutions of the Heavenly Bodies*, 1543 Francis Bacon, 1561–1626 Galileo, 1564–1642 Johannes Kepler, 1571–1630 William Harvey, 1578–1657	Erasmus, *The Praise of Folly*, 1509 Cervantes, 1547–1616 Baroque movement in the arts, ca 1550–1725 Shakespeare, 1564–1616 Rubens, 1577–1640 Michel de Montaigne, *Essays,* 1598 Diego Velazquez, 1599–1660
Huguenot revolt in France, 1625	Frances Bacon, *The Advancement of Learning*, 1605 Robert Boyle, 1627–1691 Anton Leeuwenhoek, 1632–1723	Rembrandt van Rijn, 1606–1669 Golden Age of Dutch culture, 1625–1675 Jan Vermeer, 1632–1675 Jean Baptiste Racine, 1639–1699
Patriarch Nikon's reforms split Russian Orthodox church, 1652 Test Act in England excludes Roman Catholics from public office, 1673 Revocation of Edict of Nantes, 1685 James II attempts to restore Roman Catholicism as state religion, 1685–1688 Montesquieu, 1689–1755 Locke, *Second Treatise on Civil Government*, 1690 Pierre Bayle, *Historical and Critical Dictionary*, 1697	Jethro Tull (1674–1741) encourages innovation in English agriculture Newton, *Principia Mathematica*, 1687 Newcomen develops steam engine, 1705	Construction of baroque palaces and remodeling of capital cities throughout central and eastern Europe, ca 1650–1725 J.S. Bach, 1685–1750 Fontenelle, *Conversations on the Plurality of Worlds*, 1686 The Enlightenment, ca 1690–1790 Voltaire, 1694–1778

	Government	Society and Economy
1700	War of the Spanish Succession, 1701–1713 Peace of Utrecht, 1713 Frederick William I of Prussia, r. 1713–1740 Louis XV of France, r. 1715–1774 Maria Theresa of Austria, r. 1740–1780 Frederick the Great of Prussia, r. 1740–1786	Foundation of St. Petersburg, 1701 Last appearance of bubonic plague in Western Europe, ca 1720 Enclosure movement in England, ca 1730–1830 Jeremy Bentham, 1748–1823
1750	Seven Years' War, 1756–1763 Catherine the Great of Russia, r. 1762–1796 Partition of Poland, 1772–1795 Louis XVI of France, r. 1774–1792 American Revolution, 1776–1783 Beginning of the French Revolution, 1789	Start of general European population increase, ca 1750 Growth of illegitimate births, ca 1750–1850 Adam Smith, *The Wealth of Nations*, 1776 Thomas Malthus, *Essay on the Principle of Population*, 1798
1800	Napoleonic era, 1799–1815 Congress of Vienna, 1814–1815 "Battle of Peterloo," Great Britain, 1819	European economic imperialism, ca 1816–1880
1825	Greece wins independence, 1830 Revolution in France, 1830 Great Britain: Reform Bill of 1832; Poor Law reform, 1834; Chartist movement and repeal of Corn Laws, 1838–1848 British complete occupation of India, 1848 Revolutions in Europe, 1848	Height of French utopian socialism, 1830s–1840s German Zollverein founded, 1834 European capitalists begin large-scale foreign investment, 1840s Great Famine in Ireland, 1845–1851 Marx, *Communist Manifesto*, 1848
1850	Second Empire in France, 1852–1870 Crimean War, 1853–1856 Unification of Italy, 1859–1870 Civil War, United States, 1861–1865 Bismarck in power, Germany, 1862–1890 Unification of Germany, 1864–1871 Second Reform Bill, Great Britain, 1867 Third Republic in France, 1870–1940	Crédit Mobilier founded in France, 1852 Japan opened to European influence, 1853 Mill, *On Liberty*, 1859 Emancipation of the serfs, Russia, 1861 First Socialist International, 1864–1871 Marx, *Das Capital*, 1867
1875	Congress of Berlin, 1878 European "scramble for Africa," 1880–1900 Indian National Congress formed, 1883 Third Reform Bill, Great Britain, 1884 Berlin conference on Africa, 1884 Dreyfus affair in France, 1894–1899 Spanish-American War, 1898 Boer War, 1899–1902	Full property rights for women, Great Britain, 1882 Social welfare legislation, Germany, 1883–1889 Second Socialist International, 1889–1914 Witte directs modernization of Russian economy, 1892–1899

Religion and Philosophy	Science and Technology	Arts and Letters
John Wesley, 1703–1791 David Hume, 1711–1776 Diderot, 1713–1784 Condorcet, 1743–1794		
David Ricardo, 1772–1823 Charles Fourier, 1772–1837 Papacy dissolves the Jesuits, 1773 Church reforms of Joseph II in Austria, 1780s Reorganization of the church in France, 1790s	James Hargreaves invents spinning jenny, ca 1765 Richard Arkwright invents water frame, ca 1765 James Watt's steam engine promotes industrial breakthroughs, 1780s War widens the gap in technology between Britain and the continent, 1792–1815 Jenner's smallpox vaccine, 1796	Publication of the *Encyclopedia*, edited by Diderot and d'Alembert, 1751–1765 W. A. Mozart, 1756–1791 Rousseau, *The Social Contract*, 1762 Ludwig van Beethoven, 1170–1827 Wordsworth, 1770–1850 Romantic movement in the arts, ca 1790–1850 Wollstonecraft, *A Vindication of the Rights of Women*, 1792
Napoleon sings Concordat with Pope Pius VII regulating Catholic church in France, 1801 Herbert Spencer, 1820–1903		
Comte, *System of Positive Philosophy*, 1830–1842 Friedrich List, *National System of Political Economy*, 1841 Friedrich Nietzsche, 1844–1900 Georges Sorel, 1847–1922	First railroad, Great Britain, 1825 Michael Faraday's studies in electromagnetism, 1830–1840s	Balzac, *The Human Comedy*, 1829–1841 Delacroix, *Liberty Leading the People*, 1830 Victor Hugo, *Hunchback of Notre Dame*, 1831
Decline in church attendance among working classes, ca 1850–1914 Pope Pius IX, *Syllabus of Errors*, denounces modern thoughts, 1864 Doctrine of papal infallibility, 1870	Modernization of Paris, ca 1850–1870 Great Exhibition, London, 1851 Darwin, *Origin of Species*, 1859 Louis Pasteur develops germ theory of disease, 1860s Suez Canal opened, 1869 Dmitri Mendeleev develops the periodic table, 1869	Realism in art and literature, ca 1850–1870 Freud, 1856–1939 Flaubert, *Madame Bovary*, 1857 Tolstoy, *War and Peace*, 1869 Impressionism in art, ca 1870–1900 Eliot (Mary Ann Evans), *Middlemarch*, 1872
Growth of public education in France, ca 1880–1900 Growth of mission schools in Africa, 1890–1914	Emergence of modern immunology, ca 1875–1900 Trans-Siberian Railroad, 1890s Marie Curie, discovery of radium, 1898 Electrical industry: lightening and streetcars, 1880–1900	Zola, *Germinal*, 1885 Rudyard Kipling, "The White Man's Burden," 1899

	Government	Society and Economy
1900	Russo-Japanese War, 1904–1905 Revolution in Russia, 1905 Balkin wars, 1912–1913	Women's suffrage movement, England, ca 1900–1914 Social welfare legislation, France, 1904, 1910; England, 1906–1914 Agrarian reforms in Russia, 1907–1912
1914	World War One, 1914–1918 *Lusitania* sinks, 1915 Easter Rebellion, 1916 U.S. declares war on Germany, 1917 Bolshevik Revolution, 1917–1918 Treaty of Versailles, 1919	Planned economies in Europe, 1914 Auxiliary Service Law in Germany, 1916 Bread riots in Russia, March 1917
1920	Mussolini seizes power, 1922 Forced collectivization in the Soviet Union, 1929 Stalin uses police terrorism, ca 1929–1939 Hitler becomes chancellor of Germany, 1933 Rome-Berlin Axis, 1936 Nazi-Soviet Non-Aggression Pact, 1939 World War Two begins, 1939	New Economic Policy in the Soviet Union, 1921 Dawes Plan for reparations and recovery, 1924 The Great Depression, 1929–1939 Rapid industrialization in Soviet Union, 1930s Roosevelt's "New Deal," 1933 National Recovery Administration, 1935
1940	Japan bombs Pearl Harbor, 1941 War in Europe ends, 1945 United Nations, 1945 Cold War era begins, 1947 Fall of colonial empires, 1947–1962 Communist government in China, 1949 Korean War, 1950–1953 "De-Stalinization" in Soviet Union, 1955–1962	The Holocaust, 1941–1945 Marshall Plan, 1947 Organization of European Economic Cooperation, 1948 European economic progress, ca 1950–1969 European Coal and Steel Community, 1952 European Economic Community, 1957
1960	The Berlin Wall, 1961 Cuban missile crisis, 1962 United States in Vietnam, ca 1961–1973 Student rebellion in France, 1968 Détente, 1970s Soviet intervention in Afghanistan, 1979	Civil rights movement in United States, 1960s Collapse of postwar monetary system, 1971 OPEC oil price increases, 1973 and 1979 Stagflation, 1970s International Women's Movement, 1970s
1980	U.S. military buildup, 1980s Solidarity in Poland, 1980 Gorbachev begins reforms in the Soviet Union, 1985 Revolutions in Eastern Europe, 1989–1990 End of Soviet Union, 1991	Growth of debt, 1980s Gorbachev implements perestroika, 1985 Economic crisis in Poland, 1988 Unification of East and West Germany, 1989

Religion and Philosophy	Science and Technology	Arts and Letters
Separation of church and state, France, 1901–1905 Jean-Paul Sartre, 1905–1980	Max Planck develops quantum theory, ca 1900 First airplane flight, 1903 Einstein develops relativity theory, 1905–1910	"Modernism" ca 1900–1929 Conrad, *Heart of Darkness,* 1902 Cubism in art, ca 1905–1930 Marcel Proust, *Remembrance of Things Past,* 1913–1927
Schweitzer, *Quest of the Historical Jesus,* 1906	Submarine warfare, 1915 Ernest Rutherford splits the atom, 1919	Oswald Spengler, *The Decline of the West,* 1918
Emergence of modern existentialism, 1920s Wittgenstein, *Essay on Logical Philosophy,* 1922 Revival of Christianity, 1920s and 1930s	"Heroic age of physics," 1920s First major public broadcasts in Great Britain and the United States, 1920 Werner Heisenberg, "principle of uncertainty," 1927 Talking movies, 1930 Radar system in England, 1939	Walter Gropius, the Bauhaus, 1920s Dadaism and Surrealism in art, 1920s Virginia Woolf, *Jacob's Room,* 1922 James Joyce, *Ulysseus,* 1922 T. S. Eliot, *The Waste Land,* 1922 Erich Remarque, *All Quiet on the Western Front,* 1929 Pablo Picasso, *Guernica,* 1937
Simone de Beauvoir, *The Second Sex,* 1949 Communists fail to break Catholic Church in Poland, 1950s	J. Robert Oppenheimer, 1904–1967 "Big Science" in the United States, ca 1940–1970 U.S. drops atomic bombs on Japan, 1945 James Watson and Francis Crick discover structure of DNA molecule, 1953 Russian satellite in orbit, 1957	Cultural purge in Soviet Union, 1946–1952 Ludwig Mies van der Rohe, Lake Shore Apartments, 1948–1951 George Orwell, *1984,* 1949 Boris Pasternak, *Doctor Zhivago,* 1956 The "beat" movement in the United States, late 1950s
Catholic Church opposes the legalization of divorce and abortion, 1970 to present Pope John Paul II electrifies Poland, 1979	European Council for Nuclear Research (CERN), 1960 Space race, 1960s Russian cosmonaut first to orbit globe, 1961 American astronaut first person on the moon, 1969	The Beatles, 1960s Alexander Solzhenitsyn, *One Day in the Life of Ivan Denisovitch,* 1962 Betty Friedan, *The Feminine Mystique,* 1963 J.J. Servan-Schreiber, *The American Challenge,* 1967
Revival of religion in Soviet Union, 1985 to present	Reduced spending on Big Science, 1980s Computer revolution continues, 1980s and 1990s	Solzhenitsyn returns to Russia, 1994

Index

Z